CANADA

Lake Superior

Duluth

nesota

eapolis ★ St. Paul

Wisconsin

Milwaukee
Madison ★
Lansing
Detroit

Michigan

Lake Michigan

Lake Huron

Lake Erie

Lake Ontario

Buffalo

Maine

Augusta ★

Vermont

Montpelier ★

New Hampshire

Concord ★

Albany ★

New York

Boston ★ Massachusetts

Providence ★
Hartford ★

Rhode Island

Connecticut

Iowa

Des Moines ★

aha

Kansas
City ★

Illinois

Springfield ★

Indiana

Indianapolis ★

Cincinnati ●

Chicago ●

Cleveland ●

Pennsylvania

Harrisburg ★

Pittsburgh ●

Ohio

Columbus ●

Frankfort ★

Ohio

Kentucky

Nashville ★

Tennessee

Memphis ●

Little Rock ★

Arkansas

Tennessee

Mississippi

Birmingham ●

Alabama

Mississippi   Montgomery ★

Jackson ★

Louisiana

Baton Rouge ★
New Orleans ●

*Gulf of
Mexico*

New York ●

Trenton ●

Philadelphia ●

New Jersey

Baltimore ●
Annapolis ★

Dover ★

Delaware

Washington, D.C. ⊛

Maryland

West
Virginia

Charleston ★

Richmond ★

Norfolk ●

Virginia

Raleigh ★

North Carolina

Charlotte ●

South Carolina

Columbia ★

Atlanta ★

Georgia

Savannah ●

A P P A L A C H I A N   M O U N T A I N S

ATLANTIC
OCEAN

40°N

30°N

Tallahassee ★

Florida

Orlando ●

Tampa ●

Miami ●

BAHAMAS

N

100   200 mi.

100   200 km

90°W   80°W

NITED STATES OF AMERICA

WORLDMARK
ENCYCLOPEDIA
OF THE STATES

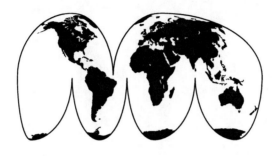

ISSN 1531-1627

WORLDMARK ENCYCLOPEDIA OF THE STATES, SEVENTH EDITION

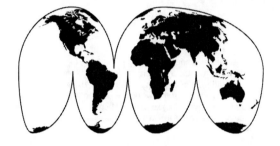

Volume 1

Alabama to Montana

 GALE
CENGAGE Learning

Detroit • New York • San Francisco • New Haven, Conn • Waterville, Maine • London

Worldmark Encyclopedia of the States, Seventh Edition
Timothy L. Gall, Editor in Chief

Project Editor
Mary Rose Bonk

Editorial
Jennifer Greve,
Kimberly Lewis,
Kate Potthoff

Imaging
Christine O'Bryan

Product Design
Jennifer Wahi

Manufacturing
Rita Wimberly

ISBN 1-4144-1058-1 (set)
ISBN 1-4144-1121-9 (v.1)
ISBN 1-4144-1122-7 (v.2)
ISSN 1531-1627 (set)

This title is also available as an e-book
ISBN 1-4144-1114-6
Contact your Gale sales representative for ordering information.

Printed in the United States of America
5 6 7 8   14 13

CONTENTS

PREFACE

In 1980, editor and publisher Moshe Y. Sachs set out to create the *Worldmark Encyclopedia of the Nations,* a new kind of reference work that would view every nation of the world as if through a "world mirror" and not from the perspective of any one country or group of countries. In 1981, a companion volume, the *Worldmark Encyclopedia of the States,* was introduced. It was selected as an "Outstanding Reference Source" by the Reference Sources Committee of the American Library Association, Reference and Adult Services Division. Gale now offers a revised and updated seventh edition of the *Worldmark Encyclopedia of the States.*

The fitness of the United States of America as a subject for encyclopedic study is plain. No discussion of world politics, economics, culture, technology, or military affairs would be complete without an intensive examination of the American achievement. What is not so obvious is why the editors chose to present this work as an encyclopedia of the *states* rather than of the United States. In so doing, they emphasize the fact that the United States is a federal union of separate states with divergent histories, traditions, resources, laws, and economic interests.

Every state, large or small, is treated in an individual chapter, within a framework of 50 standard subject headings; generally, the more populous the state, the longer the article. The District of Columbia and the Commonwealth of Puerto Rico each have their own chapters, and two additional articles describe in summary the other Caribbean and Pacific dependencies. The concluding chapter is an overview of the nation as a whole. Supplementing this textual material are tables of conversions and abbreviations, a glossary, and more than 50 black-and-white maps prepared especially for this encyclopedia.

Publication of this encyclopedia was a collective effort that enlisted the talents of scholars, government agencies, editor-writers, artists, cartographers, typesetters, proofreaders, and many others. Perhaps only those involved in the production of reference books fully appreciate how complex that endeavor can be. Readers customarily expect that a reference book will be correct in every particular; and yet, by the time it has been on the shelves for a few months, a conscientious editor may already have a long list of improvements and corrections to be made in a subsequent edition. We invite you, the reader, to add your suggestions to our list.

Send comments to:

Worldmark Encyclopedia oft he States
Gale
27500 Drake Road
Farmington Hills, MI 48331

The Editors

GUIDE TO STATE ARTICLES

All information contained within a state article is uniformly keyed by means of small superior numerals to the left of the subject headings. A heading such as "Population," for example, carries the same key numeral (6) in every article. Thus, to find information about the population of Alabama, consult the table of contents for the page number where the Alabama article begins and look for section 6 thereunder.

Introductory matter for each state includes:

Origin of state name
Nickname
Capital
Date and order of statehood
Song
Motto
Flag
Official seal
Symbols (animal, tree, flower, etc.)
Legal holidays
Time zone

SUBJECT HEADINGS IN NUMERICAL ORDER

1	Location, size, and extent	27	Mining
2	Topography	28	Energy and power
3	Climate	29	Industry
4	Flora and fauna	30	Commerce
5	Environmental protection	31	Consumer protection
6	Population	32	Banking
7	Ethnic groups	33	Insurance
8	Languages	34	Securities
9	Religions	35	Public finance
10	Transportation	36	Taxation
11	History	37	Economic policy
12	State government	38	Health
13	Political parties	39	Social welfare
14	Local government	40	Housing
15	State services	41	Education
16	Judicial system	42	Arts
17	Armed forces	43	Libraries and museums
18	Migration	44	Communications
19	Intergovernmental cooperation	45	Press
20	Economy	46	Organizations
21	Income	47	Tourism, travel, and recreation
22	Labor		
23	Agriculture	48	Sports
24	Animal husbandry	49	Famous persons
25	Fishing	50	Bibliography
26	Forestry		

SUBJECT HEADINGS IN ALPHABETICAL ORDER

Agriculture	23	Intergovernmental cooperation	19
Animal husbandry	24	Judicial system	16
Armed forces	17	Labor	22
Arts	42	Languages	8
Banking	32	Libraries and museums	43
Bibliography	50	Local government	14
Climate	3	Location, size, and extent	1
Commerce	30	Migration	18
Communications	44	Mining	27
Consumer protection	31	Organizations	46
Economic policy	37	Political parties	13
Economy	20	Population	6
Education	41	Press	45
Energy and power	28	Public finance	35
Environmental protection	5	Religions	9
Ethnic groups	7	Securities	34
Famous persons	49	Social welfare	39
Fishing	25	Sports	48
Flora and fauna	4	State government	12
Forestry	26	State services	15
Health	38	Taxation	36
History	11	Topography	2
Housing	40	Tourism, travel, and recreation	47
Income	21	Transportation	10
Industry	29		
Insurance	33		

EXPLANATION OF SYMBOLS

A fiscal split year is indicated by a stroke (e.g. 1994/95).
A dollar sign ($) stands for US$ unless otherwise indicated.
Note that 1 billion = 1,000 million = 10^9.
The use of a small dash (e.g., 1990–94) normally signifies the full period of calendar years covered (including the end year indicated).

NOTES

GENERAL NOTE: In producing the seventh edition of *Worldmark Encyclopedia of the States*, the editors were aided by the wealth of information now available from state governments on the World Wide Web. The information included in this volume from postings by state agencies was supplemented by data from The Council of State Governments, the Census Bureau, the Bureau of Economic Analysis, the National Center for Education Statistics, the Bureau of Justice Statistics, the Department of Energy, the National Science Board, the National Center for Health Statistics, the Federal Highway Administration, the Department of Defense, the Department of Veterans Affairs, the Department of the Interior, the Federal Deposit Insurance Corporation, and a wide variety of additional federal agencies and offices. This state and federal information was indispensable to *Worldmark* editors in revising state articles. Space does not permit listing of the hundreds of additional documents from private sources which were consulted for each state's entry. Listed below are notable sources of data which were used in revising a majority of entries.

MAPS: The maps of the states were produced by the University of Akron Laboratory for Cartographic and Spatial Analysis under the direction of Joseph W. Stoll. The maps originated from the United States Geological Survey 1:2,000,000 Digital Line Graphs (DLG). Additional sources used to determine and verify the positioning of text and symbols include 1990 United States Census Data, USGS 1:500,000 Topographic State Maps, brochures and maps from the state visitor bureaus, and the *Rand McNally United States Road Atlas*. For definitions of abbreviations used on the maps please refer to the section entitled "Abbreviations and Acronyms" appearing on page xi.

WEIGHTS AND MEASURES: Recognizing the trend toward use of the metric system throughout the United States, the text provides metric equivalents for customary measures of length and area, and both Fahrenheit and Centigrade expressions for temperature. Production figures are expressed exclusively in the prevailing customary units.

LOCATION, SIZE, AND EXTENT: The lengths of interstate boundary segments and the total lengths of state boundaries appear in roman type when derived from official government sources; italic type indicates data derived from other sources. Discrepancies in the boundary lengths of neighboring states as specified by official sources arise from divergent methodologies of measurement.

FLORA AND FAUNA: Discussions of endangered species are based on the *List of Endangered and Threatened Wildlife and Plants* maintained by the Fish and Wildlife Service of the US Department of the Interior, and on data supplied by the states.

POPULATION: Population figures are from data released by the US Census Bureau's Population Estimates Program as of 2006. These data can be found at http://eire.census.gov/popest/estimates.php together with a wide variety of additional economic and demographic data collected by the US Department of Commerce and other related federal agencies. Tables of counties, county seats, county areas, and estimates of county populations as of 2006 accompany the articles on the 14 most populous states; the editors regret that space limitations prevented the publication of such a table for each state. Because of rounding of numbers, county areas in these tables may not equal the total.

LANGUAGES: Examples of lexical and pronunciation patterns cited in the text are meant to suggest the historic development of principal linguistic features and should not be taken as a comprehensive statement of current usage. Data on languages spoken in the home were obtained from "Languages Spoken at Home: 2000" issued online at http://factfinder.census.gov by the US Census Bureau.

TRANSPORTATION: Transportation statistics were compiled from the *Transportation Profile* for each of the states and the District of Columbia published by the Bureau of Transportation Statistics, US Department of Transportation.

JUDICIAL SYSTEM: *Uniform Crime Reports for the United States*, published annually by the Federal Bureau of Investigation and embodying the FBI Crime Index (tabulations of offenses known to the police), was the principal source for the crime statistics cited in the text.

ARMED FORCES: The number of veterans of US military service are as reported by Census Bureau as of 2006. Additional data came from the *State Summary* reports prepared by the Office of Public Affairs, Media Relations, Department of Veterans Affairs.

INCOME: Data on income was extracted in part from *State BEARFACTS 1994 – 2004* published online at http://www.bea.gov/bea/regional/bearfacts by the Bureau of Economic Analysis of the US Department of Commerce.

LABOR: Statistics on the labor force and union membership were obtained from Bureau of Labor Statistics, United States Department of Labor and are available online at http://www.bls.gov.

ENERGY AND POWER: Data for proved reserves and production of fossil fuels were derived from publications of the American Gas Association, American Petroleum Institute, National Coal Association, and US Department of Energy. Data on nuclear power facilities were obtained from the Nuclear Information and Resource Service and from state sources.

INSURANCE: The principal statistical sources for information on insurance were annual publications of the Insurance Information Institute and the American Council of Life Insurance.

PUBLIC FINANCE: Tables of state government revenues and expenditures were obtained from *2004 State Government Tax Collections* and *State Government Finances: 2004* issued by the US Census Bureau and available online at http://www.census.gov/govs/www/statetax02.html and http://www.census.gov/govs.state. Additional information came from the official web sites of the individual states.

HEALTH: The principal statistical sources for hospitals and medical personnel were annual publications of the American Dental Association, American Hospital Association, and American Medical Association.

LIBRARIES AND MUSEUMS: In most cases, library and museum names are listed in the *American Library Directory* by R. R. Bowker, and the *Official Museum Directory,* compiled by the National Register Publishing Co. in cooperation with the American Association of Museums.

PRESS: Circulation data follow the 2005 *Editor & Publisher International Yearbook.*

FAMOUS PERSONS: Entries are current through July 2006. Where a person described in one state is known to have been born in another, the state of birth follows the personal name, in parentheses.

BIBLIOGRAPHY: Bibliographies are intended as a guide to landmark works on each state for further research and not as a listing of sources in preparing the articles. Such listings would have far exceeded space limitations.

CONVERSION TABLES*

LENGTH
1 centimeter ....0.3937 inch
1 centimeter ....0.03280833 foot
1 meter (100 centimeters) ....3.280833 feet
1 meter ....1.093611 US yards
1 kilometer (1,000 meters) ....0.62137 statute mile
1 kilometer ....0.539957 nautical mile
1 inch ....2.540005 centimeters
1 foot (12 inches) ....30.4801 centimeters
1 US yard (3 feet) ....0.914402 meter
1 statute mile (5,280 feet; 1,760 yards) ....1.609347 kilometers
1 British mile ....1.609344 kilometers
1 nautical mile (1.1508 statute miles
or 6,076.10333 feet) ....1.852 kilometers
1 British nautical mile (6,080 feet) ....1.85319 kilometers

AREA
1 sq centimeter ....0.154999 sq inch
1 sq meter (10,000 sq centimeters) ....10.76387 sq feet
1 sq meter ....1.1959585 sq yards
1 hectare (10,000 sq meters) ....2.47104 acres
1 sq kilometer (100 hectares) ....0.386101 sq mile
1 sq inch ....6.451626 sq centimeters
1 sq foot (144 sq inches) ....0.092903 sq meter
1 sq yard (9 sq feet) ....0.836131 sq meter
1 acre (4,840 sq yards) ....0.404687 hectare
1 sq mile (640 acres) ....2.589998 sq kilometers

VOLUME
1 cubic centimeter ....0.061023 cubic inch
1 cubic meter
(1,000,000 cubic centimeters) ....35.31445 cubic feet
1 cubic meter ....1.307943 cubic yards
1 cubic inch ....16.387162 cubic centimeters
1 cubic foot (1,728 cubic inches) ....0.028317 cubic meter
1 cubic yard (27 cubic feet) ....0.764559 cubic meter

LIQUID MEASURE
1 liter ....0.8799 imperial quart
1 liter ....1.05671 US quarts
1 hectoliter ....21.9975 imperial gallons
1 hectoliter ....26.4178 US gallons
1 imperial quart ....1.136491 liters
1 US quart ....0.946333 liter
1 imperial gallon ....0.04546 hectoliter
1 US gallon ....0.037853 hectoliter

WEIGHT
1 kilogram (1,000 grams) ....35.27396 avoirdupois ounces
1 kilogram ....32.15074 troy ounces
1 kilogram ....2.204622 avoirdupois pounds
1 quintal (100 kg) ....220.4622 avoirdupois pounds
1 quintal ....1.9684125 hundredweights
1 metric ton (1,000 kg) ....1.102311 short tons
1 metric ton ....0.984206 long ton

1 avoirdupois ounce ....0.0283495 kilogram
1 troy ounce ....0.0311035 kilogram
1 avoirdupois pound ....0.453592 kilogram
1 avoirdupois pound ....0.00453592 quintal
1 hundred weight (cwt., 112 lb) ....0.50802 quintal
1 short ton (2,000 lb) ....0.907185 metric ton
1 long ton (2,240 lb) ....1.016047 metric tons

ELECTRIC ENERGY
1 horsepower (hp) ....0.7457 kilowatt
1 kilowatt (kw) ....1.34102 horsepower

TEMPERATURE
Celsius (C) ....Fahrenheit−32 x 5/9
Fahrenheit (F) ....9/5 Celsius + 32

BUSHELS

	LB	METRIC TON	BUSHELS PER METRIC TON
Barley (US)	48	0.021772	45.931
(UK)	50	0.022680	44.092
Corn (UK, US)	56	0.025401	39.368
Linseed (UK)	52	0.023587	42.396
(Australia, US)	56	0.025401	39.368
Oats (US)	32	0.014515	68.894
(Canada)	34	0.015422	64.842
Potatoes (UK, US)	60	0.027216	36.743
Rice (Australia)	42	0.019051	52.491
(US)	45	0.020412	48.991
Rye (UK, US)	56	0.025401	39.368
(Australia)	60	0.027216	36.743
Soybeans (US)	60	0.027216	36.743
Wheat (UK, US)	60	0.027216	36.743

BAGS OF COFFEE

	LB	KG	BAGS PER METRIC TON
Brazil, Columbia Mexico, Venezuela	132.28	60	16.667
El Salvador	152.12	69	14.493
Haiti	185.63	84.2	11.876

BALES OF COTTON

	LB	METRIC TON	BALES PER METRIC TON
India	392	0.177808	5.624
Brazil	397	0.180000	5.555
US (net)	480	0.217724	4.593
US (gross)	500	0.226796	4.409

PETROLEUM
One barrel = 42 US gallons = 34.97 imperial gallons = 158.99 liters = 0.15899 cubic meter (or 1 cubic meter = 6.2898 barrels).

*Includes units of measure cited in the text, as well as certain other units employed in parts of the English-speaking world.

ABBREVIATIONS AND ACRONYMS

AD—Anno Domini
AFDC—Aid to Families with Dependent Children
AFL–CIO—American Federation of Labor-
    Congress of Industrial Organizations
AM—before noon
AM—amplitude modulation
American Ind.—American Independent Party
Amtrak—National Railroad Passenger Corp.
b.—born
BC—Before Christ
Btu—British thermal unit(s)
bu—bushel(s)
c.—circa (about)
C—Celsius (Centigrade)
CIA—Central Intelligence Agency
cm—centimeter(s)
Co.—company
comp.—compiler
Conrail—Consolidated Rail Corp.
Corp.—corporation
Cr.—creek
CST—Central Standard Time
cu—cubic
cwt—hundredweight(s)
d.—died
D—Democrat
e—evening
E—east
ed.—edition, editor
e.g.—exempli gratia (for example)
EPA—Environmental Protection Agency
est.—estimated
EST—Eastern Standard Time
et al.—et alii (and others)

etc.—et cetera (and so on)
F—Fahrenheit
FBI—Federal Bureau of Investigation
FCC—Federal Communications Commission
FM—frequency modulation
For.—forest
Ft.—fort
ft—foot, feet
GDP—gross domestic product
gm—gram
GMT—Greenwich Mean Time
GNP—gross national product
GRT—gross registered tons
Hist.—historic
I—interstate (highway)
i.e.—id est (that is)
in—inch(es)
Inc.—incorporated
Ind. Res.—Indian Reservation
Is.—isle, island
Jct.—junction
K—kindergarten
kg—kilogram(s)
km—kilometer(s)
km/hr—kilometers per hour
kw—kilowatt(s)
kwh—kilowatt-hour(s)
lb—pound(s)
m—meter(s); morning
m^3—cubic meter(s)
Mem.—memorial
mi—mile(s)
Mil. Res.—military reservation
Mon.—monument

mph—miles per hour
MST—Mountain Standard Time
Mt.—mount
Mtn.—mountain
mw—megawatt(s)
N—north
NA—not available
Natl.—National
Natl. Mon.—national monument
NATO—North Atlantic Treaty Organization
NCAA—National Collegiate Athletic Association
n.d.—no date
N.F.—national forest
N.P.—national park
N.W.R.—national wildlife refuge
oz—ounce(s)
PM—after noon
PST—Pacific Standard Time
r.—reigned
R—Republican
Ra.—range
Res.—reservoir, reservation
rev. ed.—revised edition
s—south
S—Sunday
Soc.—Socialist
S.P.—senic point
sq—square
St.—saint, state
UN—United Nations
US—United States
USIA—United States Information Agency
w—west
W.M.A.—wildlife management area

NAMES OF STATES AND OTHER SELECTED AREAS

	Standard Abbreviation(s)	Postal Abbreviation		Standard Abbreviation(s)	Postal Abbreviation
Alabama	Ala.	AL	Nebraska	Nebr. (Neb.)	NE
Alaska	*	AK	Nevada	Nev.	NV
Arizona	Ariz.	AZ	New Hampshire	N.H.	NH
Arkansas	Ark.	AR	New Jersey	N.J.	NJ
California	Calif.	CA	New Mexico	N.Mex. (N.M.)	NM
Colorado	Colo.	CO	New York	N.Y.	NY
Connecticut	Conn.	CT	North Carolina	N.C.	NC
Delaware	Del.	DE	North Dakota	N.Dak. (N.D.)	ND
District of Columbia	D.C.	DC	Ohio	*	OH
Florida	Fla.	FL	Oklahoma	Okla.	OK
Georgia	Ga.	GA	Oregon	Oreg. (Ore.)	OR
Hawaii	*	HI	Pennsylvania	Pa.	PA
Idaho	*	ID	Puerto Rico	P.R.	PR
Illinois	Ill.	IL	Rhode Island	R.I.	RI
Indiana	Ind.	IN	South Carolina	S.C.	SC
Iowa	*	IA	South Dakota	S.Dak. (S.D.)	SD
Kansas	Kans. (Kan.)	KS	Tennessee	Tenn.	TN
Kentucky	Ky.	KY	Texas	Tex.	TX
Louisiana	La.	LA	Utah	*	UT
Maine	Me.	ME	Vermont	Vt.	VT
Maryland	Md.	MD	Virginia	Va.	VA
Massachusetts	Mass.	MA	Virgin Islands	V.I.	VI
Michigan	Mich.	MI	Washington	Wash.	WA
Minnesota	Minn.	MN	West Virginia	W.Va.	WV
Mississippi	Miss.	MS	Wisconsin	Wis.	WI
Missouri	Mo.	MO	Wyoming	Wyo.	WY
Montana	Mont.	MT	*No standard abbreviation		

GLOSSARY

ANTEBELLUM: before the US Civil War.

BLUE LAWS: laws forbidding certain practices (e.g., conducting business, gaming, drinking liquor), especially on Sundays.

CAPITAL BUDGET: a financial plan for acquiring and improving buildings or land, paid for by the sale of bonds.

CAPITAL PUNISHMENT: punishment by death.

CIVILIAN LABOR FORCE: all persons 16 years of age or older who are not in the armed forces and who are now holding a job, have been temporarily laid off, are waiting to be reassigned to a new position, or are unemployed but actively looking for work.

CLASS I RAILROAD: a railroad having gross annual revenues of $83.5 million or more in 1983.

COMMERCIAL BANK: a bank that offers businesses and individuals a variety of banking services, including the right of withdrawal by check.

COMPACT: a formal agreement, covenant, or understanding between two or more parties.

CONSOLIDATED BUDGET: a financial plan that includes the general budget, federal funds, and all special funds.

CONSTANT DOLLARS: money values calculated so as to eliminate the effect of inflation on prices and income.

CONTINENTAL CLIMATE: the climate typical of the US interior, having distinct seasons, a wide range of daily and annual temperatures, and dry, sunny summers.

COUNCIL-MANAGER SYSTEM: a system of local government under which a professional administrator is hired by an elected council to carry out its laws and policies.

CREDIT UNION: a cooperative body that raises funds from its members by the sale of shares and makes loans to its members at relatively low interest rates.

CURRENT DOLLARS: money values that reflect prevailing prices, without excluding the effects of inflation.

DEMAND DEPOSIT: a bank deposit that can be withdrawn by the depositor with no advance notice to the bank.

ELECTORAL VOTES: the votes that a state may cast for president, equal to the combined total of its US senators and representatives and nearly always cast entirely on behalf of the candidate who won the most votes in that state on Election Day.

ENDANGERED SPECIES: a type of plant or animal threatened with extinction in all or part of its natural range.

FEDERAL POVERTY LEVEL: a level of money income below which a person or family qualifies for US government aid.

FISCAL YEAR: a 12-month period for accounting purposes.

FOOD STAMPS: coupons issued by the government to low-income persons for food purchases at local stores.

GENERAL BUDGET: a financial plan based on a government's normal revenues and operating expenses, excluding special funds.

GENERAL COASTLINE: a measurement of the general outline of the US seacoast. See also TIDAL SHORELINE.

GREAT AWAKENING: during the mid–18th century, a Protestant religious revival in North America, especially New England.

GROSS STATE PRODUCT: the total value of goods and services produced in the state.

GROWING SEASON: the period between the last 32°f (0°c) temperature in spring and the first 32°f (0°c) temperature in autumn.

HOME-RULE CHARTER: a document stating how and in what respects a city, town, or county may govern itself.

INSTALLED CAPACITY: the maximum possible output of electric power at any given time.

MAYOR-COUNCIL SYSTEM: a system of local government under which an elected council serves as a legislature and an elected mayor is the chief administrator.

MEDICAID: a federal-state program that helps defray the hospital and medical costs of needy persons.

MEDICARE: a program of hospital and medical insurance for the elderly, administered by the federal government.

METROPOLITAN AREA: in most cases, a city and its surrounding suburbs.

NO-FAULT INSURANCE: an automobile insurance plan that allows an accident victim to receive payment from an insurance company without having to prove who was responsible for the accident.

NORTHERN, NORTH MIDLAND: major US dialect regions.

OMBUDSMAN: a public official empowered to hear and investigate complaints by private citizens about government agencies.

PER CAPITA: per person.

POCKET VETO: a method by which a state governor (or the US president) may kill a bill by taking no action on it before the legislature adjourns.

PROVED RESERVES: the quantity of a recoverable mineral resource (such as oil or natural gas) that is still in the ground.

PUBLIC DEBT: the amount owed by a government.

RELIGIOUS ADHERENTS: the followers of a religious group, including (but not confined to) the full, confirmed, or communicant members of that group.

RETAIL TRADE: the sale of goods directly to the consumer.

REVENUE SHARING: the distribution of federal tax receipts to state and local governments.

RIGHT-TO-WORK LAW: a measure outlawing any attempt to require union membership as a condition of employment.

SAVINGS AND LOAN ASSOCIATION: a bank that invests the savings of depositors primarily in home mortgage loans.

SERVICE INDUSTRIES: industries that provide services (e.g., health, legal, automotive repair) for individuals, businesses, and others.

SOCIAL SECURITY: as commonly understood, the federal system of old age, survivors, and disability insurance.

SOUTHERN, SOUTH MIDLAND: major US dialect regions.

STOLPORT: an airfield for short-takeoff-and-landing (STOL) aircraft, which require runways shorter than those used by conventional aircraft.

SUNBELT: the southernmost states of the United States, extending from Florida to California.

SUPPLEMENTAL SECURITY INCOME: a federally administered program of aid to the aged, blind, and disabled.

TIDAL SHORELINE: a detailed measurement of the US seacoast that includes sounds, bays, other outlets, and offshore islands.

TIME DEPOSIT: a bank deposit that may be withdrawn only at the end of a specified time period or upon advance notice to the bank.

VALUE ADDED BY MANUFACTURE: the difference, measured in dollars, between the value of finished goods and the cost of the materials needed to produce them.

WHOLESALE TRADE: the sale of goods, usually in large quantities, for ultimate resale to consumers.

EDITORIAL STAFF

Editor in Chief: Timothy L. Gall
Senior Editors: Jeneen M. Hobby, Karen Ellicott, George Vukmanovich
Graphics Editor: Daniel Mehling
Associate Editors: Rachel Babura, Susan Bevan Gall, James Henry, Daniel M. Lucas, Maura E. Malone, Michael A. Parris, Seth E. Rosenberg, Gail Rosewater, Susan Stern, Jeanne-Marie Stumpf, Kimberly Tilly, Rosalie Wieder, Sarah Wang, Daiva Ziedonis
Proofreaders: Jane Hoehner, Deborah A. Ring
Cartography: University of Akron Laboratory for Cartographic and Spatial Analysis: Joseph W. Stoll, Supervisor; Scott Raypholtz; Mike Meyer

CONTRIBUTORS
TO THE FIRST EDITION

ALLEN, HAROLD B. Emeritus Professor of English and Linguistics, University of Minnesota (Minneapolis–St. Paul). LANGUAGES.

BASSETT, T. D. SEYMOUR. Former University Archivist, University of Vermont (Burlington). VERMONT.

BENSON, MAXINE. Curator of Document Resources, Colorado Historical Society. COLORADO.

BROWN, RICHARD D. Professor of History, University of Connecticut (Storrs). MASSACHUSETTS.

CASHIN, EDWARD J. Professor of History, Augusta College. GEORGIA.

CHANNING, STEVEN A. Professor of History, University of Kentucky (Lexington). KENTUCKY.

CLARK, CHARLES E. Professor of History, University of New Hampshire (Durham). MAINE.

COGSWELL, PHILIP, JR. Forum Editor, *The Oregonian.* OREGON.

CONLEY, PATRICK T. Professor of History and Law, Providence College. RHODE ISLAND.

CORLEW, ROBERT E. Dean, School of Liberal Arts, Middle Tennessee State University (Murfreesboro). TENNESSEE.

CREIGH, DOROTHY WEYER. Author and historian; member, Nebraska State Board of Education. NEBRASKA.

CUNNINGHAM, JOHN T. Author and historian. NEW JERSEY.

FISHER, PERRY. Director, Columbia Historical Society. DISTRICT OF COLUMBIA.

FRANTZ, JOE B. Professor of History, University of Texas (Austin). TEXAS.

GOODELL, LELE. Member, Editorial Board, *Hawaiian Journal of History.* HAWAII (in part).

GOODRICH, JAMES W. Associate Director, State Historical Society of Missouri. MISSOURI.

HAMILTON, VIRGINIA. Professor of History, University of Alabama (Birmingham). ALABAMA.

HAVIGHURST, WALTER. Research Professor of English Emeritus, Miami University (Oxford). OHIO.

HINTON, HARWOOD P. Editor, *Arizona and the West,* University of Arizona (Tucson). ARIZONA.

HOOGENBOOM, ARI. Professor of History, Brooklyn College of the City University of New York. PENNSYLVANIA.

HOOVER, HERBERT T. Professor of History, University of South Dakota (Vermillion). SOUTH DAKOTA.

HUNT, WILLIAM R. Historian; former Professor of History, University of Alaska. ALASKA.

JENSEN, DWIGHT. Author and historian. IDAHO.

JENSEN, RICHARD J. Professor of History, University of Illinois (Chicago). ILLINOIS.

LARSON, ROBERT W. Professor of History, University of Northern Colorado (Greeley). NEW MEXICO.

MAPP, ALF J., JR. Author, lecturer, and historian; Professor of English, Creative Writing, and Journalism, Old Dominion University (Norfolk). VIRGINIA.

MAY, GEORGE S. Professor of History, Eastern Michigan University (Ypsilanti). MICHIGAN.

MEYER, GLADYS. Professor emeritus, Columbia University. ETHNIC GROUPS.

MOODY, ERIC N. Historian, Nevada Historical Society. NEVADA.

MUNROE, JOHN A. H. Rodney Sharp Professor of History, University of Delaware. DELAWARE.

MURPHY, MARIAM. Associate Editor, *Utah Historical Quarterly.* UTAH.

O'BRIEN, KATHLEEN ANN. Project Director, Upper Midwest Women's History Center for Teachers. MINNESOTA.

PADOVER, SAUL K. Distinguished Service Professor Emeritus, Graduate Faculty, New School (New York City). UNITED STATES OF AMERICA.

PECKHAM, HOWARD H. Professor emeritus, University of Michigan. INDIANA.

PRYOR, NANCY. Research consultant and librarian, Washington State Library. WASHINGTON.

RAWLS, JAMES J. Instructor of History, Diablo Valley College (Pleasant Hill). CALIFORNIA.

RICE, OTIS K. Professor of History, West Virginia Institute of Technology (Montgomery). WEST VIRGINIA.

RICHMOND, ROBERT W. Assistant Executive Director, Kansas State Historical Society. KANSAS.

RIGHTER, ROBERT W. Assistant Professor of History, University of Wyoming (Laramie). WYOMING.

ROTH, DAVID M. Director, Center for Connecticut Studies, Eastern Connecticut State College (Willimantic). CONNECTICUT.

SCHEFFER, BARBARA MOORE. Feature Writer. OKLAHOMA (in part).

SCHEFFER, WALTER F. Regents' Professor of Political Science and Director, Graduate Program in Public Administration, University of Oklahoma (Norman). OKLAHOMA (in part).

SCHMITT, ROBERT C. Hawaii State Statistician. HAWAII (in part).

SCUDIERE, PAUL J. Senior Historian, New York State Education Department. NEW YORK.

SKATES, JOHN RAY. Professor of History, University of Southern Mississippi (Hattiesburg). MISSISSIPPI.

SMITH, DOUG. Writer, *Arkansas Gazette* (Little Rock). ARKANSAS.

STOUDEMIRE, ROBERT H. Professor of State and Local Government and Senior Research Associate, Bureau of Governmental Research, University of South Carolina (Columbia). SOUTH CAROLINA.

SULLIVAN, LARRY E. Librarian, New York Historical Society. MARYLAND.

TAYLOR, JOE GRAY. Professor of History, McNeese State University (Lake Charles). LOUISIANA.

TEBEAU, CHARLTON W. Emeritus Professor of History, University of Miami. FLORIDA.

THOMPSON, WILLIAM FLETCHER. Director of Research, State Historical Society of Wisconsin. WISCONSIN.

VIVO, PAQUITA. Author and consultant. PUERTO RICO.

WALL, JOSEPH FRAZIER. Professor of History, Grinnell College. IOWA.

WALLACE, R. STUART. Assistant Director/Editor, New Hampshire Historical Society. NEW HAMPSHIRE.

WATSON, HARRY L. Assistant Professor of History, University of North Carolina (Chapel Hill). NORTH CAROLINA.

WEAVER, KENNETH L. Associate Professor of Political Science, Montana State University (Bozeman). MONTANA.

WILKINS, ROBERT P. Professor of History, University of North Dakota (Grand Forks). NORTH DAKOTA.

WOODS, BOB. Editor, *Sierra Club Wildlife Involvement News.* FLORA AND FAUNA.

ALABAMA

State of Alabama

ORIGIN OF STATE NAME: Probably after the Alabama Indian tribe. **NICKNAME:** The Heart of Dixie. **CAPITAL:** Montgomery. **ENTERED UNION:** 14 December 1819 (22nd). **SONG:** "Alabama." **MOTTO:** *Aldemus jura nostra defendere* (We dare defend our rights). **COAT OF ARMS:** Two eagles, symbolizing courage, support a shield bearing the emblems of the five governments (France, England, Spain, Confederacy, US) that have held sovereignty over Alabama. Above the shield is a sailing vessel modeled upon the ships of the first French settlers of Alabama; beneath the shield is the state motto. **FLAG:** Crimson cross of St. Andrew on a square white field. **OFFICIAL SEAL:** The map of Alabama, including names of major rivers and neighboring states, surrounded by the words "Alabama Great Seal." **BIRD:** Yellowhammer. **FISH:** Tarpon. **FLOWER:** Camellia. **TREE:** Southern (longleaf) pine. **GEM:** Star Blue Quartz. **LEGAL HOLIDAYS:** New Year's Day, 1 January; Birthdays of Robert E. Lee and Martin Luther King, Jr., 3rd Monday in January; George Washington's/Thomas Jefferson's Birthdays, 3rd Monday in February; Mardi Gras, February or March; Confederate Memorial Day, 4th Monday in April; Jefferson Davis's Birthday, 1st Monday in June; Independence Day, 4 July; Labor Day, 1st Monday in September; Columbus Day/American Indian Heritage Day, 2nd Monday in October; Veterans Day, 11 November; Thanksgiving Day, 4th Thursday in November; Christmas Day, 25 December. **TIME:** 6 AM CST = noon GMT.

¹LOCATION, SIZE, AND EXTENT

Located in the eastern south-central United States, Alabama ranks 29th in size among the 50 states.

The total area of Alabama is 51,705 sq mi (133,915 sq km), of which land constitutes 50,767 sq mi (131,486 sq km) and inland water, 938 sq mi (2,429 sq km). Alabama extends roughly 200 mi (320 km) E–W; the maximum N–S extension is 300 mi (480 km). Alabama is bordered on the N by Tennessee; on the E by Georgia (with part of the line formed by the Chattahoochee River); on the S by Florida (with part of the line defined by the Perdido River) and the Gulf of Mexico; and on the W by Mississippi (with the northernmost part of the line passing through the Tennessee River).

Dauphin Island, in the Gulf of Mexico, is the largest offshore island. The total boundary length of Alabama is 1,044 mi (1,680 km). The state's geographic center is in Chilton County, 12 mi (19 km) SW of Clanton.

²TOPOGRAPHY

Alabama is divided into four major physiographic regions: the Gulf Coastal Plain, Piedmont Plateau, Ridge and Valley section, and Appalachian (or Cumberland) Plateau. The physical characteristics of each province have significantly affected settlement and industrial development patterns within the state.

The coastal plain, comprising the southern half of Alabama, consists primarily of lowlands and low ridges. Included within the coastal plain is the Black Belt—historically, the center of cotton production and plantation slavery in Alabama—an area of rich, chalky soil that stretches across the entire width of central Alabama. Just to the north, the piedmont of east-central Alabama contains rolling hills and valleys. Alabama's highest elevation, Cheaha Mountain, 2,405 ft (733 m) above sea level, is located at

the northern edge of this region. North and west of the piedmont is a series of parallel ridges and valleys running in a northeast-southwest direction. Mountain ranges in this area include the Red, Shades, Oak, Lookout, and other noteworthy southern extensions of the Appalachian chain; elevations of 1,200 ft (366 m) are found as far south as Birmingham. The Appalachian Plateau covers most of northwestern Alabama, with a portion of the Highland Rim in the extreme north near the Tennessee border. The floodplain of the Tennessee River cuts a wide swath across both these northern regions. The lowest point in the state is at sea level at the Gulf of Mexico. The mean elevation of the state is approximately 500 ft (153 m).

The largest lake wholly within Alabama is Guntersville Lake, covering about 108 sq mi (280 sq km) and formed during the development of the Tennessee River region by the Tennessee Valley Authority (TVA). The TVA lakes—also including Wheeler, Pickwick, and Wilson—are all long and narrow, fanning outward along a line that runs from the northeast corner of the state westward to Florence. Wetlands cover about 10% of the state.

The longest rivers are the Alabama, extending from the mid-central region to the Mobile River for a distance of about 160 mi (260 km); the Tennessee, which flows across northern Alabama for about the same distance; and the Tombigbee, which flows south from north-central Alabama for some 150 mi (240 km). The Alabama and Tombigbee rivers, which come together to form the Mobile River, and the Tensaw River flow into Mobile Bay, an arm of the Gulf of Mexico. The Mobile River, which has its source in Tickanetley Creek, Georgia, has a total length of 774 mi (1,246 km) and is the twentieth longest river in the country.

About 450 million years ago, Alabama was covered by a warm, shallow sea. Over millions of years, heavy rains washed gravel, sand, and clay from higher elevations onto the rock floor of the sea to help form the foundation of modern Alabama. The skeletons and shells of sea animals, composed of limy material from rocks that had been worn away by water, settled into great thicknesses of limestone and dolomite. Numerous caves and sinkholes formed as water slowly eroded the limestone subsurface of northern Alabama. Archaeologists believe that Russell Cave, in northeastern Alabama, was the earliest site of human habitation in the southeastern US. Other major caves in northern Alabama are Manitou and Sequoyah; near Childersburg is DeSoto Caverns, a huge onyx cave once considered a sacred place by Creek Indians.

Wheeler Dam on the Tennessee River is now a national historic monument. Other major dams include Guntersville, Martin, Millers Ferry, Jordan, Mitchell, and Holt.

3 CLIMATE

Alabama's three climatic divisions are the lower coastal plain, largely subtropical and strongly influenced by the Gulf of Mexico; the northern plateau, marked by occasional snowfall in winter; and the Black Belt and upper coastal plain, lying between the two extremes. Among the major population centers, Birmingham has an annual average temperature of 63°F (17°C), with an average July daily maximum of 90°F (32°C) and a normal January daily minimum of 33°F (1°C). Montgomery has an annual average of 65°F (18°C), with a normal July daily average maximum of 92°F (33°C) and a normal January daily minimum of 37°F (2°C). The average in Mobile is 67°F (19°C), with a normal July daily maximum of 91°F (33°C) and a normal January daily minimum of 41°F (5°C). The record low temperature for the state is -27°F (-33°C), registered at New Market, in the northeastern corner, on 30 January 1966; the all-time high is 112°F (44°C), registered at Centerville, in the state's midsection, on 5 September 1925. Mobile, one of the rainiest cities in the United States, recorded an average precipitation of 66.3 in (168 cm) a year between 1971 and 2000.

Its location on the Gulf of Mexico leaves the coastal region open to the effects of hurricanes. In August 2005, Hurricane Katrina swept through the region, causing two deaths in Mobile, extensive flooding, and power outages for over 300,000 people.

4 FLORA AND FAUNA

Alabama was once covered by vast forests of pine, which still form the largest proportion of the state's forest growth. Alabama also has an abundance of poplar, cypress, hickory, oak, and various gum trees. Red cedar grows throughout the state; southern white cedar is found in the southwest, hemlock in the north. Other native trees include hackberry, ash, and holly, with species of palmetto and palm in the Gulf Coast region. There are more than 150 shrubs, mountain laurel and rhododendron among them. Cultivated plants include wisteria and camellia, the state flower.

In a state where large herds of bison, elk, bear, and deer once roamed, only the white-tailed deer remains abundant. Other mammals still found are the Florida panther, bobcat, beaver, muskrat, and most species of weasel. The fairly common raccoon, opossum, rabbit, squirrel, and red and gray foxes are also native, while nutria and armadillo have been introduced to the state. Alabama's birds include golden and bald eagles, osprey and various other hawks, yellowhammers or flickers (the state bird), and black and white warblers; game birds include quail, duck, wild turkey, and geese. Freshwater fish such as bream, shad, bass, and sucker

are common. Along the Gulf Coast there are seasonal runs of tarpon (the state fish), pompano, redfish, and bonito.

In April 2006, a total of 96 species occurring within the state were on the threatened and endangered species list of the US Fish and Wildlife Service. These included 79 animals, the Alabama beach mouse, gray bat, Alabama red-belly turtle, finback and humpback whales, bald eagle, and wood stork among them, and 17 plant species.

5 ENVIRONMENTAL PROTECTION

Under the 1982 Alabama Environmental Management Act, the Alabama Environmental Management Commission was created and the Alabama Department of Environmental Management (ADEM) was established. The ADEM absorbed several commissions, programs, and agencies that had been responsible for Alabama's environment.

The Environmental Management Commission, whose seven members are appointed to six-year terms by the governor and approved by the Alabama Senate, is charged with managing the state's land, air, and water resources. The ADEM administers all major federal environmental requirements including the Clean Air Act, Safe Drinking Water Act, and solid and hazardous waste laws. The most active environmental groups in the state are the Alabama Environmental Council, Sierra Club, League of Women Voters, Alabama Audubon Council, and Alabama Rivers Alliance.

Major concerns of environmentalists in the state are the improvement of land-use planning and the protection of groundwater. Another issue is the transportation, storage, and disposal of hazardous wastes. In 2003, the US Environmental Protection Agency (EPA) database listed 258 hazardous waste sites. As of 2006, 13 of these sites were on the National Priorities List; Alabama Plating Co. and Capitol City Plume were proposed sites. One of the nation's five largest commercial hazardous waste sites is in Emelle, in Sumter County. In 2005, the EPA allotted over $2.6 million through the Superfund program for the cleanup of hazardous waste sites in the state. Alabama's solid waste stream is about 4.500 million tons a year (1.10 tons per capita). There are 108 municipal landfills and 8 curbside recycling programs in the state. Air quality is generally satisfactory. But in 2003, 118.4 million lb of toxic chemicals were released by the state. In 2005, federal EPA grants awarded to the state included over $20 million for clean water projects.

6 POPULATION

Alabama ranked 23rd in population among the 50 states in 2005 with an estimated total of 4,557,808, an increase of 2.5% since 2000. Between 1990 and 2000, Alabama's population grew from 4,040,587 to 4,447,100, an increase of 10.1%. The population is projected to reach 4,663,111 by 2015 and 4,800,092 by 2025.

In 2004 the median age was 37. Persons under 18 years old accounted for 24.2% of the population, while 13.2% was age 65 or older.

Alabama experienced its greatest population growth between 1810 and 1820, following the defeat of the Creek Nation by General Andrew Jackson and his troops. Population in what is now Alabama boomed from 9,046 in 1810 to 127,901 in 1820, as migrants from older states on the eastern seaboard poured into the territory formerly occupied by the Creek Indians. Thousands of

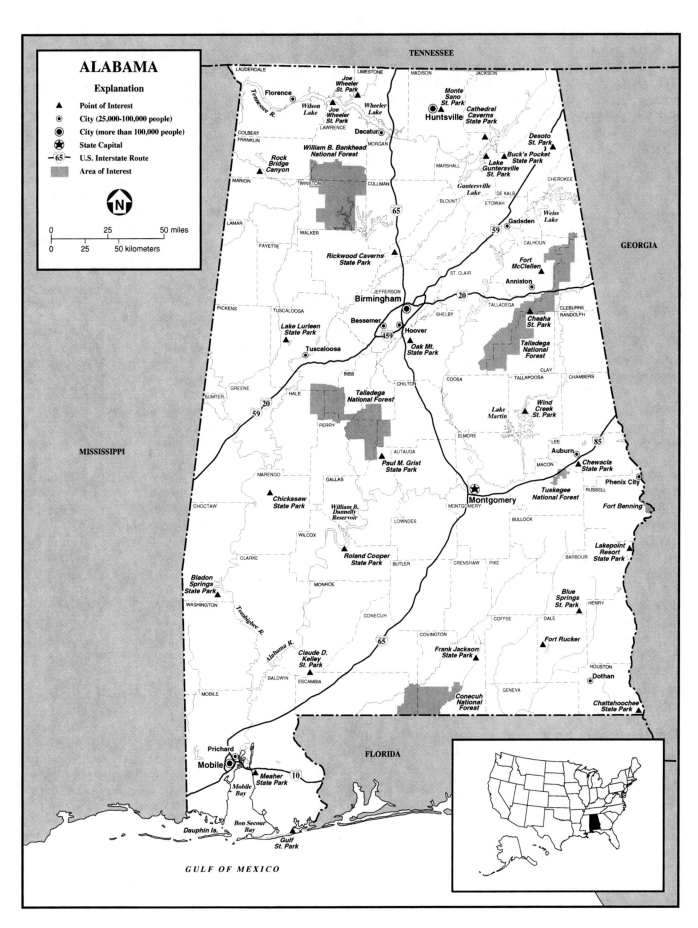

farmers, hoping to find fertile land or to become wealthy cotton planters, brought their families and often their slaves into the young state, more than doubling Alabama's population between 1820 and 1830. By 1860, Alabama had almost 1,000,000 residents, nearly one-half of whom were black slaves. The Civil War brought Alabama's population growth almost to a standstill, largely because of heavy losses on the battlefield. The total population gain between 1860 and 1870 was only about 30,000, whereas between 1870 and 1970, Alabama's population rose by 150,000–300,000 every decade. During the 1980s the population increased 148,000.

In 2004, Alabama had a population density of 89.3 persons per sq mi. First in size among Alabama's metropolitan areas comes greater Birmingham, which had an estimated 1,082,193 residents in July 2004. Other major metropolitan areas were Greater Mobile, 400,526; Greater Montgomery, 355,181; and Greater Huntsville, 362,459. The city of Birmingham proper was Alabama's largest city, with an estimated 233,149 residents in 2004; Montgomery had 200,983, and Mobile had 192,759.

7 ETHNIC GROUPS

Alabama's population is largely divided between whites of English and Scotch-Irish descent and blacks descended from African slaves. The 2000 census counted about 22,430 American Indians (up from 17,000 in 1990), or 0.5% of the total population, mostly of Creek or Cherokee descent. Creek Indians are centered around the small community of Poarch in southern Alabama; most of the Cherokee live in the northeastern part of the state, where the Cherokee reservation had 12,294 residents as of 2000. In 2004, 0.5% of Alabama's population was American Indian.

The black population of Alabama in 2000 numbered 1,155,930, or about 26% of the total population. In 2004, the black population of Alabama amounted to 26.4% of the total population. As before the Civil War, rural blacks are most heavily represented in the Black Belt of central Alabama.

In 2000, the Asian population totaled 31,346, or less than 1% of the total, and Pacific Islanders numbered 1,409; in the same year, the population of Hispanic or Latino descent totaled 75,830, up from 43,000 in 1990, an increase from 1% to 1.7% of the total population within the decade. In 2000, Alabama had 6,900 Asian Indians (up from 3,686 in 1990), 4,116 Koreans, and 6,337 Chinese (up from 3,529 in 1990). All told, the foreign born numbered 87,772 (2% of the state's population) in 2000, up from 1% 10 years earlier. Among persons reporting a single ancestry group, the leaders were Irish, 343,254 (down from 617,065 in 1990), and English, 344,735 (down from 479,499 in 1990). In 2004, 0.8% of the population of Alabama was Asian, 2.2% of the population was of Hispanic or Latino origin, and 0.9% of the population reported origins of two or more races.

Alabama's Cajuns, of uncertain racial origin (Anglo-Saxon, French, Spanish, Choctaw, Apache, and African elements may all be represented), are ethnically unrelated to the Cajuns of Louisiana. Thought to number around 10,000, they live primarily in the pine woods area of upper Mobile and lower Washington counties. Many Alabama Cajuns suffer from poverty, poor health, and malnutrition.

8 LANGUAGES

Four Indian tribes—the Creek, Chickasaw, Choctaw, and Cherokee—occupied the four quarters of Alabama as white settlement began, but by treaty agreement they were moved westward between 1814 and 1835, leaving behind such place-names as Alabama, Talladega, Mobile, and Tuscaloosa.

Alabama English is predominantly Southern, with a transition zone between it and a smaller area into which South Midland speech was taken across the border from Tennessee. Some features common to both dialects occur throughout the state, such as *croker sack* (burlap bag), *batter cakes* (made of cornmeal), harp (harmonica), and *snap beans*. In the major Southern speech region are found the decreasing loss of final /r/, the /boyd/ pronunciation of *bird*, *soft peach* (freestone), *press peach* (clingstone), *mosquito hawk* (dragonfly), *fire dogs* (andirons), and *gopher* (burrowing turtle). In the northern third of the state are found South Midland *arm* and *barb* rhyming with *form* and *orb*, *redworm* (earthworm), *peckerwood* (woodpecker), *snake doctor* and *snake feeder* (dragonfly), *tow sack* (burlap bag), *plum peach* (clingstone), *French harp* (harmonica), and *dog irons* (andirons).

Alabama has experienced only minor foreign immigration, and in 2000, 96.1% of all residents five years old or older spoke only English at home, a slight decrease over the 97.1% recorded in 1990.

The following table gives selected statistics from the 2000 Census for language spoken at home by persons five years old and over. The category "African languages" includes Amharic, Ibo, Twi, Yoruba, Bantu, Swahili, and Somali.

LANGUAGE	NUMBER	PERCENT
Population 5 years and over	**4,152,278**	**100.0**
Speak only English	3,989,795	96.1
Speak a language other than English	162,483	3.9
Speak a language other than English	**162,483**	**3.9**
Spanish or Spanish Creole	89,729	2.2
German	14,905	0.4
French (incl. Patois, Cajun)	13,656	0.3
Chinese	5,271	0.1
Vietnamese	4,561	0.1
Korean	4,029	0.1
Arabic	2,620	0.1
African languages	2,306	0.1
Japanese	2,201	0.1
Italian	2,158	0.1

9 RELIGIONS

Although predominantly Baptist today, Alabama was officially Roman Catholic throughout most of the 18th century, under French and Spanish rule. A century passed between the building of the first Catholic Church in 1702 and the earliest sustained efforts by Protestant evangelists. The first Baptist church in the state, the Flint River Church in Madison County, was organized in 1808; the following year, the Old Zion Methodist Church was founded in the Tombigbee area.

During the second decade of the 19th century, settlers from the southeastern states brought the influence of the Great Revival to Alabama, along with the various Methodist, Presbyterian, and Baptist sects that had developed in its wake. The first black church in Alabama probably dates from 1820. As in other southern states, black slaves who had previously attended the churches of their masters formed their own churches after the Civil War. One of the earliest of these, the Little Zion Methodist Church, was established in 1867 in Mobile. Most freed blacks became Baptists, however.

The vast majority of congregations in the state belong in the category of Evangelical Protestants. As of 2000, the Southern Baptist Convention was the fastest growing and the largest denomination within the state, with 1,380,121 adherents and 3,148 congregations, representing an increase of 83 congregations since 1990. In 2002, an additional 24,454 members joined the Southern Baptist Convention. In 2003, the United Methodist Church claimed 306,289 adherents with 1,505 congregations in all state conferences (which include some congregations in West Florida). In 2004, there were 140,365 Roman Catholics in the state. The Church of Christ had 119,049 adherents in 2000 and 895 congregations. The same year there were an estimated 9,100 Jews. About 45.2% of the population did not specify a religious affiliation.

The national headquarters of the Women's Missionary Union of the Southern Baptist Conference is located in Birmingham. The organization was founded in 1888 and is one of the largest Protestant women's mission organizations in the world, with about 1 million members.

¹⁰TRANSPORTATION

The first rail line in the state—the Tuscumbia Railroad, chartered in 1830—made its first run, 44 mi (71 km) around the Muscle Shoals from Tuscumbia to Decatur, on 15 December 1834. By 1852, however, Alabama had only 165 mi (266 km) of track, less than most other southern states. Further development awaited the end of the Civil War. Birmingham, as planned by John T. Milner, chief engineer of the South and North Railroad, was founded in 1871 as a railroad intersection in the midst of Alabama's booming mining country; it subsequently became the state's main rail center, followed by Mobile. As of 2003, Alabama had 3,735 total rail mi (6,013 km) of track, of which the state's five Class I railroads accounted for 2,900 rail mi (4,690 km). In that same year, coal accounted for the largest portion of all commodities (by weight) shipped by rail. As of 2006, Amtrak passenger service connected Birmingham, Anniston, and Tuscaloosa with Washington and New Orleans. Other passenger service included a route connecting Mobile with Jacksonville, Florida and New Orleans.

In settlement days the principal roads into Alabama were the Federal Road, formerly a Creek horse path, from Georgia and South Carolina; and the Natchez Trace, bought by the federal government (1801) from the Choctaw and Chickasaw, leading from Kentucky and Tennessee. Throughout most of the 19th century, road building was in the hands of private companies. Only after the establishment of a state highway department in 1911 and the securing of federal aid for rural road building in 1916 did Alabama begin to develop modern road systems.

As of 2004 there were 95,483 mi (151,778 km) of public streets, roads, and highways. In the same year, the state had 1.677 million registered automobiles, 2.778 million trucks of all types, and some 3,000 buses. There were 3.613 million licensed drivers in 2004. Most of the major interstate highways in Alabama intersect at Birmingham: I-65, running from the north to Montgomery and Mobile; and I-59 from the northeast and I-20 from the east, which, after merging at Birmingham, run southwestward to Tuscaloosa and into Mississippi. Route I-85 connects Montgomery with Atlanta; and I-10 connects Mobile with New Orleans and Tallahassee, FL.

The coming of the steamboat to Alabama waters, beginning in 1818, stimulated settlement in the Black Belt; however, the high price of shipping cotton by water contributed to the eventual displacement of the steamboat by the railroad. Thanks to the Tennessee Valley Authority, the Tennessee River has been transformed since the 1930s into a year-round navigable waterway, with three locks and dams in Alabama. The 234-mi (377-km), $2-billion Tennessee-Tombigbee project, which opened in 1985, provided a new barge route, partly through Alabama, from the Midwest to the Gulf of Mexico, for which the US Army Corps of Engineers cut a 39-mi (63-km) canal and built 10 locks and dams. This was not only the largest civilian engineering project in the United States during the early 1980s but also by far the largest earth-moving project in US history, displacing more earth than was moved to build the Panama Canal.

The Alabama-Coosa and Black Warrior–Tombigbee systems also have been made navigable by locks and dams. River barges are used to carry bulk cargoes. There are 1,270 mi (2,043 km) of navigable inland waterways and 50 mi (80 km) of Gulf coast. The only deepwater port is Mobile, with a large oceangoing trade. As of 2004, Mobile was the 11th-busiest port in the United States, handling a total of 56.211 million tons. Total waterborne tonnage for the state in 2003 was 72.65 million tons. The Alabama State Docks also operates a system of 10 inland docks; and there are several privately run inland docks.

In 2005, Alabama had a total of 277 public and private-use aviation-related facilities. This included 182 airports, 90 heliports, one STOLport (Short Take-Off and Landing), and four seaplane bases. The state's largest and busiest airport is Birmingham International Airport. In 2004, the airport had 1,498,651 enplanements.

¹¹HISTORY

The region now known as Alabama has been inhabited for some 9,000–10,000 years. The earliest evidence of human habitation, charcoal from an ancient campfire at Russell Cave in northeastern Alabama, is about 9,000 years old. These early peoples, probably descended from humans who crossed from Asia to North America via the Bering Strait, moved from caves and open campsites to permanent villages about AD 1000. Some of their descendants, popularly called Mound Builders, erected huge earthen temple mounds and simple huts along Alabama's rivers, beginning around 1100. Moundville (near Tuscaloosa), one of the most important Mound Builder sites in the southeastern US, includes 20 "platform mounds" for Indian buildings, dating from 1200 to 1500. When the first Europeans arrived, Alabama was inhabited by Indians, half of them either Creek or members of smaller groups living within the Creek confederacy. The Creeks resided in central and eastern Alabama; Cherokee Indians inhabited northeastern Alabama, the Chickasaws lived in the northwest, and the Choctaws settled in the southwest.

During the 16th century, five Spanish expeditions entered Mobile Bay or explored the region now called Alabama. The most extensive was that of Hernando de Soto, whose army marched from the Tennessee Valley to the Mobile Delta in 1540. In 1702, two French naval officers—Pierre Le Moyne, Sieur d'Iberville; and Jean Baptiste Le Moyne, Sieur de Bienville—established Ft. Louis de la Mobile, the first permanent European settlement in present-day Alabama. Mobile remained in French hands until 1763, when it was turned over to the British under the terms of the Treaty of Paris. Because a British garrison held Mobile during the American Revolution, that city was captured in 1780 by the forces of Spain, an ally of the rebellious American colonists. In 1803, the United States claimed the city as part of the Louisiana Purchase, but in vain. Spanish control of Mobile lasted until the city was again seized during the War of 1812, this time by American troops in 1813. West Florida, including Mobile, was the only territory added to the United States as a result of that war.

At the start of the 19th century, Indians still held most of present-day Alabama. War broke out in 1813 between American settlers and a Creek faction known as the Red Sticks, who were determined to resist white encroachment. After General Andrew Jackson and his Tennessee militia crushed the Red Sticks in 1814 at the Battle of Horseshoe Bend in central Alabama, he forced the Creek to sign a treaty ceding some 40,000 sq mi (103,600 sq km) of land to the United States, thereby opening about three-fourths of the present state to white settlement. By 1839, nearly all Alabama Indians had been removed to Indian Territory.

From 1814 onward, pioneers, caught up by what was called "Alabama fever," poured out of the Carolinas, Virginia, Georgia, Tennessee, and Kentucky into what Andrew Jackson called "the best unsettled country in America." Wealthy migrants came in covered wagons, bringing their slaves, cattle, and hogs. But the great majority of pioneers were ambitious farmers who moved to the newly opened area in hopes of acquiring fertile land on which to grow cotton. Cotton's profitability had increased enormously with the invention of the cotton gin. In 1817, Alabama became a territory; on 2 August 1819, a state constitution was adopted; and on the following 14 December, Alabama was admitted to statehood. Alabama, then as now, was sparsely populated. In 1819, its residents comprised 1.3% of the US population. That percentage had grown to only 2% in 1980, but by 2004, the percentage had increased to 6.5%.

During the antebellum era, 95% of white Alabamians lived and worked in rural areas, primarily as farmers. Although "Cotton was king" in 19th-century Alabama, farmers also grew corn, sorghum, oats, and vegetables, as well as razorback hogs and cattle. By 1860, 80% of Alabama farmers owned the land they tilled. Only about 33% of all white Alabamians were slave owners. Whereas in 1820 there were 85,451 free whites and 41,879 slaves, by 1860 the number of slaves had increased to 435,080, constituting 45% of the state population. Large planters (owners of 50 slaves or more) made up less than 1% of Alabama's white population in 1860. However, they owned 28% of the state's total wealth and occupied 25% of the seats in the legislature. Although the preponderance of the wealth and the population in Alabama was located in the north, the success of Black Belt plantation owners at forging coalitions with industrialists enabled planters to dominate state politics both before and after the Civil War. The planters led the secessionist movement, and most other farmers, fearing the consequences of an end to slavery, eventually followed suit. However, 2,500 white Alabamians served in the Union Army and an estimated 8,000–10,000 others acted as Union scouts, deserted Confederate units, or hid from conscription agents.

Alabama seceded from the Union in January 1861 and shortly thereafter joined the Confederate States of America. The Confederacy was organized in Alabama's Senate chamber in Montgomery, and Jefferson Davis was inaugurated president on the steps of the capitol. Montgomery served as capital of the Confederacy until May, when the seat of government was moved to Richmond, VA.

Remote from major theaters of war, Alabama experienced only occasional Union raids during the first three years of the conflict. In the summer of 1864, however, Confederate and Union ships fought a major naval engagement in Mobile Bay, which ended in surrender by the outnumbered southern forces. During the Confederacy's dying days in the spring of 1865, federal troops swept through Tuscaloosa, Selma, and Montgomery. Their major goal, Selma, one of the Confederacy's main industrial centers, was left almost as heavily devastated as Richmond or Atlanta. Estimates of the number of Alabamians killed in the Civil War range from 25,000 upward.

During Reconstruction, Alabama was under military rule until it was readmitted to the Union in 1868. For the next six years, Republicans held most top political positions in the state. With the help of the Ku Klux Klan, Democrats regained political control of the state in November 1874.

Cotton remained the foundation of the Alabama economy in the late 19th and early 20th centuries. However, with the abolition of slavery it was now raised by sharecroppers—white and black landless farmers who paid for the land they rented from planters with the cotton they harvested. Alabama also attempted to create a "New South" in which agriculture would be balanced by industry. In the 1880s and 1890s, at least 20 Alabama towns were touted as ironworking centers. Birmingham, founded in 1871, became the New South's leading industrial center. Its promoters invested in pig iron furnaces, coal mines, steel plants, and real estate. Small companies merged with bigger ones, which were taken over, in turn, by giant corporations. In 1907, Birmingham's Tennessee Coal, Iron, and Railroad Co. was purchased by the nation's largest steelmaker, US Steel.

Another major Alabama enterprise was cotton milling. By 1900, 9,000 men, women, and children were employed in Alabama mills; most of these white workers were farm folk who had lost their land after the Civil War because of mounting debts and low cotton prices. Wages in mills were so low that entire families had to work hours as long as those they had endured as farmers.

The rise in the rate of farm tenancy produced a corresponding increase in social and political unrest. Discontented farmers and factory workers allied during the 1890s in the Populist Party in an attempt to overthrow the Bourbon Democrats, who had dominated Alabama politics for two decades. Although a number of Populists were elected to the Alabama legislature, no Populist candidate succeeded in winning the governorship, primarily because Democrats manipulated the black vote to their own advantage. In 1901, Alabama adopted a new state constitution containing numerous restrictions on voting, supposedly to end vote manipulation and restore honest elections. The tangible result of these new rules was to disenfranchise almost all Alabama black voters and thousands of poor whites. For example, the total number of blacks registered in 14 counties fell from 78,311 in 1900 to 1,081 in 1903. As recently as 1941, fewer than 25% of Alabama adults were registered voters. In 1960, no blacks voted in Lowndes or Wilcox counties, which were 80% and 78% black, respectively.

As one of the poorest states in the country, Alabama benefited disproportionately from the New Deal. Yet, like other southern states, Alabama viewed the expansion of the national government's role with mixed feelings. Alabamians embraced federal aid, even lobbying for military bases, while seeing federal power as a threat to the "southern way of life," which included racial segregation.

During the 1950s and 1960s, national attention focused on civil rights demonstrations in Alabama, including the Montgomery bus boycott of 1955, the Birmingham and University of Alabama demonstrations of 1963, and the voting rights march from Selma to Montgomery in 1965. The primary antagonists were Dr. Martin Luther King Jr., head of the Southern Christian Leadership Conference, and Governor George C. Wallace, an opponent of integration. These black protests and the sometimes violent reactions to them, such as the 1963 bombing of a church in Birmingham in which four young black girls—Denise McNair, Cynthia Wesley, Carole Rosamond Robertson, and Addie Mae Collins—were killed, helped influence the US Congress to pass the Civil Rights Act of 1964 and the Voting Rights Act of 1965. Four former Ku Klux Klansmen were suspects in the church bombing: Robert E. Chambliss, Bobby Frank Cherry, Herman Frank Cash, and Thomas E. Blanton Jr. In 1977, Robert Chambliss was convicted of the murders and was sentenced to a life term. He died in prison in 1985. Suspect Herman Cash died in 1994, without having been charged of the crime. Blanton and Cherry were indicted on four counts each of first-degree and reckless murder in 2000. Cherry was subsequently ruled mentally incompetent to stand trial, but Blanton was convicted of four counts of first-degree murder in 2001, and sentenced to four life terms. Cherry was later deemed competent to stand trial, and in 2002, he was convicted and sentenced to an automatic life term in prison. Cherry died in 2004.

Once the most tightly segregated city in the nation, Birmingham has become thoroughly integrated in public facilities, and in 1979 the city elected its first black mayor, Richard Arrington. The civil rights era brought other momentous changes to Alabama. Hundreds of thousands of black voters are now an important force in state politics. Blacks attend school, colleges, and universities of their choice and enjoy equal access to all public facilities. On the whole, new racial attitudes among most whites have contributed to a vast improvement in the climate of race relations since 1960. Indeed, a significant amount of black support contributed to Wallace's election to a fourth term as governor in 1982. When he died in September 1998 he was given a full state funeral and his family received condolences from black leaders. In 1984 there were 314 black elected officials, including 25 mayors, 19 lawmakers in the Alabama state legislature, and an associate justice of the state supreme court. In 1990, 704 blacks held elective office, and by 2001, the number had increased to 756.

In many respects Alabama has resisted change more successfully than any other state in the Deep South. The state's tax system remains the most regressive in the country. In 1982, the state legislature passed a law prohibiting taxation at market value of land owned by timber companies (timber comprises the state's largest industry). Alabama does not use property taxes to fund schools; instead, public education revenue is derived principally from state income tax (54.6% in 2004) and sales tax (31.9% in 2004). In the late 1990s, the state worked to increase teachers' salaries and bring other measures in line with national education statistics. Alabama has had one of the highest infant mortality rates in the nation, owing in part to widespread poverty. (Alabama and West Virginia were tied for 43rd out of the 50 states in terms of general health and health care in 2004.) Though Alabama's poverty rate steadily declined during the last decades of the 1900s, it remained among the nation's poorer states. In 1969, 25.4% of Alabamians lived below federal poverty levels. By 1989 the figure dropped to 18.3%, and in 1998, it decreased to an estimated 15%, which was still the 13th-highest rate in the nation. By the end of the millennium, 16% of Alabamians lived in poverty, compared to 12.4% of the US population. Alabama is the only state to tax residents earning less than $5,000 a year. The poorest families in the state pay about 11% of their earnings in income, sales, and other local taxes.

A strange turn of events in 1986 resulted in the election of the first Republican governor since Reconstruction. The Democratic candidate, state attorney general Charles Graddick, was stripped of his party's nomination by a federal panel because of crossover Republican voting in the Democratic primary. His replacement, Lieutenant Governor Bill Baxley, lost the election to a little-known pro-business Republican and former Baptist preacher, Guy Hunt. Hunt was reelected in 1990 but was confronted early in his second term with accusations of financial misdeeds, including personal use of official resources and mismanagement of public funds. In 1992, Hunt was indicted on 13 separate felony counts. The following year, he was found guilty of fraud and conspiracy charges and forced to resign the governorship, becoming the fourth governor in the nation's history to be convicted of criminal charges while in office.

In 1999, Alabama received the second largest surplus in the history of the state; the $57 million budget surplus was credited to tight controls over agency spending. In 2003, the state had a $675 million budget deficit, and Governor Bob Riley proposed a $1.2 billion tax increase, raising individual and corporate taxes by $461 million and local and state property taxes by $465 million. In a September 2003 referendum, Alabama voters rejected Riley's tax increase; only 33% of voters cast their ballots in favor of the plan.

Alabama was severely affected by Hurricane Katrina in August 2005. An original six Alabama counties (Baldwin, Mobile, Washington, Clarke, Choctaw, and Sumter) were declared by President George W. Bush to be federal disaster areas. Later, President Bush approved Governor Riley's request to add more Alabama counties to the federal disaster relief list: residents of Greene, Hale, Pickens, and Tuscaloosa were deemed eligible for individual assistance, and Hale, Jefferson, Marengo, and Tuscaloosa counties were deemed eligible for infrastructure assistance due to storm damage.

12 STATE GOVERNMENT

Alabama has had six constitutions, the most recent one dating from 1901. By January 2005 that document had been amended 766 times. In 2002, amid calls for a constitutional convention, voters approved a constitutional amendment providing that no constitution could be adopted without voter approval.

Alabama's bicameral legislature consists of a 35-seat Senate and a 105-seat House of Representatives, all of whose members are elected at the same time for four-year terms. Legislative sessions are held each year, convening on the second Tuesday in January in general election years, on the first Tuesday in March in years following general election years, and on the first Tuesday in February all other years. (There is a legal provision for an organizational session prior to the stated convening date—on the second Tuesday in January for ten calendar days in the year following a general election.) Session length is limited to 30 legislative days in 105 calendar days. Only the governor may call special sessions, which are limited to 12 legislative days in 30 calendar days. Senators must be at least 25 years old; representatives, 21. Legislators must have resided in the state for at least three years before election and in the district forat least one year. Under federal pressure, in 1983 the legislature approved a reapportionment plan, effective in 1986, that was expected to increase black representation. In 2004, Alabama's legislators received a per diem salary of $10 during regular sessions; each member was also paid $50 per diem for the performance of his or her duties as a member of any authorized interim legislative committee or subcommittee, and $75 for attendance for any other legislative business. Legislators in 2004 received living expenses in the amount of $2,280 per month plus $50 per day for the three days per week that the legislature actually meets. Legislators' terms of office begin on the day after election and expire on the day after election four years later.

State elected officials are the governor and lieutenant governor (separately elected), secretary of state, attorney general, treasurer, auditor, and commissioner of agriculture and industries. The governor, who serves for four years, must be at least thirty years old and must have been a US citizen for ten years and a citizen of the state for seven. The governor is limited to a maximum of two consecutive terms. As of December 2004, Alabama's governor earned a salary of $96,361, and was entitled to reimbursement of travel expenses.

A bill becomes a law when it is passed by at least a majority of a quorum of both houses and is either signed by the governor, left unsigned for six days (Sundays excluded) while the legislature is in session, or passed over the governor's veto by a majority of the elected members of each house. A bill must pass both houses in the same form. The governor may pocket veto a measure submitted fewer than five days before adjournment by not signing it within 10 days after adjournment. The governor may amend one or more provisions of any bill, but the legislature may override them by a majority vote. The governor does not have the line-item veto.

The submission of a constitutional amendment to the electorate requires the approval of three-fifths of the membership of each house, but such amendments can also be adopted by constitutional convention. Amendments are ratified by a majority vote of the electorate.

Voters in Alabama must be US citizens, state and county citizens, and at least 18 years old. Restrictions apply to convicted felons and those declared mentally incompetent by the court.

[13] POLITICAL PARTIES

The major political parties in Alabama are the Democratic and Republican parties, each affiliated with the national party organization. The Republicans are weak below the federal-office level.

Pre–Civil War political divisions in the state reflected those found elsewhere in the South. Small and subsistence farmers, especially in the northern hill country and pine forest areas, tended to be Jacksonian Democrats, while the planters of the Black Belt and the river valleys often voted Whig. After a period of Radical Republican rule during Reconstruction, the Bourbon Democrats, whose party then served largely the interests of wealthy proper-

Alabama Presidential Vote by Political Parties, 1948–2004

YEAR	ELECTORAL VOTE	ALABAMA WINNER	DEMOCRAT	REPUBLICAN	STATES' RIGHTS DEMOCRAT	PROHIBITION	PROGRESSIVE
1948	11	Thurmond (SRD)	—	40,930	171,443	1,026	1,522
1952	11	Stevenson (D)	275,075	149,231	—	1,814	
					UNPLEDGED		
1956	11	Stevenson (D)	279,542	195,694	20,323	—	—
					NAT'L STATES' RIGHTS		
1960	11	*Kennedy (D)	318,303	236,110	4,367	—	—
					UNPLEDGED DEMOCRAT		
1964	10	Goldwater (R)	—	479,085	210,782	—	—
					AMERICAN IND.	AM. IND. DEMOCRAT	
1968	10	Wallace (AI)	195,918	146,591	687,664	3,814	10,518
					AMERICAN		
1972	9	*Nixon (R)	256,923	728,701	11,928	8,559	—
					AMERICAN IND.		COMMUNIST
1976	9	*Carter (D)	659,170	504,070	9,198	6,669	1,954
1980	9	*Reagan (R)	636,730	654,192	—	—	—
					LIBERTARIAN		
1984	9	*Reagan (R)	551,899	872,849	9,504	—	—
1988	9	*Bush (R)	549,506	815,576	8,460	3,311	—
							IND. (Perot)
1992	9	Bush (R)	690,080	804,283	5,737	2,161	183,109
1996	9	Dole (R)	662,165	769,044	5,290	—	92,149
						IND. (Buchanan)	IND. (Nader)
2000	9	*Bush, G. W. (R)	692,611	941,173	5,893	6,351	18,323
					IND. (Badnarik)	IND. (Peroutka)	
2004	9	*Bush, G. W. (R)	693,933	1,176,394	3,529	1,994	6,701

*Won US presidential election.

ty owners, business people, and white supremacists, ran the state for the rest of the century, despite a challenge in the 1890s by the Populist Party.

On two occasions, 1948 and 1964, the Alabama Democratic Party bolted the national Democratic ticket, each time because of disagreement over civil rights. Barry Goldwater in 1964 was the first Republican presidential candidate in the 20th century to carry Alabama. In 1968, George Wallace carried Alabama overwhelmingly on the American Independent Party slate.

In the 2004 presidential elections, incumbent president Republican George W. Bush carried the state, winning 62.5% of the vote to Democrat John Kerry's 36.8%. Bush increased his margin of victory in 2004; in 2000, Bush won 57% of the vote to Democrat Al Gore's 42%. In 2004 there were 2,597,000 registered voters; there is no party registration. The state had nine electoral votes in the 2004 presidential election. US Senator Richard Shelby was reelected as a Democrat in 1992, but switched his affiliation to Republican on 9 November 1994, the day after the Republicans swept into power in the Senate. He was reelected in 1998 and in 2004, when he won 67.5% of the vote. In 1996 Democratic Senator Howell Heflin retired, and his seat was won by Republican Jeff B. Sessions. Sessions was reelected in 2002. Alabama's delegation of US Representatives following the 2004 elections consisted of two Democrats and five Republicans.

During the 20th century, the Democratic Party commanded virtually every statewide office, major and minor. Democrat James Folsom was elected Lieutenant Governor in 1990 and became governor in April of 1993 when Governor Guy Hunt was convicted of illegally using money from his inauguration for personal expenses. Folsom lost his election bid for governor to Fob James Jr. in 1994. James had served as governor of the state from 1979 to 1983 as a Democrat, but he switched party affiliations for the 1994 election and upset Folsom in a narrow victory. In the 1998 election Democrat Don Siegelman was elected to the governor's office. In 2002, Republican Bob Riley was elected governor, after serving six years in the US House of Representatives. The Alabama legislature in 2005 consisted of 25 Democrats and 10 Republicans in the Senate and 63 Democrats and 42 Republicans in the House.

14 LOCAL GOVERNMENT

In 2005, Alabama had 67 counties, 451 municipalities, and 128 public school districts. There were 525 special districts, including the Northeast Mississippi–Northwest Alabama Railroad Authority, the Alabama Housing Finance Authority, and the Alabama Highway Authority. Counties are governed by county commissions, usually consisting of three to seven commissioners, elected by district. Other county officials include judges of probate, clerk, tax assessor and collector, sheriff, and superintendent of education. The oldest county in the state is Washington, established in 1800. The newest county, Houston, was established in 1903.

Mayor-council is the most common form of municipal government. But until the late 1970s, the predominant form of municipal government, especially in the larger cities, was the commission, whose members are elected either at-large or by district. Partly in response to court orders requiring district elections in order to permit the election of more black officials, after the 1970s there was a trend toward the mayor-council form, although the US Supreme Court ruled in May 1980 that Mobile may elect its public officials at-large. Elections for municipal officers are held every four years.

An alteration in local government had a significant effect on the racial climate in Birmingham during the 1960s, when the Young Men's Business Club led a movement to change to the mayor-council system, in order to oust a commission (including Eugene "Bull" Connor as public safety commissioner) that for nearly a decade had reacted negatively to every black demand. After a narrow vote in favor of the change, a moderate was elected mayor in April 1963, but the former commissioners then contested the initial vote that had changed the system. At the height of Birmingham's racial troubles, both the former commissioners and the newly elected council claimed to govern Birmingham, but neither did so effectively. When peace came, it was as the result of an unofficial meeting held between local black leaders and 77 of the city's most influential whites, with federal officials serving as mediators. Although the council, like the commissioners, publicly opposed these negotiations, once they were over and the council's election confirmed, the new moderate leadership permitted peaceful racial accommodation to go forward. In addition to the mayor-council and commission forms of administration, some municipalities employ city managers.

In 2005, local government accounted for about 188,349 full-time (or equivalent) employment positions.

15 STATE SERVICES

To address the continuing threat of terrorism and to work with the federal Department of Homeland Security, homeland security in Alabama operates under the authority of state statute. The state Director of Homeland Security is designated as the state homeland security adviser.

Alabama's Ethics Commission administers the state's ethics law, makes financial disclosure records available to the public, and receives monthly reports from lobbyists. Educational services are administered primarily by the Department of Education and the Alabama Commission on Higher Education. The Alabama Public Library Service supports and promotes the development of public libraries. The Department of Aeronautics, Department of Transportation, and Public Service Commission (PSC) administer transportation services; the PSC supervises, regulates, and controls all transportation companies doing business in the state. Driver's licenses are issued by the Department of Public Safety.

Health and welfare services are offered primarily through the Department of Public Health, Department of Mental Health and Mental Retardation, Department of Veterans Affairs, Department of Youth Services, and Department of Senior Services. Planning for the state's future health-care needs is carried out by the Health Planning and Development Agency.

Public protection services are administered by the Military Department, Department of Corrections, and Department of Public Safety, among other agencies. Numerous government bodies offer resource protection services: the Department of Conservation and Natural Resources, Department of Environmental Management, Alabama Forestry Commission, Oil and Gas Board, Surface Mining Commission, and Soil and Water Conservation Committee.

¹⁶JUDICIAL SYSTEM

The Alabama Supreme Court is the highest court in the state, consisting of a chief justice and eight associate justices, all elected for staggered six-year terms. It issues opinions on constitutional issues and hears cases appealed from the lower courts. The court of civil appeals has exclusive appellate jurisdiction in all suits involving sums up to $10,000. Its three judges are elected for six-year terms, and the one who has served the longest is the presiding judge. The five judges of the court of criminal appeals are also elected for six-year terms; they choose the presiding judge by majority vote.

Circuit courts, which encompassed 131 judgeships in 1999, have exclusive original jurisdiction over civil actions involving sums of more than $5,000, and over criminal prosecutions involving felony offenses. They also have original jurisdiction, concurrent with the district courts, in all civil matters exceeding $500. They have appellate jurisdiction over most cases from district and municipal courts. A system of district courts staffed by judges who serve six-year terms replaced county and juvenile courts as of January 1977. Municipal court judges are appointed by the municipality.

As of 31 December 2004, a total of 25,887 prisoners were held in Alabama's state and federal prisons, a decrease (from 27,913) of 7.3% from the previous year. As of year-end 2004, a total of 1,748 inmates were female, down 12.7% (from 2,003) the year before. Among sentenced prisoners (one year or more), Alabama had an incarceration rate of 556 per 100,000 population.

According to the Federal Bureau of Investigation, Alabama in 2004 had a violent crime rate (murder/nonnegligent manslaughter; forcible rape; robbery; aggravated assault) of 426.6 reported incidents per 100,000 population, or a total of 19,324 reported incidents. Crimes against property (burglary; larceny/theft; and motor vehicle theft) in that same year totaled 182,340 reported incidents or 4,025 reported incidents per 100,000 people. Alabama has a death penalty, which can be carried out by lethal injection or electrocution, depending upon the prisoner's request. From 1976 through May 2006, the state executed 34 persons; there were four executions in 2005. There were no executions from January to April 2006. As of 1 January 2006, there were 190 inmates on death row.

In 2003, Alabama spent $261,678,684 on homeland security, an average of $57 per state resident.

¹⁷ARMED FORCES

The US Department of Defense had 11,845 active military personnel in Alabama in 2004, and civilian personnel numbered 15,789. The major installation in terms of expenditures was the US Army's Redstone Arsenal at Huntsville. Redstone is the center of the Army's missile and rocket programs and contains the George C. Marshall Space Flight Center of the National Aeronautics and Space Administration, which directs all private contractors for the space program. Among the spacecraft developed there were the Redstone rocket, which launched the first US astronaut; *Explorer I*, the first US earth-orbiting satellite; and the Saturn rocket, which boosted the Apollo missions to the moon. In 2004, Redstone had 8,753 civilian employees, the highest number in the state. Other installations include Ft. Rucker (near Enterprise); the Anniston Army Depot; Maxwell Air Force Base (Montgomery), site of the US Air University and Air War Colleges, and national headquar-

ters for the Civil Air Patrol; and Gunter Air Force Base (also in Montgomery). The most military personnel in the state, 5,801, were stationed at Ft. Rucker (Army) in 2004. Reserve and National Guard numbered 4,577. During 2004, Alabama firms received defense contract awards totaling over $5.8 billion. That year the Defense Department payroll was about $3.2 billion, including retired military pay.

There were 426,322 veterans of US military service in Alabama as of 2003, of whom 50,383 served in World War II; 47,411 in the Korean conflict; 124,673 during the Vietnam era; and 71,523 in the Gulf War. In 2004, the Veterans Administration expended more than $1.3 billion in pensions, medical assistance, and other major veterans' benefits.

As of 31 October 2004, the Alabama Department of Public Safety employed 680 full-time sworn officers.

¹⁸MIGRATION

After 1814, Alabama was the mecca of a great migratory wave, mainly of whites of English and Scotch-Irish descent (some with their black slaves) from Virginia, Georgia, and the Carolinas. Since the Civil War, migration to Alabama has been slight. Many blacks left Alabama from World War I (1914–18) through the 1960s to seek employment in the East and Midwest, and the proportion of blacks in Alabama's population fell from 35% in 1940 to 26% in 1998, where it remained through mid-2002. Overall, Alabama may have lost as many as 944,000 residents through migration between 1940 and 1970, but enjoyed a net gain from migration of over 143,000 between 1970 and 1990, and an additional 114,000 in domestic and 13,000 in international migration between 1990 and 1998. In the period 2000–05, net international migration was 25,936 and net internal was 10,521, for a net gain of 36,457 people.

¹⁹INTERGOVERNMENTAL COOPERATION

Among the interstate compacts and commissions in which Alabama participates are the Gulf States Marine Fisheries Commission, Interstate Mining Compact Commission, Interstate Oil and Gas Compact, Southeastern Forest Fire Protection Compact, Southern Growth Policies Board, Southern Regional Education Board, Historic Chattahoochee Compact, and the Tennessee-Tombigbee Waterway Development Authority. In 1997, the state began two new water resources projects: the Alabama-Coosa-Tallapoosa (ACT) River Basin Compact between Alabama and Georgia, and the Apalachicola-Chattahoochee-Flint (ACF) River Basin Compact among Alabama, Florida, and Georgia. The Office of State Planning and Federal Programs coordinates planning efforts by all levels of government. During fiscal year 2005, Alabama received federal grants amounting to $5.22 billion. For fiscal year 2006, federal grants to Alabama were estimated at $5.205 billion, and for fiscal year 2007, at $5.383 billion.

²⁰ECONOMY

Cotton dominated Alabama's economy from the mid-1800s to the 1870s, when large-scale industrialization began. The coal, iron, and steel industries were the first to develop, followed by other resource industries such as textiles, clothing, paper, and wood products. Although Alabama's prosperity has increased, particularly in recent decades, the state still lags in wage rates and per capita income. One factor that has hindered the growth of the state's economy is declining investment in resource industries owned by large corporations outside the state. Between 1974 and 1983, manufacturing grew at little more than half the rate of all state goods and services. Industries such as primary metals and apparel, once mainstays of Alabama's economy, were clearly losing importance.

In 2004, Alabama's gross state product (GSP) was $139.8 billion, of which manufacturing (durable and nondurable goods) accounted for $23.4 billion or 16.7% of GSP, followed by real estate, rental, and leasing at $14.3 billion or 10.2% of GSP, and health care and social assistance at $9.668 billion or 6.9% of GSP. As Alabama's traditional industries have declined, the role played by small business as an engine for economic growth has increased. As of 2004, of the 86,651 businesses that had employees, an estimated 84,277 or 97.3% were small businesses. However, new business creation did not offset business terminations that year. While an estimated 9,413 new employer businesses were created in 2004, up 4.4% from 2003, business terminations that same year totaled 10,104. There were 325 business bankruptcies in 2004, up 13.2% from the previous year. In 2005, Alabama had one of the nation's highest overall personal bankruptcy filings rates, at 939 (Chapter 7 and Chapter 13) per 100,000 people, ranking the state at number two, behind Tennessee.

21 INCOME

In 2005 Alabama had a gross state product (GSP) of $150 billion which accounted for 1.2% of the nation's gross domestic product and placed the state at number 25 in highest GSP among the 50 states and the District of Columbia.

According to the Bureau of Economic Analysis, in 2004 Alabama had a per capita personal income (PCPI) of $27,695. This ranked 41st in the United States and was 84% of the national average of $33,050. The 1994–2004 average annual growth rate of PCPI was 4.1%. Total personal income (TPI) was $125,329,964,000, which ranked 24th in the United States and represented an increase of 5.7% from 2003, compared to a national change of 6.0%. The 1994–2004 average annual growth rate of TPI was 4.7%. Earnings of persons employed in Alabama increased from $87,574,951,000 in 2003 to $93,039,492,000 in 2004, an increase of 6.2%. The 2003–04 national change was 6.3%.

The US Census Bureau reports that the three-year average median household income for 2002 to 2004 in 2004 dollars was $38,111, compared to a national average of $44,473. During the same period an estimated 15.5% of the population was living below the poverty line, as compared to 12.4% nationwide.

22 LABOR

According to the Bureau of Labor Statistics (BLS), in April 2006 the seasonally adjusted civilian labor force in Alabama numbered 2,173,500, with approximately 78,500 workers unemployed, yielding an unemployment rate of 3.6%, compared to the national average of 4.7% for the same period. Preliminary data for the same period placed nonfarm employment at 1,975,700. Since the beginning of the BLS data series in 1976, the highest unemployment rate recorded in Alabama was 14.4% in December 1982. The historical low was 3.3% in March 2006. Preliminary nonfarm employment data by occupation for April 2006 showed that approximately 5.6% of the labor force was employed in construction;

19.4% in trade, transportation, and public utilities; 4.9% in financial activities; 10.9% in professional and business services; 10.3% in education and health services; 8.5% in leisure and hospitality services; and 18.4% in government. Data for manufacturing was not available.

In 1871, James Thomas Rapier, a black Alabamian who would later serve a term as a US representative from the state, organized the first black labor union in the South, the short-lived Labor Union of Alabama. The Knights of Labor began organizing in the state in 1882. A serious obstacle to unionization and collective bargaining was the convict leasing system, which was not ended officially until 1923, and in practice, not until five years later. In 1888, the Tennessee Coal, Iron, and Railroad Co. (later taken over by US Steel) was granted an exclusive 10-year contract to use the labor of all state convicts, paying the state $9–18 per person per month.

Child labor was also exploited. Alabama had limited a child's working day to eight hours in 1887, but a Massachusetts company that was building a large mill in the state secured the repeal of that law in 1895. A weaker measure passed 12 years later limited a child's workweek to 60 hours and set the minimum working age at 12.

The US Department of Labor's Bureau of Labor Statistics reported that in 2005, a total of 195,000 of Alabama's 1,909,000 employed wage and salary workers were formal members of a union. This represented 10.2% of those so employed, up from 9.7% in 2004, but below the national average of 12%. Overall in 2005, a total of 223,000 workers (11.7%) in Alabama were covered by a union or employee association contract, which includes those workers who reported no union affiliation. Alabama is one of 22 states with a right-to-work law. Unions were especially strong in the northern industrial cities and in Mobile.

As of 1 March 2006, Alabama did not have a state-mandated minimum wage law, leaving employees in that state to be covered under federal minimum wage statutes. In 2004, women in the state accounted for 46.6% of the employed civilian labor force.

23 AGRICULTURE

Alabama ranked 25th among the 50 states in farm marketing in 2005 with $3.89 billion, of which only $716 million came from crops.

There was considerable diversity in Alabama's earliest agriculture. By the mid-19th century, however, cotton had taken over, and production of other crops dropped so much that corn and other staples, even work animals, were often imported. In 1860, cotton was grown in every county, and one-crop agriculture had already worn out much of Alabama's farmland.

Diversification began early in the 20th century, a trend accelerated by the destructive effects of the boll weevil on cotton growing. In 2004, only 595,000 acres (223,000 hectares) were planted in cotton, compared to 3,500,000 acres (1,400,000 hectares) in 1930. As of 2004 there were some 44,000 farms in Alabama, occupying approximately 8.7 million acres (3.5 million hectares), or roughly 30% of the state's land area. Soybeans and livestock are raised in the Black Belt; peanuts in the southeast; vegetables, livestock, and timber in the southwest; and cotton and soybeans in the Tennessee River Valley.

In 2004, Alabama ranked third in the United States in production of peanuts, with 557,200,000 lb (253,273,000 kg), worth about $10,311,000. Other crops included soybeans, 6,650,000 bushels, $36,243,000; corn for fresh market, 23.9 million bushels, $57,564,000; wheat, 2,880,000 bushels, $10,224,000; tomatoes for fresh market, 342,000 hundredweight (15.5 million kg), $11,901,000; sweet potatoes, 380,000 hundredweight (17.3 million kg), $7.9 million; and pecans, 1,000,000 lb (450,000 kg), $1.3 million. The 2004 cotton crop of 820,000 bales was valued at $205,066,000.

24 ANIMAL HUSBANDRY

The principal livestock-raising regions of Alabama are the far north, the southwest, and the Black Belt, where the lime soil provides excellent pasturage. In 2003 Alabama produced an estimated 522.2 million lb (237.4 million kg) of cattle and calves, valued at $371.5 million, and an estimated 48.7 million lb (22.1 million kg) of hogs, valued at $20 million. There were 1,360,000 cattle and an estimated 180,000 hogs and pigs on Alabama farms and ranches in 2004. According to preliminary figures, 18,000 milk cows yielded 252 million lb (114.5 million kg) of milk in 2003.

Alabama is a leading producer of chickens, broilers, and eggs. In broiler production, the state was surpassed only by Georgia and Arkansas in 2003, with an estimated 5.4 billion lb (2.5 billion kg), valued at $1.8 billion. That year, Alabama ranked fourth in chicken production, with over 76.38 million lb (34.7 million kg), worth $5.2 million. Egg production totaled 2.19 billion, worth $295.6 million.

25 FISHING

In 2004, Alabama's commercial fish catch was about 26.6 million lb (12.1 million kg), worth $37 million. The principal fishing port is Bayou La Batre, which brought in about 19.1 million lb (8.7 million kg), worth $28.4 million. Alabama ranked fifth in the Gulf region for volume of shrimp landings with a total of 16.1 million lb (7.3 million kg).

Catfish farming is of growing importance. As of January 2005, there were 230 catfish farms (down from 370 in 1990) covering 25,100 acres (10,200 hectares) of water surface, with an average farm size of about 109 acres (44 hectares). In early 2006, Alabama growers had an inventory of 302.4 million stocker-size and 166 million fingerling/fry catfish.

As of 2003, there were 69 processing and 26 wholesaling plants in the state, with a combined total of about 1,649 employees. The commercial fishing fleet had about 1,775 boats and vessels in 2001.

There were 486,877 sport fishing licenses issued in Alabama in 2004.

26 FORESTRY

Forestland in Alabama, predominantly pine, covering 22,981,000 acres (9,302,000 hectares), was over 3% of the nation's total in 2004. Nearly all of that was classified as commercial timberland, and 21,757,000 acres (8,805,000 hectares) privately owned. Four national forests covered a gross acreage of 1,288,000 acres (521,250 hectares) in 2003. Production of softwood and hardwood lumber totaled 2.72 billion board feet in 2004 (seventh in the United States).

Alabama has a program in place, called TREASURE Forest, to recognize and certify sustainable forestry management on private lands. This program has already certified over 1.57 million acres (635,000 hectares).

27 MINING

In 2004, Alabama's nonfuel mineral output was valued at $972 million, according to the US Geological Survey, and consisted entirely of industrial minerals. This was an 8% increase from 2003 and followed a 6.8% increase from 2002 to 2003, making the state 18th out of the 50 states in nonfuel mineral production. In 2004, the state accounted for over 2% of all nonfuel mineral production in the United States. The top four nonfuel mineral commodities in 2004 (by value) were cement, crushed stone, lime, and construction grade sand and gravel. These four products accounted for almost 93% of nonfuel mineral output, with cement and crushed stone alone accounting for 69% of production.

According to figures for 2004, Alabama produced: 4.8 million metric tons of portland cement valued at an estimated $320 million; 2.12 million metric tons of common clay worth $29.6 million; 49.1 million metric tons of crushed stone valued at $303 million; 2.280 million metric tons of lime valued at $164 million; and 14.7 million metric tons construction sand and gravel valued at $65.3 million.

Other industrial minerals produced in the state included chalk, building stone (limestone and sandstone), bauxite clays, salt (solution recovery), silicon, and recovered sulfur.

28 ENERGY AND POWER

As of 2003, Alabama had 63 electrical power service providers, of which 36 were publicly owned and 23 were cooperatives. Of the remainder, one was federally operated, while the other was investor owned. As of that same year there were nearly 2.340 million retail customers. Of that total, over 1.363 million received their power from the state's only investor-owned service provider. Cooperatives accounted for 499,615 customers, while publicly owned providers had 476,247 customers.

Total net summer generating capability by the state's electrical generating plants in 2003 stood at 30.162 million kW, with total production that same year at 137.487 billion kWh. Of the total amount generated, 92.3% came from electric utilities, with the remainder coming from independent producers and combined heat and power service providers. The largest portion of all electric power generated, 76.696 billion kWh (55.8%), came from coal-fired plants, with nuclear fueled plants in second place at 31.676 billion kWh (23%).

As of 2006, Alabama had two operating nuclear power plants: the Browns Ferry plant, which is operated by the Tennessee Valley Authority, and the Joseph M Farley facility, which is operated by the Alabama Power Company's wholly owned subsidiary, the Southern Nuclear Operations Company.

Significant petroleum finds in southern Alabama date from the early 1950s. As of 2004, the state had proven crude oil reserves of 53 million barrels, or less than 1% of all US reserves, while output that same year averaged 20,000 barrels per day. Including federal offshore domains, Alabama that year ranked 18th (17th excluding federal offshore) in reserves and 16th (15th excluding federal offshore) among the 31 producing states. In 2004 Alabama had 824 producing oil wells, accounting for less than 1% of all US production. As of 2005, the state's three refineries had a combined crude oil distillation capacity of 113,500 barrels per day.

In 2004, Alabama had 5,526 producing natural gas and gas condensate wells. In that same year, marketed gas production (all gas produced excluding gas used for repressuring, vented and flared, and nonhydrocarbon gases removed) totaled 316 billion cu ft (8.9 billion cu m). As of 31 December 2004, proven reserves of dry or consumer-grade natural gas totaled 4,120 billion cu ft (117 billion cu m).

Alabama in 2004, had 49 producing coal mines, 41 of which were surface mines and 8 were underground. Coal production that same year totaled 22,271,000 short tons, up from 20,118,000 short tons in 2003. Of the total produced, underground mines in 2004 accounted for 16,114,000 short tons. Recoverable coal reserves in 2004 totaled 341 million short tons. One short ton equals 2,000 lb (0.907 metric tons).

29INDUSTRY

Alabama's manufacturing boom began in the 1870s with the exploitation of the coal and iron fields in the north, which quickly transformed Birmingham into the leading industrial city in the South, producing pig iron more cheaply than its American and English competitors. An important stimulus to manufacturing in the north was the development of ports and power plants along the Tennessee River. Although Birmingham remains highly dependent on steel, the state's manufacturing sector has diversified considerably since World War II (1939–45).

According to the US Census Bureau's Annual Survey of Manufactures (ASM) for 2004, Alabama's manufacturing sector covered some 20 product subsectors. The shipment value of all products manufactured in the state that same year was $76.095 billion. Of that total, the manufacturing of transportation equipment accounted for the largest portion, at $10.047 billion. It was followed by chemical manufacturing at $8.557 billion, primary metal manufacturing at $8.322 billion, food manufacturing at $8.019 billion, and paper manufacturing at $6.211 billion.

In 2004, a total of 259,058 people in Alabama were employed in the state's manufacturing sector, according to the ASM. Of that total, 200,645 were production workers. In terms of total employment, the food manufacturing industry accounted for the largest portion of all manufacturing employees at 35,549, with 28,186 actual production workers. It was followed by transportation equipment manufacturing with 26,868 employees (21,304 actual production workers); fabricated metal product manufacturing with 23,394 employees (17,211 actual production workers); wood product manufacturing with 19,269 employees (15,409 actual production workers); plastics and rubber products manufacturing with 17,136 employees (14,036 actual production workers); and primary metal manufacturing with 16,438 employees (12,764 actual production workers).

ASM data for 2004 showed that Alabama's manufacturing sector paid $9.357 billion in wages. Of that amount, the transportation equipment manufacturing sector accounted for the largest portion at $1.145 billion. It was followed by food manufacturing at $880.272 million; fabricated metal product manufacturing at $868.126 million; primary metal manufacturing at $805.290 million; and paper manufacturing at $709.987 million.

30COMMERCE

According to the 2002 Census of Wholesale Trade, Alabama's wholesale trade sector had sales that year totaling $43.6 billion from 5,747 establishments. Wholesalers of durable goods accounted for 3,800 establishments, followed by nondurable goods wholesalers at 1,579 and electronic markets, agents, and brokers accounting for 376 establishments. Sales by durable goods wholesalers in 2002 totaled $16.4 billion, while wholesalers of nondurable goods saw sales of $22.3 billion. Electronic markets, agents, and brokers in the wholesale trade industry had sales of $4.8 billion.

In the 2002 Census of Retail Trade, Alabama was listed as having 19,608 retail establishments with sales of $43.7 billion. The leading types of retail businesses by number of establishments were: gasoline stations (2,978); motor vehicle and motor vehicle parts dealers (2,643); clothing and clothing accessory stores (2,379); and food and beverage stores (1,996). In terms of sales, motor vehicle and motor vehicle parts stores accounted for the largest share of retail sales at $11.9 billion, followed by general merchandise stores at $7.6 billion; food and beverage stores at $6.08 billion; and gasoline stations at $4.3 billion. A total of 222,416 people were employed in the retail sector in Alabama for that year.

Exporters located in Alabama exported $10.7 billion in merchandise during 2005.

31CONSUMER PROTECTION

The Office of Consumer Affairs, established in 1972, was transferred to the Office of the Attorney General in 1979. The major duties of the office are to enforce the state's Deceptive Trade Practices Act and other criminal and civil laws to combat consumer fraud, and to offer programs in consumer education. In response to a myriad of inquiries, complaints, and fraudulent schemes, recent attorneys general have expanded the division's role in their administrations, and it has become one of the most effective arms of the attorney general's law enforcement efforts. The Office of Consumer Affairs also acts as a mediator or negotiator in response to approximately 3,000 consumer complaints received each year, three-quarters of which are registered by residents over age 65.

When dealing with consumer protection issues, the state's Attorney General's Office can initiate civil and criminal proceedings; represent the state before state and federal regulatory agencies; administer consumer protection and education programs; handle formal consumer complaints; and exercise broad subpoena powers. In antitrust actions, the Attorney General's Office can act on behalf of those consumers who are incapable of acting on their own; initiate damage actions on behalf of the state in state courts; and initiate criminal proceedings. However, the state's Attorney General cannot represent counties, cities and other governmental entities in recovering civil damages under state or federal law.

The Office of the Attorney General's Office of Consumer Affairs is located in the state capitol of Montgomery.

32BANKING

As of June 2005, Alabama had 160 insured banks, savings and loans, and saving banks, in addition to 71 state-chartered and 88 federally chartered credit unions (CUs). Excluding the CUs, the Birmington-Hoover market area accounted for the largest portion of the state's financial institutions and deposits in 2004, with 41 institutions and $19.824 billion in deposits. As of June 2005, CUs accounted for 4.7% of all assets held by all financial institutions in the state, or some $10.704 billion. Banks, savings and loans, and savings banks collectively accounted for the remaining 95.3%, or $214.840 billion in assets held.

The median net interest margin (NIM—the difference between the lower rates offered to savers and the higher rates charged on loans) of the state's insured institutions in fourth quarter 2005 stood at 4.25%, up from 4.12% for all of 2004 and 4.02% for all of 2003. The median percentage of past-due/nonaccrual loans compared to total loans stood at 1.59% as of fourth quarter 2005, down from 1.99% for all of 2004 and 2.68% for all of 2003.

The regulation of Alabama's state-chartered banks and other state-chartered financial institutions is the responsibility of the Alabama Banking Department.

³³INSURANCE

In 2004 there were 6.2 million individual life insurance policies in force with a total value of $188.7 billion; total value for all categories of life insurance (individual, group, and credit) was $283.5 billion. The average coverage amount is $30,300 per policy holder. Death benefits paid that year totaled $986.2 million.

As of 2003, there were 22 property and casualty and 16 life and health insurance companies incorporated or organized in the state. In 2004, direct premiums for property and casualty insurance amounted to about $5.95 billion. That year, there were 41,912 flood insurance policies in force in the state, with a total value of $5.87 billion. There were also 3,169 beach and windstorm insurance policies in force against hurricane and other windstorm damage, with a total value of $317.69 million.

In 2004, 55% of state residents held employment-based health insurance policies, 3% held individual policies, and 26% were covered under Medicare and Medicaid; 14% of residents were uninsured. In 2003, employee contributions for employment-based health coverage averaged about 20% for single coverage and 28% for family coverage. Alabama does not offer extended health benefits in connection with the Consolidated Omnibus Budget Reconciliation Act (COBRA, 1986), a health insurance extension program for those who lose employment-based coverage due to termination or reduction of work hours.

In 2003, there were over 3 million auto insurance policies in effect for private passenger cars. Required minimum coverage includes bodily injury liability of up to $20,000 per individual and $40,000 for all persons injured, as well as property damage liability of $10,000. In 2003, the average expenditure per vehicle for insurance coverage was $655.42.

³⁴SECURITIES

Alabama has no securities exchanges. In 2005, there were 1,050 personal financial advisers employed in the state and 1,580 securities, commodities, and financial services sales agents. In 2004, there were over 59 publicly traded companies within the state, with over 28 NASDAQ companies, 17 NYSE listings, and 4 AMEX listings. In 2006, the state had two Fortune 500 companies; Regions Financial ranked first in the state and 354th in the nation with revenues of over $6.1 billion, followed by Saks. AmSouth Bancorp, Vulcan Materials, and Torchmark were in the Fortune 1,000. All five of these NYSE companies are based in Birmingham.

³⁵PUBLIC FINANCE

The Division of the Budget within the Department of Finance prepares and administers the state budget, which the governor submits to the legislature for amendment and approval. The fiscal year runs from 1 October through 30 September, making Alabama one of only four states in which the fiscal year (FY) does not begin in July. General funds for fiscal year 2006 were estimated

Alabama—State Government Finances

(Dollar amounts in thousands. Per capita amounts in dollars.)

	AMOUNT	PER CAPITA
Total Revenue	21,568,441	4,766.51
General revenue	17,616,091	3,893.06
Intergovernmental revenue	6,871,334	1,518.53
Taxes	7,018,242	1,550.99
General sales	1,892,560	418.25
Selective sales	1,783,002	394.03
License taxes	397,429	87.83
Individual income tax	2,243,537	495.81
Corporate income tax	292,051	64.54
Other taxes	409,663	90.53
Current charges	2,667,878	589.59
Miscellaneous general revenue	1,058,637	233.95
Utility revenue	–	–
Liquor store revenue	172,430	38.11
Insurance trust revenue	3,779,920	835.34
Total expenditure	19,544,560	4,319.24
Intergovernmental expenditure	4,164,719	920.38
Direct expenditure	15,379,841	3,398.86
Current operation	10,740,445	2,373.58
Capital outlay	1,644,475	363.42
Insurance benefits and repayments	1,745,203	385.68
Assistance and subsidies	1,013,301	223.93
Interest on debt	236,417	52.25
Exhibit: Salaries and wages	3,141,319	694.21
Total expenditure	19,544,560	4,319.24
General expenditure	17,621,702	3,894.30
Intergovernmental expenditure	4,164,719	920.38
Direct expenditure	13,456,983	2,973.92
General expenditures, by function:		
Education	7,617,223	1,683.36
Public welfare	4,568,332	1,009.58
Hospitals	1,100,506	243.21
Health	814,615	180.03
Highways	1,199,566	265.10
Police protection	130,234	28.78
Correction	397,943	87.94
Natural resources	237,615	52.51
Parks and recreation	23,014	5.09
Government administration	433,653	95.83
Interest on general debt	236,417	52.25
Other and unallocable	862,584	190.63
Utility expenditure	–	–
Liquor store expenditure	177,655	39.26
Insurance trust expenditure	1,745,203	385.68
Debt at end of fiscal year	6,363,885	1,406.38
Cash and security holdings	29,992,119	6,628.09

Abbreviations and symbols: – zero or rounds to zero; (NA) not available; (X) not applicable.

SOURCE: *U.S. Census Bureau, Governments Division, 2004 Survey of State Government Finances,* January 2006.

at nearly $7.8 billion for resources and $6.7 billion for expenditures. In fiscal year 2004, federal government grants to Alabama were $7.0 billion. For fiscal year 2007, federal funding for the State Children's Health Insurance Program (SCHIP) and the HOME Investment Partnership Program was increased.

[36]TAXATION

In 2005, Alabama collected $7,800 million in tax revenues, or $1,711 per capita, which placed it 44th among the 50 states in per capita tax burden. The national average was $2,192 per capita. Property taxes accounted for 3.0% of the total, sales taxes 26.1%, selective sales taxes 25.1%, individual income taxes 32.5%, corporate income taxes 5.1%, and other taxes 8.3%.

As of 1 January 2006, Alabama had three individual income tax brackets ranging from 2.0 to 5.0%. The state taxes corporations at a flat rate of 6.5%.

In 2004, state and local property taxes amounted to $1,440,385,000, or $367 per capita. The per capita amount ranks the state as having the lowest property taxes in the nation. Local governments collected $1,440,385,000 of the total and the state government, $221,470,000.

Alabama taxes retail sales at a rate of 4%. In addition to the state tax, local taxes on retail sales can reach as much as 7%, making for a potential total tax on retail sales of 11%. Food purchased for consumption off-premises is taxable. The tax on cigarettes is 42.5 cents per pack, which ranks 39th among the 50 states and the District of Columbia. Alabama taxes gasoline at 18 cents per gallon. This is in addition to the 18.4 cents per gallon federal tax on gasoline.

According to the Tax Foundation, for every federal tax dollar sent to Washington in 2004, Alabama citizens received $1.71 in federal spending, which ranks the state sixth-highest nationally.

[37]ECONOMIC POLICY

Alabama seeks to attract out-of-state business by means of tax incentives and plant-building assistance. The Alabama Development Office (ADO) plans for economic growth through industrial development. It also extends loans, issues bonds, and offers other forms of financing to growing companies, to firms that create permanent jobs, and to small businesses. The International Trade Division of the ADO provides a variety of services to help Alabama companies export. In 1987 the Alabama Enterprise Zone Program was passed. As of 2006, 27 Enterprise Zones had been authorized across the state in areas considered to have depressed economies, each zone offering packages of local tax and nontax incentives to encourage businesses to locate in the area. As of 2006, qualified new and expanding businesses in eligible industries were able to receive a corporate income tax credit of up to 5% of capital costs per year for up to 20 years. Small businesses may qualify if they create 15 jobs and invest $1 million. Other new projects or expansions qualify if they create 20 jobs and invest $2 million. All companies must pay wages of at least $8 an hour or have an average total compensation of $10 per hour. Alabama's target industries in 2006 were automobiles, aviation, electronics, plastics, and wood and wood products. The Alabama Industrial Development Training Institute, within the Department of Education, provides job training especially designed to suit the needs of high-technology industries. Alabama offers zero-interest loans and grants to rural

economic development projects. In an effort to attract new industries or help existing companies grow, the state helps counties and municipalities pay for site improvements, and assists communities in financing infrastructures such as water and sewer lines or access roads. The Alabama Commerce Commission promotes legislation that protects and nurtures the Alabamian economy, including infrastructural projects on the state's roads, bridges, and docks. In 2000, the Alabama Commission on Environmental Initiatives was created by executive order and charged with developing a program for improving the environmental quality of the state. In 2002, a Brownfields Redevelopment Program was introduced.

In September 2005, in the aftermath of Hurricane Katrina which devastated the Gulf Coast region, President George W. Bush announced he would create a Gulf Opportunity Zone for Louisiana, Mississippi, and Alabama. Businesses would be able to double (to $200,000) the amount they could deduct from their taxes for investments in new equipment. The act also provided a 50% bonus depreciation and made loan guarantees available. Congress passed the Gulf Opportunity Zone Act in December 2005, providing a number of tax incentives to encourage the rebuilding of areas ravaged by Hurricanes Katrina, Rita, and Wilma.

[38]HEALTH

The infant mortality rate in October 2005 was estimated at 8.8 per 1,000 live births. The birth rate in 2003 was 13.2 per 1,000 population. The abortion rate stood at 14.3 per 1,000 women in 2000. In 2003, about 83.8% of pregnant woman received prenatal care beginning in the first trimester. In 2004, approximately 82% of children received routine immunizations before the age of three.

The crude death rate in 2003 was 10.4 deaths per 1,000 population, representing the highest rate in the nation for that year. As of 2002, the death rates for all the major causes of death were higher than the national averages. The rates that year (per 100,000 resident population) were: heart disease, 294.1; cancer, 216.2; cerebrovascular diseases, 71.3; diabetes, 33.1; and chronic lower respiratory diseases, 51.9. The mortality rate from HIV infection was 4.2 per 100,000 population, lower than the national average of 4.9 per 100,000 population for 2002. In 2004, the reported AIDS case rate was about 10.3 per 100,000 population. In 2002, about 61% of the population was considered overweight or obese, representing the second-highest percentage in the nation (following West Virginia). As of 2004, Alabama ranked seventh in the nation for the percentage of smokers, with about 24.8%.

In 2003, Alabama had 107 community hospitals with about 15,600 beds. There were about 709,000 patient admissions that year and 8.9 million outpatient visits. The average daily inpatient census was about 9,700 patients. The average cost per day for hospital care was $1,166. Also in 2003, there were about 228 certified nursing facilities in the state, with 26,369 beds and an overall occupancy rate of about 89.4%. In 2004, it was estimated that about 69.2% of all state residents had received some type of dental care within the year. Alabama had 216 physicians per 100,000 resident population in 2004 and 818 nurses per 100,000 in 2005. In 2004, there was a total of 1,971 dentists in the state.

About 26% of state residents was enrolled in Medicaid and Medicare programs in 2004. Approximately 14% of the state was uninsured in 2004. In 2003, state health care expenditures totaled $5 million.

39 SOCIAL WELFARE

In 2004, about 119,000 people received unemployment benefits, with an average weekly unemployment benefit of $177. In fiscal year 2005, the estimated average monthly participation in the food stamp program included about 558,596 persons (222,132 households); the average monthly benefit was about $91.91 per person. That year, the total benefits paid through the state for the food stamp program was about $616 million.

Temporary Assistance for Needy Families (TANF), the system of federal welfare assistance that officially replaced Aid to Families with Dependent Children (AFDC) in 1997, was reauthorized through the Deficit Reduction Act of 2005. TANF is funded through federal block grants that are divided among the states based on an equation involving the number of recipients in each state. Alabama's TANF program is called the Family Assistance Program (FA). In 2004 the state program had 45,000 recipients; state and federal expenditures on this TANF program in fiscal year 2003 totaled $50 million.

In December 2004, Social Security benefits were paid to 884,410 Alabamians. This number included 484,310 retired workers, 98,650 widows and widowers, 159,300 disabled workers, 47,110 spouses, and 95,040 children. Social Security beneficiaries represented 19.5% of the total state population and 92.6% of the state's population age 65 and older. Retired workers received an average monthly payment of $912; widows and widowers, $823; disabled workers, $866; and spouses, $451. Payments for children of retired workers averaged $458 per month; children of deceased workers, $590; and children of disabled workers, $261. Also in December 2004, Federal Supplemental Security Income payments went to 163,002 Alabama residents, averaging $374 a month. About $26,000 of state-administered supplemental payments was distributed to 434 residents.

40 HOUSING

In 2004, there were an estimated 2,058,951 housing units in Alabama, of which 1,755,332 were occupied. In the same year, about 71.9% of all housing units were owner-occupied. It was estimated that about 96,954 households across the state were without telephone service, 6,757 lacked complete plumbing facilities, and 5,212 lacked complete kitchen facilities. About 67.3% of all housing units were detached, single-family homes; 14.6% were mobile homes. The average household had 2.51 members.

Approximately 27,400 new privately owned units were authorized in 2004. The median home value that year was $94,671. The median monthly housing cost for mortgage owners was $872, while the median cost for renters was $519. In September 2005, the state was awarded grants of $299,963 from the US Department of Housing and Urban Development (HUD) for rural housing and economic development programs. For 2006, HUD allocated to the state over $25.8 million in community development block grants. Also in 2006, HUD offered an additional $74 million to the state in emergency funds to rebuild housing that was destroyed by Hurricanes Katrina, Rita, and Wilma in late 2005.

The Fairhope Single Tax Corporation, near Point Clear, was founded in 1893 by individuals seeking to put into practice the economic theories of Henry George. Incorporated under Alabama law in 1904, this oldest and largest of US single-tax experiments continues to lease land in return for the payment of a rent (the "single tax") based on the land's valuation; the combined rents are used to pay taxes and to provide and improve community services.

41 EDUCATION

In 2004, 82.4% of Alabamians age 25 and older were high school graduates. Some 22.3% had obtained a bachelor's degree or higher.

The total enrollment for fall 2002 in Alabama's public schools stood at 740,000. Of these, 534,000 attended schools from kindergarten through grade eight, and 206,000 attended high school. Approximately 59.9% of the students were white, 36.4% were black, 2.1% were Hispanic, 0.9% were Asian/Pacific Islander, and 0.8% were American Indian/Alaskan Native. Total enrollment was estimated at 734,000 in fall 2003 and was expected to be 709,000 by fall 2014, a decline of 4.1% during the period 2002 to 2014. There were 73,105 students enrolled in 408 private schools in fall 2003. Expenditures for public education in 2003/04 were estimated at $5.4 billion. Since 1969, the National Assessment of Educational Progress (NAEP) has tested public school students nationwide. The resulting report, *The Nation's Report Card*, stated that eighth graders in Alabama scored 262 out of 500 in 2005 compared with the national average of 278.

As of fall 2002, there were 246,414 students enrolled in college or graduate school. Minority students comprised 31.5% of total postsecondary enrollment that same year. As of 2005, Alabama had 75 degree-granting institutions. The largest state universities are Auburn University and the three University of Alabama campuses, including Birmingham, Huntsville, and the main campus in Tuscaloosa. Tuskegee University, founded as a normal and industrial school in 1881 under the leadership of Booker T. Washington, has become one of the nation's most famous predominantly black colleges.

42 ARTS

The Alabama State Council on the Arts, established by the legislature in 1966, provides aid to local nonprofit arts organizations. The Alabama Humanities Foundation was established in 1974. In 2005, the National Endowment for the Humanities awarded 10 grants totaling $1,020,965 to Alabama organizations and the National Endowment for the Arts awarded 18 grants totaling $910,100 to Alabama arts organizations. The Alabama Center for Traditional Culture, established in 1990, works in conjunction with the state council to promote and preserve local arts and culture. The Alabama Jazz and Blues Federation, also established in 1990, has been very active in offering monthly jam sessions for artists, an annual summer festival, and several concerts throughout the year.

The Alabama Shakespeare Festival State Theater performs in Montgomery and as of 2006 was noted as the sixth-largest Shakespeare festival worldwide. The festival hosts over 300,000 annual visitors that travel from over 60 countries and all 50 states. The Birmingham International Festival (BIF) was founded in 1951 and works to promote mutual understanding among cultures through art, education, and economic development programs. Working to fulfill their mission the BIF highlights a different country each year.

Alabama is also home to the Huntsville Symphony Orchestra, the Montgomery Symphony Orchestra, and the Tuscaloosa Symphony Orchestra. Among several dance organizations in the state, the Alabama Ballet, founded in 1981, is notable for establishing a professional affiliation with the University of Alabama at Birmingham, thus expanding opportunities for both students and audiences of dance.

As of 2006, the Tennessee Valley Old Time Fiddlers Convention was held annually in October at Athens State College. The annual event began in mid-1960s, showcasing "old time" music. Every June, the annual Hank Williams Memorial Celebration is held near the country singer's birthplace at the Olive West Community. As of 2006, there were opera groups in both Huntsville and Mobile.

43 LIBRARIES AND MUSEUMS

For the fiscal year ending September 2001, Alabama had 207 public library systems, with a total of 283 libraries, of which 77 were branches. The state's public libraries that same year had a combined total of 8,801,000 volumes of books and serial publications, and a total circulation of 15,988,000. The system also had 269,000 audio and 244,000 video items, 8,000 electronic format items (CD-ROMs, magnetic tapes, and disks), and 17 bookmobiles. The University of Alabama had 1,896,687 volumes, while the Birmingham Public Library had 19 branches and 973,936 volumes. The Alabama Department of Archives and History Library, at Montgomery, had 260,000 volumes and several special collections on Alabama history and government. Collections on aviation and space exploration in Alabama's libraries, particularly its military libraries, may be the most extensive in the United States outside of Washington, DC. In 1997 the Alabama Public Library Service and its regional library for the blind and physically handicapped had over 480,000 books, videos, and audiotapes, including more than 25,000 books in Braille. Memorabilia of Wernher von Braun are in the library at the Alabama Space and Rocket Center at Huntsville; the Redstone Arsenal's Scientific Information Center holds over 227,000 volumes and 1,800,000 technical reports. Total income for the public library system in 2003 was $64,927,000, including $908,978 in federal grants and $4,479,963 in state grants. State libraries spent 64.2% of that income on staff.

Alabama had 81 museums in 2000. The most important art museum is the Birmingham Museum of Art. Other museums include the George Washington Carver Museum at Tuskegee Institute, the Women's Army Corps Museum and Military Police Corps Museum at Ft. McClellan, the US Army Aviation Museum at Ft. Rucker, the Pike Pioneer Museum at Troy, the Museum of the City of Mobile, and the Montgomery Museum of Fine Arts. Also in Montgomery are Old Alabama Town and the F. Scott and Zelda Fitzgerald home. Russell Cave National Monument has an archaeological exhibit. In Florence is the W. C. Handy Home; at Tuscumbia, Helen Keller's birthplace, Ivy Green.

44 COMMUNICATIONS

In 2004, 92.2% of Alabama's occupied housing units had telephones. In addition, by June of that same year there were 2,301,847 mobile wireless telephone subscribers. In 2003, 53.9% of Alabama households had a computer and 45.7% had Internet access. By June 2005, there were 454,546 high-speed lines in Alabama,

408,937 residential and 45,609 for business. A total of 44,371 Internet domain names had been registered in Alabama by 2000.

During 2005, Alabama had 93 major operating radio stations (19 AM, 74 FM) and 22 major television stations. In 2000, 69% of television households in the Birmingham area subscribed to cable television.

45 PRESS

The earliest newspaper in Alabama, the short-lived *Mobile Centinel (sic),* made its first appearance on 23 May 1811. The oldest newspaper still in existence in the state is the *Mobile Register,* founded in 1813.

As of 2005 Alabama had 21 morning dailies; 3 evening dailies; and 20 Sunday papers. The following table shows the leading dailies with their 2005 circulations:

AREA	NAME	DAILY	SUNDAY
Birmingham	*News** (m,S)	167,889	184,036
	Post–Herald (m)	150,353	
Huntsville	*Times** (e,S)	53,145	74,401
Mobile	*Register**(m,S)	88,253	111,778
Montgomery	*Advertiser* (m,S)	48,389	58,429
Tuscaloosa	*News* (m,S)	34,332	36,205

*Owned by the Alabama Group of Advance Publications

In 2005, there were 97 weekly publications in Alabama. Of these, 73 are paid weeklies, 3 are free weeklies, and 21 are combined weeklies. The total circulation of paid weeklies (416,280) and free weeklies (192,402) is 608,682. Of the combined weeklies in the United States, the Columbiana/Shelby counties *Reporter* ranked 25th with a circulation of 32,497.

46 ORGANIZATIONS

In 2006, there were over 2,900 nonprofit organizations registered within the state, of which 2,063 were registered as charitable, educational, or religious organizations. National associations with headquarters in Alabama include Civitan International in Birmingham; and Klanwatch and the Southern Poverty Law Center, both in Montgomery. The last-named is one of the major civil rights organizations active in Alabama, along with the Southern Christian Leadership Conference (SCLC) and the National Association for the Advancement of Colored People (NAACP). The League of the South, a national organization founded in 1994 as a political, economic, and civil rights advocacy organization, has its national headquarters in Killen. Two branches of the Ku Klux Klan are also active in Alabama.

The American Council on Alcohol Problems is based in Birmingham, which also hosts the central offices of the fourth district of Alcoholics Anonymous World Wide Services.

State cultural organizations include the Alabama Historical Association and Alabama Preservation Alliance, both in Montgomery. Sports and recreation associations based in the state include the American Baseball Foundation, the National Speleological Society, the Kampground Owners Association, and the Bass Anglers Sportsman Society. Regional wildlife groups include the Alabama Mookee Association, the Alabama Santa Gertrudis Association, and the Alabama National Wild Turkey Federation, which has several chapters throughout the state.

47TOURISM, TRAVEL, AND RECREATION

In 2004, some 20 million people visited Alabama, spending $5.5 billion. With a statewide impact of 157,000 jobs, tourism is an important industry for Alabama. An estimated 73% of all tourists choose destinations in one of six counties: Baldwin, Jefferson, Madison, Mobile, Montgomery, and Tuscaloosa. In 2005, the number of visitors to Alabama increased as people fled Louisiana and Florida due to the severe hurricane season.

A top tourist attraction is the Alabama Space and Rocket Center at Huntsville, home of the US Space Camp. Other attractions include many antebellum houses and plantations: Magnolia Grove (a state shrine) at Greensboro; Gaineswood and Bluff Hall at Demopolis; Arlington in Birmingham; Oakleigh at Mobile; Sturdivant Hall at Selma; Shorter Mansion at Eufaula; and the first White House of the confederacy at Montgomery. Racing fans can visit the Talledega Super Speedway and the Motorsports Hall of Fame.

The celebration of Mardi Gras in Mobile, which began in 1704, predates that in New Orleans and now occupies several days before Ash Wednesday. Gulf beaches are a popular attraction and Point Clear, across the bay from Mobile, has been a fashionable resort, especially for southerners, since the 1840s. The state fair is held at Birmingham every October.

During 2004, Baldwin and Jefferson counties were the biggest tourist beneficiaries; home to Alabama's four national park sites, which include Tuskegee Institute National Historic Site and Russell Cave National Monument, an almost continuous archaeological record of human habitation from at least 7000 BC to about AD 1650. Tannehill Historical State Park features ante- and postbellum dwellings, a restored iron furnace over a century old, and a museum of iron and steel. There were some 500,000 visitors to Alabama's state parks that year.

The Alabama Deep Sea Fishing Rodeo at Dauphin Island also attracts thousands of visitors. Alabama's Robert Trent Jones Golf Trail is a major tourist attraction, with seven championship courses located from Huntsville to Mobile.

48SPORTS

Alabama is home to a number of professional teams in various sports. The Birmingham Power was a member of the National Women's Basketball League until 2005, and the Birmingham Steeldogs are an Arena League 2 football squad. There are minor league baseball clubs in Birmingham, Mobile, and Huntsville, and minor league hockey teams in Birmingham, Huntsville, and Mobile. Two major professional stock car races, Aaron's 499 and the UAW-Ford 500, are held at the Talladega Speedway. Dog racing was legalized in Mobile in 1971. Four of the major hunting-dog competitions in the United States are held annually in the state.

Football reigns supreme among collegiate sports. The University of Alabama finished number one in 1961, 1964, 1965 (against Michigan State), 1978 (against University of Southern California), 1979, and 1992 and is a perennial top-10 entry. Competing in the Southeastern Conference, Alabama's Crimson Tide won the Sugar Bowl in 1962, 1964, 1967, 1978, 1979, 1980, and 1993; the Orange Bowl in 1943, 1953, 1963, and 1966; the Cotton Bowl in 1942 and 1981; the Sun Bowl in 1983 and 1988; and the Independence Bowl in 2001. The Crimson Tide have won a total of 12 national championships and 21 SEC titles. Auburn University, which also competes in the Southeastern Conference, won the Sugar Bowl in 1984; the Florida Citrus Bowl in 1982 and 1987; the Gator Bowl in 1954, 1971, and 1972; and the Sun Bowl in 1968. The Tigers have won 14 bowl games, 6 SEC titles, and have produced 2 Heisman trophy winners (Pat Sullivan and Bo Jackson). The Blue-Gray game, an all-star contest, is held at Montgomery on Christmas Day, and the Senior Bowl game is played in Mobile in January. Additionally, Alabama-Huntsville won National Collegiate Athletic Association Division II hockey championships in 1996, 1997, and 1998.

Boat races include the annual Dauphin Island Race, the largest one-day sailing race in the United States. The Alabama Sports Hall of Fame is located at Birmingham.

Some of the most notable athletes born in Alabama are Willie Mays, Hank Aaron, Jesse Owens, and Bo Jackson.

49FAMOUS ALABAMIANS

William Rufus De Vane King (b.North Carolina, 1786–1853) served as a US senator from Alabama and as minister to France before being elected US vice president in 1852 on the Democratic ticket with Franklin Pierce; he died six weeks after taking the oath of office. Three Alabamians who served as associate justices of the US Supreme Court were John McKinley (b.Virginia, 1780–1852), John A. Campbell (b.Georgia, 1811–89), and Hugo L. Black (1886–1971). Campbell resigned from the court in 1861, later becoming assistant secretary of war for the Confederacy; Black, a US senator from 1927 to 1937, served one of the longest terms (1937–71) in the history of the court and is regarded as one of its most eminent justices.

Among the most colorful figures in antebellum Alabama was William Lowndes Yancey (b.Georgia, 1814–63), a fiery orator who was a militant proponent of slavery, states' rights, and eventually secession. During the early 20th century, a number of Alabamians became influential in national politics. Among them were US senators John Hollis Bankhead (1842–1920) and John Hollis Bankhead Jr. (1872–1946); the latter's brother, William B. Bankhead (1874–1940), who became speaker of the US House of Representatives in 1936; and US Senator Oscar W. Underwood (b.Kentucky, 1862–1929), a leading contender for the Democratic presidential nomination in 1912 and 1924. Other prominent US senators from Alabama have included (Joseph) Lister Hill (1894–1984) and John Sparkman (1899–1985), who was the Democratic vice presidential nominee in 1952. Alabama's most widely known political figure is George Corley Wallace (1919–98), who served as governor in 1963–67 and 1971–79 and was elected to a fourth term in 1982. Wallace, an outspoken opponent of racial desegregation in the 1960s, was a candidate for the Democratic presidential nomination in 1964; four years later, as the presidential nominee of the American Independent Party, he carried five states. While campaigning in Maryland's Democratic presidential primary on 15 May 1972, Wallace was shot and paralyzed from the waist down by a would-be assassin. In 1976, Wallace made his fourth and final unsuccessful bid for the presidency.

Civil rights leader Martin Luther King Jr. (b.Georgia, 1929–68), winner of the Nobel Peace Prize in 1964, first came to national prominence as leader of the Montgomery bus boycott of 1955; he also led demonstrations at Birmingham in 1963 and at Selma in 1965. His widow, Coretta Scott King (1927–2006), is a native Alabamian. Federal judge Frank M. Johnson Jr. (1918–99) has made several landmark rulings in civil rights cases.

Helen Keller (1880–1968), deaf and blind as the result of a childhood illness, was the first such multihandicapped person to earn a college degree; she later became a world-famous author and lecturer. Another world figure, black educator Booker T. Washington (b.Virginia, 1856–1915), built Alabama's Tuskegee Institute from a school where young blacks were taught building, farming, cooking, brickmaking, dressmaking, and other trades into an internationally known agricultural research center. Tuskegee's most famous faculty member was George Washington Carver (b.Missouri, 1864–1943), who discovered some 300 different peanut products, 118 new ways to use sweet potatoes, and numerous other crop varieties and applications. Among Alabama's leaders in medicine was Dr. William Crawford Gorgas (1854–1920), head of sanitation in Panama during the construction of the Panama Canal; he later served as US surgeon general. Brought to the United States after World War II (1939–45), the internationally known scientist Wernher von Braun (b.Germany, 1912–77) came to Alabama in 1950 to direct the US missile program.

Two Alabama writers, (Nelle) Harper Lee (b.1926) and Edward Osborne Wilson (b.1929), have won Pulitzer Prizes. Famous musicians from Alabama include blues composer and performer W(illiam) C(hristopher) Handy (1873–1958), singer Nat "King" Cole (1917–65), and singer-songwriter Hank Williams (1923–53). Alabama's most widely known actress was Tallulah Bankhead (1903–68), the daughter of William B. Bankhead.

Among Alabama's sports figures are track and field star Jesse Owens (James Cleveland Owens, 1913–80), winner of four gold medals at the 1936 Olympic Games in Berlin; boxer Joe Louis (Joseph Louis Barrow, 1914–81), world heavyweight champion from 1937 to 1949; and baseball stars Leroy Robert "Satchel" Paige (1906?–82), Willie Mays (b.1931), and (Louis) Henry Aaron (b.1934), all-time US home-run leader.

50 BIBLIOGRAPHY

Arsenault, Raymond. *Freedom Riders: 1961 and the Struggle for Racial Justice.* New York: Oxford University Press, 2006.

Council of State Governments. *The Book of the States, 2006 Edition.* Lexington, Ky.: Council of State Governments, 2006.

Flynt, Wayne. *Alabama in the Twentieth Century.* Tuscaloosa: University of Alabama Press, 2004.

Gaillard, Frye. *Cradle of Freedom: Alabama and the Movement that Changed America.* Tuscaloosa: University of Alabama Press, 2004.

Jordan, Jeffrey L. *Interstate Water Allocation in Alabama, Florida, and Georgia.* Gainesville: University Press of Florida, 2006.

Lofton, J. Mack. *Voices from Alabama: A Twentieth-Century Mosaic.* Tuscaloosa: University of Alabama Press, 1993.

Norman, Corrie E., and Don S. Armentrout (eds.). *Religion in the Contemporary South: Changes, Continuities, and Contexts.* Knoxville: University of Tennessee Press, 2005.

Suitts, Steve. *Hugo Black of Alabama: How His Roots and Early Career Shaped the Great Champion of the Constitution.* Montgomery: NewSouth Books, 2005.

US Dept. of Commerce, Economics and Statistics Administration, US Census Bureau. *Alabama, 2000. Summary Social, Economic, and Housing Characteristics: 2000 Census of Population and Housing.* Washington, D.C.: US Government Printing Office, 2003.

ALASKA

State of Alaska

ORIGIN OF STATE NAME: From the Aleut word *"alyeska,"* meaning "great land." **NICKNAME:** Land of the Midnight Sun; The Last Frontier. **CAPITAL:** Juneau. **ENTERED UNION:** 3 January 1959 (49th). **SONG:** "Alaska's Flag." **MOTTO:** North to the Future. **FLAG:** On a blue field, eight gold stars form the Big Dipper and the North Star. **OFFICIAL SEAL:** In the inner circle symbols of mining, agriculture, and commerce are depicted against a background of mountains and the northern lights. In the outer circle are a fur seal, a salmon, and the words "The Seal of the State of Alaska." **BIRD:** Willow ptarmigan. **FISH:** King salmon. **FLOWER:** Wild forget-me-not. **TREE:** Sitka spruce. **GEM:** Jade. **LEGAL HOLIDAYS:** New Year's Day, 1 January; Martin Luther King Jr. Day, 3rd Monday in January; Presidents' Day, 3rd Monday in February; Seward's Day, last Monday in March; Memorial Day, last Monday in May; Independence Day, 4 July; Labor Day, 1st Monday in September; Alaska Day, 18 October; Veterans' Day, 11 November; Thanksgiving Day, 4th Thursday in November; Christmas Day, 25 December. **TIME:** 3 AM Alaska Standard Time, 2 AM Hawaii-Aleutian Standard Time = noon GMT.

¹LOCATION, SIZE, AND EXTENT

Situated at the northwest corner of the North American continent, Alaska is separated by Canadian territory from the coterminous 48 states. Alaska is the largest of the 50 states, with a total area of 591,004 sq mi (1,530,699 sq km). Land takes up 570,833 sq mi (1,478,456 sq km) and inland water, 20,171 sq mi (52,243 sq km). Alaska is more than twice the size of Texas, the next largest state, and occupies 16% of the total US land area; the E–W extension is 2,261 mi (3,639 km); the maximum N–S extension is 1,420 mi (2,285 km).

Alaska is bounded on the N by the Arctic Ocean and Beaufort Sea; on the E by Canada's Yukon Territory and province of British Columbia; on the S by the Gulf of Alaska, Pacific Ocean, and Bering Sea; and on the W by the Bering Sea, Bering Strait, Chukchi Sea, and Arctic Ocean.

Alaska's many offshore islands include St. Lawrence, St. Matthew, Nunivak, and the Pribilof group in the Bering Sea; Kodiak Island in the Gulf of Alaska; the Aleutian Islands in the Pacific; and some 1,100 islands constituting the Alexander Archipelago, extending SE along the Alaska panhandle.

The total boundary length of Alaska is 8,187 mi (13,176 km), including a general coastline of 6,640 mi (10,686 km); the tidal shoreline extends 33,904 mi (54,563 km). Alaska's geographic center is about 60 mi (97 km) NW of Mt. McKinley. The northern-most point in the United States—Point Barrow, at 71°23′30″N, 156°28′30″W—lies within the state of Alaska, as does the westernmost point—Cape Wrangell on Attu Island in the Aleutians, at 52°55′30″N, 172°28′E. Little Diomede Island, belonging to Alaska, is less than 2 mi (3 km) from Big Diomede Island, belonging to Russia.

²TOPOGRAPHY

Topography varies sharply among the six distinct regions of Alaska. In the southeast is a narrow coastal panhandle cut off from the main Alaskan landmass by the St. Elias Range. This region, featuring numerous mountain peaks of 10,000 ft (3,000 m) in elevation, is paralleled by the Alexander Archipelago. South-central Alaska, which covers a 700-mi (1,100-km) area along the Gulf of Alaska, includes the Kenai Peninsula and Cook Inlet, a great arm of the Pacific penetrating some 200 mi (320 km) to Anchorage. The southwestern region includes the Alaska Peninsula, filled with lightly wooded, rugged peaks; and the 1,700-mi (2,700-km) sweep of the Aleutian islands, barren masses of volcanic origin. Western Alaska extends from Bristol Bay to the Seward Peninsula, an immense tundra dotted with lakes and containing the deltas of the Yukon and Kuskokwim rivers, the longest in the state at 1,900 mi (3,058 km) and 680 mi (1,094 km), respectively. The Yukon River also ranks third among the nation's longest rivers; its source is McNeil River in Canada. Interior Alaska extends north of the Alaska Range and south of the Brooks Range, including most of the drainage of the Yukon and its major tributaries, the Tanana and Porcupine rivers. The Arctic region extends from Kotzebue, north of the Seward Peninsula, east to Canada. From the northern slopes of the Brooks Range, the elevation falls to the Arctic Ocean. The mean elevation of the state is approximately 1,900 ft (580 m).

The 11 highest mountains in the United States—including the highest in North America, Mt. McKinley (20,320 ft/6,198 m), located in the Alaska Range—are in the state, which also contains half the world's glaciers; the largest, Malaspina, covers more area than the entire state of Rhode Island. Ice fields cover 4% of the state. Alaska has more than three million lakes larger than 20 acres (8 hectares), and more than one-fourth of all the inland water wholly within the United States lies inside the state's borders. The largest lake is Iliamna, occupying about 1,000 sq mi (2,600 sq km). The lowest point of the state is at sea level at the Pacific Ocean.

The most powerful earthquake in recorded US history, measuring 8.5 on the Richter scale, struck the Anchorage region on 27 March 1964, resulting in 114 deaths and $500 million in property damage in Alaska and along the US West Coast.

³CLIMATE

Americans, who called Alaska "Seward's icebox" when it was first purchased from the Russians, were unaware of the variety of climatic conditions within its six topographic regions. Although minimum daily winter temperatures in the Arctic region and in the Brooks Range average -20°F (-29°C) and the ground at Point Barrow is frozen permanently to 1,330 ft (405 m), summer maximum daily temperatures in the Alaskan lowlands average above 60°F (16°C) and have been known to exceed 90°F (32°C). The southeastern region is moderate, ranging from a daily average of 30°F (-1°C) in January to 56°F (13°C) in July; the south-central zone has a similar summer range, but winters are somewhat harsher, especially in the interior. The Aleutian Islands have chilly, damp winters and rainy, foggy weather for most of the year; western Alaska is also rainy and cool. The all-time high for the state was 100°F (38°C), recorded at Ft. Yukon on 27 June 1915; the reading of -79.8°F (-62°C), registered at Prospect Creek Camp in the northwestern part of the state on 23 January 1971, is the lowest temperature ever officially recorded in the United States.

The annual normal daily mean temperature in Juneau is 41.5°F (5.3°C). Juneau receives an annual average precipitation of 55.2 in (140 cm), with an average of 99 in (251 cm) of snowfall recorded at the airport there each year. The entire southeastern region of Alaska has a wide range of microclimates with varying levels of precipitation; Juneau's metropolitan area precipitation ranges from 40 in (102 cm) to over 100 in (254 cm) per year. Parts of Alaska are prone to wildfires, which burned about 4.4 million acres statewide in 2005.

⁴FLORA AND FAUNA

Life zones in Alaska range from grasslands, mountains, and tundra to thick forests, in which Sitka spruce (the state tree), western hemlock, tamarack, white birch, and western red cedar predominate. Various hardy plants and wild flowers spring up during the short growing season on the semiarid tundra plains. Some species of poppy and gentian are endangered.

Mammals abound amid the wilderness. Great herds of caribou migrate across some northern areas of the state. Moose move within ranges they establish, but do not migrate seasonally or move in herds as do caribou. Reindeer were introduced to Alaska as herd animals for Alaska Natives, and there are no free-ranging herds in the state. Kodiak, polar, black, and grizzly bears, Dall sheep, and an abundance of small mammals are also found. The sea otter and musk ox have been successfully reintroduced. Round Island, along the north shore of Bristol Bay, has the world's largest walrus rookery. North America's largest population of bald eagles nest in Alaska, and whales migrate annually to the icy bays. Pristine lakes and streams are famous for trout and salmon fishing. In all, 386 species of birds, 430 fishes, 105 mammals, 7 amphibians, and 3 reptiles have been found in the state.

Izembek Lagoon, at the tip of the Alaskan Peninsula, contains what is considered to be the most extensive eelgrass meadow in the world. The area is a staging and nesting ground for hundreds of thousands of migratory birds and ducks. At least 39 species of fish visit the site as a spawning ground.

In April 2006, a total of 12 species occurring within the state were on the threatened and endangered species list of the US Fish and Wildlife Service. These included 11 endangered animals, such as the Eskimo curlew, short-tailed albatross, leatherback sea turtle, Steller sea-lion, and bowhead, finback, and humpback whales. Three species listed as threatened included the spectacled eider, Steller's aider, and Steller sea-lion. Numerous species considered endangered in the coterminous US remain common in Alaska, however.

⁵ENVIRONMENTAL PROTECTION

In 1997, Alaska's number one environmental health problem was the unsafe water and sanitation facilities in over 135 of Alaska's communities—mostly Alaska Native villages. The people of these communities must carry their water from streams or watering points to their homes; people must use "honey buckets" or privies for disposal of human waste; and solid waste lagoons are usually a collection of human waste, trash, and junk, infested with flies and other carriers of disease. The government of Alaska, under then-governor Tony Knowles, established a goal of "putting the honey bucket in museums" as of 2005. To accomplish this goal, in 1993 Knowles established the "Rural Sanitation Task Force" to guide the effort and has committed approximately $40 million per year in state and federal funds to finance new water, sewer, and solid waste facilities. In 2005, federal EPA grants awarded to the state included over $49 million for the development and construction of water and wastewater systems.

A tremendous backlog of contaminated sites from World War II (1939–45) military installations exists, and some of these sites many years later were discovered to be the source of contamination of groundwater, drinking water, and fisheries habitat. The US Environment Protection Agency (EPA) database listed 86 hazardous waste sites in Alaska in 2003. As of 2006, six of these sites were on the National Priorities List, five of which were military installations. The Standard Steel & Metal Salvage Yard of the US Department of Transportation had been deleted from the list that year. Sites have been identified and prioritized, and an aggressive state/federal cleanup effort is underway. Two former pulp mill sites in southeast Alaska are also the subject of major cleanup efforts. In 2005, the EPA spent $179,975 through the Superfund program for the cleanup of hazardous waste sites in the state.

Alaskan wetlands, which cover about 170 million acres, serve as resting and nesting grounds for over 13 million ducks and geese and 100 million shorebirds. Freshwater wetlands, primarily peatlands or marshes, bogs, fens, tundra, and meadows, cover about 110 million acres. Protection of coastal wetlands is shared by local, state, and rural regional governments. Izembek Lagoon National Wildlife Refuge, located at the westernmost tip of the Alaskan Peninsula, was designated as a Ramsar Wetland of International Importance in 1986.

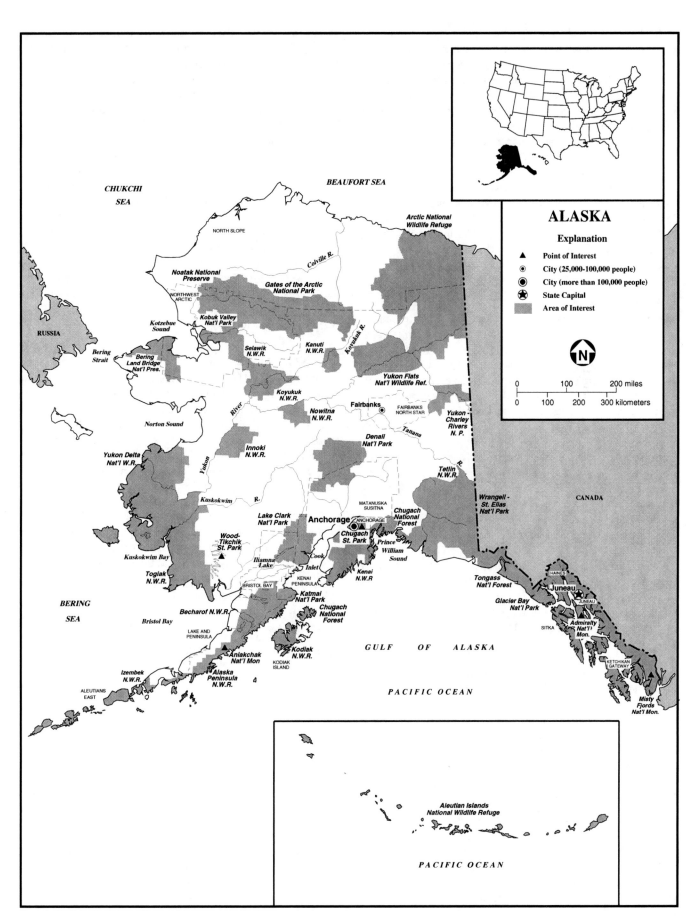

CHUKCHI
SEA

BEAUFORT SEA

Arctic National
Wildlife Refuge

NORTH SLOPE

Colville R.

Noatak National
Preserve

Gates of the Arctic
National Park

NORTHWEST
ARCTIC

Kotzebue
Sound

Kobuk Valley
Nat'l Park

Kanuti
N.W.R.

RUSSIA

Selawik
N.W.R.

Koyukuk R.

Bering
Strait

Bering
Land Bridge
Nat'l Pres.

Yukon Flats
Nat'l Wildlife Ref.

Koyukuk
N.W.R.

Nowitna
N.W.R.

Fairbanks

FAIRBANKS
NORTH STAR

Yukon-
Charley
Rivers
N. P.

Norton Sound

River

Innoki
N.W.R.

Denali
Nat'l Park

Tanana

Yukon Delta
Nat'l W.R.

Yukon

Tetlin
N.W.R.

R.

CANADA

Kuskokwim   R.

Lake Clark
Nat'l Park

MATANUSKA
SUSITNA

Chugach
National
Forest

Wrangell -
St. Elias
Nat'l Park

Wood-
Tikchik
St. Park

Anchorage

ANCHORAGE

Chugach
St. Park

Prince
William
Sound

Kuskokwim Bay

Iliamna
Lake

Cook

Inlet

Kenai
N.W.R

Togiak
N.W.R.

KENAI
PENINSULA

Tongass
Nat'l Forest

Juneau

BERING

SEA

Becharof N.W.R.

BRISTOL BAY

Katmai
Nat'l Park

Chugach
National
Forest

Glacier Bay
Nat'l Park

HAINES

JUNEAU

Bristol Bay

LAKE AND
PENINSULA

Kodiak
N.W.R.

GULF   OF   ALASKA

SITKA

Admiralty
Nat'l
Mon.

Izembek
N.W.R.

Aniakchak
Nat'l Mon

Alaska
Peninsula
N.W.R.

KODIAK
ISLAND

PACIFIC OCEAN

KETCHIKAN
GATEWAY

ALEUTIANS
EAST

Misty
Fjords
Nat'l Mon.

ALASKA

Explanation

▲ Point of Interest
⊙ City (25,000-100,000 people)
◉ City (more than 100,000 people)
★ State Capital
Area of Interest

N

| 0 | | 100 | | 200 miles |
| 0 | 100 | 200 | 300 kilometers |

Aleutian Islands
National Wildlife Refuge

PACIFIC OCEAN

The 1989 Exxon Valdez oil spill highlighted the need for better prevention and response abilities. Since then these capabilities have been increased through stronger laws and more clearly defined roles among all the various governments and communities and greatly enhanced state regulatory agency capabilities. State-of-the-art tugs now escort tankers in Prince William Sound; these tankers are constantly monitored to ensure that they stay on course, and their crews have been increased to ensure redundancy of critical positions.

Oil development on the North Slope and in Cook Inlet, mining throughout the state, and timber harvesting largely in the southern regions remain areas of focus for environmental protection, as do winter violations of air quality standards for carbon monoxide in Anchorage and Fairbanks. In 2003, 539.6 million lb of toxic chemicals were released by the state, the highest amount of any state in the nation.

6 POPULATION

Alaska, with a land area one-fifth the size of the conterminous United States, ranked 47th in population in 2005 with an estimated total of 663,661, an increase of 5.9% since 2000. Between 1990 and 2000, Alaska's population grew from 550,043 to 626,932, or 14%. The state is projected to have a population of 732,544 by 2015 and 820,881 by 2025. Regions of settlement and development constitute less than 1% of Alaska's total land area. The population density was 1.2 persons per sq mi in 2004, making Alaska the nation's most sparsely settled state.

Historically, population shifts in Alaska have directly reflected economic and political changes. The Alaska gold rush of the 1890s resulted in a population boom from 32,052 in 1890 to 63,592 a decade later; by the 1920s, however, mining had declined and Alaska's population had decreased to 55,036. The region's importance to US national defense during the 1940s led to a rise in population from 72,524 to 128,643 during that decade. Oil development, especially the construction of the Alaska pipeline, brought a 78% population increase between 1960 and 1980. Almost all of this gain was from migration.

The state's population is much younger than that of the nation as a whole. The median age was 33.4 in 2004, compared with the national average of 36.2, and only 6.4% of all Alaskans were 65 years of age or older, while 28.7% were under 18 years old (compared with the national average of 25%). Alaska is one of the few states where men outnumber women; as of 2004, women accounted for 48.3% of Alaskan residents.

About half of Alaska's residents live in and around Anchorage, whose population was estimated at 272,687 in 2004. The 2004 estimated population of Fairbanks was 85,930. Less than one-quarter of the population lives in Western Alaska.

7 ETHNIC GROUPS

In 2000 Native Americans accounted for 15.6% of Alaska's population—the highest percentage of any state. In 2004, that figure was 15.8% of Alaska's population. American Indians, primarily Athabaskan (14,520) and Tlingit-Haida (14,825) living in southeastern Alaska (Alaska Panhandle), numbered around 29,345 in 2000. There are also small numbers of Tsimshian living in this area. Eskimos (45,919) and Aleuts (11,941), the other native peoples, live mostly in scattered villages to the north and northwest. Taken together, Alaska Natives were estimated in 2000 to number about 98,043, up from 86,000 (16%) in 1996. The Native Claims Settlement Act of 1971 gave 13 native corporations nearly $1 billion in compensation for exploration, mining, and drilling rights, and awarded them royalties on oil and the rights to nearly 12% of Alaska's land area.

In 2000, the black population was 21,787, or 3.5% of the total population, down slightly from 22,000 in 1990. In 2004, the black population was 3.6% of the total population. Among those of Asian origin in 2000 were 12,712 Filipinos, 1,414 Japanese, and 4,573 Koreans; in the same year, the total Asian population was 25,116 and Pacific Islanders numbered 3,309. In 2004, the Asian population was 4.5% of the total population. In 2000, of Alaska's total population, about 25,852 individuals was of Hispanic or Latino origin, with 13,334 of those claiming Mexican ancestry (up from 6,888 in 1990). In 2004, 4.9% of the population claimed Hispanic or Latino origin, and 4.7% of the population claimed origin of two or more races. Foreign-born persons numbered 37,170, or 5.9% of the population (up from 4.4% in 1990).

8 LANGUAGES

From the Tlingit, Haida, and Tsimshian groups of lower Alaska almost no language influence has been felt, save for *hooch* (from Tlingit *hoochino*); but some native words have escaped into general usage, notably Eskimo *mukluk* and Aleut *parka*. Native placenames abound: Skagway and Ketchikan (Tlingit), Kodiak and Katmai (Eskimo), and Alaska and Akutan (Aleut).

In 2000, 85.7% of the population five years old and older was reported to speak only English in the home, a decrease over 87.9% recorded in 1990.

The following table gives selected statistics from the 2000 Census for language spoken at home by persons five years old and over. The category "Other Native North American languages" includes Apache, Cherokee, Choctaw, Dakota, Keres, Pima, and Yupik. The category "Other Pacific Island languages" includes Chamorro, Hawaiian, Ilocano, Indonesian, and Samoan.

LANGUAGE	NUMBER	PERCENT
Population 5 years and over	**579,740**	**100.0**
Speak only English	496,982	85.7
Speak a language other than English	82,758	14.3
Speak a language other than English	**82,758**	**14.3**
Other Native North American languages	30,121	5.2
Spanish or Spanish Creole	16,674	2.9
Tagalog	8,934	1.5
Korean	4,369	0.8
German	3,574	0.6
Russian	2,952	0.5
Other Pacific Island languages	2,591	0.4
French (incl. Patois, Cajun)	2,197	0.4
Japanese	1,392	0.2
Chinese	1,295	0.2

9 RELIGIONS

The largest religious organization in the state is the Roman Catholic Church, which had 52,892 members and 78 parishes in 2004; the Anchorage archdiocese reported about 29,693 members. In 2006, the Latter-day Saints (Mormons), reported a statewide membership of 27,600 members, with 73 congregations; a small local temple was built in Anchorage in 1999. As of 2000, the Southern

Baptists have been one of the largest Protestant denominations, with 22,959 adherents and 68 congregations; there were 526 new members in the Southern Baptist Convention in 2002.

Many Aleuts were converted to the Russian Orthodox religion during the 18th century, and small Russian Orthodox congregations are still active on the Aleutian Islands, in Kodiak and southeastern Alaska, and along the Yukon River. The Orthodox Church in America—Territorial Dioceses had 20,000 adherents and 46 congregations in 2000.

The next largest denominations (with 2000 data) include the Assembly of God, 11,638; Independent, Non-Charismatic Churches, 7,600; and Episcopalians, 6,693. There were about 3,525 Jews and 1,381 Muslims. About 65.7% of the population did not specify a religious affiliation.

10 TRANSPORTATION

The first rail transportation networks in Alaska were constructed to serve mining interests. The 110-mi (177-km) White Pass and Yukon Railway (WP&YRR), originally constructed during the Klondike gold rush and completed in 1900, constituted the key link between tidewater at Skagway, the Yukon River, and the gold fields. Today, this line runs as a summer-only tourist attraction and provides service between Skagway and Fraser, British Columbia. Shortly after the turn of the century, the Guggenheims financed the construction of the Copper River & Northwestern Railway, which connected Cordova and McCarthy to service the Kennicott Copper Mining Company.

Regular passenger and freight railroad service began in 1923, when the Alaska Railroad began operation. The Alaska Railroad links communities between Whittier, Seward, Anchorage, and Fairbanks. As of 2003, this railroad of 466 route mi (750 km) was not connected to any other North American line (although rail-barge service provides access to the rest of the US rail network). The Alaska Railroad was federally operated until 1985, when it was bought by the state government for $22.3 million. The railroad carries volumes of coal from Healy north to Fairbanks (600,000 tons/year) and south to Seward for export (800,000 tons/year). The railroad also carries large volumes of gravel to Anchorage (more than two million tons from Palmer in the mid-1990s) and petroleum products (more than one million tons from Mapco's North Pole refinery) to Anchorage and various military bases in the area. The railroad is increasing summer passenger travel, often by hauling dome/dining rail cars owned by tour companies.

The Alaska Highway, which extends 1,523 mi (2,451 km) from Dawson Creek, British Columbia, to Fairbanks, is the only total road link with the rest of the United States. In-state roads are few and far between: although Fairbanks, Anchorage, and Seward are linked, Juneau, the state capital, has no road link. In total, there were 14,107 mi (22,712 km) of roads in use in 2004, including more than 1,800 mi (2,896 km) of roads in national parks and forests. During that same year, the state had around 669,000 registered vehicles and 482,532 licensed drivers. The largest public transit system, that of Anchorage, accommodated over three million unlinked passenger trips annually in the mid-1990s.

The Alaska Marine Highway System (AMHS) provides year-round scheduled ferry service to over 30 communities throughout southeast and southwest Alaska. Service extends from Bell-ingham, Washington, and Prince Rupert, British Columbia. This ferry system extends over 3,500 route mi (5,632 km) and connects communities with each other, with regional centers, and with the continental road system.

Water transport in Alaska is dominated by Valdez, which annually ships about 100 million tons of crude petroleum from the Trans-Alaska Pipeline Terminal. In 2004, total cargo volume for the Port of Valdez totaled 46.758 million tons, making it the 18th-busiest port in the United States. Kenai/Nikishka is the state's second-largest freight-handling port and also has petroleum as its principal commodity. Anchorage is the state's largest general cargo port, with over three million tons per year. In 2004, Alaska had 5,497 mi (8,850 km) of navigable inland waterways. Waterborne shipments for the state in 2003 totaled 65.353 million tons.

Air travel is the primary means of intrastate transportation, with regional carriers serving remote communities. In 2005, Alaska had a total of 678 public- and private-use aviation-related facilities. This included 517 airports, 37 heliports, and 124 seaplane bases. The state has three major international airports, at Anchorage, Fairbanks, and Juneau, the state's capital. Anchorage International Airport (AIA) is a major refueling stop for international freight airplanes and is a freight hub for Federal Express and United Parcel Service. In 2004, Anchorage International had 2,439,969 passenger enplanements. Fairbanks International in that same year had 420,394 enplanements, while Juneau International had 377,505.

11 HISTORY

At some time between 10,000 and 40,000 years ago, the ancestors of all of America's aboriginal peoples trekked over a land bridge that connected northeastern Siberia with northwestern America. These early hunter-gatherers dispersed, eventually becoming three distinct groups: Aleut, Eskimo, and Indian.

Ages passed before overseas voyagers rediscovered Alaska. Separate Russian parties led by Aleksei Chirikov and Vitas Bering (who had sailed in 1728 through the strait that now bears his name) landed in Alaska in 1741. Within a few years, the discoverers were followed by the exploiters, who hunted the region's fur-bearing animals. In 1784, the first permanent Russian settlement was established on Kodiak Island: 15 years later, the Russian American Company was granted a monopoly over the region. Its manager, Aleksandr Baranov, established Sitka as the company's headquarters. In 1802, the Tlingit Indians captured Sitka, but two years later lost the town and the war with the Russian colonizers. Fluctuations in the fur trade, depletion of the sea otter, and the Russians' inability to make their settlements self-sustaining limited their development of the region. Increasingly, the czarist government viewed the colonies as a drain on the treasury. In 1867, as a result of the persistence of Secretary of State William H. Seward, a devoted American expansionist, Russia agreed to sell its American territories to the United States for $7,200,000. From 1867 until the first Organic Act of 1884, which provided for a federally appointed governor, Alaska was administered first by the US Army, then by the US Customs Service.

The pace of economic development quickened after the discovery of gold in 1880 at Juneau. Prospectors began moving into the eastern interior after this success, leading to gold strikes on Forty

Mile River in 1886 and at Circle in 1893. But it was the major strike in Canada's Klondike region in 1896 that sparked a mass stampede to the Yukon Valley and other regions of Alaska, including the Arctic. The gold rush led to the establishment of permanent towns in the interior for the first time.

Subsequent development of the fishing and timber industries increased Alaska's prosperity and prospects, although the region suffered from a lack of transportation facilities. A significant achievement came in 1914, when construction started on the Alaska Railroad connecting Seward, a new town with an ice-free port, with Anchorage and Fairbanks. Politically there were advances as well. In 1906, Alaskans were allowed to elect a nonvoting delegate to Congress for the first time. Congress granted territorial status to the region in 1912, and the first statehood bill was introduced in Congress four years later.

Mineral production declined sharply after 1914. Population declined too, and conditions remained depressed through the 1920s, although gold mining was helped by a rise in gold prices in 1934. World War II (1939–45) provided the next great economic impetus for Alaska; the Aleutian campaign that followed the Japanese invasion of the islands, though not as pivotal as the combat in other areas of the Pacific, did show American policymakers that Alaska's geography was in itself an important resource. Thus the spurt of federal construction and movement of military personnel continued even after the war ended, this time directed at the Soviet Union—only 40 mi (64 km) across the Bering Strait—rather than Japan.

The US government built the Alaska Highway and many other facilities, including docks, airfields, and an extension of the Alaska Railroad. Population soared as thousands of civilian workers and military personnel moved to the territory. The newcomers added impetus to a new movement for statehood, and the Alaska Statehood Act was adopted by Congress in June 1958 and ratified by Alaska voters that August. On 3 January 1959, President Dwight Eisenhower signed the proclamation that made Alaska the 49th state.

In 1971, the Native Claims Settlement Act provided an extensive grant to the state's natives but also precipitated a long federal-state controversy over land allocations. A major oil field was discovered in 1968, and in 1974, over the opposition of many environmentalists, construction began on the 789-mi (1,270-km) Trans-Alaska Pipeline from Prudhoe Bay to Valdez. The oil that began flowing through the pipeline in 1977 made Alaska almost immediately one of the nation's leading energy producers.

Alaska's extraordinary oil wealth enabled it to embark on a heavy program of state services and to abolish the state income tax. However, state spending failed to stimulate the private sector to the degree expected. Further, the state's dependence on oil—82% of its revenue came from oil industry taxes and royalties—became a disadvantage when overproduction in the Middle East drove the price of oil down from $36 a barrel at the peak of Alaska's oil boom in 1980–81 to $13.50 a barrel in 1988. In 1986, the state's revenues had declined by two-thirds. Alaska lost 20,000 jobs between 1985 and 1989. The economy's collapse forced 10,000 properties into foreclosure in those years. At the same time, the state rapidly depleted its oil reserves. In 1981, the Interior Department estimated that 83 billion barrels of undiscovered oil existed. By 1989, that estimate had dropped to 49 billion barrels.

On 24 March 1989, the *Exxon Valdez*, a 987-ft (300-m) oil tanker, hit a reef and ran aground. The tanker spilled 11 million gallons of crude oil. The oil eventually contaminated 1,285 mi (2,068 km) of shoreline, fouling Prince William Sound and its wildlife sanctuary, the Gulf of Alaska, and the Alaska Peninsula. In the settlement of the largest environmental suit in US history brought by the state and federal governments, Exxon was fined $1.025 billion in civil and criminal penalties. By 1992, Exxon had spent some $2 billion cleaning up Prince William Sound and paid another $300 million in compensation for losses. Ten years after the spill, a $100-million response system was in place to prevent future disasters and every tanker that departed the Valdez terminal in Prince William Sound was escorted by tugboats.

In the early 1990s, oil production in Prudhoe Bay was declining, a development that forced Governor Tony Knowles to implement cutbacks in state spending and brought a renewal of proposals to open areas of the nearly 20-million acre (8.1 million hectare) Arctic National Wildlife Refuge (ANWR) to commercial development. A congressional bill introduced in October 1999 by Alaskan senator Frank Murkowski and backed by the state's other members of Congress, would allow oil and gas, tourism, and residential development in the refuge, which is often called "America's Serengeti" for its wealth and diversity of wildlife. As the Republican-dominated Congress considered the bill in 2000 and after, conservationists rallied against it. In November 2002, Murkowski was elected governor of Alaska and continued his support for oil drilling in ANWR. The US Senate has continually voted to reject drilling in ANWR, but the US House of Representatives has voted in favor. In August 2005, President George W. Bush signed the first national energy legislation in more than a decade, and signaled the law would help wean the United States off foreign sources of oil by encouraging the domestic production of oil and natural gas and the use of cleaner-burning, domestic energy sources such as nuclear power, ethanol, and liquefied natural gas. The legislation dropped an amendment regarding the long-standing contentious issue of drilling in ANWR, which had blocked passage of earlier versions. As early as October 2005, however, the Senate Energy Committee voted to open ANWR to oil drilling as part of a broad budget bill to fund the federal government; the issue is far from being resolved.

12 STATE GOVERNMENT

Under Alaska's first and only constitution—adopted in 1956, effective since the time of statehood and amended 29 times by January 2005—the House of Representatives consists of 40 members elected for two-year terms; the Senate has 20 members elected for staggered four-year terms. The minimum age is 21 for a representative, 25 for a senator; legislators must have resided in the state for at least three years before election and in the district at least one year. Annual legislative sessions begin in January and are limited to 121 calendar days. Special sessions, limited to 30 calendar days, may be called by a two-thirds vote of the members. As of 2004, legislators' salaries were $24,012. Legislators receive reimbursement for living expenses at the rate of $204 per day.

Alaska's executive branch, modeled after New Jersey's, features a strong governor who appoints most cabinet members and judges subject to legislative confirmation. The lieutenant governor (elected jointly with the governor) is the only other elected executive. The governor must be at least 30 years old, and must have been a US citizen for seven years and an Alaska resident for seven years. The term of office is four years, and the governor is limited to two consecutive terms. The qualifications for the lieutenant governor are the same as for the governor. As of December 2004, the governor's salary was $85,766.

After a bill has been passed by the legislature, it becomes law if signed by the governor; if left unsigned for 15 days (Sundays excluded) while the legislature is in session, or for 20 days after it has adjourned; or if passed by a two-thirds vote of the elected members of the combined houses over a gubernatorial veto (to override a veto of an appropriations bill requires a three-fourths vote). Constitutional amendments require a two-thirds vote of the legislature and ratification by the electorate. Voters must be 18 years old (within 90 days of registration), US citizens, and not registered to vote in another state. Restrictions apply to convicted felons and those declared mentally incompetent by the court.

Between 1993 and 1995, the Constitutional Revision Task Force studied alternatives to existing methods of revising the state constitution, recommending the appointment of a permanent advisory commission to submit proposals to the state legislature. In 2002 voters rejected a proposal that called for a constitutional convention.

13 POLITICAL PARTIES

When Congress debated the statehood question in the 1950s, it was assumed that Alaska would be solidly Democratic, but this expectation has not been borne out; as of 2004 there were 472,000 registered voters, of which only nearly 16% were Democratic, while 25% were Republican and 59% were unaffiliated or members of other parties.

In 1990, a member of the Alaskan Independent party, Walter J. Hickel, was elected governor. Democrat Tony Knowles won the governorship in the November 1994 election and was reelected in 1998. Two Republicans, Frank Murkowski and Ted Stevens, were reelected to the US Senate in 1998 and 2002, respectively. Murkowski was elected Alaska's governor in 2002; he appointed his daughter Lisa to the US Senate to fill his vacancy when he assumed the office of governor; Lisa Murkowski then won election in the 2004 Senate race, with 48.6% of the vote to Democrat Tony Knowles 45.6%.

In 2004, Alaska's incumbent US Representative, Republican Don Young, was reelected with 71% of the vote. In presidential elections since 1968, Alaskans have voted Republican 10 consecutive times. Alaskans reelected incumbent Republican George W. Bush with 61.8% of the vote in 2004 (an increase from 59% in 2000) to Democrat John Kerry's 35.0%. The state had three electoral votes in the 2004 presidential election. Alaska's state legislature in 2005 consisted of 8 Democrats and 11 Republicans in the Senate, and 14 Democrats and 26 Republicans in the House. Twelve women held statewide elected office in 2003.

14 LOCAL GOVERNMENT

Alaska has 12 borough governments, which function much in the same way that county governments do in other states. Each borough has its own administrative assembly. There are also four consolidated city-borough governments: Anchorage, Juneau, Sitka, and Yakutat. Alaska is divided into 149 municipalities, ranging from the geographically small Bristol Bay (519 sq mi or 1,344 sq km) to the expansive North Slope (87,860 sq mi or 227,557 sq mi). Most municipalities were governed by elected mayors and councils, and there are more than 100 village councils. There are 53 public school districts in Alaska. The state has 14 special districts. For census purposes, Alaska is divided into 27 county equivalents.

In 1971 land claims were settled, returning 44 million acres of federal land to Alaska's native population. Through the US Bureau of Indian Affairs, native communities receive varying levels of assistance including help in setting up villages in accordance with governing laws. In 2002, there were 12 Alaska Native Regional Corporations.

In 2005, local government accounted for about 27,167 full-time (or equivalent) employment positions.

15 STATE SERVICES

To address the continuing threat of terrorism and to work with the federal Department of Homeland Security, homeland security in Alaska operates under the authority of the governor and state statute; the adjutant general was designated as the state homeland security adviser.

By law, Alaska's government may contain no more than 20 administrative departments. As of 2006 departments in Alaska were: Administration; Commerce, Community, and Economic Development; Corrections; Education and Early Development; Environmental Conservation; Fish and Game; Health and Social Services; Labor and Workforce Development; Law; Military and Veterans Affairs; Natural Resources; Public Safety; Revenue; and Transportation and Public Facilities. In addition, the state has an ombudsman with limited powers to investigate citizen complaints against state agencies.

16 JUDICIAL SYSTEM

The Alaska Supreme Court, consists of a chief justice and four associate justices, and hears appeals for civil matters from the 15 superior courts, whose 40 judges are organized among the four state

---

Alaska Presidential Vote by Major Political Parties, 1960–2004

YEAR	ELECTORAL VOTE	ALASKA WINNER	DEMOCRAT	REPUBLICAN
1960	3	Nixon (R)	29,809	30,953
1964	3	*Johnson (D)	44,329	22,930
1968	3	*Nixon (R)	35,411	37,600
1972	3	*Nixon (R)	32,967	55,349
1976	3	Ford (R)	44,058	71,555
1980	3	*Reagan (R)	41,842	86,112
1984	3	*Reagan (R)	62,007	138,377
1988	3	*Bush (R)	72,584	119,251
1992**	3	Bush (R)	78,294	102,000
1996***	3	Dole (R)	80,380	122,746
2000	3	*Bush, G. W. (R)	79,004	167,398
2004	3	*Bush, G. W. (R)	111,025	190,889

*Won US presidential election.
**IND. candidate Ross Perot received 73,481 votes.
***IND. candidate Ross Perot received 26,333 votes.

judicial districts, and for criminal matters from the three-member court of appeals. The superior court has original jurisdiction in all civil and criminal matters, and it hears appeals from the district court. The lowest court is the district court, of which there are 56 in four districts. All judges are appointed by the governor from nominations made by the Judicial Council, but are thereafter subject to voter approval. Supreme court justices serve terms of ten years, while court of appeals and superior court judges serve terms of eight years. District judges serve terms of four years.

As of 31 December 2004, a total of 4,554 prisoners were held in Alaska's state and federal prisons, an increase from 4,527 of 0.6% from the previous year. As of year-end 2004, a total of 397 inmates were female, up from 392 or 1.3% from the year before. Among sentenced prisoners (one year or more), Alaska had an incarceration rate of 398 per 100,000 population in 2004.

According to the Federal Bureau of Investigation, in 2004 Alaska had a violent crime rate (murder/nonnegligent manslaughter; forcible rape; robbery; aggravated assault) of 634.5 reported incidents per 100,000 population, or a total of 4,159 reported incidents. Crimes against property (burglary; larceny/theft; and motor vehicle theft) in that same year totaled 22,172 reported incidents or 3,382.8 reported incidents per 100,000 people. Alaska does not have a death penalty.

In 2003, Alaska spent $207,159,311 on homeland security, an average of $296 per state resident.

17 ARMED FORCES

A huge buildup of military personnel occurred after World War II (1939–45), as the Cold War with the Soviet Union led the United States to establish the Distant Early Warning (DEW) System, Ballistic Missile Early Warning System, and Joint Surveillance System in the area. Later years saw a cutback in personnel, however, from a high of 40,214 in 1962 to 15,906 in 2002, 9,136 of them in the Air Force. Anchorage is the home of both the largest Army base, Fort Richardson (Anchorage), and the largest Air Force base, Elmendorf (Anchorage). These bases had the most active-duty military personnel and civilian personnel in the state, 7,140 and 1,133, respectively. In the Aleutians are several Navy facilities and the Shemya Air Force Base. In 2004, there were 21,002 active duty military personnel, 1,513 in the National Guard, and 3,527 civilian personnel. Alaska firms received defense contracts worth $1.2 billion in 2004. In that same year, the Defense Department payroll was about $1.2 billion, including retired military pay.

There were 67,299 veterans of US military service in Alaska as of 2003, of whom 3,475 served in World War II; 3,612 in the Korean conflict; 23,948 during the Vietnam era; and 15,678 during 1990–2000 (in the Gulf War). Expenditures on veterans amounted to $230 million in 2004.

The Alaska State Troopers provide police protection throughout the state, except in the larger cities, where municipal police forces have jurisdiction. As of 31 October 2004, the Alaska State Troopers employed 353 full-time sworn officers.

18 MIGRATION

The earliest immigrants to North America, more than 10,000 years ago, likely came to Alaska via a land bridge across what is now the Bering Strait. The Russian fur traders who arrived during the 1700s found Aleuts, Eskimos, and American Indians already established there. Despite more than a century of Russian sovereignty over the area, however, few Russians came, and those that did returned to the mother country with the purchase of Alaska by the United States in 1867. Virtually all other migration to Alaska has been from the continental US—first during the gold rush of the late 19th century and most recently during the oil boom of the 1970s. Between 1970 and 1983, Alaska's net gain from migration was 78,000, but Alaska suffered net losses in domestic migration of over 37,500 from 1985 to 1990, and 21,000 from 1990 and 1998.

Mobility is a way of life in Alaska. Urbanization increased with migration during the 1980s; the urban population increased from 64.5% of the total population in 1980 to 67.5% in 1990. In the 1990s, migration added 17,000 people to the state. In 1998, Alaska admitted 1,008 immigrants. Between 1995 and 1998, the population increased 2.1%. In the period 2000–05, net international migration was 5,800 and net internal migration was -4,619, for a net gain of 1,181 people.

19 INTERGOVERNMENTAL COOPERATION

Alaska participates with Washington, Oregon, and California in the Pacific States Marine Fisheries Commission. Alaska also belongs to other Western regional agreements covering energy, corrections, radioactive waste, and education. The most important federal-state effort, the Joint Federal-State Land Use Planning Commission, was involved with the Alaska lands controversy throughout the 1970s. The Interstate Oil and Gas Compact was enacted in 1980. In 1990, Alaska also joined the Western States/British Columbia Oil Spill Tax Force. Federal grants to Alaska amounted to $2.3 billion in fiscal year 2001; following a national trend, they declined markedly thereafter, to $1.634 billion in fiscal year 2005, an estimated $1.751 billion in fiscal year 2006, and an estimated $1.849 billion in fiscal year 2007.

20 ECONOMY

When Alaska gained statehood in 1959, its economy was almost totally dependent on the US government. Fisheries, limited mining (mostly gold and gravel), and some lumber production made up the balance. That all changed with development of the petroleum industry during the 1970s. Construction of the Trans-Alaska Pipeline brought a massive infusion of money and people into the state. Construction, trade, and services boomed—only to decline when the pipeline was completed.

One area of growth in the 1980s and early 1990s was the Alaska groundfish industry. Commercial fishing is one of the bulwarks of the Alaska economy. The seafood industry had wholesale values of more than $3 billion in 1990, and Alaska's fishery accounts for 50% of the total annual US catch. The volume of Alaska groundfish catches rose from 69 million lb (31.3 million kg) in 1980 to 4.8 billion lb (2.2 billion kg) in 1990. Employment in seafood harvesting grew from 45,000 in 1980 to 54,000 in 1991, although the boom has slowed somewhat since.

The tourism industry attracted over 1.1 million visitors in 2000, and contrary to national trends, continued to expand into 2002. The number of inbound cruise ship visitors, for example, increased 14% from summer 2001 to summer 2002. As of 2005, tourism had become the state's second-largest private-sector employer, generating $640 million in payroll and 30,700 jobs. Overall, tourism brings in more than $1 billion annually to the state. Other important industries include timber, mining (including gold, coal, silver, and zinc), and agriculture. From 1997 to 2002, increased environmental regulations and foreign competition from, particularly, Chile and Norway contributed to a decline in employment in the traditional seafood-packing industry of more than 15%. On the other hand, employment in both state and local government and in the hotels and lodging industry increased by almost 15%. Employment in the oil and gas extraction sector increased by about 5% from 1997 to 2002, while employment with the federal government decreased almost 3%. In 2006, rising oil prices, reflecting political instability among suppliers such as Nigeria, Iraq, and possibly Iran, were expected to benefit the Alaskan economy.

In 2004, Alaska's gross state product (GSP) was $34.023 billion, of which the mining sector (including oil extraction) accounted for $7.328 billion or 21.5% of GSP, followed by real estate, rental and leasing at $3.209 billion, or 9% of GSP. The manufacturing sector contributed $725 million, or just over 2% of GSP in 2004. As in other states, small business plays an important role in the state's economy. In 2004, the state had an estimated 63,497 small businesses. Of the 16,975 firms that year with employees, 16,443 or 96.9% were considered small businesses. However, the creation of new businesses fell 24.3% from 2003 to 2004. Business terminations in 2004 totaled 2,650, up 5.7% from 2003, although business bankruptcies in 2004 fell 47.1% (to 64) that year. In 2005, Alaska had the lowest personal bankruptcy rate in the United States. The combined Chapter 7 and Chapter 13 bankruptcy rate in the state stood at 216 filings per 100,000 people.

21 INCOME

In 2005 Alaska had a gross state product (GSP) of $40 billion, which accounted for 0.3% of the nation's gross domestic product and placed the state at number 46 in highest GSP among the 50 states and the District of Columbia.

According to the Bureau of Economic Analysis, in 2004 Alaska had a per capita personal income (PCPI) of $34,000. This ranked 17th in the United States and was 103% of the national average of $33,050. The 1994–2004 average annual growth rate of PCPI was 3.1%. Alaska had a total personal income (TPI) of $22,363,425,000, which ranked 48th in the United States and reflected an increase of 4.4% from 2003. The 1994–2004 average annual growth rate of TPI was 4.0%. Earnings of persons employed in Alaska increased from $17,903,311,000 in 2003 to $19,099,127,000 in 2004, an increase of 6.7%. The 2003–04 national change was 6.3%.

The US Census Bureau reports that the three-year average median household income for 2002–04 in 2004 dollars was $54,627, compared to a national average of $44,473. During the same period an estimated 9.2% of the population was below the poverty line as compared to 12.4% nationwide.

22 LABOR

According to the Bureau of Labor Statistics (BLS), in April 2006 the seasonally adjusted civilian labor force in Alaska numbered 342,300, with approximately 24,000 workers unemployed, yielding an unemployment rate of 7%, compared to the national average of 4.7% for the same period. Preliminary data for the same

period placed nonfarm employment at 313,800. Since the beginning of the BLS data series in 1976, the highest unemployment rate recorded in Alaska was 11.5% in July 1986. The historical low was 5.9% in September 1999. Preliminary nonfarm employment data by occupation for April 2006 showed that approximately 6.1% of the labor force was employed in construction; 20.4% in trade, transportation, and public utilities; 4.7% in financial activities; 7.5% in professional and business services; 11.4% in education and health services; 9.9% in leisure and hospitality services; and 26% in government. Data for manufacturing was unavailable.

The US Department of Labor's Bureau of Labor Statistics reported that in 2005, a total of 63,000 of Alaska's 275,000 employed wage and salary workers were formal members of a union. This represented 22.8% of those so employed, up from 20.1% in 2004, above the national average of 12%. Overall in 2005, a total of 66,000 workers (24.1%) in Alaska were covered by a union or employee association contract, which includes those workers who reported no union affiliation. Alaska is one of 28 states that does not have a right-to-work law. It is also one out of only five states with a union membership rate of over 20%.

As of 1 March 2006, Alaska had a state-mandated minimum wage rate of $7.15 per hour. In 2004, women accounted for 46% of the employed civilian labor force.

The International Brotherhood of Teamsters is especially strong in the state, covering a range of workers from truck drivers to school administrators.

23 AGRICULTURE

A short but intense growing season provides good potential for Alaska commercial agriculture, although the expense of getting agricultural products to market is a limiting factor. International export opportunities are being developed. Alaska's 620 farms covered 900,000 acres (364,000 hectares) in 2004. Commodities including hay, potatoes, lettuce, cabbage, carrots, beef, pork, dairy products, and greenhouse and nursery items are commonly produced. In 2004, hay production was 28,000 tons, valued at $6,440,000; potatoes, 177,000 hundredweight (8 million kg), $3,469,000; and barley for grain, 145,000 tons, $500,000. The leading farming regions of Alaska are the Matanuska Valley, northeast of Anchorage, and Delta Junction, north of Fairbanks.

24 ANIMAL HUSBANDRY

Dairy and livestock products account for about 55% of Alaska's agricultural receipts. In 2003, an estimated 16.7 million lb (7.6 million kg) of milk were produced. Milk cows numbered 1,300 in 2003. Meat and poultry production is negligible by national standards.

25 FISHING

In 2005 Alaska was the leading commercial fishing state in terms of volume and value. The total catch was over 5.3 billion lb (2.4 billion kg), valued at over $1.711 billion. Landings at the port of Dutch Harbor–Unalaska had the highest volume of all US domestic ports (886.4 million lb/402.9 million kg) and the second highest catch in terms of value ($155 million). The Kodiak port ranked fourth in the nation in volume (312.6 million lb/142 million kg) and fourth in value ($91 million).

According to 2004 figures, the salmon catch, the staple of the industry, amounted to 697.8 million lb (317.1 million kg), valued at $225.3 million and representing 94% of total US salmon landings. The distribution of Alaska salmon landings by species that year was pink, 43%; sockeye, 36%; chum, 14%; coho, 5%; and chinook, 2%. Landings of pollock amounted to 3.4 billion lb (1.5 billion kg), and the Pacific cod catch came to about 586.7 million lb (266.7 million kg). The Alaskan catch of sea herring (at 70.8 million lb/32.2 million kg) accounted for 94% of thePacific coast catch. Alaska had the nation's third largest catch of dungeness crab, a major export item for the state.

As of 2003, Alaska had 306 processing and wholesale plants with an average of 8,077 employees. In 2002, the commercial fishing fleet had 14,035 boats and vessels.

Anglers are also attracted by Alaska's abundant stocks of salmon and trout. There were about 468,735 sport anglers licensed in Alaska in 2004.

26 FORESTRY

In 2004, Alaska's forested area was 127,380,000 acres (51,550,000 hectares), far more than any other state. However, the area of harvestable timberland was only 11,865,000 acres (4,801,000 hectares). Some 35,875,000 acres (14,519,000 hectares) of forestland were privately held in 2004. Alaska contains the nation's largest national forests, Tongass in the southeast (17.4 million acres—7 million hectares) and Chugach along the Gulf Coast (6.9 million acres—2.8 million hectares).

Timber companies harvest logs from the two national forests, with the majority from the Tongass National Forest. The timber is made available for harvest through a competitive bidding process. Timber removals in 2003 totaled 140 million cu ft.

27 MINING

Preliminary data from the US Geological Survey put the value of Alaska's nonfuel mineral production in 2004 at an estimated $1.32 billion, up about 22% over 2003 and up almost 2% from 2002 to 2003. Metallic minerals accounted for 94% of Alaska's total nonfuel mineral production in 2004, most of it the result of zinc, lead, and silver production at the Red Dog Mine in the northwestern part of the state and the Greens Creek Mine in southeastern Alaska (southwest of Juneau), and of gold production at the Fort Knox Mine near Fairbanks and the Greens Creek Mine. Overall, Alaska retained its 12th ranked position among the 50 states in total nonfuel mineral output, accounting for 3% of US production.

According to preliminary figures for 2004, Alaska produced 2.8 million metric tons of crushed stone, valued at $16.5 million, and 10.2 million metric tons of sand and gravel, valued at $58 million. Gold and silver production in 2002 (the latest year for which data was available) totaled 16,900 kg and 559,000 kg, respectively, and was valued at $170 million and $83.1 million, respectively.

Although reported placer gold production was limited, it did reflect an increase in output in 2004 of up to 873 kg. In 2003, reported production totaled 734 kg.

The Alaska Department of Natural Resources (DNR) presents reclamation awards to mining firms for exemplary work in return-ing disturbed ground to useful condition as required by state law. In 2004, the award was given to two employees from Taiga Mining Co for work on Bear Creek and its Dry and Ida creek tributaries.

28 ENERGY AND POWER

As of 2003, Alaska had 73 electrical power service providers, of which 34 were publicly owned, 21 were investor owned and 18 were cooperatives. As of that same year, there were 290,842 retail customers. Of that total, over 207,630 received their power from cooperatives. Publicly owned service providers accounted for 56,553 customers, while investor owned providers had 26,659 customers.

Total net summer generating capability by the state's electric-generating plants in 2003 stood at 1.896 million kW, with total production that same year at 6.388 billion kWh. Of the total amount generated, 89.5% came from electric utilities, with the remainder coming from independent producers and combined heat and power service providers. The largest portion of all electric power generated, 3.354 billion kWh (52.9%), came from natural gas-fired plants, with hydroelectric plants in second place at 1.582 billion kWh (25%). Petroleum fueled plants accounted for 13.4% of all power produced, while coal accounted for 8.7%. Alaska had no nuclear power plants.

As of 2004, Alaska had proven crude oil reserves of 4,327 million barrels, or 20% of all US reserves, while output that same year averaged 908,000 barrels per day. Including federal offshore domains, Alaska that year ranked third (second excluding federal offshore) in reserves and in output among the 31 producing states. Alaska had 1,924 producing oil wells and accounted for 17% of all US production. The Trans-Alaska Pipeline runs 789 mi (1,270 km) from the North Slope oil fields to the port of Valdez on the southern coast. Most of Alaska's energy products are produced and refined locally. As of 2005, the state's six refineries had a combined crude distillation capacity of about 374,000 barrels per day.

In 2004, Alaska had 224 producing natural gas and gas condensate wells. In that same year, marketed gas production (all gas produced excluding gas used for repressuring, vented and flared, and nonhydrocarbon gases removed) totaled 471.899 billion cu ft (13.4 billion cu m). As of 31 December 2004, proven reserves of dry or consumer-grade natural gas totaled 8,407 billion cu ft (238.7 billion cu m).

Alaska in 2004, had only one producing coal mine, which was a surface operation. Coal production that same year totaled 1,512,000 short tons, up from 1,081,000 short tons in 2003. The state's sole coal mine was located at Healy.

29 INDUSTRY

Alaska's manufacturing sector is primarily centered on the manufacture of food products, particularly seafood, although there is some petroleum refining, apparel manufacturing, and lumber processing.

According to the US Census Bureau's Annual Survey of Manufactures (ASM) for 2004, Alaska's manufacturing sector had a total shipment value of $50.680 million. Of that total, the manufacturing of food products accounted for $31.039 million.

In 2004, a total of 10,262 people in Alaska were employed in the state's manufacturing sector, according to the ASM. Of that total,

8,696 were actual production workers. In the food manufacturing industry that same year, there were 7,289 production workers, of which 6,486 were actually involved in the production process.

ASM data for 2004 showed that Alaska's manufacturing sector paid $351.542 million in wages. Of that amount, the food-manufacturing sector accounted for $207.230 million.

³⁰COMMERCE

According to the 2002 Census of Wholesale Trade, Alaska's wholesale trade sector had sales that year totaling $3.6 billion from 740 establishments. Wholesalers of durable goods accounted for 393 establishments, followed by nondurable goods wholesalers at 308 and electronic markets, agents, and brokers accounting for 39 establishments. Sales by durable goods wholesalers in 2002 totaled $1.6 billion, while wholesalers of nondurable goods saw sales of $1.7 billion. Electronic markets, agents, and brokers in the wholesale trade industry had sales of $181.7 million.

In the 2002 Census of Retail Trade, Alaska was listed as having 2,661 retail establishments with sales of $7.4 billion. The leading types of retail businesses by number of establishments were: miscellaneous store retailers (458); food and beverage stores (384); motor vehicle and motor vehicle parts dealers (302); clothing and clothing accessories stores (259); and sporting goods, hobby, book, and music stores (247). In terms of sales, general-merchandise stores accounted for the largest share of retail sales at $1.8 billion, followed by motor vehicle and motor vehicle parts dealers at $1.7 billion, and food and beverage stores at $1.2 billion. A total of 32,984 people were employed by the retail sector in Alaska that year.

During 2005, Alaskan exporters sold $3.5 billion of merchandise. Many of Alaska's resource products, including the salmon and crab catch, pass through the Seattle customs district. By federal law, Alaskan petroleum cannot be exported to other countries, a provision many Alaskans would like to see repealed. Around one-third of Alaska's manufactured goods were exported to other countries, with paper and food products being major items.

³¹CONSUMER PROTECTION

Consumer protection in Alaska is the responsibility of the Consumer Protection Unit of the Department of Law, which falls under the Office of the Attorney General and provides consumers with information, investigates business and trade practices, and enforces statutes prohibiting unfair, false, misleading, or deceptive acts and practices.

When dealing with consumer protection issues, the state's Attorney General's Office can initiate civil and criminal proceedings; represent the state before state and federal regulatory agencies; administer consumer protection and education programs; handle formal consumer complaints; and exercise broad subpoena powers. In antitrust actions, the Attorney General's Office can act on behalf of those consumers who are incapable of acting on their own; initiate damage actions on behalf of the state in state or federal courts; and initiate criminal proceedings. However, the state's Attorney General cannot represent counties, cities, and other governmental entities in recovering civil damages under state or federal law.

The offices of the Consumer Protection Unit are located in Anchorage.

³²BANKING

As of June 2005, Alaska had seven insured banks, savings and loans, and saving banks, in addition to one state-chartered and eleven federally chartered credit unions (CUs). Excluding the CUs, Anchorage and Fairbanks each accounted for five and six financial institutions, respectively in 2004. Unlike other states, CUs play a major role in the state's financial industry. As of June 2005, CUs accounted for 49.3% of all assets held by all financial institutions in the state, or some $3.909 billion. Banks, savings and loans, and savings banks collectively accounted for the remaining $4.020 billion in assets held.

Alaska's state-chartered banks are under the regulatory authority of the Department of Community and Economic Development's Division of Banking, Securities, and Corporations, including the Denali State Bank and the Northrim Bank. As of 2003, approximately 18.72% of all bank assets in Alaska were held in state-chartered institutions. The state's federally chartered banks are under the regulatory authority of the Office of the Comptroller of the Currency.

As of 2004, the state's median net interest margin (the difference between the lower rates offered to savers and the higher rates charged on loans) stood at 4.88%, up from 4.86% in 2003.

³³INSURANCE

In 2004, there were 178,000 individual life insurance policies in force, with a total value of $27.7 billion; total value for all categories of life insurance (individual, group, and credit) was $41.2 billion. The average coverage amount is $156,000 per policy holder. Death benefits paid that year totaled $80.5 million.

As of 2003, there were no life insurance companies based on Alaska, but seven property and casualty insurance companies were domiciled there. Direct premiums for property and casualty insurance amounted to $1.4 billion in 2004. That year, there were 2,429 flood insurance policies in force in the state, with a total value of $410.8 million.

In 2004, 52% of state residents held employment-based health insurance policies, 4% held individual policies, and 21% were covered under Medicare and Medicaid; 18% of residents were uninsured. In 2003, employee contributions for employment-based health coverage averaged are 11% for single coverage and 17% for family coverage, representing one of the lowest employee contribution rates in the country. Alaska does not offer extended health benefits in connection with the Consolidated Omnibus Budget Reconciliation Act (COBRA, 1986), a health insurance extension program for those who lose employment-based coverage due to termination or reduction of work hours.

In 2003, there were 375,498 auto insurance policies in effect for private passenger cars. Required minimum coverage includes bodily injury liability of up to $50,000 per individual and $100,000 for all persons injured, as well as property damage liability of $25,000. In 2003, the average expenditure per vehicle for insurance coverage was $937.32, which ranked as the tenth-highest average in the nation.

The insurance industry is regulated by the Department of Commerce and Economic Development's Division of Insurance.

³⁴SECURITIES

There are no securities exchanges in Alaska. In 2005, there were 260 securities, commodities, and financial services sales agents. In 2004, there were over six publicly traded companies within the state, with over three NASDAQ companies: Alaska Communications Systems Group, Inc.; General Communications, Inc.; and Northern Bank.

The Alaska Securities Act of 1959 serves as the foundation for the regulation of the sale of securities through a triple-tiered system of registration for brokers and dealers, as well as through antifraud provisions.

³⁵PUBLIC FINANCE

Alaska's annual budget is prepared by the Division of Budget and Management within the Office of the Governor, and is submitted by the governor to the legislature for amendment and approval. The fiscal year (FY) runs from 1 July through 30 June. Alaska's budget process is by and large timely, as is its financial reporting, with good audit results. The state depends on petroleum-based revenues. In 2006, general funds were estimated at nearly $3.9 billion for resources and $3.9 billion for expenditures. In 2004, federal government grants to Alaska were $3.2 billion. In 2007, federal funding for the construction of an Alaska Region Research Vessel for studying changes in the ocean around Alaska is provided, as well as more funding for the Indian Health Service and Pacific Coastal Salmon Recovery Fund (PCSRF), for tribal efforts at habitat restoration, and funding for the National Oceanic and Atmospheric Administration's (NOAA) Coastal Zone Management Program.

³⁶TAXATION

In 2005, Alaska collected $1,851 million in tax revenues or $2,787 per capita, which placed it eighth among the 50 states in per capita tax burden. The national average was $2,192 per capita. Property taxes accounted for 2.3% of the total; selective sales taxes, 10.3%; corporate income taxes, 31.8%; and other taxes 55.6%.

As of 1 January 2006, Alaska had no state income tax, a distinction it shared with Wyoming, Washington, Nevada, Florida, Texas, and South Dakota. The state taxes corporations at rates ranging from 1.0 to 9.4% depending on tax bracket.

In 2004, state and local property taxes amounted to $859,056,000, or $1,306 per capita. The per capita amount ranks the state 12th highest nationally. Local governments collected $811,688,000 of the total and the state government, $47,368,000.

Alaska does not tax retail sales. However, Alaskan cities and boroughs may levy local sales taxes from 1% to 6%. Food purchased for consumption off-premises is taxable. As of 2004, the tax on cigarettes is 160 cents per pack, which ranks seventh among the 50 states and the District of Columbia. Alaska taxes gasoline at 8 cents per gallon. This is in addition to the 18.4 cents per gallon federal tax on gasoline.

Alaska—State Government Finances

(Dollar amounts in thousands. Per capita amounts in dollars.)

	AMOUNT	PER CAPITA
Total Revenue	8,847,705	13,446.36
General revenue	6,625,657	10,069.39
Intergovernmental revenue	2,193,578	3,333.71
Taxes	1,338,707	2,034.51
General sales	–	–
Selective sales	168,392	255.91
License taxes	83,738	127.26
Individual income tax	–	–
Corporate income tax	339,564	516.05
Other taxes	747,013	1,135.28
Current charges	377,517	573.73
Miscellaneous general revenue	2,715,855	4,127.44
Utility revenue	14,161	21.52
Liquor store revenue	–	–
Insurance trust revenue	2,207,887	3,355.45
Total expenditure	8,089,240	12,293.68
Intergovernmental expenditure	1,049,706	1,595.30
Direct expenditure	7,039,534	10,698.38
Current operation	4,529,620	6,883.92
Capital outlay	886,846	1,347.79
Insurance benefits and repayments	1,165,261	1,770.91
Assistance and subsidies	206,582	313.95
Interest on debt	251,225	381.80
Exhibit: Salaries and wages	1,199,170	1,822.45
Total expenditure	8,089,240	12,293.68
General expenditure	6,834,832	10,387.28
Intergovernmental expenditure	1,049,706	1,595.30
Direct expenditure	5,785,126	8,791.98
General expenditures, by function:		
Education	1,707,847	2,595.51
Public welfare	1,471,607	2,236.48
Hospitals	23,043	35.02
Health	118,307	179.80
Highways	828,835	1,259.63
Police protection	61,681	93.74
Correction	176,642	268.45
Natural resources	247,000	375.38
Parks and recreation	9,527	14.48
Government administration	432,840	657.81
Interest on general debt	242,443	368.45
Other and unallocable	1,515,060	2,302.52
Utility expenditure	89,147	135.48
Liquor store expenditure	–	–
Insurance trust expenditure	1,165,261	1,770.91
Debt at end of fiscal year	5,730,403	8,708.82
Cash and security holdings	45,325,821	68,884.23

Abbreviations and symbols: – zero or rounds to zero; (NA) not available; (X) not applicable.

SOURCE: *U.S. Census Bureau, Governments Division, 2004 Survey of State Government Finances,* January 2006.

According to the Tax Foundation, for every federal tax dollar sent to Washington in 2004, Alaska citizens received $1.87 in federal spending, which ranks the state second-highest nationally.

³⁷ECONOMIC POLICY

The Alaska Industrial Development and Export Authority (AID-EA), a public corporation of the state, provides long-term financing for capital investments and loans for most commercial and industrial activities, including manufacturing, small business, tourism, mining, commercial fishing, and other enterprises. In

1985 its mission was extended to provide financing for infrastructural projects to support private enterprise in Alaska. In 2000, economic development projects included the Gateway Alaska project, which undertook reconstruction of the Ted Stevens Anchorage International Airport and surrounding roads. Under the AIDEA's Conduit Revenue Bond Program, designed to facilitate access to the state bond market, Hope Community Resources in 2002 was able to borrow to expand its facilities for providing services for the developmentally disabled. In 1999, the Rural Development Initiative Fund, created in 1992 to help small businesses not eligible for traditional commercial finance, was transferred to the AIDEA. The AIDEA also has oversight over the Alaska Energy Authority which was created in 1976 and has responsibility for two major programs, the Alaska Rural Energy Plan and the Statewide Energy Plan. The rural population poses a challenge to economic development of the state, which the state government has begun to address by broadening the utilities infrastructure and by subsidizing energy costs. The Alaska Science and Technology Foundation (ASTF), created in 1988, has as its mission the improvement of the state economy through investments in science and technology. The state imposes no taxes on income, sales, gross receipts or inventories. It offers an investment tax credit for the development of gas-processing projects and for the mining of minerals and other natural deposits, except oil and gas.

In 2004, the Office of Economic Development (OED) was established. The OED facilitates economic development and employment opportunities, particularly in rural Alaska. The OED offers specialized assistance in the tourism, fisheries, and minerals development sectors.

[38] HEALTH

The infant mortality rate in October 2005 was estimated at 5.8 per 1,000 live births. The birth rate in 2003 was 15.6 per 1,000 population. The abortion rate stood at 11.7 per 1,000 women in 2000. In 2003, about 79.8% of pregnant woman received prenatal care beginning in the first trimester. In 2004, approximately 75% of children received routine immunizations before the age of three.

The crude death rate in 2003 was 4.9 deaths per 1,000 population. As of 2002, the death rates for major causes of death (per 100,000 resident population) were: heart disease, 88.1; cancer, 111.1; cerebrovascular diseases, 24.5; chronic lower respiratory diseases, 22.1; and diabetes, 13.4. The death rates for heart disease and diabetes represent the lowest in the nation. However, Alaska has the second-highest suicide rate (after Wyoming), with 20.5 per 100,000 residents. The state also has one of the highest rates for accidental deaths at 53.7 per 100,000. The 2002 mortality rate from HIV infection was not available. In 2004, the reported AIDS case rate was 8.4 per 100,000 population. In 2002, about 59.5% of the population was considered overweight or obese, representing the fifth-highest percentage in the nation. As of 2004, about 24.7% of state residents were smokers.

In 2003, Alaska had 19 community hospitals, with about 1,500 beds. There were about 46,000 patient admissions that year and 1.4 million outpatient visits. The average daily inpatient census was about 800 patients. The average cost per day for hospital care was $1,952. Also in 2003, there were about 15 certified nursing facilities in the state, with 821 beds and an overall occupancy rate of about 76.8%. In 2004, it was estimated that about 69.6% of all state residents had received some type of dental care within the past year. Alaska had 217 physicians per 100,000 resident population in 2004 and 761 nurses per 100,000 in 2005. In 2004, there was a total of 490 dentists in the state.

About 21% of state residents were enrolled in Medicaid and Medicare programs in 2004. Approximately 18% of the state population was uninsured in 2004. In 2003, state health care expenditures totaled $1.2 million.

Alaska's Pioneer Homes, operated by the state's Department of Administration, are residential facilities for Alaskans over 65 (with at least one year of residency in the state) that offer five levels of care, from independent living to full medical care, including Alzheimer's disease units. As of 1997, a total of 600 residents were being served at six locations.

[39] SOCIAL WELFARE

In 2004, about 46,000 people received unemployment benefits, with an average weekly unemployment benefit of $194. In fiscal year 2005, the estimated average monthly participation in the food stamp program included about 55,567 persons (20,224 households); the average monthly benefit was about $120.58 per person. That year, the total benefits paid through the state for the food stamp program totaled $80.4 million.

Temporary Assistance for Needy Families (TANF), the system of federal welfare assistance that officially replaced Aid to Families with Dependent Children (AFDC) in 1997, was reauthorized through the Deficit Reduction Act of 2005. TANF is funded through federal block grants that are divided among the states based on an equation involving the number of recipients in each state. Alaska's TANF program is called the Alaska Temporary Assistance Program (ATAP). In 2004, the state program had 14,000 recipients; state and federal expenditures on this TANF program totaled $59 million in 2003.

In December 2004, Social Security benefits were paid to 63,440 Alaskans. This number included 37,150 retired workers, 5,260 widows and widowers, 9,380 disabled workers, 2,920 spouses, and 8,730 children. Social Security beneficiaries represented 9.6% of the total state population and 92.3% of the state's population age 65 and older. Retired workers received an average monthly payment of $920; widows and widowers, $840; disabled workers, $868; and spouses, $419. Payments for children of retired workers averaged $418 per month; children of deceased workers, $605; and children of disabled workers, $231. Federal Supplemental Security Income payments in December 2004 went to 10,781 Alaska residents, averaging $387 a month. About $4.3 million of state-administered supplemental payments was distributed to 14,980 residents.

In 1979, Alaska became the first state to withdraw its government workers from the Social Security system.

[40] HOUSING

Despite the severe winters, housing designs in Alaska do not differ notably from those in other states. Builders do usually provide thicker insulation in walls and ceilings, but the high costs of construction have not encouraged more energy-efficient adaptation to the environment. In 1980, the state legislature passed several measures to encourage energy conservation in housing and in public buildings. In native villages, traditional dwellings like the half-buried huts of the Aleuts and others have long since given way to conventional, low-standard housing. In point of fact, Alaska's Eskimos never built snow houses, as did those of Canada; in the Eskimo language, the word *igloo* refers to any dwelling.

In 2004, there were an estimated 271,533 housing units, of which 228,358 were occupied. Alaska had the second-smallest housing stock in the nation, (above Wyoming). The same year, about 65.5% of all occupied units were owner-occupied. About 61% of all units were single-family, detached dwellings. It was estimated that about 5,542 units statewide were without telephone service, while 6,017 lacked complete plumbing facilities and 5,489 lacked complete kitchen facilities. The average household had 2.78 members.

From 1970 to 1978, 43,009 building permits were issued, as construction boomed during the years of pipeline building. In 2004, the state authorized 3,100 new privately owned housing units. The median home value was $179,304. The median monthly cost for mortgage owners was $1,421, while the median monthly rental cost was $808. In September 2005, the state was awarded grants of $150,000 from the US Department of Housing and Urban Development (HUD) for rural housing and economic development programs. For 2006, HUD allocated to the state over $2.5 million in community development block grants.

The Alaska State Housing Authority acts as an agent for federal and local governments in securing financial aid for construction and management of low-rent and moderate-cost homes.

41 EDUCATION

As of 2004, 90.2% of the population 25 years or older had completed high school. Some 25.5% had obtained a bachelor's degree or higher.

Enrollment in public schools was 134,000 in the fall of 2002. Of these, 94,000 attended schools from kindergarten through grade eight, and 40,000 attended high school. Approximately 58.9% of the students were white, 4.7% were black, 3.9% were Hispanic, 6.5% were Asian/Pacific Islander, and 26% were American Indian/Alaskan Native. Total enrollment was estimated at 134,000 in fall 2003 and expected to be 145,000 by fall 2014, a 7.7% increase during the period 2002–14. There were 6,177 students enrolled in 75 private schools in fall 2003. Expenditures for public education in 2003/04 were estimated at $1.6 billion or $10,114 per student, the eighth-highest among the 50 states. Since 1969, the National Assessment of Educational Progress (NAEP) has tested public school students nationwide. The resulting report, *The Nation's Report Card,* stated that in 2005, eighth graders in Alaska scored 279 out of 500 in mathematics, compared with the national average of 278.

The University of Alaska is the state's leading higher-educational institution. The main campus, established in 1917, is at Fairbanks; satellite campuses are located in Anchorage and Juneau. Private institutions include Sheldon Jackson College, Alaska Bible College (a theological seminary), and Alaska Pacific University. The University of Alaska's Rural Education Division has a network of education centers. As of fall 2002, there were 29,546 students enrolled in college or graduate school; minority students comprised 24.3% of total postsecondary enrollment. As of 2005, Alaska had eight degree-granting institutions.

42 ARTS

The Alaska Council on the Arts (ASCA), founded in 1966, sponsors tours by performing artists, supports artists' residencies in the schools, aids local arts projects, and purchases the works of living Alaskans for display in state buildings. In 2005, the National Endowment for the Humanities awarded seven grants totaling $1,077,348 to Alaska organizations. In 2005, the National Endowment for the Arts awarded 11 grants totaling $698,500 to Alaska arts organizations. Alaska is also a member state of the regional Western States Arts Federation (WESTAF).

Symphony orchestras are located in Fairbanks, Juneau, and Anchorage.The Anchorage Symphony Orchestra was founded in 1945. Anchorage also has a civic opera, incorporated in 1962. The annual Alaska Folk Festival in Juneau (est. 1975) held its 32nd festival in 2006. It is one of the largest cultural/musical festivals in the state, drawing over 10,000 people each year by providing such activities as folk music performances, dance workshops, and family concerts.

43 LIBRARIES AND MUSEUMS

For the fiscal year ending in June 2001, Alaska had 86 public library systems, with a total of 103 libraries, of which 17 were branches. The public systems had a combined book and serial publications stock of 2,264,000 volumes and a total circulation of 3,628,000 that same year. The system also had 87,000 audio and 101,000 video items, 3,000 electronic format items (CD-ROMs, magnetic tapes, and disks), and two bookmobiles. Facilities were located in seven boroughs and in most larger towns. Anchorage had the largest public library system, with five branches and 554,686 volumes in 1998. Also notable are the State Library in Juneau and the library of the University of Alaska at Fairbanks (with 954,510 and 60,000 volumes, respectively). Total operating income for the public library system in 2001 was $23,681,000; including $787,000 in state grants.

Alaska had 44 museums in 2000. The Alaska State Museum in Juneau offers an impressive collection of native crafts and Alaskan artifacts. Sitka National Historical Park features Indian and Russian items, and the nearby Museum of Sheldon Jackson College holds important native collections. Noteworthy historical and archaeological sites include the Totem Heritage Center in Ketchikan. Anchorage has the Anchorage Museum of History and Art and the Alaska Zoo.

44 COMMUNICATIONS

Considering the vast distances traveled and the number of small, scattered communities, the US mail is a bargain for Alaskans. In 2004, 95.6% of the state's residences had telephones. In addition, by June of that same year there were 307,323 mobile wireless telephone subscribers. In 2003, 72.7% of Alaska households had a computer and 67.6% had Internet access. By June 2005, there were 95,763 high-speed lines in Alaska (80,556 residential and 5,207 for business). A total of 13,558 Internet domain names had been registered in Alaska as of 2000.

There were 41 major radio stations (13 AM, 28 FM) in 2005, along with 15 television stations. Prime Cable of Alaska is the state's major cable carrier.

⁴⁵PRESS

Alaska's most widely read newspaper, among its seven dailies and five Sunday papers, is the *Anchorage Daily News*. Below are the leading newspapers with their circulations.

Anchorage Daily News	(m) 76,231	(S) 82,179
Fairbanks Daily News-Miner	(m) 16,127	(S) 21,557

There are about 30 publishers in Alaska, including the University of Alaska Press, Denali Press, Alaska Geographic, Rainforest Publishers, and Inside Passage Press. *Alaska Business Monthly, Alaska* magazine, and *Alaska Outdoors* are popular statewide magazines.

In 2005, there were 18 weekly publications in Alaska, 11 paid weeklies, 2 free weeklies, and 5 combined weeklies. The total circulation of paid weeklies (45,634) and free weeklies (37,949) is 83,583.

⁴⁶ORGANIZATIONS

In 2006, there were over 1,030 nonprofit organizations registered within the state, of which about 708 were registered as charitable, educational, or religious organizations. The largest statewide organization, the Alaska Federation of Natives, with headquarters in Anchorage, represents the state's Eskimos, Aleuts, and American Indians. The Maniilaq Association, based in Kotzebue, is another tribal organization serving native Eskimos. Alutiiq Heritage Foundation is based in Kodiak. Ketchikan Indian Community is a social services organization for Alaskan natives.

The Alaska Oil and Gas Association is one of several local professional and business associations. Environmental groups include the Alaska Conservation Alliance, the Alaska Conservation Foundation, the Alaska Geographic Society, and the Alaska Wildlife Alliance. Arts and culture are represented in part by the Alaska Historical Society. The International Association for Spiritual Consciousness, which promotes such practices as meditation and yoga, is based in Anchorage.

⁴⁷TOURISM, TRAVEL, AND RECREATION

With thousands of miles of unspoiled scenery and hundreds of mountains and lakes, Alaska has vast tourist potential. In fact, tourism has become the second-largest private-sector employer in the state. Alaska's tourism industry is estimated at over $1 billion per year. The industry, directly and indirectly, generates an annual average of 23,000 jobs and $640 million in payroll (not including employment on cruise ships). In 2004, some 52,000 visitors came from overseas. Alaska had the highest rate of growth in travel and tourism, a rise of 4.3%.

The Far North region of Alaska is home to many native Inuit (Eskimo) groups. The city of Nome is home to the famous Iditarod Trail Seld Dog Race. The Southwest region (Kodiak) exhibits the Russian influence, as seen in its Orthodox churches. Popular cities

visited by tourists are, Juneau, Fairbanks, Ketchican, and Skagway. Tourists can travel by rail to the interior regions. There are many popular gold-mining sites, nature preserves, historic towns dating from the days of the gold rush, and glaciers.

Cruise travel along the Gulf of Alaska is one of the fastest growing sectors in the tourist trade. Sportfishing and outdoor adventure opportunities have also become popular. Millions of visitors travel to the state's national parks, preserves, historical parks, and monuments, which totaled 52.9 million acres (21.7 million hectares) in 1999. Denali State Park is home to Mt. McKinley, the highest peak in North America. Another popular tourist destination is Glacier Bay National Monument.

⁴⁸SPORTS

There are no major professional sports teams in Alaska, but there is a minor league hockey team in Anchorage. In addition, college hockey teams, such as the University of Alaska–Fairbanks, are involved at the National Collegiate Athletic Association Division I level. Sports in Alaska generally revolve around the outdoors, including skiing, fishing, hiking, mountain biking, and camping. Perhaps the biggest sporting event in the state is the Iditarod Trail Sled Dog Race, covering 1,159 mi (1,865 km) from Anchorage to Nome. The race is held in March, and both men and women compete. With a $50,000 purse, it is the most lucrative sled dog race in the world.

Other annual sporting events include the Great Alaska Shootout, in which college basketball teams from around the country compete in Anchorage in November, and the World Eskimo-Indian Olympics in Fairbanks in July.

⁴⁹FAMOUS ALASKANS

Alaskan's best-known federal officeholder was Ernest Gruening (b.New York, 1887–1974), a territorial governor from 1939 to 1953 and US senator from 1959 to 1969. Alaska's other original US senator was E. L. "Bob" Bartlett (1904–68). Walter Hickel (b.Kansas, 1919), the first Alaskan to serve in the US cabinet, left the governorship in 1969 to become secretary of the interior. Among historical figures, Vitus Bering (b.Denmark, 1680–1741), a seaman in Russian service who commanded the discovery expedition in 1741, and Aleksandr Baranov (b.Russia, 1746–1819), the first governor of Russian America, are outstanding. Secretary of State William H. Seward (b.New York, 1801–72), who was instrumental in the 1867 purchase of Alaska, ranks as the state's "founding father," although he never visited the region.

Sheldon Jackson (b.New York, 1834–1909), a Presbyterian missionary, introduced the reindeer to the region and founded Alaska's first college in Sitka. Carl Ben Eielson (1897–1929), a famed bush pilot, is a folk hero. Benny Benson (1913–72), born at Chignik, designed the state flag at the age of 13.

⁵⁰BIBLIOGRAPHY

Borneman, Walter R. *Alaska: Saga of a Bold Land*. New York: HarperCollins, 2003.

Council of State Governments. *The Book of the States, 2006 Edition*. Lexington, Ky.: Council of State Governments, 2006.

Haycox, Stephen W., and Mary Childers Mangusso (eds.). *An Alaska Anthology: Interpreting the Past.* Seattle: University of Washington Press, 1996.

Hedin, Robert, and Gary Holthaus (eds.). *The Great Land: Reflections on Alaska.* Tucson: University of Arizona Press, 1994.

Kizzia, Tom. *The Wake of the Unseen Object: Among the Native Cultures of Bush Alaska.* New York: Henry Holt, 1992.

McBeath, Gerald A. *Alaska Politics and Government.* Lincoln: University of Nebraska Press, 1994.

O'Neill, Daniel T. *A Land Gone Lonesome: An Inland Voyage along the Yukon River.* New York: Counterpoint, 2006.

Ripley, Kate. *Best Places Alaska.* 3rd ed. Seattle: Sasquatch Books, 2003.

Ryan, Alan (ed.). *The Reader's Companion to Alaska.* San Diego, Calif.: Harcourt Brace, 1997.

Salisbury, Gay. *The Cruelest Miles: The Heroic Story of Dogs and Men in a Race against an Epidemic.* New York: W.W. Norton, 2003.

US Department of Commerce, Economics and Statistics Administration, US Census Bureau. *Alaska, 2000. Summary Social, Economic, and Housing Characteristics: 2000 Census of Population and Housing.* Washington, D.C.: US Government Printing Office, 2003.

ARIZONA

State of Arizona

ORIGIN OF STATE NAME: Probably from the Pima or Papago Indian word *arizonac*, meaning "place of small springs." **NICKNAME:** The Grand Canyon State. **CAPITAL:** Phoenix. **ENTERED UNION:** 14 February 1912 (48th). **SONG:** "Arizona;" "Arizona March Song." **MOTTO:** *Ditat Deus* (God enriches). **FLAG:** A copper-colored five-pointed star symbolic of the state's copper resources rises from a blue field; six yellow and seven red segments radiating from the star cover the upper half. **OFFICIAL SEAL:** Depicted on a shield are symbols of the state's economy and natural resources, including mountains, a rising sun, and a dam and reservoir in the background; irrigated farms and orchards in the middle distance; a quartz mill, a miner, and cattle in the foreground; and the state motto. The words "Great Seal of the State of Arizona 1912" surround the shield. **BIRD:** Cactus wren. **FLOWER:** Blossom of the saguaro cactus. **TREE:** Palo verde. **LEGAL HOLIDAYS:** New Year's Day, 1 January; Martin Luther King Jr./Civil Rights Day, 3rd Monday in January; Lincoln/Washington/ Presidents' Day, 3rd Monday in February; Memorial Day, last Monday in May; Independence Day, 4 July; Labor Day, 1st Monday in September; Columbus Day, 2nd Monday in October; Veterans Day, 11 November; Thanksgiving Day, 4th Thursday in November; Christmas Day, 25 December. **TIME:** 5 AM MST = noon GMT. Arizona does not observe daylight savings time.

¹LOCATION, SIZE, AND EXTENT

Located in the Rocky Mountains region of the southwestern United States, Arizona ranks sixth in size among the 50 states.

The total area of Arizona is 114,000 sq mi (295,260 sq km), of which land takes up 113,508 sq mi (293,986 sq km) and inland water 492 sq mi (1,274 sq km). Arizona extends about 340 mi (547 km) E–W; the state's maximum N–S extension is 395 mi (636 km).

Arizona is bordered on the N by Utah and on the E by New Mexico (with the two borders joined at Four Corners, the only point in the United States common to four states); on the S by the Mexican state of Sonora; and on the W by the Mexican state of Baja California Norte, California, and Nevada (with most of the line formed by the Colorado River). The total boundary length of Arizona is 1,478 mi (2,379 km). The state's geographic center is in Yavapai County, 55 mi (89 km) ESE of Prescott.

²TOPOGRAPHY

Arizona is a state of extraordinary topographic diversity and beauty. The Colorado Plateau, which covers two-fifths of the state in the north, is an arid upland region characterized by deep canyons, notably the Grand Canyon, a vast gorge more than 200 mi (320 km) long, up to 18 mi (29 km) wide, and more than 1 mi (1.6 km) deep. Also within this region are the Painted Desert and Petrified Forest, as well as Humphreys Peak, the highest point in the state, at 12,633 ft (3,853 m). The mean elevation of the state is approximately 4,100 ft (1,251 m).

The Mogollon Rim separates the northern plateau from a central region of alternating basins and ranges with a general northwest–southeast direction. Ranges in the Mexican Highlands in the southeast include the Chiricahua, Dos Cabezas, and Pinaleno mountains. The Sonora Desert, in the southwest, contains the lowest point in the state, 70 ft (21 m) above sea level, on the Colorado River near Yuma.

The Colorado is the state's major river, flowing southwest from Glen Canyon Dam on the Utah border through the Grand Canyon and westward to Hoover Dam, then turning south to form the border with Nevada and California. Tributaries of the Colorado include the Little Colorado and Gila rivers. Arizona has few natural lakes, but there are several large artificial lakes formed by dams for flood control, irrigation, and power development. These include Lake Mead (shared with Nevada), formed by Hoover Dam; Lake Powell (shared with Utah); Lake Mohave and Lake Havasu (shared with California), formed by David Dam and Parker Dam, respectively; Roosevelt Lake, formed by Theodore Roosevelt Dam; and the San Carlos Lake, created by Coolidge Dam.

³CLIMATE

Arizona has a dry climate, with little rainfall. Temperatures vary greatly from place to place, season to season, and day to night. Average daily temperatures at Yuma, in the southwestern desert range from 48° to 69°F (8° to 20°C) in January, and from 81° to 107°F (27° to 41°C) in July. At Flagstaff, in the interior uplands, average daily January temperatures range from 15° to 42°F (-9° to 5°C), and average daily July temperatures range from 50° to 82°F (10° to 27°C). The maximum recorded temperature was 128°F (53°C), registered at Lake Havasu City on 29 June 1994; the minimum, -40°F (-40°C), was set at Hawley Lake on 7 January 1971.

The highest elevations of the state, running diagonally from the southeast to the northwest, receive between 25 and 30 in (63–76 cm) of precipitation a year, and the rest, for the most part, between 7 and 20 in (18–51 cm). Average annual precipitation at Phoenix is about 7.7 in (19 cm). The driest area is the extreme southwest, which receives less than 3 in (8 cm) a year. Snow, sometimes as much as 100 in (254 cm), falls on the highest peaks each winter but is rare in the southern and western lowlands.

The greatest amount of sunshine is registered in the southwest, with the proportion decreasing progressively toward the northeast; overall, the state receives more than 80% of possible sunshine, among the highest in the United States, and Phoenix's 86% is higher than that of any other major US city.

4 FLORA AND FAUNA

Generally categorized as desert, Arizona's terrain also includes mesa and mountains; consequently, the state has a wide diversity of vegetation. The desert is known for many varieties of cacti, from the saguaro, whose blossom is the state flower, to the cholla and widely utilized yucca. Desert flowers include the night-blooming cereus; among medicinal desert flora is the jojoba, also harvested for its oil-bearing seeds. Below the tree line (about 12,000 ft, or 3,658 m) the mountains are well timbered with varieties of spruce, fir, juniper, ponderosa pine, oak, and piñon. Rare plants, some of them endangered or threatened, include various cacti of commercial or souvenir value.

Arizona's fauna range from desert species of lizards and snakes to the deer, elk, and antelope of the northern highlands. Mountain lion, jaguar, coyote, and black and brown bears are found in the state, along with the badger, black-tailed jackrabbit, and gray fox. Small mammals include various cottontails, mice, and squirrels; prairie dog towns dot the northern regions. Rattlesnakes are abundant, and the desert is rife with reptiles such as the collared lizard and chuckwalla. Native birds include the thick-billed parrot, white pelican, and cactus wren (the state bird).

In April 2006, a total of 53 species occurring within the state were on the threatened and endangered species list of the US Fish and Wildlife Service. These included 35 animals (vertebrates and invertebrates) and 18 plant species. Arizona counts the desert tortoise and lesser long-nosed bat among its threatened wildlife. Officially listed as endangered or threatened were the southern bald eagle, masked bobwhite (quail), Sonoran pronghorn, ocelot, jaguar, black-footed ferret, four species of chub, two species of gray wolf, woundfin, Apache trout, Gila topminnow, Gila trout, and southwestern willow flycatcher.

5 ENVIRONMENTAL PROTECTION

Aside from Phoenix, whose air quality is poorer than that of most other US cities, Arizona has long been noted for its clear air, open lands, and beautiful forests. The main environmental concern of the state is to protect these resources in the face of growing population, tourism, and industry.

State agencies with responsibility for the environment include the State Land Department, which oversees natural resource conservation and land management; the Game and Fish Commission, which administers state wildlife laws; the Department of Health Services, which supervises sewage disposal, water treatment, hazardous and solid waste treatment, and air pollution prevention programs; and the Department of Water Resources, formed in 1980, which is concerned with the development, management, use, and conservation of water. The Department of Water Resources created five zones to monitor water use by about 80% of the population (using about 75% of the state's water). The Rural Arizona Watershed Alliance, representing the remaining 20% of its population who reside in the rural areas making up 85% of Arizona's land mass, has been funded by the legislature since 1999/2000 to undertake statewide planning for water resource use and allocation. In 2005, federal EPA grants awarded to the state included $9.4 million for safe drinking water projects and a $7.3 million grant for water pollution control projects.

Legislation enacted in 1980 attempts to apportion water use among cities, mining, and agriculture, the last of which, through irrigation, accounts for the largest share of the state's annual water consumption. Less than 1% of Arizona's land is wetlands. In 2003, 48.2 million lb of toxic chemicals were released by the state. In 2003, the US EPA database listed 167 hazardous waste sites in Arizona, nine of which were on the National Priorities List as of 2006, including the Tucson International Airport area. In 2005, the EPA spent over $4.8 million through the Superfund program for the cleanup of hazardous waste sites in the state.

6 POPULATION

The state ranked 17th in population in the United States with an estimated total of 5,939,292 in 2005, an increase of 15.8% since 2000. Between 1990 and 2000, Arizona's population grew from 3,665,228 to 5,130,632, the fifth-largest increase and second-largest percentage gain (40%) among the 50 states. The population is projected to reach 7.4 million by 2015 and 9.5 million by 2025.

Population density was 50.6 persons per sq mi in 2004. The median age was 34.1. Arizonans who were 65 years of age or older accounted for 12.7% of the population in 2004. Persons under 18 years old accounted for 26.9%.

Three out of four Arizonans live in urban areas. The largest metropolitan area is Phoenix-Mesa-Scottsdale, with a 2004 estimated population of 3,715,360, and Tucson, with an estimated 907,059. The largest cities proper are Phoenix, with a 2004 estimated population of 1,418,041; Tucson, 512,023; Mesa, 437,454; Glendale, 235,591; and Chandler, 223,991. More than half the state's population resides in Maricopa County, which includes every leading city except Tucson. Phoenix was the nation's sixth-largest city in 2004.

7 ETHNIC GROUPS

Arizona has by far the nation's greatest expanse of American Indian lands: the state's 22 reservations have a combined area of 19.1 million acres (7.7 million hectares), 26% of the total state area. In 2000, Arizona had the nation's third-highest American Indian population, 255,879, or 5% of the state total population. The 5% figure was unchanged in 2004.

The largest single American Indian nation, the Navaho, with a population of 104,565 in 2000, is located primarily in the northeastern part of the state. The Navaho reservation, covering 14,221 sq mi (36,832 sq km) within Arizona, extends into Utah and New Mexico and comprises desert, mesa, and mountain terrain. Herders by tradition, the people are also famous for their crafts. The reservation's total American Indian population in 2000 was 173,631, up 21% from 143,405 in 1990. Especially since 1965, the Navaho have been active in economic development; reservation resources in uranium and coal have been leased to outside corporations, and loans from the US Department of Commerce have made possible roads, telephones, and other improvements. There are at least 12 and perhaps 17 other tribes (depending on definition). After the Navaho, the leading tribes are the Papago in the south, Apache in the east, and Hopi in the northeast. The Hopi reservation had a population of 6,946 in 2000.

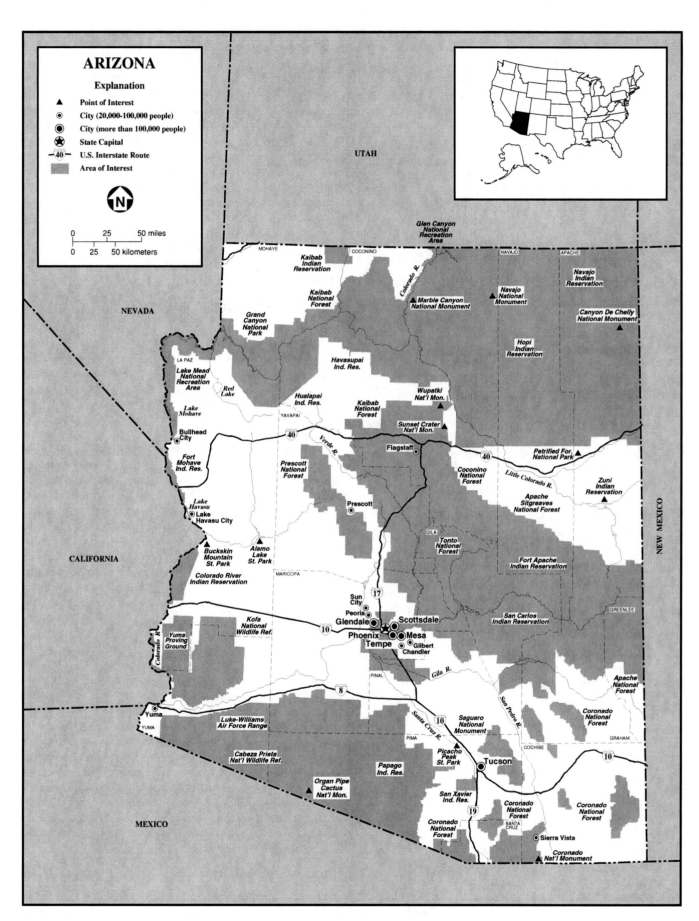

The southern part of Arizona has most of the state's largest ethnic majority, a Hispanic and Latino population estimated at 1,295,617 in 2000, or 25.3% of the total population (up from the 1990 figure of 668,000, or 18% of the population). In 2004, the percentage of the population reporting Hispanic or Latino origin had risen to 28% of the total population. There are some old, long-settled Spanish villages, but the bulk of Hispanics (1,065,578) are of Mexican origin. Raul Castro, a Mexican-American, served as governor in 1975–77. There were an estimated 158,873 blacks as of 2000. In 2004, 3.5% of the population was black. Filipinos, Chinese, Japanese, and other Asians made up 1.8% of the population in 2000; by 2004, that figure had risen to 2.1% of the total population. In 2004, 1.5% of the population reported origin of two or more races.

8 LANGUAGES

With the possible exception of the Navaho word *hogan* (earth-and-timber dwelling), the linguistic influence of Arizona's Papago, Pima, Apache, Navaho, and Hopi tribes is almost totally limited to some place-names: Arizona itself, Yuma, Havasu, Tucson, and Oraibi. American Indian loan-words spreading from Arizona derive from the Nahuatl speech of the Mexican Aztecs—for example, *coyote, chili, mesquite, and tamale*. Spanish, dominant in some sections, has provided English *mustang, ranch, stampede, rodeo, marijuana, bonanza, canyon, mesa, patio, and fiesta*.

English in the state represents a blend of North Midland and South Midland dialects without clear regional differences, although new meanings developed in the north and east for *meadow* and in the southern strip for *swale* as terms for flat mountain valleys. The recent population surge from eastern states has produced an urban blend with a strong northern flavor. In 2000, 3,523,487 Arizonans—74.1% of all residents five years old and older—spoke only English at home, a decrease from the 79.2% reported in 1990.

The following table gives selected statistics from the 2000 Census for language spoken at home by persons five years old and over. The category "Other Native North American languages" includes Apache, Cherokee, Choctaw, Dakota, Keres, Pima, and Yupik.

LANGUAGE	NUMBER	PERCENT
Population 5 years and over	**4,752,724**	**100.0**
Speak only English	3,523,487	74.1
Speak a language other than English	1,229,237	25.9
Speak a language other than English	**1,229,237**	**25.9**
Spanish or Spanish Creole	927,395	19.5
Navajo	89,951	1.9
Other Native North American languages	30,109	0.6
German	25,103	0.5
Chinese	17,111	0.4
French (incl. Patois, Cajun)	15,663	0.3
Tagalog	10,049	0.2
Vietnamese	9,999	0.2
Italian	8,992	0.2
Korean	7,689	0.2

9 RELIGIONS

The first religions of Arizona were the sacred beliefs and practices of the American Indians. Catholic missionaries began converting Arizona Indians (Franciscans among the Hopi, and Jesuits among the Pima) to the Christian faith in the late 17th century. By the late 18th century, the Franciscans were the main missionary force, and the Roman Catholic Church was firmly established. In 2004, the state had 906,692 Catholics in 161 parishes.

The Church of Jesus Christ of Latter-day Saints (Mormons) constitutes the second-largest Christian denomination, with a statewide membership of 346,677 in 701 congregations in 2006, up from 251,974 adherents in 643 congregations in 2000. Mormons were among the state's earliest Anglo settlers. Other major Christian denominations include the Southern Baptist Convention, which had 138,516 statewide adherents in 2000 and reported 3,155 newly baptized members in 2002. The Assemblies of God reported 82,802 members in 2000, while the United Methodist Church had 53,232. Also in 2000, Arizona's estimated Jewish population was 81,675. There were about 11,857 Muslims. There were also about 25 Buddhist and 9 Hindu congregations. About 60% of the population did not specify a religious affiliation.

The city of Sedona has become known for its community of believers in New Age religious movements.

10 TRANSPORTATION

Until the last decade of the 19th century, the principal reason for the development of transportation in Arizona was to open routes to California. The most famous early road was El Camino de Diablo (The Devil's Highway), opened by the missionary Eusebio Kino in 1699. The first wagon road across Arizona was the Gila Trail (Cooke's Wagon Road), opened in 1846 as a southern route to California; Beale's Road was inaugurated in 1857. Also in 1857, the first stagecoach began operations. Until the coming of the railroads in the 1880s, however, the bulk of territorial commerce was by water transport on the Colorado River. Railroad construction reached its peak in the 1920s and declined rapidly thereafter.

Railroad trackage totaled 1,836 rail mi (2,956 km) in 2003, with 10 railroads operating in the state. The state's two Class I railroads, the Burlington Northern Santa Fe and the Union Pacific, controlled 1,261 rail miles in 2003. In that same year, the top rail commodities (by weight) originating from within the state were glass and stone products, while coal was the top rail commodity (by weight) terminating in the state. As of 2006, Amtrak provided limited passenger service through Flagstaff, Kingman, and other cities in the north, and through Tucson and Yuma on its southern route.

In 2004, the state had 58,112 mi (93,544 km) of public streets and roads. Interstate highways in Arizona totaled 1,168 mi (1,879 km). Of the approximately 3.944 million motor vehicles registered in 2004, there were some 2.038 million automobiles, 1.697 million trucks of all types, and around 1,000 buses. There were 3,783,927 licensed drivers in 2004.

In 2005, Arizona had a total of 299 public- and private-use aviation-related facilities. This included 190 airports, 108 heliports, and 1 STOLport (Short Take-Off and Landing). The state's leading air terminal was Phoenix Sky Harbor International Airport. In 2004, the airport had total passenger enplanements of 19,336,099, making it the seventh-busiest airport in the United States. Tucson International Airport was Arizona's second-largest airport, with 1,863,790 enplanements in that same year.

11 HISTORY

Evidence of a human presence in Arizona dates back more than 12,000 years. The first Arizonans—the offshoot of migrations across the Bering Strait—were large-game hunters: their remains have been found in the San Pedro Valley in the southeastern part of the state. By AD 500, their descendants had acquired a rudimentary agriculture from what is now Mexico and divided into several cultures. The Basket Makers (Anasazi) flourished in the northeastern part of the state; the Mogollon hunted and foraged in the eastern mountains; the Hokoham, highly sophisticated irrigators, built canals and villages in the central and southern valleys: and the Hakataya, a less-advanced river people, lived south and west of the Grand Canyon. For reasons unknown—a devastating drought is the most likely explanation—these cultures were in decay and the population much reduced by the 14th century. Two centuries later, when the first Europeans arrived, most of the natives were living in simple shelters in fertile river valleys, dependent on hunting, gathering, and small-scale farming for subsistence. These Arizona Indians belonged to three linguistic families: Uto-Aztecan (Hopi, Paiute, Chemehuevi, Pima-Papago), Yuman (Yuma, Mohave, Cocopa, Maricopa, Yavapai, Walapai, Havasupai), and Athapaskan (Navaho-Apache). The Hopi were the oldest group, their roots reaching back to the Anasazi; the youngest were the Navaho-Apache, migrants from the Plains, who were not considered separate tribes until the early 18th century.

The Spanish presence in Arizona involved exploration, missionary work, and settlement. Between 1539 and 1605, four expeditions crossed the land, penetrating both the upland plateau and the lower desert in ill-fated attempts to find great riches. In their footsteps came Franciscans from the Rio Grande to work among the Hopi, and Jesuits from the south, led by Eusebio Kino in 1692, to proselytize among the Pima. Within a few years, Kino had established a major mission station at San Xavier del Bac, near present-day Tucson. In 1736, a rich silver discovery near the Pima village of Arizona, about 20 mi (32 km) southwest of present-day Nogales, drew Spanish prospectors and settlers northward. To control the restless Pima, Spain in 1752 placed a military outpost, or presidio, at Tubac on the Santa Cruz River north of Nogales. This was the first major European settlement in Arizona. The garrison was moved north to the new fort at Tucson, also on the Santa Cruz, in 1776. During these years, the Spaniards gave little attention to the Santa Cruz settlements, administered as part of the Mexican province of Sonora, regarding them merely as way stations for colonizing expeditions traveling overland to the highly desirable lands of California. The end of the 18th century and the beginning of the 19th were periods of relative peace on the frontier; mines were developed and ranches begun. Spaniards removed hostile Apache bands onto reservations and made an effort to open a road to Santa Fe.

When Mexico revolted against Spain in 1810, the Arizona settlements were little affected. Mexican authorities did not take control at Arizpe, the Sonoran capital, until 1823. Troubled times followed, characterized by economic stagnation, political chaos, and renewed war with the Apache. Sonora was divided into *partidos* (counties), and the towns on the Santa Cruz were designated as a separate *partido*, with the county seat at Tubac. The area north of the Gila River, inhabited only by American Indians, was vaguely claimed by New Mexico. With the outbreak of the Mexican War in 1846, two US armies marched across the region: Col. Stephen W. Kearny followed the Gila across Arizona from New Mexico to California, and Lt. Col. Philip Cooke led a Mormon battalion

westward through Tucson to California. The California Gold Rush of 1849 saw thousands of Americans pass along the Gila toward the new El Dorado. In 1850, most of present-day Arizona became part of the new US Territory of New Mexico; the southern strip was added by the Gadsden Purchase in 1853.

Three years later, the Sonora Exploring and Mining Co. organized a large party, led by Charles D. Poston, to open silver mines around Tubac. A boom followed, with Tubac becoming the largest settlement in the valley; the first newspaper, the *Weekly Arizonian,* was launched there in 1859. The great desire of California for transportation links with the rest of the Union prompted the federal government to chart roads and railroad routes across Arizona, erect forts there to protect Anglo travelers from the Arizona Indians, and open overland mail service. Dissatisfied with their representation at Santa Fe, the territorial capital, Arizona settlers joined those in southern New Mexico in 1860 in an abortive effort to create a new territorial entity. The outbreak of the Civil War in 1861 saw the declaration of Arizona as Confederate territory and abandonment of the region by the Union troops. A small Confederate force entered Arizona in 1862 but was driven out by a volunteer Union army from California. On 24 February 1863, President Abraham Lincoln signed into law a measure creating the new Territory of Arizona. Prescott became the capital in 1864, Tucson in 1867, Prescott again in 1877, and finally Phoenix in 1889.

During the early years of territorial status, the development of rich gold mines along the lower Colorado River and in the interior mountains attracted both people and capital to Arizona, as did the discovery of silver bonanzas in Tombstone and other districts in the late 1870s. Additional military posts were constructed to protect mines, towns, and travelers. This activity, in turn, provided the basis for a fledgling cattle industry and irrigated farming. Phoenix, established in 1868, grew steadily as an agricultural center. The Southern Pacific Railroad, laying track eastward from California, reached Tucson in 1880, and the Atlantic and Pacific (later acquired by the Santa Fe), stretching west from Albuquerque through Flagstaff, opened service to California in 1883. By 1890, copper had replaced silver as the principal mineral extracted in Arizona. In the Phoenix area, large canal companies began wrestling with the problem of supplying water for commercial agriculture. This problem was resolved in 1917 with the opening of the Salt River Valley Project, a federal reclamation program that provided enormous agricultural potential.

As a creature of the Congress, Arizona Territory was presided over by a succession of governors, principally Republicans, appointed in Washington. In reaction, the populace was predominantly Democratic. Within the territory, a merchant-capitalist class, with strong ties to California, dominated local and territorial politics until it was replaced with a mining-railroad group whose influence continued well into the 20th century. A move for separate statehood began in the 1880s but did not receive serious attention in Congress for another two decades. In 1910, after Congress passed an enabling act that allowed Arizona to apply for statehood, a convention met at Phoenix and drafted a state constitution. On 14 February 1912, Arizona entered the Union as the 48th state.

During the first half of the 20th century, Arizona shook off its frontier past. World War I (1914–18) spurred the expansion of the copper industry, intensive agriculture, and livestock production.

Goodyear Tire and Rubber established large farms in the Salt River Valley to raise pima cotton. The war boom also generated high prices, land speculation, and labor unrest; at Bisbee and Jerome, local authorities forcibly deported more than 1,000 striking miners during the summer of 1917. The 1920s brought depression: banks closed, mines shut down, and agricultural production declined. To revive the economy, local boosters pushed highway construction, tourism, and the resort business. Arizona also shared in the general distress caused by the Great Depression of the 1930s and received large amounts of federal aid for relief and recovery. A copper tariff encouraged the mining industry, additional irrigation projects were started, and public works were begun on Indian reservations, in parks and forests, and at education institutions. Prosperity returned during World War II (1939–45) as camps for military training, prisoners of war, and displaced Japanese Americans were built throughout the state. Meat, cotton, and copper markets flourished, and the construction of processing and assembly plants suggested a new direction for the state's economy.

Arizona emerged from World War II as a modern state. War industries spawned an expanding peacetime manufacturing boom that soon provided the principal source of income, followed by tourism, agriculture, and mining. During the 1950s, the political scene changed. Arizona Republicans captured the governorship, gained votes in the legislature, won congressional seats, and brought a viable two-party system to the state. The rise of Barry Goldwater of Phoenix to national prominence further encouraged Republican influence. Meanwhile, air conditioning improved the quality of life, prompting a significant migration to the state.

But prosperity did not reach into all sectors. While the state ranked as only the 19th poorest in the nation in 1990 (with a poverty rate of 13.7%), by 1998, it ranked sixth-poorest, with a poverty rate of 16.6%. Although the poverty rate in Arizona subsequently declined (to 13.9% in 2004), from 2000 to 2004 the Arizona poverty rate climbed two full percentage points, double the national average.

For many years Arizona had seen its water diverted to California. In 1985, however, the state acted to bring water from the Colorado River to its own citizens by building the Central Arizona Project (CAP). The CAP was a $3 billion network of canals, tunnels, dams and pumping stations which had the capacity to bring 2.8 million acre-feet of water a year from the Colorado River to Arizona's desert lands, cities, and farms. By 1994, however, many considered the project to be a failure, as little demand existed for the water it supplied. Farmers concluded that water-intensive crops such as cotton were not profitable, and Arizona residents complained that the water provided by the CAP was dirty and undrinkable.

Arizona politics in the recent past have been rocked by the discovery of corruption in high places. In 1988, Governor Evan Mecham was impeached on two charges of official misconduct. In 1989, Senators John McCain and Dennis DeConcini were indicted for interceding in 1987 with federal bank regulators on behalf of Lincoln Savings and Loan Association. Lincoln's president, Charles Keating Jr., had contributed large sums to the Senators' reelection campaigns. In 1990, Peter MacDonald, the leader of the Navajo Nation, was convicted in the Navajo Tribal Court of soliciting $400,000 in bribes and kickbacks from corporations and individuals who sought to conduct business with the tribe in the

1970s and 1980s. A year later, seven members of the Arizona state legislature were charged with bribery, money laundering, and filing false election claims, the result of a sting operation. The legislators were videotaped accepting thousands of dollars from a man posing as a gaming consultant in return for agreeing to legalize casino gambling.

The most recent in Arizona's series of political scandals was the investigation and 1996 indictment of Governor Fife Symington on 23 counts of fraud and extortion in connection with his business ventures before he became governor in 1991, and his filing of personal bankruptcy. The case went to trial in May 1997. Convicted of fraud, Symington was replaced by secretary of state Jane Hull, also a Republican. In 1998 gubernatorial elections, Hull was elected in her own right. Democrat Janet Napolitano was elected governor in 2002. In 2003, the Arizona Supreme Court decided to individually review the 27 death sentences imposed by judges rather than juries, which was a practice deemed unconstitutional by the US Supreme Court.

12 STATE GOVERNMENT

The current constitution of Arizona, drafted in 1910 at the height of the Progressive era, contained reform provisions that were very advanced for the time; initiative, referendum, workers' compensation, short terms for elected officials, suffrage for women, and the barring of trusts and monopolies from the state. The constitution was adopted in 1911 and had been amended 136 times by January 2005.

Legislative authority is vested in a 30-member Senate and a 60-member House of Representatives. Legislative sessions are annual, begin in January, and must adjourn no later than the Saturday of the week during which the 100th day of the session falls. Special sessions, which are not limited in duration, may be called by petition of two-thirds of the membership of each house. All senators and representatives serve two-year terms and are chosen at the general election in November of each even-numbered year. A legislator must be a US citizen, at least 25 years old, an Arizona resident for at least three years, and a member of the district for at least a year. The legislative salary in 2004 was $24,000.

Chief executive officials elected statewide include the governor, secretary of state (the designated successor to the governor, as there is no lieutenant governor), treasurer, attorney general, and superintendent of public instruction, all of whom serve four-year terms. The governor is limited to a maximum of two consecutive terms. The five members of the Corporation Commission, which regulates public services and utilities, are elected for a four-year term with the possibility of reelection to a second consecutive four-year term; the state mine inspector is elected for two years. Candidates for executive office must have been US citizens for at least 10 years, must be at least 25 years old, and must have been a citizen of Arizona for at least 5 years. As of December 2004, the governor's salary was $95,000.

Bills may originate in either house of the legislature and must be passed by both houses and approved by the governor in order to become law. A two-thirds vote of the elected members in each house is necessary to override the governor's veto. If the governor fails to sign or veto a bill, it becomes law after five days (Sundays excluded) or ten days after the legislature has adjourned. Under the initiative procedure, legislation and proposed constitutional amendments can be placed on the ballot by petition. The petition must be signed by 15% of total votes cast for all candidates for governor at the last election. Constitutional amendments proposed in the legislature are ratified by a majority vote of the electorate.

In order to vote in Arizona, a person must be 18 years old, a US citizen, a resident of the state for at least 29 days prior to the upcoming election. Restrictions apply to convicted felons and those declared mentally incapacitated by the court.

[13] POLITICAL PARTIES

Of Arizona's 17 territorial governors, all of whom were federally appointed, 14 were Republicans and 3 were Democrats. Statehood meant a prolonged period of Democratic dominance. From 1912 through 1950, the state had nine Democratic and three Republican governors; during that period, Republicans held the statehouse for only six years.

Republican Party fortunes improved dramatically after 1950, largely because of the rise to state and national prominence of a conservative Republican, Barry Goldwater, first elected to the US Senate in 1952. From 1951 to 1994, eight Republican governors led the state for a total of 26 years, and five Democratic governors for 18 years. Several Arizona Republicans were appointed to high office during the Richard Nixon years, and in 1973, another Republican, John J. Rhodes, became minority leader in the US House of Representatives. Democrat and former governor Bruce Babbitt was named secretary of the interior for the Bill Clinton administration in 1992.

In 1992, Bill Clinton ended 40 years of Republican presidential victories in Arizona, becoming the first Democratic winner since 1952, with 47% of the vote to Republican Bob Dole's 44% and Independent Ross Perot's 8%. In 2000, the pendulum swung back to the Republican side, with Republican George W. Bush winning 51% of the vote to Democrat Al Gore's 45% and the Green Party candidate Ralph Nader's 3%. In 2004, Bush won reelection, with

55% of the vote to Democrat John Kerry's 45%. In 2004 there were 2,643,000 registered voters. Of registered voters in 2001, 38% were Democratic, 43% Republican, and 19% unaffiliated or members of other parties. The state had 10 electoral votes in 2004, an increase over 8 in the 2000 presidential election.

Democrat Dennis DeConcini won reelection to the US Senate in 1988; he retired in 1994, and his seat was won by Republican Jon Kyl, who was reelected in 2000. Republican John McCain was reelected senator in 1992, 1998, and 2004; McCain ran for the presidency in 2000 but dropped his bid. Following the November 1994 election, Arizona's delegation of US Representatives went from three Democrats and three Republicans to one Democrat and five Republicans; in the 109th Congress (2005–06), Arizona's congressional delegation was made up of six Republicans and two Democrats in the House. Arizonans elected a Democrat, Janet Napolitano, as governor in 2002; she was the first female governor to be elected back-to-back behind another female governor, Jane Dee Hull. In 2005, Arizona's state legislature consisted of 18 Republicans and 12 Democrats in the Senate, and 39 Republicans and 21 Democrats in the state House. In 2003 there were 25 women serving in the state legislature.

[14] LOCAL GOVERNMENT

Each of Arizona's 15 counties has a sheriff, county attorney, county recorder, treasurer, assessor, superintendent of schools, and three or five supervisors, each elected to a four-year term. Counties act as agents of the state.

Other local governmental units are cities, charter cities, and towns (communities with populations under 3,000). Towns generally follow the council-mayor form of government. All of Arizona's largest cities are charter cities. In 2005, there were 87 municipal governments and 305 special districts. The state had 410 school districts.

Each of the 21 Indian reservations in Arizona has a tribal coun-

Arizona Presidential Vote by Political Party, 1948–2004

YEAR	ELECTORAL VOTE	ARIZONA WINNER	DEMOCRAT	REPUBLICAN	PROGRESSIVE
1948	4	*Truman (D)	95,251	77,597	3,310
1952	4	*Eisenhower (R)	108,528	152,042	—
1956	4	*Eisenhower (R)	112,880	176,990	—
1960	4	Nixon (R)	176,781	221,241	—
1964	5	Goldwater (R)	237,753	242,535	—
					AMERICAN IND.
1968	5	*Nixon (R)	170,514	266,721	46,573
					AMERICAN
1972	6	*Nixon (R)	198,540	402,812	21,208
1976	6	Ford (R)	295,602	418,642	7,647
1980	6	*Reagan (R)	246,843	529,688	18,784
1984	7	*Reagan (R)	333,854	681,416	10,585
1988	7	*Bush (R)	454,029	702,541	13,351
					IND. (Perot)
1992	8	Bush (R)	543,086	572,086	353,741
1996	8	*Clinton (D)	653,288	622,073	112,072
					GREEN
2000	8	*Bush, G. W. (R)	685,341	781,652	45,645
					LIBERTARIAN
2004	10	*Bush, G. W. (R)	893,524	1,104,294	11,856

*Won US presidential election.

cil or board with members elected by the people.

In 2005, local government accounted for about 212,570 full-time (or equivalent) employment positions.

15 STATE SERVICES

To address the continuing threat of terrorism and to work with the federal Department of Homeland Security, homeland security in Arizona operates under the authority of the governor; the emergency management director heads the Arizona Office of Homeland Security and is appointed by the governor.

The Arizona Department of Education regulates the school system. The Arizona Board of Regents governs the state's three public universities. A commission for postsecondary education provides students with financial aid, and school information. The Department of Transportation administers the state's highway and air-transport systems, among other functions. The Department of Financial Institutions supervises the financial institutions and enterprises of the state.

The Department of Health Services operates programs for environmental health, behavioral health (including alcohol abuse, drug abuse, and mental-illness treatment facilities), and family health services. The National Guard falls under the jurisdiction of the Department of Emergency and Military Affairs, while prisons and rehabilitation programs are administered by the State Department of Corrections. The Department of Public Safety oversees the state highway patrol.

Natural resources are the responsibility of several agencies, including the Game and Fish Commission, Department of Mines and Mineral Resources, Oil and Gas Conservation Commission, Parks Board, and Department of Water Resources. The Department of Economic Security handles employment services and public-assistance programs.

16 JUDICIAL SYSTEM

The Supreme Court is the highest court in Arizona and has administrative responsibility over all other courts in the state. The five supreme court justices, appointed by the governor for staggered six-year terms, choose a chief justice and vice-chief justice to preside over the court.

The Court of Appeals, established in 1964, is organized in two geographical divisions which together have 22 judges. Appeals court judges are appointed for terms of six years.

The superior court is the general trial court of the state, and there must be at least one superior court judge in every Arizona county. In 1999, there were 136 superior court judges, plus 2 part-time judges, in the state's 15 counties. In counties with populations over 150,000, superior court judges are appointed by the governor; they hold office for terms ending 60 days following the next regular general election after expiration of a two-year term. Those seeking retention run at the next general election on a nonpartisan ballot. In counties with a population under 150,000, superior court judges are elected by nonpartisan ballot to four-year terms.

Counties are divided into precincts, each of which has a justice court. Every incorporated city and town has a police court. The jurisdiction of justice courts and police courts is limited to minor civil and criminal cases. Local judges are elected for terms of four years.

As of 31 December 2004, a total of 32,515 prisoners were held in Arizona's state and federal prisons, an increase (from 31,170) of 4.3% from the previous year. As of year-end 2004, a total of 2,765 inmates were female, up (from 2,656) 4.1% from the year before. Among sentenced prisoners (one year or more), Arizona had an incarceration rate of 534 per 100,000 population in 2004.

According to the Federal Bureau of Investigation, Arizona in 2004 had a violent crime rate (murder/nonnegligent manslaughter; forcible rape; robbery; aggravated assault) of 504.1 reported incidents per 100,000 population, or a total of 28,952 reported incidents. Crimes against property (burglary; larceny/theft; and motor vehicle theft) that same year totaled 306,747 reported incidents or 5,340.5 reported incidents per 100,000 people. Arizona has a death penalty, which can be carried out by lethal injection or lethal gas, depending upon the prisoner's request. However, if the inmate was sentenced prior to 15 November 1992, execution is by lethal gas. From 1976 through 5 May 2006 the state executed 22 persons. As of May 2006, the most recent had been in November 2000. As of 1 January 2006, there were 125 inmates on death row.

In 2003, Arizona spent $258,260,247 on homeland security, an average of $49 per state resident.

17 ARMED FORCES

In 2004, 27,026 active-duty federal military personnel were stationed at five military installations in Arizona, with 5,319 National Guard, and 6,140 civilian employees in the state. Major military installations include the Army's Fort Huachuca at Sierra Vista, with the most military personnel in the state, 7,016. The Air Force's Williams base near Phoenix closed in 1993, but remaining are the Luke and Davis-Monthan bases, near Phoenix and Tucson, respectively. There is also the Marine Corps' Yuma Air Station. Defense Department expenditures in Arizona were approximately $11.0 billion in 2004, $8.4 billion for contracts (sixth in the nation), and about $2.6 billion for payroll, including retired military pay.

There were 555,223 veterans of US military service in Arizona as of 2003, of whom 84,587 served in World War II; 66,564 in the Korean conflict; 155,908 during the Vietnam era; and 83,907 in the Gulf War. On 10 September 1992, Nathan E. Cook, the last veteran of the Spanish-American War (1898–1902), died in Phoenix at the age of 106. In 2004, total Veterans Affairs expenditures amounted to $1.4 billion.

As of 31 October 2004, the Arizona Department of Public Safety employed 1,133 full-time sworn officers.

18 MIGRATION

Arizona's first migrants were the ancient peoples who came from Asia across the Bering Strait more than 12,000 years ago. Hispanic settlers began arriving in the late 17th century. Anglo migration, especially from the South, became significant as the United States developed westward to California, and increased at an even faster rate with the building of the railroads during the 1880s. Migration has accelerated since World War II (1939–45), and Arizona showed a net gain of 519,000 in domestic migration and 96,000 in international migration from 1990 to 1998. Mexico is the main source of foreign immigrants. In the 1980s, half of Arizona's total population increase was from migration; about 530,000 persons moved there during that time. By 1998, Arizona's Hispanic population numbered 963,000; those of Hispanic origin numbered 1,034,000. In 1998, 6,211 immigrants from foreign countries arrived in Arizona, of whom 3,209 were from Mexico. Arizona's total population increased 27.4% between 1990 and 1998. In the period 2000–05, net international migration was 168,078 and net internal migration was 408,160, for a net gain of 576,238 people.

[19] INTERGOVERNMENTAL COOPERATION

Arizona is a signatory to a boundary agreement with California (1963) and Nevada; and to such interstate accords as the Colorado River Compact, Desert Pacific Economic Region Compact, Interstate Compact for Juveniles, Interstate Oil and Gas Compact, Upper Colorado River Basin Compact, Western Interstate Commission for Higher Education, Wildlife Violator Compact, and Western Interstate corrections, nuclear, and education compacts.

The most important federal project in the state has been the Central Arizona Project, approved by Congress in 1968 and designed to divert water from the Colorado River to the Phoenix and Tucson areas for agriculture, energy, and other purposes. Federal grants totaled $6.617 billion in fiscal year 2005, an estimated $7.156 billion in fiscal year 2006, and an estimated $7.631 billion in fiscal year 2007.

[20] ECONOMY

Mining and cattle-raising were the principal economic activities in Arizona during the territorial period. With the introduction of irrigation in the early 1900s, farming assumed a greater importance. Improvements in transportation later in the 20th century led to the development of manufacturing and tourism.

Arizona's economy compiled an impressive growth record during the 1970s and early 1980s. Between 1973 and 1983, the state population increased by 39% (fourth in the United States). Nonfarm wage and salary employment grew by 49% (fifth in the United States), and total personal income by 218% (sixth in the United States). Overexpansion brought a slowdown in the late 1980s, and in the national recession of 1991, Arizona's annual job creation rate dropped from 3% to 0. However, economic recovery was rapid and Arizona's annual job creation rate rose to a peak of about 8% in 1994 and continued above 4% until the recession of 2001, when job growth turned negative, and only grew 0.2% in 2002. In addition to substantial layoffs in the manufacturing, transportation and utilities, and finance, insurance, and real estate sectors, the state budget crunch prompted scheduled layoffs in the government for fiscal 2004. Total assets in Arizona's financial institutions, which had grown from $38.8 billion in September 1998 to $65.3 billion by September 2001 (+68.3%), fell to $46.8 billion (-28.3%) as of September 2002.

In 2004, state gross product (GSP) totaled $199.953 billion, of which the real estate sector accounted for the largest single portion at $26.327, or 13% of GSP. This was followed by manufacturing, at $23.55 billion (11.7% of GSP); healthcare services, at $13.382 billion (6.7% of GSP); and construction, at $12.273 billion (6% of GSP). Small businesses account for a large portion of Arizona's employed workforce. In 2004, of the 110,153 businesses with employees, 97.2% of that total, or 107,018, consisted of small businesses. For that same year, a total of 12,421 new businesses were formed, down 6.8% from 2003. Business terminations totaled 17,553 in 2004, up 13.3% from the previous year,

although business bankruptcies fell 31.5% to 480 in that year. Personal bankruptcy filing rates in 2005 ranked the state around the middle nationally. In that year, the personal bankruptcy filing rate (Chapter 7 and Chapter 13) came to 570 filings per 100,000 people, putting the state 23rd.

[21] INCOME

In 2005 Arizona had a gross state product (GSP) of $216 billion, which accounted for 1.7% of the nation's gross domestic product and placed the state at number 22 in highest GSP among the 50 states and the District of Columbia.

According to the Bureau of Economic Analysis, in 2004 Arizona had a per capita personal income (PCPI) of $28,658. This ranked 39th in the United States and was 87% of the national average of $33,050. The 1994–2004 average annual growth rate of PCPI was 4.1%. Arizona had a total personal income (TPI) of $164,495,305,000, which ranked 22nd in the United States and reflected an increase of 8.4% from 2003. The 1994–2004 average annual growth rate of TPI was 7.3%. Earnings of persons employed in Arizona increased from $114,663,260,000 in 2003 to $125,262,159,000 in 2004, an increase of 9.2%. The 2003–04 national change was 6.3%.

The US Census Bureau reports that the three-year average median household income for 2002–04 in 2004 dollars was $42,590, compared to a national average of $44,473. During the same period an estimated 13.8% of the population was below the poverty line, as compared to 12.4% nationwide.

[22] LABOR

According to the Bureau of Labor Statistics (BLS), in April 2006 the seasonally adjusted civilian labor force in Arizona numbered 2,948,600, with approximately 127,600 workers unemployed, yielding an unemployment rate of 4.3%, compared to the national average of 4.7% for the same period. Preliminary data for the same period placed nonfarm employment at 2,612,600. Since the beginning of the BLS data series in 1976, the highest unemployment rate recorded in Arizona was 11.5% in February 1983. The historical low was 3.9% in December 2000. Preliminary nonfarm employment data by occupation for April 2006 showed that approximately 8.1% of the labor force was employed in construction; 7.0% in manufacturing; 19.4% in trade, transportation, and public utilities; 6.8% in financial activities; 15.0% in professional and business services; 10.8% in education and health services; 10.2% in leisure and hospitality services; and 15.5% in government.

Organized labor has a long history in Arizona. A local of the Western Federation of Miners was founded in 1896, and labor was a powerful force at the constitutional convention in 1910. Nevertheless, the state's workforce is much less organized than that of the nation as a whole.

The US Department of Labor's Bureau of Labor Statistics reported that in 2005, a total of 145,000 of Arizona's 2,366,000 employed wage and salary workers were formal members of a union. This represented 6.1% of those so employed, down from 6.3% in 2004 and well below the national average of 12%. Overall in 2005, a total of 181,000 workers (7.7%) in Arizona were covered by a union or employee association contract, which includes those workers who reported no union affiliation. Arizona is one of 22 states with a right-to-work law.

As of 1 March 2006, Arizona did not have a state-mandated minimum wage law, leaving employees in that state covered under federal minimum wage statutes. In 2004, women in the state accounted for nearly 45% of the employed civilian labor force.

23 AGRICULTURE

Arizona's agricultural output (including livestock products) was valued at $3.18 billion in 2005 (29th in the United States). Cash receipts from crops alone amounted to $1.7 billion.

In 2004, there were about 10,200 farms covering 24.7 million acres (10.7 million hectares), or about 39% of the state's total area, but only 1,961,000 acres (389,000 hectares), or 1.3% of the state, were actually farmed for crops. Arizona's farmed cropland is intensely cultivated and highly productive. In 2004, Arizona was second among all states in cotton yield per acre (1,371 lb per acre). About 95% of all farmland is dependent on irrigation provided by dams and water projects.

Cotton is the leading cash crop in Arizona. In 2004 the state produced 680,000 bales of Upland cotton on 238,000 acres (96,000 hectares), with a total value of $163,200,000. Arizona also produced 6,000 bales of American-Pima cotton on 3,000 acres (1,200 hectares) valued at $2,857,000. Vegetables, especially head lettuce, accounted for a value of $858,010,000 in 2004. Hay is also an important item; total hay production was 2,119,000 tons in 2004, for a value of $208,269,000. Other crops are wheat, sorghum, barley, grapes, and citrus fruits.

24 ANIMAL HUSBANDRY

The total inventory of cattle and calves was an estimated 910,000 in 2005, with a value of $928.2 million. In 2005, the state had an estimated 100,000 sheep and lambs. In 2004, the state had 136,000 hogs and pigs valued at $14.9 million.

A total of 3.5 billion lb (1.6 billion kg) of milk was produced in 2003.

25 FISHING

Arizona has no commercial fishing. Sports fishing, however, is popular with residents and tourists. In 2004, the state had about 361,958 licensed sport fishermen. The Alchesay and the Williams Creek National Fish Hatcheries, located on the Fort Apache Indian Reservation in east central Arizona, have played a leading role in the recovery of the threatened Apache trout. Rainbow, cutthroat, brown, and brook trout are raised for stocking, primarily on American Indian lands in Arizona, western New Mexico, and southern Colorado. The coldwater Willow Beach National Hatchery, located downriver from Hoover Dam on the Arizona side of the Colorado River, raises rainbow trout. Approximately 750,000 trout are stocked annually in the Colorado River. The Pinetop Fish Health Center is a federally sponsored research and technology center.

26 FORESTRY

The lumber industry in Arizona began during the 19th century, when the building of the transcontinental railroad created a demand for railroad ties. Production of lumber from Arizona's forests remained strong until the 1990s, when the primary emphasis shifted to conservation and recreation. Lumber production in 2004 was 65 million board feet.

The main forest regions stretch from the northwest to the southeast, through the center of the state. Altogether, in 2003 there were 19,427,000 acres (7,862,000 hectares) of forestland in Arizona, over 25% of the state's area and 2.6% of total US forestland. Commercial timberland accounted for only 3,527,000 acres (1,427,000 hectares). National forests covered 11,891,000 acres (4,812,000 hectares) as of 2003. Lumber production remains an important emphasis on the Kaibab, Coconino, and Apache-Sitgreaves National Forests, and on the Hualapai, Navajo, Ft. Apache, and San Carlos Apache Indian Reservations. The Rodeo-Chediski fire in 2002 burned over 400,000 acres (162,000 hectares).

27 MINING

Arizona ranked third in nonfuel mineral production by value in 2004. According to the US Geological Survey, nonfuel mineral production in Arizona during 2004 was valued at $3.3 billion, up almost 53% from the 2003s total of $2.18 billion, and up 11.8% from 2002 to 2003. Copper represented about 64% of the nonfuel mineral production by value in 2004, followed by construction sand and gravel, molybdenum concentrates, portland cement, crushed stone, and lime. The sharp increases in nonfuel mineral output by value mostly reflected increasing prices for copper and molybdenum, and to a lesser extent increases in construction sand and gravel, portland cement, and crushed stone. Copper output by volume in 2004, actually fell by around 2.5%, and molybdenum concentrate production increased only 2% that same year, although by value, output was over three times that of 2003.

Production and values in 2004 for the principal minerals are as follows: copper, 723,000 metric tons ($2.13 billion); construction sand and gravel, 79.6 million metric tons ($430 million); and crushed stone, 11.1 million metric tons ($57.2 million).

Arizona continued to lead the country in copper and molybdenum concentrate production in 2004, producing over 62% of all copper mined and produced in the United States. Arizona also ranked second in gemstones (by value); third in perlite, and in construction sand and gravel. The state ranked seventh in silver output and tenth in gold production.

Population growth and freeway construction projects in metropolitan Phoenix have contributed to Arizona's ranking as the nation's third-largest producer of sand and gravel.

28 ENERGY AND POWER

As of 2003, Arizona had 45 electrical power service providers, of which 28 were publicly owned and 9 were cooperatives. Of the remainder, three were federally operated, while five were investor owned. As of that same year there were over 2.422 million retail customers. Of that total, over 1,381,302 received their power from the state's five investor-owned service providers. Cooperatives accounted for 148,880 customers, while publicly owned providers had 872,381 customers.

Total net summer generating capability by the state's electrical generating plants in 2003 stood at 25.510 million kW, with total production that same year at 94.396 billion kWh. Of the total amount generated, 85.1% came from electric utilities, with the remainder from independent producers and combined heat and power service providers. The largest portion of all electric power generated, 38.091 billion kWh (40.4%), came from coal-fired plants, with nuclear fueled plants in second place, at 28.851 billion kWh (30.3%).

As of 2006, Arizona had one nuclear power–generating plant, the three unit Palo Verde facility near Wintersburg in Maricopa County.

Arizona's fossil-fuel potential remains largely undeveloped, though oil and natural-gas exploration began in the 1980s. As of 2004, the state had proven crude oil reserves of less than 1% of all US reserves, while output that same year averaged 142 barrels per day, most of which came from so-called "stripper wells," wells that produce under 10 barrels per day. Including federal offshore domains, Arizona that year ranked 31st (30th excluding federal offshore) among the 31 producing states. In 2004 the state had 18 producing oil wells and accounted for less than 1% of all US production. As of 2005, there were no refineries in Arizona.

In 2004, Arizona had six producing natural gas and gas condensate wells. In that same year, marketed gas production (all gas produced excluding gas used for repressuring, vented and flared, and nonhydrocarbon gases removed) totaled 331 million cu ft (9.4 million cu m). There is no data on the state's proven reserves of natural gas.

Arizona in 2004, had two producing coal mines, both of which were surface operations. Coal production that year totaled 12,731,000 short tons, up from 12,059,000 short tons in 2003.

Energy resource development in the state is encouraged by the Department of Mines and Mineral Resources, Oil and Gas Conservation Commission, and Department of Water Resources.

29INDUSTRY

Manufacturing, which has grown rapidly since World War II (1939–45), became the state's leading economic activity in the 1970s. Factors contributing to this growth included a favorable tax structure, available labor, plentiful electric power, and low land costs. The major manufacturing centers are the Phoenix and Tucson areas.

According to the US Census Bureau's Annual Survey of Manufactures (ASM) for 2004, Arizona's manufacturing sector covered some 17 product subsectors. The shipment value of all products manufactured in the state that same year was $41.644 billion. Of that total, the manufacturing of computer and electric products accounted for the largest portion, at $11.587 billion. It was followed by the manufacture of transportation equipment at $9.437 billion, fabricated metal products at $3.208 billion, and food manufacturing at $3.146 billion.

In 2004, a total of 158,004 people in Arizona were employed in the state's manufacturing sector, according to the ASM. Of that total, 95,923 were production workers. In terms of total employment, the transportation equipment manufacturing sector accounted for the largest portion of all manufacturing employees at 30,334, with 12,981 actual production workers. It was followed by computer and electronic product manufacturing, with 27,129 employees (12,357 actual production workers); fabricated metal product manufacturing at 17,218 employees (12,230 actual production workers); wood product manufacturing with 10,508 employees (7,809 actual production workers); and food manufacturing at 9,386 employees (6,824 actual production workers).

ASM data for 2004 showed that Arizona's manufacturing sector paid $7.240 billion in wages. Of that amount, the transportation equipment manufacturing sector accounted for the largest portion at $1.994 billion. It was followed by computer and electronic product manufacturing at $880.272 million and fabricated metal product manufacturing at $688.006 million.

Principal manufacturers of electronic and technology-intensive equipment in Arizona include: Motorola, Allied Signal Aerospace, Honeywell, Hughes Missile Systems Co., and Intel. Intel expanded its operations in Arizona with the construction of a $1.3 billion plant in 1994. While high-tech manufacturing actually declined in Arizona in 1998 and early 1999, in part because of the Asian financial crisis, the state's low-tech manufacturing improved.

30COMMERCE

According to the 2002 Census of Wholesale Trade, Arizona's wholesale trade sector had sales that year totaling $60.9 billion from 6,651 establishments. Wholesalers of durable goods accounted for 4,154 establishments, followed by nondurable goods wholesalers at 1,950, and electronic markets, agents, and brokers accounting for 547 establishments. Sales data for durable and nondurable goods wholesalers, as well as for electronic markets, agents, and brokers, was unavailable. Most wholesale establishments were concentrated in Maricopa and Pima counties.

In the 2002 Census of Retail Trade, Arizona was listed as having 17,238 retail establishments, with sales of $56.4 billion. The leading types of retail businesses by number of establishments were: miscellaneous store retailers (2,463); clothing and clothing accessories stores (2,426); motor vehicle and motor vehicle parts dealers (1,966); and gasoline stations (1,866). In terms of sales, motor vehicle and motor vehicle parts stores accounted for the largest share of retail sales, at $16.05 billion, followed by food and beverage stores at $8.1 billion; gasoline stations at $4.9 billion; and building material/garden equipment and supplies dealers at $3.7 billion. A total of 268,584 people were employed by the retail sector in Arizona that year.

Exporters located in Arizona exported $14.9 billion in merchandise during 2005.

31CONSUMER PROTECTION

Consumer protection in Arizona is the responsibility of the Public Advocacy Division of the state's Office of the Attorney General. Under the state's Consumer Fraud Act, the Arizona attorney general has primary enforcement powers regarding consumer protection, although enforcement may be delegated to County Attorneys. In addition, private citizens, under the Consumer Fraud Act, may also initiate legal action within one year from the date, from which the claim arises.

When dealing with consumer protection issues, the state's attorney general can initiate civil (but not criminal) proceedings, and is responsible for the administration of consumer protection and education programs and the handling of consumer complaints. However, the Attorney General's Office cannot represent the state before state regulatory agencies and has limited subpoena powers that can only be used in antitrust actions. In those actions, the attorney general can act on behalf of those consumers who are incapable of acting on their own; can initiate damage actions on behalf of the state in state courts; can initiate criminal proceedings; and can represent counties, cities, and other governmental entities in recovering civil damages under state or federal law.

The Attorney General's Office has locations in Phoenix and Tucson. County Attorney's Offices are located in the cities of Clifton, Flagstaff, Florence, Globe, Holbrook, Kingman, Nogales, Parker, Prescott, Safford, St. Johns, and Yuma.

³²BANKING

As of June 2005, Arizona had 51 insured banks, savings and loans, and saving banks, along with 28 state-chartered and 35 federally chartered credit unions (CUs). Excluding the CUs, the Phoenix-Mesa-Scottsdale market area had 65 financial institutions in 2004, followed by Tucson at 21, Prescott at 12, Yuma at 9, and Flagstaff at 8. As of June 2005, CUs accounted for 12.8% of all assets held by all financial institutions in the state, or some $10.841 billion. Banks, savings and loans, and savings banks collectively accounted for the remaining 87.2% or $74.020 billion in assets held.

Arizona has a high percentage of new banking institutions. As of the fourth quarter of 2005, 11 were less than 3 years old. For the same period, the median net interest margin (the difference between the lower rates offered to savers and the higher rates charged on loans) was 5.38%. The state's median annualized return on average assets (ROA) ratio (the measure of earnings in relation to all resources) was 1.19%.

State-chartered financial institutions in Arizona are regulated by the Department of Banking. Nationally or federally chartered financial institutions either are under the Office of the Comptroller of the Currency (banks), the Office of Thrift Supervision, or the National Credit Union Administration. Federally regulated institutions in Arizona include the Bank of America, Bank One, Wells Fargo Bank, Desert Schools Federal Credit Union, and Arizona Federal Credit Union.

³³INSURANCE

In 2004 there were 1.79 million individual life insurance policies in force with a total value of $203.9 billion; total value for all categories of life insurance (individual, group, and credit) was $309 billion. The average coverage amount was $113,800 per policy holder. Death benefits paid that year totaled $874 million.

As of 2003, there were 50 property and casualty and 262 life and health insurance companies incorporated or organized in the state. Direct premiums for property and casualty insurance amounted to $7.5 billion in 2004. That year, there were 29,078 flood insurance policies in force in the state, with a total value of $4.97 billion.

In 2004, 48% of state residents held employment-based health insurance policies, 6% held individual policies, and 27% were covered under Medicare and Medicaid; 17% of residents were uninsured. In 2003, employee contributions for employment-based health coverage averaged at 18% for single coverage and 30% for family coverage. For family coverage, an average employee contribution rate of 30% was one of the highest in the country. Arizona does not offer extended health benefits in connection with the Consolidated Omnibus Budget Reconciliation Act (COBRA), a health insurance extension program for those who lose employment-based coverage due to termination or reduction of work hours.

In 2003, there were over 3.3 million auto insurance policies in effect for private passenger cars. Required minimum coverage includes bodily injury liability of up to $25,000 per individual and $30,000 for all persons injured, as well as property damage liability of $10,000. In 2003, the average expenditure per vehicle for insurance coverage was $920.38.

The Department of Insurance regulates the state's insurance industry and examines and licenses agents, and brokers.

³⁴SECURITIES

The Arizona Stock Exchange (AZX), originally established by Steve Wunsch in 1990 as the Wunsch Auction System, was an electronic call market that traded equity securities, including many Arizona-based companies. However, the AZX closed in 2001 due to lack of volume.

In 2005, there were 2,590 personal financial advisers employed in the state. In 2004, there were over 133 publicly traded companies within the state, with over 45 NASDAQ companies, 17 NYSE listings, and 7 AMEX listings. In 2006, the state had four Fortune 500 companies; Avnet (Phoenix) ranked first in the state and 212th in the nation with revenues of over $11 billion, followed by Phelps Dodge (Phoenix), Allied Waste Industries (Scottsdale), and US Airways Group (Tempe), all of which are NYSE companies. PetSmart (Phoenix), a NASDAQ listing, made the Fortune 1,000 list, at 518th in the nation.

³⁵PUBLIC FINANCE

The governor's budgets are prepared in the Office of Strategic Planning and Budgeting (OSPB). During the 1990's, Arizona moved from an annual to a biennial budget format. Agency requests are submitted to the OSPB by September 1, and agency hearings are held in November and December. The governor's budget is submitted in January and the legislature is expected to pass the budget in the period January to April. With rebounding tourism dollars, cost cutting, and strong population increases Arizona's fiscal picture has improved. Fiscal year 2006 general funds were estimated at nearly $9.3 billion for resources and $8.2 billion for expenditures. In fiscal year 2004, federal government grants to Arizona were $8.3 billion. For fiscal year 2007, federal funding for border station improvements was authorized, as was increased funding for research on water purification technology under the Water 2025 program.

³⁶TAXATION

In 2005, Arizona collected $11,008 million in tax revenues, or $1,854 per capita, which placed it 40th among the 50 states in per capita tax burden. The national average was $2,192 per capita. Property taxes accounted for 3.4% of the total; sales taxes, 47.3%; selective sales taxes, 13.5%; individual income taxes, 25.9%; corporate income taxes, 6.4%; and other taxes 3.5%.

As of 1 January 2006, Arizona had five individual income tax brackets ranging from 2.87% to 5.04%. The state taxes corporations at a flat rate of 6.968%.

In 2004, state and local property taxes amounted to $4,867,990,000, or $848 per capita. The per capita amount ranks the state 35th highest nationally. Local governments collected $4,521,563,000 of the total and the state government, $346,427,000.

Arizona taxes retail sales at a rate of 5.60%. In addition to the state tax, local taxes on retail sales can reach as high as 4.50%, making for a potential total tax on retail sales of 10.10%. Food purchased for consumption off-premises is tax exempt. The tax on cigarettes is 118 cents per pack, which ranks 16th among the 50 states and the District of Columbia. Arizona taxes gasoline at 18 cents per gallon. This is in addition to the 18.4 cents per gallon federal tax on gasoline.

According to the Tax Foundation, for every federal tax dollar sent to Washington in 2004, Arizona citizens received $1.30 in federal spending.

Arizona—State Government Finances

(Dollar amounts in thousands. Per capita amounts in dollars.)

	AMOUNT	PER CAPITA
Total Revenue	23,753,397	4,138.22
General revenue	18,949,181	3,301.25
Intergovernmental revenue	6,987,389	1,217.32
Taxes	9,606,318	1,673.57
General sales	4,719,642	822.24
Selective sales	1,351,095	235.38
License taxes	289,803	50.49
Individual income tax	2,315,865	403.46
Corporate income tax	525,650	91.58
Other taxes	404,263	70.43
Current charges	1,169,721	203.78
Miscellaneous general revenue	1,185,753	206.58
Utility revenue	25,446	4.43
Liquor store revenue	–	–
Insurance trust revenue	4,778,770	832.54
Total expenditure	21,748,803	3,788.99
Intergovernmental expenditure	7,544,080	1,314.30
Direct expenditure	14,204,723	2,474.69
Current operation	9,930,123	1,729.99
Capital outlay	1,460,258	254.40
Insurance benefits and repayments	2,179,136	379.64
Assistance and subsidies	394,561	68.74
Interest on debt	240,645	41.92
Exhibit: Salaries and wages	2,627,433	457.74
Total expenditure	21,748,803	3,788.99
General expenditure	19,541,494	3,404.44
Intergovernmental expenditure	7,544,080	1,314.30
Direct expenditure	11,997,414	2,090.14
General expenditures, by function:		
Education	7,149,182	1,245.50
Public welfare	5,162,214	899.34
Hospitals	59,012	10.28
Health	1,133,082	197.40
Highways	1,891,625	329.55
Police protection	188,754	32.88
Correction	790,485	137.72
Natural resources	238,297	41.52
Parks and recreation	167,668	29.21
Government administration	484,420	84.39
Interest on general debt	237,435	41.36
Other and unallocable	2,039,320	355.28
Utility expenditure	28,173	4.91
Liquor store expenditure	–	–
Insurance trust expenditure	2,179,136	379.64
Debt at end of fiscal year	6,773,923	1,180.13
Cash and security holdings	38,840,515	6,766.64

Abbreviations and symbols: – zero or rounds to zero; (NA) not available; (X) not applicable.

SOURCE: *U.S. Census Bureau, Governments Division, 2004 Survey of State Government Finances,* January 2006.

37 ECONOMIC POLICY

The Department of Commerce has primary responsibility for attracting business and industry to Arizona, aiding existing business and industry, and assisting companies engaged in international trade. Its programs emphasize job opportunities, energy conservation, support of small businesses, and development of the film industry. The Commerce and Economic Development Commission (CEDC), a six-member agency chaired by the director of the Department of Commerce, was established in 1989 as the state economic policy and planning board. Its budget is provided by two scratch games in the Arizona lottery. Economic development programs supported at least in part by the state include the Arizona Enterprise Zone (EZ) Program, which offers tax reductions and exemptions for investment in areas where poverty and/or unemployment are high; the Military Reuse Zone (MRZ) program, established 1992, which offers incentives for investments to retool military installations for civilian use; the Tucson Empowerment Zone Tax Incentive Plan, a $17 billion tax incentive program designed after Tucson won designation by the federal government as an empowerment zone; the Arizona Job Training Program, which designs job training programs; the Economic Strengths Program (ESP), which provides grants for road construction; Waste Reduction Assistance (WRA); the Waste Reduction Initiative Through Education (WRITE); the Private Activity Bonds (PAB) Program, which in 1986 replaced the Industrial Development Bond Program, and which offers finance in favorable terms for the construction of industrial and manufacturing facilities, student loans, housing, private utility projects, and some municipal projects; the Lease Excise Tax Program, which offered tax abatements to businesses that lease, rather than own, city property; and the IT Training Tax Credit, which offered training for up to 20 employees in information technology (IT) skills. As of 2006, the state had also designated seven Foreign Trade Zones (FTZs), which were accorded treatment as territory outside of the state's tax jurisdiction. Other tax incentives offered by Arizona include a 10% Pollution Control Tax credit on real and personal property used to control pollution; a schedule of tax credits for research and development expenditures; and accelerated depreciation for capital investments.

38 HEALTH

The infant mortality rate in October 2005 was estimated at 6.9 per 1,000 live births. The birth rate in 2003 was 16.3 per 1,000 population, the third-highest in the nation (following Utah and Texas). The abortion rate stood at 16.5 per 1,000 women in 2000. In 2003, about 76.6% of pregnant woman received prenatal care beginning in the first trimester. In 2004, approximately 79% of children received routine immunizations before the age of three.

The crude death rate in 2003 was 7.8 deaths per 1,000 population. As of 2002, the death rates for major causes of death (per 100,000 resident population) were: heart disease, 198.9; cancer, 171.5; cerebrovascular diseases, 46.5; chronic lower respiratory diseases, 47.2; and diabetes, 22.6. The mortality rate from HIV infection was 3 per 100,000 population. In 2004, the reported AIDS case rate was at about 9.8 per 100,000 population. In 2002, about 54.1% of the population was considered overweight or obese. As of 2004, about 18.5% of state residents were smokers.

In 2003, Arizona had 61 community hospitals with about 10,800 beds. There were about 603,000 patient admissions that year and 6.7 million outpatient visits. The average daily inpatient census was about 7,300 patients. The average cost per day for hospital care was $1,570. Also in 2003, there were about 135 certified nursing facilities in the state, with 16,451 beds and an overall occupancy rate of about 80.5%. In 2004, it was estimated that about 68.6% of all state residents had received some type of dental care within the year. Arizona had 225 physicians per 100,000 resident population in 2004 and 522 nurses per 100,000 in 2005. In 2004, there was a total of 2,976 dentists in the state.

About 27% of state residents were enrolled in Medicaid and Medicare programs in 2004. Approximately 17% of the state population was uninsured in 2004. In 2003, state healthcare expenditures totaled $5.5 million.

39 SOCIAL WELFARE

In 2004, about 96,000 people received unemployment benefits with the average weekly unemployment benefit at $177. In fiscal year 2005, the estimated average monthly participation in the food stamp program included about 550,291 persons (220,498 households); the average monthly benefit was about $95.98 per person. That year, the total benefits paid through the state for the food stamp program was about $633.8 million.

Temporary Assistance for Needy Families (TANF), the system of federal welfare assistance that officially replaced Aid to Families with Dependent Children (AFDC) in 1997, was reauthorized through the Deficit Reduction Act of 2005. TANF is funded through federal block grants that are divided among the states based on an equation involving the number of recipients in each state. Arizona's TANF program is called EMPOWER (Employing and Moving People Off Welfare and Encouraging Responsibility). In 2004, the state program had 115,000 recipients; state and federal expenditures on the TANF program totaled $175 million in fiscal year 2003.

In December 2004, Social Security benefits were paid to 888,460 Arizona residents. This number included 578.590 retired workers, 76,490 widows and widowers, 114,250 disabled workers, 49,760 spouses, and 69,370 children. Social Security beneficiaries represented 15.5% of the total state population and 86.3% of the state's population age 65 and older. Retired workers received an average monthly payment of $973; widows and widowers, $930; disabled workers, $924; and spouses, $482. Payments for children of retired workers averaged $467 per month; children of deceased workers, $605; and children of disabled workers, $262. Federal Supplemental Security Income payments in December 2004 went to 94,400 Arizona residents, averaging $406 a month. An additional $23,000 in state-administered supplemental payments was distributed to 457 residents.

40 HOUSING

In 2004, there were an estimated 2,458,231 housing units, of which 2,131,534 were occupied. In the same year, 68.7% of all housing units were owner-occupied. It was estimated that about 101,678 units statewide were without telephone service, 14,897 lacked complete plumbing facilities, and 11,543 lacked complete kitchen facilities. About 59% of all units were single-family detached homes; about 13.2% were mobile homes. The average household had 2.64 members.

From 1980 to 1990, the housing boom in Arizona caused the number of housing units to increase by 55%. About 27.6% of all housing structures in Arizona were built in 1995 or later. In 2004, the median value of a home was $145,741. The median monthly cost for mortgage owners was $1,130; the median cost monthly cost for renters was $691. Approximately 90,600 new units were authorized in 2004. In September 2005, the state was awarded grants of over $2 million from the US Department of Housing and Urban Development (HUD) for rural housing and economic development programs. For 2006, HUD allocated to the state over $12.1 million in community development block grants.

41 EDUCATION

In 2004, 84.4% of Arizonans 25 years old and over were high school graduates. Some 28% had obtained a bachelor's degree or higher.

The first public school in the state opened in 1871 at Tucson, with 1 teacher and 138 students. In the fall of 2002, total enrollment in public schools was 938,000. Of these, 660,000 attended schools from kindergarten through grade eight, and 277,000 attended high school. Approximately 49.2% of the students were white, 4.8% were black, 37.2% were Hispanic, 2.2% were Asian/Pacific Islander, and 6.6% were American Indian/Alaskan Native. Total enrollment was estimated at 949,000 in fall 2003 and expected to be 1,074,000 by fall 2014, an increase of 14.5% during the period 2002–14. There were 46,366 students enrolled in 292 private schools in fall 2003. Expenditures for public education in 2003/04 were estimated at $6.7 billion or $6,036 per student, the third-lowest among the 50 states. Since 1969, the National Assessment of Educational Progress (NAEP) has tested public school students nationwide. The resulting report, *The Nation's Report Card,* stated that in 2005 eighth graders in Arizona scored 274 out of 500 in mathematics compared with the national average of 278.

As of fall 2002, there were 401,605 students enrolled in college or graduate school; minority students comprised 28.8% of total postsecondary enrollment. As of 2005, Arizona had 74 degree-granting institutions. The leading public higher educational institutions, the University of Arizona at Tucson and Arizona State University (originally named the Arizona Territorial Normal School) at Tempe, were both established in 1885. Thunderbird, The Garvin School of International Management, a private institution, is located in Glendale.

42 ARTS

The Arizona Commission on the Arts was established as a permanent state agency in 1967. The Arizona Humanities Council was established in 1973. In 2005, the National Endowment for the Arts (NEA) awarded 18 grants totaling $977,400 to Arizona arts organizations; the National Endowment for the Humanities (NEH) awarded 11 grants totaling $1,241,940. State arts programs are also supported by the Arizona Arts Endowment Fund (also called Arizona ArtShare), which was established in 1996. Arizona is also a member state of the Western States Art Federation (WESTAF).

Arizona has traditionally been a center for American Indian folk arts and crafts. The Arizona State Museum (Tucson), Colorado River Indian Tribes Museum (Parker), Heard Museum of

Anthropology and Primitive Art (Phoenix), Mohave Museum of History and Arts (Kingman), Navajo Tribal Museum (Window Rock), and Pueblo Grande Museum (Phoenix) all display Indian creations, both historic and contemporary. Modern Arizona artists are featured at the Tucson Museum of Art and the Yuma Art Center.

Musical and dramatic performances are presented in Phoenix, Tucson, Scottsdale, and other major cities. One of Arizona's oldest arts organization and one of the longest-running theaters nationwide, the Phoenix Theatre celebrated its 85th season in 2005. Ballet Arizona, based in Phoenix, celebrated 20 years of performance during its 2005/06 season. The Arizona Opera Company and the Arizona Theatre Company perform both in Tucson and Phoenix. As of 2006, there were two major orchestras, the Phoenix Symphony, founded in 1947, and the Tucson Symphony Orchestra, founded in 1928, one of the oldest symphonies in the Southwest. The annual Grand Canyon Music Festival (est. 1984) features the finest in both classical and folk music.

43 LIBRARIES AND MUSEUMS

For the fiscal year ending in June 2001, Arizona had 35 public library systems, with a total of 176 libraries, of which 148 were branches. Also that year, the system had a combined book and serial publications stock of 8,760,000 volumes, and a total circulation of 33,066,000. The system also had 364,000 audio and 484,000 video items, 38,000 electronic format items (CD-ROMs, magnetic tapes, and disks), and 15 bookmobiles. Principal public libraries included the Phoenix Public Library and the State Library and Department of Archives in Phoenix, and the Arizona Historical Society Library in Tucson. The largest university libraries are located at the University of Arizona and Arizona State University. Total operating income for the public library system amounted to $118,286,000 in fiscal year 2001, including $682,000 in federal grants and $652,000 in state grants.

Arizona has more than 120 museums and historic sites. Attractions in Tucson include the Arizona State Museum, University of Arizona Museum of Art, Arizona Historical Society, Arizona-Sonora Desert Museum, Flandreau Planetarium, and Gene C. Reid Zoological Park. Phoenix has the Heard Museum (anthropology and primitive art), Arizona Mineral Resources Museum, Phoenix Art Museum, Phoenix Zoo, Pueblo Grande Museum, and Desert Botanical Garden. The Museum of Northern Arizona and Lowell Observatory are in Flagstaff. Kitt Peak National Observatory is in Tucson.

Archaeological and historical sites include the cliff dwellings at the Canyon de Chelly, Casa Grande Ruins, Montezuma Castle, Tonto, and Tuzigoot national monuments; the town of Tombstone, the site of the famous O. K. Corral gunfight in the early 1880s; and the restored mission church at Tumacacori National Monument and San Xavier del Bac Church near Tucson.

44 COMMUNICATIONS

Over 91.8% of housing units had telephones in 2004. In addition, by June of that same year there were 3,079,657 mobile wireless telephone subscribers. In 2003, 64.3% of Arizona households had a computer and 55.2% had Internet access. By June 2005, there were 860,082 high-speed lines in Arizona, 783,322 residential and

76,760 for business. A total of 131,164 Internet domain names had been registered in Arizona as of 2000.

There were 70 major radio stations broadcasting in Arizona in 2005 (15 AM and 55 FM). The state also had 15 major television stations in 2005. In 1999, 59% of Phoenix's 1,390,750 television households received cable.

45 PRESS

The *Weekly Arizonian,* started in 1859, was the first newspaper in the state. The *Daily Arizona Miner,* the state's first daily, was founded at Prescott in 1866. In 2004, *The Arizona Republic* was the 15th largest newspaper in the country, based on daily circulation rates. As of 2005 there were 10 morning dailies and 6 evening dailies; 11 dailies had Sunday editions.

The following table shows 2005 circulations for leading dailies:

AREA	NAME	DAILY	SUNDAY
Phoenix	*Arizona Republic* (m,S)	413,268	530,751
Tucson	*Arizona Daily Star* (m,S)	100,824	161,957
	Citizen (e)	30,090	

In 2005, there were 68 weekly publications in Arizona, including 29 paid weeklies, 27 free weeklies, and 12 combined weeklies. The total circulation of paid weeklies (180,610) and free weeklies (531,432) is 712,042. Tucson's *Shopper,* with a circulation of 328,149, ranked 20th in the nation among publications of its type.

Among the most notable magazines and periodicals published in Arizona were *Phoenix Magazine, Phoenix Living,* and *Arizona Living,* devoted to the local and regional life-style; *American West,* dedicated to the Western heritage; *Arizona and the West,* published quarterly by the University of Arizona Library in Tucson; and *Arizona Highways,* a beautifully illustrated monthly published by the Department of Transportation in Phoenix.

46 ORGANIZATIONS

In 2006, there were over 2,880 nonprofit organizations registered within the state, of which about 2,069 were registered as charitable, educational, or religious organizations. Among the organizations headquartered in Arizona are the National Foundation for Asthma (Tucson), the American Bicycle Association (Chandler), the American Federation of Astrologers (Tempe), the American Rock Art Research Association (Tucson), the Muscular Dystrophy Association (Tucson), the Western National Parks Association (Tucson), the Make-A-Wish Foundation of America (Phoenix), Safari Club International (Tucson), and the United States Handball Association (Tucson). The national Fisher-Price Collector's Club is based in Mesa.

The National Native American Cooperative in Tucson and the Association of American Cultures serves local and national members who strive to preserve and promote interest in native arts and cultures. The desert Bluegrass Association is another regional arts association. The Desert Botanical Garden in Phoenix presents tours of the gardens and a museum as well as offering seminars on the flora of arid lands. Offices for the Messianic Jewish Movement International are based in Chandler.

47 TOURISM, TRAVEL, AND RECREATION

Tourism and travel is a leading industry in Arizona. In 2004, tourism and travel accounted for more than $13.76 billion in direct sales. There were 27.8 million domestic visitors and 900,000 from overseas.

There are 22 national parks and monuments located entirely within Arizona. By far the most popular is Grand Canyon National Park. Petrified Forest National Park and Saguaro National Monument are also popular national parks. There are also 14 state parks that regularly attract over a million visitors per year.

Arizona offers excellent camping on both public and private land, and there are many farm vacation sites and dude ranches, particularly in the Tucson and Wickenburg areas. Popular for sightseeing and shopping are the state's American Indian reservations, particularly those of the Navaho and Hopi. Boating and fishing on Lake Mead, Lake Powell, Lake Mohave, Lake Havasu (people can revisit the original London Bridge), the Colorado River, and the Salt River lakes are also attractions. The Hoover Dam is located on the Arizona-Nevada border. The red rock country of Sedona is a popular destination. The nearby city of Jerome is a real ghost town. Winter visitors can ski and enjoy other winter sports in Flagstaff in an area called the Snow Bowl. Biosphere 2 in Oracle is another popular tourist attraction. Tourists interested in architecture can visit Frank Lloyd Wright's workshop, Taliesin West, in Carefree. In the late winter and early spring, many Major League Baseball teams conduct their spring training at camps in Arizona. Visitors can watch practice games and visit with the players. For auto racing fans, NASCAR also has a big presence in Arizona.

[48] SPORTS

There are five major professional teams in Arizona, all in Phoenix: the Cardinals of the National Football League, the Suns of the National Basketball Association, the Coyotes of the National Hockey League, the Mercury of the Women's National Basketball Association, and the Diamondbacks of Major League Baseball. The Diamondbacks captured the World Series in 2001. There is a minor league hockey team, also in Phoenix. Several Major League Baseball teams hold spring training in Arizona, and there is a minor league team in Tucson, as well as several rookie league teams throughout the state. There is horse racing at Turf Paradise in Phoenix, and dog racing at Phoenix, Tucson, and Yuma. Auto racing is held at Manzanita Raceway and International Raceway, in Phoenix. Phoenix International Raceway also hosts NASCAR Nextel Cup and Busch Series events. Both Phoenix and Tucson have hosted tournaments on the Professional Golfers Association's nationwide tour.

The first organized rodeo that awarded prizes and charged admission was held in Prescott on 4 July 1988, and rodeos continue to be held throughout the state.

Both Arizona State and the University of Arizona joined the Pacific 10 Conference in 1978. The Sun Devils won the Rose Bowl in their first appearance in 1987, and also appeared in 1997. The Wildcats captured National Collegiate Athletic Association (NCAA) Division I baseball championships in 1975, 1980, and 1986, and the NCAA Division I men's basketball championship in 1997. The men's basketball team at the University of Arizona has reached the NCAA Tournament for 22 consecutive years. The Sun Devils won the baseball championship in 1981. College football's Fiesta Bowl is held annually at Sun Devil Stadium in Tempe, the home stadium for the Arizona State football team.

Other annual sporting events include the Thunderbird Balloon Classic in Scottsdale in November.

[49] FAMOUS ARIZONIANS

Although Arizona entered the Union relatively late (1912), many of it citizens have achieved national prominence, especially since World War II (1939–45). William H. Rehnquist (b.Wisconsin, 1924–2005) was appointed associate justice of the US Supreme Court in 1971 and chief justice in 1986; in 1981 Sandra Day O'Connor (b.Texas, 1930) became the first woman to serve on the Supreme Court. Arizona natives who became federal officeholders include Lewis Douglas (1894–1974), a representative who served as director of the budget in 1933–34 and ambassador to the Court of St. James's from 1947 to 1950; Stewart L. Udall (b.1920), secretary of the interior, 1961–69; and Richard B. Kleindienst (1923–2000), attorney general, 1972–73, who resigned during the Watergate scandal. Another native son was Carl T. Hayden (1877–1972), who served in the US House of Representatives from statehood in 1912 until 1927 and in the US Senate from 1927 to 1969, thereby setting a record for congressional tenure. Barry Goldwater (1909–98), son of a pioneer family, was elected to the US Senate in 1952, won the Republican presidential nomination in 1964, and returned to the Senate in 1968. His Republican colleague, John J. Rhodes (b.Kansas, 1916–2003), served in the US House of Representatives for 30 years and was House minority leader from 1973 to 1980. Raul H. Castro (b.Mexico, 1916), a native of Sonora, came to the United States in 1926, was naturalized, served as Arizona governor from 1975 to 1977, and has held several ambassadorships to Latin America. Morris K. Udall (1922–98), first elected to the US House of Representatives in 1960, contended for the Democratic presidential nomination in 1976.

Prominent state officeholders include General John C. Frémont (b.Georgia, 1813–90), who was territorial governor of Arizona from 1878 to 1883, and George W. P. Hunt (1859–1934), who presided over the state constitutional convention in 1910 and was elected governor seven times during the early decades of statehood. Eusebio Kino (b.Italy, 1645?–1711) was a pioneer Jesuit who introduced missions and European civilization to Arizona. Also important to the state's history and development were Charles D. Poston (1825–1902), who in the late 1850s promoted settlement and separate territorial status for Arizona; Chiricahua Apache leaders Cochise (1812?–74) and Geronimo (1829–1909), who, resisting the forced resettlement of their people by the US government, launched a series of raids that occupied the Army in the Southwest for over two decades; Wyatt Earp (b.Illinois, 1848–1929), legendary lawman of Tombstone during the early 1880s; John C. Greenway (1872–1926), copper magnate and town builder who was a nominee on the Democratic ticket in 1924 for US vice president; and Frank Luke Jr. (1897–1918), a World War I flying ace who was the first American airman to receive the Medal of Honor.

Distinguished professional people associated with Arizona have included James Douglas (b.Canada, 1837–1918), metallurgist and developer of the Bisbee copper district; Percival Lowell (b.Massachusetts, 1855–1916), who built the Lowell Observatory in Flagstaff; and Andrew Ellicott Douglass (b.Vermont, 1867–1962), astronomer, university president, and inventor of dendrochronology, the science of dating events and environmental variations through the study of tree rings and aged wood. Cesar Chavez (1927–93) was president of the United Farm Workers of America.

Writers whose names have been associated with Arizona include novelist Harold Bell Wright (b.New York, 1872–1944), who lived for an extended period in Tucson; Zane Grey (b.Ohio, 1875–1939), who wrote many of his Western adventure stories in his summer home near Payson; and Joseph Wood Krutch (b.Tennessee, 1893–1970), an essayist and naturalist who spent his last two decades in Arizona. Well-known performing artists from Arizona include singers Marty Robbins (1925–70), and Linda Ronstadt (b.1946). Joan Ganz Cooney (b.1929), president of the Children's Television Workshop, was one of the creators of the award-winning children's program, *Sesame Street*.

⁵⁰BIBLIOGRAPHY

Alampi, Gary (ed.). *Gale State Rankings Reporter.* Detroit: Gale Research, Inc., 1994.

Bischoff, Matt C. *Touring Arizona Hot Springs.* Helena, Mont.: Falcon, 1999.

Busby, Mark (ed.). *The Southwest.* Vol. 8 in *The Greenwood Encyclopedia of American Regional Cultures.* Westport, Conn.: Greenwood Press, 2004.

Cities of the United States. 5th ed. Farmington Hills, Mich.: Thomson Gale, 2005.

Council of State Governments. *The Book of the States, 2006 Edition.* Lexington, Ky.: Council of State Governments, 2006.

Eichholz, Alice. *Red Book: American State, County, and Town Sources.* 3rd ed. Provo, Utah: Ancestry, 2004.

FDIC, Division of Research and Statistics. *Statistics on Banking: A Statistical Profile of the United States Banking Industry.* Washington, D.C.: Federal Deposit Insurance Corporation, 1993.

Goldwater, Barry. *Arizona.* New York: Random House, 1978.

Parzybok, Tye W. *Weather Extremes in the West.* Missoula, Mont.: Mountain Press, 2005.

Preston, Thomas. *Intermountain West: Idaho, Nevada, Utah, and Arizona.* Vol. 2 of *The Double Eagle Guide to 1,000 Great Western Recreation Destinations.* 2nd ed. Billings, Mont.: Discovery Publications, 2003.

Sheridan, Thomas E. *Arizona: A History.* Tucson: University of Arizona Press, 1995.

US Department of Commerce, Economics and Statistics Administration, US Census Bureau. *Arizona, 2000. Summary Social, Economic, and Housing Characteristics: 2000 Census of Population and Housing.* Washington, D.C.: US Government Printing Office, 2003.

ARKANSAS

State of Arkansas

ORIGIN OF STATE NAME: French derivation of *Akansas* or *Arkansas,* a name given to the Quapaw Indians by other tribes. **NICKNAME:** The Natural State. **CAPITAL:** Little Rock. **ENTERED UNION:** 15 June 1836 (25th). **SONG:** "Arkansas." **MOTTO:** *Regnat populus* (The people rule). **COAT OF ARMS:** In front of an American eagle is a shield displaying a steamboat, plow, beehive, and sheaf of wheat, symbols of Arkansas's industrial and agricultural wealth. The angel of mercy, the goddess of liberty encircled by 13 stars, and the sword of justice surround the eagle, which holds in its talons an olive branch and three arrows, and in its beak a banner bearing the state motto. **FLAG:** On a red field, 25 stars on a blue band border, a white diamond containing the word "Arkansas" and four blue stars. **OFFICIAL SEAL:** Coat of arms surrounded by the words "Great Seal of the State of Arkansas." **BIRD:** Mockingbird. **FLOWER:** Apple blossom. **TREE:** Pine. **GEM:** Diamond. **LEGAL HOLIDAYS:** New Year's Day, 1 January; Robert E. Lee's birthday, 19 January; Birthdays of Martin Luther King Jr. and Robert E. Lee, 3rd Monday in January; George Washington's Birthday and Daisy Gatson Bates Day, 3rd Monday in February; Memorial Day, last Monday in May; Independence Day, 4 July; Labor Day, 1st Monday in September; Veterans' Day, 11 November; Thanksgiving Day, 4th Thursday in November; Christmas Eve, 24 December; Christmas Day, 25 December. **TIME:** 6 AM CST = noon GMT.

¹LOCATION, SIZE, AND EXTENT

Located in the western south-central United States, Arkansas ranks 27th in size among the 50 states.

The total area of Arkansas is 53,187 sq mi (137,754 sq km), of which land takes up 52,078 sq mi (134,882 sq km), and inland water, 1,109 sq mi (2,872 sq km). Arkansas extends about 275 mi (443 km) E–W and 240 mi (386 km) N–S.

Arkansas is bordered on the N by Missouri; on the E by Missouri, Tennessee, and Mississippi (with part of the line passing through the St. Francis and Mississippi rivers); on the S by Louisiana; on the SW by Texas (with part of the line formed by the Red River), and on the W by Oklahoma. The total boundary length of Arkansas is 1,168 mi (1,880 km). The state's geographic center is in Pulaski County, 12 mi (19 km) NW of Little Rock.

²TOPOGRAPHY

The Boston Mountains (an extension of the Ozark Plateau, sometimes called the Ozark Mountains) in the northwest and the Ouachita Mountains in the west-central region not only constitute Arkansas's major uplands but also are the only mountain chains between the Appalachians and the Rockies. Aside from the wide valley of the Arkansas River, which separates the two chains, the Arkansas lowlands belong to two physiographic regions: the Mississippi Alluvial Plain and the Gulf Coastal Plain. The highest elevation in Arkansas, at 2,753 ft (840 m), is Magazine Mountain, standing north of the Ouachitas in the Arkansas River Valley. The state's lowest point, at 55 ft (17 m), is on the Ouachita River in south-central Arkansas. The mean elevation of the state is approximately 650 ft (198 m).

Arkansas's largest lake is the artificial Lake Ouachita, covering 63 sq mi (163 sq km); Lake Chicot, in southeastern Arkansas, and oxbow of the Mississippi River, is the state's largest natural lake, with a length of 18 mi (29 km). Bull Shoals Lake, occupying 71

sq mi (184 sq km), is shared with Missouri. Principal rivers include the Mississippi, forming most of the eastern boundary; the Arkansas (the sixth longest river in the country), beginning in Colorado and flowing 1,450 mi (2,334 km) through Kansas and Oklahoma and across central Arkansas to the Mississippi; and the Red, White, Ouachita, and St. Francis rivers, all of which likewise drain south and southeast into the Mississippi. Numerous springs are found in Arkansas, of which the best known are Mammoth Springs, near the Missouri border, one of the largest in the world, with a flow rate averaging nine million gal (34 million l) an hour, and Hot Springs in the Ouachitas.

Crowley's Ridge, a unique strip of hills formed by sedimentary deposits and windblown sand, lies west of and parallel to the St. Francis River for about 180 mi (290 km). The ridge is rich in fossils and has an unusual diversity of plant life.

³CLIMATE

Arkansas has a temperate climate, warmer and more humid in the southern lowlands than in the mountainous regions. At Little Rock, the normal daily temperature ranges from 40°F (4°C) in January to 82°F (27°C) in July. A record low of -29°F (-34°C) was set on 13 February 1905 at the Pond weather station, and a record high of 120°F (49°C) was recorded on 10 August 1936 at the Ozark station.

Average yearly precipitation is approximately 45 in (114 cm) in the mountainous areas and greater in the lowlands; Little Rock receives an annual average of 50.5 in (128 cm). Snowfall in the capital averages 5.1 in (12 cm) a year.

⁴FLORA AND FAUNA

Arkansas has at least 2,600 native plants, and there are many naturalized exotic species. Cypresses, water oak, hickory, and ash grow in the Mississippi Valley, while the St. Francis Valley is home to the rare cork tree. Crowley's Ridge is thick with tulip trees and beeches. A forest belt of oak, hickory, and pine stretches across south-central and southwestern Arkansas, including the Ozark and Ouachita mountains. The Mexican juniper is common along the White River's banks. The state has at least 26 native varieties of orchid; the passion flower is so abundant that it was once considered for designation as the state flower, but the apple blossom was finally chosen instead.

Arkansas's native animals include 15 varieties of bat and 3 each of rabbit and squirrel. Common throughout the state are mink, armadillo, white-tailed deer, and eastern chipmunk. The only remaining native population of black bears is found in the White River National Wildlife Refuge and the Trusten Holder Wildlife Management Area. These two sites are part of the Cache-Lower White River area, which has been designated as a Ramsar Wetland of International Importance for the role it plays as a wintering habitat for migratory birds. Among 300 native birds are such game birds as the eastern wild turkey, mourning dove, and bobwhite quail. Among local fish are catfish, gar, and the unusual paddle fish. Arkansas counts 20 frog and toad species, 23 varieties of salamander, and 36 kinds of snake.

In April 2006, a total of 29 species occurring within the state were on the threatened and endangered species list of the US Fish and Wildlife Service. These included 23 animals (vertebrates and invertebrates) and 6 plant species. The Arkansas Game and Fish Commission lists the leopard darter and fat pocketbook pearly mussel as threatened species. The bald eagle is listed as endangered, along with the Indiana and gray bats, cave crayfish, pink mucket, several species of mussel, pallid sturgeon, least tern, and red-cockaded woodpecker. Among endangered or threatened plants are the Missouri bladderpod, pondberry, eastern prairie fringed orchid, and running buffalo clover. In 1983, Arkansas established the Non-Game Preservation Committee to promote sound management, conservation, and public awareness of the state's nongame animals and native plants.

5 ENVIRONMENTAL PROTECTION

In 1949, the Arkansas General Assembly created the Arkansas Pollution Control Commission. This legislation was amended in later years to be known as the Arkansas Water and Air Pollution Control Act. Under an extensive reorganization of state government in 1971, the Arkansas Department of Pollution Control and Ecology (ADPC & E) was created as a cabinet-level agency and the commission was renamed the Arkansas Pollution Control and Ecology Commission. (In 1996, the Arkansas General Assembly voted to change the name of the department to the Arkansas Department of Environmental Quality—ADEQ, effective 31 March 1999.) Although the terms are frequently confused or used interchangeably by persons not connected with either governmental unit, the commission and the department are two separate, but related, entities. The commission, with guidance from the governor and the Arkansas General Assembly, determines the environmental policies for the state, and the department employees are responsible for implementing those policies..

The initial authority to regulate water and air sources has been expanded to open-cut mining, solid waste, hazardous waste, recycling, and underground storage tanks. In 2001, an ADEQ focus on recycling waste oil resulted in a 91% increase in the amount of waste oil recycled, from 21,189 tons in 2000 to 41,500 tons in 2001. In 2002, ADEQ turned its attention to recycling of wood waste.

In 1987, the state adopted some of the first "ecoregion" water-quality standards in the nation. These standards recognize the distinct physical, chemical, and biological properties of the six geographical regions of the state and establish separate water quality standards within each region. In 2005, federal Environment Protection Agency (EPA) grants awarded to the state included $8.9 million for safe drinking water projects. A grant in excess of $4.6 million was awarded for water pollution prevention projects.

The EPA delegated responsibility for its clean-air programs to ADEQ. These programs include New Source Performance Standards (NSPS), National Emission Standards for Hazardous Air Pollutants (NESHAPS), Prevention of Significant Deterioration (PSD), and State Implementation Plan (SIP). In 2003, 40.6 million lb of toxic chemicals were released by the state.

Citizen's groups actively involved with environmental issues include: the Arkansas Native Plant Society, Arkansas Audubon Society, Arkansas Canoe Club, Arkansas Herpetological Society, Arkansas Wildlife Federation, Audubon Society of Central Arkansas, League of Women Voters, Ozark Society, Sierra Club—Arkansas Chapter, and National Water Center. The Arkansas Environmental Federation presents industry's viewpoints on environmental issues.

The Buffalo River, designated as a national river, flows through northern Arkansas. One of the wildest areas in the state is the 113,000-acre (46,000-hectare) White River Refuge, which contains more than 100 small lakes. About 8% of the state is wetland. The wetlands of the Cache–Lower White River were designated as Ramsar Wetlands of International Importance in 1989. The site includes two national wildlife refuges, managed by the federal government, and three wildlife management areas, managed by the state. The Arkansas Natural Heritage Commission was established in 1975 for, among other purposes, the preservation of rivers and natural areas and to serve as a source of information on plant and animal species of Arkansas.

In 2003, the EPA database listed 78 hazardous waste sites in Arkansas, 10 of which were on the National Priorities List as of 2006. Jacksonville Municipal Landfill and the Rogers Road Municipal Landfill (also in Jacksonville) were both deleted from the list in 2006. In 2005, the EPA spent over $6.3 million through the Superfund program for the cleanup of hazardous waste sites in the state.

6 POPULATION

Arkansas ranked 32nd in population in the United States with an estimated total of 2,779,154 in 2005, an increase of 4% since 2000. Between 1990 and 2000, Arkansas's population grew from 2,350,725 to 2,673,400, an increase of 13.7%. The population is projected to reach 2.96 million by 2015 and 3.15 million by 2025. The average population density in 2004 was 52.9 per sq mi.

As of 2004, 13.8% of the population was age 65 or over (compared with a national average of 12.4%), partially reflecting the large number of retirees who settled in the state during the early

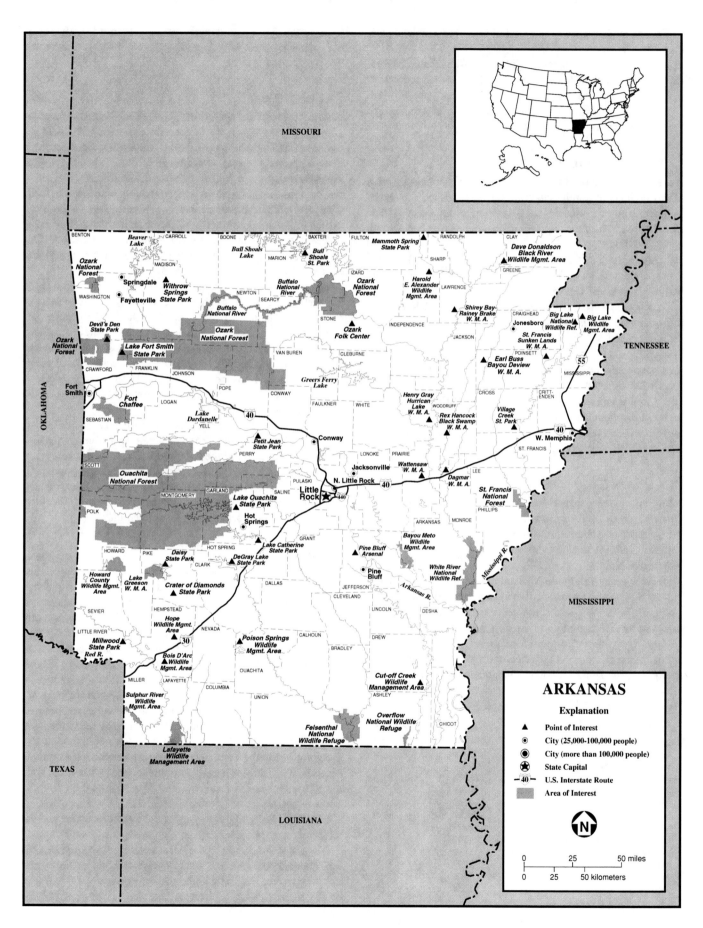

MISSOURI

OKLAHOMA

TENNESSEE

TEXAS

MISSISSIPPI

LOUISIANA

BENTON
CARROLL
Beaver Lake
Ozark National Forest
Springdale
Fayetteville
WASHINGTON
Devil's Den State Park
Ozark National Forest
CRAWFORD
Fort Smith
Fort Chaffee
SEBASTIAN
Lake Fort Smith State Park
FRANKLIN
LOGAN
JOHNSON
SCOTT
POLK
Ouachita National Forest
MONTGOMERY
HOWARD
PIKE
Howard County Wildlife Mgmt. Area
Lake Greeson W. M. A.
SEVIER
LITTLE RIVER
Millwood State Park
Red R.
Bois D'Arc Wildlife Mgmt. Area
MILLER
Sulphur River Wildlife Mgmt. Area
LAFAYETTE
COLUMBIA
Lafayette Wildlife Management Area

MADISON
NEWTON
Withrow Springs State Park
Buffalo National River
Buffalo River
Ozark National Forest
SEARCY
VAN BUREN
Lake Dardanelle
YELL
40
Petit Jean State Park
PERRY
Ouachita National Forest
GARLAND
Lake Ouachita State Park
Hot Springs
HOT SPRING
Lake Catherine State Park
Daisy State Park
DeGray Lake State Park
CLARK
Crater of Diamonds State Park
Lake Greeson W. M. A.
HEMPSTEAD
Hope Wildlife Mgmt. Area
NEVADA
Poison Springs Wildlife Mgmt. Area
OUACHITA
CALHOUN
Felsenthal National Wildlife Refuge
UNION

BOONE
BAXTER
FULTON
Bull Shoals Lake
Bull Shoals St. Park
MARION
Buffalo National River
Mammoth Spring State Park
IZARD
Ozark National Forest
STONE
Ozark Folk Center
CLEBURNE
Greers Ferry Lake
CONWAY
FAULKNER
WHITE
Conway
LONOKE
PRAIRIE
Jacksonville
PULASKI
N. Little Rock
Little Rock
440
SALINE
GRANT
Pine Bluff Arsenal
JEFFERSON
Pine Bluff
CLEVELAND
LINCOLN
DESHA
DREW
BRADLEY
Cut-off Creek Wildlife Management Area
ASHLEY
Overflow National Wildlife Refuge
CHICOT

RANDOLPH
CLAY
Dave Donaldson Black River Wildlife Mgmt. Area
GREENE
SHARP
Harold E. Alexander Wildlife Mgmt. Area
LAWRENCE
Shirey Bay-Rainey Brake W. M. A.
CRAIGHEAD
Jonesboro
Big Lake National Wildlife Ref.
Big Lake Wildlife Mgmt. Area
St. Francis Sunken Lands W. M. A.
POINSETT
55
Earl Buss Bayou Deview W. M. A.
JACKSON
INDEPENDENCE
WOODRUFF
CROSS
CRITTENDEN
40
W. Memphis
ST. FRANCIS
Henry Gray Hurricane Lake W. M. A.
Rex Hancock Black Swamp W. M. A.
Village Creek St. Park
Wattensaw W. M. A.
Dagmar W. M. A.
LEE
St. Francis National Forest
PHILLIPS
MONROE
ARKANSAS
Bayou Meto Wildlife Mgmt. Area
White River National Wildlife Ref.
Arkansas R.
Mississippi R.

1980s. The median age was 36.6, and 24.6% of the population was under 18 years old.

The largest city in Arkansas is Little Rock, which had a 2004 estimated population of 184,081. The Little Rock–North Little Rock metropolitan area had an estimated 636,636 residents in 2004. Other major cities with large populations include Ft. Smith, North Little Rock, Pine Bluff, and Fayetteville.

7 ETHNIC GROUPS

Arkansas's population is predominantly white, composed mainly of descendants of immigrants from the British Isles. The largest minority group consists of black Americans, estimated at 418,950 in 2000, or 15.7% of the population. That percentage had risen to 15.8% by 2004. The American Indian population was estimated at 17,808 in 2000. In 2004, 0.7% of the population was American Indian. About 86,866 Arkansans, or 3.2% of the total population, was of Hispanic or Latino origin, nearly double the 1990 figure of 44,000 (1.9%). That figure had risen to 4.4% by 2004. In 2000 the Asian population was estimated at 20,220, and Pacific Islanders numbered 1,668. In 2004, the Asian population was 0.9% and Native Hawaiians and other Pacific Islanders made up 0.1% of the total population. The 2000 census listed 3,974 Vietnamese (up from 1,788 in 1990), 3,126 Chinese (1,575 in 1990), 2,489 Filipinos, 3,104 Asian Indians (1,202 in 1990), and 1,036 Japanese. The foreign-born population numbered 73,690, or 2.8% of all Arkansas residents, up from 24,867, or 1%, in 1990. In 2004, 1.2% of the total population reported origin of two or more races.

8 LANGUAGES

A few place-names, such as Arkansas itself, Choctaw, Caddo, and Ouachita, attest to the onetime presence of American Indians in the Territory of Arkansas, mostly members of the Caddoan tribe, with the Cherokee the most influential.

Arkansas English is essentially a blend of Southern and South Midland speech, with South Midland dominating the mountainous northwest; and Southern, the southeastern agricultural areas. Common in the east and south are *redworm* (earthworm) and *mosquito hawk* (dragonfly). In the northwest appear South Midland *whirlygig* (merry-go-round) and *sallet* (garden greens).

The following table gives selected statistics from the 2000 Census for language spoken at home by persons five years old and over. The category "Other Pacific Island languages" includes Chamorro, Hawaiian, Ilocano, Indonesian, and Samoan.

LANGUAGE	NUMBER	PERCENT
Population 5 years and over	**2,492,205**	**100.0**
Speak only English	2,368,450	95.0
Speak a language other than English	123,755	5.0
Speak a language other than English	**123,755**	**5.0**
Spanish or Spanish Creole	82,465	3.3
German	7,444	0.3
French (incl. Patois, Cajun)	7,312	0.3
Vietnamese	3,467	0.1
Chinese	2,529	0.1
Laotian	2,502	0.1
Tagalog	1,627	0.1
Korean	1,250	0.1
Japanese	1,193	0.0
Other Pacific Island languages	1,185	0.0
Italian	1,106	0.0

In 2000, 2,368,450 Arkansans (95% of the residents five years old or older) spoke only English at home, a decrease from the 97.2% recorded in 1990.

9 RELIGIONS

Although French Roman Catholic priests had worked as missionaries among the American Indians since the early 18th century, the state's first mission was founded among the Cherokee by a Congregationalist, Cephas Washburn, in 1820. When the Cherokee were removed to Indian Territory (present-day Oklahoma), the mission moved there as well, remaining active through the Civil War. William Patterson may have been the first Methodist to preach in Arkansas, around 1800, in the area of Little Prairie: the first Methodist circuit, that of Spring River, was organized in 1815. The first Baptist church was likely that of the Salem congregation, begun in 1818 near what is now Pocahontas.

The vast majority of religious adherents in the state belong to Evangelical Protestant congregations. The largest denomination is the Southern Baptist Convention, which had 685,301 adherents in 1,372 congregations in 2000; there were 13,119 newly baptized members in 2002. In 2000, the American Baptist Association had 115,916 adherents and 570 congregations and the Baptist Missionary Association of America had 87,244 adherents and 359 congregations. The Churches of Christ claimed 86,342 adherents in 754 congregations that same year.

The leading mainline Protestant group in 2000 was the United Methodist Church, with 179,383 adherents in 747 congregations. By 2004, however, the United Methodist Church reported a statewide membership of 138,987. The Roman Catholic population of Arkansas in 2004 was 106,051 with 88 parishes. The estimated Jewish population in 2000 was 1,600 people. About 42.9% of the population did not specify a religious affiliation.

10 TRANSPORTATION

Although railroad construction began in the 1850s, it was not until after the Civil War (1861–65) that any lines were completed. The most important railroad, the St. Louis, Iron Mountain, and Southern line, reached Little Rock in 1872 and was subsequently acquired by financier Jay Gould, who added the Little Rock and Ft. Smith line to it in 1882. By 1890, the state had about 2,200 mi (3,500 km) of track. In 1974, trackage totaled 3,559 mi (5,728 km). As of 2003, Arkansas had a total of 3,484 rail mi (5,609 km) of track, of which the three Class I roads that served the state accounted for 2,607 rail miles (4,197 km). In that same year, nonmetallic minerals were the top commodity carried by rail in the state, for shipments originating within the state. For rail shipments terminating within the state, coal (by weight) was the top commodity. As of 2006, Amtrak passenger trains serviced Little Rock, Walnut Ridge, Malvern, Arkadelphia, and Texarkana en route from St. Louis to Dallas.

Intensive road building began in the 1920s, following the establishment of the State Highway Commission and the inauguration of a gasoline tax. By 2004, Arkansas had 98,606 mi (158,755 km) of public roads, streets, and highways. During that same year, there were some 950,000 automobiles and around 938,000 trucks of all types registered in Arkansas. In 2004, there were 1,862,430 licensed drivers in the state.

Beginning in the 1820s, steamboats replaced keelboats and flatboats on Arkansas rivers. Steamboat transportation reached its peak during 1870–90, when it was supplanted by the railroads that were opened during the same two decades. Development of the Arkansas River, completed during the early 1970s, made the waterway commercially navigable all the way to Tulsa. In 2004, Arkansas had 1,860 mi (2,994 km) of navigable inland waterways. Waterborne shipments in 2003 totaled 15.083 million tons.

In 2005, Arkansas had a total of 321 public- and private-use aviation-related facilities. This included 238 airports, and 83 heliports. The principal airport in the state is Adams Field at Little Rock. In 2004, the airport had 1,138,249 enplanements.

11 HISTORY

Evidence of human occupation of Arkansas reaches back to about 10,000 BC. The bluff dwellers of the Ozark Plateau were among the first human beings to live in what is now Arkansas, making their homes in caves and beneath overhanging rock cliffs along the banks of the upper White River. Farther south are the remains of another primitive people, the Mound Builders. The most significant of the Stone Age monuments they left are those of the Toltec group in Lonoke County, some 25 mi (40 km) southeast of Little Rock. Eventually, both ancient peoples vanished, for reasons that remain unclear.

Foremost among the American Indian tribes in Arkansas were the Quapaw (meaning "downstream people" or "South Wind people"), agriculturists who had migrated to southern Arkansas in the early 16th century; the Caddo, fighters from Texas, who claimed the western region between the Red and Arkansas rivers; the warlike Osage, who hunted north of the Arkansas River and in present-day Missouri; and the Choctaw. Another prominent tribe, the Cherokee, arrived in the early 19th century, after federal and state authorities had taken their land east of the Mississippi and driven them westward. Nearly all these American Indians had been expelled to what is now Oklahoma by the time Arkansas became a state.

The first Europeans to set foot in Arkansas were Spaniards, led by Hernando de Soto. They crossed the Mississippi River, probably near present-day Helena, in spring 1541, roamed the land for a year or so, and then returned to the mighty river, where De Soto was buried in 1542. More than 100 years later, in 1673, a small band of Frenchmen led by Jacques Marquette, a Jesuit missionary, and Louis Jolliet, a fur trader and explorer, ended their voyage down the Mississippi at the mouth of the Arkansas River and returned north after being advised by friendly American Indians that hostile tribes lay to the south. Nine years later, Robert Cavelier, Sieur de la Salle, led an expedition from Canada down the Mississippi to the Gulf of Mexico, stopping at Indian villages in Arkansas along the way and, on 9 April 1682, claiming all the Mississippi Valley for his king, Louis XIV.

Henri de Tonti, who had been second in command to La Salle, came back to Arkansas in 1686 to claim a land grant at the confluence of the Arkansas and White rivers, a few miles inland from the Mississippi. He left six men there; the log house they built was the beginning of Arkansas Post, the first permanent white settlement in the lower Mississippi Valley. Though tiny and isolated, Arkansas Post upheld the French claim to the Mississippi Valley

until 1762, when France ceded the territory to Spain. Restored to France in 1800, the territory was sold to the United States in the Louisiana Purchase of 1803. White settlers soon began arriving in Arkansas, and in 1806, the Louisiana territorial legislature created the District of Arkansas as a separate entity. When the Louisiana Purchase was further subdivided, Arkansas became part of the Missouri Territory. In 1819, Arkansas gained territorial status in its own right, and its boundaries were fixed by Congress. The territorial capital was moved from Arkansas Post to Little Rock in 1821. By 1835, Arkansas Territory had a population of 52,240, including 9,838 slaves. It was admitted to the Union in 1836 as a slave state, paired with the free state of Michigan in accordance with the Missouri Compromise.

Increasing numbers of slaves were brought into the largely agricultural state as the cultivation of cotton spread. Arkansas, like the rest of the South, was headed for secession, although it waited to commit itself until the Civil War (1861–65) had begun. There was considerable Union sentiment in the state, especially in the hilly northern and western counties, which lacked the large plantations and the slaves of southern and eastern Arkansas. But the pro-Union sympathies crumbled after Confederate guns fired on Ft. Sumter, SC, and the secession convention was held at Little Rock on 6 May 1861. The final vote to leave the Union was 69–1: the lone holdout was Isaac Murphy of Madison County, who became the first Unionist Democrat governor at the end of the war.

The largest Civil War battle fought in Arkansas, and one of the most significant battles of the war west of the Mississippi, was at Pea Ridge, in the northwest corner of the state. After three days of fighting, the Union forces retreated, and then the Confederate forces relinquished the field. By September 1863, the Union Army had taken Little Rock, and the Confederate capital was moved to Washington, in Hempstead County, until the conclusion of hostilities in 1865. Like virtually all white southerners, Arkansas's white majority hated the postwar Reconstruction government and repudiated it thoroughly at the first opportunity. Reconstruction officially ended in 1874, when the reenfranchised white Democratic majority adopted a new state constitution, throwing out the carpetbagger constitution of 1868. The most colorful figure in postwar Arkansas was federal judge Isaac C. Parker, known as the Hanging Judge. From his court at Ft. Smith, he had sole jurisdiction over Indian Territory, which had become a gathering place for the nation's worst cutthroats. Parker and his deputy marshals fought them relentlessly. From 1875 through 1896, the judge hanged 79 men on his Ft. Smith gallows. The struggle was not one-sided: 65 of Parker's deputy marshals were killed.

Industrialization, urbanization, and modernization did not come to Arkansas until after the depression of the 1930s. Following World War II (1939–45), the state became the first in the South to integrate its public colleges and universities. Little Rock's school board decided in 1954 to comply with the US Supreme Court's desegregation decision. Nevertheless, in September 1957, Governor Orval E. Faubus called out the National Guard to block the integration of Central High School at Little Rock. US President Dwight D. Eisenhower enforced a federal court order to integrate the school by sending in federal troops. The 1957 crisis brought years of notoriety to Arkansas, as Faubus, then in his second term, was elected to a third term and then to three more.

By the end of the Faubus administration, the public mood had changed, and the contrast between Faubus and his successor could not have been greater. Winthrop Rockefeller, millionaire scion of a famous family, moved to Arkansas from New York in the early 1950s, established himself as a gentleman rancher, and devoted himself to luring industry into his adopted state and building a Republican Party organization in one of the most staunchly Democratic states in the Union. Elected governor in 1966, Rockefeller thus became the first Republican to capture the Arkansas statehouse since Reconstruction. The specific accomplishments of his two terms were relatively few—he and the Democratic-controlled legislature warred incessantly—but he helped immeasurably in bringing a new image and a new spirit to the state.

Rockefeller's successors have continued the progressive approach he took. Governor Bill Clinton, who became US president in 1992, introduced a number of reforms. These included investment tax credits to help corporations modernize their facilities and thereby to create jobs. Clinton also signed a "bare bones" health insurance law, which dropped state requirements for some of the more costly coverages and thus made health insurance affordable for small businesses. He increased expenditures for education and passed legislation requiring competency tests for teachers. But Clinton, like other governors before him, remained hampered in his efforts to improve Arkansas's economy and standard of living by the state constitutional requirement that any increase in the state income tax obtain approval of two-thirds of the legislature. Arkansas continued to rank among the poorest states in the nation, with a per capita income in 1990 of only $14,000 (46th among the states). By 1998, its ranking had improved, with 14.8% of its people living below poverty level, making it the 12th poorest state in the nation. In 2002–03, Arkansas had an 18.8% poverty rate; that percentage dropped to 16.4% in 2003–04. The US poverty rate in 2004 was 12.7%, up from 12.5% in 2003. Arkansas's poverty rate contributes to its status as an unhealthy state: Arkansas was ranked 46th on the United Health Foundation's state health ratings in 2004.

In 1994, a federal special prosecutor began to investigate the actions of several members of Little Rock's Rose law firm, in which First Lady Hillary Rodham Clinton had been a partner, in connection with the failed Whitewater real estate venture. Governor Jim Guy Tucker resigned from office in July 1996 after his conviction on fraud and conspiracy charges stemming from his bank dealings. In March 2000, independent counsel Robert Ray began filing final reports detailing the six-year investigation into Whitewater, and that September, he issued a report finding that neither President Bill Clinton nor First Lady Hillary Clinton had knowingly participated in any criminal conduct. Susan McDougal, with her husband a controlling partner in the Whitewater land deal, found guilty of fraud in 1996, was pardoned by President Clinton in January 2001, just before he left office.

While the state was rocked by political scandal in the 1990s, it also coped with tragic school shootings. On 24 March 1998, two students (ages 11 and 13) went on a rampage in a Jonesboro school, killing four students and a teacher, and wounding ten others. Another shooting occurred in the small community of Prairie Grove on 11 May 2000, when a seventh-grade student left school in a rage and later engaged in an exchange of gunfire with an officer nearby; both were injured. While the nation wrestled with the problem of violence in its schools and the issue of gun control, for Arkansas residents it was a problem that was too close to home.

12 STATE GOVERNMENT

Arkansas's fifth constitution, enacted in 1874, has survived several efforts to replace it with a more modern charter. In November 1980, voters turned down yet another proposed new constitution. In May 1995, the Governor's Task Force for a New Constitution was appointed in anticipation of a proposed 1996 constitutional convention. However, in December 1995, a referendum authorizing the convention was defeated by the voters. The constitution had been amended 91 times by January 2005. Eight of the approved amendments have been superseded and are not printed in the current edition of the constitution. The total adopted does not include five amendments proposed and adopted since statehood.

Arkansas's bicameral legislature, the general assembly, consists of a 35-member Senate and a 100-member House of Representatives. Regular legislative sessions are held in odd-numbered years, begin in January, and are limited to 60 calendar days. Senators serve four-year terms and must be at least 25 years old; representatives serve for two years and must be at least 21. Each legislator must be a US citizen and have resided for at least two years in the state and one year in the county or district prior to election. Legislators' salaries in 2004 were $13,751 per biennial session.

The executive officers elected statewide are the governor, lieutenant governor, secretary of state, treasurer, auditor, and attorney general, all of whom serve four-year terms. The governor is limited to a maximum of two consecutive elected terms. The governor and lieutenant governor, who run separately, must be US citizens, be at least 30 years old, and have resided in Arkansas for seven years. As of December 2004 the governor's salary was $75,296.

A bill passed by a majority in both houses of the legislature becomes law if signed by the governor, if passed over his veto by a majority of all elected members of each house, or if neither signed nor returned by the governor within five days (Sundays excepted) when the legislature is in session or 20 days (Sundays included) after session adjournment. Under an initiative procedure, 8% of those who voted for governor in the last election may propose a law, and 10% of the voters (for governor at the last election) may initiate a constitutional amendment; initiative petitions must be filed at least four months before the general election in order to be voted upon at that time. A referendum on any measure passed by the General Assembly or any item of an appropriations bill or other measure may be petitioned by 6% of the voters; referendum petitions must be filed within 90 days of the session in which the act in question was passed. A successful referendum measure may be repealed by a two-thirds vote of all elected members of the General Assembly. Constitutional amendments may also be proposed by the General Assembly (and approved by a majority vote of both houses) or by constitutional convention. Proposed amendments must be ratified by a majority of voters.

To vote in Arkansas, one must be a US citizen, at least 18 years old, a state resident, and not able to claim the right to vote in another jurisdiction. Restrictions apply to convicted felons.

Arkansas Presidential Vote by Political Parties, 1948–2004

YEAR	ELECTORAL VOTE	ARKANSAS WINNER	DEMOCRAT	REPUBLICAN	STATES' RIGHTS DEMOCRAT
1948	9	*Truman (D)	149,659	50,959	40,068
1952	8	Stevenson (D)	226,300	177,155	—
					CONSTITUTION
1956	8	Stevenson (D)	213,277	186,287	7,008
					NAT'L STATES' RIGHTS
1960	8	*Kennedy (D)	215,049	184,508	28,952
1964	6	*Johnson (D)	314,197	243,264	2,965
					AMERICAN IND.
1968	6	Wallace (AI)	188,228	190,759	240,982
					AMERICAN
1972	6	*Nixon (R)	199,892	448,541	2,887
1976	6	*Carter (D)	498,604	267,903	—
					LIBERTARIAN
1980	6	*Reagan (R)	398,041	403,164	8,970
1984	6	*Reagan (R)	388,646	534,774	2,2221
1988	6	*Bush (R)	349,237	466,578	3,297
					IND. (Perot)
1992	6	*Clinton (D)	505,823	337,324	99,132
1996	6	*Clinton (D)	475,171	325,416	69,884
					GREEN
2000	6	*Bush, G. W. (R)	422,768	472,940	13,421
					POPULIST PARTY OF ARKANSAS (Nader)
2004	6	*Bush, G. W. (R)	469,953	572,898	6,171

*Won US presidential election.

13 POLITICAL PARTIES

The principal political groups in Arkansas are the Democratic Party and the Republican Party, each affiliated with the national party organizations.

Before the Civil War (1861–65), politics in Arkansas were fraught with violence. Republicans ruled during Reconstruction, which officially ended in Arkansas after the constitution of 1874 had been adopted by the new Democratic majority. During the election of 1872, the Liberal Republicans, nicknamed Brindletails, opposed the Radical Republicans, or Minstrels. After the Minstrel candidate, Elisha Baxter, was elected, he proved so independent a governor that some of the party leaders who had supported him attempted to oust him through a court order in April 1874, declaring his defeated opponent, Joseph Brooks, the winner. Supported by a militia of about 300 blacks under white command, Brooks took over the statehouse; Baxter, bolstered by his own 300-man black army, set up his headquarters three blocks away. The so-called Brooks-Baxter War finally ended with President Ulysses S. Grant's proclamation of Baxter as the lawful governor. Baxter did not seek reelection-instead Augustus H. Garland was elected, the first of a long series of Bourbon Democrats who were to rule the state well into the 20th century.

After Reconstruction, blacks in Arkansas continued to vote and to be elected to public office; under what became known as the fusion principle, black Republican and white Democratic leaders in the Plantation Belt often agreed not to oppose each other's candidates. Segregation in public places was still outlawed, and Little Rock was perhaps the most integrated city in the South. During the 1890s, however, as in the rest of the South, Democrats began to pass laws imposing segregation and disfranchising blacks as well as poor whites. In 1906, the Democrats instituted a nominating primary for whites only.

On the rocky path to progressive government, Arkansans elected several governors who stand out as progressive: George Donaghey (1909–13), Charles Brush (1917–21), Thomas McRae (1921–25), Carl Bailey (1935–39), and Sidney McMath (1948–53). Although elected to the governorship as a progressive in 1954, McMath's protégé Orval Faubus took a segregationist stand in 1957. In subsequent years, poor whites tended to support Faubus, while blacks and more affluent whites opposed him. Faubus's successor, progressive Republican Winthrop Rockefeller, was strongly supported by blacks. Rockefeller was followed by three more progressives, all Democrats: Dale Bumpers, David Pryor, and—after Bumpers and Pryor had graduated to the US Senate—Bill Clinton. In a major upset, Clinton was defeated in 1980 by Republican Frank White, but he recaptured the statehouse in 1982 and won reelection in 1984, 1986, and 1990. Clinton ran for and won the presidency in 1992 with a plurality of 53% in Arkansas. Clinton won presidential reelection in 1996, gaining 54% of the vote, against 37% for Republican challenger Bob Dole and 8% for Independent Ross Perot. In the 2000 presidential election, George W. Bush won 51% of the vote to Al Gore's 45% and 2% for Green Party candidate Ralph Nader; in 2004, Bush was reelected with 54% of the vote to Democrat John Kerry's 37%. In 2004 there were 1,686,000 registered voters; there is no party registration in the state. The state had six electoral votes in the 2004 presidential election.

On 8 November 1994, Democratic governor Jim Guy Tucker was one of the few of his party nationwide to resist a Republican challenge. However, in 1996 Tucker was forced to resign following his conviction on charges related to the Whitewater prosecution, and the governorship was assumed by Lieutenant Governor Mike

Huckabee. Huckabee was elected in his own right in 1998 and re-elected in 2002.

In 1996, the vacated US Senate seat of Democrat David Pryor was won by US Representative Tim Hutchinson, a Republican. Hutchinson was the first Republican ever to be popularly elected to the US Senate from Arkansas. In 1998 Democrat Blanche Lincoln was voted into office, only the second woman in Arkansas history to be elected to the Senate; she was reelected with 56% of the vote in 2004. Democrat Mark Pryor, son of David Pryor, was elected to the US Senate in 2002. Arkansas's US representatives following the 2006 elections included one Republican and three Democrats. As of 2006, the state legislature had 27 Democrats and 8 Republicans in the Senate, and 72 Democrats and 28 Republicans in the House. As of 2006, there were 23 women serving in the state legislature.

¹⁴LOCAL GOVERNMENT

There are 75 counties in Arkansas, 10 of them with 2 county seats. Each county is governed by a quorum court, consisting of between 9 and 15 justices of the peace, elected for 2-year terms; the county judge, who presides, does not vote but has veto power, which may be overridden by a three-fifths vote of the total membership. Elected county officials, who serve two-year terms, include the sheriff, assessor, coroner, treasurer, and county supervisor. In 2005, Arkansas had 499 municipalities, administered under the mayor-council or city-manager form of government. There were 704 special districts and 310 public school districts.

In 2005, local government accounted for about 105,930 full-time (or equivalent) employment positions.

¹⁵STATE SERVICES

To address the continuing threat of terrorism and to work with the federal Department of Homeland Security, homeland security in Arkansas operates under the authority of the governor; the emergency management director is designated as the state homeland security adviser.

Educational services in Arkansas are administered primarily by the Department of Education and the Department of Higher Education. The State Highway and Transportation Department has primary responsibility for roads, rails, and public transit; the offices of motor vehicle registration and driver services are in the Department of Finance and Administration. The Department of Information Systems governs the state's computer links, while the Department of Parks and Tourism encourages visitors.

Health and welfare services are under the jurisdiction of the Department of Health and Human Services. Public protection is provided primarily through the Department of Emergency Management, State Police, National Guard, and Civil Air Patrol, as well as the Department of Correction, which operates prisons and work-release centers. The Public Service Commission regulates utilities in the state.

¹⁶JUDICIAL SYSTEM

Arkansas's highest court is the Arkansas Supreme Court, which consists of a chief justice and six associate justices, elected for staggered eight-year terms. An appeals court of 12 judges, also elected for eight-year terms, was established in 1978.

Arkansas's courts of original jurisdiction are the circuit courts (law) and the chancery courts (equity), of which there are 24 circuits each. In 1999, there were 30 circuit court judges serving four-year terms and 33 chancery probate court judges serving six-year terms. An additional 43 judges were serving both circuit and chancery courts. Courts of limited jurisdiction include justice of the peace, county, municipal, and police courts, and courts of common pleas.

As of 31 December 2004, a total of 13,807 prisoners were held in state and federal prisons in Arkansas, an increase from 13,315, or 3.7%, from the previous year. As of year-end 2004, a total of 962 inmates were female, up from 866, or 11.1%, from the year before. Among sentenced prisoners (one year or more), Arkansas had an incarceration rate of 495 per 100,000 population in 2004.

According to the Federal Bureau of Investigation, Arkansas in 2004 had a violent crime rate (murder/nonnegligent manslaughter; forcible rape; robbery; aggravated assault) of 499.1 reported incidents per 100,000 population, or a total of 13,737 reported incidents. Crimes against property (burglary; larceny/theft; and motor vehicle theft) in that same year totaled 110,464 reported incidents, or 4.13 reported incidents per 100,000 people. Arkansas has a death penalty, which can be carried out by lethal injection or electrocution, depending upon the prisoner's request. As of 1976, the state has executed 27 persons; there was one execution in 2005. As of 1 January 2006, there were 38 death row inmates.

In 2003, Arkansas spent $105,532,650 on homeland security, an average of $38 per state resident.

¹⁷ARMED FORCES

As of 2004, there were five military installations in Arkansas, the principal ones being Little Rock Air Force Base with the most active-duty military personnel in the state (6,156), and the Army's Pine Bluff Arsenal, with the most civilian employees (1,065). Military personnel in the state numbered 7,676 in 2004, Reserve and National Guard numbered 2,554, and there were 1,714 civilian employees. Firms in the state received $493 million in defense contract awards in 2004, while the Defense Department payroll was about $1.2 billion, including retired military pay.

There were 268,353 veterans of US military service in Arkansas as of 2003, of whom 36,703 served in World War II; 28,509 in the Korean conflict; 79,280 during the Vietnam era; and 42,007 during 1990–2000 (in the Gulf War). US Veterans Administration spending in Arkansas was $1.0 billion in 2004.

In June 2003, the Arkansas State Police had 559 full-time sworn officers.

¹⁸MIGRATION

Near the end of the 18th century, American Indians from east of the Mississippi, displaced by white settlement, entered the area now known as Arkansas. However, as the availability of cheap land in Louisiana Territory drew more and more white settlers—in particular, veterans of the War of 1812, who had been promised

160-acre (65-hectare) tracts—the Indians were pressured to cross the border from Arkansas to present-day Oklahoma.

After the end of the Mexican War, thousands of Arkansans immigrated to Texas, and others were attracted to California in 1849 by the gold rush. Because of a law passed in 1859 requiring free blacks to leave the state by the end of the year or risk being enslaved, Arkansas's population of free blacks dropped from 682 in 1858 to 144 in 1860. During Reconstruction, the state government encouraged immigration by both blacks and whites. Literature sent out by the Office of State Lands and Migration, under the tenure of William H. Grey, a black leader, described the state as a new Africa. Railroads, seeking buyers for the lands they had acquired through government grants, were especially active in encouraging immigration after Reconstruction. Later immigrants included Italians and, in the early 1900s, Germans.

During the Depression era (1930s) and thereafter, Arkansas lost a substantial proportion of its farm population, and many blacks left the state for the industrial cities of the Midwest and the east and west coasts. The net loss from migration totaled 919,000 between 1940 and 1970. Between 1970 and 1980, however, the state gained 180,000 residents through migration, as the Ozarks became one of the fastest-growing rural areas in the United States. The state experienced a small net decline of 2,000 in migration between 1980 and 1983. Net migration from 1985 to 1990 amounted to a gain of nearly 36,600. Between 1990 and 1998, there were net gains of 106,000 in domestic migration and 9,000 in international migration. In 1998, Arkansas admitted 914 immigrants. Between 1990 and 1998, the state's overall population increased by 8%. In the period 2000–05, net international migration was 21,947 and net internal migration was 35,664, for a net gain of 57,611 people.

[19] INTERGOVERNMENTAL COOPERATION

Among the many interstate agreements in which Arkansas participates are the Arkansas River Basin Compact of 1970 (with Oklahoma), Arkansas-Mississippi Great River Bridge Construction Compact, Bi-State Criminal Justice Center Compact, Central Interstate Low-Level Radioactive Waste Compact, Interstate Mining Compact Commission, Interstate Oil and Gas Compact, Red River Compact, South Central Interstate Forest Fire Protection Compact, Southern Growth Policies Board, Southern Regional Education Board, and Southern States Energy Board. There are boundary agreements with Mississippi, Missouri, and Tennessee. In fiscal year 2005, Arkansas received federal grants totaling $3.818 billion, an estimated $3.776 billion in fiscal year 2006, and an estimated $4.016 billion in fiscal year 2007.

[20] ECONOMY

During the 19th century, Arkansas's economic growth was hindered by credit problems. When the state's two central banks, the Arkansas State Bank and the Real Estate Bank, failed during the 1840s, the government defaulted on bonds issued by the latter and amended the constitution to prohibit all banking in Arkansas. Although banking was restored after the Civil War (1861–65), the state defaulted on its obligations once more in 1877, this time following a decision by the Arkansas supreme court that $10 million worth of railroad bonds issued during Reconstruction were

unconstitutional. Not until 1917 did New York banks again accept Arkansas securities.

Cotton dominated Arkansas's agricultural economy until well into the 20th century, when rice, soybeans, poultry, and fish farming diversified the output. Coal mining began in the 1870s, bauxite mining near the turn of the century, and oil extraction in the 1920s. Lumbering developed in the last quarter of the 19th century, reached its peak about 1909, and then declined until the 1920s, when reforestation started. Industrialization was limited however, and resources were generally shipped out of state for processing. Not until the 1950s did Arkansas enjoy significant success in attracting industry, thanks in large part to the efforts of Winthrop Rockefeller.

By the 1990s, principal industries in Arkansas had become manufacturing, dominated by lumber and wood products companies; agriculture; forestry; and tourism. Fifty-seven Fortune 500 parent firms are found in Arkansas, including Wal-Mart Stores, Tyson Foods, Dillard Department Stores, Beverly Enterprises, and Alltel. Other important corporations include Jacuzzi, Riceland Foods, Maybelline, Whirlpool, International Paper, American Greetings, and Georgia Pacific. Stephens Inc., in Little Rock, is the largest off-Wall Street investment firm in the country. Growth in gross state product (GSP) rose to 6% in 1999, but fell to 2.8% in 2000 and 1.7% in 2001. Contributing to Arkansas's GSP of $80.902 billion in 2004 were manufacturing (durable and nondurable goods) at $14.85 billion (18.3% of GSP); real estate at $7.417 (9% of GSP); and healthcare and social assistance at $6.150 billion (7.6% of GSP). In 2004, of the 61,778 firms that had employees, a total of 60,007, or 97.1%, were small businesses. In addition, the number of self-employed persons in that same year rose 8.6%, from 149,093 in 2003 to 161,842 in 2004. New business rose from 8.3%in 2003 to 7,852 in 2004, surpassing business terminations that same year of 6,481. In addition, business bankruptcies in 2004 totaled 376, down 12.4% from 2003. In 2005, personal bankruptcies (Chapter 7 and Chapter 13) totaled 881 per 100,000 people, ranking Arkansas as the seventh in the United States.

[21] INCOME

In 2005, Arkansas had a gross state product (GSP) of $87 billion, which accounted for 0.7% of the nation's gross domestic product and placed the state at number 34 in highest GSP among the 50 states and the District of Columbia.

According to the Bureau of Economic Analysis, in 2004 Arkansas had a per capita personal income (PCPI) of $25,814. This ranked 49th in the United States and was 78% of the national average of $33,050. The 1994–2004 average annual growth rate of PCPI was 4.1%. Arkansas had a total personal income (TPI) of $70,987,900,000, which ranked 34th in the United States and reflected an increase of 7.0% from 2003. The 1994–2004 average annual growth rate of TPI was 5.1%. Earnings of persons employed in Arkansas increased from $49,196,825,000 in 2003 to $52,896,830,000 in 2004, an increase of 7.5%. The 2003–04 national change was 6.3%.

The US Census Bureau reports that the three-year average median household income for 2002–04 in 2004 dollars was $33,948, compared to a national average of $44,473. During the same period, an estimated 17.6% of the population was below the poverty line, as compared to 12.4% nationwide.

22 LABOR

According to the Bureau of Labor Statistics (BLS), in April 2006 the seasonally adjusted civilian labor force in Arkansas numbered 1,398,400, with approximately 71,800 workers unemployed, yielding an unemployment rate of 5.1%, compared to the national average of 4.7% for the same period. Preliminary data for the same period placed nonfarm employment at 1,189,400. Since the beginning of the BLS data series in 1976, the highest unemployment rate recorded in Arkansas was 10.2% in March 1983. The historical low was 4.1% in September 2000. Preliminary nonfarm employment data by occupation for April 2006 showed that approximately 4.6% of the labor force was employed in construction; 16.5% in manufacturing; 20.8% in trade, transportation and public utilities; 4.4% in financial activities; 9.6% in professional and business services; 12.5% in education and health services; 8% in leisure and hospitality services; and 17.4% in government.

Chartered in 1865, the Little Rock Typographical Union, consisting of *Arkansas Gazette* employees, was the first labor union in the state. The United Mine Workers (UMW) was established in the Ft. Smith area by 1898; six years later, the UMP led in the founding of the Arkansas Federation of Labor. Between 1904 and World War I (1914–18), a series of progressive labor laws was enacted, including a minimum wage, restrictions on child labor, and prohibitions against blacklisting and payment of wages in scrip. Union strength waned after the war, however, and the labor movement is not a powerful force in the state today.

The US Department of Labor's Bureau of Labor Statistics reported that in 2005, a total of 54,000 of Arkansas' 1,138,000 employed wage and salary workers were formal members of a union. This represented 4.8% of those so employed. This was unchanged from 2004, and below the national average of 12%. Overall in 2005, a total of 68,000 workers (6%) in Arkansas were covered by a union or employee association contract, which included those workers who reported no union affiliation. As of 1 January 2006 Arkansas was one of 22 states with a right-to-work law.

As of 1 March 2006, Arkansas had a state-mandated minimum wage rate of $5.15 per hour. In 2004, women in the state accounted for 45.6% of the employed civilian labor force.

23 AGRICULTURE

Farm marketing's in Arkansas were over $6 billion in 2005 (11th in the United States), with crops and livestock accounting for about 35% and 65%, respectively. The state is the nation's leading producer of rice and is among the leaders in cotton, soybeans, and grain sorghum.

Cotton was first grown in the state about 1800, along the river valleys. Confined mainly to slaveholding plantations before the Civil War (1861–65), cotton farming became more widespread in the postwar period, expanding into the hill country of the northwest and eventually into the deforested areas of the northeast, which proved to be some of the most fertile farmland in the nation. As elsewhere in the postbellum South, sharecropping by tenant farmers predominated well into the 20th century, until mechanization and diversification gradually brought an end to the

system. Rice was first grown commercially in the early 1900s; by 1920, Arkansas had emerged as a poultry and soybean producer.

During 2004, Arkansas produced 124,425,000 bushels of soybeans, valued at $690,559,000; 32,860,000 bushels of wheat, worth $115,010,000; 3,570,000 tons of hay, worth $166,180,000; and 4,704,000 bushels of sorghum for grain, valued at $10,142,000. The rice harvest in 2004 was 96,600,000 hundredweight (4.39 million kg), worth $768,196,000. The cotton crop in 2004, 2,085,000 bales, was worth $488,390,000.

24 ANIMAL HUSBANDRY

Poultry farms are found throughout Arkansas, but especially in the northern and western regions. Broiler production accounts for over 40% of the state's agricultural receipts. Arkansas was the second-highest broiler-producing state in the United States in 2003 (after Georgia); 5.4 billion lb (2.5 billion kg) of broilers were valued at $2 billion.

In 2004, it was estimated that Arkansas produced 3.5 billion eggs. In 2003 Arkansas produced 477 million lb (217 million kg) of turkey, valued at $176.5 million and 125.9 million lb (57.2 million kg) of chickens, valued at $8.8 million.

The yield of the state's 29,000 milk cows in 2003 was 352 million lb (160 million kg) of milk. In 2005, Arkansas had an estimated 1.9 million cattle and calves valued at $1.5 billion. In 2004, Arkansas had an estimated 330,000 hogs and pigs valued at $32.3 million.

25 FISHING

As of 2005, the state ranked second only to Mississippi in catfish farming. As of 1 January 2005, there were 153 catfish operations covering 31,500 acres (14,300 hectares) of water surface, with 100.6 million stocker-size and 184 million fingerling/fry catfish in early 2006. Some producers rotate fish crops with row crops, periodically draining their fish ponds and planting grains in the rich and well-fertilized soil. Most public fishing areas are frequently stocked with trout. Arkansas had 685,634 licensed anglers in 2004. There are three national fish hatcheries in Arkansas.

26 FORESTRY

Forestland comprised 18,771,000 acres (7,596,000 hectares), 56% of the state's total land area, in 2003. Of that total, 18,373,000 acres (7,435,000 hectares) were commercial timberland. The southwest and central plains, the state's timber belt, constitute one of the most concentrated sources of yellow pine in the United States. Lumber production in 2004 totaled 2.9 billion board feet, third in the United States. Three national forests in Arkansas covered a total of 3,540,000 acres (1,432,638 hectares) in 2003.

27 MINING

According to the US Geological Survey, the value of nonfuel mineral production in Arkansas in 2004 totaled $518 million, an increase of 13.8% from 2003. Bromine, crushed stone, cement (portland and masonry), and construction sand and gravel were the top four nonfuel minerals produced by value, respectively, and accounted for 92% of all nonfuel mineral output by value in the state for 2004. Overall, Arkansas accounted for more than 1% of all US nonfuel mineral output.

A total of 32.9 million metric tons of crushed stone were produced in 2004 (valued at $162 million), as well as 9.37 million metric tons of construction sand and gravel with a value of $53.5 million.

Arkansas in 2004 continued to be the leading bromine-producing state, accounting for most US production. Michigan was the only other state to produce bromine. Also in that year, Arkansas, remained the only state that produced silica stone. A total of 655 metric tons was produced, with a value of $3.66 million. The state also ranked fifth in gemstones in 2004, with output valued at $590,000.

28 ENERGY AND POWER

As of 2003, Arkansas had 39 electrical power service providers, of which 15 were publicly owned and 17 were cooperatives. Of the remainder, four were investor owned and three were owners of independent generators that sold directly to customers. As of that same year there were over 1.415 million retail customers. Of that total, over 832,486 received their power from investor-owned service providers. Cooperatives accounted for 419,184 customers, while publicly owned providers had 164,252 customers.

Total net summer generating capability by the state's electrical generating plants in 2003 stood at 13.548 million kW, with total production that same year at 50.401 billion kWh. Of the total amount generated, 82.6% came from electric utilities, with the remainder coming from independent producers and combined heat and power service providers. The largest portion of all electric power generated, 23.504 billion kWh (46.6%), came from coal-fired plants, with nuclear fueled plants in second place at 14.869 billion kWh (29.1%). Natural gas–fired plants accounted for 14.5% of all power generated, with hydroelectric and other renewable fueled plants at 3.7%.

As of 2006, Arkansas had one operating nuclear power facility, the Arkansas Nuclear One power plant in Pope County.

As of 2004, Arkansas had proven crude oil reserves of 51 million barrels, or less than 1% of all US reserves, while output that same year averaged 18,000 barrels per day. Including federal offshore domains, the state that year ranked 19th (18th excluding federal offshore) in reserves and 17th (16th excluding federal offshore) among the 31 producing states. In 2004, Arkansas had 6,660 producing oil wells and accounted for less than 1% of all US production. As of 2005, the state's two small refineries had a crude oil distillation capacity of 76,800 barrels per day.

In 2004, Arkansas had 3,460 producing natural gas and gas condensate wells. In 2003 (the latest year for which data was available) marketed gas production (all gas produced excluding gas used for repressuring, vented and flared, and nonhydrocarbon gases removed) totaled 169.599 billion cu ft (4.8 billion cu m). As of 31 December 2004, proven reserves of dry or consumer-grade natural gas totaled 1,835 billion cu ft (52.1 billion cu m).

Arkansas in 2004 had two producing coal mines, one surface and one underground. Coal production that year totaled 7,000 short tons, down from 8,000 short tons in 2003. Of the total produced in 2004, the surface mine accounted for 6,000 short tons.

29 INDUSTRY

Manufacturing in Arkansas is diverse, ranging from blue jeans to bicycles, though resource industries such as rice processing and woodworking still play a major role.

According to the US Census Bureau Annual Survey of Manufactures (ASM) for 2004, the state's manufacturing sector covered some 19 product subsectors. The shipment value of all products manufactured in the state that same year was $54.547 billion. Of that total, the food manufacturing sector accounted for the largest portion, at $14.064 billion. It was followed by primary metal manufacturing, at $5.419 billion; transportation equipment manufacturing, at $4.122 billion; paper manufacturing, at $3.858 billion; and fabricated metal product manufacturing, at $3.844 billion.

In 2004, a total of 193,746 people in Arkansas were employed in the state's manufacturing sector, according to the ASM. Of that total, 155,852 were production workers. In terms of total employment, the food manufacturing industry accounted for the largest portion of all manufacturing employees at 49,972, with 43,043 actual production workers. It was followed by fabricated metal product manufacturing, with 16,558 employees (11,808 actual production workers); plastics and rubber products manufacturing, with 15,078 employees (12,160 actual production workers); transportation equipment manufacturing, with 15,004 employees (12,287 actual production workers); and machinery manufacturing, with 14,324 employees (10,274 actual production workers).

ASM data for 2004 showed that the state's manufacturing sector paid $6.391 billion in wages. Of that amount, the food manufacturing sector accounted for the largest portion, at $1.259 billion. It was followed by fabricated metal product manufacturing, at $610.668 million; plastics and rubber products manufacturing, at $537.290 million; paper manufacturing, at $524.614 million; and transportation equipment manufacturing, at $512.188 million.

30 COMMERCE

According to the 2002 Census of Wholesale Trade, the state's wholesale trade sector had sales that year totaling $34.4 billion from 3,498 establishments. Wholesalers of durable goods accounted for 2,156 establishments, followed by nondurable goods wholesalers at 1,152 and electronic markets, agents, and brokers accounting for 190 establishments. Sales by durable goods wholesalers in 2002 totaled $10.1 billion, while wholesalers of nondurable goods saw sales of $17.5 billion. Electronic markets, agents, and brokers in the wholesale trade industry had sales of $6.7 billion.

In the 2002 Census of Retail Trade, Arkansas was listed as having 12,141 retail establishments with sales of $25.6 billion. The leading types of retail businesses by number of establishments were: motor vehicle and motor vehicle parts dealers (1,783); gasoline stations (1,695); miscellaneous store retailers (1,404) food and beverage stores (1,354); clothing and clothing accessories stores (1,201); and building material/garden equipment and supplies dealers (1,095). In terms of sales, motor vehicle and motor vehicle parts stores accounted for the largest share of retail sales at $7.09 billion, followed by general merchandise stores at $5.2 billion; gasoline stations at $3.02 billion; and food and beverage stores at $2.8 billion. A total of 134,197 people were employed by the retail sector in Arkansas that year.

During 2005, exports of goods from the state were valued at $3.8 billion, ranking the state 36th in the nation.

31 CONSUMER PROTECTION

Under the mandate of Consumer Protection Act of 1971, the Consumer Protection Division (CPD) of the Office of the Attorney General has principal responsibility for consumer affairs. The CPD serves as a central coordinating agency for individual consumer complaints, conducts investigations, acts as an advocate and mediator in resolving complaints, and prosecutes civil cases on behalf of Arkansas citizens.

When dealing with consumer protection issues, the state's Attorney General can initiate civil (but not criminal) proceedings; represent the state before state and federal regulatory agencies; administer consumer protection and education programs; and handle consumer complaints. However, the Attorney General's Office has limited subpoena powers. In antitrust actions, the attorney general can act on behalf of consumers who are incapable of acting on their own and may initiate damage actions on behalf of the state in state courts.

The office of the Consumer Protection Division is located in Little Rock.

32 BANKING

In 1836, the first year of statehood, the legislature created the Arkansas State Bank, and the Real Estate Bank, which were intended to promote the plantation system. Fraud, mismanagement, and the consequences of the financial panic of 1837 ruined both banks and led to the passage in 1846 of a constitutional amendment prohibiting the incorporation of any lending institution in Arkansas. Money grew scarce, with credit being rendered largely by suppliers and brokers to farmers and planters until after the Civil War (1861–65), when the prohibition was removed.

As of June 2005, Arkansas had 163 insured banks, savings and loans, and saving banks, plus 72 credit unions (CUs), all of which were federally chartered. Excluding the CUs, the Memphis market area (which includes portions of Tennessee, Arkansas and Mississippi) had 52 financial institutions in 2004, with deposits of $26.946 billion, followed by the Little Rock/North Little Rock area, with 37 institutions and $9.799 billion in deposits. As of June 2005, CUs accounted for only 3.6% of all assets held by all financial institutions in the state, or some $1.584 billion. Banks, savings and loans, and savings banks collectively accounted for the remaining 96.4% ($42.280 billion) in assets held.

As of the early 1980s, the Arkansas usury law imposed a 10% ceiling on interest rates (one of the most rigid in the United States); which the US Supreme Court upheld in 1981. The rise of the federal rate above that limit, beginning in mid-1979, caused a considerable outflow of capital from Arkansas. The Arkansas Usury Law was changed in December 1992 with the Interest Rate Control Amendment, which set the maximum interest rate on general loans at 5% above the Federal Reserve Discount Rate. The Arkansas Supreme Court interpreted the amendment to mean that the rate on consumer loans would be 5% above the discount rate, up to 17%. Although many institutions offered higher interest rates anyway, the ability to do so was formalized in the Financial Modernization Act of 1999. Opposition to usury came primarily from religious factions and labor unions, but low levels of investment during the 1990s motivated the Arkansas government to change the law. State-chartered banks in Arkansas are regulated by the Arkansas State Bank Department.

In 2005, Arkansas experienced strong economic growth in 2005, which benefited the state's financial community as institutions based in the state experienced record net income growth, due mainly to increased net operating income. In 2004, median net interest margins (NIMs—the difference between the lower rates offered to savers and the higher rates charged on loans) for Arkansas' insured institutions stood at 4.14%, up from 4.13% in 2003.

33 INSURANCE

In 2004 there were 1.77 million individual life insurance policies in force with a total value of $83.9 billion; total value for all categories of life insurance (individual, group, and credit) was $136.2 billion. The average coverage amount is $47,400 per policy holder. Death benefits paid that year totaled $461.6 million.

As of 2003, there were 11 property and casualty and 38 life and health insurance companies incorporated or organized in the state. Direct premiums for property and casualty insurance amounted to $3.69 billion in 2004. That year, there were 15,067 flood insurance policies in force in the state, with a total value of $1.3 billion.

In 2004, 46% of state residents held employment-based health insurance policies, 5% held individual policies, and 30% were covered under Medicare and Medicaid; 17% of residents were uninsured. In 2003, employee contributions for employment-based health coverage averaged at 21% for single coverage and 29% for family coverage. The state offers a 120-day health benefits expansion program for small-firm employees in connection with Consolidated Omnibus Budget Reconciliation Act (COBRA, 1986), a health insurance program for those who lose employment-based coverage due to termination or reduction of work hours.

In 2003, there were over 1.8 million auto insurance policies in effect for private passenger cars. Required minimum coverage includes bodily injury liability of up to $25,000 per individual and $50,000 for all persons injured, as well as property damage liability of $25,000. In 2003, the average expenditure per vehicle for insurance coverage was $698.28.

34 SECURITIES

There are no securities exchanges in Arkansas. In 2005, there were 570 personal financial advisers employed in the state and 1,420 securities, commodities, and financial services sales agents. In 2004, there were over 30 publicly traded companies within the state, with over 14 NASDAQ companies, 9 NYSE listings, and 1 AMEX listing. In 2006, the state had five Fortune 500 companies; Wal-Mart Stores (Bentonville) ranked first in the state and second in the nation with revenues of over $315 billion, followed by Tyson Foods (Springdale), Murphy Oil (El Dorado), Alltel (Little Rock), and Dillard's (Little Rock). All five of these companies were listed on the NYSE.

35 PUBLIC FINANCE

Under the 1874 constitution, state expenditures may not exceed revenues. The mechanism adopted each biennium to prevent deficit spending is a Revenue Stabilization Act. This Act provides the funding for state appropriations by assigning levels of funding priority to the appropriations. All higher level appropriations must

---

Arkansas—State Government Finances

(Dollar amounts in thousands. Per capita amounts in dollars.)

	AMOUNT	PER CAPITA
Total Revenue	14,225,176	5,172.79
General revenue	11,679,719	4,247.17
Intergovernmental revenue	4,041,889	1,469.78
Taxes	5,580,678	2,029.34
General sales	2,149,527	781.65
Selective sales	784,503	285.27
License taxes	187,876	68.32
Individual income tax	1,685,585	612.94
Corporate income tax	181,830	66.12
Other taxes	591,357	215.04
Current charges	1,543,848	561.40
Miscellaneous general revenue	513,304	186.66
Utility revenue	–	–
Liquor store revenue	–	–
Insurance trust revenue	2,545,457	925.62
Total expenditure	12,674,325	4,608.85
Intergovernmental expenditure	3,233,499	1,175.82
Direct expenditure	9,440,826	3,433.03
Current operation	7,074,989	2,572.72
Capital outlay	1,005,560	365.66
Insurance benefits and repayments	991,592	360.58
Assistance and subsidies	245,563	89.30
Interest on debt	123,122	44.77
Exhibit: Salaries and wages	1,528,630	555.87
Total expenditure	12,674,325	4,608.85
General expenditure	11,682,733	4,248.27
Intergovernmental expenditure	3,233,499	1,175.82
Direct expenditure	8,449,234	3,072.45
General expenditures, by function:		
Education	4,730,047	1,720.02
Public welfare	2,995,212	1,089.17
Hospitals	532,800	193.75
Health	316,062	114.93
Highways	1,116,310	405.93
Police protection	79,800	29.02
Correction	351,786	127.92
Natural resources	225,132	81.87
Parks and recreation	83,065	30.21
Government administration	476,279	173.19
Interest on general debt	123,122	44.77
Other and unallocable	653,118	237.50
Utility expenditure	–	–
Liquor store expenditure	–	–
Insurance trust expenditure	991,592	360.58
Debt at end of fiscal year	3,749,282	1,363.38
Cash and security holdings	18,988,203	6,904.80

Abbreviations and symbols: – zero or rounds to zero; (NA) not available; (X) not applicable.

SOURCE: *U.S. Census Bureau, Governments Division, 2004 Survey of State Government Finances,* January 2006.

---

be fully funded before any lower level appropriations are funded. In the event of insufficient revenues to fund appropriations, each agency reduces its spending to correspond to the general revenues allocated to the agency. Efforts to install a statewide Web-based information system met with technical and training difficulties that had slowly been rectified as of 2006. Fiscal year 2006 general funds were estimated at nearly $3.8 billion for resources and $3.8 billion for expenditures. In fiscal year 2004, federal government grants to Arkansas were nearly $4.7 billion. For fiscal year 2007, federal funding for the State Children's Health Insurance Program (SCHIP) and the HOME Investment Partnership Program was increased.

36 TAXATION

In 2005, Arkansas collected $6,552 million in tax revenues ($2,358 per capita), which placed it 18th among the 50 states in per capita tax burden. The national average was $2,192 per capita. Property taxes accounted for 8.5% of the total; sales taxes, 39.3%; selective sales taxes, 13.5%; individual income taxes, 28.6%; corporate income taxes, 4.2%; and other taxes, 5.9%.

As of 1 January 2006, Arkansas had six individual income tax brackets of 1.0–7.0%. The state taxes corporations at rates of 1.0–6.5%, depending on tax bracket.

In 2004, state and local property taxes amounted to $1,100,938,000 ($400 per capita). The per capita amount ranks the state 49th among the 50 states. Local governments collected $580,614,000 of the total and the state government, $520,324,000. Although local property taxes are the lowest in the nation, state property tax collections are unusually high.

Arkansas taxes retail sales at a rate of 6%. In addition to the state tax, local taxes on retail sales can reach as much as 5.50%, making for a potential total tax on retail sales of 11.50%. Food purchased for consumption off-premises is taxable. The tax on cigarettes is 59 cents per pack, which ranks 32nd among the 50 states and the District of Columbia. Arkansas taxes gasoline at 21.5 cents per gallon. This is in addition to the 18.4 cents per gallon federal tax on gasoline.

According to the Tax Foundation, for every federal tax dollar sent to Washington in 2004, Arkansas citizens received $1.47 in federal spending.

37 ECONOMIC POLICY

First as chairman of the Arkansas Industrial Development Commission and later as governor of the state (1967–71), Winthrop Rockefeller succeeded in attracting substantial and diverse new industries to Arkansas. In 1979, Governor Bill Clinton formed the Department of Economic Development from the former Arkansas Industrial Development Commission for the purpose of stimulating the growth of small business and finding new export markets. The Arkansas Development Finance Authority was created in 1985 in order to support small-scale economic development of new businesses, mortgages, education, and health care. The Economic Development Commission offers such incentives to new businesses as an Enterprise Zone Program, income tax credit, sales and use tax refunds, among others. In 2003, the legislature passed the Consolidated Incentive Act which combined six previous economic development incentive programs into one package, plus added some additional incentives for investment and regional development. The six programs consolidated in the Act were the Enterprise Zone program (Advantage Arkansas), which provides incentives for investments in areas with high poverty and/or unemployment); the Economic Investment Tax Credit program (InvestArk Program); the Economic Development Incentives Act (CreateRebate); the Arkansas Economic Development Act (AEDA), which offers tax reductions for investments of at least $5 million dollars creating at least 100 new permanent jobs; plus incentive programs for improvements in energy technology and biotechnology. By the act, companies would be allowed to sell tax credits earned in order to realize the benefits earlier. The act seeks to promote regional development by rewarding counties which enter into binding compacts with each other to further economic development.

In 2006, the rubber and plastics industry was a targeted industry for the state, due, in part, to the influx of a large number of automotive parts suppliers to the state. Arkansas is home to approximately 200 plastics and rubber companies. Because of its central location in the country, halfway between Canada and Mexico and between the two US coasts, Arkansas provides a valuable transportation advantage. A billion-dollar program to improve approximately 380 mi (600 km) of interstate highways was scheduled to be completed in 2005.

38 HEALTH

The infant mortality rate in October 2005 was estimated at 7.6 per 1,000 live births. The birth rate in 2003 was 14 per 1,000 population. The abortion rate stood at 9.8 per 1,000 women in 2000. In 2003, about 81.3% of pregnant woman received prenatal care beginning in the first trimester. In 2004, approximately 82% of children received routine immunizations before the age of three.

The crude death rate in 2003 was 10.2 deaths per 1,000 population. As of 2002, the death rates for major causes of death (per 100,000 resident population) were: heart disease, 307.4; cancer, 231.8; cerebrovascular diseases, 82.4 (the highest in the nation); chronic lower respiratory diseases, 53.2; and diabetes, 29.3. The mortality rate from HIV infection was 3 per 100,000 population. In 2004, the reported AIDS case rate was at about 6.7 per 100,000 population. In 2002, about 58.9% of the population was considered overweight or obese. As of 2004, Arkansas ranked sixth in the nation for the highest percentage of resident smokers, with 25.5%.

In 2003, Arkansas had 88 community hospitals with about 9,900 beds. There were about 388,000 patient admissions that year and 4.6 million outpatient visits. The average daily inpatient census was about 5,700 patients. The average cost per day for hospital care was $1,130. Also in 2003, there were about 242 certified nursing facilities in the state with 24,791 beds and an overall occupancy rate of about 72.6%. In 2004, it was estimated that about 60.9% of all state residents had received some type of dental care within the year. Arkansas had 205 physicians per 100,000 resident population in 2004 and 729 nurses per 100,000 in 2005. In 2004, there was a total of 1,120 dentists in the state.

About 30% of state residents were enrolled in Medicaid and Medicare programs in 2004; the state had the third-highest per-

centage of Medicare recipients in the nation (following West Virginia and Maine). Approximately 17% of the state population was uninsured in 2004. In 2003, state health care expenditures totaled $3 million.

39 SOCIAL WELFARE

In 2004, about 85,000 people received unemployment benefits, with an average weekly unemployment benefit of $228. In fiscal year 2005, the estimated average monthly participation in the food stamp program included about 373,764 persons (152,916 households); the average monthly benefit was about $89.47 per person. That year, the total benefits paid through the state for the food stamp program was about $401.2 million.

Temporary Assistance for Needy Families (TANF), the system of federal welfare assistance that officially replaced Aid to Families with Dependent Children (AFDC) in 1997, was reauthorized through the Deficit Reduction Act of 2005. TANF is funded through federal block grants that are divided among the states based on an equation involving the number of recipients in each state. Arkansas's TANF program is called Transitional Employment Assistance (TEA). In 2004, the state program had 22,000 recipients; state and federal expenditures on this TANF program totaled $22 million fiscal year 2003.

In December 2004, Social Security benefits were paid to 546,080 Arkansas residents. This number included 310,790 retired workers, 58,020 widows and widowers, 95,960 disabled workers, 28,060 spouses, and 53,240 children. Social Security beneficiaries represented 20.1% of the total state population and 93.1% of the state's population age 65 and older. Retired workers received an average monthly payment of $888; widows and widowers, $795; disabled workers, $846; and spouses, $429. Payments for children of retired workers averaged $451 per month; children of deceased workers, $554; and children of disabled workers, $249. Federal Supplemental Security Income payments in December 2004 went to 87,928 Arkansas residents, averaging $361 a month.

40 HOUSING

In 2004, there were an estimated 1,233,203 housing units in Arkansas, of which 1,099,086 were occupied. In the same year, 65.5% of all housing units were owner-occupied. It was estimated that about 98,716 units were without telephone service, 1,709 lacked complete plumbing facilities, and 5,662 lacked complete kitchen facilities. Though most units relied on gas and electricity for heating fuels, about 40,890 households used wood for a primary heating source. About 69% of all units were single-family, detached homes; 12.7% were mobile homes. The average household had 2.43 members.

The Department of Housing and Urban Development awarded $39.6 million in grants to the Arkansas state program in 2002, including $24.9 million in community development block grants. About 15,900 new housing units were authorized in 2004. The median home value in 2004 was $79,006, the lowest in the country. The median monthly cost for mortgage owners was $773 while the monthly cost for renters was at a median of $517. In September 2005, the state was awarded grants of $680,321 from the US Department of Housing and Urban Development (HUD) for rural housing and economic development programs. For 2006, HUD allocated to the state over $19.3 million in community development block grants.

41 EDUCATION

In 2004, 79.2% of all Arkansans 25 years of age and older were high school graduates. Some 18.8% had obtained a bachelor's degree or higher.

In some ways, Little Rock was an unlikely site for the major confrontation over school integration that occurred in 1957. The school board had already announced its voluntary compliance with the Supreme Court's desegregation decision, and during Governor Faubus's first term (1955–56), several public schools in the state had been peaceably integrated. Nevertheless, on 5 September 1957, Faubus, claiming that violence was likely, ordered the National Guard to seize Central High School to prevent the entry of nine black students. When a mob did appear following the withdrawal of the National Guardsmen in response to a federal court order later that month, President Dwight Eisenhower dispatched federal troops to Little Rock, and they patrolled the school grounds until the end of the 1958 spring semester. Although Faubus's stand encouraged politicians in other southern states to resist desegregation, in Arkansas integration proceeded at a moderate pace. By 1980, Central High School had a nearly equal balance of black and white students, and the state's school system was one of the most integrated in the South.

Public school enrollment in fall 2002 totaled 451,000. Of these, 319,000 attended schools from kindergarten through grade eight, and 132,000 attended high school. Approximately 69.9% of the students were white, 23.1% were black, 5.3% were Hispanic, 1.1% were Asian/Pacific Islander, and 0.6% were American Indian/Alaskan Native. Total enrollment was estimated at 449,000 in fall 2003 and expected to be 449,000 by fall 2014, a decrease of 0.5% during the period 2002 to 2014. There were 27,500 students enrolled in 189 private schools in fall 2003. Expenditures for public education in 2003/04 were estimated at $3.5 billion. Since 1969, the National Assessment of Educational Progress (NAEP) has tested public school students nationwide. The resulting report, *The Nation's Report Card,* stated that in 2005, eighth graders in Arkansas scored 272 out of 500 in mathematics compared with the national average of 278.

As of fall 2002, there were 127,372 students enrolled in college or graduate school; minority students comprised 21.4% of total postsecondary enrollment. As of 2005, Arkansas had 47 degree-granting institutions. The largest institution of higher education in the state is the University of Arkansas at Fayetteville (established in 1871). The state university system also has campuses at Fort Smith, Little Rock, Monticello, and Pine Bluff, as well as a medical school. Student aid is provided by the State Scholarship Program within the Department of Higher Education, by the Arkansas Student Loan Guarantee Foundation, and by the Arkansas Rural Endowment Fund, Inc.

42 ARTS

The Arkansas Arts Council was established in 1971 as one of seven agencies of the Department of Arkansas Heritage, which include the Arkansas Historic Preservation Program, the Arkansas Natural Heritage Commission, the Delta Cultural Center, the Historic Arkansas Museum, the Mosaic Templars Cultural Center, and the Old State House Museum. Major funding comes from the state and the National Endowment for the Arts. In 2005, the National Endowment for the Arts awarded seven grants totaling $616,200 to Arkansas arts organizations, and the National Endowment for the Humanities awarded eight grants totaling $1,739,430 to Arkansas organizations. Arkansas is also affiliated with the regional Mid-America Arts Alliance.

Little Rock is the home of the Arkansas Symphony Orchestra (ASO). The ASO celebrated 41 years of performance with its 2006/07 season. Little Rock is also home to the Arkansas Festival Ballet, the Arkansas Repertory Theater, and the Arkansas Arts Center, which holds art exhibits and classes, as well as children's theater performances.

The best-known center for traditional arts and crafts is the Ozark Folk Center at Mountain View. The Ozark Folk Center offers workshops in music and crafts as well as weekly evening concerts that focus on preserving "mountain music" from the Ozark region. As of 2006, the Annual Arkansas Folk Festival was held in Mountain View in April. The Regional Studies Center of Lyon College at Batesville presents an annual Ozark history and culture program.

43 LIBRARIES AND MUSEUMS

In calendar year 2001, Arkansas had 35 public library systems, with a total of 209 libraries, of which 169 were branches. In that same year, the state's public libraries held 5,497,000 volumes of books and serial publications, while total circulation amounted to 10,452,000. The system also had 112,000 audio and 101,000 video items, 5,000 electronic format items (CD-ROMs, magnetic tapes, and disks), and five bookmobiles. Important collections include those of the University of Arkansas at Fayetteville (1,556,572 volumes), Arkansas State University at Jonesboro (544,326), the Central Arkansas Library System of Little Rock (528,982), and the News Library of the Arkansas Gazette, also in Little Rock. The total operating income of the public library system was $38,704,000 in 2001. Arkansas received $72,000 in federal grants, while state grants that year came to $4,106,000. The state spent 59.3% of this income on staff and 17.7% on the collection.

There were 78 museums in 2000 and a number of historic sites. Principal museums include the Arkansas Arts Center and the Museum of Science and History, both at Little Rock; the Arkansas State University Museum at Jonesboro; and the University of Arkansas Museum at Fayetteville, specializing in archaeology, anthropology, and the sciences. Also of interest are the Stuttgart Agricultural Museum; the Arkansas Post County Museum at Gillett, whose artifacts are housed in re-created plantation buildings; Hampson Museum State Park, near Wilson, which has one of the largest collections of Mound Builder artifacts in the United States; the Mid-American Museum at Hot Springs, which has visitor-participation exhibits; and the Saunders Memorial Museum at Berryville, with an extensive collection of firearms.

Civil War battle sites include the Pea Ridge National Military Park, the Prairie Grove Battlefield State Park, and the Arkansas Post National Memorial. The Ft. Smith National Historic Site includes buildings and museums from the days when the town was a military outpost on the border of Indian Territory.

⁴⁴COMMUNICATIONS

In 2004, 88.6% of the state's occupied housing units had telephones, the lowest rate in the nation. In addition, by June of that same year there were 307,323 mobile wireless telephone subscribers. In 2003, 50.0% of Arkansas households had a computer and 42.2% had Internet access, the second-lowest in the nation (after Mississippi) for both categories. By June 2005, there were 258,564 high-speed lines in Arkansas, 236,325 residential and 22,239 for business.

There were 63 major radio stations (7 AM, 56 FM) and 17 major television stations in 2005. A total of 23,195 Internet domain names had been registered in Arkansas as of 2000.

⁴⁵PRESS

The first newspaper in Arkansas, the *Arkansas Gazette,* established at Arkansas Post in 1819 by William E. Woodruff, ceased publication in 1991. In 2005, there were 14 morning dailies, 14 evening papers, and 16 Sunday papers. In 1992, Little Rock's two major dailies, the *Arkansas Democrat* and the *Democrat Gazette,* merged.

The following table shows the 2005 circulations of the leading dailies:

AREA	NAME	DAILY	SUNDAY
Fort Smith	*Southwest Times Record* (m, S)	37,462	43,322
Jonesboro	*Jonesboro Sun* (m, S)	23,156	26,481
Little Rock	*Arkansas Democrat-Gazette* (m, S)	182,391	280,529
Springdale-Rogers	*Morning News* (m, S)	37,669	43,289

In 2005, there were 97 weekly publications in Arkansas. Of these there are 87 paid weeklies, 2 free weeklies, and 8 combined weeklies. The total circulation of paid weeklies (288,228) and free weeklies (43,482) is 331,710.

⁴⁶ORGANIZATIONS

In 2006, there were over 2,190 nonprofit organizations registered within the state, of which about 1,478 were registered as charitable, educational, or religious organizations. Among the national organizations with headquarters in Arkansas are the American Crossbow Association in Huntsville; the American Fish Farmers Federation in Lonoke; and the Ozark Society, the American Parquet Association, the Federation of American Hospitals, and the Civil War Round Table Associates, all located in Little Rock. The national headquarters of the Knights of the Ku Klux Klan is in Harrison.

The Association of Community Organizations for Reform Now (ACORN) was founded in Little Rock in 1970 and has since spread to some 20 other states, becoming one of the most influential citizens' lobbies in the United States. Heifer Project International, a social welfare organization that provides agricultural and community development assistance in third world countries, is headquartered in Little Rock. The Arkansas Arts Council and the Historic Preservation Alliance of Arkansas are based in Little Rock.

⁴⁷TOURISM, TRAVEL, AND RECREATION

In 2004, Arkansas received 218,000,000 visitors and generated 57,300 jobs in the travel industry. Pulaski and Garland counties accounted for the most visited by tourists.

Leading attractions in Arkansas are the mineral waters and recreational facilities at Hot Springs, Eureka Springs, Mammoth Spring, and Heber Springs. The Crater of Diamonds, near Murfreesboro, is the only known public source of natural diamonds in North America. For a fee, visitors may hunt for diamonds and keep any they find; more than 100,000 diamonds have been found in the area since 1906, of which the two largest are the 40.42-carat Uncle Sam and the 34.25-carat Star of Murfreesboro. The World's Championship Duck Calling Contest is held at the beginning of the winter duck season in Stuttgart. The city of Hamburg hosts the Armadillo Festival.

In support of the industry, the Arkansas Tourism Development Act of 1999 provides incentives for qualified new or expanding tourism facilities and attractions. The program applies to cultural or historical sites; recreational or entertainment facilities; natural, theme, and amusement parks; plays and musicals; and gardens. To qualify, the project must cost more than $500,000 and have a positive effect on the state. The state has 14 tourist information centers. In 2002, the state had some 19.9 million visitors with travel expenditures reaching over $3.9 billion (a 2.8% increase from 2000). The new William Jefferson Clinton Presidential Library in Little Rock has the largest collection of presidential artifacts. The University of Alabama recently opened the Clinton School of Public Service.

⁴⁸SPORTS

Arkansas has no major professional sports teams but it does have a minor league baseball team, the Travelers. Oaklawn Park in Hot Springs has a 62-day thoroughbred-racing season each spring, and dog races are held in West Memphis from April through November. Several major rodeos take place in summer and fall, including the Rodeo of the Ozarks in Springdale in early July.

The University of Arkansas has competed in the Southeastern Conference since 1990, when it ended its 76-year affiliation with the Southwest Conference. The Razorback football team won the Cotton Bowl in 1947, 1965, 1976, and 2000; the Orange Bowl in 1978; the Sugar Bowl in 1969; and the Bluebonnet Bowl in 1982. The men's basketball team won the National Collegiate Athletic Association (NCAA) Division I basketball championship in 1994; won or shared the Southwest Conference championship in 1977, 1978, 1979, 1981, and 1982; and won the Southeastern Conference in 1994 and 2000.

⁴⁹FAMOUS ARKANSANS

Arkansas has produced one president of the United States, William Jefferson Clinton (b.1946). Clinton, a Democrat, defeated President George H. W. Bush in the 1992 presidential election and was reelected in 1996. Clinton's wife is the former Hillary Rodham (b.Illinois, 1947). Arkansas has yet to produce a vice president or a Supreme Court justice, although one Arkansan came close to reaching both offices: US Senator Joseph T. Robinson (1872–1937) was the Democratic nominee for vice president in 1928, on the ticket with Al Smith; later, he was Senate majority leader under

President Franklin D. Roosevelt. At the time of his death, Robinson was leading the fight for Roosevelt's bill to expand the Supreme Court's membership and had reportedly been promised a seat on the court if the bill passed. Robinson's colleague, Hattie W. Caraway (b.Tennessee, 1878–1950), was the first woman elected to the US Senate, serving from 1931 to 1945.

After World War II (1939–45), Arkansas's congressional delegation included three men of considerable power and fame: Senator John L. McClellan (1896–1977), investigator of organized labor and organized crime and champion of the Arkansas River navigation project; Senator J. William Fulbright (b.Missouri, 1905–95), chairman of the Senate Foreign Relations Committee; and Representative Wilbur D. Mills (1909–92), chairman of the House Ways and Means Committee until scandal ended his political career in the mid-1970s.

Other federal officeholders include Brooks Hays (1898–1981), former congressman and special assistant to Presidents John F. Kennedy and Lyndon B. Johnson, as well as president of the Southern Baptist Convention, the nation's largest Protestant denomination; and Frank Pace Jr. (1912–88), secretary of the Army during the Truman administration.

General Douglas MacArthur (1880–1964), supreme commander of Allied forces in the Pacific during World War II, supervised the occupation of Japan and was supreme commander of UN troops in Korea until relieved of his command in April 1951 by President Harry Truman.

Orval E. Faubus (1910–94) served six terms as governor (a record), drew international attention during the 1957 integration crisis at Little Rock Central High School, and headed the most powerful political machine in Arkansas history. Winthrop Rockefeller (b.New York, 1917–73) was Faubus's most prominent successor. At the time of his election in 1978, Bill Clinton was the nation's youngest governor.

Prominent business leaders include the Stephens brothers, W. R. "Witt" (1907–91) and Jackson T. (1923–2005), whose Stephens, Inc., investment firm in Little Rock is the largest off Wall Street; and Kemmons Wilson (1913–2003), founder of Holiday Inns.

Other distinguished Arkansans are Edward Durrell Stone (1902–78), renowned architect; C. Vann Woodward (1908–99), Sterling Professor Emeritus of History at Yale University; and the Right Reverend John M. Allin (1921–98), presiding bishop of the Episcopal Church of the United States. John H. Johnson (1918–2005), publisher of the nation's leading black-oriented magazines—*Ebony, Jet,* and others—is an Arkansan, as is Helen Gurley Brown (b.1922), former editor of *Cosmopolitan.*

Harry S. Ashmore (b.South Carolina, 1916–98) won a Pulitzer Prize for his *Arkansas Gazette* editorials calling for peaceful integration of the schools during the 1957 crisis; the *Gazette* itself won a Pulitzer for meritorious public service that year. Paul Greenberg (b.Louisiana, 1937), of the *Pine Bluff Commercial,* is another Pulitzer Prize-winning journalist. John Gould Fletcher (1886–1950) was a Pulitzer Prize-winning poet. Other Arkansas writers include Dee Brown (b.Louisiana, 1908–2002), Maya Angelou (b.Missouri, 1928), Charles Portis (b.1933), and Eldridge Cleaver (1935–98).

Arkansas planter Colonel Sanford C. Faulkner (1803–74) is credited with having written the well-known fiddle tune "The Arkansas Traveler" and its accompanying dialogue. Perhaps the best-known country music performers from Arkansas are Johnny Cash (1932–2003) and Glen Campbell (b.1938). Film stars Dick Powell (1904–63) and Alan Ladd (1913–64) were also Arkansans.

Notable Arkansas sports personalities include Jerome Herman "Dizzy" Dean (1911–74) and Bill Dickey (1907–93), both members of the Baseball Hall of Fame; Brooks Robinson (b.1937), considered by some the best-fielding third baseman in baseball history; and star pass-catcher Lance Alworth (b.Mississippi, 1940), a University of Arkansas All-American and member of the Professional Football Hall of Fame.

⁵⁰BIBLIOGRAPHY

Alampi, Gary (ed.). *Gale State Rankings Reporter.* Detroit: Gale Research, Inc., 1994.

Angelou, Maya. *The Collected Autobiographies of Maya Angelou.* New York: Modern Library, 2004.

———. *I Know Why the Caged Bird Sings.* N. Y.: Bantam, 1971.

Bumpers, Dale. *The Best Lawyer in a One-Lawyer Town: A Memoir.* New York: Random House, 2003.

Cities of the United States. 5th ed. Farmington Hills, Mich.: Thomson Gale, 2005.

Clinton, Bill. *My Life.* New York: Alfred A. Knopf, 2004.

Council of State Governments. *The Book of the States, 2006 Edition.* Lexington, Ky.: Council of State Governments, 2006.

FDIC, Division of Research and Statistics. *Statistics on Banking: A Statistical Profile of the United States Banking Industry.* Washington, D.C.: Federal Deposit Insurance Corporation, 1993.

Gatewood, Willard B., and Jeannie Whayne (eds.). *The Arkansas Delta: Land of Paradox.* Fayetteville: University of Arkansas Press, 1993.

Hamilton, Nigel. *Bill Clinton: An American Journey.* New York: Random House, 2003.

McDougal, Jim, and Curtis Wilkie. *Arkansas Mischief: the Birth of a National Scandal.* N.Y.: Henry Holt, 1998.

Newman, Katherine S. *Rampage: The Social Roots of School Shootings.* New York: Basic Books, 2004.

Norman, Corrie E., and Don S. Armentrout (eds.) *Religion in the Contemporary South: Changes, Continuities, and Contexts.* Knoxville: University of Tennessee Press, 2005.

Paulson, Alan C. *Roadside History of Arkansas.* Missoula, Mont.: Mountain Press, 1998.

Polakow, Amy. *Daisy Bates: Civil Rights Crusader.* North Haven, Conn.: Linnet Books, 2003.

US Department of Commerce, Economics and Statistics Administration, US Census Bureau. *Arkansas, 2000. Summary Social, Economic, and Housing Characteristics: 2000 Census of Population and Housing.* Washington, D.C.: US Government Printing Office, 2003.

US Department of Education, National Center for Education Statistics. Office of Educational Research and Improvement. *Digest of Education Statistics, 1993.* Washington, D.C.: US Government Printing Office, 1993.

US Department of the Interior, US Fish and Wildlife Service. *Endangered and Threatened Species Recovery Program.* Washington, D.C.: US Government Printing Office, 1990.

Whayne, Jeannie M. *A New Plantation South: Land, Labor, and Federal Favor in Twentieth-Century Arkansas.* Charlottesville: University Press of Virginia, 1996.

CALIFORNIA

State of California

ORIGIN OF STATE NAME: Probably from the mythical island California in a 16th-century romance by Garci Ordóñez de Montalvo. **NICKNAME:** The Golden State. **CAPITAL:** Sacramento. **ENTERED UNION:** 9 September 1850 (31st). **SONG:** "I Love You, California." **MOTTO:** *Eureka* (I have found it). **FLAG:** The flag consists of a white field with a red star at upper left and a red stripe and the words "California Republic" across the bottom; in the center, a brown grizzly bear walks on a patch of green grass. **OFFICIAL SEAL:** In the foreground is the goddess Minerva; a grizzly bear stands in front of her shield. The scene also shows the Sierra Nevada, San Francisco Bay, a miner, a sheaf of wheat, and a cluster of grapes, all representing California's resources. The state motto and 31 stars are displayed at the top. The words "The Great Seal of the State of California" surround the whole. **BIRD:** California valley quail. **FISH:** South Fork golden trout. **FLOWER:** Golden poppy. **TREE:** California redwood. **GEM:** Benitoite. **LEGAL HOLIDAYS:** New Year's Day, 1 January; Birthday of Martin Luther King Jr., 3rd Monday in January; Lincoln's Birthday, 12 February; Presidents' Day, 3rd Monday in February; Cesar Chavez Day, 31 March; Memorial Day, last Monday in May; Independence Day, 4 July; Labor Day, 1st Monday in September; Columbus Day, 2nd Monday in October; Veterans' Day, 11 November; Thanksgiving Day, 4th Thursday in November; Christmas Day, 25 December. **TIME:** 4 AM PST = noon GMT.

¹LOCATION, SIZE, AND EXTENT

Situated on the Pacific coast of the southwestern United States, California is the nation's third-largest state (after Alaska and Texas).

The total area of California is 158,706 sq mi (411,048 sq km), of which land takes up 156,299 sq mi (404,814 sq km) and inland water, 2,407 sq mi (6,234 sq km). California extends about 350 mi (560 km) E–W; its maximum N–S extension is 780 mi (1,260 km).

California is bordered on the N by Oregon; on the E by Nevada; on the SE by Arizona (separated by the Colorado River); on the S by the Mexican state of Baja California Norte; and on the W by the Pacific Ocean.

The eight Santa Barbara islands lie from 20 to 60 mi (32–97 km) off California's southwestern coast; the small islands and islets of the Farallon group are about 30 mi (48 km) W of San Francisco Bay. The total boundary length of the state is 2,050 mi (3,299 km), including a general coastline of 840 mi (1,352 km); the tidal shoreline totals 3,427 mi (5,515 km). California's geographic center is in Madera County, 38 mi (61 km) E of the city of Madera.

²TOPOGRAPHY

California is the only state in the United States with an extensive seacoast, high mountains, and deserts. The extreme diversity of the state's landforms is best illustrated by the fact that Mt. Whitney (14,494 ft/4,419 m), the highest point in the contiguous US, is situated no more than 80 mi (129 km) from the lowest point in the entire country, Death Valley (282 ft/86 m, below sea level). The mean elevation of the state is about 2,900 ft (885 m).

California's principal geographic regions are the Sierra Nevada in the east, the Coast Ranges in the west, the Central Valley between them, and the Mojave and Colorado deserts in the south-

east. The mountain-walled Central Valley, more than 400 mi (640 km) long and about 50 mi (80 km) wide, is probably the state's most unusual topographic feature. It is drained in the north by the Sacramento River, about 320 mi (515 km) long, and in the south by the San Joaquin River, about 350 mi (560 km). The main channels of the two rivers meet at and empty into the northern arm of San Francisco Bay, flowing through the only significant break in the Coast Ranges, a mountain system that extends more than 1,200 mi (1,900 km) alongside the Pacific. Lesser ranges, including the Siskiyou Mountains in the north and the Tehachapi Mountains in the south, link the two major ranges and constitute the Central Valley's upper and lower limits.

California has 41 mountains exceeding 10,000 ft (3,050 m). After Mt. Whitney, the highest peaks in the state are Mt. Williamson, in the Sierra Nevada, at 14,375 ft (4,382 m) and Mt. Shasta (14,162 ft/4,317 m), an extinct volcano in the Cascades, the northern extension of the Sierra Nevada. Lassen Peak (10,457 ft/3,187 m), also in the Cascades, is a dormant volcano.

Beautiful Yosemite Valley, a narrow gorge in the middle of the High Sierra, is the activity center of Yosemite National Park. The Coast Ranges, with numerous forested spurs and ridges enclosing dozens of longitudinal valleys, vary in height from about 2,000 to 7,000 ft (600–2,100 m).

Melted snow from the Sierra Nevada feeds the state's principal rivers, the Sacramento and San Joaquin. The Coast Ranges are drained by the Klamath, Eel, Russian, Salinas, and other rivers. In the south, most rivers are dry creek beds except during the spring flood season; they either dry up from evaporation in the hot summer sun or disappear beneath the surface, like Death Valley's Amargosa River. The Salton Sea, in the Imperial Valley of the southeast, is the state's largest lake, occupying 374 sq mi (969 sq km). This saline sink was created accidentally in the early 1900s when

Colorado River water, via an irrigation canal, flooded a natural depression 235 ft (72 m) below sea level in the Imperial Valley. Lake Tahoe, in the Sierra Nevada at the angle of the California-Nevada border, covers 192 sq mi (497 sq km).

The California coast is indented by two magnificent natural harbors, San Francisco Bay and San Diego Bay, and two smaller bays, Monterey and Humboldt. Two groups of islands lie off the California shore: the Santa Barbara Islands, situated west of Los Angeles and San Diego; and the rocky Farallon Islands, off San Francisco.

The Sierra Nevada and Coast Ranges were formed more than 100 million years ago by the uplifting of the earth's crust. The Central Valley and the Great Basin, including the Mojave Desert and Death Valley, were created by sinkage of the earth's crust; inland seas once filled these depressions but evaporated over eons of time. Subsequent volcanic activity, erosion of land, and movement of glaciers until the last Ice Age subsided some 10,000 years ago and gradually shaped the present topography of California. The San Andreas Fault, extending from north of San Francisco Bay for more than 600 mi (970 km) southeast to the Mojave Desert, is a major active earthquake zone and was responsible for the great San Francisco earthquake of 1906. Damage from that earthquake amounted to $24 million, with an additional $350–500 in fire losses (total losses would amount to about $6 billion in current dollars). More recently, the 1994 earthquake in Northridge caused damage estimated at $13–20 billion, making it the costliest earthquake in US history.

Because water is scarce in the southern part of the state and because an adequate water supply is essential both for agriculture and for industry, more than 1,000 dams and reservoirs have been built in California. By 1993, there were 1,336 reservoirs in the state. Popular reservoirs for recreation are located along the tributaries of the Sacramento and San Joaquín rivers. Clair Lake Eagle, also known as Trinity Lake, is located on the Trinity River. The reservoir has a surface area of 16,400 acres (6,640 hectares). Lake Shasta, located on the Sacramento River, has a surface area of 15,800 acres (6,397 hectares). Lake Berryessa, located on Putah Creek, has a surface area of 19,250 acres (7,794 hectares). Lake New Melones, located on the Stanislaus River, has a surface area of 12,500 acres (5,061 hectares). The San Luis Reservoir, fed by the California Aqueduct, has a surface area of 12,500 acres (5,061 hectares). Don Pedro Lake, located on the Toulumme River, has a surface area of 13,000 acres (5,263 hectares).

³CLIMATE

Like its topography, California's climate is varied and tends toward extremes. Generally there are two seasons—a long, dry summer, with low humidity and cool evenings, and a mild, rainy winter—except in the high mountains, where four seasons prevail and snow lasts from November to April. The one climatic constant for the state is summer drought.

California has four main climatic regions. Mild summers and winters prevail in central coastal areas, where temperatures are more equable than virtually anywhere else in the United States; in the area between San Francisco and Monterey, for example, the difference between average summer and winter temperatures is seldom more than 10°F (6°C). During the summer there are heavy fogs in San Francisco and all along the coast. Mountainous regions are characterized by milder summers and colder winters, with markedly low temperatures at high elevations. The Central Valley has hot summers and cool winters, while the Imperial Valley is marked by very hot, dry summers, with temperatures frequently exceeding 100°F (38°C).

Average annual temperatures for the state range from 47°F (8°C) in the Sierra Nevada to 73°F (23°C) in the Imperial Valley. The highest temperature ever recorded in the United States was 134° (57°C), registered in Death Valley on 10 July 1913. Death Valley has the hottest average summer temperature in the Western Hemisphere, at 98°F (37°C). The state's lowest temperature was -45°F (-43°C), recorded on 20 January 1937 at Boca, near the Nevada border.

Among the major population centers, Los Angeles has an average annual temperature of 65°F (18°C), with an average January minimum of 48°F (9°C) and an average July maximum of 73°F (27°C). San Francisco has an annual average of 57°F (13°C), with a January average minimum of 46°F (7°C) and a July average maximum of 66°F (18°C). The annual average in San Diego is 64°F (18°C), the January average minimum 48°F (8°C), and the July average maximum 76°F (24°C). Sacramento's annual average temperature is 61°F (16°C), with January minimums averaging 38°F (3°C) and July maximums of 93°F (34°C).

Annual precipitation varies from only 2 in (5 cm) in the Imperial Valley to 68 in (173 cm) at Blue Canyon, near Lake Tahoe. San Francisco has an average annual precipitation of 20.4 in (51 cm), Sacramento 17.4 in (44 cm), Los Angeles 14 in (35 cm), and San Diego 9.9 in (25 cm). The largest one-month snowfall ever recorded in the United States—390 in (991 cm)—fell in Alpine County in January 1911. Snow averages between 300 and 400 in (760 to 1,020 cm) annually in the high elevations of the Sierra Nevada, but is rare in the coastal lowlands.

Sacramento has the greatest percentage (78%) of possible annual sunshine among the state's largest cities; San Diego has 68% and San Francisco 66%. San Francisco is the windiest, with an average annual wind speed of 11 mph (18 km/hr). Topical rainstorms occur often in California during the winter. Part of California are also prone to wildfires. In 2003, wildfires burned in southern California from late October through early November causing 22 deaths. Damage included to 743,000 acres of burned brush and timber and over 3,700 destroyed homes, with a total cost of damage at over $2.5 billion.

⁴FLORA AND FAUNA

Of the 48 conterminous states, California embraces the greatest diversity of climate and terrain. The state's six life zones are the lower Sonoran (desert); upper Sonoran (foothill regions and some coastal lands); transition (coastal areas and moist northeastern counties); and the Canadian, Hudsonian, and Arctic zones, comprising California's highest elevations.

Plant life in the arid climate of the lower Sonoran zone features a diversity of native cactus, mesquite, and paloverde. The Joshua tree (Yucca brevifolia) is found in the Mojave Desert. Flowering plants include the dwarf desert poppy and a variety of asters. Fremont cottonwood and valley oak grow in the Central Valley. The upper Sonoran zone includes the unique chaparral belt, charac-

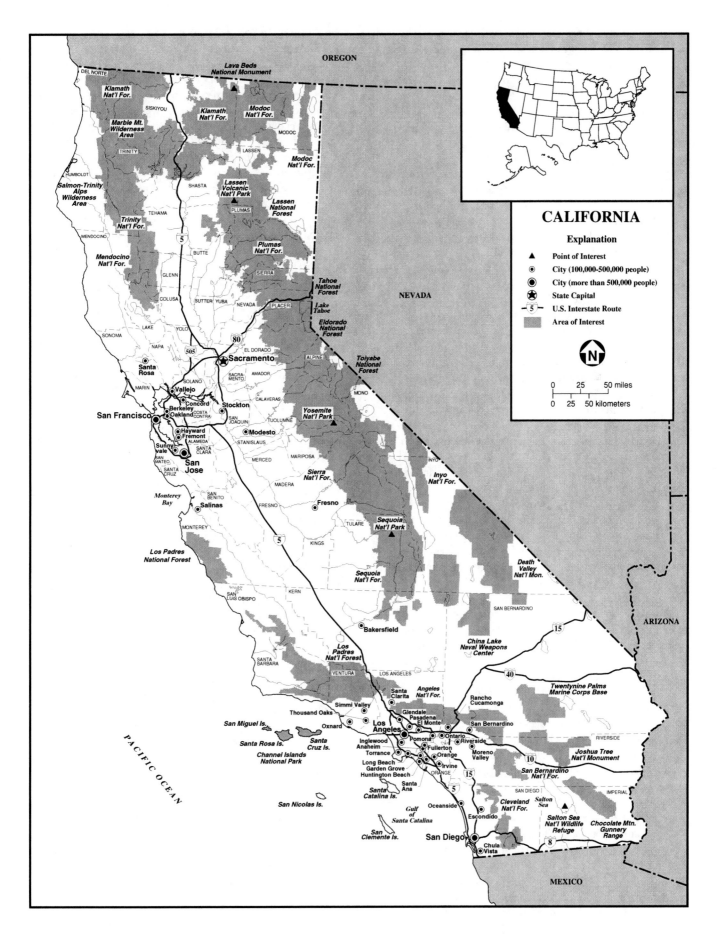

terized by forests of small shrubs, stunted trees, and herbaceous plants. Nemophila, mint, phacelia, viola, and the golden poppy (Eschscholtzia californica)—the state flower—also flourish in this zone, along with the lupine, more species of which occur here than anywhere else in the world.

The transition zone includes most of the state's forests, with such magnificent specimens as the redwood (Sequoia sempervirens) and "big tree" or giant sequoia (Sequoia gigantea), among the oldest living things on earth (some are said to have lived at least 4,000 years). Tanbark oak, California laurel, sugar pine, madrona, broad-leaved maple, and Douglas fir are also common. Forest floors are carpeted with swordfern, alumroot, barrenwort, and trillium, and there are thickets of huckleberry, azalea, elder, and wild currant. Characteristic wild flowers include varieties of mariposa, tulip, and tiger and leopard lilies.

The high elevations of the Canadian zone are abundant with Jeffrey pine, red fir, and lodgepole pine. Brushy areas are covered with dwarf manzanita and ceanothus; the unique Sierra puffball is also found here. Just below timberline, in the Hudsonian zone, grow the whitebark, foxtail, and silver pines. At approximately 10,500 ft (3,200 m) begins the Arctic zone, a treeless region whose flora includes a number of wild flowers, including Sierra primrose, yellow columbine, alpine buttercup, and alpine shooting star.

Common plants introduced into California include the eucalyptus, acacia, pepper tree, geranium, and Scotch broom. Among the numerous species found in California that are federally classified as endangered are the Contra Costa wallflower, Antioch Dunes evening primrose, Solano Grass, San Clemente Island larkspur, salt marsh bird's beak, McDonald's rock-cress, and Santa Barbara Island Liveforever.

Mammals found in the deserts of the lower Sonoran zone include the jackrabbit, kangaroo rat, squirrel, and opossum. The Texas night owl, roadrunner, cactus wren, and various species of hawk are common birds, and the sidewinder, desert tortoise, and horned toad represent the area's reptilian life. The upper Sonoran zone is home to such mammals as the antelope, brown-footed woodrat, and ring-tailed cat. Birds distinctive to this zone are the California thrasher, bush tit, and California condor.

Animal life is abundant amid the forests of the transition zone. Colombian black-tailed deer, black bear, gray fox, cougar, bobcat, and Roosevelt elk are found. Garter snakes and rattlesnakes are common, as are such amphibians as the water-puppy and redwood salamander. The kingfisher, chickadee, towhee, and hummingbird represent the bird life of this region.

Mammals of the Canadian zone include the mountain weasel, snowshoe hare, Sierra chickaree, and several species of chipmunk. Conspicuous birds include the blue-fronted jay, Sierra hermit thrush, water ouzel, and Townsend solitaire. Birds become scarcer as one ascends to the Hudsonian zone, and the wolverine is now regarded as rare. Only one bird is native to the high Arctic region—the Sierra rosy finch—but others often visit, including the hummingbird and Clark nutcracker. Principal mammals of this region are also visitors from other zones; the Sierra coney and white-tailed jackrabbit make their homes here. The bighorn sheep also lives in this mountainous terrain; the bighorn sheep has been listed as endangered by the US Fish and Wildlife Service. Among fauna found throughout several zones are the mule deer,

coyote, mountain lion, red-shafted flicker, and several species of hawk and sparrow.

Aquatic life in California is abundant, from the state's mountain lakes and streams to the rocky Pacific coastline. Many trout species are found, among them rainbow, golden, and Tahoe; migratory species of salmon are also common. Deep-sea life forms include sea bass, yellowfin tuna, barracuda, and several types of whale. Native to the cliffs of northern California are seals, sea lions, and many types of shorebirds, including several migratory species.

The Resources Agency of California's Department of Fish and Game is especially active in listing and providing protection for rare, threatened, and endangered fauna. Joint efforts by state and federal wildlife agencies have established an ambitious, if somewhat controversial, recovery program to revitalize the dwindling population of the majestic condor, the largest bird native to the United States.

In April 2006, a total of 303 species occurring within the state were on the threatened and endangered species list of the US Fish and Wildlife Service. These included 124 animals (vertebrates and invertebrates) and 179 plant species. Endangered animals include the San Joaquin kit fox, Point Arena mountain beaver, Pacific pocket mouse, salt marsh harvest mouse, Morro Bay kangaroo rat (and five other species of kangaroo rat), Amargosa vole, California least tern, California condor, San Clemente loggerhead shrike, San Clemente sage sparrow, San Francisco garter snake, five species of salamander, three species of chub, and two species of pupfish. Eleven butterflies listed as endangered and two as threatened on the federal list are California species. Among threatened animals are the coastal California gnatcatcher, Paiute cutthroat trout, southern sea otter, and northern spotted owl.

5 ENVIRONMENTAL PROTECTION

Efforts to preserve natural wilderness areas in California go back at least to 1890, when the US Congress created three national parks in the Sierra Nevada: Sequoia, Grant (now part of Kings Canyon), and Yosemite. Three years later, some 4 million acres (1.6 million hectares) of the Sierra Nevada were set aside in national forests. In 1892, naturalist John Muir and other wilderness lovers founded the Sierra Club which, with other private groups of conservationists, has been influential in saving the Muir Woods and other stands of redwoods from the lumbermen's axes. Over the next century, numerous other natural areas were designated national parklands. Among the most recent were Death Valley National Park (1994), Joshua Tree National Park (1994), and "Rosie the Riveter" World War II Home Front National Historical Park (2000).

California is home to four Ramsar Wetlands of International Importance. Bolinas Lagoon, located at Point Reyes peninsula northwest of San Francisco, was designated in 1998, primarily for its role as a wintering habitat for migratory birds. This area is owned and managed jointly by the County of Marin and the Golden Gate National Recreational Area under the Bolinas Lagoon Resource Management Plan, which was developed in 1981 and updated in 1996. Damage and erosion to the area caused by various sport and recreation activities is a primary concern for conservation of this area, as is the threat of oil and sewage spills. Tomales Bay, adjacent to the Point Reyes National Seashore, was designated in 2002. This area supports rare eelgrass beds, a well developed coastal sand dune system, and over 21,000 migratory birds per year. The site is managed by both private and public ownership through the efforts of the Point Reyes National Seashore, the Golden Gate Recreation Area, and the Marin Agricultural Land Trust. The Grassland Ecological Area in the Central Valley of the San Joaquin River basin was designated in February 2005. This is the largest single freshwater wetland in the state, but the site has been threatened through plans for urban development. Some conservation issues of this site are handled under the Central Valley Project Improvement Act of 1992. The Tijuana River National Estuarine Research Reserve, located near the border of Mexico, was also designated in February 2005. This site is managed through the joint efforts of the US Fish and Wildlife Service and the California State Department of Parks and Recreation.

California's primary resource problem is water: the southern two-thirds of the state account for about 75% of annual water consumption but only 30% of the supply. Water has been diverted from the Sierra Nevada snow runoff and from the Colorado River to the cities and dry areas largely by means of aqueducts, some 700 mi (1,100 km) of which have been constructed in federal and state undertakings. In 1960, California embarked on one of the largest public works programs ever undertaken in the United States when voters approved a bond issue to construct the California Water Project, designed to deliver 1.4 trillion gallons of water annually to central and southern California for residential, industrial, and agricultural use. Other purposes of the project were to provide flood control, generate electric power, and create recreation areas.

Maintaining adequate water resources continued to be a problem in the 1990s. As the result of a US Supreme Court decision, southern California lost close to 20% of its water supply in December 1985, when a portion of the water it had been permitted to draw from the Colorado River was diverted to Arizona. In 1982, California voters turned down a proposal to build a canal that would have delivered water that flows into San Francisco Bay to southern California; no other plans to cope with the impending shortage were approved at that time. In December 1994 the state and federal governments joined together to form the Bay Delta Accord, intended to restore the environmentally threatened San Francisco Bay area through a combination of better conservation efforts and public and private investment. In November 1996 voters approved a bond issue valued at nearly $1 billion to implement the Accord.

Air pollution has been a serious problem since July 1943, when heavy smog enveloped Los Angeles for the first time; smog conditions in October 1954 forced the closing of the city's airport and harbor. Smog is caused by an atmospheric inversion of cold air that traps unburned hydrocarbons at ground level; perhaps two-thirds of the smog particles are created by automobile exhaust emissions. In 1960, the state legislature passed the first automobile antismog law in the nation, requiring that all cars be equipped with antismog exhaust devices within three years. (Federal laws controlling exhaust emissions on new cars came into effect in the 1970s.) The city's smog problem has since been reduced to manageable proportions, but pollution problems from atmospheric inversions still persist there and in other California cities. Nonetheless there is reason for optimism—in 1996, for example, Southern California had the best air quality ever measured in the post–World War II era. A key factor was introduction of a reformulated gasoline

touted as the cleanest-burning in the world, which reduced polluting emissions by 15% when put into use in 1996. The state inspection-and-maintenance program is also being reformed and updated, focusing on the small number of cars linked to as much as 50% of vehicular pollution in the state.

In early 1995, the Environmental Protection Agency (EPA) approved a California ozone-reduction plan that ordered car manufacturers to design and produce cars that will be 50% to 84% cleaner than the ones sold in 1990. In 1998 new regulations were introduced to give tax credits to Californians who drove very low emission vehicles. In 2001 regulators proposed offering credits for use of a shared fleet of vehicles. California's plan that 10% of the 2003 cars offered for sale would be zero emission vehicles (ZEV) was not realized. In 2003, 57.9 million lb of toxic chemicals were released by the state.

State land-reclamation programs have been important in providing new agricultural land and controlling flood damage. One of the earliest such programs, begun shortly before 1900, reclaimed 500,000 acres (200,000 hectares) by means of a network of dams, dikes, and canals in the swampy delta lying within the fork of the Sacramento and San Joaquin rivers. In 1887, a state law created irrigation districts in the southeastern region; the Imperial Valley was thus transformed from a waterless, sandy basin into some of the most productive agricultural land in the United States.

Flood control was one of the main purposes of the $2.6 billion Feather River Project in the Central Valley, completed during the 1970s. Ironically, in the western portion of the Central Valley, farmland is now threatened by irrigation water tainted by concentrated salts and other soil minerals, for which current drainage systems are inadequate. One drainage system, the San Luis Drain, originally intended to carry the water to San Francisco Bay, was stopped short of completion and goes only as far as the Kesterson National Wildlife Refuge, where, according to the US Fish and Wildlife Service, the tainted water has caused birth defects in birds.

In the 1980s, the state legislature enacted stringent controls on toxic waste. California has also been a leader in recycling waste products, for example, using acid waste from metal-processing plants as a soil additive in citrus orchards. In 2003, the US Environment Protection Agency (EPA) database listed 903 hazardous waste sites in California, 93 of which were on the National Priorities List as of 2006. National Priority List sites included 18 military sites, 4 sites in the San Fernando Valley, 4 sites in the San Gabriel Valley, 2 sites owned by Intel Corp., 1 site owned by Hewlett-Packard, and the Jet Propulsion Laboratory of the National Aeronautics and Space Administration (NASA). California ranks third in the nation for the most National Priority List sites, following New Jersey and Pennsylvania. In 2005, the EPA spent over $25 million through the Superfund program for the cleanup of hazardous waste sites in the state. Also in 2005, federal EPA grants awarded to the state included $85 million for a safe drinking water revolving loan fund and $82 million for a water pollution control revolving loan fund.

The California Department of Water Resources is responsible for maintaining adequate groundwater levels, enforcing water-quality standards, and controlling floodwaters. The state Department of Conservation has overall responsibility for conservation and protection of the state's soil, mineral, petroleum, geothermal, and marine resources. The California Coastal Commission, created in 1972, is designated by federal law to review projects that effect California's coastline, including offshore oil leasing, which has become a source of concern in recent years.

6 POPULATION

California ranked first in population among the 50 states in 2005 with an estimated total of 36,132,147, an increase of 6.7% since 2000. California replaced New York as the decennial census leader in 1970, with a total of 19,971,069 residents, and has lengthened its lead ever since. Between 1990 and 2000, California's population grew from 29,760,021 to 33,871,648, an increase of 13.8%. The population is projected to reach 40.1 million by 2015 and 44.3 million by 2025.

In 2004 the median age was 34.2. Persons under 18 years old accounted for 26.7% of the population while only 10.7% was age 65 or older (lower than the national average of 12.4% at 65 or older).

When Europeans first arrived in California, at least 300,000 American Indians lived in the area. By 1845, the Indian population had been reduced to about 150,000. Although Spanish missions and settlements were well established in California by the late 18th century, the white population numbered only about 7,000 until the late 1840s. The Gold Rush brought at least 85,000 adventurers to the San Francisco Bay area by 1850, however, and the state's population increased rapidly thereafter. California's population grew to 379,994 by 1860 and had passed the 1 million mark within 30 years. Starting in 1890, the number of state residents just about doubled every two decades until the 1970s, when

the population increased by 18.5%, down from the 27.1% increase of the 1960s. However, the total growth rate during the 1980s was 25.7%, reflecting a population increase of over 6 million.

More than 90% of California's residents live in metropolitan areas. The population density in 2004 was 230.2 persons per sq mi, up from 190.8 per sq mi in 1990. Between 1997 and 2002 the largest population growth occurred mainly in the Central Valley and foothill counties, and in Riverside and San Bernardino Counties in Southern California. The five counties of Los Angeles, Orange, Riverside, San Bernardino, and San Diego accounted for 55% of California's total population in 2002, and 52% of the total increase in population since 1997. The city of Los Angeles, ranking as the second-largest city in the nation, had an estimated 2004 population of 3,845,541; San Diego (seventh in the nation), 1,263,756; San Jose (10th), 904,522; San Francisco (14th), 744,230; Long Beach, 476,564; Fresno, 457,719; Sacramento, 454,330; Oakland, 397,976; Santa Ana, 342,715; and Anaheim, 333,776.

Los Angeles, which expanded irregularly and lacks a central business district, nearly quadrupled its population from 319,000 in 1910 to 1,240,000 in 1930, and then doubled it to 2,479,000 by 1960. A major component of the city's population growth was the upsurge in the number of blacks after World War II, especially between 1960 and 1970, when the number of blacks increased from 335,000 to 504,000, many of them crowded into the deteriorating Watts section.

In 1999, the Los Angeles–Long Beach–Santa Ana urban complex, with a total estimated population of 12,925,330, was the second most populous metropolitan area in the United States (after that of New York). Other estimates for that year include the San

California—Counties, County Seats, and County Areas and Populations

COUNTY	COUNTY SEAT	LAND AREA (SQ MI)	POPULATION (2005 EST.)	COUNTY	COUNTY SEAT	LAND AREA (SQ MI)	POPULATION (2005 EST.)
Alameda	Oakland	735	1,448,905	Placer	Auburn	1,416	317,028
Alpine	Markleeville	739	1,159	Plumas	Quincy	2,573	21,477
Amador	Jackson	589	38,471	Riverside	Riverside	7,214	1,946,419
Butte	Oroville	1,646	214,185	Sacramento	Sacramento	971	1,363,482
Calaveras	San Andreas	1,021	46,871	San Benito	Hollister	1,388	55,936
Colusa	Colusa	1,153	21,095	San Bernardino	San Bernardino	20,064	1,963,535
Contra Costa	Martinez	730	1,017,787	San Diego	San Diego	4,212	2,933,462
Del Norte	Crescent City	1,007	28,705	San Francisco	San Francisco*	46	739,426
El Dorado	Placerville	1,715	176,841	San Joaquin	Stockton	1,415	664,116
Fresno	Fresno	5,978	877,584	San Luis Obispo	San Luis Obispo	3,308	255,478
Glenn	Willows	1,319	27,759	San Mateo	Redwood City	447	699,610
Humboldt	Eureka	3,579	128,376	Santa Barbara	Santa Barbara	2,748	400,762
Imperial	El Centro	4,173	155,823	Santa Clara	San Jose	1,293	1,699,052
Inyo	Independence	10,223	18,156	Santa Cruz	Santa Cruz	446	249,666
Kern	Bakersfield	8,130	756,825	Shasta	Redding	3,786	179,904
Kings	Hanford	1,392	143,420	Sierra	Downieville	959	3,434
Lake	Lakeport	1,262	65,147	Siskiyou	Yreka	6,281	45,259
Lassen	Susanville	4,553	34,751	Solano	Fairfield	834	411,593
Los Angeles	Los Angeles	4,070	9,935,475	Sonoma	Santa Rosa	1,604	466,477
Madera	Madera	2,145	142,788	Stanislaus	Modesto	1,506	505,505
Marin	San Rafael	523	246,960	Sutter	Yuba City	602	88,876
Mariposa	Mariposa	1,456	18,069	Tehama	Red Bluff	2,953	61,197
Mendocino	Ukiah	3,512	88,161	Trinity	Weaverville	3,190	13,622
Merced	Merced	1,944	241,706	Tulare	Visalia	4,808	410,874
Modoc	Alturas	4,064	9,524	Tuolumne	Sonora	2,234	59,380
Mono	Bridgeport	3,019	12,509	Ventura	Ventura	1,862	796,106
Monterey	Salinas	3,303	412,104	Yolo	Woodland	1,014	184,932
Napa	Napa	744	132,764	Yuba	Marysville	640	67,153
Nevada	Nevada City	960	98,394	**TOTALS**		156,296	36,132,147
Orange	Santa Ana	798	2,988,072				

Francisco–Oakland–Fremont area, 4,153,870; metropolitan San Diego, 2,931,714; and metropolitan Sacramento, 2,016,702.

7 ETHNIC GROUPS

In 2000, California's foreign-born population numbered 8,864,255, or 26% of the state's total population, the largest percentage among the 50 states. Nearly one-third of all foreign-born persons in the United States live in California. Latin Americans account for about half of foreign-born Californians, while Asians account for another third. As of 2002, nearly four-fifths of foreign-born Californians lived in the metropolitan areas of Los Angeles (5.1 million) and San Francisco (1.9 million).

The westward movement of American settlers in the third quarter of the 19th century, followed by German, Irish, North Italian, and Italian Swiss immigrants, overshadowed but did not obliterate California's Spanish heritage. In 2000, 10,966,556 (32.4%) of the state's residents was of Hispanic or Latino origin, up from 7,688,000 (25.8%) in 1990, and more than the total for any other state. In 2004, 34.7% of the total population was of Hispanic or Latino origin. The census of 2000 recorded that the majority— 8,455,926, up from 5,322,170 in 1990—were Mexican-Americans; there were also 140,570 Puerto Ricans and 72,286 Cubans. After World War II, the Hispanic communities of Los Angeles, San Diego, and other southern California cities developed strong political organizations. Increasing numbers of Mexican-Americans have won local, state, and federal elective office, though their potential remains unrealized.

In 2000 California had the largest Asian population of any state: 3,697,513 (up from 2,846,000 in 1990), or 10.9% of the state's total population (the second-highest percentage in the nation). In 2004, the Asian population was 12.1% of the total population. In 2000 there were 116,961 Pacific Islanders (including more native Hawaiians than in any state except Hawaii). In 2004, 0.4% of the population was Native Hawaiian or other Pacific Islander. Chinese workers were first brought to California between 1849 and 1882, when the Chinese Exclusion Act was passed by Congress. In 2000 the Chinese constituted the largest group among California's Asian population, numbering 980,642, or 2.9% of the population. The nation's oldest and largest Chinatown is in San Francisco. Although Chinese-Americans, as they prospered, moved to suburban areas, the seats of the powerful nationwide and worldwide merchant and clan associations are in that city. Los Angeles also has a Chinese district.

The Japanese, spread throughout the western seaboard states, were engaged mainly in agriculture, along with fishing and small business, until their removal and internment during World War II. After the war, some continued in market gardening and other family agriculture, but most, deprived of their landholdings, entered urban occupations, including the professions; many dispersed to other regions of the country. In 2000 there were 288,854 Japanese in California, down from 353,251 in 1990.

After the Chinese, the most populous Asian group in California in 2000 was the Filipino community, with 918,678, or 2.7% of the total state population. In 2000 California also had 345,882 Koreans, 447,032 Vietnamese (up from 242,946 in 1990), 314,819 Asian Indians (up from 112,560), 55,456 Laotians, 20,571 native

Hawaiians (down from 43,418 in 1990), 37,498 Samoans, and 20,918 Guamanians.

American Indians and Alaska Natives numbered around 333,346 in 2000 (up from 242,000 in 1990), the greatest number of any state in the country. The figure for American Indians includes Indians native to California and many others coaxed to resettle there under a policy that sought to terminate tribal status. Along with the remaining indigenous tribes in California, there is also a large urban Indian population, especially in Los Angeles, which has more Indians than any other US city. Many of the urban Indians were unprepared for the new kind of life and unable to earn an adequate living; militant Indians have made dramatic, but on the whole unsuccessful, protests aimed at bettering their condition. In 2004, American Indians and Alaska Natives accounted for 1.2% of the population.

Black Americans constitute a smaller proportion of California's population than that of the nation as a whole: less than 7% in 2000. Nevertheless, California still had the fifth-largest black population, numbering 2,263,882. In 2004, 6.8% of the population was black. Considerable migration of blacks took place during World War II, when defense industries on the West Coast offered new opportunities.

8 LANGUAGES

The speakers of Russian, Spanish, and English who first came to what is now California found an amazing diversity of American Indian cultures, ranging from the Wiyot in the north to the Yokuts in the Central Valley and the Diegueño in the south, and of Indian languages, representing four great language families: Athapaskan, Penutian, Kokan-Siouan, and Aztec. Yet, except for place names such as Shasta, Napa, and Yuba, they have not lent any of their words to California speech.

As in much of the West, California English is a composite of the eastern dialects and subdialects brought by the continuing westward migration from the eastern states, first for gold and timber, then for farming, for diversified manufacture, for Hollywood, and for retirement. The interior valley is Midland-oriented, with such retained terms as *piece* (a between-meals lunch), *quarter till, barn lot* (barnyard), *dog irons* (andirons), and *snake feder and snake doctor* (dragonfly), but generally, in both northern and southern California, Northern dominates the mixture of North Midland and South Midland speech in the same communities. Northern *sick to the stomach*, for example, dominates Midland *sick at* and *sick in*, with a 46% frequency; Northern *angleworm* has 53% frequency, as compared with 21% for Midland *fishworm*; and Northern *string beans* has 80% frequency, as compared with 17% North Midland *green beans* and South Midland and Southern *snap beans*. Northern *comforter* was used by 94% of the informants interviewed in a state survey; Midland *comfort* by only 21%. Dominant is Northern /krik/ as the pronunciation of *creek*, but Midland *bucket* has a greater frequency than Northern *pail*, and the Midland /greezy/ for *greasy* is scattered throughout the state. Similarly, the distinction between the /wh/ in *wheel* and the /w/ of *weal* is lost in the use of simple /w/ in both words, and *cot* and *caught* sound alike, as do *caller* and *collar*.

There are some regional differences. San Francisco, for instance has *sody* or *soda water* for a soft drink; there the large sandwich is a *grinder*, while in Sacramento it is either a *poor Joe* or a *submarine*. Notable is the appearance of *chesterfield* (meaning sofa or davenport), found in the Bay region and from San Jose to Sacramento; this sense is common in Canada but now found nowhere else in the United States. Boonville, a village about 100 mi (160 km) north of San Francisco, is notorious for "Boontling," a local dialect contrived in the mid-19th century by Scotch-Irish settlers who wanted privacy and freedom from obscenities in their conversation. Now declining in use, Boontling has about 1,000 vocabulary replacements of usual English words, together with some unusual pronunciations and euphemisms.

As the nation's major motion picture, radio, and television entertainment center, Los Angeles has influenced English throughout the nation—even the world—by making English speakers of many dialects audible and visible and by making known new terms and new meanings. It has thus been instrumental in reducing dialectal extremes and in developing increased language awareness.

California's large foreign-language populations have posed major educational problems. In 1974, a landmark San Francisco case, *Lau v. Nichols*, brought a decision from the US Supreme Court that children who do not know English should not thereby be handicapped in school, but should receive instruction in their native tongue while learning English. California's Chacon-Moscone law required native-language instruction, but the law expired in 1987. In 1997, a federal judge ruled against an injunction that had blocked English immersion classes in Orange County. The ruling ended the bilingual education program in the school district and opened the possibility for a statewide vote in June 1998 to decide if non-English-speaking students will be permitted to learn English upon entering public schools. On 2 June 1998 California voters enacted Proposition 227, which called for students to be taught English by being submerged in English-language classrooms.

In 2000, 19,014,873 Californians, or 60.5% of the population five years old or over, reported speaking only English at home, down from 68.5% in 1990.

The following table gives selected statistics from the 2000 Census for language spoken at home by persons five years old and over.

LANGUAGE	NUMBER	PERCENT
Population 5 years and over	**31,416,629**	**100.0**
Speak only English	19,014,873	60.5
Speak a language other than English	12,401,756	39.5
Speak a language other than English	**12,401,756**	**39.5**
Spanish or Spanish Creole	8,105,505	25.8
Chinese	815,386	2.6
Tagalog	626,399	2.0
Vietnamese	407,119	1.3
Korean	298,076	0.9
Armenian	155,237	0.5
Japanese	154,633	0.5
Persian	154,321	0.5
German	141,671	0.5
French (incl. Patois, Cajun)	135,067	0.4
Russian	118,382	0.4

9 RELIGIONS

The first Roman Catholics in California were Spanish friars, who established 21 Franciscan missions from San Diego to Sonoma between 1769 and 1823. After an independent Mexican government began to secularize the missions in 1833, the American Indian population at the missions declined from about 25,000 to only about 7,000 in 1840. With the American acquisition of California in 1848, the Catholic Church was reorganized to include the archdiocese of San Francisco. The Church also maintains an archdiocese in Los Angeles.

Protestant ministers accompanied migrant miners during the gold rush, founding 32 churches in San Francisco by 1855. These early Protestants included Baptists, Congregationalists, Methodists, Presbyterians, and Episcopalians; a group of Mormons had arrived by ship via Cape Horn in 1846. The Midwesterners who began arriving in large numbers in the 1880s were mostly Protestants, who settled in southern California. By 1900, the number of known Christians in the state totaled 674,000, out of a population of nearly 1,500,000.

Small Jewish communities were established throughout California by 1861, and in 1880, the Jewish population was estimated at 18,580.

The mainstream religions did not satisfy everybody's needs, however, and in the early 20th century, many dissident sects sprang up, including such organizations as Firebrands for Jesus, the Psychosomatic Institute, the Mystical Order of Melchizedek, the Infinite Science Church, and Nothing Impossible, among many others.

Perhaps the best-known founder of a new religion was Canadian-born Aimee Semple McPherson, who preached her Foursquare Gospel during the 1920s at the Angelus Temple in Los Angeles, won a large radio audience and thousands of converts, and established 240 branches of her church throughout the state before her death in 1944. She was typical of the many charismatic preachers of new doctrines who gave—and still give—California its exotic religious flavor. The Foursquare Church national office is still located in Los Angeles. Since World War II, religions such as Zen Buddhism and Scientology have won enthusiastic followings, along with various cults devoted to self-discovery and self-actualization.

Nevertheless, the majority of religious adherents in California continue to follow traditional faiths. In 2004, there were 10,496,697 Roman Catholics in 1,070 parishes. The next largest religion is Judaism, with about 994,000 adherents in 425 congregations in 2000. In 2006, the Latter-day Saints reported a statewide membership of 761,763 adherents in 1,386 congregations; new Mormon temples were built in Redlands in 2003 and in Newport Beach in 2005. The largest Protestant churches in the state, as of 2000, include Southern Baptist, 471,119; Assembly of God, 310,522; Presbyterian Church USA, 229,918, and the United Methodist Church, 228,844. In 2000, there were 489 Buddhist, 131, Hindu, and 163 Muslim congregations in the state. About 53.9% of the population did not specify a religious affiliation.

The Church of Scientology in Los Angeles, established in 1954 by the religion's founder L. Ron Hubbard, is the religion's largest facility, which also serves as a training center for leaders. The Church of Scientology reportedly sponsors about 3,200 churches worldwide in 154 countries. There were 11 congregations in the state of California in 2006.

The Crystal Cathedral, opened in 1980 in Garden Grove, California, is the home base for the international Crystal Cathedral Ministries and the internationally televised *Hour of Power*. Dr.

Robert H. Schuller, a minister of the Reformed Church in America, presides over a congregation of over 10,000 members.

The national office of the American Druze Society is in Eagle Rock. A national headquarters for Jews for Jesus is located in San Francisco, and the national headquarters of Soka Gakkai International is in Santa Monica. The international headquarters of the Rosicrucian Fellowship is in Oceanside.

¹⁰TRANSPORTATION

California has—and for decades has had—more motor vehicles than any other state, and ranked second only to Texas in interstate highway mileage in 2004. An intricate 8,300-mi (13,400-km) network of urban interstate highways, expressways, and freeways is one of the engineering wonders of the modern world, but the traffic congestion in the state's major cities during rush hours may well be the worst in the country.

In pioneer days, the chief modes of transportation were sailing ships and horse-drawn wagons; passage by sea from New York took three months, and the overland route from Missouri was a six-week journey. The gold rush spurred development of more rapid transport. The state's first railroad, completed in 1856, was a 25-mi (40-km) line from Sacramento northeast to Folsom, in the mining country. The Central Pacific–Union Pacific transcontinental railroad, finished 13 years later, would give California a direct rail line to the eastern US. In 1876, the Southern Pacific (the successor to the Central Pacific) completed a line from Sacramento to Los Angeles and another line to Texas the following year. Other railroads took much longer to build; the coastal railroad from San Francisco to Los Angeles was not completed until 1901, and another line to Eureka was not finished until 1914. The railroads dominated transportation in the state until motor vehicles came into widespread use in the 1920s.

As of 2003, California had 7,283 rail mi (11,725 km) of track, with over 76% of all railroad right-of-ways in the state operated by Class I railroads, the Burlington Northern Santa Fe Railway and the Union Pacific. As of 2006, Amtrak passenger trains connected the state's major population centers through three east–west routes via its California Zephyr (Chicago to Oakland), Southwest Chief (Chicago to Los Angeles) and Sunset Limited (Los Angeles to Orlando/Jacksonville, Florida) trains, and by four north–south routes that linked: Sacramento with San Jose, Oakland and Auburn (Capitol Corridor); Sacramento/Oakland with Bakersfield (San Joaquins); and Los Angeles to Seattle (Coast Starlight); and ran along the coast from Paso Robles to Los Angeles and San Diego (Pacific Surfliner).

Urban transit began in San Francisco in 1861 with horse-drawn streetcars. Cable-car service was introduced in 1873. A few cable cars are still in use, mainly for the tourist trade. The 71-mi (114-km) Bay Area Rapid Transit System (BART) was completed in the 1970s, despite many mechanical problems and costly delays. BART connects San Francisco with Oakland by high-speed, computerized subway trains via a 3.6-mi (5.8-km) tunnel under San Francisco Bay and runs north–south along the San Francisco peninsula.

Public transit in the Los Angeles metropolitan area was provided by electric trolleys beginning in 1887. By the early 1930s, the Los Angeles Railway carried 70% of the city's transit passengers,

and in 1945, its trolleys transported 109 million passengers. Competition from buses, which provided greater mobility, but aggravated the city's smog and congestion problems, forced the trolleys to end service in 1961. During the late 1980s, plans were developed for a commuter rail transportation system in the Southern California region. In 1992, the first three lines of the Metrolink system began operation. By 1995, six Metrolink lines were serving the counties of Los Angeles, Orange, Riverside, San Bernardino, and Ventura.

California's extensive highway system had its beginning in the mid-19th century, when stagecoaches began hauling freight to the mining camps from San Francisco, Sacramento, and San Jose. In the early 1850s, two stagecoach lines, Adams and Wells Fargo, expanded their routes and began to carry passengers. By 1860, some 250 stagecoach companies were operating in the state. The decline of stagecoach service corresponded with the rise of the railroads. In 1910, at a time when only 36,000 motor vehicles were registered in the state, the California Highway Commission was established. Among its first acts was the issuance of $18 million in bonds for road construction, and the state's first paved highway was constructed in 1912. The number of automobiles surged to 604,000 by 1920. In 1929, about 1 of every 11 cars in the United States belonged to a Californian. Ironically in view of the state's subsequent traffic problems, the initial effect of the automobile was to disperse the population to outlying areas, thus reducing traffic congestion in the cities.

The Pasadena Freeway, the first modern expressway in California, opened in 1941. During the 1960s and 1970s, the state built a complex toll-free highway network linking most cities of more than 5,000 population, tying in with the federal highway system, and costing more than $10 billion. Local, state, and federal authorities combined spent over $9.3 billion on California highways in 1997, nearly $2 billion of that amount for maintenance. Also in 1997, federal aid to California from the Federal Highway Administration fund totaled about $2 billion.

By providing easy access to beach and mountain recreation areas, the new freeways, in combination with the favorable climate and low price of gasoline, further encouraged the use of the automobile and led to massive traffic tie-ups, contributed to the decline of public transit, and worsened the coastal cities' air-pollution problems. Los Angeles County claims more automobiles, more miles of streets, and more intersections than any other city in the United States. The greatest inducement to automobile travel in and out of San Francisco was the completion in 1936 of the 8-mi (13-km) San Francisco–Oakland Bay Bridge. The following year saw the opening of the magnificent Golden Gate Bridge, which at 4,200 ft (1,280 m) was the world's longest suspension bridge until New York's Verrazano–Narrows Bridge opened to traffic in 1964.

In 2004, California had 169,791 mi (273,363 km) of public roads. In that same year, the state registered approximately 31.501 million motor vehicles, including 19.057 million automobiles, 11.799 million trucks of all types, and some 36,000 buses. California also leads the nation in private and commercial motorcycle registrations, at around 611,000. There were 22,761,088 licensed California drivers in 2004.

The large natural harbors of San Francisco and San Diego monopolized the state's maritime trade until 1912, when Los Angeles began developing port facilities at San Pedro by building a breakwater that eventually totaled 8 mi (13 km) in length. In 1924, Los Angeles surpassed San Francisco in shipping tonnage handled and became one of the busiest ports on the Pacific coast. In 2004, the port at Long Beach handled 80.066 million tons of cargo, making it the fifth-busiest port in the United States. The port at Los Angeles handled 51.931 million tons in that same year and was the nation's 14th busiest port. Other main ports and their 2004 cargo quantities include: Richmond, 24.743 million tons; Oakland, 15.541 million tons; and San Diego, with 3.170 million tons. In 2004, California had 286 mi (460 km) of navigable inland waterways. In 2003 waterborne shipments totaled 193.378 million tons.

In 2005, California had a total of 933 public and private-use aviation-related facilities. This included 535 airports, 385 heliports, two STOLports (Short Take-Off and Landing), and 11 seaplane bases. California had seven airports that ranked among the top 50 busiest airports in the United States in 2004. The state's most active air terminal that year was Los Angeles International Airport, with a total of 28,925,341 enplanements, making it the nation's third busiest airport, behind Atlanta Hartsfield and Chicago O'Hare International. San Francisco International was the state's second busiest airport with 15,605,822 enplanements, which made it the 13th busiest in the United States. San Diego International, Metropolitan Oakland International, Norman Y. Mineta–San Jose International, Sacramento International, and John Wayne Airport–Orange County were the state's third, fourth, fifth, sixth, and seventh busiest air terminals, and the nation's 29th, 31st, 37th, 41st, and 42nd busiest air terminals, respectively that year.

11 HISTORY

The region now known as California has been populated for at least 10,000 years, and possibly far longer. Estimates of the prehistoric American Indian population have varied widely, but it is clear that California was one of the most densely populated areas north of Mexico. On the eve of European discovery, at least 300,000 Indians lived there. This large population was divided into no fewer than 105 separate tribes or nations speaking at least 100 different languages and dialects, about 70% of which were as mutually unintelligible as English and Chinese. No area of comparable size in North America, and perhaps the world, contained a greater variety of native languages and cultures than did aboriginal California.

In general, the California tribes depended for their subsistence on hunting, fishing, and gathering the abundant natural food resources. Only in a few instances, notably along the Colorado River, did the Indians engage in agriculture. Reflecting the mild climate of the area, their housing and dress were often minimal. The basic unit of political organization was the village community, consisting of several small villages, or the family unit. For the most part, these Indians were sedentary people: they occupied village sites for generations, and only rarely warred with their neighbors.

European contact with California began early in the Age of Discovery, and was a product of the two great overseas enterprises of 16th-century Europe: the search for a western passage to the East and the drive to control the riches of the New World. In 1533, Hernán Cortés, Spanish conqueror of the Aztecs, sent a naval expedition northward along the western coast of Mexico in search of new wealth. The expedition led to the discovery of Baja California (now part of Mexico), mistakenly described by the pilot of the

voyage, Fortún Jiménez, as an island. Two years later, Cortés established a settlement on the peninsula at present-day La Paz, but because Baja California seemed barren of any wealth, the project was soon abandoned. The only remaining interest in California was the search for the western mouth of the transcontinental canal—a mythical waterway the Spanish called the Strait of Anian. In 1542, Juan Rodriquez Cabrillo led a voyage of exploration up the western coast in a futile search for the strait. On 28 September, Cabrillo landed at the bay now known as San Diego, thus becoming the first European discoverer of Alta (or Upper) California.

European interest in the Californias waned in the succeeding decades, and California remained for generations beyond the periphery of European activity in the New World. Subsequent contact was limited to occasional landfalls by Manila galleons, such as those of Pedro de Unamuno (1587) and Sebastián Cermeno (1595), and the tentative explorations of Sebastián Vizcaino in 1602–03.

Spanish interest in California revived during the late 18th century, largely because Spain's imperial rivals were becoming increasingly aggressive. For strategic and defensive reasons, Spain decided to establish permanent settlements in the north. In 1769, José de Gálvez, visitor-general in New Spain, selected the president of the Franciscan missions in Baja California, Father Junipero Serra, to lead a group of missionaries on an expedition to Alta California. Accompanying Serra was a Spanish military force under Gaspar de Portolá. The Portolá-Serra expedition marks the beginning of permanent European settlement in California. Over the next half-century, the 21 missions established by the Franciscans along the Pacific coast from San Diego to San Francisco formed the core of Hispanic California. Among the prominent missions were San Diego de Alcalá (founded in 1769), San Francisco de Asis (1776), Santa Barbara (1786), and San José (1797). During most of the Spanish period, Mission San Carlos Borromeo (1770), at Carmel, was the ecclesiastical headquarters of the province, serving as the residence of the president-general of the Alta California missions.

These missions were more than just religious institutions. The principal concern of the missionaries was to convert the Indians to Christianity—a successful enterprise, if the nearly 88,000 baptisms performed during the mission period are any measure. The Franciscans also sought to bring about a rapid and thorough cultural transformation. The Indians were taught to perform a wide variety of new tasks: making bricks, tiles, pottery, shoes, saddles, wine, candles, and soap; herding horses, cattle, sheep, and goats; and planting, irrigating, and harvesting. In addition to transforming the way of life of the California Indians, the missions also reduced their number by at least 35,000. About 60% of this decline was due to the introduction of new diseases, especially diseases that were nonepidemic and sexually tranmitted.

Spain also established several military and civilian settlements in California. The four military outposts, or presidios, at San Diego (1769), Monterey (1770), San Francisco (1776), and Santa Barbara (1783) served to discourage foreign influence in the region and to contain Indian resistance. The presidio at Monterey also served as the political capital, headquarters for the provincial governors appointed in Mexico City. The first civilian settlement, or pueblo, was established at San José de Guadalupe in 1777, with 14 families from the Monterey and San Francisco presidios. The pueblo settlers, granted supplies and land by the government, were expected to provide the nearby presidios with their surplus agricultural products. The second pueblo was founded at Los Angeles (1781), and a third, Branciforte, was established near present-day Santa Cruz in 1797.

During the 40 years following the establishment of the Los Angeles pueblo, Spain did little to strengthen its outposts in Alta California. The province remained sparsely populated and isolated from other centers of Hispanic civilization. During these years, the Spanish-speaking population of 600 grew nearly fivefold, but this expansion was almost entirely due to natural increase rather than immigration.

Spanish control of California ended with the successful conclusion of the Mexican Revolution in 1821. For the next quarter-century, California was a province of the independent nation of Mexico. Although California gained a measure of self-rule with the establishment of a provincial legislature, the real authority still remained with the governor appointed in Mexico City. The most important issues in Mexican California were the secularization of the missions, the replacement of the Franciscans with parish or "secular" clergy, and the redistribution of the vast lands and herds the missions controlled. Following the secularization proclamation of Governor José Figueroa in 1834, the Mexican government authorized more than 600 rancho grants in California to Mexican citizens. The legal limit of an individual grant was 11 square leagues (about 76 sq mi/197 sq km), but many large landholding families managed to obtain multiple grants.

The rancho economy, like that of the missions, was based on the cultivation of grain and the raising of huge herds of cattle. The rancheros traded hides and tallow for manufactured goods from foreign traders along the coast. As at the missions, herding, slaughtering, hide tanning, tallow rendering, and all the manual tasks were performed by Indian laborers. By 1845, on the eve of American acquisition, the non-Indian population of the region stood at about 7,000.

During the Mexican period, California attracted a considerable minority of immigrants from the United States. Americans first came to California in the late 18th century in pursuit of the sea otter, a marine mammal whose luxurious pelts were gathered in California waters and shipped to China for sale. Later, the hide and tallow trade attracted Yankee entrepreneurs, many of whom became resident agents for American commercial firms. Beginning in 1826, with the arrival overland of Jedediah Strong Smith's party of beaver trappers, the interior of California also began to attract a growing number of Americans. The first organized group to cross the continent for the purpose of settlement in California was the Bidwell-Bartleson party of 1841. Subsequent groups of overland pioneers included the ill-fated Donner party of 1846, whose members, stranded by a snowstorm near the Sierra Nevada summit, resorted to cannibalism, which allowed 47 of the 87 travelers to survive.

Official American efforts to acquire California began during the presidency of Andrew Jackson in the 1830s, but it was not until the administration of James K. Polk that such efforts were successful. Following the American declaration of war against Mexico on 13 May 1846, US naval forces, under command of Commodores John D. Sloat and Robert F. Stockton, launched an assault along the Pacific coast, while a troop of soldiers under Stephen W. Ke-

arny crossed overland. On 13 January 1847, the Mexican forces in California surrendered. More than a year later, after protracted fighting in central Mexico, a treaty of peace was signed at Guadalupe-Hidalgo on 2 February 1848. Under the terms of the treaty, Mexico ceded California and other territories to the United States in exchange for $15 million and the assumption by the United States of some $3 million in claims by Mexican citizens.

Just nine days before the treaty was signed, James Wilson Marshall discovered gold along the American River in California. The news of the gold discovery, on 24 January 1848, soon spread around the globe, and a massive rush of people poured into the region. By the end of 1848, about 6,000 miners had obtained $10 million worth of gold. During 1849, production was two or three times as large, but the proceeds were spread among more than 40,000 miners. In 1852, the peak year of production, about $80 million in gold was mined in the state, and during the century following its discovery, the total output of California gold amounted to nearly $2 billion.

California's census population quadrupled during the 1850s, reaching nearly 380,000 by 1860, and continued to grow at a rate twice that of the nation as a whole in the 1860s and 1870s. The new population of California was remarkably diverse. The 1850 census found that nearly a quarter of all Californians were foreign-born, while only a tenth of the national population had been born abroad. In succeeding decades, the percentage of foreign-born Californians increased, rising to just under 40% during the 1860s.

One of the most serious problems facing California in the early years of the gold rush was the absence of adequate government. Miners organized more than 500 "mining districts" to regulate their affairs; in San Francisco and other cities, "vigilance committees" were formed to combat widespread robbery and arson. The US Congress, deadlocked over the slavery controversy, failed to provide any form of legal government for California from the end of the Mexican War until its admission as a state in the fall of 1850. Taking matters into their own hands, 48 delegates gathered at a constitutional convention in Monterey in September 1849 to draft a fundamental law for the state. The completed constitution contained several unique features, but most of its provisions were based on the constitutions of Iowa and New York. To the surprise of many, the convention decided by unanimous vote to exclude slavery from the state. After considerable debate, the delegates also established the present boundaries of California. Adopted on 10 October, the constitution was ratified by the voters on 13 November 1849; at the same time, Californians elected their first state officials. California soon petitioned Congress for admission as a state, having bypassed the preliminary territorial stage, and was admitted after southern objections to the creation of another free state were overcome by adoption of the stringent new Fugitive Slave Law. On 9 September 1850, President Millard Fillmore signed the admission bill, and California became the 31st state to enter the union.

The early years of statehood were marked by racial discrimination and considerable ethnic conflict. Indian and white hostilities were intense; the Indian population declined from an estimated 150,000 in 1845 to less than 30,000 by 1870. In 1850, the state legislature enacted a foreign miners' license tax, aimed at eliminating competition from Mexican and other Latin American miners.

The Chinese, who replaced the Mexicans as the state's largest foreign minority, soon became the target of a new round of discrimination. By 1852, 25,000 Chinese were in California, representing about a tenth of the state's population. The legislature enacted new taxes aimed at Chinese miners, and passed an immigration tax (soon declared unconstitutional) on Chinese immigrants.

Controversy also centered on the status of the Mexican ranchos, those vast estates created by the Mexican government that totaled more than 13 million acres (5 million hectares) by 1850. The Treaty of Guadalupe-Hidalgo had promised that property belonging to Mexicans in the ceded territories would be "inviolably protected." Nevertheless, in the early years of statehood, thousands of squatters took up residence on the rancho lands. Ultimately, about three-fourths of the original Mexican grants were confirmed by federal commissions and courts; however, the average length of time required for confirmation was 17 years. During the lengthy legal process, many of the grantees either sold parts of their grants to speculators or assigned portions to their attorneys for legal fees. By the time title was confirmed, the original grantees were often bankrupt and benefited little from the decision.

Despite the population boom during the gold rush, California remained isolated from the rest of the country until completion of the transcontinental railroad in 1869. Under terms of the Pacific Railroad Act of 1862, the Central Pacific was authorized by Congress to receive long-term federal loans and grants of land, about 12,500 acres per mi (3,100 hectares per km) of track, to build the western link of the road. The directors of the California corporation—Leland Stanford, Collis P. Huntington, Charles Crocker, and Mark Hopkins, who became known as the Big Four—exercised enormous power in the affairs of the state. Following completion of the Central Pacific, the Big Four constructed additional lines within California, as well as a second transcontinental line, the Southern Pacific, providing service from southern California to New Orleans.

To a degree unmatched anywhere in the nation, the Big Four established a monopoly of transportation in California and the Far West. Eventually the Southern Pacific, as the entire system came to be known after 1884, received from the federal government a total of 11,588,000 acres (4,690,000 hectares), making it the largest private landowner in the state. Opponents of the railroad charged that it had established not only a transportation monopoly but also a corrupt political machine and a "land monopoly" in California. Farmers in the San Joaquin Valley became involved in a protracted land dispute with the Southern Pacific, a controversy that culminated in a bloody episode in 1880, known as the Battle of Mussel Slough, in which seven men were killed. This incident, later dramatized by novelist Frank Norris in *The Octopus* (1901), threw into sharp relief the hostility between many Californians and the state's largest corporation.

In the late 19th century, California's economy became more diversified. The early dependence on gold and silver mining was overcome through the development of large-scale irrigation projects and the expansion of commercial agriculture. Southern California soon was producing more than 65% of the nation's orange crop, and more than 90% of its lemons. The population of southern California boomed in the 1880s, fueled by the success of the new citrus industry, an influx of invalids seeking a warmer climate, and a railroad rate war between the Southern Pacific and the newly completed Santa Fe. For a time, the tariff from Kansas City to Los Angeles fell to a dollar a ticket. Real estate sales in Los Angeles County alone exceeded $200 million in 1887.

During the early 20th century, California's population growth became increasingly urban. Between 1900 and 1920, the population of the San Francisco Bay area doubled, while residents of metropolitan Los Angeles increased fivefold. On 18 April 1906, San Francisco's progress was interrupted by the most devastating earthquake ever to strike California. The quake and the fires that raged for the following three days killed at least 452 people, razed the city's business section, and destroyed some 28,000 buildings. The survivors immediately set to work to rebuild the city, and completed about 20,000 new buildings within three years.

By 1920, the populations of the two urban areas were roughly equal, about 1 million each. As their population grew, the need for additional water supplies became critical, and both cities became involved in bitter "water fights" with other state interests. Around 1900, San Francisco proposed the damming of the Tuolumne River at the Hetch Hetchy Valley to form a reservoir for the city's water system. Conservationist John Muir and the Sierra Club objected strongly to the proposal, arguing that the Hetch Hetchy was as important a natural landmark as neighboring Yosemite Valley. The conservationists lost the battle, and the valley was flooded. (The dam there is named for Michael O'Shaughnessy, San Francisco's city engineer from 1912 to 1932 and the builder of many of California's water systems.) When Los Angeles began its search for new water supplies, it soon became embroiled in a long controversy over access to the waters of the Owens River. The city constructed a 250-mi (400-km) aqueduct that eventually siphoned off nearly the entire flow of the river, thus jeopardizing the agricultural development of Owens Valley. Residents of the valley dramatized their objection to the project by dynamiting sections of the completed aqueduct.

Important movements for political reform began simultaneously in San Francisco and Los Angeles in the early 20th century. Corruption in the administration of San Francisco Mayor Eugene Schmitz led to a wide-ranging public investigation and to a series of trials of political and business leaders. Meanwhile, in Los Angeles, a coalition of reformers persuaded the city to adopt a new charter with progressive features such as initiative, referendum, and recall. Progressive Republican Hiram Johnson won the governorship in 1910, and reformers gained control of both houses of the state legislature in 1911. Subsequent reform legislation established effective regulation of the railroads and other public utilities, greater governmental efficiency, female suffrage, closer regulation of public morality, and workers' compensation.

During the first half of the 20th century, California's population growth far outpaced that of the nation as a whole. The state's climate, natural beauty, and romantic reputation continued to attract many, but new economic opportunities were probably most important. In the early 1920s, major discoveries of oil were made in the Los Angeles Basin, and for several years during the decade, California ranked first among the states in production of crude oil. The population of Los Angeles County more than doubled during the decade, rising to 2,208,492 by 1930. Spurred by the availability and low price of petroleum products and by an ever expanding system of public roadways, Los Angeles also became the most thoroughly motorized and automobile-conscious city in the world. By 1925, Los Angeles had one automobile for every three persons, more than twice the national average.

Even during the 1930s, when California shared in the nationwide economic depression, hundreds of thousands of refugees streamed into the state from the dust bowl of the southern Great Plains. The film industry, which offered at least the illusion of prosperity to millions of Americans, continued to prosper during the depression. By 1940 there were more movie theaters in the United States than banks, and the films they showed were almost all California products.

Politics in the Golden State in the 1930s spawned splinter movements like the Townsend Plan and the "Ham'n' Eggs" Plan, both of which advocated cash payments for the elderly. In 1934, Socialist author Upton Sinclair won the Democratic gubernatorial nomination with a plan called End Poverty in California (EPIC), but he lost the general election to the Republican incumbent, Frank Merriam.

During World War II, the enormous expansion of military installations, shipyards, and aircraft plants attracted millions of new residents to California. The war years also saw an increase in the size and importance of ethnic minorities. By 1942, only Mexico City had a larger urban Mexican population than Los Angeles. During the war, more than 93,000 Japanese-Americans in California—most of whom were US citizens and American born—were interned in "relocation centers" throughout the Far West.

California continued to grow rapidly during the postwar period, as agricultural, aerospace, and service industries provided new economic opportunities. Politics in the state were influenced by international tensions, and the California legislature expanded the activities of its Fact-Finding Committee on Un-American Activities. The University of California became embroiled in a loyalty-oath controversy, culminating in the dismissal in 1950 of 32 professors who refused to sign an anticommunist pledge. Blacklisting became common in the film industry. The early 1950s saw the rise to the US vice presidency of Richard Nixon, whose early campaigns capitalized on fears of communist subversion.

In 1958 Congress decided that some Native American tribes could no longer be considered as such; the move denied these groups—38 of them in California—federal benefits. More than 40 years later, one group, the Miwok, sought to regain official status. Calling themselves the Federated Indians of the Graton Rancheria, the 360 remaining members aimed to restore their culture and heritage. Promising a no-gambling policy, the federation was recognized in 1999 by the US House of Representatives, which said it was righting a wrong. If the bill were approved by the Senate, the tribe would receive health, education, and economic benefits. They could also reclaim tribal lands in northern California, as long as there were no adverse claims to the property.

At the beginning of 1963, California (according to census estimates) became the nation's most populous state; its population continued to increase at a rate of 1,000 net migrants a day through the middle of the decade. By 1970, however, California's growth rate had slowed considerably. During the 1960s, the state was beset by a number of serious problems that apparently discouraged would-be immigrants. Economic opportunity gave way to recessions and high unemployment. Such rapid-growth industries as aerospace experienced a rapid decline in the late 1960s and early 1970s. Pollution of air and water called into question the quality of the California environment. The traditional romantic image of California was overshadowed by reports of mass murders, bizarre religious cults, extremist social and political movements, and racial and campus unrest. Nevertheless, the state's population has continued to grow. According to government figures, California had a population of 31.6 million in 1995, making it the most populous state in the nation. By 2000, its population was estimated at 33.8 million, and officials believed the state would retain its status of most populated through the year 2025.

The political importance of California's preeminence in population can be measured in the size of its congressional delegation and electoral votes. Defeated in his quest for the presidency in 1960, former vice president Nixon in 1968 became the first native Californian to win election to the nation's highest office. Both Ronald Reagan, governor of the state from 1967 to 1975, and Edmund G. Brown Jr., elected governor in 1974 and reelected in 1978, were active candidates for the US presidency in 1980. Reagan was the Republican presidential winner that year and in 1984.

Assisted by the Reagan administration's military buildup, which invested billions of dollars into California manufacturers of bombers, missiles, and spacecraft as well as into its military bases, the California economy rebounded in the early and mid-1980s, bringing increases in total output, personal income, and employment which surpassed the national average. By the late 1980s and early 1990s, however, a recession and cuts in military spending, combined with existing burdens of expensive commercial and residential real estate, strict environmental regulations, and the effects of a savings and loan scandal, produced a dramatic economic decline. In 1992, the state's unemployment rate climbed to 10.1%. Jobs in the California aerospace and manufacturing sector dropped by 24%. For the first time in the state's history, substantial numbers of Californians migrated—over a million left between 1991 and 1994. Although such factors as air pollution, traffic congestion, and earthquakes were cited as reasons for this exodus, research has shown that most left in search of better job opportunities.

California's economic woes were matched by civil disorders. In 1991, an onlooker released a seven-minute videotape showing a group of police officers beating Rodney King, a black motorist, with nightsticks. The driver had pulled over after giving chase. In a jury trial which took place in a mostly white suburb northwest of Los Angeles, four police officers who had been charged with unnecessary brutality were acquitted. The verdict set off riots in South Central Los Angeles, killing 60 people and causing an estimated $1 billion in property damage.

In the late 1980s and early 1990s, California was also hit by two severe earthquakes. The first, which struck the San Francisco area in 1989, measured 7.1 on the Richter scale. The quake caused the collapse of buildings, bridges, and roadways, including the upper level of Interstate Highway 880 in Oakland and a 30-ft section of the Bay Bridge. As many as 270 people were killed and 100,000 houses were damaged. The quake caused $5–7 billion worth of property damage. In 1994, an earthquake measuring 6.7 on the Richter scale occurred 20 mi northwest of downtown Los Angeles. Three major overpasses ruptured and 680,000 people were left without electricity. The quake produced $13–20 million in property damage.

In 1994, anger over illegal immigration led to passage of Proposition 187, which would bar illegal aliens from welfare, education, and nonemergency health services. The measure was approved by a 59 to 41% margin. Passage of the measure prompted immediate challenges in the courts by the opposition. The following year, Governor Pete Wilson signed an executive order limiting the application of affirmative action in hiring and contracting by the state. He also approved the elimination of affirmative action in university admissions, a policy implemented by the Board of Regents and effective as of January 1997. After most of Proposition 187 was ruled unconstitutional in a US district court, in 1999 Governor Gray Davis agreed to end the legal battle over the controversial measure. The only part that survived was a provision strengthening the penalties for manufacture and use of false documents to conceal illegal immigrant status. While the governor said he was reluctant to go against the will of the majority of voters, civil rights groups had successfully challenged most of the language in the proposition. Further, by the time Davis agreed to stop defending the measure, federal laws had accomplished much of the intent of Proposition 187. All states were by then required to deny welfare benefits and all health benefits (except emergency care) to anyone who could not verify their presence in the United States was legal.

In November 1996, the California Civil Rights Initiative (Proposition 209) passed with 55% of the vote, banning the use of racial and sex-based preferences in state-run affirmative action programs. Three weeks later, a federal judge blocked the enforcement of the initiative, claiming that it might be unconstitutional. In April 1997, however, a federal appeals court upheld the constitutionality of Proposition 209.

In mid-2000, Governor Gray Davis signed the state's $99.4-billion budget, which included a $1.35 billion education reform program. The state's goals for its school system included recruiting 300,000 new teachers by 2010, retaining and rewarding good teachers, placing computers and Internet connections in classrooms, and raising student achievement by awarding state-funded college scholarships to top students. The package was considered one of the most comprehensive education reform plans in the nation.

Some observers believed California's biggest struggle in the 21st century would be over water. In 2000, California and six other states were on the verge of a historic agreement that would give Southern California a 15-year deadline to cut its use of the Colorado River. Municipalities began discussing ways to turn waste water into drinking water. In June Governor Gray Davis, Secretary of the Interior Bruce Babbitt, and Senator Dianne Feinstein announced the CALFED Bay-Delta Program, calling it an "unprecedented effort" between state and federal governments, local agencies, the public, and private businesses to build a framework for managing water. Highlights of the plan included multimillion dollar investments in ecosystem restoration projects, projects to increase water-storage capacity, loan and grant programs for agricultural and urban water use efficiency, water-recycling capitol improvement projects, and improving water supply reliability through integration of storage, conveyance, water-use efficiency, water quality, and water transfer programs.

Beginning in 2000, California experienced an energy crisis that saw electricity prices spike to their highest levels in 2001. Prices went from $12 per megawatt hour in 1998 to $200 in December 2000 and $250 in January 2001, and at times a megawatt hour cost $1000. A series of rolling blackouts in various areas occurred during 2001. California subsequently signed $40 billion in long-term power contracts, which were seen as assuring the state's power supply at reasonable rates, but after the crisis, when electricity rates fell, they proved to be very costly. Governor Davis pledged to fight the energy companies accused of profiting from the crisis, including the Enron Corporation, and in March 2003, the Federal Energy Regulatory Commission issued a ruling that companies would have to pay $3.3 billion in refunds for gaming the state's energy markets. California claimed it was owed $9 billion in refunds.

Gray Davis was reelected governor in 2002, but by 2003, his popularity ratings had dropped dramatically, due in part to the state's $38 billion budget deficit and the 2000–01 energy crisis, and a gubernatorial recall election was approved for 7 October 2003. One hundred thirty-five candidates were certified as candidates in the election, including Hollywood movie star and political novice Arnold Schwarzenegger. Lieutenant Governor Cruz Bustamante, although indicating Davis should stay in office, was running in the election in order to give voters the choice of voting for a strong Democratic candidate. In the first gubernatorial recall in California history, and only the second in US history, Davis was recalled with 55.4% of the vote in favor of the recall. Although dogged by charges of sexual harassment, Republican Arnold Schwarzenegger was elected to replace him.

Once he came to office, Schwarzenegger repealed an unpopular increase in vehicle license fees, and took steps to easing the state's budget woes. He proposed floating $15 in bonds, urged passage of a constitutional amendment to limit state spending, and promised an overhaul of workers' compensation. In a March 2004 election, Proposition 57, authorizing the $15 billion bond sale, and Proposition 58, mandating balanced budgets, overwhelmingly passed with 63.3% and 71% in favor, respectively. In April 2004, Schwarzenegger signed a workers' compensation reform bill into law. In September 2005, Schwarzenegger announced he would run for reelection.

12 STATE GOVERNMENT

The first state constitution, adopted in 1849, outlawed slavery and was unique in granting property rights to married women in their own name. A new constitution, drafted in 1878 and ratified the following year, sought to curb legislative abuses—even going so far as to make lobbying a felony—and provided for a more equitable system of taxation, stricter regulation of the railroads, and an eight-hour workday. Of the 152 delegates to the 1878 constitutional convention, only two were natives of California, and 35 were foreign born; no Spanish-speaking persons or Indians were included. This second constitution, as amended, is the basic document of state government today.

In April 1994 the California Constitutional Revision Commission was appointed to make recommendations to the governor and legislature for constitutional revisions affecting budget process, governmental structure, local government duties, and other areas. The Commission made its final report in 1996, on schedule. As of January 2005, the California constitution had been amended 513 times.

The California legislature consists of a 40-member Senate and an 80-member assembly. Senators are elected to four-year terms, half of them every two years, and assembly members are elected to two-year terms. As a result of a 1972 constitutional amendment, the legislature meets in a continuous two-year session, thus eliminating the need to reintroduce or reprint bills proposed in the first year of the biennium. Each session begins with an organizational meeting in December of even-numbered years; then, following a brief recess, the legislature reconvenes on the first Monday in January (of the odd-numbered year) and continues in session until 30 November of the next even-numbered year. Members of the Senate and assembly must be over 18 years old, and must have been US citizens and residents of the state for at least three years and residents of the districts they represent for at least one year prior to election. Legislative salaries in 2004 were $99,000 annually, unchanged from 1999.

Bills, which may be introduced by either house, are referred to committees, and must be read before each house three times. Legislation must be approved by an absolute majority vote of each house, except for appropriations bills, certain urgent measures, and proposed constitutional amendments, which require a two-thirds vote for passage. Gubernatorial vetoes may be overridden by two-thirds vote of the elected members in both houses. In the 1973/74 session, the legislature overrode a veto for the first time since 1946, but overrides have since become more common.

Constitutional amendments and proposed legislation may also be placed on the ballot through the initiative procedure. For a constitutional amendment, petitions must be signed by at least 8% of the number of voters who took part in the last gubernatorial election; for statutory measures, 5%. In each case, a simple majority vote at the next general election is required for passage.

Officials elected statewide include the governor and lieutenant governor (who run separately), secretary of state, attorney general, controller, treasurer, and superintendent of public instruction. Each serves a four-year term, without limitation. As chief executive officer of the state, the governor is responsible for the state's policies and programs, appoints department heads and members of state boards and commissions, serves as commander in chief of the California National Guard, may declare states of emergency, and may grant executive clemency to convicted criminals. In general, if the governor fails to sign or veto a bill within 12 days (excluding Saturdays, Sundays, and holidays), it becomes law. A candidate for governor must be at least 18 years old, a five-year citizen of the United States, and a five-year resident of California. The governor is limited to a maximum of two consecutive terms. The governor's annual salary as of December 2004 was $175,000.

The lieutenant governor acts as president of the Senate and may assume the duties of the governor in case of the latter's death, resignation, impeachment, inability to discharge the duties of the office, or absence from the state. To vote in California, one must be a US citizen, at least 18 years old, and a resident of the state. Restrictions apply to convicted felons and those declared mentally incompetent by the court.

California Presidential Vote by Political Parties, 1948–2004

YEAR	ELECTORAL VOTE	CALIFORNIA WINNER	DEMOCRAT	REPUBLICAN	STATES' RIGHTS	PROGRESSIVE	SOCIALIST	PROHIBITION
1948	25	*Truman (D)	1,913,134	1,895,269	1,228	190,381	3,459	16,926
					CONSTITUTION		SOC. LABOR	
1952	32	*Eisenhower (R)	2,197,548	2,897,310	3,504	24,692	273	16,117
1956	32	*Eisenhower (R)	2,420,135	3,027,668	6,087	—	300	11,119
1960	32	Nixon (R)	3,224,099	3,259,722	—	—	1,051	21,706
1964	40	*Johnson (D)	4,171,877	2,879,108	—	—	489	—
					AMERICAN IND.		PEACE AND FREEDOM	
1968	40	*Nixon (R)	3,244,318	3,467,664	487,270	—	27,707	—
						AMERICAN	PEOPLE'S	LIBERTARIAN
1972	45	*Nixon (R)	3,475,847	4,602,096	—	232,554	55,167	980
						COMMUNIST		
1976	45	Ford (R)	3,742,284	3,882,244	51,096	12,766	41,731	56,388
						CITIZENS	PEACE AND FREEDOM	
1980	45	*Reagan (R)	3,039,532	4,444,044	—	9,687	60,059	17,797
1984	47	*Reagan (R)	3,922,519	5,467,009	39,265	NEW ALLIANCE	26,297	49,951
1988	47	*Bush (R)	4,702,233	5,054,917	27,818	31,181	—	70,105
						IND. (Perot)		
1992	54	*Clinton (D)	5,121,325	3,630,574	12,711	2,296,006	18,597	48,139
							GREEN (Nader)	
1996	54	*Clinton (D)	5,119,835	3,828,380	—	697,847	237,016	73,600
					REFORM			
2000	54	Gore (D)	5,861,293	4,567,429	44,987		418,707	45,520
					AMERICAN IND. (Peroutka)	PEACE AND FREEDOM (Peltier)	GREEN (Cobb)	
2004	55	Kerry (D)	6,745,485	5,509,826	26,645	27,607	40,771	50,165

*Won US presidential election.

13 POLITICAL PARTIES

As the state with the largest number of US representatives (53 in 2005) and electoral votes (55 in 2004), California plays a key role in national and presidential politics. In 2004 there were 16,557,000 registered voters; an estimated 44% were Democratic, 35% Republican, and 21% unaffiliated or members of other parties.

In 1851, the year after California entered the Union, the state Democratic Party was organized. But the party soon split into a pro-South faction, led by US Senator William Gwin, and a pro-North wing, headed by David Broderick. A political leader in San Francisco, Broderick became a US senator in 1857 but was killed in a duel by a Gwin stalwart two years later. This violent factionalism helped switch Democratic votes to the new Republican Party in the election of 1860, giving California's four electoral votes to Abraham Lincoln. This defeat, followed by the Civil War, demolished Senator Gwin's Democratic faction, and he fled to exile in Mexico.

The Republican party itself split into liberal and conservative wings in the early 1900s. Progressive Republicans formed the Lincoln-Roosevelt League to espouse political reforms, and succeeded in nominating and electing Hiram Johnson as governor on the Republican ticket in 1910. The following year, the legislature approved 23 constitutional amendments, including the initiative, referendum, recall, and other reform measures. Johnson won reelection on a Progressive Party line in 1915. After Johnson's election to the US Senate in 1916, Republicans (both liberal and conservative) controlled the state House uninterruptedly for 22 years, from 1917 to 1939. Democratic fortunes sank so low that in 1924 the party's presidential candidate, John W. Davis, got only 8% of the state's votes, leading humorist Will Rogers to quip, "I don't belong to any organized political party—I am a California Democrat." An important factor in the Progressive Republicans' success was the cross-filing system, in effect from 1913 to 1959, which blurred party lines by permitting candidates to appear on the primary ballots of several parties. This favored such Republican moderates as Earl Warren, who won an unprecedented three terms as governor—in 1946, he won both Republican and Democratic party primaries—before being elevated to US chief justice in 1953.

Political third parties have had remarkable success in California since the secretive anti-foreign, anti-Catholic Native American Party (called the Know-Nothings because party members were instructed to say they "knew nothing" when asked what they stood for) elected one of their leaders, J. Neely Johnson, as governor in 1855. The Workingmen's Party of California, as much anti-Chinese as it was antimonopolist and prolabor, managed to elect about one-third of the delegates to the 1878 constitutional convention. The most impressive third-party triumph came in 1912, when the Progressive Party's presidential candidate, Theodore Roosevelt, and vice presidential nominee, Governor Hiram Johnson, defeated both the Republican and Democratic candidates among state voters. The Socialist Party also attracted support in the early 20th century. In 1910, more than 12% of the vote went to the Socialist candidate for governor, J. Stitt Wilson. Two years later, Socialist congressional nominees in the state won 18% of the vote, and a Socialist assemblyman was elected from Los Angeles. In 1914, two Socialist assemblymen and one state senator were elected. During the depression year of 1934, the Socialist Party

leader and author Upton Sinclair won the Democratic nomination for governor on his End Poverty In California program and received nearly a million votes, while losing to Republican Frank Merriam. Nonparty political movements have also won followings: several southern California congressmen were members of the ultraconservative John Birch Society during the 1960s, and in 1980 the Grand Dragon of the Ku Klux Klan won the Democratic Party nomination for a US House seat. Even when they lost decisively, third parties have won enough votes to affect the outcome of elections. In 1968, for example, George Wallace's American Independent Party received 487,270 votes, while Republican presidential candidate Richard Nixon topped Democrat Hubert Humphrey by only 223,346. In 1992, Ross Perot picked up 20.6% of the vote. In 2000, Green Party candidate Ralph Nader won 4% of the vote, or 405,722 votes.

Even with a historic advantage in voter registration, however, the Democrats managed to carry California in presidential elections only three times between 1948 and 1992, and to elect only two governors—Edmund G. "Pat" Brown (in 1958 and 1962) and his son, Edmund G. "Jerry" Brown Jr. (in 1974 and 1978)—during the same period. Three times Californians gave their electoral votes to a California Republican, Richard Nixon, though they turned down his bid for governor in 1962. They elected one former film actor, Republican George Murphy, as US senator in 1964, and another, Republican Ronald Reagan, as governor in 1966 and 1970 and as president in 1980 and 1984. Democratic nominee Bill Clinton garnered 51% of the popular vote in 1996, while Republican Bob Dole received 38% and Independent Ross Perot picked up just under 7%. In the 2000 presidential election, Democrat Al Gore carried the state, with 54% of the vote to George W. Bush's 42%; in 2004, Democrat John Kerry won 54.6% of the California vote to incumbent president George W. Bush's 44.3%. (Bush won on the national level.) In 1998, Democrat Gray Davis, formerly lieutenant governor, was elected to be the state's 37th governor by 58% of voters. He won reelection in 2002, but was recalled in October 2003, the second governor to be recalled in US history. An electricity crisis in 2001 and a massive state budget deficit in 2003 contributed to his recall. He was succeeded by Republican Arnold Schwarzenegger.

Both US senators in 2005 were women: Democrat Barbara Boxer, who won reelection to a third term in 2004; and Dianne Feinstein, elected in 1992 to replace Senator Pete Wilson (who was elected governor in 1990) and reelected in 1994 to serve her first full (six-year) term. She was reelected once again in 2000, with 56% of the vote. California's delegation of US representatives to the 109th Congress (2005–06) consisted of 33 Democrats and 20 Republicans. Democrat Nancy Pelosi was elected House Minority Leader in 2003. After 2004 elections, the Democrats kept control of the state Senate (25–15) and House (48–32).

Minority groups of all types are represented in California politics. In mid-2003, there were 31 women, 24 Latino members, and 6 black members in the state legislature. Two of the most prominent black elected officials include Los Angeles Mayor Thomas Bradley, who served from 1973–90, and San Francisco Mayor Willie L. Brown Jr., who began his first term in 1996 and won reelection in 1999. Organized groups of avowed homosexuals began to play an important political role in San Francisco during the 1970s.

14 LOCAL GOVERNMENT

As of 2005, California had 58 counties, 475 municipal governments, 2,830 special districts, and 985 public school districts. County government is administered by an elected board of supervisors, which also exercises jurisdiction over unincorporated towns within the county. Government operations are administered by several elected officials, the number varying according to the population of the county. Most counties have a district attorney, assessor, treasurer–tax collector, superintendent of schools, sheriff, and coroner. Larger counties may also have an elected planning director, public defender, public works director, purchasing agent, and social welfare services director.

Municipalities are governed under the mayor-council, council-manager, or commission system. Most large cities are run by councils of from 5 to 15 members, elected to four-year terms, the councils being responsible for taxes, public improvements, and the budget. An elected mayor supervises city departments and appoints most city officials. Other elected officials usually include the city attorney, treasurer, and assessor. Los Angeles and San Francisco have the mayor-council form of government, but in San Francisco, the city and county governments are consolidated under an elected board of supervisors, and the mayor appoints a manager who has substantial authority. San Diego and San Jose each have an elected mayor and city manager chosen by an elected city council.

The state's direct primary law had a salutary effect on local politics by helping end the power of political machines in the large cities. In 1910, Los Angeles voters adopted the nonpartisan primary and overthrew the corrupt rule of Mayor A. C. Harper in favor of reformer George Alexander. At the same time, voters were revolting against bossism and corruption in San Francisco, Sacramento, Oakland, and other cities.

In 2005, local government accounted for about 1,384,276 full-time (or equivalent) employment positions.

15 STATE SERVICES

To address the continuing threat of terrorism and to work with the federal Department of Homeland Security, homeland security in California operates under executive order; a Homeland Security Director is appointed to oversee the state's homeland security activities, which include enhanced highway patrol operations and the California Anti-Terrorism Information Center.

In accordance with the Political Reform Act of 1974, the Fair Political Practices Commission investigates political campaign irregularities, regulates lobbyists, and enforces full disclosure of political contributions and public officials' assets and income.

Educational services are provided by the Department of Education, which administers the public school system. The department, which is headed by the superintendent of public instruction, also regulates special schools for blind, deaf, and disabled children. The University of California system is governed by a board of regents headed by the governor.

Transportation services are under the direction of the California Department of Transportation (CALTRANS), which oversees mass transit lines, highways, and airports. Intrastate rate regulation of pipelines, railroads, buses, trucks, airlines, and waterborne transportation is the responsibility of the Public Utilities Commission, which also regulates gas, electric, telephone, water, sewer, and steam-heat utilities. The Department of Motor Vehicles licenses drivers, road vehicles, automotive dealers, and boats.

Health and welfare services are provided by many state departments, most of which are part of the Health and Human Services Agency. The Department of Health Services provides health care for several millions of persons through the state's Medi-Cal program. The department's public health services include controlling infectious disease, conducting cancer research, safeguarding water quality, and protecting the public from unsafe food and drugs. The department also has licensing responsibility for hospitals, clinics, and nursing homes. Care for the mentally ill is provided through the Department of Mental Health by means of state hospitals and community outpatient clinics. Disabled people receive counseling, vocational training, and other aid through the Department of Rehabilitation. Needy families receive income maintenance aid and food stamps from the Department of Social Services. Senior citizens can get help from the Department of Aging, which allocates federal funds for the elderly. The Commission on the Status of Women reports to the legislature on women's educational and employment needs, and on statutes or practices that infringe on their rights. The Youth Authority, charged with the rehabilitation of juvenile offenders, operates training schools and conservation camps. The Department of Alcohol and Drug Programs coordinates prevention and treatment activities.

Public protection services are provided by the Army and Air National Guard, and by the Youth and Adult Correctional Agency, which maintains institutions and programs to control and treat convicted felons and narcotics addicts. The California Highway Patrol has its own separate department within the Business, Transportation and Housing Agency. This agency also includes the Department of Housing and Community Development. The State and Consumer Services Agency has jurisdiction over the Department of Consumer Affairs, the California State Teachers' Retirement System (CalSTRS), and several other state departments. A state innovation was the establishment in 1974 of the Seismic Safety Commission to plan public safety programs in connection with California's continuing earthquake problem.

Programs for the preservation and development of natural resources are centralized in the Resources Agency. State parks and recreation areas are administered by the Department of Parks. California's vital water needs are the responsibility of the Department of Water Resources. In 1975, as a result of a national oil shortage, the state established the Energy Resources Conservation and Development Commission to develop contingency plans for dealing with fuel shortages, to forecast the state's energy needs, and to coordinate programs for energy conservation (it now exists as the California Energy Commission). The Department of Conservation provides employment opportunities for young people in conservation work.

The Department of Industrial Relations has divisions dealing with fair employment practices, occupational safety and health standards, and workers' compensation. The Employment Development Department provides unemployment and disability benefits and operates job-training and work-incentive programs. The California Environmental Protection Agency (CalEPA) guards the natural environment.

16 JUDICIAL SYSTEM

California has a complex judicial system and a very large correctional system.

The state's highest court is the Supreme Court, which may review appellate court decisions and superior court cases involving the death penalty. The high court has a chief justice and six associate justices, all of whom serve 12-year terms. Justices are appointed by the governor, confirmed or disapproved by the Commission on Judicial Appointments (headed by the chief justice), and then submitted to the voters for ratification. The chief justice also chairs the Judicial Council, which seeks to expedite judicial business and to equalize judges' caseloads.

Courts of appeal, organized in six appellate districts, review decisions of superior courts and, in certain cases, of municipal and justice courts. There were 93 district appeals court judgeships in 1999. All district court judges are appointed by the governor, reviewed by the Commission on Judicial Appointments, and subject to popular election for 12-year terms.

Superior courts in each of the 58 county seats have original jurisdiction in felony, juvenile, probate, and domestic relations cases, as well as in civil cases involving more than $15,000. They also handle some tax and misdemeanor cases and appeals from lower courts. Municipal courts, located in judicial districts with populations of more than 40,000, hear misdemeanors (except those involving juveniles) and civil cases involving $15,000 or less. In districts with less than 40,000 population, justice courts have jurisdiction similar to that of municipal courts. All trial court judges are elected to six-year terms.

As of 31 December 2004, a total of 166,556 prisoners were held in California's state and federal prisons, an increase (from 164,487) of 1.3% from the previous year. As of year-end 2004, a total of 11,188 inmates were female, up 5% (from 10,656) from the year before. Among sentenced prisoners (one year or more), California had an incarceration rate of 456 per 100,000 population in 2004.

According to the Federal Bureau of Investigation, California in 2004 had a violent crime rate (murder/nonnegligent manslaughter; forcible rape; robbery; aggravated assault) of 551.8 reported incidents per 100,000 population, or a total of 198,070 reported incidents. Crimes against property (burglary; larceny/theft; and motor vehicle theft) in that same year totaled 1,227,194 reported incidents or 3,419 reported incidents per 100,000 people. California has a death penalty, which can be carried out by lethal injection or electrocution, depending upon the prisoner's request. From 1976 through 5 May 2006 the state has executed 13 persons; there were 2 executions in 2005 and 1 in 2006 (as of 5 May). As of 1 January 2006, there were 649 death row inmates, the most of any state in the nation.

In 2003, California spent $1,158,362,732 on homeland security, an average of $34 per state resident.

17 ARMED FORCES

California leads the 50 states in defense contracts received, numbers of National Guardsmen and military veterans, veterans' benefit payments, and funding for police forces.

In 2004, the US Department of Defense had 173,318 active-duty military personnel, 19,026 Reserve and National Guard personnel, and 49,870 civilian personnel in California. Army military personnel totaled 9,063; the Navy (including Marines), 130,887; and the Air Force, 30,918.

Army bases are located at Oakland and San Francisco, and naval facilities in the San Diego area. There are weapons stations at Concord and Seal Beach, and supply depots at Oakland and San Pedro. The Marine Corps training base, Camp Pendleton, is at Oceanside. The Air Force operates four main bases—Beale Air Force Base (AFB) at Marysville, home for the U-2 reconnaissance aircraft, the T-38 jet trainer, the KC-135 tanker, and the GLOBAL HAWK, the Air Force's high-altitude reconnaissance platform; Edwards AFB at Rosamond, in California's Mojave Desert, which has two unique natural resources that help make it the premier flight test facility in the world; Rogers and Rosamond dry lakebeds; Travis AFB at Fairfield, which handles more cargo and passengers than any other military air terminal in the United States and is the West Coast terminal for aeromedical evacuation aircraft returning sick or injured patients from the Pacific area; and Vandenberg AFB at Lompoc, headquarters for the 30th Space Wing, which manages Department of Defense space and missile testing, places satellites into polar orbit from the West Coast, and is also home to the Western Launch and Test Range (WLTR). There are also numerous smaller installations. In 2004, California companies were awarded $27.8 billion in defense contracts, the highest in the nation, and amounting to over 13% of the US total. Defense Department expenditures in California that year included another $15.0 billion for payroll (including retired military pay), second only to Virginia.

There were 2,310,968 veterans of US military service in California as of 2003, of whom 333,489 served in World War II; 253,834 in the Korean conflict; 707,737 during the Vietnam era; and 334,111 during 1990–2000 (in the Gulf War). US Veterans Administration spending in Californian exceeded $5.6 billion in 2004.

California's military forces consist of the Army and Air National Guard, the naval and state military reserve (militia), and the California Cadet Corps. As of 31 October 2004, the California Highway Patrol employed 7,065 full-time sworn officers.

18 MIGRATION

A majority of Californians today are migrants from other states. The first great wave of migration, beginning in 1848, brought at least 85,000 prospectors by 1850. Perhaps 20,000 of them were foreign born, mostly from Europe, Canada, Mexico, and South America, as well as a few from the Hawaiian Islands and China. Many thousands of Chinese were brought in during the latter half of the 19th century to work on farms and railroads. When Chinese immigration was banned by the US Congress in 1882, Japanese migration provided farm labor. These ambitious workers soon opened shops in the cities and bought land for small farms. By 1940, about 94,000 Japanese lived in California. During the Depression of the 1930s, approximately 350,000 migrants came to California, most of them looking for work. Many thousands of people came there during World War II to take jobs in the burgeoning war industries; after the war, some 300,000 discharged servicemen settled in the state. All told, between 1940 and 1990 California registered a net gain from migration of 12,426,000, representing well over half of its population growth during that period.

In the 1990s, California registered net losses in domestic migration, peaking with a loss of 444,186 in 1993–94. Altogether, net losses in domestic migration between 1990 and 1998 totaled 2,082,000 people. During the same period, net gains in international migration totaled 2,019,000. As of 1996, nearly 22% of all foreign immigrants in the United States were living in California, a higher proportion than in any other state. Although the 1970s brought an influx of refugees from Indochina, and, somewhat later, from Central America, the bulk of postwar foreign immigration has come from neighboring Mexico. At first, Mexicans—as many as 750,000 a year—were imported legally to supply seasonal labor for California growers. Later, hundreds of thousands, perhaps even millions, of illegal Mexican immigrants crossed the border in search of jobs and then, unless they were caught and forcibly repatriated, stayed on. Counting these state residents for census purposes is extremely difficult, since many of them are unwilling to declare themselves for fear of being identified and deported. As of 1990, California's foreign-born population was reported at 8,055,000, or 25% of the state's total. As of 1994, the number of undocumented immigrants was estimated at between 1,321 and 1,784—the most any state and close to 40% of the total number thought to be residing in the United States. As of 1998, California was the intended residence of 170,126 foreign immigrants (more than any other state and 26% of the United States total that year), of these, 62,113 were from Mexico.

Intrastate migration has followed two general patterns: rural to urban until the mid-20th century, and urban to suburban, thereafter. In particular, the percentage of blacks increased in Los Angeles, San Francisco, and San Diego between 1960 and 1970 as they settled or remained in the cities while whites moved out, into the surrounding suburbs. In the 1970s and 1980s, the percentage of blacks in Los Angeles and San Francisco decreased slightly; in San Diego, the percentage of blacks increased from 8.9% to 9.4%. By 1997, blacks represented 8.3% of the Los Angeles metropolitan population, 8.8% of the San Francisco metropolitan population, but only 6.4% of the San Diego metropolitan population, a 3% decrease from the 1980s. California's net gain from migration during 1970–80 amounted to about 1,573,000. In the 1980s, migration accounted for 54% of the net population increase, with about 2,940,000 new residents. Between 1990 and 1998, the state's overall population increased by 9.7%. In the period 2000–05, net international migration was 1,415,879 and net internal migration was -664,460, for a net gain of 751,419 people.

19 INTERGOVERNMENTAL COOPERATION

The Colorado River Board of California represents the state's interests in negotiations with the federal government and other states over utilization of Colorado River water and power resources. California also is a member of the Colorado River Crime Enforcement Compact, California-Nevada Compact for Jurisdiction on Interstate Waters, the Klamath River Compact Commission (with Oregon), and the Tahoe Regional Planning Agency (with Nevada). Regional agreements signed by the state include the Pacific States Marine Fisheries Commission, Western Interstate Commission for Higher Education, Western Interstate Corrections Compact,

and Western Interstate Energy Compact. The Arizona-California boundary accord dates from 1963. California also is a member of the Commission of the Californias, along with the State of Baja California Norte and the territory of Baja California Sur, both in Mexico. During 2005, federal grants to California amounted to $43.965 billion, the most received by any state. In 2006, California received an estimated $42.467 billion in federal grants, and an estimated $43.293 billion in 2007.

20 ECONOMY

California leads the 50 states in economic output and total personal income. In the 1960s, when it became the nation's most populous state, California also surpassed Iowa in agricultural production and New York in value added by manufacturing.

The gold rush of the mid-19th century made mining (which employed more people than any other industry in the state until 1870) the principal economic activity and gave impetus to agriculture and manufacturing. Many unsuccessful miners took up farming or went to work for the big cattle ranches and wheat growers. In the 1870s, California became the most important cattle-raising state and the second-leading wheat producer. Agriculture soon expanded into truck farming and citrus production, while new manufacturing industries began to produce ships, metal products, lumber, leather, cloth, refined sugar, flour, and other processed foods. Manufacturing outstripped both mining and agriculture to produce goods valued at $258 million by 1900, and 10 times that by 1925. Thanks to a rapidly growing workforce, industrial output continued to expand during and after both world wars, while massive irrigation projects enabled farmers to make full use of the state's rich soil and favorable climate.

By the late 1970s, one of every four California workers was employed in high-technology industry. California has long ranked first among the states in defense procurement, and in 1997, defense contracts awarded to southern California firms surpassed the combined totals of New York and Texas.

From its beginnings in the late 18th century, California's wine industry has grown to encompass more than 700 wineries, which is over 50% of all the wineries in the United States. In addition, the state accounts for approximately 95% of all US wine output, followed by New York and Ohio. California's Central Valley accounts for 75% to 80% of the state's wine output.

A highly diversified economy made California less vulnerable to the national recession of the early 1980s than most other states. During the first half of the 1980s, the state generally outperformed the national economy. In 1984, California enjoyed an estimated increase of 12.1% in personal income and a 6.1% increase in non-agricultural employment, and reduced the unemployment rate from 9.7% to an estimated 7.8%. The boom was short-lived, however. Cuts in the military budget in the late 1980s, a decline in Japanese investment, and the national recession in the early 1990s had a devastating impact on the state, particularly on southern California. Unemployment in 1992 rose to 9.1%, up from 5.1% in 1989. The aerospace and construction industries suffered disproportionately. Employment in aerospace declined 22.3% between May of 1990 and September of 1992; construction lost 20% of its jobs in the same period.

Stock market growth in the high-technology sector led California's growth during the late 1990s. The gross state product (GSP) in 1997 was approximately $1 trillion. Annual growth rates in 1998 and 1999 averaged 7.75% in 1998 and 1999, and soared to 9.6% in 2000. The national recession of 2002, however, brought the growth rate down to 2.2%. While employment in southern California continued to expand, the San Francisco Bay area, severely impacted by the decline in the high-tech manufacturing and software sectors, the bursting of the dot.com bubble in the stock market, and the collapse of the venture capital market, experienced its worst recession in 50 years. In 2002, recovery remained elusive, and in 2003, the state faced a projected $38 billion budget deficit that was the main issue in an unprecedented campaign to the recall the governor.

Total GSP in 2004 was $1.55 trillion, of which the real estate sector was the largest component, accounting for $240.370 billion, or 13.1% of GSP. This was followed by manufacturing (durable and nondurable goods) at $175.852 billion (11.3% of GSP), and by professional and technical services at $121.686 billion (7.8% of GSP). In 2004, the state had more than 3.3 million small businesses. Of the 1,077,390 firms that had employees that same year, an estimated 1,068,602 (or 99.2%) were small firms. In 2004, a total of 117,016 new businesses were formed in California, up 3.1% from 2003. However, business terminations that year totaled 143,115, up 1.9% from 2003. Business bankruptcies fell 16.7% in 2004 from the year before to 3,748. The personal bankruptcy (Chapter 7 and Chapter 13) filing rate in 2005 totaled 391 filings per 100,000 people, ranking the state 41st.

21 INCOME

In 2005 California had a gross state product (GSP) of $1,622 billion, which accounted for 13.1% of the nation's gross domestic product and placed the state first in GSP among the 50 states and the District of Columbia.

According to the Bureau of Economic Analysis, in 2004 California had a per capita personal income (PCPI) of $35,219. This ranked 12th in the United States and was 107% of the national average of $33,050. The 1994–2004 average annual growth rate of PCPI was 4.3%. California had a total personal income (TPI) of $1,262,306,032,000, which ranked first in the United States and reflected an increase of 6.6% from 2003. The 1994–2004 average annual growth rate of TPI was 5.6%. Earnings of persons employed in California increased from $939,640,136,000 in 2003 to $1,008,113,229,000 in 2004, an increase of 7.3%. The 2003–04 national change was 6.3%.

The US Census Bureau reports that the three-year average median household income for 2002–04 in 2004 dollars was $49,894, compared to a national average of $44,473. During the same period, an estimated 13.2% of the population was below the poverty line, as compared to 12.4% nationwide.

22 LABOR

California has the largest workforce in the nation and the greatest number of employed workers. During the 1970s, California's workforce also grew at a higher annual rate than that of any other state.

According to the Bureau of Labor Statistics (BLS), in April 2006 the seasonally adjusted civilian labor force in California numbered 17,735,300, with approximately 870,400 workers unemployed, yielding an unemployment rate of 4.9%, compared to the national average of 4.7% for the same period. Preliminary data for the same period placed nonfarm employment at 14,951,100. Since the beginning of the BLS data series in 1976, the highest unemployment rate recorded in California was 11%, in February 1983. The historical low was 4.7% in February 2001. Preliminary nonfarm employment data by occupation for April 2006 showed that approximately 6.1% of the labor force was employed in construction; 10% in manufacturing; 18.9% in trade, transportation, and public utilities; 6.2% in financial activities; 14.6% in professional and business services; 10.7% in education and health services; 10.1% in leisure and hospitality services; and 16.2% in government.

The labor movement in California was discredited by acts of violence during its early years. On 1 October 1910, a bomb explosion at a *Los Angeles Times* plant killed 21 workers, resulting in the conviction and imprisonment of two labor organizers a year later. Another bomb explosion, this one killing 10 persons in San Francisco on 22 July 1916, led to the conviction of two radical union leaders, Thomas Mooney and Warren Billings. The death penalty for Mooney was later commuted to life imprisonment (the same sentence Billings had received), and after evidence had been developed attesting to his innocence, he was pardoned in 1939. These violent incidents led to the state's Criminal Syndicalism Law of 1919, which forbade "labor violence" and curtailed militant labor activity for more than a decade.

Unionism revived during the depression of the 1930s. In 1934, the killing of two union picketers by San Francisco police during a strike by the International Longshoremen's Association led to a three-day general strike that paralyzed the city, and the union eventually won the demand for its own hiring halls. In Los Angeles, unions in such industries as automobiles, aircraft, rubber, and oil refining obtained bargaining rights, higher wages, and fringe benefits during and after World War II. In 1958, the California Labor Federation was organized, and labor unions have since increased both their membership and their benefits.

The US Department of Labor's Bureau of Labor Statistics reported that in 2005, a total of 2,424,000 of California's 14,687,000 employed wage and salary workers were formal members of a union. This represented 16.5% of those so employed, unchanged from 2004, and above the national average of 12%. Overall in 2005, a total of 2,610,000 workers (17.8%) in California were covered by a union or employee association contract, which included those workers who reported no union affiliation. California does not have a right-to-work law.

As of 1 March 2006, California had a state-mandated minimum wage rate of $6.75 per hour. However, the city of San Francisco has its own mandated minimum wage rate of $8.50 per hour. In 2004, women in the state accounted for 44.8% of the employed civilian labor force.

Of all working groups, migrant farm workers have been the most difficult to organize because their work is seasonal and because they are largely members of minority groups, mostly Mexicans, with few skills and limited job opportunities. During the 1960s, a Mexican American "stoop" laborer named Cesar Chavez established the National Farm Workers Association (later the United Farm Workers Organizing Committee, and now the United Farm Workers of America), which, after a long struggle, won bargaining rights from grape, lettuce, and berry growers in the San Joaquin Valley. Chavez's group was helped by a secondary boycott against these California farm products at some grocery stores throughout the United States. When his union was threatened by the rival Teamsters Union in the early 1970s, Chavez got help from the AFL-CIO and from Governor Jerry Brown, who in 1975 pushed through the state legislature a law mandating free elections so agricultural workers could determine which union they wanted to represent them. The United Farm Workers and Teamsters formally settled their jurisdictional dispute in 1977.

23 AGRICULTURE

California has led the United States in agriculture for nearly 50 years with a diverse economy of over 250 crop and livestock commodities. With only 4% of the nation's farms and 3% of the nation's farm acreage, the state accounts for over 13% of US gross cash farm receipts. Famous for its specialty crops, California produces virtually all (99% or more) of the following crops grown commercially in the United States: almonds, artichokes, avocados, clovers, dates, figs, kiwifruit, olives, persimmons, pistachios, prunes, raisins, and English walnuts. California's total cash farm receipts for 2005 amounted to $31.9 billion.

Agriculture has always thrived in California. The Spanish missions and Mexican ranchos were farming centers until the mid-19th century, when large ranches and farms began to produce cattle, grain, and cotton for the national market. Wheat was a major commodity by the 1870s, when the citrus industry was established and single-family farms in the fertile Central Valley and smaller valleys started to grow large quantities of fruits and vegetables. European settlers planted vineyards on the slopes of the Sonoma and Napa valleys, beginning California's wine industry, which today produces over 90% of US domestic wines. Around 1900, intensive irrigation transformed the dry, sandy Imperial Valley in southeastern California into a garden of abundance for specialty crops. Since World War II, corporate farming, or agribusiness, has largely replaced small single-family farms. Today, the state grows approximately 55% of all fruits and vegetables marketed in the United States.

In 2004, California devoted nearly one-third (27.7 million acres/11.2 million hectares) of its 100 million acres (40.4 million hectares) to agricultural production with 77,000 farms comprising 26.7 million acres (10.8 million hectares. Some 25% of all farmland represents crop growth, and currently 10% of all cropland uses irrigation.

Irrigation is essential for farming in California. Agriculture consumes 28% of the state's annual water supply. A major irrigation system was implemented, including the Colorado River Project, which irrigated 500,000 acres (200,000 hectares) in the Imperial Valley in 1913; the Central Valley Project, completed by 1960, which harnessed the runoff of the Sacramento River; and the Feather River Project, also in the Central Valley, which was finished during the 1970s. Largest of all is the California Water

Project, begun in 1960 and completed in 1973. During 1983, this project delivered 1.3 million acre-feet of water.

On 16 June 1980, the US Supreme Court ended 13 years of litigation by ruling that federally subsidized irrigation water in the Imperial Valley could not be limited to family farms of fewer than 160 acres (56 hectares) but must be made available to all farms regardless of size; the ruling represented a major victory for agribusiness interests.

The leading crops in 2004 (by value) included greenhouse and nursery products, grapes, and almonds. These three commodities accounted for 26% of the state's crop receipts that year. Other important crops include cotton, lettuce, hay, tomatoes, flowers and foliage, strawberries, oranges, rice, broccoli, walnuts, carrots, celery, and cantaloupe.

California was the top agricultural exporter in the United States with nearly $9.2 billion in 2004. Leading agricultural exports in 2004 included vegetables ($2.4 billion), fruits ($2.0 billion), and tree nuts ($1.7 billion). Japan accounts for more than 25% of all California agricultural exports, and the entire Pacific Rim accounts for more than half its total exports. Export markets hold the greatest potential for expanding sales of California agriculture products.

24 ANIMAL HUSBANDRY

In 2005, farm marketings from livestock and dairy products amounted to almost $8.3 billion, or 7% of the US total, second only to Texas.

In 2005 there were an estimated 5.4 million cattle and calves in California valued at $6.1 billion. There were 140,000 hogs and pigs on California farms and ranches in 2004, valued at $18.2 million. In 2003 California produced 49.7 million lb (22.6 million kg) of sheep and lambs for a gross income of $69.8 million.

In 2003, California was the leading milk producer among the 50 states, with 35.4 billion lb (16.1 billion kg) of milk produced. Milk cows, raised mainly in the southern interior, totaled 1.69 million head in the same year.

California ranked fourth among the 50 states in egg production in 2003, with an output of 5.38 billion eggs. In 2003, California produced 418.7 million lb (190.3 million kg) of turkey, which was valued at $150.7 million.

25 FISHING

The Pacific whaling industry, with its chief port at San Francisco, was important to the California economy in the 19th century, and commercial fishing is still central to the food-processing industry. In 2004, California ranked fifth in the nation in commercial fishing volume, with a catch of 378.6 million lb (172 million kg), valued at $139 million. Los Angeles ranked 17th among fishing ports (in terms of volume), with landings totaling 92.4 million lb (42 million kg).

In 2004, California accounted for 97% of US landings of chub mackerel. Salmon landings totaled 7 million lb (3.2 million kg), the fourth-largest volume in the nation, with a value of $17.7 million. The state was also second in volume of dungeness crab landings with 24.8 million lb (11.3 million kg). California was the leading state in squid catch at 87.3 million lb (40.6 million kg). In 2003, there were 364 processing and wholesale plants in the state. In 2002, the California fishing fleet numbered 2,198 boats and vessels.

Deep-sea fishing is a popular sport. World records for giant sea bass, California halibut, white catfish, and sturgeon have been set in California. There were 2,024,709 anglers licensed in the state in 2004, when recreational fishers caught an estimated 13.2 million (6 million kg) of fish.

²⁶FORESTRY

California has more forests than any other state except Alaska. Forested lands in 2003 covered 40,233,000 acres (16,282,000 hectares), 40% of the total land area.

Forests are concentrated in the northwestern part of the state and in the eastern Sierra Nevada. Commercial forestland in private hands was estimated at 17,781,000 acres (7,196,000 hectares) in 2003; an additional 18,515,000 acres (7,493,000 hectares) was US Forest Service lands, and 2,208,000 acres (893,600 hectares) was regulated by the Bureau of Land Management. In 2004, lumber production totaled 2.9 billion board feet (fifth in the United States), mostly such softwoods as fir, pine, cedar, and redwood.

About half of the state's forests are protected as national forests and state parks or recreational areas. Although stands of coast redwood trees have been preserved in national and state parks since the late 19th century, only about 46% of the original 2 million acres (800,000 hectares) of redwoods between Monterey Bay and southern Oregon remain.

Reforestation of public lands is supervised by the National Forest Service and the California Department of Forestry. In 1924–25, more than 1.5 million redwood and Douglas fir seedlings were planted in the northwestern corner of the state. During the 1930s, the Civilian Conservation Corps replanted trees along many mountain trails, and the California Conservation Corps performed reforestation work in the 1970s.

As of 2005, there were 21 national forests in California. The total area within their boundaries in California amounted to 24,430,000 acres (9,886,821 hectares), of which 85% was National Forest System land.

²⁷MINING

According to data compiled by the US Geological Survey, California was the leading state in the nation in the production, by value, of nonfuel minerals during 2004, accounting for more than 8% of the US total. The value of the nonfuel mineral commodities produced in the state during the year was valued at $3.76 billion, an increase of almost 10% from 2003. Industrial minerals accounted for nearly 99% of nonfuel mineral production, by value, with the rest supplied (in descending value) by gold, silver, and iron ore.

In 2004, California remained the only state to produce boron minerals (1.21 million metric tons, valued at $626 million) and led the nation in the production of construction sand and gravel (166 million metric tons, valued at $1.280 billion), accounting for over 13% of all US production (by volume) and nearly 19.5% by value. Construction sand and gravel also constituted California's leading nonfuel mineral, accounting for about 34% of the state's nonfuel mineral production by value. Cement (portland and masonry) was the second-leading nonfuel mineral, followed by boron minerals, crushed stone, diatomite, and soda ash. Together

these six commodities accounted for almost 94% of the state's total industrial mineral output by value. Portland cement production by California in 2004 totaled 11.9 million metric tons, with an estimated value of $1 billion.

Although gold prices rose in 2004, gold production (by recoverable content of ores) in California fell in 2004 to 3,260 kg ($43 million) from 4,270 kg ($50.1 million) in 2003 and 9,180 kg ($91.9 million) in 2002. In that same year, there were only four major operating gold mines in the state. However, all production came not from mining but from heap leaching. From 1999 through 2004, gold production in the state had fallen nearly 85%. Silver output (by recoverable content of ores) in 2004 totaled 801 kg ($172,000), down from 957 kg ($151,000) in 2003 and 3,400 kg ($506,000) in 2002. All silver production in the state was the by-product of gold production. Silver accounted for less than 1% of all metal output in California.

In 2004, California had about 1,156 mines actively producing nonfuel minerals, which employed about 11,000 people. At the beginning of 2002, the Division of Mines and Geology was renamed the California Geological Survey (CGS). The CGS grants mining permits. Among the programs it oversees are Mineral Resources and Mineral Hazards Mapping, Seismic Hazards Mapping, Timber Harvest Enforcement, and Watershed Restoration. Siting and permitting of mining operations throughout California often generate local controversies. The leading issues involve intense land-use competition and wide-ranging environmental concerns, along with the typical noise, dust, and truck-traffic issues in populated areas.

²⁸ENERGY AND POWER

California had 87 electrical power service providers, of which 35 were publicly owned and 23 were cooperatives. Of the remainder, six were investor owned, one was federally operated, and 22 were owners of independent generators that sold directly to customers. As of that same year there were 13,999,457 retail customers. Of that total, 10,788,096 received their power from investor-owned service providers. Cooperatives accounted for 14,659 customers, while publicly owned providers had 3,128,465 customers. There were 48 federal customers and 25 were independent generator or "facility" customers.

Total net summer generating capability by the state's electrical generating plants in 2003 stood at 57.850 million kW, with total production that same year, at 192.788 billion kWh. Of the total amount generated, 42.4% came from electric utilities, with the remainder coming from independent producers and combined heat and power service providers. The largest portion of all electric power generated, 91.432 billion kWh (47.4%), came from natural gas-fired plants, with hydroelectric plants in second place, at 36.370 billion kWh (18.9%), and nuclear fueled–plants in third at 35.593 billion kWh (18.5%). Other renewable power sources accounted for 12.3% of all power generated, with coal and petroleum fired plants at 1.2% each.

California utilities own and operate coal-fired power plants across the southwest. This electricity shows up as "imports" in federal accounting. California utilities buy electricity from out-of-state suppliers if it is less expensive than in-state operation.

As of 2006, California had two operating nuclear power facilities: Pacific Gas and Electric Co's Diablo Canyon nuclear power plant near San Luis Obispo; and the San Onofre facility, near San Clemente, which is operated by the Southern California Edison Co. The two facilities had a combined total of four reactors.

In 2003, retail sales of electric power in the state totaled 238.710 billion kWh, of which roughly 45.3% went to commercial businesses, 33.8% to home consumers, and 20.6% to industries.

Crude oil was discovered in Humboldt and Ventura counties as early as the 1860s with the first year of commercial production occurring in 1876. It was not until the 1920s, however, that large oil strikes were made at Huntington Beach, near Los Angeles, and at Santa Fe Springs and Signal Hill, near Long Beach. These fields added vast pools of crude oil to the state's reserves, which were further augmented in the 1930s by the discovery of large offshore oil deposits in the Long Beach area.

The state's attempts to retain rights to tideland oil reserves as far as 30 mi (48 km) offshore were denied by the US Supreme Court in 1965. State claims were thus restricted to Monterey Bay and other submerged deposits within a 3-mi (5-km) offshore limit. In 1994, however, California banned any further oil drilling in state offshore waters because of environmental concerns, high operating costs, and resource limitations.

As of 2004, California had proven crude oil reserves of 3,376 million barrels, or 16% of all proven US reserves, while output that same year averaged 656,000 barrels per day. Including federal offshore domains, the state that year ranked fourth (third excluding federal offshore) in both proven reserves and production among the 31 producing states. In 2004 California had 47,065 producing oil wells and accounted for 12% of all US production. As of 2005, the state's 21 refineries had a combined crude oil distillation capacity of 2,004,788 barrels per day.

In 2004, California had 1,272 producing natural gas and gas condensate wells. In that same year, marketed gas production (all gas produced excluding gas used for repressuring, vented and flared, and nonhydrocarbon gases removed) totaled 319.919 billion cu ft (9.08 billion cu m). As of 31 December 2004, proven reserves of dry or consumer-grade natural gas totaled 2,634 billion cu ft (7.8 billion cu m).

29 INDUSTRY

California is the nation's leading industrial state, ranking first in almost every general manufacturing category: number of establishments, number of employees, total payroll, value added by manufacture, value of shipments, and new capital spending. Specifically, California ranks among the leaders in machinery, fabricated metals, agricultural products, food processing, computers, aerospace technology, and many other industries.

With its shipyards, foundries, flour mills, and workshops, San Francisco was the state's first manufacturing center. The number of manufacturing establishments in California nearly doubled between 1899 and 1914, and the value of manufactures increased almost tenfold from 1990 to 1925. New factories for transportation equipment, primary metal products, chemicals and food products sprang up in the state during and after World War II. Second to New York State in industrial output for many years, California finally surpassed that state in most manufacturing categories in the 1972 Census of Manufacturers.

California's industrial workforce is mainly located in the two major manufacturing centers: almost three-fourths work in either the Los Angeles–Long Beach–Orange County area or the San Francisco–Oakland–San Jose area. Although the state workforce has a wide diversity of talents and products, the majority produces food, electronic and other electrical equipment, transportation equipment, apparel, and fabricated and industrial machinery.

According to the US Census Bureau's Annual Survey of Manufactures (ASM) for 2004, California's manufacturing sector covered some 21 product subsectors. The shipment value of all products manufactured in the state that same year was $388.332 billion. Of that total, computer and electronic product manufacturing accounted for the largest portion, at $78.161 billion. It was followed by food manufacturing at $49.392 billion; transportation equipment manufacturing at $38.038 billion; petroleum and coal products manufacturing at $31.399 billion; and chemical product manufacturing at $31.270 billion.

In 2004, a total of 1,440,882 people in California were employed in the state's manufacturing sector, according to the ASM. Of that total, 895,157 were production workers. In terms of total employment, the computer and electronic product manufacturing industry accounted for the largest portion of all manufacturing employees at 252,241, with 94,978 actual production workers. It was followed by food manufacturing with 155,807 employees (113,717 actual production workers); fabricated metal product manufacturing at 146,249 employees (105,686 actual production workers); transportation equipment manufacturing with 130,966 employees (72,185 actual production workers); and miscellaneous manufacturing at 107,492 employees (62,521 actual production workers).

ASM data for 2004 showed that California's manufacturing sector paid $65.248 billion in wages. Of that amount, the computer and electronic product manufacturing sector accounted for the largest share at $15.889 billion. It was followed by transportation equipment manufacturing at $7.688 billion; fabricated metal product manufacturing at $5.798 billion; food manufacturing at $5.275 billion; and miscellaneous manufacturing at $4.593 billion.

30 COMMERCE

According to the 2002 Census of Wholesale Trade, California's wholesale trade sector had sales that year totaling $655.9 billion from 58,770 establishments. Wholesalers of durable goods accounted for 34,865 establishments, followed by nondurable goods wholesalers at 20,719 and electronic markets, agents, and brokers accounting for 3,186 establishments. Sales by durable goods wholesalers in 2002 totaled $389.8 billion, while wholesalers of nondurable goods saw sales of $211.7 billion. Electronic markets, agents, and brokers in the wholesale trade industry had sales of $54.3 billion.

In the 2002 Census of Retail Trade, California was listed as having 108,941 retail establishments with sales of $359.1 billion. The leading types of retail businesses by number of establishments were: clothing and clothing accessories stores (17,067); food and beverage stores (16,145); miscellaneous store retailers (13,219); motor vehicle and motor vehicle parts dealers (11,225); and health and personal care stores (8,453). In terms of sales, motor vehicle and motor vehicle parts dealers accounted for the largest share of retail sales at $95.9 billion, followed by food and beverage stores at $60.2 billion; general merchandise stores at $46.6 billion; and building material/garden equipment and supplies dealers at $26.7 billion. A total of 1,525,113 people were employed by the retail sector in California that year.

Foreign trade is important to the California economy. In 2005, goods exported from California were valued at $116.8 billion. The state's major markets are Japan, Canada, South Korea, Mexico, the European Community, and the industrializing countries of East Asia.

Leading exports include data-processing equipment, electrical tubes and transistors, scientific equipment, measuring instruments, optical equipment, and aircraft parts and spacecraft. The state's leading agricultural export is cotton.

California's customs districts are the ports of Los Angeles, San Francisco, and San Diego. San Francisco and San Jose have been designated as federal foreign-trade zones, where imported goods may be stored duty-free for reshipment abroad, or customs duties avoided until the goods are actually marketed in the United States.

31 CONSUMER PROTECTION

Numerous California state and local government agencies protect, promote, and serve the interests of consumers.

The California Department of Consumer Affairs comprises 40 entities (nine bureaus, one program, 24 boards, 3 committees, 1 commission, 1 office, and 1 task force) that license more than 100 business and 200 professions (including automotive repair facilities, doctors and dentists, cosmetologists and contractors). These state entities establish minimum qualifications and levels of competency for licensure; license, register, or certify practitioners; investigate complaints; and discipline violators.

The California Department of Consumer Affairs also administers the Consumer Affairs Act (consumer information, education, complaints, and advocacy), the Arbitration Certification Program (auto warranty dispute resolution), and the Dispute Resolution Programs Act (funding of local dispute resolution programs). It helps carry out the Small Claims Act by publishing materials for those who administer and use the Small Claims Court, and by training small claims advisors and attorneys who serve as judges.

Other state agencies that serve consumers include the Department of Fair Employment and Housing (unlawful employment and housing discrimination), the Department of Real Estate (licensing of real estate brokers and sales agents), the Department of Corporations (licensing of personal finance companies, and a new service dedicated to combat investment fraud on the Internet), and the Department of Insurance (licensing and conduct of insurance companies).

Consumers are also assisted by a variety of state and local law enforcement agencies that enforce the state's laws on false and deceptive advertising, unfair and deceptive trade practices, unfair competition, and other laws. These agencies include the California attorney general, the district attorneys of most counties, the city attorneys of San Francisco, Los Angeles, and San Diego counties, and county consumer affairs departments.

When dealing with consumer protection issues, the state's attorney general can initiate civil and criminal proceedings; is responsible for the administration of consumer protection and education programs and the handling of consumer complaints; and has broad subpoena powers. However, the Attorney General's office cannot represent the state before state regulatory agencies. In antitrust actions, the attorney general can act on behalf of those consumers who are incapable of acting on their own; initiate damage actions on behalf of the state in state courts; and initiate criminal proceedings.

The Office of the Attorney General, the California Department of Consumer Affairs, and the Consumer Affairs Bureau of Automotive Repair are located in Sacramento. County government consumer and environmental protection offices are located in Fairfield, Fresno, Los Angeles, Martinez, Modesto, Napa, Redwood City, Salinas, San Diego, San Francisco, San Jose, San Luis Obispo, San Rafael, Santa Barbara, Santa Cruz, Ventura, and West Santana. City government offices are located in Bakersfield, Los Angeles, San Diego, and Santa Monica.

32 BANKING

In 1848, California's first financial institution, the Miners' Bank, was founded in San Francisco. Especially since 1904, when A. P. Giannini founded the Bank of Italy, now known as the Bank of America, California banks have pioneered in branch banking for families and small businesses. Today, California is among the leading states in branch banking, savings and loan associations, and credit union operations.

As of June 2005, California had 300 insured banks, savings and loans, and saving banks, plus 212 state-chartered and 353 federally chartered credit unions (CUs). Excluding the CUs, the Los Angeles–Long Beach–Santa Ana market area had 160 financial institutions in 2004 with $271.957 billion in deposits, followed by the San Francisco–Oakland–Fremont area with 85 institutions and $170.866 billion in deposits. As of June 2005, CUs accounted for 10.5% of all assets held by all financial institutions in the state, or some $107.169 billion. Banks, savings and loans, and savings banks collectively accounted for the remaining 89.5%, or $917.960 billion in assets held.

In 2004, the median net interest margin (the difference between the lower rates offered to savers and the higher rates charged on loans) for California's insured institutions stood at 4.37%, up from 4.36% in 2003.

Until 30 June 1997, the State Banking Department administered laws and regulations governing state-chartered banks, foreign banks, trust companies, issuers of payment instruments, issuers of travelers' checks, and transmitters of money abroad. On 1 July 1997, a new department began supervising all of California's depository institutions. The Department of Financial Institutions now supervises over 700 commercial banks, credit unions, industrial loan companies, savings and loans, and other licensees formerly supervised by the State Banking Department. Federally chartered financial institutions are regulated by the office of the comptroller of the Currency (banks), the office of Thrift Supervision, or the National Credit Union Administration.

³³INSURANCE

Insurance companies provide a major source of California's investment capital by means of premium payments collected from policyholders. Life insurance companies also invest heavily in real estate; in 2001, life insurance firms owned $5,101.7 billion in real estate, and held an estimated $41.8 billion in mortgage debt on California properties.

In 2004, there were 11 million individual life insurance policies in force with a total value of $1.56 trillion; total value for all categories of life insurance (individual, group, and credit) was over $2.2 trillion. The average coverage amount is $145,000 per policy holder. Death benefits paid that year totaled $5 billion.

In 2003, there were 28 life and health and 136 property and casualty companies domiciled in California. Direct premiums for property and casualty insurance amounted to $56.8 billion in 2004; the highest amount of the 50 states. That year, there were 261,693 flood insurance policies in force in the state, with a total value of $48.6 billion. Also in 2004, there were $722.3 million in direct premiums in earthquake insurance written, representing about 45% of the US total. About $44.9 billion of coverage was offered through FAIR plans, which are designed to offer coverage for some natural circumstances, such as wind and hail, in high risk areas. In California, FAIR plans include coverage for those areas prone to brush fires.

In 2004, 49% of state residents held employment-based health insurance policies, 6% held individual policies, and 25% were covered under Medicare and Medicaid; 19% of residents were uninsured. California ranks fourth in the nation for the number of uninsured residents. In 2003, employee contributions for employment-based health coverage averaged at 14% for single coverage and 25% for family coverage. The state offers an 18-month expansion for small-firm employees program in connection with the Consolidated Omnibus Budget Reconciliation Act (COBRA, 1986), a health insurance program for those who lose employment-based coverage due to termination or reduction of work hours.

In 2003, there were over 21.2 million auto insurance policies in effect for private passenger cars. Required minimum coverage includes bodily injury liability of up to $15,000 per individual and $30,000 for all persons injured, as well as property damage liability of $5,000. In 2003, the average expenditure per vehicle for insurance coverage was $821.11.

³⁴SECURITIES

California's Pacific Exchange (PCX) was founded as the San Francisco Stock and Bond Exchange in 1882. A 1957 merger with the Los Angeles Oil Exchange created the Pacific Coast Stock Exchange, which became known as the Pacific Exchange in 1999. The Pacific exchange was the first in the world to operate an electronic trading system and the first in the United States to demutualize in 1999 by establishing PCX Equities, Inc. The two trading floors of the Pacific Exchange, in Los Angeles and San Francisco, closed in 2001 and 2002 respectively. In 2003, the organization established PCX Plus, an electronic options trading. In 2005, PCX Holdings (the parent company of the Pacific Exchange and PCX Equities) was acquired by Archipelago Holdings which established the Archipelago Exchange (ArcaEx), the first all-electronic stock market

in the United States. In 2006, Archipelago Holdings was acquired by the NYSE Group, which established operations of NYSE Arca.

In 2005, there were 12,210 personal financial advisers employed in the state and 35,010 securities, commodities, and financial services sales agents. In 2004, there were over 1,730 publicly traded companies within the state, with over 856 NASDAQ companies, 203 NYSE listings, and 75 AMEX listings. In 2006, the state had 52 Fortune 500 companies; Chevron (in San Ramon) ranked first in the state and fourth in the nation with revenues of over $189 billion, followed by Hewlett-Packard (Palo Alto), McKesson (San Francisco), and Wells Fargo (San Francisco), which were all listed

California—State Government Finances

(Dollar amounts in thousands. Per capita amounts in dollars.)

	AMOUNT	PER CAPITA
Total Revenue	229,289,356	6,397.23
General revenue	154,484,882	4,310.16
Intergovernmental revenue	49,555,933	1,382.62
Taxes	85,721,483	2,391.65
General sales	26,506,911	739.55
Selective sales	7,477,277	208.62
License taxes	5,744,089	160.26
Individual income tax	36,398,983	1,015.54
Corporate income tax	6,925,916	193.23
Other taxes	2,668,307	74.45
Current charges	11,386,550	317.69
Miscellaneous general revenue	7,820,916	218.21
Utility revenue	4,367,289	121.85
Liquor store revenue	—	—
Insurance trust revenue	70,437,185	1,965.21
Total expenditure	203,814,714	5,686.48
Intergovernmental expenditure	80,132,150	2,235.71
Direct expenditure	123,682,564	3,450.77
Current operation	82,253,414	2,294.89
Capital outlay	7,542,690	210.44
Insurance benefits and repayments	27,194,376	758.73
Assistance and subsidies	2,128,418	59.38
Interest on debt	4,563,666	127.33
Exhibit: Salaries and wages	20,841,748	581.49
Total expenditure	203,814,714	5,686.48
General expenditure	171,078,543	4,773.13
Intergovernmental expenditure	80,132,150	2,235.71
Direct expenditure	90,946,393	2,537.43
General expenditures, by function:		
Education	59,777,134	1,667.80
Public welfare	46,898,712	1,308.48
Hospitals	5,168,694	144.21
Health	9,525,062	265.75
Highways	7,857,947	219.24
Police protection	1,273,619	35.53
Correction	5,875,717	163.93
Natural resources	3,626,925	101.19
Parks and recreation	811,686	22.65
Government administration	8,298,729	231.54
Interest on general debt	4,141,666	115.55
Other and unallocable	17,822,652	497.26
Utility expenditure	5,541,795	154.62
Liquor store expenditure	—	—
Insurance trust expenditure	27,194,376	758.73
Debt at end of fiscal year	102,812,905	2,868.50
Cash and security holdings	435,841,104	12,160.07

Abbreviations and symbols: – zero or rounds to zero; (NA) not available; (X) not applicable.

SOURCE: *U.S. Census Bureau, Governments Division, 2004 Survey of State Government Finances*, January 2006.

on NYSE, and Intel (Santa Clara), listed on NASDAQ. Hewlett-Packard ranked at 11th in the nation of Fortune 500 companies and McKesson ranked at 16th.

35 PUBLIC FINANCE

California has the largest state budget in the nation. The Governor's Budget is prepared by the Department of Finance (DOF) and presented by the governor to the legislature for approval. The state's fiscal year (FY) begins 1 July and ends 30 June. The Governor's Budget is the result of a process that begins more than one year before the budget becomes law. When presented to the legislature by 10 January of each year, the Governor's Budget incorporates revenue and expenditure estimates based upon the most current information available through late December. The DOF proposes adjustments to the Governor's Budget through "Finance Letters" in March. These adjustments are to update proposals made in January or to submit any new proposal of significant importance that has arisen since the fall process. By 14 May, the DOF submits revised expenditure and revenue estimates for both the current and budget years to the legislature. This revision, known as the May Revision, incorporates changes in enrollment, caseload, and population estimates. The constitution requires that the governor submit a balanced budget and it is a statutory requirement that the governor sign a balanced budget. The legislature is supposed to adopt a budget by June 15, but California law requires a two-thirds supermajority to pass the budget. California's budget process can be viewed as a casualty of California's initiative process, impeding elected officials' by reducing flexibility within the budget. Fiscal year 2006 general funds were estimated at $97.3 billion for resources and $90.3 billion for expenditures. In fiscal year 2004, federal government grants to California were $54.5 billion. For fiscal year 2007, federal funds are provided or increased for many projects, including: transportation system improvements; watershed and dam safety and improvements; to the CALFED Bay-Delta Program to address issues of water quality and supply; design and construction at Calexico, California of the Calexico West Border Station; and a US coastal tsunami detection and warning system.

36 TAXATION

In 2005, California collected $98,435 million in tax revenues or $2,724 per capita, which placed it ninth among the 50 states in per capita tax burden. The national average was $2,192 per capita. Property taxes accounted for 2.2% of the total; sales taxes, 30.4%; selective sales taxes, 7.8%; individual income taxes, 43.7%; corporate income taxes, 8.8%; and other taxes, 7.0%.

As of 1 January 2006, California had six individual income tax brackets ranging from 1.0 to 9.3%. The state taxes corporations at a flat rate of 8.84%.

In 2004, state and local property taxes amounted to $34,499,304,000, or $963 per capita. California property tax collections are slightly below average for the 50 states. Local governments collected $32,419,978,000 of the total, and the state government, $2,079,326,000.

California taxes retail sales at a rate of 6.25%. In addition to the state tax, local taxes on retail sales can reach as much as 2.65%, making for a potential total tax on retail sales of 8.90%. Food pur-

chased for consumption off-premises is tax exempt. The tax on cigarettes is 87 cents per pack, which ranks 23rd among the 50 states and the District of Columbia. California taxes gasoline at 18 cents per gallon. This is in addition to the 18.4 cents per gallon federal tax on gasoline.

According to the Tax Foundation, for every federal tax dollar sent to Washington in 2004, California citizens received only 79 cents in federal spending, down from 93 cents in 1992.

37 ECONOMIC POLICY

The California Trade and Commerce Agency was created by Governor Pete Wilson as a cabinet-level agency that consolidated the former Department of Commerce, the World Trade Commission, and the state's overseas offices. In 2001, under Governor Gray Davis, it became the Technology, Trade and Commerce Agency (TTCA). The TTCA is the state's lead agency for promoting economic development, job creation, and business retention. The agency oversees all state economic development efforts, international commerce, and tourism. Some of the array of agencies coordinated by the TTCA include the California Infrastructure and Economic Development Bank (I-Bank), which helps local governments and businesses secure capital for infrastructural and nonprofit projects; the California Export Finance Office (CEFO), which provides loan guarantees to financial institutions lending to small and medium-sized California exporters; the Small Business Loan Guarantee Program (SBLGP); and the California Financing Coordination Committee (CFCC), which consists of state and federal agencies that work together to coordinate and streamline infrastructure financing in local communities.

In fulfilling its mission to improve California's business climate, the agency works closely with domestic and international businesses, economic development corporations, chambers of commerce, regional visitor and convention bureaus, and the various permit-issuing state and municipal government agencies.

The International Trade and Investment Division is headquarters for California's international offices and the Offices of Foreign Investment, Export Finance, and Export Development. The Agency also houses the Tourism Division, and the Economic Development Division, which includes the Offices of Business Development, Small Business, Strategic Technology, Permit Assistance, Major Corporate Projects, and the California Film Commission.

California offers a broad array of state economic development incentives, including a business assistance program that offers guidance through the regulatory and permitting processes. California has a statewide network of small business development centers, and has an enterprise zone program with 39 zones offering various tax credits, deductions, and exemptions. The zones focus on rural and economically distressed areas. There are ten foreign trade zones in the state, and an Office of Foreign Investment with incentives to attract foreign companies.

Among the development projects being pursued is the State Theatrical Arts Resources (STAR) program, begun in 2001 as a continuation of the successful Film California First program of 2000. The STAR program seeks to support California's $33 billion filmmaking industry, and in 2003, the government announced the completion of eight distinctive filming locations. In 2003, the Governor introduced a Build California program aimed at expediting the construction of schools, housing, roads, and other infrastructural projects as a means of reviving the state economy. In 2002, the TTCA gave its support to a national campaign called Back on Track America which aimed at helping small businesses through the country's economic downturn. In 2003, the government announced that outstanding loans under the SBLGP, created in 1999, had surpassed $200 million. Through the Goldstrike partnership, the Office of Strategic Technology supports the growth of high technology in California. The conversion of former military bases to new manufacturing and commercial sites is also a priority of the state government. Among the development projects announced in 2003 was $10 million in low-cost state financing, arranged through the I-Bank, for Sacramento County to be used for the economic development of the former McClennan and Mather air force bases.

Although California's high cost of living may be a disincentive to doing business in the state, Governor Arnold Schwarzenegger, upon coming to office in 2003, embarked upon a billboard advertising campaign through the California Commission for Jobs and Economic Growth featuring the slogan: "Arnold Says: California Wants Your Business." The ad was placed on billboards in major metropolitan areas of competing states, including in New York's Time Square, to stave off efforts by states to lure away California companies by underlining the positive aspects of conducting business in the state. The governor's message was also readapted for a trade mission to Japan to promote the business climate on an international level.

[38] HEALTH

The infant mortality rate in October 2005 was estimated at 5 per 1,000 live births. The birth rate in 2003 was 15.2 per 1,000 population. The abortion rate stood at 31.2 per 1,000 women in 2000. In 2003, about 87.3% of pregnant woman received prenatal care beginning in the first trimester. In 2004, approximately 81% of children received routine immunizations before the age of three.

The crude death rate in 2002 was 6.7 deaths per 1,000 population. That year, the death rates for major causes of death (per 100,000 resident population) were: heart disease, 195.9; cancer, 154.2; cerebrovascular diseases, 50.2; chronic lower respiratory diseases, 36.1; and diabetes, 19.4. The mortality rate from HIV infection was 4.1 per 100,000 population. In 2004, the reported AIDS case rate was about 13 per 100,000 population. In 2002, about 54.6% of the population was considered overweight or obese. As of 2004, only about 14.8% of state residents were smokers.

In 2003, California had 370 community hospitals with about 74,300 beds. There were about 3.4 million patient admissions that year and 48 million outpatient visits. The average daily inpatient census was about 51,500 patients. The average cost per day for hospital care was $1,763. Also in 2003, there were about 1,342 certified nursing facilities in the state with 129,658 beds and an overall occupancy rate of about 83%. In 2004, it was estimated that about 70.5% of all state residents had received some type of dental care within the year. California had 261 physicians per 100,000 resident population in 2004 and 626 nurses per 100,000 in 2005. In 2004, there were a total of 26,692 dentists in the state.

In 2005, University of California at Los Angeles (UCLA) Medical Center in Los Angeles ranked 5 on the Honor Roll of Best Hospitals 2005 by *U.S. News & World Report.* In the same report, it ranked 8 in the nation for best cancer care. The University of California, San Francisco Medical Center ranked 10 on the Honor Roll. Stanford Hospital and Clinics ranked 16 on the Honor Roll and 11 for best care in heart disease and heart surgery. The Lucile Packard Children's Hospital at Stanford, Mattel Children's Hospital at UCLA, Children's Hospital Los Angeles, and University of California San Francisco Medical Center all ranked within the top 20 for best pediatric care.

Medi-Cal is a statewide program that pays for the medical care of persons who otherwise could not afford it. California has also been a leader in developing new forms of health care, including the health maintenance organization (HMO), which provides preventive care, diagnosis, and treatment for which the patient pays a fixed annual premium.

About 28% of state residents were enrolled in Medicaid programs in 2003; with this percentage, the state was tied with the District of Columbia and Tennessee at the second-highest percentage of Medicaid recipients in the country (after Maine). Approximately 19% of the state population was uninsured in 2004. In 2003, state health care expenditures totaled $38.5 million.

[39] SOCIAL WELFARE

In 2004, about 1.1 million people received unemployment benefits, with the average weekly unemployment benefit at $260. In fiscal year 2005, the estimated average monthly participation in the food stamp program included about 1,990,919 persons (785,385 households); the average monthly benefit was about $96.80 per person. That year, the total of benefits paid through the state for the food stamp program was over $2.3 billion.

Temporary Assistance for Needy Families (TANF), the system of federal welfare assistance that officially replaced Aid to Families with Dependent Children (AFDC) in 1997, was reauthorized through the Deficit Reduction Act of 2005. TANF is funded through federal block grants that are divided among the states based on an equation involving the number of recipients in each state. California's TANF program is called CALWORKS (California Work Opportunity and Responsibility to Kids). In 2004, the state program had 1,103,000 recipients; state and federal expenditures on this TANF program totaled $3.4 billion in 2003.

In December 2004, Social Security benefits were paid to 4,411,970 California residents. This number included 2,838,010 retired workers, 407,540 widows and widowers, 531,490 disabled workers, 281,740 spouses, and 352,190 children. Social Security beneficiaries represented 12.3% of the total state population and 83.9% of the state's population age 65 and older. Retired workers received an average monthly payment of $957; widows and widowers, $926; disabled workers, $910; and spouses, $459. Payments for children of retired workers averaged $450 per month; children of deceased workers, $638; and children of disabled workers, $276. Federal Supplemental Security Income payments in December 2004 went to 1,183,002 Californians, averaging $559 a month.

[40] HOUSING

The earliest homes in southern California were Spanish colonial structures renowned for their simplicity and harmony with the landscape. These houses were one-story high and rectangular in plan, with outside verandas supported by wooden posts; their thick adobe walls were covered with whitewashed mud plaster. In the north, the early homes were usually two stories high, with thick adobe walls on the ground floor, balconies at the front and back, and tile roofing. Some adobe houses dating from the 1830s still stand in coastal cities and towns, particularly Monterey.

During the 1850s, jerry-built houses of wood, brick, and stone sprang up in the mining towns, and it was not until the 1870s that more substantial homes, in the Spanish mission style, were built in large numbers in the cities. About 1900, the California bungalow, with overhanging eaves and low windows, began to sweep the state and then the nation. The fusion of Spanish adobe structures and traditional American wooden construction appeared in the 1930s, and "California-style" houses gained great popularity throughout the West. Adapted from the functional international style of Frank Lloyd Wright and other innovative architects, modern domestic designs, emphasizing split-level surfaces and open interiors, won enthusiastic acceptance in California. Wright's finest California homes include the Freeman house in Los Angeles and the Millard house in Pasadena. One of Wright's disciples, Viennese-born Richard Neutra, was especially influential in adapting modern design principles to California's economy and climate.

Between 1960 and 1990, some 6.3 million houses and apartments were built in the state, comprising more than 56% of California housing stock. Housing construction boomed at record rates during the 1970s but slowed down at the beginning of the 1980s because rising building costs and high mortgage interest rates made it difficult for people of moderate means to enter the housing market. The total number of housing units in the state increased by 53% during 1940–50; 52% in 1950–60; 28% in 1960–70; 33% in 1970–80; and 20% in 1980–90.

Of the state's estimated 12,804,702 housing units in 2004, 11,972,158 were occupied; about 58.6% were owner occupied. That year, California ranked as having the most housing units among the 50 states and the District of Columbia; the state also ranked as having the third-lowest percentage of owner-occupied units. It was estimated that about 253,281 units were without telephone service, 54,412 lacked complete plumbing facilities, and 91,851 lacked complete kitchen facilities. While most homes used gas or electricity as a heating fuel, about 261,527 households relied on wood and about 9,112 employed solar heating. About 57.5% of all units were single-family, detached homes; about 11% of dwellings were in buildings with 20 or more units. The average household had 2.93 members.

California ranked first in the nation for highest home values in 2004, when the median value of a one-family home was $391,102. The median monthly cost for mortgage owners was about $1,733 while the cost for renters was at a median of about $914. In 2004, the state authorized construction of 207,400 privately owned housing units.

California housing policies have claimed national attention on several occasions. In 1964, state voters approved Proposition 14, a measure repealing the Fair Housing Act and forbidding any future restrictions on the individual's right to sell, lease, or rent to anyone of his own choosing. The measure was later declared unconstitutional by state and federal courts. In March 1980, a Los Angeles city ordinance banned rental discrimination on the basis of age. A municipal court judge had previously ruled it was illegal for a landlord to refuse to rent an apartment to a couple simply because they had children. Ordinances banning age discrimination had previously been enacted in the cities of San Francisco, Berkeley, and Davis and in Santa Monica and Santa Clara counties.

In September 2005, the state was awarded grants of over $1.3 million from the US Department of Housing and Urban Development (HUD) for rural housing and economic development programs. For 2006, HUD allocated to the state over $43 million in community development block grants.

41 EDUCATION

The history of public education in California goes back at least to the 1790s, when the governor of the Spanish colony assigned retired soldiers to open one-room schools at the Franciscan mission settlements of San Jose, Santa Barbara, San Francisco, San Diego, and Monterey. Most of these schools, and others opened during the next three decades, were short-lived, however. During the 1830s, a few more schools were established for Spanish children, including girls, who were taught needlework. Easterners and Midwesterners who came to California in the 1840s laid the foundation for the state's present school system. The first American school was opened in an old stable at the Santa Clara mission in 1846, and the following year a schoolroom was established in the Monterey customhouse. San Francisco's first school was founded in April 1848 by a Yale graduate, Thomas Douglass, but six weeks later, caught up in Gold Rush fever, he dropped his books and headed for the mines. Two years after this inauspicious beginning, the San Francisco city council passed an ordinance providing for the first free public school system in California. Although the first public high school was opened in San Francisco in 1856, the California legislature did not provide for state financial support of secondary schools until 1903.

The state's first colleges, Santa Clara College (now the Santa Clara University), founded by Jesuits, and California Wesleyan (now the University of the Pacific), located in Stockton, both opened in 1851. A year later, the Young Ladies' Seminary (now Mills College) was founded at Benicia. The nucleus of what later became the University of California was established at Oakland in 1853 and moved to nearby Berkeley in 1873. Subsequent landmarks in education were the founding of the University of Southern California (USC) at Los Angeles in 1880 and of Stanford University in 1885, the opening of the first state junior colleges in 1917, and the establishment in 1927 of the Department of Education, which supervised the vast expansion of the California school system in the years following.

In 2004, 81.3% of Californians age 25 and older were high school graduates. Some 31.7% had obtained a bachelor's degree or higher. The total enrollment for fall 2002 in California's public schools stood at 6,356,000. Of these, 4,529,000 attended schools from kindergarten through grade eight, and 1,828,000 attended high school. Approximately 32.9% of the students were white, 8.2% were black, 46.7% were Hispanic, 11.3% were Asian/Pacific Islander, and 0.8% were American Indian/Alaskan Native. Total enrollment was estimated at 6,399,000 in fall 2003 and expected to be 7,268,000 by fall 2014, an increase of 14.3% during the period 2002 to 2014. There were 623,105 students enrolled in 3,377 private schools in fall 2003. Expenditures for public education in

2003/04 were estimated at $60 billion or $7,748 per student. Since 1969, the National Assessment of Educational Progress (NAEP) has tested public school students nationwide. The resulting report, *The Nation's Report Card,* stated that in 2005 eighth graders in California scored 269 out of 500 in mathematics compared with the national average of 278.

As of fall 2002, there were 2,474,024 students enrolled in institutions of higher education; minority students comprised 51.2% of total postsecondary enrollment. As of 2005, California had 401 degree-granting institutions. The University of California has its main campus at Berkeley and branches at Davis, Irvine, Los Angeles (UCLA), Merced, Riverside, San Diego, San Francisco, Santa Barbara, and Santa Cruz. The Hastings College of Law is also part of the UC system. The California state college and university system is not be confused with the University of California. California's state universities include those at Los Angeles, Sacramento, San Diego, San Francisco, and San Jose; locations of state colleges include Bakersfield, San Bernardino, and Stanislaus. Privately endowed institutions with the largest student enrollments are the University of Southern California (USC) and Stanford University. Other independent institutions are Occidental College in Los Angeles, Mills College at Oakland, Whittier College, the Claremont consortium of colleges (including Harvey Mudd College, Pomona College, and Claremont McKenna College), and the California Institute of Technology at Pasadena. California has several Roman Catholic colleges and universities, including Loyola Marymount University of Los Angeles.

The California Student Aid Commission administers financial aid. All recipients must have been California residents for at least 12 months.

42 ARTS

The arts have always thrived in California, at first in the Franciscan chapels with their religious paintings and church music, later in the art galleries, gas-lit theaters, and opera houses of San Francisco and Los Angeles, and now in seaside artists' colonies, regional theaters, numerous concert halls, and, not least, the motion picture studios of Hollywood.

In the mid-19th century, many artists came from the East to paint Western landscapes, and some stayed on in California. The San Francisco Institute of Arts was founded in 1874; the E. B. Crocker Art Gallery was established in Sacramento in 1884; and the Monterey-Carmel artists' colony sprang up in the early years of the 20th century. Other art colonies developed later in Los Angeles, Santa Barbara, Laguna Beach, San Diego, and La Jolla. Notable art museums and galleries include the Los Angeles County Museum of Art (founded in 1910), Huntington Library, Art Gallery and Botanical Gardens at San Marino (1919), Norton Simon Museum of Art at Pasadena (1924), and the San Diego Museum of Art (1922). The San Francisco Museum of Modern Art opened in 1935 as the San Francisco Museum of Art; the word "Modern" was added to the museum's title in 1975. In 2006, the museum featured an exhibition titled "1906 Earthquake: A Disaster in Pictures," which showcased approximately 100 photographs commemorating the centennial of the San Francisco earthquake of 1906.

The theater arrived in California as early as 1846 in the form of stage shows at a Monterey amusement hall. The first theater building was opened in 1849 in Sacramento by the Eagle Theater Company. Driven out of Sacramento by floods, the company soon found refuge in San Francisco; by 1853, that city had seven theaters. During the late 19th century, many famous performers, including dancer Isadora Duncan and actress Maude Adams, began their stage careers in California. Today, California theater groups with national reputations include the Berkeley Repertory Theater, Mark Taper Forum in Los Angeles, Old Globe Theater of San Diego, and the American Conservatory Theater of San Francisco. The American Conservatory Theater (ACT) of San Francisco was founded in 1965 and opened its first season at the Geary Theater in 1967. ACT celebrated 40 years of performing during its 2006/07 season

The motion picture industry did not begin in Hollywood—the first commercial films were made in New York City and New Jersey in the 1890s—but within a few decades this Los Angeles suburb had become synonymous with the new art form. California became a haven for independent producers escaping an East Coast monopoly on patents related to filmmaking. (If patent infringements were discovered, the producer could avoid a lawsuit by crossing the border into Mexico.) In 1908, an independent producer, William Selig, completed in Los Angeles a film he had begun in Chicago, *The Count of Monte Cristo,* which is now recognized as the first commercial film produced in California. He and other moviemakers opened studios in Los Angeles, Santa Monica, Glendale, and, finally, Hollywood, where the sunshine was abundant, land was cheap, and the workforce plentiful. These independent producers developed the full-length motion picture and the star system, utilizing the talents of popular actors like Mary Pickford, Douglas Fairbanks, and Charlie Chaplin again and again. In 1915, D. W. Griffith produced the classic "silent," *The Birth of a Nation,* which was both a popular and an artistic success. Motion picture theaters sprang up all over the country, and an avalanche of motion pictures was produced in Hollywood by such increasingly powerful studios as Warner Brothers, Fox, and Metro-Goldwyn-Mayer. Hollywood became the motion picture capital of the world. By 1923, film production accounted for one-fifth of the state's annual manufacturing value; in 1930, the film industry was one of the 10 largest in the United States.

Hollywood flourished by using the latest technical innovations and by adapting itself to the times. Sound motion pictures achieved a breakthrough in 1927 with *The Jazz Singer,* starring Al Jolson; color films appeared within a few years; and Walt Disney originated the feature-length animated cartoon with *Snow White and the Seven Dwarfs* (1937). Whereas most industries suffered drastically from the depression of the 1930s, Hollywood prospered by providing, for the most part, escapist entertainment on a lavish scale. The 1930s saw the baroque spectacles of Busby Berkeley, the inspired lunacy of the Marx Brothers, and the romantic historical drama *Gone with the Wind* (1939). During World War II, Hollywood offered its vast audience patriotic themes and pro-Allied propaganda.

In the postwar period, the motion picture industry fell on hard times because of competition from television, but it recovered fairly quickly by selling its old films to television and producing new ones specifically for home viewing. In the 1960s, Hollywood replaced New York City as the main center for the production of television programs. Fewer motion pictures were made, and those that were produced were longer and more expensive, including such top box-office attractions as *The Sound of Music* (1965), *Star Wars* (1977), *E.T.—The Extra-Terrestrial* (1982), *Jurassic Park* (1993), *Independence Day* (1996), *Titanic* (1997), *Armageddon* (1998), *The Matrix Reloaded* (2003), and Stephen Spielberg's version of *War of the Worlds* (2005). No longer are stars held under exclusive contracts, and the power of the major studios has waned as the role of independent filmmakers like Francis Ford Coppola, Steven Spielberg, and George Lucas has assumed increased importance.

Among the many composers who came to Hollywood to write film music were Irving Berlin, George Gershwin, Kurt Weill, George Antheil, Ferde Grofe, Erich Korngold, and John Williams; such musical luminaries as Igor Stravinsky and Arnold Schoenberg were longtime residents of the state. Symphonic music is well established. In addition to the renowned Los Angeles Philharmonic, whose permanent conductors have included Zubin Mehta and Carlo Maria Giulini, there are the San Francisco Symphony and other professional symphonic orchestras in Oakland and San Jose. Many semiprofessional or amateur orchestras have been organized in other communities. Resident opera companies include the San Francisco Opera (1923) and the San Diego Opera. Annual musical events include the Sacramento and Monterey jazz festivals and summer concerts at the Hollywood Bowl. As of 2006, the Monterey Jazz Festival, celebrating its 49th anniversary, was noted as the longest running jazz festival in the world.

California has also played a major role in the evolution of popular music since the 1960s. The "surf sound" of the Beach Boys dominated California pop music in the mid-1960s. By 1967, the "acid rock" of bands like the Grateful Dead, Jefferson Airplane (later Jefferson Starship), and the Doors had started to gain national recognition, and that year the heralded "summer of love" in San Francisco attracted young people from throughout the country. It was at the Monterey International Pop Festival, also in 1967, that Jimi Hendrix began his rise to stardom. During the 1970s, California was strongly identified with a group of resident singer-songwriters, including Neil Young, Joni Mitchell, Randy Newman, Jackson Browne, and Warren Zevon, who brought a new sophistication to rock lyrics. Los Angeles is a main center of the popular music industry, with numerous recording studios and branch offices of the leading record companies. Los Angeles-based Motown Industries, the largest black-owned company in the United States, is a major force in popular music.

California has nurtured generations of writers, many of whom moved there from other states. In 1864, Mark Twain, a Missourian, came to California as a newspaperman. Four years later, New York–born Bret Harte published his earliest short stories, many set in mining camps, in San Francisco's *Overland Monthly*. The writer perhaps most strongly associated with California is Nobel Prize-winner John Steinbeck, a Salinas native. Hollywood's film industry has long been a magnet for writers, and San Francisco in the 1950s was the gathering place for a group, later known as the Beats (or "Beat Generation"), that included Jack Kerouac and Allen Ginsberg. The City Lights Bookshop, owned by poet Lawrence Ferlinghetti, was the site of readings by Beat poets during this period.

In 2005, the California Arts Council and other arts organizations received 303 grants totaling $8,459,000 from the National Endowment for the Arts, and California organizations received 87 grants totaling $10,903,937 from the National Endowment for the Humanities. The California Arts Council also used state financial resources to promote arts organizations. The California Council for the Humanities has offices in San Diego, San Francisco, and Los Angeles. California is also a member state of the regional Western States Arts Federation. A California law, effective 1 January 1977, was the first in the nation to provide living artists with royalties on the profitable resale of their work.

43 LIBRARIES AND MUSEUMS

For the fiscal year ending in June 2001, California had 179 public library systems, with 1,063 libraries, of which 897 were branches. The state's public library system that same year held 67,219,000 volumes of books and serial publications and had a circulation of 172,337,000. The system also had 2,734,000 audio and 2,095,000 video items, 110,000 electronic format items (CD-ROMs, magnetic tapes, and disks), and 61 bookmobiles. California has three of the largest public library systems in the nation, along with some of the country's finest private collections. In 1998, the Los Angeles Public Library System had 5,811,492 volumes; the San Francisco Public Library, 2,137,618; and the San Diego Public Library, 2,670,375. Public library operating income came to $890,188,000 in fiscal year 2001, including $3,832,000 in federal grants and $77,456,000 in state grants. While California's public libraries had the second largest income of all states, spending per capita was mediocre.

Outstanding among academic libraries is the University of California's library at Berkeley, with its Bancroft collection of Western Americana. Stanford's Hoover Institution has a notable collection of research materials on the Russian Revolution, World War I, and worldwide relief efforts thereafter. Numerous rare books, manuscripts, and documents are held in the Huntington Library in San Marino.

California has nearly 576 museums and over 50 public gardens. Outstanding museums include the California Museum of Science and Industry, Los Angeles County Museum of Art, and Natural History Museum, all in Los Angeles; the San Francisco Museum of Modern Art, Fine Arts Museums of San Francisco, and Asian Art Museum of San Francisco; the San Diego Museum of Man; the California State Indian Museum in Sacramento; the Norton Simon Museum in Pasadena; and the J. Paul Getty Museum at Malibu. Among historic sites are Sutter's Mill, northeast of Sacramento, where gold was discovered in 1848, and a restoration of the Mission of San Diego de Alcala, where in 1769 the first of California's Franciscan missions was established. San Diego has an excellent zoo, and San Francisco's Strybing Arboretum and Botanical Gardens has beautiful displays of Asian, Mediterranean, and California flora.

44 COMMUNICATIONS

Mail service in California, begun in 1851 by means of mule-drawn wagons, was soon taken over by stagecoach companies. The need for speedier delivery led to the founding in April 1860 of the Pony Express, which operated between San Francisco and Missouri. On the western end, relays of couriers picked up mail in San Francisco, carried it by boat to Sacramento, and then conveyed it on horseback to St. Joseph, Missouri, a hazardous journey of nearly

2,000 mi (3,200 km) within 10 days. The Pony Express functioned for only 16 months, however, before competition from the first transcontinental telegraph line (between San Francisco and New York) put it out of business; telegraph service between San Francisco and Los Angeles had begun a year earlier.

California was third among US households in 2004 in having telephones, with fully 96.0% of the state's occupied housing units. In addition, by June of that same year, there were 21,575,797 mobile wireless telephone subscribers. In 2003, 66.3% of California households had a computer and 59.6% had Internet access. By June 2005, there were 6,045,283 high-speed lines in California, 5,378,549 residential and 666,734 for business.

The state's first radio broadcasting station, KQW in San Jose, began broadcasting speech and music on an experimental basis in 1912. California stations pioneered in program development with the earliest audience-participation show (1922) and the first "soap opera," *One Man's Family* (1932). When motion picture stars began doubling as radio performers in the 1930s, Hollywood emerged as a center of radio network broadcasting. Similarly, Hollywood's abundant acting talent, experienced film crews, and superior production facilities enabled it to become the principal production center for television programs from the 1950s onward.

In 2005 there were 241 FM and 81 AM major radio stations and 67 major television stations. California ranks second in the United States (after Texas) in the number of commercial television stations and of radio stations.

In 1999, Los Angeles alone had 3,392,820 cable television households (65% of television-owning households); second only to the New York City area. The Sacramento-Stockton-Modesto area had 64% cable penetration of 1,19,820 television households. The San Francisco-Oakland-San Jose area had cable in 72% of its TV-owning homes, and San Diego, in 83%.

A total of 1,511,571 Internet domain names had been registered in California as of 2000, the most of any state.

45 PRESS

In 2005 there were 68 morning dailies and 23 evening dailies; 61 newspapers had Sunday editions.

The following table shows California's leading newspapers, with their 2005 circulations:

AREA	NAME	DAILY	SUNDAY
Fresno	*Fresno Bee* (m,S)	160,143	191,205
Long Beach–			
Huntington Beach	*Press-Telegram* (m,S)	96,967	109,296
Los Angeles	*Times* (m,S)	902,164	1,292,274
	Investor's Business Daily (m)	191,846	
	Daily News (m,S)	178,404	200,458
	La Opinion (Spanish, m,S)	124,990	68,965
Oakland	*Oakland Tribune* (m,S)	51,994	65,705
Orange County–			
Santa Ana	*Orange County Register* (m,S)	303,418	371,046
Riverside	*Press-Enterprise* (m,S)	182,790	186,790
Sacramento	*Sacramento Bee* (m,S)	293,705	346,742
San Diego	*San Diego Union-Tribune* (m,S)	366,740	433,973
San Francisco	*San Francisco Chronicle* (a,S)	505,022	540,314
	Examiner (e,S)	95,800	552,400
San Jose	*San Jose Mercury-News* (m,S)	263,067	298,067

Investor's Business Daily has nationwide circulation. In 2004, the *Los Angeles Times* was the fourth-largest daily newspaper in the country, based on circulation. It ranked second in the nation for Sunday circulation the same year. The San Francisco *Chronicle* had the 11th-largest daily circulation and the 16th-largest Sunday circulation in 2004. San Francisco has long been the heart of the influential Hearst newspaper chain.

In 2005, there were 305 weekly publications in California. Of these there are 123 paid weeklies, 111 free weeklies, and 71 combined weeklies. The total circulation of paid weeklies (863,732) and free weeklies (2,590,133) is 3,453,865. Among the Top Fifty Shopper Publications in the United States, California's statewide *Pennysaver* ranked first, with a circulation of 5,000,000. The Beverley Hills *Courier* ranked 11th by circulation among the combined weeklies in the United States.

In August 1846, the state's first newspaper, the *Californian*, printed (on cigarette paper—the only paper available) the news of the US declaration of war on Mexico. The *Californian* moved to San Francisco in 1847 to compete with a new weekly, the *California Star*. When gold was discovered, both papers failed to mention the fact and both soon went out of business as their readers headed for the hills. On the whole, however, the influx of gold seekers was good for the newspaper business. In 1848, the *Californian* and the *Star* were resurrected and merged into the *Alta Californian*, which two years later became the state's first daily newspaper; among subsequent contributors were Mark Twain and Bret Harte. Four years later there were 57 newspapers and periodicals in the state.

The oldest continuously published newspapers in California are the *Sacramento Bee* (founded in 1857), San Francisco's *Examiner* (1865) and *Chronicle* (1868), and the *Los Angeles Times* (1881). *Times* owner and editor Harrison Gray Otis quickly made his newspaper preeminent in Los Angeles, a tradition continued by his son-in-law, Henry Chandler, and by the Otis-Chandler family today. Of all California's dailies, the *Times* is the only one with a depth of international and national coverage to rival the major East Coast papers. In 1887, young William Randolph Hearst took over his father's *San Francisco Daily Examiner* and introduced human interest items and sensational news stories to attract readers. The *Examiner* became the nucleus of the Hearst national newspaper chain, which later included the *News-Call Bulletin* and *Herald Examiner* in Los Angeles. The *Bulletin*, like many other newspapers in the state, ceased publication in the decades following World War II because of rising costs and increased competition for readers and advertisers.

California has more book publishers—about 225—than any state except New York. Among the many magazines published in the state are *Architectural Digest, Bon Appetit, Motor Trend, PC World, Runner's World,* and *Sierra*.

46 ORGANIZATIONS

Californians belong to thousands of nonprofit societies and organizations, many of which have their national headquarters in the state. In 2006, there were over 25,450 nonprofit organizations registered within the state, of which about 19,002 were registered as charitable, educational, or religious organizations.

National service organizations operating out of California include the National Assistance League and the Braille Institute of America, both in Los Angeles, and Knights of the Round Table International, Pasadena. Gamblers Anonymous has its international service office in Los Angeles. Some national social and civic organizations are based in the state, such as the Red Hat Society and Clowns Without Borders–USA.

Environmental and scientific organizations include the Sierra Club, Friends of the Earth, and Save-the-Redwoods League, all with headquarters in San Francisco; Animal Protection Institute of America, Sacramento; Geothermal Resources Council, Davis; and Seismological Society of America, Berkeley.

Among entertainment-oriented organizations centered in the state are the Academy of Motion Picture Arts and Sciences and the Academy of Television Arts and Sciences, both in Beverly Hills; Directors Guild of America and Writers Guild of America (West), both in Los Angeles; Screen Actors Guild and American Society of Cinematographers, both in Hollywood; the American Society of Music Arrangers and Composers, in Encino; the GRAMMY Foundation in Santa Monica; and the National Academy of Recording Arts and Sciences, Burbank. There are also several fan clubs for actors, singers, and other entertainment artists. Other commercial and professional groups are the Institute of Mathematical Statistics, San Carlos; Manufacturers' Agents National Association, Irvine; National Association of Civil Service Employees, San Diego; American Society of Zoologists, Thousand Oaks. and Pacific Area Travel Association, San Francisco.

The many national sports groups with California headquarters include the Association of Professional Ball Players of America (baseball), Garden Grove; US Hang Gliding Association, Los Angeles; National Hot Rod Association, North Hollywood; Professional Karate Association, Beverly Hills; United States Youth Soccer Association, Castro Valley; Soaring Society of America, Santa Monica; International Softball Congress, Anaheim Hills; American Surfing Association, Huntington Beach; and US Swimming Association, Fresno.

There are numerous state, regional, and local organizations dedicated to arts and culture. These include the California Arts Council, California Council for the Humanities, the Pacific Arts Association, and the California Hispanic Cultural Society. The Guitar Foundation of America is based in Claremont. The Jack London Research Center, the George Sand Association, and the Eugene O'Neill Society are headquartered in the state. Religious groups with central bases in the state include the American Druze Society, Jews for Jesus, and the Church of Scientology. There are also a number of regional conservation, environmental, and agricultural organizations. California also hosts the National Investigations Committee on UFOs, Van Nuys.

47 TOURISM, TRAVEL, AND RECREATION

California is one of the leading travel destination in the United States. In 2004, tourism was the state's third-largest employer, with direct travel spending in the state reaching $82.5 billion that year. In 2003, California led the nation in travel and tourism with a payroll of $19.7 billion. In support of the industry, the state adopted the California Tourism Marketing Act in 1995. This marketing referendum of California businesses established the California Travel and Tourism Commission (CTTC) and a statewide marketing fund derived from mandatory assessments. The success of the California Tourism Program, a joint venture between the CTTC and the California Division of Tourism, is a model for other states.

In 2003, 85% of tourists were Californians themselves. The state also hosted 4 million international visitors that year, with 693,000 from the United Kingdom; 590,000 from Japan; 303,000 from South Korea; 260,000 from Australia and New Zealand; and 238,000 from Germany. Nearly 440,000 travelers traveled by air from Mexico, and another 3 million came by car; some 890,000 were from Canada. There are 11 official California Welcome Centers within the state; 5 international travel trade offices operate, in Brazil, Australia, Germany, Japan, and the United Kingdom.

While the state's mild, sunny climate and varied scenery of seacoast, mountains, and desert lure many visitors, the San Francisco and Los Angeles metropolitan areas offer the most popular tourist attractions. San Francisco's Fisherman's Wharf, Chinatown, and Ghirardelli Square are popular for shopping and dining; tourists also frequent the city's unique cable cars, splendid museums, Opera House, and Golden Gate Bridge. The Golden Gate National Recreation Area, comprising 68 sq mi (176 sq km) on both sides of the entrance to San Francisco Bay, includes Fort Point in the Presidio park, Alcatraz Island (formerly a federal prison) in the bay, the National Maritime Museum with seven historic ships, and the Muir Woods, located 17 mi (27 km) north of the city. South of the city, the rugged coastal scenery of the Monterey peninsula attracts many visitors; to the northeast, the wineries of the Sonoma and Napa valleys offer their wares for sampling and sale.

Spending by travelers averages $1.4 billion per county, but Los Angeles County hosts the greatest number of tourist and receives approximately $17.9 billion in direct tourist spending. The Los Angeles area has the state's principal tourist attractions: the Disneyland amusement center at Anaheim, and Hollywood, which features visits to motion picture and television studios and sightseeing tours of film stars' homes in Beverly Hills. One of Hollywood's most popular spots is Mann's (formerly Grauman's) Chinese Theater, where the impressions of famous movie stars' hands and feet (and sometimes paws or hooves) are embedded in concrete. The New Year's Day Tournament of Roses at Pasadena is an annual tradition. Southwest of Hollywood, the Santa Monica Mountain National Recreation Area was created by Congress in 1978 as the country's largest urban park, covering 150,000 acres (61,000 hectares). The Queen Mary ocean liner, docked at Long Beach, is now a marine-oceanographic exposition center and hotel-convention complex. The Ronald Reagan Presidential Library is in Simi Valley.

The rest of the state offers numerous tourist attractions, including some of the largest and most beautiful national parks in the United States. In the north are Redwood National Park and Lassen Volcanic National Park. In east-central California, situated in the Sierra Nevada, are Yosemite National Park, towering Mt. Whitney in Sequoia National Park, and Lake Tahoe on the Nevada border. About 80 mi (129 km) east of Mt. Whitney is Death Valley. Among the popular tourist destinations in southern California are the zoo and Museum of Man in San Diego's Balboa Park and the Mission San Juan Capistrano, to which, according to tradition, the swallows return each spring. The San Simeon mansion and estate of the late William Randolph Hearst are now state historical monuments.

48 SPORTS

There are considerably more professional sports teams in California than in any other state. California has everything from baseball to hockey to soccer to women's basketball. The Major League Baseball teams are the Los Angeles Dodgers, the San Francisco Giants, the San Diego Padres, the Oakland Athletics, and the Los Angeles Angels of Anaheim. The Oakland Raiders, the San Francisco 49ers, and the San Diego Chargers play in the National Football League. In basketball the Los Angeles Lakers, the Los Angeles Clippers, the Golden State Warriors, and the Sacramento Kings play in the National Basketball Association. The Los Angeles Sparks and Sacramento Monarchs are in the Women's National Basketball Association. The Los Angeles Kings, the Anaheim Mighty Ducks, and the San Jose Sharks are members of the National Hockey League. The Major League Soccer teams are the Los Angeles Galaxy and San Jose Earthquakes.

Since moving from Brooklyn, New York, in 1959, the Dodgers have won the National League Pennant 10 times, going on to win the World Series in 1959, 1963, 1965, 1981, and 1988. The Athletics won the American League Pennant six times, going on to win the World Series in 1972, 1973, 1974, and 1980. The Giants, who moved from New York City in 1959, won the National League Pennant in 1962, 1989, and 2002, losing all three World Series. The Padres won the National League Pennant in 1984 and lost the World Series. They returned to the World Series after claiming the National League Pennant in 1999, but lost again. The Anaheim Angels (formerly the California Angels and currently the Los Angeles Angels of Anaheim) won the 2002 World Series.

The Lakers won the National Basketball Association (NBA) Championship in 1972, 1980, 1982, 1985, 1987, 1988, and from 2000 through 2002. The Warriors won the Championship in 1975. The Los Angeles Rams, who moved to St. Louis in 1996, played in NFL title games in 1949, 1950, 1951, 1955, 1974, 1975, 1976, 1978, and 1978. They won in 1951, and lost the Super Bowl in 1980. The Raiders won the Super Bowl three times: twice from Oakland, in 1977 and 1981, and once from Los Angeles, in 1984. The Raiders returned to Oakland in 1996. They were defeated by the Tampa Bay Buccaneers in the 2003 Super Bowl. The 49ers were the 1980s' most successful NFL team, winning the Super Bowl in 1982, 1985, 1989, 1990, and 1995. The Kings became the first California hockey team to make it to the Stanley Cup Finals in 1993, but they lost to the Montreal Canadians.

Another popular professional sport is horse racing at such well-known tracks as Santa Anita and Hollywood Park. Because of the equitable climate, there is racing virtually all year round. The California Speedway, in Fontana, hosts two NASCAR Cup Series races each year, and the Infineon Raceway hosts one NASCAR Nextel Cup event.

California's universities have fielded powerhouse teams in collegiate sports. The University of Southern California's (USC) baseball team won five consecutive national championships between 1970 and 1974. Its football team was number one in the nation in 1928, 1931, 1932, 1962, 1967, 1972, and 2004, and was a conational champion in 1974, 1978, and 2003. USC has won the Rose Bowl over 20 times, most recently in 2004. The University of California at Los Angeles (UCLA) basketball team won 10 National Collegiate Athletic Association (NCAA) titles, while the Bruins football team won Rose Bowls in 1966, 1976, 1983, 1984, and 1986.

Additionally, Stanford has won six Rose Bowl titles and University of California at Berkeley, three. Stanford also won the NCAA men's basketball championship in 1942, and the women's championships in 1990 and 1992. University of California at Berkeley won the men's title in 1959. All four schools compete in the PAC-10 Conference.

Among the famous athletes born in California are Joe DiMaggio, Venus and Serena Williams, Mark McGwire, Tiger Woods, and Jeff Gordon.

49 FAMOUS CALIFORNIANS

Richard Milhous Nixon (1913–94) is the only native-born Californian ever elected to the presidency. Following naval service in World War II, he was elected to the US House of Representatives in 1946, then to the US Senate in 1950. He served as vice president during the Dwight Eisenhower administration (1953–61) but failed, by a narrow margin, to be elected president as the Republican candidate in 1960. Returning to his home state, Nixon ran for the California governorship in 1962 but was defeated. The next year he moved his home and political base to New York, from which he launched his successful campaign for the presidency in 1968. As the nation's 37th president, Nixon withdrew US forces from Vietnam while intensifying the US bombing of Indochina, established diplomatic relations with China, and followed a policy of détente with the Soviet Union. In 1972, he scored a resounding reelection victory, but within a year his administration was beset by the Watergate scandal. On 9 August 1974, after the House Judiciary Committee had voted articles of impeachment, Nixon became the first president ever to resign the office.

The nation's 31st president, Herbert Hoover (b.Iowa, 1874–1964), moved to California as a young man. There he studied engineering at Stanford University and graduated with its first class (1895) before beginning the public career that culminated in his election to the presidency on the Republican ticket in 1928. Former film actor Ronald Reagan (b.Illinois, 1911–2004) served two terms as state governor (1967–75) before becoming president in 1981. He was elected to a second presidential term in 1984.

In 1953, Earl Warren (1891–1974) became the first Californian to serve as US chief justice (1953–69). Warren, a native of Los Angeles, was elected three times to the California governorship and served in that office (1943–53) longer than any other person. Following his appointment to the US Supreme Court by President Eisenhower, Warren was instrumental in securing the unanimous decision in *Brown v. Board of Education of Topeka* (1954) that racial segregation was unconstitutional under the 14th Amendment. Other cases decided by the Warren court dealt with defendants' rights, legislative reapportionment, and First Amendment freedoms.

Before the appointment of Earl Warren, California had been represented on the Supreme Court continuously from 1863 to 1926. Stephen J. Field (b.Connecticut, 1816–99) came to California during the gold rush, practiced law, and served as chief justice of the state supreme court from 1859 to 1863. Following his appointment to the highest court by President Abraham Lincoln, Field served what was at that time the longest term in the court's history (1863–97). Joseph McKenna (b.Pennsylvania, 1843–1926) was appointed to the Supreme Court to replace Field upon his retirement. McKenna, who moved with his family to California in 1855, became US attorney general in 1897, and was then elevated by President William McKinley to associate justice (1898-1925).

Californians have also held important positions in the executive branch of the federal government. Longtime California resident Victor H. Metcalf (b.New York, 1853-1936) served as Theodore Roosevelt's secretary of commerce and labor. Franklin K. Lane (b.Canada, 1864-1921) was Woodrow Wilson's secretary of the interior, and Ray Lyman Wilbur (b.Iowa, 1875-1949) occupied the same post in the Herbert Hoover administration. Californians were especially numerous in the cabinet of Richard Nixon. Los Angeles executive James D. Hodgson (b.Minnesota, 1915) was secretary of labor; former state lieutenant governor Robert H. Finch (b.Arizona, 1925-95) and San Francisco native Caspar W. Weinberger (1917-2006) both served terms as secretary of health, education, and welfare; and Claude S. Brinegar (b.1926) was secretary of transportation. Weinberger and Brinegar stayed on at their respective posts in the Gerald Ford administration; Weinberger later served as secretary of defense under Ronald Reagan. An important figure in several national administrations, San Francisco-born John A. McCone (1902-91) was chairman of the Atomic Energy Commission (1958-60) and director of the Central Intelligence Agency (1961-65).

John Charles Frémont (b.Georgia, 1813-90) led several expeditions to the West, briefly served as civil governor of California before statehood, became one of California's first two US senators (serving only until 1851), and ran unsuccessfully as the Republican Party's first presidential candidate, in 1856. Other prominent US senators from the state have included Hiram Johnson (1866-1945), who also served as governor from 1911 to 1917; William F. Knowland (1908-74); and, more recently, former college president and semanticist Samuel Ichiye Hayakawa (b.Canada, 1906-92) and former state controller Alan Cranston (1914-2001). Governors of the state since World War II include Reagan, Edmund G. "Pat" Brown (1905-96), fourth-generation Californian Edmund G. "Jerry" Brown Jr. (b.1938), and George Deukmejian (b.New York, 1928). Other prominent state officeholders are Rose Elizabeth Bird (b.Arizona, 1936-99), the first woman to be appointed chief justice of the state supreme court, and Wilson Riles (b.Louisiana, 1917), superintendent of public instruction, and the first black Californian elected to a state constitutional office. Prominent among mayors are Thomas Bradley (b.Texas, 1917-98) of Los Angeles, Pete Wilson (b.Illinois, 1933) of San Diego, Dianne Feinstein (b.1933) of San Francisco, and Janet Gray Hayes (b.Indiana, 1926) of San Jose.

Californians have won Nobel Prizes in five separate categories. Linus Pauling (b.Oregon, 1901-94), professor at the California Institute of Technology (1927-64) and at Stanford (1969-74), won the Nobel Prize for chemistry in 1954 and the Nobel Peace Prize in 1962. Other winners of the Nobel Prize in chemistry are University of California (Berkeley) professors William Francis Giauque (b.Canada, 1895-1982), in 1949; Edwin M. McMillan (1907-91) and Glenn T. Seaborg (b.Michigan, 1912-99), who shared the prize in 1951; and Stanford Professor Henry Taube (b.Canada, 1915-2005), in 1983. Members of the Berkeley faculty who have won the Nobel Prize for physics include Ernest Orlando Lawrence (b.South Dakota, 1901-58), in 1939; Emilio Segré (b.Italy, 1905-89) and Owen Chamberlain (1920-2006), who shared the prize

in 1959; and Luis W. Alvarez (1911-88), in 1968. Stanford professor William Shockley (b.England, 1910-89) shared the physics prize with two others in 1956; William A. Fowler (b.Pennsylvania, 1911-95), professor at the California Institute of Technology, won the prize in 1983. The only native-born Californian to win the Nobel Prize for literature was novelist John Steinbeck (1902-68), in 1962. Gerald Debreu (b.France, 1921-2004), professor at the University of California at Berkeley, won the 1983 prize for economics.

Other prominent California scientists are world-famed horticulturist Luther Burbank (b.Massachusetts, 1849-1926) and nuclear physicist Edward Teller (b.Hungary, 1908-2003). Naturalist John Muir (b.Scotland, 1838-1914) fought for the establishment of Yosemite National Park. Influential California educators include college presidents David Starr Jordan (b.New York, 1851-1931) of Stanford, and Robert Gordon Sproul (1891-1975) and Clark Kerr (b.Pennsylvania, 1911-2003) of the University of California.

Major figures in the California labor movement were anti-Chinese agitator Denis Kearney (b.Ireland, 1847-1907); radical organizer Thomas Mooney (b.Illinois, 1882-1942); and Harry Bridges (b.Australia, 1901-90), leader of the San Francisco general strike of 1934. The best-known contemporary labor leader in California is Cesar Chavez (b.Arizona, 1927-93).

The variety of California's economic opportunities is reflected in the diversity of its business leadership. Prominent in the development of California railroads were the men known as the Big Four: Charles Crocker (b.New York, 1822-88), Mark Hopkins (b.New York, 1813-78), Collis P. Huntington (b.Connecticut, 1821-1900), and Leland Stanford (b.New York, 1824-93). California's long-standing dominance in the aerospace industry is a product of the efforts of such native Californians as John Northrop (1895-1981) and self-taught aviator Allen Lockheed (1889-1969), along with Glenn L. Martin (b.Iowa, 1886-1955); the San Diego firm headed by Claude T. Ryan (b.Kansas, 1898-1982), built the monoplane, *Spirit of St. Louis,* flown by Charles Lindbergh across the Atlantic in 1927. Among the state's banking and financial leaders was San Jose native Amadeo Peter Giannini (1870-1949), founder of the Bank of America. Important figures in the development of California agriculture include Edwin T. Earl (1856-1919), developer of the first ventilator-refrigerator railroad car, and Mark J. Fontana (b.Italy, 1849-1922), whose California Packing Corp., under the brand name of Del Monte, became the largest seller of canned fruit in the United States. Leaders of the state's world-famous wine and grape-growing industry include immigrants Ágostan Haraszthy de Mokcsa (b.Hungary, 1812?-69), Charles Krug (b.Prussia, 1830-94), and Paul Masson (b.France, 1859-1940), as well as two Modesto natives, brothers Ernest (b.1910) and Julio (1911-93) Gallo. It was at the mill of John Sutter (b.Baden, 1803-80) that gold was discovered in 1848.

Leading figures among the state's newspaper editors and publishers were William Randolph Hearst (1863-1951), whose publishing empire began with the *San Francisco Examiner,* and Harrison Gray Otis (b.Ohio, 1837-1917), longtime owner and publisher of the *Los Angeles Times.* Pioneers of the state's electronics industry include David Packard (b.Colorado, 1912-96) and William R. Hewlett (b.Michigan, 1913-2001); Stephen Wozniak (b.1950) and Steven Jobs (b.1955) were cofounders of Apple Computer. Other prominent business leaders include clothier Levi

Strauss (b.Germany, 1830–1902), paper producer Anthony Zellerbach (b.Germany, 1832–1911), cosmetics manufacturer Max Factor (b.Poland, 1877–1938), and construction and manufacturing magnate Henry J. Kaiser (b.New York, 1882–1967).

California has been home to a great many creative artists. Native California writers include John Steinbeck, adventure writer Jack London (1876–1916), novelist and dramatist William Saroyan (1908–81), and novelist-essayist Joan Didion (b.1934). One California-born writer whose life and works were divorced from his place of birth was Robert Frost (1874–1963), a native of San Francisco. Many other writers who were residents but not natives of the state have made important contributions to literature. Included in this category are Mark Twain (Samuel Langhorne Clemens, b.Missouri, 1835–1910); local colorist Bret Harte (b.New York, 1836–1902); author-journalist Ambrose Bierce (b.Ohio, 1842–1914); novelists Frank Norris (b.Illinois, 1870–1902), Mary Austin (b.Illinois, 1868–1934), and Aldous Huxley (b.England, 1894–1963); novelist-playwright Christopher Isherwood (b.England, 1904–86); and poets Robinson Jeffers (b.Pennsylvania, 1887–1962) and Lawrence Ferlinghetti (b.New York, 1920). California has been the home of several masters of detective fiction, including Raymond Chandler (b.Illinois, 1888–1959), Dashiell Hammett (b.Connecticut, 1894–1961), Erle Stanley Gardner (b.Massachusetts, 1889–1970), creator of Perry Mason, and Ross Macdonald (1915–83). Producer-playwright David Belasco (1853–1931) was born in San Francisco.

Important composers who have lived and worked in California include natives Henry Cowell (1897–1965) and John Cage (1912–92), and immigrants Arnold Schoenberg (b.Austria, 1874–1951), Ernest Bloch (b.Switzerland, 1880–1959), and Igor Stravinsky (b.Russia, 1882–1971). Immigrant painters include landscape artists Albert Bierstadt (b.Germany, 1830–1902) and William Keith (b.Scotland, 1839–1911), as well as abstract painter Hans Hofmann (b.Germany, 1880–1966). Contemporary artists working in California include Berkeley-born Elmer Bischoff (b.1916–91), Wayne Thiebaud (b.Arizona, 1920), and Richard Diebenkorn (b.Oregon, 1922–93). San Francisco native Ansel Adams (1902–84) is the best known of a long line of California photographers that includes Edward Curtis (b.Wisconsin, 1868–1952), famed for his portraits of American Indians, and Dorothea Lange (b.New Jersey, 1895–1965), chronicler of the 1930s migration to California.

Many of the world's finest performing artists have also been Californians: Violinist Ruggiero Ricci (b.1918) was born in San Francisco, while fellow virtuosos Yehudi Menuhin (b.New York, 1916–99) and Isaac Stern (b.Russia, 1920–2001) were both reared in the state. Another master violinist, Jascha Heifetz (b.Russia, 1901–84), made his home in Beverly Hills. California jazz musicians include Dave Brubeck (b.1920) and Los Angeles-reared Stan Kenton (b.Kansas, 1912–79).

Among the many popular musicians who live and record in the state are California natives David Crosby (b.1941), Randy Newman (b.1943), and Beach Boys Brian (b.1942) and Carl (1946–98) Wilson.

The list of talented and beloved film actors associated with Hollywood is enormous. Native Californians on the screen include child actress Shirley Temple (Mrs. Charles A. Black, b.1928) and such greats as Gregory Peck (1916–2003) and Marilyn Monroe (Norma Jean Baker, 1926–62). Other longtime residents of the state include Douglas Fairbanks (b.Colorado, 1883–1939), Mary Pickford (Gladys Marie Smith, b.Canada, 1894–1979), Harry Lillis "Bing" Crosby (b.Washington, 1904–77), Cary Grant (Archibald Leach, b.England, 1904–86), John Wayne (Marion Michael Morrison, b.Iowa, 1907–79), Bette Davis (b.Massachusetts, 1908–89), and Clark Gable (b.Ohio, 1901–60). Other actors born in California include Clint Eastwood (b.1930), Robert Duvall (b.1931), Robert Redford (b.1937), Kevin Costner (b.1955), and Dustin Lee Hoffman (b.1937).

Hollywood has also been the center for such pioneer film producers and directors as D. W. Griffith (David Lewelyn Wark Griffith, b.Kentucky, 1875–1948), Cecil B. DeMille (b.Massachusetts, 1881–1959), Samuel Goldwyn (b.Poland, 1882–1974), Frank Capra (b.Italy, 1897–1991), and master animator Walt Disney (b.Illinois, 1901–66).

California-born athletes have excelled in every professional sport. A representative sampling includes Baseball Hall of Famers Joe Cronin (1906–1984), Vernon "Lefty" Gomez (1908–89), and Joe DiMaggio (1914–99), along with tennis greats John Donald "Don" Budge (1915–2000), Richard A. "Pancho" Gonzales (1928–95), Maureen "Little Mo" Connelly (1934–69), and Billie Jean (Moffitt) King (b.1943); Gene Littler (b.1930) in golf, Frank Gifford (b.1930) and Orenthal James "O. J." Simpson (b.1947) in football, Mark Spitz (b.1950) in swimming, and Bill Walton (b.1952) in basketball. Robert B. "Bob" Mathias (b.1930) won the gold medal in the decathlon at the 1948 and 1952 Olympic Games.

50 BIBLIOGRAPHY

Cochrane, Michelle. *When AIDS Began: San Francisco and the Making of an Epidemic*. New York: Routledge, 2004.

Council of State Governments. *The Book of the States, 2006 Edition*. Lexington, Ky.: Council of State Governments, 2006.

Dawson, Robert, and Gray Brechin. *Farewell, Promised Land: Waking from the California Dream*. Berkeley: University of California Press, 1999.

Fradkin, Philip L. *The Great Earthquake and Firestorms of 1906: How San Francisco Nearly Destroyed Itself*. Berkeley: University of California Press, 2005.

Hohm, Charles F. (ed.). *California's Social Problems*. New York: Longman, in collaboration with the California Sociological Association, 1997.

Klett, Mark. *Yosemite in Time: Ice Ages, Tree Clocks, Ghost Rivers*. San Antonio, Tex.: Trinity University Press, 2005.

McCarthy, Kevin F., and Georges Vernez. *Immigration in a Changing Economy: California's Experience*. Santa Monica, Calif.: Rand, 1997.

Orsi, Richard J. *Sunset Limited: The Southern Pacific Railroad and the Development of the American West, 1850–1930*. Berkeley: University of California Press, 2005.

Parzybok, Tye W. *Weather Extremes in the West*. Missoula, Mont.: Mountain Press, 2005.

Preston, Thomas. *Pacific Coast: Washington, Oregon, California*. 2nd ed. Vol. 1 in *The Double Eagle Guide to 1,000 Great Western Recreation Destinations*. Billings, Mont.: Discovery Publications, 2003.

Righter, Robert W. *The Battle over Hetch Hetchy: America's Most Controversial Dam and the Birth of Modern Environmentalism.* New York: Oxford University Press, 2005.

Starr, Kevin. *California: A History.* New York: Modern Library, 2005.

———. *The Dream Endures: California Enters the 1940s.* New York: Oxford University Press, 1997.

Storer, Tracy Irwin. *Sierra Nevada Natural History.* Rev. ed. Berkeley: University of California Press, 2004.

Thomson, David. *The Whole Equation: A History of Hollywood.* New York: Alfred A. Knopf, 2005.

US Department of Commerce, Economics and Statistics Administration, US Census Bureau. *California, 2000. Summary Social, Economic, and Housing Characteristics: 2000 Census of Population and Housing.* Washington, D.C.: US Government Printing Office, 2003.

Williams, James C. *Energy and the Making of Modern California.* Akron, Ohio: University of Akron Press, 1997.

Winchester, Simon. *A Crack in the Edge of the World: America and the Great California Earthquake of 1906.* New York: HarperCollins, 2005.

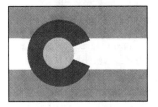

COLORADO

State of Colorado

ORIGIN OF STATE NAME: From the Spanish word *colorado*, meaning red or reddish brown. The Colorado River often runs red during flood stages. **NICKNAME:** The Centennial State. **CAPITAL:** Denver. **ENTERED UNION:** 1 August 1876 (38th). **SONG:** "Where the Columbines Grow." **MOTTO:** *Nil sine numine* (Nothing without providence). **COAT OF ARMS:** The upper portion of a heraldic shield shows three snow-capped mountains surrounded by clouds; the lower portion has a miner's pick and shovel crossed. Above the shield are an eye of God and a Roman fasces, symbolizing the republican form of government; the state motto is below. **FLAG:** Superimposed on three equal horizontal bands of blue, white, and blue is a large red "C" encircling a golden disk. **OFFICIAL SEAL:** The coat of arms surrounded by the words "State of Colorado 1876." **BIRD:** Lark bunting. **FISH:** Greenback cutthroat trout. **FLOWER:** Columbine. **TREE:** Blue spruce. **GEM:** Aquamarine. **LEGAL HOLIDAYS:** New Year's Day, 1 January; Birthday of Martin Luther King Jr., 3rd Monday in January; Lincoln's Birthday, 12 February; Washington's Birthday, 3rd Monday in February; Cesar Chavez Day, 31 March; Memorial Day, last Monday in May; Independence Day, 4 July; Colorado Day, 1st Monday in August; Labor Day, 1st Monday in September; Columbus Day, 2nd Monday in October; Election Day, 1st Tuesday after 1st Monday in November in even-numbered years; Thanksgiving Day, 4th Thursday in November; Christmas Day, 25 December. **TIME:** 5 AM MST = noon GMT.

¹LOCATION, SIZE, AND EXTENT

Located in the Rocky Mountain region of the United States, Colorado ranks eighth in size among the 50 states.

The state's total area is 104,091 sq mi (269,596 sq km), of which 103,595 sq mi (268,311 sq km) consists of land and 496 sq mi (1,285 sq km) comprises inland water. Shaped in an almost perfect rectangle, Colorado extends 387 mi (623 km) E–W and 276 mi (444 km) N–S.

Colorado is bordered on the N by Wyoming and Nebraska; on the E by Nebraska and Kansas; on the s by Oklahoma and New Mexico; and on the w by Utah (with the New Mexico and Utah borders meeting at Four Corners). The total length of Colorado's boundaries is 1,307 mi (2,103 km). The state's geographic center lies in Park County, 30 mi (48 km) NW of Pikes Peak.

²TOPOGRAPHY

With a mean average elevation of 6,800 ft (2,074 m), Colorado is the nation's highest state. Dominating the state are the Rocky Mountains. Colorado has 54 peaks 14,000 ft (4,300 m) or higher, including Elbert, the highest in the Rockies at 14,433 ft (4,402 m), and Pikes Peak, at 14,110 ft (4,301 m), one of the state's leading tourist attractions.

The entire eastern third of the state is part of the western Great Plains, a high plateau that rises gradually to the foothills of the Rockies. Colorado's lowest point, 3,350 ft (1,022 m), on the Arkansas River, is located in this plateau region. Running in a ragged north–south line, slightly west of the state's geographic center, is the Continental Divide, which separates the Rockies into the Eastern and Western slopes. The Eastern Slope Front (Rampart) Range runs south from the Wyoming border and just west of Colorado Springs. Also on the Eastern Slope are the Park, Mosquito, Medi-

cine Bow, and Laramie mountains. Western Slope ranges include the Sawatch, Gore, Elk, Elkhead, and William Fork mountains. South of the Front Range, crossing into New Mexico, is the Sangre de Cristo Range, separated from the San Juan Mountains to its west by the broad San Luis Valley. Several glaciers, including Arapahoe, St. Mary's, Andrews, and Taylor, are located on peaks at or near the Continental Divide. Colorado's western region is mostly mesa country: broad, flat plateaus accented by deep ravines and gorges, with many subterranean caves. Running northwest from the San Juans are the Uncompahgre Plateau, Grand Mesa, Roan Plateau, Flat Tops, and Danforth Hills. The Yampa and Green gorges are located in the northwestern corner of the state.

Blue Mesa Reservoir in Gunnison County is Colorado's largest lake. Six major river systems originate in Colorado: the Colorado River, which runs southwest from the Rockies to Utah; the South Platte, northeast to Nebraska; the North Platte, north to Wyoming; the Rio Grande, south to New Mexico; and the Arkansas and Republican, east to Kansas. Dams on these rivers provide irrigation for the state's farmland and water supplies for cities and towns. Eighteen hot springs are still active in Colorado; the largest is at Pagosa Springs.

³CLIMATE

Abundant sunshine and low humidity typify Colorado's highland continental climate. Winters are generally cold and snowy, especially in the higher elevations of the Rocky Mountains. Summers are characterized by warm, dry days and cool nights.

The average annual temperature statewide ranges from 54°F (12°C) at Lamar and at John Martin Dam to about 32°F (0°C) at the top of the Continental Divide; differences in elevation account for significant local variations on any given day. Denver's annual average is 51°F (10°C); normal temperatures range from 16° to

43°F (-9° to 6°C) in January and from 59° to 88°F (15° to 31°C) in July. Bennett recorded the highest temperature in Colorado, 118°F (48°C), on 11 July 1888; the record low was -61°F (-52°C), in Moffat County, on 1 February 1985.

Annual precipitation ranges from a low of 7 in (18 cm) in Alamosa to a high of 25 in (64 cm) in Crested Butte, with Denver receiving about 15.8 in (40 cm) during 1971–2000. Denver's snowfall averages 60.3 in (153.2 cm) yearly. The average snowfall at Cubres in the southern mountains is nearly 300 in (762 cm); less than 30 mi (48 km) away at Manassa, snowfall is less than 25 in (64 cm). On 14–15 April 1921, Silver Lake had 76 in (193 cm) of snowfall, the highest amount ever recorded in North America during a 24-hour period.

⁴FLORA AND FAUNA

Colorado's great range in elevation and temperature contributes to a variety of vegetation, distributed among five zones: plains, foothills, montane, subalpine, and alpine. The plains teem with grasses and as many as 500 types of wildflowers. Arid regions contain two dozen varieties of cacti. Foothills are matted with berry shrubs, lichens, lilies, and orchids, while fragile wild flowers, shrubs, and conifers thrive in the montane zone. Aspen and Engelmann spruce are found up to the timberline. As of 2003, 13 plant species were listed as threatened or endangered, including three species of cacti, two species of milk-vetch, Penland beardtongue, and Colorado butterfly plant.

Colorado has counted as many as 747 nongame wildlife species and 113 sport-game species. Principal big-game species are the elk, mountain lion, Rocky Mountain bighorn sheep (the state animal), antelope, black bear, and white-tailed and mule deer; the mountain goat and the moose—introduced in 1948 and 1975, respectively—are the only nonnative big-game quarry. The lark bunting is the state bird; blue grouse and mourning doves are numerous, and 28 duck species have been sighted. Colorado has about 100 sport-fish species. Scores of lakes and rivers contain bullhead, kokanee salmon, and a diversity of trout. Rare Colorado fauna include the golden trout, white pelican, and wood frog. In April 2006, a total of 30 species occurring within the state were on the threatened and endangered species list of the US Fish and Wildlife Service. These included 17 animal (vertebrates and invertebrates) and 13 plant species. The Mexican spotted owl and bald eagle are among threatened species. The razorback sucker, gray wolf, whooping crane, black-footed ferret, southwestern willow flycatcher, and bonytail chub are among endangered species.

⁵ENVIRONMENTAL PROTECTION

The Department of Natural Resources and the Department of Health share responsibility for state environmental programs. The first efforts to protect Colorado's natural resources were the result of federal initiatives. On 16 October 1891, US president Benjamin Harrison set aside the White River Plateau as the first forest reserve in the state. Eleven years later, President Theodore Roosevelt incorporated six areas in the Rockies as national forests. By 1906, 11 national forests covering about one-fourth of the state had been created. Mesa Verde National Park, founded in 1906, and Rocky Mountain National Park (1915) were placed under the direct control of the National Park Service. In 1978, Colorado became the first state in the United States to encourage taxpayers to allocate part of their state income tax refunds to wildlife conservation. In addition, a state lottery was approved in the late 1980s, with proceeds approved for Great Outdoors Colorado (GOCO) to be used for parks improvement and wildlife and resource management.

Air pollution, water supply problems, and hazardous wastes head the list of Colorado's current environmental concerns. The Air Quality Control Commission, within the Department of Health, has primary responsibility for air pollution control. Because of high levels of carbon monoxide, nitrogen dioxide, and particulates in metropolitan Denver, Colorado Springs, Pueblo, and other cities, a motor vehicle emissions inspection system was inaugurated in January 1982 for gasoline-powered vehicles and in January 1985 for diesel-powered vehicles. The high altitudes of Colorado almost double auto emissions compared to auto emissions at sea level. The high level of particulates in the air is a result of frequent temperature inversions along Colorado's Front Range. The state has launched an aggressive campaign to improve air quality. Cars must use oxygenated fuels and pass tough vehicle emissions controls, and driving is discouraged on high-pollution days. In 2003, 22.5 million lb of toxic chemicals were released by the state.

Formal efforts to ensure the state's water supply date from the Newlands Reclamation Act of 1902, a federal program designed to promote irrigation projects in the semiarid plains areas; its first effort, the Uncompahgre Valley Project, reclaimed 146,000 acres (59,000 hectares) in Montrose and Delta counties. One of the largest undertakings, the Colorado–Big Thompson Project, started in the 1930s, diverts a huge amount of water from the Western to the Eastern Slope. Colorado's efforts to obtain water rights to the Vermejo River in the Rockies were halted in 1984 by the US Supreme Court, which ruled that New Mexico would retain these rights. Some 98% of Colorado's drinking water complies with federal and state standards. The Colorado Department of Health works with local officials to ensure federal standards for drinking water are met. Isolated aquifers are generally in good condition in Colorado, though a few are contaminated. Colorado's groundwater quality is generally high.

Colorado's rapid population growth during the 1970s and early 1980s taxed an already low water table, especially in the Denver metropolitan area. The Department of Natural Resource's Water Conservation Board and Division of Water Resources are responsible for addressing this and other water-related problems.

The Department of Health has primary responsibility for hazardous waste management. From 1984 until the mid-1990s, the department, along with federal agencies, undertook the cleanup of nearly 7,000 contaminated sites in Grand Junction and other parts of Mesa County; these sites, homes and properties, were contaminated during the 1950s and 1960s by radioactive mill tailings that had been used as building material and that were not considered hazardous at the time. (It is now known that the low-level radiation emitted by the mill tailings can cause cancer and genetic damage.) In the fall of 1984, Aspen was placed on the federal US Environment Protection Agency (EPA) list of dangerous waste sites because potentially hazardous levels of cadmium, lead, and zinc were found in Aspen's streets, buildings, and water. Cadmium, lead, and zinc mill tailings had been used as filling material during the construction of the popular resort. Also in the mid-1980s, Rocky Flats, a former plutonium production site near Golden, was

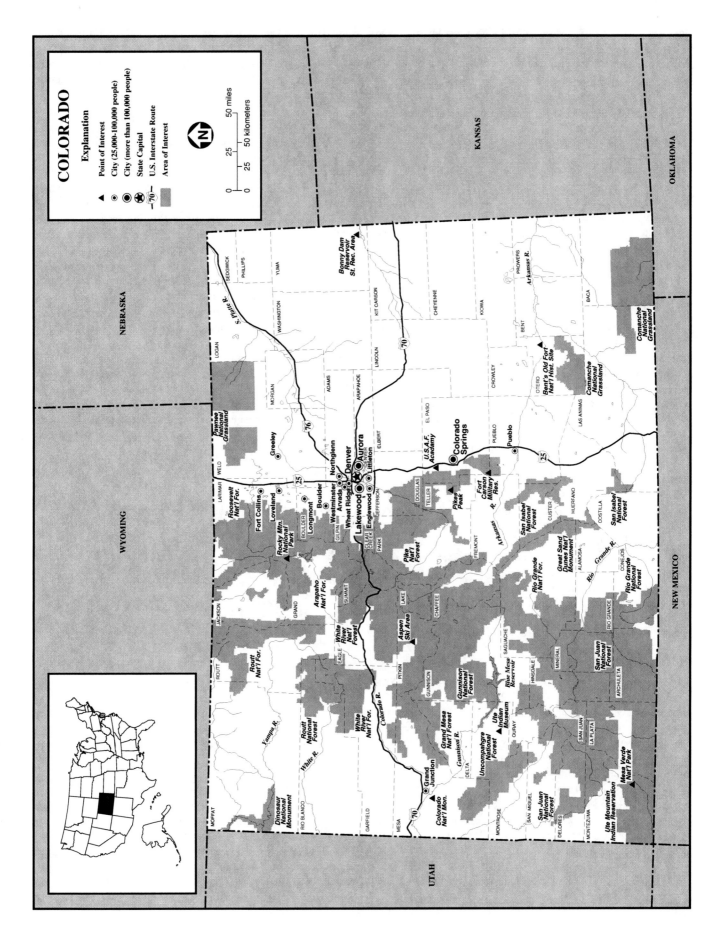

closed and a major cleanup was begun; by 2003, all plutonium and uranium had been removed. During 2004 and 2005 the buildings at Rocky Flats were scheduled to be demolished. Rocky Flats National Wildlife Refuge was planned for the site when the demolition was complete. (The site had been the focus of many protests during the 1970s, and has been a major newsmaker since the start of the cleanup. In 2003, the EPA database listed 202 hazardous waste sites in Colorado, 17 of which were on the National Priorities List as of 2006, including the Rocky Mountain Arsenal (US Army), Denver Radium Site, and Uravan Uranium Project site of Union Carbide Corp. In 2005, the EPA spent over $22.9 million through the Superfund program for the cleanup of hazardous waste sites in the state. Also in 2005, federal EPA grants awarded to the state included $13.7 million for a cleanwater revolving loan fund.

Some 1.5% of the state's land is covered with wetlands, a 50% decrease over the last two centuries.

6 POPULATION

Colorado ranked 22nd in population in the United States, with an estimated total of 4,656,177 in 2005, an increase of 8.4% since 2000. Between 1990 and 2000, Colorado's population grew from 3,294,394 to 4,301,261, an increase of 30.6%. This was the third-largest percentage increase in the country for this period (exceeded only by Nevada and Arizona) and the eighth-largest gain in population size. The population was projected to reach 5 million by 2015 and 5.5 million by 2025.

Colorado rose from 30th in population in 1970 to 28th in 1980 and 26th in 1990, with a 14% increase during the 1980s. The population density in 2004 was 44.4 people per sq mi. The estimated median age in 2004 was 34.5 years; 9.8% of the population was over 65 and persons under 18 years old accounted for 25.6% of the population.

Denver is the state's largest city and was, in 2004, the 25th largest US city. Its estimated 2004 population was 556,835, but its metropolitan area (including Aurora) exceeded 2,330,146, or about half the state's population, in 2004. Other major cities, with their estimated 2004 population figures, are Colorado Springs, 369,363; Aurora, 291,843; Lakewood, 141,301; Fort Collins, 126,967; Westminster, 104,759; and Pueblo, 103,621.

7 ETHNIC GROUPS

Once the sole inhabitants of the state, American Indians in 2000 numbered 44,241, up from 28,000 in 1990. In 2004, American Indians accounted for 1.1% of the total population. The black population is also small, 165,063, or 3.8% in 2000; the percentage for Denver, however, was considerably higher (11.1% in 2000). In 2004, the black population was 4.1% of the total population. Of far greater importance to the state's history, culture, and economy are its Hispanic and Latino residents, of whom there were 735,601 in 2000 (17.1%), up from 424,000 (under 13%) in 1990. Among residents of Denver, 31.7% were Hispanic or Latino in 2000. In 2004, 19.1% of the state's residents was of Hispanic or Latino origin. Of over 95,213 Asians (2.2%), up from 60,000 in 1990, 11,571 were Japanese (down from 15,198 in 1990); 16,395, Korean (up from 12,490 in 1990); 15,457, Vietnamese (more than double the 1990 total of 6,679); 15,658, Chinese (up from 9,117 in 1990); and 8,941, Filipino. In 2004, 2.5% of the population was Asian. The

population of Pacific Islanders was estimated at 4,621 in 2000. In 2004, the percentage of Pacific Islanders in Colorado was 0.1%. In all, 369,903 residents, or 8.6% of the state population, were foreign born in 2000. In 2004, 1.8% of the population reported origin of two or more races.

8 LANGUAGES

The first whites to visit Colorado found Arapaho, Kiowa, Comanche, and Cheyenne Indians roaming the plains and often fighting the Ute Indians in the mountains. Despite this diverse heritage, Indian place-names are not numerous: Pagosa Springs, Uncompahgre, Kiowa, and Arapahoe.

Colorado English is a mixture of the Northern and Midland dialects, in proportions varying according to settlement patterns. Homesteading New Englanders in the northeast spread *sick to the stomach, pail,* and *comforter* (tied and filled bedcover), which in the northwest and the southern half are Midland *sick at the stomach, bucket,* and *comfort.* South Midland *butter beans* and *snap beans* appear in the eastern agricultural strip. Denver has *slat fence,* and *Heinz dog* (mongrel). In the southern half of the state, the large Spanish population has bred many loanwords such as *arroyo* (small canyon or gulley) and *penco* (pet lamb).

In 2000, 3,402,266 Coloradans, amounting to 84.9% of the residents five years old and older, spoke only English at home, down from 89.5% in 1990.

The following table gives selected statistics from the 2000 Census for language spoken at home by persons five years old and over.

LANGUAGE	NUMBER	PERCENT
Population 5 years and over	**4,006,285**	**100.0**
Speak only English	3,402,266	84.9
Speak a language other than English	604,019	15.1
Speak a language other than English	**604,019**	**15.1**
Spanish or Spanish Creole	421,670	10.5
German	30,824	0.8
French (incl. Patois, Cajun)	18,045	0.5
Vietnamese	12,499	0.3
Korean	12,045	0.3
Chinese	11,333	0.3
Russian	10,737	0.3
Japanese	6,605	0.2
Italian	5,703	0.1
Polish	5,064	0.1
Tagalog	5,013	0.1
Arabic	4,998	0.1

9 RELIGIONS

The Spanish explorers who laid claim to (but did not settle in) Colorado were Roman Catholic, but the first American settlers were mostly Methodists, Lutherans, and Episcopalians. Some evangelical groups sought to proselytize the early mining camps during the mid-19th century.

Roman Catholics comprise the single largest religious group in the state, with 627,753 adherents in 2006 parishes in 2004. The United Methodist Church, which was the second-largest Protestant denomination in 1990, slipped down to fourth in 2000, with 77,286 adherents in 222 congregations. The second-largest group is the Latter-Day Saints, with 126,118 adherents in 275 congregations as of 2006. The Southern Baptist Convention had 85,083 adherents in 243 congregations in 2000; there were 1,898 newly baptized members in 2002.

There were about 72,000 adherents in the Jewish community in 2000. The same year, there were about 72 Buddhist, 7 Hindu, and 12 Muslim congregations in the state. About 60.5% of the population did not specify a religious affiliation.

The World Evangelical Fellowship is headquartered in Colorado Springs. The national headquarters of Promise Keepers, primarily a Christian men's organization, is in Denver. A Youth for Christ national service center is located in Englewood.

10 TRANSPORTATION

As the hub of the Rocky Mountain states, Colorado maintains extensive road and rail systems.

Because of its difficult mountainous terrain, Colorado was bypassed by the first transcontinental railroads. In 1870, however, the Denver Pacific built a line from Denver to the Union Pacific's cross-country route at Cheyenne, Wyoming. Several intrastate lines were built during the 1870s, connecting Denver with the mining towns. In particular, the Denver and Rio Grande built many narrow-gauge lines through the mountains. Denver finally became part of a main transcontinental line in 1934. As of 2003, there were 3,645 rail mi (5,868 km) of track in the state, utilized by 14 railroads. This included two Class I railroads. As of 2006, two Amtrak trains, the California Zephyr and the Southwest Chief, provided service to nine cities in Colorado.

Colorado has an extensive network of roads, including 29 mountain passes. As of 2004 there were 87,096 mi (140,225 km) of roadway in Colorado. The major state roads are Interstate 70, US 40, and US 50 crossing the state from east to west, and Interstate 25 running north–south along the Front Range of the Rocky Mountains between Raton Pass and Cheyenne, Wyoming. Interstate 76 connects Denver on a northeasterly diagonal with Nebraska's I-80 to Omaha.

Of the approximately 1.990 million motor vehicles registered in 2004, there were some 880,000 automobiles, 1.096 million trucks of all types, and 2,000 buses. There were 3,205,054 licensed drivers in that same year.

In 2005, Colorado had a total of 437 public and private-use aviation-related facilities. This included 259 airports, 172 heliports, and 6 STOLports (Short Take-Off and Landing). Denver International Airport (DIA) replaced the former Stapleton International Airport in 1994 as the state's largest and busiest. In 2004, DIA handled 20,407,002 enplanements, making it the fifth busiest airport in the United States. In addition to DIA, Centennial Airport (formerly Arapahoe County Airport), located in suburban Denver, is the Rocky Mountain region's busiest general aviation airport, and in 2003, it ranked as the second-busiest such airport in the nation. General-aviation airports handle unscheduled flights, such as business and private aircraft.

11 HISTORY

A hunting people lived in eastern Colorado at least 20,000 years ago, but little is known about them. The Basket Makers, who came to southwestern Colorado after 100 BC, grew corn and squash and lived in pit houses. By AD 800, there were Pueblo tribes who practiced advanced forms of agriculture and pottery making. From the 11th through the 13th centuries (when they migrated southward), the Pueblo Indians constructed elaborate apartment-like dwellings in the cliffs of the Colorado canyons and planted their crops both on the mesa tops and in the surrounding valleys.

In the 1500s, when Spanish conquistadors arrived in the Southwest, northeastern Colorado was dominated by the Cheyenne and Arapaho, allied against the Comanche and Kiowa to the south. These plains-dwellers also warred with the mountain-dwelling Ute Indians, who were divided into the Capote, Moache, and Wiminuche in the southwest; the Yampa, Grand River, and Uintah in the northwest; and the Tabeguache and Uncompahgre along the Gunnison River.

The exact date of the first Spanish entry into the region now called Colorado is undetermined; the explorer Juan de Onate is believed to have traveled into the southeastern area in 1601. More than a century later, in 1706, Juan de Uribarri claimed southeastern Colorado for Spain, joining it with New Mexico. Meanwhile, French traders did little to stake out their claim to the Colorado region, which included most of the area east of the Rocky Mountains. In 1763, France formally ceded the Louisiana Territory to Spain, which returned it to the French in 1801. Two years later, as part of the Louisiana Purchase, Colorado east of the Rockies became US land; the rest of Colorado still belonged to Spain.

Formal boundaries had never been demarcated between the lands of French Louisiana and Spanish New Mexico. In 1806, the US government sent out a group led by Lt. Zebulon M. Pike to explore this southwestern border. Pike's group reached Pueblo on 23 November 1806 and then attempted without success to scale the peak that now bears his name. Not until 1819 did the United States and Spain agree to establish the boundary along the Arkansas River and then northward along the Continental Divide. The following year, Maj. Stephen Long explored this new border, and Dr. Edwin James made the first known ascent of Pikes Peak.

Eastern Colorado remained a wilderness for the next few decades, although traders and scouts like Charles and William Bent, Kit Carson, and Jim Bridger did venture into the largely uncharted and inhospitable land, establishing friendly relations with the Colorado Indians. It was in 1840 at Bent's Fort, the area's major trading center, that the four major eastern tribes ended their warfare and struck an alliance, a bond that lasted through their later struggle against the white settlers and US government. Between 1842 and 1853, John C. Frémont led five expeditions into the region, the first three for the US government. In 1842, he traveled along the South Platte River; on the next two trips, he crossed the Rockies. In his fourth expedition, he and a few of his party barely survived severe winter conditions. Finally, in 1853, Frémont led an expedition over a route traveled by Capt. John Gunnison earlier that year, through the San Luis Valley over Cochetopa Pass and along the Gunnison River. The 1853 trips were made five years after western and southern Colorado had come into US possession through the Mexican War.

The magnet that drew many Americans to Colorado was the greatly exaggerated report of a gold strike in Cherry Creek (present-day Denver) in July 1858. Within a year, thousands of prospectors had crossed the plains to seek their fortune. Many were disappointed and headed back east, but those who stayed benefited from a second strike at North Clear Creek, some 40 mi (64 km) to the west. The subsequent boom led to the founding of such mining towns as Central City, Tarryall, Golden, Blackhawk, Boulder, Nevadaville, Colorado City, and Gold Hill. By 1860, the population exceeded 30,000. A bill to organize a territory called Colorado, along the lines of the state's present-day boundaries, was passed by the US Congress on 28 February 1861. Colorado City, Golden, and Denver served, at various times, as the territorial capital until 1867 when Denver was selected as the permanent site. Colorado sided with the Union during the Civil War, though some settlers fought for the Confederacy. Union troops from Colorado helped defeat a contingent led by Confederate Gen. Henry H. Sibley at La Glorieta Pass in New Mexico in 1862.

The 1860s also saw the most serious conflict between Indians and white settlers in Colorado history. Cheyenne and Arapaho chiefs had ceded most of their tribal holdings to the US government in 1861. Sent to a reservation in the Arkansas Valley, these nomadic tribes were expected to farm the land. Unsuccessful at farming, the Indians rebelled against the poor rations supplied them by the US government and sought to resume a nomadic lifestyle, hunting buffalo, raiding towns, and attacking travelers along the Overland and Sante Fe trails. Col. John Chivington was placed in charge of controlling the Indian unrest in the summer of 1864 as Territorial Governor John Evans departed for Washington, DC, leaving the situation in the hands of the military. On 29 November of that year, Chivington led his forces to Sand Creek, on the reservation's northeastern border, where they brutally massacred perhaps 200 Indian men, women, and children who thought they were under the protection of US military forces at nearby Ft. Lyon. Five more years of warfare followed, with the Indians finally defeated at Beecher Island (1868) and Summit Spring (1869). By 1874, most Plains Indians were removed to reservations in what is now Oklahoma. After gold and silver were discovered in areas belonging to the Ute in 1873, they too were forced off the land. By 1880, a series of treaties limited the Ute to a small reservation in the barren mesa country.

The first bill to admit Colorado to statehood was vetoed in 1866 by President Andrew Johnson, who at that time was in the midst of an impeachment fight and feared the entry of two more Republicans into the US Senate. Colorado finally entered the Union as the 38th state on 1 August 1876, less than a month after the nation's 100th birthday and during the presidency of Ulysses S. Grant.

In the early years of statehood, silver strikes at Leadville and Aspen brought settlers and money into Colorado. Rail lines, smelters, and refineries were built, and large coalfields were opened up. The High Plains attracted new farmers, and another new industry, tourism, emerged. As early as the 1860s, resorts had opened near some of the state's mineral springs. By the mid-1870s, scenic canyons and towns became accessible by train. One of the first major spas, Colorado Springs, recorded 25,000 tourists in 1878, and by the mid-1880s, Denver was accommodating up to 200,000 visitors a year. Colorado's boom years ended with a depression during the early 1890s. Overproduction of silver coupled with the US government's decision to adopt a gold standard in 1893 wiped out the silver market, causing the closing of mines, banks, and some businesses. Coinciding with this economic disaster was a drought that led to the abandonment of many farms. A more positive development was a gold find at Cripple Creek in 1891.

By the dawn of the 20th century, farmers were returning to the land and making better use of it. Immigrants from Germany and Russia began to grow sugar beets in the Colorado, Arkansas, and South Platte river valleys. Huge reclamation projects brought water to semiarid cropland, and dry-land farming techniques also helped increase yields. The development of the automobile and good roads opened up more of the mountain areas, bringing a big boom in tourism by the 1920s.

Following World War I, the agricultural and mining sectors fell into depression. From 1920 to 1940, statewide employment declined and the population growth rate lagged behind that of the United States as a whole. World War II (1939–45) brought military training camps, airfields, and jobs to the state. Colorado also became the site of several major prisoner-of-war (POW) camps as well as relocation centers for Japanese Americans (Nisei), especially the northeastern and southeastern areas of the state. After the war, the expansion of federal facilities in Colorado led to new employment opportunities. The placement of both the North American Air Defense Command and the US Air Force Academy in Colorado Springs helped stimulate the growth of defense, federal research, and aerospace-related industries in the state. As these and other industries grew, so too did Colorado's population and income: between 1960 and 1983, the state's population growth rate was more than twice that of the nation as a whole; and between 1970 and 1983, Colorado moved from 18th to 9th among the states in personal income per capita. The construction of the Air Force Space Operations Center at Colorado Springs, announced in 1983, also contributed Colorado's economic and population growth.

In the 1970s and early 1980s, Colorado experienced a boom in its oil, mining, and electronics industries. Prosperity attracted immigrants from other states, and for about a decade Colorado's population increased at an average of 3% a year. The economy began to shrink, however, in the mid-1980s with the drop in oil prices and the closing of mines, culminating in a full-scale recession by 1987. The economy rebounded by the early 1990s, spurred by an educated workforce and the low cost of doing business in the state. Industry in the state became more diverse, now including oil and gas, telecommunications, retail, and, very importantly, high technology. In 1998, the state ranked ninth nationally in per capita personal income, and by 1999 its unemployment rate, just 2.9%, was among the lowest in the country. Due to the 2001 economic recession in the United States and its aftermath, the Colorado unemployment rate stood at 5.8% in May 2003, below the national average of 6.1% but still causing difficulties for the state's economy. As of September 2005, Colorado's unemployment rate was 5.1%, exactly equal to the national unemployment rate.

On 20 April 1999, the affluent Denver suburb of Littleton made headlines around the world after two teenaged gunmen entered Columbine High School and went on a shooting rampage, killing 12 students and one teacher before turning their guns on themselves. Several others were injured. The tragic event escalated the national debate on gun control and reopened the discussion about what effect media violence has on the nation's youth.

Major challenges facing Colorado in the 1990s and into the 2000s included industrial pollution of its air and water, overcrowding on the Rockies eastern slope (home to four-fifths of its population), and water shortages. By spring 2000 one issue emerged that encompassed many of the problems Coloradans faced: the practice of open-pit gold mining. Gaping holes, forged by explosives and chemicals, had been created by mining companies across western states since 1980. According to environmentalists and other concerned citizens, the cost-efficient method for extracting the precious metal from stone had come at a price: cyanide, used to dissolve gold in the mines, leached into streams and rivers; and mishaps occurred, including the accidental cyanide release that contaminated 17 mi (27 km) of Colorado's Alamosa River in the early 1990s, the costliest mining disaster in US history. Banning open-pit mining had gained wide public support in the months preceding the 2000 election, when organizers hoped to place the initiative on the ballot. Although about 72% of Colorado voters were thought to be in agreement with the ban, the initiative failed to make the ballot in November 2000.

Colorado was among the western states ravaged by wildfires during the summer of 2000, the worst fire season since 1988. In the summer of 2002, wildfires burned over 7.1 million acres of public and private land. The Hayman fire of 2002 was called the largest wildfire in Colorado history. The Hayman fire burned 138,577 acres of Colorado land thirty miles southwest of Denver. Another major 2002 wildfire was the Missionary Ridge fire: it burned 72,964 acres of land north and northeast of Durango.

12 STATE GOVERNMENT

Colorado's state constitution, ratified on 1 July 1876, is a complex and extremely detailed document specifying the duties and structure of state and local government. Despite numerous amendments (145 by January 2005) and revisions, some anachronistic legislation has remained on the books.

The General Assembly, which meets annually from the second Wednesday of January into May (for a maximum of 120 calendar days), consists of a 35-member Senate and 65-member House of Representatives. The legislature may call special sessions by request of two-thirds of the members of each house. The governor may also call a special session of the legislature. Members of the legislature must be US citizens, at least 25 years old, and have lived in their district for at least one year. The legislative salary in 2004 was $30,000, unchanged from 1999.

The executive branch is headed by the governor, who submits the budget and legislative programs to the General Assembly, and appoints judges, department heads, boards, and commissions. The governor, who is limited to serving two consecutive terms, must be a US citizen, at least 30 years old, and have been a resident of the state for two years or more. Elected with the governor is the lieutenant governor, who assumes the governor's duties in the governor's absence. Other elective officers include the secretary of state, attorney general, and treasurer, all of whom serve four-year terms. As of December 2004, the governor's salary was $90,000, unchanged from 1999.

Bills may originate in either house of the General Assembly and become law when passed by majority vote of each house and signed by the governor; a bill may also become law if the governor fails to act on it within 10 days after receiving it (or within 30 days after the legislature has adjourned). A two-thirds vote of the elected members in each house is needed to override a gubernatorial veto.

The state constitution may be amended in several ways. An amendment may be introduced in the legislature, passed by a two-thirds majority in both houses, and submitted to the voters for approval. Alternatively, an initiative amendment, signed by a number of eligible voters equaling at least 5% of the number of votes cast for secretary of state in the previous election and then

Colorado Presidential Vote by Political Parties, 1948–2004

YEAR	ELECTORAL VOTE	COLORADO WINNER	DEMOCRAT	REPUBLICAN	PROGRESSIVE	SOCIALIST	SOC. LABOR
1948	6	*Truman (D)	267,288	239,714	6,115	1,678	—
						CONSTITUTION	
1952	6	*Eisenhower (R)	245,504	379,782	1,919	2,181	—
1956	6	*Eisenhower (R)	263,997	394,479	—	759	3,308
						SOC. WORKERS	
1960	6	Nixon (R)	330,629	402,242	—	563	2,803
1964	6	*Johnson (D)	476,024	296,767	—	2,537	—
					AMERICAN IND.		
1968	6	*Nixon (R)	335,174	409,345	60,813	235	3,016
					AMERICAN		
1972	7	*Nixon (R)	329,980	597,189	17,269	666	4,361
							LIBERTARIAN
1976	7	Ford (R)	460,801	584,278	397	1,122	5,338
					STATESMAN	**CITIZENS**	
1980	7	*Reagan (R)	368,009	652,264	1,180	5,614	25,744
1984	8	Reagan (R)	454,975	821,817	**NEW ALLIANCE**	—	11,257
1988	8	*Bush (R)	621,453	728,177	2,491	—	15,482
					IND. (Perot)		
1992	8	*Clinton (D)	629,681	562,850	366,010	1,608	8,669
						GREEN (Nader)	
1996	8	Dole (R)	671,152	691,848	99,629	25,070	12,392
					FREEDOM (Buchanan)		
2000	8	*Bush, G. W. (R)	738,227	883,748	10,465	91,434	12,799
					AMERICAN CONSTITUTION (Peroutka)	**COLORADO REFORM** (Nader)	
2004	9	*Bush, G. W. (R)	1,001,732	1,101,255	2,562	12,718	7,664

*Won US presidential election.

published in every county, may be filed no later than four months before the general election. If approved by the voters, it then becomes law.

Any US citizen 18 or older who is a resident of a Colorado state 30 days prior to an election may register to vote. Prisoners may not vote.

13 POLITICAL PARTIES

The Democratic and Republican parties are the major political organizations in Colorado. Although both parties were in existence when Colorado achieved statehood, the Republicans controlled most statewide offices prior to 1900. Since then, the parties have been more evenly balanced. Of the 2,990,000 registered voters in 2004, 30% were estimated to be Democratic, 36% Republican, and 33% unaffiliated or members of other parties. In 2000, 51% of all Coloradan voters cast their ballots for Republican George W. Bush; Democrat Al Gore won 42% of the vote; Green Party candidate Ralph Nader won 5% of the vote. In 2004, Bush won reelection with 54% to Democrat John Kerry's 48.8%. The state had nine electoral votes in the 2004 presidential election.

Following the election in November 2004, the state had one Democrat and one Republican US senator, and four Republican and three Democratic US representatives. Ben Nighthorse Campbell was elected US senator in 1992 as a Democrat. The only Native American in Congress, Campbell switched parties in March 1995. When he successfully ran for reelection in 1998, it was as a Republican. In the 2004 Senate contest, Democrat Ken Salazar defeated Republican Pete Coors, winning 51% of the vote to Coors's 47%. Republican Wayne Allard was elected to the Senate in 1996 and reelected in 2002.

Following the 2004 elections, the Democrats won narrow control of the state Senate (18 Democrats to 17 Republicans) and the state House (35 Democrats to 30 Republicans). Colorado's governor, Republican Bill Owens, was elected in 1998, succeeding Democrat Roy Romer, who had been in office for the maximum two terms. Owens was the first Republican elected to the governor's office in 28 years; he was reelected in 2002. In 2003, Colorado had the second-highest percentage of women in its state legislature, with 34% (Washington was first, with 36.7%).

14 LOCAL GOVERNMENT

As of 2005 there were 63 counties, 270 municipal governments, and 1,414 special districts. There were also 176 school districts. The administrative and policymaking body in each county is the board of county commissioners, whose three to five members (dependent on population) are elected to staggered, usually four-year, terms. Other county officials include the county clerk, treasurer, assessor, sheriff, coroner, superintendent of schools, surveyor, and attorney.

Statutory cities are those whose structure is defined by the state constitution. Power is delegated by the General Assembly to either a council-manager or mayor-council form of government. Colorado municipalities have increasingly opted for home rule, taking control of local functions from the state government. Towns, which generally have fewer than 2,000 residents, are governed by a mayor and a board of trustees. The major source of revenue for both cities and towns is the property tax.

Denver, Colorado's capital and largest city, is run by a mayor and city council; a city auditor, independently elected, serves as a check on the mayor. Denver and Broomfield have consolidated city-county governments.

In 2005, local government accounted for about 184,033 full-time (or equivalent) employment positions.

15 STATE SERVICES

To address the continuing threat of terrorism and to work with the federal Department of Homeland Security, homeland security in Colorado operates under the authority of state statute and executive order; the public safety director is designated as the state homeland security adviser.

The Department of Education, under the direction of the State Board of Education, supervises and makes policy decisions for all public elementary and secondary schools. The State Board is made up of seven elected representatives from the state's congressional districts and one member-at-large; the commissioner of education is a nonvoting secretary to the Board. The Board of Regents of the University of Colorado governs the operations of that institution. All other state-run colleges, as well as the Colorado Historical Society, Council on the Arts and Humanities, and Advanced Technology Institute, are under the jurisdiction of the Department of Higher Education.

The Department of Transportation builds, operates, and maintains state roads. The Department of Health Care Policy and Financing administers welfare, medical assistance, rehabilitation, and senior-citizens programs. Human resource planning and development are under the Department of Labor and Employment, and health conditions are monitored by the Department of Health and Environment. The Department of Human Services oversees mental health, youth services, and developmental disabilities programs. The state's correctional facilities are administered by the Department of Corrections.

All programs concerned with the protection and control of Colorado's natural resources are the responsibility of the Department of Natural Resources. Other state agencies include the Department of Agriculture, Department of Military and Veterans Affairs, Department of Regulatory Agencies, Department of Public Safety, and Department of Law.

16 JUDICIAL SYSTEM

The supreme court, the highest court in Colorado, consists of seven justices elected on a nonpartisan ballot. The number of justices may be increased to nine upon request of the court and concurrence of two-thirds of the members of the General Assembly. The justices select a chief justice, who also serves as the supervisor of all Colorado courts. The next highest court, the court of appeals, consists of 16 judges, and is confined to civil matters. The 22 district courts have original jurisdiction in civil, criminal, juvenile, mental health, domestic relations, and probate cases, except in Denver, where probate and mental health matters are heard by the probate court and all juvenile matters by the juvenile court.

All judges in state courts are appointed to two-year terms by the governor from a list of names recommended by a judicial nominating commission. The appointees must then be elected by the voters: supreme court justices for 10-year terms, appeals court judges for 8 years, and district court judges for 6.

County courts hear minor civil disputes and misdemeanors. Appeals from the Denver county courts are heard in Denver's superior court. Municipal courts throughout the state handle violations of municipal ordinances.

As of 31 December 2004, a total of 20,293 prisoners were held in Colorado's state and federal prisons, an increase from 19,671 or 3.2% from the previous year. As of year-end 2004, a total of 1,900 inmates were female, up 9.4% (from 1,736) from the year before. Among sentenced prisoners (one year or more), Colorado had an incarceration rate of 438 per 100,000 population in 2004.

According to the Federal Bureau of Investigation, Colorado in 2004 had a violent crime rate (murder/nonnegligent manslaughter; forcible rape; robbery; aggravated assault) of 373.5 reported incidents per 100,000 population, or a total of 17,185 reported incidents. Crimes against property (burglary; larceny/theft; and motor vehicle theft) in that same year totaled 180,342 reported incidents or 3,919.3 reported incidents per 100,000 people. Colorado has a death penalty, of which lethal injection is the sole method used. From 1976 through 5 May 2006, the state executed only one person, which took place in October 1997. As of 1 January 2006, there were only two inmates on death row.

In 2003, Colorado spent $125,819,023 on homeland security, an average of $28 per state resident.

17 ARMED FORCES

As of 2004, 38,234 personnel, of whom 6,455 were civilians, were stationed at the nine military facilities in the state. Additionally, there were 2,909 Reserve and National Guard personnel. The largest Army base is Ft. Carson in Colorado Springs, with 14,061 active-duty military personnel. Fort Carson is a split-based home to the 4th Infantry Division, shared with Fort Hood, Texas. This post is recognized as one of the world's premier locations to lead, train, and maintain while preparing soldiers. At the Army's Rocky Mountain Arsenal near Denver, chemical weapons have been produced and stored. Colorado Springs is the site of the US Air Force Academy. Peterson Air Force Base is also located in Colorado Springs, as is the North American Air Defense Command (NORAD). Defense contracts awarded in 2004 totaled nearly $3.1 billion, and defense payroll, including retired military pay, amounted to $3.0 billion.

There were 427,956 veterans of US military service in Colorado as of 2003, of whom 43,097 served in World War II; 37,689 in the Korean conflict; 137,790 during the Vietnam era; and 79,924 in the Gulf War. US Veterans Administration spending in Colorado totaled $1.0 billion in 2004.

As of 31 October 2004, the Colorado State Police employed 666 full-time sworn officers.

18 MIGRATION

The discovery of gold in 1858 brought an avalanche of prospectors. Some of these migrants later moved westward into the Rockies and Colorado River canyons. In 1873, another gold strike brought settlers into the Ute territory, eventually driving the Indians into a small reservation in the southwestern corner of the state. During the late 19th and early 20th centuries, the sparsely populated eastern plains were settled by farmers from Kansas and Nebraska and by immigrants from Scandinavia, Germany, and Russia. Five years

of drought, from 1933 to 1938, helped drive many rural Coloradans off the land into the cities or westward to California.

Since the end of World War II, net migration into the state has been substantial, amounting to over 880,000 between 1950 and 1990. Between 1990 and 1998, Colorado had net gains of 359,000 in domestic migration and 58,000 in international migration. In 1998, 6,513 foreign immigrants were admitted to the state. Growth has been evident in both urban and rural areas, but the largest increase has been in the Denver metropolitan area, where by 1997, 14.3% of the total population was of Hispanic origin. A number of migrant workers, mostly Mexican Americans, work seasonally in the western orchards and fields. In the 1980s, migration accounted for 27% of the net population increase, with some 117,000 persons, even though there was a net loss from migration every year from 1986 to 1990. In 1990, native Coloradoans made up 43.3% of the population. Between 1990 and 1998, Colorado's overall population increased 20.5%. In the period 2000–05, net international migration was 112,217 and net internal migration was 47,740, for a net gain of 159,957 people.

19 INTERGOVERNMENTAL COOPERATION

Among the most important interstate agreements for Coloradoans are those governing water resources. Colorado participates with New Mexico in the Animas–La Plata Project, Costilla Creek, and La Plata River compacts; with Kansas in the Arkansas River Compact of 1949; and with Nebraska in the South Platte River Compact. The Cumbres and Toltec Scenic Railroad Compact supports the tourism industry. Multistate compacts allocate water from the Colorado and Republican rivers and the Rio Grande. Colorado also is a signatory to such regional agreements as the Interstate Oil and Gas Compact and the Western Interstate Energy Compact.

The Western Interstate Commission for Higher Education has its headquarters in Boulder, and the National Conference of State Legislatures has its headquarters in Denver. Federal grants to Colorado totaled over $3.9 billion in 2001. Following a national trend, they declined to $3.375 billion in fiscal year 2005, before beginning to gradually increase to an estimated $3.464 billion in fiscal year 2006, and an estimated $3.572 billion in fiscal year 2007.

20 ECONOMY

During the late 1880s, Colorado was the nation's leading silver producer and an important source of gold. With its abundant reserves of coal, natural gas, and other minerals—and the economic potential of its vast oil-shale deposits, Colorado remains a major mining state, although the mineral industry's share of the state economy declined throughout the 20th century. Agriculture, primarily livestock, retains its historic importance.

Trade, services, government, and manufacturing were responsible for more than 75% of new jobs created between 1975 and 1985. From 1972 to 2000, Colorado's employment in advanced technology grew from 39,000 to 125,000 employees, growth in which the US government was a major factor. Mining and construction suffered the greatest losses of employment between 1982 and 1992. Mining jobs declined 53% in that decade, and construction jobs dropped 29%. Employment in services, in contrast, rose 36% in those years, and jobs in finance, insurance and real estate increased by 15%. Tourism has also expanded rapidly in all areas of the state. Colorado's economy recovered strongly in the 1990s.

By 1997, Colorado's gross state product (GSP) was nearly $130 billion. By 2000, it had grown nearly 31%, with annual growth rates of 7.9% in 1998, 8.9% in 1999, and 11.2% in 2000. In the national recession of 2001, growth slowed abruptly to 2.6% as manufacturing fell 10.2% from the year before, leaving only a net gain of 1.5% in the sector from 1997 to 2001. Recovery remained elusive in 2002, as the state posted its first annual decline in employment since 1986.

In 2004, Colorado's GSP stood at $199.969 billion, of which the real estate sector accounted for the largest portion at $27.827 billion, or 13.9% of GSP, followed by professional and technical services at $17.082 billion (8.5% of GSP), and construction at $12.194 billion (6% of GSP). Mining, which has long been a staple of the state's economy, accounted for only $3.928 billion, or 1.9% of GSP. In 2004, Colorado had an estimated 493,886 small businesses. Of the 146,379 firms in the state that had employees in that year, an estimated 142,943, or 97.7%, worked for small firms, up by 1.8% from the previous year. An estimated 23,694 new companies were formed in Colorado in 2004, up 5.8% from the previous year. Business terminations in that same year totaled 9,734, a drop of 26.5% from 2003. However, business bankruptcies rose to 786 in 2004, an increase of 42.4% from 2003. In 2005, the personal bankruptcy (Chapter 7 and Chapter 13) filing rate stood at 564 per 100,000 people, ranking Colorado 24th nationally.

21 INCOME

In 2005 Colorado had a gross state product (GSP) of $216 billion, which accounted for 1.7% of the nation's gross domestic product and placed the state at number 21 in highest GSP among the 50 states and the District of Columbia.

According to the Bureau of Economic Analysis, in 2004 Colorado had a per capita personal income (PCPI) of $36,113. This ranked 10th in the United States and was 109% of the national average of $33,050. The 1994–2004 average annual growth rate of PCPI was 4.6%. Colorado had a total personal income (TPI) of $166,187,829,000, which ranked 21st in the United States and reflected an increase of 5.8% from 2003. The 1994–2004 average annual growth rate of TPI was 6.9%. Earnings of persons employed in Colorado increased from $127,196,780,000 in 2003 to $135,124,532,000 in 2004, an increase of 6.2%. The 2003–04 national change was 6.3%.

The US Census Bureau reports that the three-year average median household income for 2002–04 in 2004 dollars was $51,022, compared to a national average of $44,473. During the same period an estimated 9.8% of the population was below the poverty line, as compared to 12.4% nationwide.

22 LABOR

According to the Bureau of Labor Statistics (BLS), in April 2006, the seasonally adjusted civilian labor force in Colorado numbered 2,636,700, with approximately 113,100 workers unemployed, yielding an unemployment rate of 4.3%, compared to the national average of 4.7% for the same period. Preliminary data for the same period placed nonfarm employment at 2,264,700. Since the beginning of the BLS data series in 1976, the highest unemployment rate recorded in Colorado was 9.1%, in November 1982. The historical low was 2.5%, in January 2001. Preliminary nonfarm

employment data by occupation for April 2006 showed that approximately 7.3% of the labor force was employed in construction; 6.6% in manufacturing; 18.5% in trade, transportation, and public utilities; 7.1% in financial activities; 14.4% in professional and business services; 10% in education and health services; 11.5% in leisure and hospitality services; and 16.1% in government.

Colorado's labor history has been marked by major disturbances in the mining industry. From 1881 to 1886, the Knights of Labor led at least 35 strikes in the mines; during the 1890s, the Western Federation of Miners struck hard-rock mines in Telluride and Cripple Creek. The United Mine Workers, who came into the state in 1899, shut down operations at numerous mines in 1900 and 1903. Violence was common in these disputes. In one well-known episode, after striking miners and their families set up a tent colony at Ludlow, near Trinidad, the governor called out the militia; in the ensuing conflict, on 20 April 1914, the miners' tents were burned, killing 2 women and 11 children, an event that touched off a rebellion in the whole area. Federal troops restored order in June, and the strike ended with promises of improved labor conditions. In 1917, the state legislature created the Colorado Industrial Commission, whose purpose is to investigate all labor disputes.

The US Department of Labor's Bureau of Labor Statistics reported that in 2005, a total of 170,000 of Colorado's 2,052,000 employed wage and salary workers were formal members of a union. This represented 8.3% of those so employed, down from 8.4% in 2004, and below the national average of 12%. Overall in 2005, a total of 193,000 workers (9.4%) in Colorado were covered by a union or employee association contract, which includes those workers who reported no union affiliation. Colorado is one of 28 states that does not have a right-to-work law.

As of 1 March 2006, Colorado had a state-mandated minimum wage rate of $5.15 per hour. In 2004, women in the state accounted for 45.3% of the employed civilian labor force.

23 AGRICULTURE

Colorado ranked 14th among the 50 states in agricultural income in 2005, with $5.65 billion, of which more than $1.36 billion came from crops.

As of 2004 there were 30,900 farms and ranches covering about 30.9 million acres (12.5 million hectares); the average farm (including ranches) was 1,000 acres (405 hectares). The major crop-growing areas are the east and east-central plains, for sugar beets, beans, potatoes, and grains; the Arkansas Valley, for grains and peaches; and the Western Slope, for grains and fruits.

Colorado ranked seventh in the United States in production of dry edible beans in 2004, with 1,039,000 hundredweight; eighth in sugar beets, with 838,000 tons; fifth in barley, with 9.1 million bushels; and first in proso millet, with 7.9 million bushels (53% of the US total). Colorado is also a leading producer of wheat, with 46.9 million bushels. Other field crops include corn, hay, and sorghum. In 2004, Colorado produced 533,800 tons of fresh market vegetables, 27 million lb (12.3 million kg) of commercial apples, and 12 million lb (5.4 million kg) of peaches. About 100 tons of tart cherries were harvested in 2004. Colorado is also a major grower of roses.

²⁴ANIMAL HUSBANDRY

A leading sheep-producing state, Colorado is also a major area for cattle and other livestock. Cattle and calves, dairy products, and hogs together accounted for 71% of agricultural receipts in 2004.

From 1858 to about 1890, cattle drives were a common sight in Colorado, as a few cattle barons had their Texas longhorns graze on public-domain lands along the eastern plains and Western Slope. This era came to an end when farmers in these regions fenced in their lands, and the better-quality shorthorns and Herefords took over the market. Today, huge tracts of pasture-land are leased from the federal government by both cattle and sheep ranchers, with cattle mostly confined to the eastern plains and sheep to the western part of the state.

Preliminary estimates of the number of cattle and calves for 2005 was 2,500,000 with an estimated total value of $2.5 billion. Colorado had an estimated 800,000 hogs and pigs in 2004 with an estimated total value of $76 million. In 2003, Colorado produced 62.6 million lb (28.5 million kg) of sheep and lambs for a gross income of $96.6 million. Colorado was estimated to have produced an estimated 2.57 million lb (1.1 million kg) of shorn wool in 2004.

Other livestock products in 2003 included chickens, at an estimated 8.7 million lb (4 million kg), and milk, estimated at 2.17 billion lb (1.0 billion kg). In the same year, the state produced an estimated 1.1 billion eggs.

²⁵FISHING

There is virtually no commercial fishing in Colorado. The many warm-water lakes lure the state's 752,060 licensed sport anglers with perch, black bass, and trout, while walleyes are abundant in mountain streams. The Hotchkiss National Fish Hatchery produces and distributes trout to stock over 80 different water areas in Colorado and New Mexico.

²⁶FORESTRY

Approximately 21,637,000 acres (8,756,494 hectares) of forested lands were located in Colorado as of 2004. In spite of this wood resource, however, commercial forestry is not a major element of the state's economy. Lumber production in 2004 was 135 million board feet. In Colorado, forestry emphasis occurs in diverse areas: traditional forest management and stewardship; urban and community forestry; resource protection (from wildfire, insects, and disease); and tree planting and care. As of 2005 Colorado had 12 national forests; gross national forest acreage as of 2003 was 16,015,000 acres (6,481,271 hectares).

²⁷MINING

According to the US Geological Survey, the value all nonfuel mineral production in Colorado for 2004 was $1.01 billion, up 50% from 2003. In 2004, Colorado ranked 17th among the 50 states in the production (by value) of nonfuel minerals, with molybdenum concentrates, construction sand and gravel, portland cement, gold and crushed stones, respectively, the top nonfuel minerals (by value) produced that year. Metals accounted for almost 52% of all nonfuel mineral production, of which (in descending order), molybdenum concentrates, gold, and silver were the top three.

In 2004 Colorado (by volume) ranked second in the nation in the production of molybdenum concentrates (out of six states) and third in soda ash (out of three states). That same year, the state ranked 4th in the production of gold and 10th in silver. Overall, the state ranked 17th among the 50 states in total nonfuel mineral production, by value, with over 2% of the national total. In 2004, Colorado mined 40.9 million metric tons of construction sand and gravel ($235 million), 11 million metric tons of crushed stone ($67.3 million), 26,000 tons of lime ($2.57 million), and 249,000,000 metric tons of common clay ($1.51 million).

²⁸ENERGY AND POWER

An abundant supply of coal, oil, and natural gas makes Colorado a major energy-producing state.

As of 2003, Colorado had 67 electrical power service providers, of which 29 were publicly owned and 28 were cooperatives. Of the remainder, two were investor owned, one was federally operated and seven were owners of independent generators that sold directly to customers. As of that same year there were 2,264,833 retail customers. Of that total, 1,365,652 received their power from investor-owned service providers. Cooperatives accounted for 508,019 customers, while publicly owned providers had 391,150 customers. There were five federal customers and seven independent generator or "facility" customers.

Total net summer generating capability by the state's electrical generating plants in 2003 stood at 10.370 million kW, with total production that same year at 46.616 billion kWh. Of the total amount generated, 88.4% came from electric utilities, with the remainder coming from independent producers and combined heat and power service providers. The largest portion of all electric power generated, 36.115 billion kWh (77.5%), came from coal-fired plants, with natural gas plants in second place, at 9.226 billion kWh (19.8%), and hydroelectric plants in third, at 1.262 billion kWh (2.7%). Other renewable power sources accounted for 0.4% of all power generated, with petroleum-fired plants at 0.1%. Colorado has no nuclear power plants.

As of 2004, Colorado had proven crude oil reserves of 225 million barrels, or 1% of all proven US reserves, while output that same year averaged 60,000 barrels per day. Including federal off-shore domains, the state that year ranked 12th (11th excluding federal offshore) in proven reserves and 12th (11th excluding federal offshore) in production among the 31 producing states. In 2004 Colorado had 6,750 producing oil wells and accounted for 1% of all US production. As of 2005, the state's two petroleum refineries had a combined crude oil distillation capacity of 87,000 barrels per day.

In 2004, Colorado had 16,718 producing natural gas and gas condensate wells. In that same year, marketed gas production (all gas produced excluding gas used for repressuring, vented and flared, and nonhydrocarbon gases removed) totaled 1,079.235 billion cu ft (30.65 billion cu m). As of 31 December 2004, proven reserves of dry or consumer-grade natural gas totaled 14,743 billion cu ft (418.7 billion cu m).

Colorado in 2004 had 13 producing coal mines, 5 of which were surface mines and 8 of which were underground. Coal production that year totaled 39,870,000 short tons, up from 35,831,000 short tons in 2003. Of the total produced in 2004, underground mines accounted for 29,608,000 short tons. Recoverable coal reserves in 2004 totaled 415 million tons. (One short ton equals 2,000 lb/0.907 metric tons.)

Colorado holds the major portion of the nation's proved oil shale reserves. Because of its ample sunshine and wind, Colorado is also well suited to renewable energy development. Among the many energy-related facilities in the state is the National Renewable Energy Laboratory in Golden.

[29]INDUSTRY

Colorado is the main manufacturing center of the Rocky Mountain states. During the 1980s and 1990s, high-technology research and manufacturing grew substantially in the state.

According to the US Census Bureau's Annual Survey of Manufactures (ASM) for 2004, Colorado's manufacturing sector covered some 17 product subsectors. The shipment value of all products manufactured in the state that same year was $33.594 billion. Of that total, food manufacturing accounted for the largest share at $6.119 billion. It was followed by computer and electric product manufacturing at $4.481 billion; beverage and tobacco product manufacturing at $2.818 billion; miscellaneous manufacturing at $2.527 billion; and transportation equipment manufacturing at $2.478 billion.

In 2004, a total of 132,925 people in Colorado were employed in the state's manufacturing sector, according to the ASM. Of that total, 87,447 were actual production workers. In terms of total employment, the computer and electronic product manufacturing industry accounted for the largest portion of all manufacturing employees at 17,690, with 9,092 actual production workers. It was followed by food manufacturing, with 16,722 employees (12,228 actual production workers); miscellaneous manufacturing, with 12,940 (7,114 actual production workers); fabricated metal product manufacturing, with 12,561 (9,151 actual production workers); and transportation equipment manufacturing, with 9,734 (7,630 actual production workers).

ASM data for 2004 showed that Colorado's manufacturing sector paid $5.950 billion in wages. Of that amount, the computer and electronic product manufacturing sector accounted for the largest share at $1.015 billion. It was followed by transportation equipment manufacturing, at $702.096 million; miscellaneous manufacturing, at $556.153 million; food manufacturing, at $498.082 million; and fabricated metal product manufacturing, at $491.239 million.

[30]COMMERCE

Colorado is the leading wholesale and retail distribution center for the Rocky Mountain states. According to the 2002 Census of Wholesale Trade, Colorado's wholesale trade sector had sales that year totaling $92.09 billion from 7,339 establishments. Wholesalers of durable goods accounted for 4,495 establishments, followed by nondurable goods wholesalers at 2,093 and electronic markets, agents, and brokers accounting for 751 establishments. Sales by durable goods wholesalers in 2002 totaled $57.4 billion, while wholesalers of nondurable goods saw sales of $26.2 billion.

Electronic markets, agents, and brokers in the wholesale trade industry had sales of $8.4 billion.

In the 2002 Census of Retail Trade, Colorado was listed as having 18,851 retail establishments with sales of $52.2 billion. The leading types of retail businesses by number of establishments were: miscellaneous store retailers (2,637); clothing and clothing accessories stores (2,463); food and beverage stores (2,243); motor vehicle and motor vehicle parts dealers (1,974); and gasoline stations (1,726). In terms of sales, motor vehicle and motor vehicle parts stores accounted for the largest share of retail sales, at $14.7 billion, followed by food and beverage stores, at $8.4 billion; general merchandise stores, at $7.7 billion; and building material/garden equipment and supplies dealers, at $4.5 billion. A total of 247,264 people were employed by the retail sector in Colorado that year.

Exporters located in Colorado exported $6.7 billion in merchandise during 2005.

[31]CONSUMER PROTECTION

Colorado Attorney General's Consumer Protection Office is responsible for enforcing the state consumer protection laws including the Colorado Consumer Protection Act, the Unfair Trade Practices Act, the Fair Debt Collection Practices Act, the Uniform Consumer Credit Code, the Credit Services Organization Act and the Rental Purchase Agreement Act. Other applicable legislation includes the Motor Vehicle Repair Act, the Lemon Law, the Unsolicited Merchandise Act, the Charitable Solicitations Act, and the Colorado Statutes Concerning Pyramid Schemes. The office also represents the interests of consumers, small business, and agriculture before the Public Utilities Commission in matters involving electric, gas, and telephone utility services.

When dealing with consumer protection issues, the state's attorney general can initiate civil and criminal proceedings; represent the state before state and federal regulatory agencies; administer consumer protection and education programs; handle consumer complaints; and has broad subpoena powers. However, the Attorney General's Office cannot represent individual residents or consumers. In antitrust actions, the attorney general can act on behalf of those consumers who are incapable of acting on their own; initiate damage actions on behalf of the state in state courts; initiate criminal proceedings; and represent counties, cities, and other governmental entities in recovering civil damages under state or federal law.

The attorney general is also responsible for the enforcement of the state's ElderWatch Program, which, in conjunction with the AARP Foundation, fights the financial abuse and fraud directed toward the state's senior citizens through consumer advocacy, referrals, and information.

The state's Consumer Protection Division, Attorney General's Office, and the ElderWatch Program are located in Denver. There are also county-level consumer protection offices in Colorado Springs, Denver, Greeley, and Pueblo.

[32]BANKING

As of June 2005, Colorado had 175 insured banks, savings and loans, and saving banks, plus 69 state-chartered and 75 federally chartered credit unions (CUs). Excluding the CUs, the Denver-Aurora market area had 87 financial institutions in 2004, followed by Colorado Springs with 43. As of June 2005, CUs accounted for 22.2% of all assets held by all financial institutions in the state, or some $11.936 billion. Banks, savings and loans, and savings banks collectively accounted for the remaining 77.8%, or $41.760 billion in assets held.

State-chartered credit unions and savings and loans are regulated by the Division of Financial Services, under the Department of Regulatory Agencies (DORA). State-chartered commercial banks are regulated by the Division of Banking. Federally chartered financial institutions are regulated by the US government through the Office of the Comptroller of the Currency (banks), the Office of Thrift Supervision or the National Credit Union Administration.

In the year ending 31 December 2005, Colorado-based banks and thrifts had a median return on assets of 1.22%, which was above the national average of 1.04% in that year. In 2004, the median net interest margin (the difference between the lower rate offered savers and the higher rate charged on loans) was 4.33%, down from 4.35% in 2003, for the state's insured institutions.

33 INSURANCE

In 2004 there were 1.9 million individual life insurance policies in force with a total value of $229.6 billion; total value for all categories of life insurance (individual, group, and credit) was $351.1 billion. The average coverage amount is $118,000 per policy holder. Death benefits paid that year totaled over $814.6 million.

As of 2003, 21 property and casualty insurance companies and 10 life and health insurance companies were domiciled in Colorado. Direct premiums for property and casualty insurance amounted to about $7.57 billion in 2004. That year, there were 15,377 flood insurance policies in force in the state, with a total value of $2.7 billion.

In 2004, 58% of state residents held employment-based health insurance policies, 6% held individual policies, and 16% were covered under Medicare and Medicaid; 17% of residents were uninsured. In 2003, employee contributions for employment-based health coverage averaged at 16% for single coverage and 26% for family coverage. The state offers an 18-month health benefits expansion program for small-firm employees in connection with the Consolidated Omnibus Budget Reconciliation Act (COBRA, 1986), a health insurance program for those who lose employment-based coverage due to termination or reduction of work hours.

In 2003, there were over 3.1 million auto insurance policies in effect for private passenger cars. Required minimum coverage includes bodily injury liability of up to $25,000 per individual and $50,000 for all persons injured in an accident, as well as property damage liability of $15,000. In 2003, the average expenditure per vehicle for insurance coverage was $922.67.

34 SECURITIES

There are no stock or commodity exchanges in Colorado. In 2005, there were 1,750 personal financial advisers employed in the state and 5,860 securities, commodities, and financial services sales agents. In 2004, there were over 261 publicly traded companies within the state, with over 91 NASDAQ companies, 32 NYSE listings, and 22 AMEX listings. In 2006, the state had 10 Fortune 500 companies; Qwest Communications (based in Denver and traded on NYSE) ranked first in the state and 160th in the nation with

revenues of over $19 billion, followed by First Data (NYSE), Trans-Montaigne (AMEX), Echostar Communications (NASDAQ), and Liberty Media (NYSE).

35 PUBLIC FINANCE

The governor's Office of State Planning and Budgeting has lead responsibility for preparing the annual budget, which is presented to the General Assembly on 1 November. The legislature is expected to adopt the budget in May for the fiscal year (FY), which runs from 1 July through 30 June. The constitution requires that the budget be balanced as submitted, as passed, and as signed into

Colorado—State Government Finances

(Dollar amounts in thousands. Per capita amounts in dollars.)

	AMOUNT	PER CAPITA
Total Revenue	23,081,951	5,015.63
General revenue	14,956,732	3,250.05
Intergovernmental revenue	4,594,664	998.41
Taxes	7,051,457	1,532.26
General sales	1,909,246	414.87
Selective sales	984,789	213.99
License taxes	337,911	73.43
Individual income tax	3,413,891	741.83
Corporate income tax	239,591	52.06
Other taxes	166,029	36.08
Current charges	1,854,660	403.01
Miscellaneous general revenue	1,455,951	316.37
Utility revenue	–	–
Liquor store revenue	–	–
Insurance trust revenue	8,125,219	1,765.58
Total expenditure	18,060,533	3,924.50
Intergovernmental expenditure	4,860,577	1,056.19
Direct expenditure	13,199,956	2,868.31
Current operation	8,485,058	1,843.78
Capital outlay	1,123,706	244.18
Insurance benefits and repayments	3,015,461	655.25
Assistance and subsidies	161,239	35.04
Interest on debt	414,492	90.07
Exhibit: Salaries and wages	2,796,221	607.61
Total expenditure	18,060,533	3,924.50
General expenditure	15,034,648	3,266.98
Intergovernmental expenditure	4,860,577	1,056.19
Direct expenditure	10,174,071	2,210.79
General expenditures, by function:		
Education	6,293,255	1,367.50
Public welfare	3,537,787	768.75
Hospitals	325,203	70.67
Health	784,349	170.44
Highways	1,374,131	298.59
Police protection	112,341	24.41
Correction	701,710	152.48
Natural resources	207,025	44.99
Parks and recreation	73,484	15.97
Government administration	465,417	101.13
Interest on general debt	408,130	88.69
Other and unallocable	751,816	163.37
Utility expenditure	10,424	2.27
Liquor store expenditure	–	–
Insurance trust expenditure	3,015,461	655.25
Debt at end of fiscal year	9,874,764	2,145.75
Cash and security holdings	47,441,031	10,308.79

Abbreviations and symbols: – zero or rounds to zero; (NA) not available; (X) not applicable.

SOURCE: *U.S. Census Bureau, Governments Division, 2004 Survey of State Government Finances*, January 2006.

law. These requirements are part of the Colorado Taxpayer's Bill of Rights (TABOR), the name for a set of amendments adopted in 1992. The TABOR limits increases in per capita spending to the inflation rate, and mandates the immediate refund to the taxpayers of any surplus, unless they vote to allocate those funds to the state. The voters may also vote for tax increases beyond the inflation rate, which they did for school spending in 2001. Fiscal year 2006 general funds were estimated at $6.8 billion for resources and $6.5 billion for expenditures. In fiscal year 2004, federal government grants to Colorado were $5.6 billion.

In the fiscal year 2007 federal budget, Colorado was slated to receive: $52 million for planning and design for a new veterans hospital in Denver; $57 million for ongoing construction of the Animas La Plata Project, which will help provide water to southwestern Colorado and northwestern New Mexico.

36TAXATION

In 2005, Colorado collected $7,648 million in tax revenues or $1,640 per capita, which placed it 47th among the 50 states in per capita tax burden. The national average was $2,192 per capita. Sales taxes accounted for 26.2% of the total; selective sales taxes, 13.8%; individual income taxes, 49.3%; corporate income taxes, 4.1%; and other taxes, 6.6%.

As of 1 January 2006, Colorado had one individual income tax bracket of 4.63%. The state taxes corporations at a flat rate of 4.63%.

In 2004, local property taxes amounted to $4,722,286,000 or $1,026 per capita. The per capita amount ranks the state 23rd nationally. Colorado does not collect property taxes at the state level.

Colorado taxes retail sales at a rate of 2.90%. In addition to the state tax, local taxes on retail sales can reach as much as 7%, making for a potential total tax on retail sales of 9.90%. Food purchased for consumption off-premises is tax exempt. The tax on cigarettes is 84 cents per pack, which ranks 24th among the 50 states and the District of Columbia. Colorado taxes gasoline at 22 cents per gallon. This is in addition to the 18.4 cents per gallon federal tax on gasoline.

According to the Tax Foundation, for every federal tax dollar sent to Washington in 2004, Colorado citizens received $0.79 in federal spending.

37ECONOMIC POLICY

The Colorado Office of Economic Development and International Trade (OEDIT) implements the state government's economic plans. In 2000, the Governor's Office of Innovation and Technology (OIT) was established, and Colorado's first secretary of technology was appointed. Colorado's economic programs are aimed at encouraging new industry, helping existing companies expand and compete, and providing assistance to small businesses and to farmers. Economic development in rural areas is a priority. It offers real estate loans to help companies purchase or expand existing buildings or to construct new buildings. It assists employers with training programs for newly created and existing jobs. Colorado seeks to aid small businesses by contributing to lenders' reserve funds for small commercial and agricultural loans, by extending to small businesses loans with fixed interest rates, by giving grants to small technology-based firms for research and devel-

opment projects, and by offering capital loans and credit to small export/import companies. The state operates a network of Small Business Development Centers (SBDCs). The SBDCs offer Leading Edge courses to train businesspeople and people seeking to start business in entrepreneurial behaviors, covering such topics as strategic planning, marketing research, marketing, and cashflow analysis. The state offers a variety of loan programs for economic development and manages a number of loan programs for farmers and agricultural producers. A limited program of grants are earmarked for agriculture feasibility studies, technology, and defense conversion programs.

Colorado's Enterprise Zone program provides tax incentives to encourage businesses to locate and expand in designated economically distressed areas of the state. There were 18 enterprise zones and subzones in Colorado in 2006. Businesses located in a zone may qualify for ten different enterprise zone tax credits and incentives to encourage job creation and investment in these zones. The OEDIT also operates a Minority Business Office, whose mission is to promote development of existing and new minority businesses across the state with emphasis on rural areas that do not have access to information and technical help. The OEDIT works with Colorado businesses, associations, universities, and others to encourage the growth and development of bioscience companies, the aerospace industry, and other emerging industries. The Colorado Tourism Office (CTO) was created to promote Colorado as a tourism and travel destination. The Colorado Economic Development Commission (EDC) approves loans and grants from an economic development fund to public and private entities throughout the state to help existing businesses expand and new companies locate to Colorado. It also implements marketing programs to support ongoing business activities.

38HEALTH

The infant mortality rate in October 2005 was estimated at 6.6 per 1,000 live births. The birth rate in 2003 was 15.2 per 1,000 population. The abortion rate stood at 15.9 per 1,000 women in 2000. In 2003, about 79.3% of pregnant woman received prenatal care beginning in the first trimester. In 2004, approximately 77% of children received routine immunizations before the age of three.

The crude death rate in 2003 was 6.5 deaths per 1,000 population. As of 2002, the death rates for major causes of death (per 100,000 resident population) were: heart disease, 142.6; cancer, 141.7; cerebrovascular diseases, 42.5; chronic lower respiratory diseases, 41; and diabetes, 14.6. The mortality rate from HIV infection was 2.3 per 100,000 population. In 2004, the reported AIDS case rate was at about 7.3 per 100,000 population. In 2002, about 51.5% of the population was considered overweight or obese. As of 2004, about 20% of state residents were smokers.

In 2003, Colorado had 68 community hospitals with about 9,500 beds. There were about 444,000 patient admissions that year and 7 million outpatient visits. The average daily inpatient census was about 6,200 patients. The average cost per day for hospital care was $1,551. Also in 2003, there were about 215 certified nursing facilities in the state with 20,127 beds and an overall occupancy rate of about 81.2%. In 2004, it was estimated that about 72.3% of all state residents had received some type of dental care within the year. Colorado had 268 physicians per 100,000 resident population in 2004 and 708 nurses per 100,000 in 2005. In 2004, there were a total of 2,980 dentists in the state.

About 16% of state residents were enrolled in Medicaid and Medicare programs in 2004. Approximately 17% of the state population was uninsured in 2004. In 2003, state health care expenditures totaled $3.3 million.

39 SOCIAL WELFARE

In 2004, about 88,000 people received unemployment benefits, with the average weekly unemployment benefit at $298. In fiscal year 2005, the estimated average monthly participation in the food stamp program included about 245,926 persons (107,405 households); the average monthly benefit was about $106.14 per person. That year, the total of benefits paid through the state for the food stamp program was about $313.2 million.

Temporary Assistance for Needy Families (TANF), the system of federal welfare assistance that officially replaced Aid to Families with Dependent Children (AFDC) in 1997, was reauthorized through the Deficit Reduction Act of 2005. TANF is funded through federal block grants that are divided among the states based on an equation involving the number of recipients in each state. Colorado's TANF program is called Colorado Works. In 2004, the state program had 38,000 recipients; state and federal expenditures on this program totaled $53 million fiscal year 2003.

In December 2004, Social Security benefits were paid to 571,470 Colorado residents. This number included 366,660 retired workers, 55,380 widows and widowers, 69,780 disabled workers, 35,840 spouses, and 43,810 children. Social Security beneficiaries represented 12.4% of the total state population and 91.3% of the state's population age 65 and older. Retired workers received an average monthly payment of $935; widows and widowers, $910; disabled workers, $887; and spouses, $471. Payments for children of retired workers averaged $489 per month; children of deceased workers, $656; and children of disabled workers, $277. Federal Supplemental Security Income payments in December 2004 went to 54,131 Colorado residents, averaging $381 a month. An additional $7.4 million of state-administered supplemental payments was distributed to 33,724 residents.

40 HOUSING

In 2004, there were an estimated 2,010,806 housing units in the state, of which 1,850,238 units were occupied; 68.6% were owner occupied. It was estimated that about 65,261 units were without telephone service, 6,527 lacked complete plumbing facilities, and 7,242 lacked complete kitchen facilities. Though most homes employed gas and electricity as heating fuel, about 3,362 units were equipped for solar power heating. About 63.4% of all units were single-family, detached homes. The average household had 2.43 members.

In 2004, 46,500 new privately owned housing units were authorized. The median home value was $211,740. The median monthly cost for mortgage owners was $1,355 while the cost for renters was at a median of $724 per month. In September 2005, the state was awarded a grant of $150,000 from the US Department of Housing and Urban Development (HUD) for rural housing and economic development programs. For 2006, HUD allocated to the state over $11 million in community development block grants.

The Denver-Boulder area is Colorado's primary region of housing growth.

41 EDUCATION

As of 2004, 86.9% of Coloradans 25 years and over were high school graduates, surpassing the national average of 84%. Some 35.5% of the adult population of Colorado had completed four or more years of college, higher than the national average of 26%

In fall 2002, Colorado's public elementary and secondary schools had 752,000 pupils. Of these, 534,000 attended schools from kindergarten through grade eight, and 217,000 attended high school. Approximately 64.5% of the students were white, 5.8% were black, 25.3% were Hispanic, 3.1% were Asian/Pacific Islander, and 1.2% were American Indian/Alaskan Native. Total enrollment was estimated at 756,000 in fall 2003 and expected to be 833,000 by fall 2014, an increase of 10.9% during the period 2002–14. There were 50,123 students enrolled in 345 private schools in fall 2003. Expenditures for public education in 2003/04 were estimated at $6.8 billion. Since 1969, the National Assessment of Educational Progress (NAEP) has tested public school students nationwide. The resulting report, *The Nation's Report Card*, stated that in 2005, eighth graders in Colorado scored 281 out of 500 in mathematics compared with the national average of 278.

As of fall 2002, there were 282,343 students enrolled in institutions of higher education; minority students comprised 19.9% of total postsecondary enrollment. As of 2005, Colorado had 75 degree-granting institutions. The oldest state school is the Colorado School of Mines, founded in Golden in 1869. Although chartered in 1861, the University of Colorado did not open until 1876; its Boulder campus is now the largest in the state. Colorado State University was founded at Ft. Collins in 1870. The University of Denver was chartered in 1864 as the Colorado Seminary of the Methodist Episcopal Church. Colorado is also the home of the United States Air Force Academy.

42 ARTS

The Colorado Council on the Arts consists of 11 members appointed by the governor. In 2005, the council and other arts organizations received 26 grants totaling $2,304,700 from the National Endowment for the Arts. The Colorado Endowment for the Humanities was established in 1974. In 2005, 12 grants totaling $738,362 were awarded to state organizations from the National Endowment for the Humanities. The Council on the Arts is affiliated with the regional Western States Art Federation. The state government also provides a sizable share of the total for the support of the artists. In 1988, arts organizations in Denver successfully supported a proposal to contribute 0.1% of the area's sales tax to the development of the arts.

From its earliest days of statehood, Colorado has been receptive to the arts. Such showplaces as the Tabor Opera House in Leadville and the Tabor Grand Opera House in Denver were among the most elaborate buildings in the Old West. Newer centers are Denver's Boettcher Concert Hall, which opened in 1978 as the home of the Denver Symphony, and the adjacent Helen G. Bonfils Theater Complex, which opened in 1980 and houses a repertory theater company. The Colorado Symphony Orchestra was established in 1989 as the successor to the Denver Symphony.

Other artistic organizations include the Colorado Opera Festival of Colorado Springs; the Central City Opera House Association, which sponsors a summer opera season in this old mining town; and the Four Corners Opera Association in Durango. The amphitheater in Red Rocks Park near Denver, formed by red sandstone rocks, provides a natural and acoustically excellent concert area. In 2006, Red Rocks Amphitheater was scheduled to host a wide range of artists including the Allman Brothers, Ben Harper, and Chicago.

Aspen FilmFest, founded in 1979, offers several festivals throughout the year promoting interest in independent filmmaking. The Aspen Music Festival and School (AMFS), founded in 1949, is an annual internationally renowned classical music festival that offers over 200 events and educational opportunities throughout the summer.

43 LIBRARIES AND MUSEUMS

As of 2001, Colorado had 116 public library systems, with a total of 243 libraries, of which 138 were branches. In that same year, the state's public libraries held nearly 11,071,000 volumes of books and serial publications and had a total circulation of 43,460,000. The system also had 489,000 audio and 441,000 video items, 20,000 electronic format items (CD-ROMs, magnetic tapes, and disks), and 14 bookmobiles. The largest system was the Denver Public Library with 1,882,487 volumes in 27 branches. The leading academic library is at the University of Colorado at Boulder, with over 2.8 million volumes. Total public library operating income came to $167,910,000 in 2001, including federal grants worth $219,000 and state grants worth $4,080,000. Operating expenditures in that same year totaled $152,465,000, of which 62.4% was spent on staff, and 16.3% on the collection.

Colorado has more than 174 museums and historic sites. One of the most prominent museums in the West is the Denver Art Museum, with its large collection of American Indian, South Seas, and Oriental art. Another major art museum is the Colorado Springs Fine Arts Center, specializing in southwestern and western American art.

Other notable museums include the Denver Museum of Natural History, University of Colorado Museum in Boulder, Western Museum of Mining and Industry in Colorado Springs, and the Colorado Ski Museum–Ski Hall of Fame in Vail. Museums specializing in state history include the Colorado Heritage Center of the Colorado Historical Society in Denver, Ute Indian Museum in Montrose, Ft. Carson Museum of the Army in the West, Bent's Old Fort National Historic Site in La Junta, Georgetown–Silver Plume Historic District, Healy House–Dexter Cabin and Tabor Opera House Museum in Leadville, and Ft. Vasquez in Platteville.

44 COMMUNICATIONS

Colorado's first mail and freight service was provided in 1859 by the Leavenworth and Pikes Peak Express. Over 95.8% of the state's occupied housing units had telephones as of 2004. In addition, by June of that same year there were 2,727,910 mobile wireless telephone subscribers. In 2003, 70.0% of Colorado households had a computer and 63% had Internet access. By June 2005, there were

659,883 high-speed lines in Colorado, 623,716 residential and 72,167 for business.

Of the 80 major radio stations in operation in 2005, 22 were AM and 58 FM. There were 20 major television stations in operation in 2005. The Denver area had cable in 61% of its 1,268,230 television-owning households in 1999. A total of 109,775 Internet domain names were registered in Colorado by 2000.

45 PRESS

As of 2005, there were 21 morning dailies, 9 afternoon dailies, and 15 Sunday papers.

The leading newspapers are as follows:

AREA	NAME	DAILY	SUNDAY
Colorado Springs	*Gazette* (m, S)	90,900	107,945
Denver	*Rocky Mountain News* (m, S)	595,512	705,593
	Denver Post (m, S)	595,512	705,593

In May 2000, long-time rivals, the *Rocky Mountain News* and *Denver Post*, in search of an antitrust exemption to preserve rival editorial voices in Denver, applied for a joint operating agreement under the Newspaper Preservation Act. In 2001, they entered into a 50-50 partnership under a joint operating agreement, whereby they operate their advertising, marketing, circulation sales, distribution, and finance departments jointly. However, under their respective editors, they continue to express distinctive points of view.

In 2004, the *Rocky Mountain News* and *Denver Post* ranked 30th and 31st, respectively, among largest daily newspaper in the country, based on circulation. They ranked 8th in the nation for their combined Sunday circulation the same year.

In 2005, there were 103 weekly publications in Colorado, 71 paid weeklies, 7 free weeklies, and 25 combined weeklies. The total circulation of paid weeklies (308,254) and free weeklies (143,350) is 451,604.

46 ORGANIZATIONS

In 2006, there were over 4,880 nonprofit organizations registered within the state, of which about 3,613 were registered as charitable, educational, or religious organizations.

Professional and trade groups with national headquarters in the state include the Geological Society of America in Boulder; National Cattlemen's Association, the American School Food Service Association, American Sheep Producers Council, College Press Service, and National Livestock Producers Association.

Colorado Springs is the home of several important sports organizations, including the US Olympic Committee, USA Basketball, USA Hockey, Professional Rodeo Cowboys Association, and the US Ski Association. The Sports Car Club of America is in Englewood.

State arts and cultural organizations include the Colorado Artists Guild, the Colorado Historical Society, the Aspen Writers Foundation, and Young Audiences of Colorado. Junior Achievement has a national office in Colorado Springs.

47 TOURISM, TRAVEL, AND RECREATION

Tourism is making a comeback in the state as a result of improved funding and attention to the industry. A major slump for the industry began in 1993, when voters discontinued the state tourism tax. This resulted in a loss of $2.3 billion per year and a 33% decrease in Colorado's market share. The legislature reinstated funding of $6 million in 1999, and in 2000 the Colorado Tourism Office (CTO) was established as a branch of the office of Economic Development and International Trade. The new CTO is led by a 13-member board of directors representing various segments of the industry.

Florida, California, Arizona, and Texas are the state's primary competitors for tourism dollars. In 2004, there were 25.8 million overnight stays, and over 24 million visitors. Tourism accounts for over 200,000 jobs within the state.

Scenery, history, and skiing combine to make Colorado a prime tourist Mecca. Vail is the most popular ski resort center, followed by Keystone and Steamboat. Skiing aside, the state's most popular attraction is the US Air Force Academy near Colorado Springs. Nearby are Pikes Peak, the Garden of the Gods (featuring unusual red sandstone formations), and Manitou Springs, a resort center. Besides its many museums, parks, and rebuilt Larimer Square district, Denver's main attraction is the US Mint. Colorado is home to over 12,050 national landmarks.

All nine national forests in Colorado are open for camping, as are the state's two national parks: Rocky Mountain, encompassing 265,000 acres (107,000 hectares) in the Front Range; and Mesa Verde, 52,000 acres (21,000 hectares) of mesas and canyons in the southwest.

Other attractions include the fossil beds at Dinosaur National Monument, Indian cliff dwellings at Mesa Verde, Black Canyon of the Gunnison, Colorado National Monument at Fruita, Curecanti National Recreation Area, Florissant Fossil Beds, Great Sand Dunes, Hovenweep National Monument, Durango-Silverton steam train, and white-water rafting on the Colorado, Green, and Yampa rivers.

48 SPORTS

There are four major professional sports teams in Colorado, all in Denver: the Broncos of the National Football League, the Nuggets of the National Basketball Association, the Avalanche of the National Hockey League, and the Colorado Rockies of Major League Baseball. The Broncos won the American Football Conference Championship in 1978, 1987, 1988, and 1990, losing each year in the Super Bowl. They won back-to-back Super Bowl titles in 1998 and 1999. The Avalanche, who moved to Denver from Quebec after the 1995 season, won the Stanley Cup in 1996. The Colorado Springs Sky Sox compete in the Pacific Coast division of minor league baseball, and the Colorado Gold Kings compete in the West Coast Hockey League.

Colorado is home to some of the world's finest alpine skiing resorts, such as Vail, Aspen, and Steamboat Springs.

The Buffaloes of the University of Colorado produced some excellent football teams in the late 1980s and early 1990s, and they were named National Champions in 1990 (with Georgia Tech). Colorado won the Orange Bowl in 1957 and 1991, the Fiesta Bowl in 1995, and the Cotton Bowl in 1996. The Buffaloes have won or shared five Big Eight titles, the last one in 1991. Since the conference expanded to the Big Twelve, the Buffaloes have won the title once, in 2001.

Jack Dempsey, the famous heavyweight boxer of the 1920s, was born in Manassa.

49 FAMOUS COLORADANS

Ft. Collins was the birthplace of Byron R. White (1917–2002), who as an associate justice of the US Supreme Court since 1962, has been the state's most prominent federal officeholder. Colorado's first US senator, Henry M. Teller (b.New York, 1830–1914), also served as secretary of the interior. Gary Hart (b.Kansas, 1937) was a senator and a presidential candidate in 1984 and 1988.

Charles Bent (b.Virginia, 1799–1847), a fur trapper and an early settler in Colorado, built a famous fort and trading post near present-day La Junta. Early explorers of the Colorado region include Zebulon Pike (b.New Jersey, 1779–1813) and Stephen Long (b.New Hampshire, 1784–1864). John Evans (1814–97) was Colorado's second territorial governor and founder of the present-day University of Denver. Ouray (1820–83) was a Ute chief who ruled at the time when mining districts were being opened. Silver magnate Horace Austin Warner Tabor (b.Vermont, 1830–99) served as mayor of Leadville and lieutenant governor of the state, spent money on lavish buildings in Leadville and Denver, but lost most of his fortune before his death. The story of Tabor and his second wife Elizabeth McCourt Doe Tabor (1862–1935), is portrayed in Douglas Moore's opera *The Ballad of Baby Doe* (1956). Willard F. Libby (1909–80), winner of the Nobel Prize for chemistry in 1960, and Edward L. Tatum (1909–75), co-winner of the 1958 Nobel Prize for physiology or medicine, were born in Colorado. Among the performers born in the state were actors Lon Chaney (1883–1930) and Douglas Fairbanks (1883–1939), and band leader Paul Whiteman (1891–1967). Singer John Denver (Henry John Deutschendorf Jr., b.New Mexico, 1943–97) was closely associated with Colorado and lived in Aspen until his death in a plane crash.

Colorado's most famous sports personality is Jack Dempsey (1895–1983), born in Manassa and nicknamed the "Manassa Mauler," who held the world heavyweight boxing crown from 1919 to 1926.

50 BIBLIOGRAPHY

Abbott, Carl, Stephen J. Leonard, and Thomas J. Noel. *Colorado: A History of the Centennial State*. 3rd ed. Boulder: University Press of Colorado, 2005.

Aylesworth, Thomas G. *The Southwest: Colorado, New Mexico, Texas*. Chicago: Chelsea House Publishers, 1996.

Council of State Governments. *The Book of the States, 2006 Edition*. Lexington, Ky.: Council of State Governments, 2006.

Cronin, Thomas E. *Colorado Politics and Government: Governing the Centennial State*. Lincoln: University of Nebraska Press, 1993.

Harris, Katherine. *Long Vistas: Women and Families on Colorado Homesteads*. Niwot: University of Colorado Press, 1993.

Hill, Alice Polk. *Colorado Pioneers in Picture and Story*. Bowie, Md.: Heritage Books, 2002.

Litvak, Dianna. *Colorado*. Santa Fe, N.M.: John Muir Publications, 1999.

Mahoney, Paul F., Thomas J. Noel, and Richard E. Stevens. *Historical Atlas of Colorado.* Norman: University of Oklahoma Press, 1994.

Preston, Thomas. *Rocky Mountains: Montana, Wyoming, Colorado, New Mexico.* 2nd ed. Vol. 3 of *The Double Eagle Guide to 1,000 Great Western Recreation Destinations.* Billings, Mont.: Discovery Publications, 2003.

US Department of Commerce, Economics and Statistics Administration, US Census Bureau. *Colorado, 2000. Summary Social, Economic, and Housing Characteristics: 2000 Census of Population and Housing.* Washington, D.C.: US Government Printing Office, 2003.

Virden, William L. *Cornerstones and Communities: A Historical Overview of Colorado's County Seats and Courthouses.* Loveland, Colo.: Rodgers and Nelsen, 2001.

Wyckoff, William. *Creating Colorado: the Making of a Western American Landscape, 1860–1940.* New Haven: Yale University Press, 1999.

CONNECTICUT

State of Connecticut

ORIGIN OF STATE NAME: From the Mahican word *quinnehtukqut,* meaning "beside the long tidal river." **NICKNAME:** The Constitution State (official in 1959); the Nutmeg State. **CAPITAL:** Hartford. **ENTERED UNION:** 9 January 1788 (5th). **SONG:** "Yankee Doodle." **MOTTO:** *Qui transtulit sustinet* (He who transplanted still sustains). **COAT OF ARMS:** On a rococo shield, three grape vines, supported and bearing fruit, stand against a white field. Beneath the shield is a streamer bearing the state motto. **FLAG:** The coat of arms appears on a blue field. **OFFICIAL SEAL:** The three grape vines and motto of the arms surrounded by the words *Sigillum reipublicæ Connecticutensis* (Seal of the State of Connecticut). **BIRD:** American robin. **FLOWER:** Mountain laurel. **TREE:** White oak. **LEGAL HOLIDAYS:** New Year's Day, 1 January; Martin Luther King Jr. Day, 3rd Monday in January; Lincoln Day, 12 February; Washington's Birthday, 3rd Monday in February; Good Friday, March or April; Memorial Day, last Monday in May; Independence Day, 4 July; Labor Day, 1st Monday in September; Columbus Day, 2nd Monday in October; Veterans' Day, 11 November; Thanksgiving Day, 4th Thursday in November; Christmas Day, 25 December. **TIME:** 7 AM EST = noon GMT.

¹LOCATION, SIZE, AND EXTENT

Located in New England in the northeastern United States, Connecticut ranks 48th in size among the 50 states.

The state's area, 5,018 sq mi (12,997 sq km), consists of 4,872 sq mi (12,619 sq km) of land and 146 sq mi (378 sq km) of inland water. Connecticut has an average length of 90 mi (145 km) E–W, and an average width of 55 mi (89 km) N–S.

Connecticut is bordered on the N by Massachusetts; on the E by Massachusetts and Rhode Island (with part of the line formed by the Pawcatuck River); on the s by New York (with the line passing through Long Island Sound); and on the w by New York. On the sw border, a short panhandle of Connecticut territory juts toward New York City. The state's geographic center is East Berlin in Hartford County. Connecticut has a boundary length of 328 mi (528 km) and a shoreline of 253 mi (407 km).

²TOPOGRAPHY

Connecticut is divided into four main geographic regions. The Connecticut and Quinnipiac river valleys form the Central Lowlands, which bisect the state in a north–south direction. The Eastern Highlands range from 500 ft (150 m) to 1,100 ft (335 m) near the Massachusetts border and from 200 ft (60 m) to 500 ft (150 m) in the southeast.

Elevations in the Western Highlands, an extension of the Green Mountains, range from 200 ft (60 m) in the south to more than 2,000 ft (600 m) in the northwest; within this region, near the Massachusetts border, stands Mt. Frissell, the highest point in the state at 2,380 ft (726 m). The Coastal Lowlands, about 100 mi (160 km) long and generally 2–3 mi (3–5 km) wide, consist of rocky peninsulas, shallow bays, sand and gravel beaches, salt meadows, and good harbors at Bridgeport, New Haven, New London, Mystic, and Stonington.

Connecticut has more than 6,000 lakes and ponds. The two largest bodies of water (both artificial) are Lake Candlewood, covering about 5,000 acres (2,000 hectares), and Barkhamsted Reservoir, a major source of water for the Hartford area. The main river is the Connecticut, New England's longest river at 407 mi (655 km), of which 69 mi (111 km) lie within Connecticut; this waterway, which is navigable as far north as Hartford by means of a 15-ft (5-m) channel, divides the state roughly in half before emptying into Long Island Sound. The lowest point of the state is at sea level at the Long Island Sound. Other principal rivers include the Thames, Housatonic, and Naugatuck.

Connecticut's bedrock geology and topography are the product of a number of forces: uplift and depression, erosion and deposit, faulting and buckling, lava flows, and glaciation. About 180 million years ago, the lowlands along the eastern border sank more than 10,000 ft (3,000 m); the resultant trough or fault extends from northern Massachusetts to New Haven Harbor and varies in width from about 20 mi (32 km) to approximately 4 mi (6 km). During the Ice Ages, the melting Wisconsin glacier created lakes, waterfalls, and sand plains, leaving thin glaciated topsoil and land strewn with rocks and boulders.

³CLIMATE

Connecticut has a generally temperate climate, with mild winters and warm summers. The January mean temperature is 27°F (-3°C) and the July mean is 70°F (21°C). Coastal areas have warmer winters and cooler summers than the interior. Norfolk, in the northwest, has a January average temperature of 19°F (-7°C) and a July average of 68°F (19°C), while Bridgeport, on the shore, has an average of 30°F (-1°C) in January and of 74°F (23°C) in July. The highest recorded temperature in Connecticut was 106°F (41°C) in Danbury, on 15 July 1995; the lowest, -32°F (-36°C), in Falls Village on 16 February 1943. The annual rainfall (1971–2000) was 46.2

in (117 cm), evenly distributed throughout the year. The state receives 25–60 in (64–150 cm) of snow each year, with the heaviest snowfall in the northwest.

Weather annals reveal a remarkable range and variety of climatic phenomena. Severe droughts were experienced in 1749, 1762, 1929–33, the early 1940s, 1948–50, and 1956–57. The worst recent drought, which occurred in 1963–66, resulted in a severe forest-fire hazard, damage to crops, and rationing of water. Downtown Hartford was inundated by a flood in March 1936. On 21 September 1938, a hurricane struck west of New Haven and followed the Connecticut Valley northward, causing 85 deaths and property losses of more than $125 million. Severe flooding occurred in 1955 and again in 1982. In the latter year, property damage exceeded $266 million.

4 FLORA AND FAUNA

Connecticut has an impressive diversity of vegetation zones. Along the shore of Long Island Sound are tidal marshes with salt grasses, glasswort, purple gerardia, and seas lavender. On slopes fringing the marshes are black grass, switch grass, marsh elder, and sea myrtle.

The swamp areas contain various ferns, abundant cattails, cranberry, tussock sedge, skunk cabbage, sweet pepperbush, spicebush, and false hellebore. The state's hillsides and uplands support a variety of flowers and plants, including mountain laurel (the state flower), pink azalea, trailing arbutus, Solomon's seal, and Queen Anne's lace. Only two plant species were listed as threatened or endangered as of April 2006: the small whorled pogonia and the sandplain gerardia.

The first Englishmen arriving in Connecticut in the 1630s found a land teeming with wildlife. Roaming the forests and meadows were black bear, white-tailed deer, red and gray foxes, timber wolf, cougar, panther, raccoon, and enough rattlesnakes to pose a serious danger. The impact of human settlement on Connecticut wildlife has been profound, however. Only the smaller mammals, such as the woodchuck, gray squirrel, cottontail, eastern chipmunk, porcupine, raccoon, and striped skunk, remain common. Snakes remain plentiful and are mostly harmless, except for the northern copperhead and timber rattlesnake. Freshwater fish are abundant, and aquatic life in Long Island Sound even more so. Common birds include the robin (the state bird), blue jay, song sparrow, wood thrush, and many species of waterfowl; visible in winter are the junco, pine grosbeak, snowy owl, and winter wren.

The Connecticut River Estuary and Tidal River Wetlands Complex, a Ramsar Wetland of International Importance, serves as a habitat for at least 18 species of wintering birds and 30 species of shorebirds. The area is also an important migration path and spawning ground for a variety of fish, including Atlantic salmon and shortnose sturgeon.

In April 2006, a total of 16 animal species occurring within the state (vertebrates and invertebrates) were listed on the threatened and endangered species list of the US Fish and Wildlife Service. Among these were five kinds of sea turtles, the bald eagle, the roseate tern, two species of whale, and the gray wolf.

5 ENVIRONMENTAL PROTECTION

The Department of Environmental Protection (DEP), established in 1971, is responsible for protecting natural resources and controlling water, air, and land pollution.

Since the Connecticut Clean Water Act was passed in 1967, upgrading of sewage treatment plants, correction of combined sewer overflows, and improved treatment, at and sewage treatment tie-ins, by industrial facilities have resulted in significant water quality improvement in many state rivers. In 1997, about 75% of the state's 900 mi (1,448 km) of major streams met federal "swimmable-fishable" standards. The Connecticut Clean Water Fund was created in 1986 to provide grants and low-interest loans to municipalities to finance more than $1 billion in municipal sewerage infrastructure improvements over 20 years. Connecticut was the first state in the country to adopt, in 1980, a comprehensive statewide groundwater quality management system. In 2005, federal Environmental Protection Agency (EPA) grants awarded to the state included of $8.3 million for a drinking water state revolving loan fund.

In 1994 the governors of Connecticut and New York formally adopted a comprehensive plan to manage Long Island Sound, an "estuary of national significance." The Tidal Wetlands Act (1969) and the Inland Wetlands and Watercourses Act (1972) put the state in the forefront in wetland protection. In 1997 the DEP estimated permitted tidal wetland losses at less than one acre per year and inland wetland losses at about 630 acres per year. Two thousand or more acres of wetlands and watercourses have been restored, so that wetlands covered about 5% of the state's land area as of 2005. The Connecticut River Estuary and Tidal River Wetlands Complex, stretching through 12 counties, was designated as a Ramsar Wetland of International Importance in 1994.

For five of six criteria for air pollutants (lead, carbon monoxide, particulates, nitrogen dioxide, sulfur dioxide), Connecticut has virtually eliminated violations of health-based federal standards, and levels of these pollutants continue to decrease. The state exceeds the national standard for ozone but has reduced the number of days the standard is exceeded each year by 60% since the early 1970s. Vehicle-related emissions of ozone precursors have been reduced by almost 50%, and the state is working closely with other northeastern and mid-Atlantic states on regional ozone reduction. In 1986, the state adopted a hazardous air pollutant regulation that covers over 850 substances. Permitting and enforcement processes and voluntary reductions have resulted in at least a 68% reduction in toxins emitted to the air. In 2003, 5.4 million lb of toxic chemicals were released by the state.

In 1987, Connecticut adopted statewide mandatory recycling. Since 1986, five regional resource recovery facilities have begun operation, while dozens of landfills closed as they became full or federal regulations prohibited continued operation. The combination of resource recovery, recycling, and reduction of waste by consumers resulted in landfill garbage declining from 1,400 lb per capita in 1986 to about 300 in 1996.

In 2003, the EPA database listed 424 hazardous waste sites in Connecticut, 14 of which were on the National Priorities List as of 2006. The Broad Brook Mill of East Windsor was a proposed site in 2006. In 2005, the EPA spent $4.6 million through the Superfund program for the cleanup of hazardous waste sites in the state.

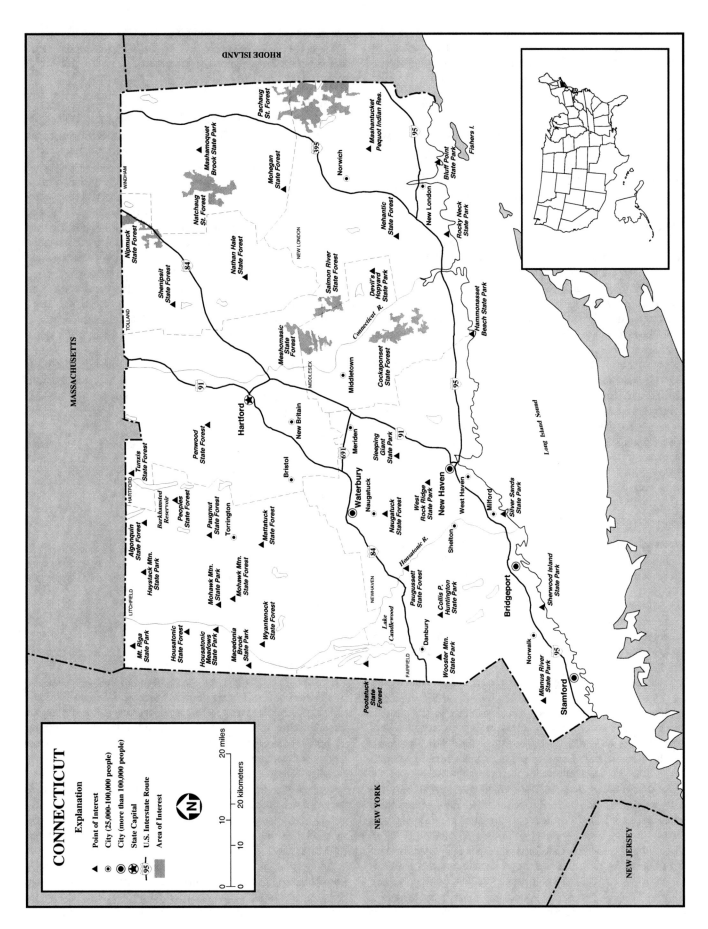

CONNECTICUT

Explanation

▲ Point of Interest

◉ City (25,000-100,000 people)

◉ City (more than 100,000 people)

★ State Capital

95 U.S. Interstate Route

Area of Interest

0   10   20 miles

0   10   20 kilometers

N

RHODE ISLAND

MASSACHUSETTS

NEW YORK

NEW JERSEY

Long Island Sound

Fishers I.

Pachaug St. Forest

Mashamoquet Brook State Park

Mohegan State Forest

Mashantucket Pequot Indian Res.

WINDHAM

Natchaug St. Forest

Norwich

New London

Bluff Point State Park

Nipmuck State Forest

Nathan Hale State Forest

NEW LONDON

Nehantic State Forest

Rocky Neck State Park

Shenipsit State Forest

84

Salmon River State Forest

Devil's Hopyard State Park

Connecticut R.

TOLLAND

Meshomasic State Forest

Hammonasset Beach State Park

91

Penwood State Forest

Hartford

New Britain

MIDDLESEX

Middletown

Cockaponset State Forest

Tunxis State Forest

HARTFORD

Meriden

691

Sleeping Giant State Park

91

Algonquin State Forest

Barkhamsted Reservoir

Peoples State Forest

Paugnut State Forest

Torrington

Mattatuck State Forest

Bristol

Waterbury

Naugatuck

Naugatuck State Forest

West Rock Ridge State Park

New Haven

West Haven

Milford

Silver Sands State Park

Haystack Mtn. State Park

Mohawk Mtn. State Park

Mohawk Mtn. State Forest

Housatonic R.

Shelton

LITCHFIELD

Wyantenock State Forest

Lake Candlewood

NEW HAVEN

Paugussett State Forest

Collis P. Huntington State Park

Sherwood Island State Park

Mt. Riga State Park

Housatonic State Forest

Housatonic Meadows State Park

Macedonia Brook State Park

Bridgeport

Danbury

FAIRFIELD

Wooster Mtn. State Park

Norwalk

Mianus River State Park

95

Pootatuck State Forest

Stamford

Connecticut DEP has been a pioneer in efforts to restore anadromous fish runs (ascending rivers) and extirpated species such as wild turkeys and fishers and to document and preserve habitats for numerous plant and animal species.

6 POPULATION

Connecticut ranked 29th in population in the United States with an estimated total of 3,510,297 in 2005, an increase of 3.1% since 2000. Between 1990 and 2000, Connecticut's population grew from 3,287,116 to 3,405,565, an increase of 3.6%. The population is projected to reach 3.63 million by 2015 and 3.69 million by 2025.

The state had a population gain of 5.8% (about 180,000 residents) for the entire decade of the 1980s, compared with a US population growth of 9.7%. One sign of the population lag was that in 1990 Connecticut had the 11th lowest birthrate in the United States, 14.5 live births per 1,000 population.

Population density in 2004 was 722.9 persons per sq mi (the fourth highest in the nation), up from 678.5 persons per sq mi in 1990. The median age of residents in 2004 was 38.9; 13.5% was age 65 or older, while 23.9% were under 18 years old.

Major cities, with 2004 population estimates, are Bridgeport, 139,910; Hartford, 124,848; New Haven, 124,829; Stamford, 120,226; and Waterbury, 108,429. The three largest cities each had a slight net growth in population between 1990 and 2002, helping to reverse their losses during the 1960s and 1970s due to an exodus to the suburbs, which had increased rapidly in population. For example, Bloomfield, to the north of Hartford, gained in population from 5,700 in 1950 to 19,023 in 1984; and Trumbell, near Bridgeport, increased from 8,641 in 1950 to 33,285 in 1984.

7 ETHNIC GROUPS

Connecticut has large populations of second-generation European descent. The biggest groups came from Italy, Ireland, Poland, and Quebec, Canada. Most of these immigrants clustered in the cities of New Haven, Hartford, Bridgeport, and New London. The number of Roman Catholic newcomers drew the hostility of many native-born residents, particularly during the decade 1910–20, when state officials deported 59 "dangerous aliens" on scant evidence of radicalism and Ku Klux Klan chapters enrolled some 20,000 members.

Since 1950, ethnic groups of non-Yankee ancestry have exercised leadership roles in all facets of Connecticut life, especially in politics. Connecticut elected a Jewish governor in 1954, and its four subsequent governors were of Irish or Italian ancestry. A wave of newcomers to the state during and after World War II consisted chiefly of blacks and Hispanics seeking employment opportunities. In 2000, the black population numbered 309,843, about 9.1% of the state total. In 2004, the black population was 10.1% of the state's total population. According to the 2000 federal census, there were also about 320,323 residents of Hispanic or Latino origin, or 9.4% of the state's total population (up from 213,000 in 1990), of whom 194,443 were Puerto Ricans (more than double the 1990 total of 93,608). In 2004, 10.6% of the population was of Hispanic or Latino origin. In 2000, Connecticut had 9,639 American Indians, up from 7,000 in 1990, 82,313 Asians, and 1,366 Pacific Islanders. In 2004, 0.3% of the population was American Indian, 3.1% was Asian, and 0.1% were Pacific Islanders. About 369,967 Connecticut residents, or 10.9% of the population, were foreign born in 2000, up from 279,000 (8.5%) in 1990. In 2004, 1.3% of the population reported origin of two or more races.

8 LANGUAGES

Connecticut English is basically that of the Northern dialect, but features of the eastern New England subdialect occur east of the Connecticut River. In the east, *half* and *calf* have the vowel of father; *box* is /bawks/ and *cart* is /kaht/; *yolk* is /yelk/; *care* and *chair* have the vowel of cat; and many speakers have the intrusive / r/, as in *swaller it* (swallow it). In the western half, *creek* is /krik/; *cherry* may be /chirry/; *on* has the vowel of *father*; an /r/ is heard after a vowel, as in *cart*. Along the Connecticut river, *butcher* is / boocher/, and *tomorrow* is pronounced /tomawro/. Along the coast, the wind may be *breezing on*, and a *creek* is a saltwater inlet. The sycamore is *buttonball*, one is *sick to his stomach*, gutters are *eavestroughs*, a lunch between meals is a *bite*, and in the northwest, an earthworm is an *angledog*.

In 2000, 2,600,601 Connecticuters (81.7% of the resident population five years old and older, down from 84.8% in 1990) spoke only English at home.

The following table gives selected statistics from the 2000 Census for language spoken at home by persons five years old and over. The category "Other Indo-European languages" includes Albanian, Gaelic, Lithuanian, and Rumanian.

LANGUAGE	NUMBER	PERCENT
Population 5 years and over	**3,184,514**	**100.0**
Speak only English	2,600,601	81.7
Speak a language other than English	583,913	18.3
Speak a language other than English	**583,913**	**18.3**
Spanish or Spanish Creole	268,044	8.4
Italian	50,891	1.6
French (incl. Patois, Cajun)	42,947	1.3
Polish	38,492	1.2
Portuguese or Portuguese Creole	30,667	1.0
Chinese	15,782	0.5
German	14,310	0.4
Other Indo-European languages	11,978	0.4
Greek	9,445	0.3
Russian	8,807	0.3
French Creole	7,856	0.2
Vietnamese	6,598	0.2

9 RELIGIONS

Connecticut's religious development began in the 1630s with the designation of the Congregational Church as the colony's "established church." The Puritan fathers enacted laws decreeing church attendance on Sundays and other appointed days, and requiring all residents to contribute to the financial maintenance of local Congregational ministers. Educational patterns, business practices, social conduct, and sexual activities were all comprehensively controlled in accordance with Puritan principles. "Blue Laws" provided penalties for offenses against God's word, such as profanation of the Sabbath and swearing, and capital punishment was mandated for adultery, sodomy, bestiality, lesbianism, harlotry, rape, and incest.

Connecticut authorities harassed and often persecuted such non-Congregationalists as Quakers, Baptists, and Anglicans. However, the church was weakened during the 18th century by increasing numbers of dissenters from the Congregational order. A coalition of dissenters disestablished the church by the Connecticut constitution of 1818. The final blow to Congregational domination came in the late 19th and early 20th centuries, with the arrival of many Roman Catholic immigrants.

Since World War I, Roman Catholics have been the most numerous religious group in the state. As of 2004, there were 1,333,044 Roman Catholics in 381 parishes. Mainline Protestants represent the second-largest category of churches and include the United Church of Christ, with 92,573 adherents in 2005, the Episcopal Church with 73,550 adherents in 186 congregations in 2000, and the United Methodist Church with 51,183 adherents in 133 congregations in 2000. The estimated number of Jewish adherents in 2000 was 108,280, and Muslims numbered about 29,647. About 42.1% of the population did not specify affiliation with a religious organization.

10 TRANSPORTATION

Because of both the state's traditional conservatism and the opposition by turnpike and steamboat companies, rail service did not fully develop until the 1840s. Hartford and New Haven were connected in 1839, and in 1850 that line was extended to Northampton, MA. In the 1840s and 1850s, a network of lines connected Hartford with eastern Connecticut communities. Railroad expansion peaked during the 1890s, when total trackage reached 1,636 mi (2,633 km). The giant in Connecticut railroading from the 1870s until its second and final collapse in 1961 was the New York, New Haven, and Hartford Railroad.

In the late 1960s, the Interstate Commerce Commission required that the assets of the bankrupt New York, New Haven, and Hartford Railroad be included in the Penn Central Transportation Company, which was formed by the merger of the New York Central and Pennsylvania Railroads. In 1970, Penn Central went bankrupt. In 1976, Penn Central's profitable assets were merged with the profitable assets of other northeast bankrupt railroads to form the Consolidated Rail Corporation (Conrail). As of 1997, Conrail had divested itself of most of its services in Connecticut, which as of 2003, was served by seven regional and short-line railroads, and one Class I railroad. As of 2003, there were 708 mi (1,140 km) of railroad in Connecticut, of which only 69 miles (111 km) were operated by the state's only Class I railroad.

In October 1970, the Connecticut Department of Transportation (CDOT) and the Metropolitan Transportation Authority of New York (MTA) entered an agreement (effective 1 January 1971) with the Trustees of Penn Central to oversee the operation of the New Haven Line Commuter Rail Service between New Haven and Grand Central Terminal in New York City and to jointly fund the operating deficit. In 1976, Conrail succeeded Penn Central as the operator of the New Haven Line and operated it until the end of 1982 when CDOT and MTA decided to operate the New Haven Line themselves.

On 1 January 1983, the Metro-North Railroad, which had been created as a subsidiary of the MTA, took over the operations of the New Haven Line in New York. CDOT and MTA continue to jointly oversee the operations of the New Haven Line service and fund the operating deficit. The costs of New Haven Line capital projects in Connecticut are funded by Connecticut, and the costs of capital projects in New York are funded by MTA. CDOT and MTA share the capital costs of rolling stock rehabilitation and acquisition. In 1985, CDOT purchased from Penn Central the Connecticut portion of the New Haven Line's main line and the three branch lines in Connecticut, including the right of way and support facilities.

On an average weekday, nearly 900 trains serve over 250,000 Metro-North customers from Connecticut and New York. In the mid-1990s, the on-time performance of New Haven Line trains ranged between 94.5% and 96.2%.

In 1990, CDOT contracted with Amtrak to operate the Shore Line East Commuter Rail Service between Old Saybrook and New Haven. Following a period of free service between 29 May and 29 June 1990, weekday only revenue service was implemented on 2 July 1990. In February of 1996, Shore Line East service was extended to New London. CDOT oversees the operation and provides the rolling stock, maintenance facilities, and funding necessary to cover the operating deficit. On an average weekday, 18 revenue trains serve about 600 customers. In the mid-1990s, the on-time performance of Shore Line East trains ranged between 90.0% and 96.3%.

Since 1971, Amtrak has provided inter-city passenger service to Connecticut on the Northeast Corridor main line (Boston–New Haven–New York City–Philadelphia–Washington, DC) and on the Springfield Line (New Haven–Hartford–Springfield).

Local bus systems provide intra-city transportation. These services are generally subsidized by the state and, in some instances, by the Federal Transit Administration. Inter-city bus service (not subsidized by the state or the federal government) is provided in over 30 municipalities by some 30 companies.

Connecticut has an extensive system of expressways, state highways, and local roads, totaling 21,144 mi (34,041 km) in 2004. Over 99% of the roads are either paved or hard-surfaced. Major highways include: I-95, the John Davis Lodge Turnpike, which crosses the entire length of the state near the shore; I-91, linking New Haven and Springfield, MA; and I-84 from the Massachusetts Turnpike, southwestward through Hartford, Waterbury, and Danbury to New York State. Over the past two decades, Connecticut has embarked on an ambitious infrastructure renewal program. Almost $2.2 billion has been expended to rehabilitate or replace over 1,866 of the 3,820 bridges that the state maintains. Approximately $927 million was used to resurface an average of 475 two-lane miles of state highway per year.

As of 2004, there were some 2.035 million automobiles, about 938,000 trucks of all types, and around 10,000 buses registered in the state. Connecticut had 2,694,574 licensed drivers during that same year.

Most of Connecticut's waterborne traffic is handled through the two major ports of New Haven and Bridgeport, which collectively handled approximately 16.5 million tons of cargo in 2004. The New London State Pier, which underwent reconstruction in the mid-1990s, unloaded its first post-renovation ship in March 1998 with Logistec Connecticut, Inc., in charge of operations. In 2004, Connecticut had 117 mi (188 km) of navigable inland waterways. Total waterborne shipments in 2003 totaled 18.579 million tons.

In 2005, Connecticut had a total of 152 public and private-use aviation-related facilities. This included 54 airports, 92 heliports, and six seaplane bases. Connecticut's principal air terminal is Bradley International Airport in Windsor Locks, located 14 mi (23 km) north of Hartford. Bradley had a total of 3,326,461 enplanements in 2004, making it the 49th-busiest airport in the United States.

11 HISTORY

The first people known to have lived in the area now called Connecticut were American Indians, whose forebears may have come to New England as many as 10,000 years ago. By the early 17th century, Connecticut had between 6,000 and 7,000 Indians organized into 16 tribes, all members of the lose Algonquian Confederation. The most warlike of these tribes were the Pequot, who apparently had migrated not long before from the Hudson River region to escape the Mohawk and had settled along the Connecticut coast. There was also a heavy concentration of Indian groups in the Connecticut River Valley, but fear of Mohawk hunting parties kept them from occupying most of western and northwestern Connecticut.

Because of their fear of the Pequot along the shore and of the Mohawk to the west, most of Connecticut's Indians sought the friendship of English newcomers in the 1630s. The Indians sold land to the English and provided instruction in New World agricultural, hunting, and fishing techniques. The impact of English settlers on Connecticut's friendly Indians was devastating, however. The Indians lost their land, were made dependents in their own territory, and were decimated by such European imports as smallpox and measles. The Pequot, who sought to expel the English from Connecticut by a series of attacks in 1636–37, were defeated during the Pequot War by a Connecticut-Massachusetts force, aided by a renegade Pequot named Uncas. By the 1770s, Connecticut's Indian population was less than 1,500.

The first recorded European penetration of Connecticut was in 1614 by the Dutch mariner Adriaen Block, who sailed from Long Island Sound up the Connecticut River, probably as far as the Enfield Rapids. The Dutch established two forts on the Connecticut River, but they were completely dislodged by the English in 1654.

The early English settlers were part of a great migration of some 20,000 English Puritans who crossed the treacherous Atlantic to New England between 1630 and 1642. The Puritans declared that salvation could be achieved only by returning to the simplicity of the early Christian Church and the truth of God as revealed in the Bible. They sailed to America in order to establish a new society that could serve as a model for the rest of Christendom. Attracted by the lushness of the Connecticut River Valley, the Puritans established settlements at Windsor (1633), Wethersfield (1634), and Hartford (1636). In 1639, these three communities joined together to form the Connecticut Colony, choosing to be governed by the Fundamental Orders, a relatively democratic framework for which the Reverend Thomas Hooker was largely responsible. (According to some historians, the Fundamental Orders comprised the world's first written constitution, hence the state nickname, adopted in 1959.) A separate Puritan colony was planted at New Haven in 1638 under the leadership of John Davenport, a Puritan minister, and Theophilus Eaton, a successful merchant.

In 1662, the Colony of Connecticut secured legal recognition by England. Governor John Winthrop Jr. persuaded King Charles II to grant a charter that recognized Connecticut's existing framework of government and established its north and south boundaries as Massachusetts and Long Island Sound and its east and west borders as Narragansett Bay and the Pacific Ocean. In 1665, New Haven reluctantly became part of the colony because of economic difficulties and fear of incorporation into Anglican New York.

Connecticut had acrimonious boundary disputes with Massachusetts, Rhode Island, New York, and Pennsylvania. The most serious disagreement was with New York, which claimed the entire area from Delaware Bay to the Connecticut River. The issue was resolved in 1683 when the boundary was set 20 mi (32 km) east of and parallel to the Hudson River, although it was not until 1881 that Connecticut, New York, and Congress established the exact line.

Connecticut functioned throughout the colonial period much like an independent republic. It was the only American colony that generally did not follow English practice in its legislative proceedings, nor did it adopt a substantial amount of English common and statute law for its legal code. Connecticut's autonomy was threatened in 1687 when Sir Edmund Andros, appointed by King James II as the governor of the Dominion of New England, arrived in Hartford to demand surrender of the 1662 charter. Connecticut leaders protected the colony's autonomy by hiding the charter in an oak tree, which subsequently became a landmark known as the Charter Oak.

With its Puritan roots and historic autonomy, Connecticut was a Patriot stronghold during the American Revolution. Tories numbered no more than 7% of the adult male population (2,000–2,500 out of a total of 38,000 males). Connecticut sent some 3,600 men to Massachusetts at the outbreak of fighting at Lexington and Concord in April 1775. Jonathan Trumbull, who served as governor from 1769 to 1784, was the only colonial governor in office in 1775 who supported the Patriots. He served throughout the Revolutionary War, during which Connecticut troops participated in most of the significant battles. Connecticut's privateers captured more than 500 British merchant vessels, and its small but potent fleet captured at least 40 enemy ships. Connecticut also produced arms and gunpowder for state and Continental forces, thus beginning an arms-making tradition that would lead to the state's unofficial designation as the "arsenal of the nation." It was also called the Provisions State, in large part because of the crucial supplies of foodstuffs it sent to General George Washington throughout the war. The state's most famous Revolutionary War figure was Nathan Hale, executed as a spy by the British in New York City in 1776.

On 9 January 1788, Connecticut became the fifth state to ratify the Constitution. Strongly Federalist during the 1790s, Connecticut ardently disagreed with the foreign policy of presidents Thomas Jefferson and James Madison, opposed the War of 1812, and even refused to allow its militia to leave the state. Connecticut's ire over the war was exacerbated by the failure of the government to offer significant help when the British attacked Essex and Stonington in the spring and summer of 1814. The politically vulnerable Federalists were defeated in 1817 by the Toleration Party. This coalition of Republicans and non-Congregationalists headed the drive for the new state constitution (1818) that disestablished the Congregational Church, a Federalist stronghold.

Long before the Civil War, Connecticut was stoutly antislavery. In the early years of independence, the General Assembly enacted legislation providing that every black born after 1 March 1784 would be free at age 25. Connecticut had a number of antislavery and abolition societies, whose members routed escaped slaves to Canada via the Underground Railroad. The state's pro-Union sentiment was reflected in the enormous support given to the Union war effort; some 55,000 Connecticut men served in the Civil War, suffering more than 20,000 casualties. Arms manufacturers such as Colt and Winchester produced desperately needed rifles and revolvers, and the state's textile, brass, and rubber firms turned out uniforms buttons, ponchos, blankets, and boots for Union troops.

The contributions by Connecticut industries to the war effort signaled the state's emergence as a manufacturing giant. Its industrial development was facilitated by abundant waterpower, the growth of capital held by banks and insurance companies, a sophisticated transportation network, and, most important, the technological and marketing expertise of the people. The first American hat factory was established in Danbury in 1780, and the nation's brass industry had its roots in Naugatuck Valley between 1806 and 1809. Connecticut clocks became known throughout the world. Micah Rugg organized the first nut and bolt factory in Marion in 1840; Elias Howe invented the first practical sewing machine in Hartford in 1843. Perhaps the most important figure in the development of Connecticut manufacturing was Eli Whitney, best known for inventing the cotton gin (1793).

Seventy-five years after Whitney's death, Connecticut was a leader in the production of hats, typewriters, electrical fixtures, machine tools, and hardware. The state's textile industry ranked sixth in the nation in 1900, with an annual output of $50 million. By 1904, Connecticut's firearms industry was producing four-fifths of the ammunition and more than one-fourth of the total value of all firearms manufactured by nongovernment factories in the United States. These great strides in manufacturing transformed Connecticut from a rural, agrarian society in the early 1800s to an increasingly urban state.

The state's contribution to the Allied forces in World War I (1914–18) more than equaled its Civil War effort. Four Liberty Loan drives raised $437 million, more than the contribution from any other state. About 66,000 Connecticuters served in the armed forces, and the state's manufacturers produced 450,000 Enfield rifles, 45,000 Browning automatic rifles, 2 million bayonets, and much other war materiel. By 1917–18, four-fifths of Connecticut's industry was involved in defense production.

The prosperity sparked by World War I continued, for the most part, until 1929. During the 1920s, Connecticuters enjoyed a rising standard of living, as the state became a national leader in the production of specialty parts for the aviation, automotive, and electric power industries. However, from 1919 to 1929, Connecticut lost 14 of its 47 cotton mills to southern states.

The stock market crash of 1929 and the subsequent depression of the 1930s hit highly industrialized Connecticut hard. By the spring of 1932, the state's unemployed totaled 150,000, and cities such as Bridgeport fell deeply in debt. The economic reversal led to significant political change: the ousting of a business-oriented Republican administration, which had long dominated the state, by a revitalized Democratic Party under the leadership of Governor Wilbur L. Cross (1931–39). During his tenure, Connecticut reorganized its state government, improved facilities in state hospitals and penal institutions, and tightened state regulations of business.

Connecticut was pulled out of the unemployment doldrums in 1939 when the state's factories were once again stimulated by defense contracts. The value of World War II (1939–45) contracts placed in Connecticut was $8 billion by May 1945, and industrial employment increased from 350,000 in 1939 to 550,000 by late 1944. Connecticut's factories turned out submarines, Navy Corsair fighter aircraft, helicopters, 80% of all ball bearings manufactured in the United States, and many thousands of small arms. Approximately 220,000 Connecticut men and women served in the US armed forces.

Since 1945, Connecticut has seen substantial population growth, economic diversification with a greater proportion of service industries, the expansion of middle-class suburbs, and an influx of black and Hispanic migrants to the major cities. Urban renewal projects in Hartford and New Haven resulted in expanded office and recreational facilities, but not much desperately needed new housing. A major challenge facing Connecticut in the 1980s was once again how to effect the social and economic integration of this incoming wave of people and industries. Providing greater economic opportunities for people living in its cities remains a challenge for Connecticut in the 2000s.

Connecticut became the nation's wealthiest state during the 1980s, achieving the highest per capita income in 1986, a position still held in 1992 when its residents' per capita income of $26,797 was 35% above the average for the United States. The state's prosperity came in part from the expansion of the military budget, as 70% of Connecticut's manufacturing sector was defense related. The end of the cold war, however, brought cuts in military spending which reduced the value of defense related contracts in Connecticut from $6 billion in 1989 to $4.2 billion in 1990. By 1992, manufacturing jobs had declined by 25% while jobs in such service industries as retail, finance, insurance and real estate increased by 23%. The total number of jobs, however, dropped by 10% during the period. Tax relief measures were taken to make manufacturing more competitive in the state. In the mid-1990s, Connecticut's economy was on the upswing, fueled in part by the recovering banking industry, and its employment outlook improved.

In the 1980s and through the 1990s, Connecticut witnessed an increasing contrast between the standard of living enjoyed by urban and suburban residents, blacks and whites, and the wealthy and the poor. In 1992, the median family income in many of the state's suburbs was nearly twice that of families living in urban areas. Governor Lowell Weicker's administration imposed a personal income tax (designed to address the inequities of the sales tax system) and implemented a program to modify state funding formulas so that urban communities received a larger share. The state also launched an effort to improve the quality of public education in relatively poor cities, to bring it in alignment with suburban schools.

While per-capita income levels remained high in the state through the rest of the decade, poverty increased. According to government figures, in 1998 Connecticut still ranked first in the nation in per capita personal income ($37,700), but the state's poverty rate, just 6% (the lowest in the nation) in 1990, had climbed to 9.2% by 1998. Per capita personal income stood at $45,506 in 2004, still highest among the states, while the poverty rate was 7.6% (the national average was 13.1%). While the state remained divided economically, it also was divided racially. Minority (black and Hispanic) populations were centered in urban Bridgeport, Hartford, and New Haven; smaller cities and suburbs remained predominately white.

Like many states across the nation, Connecticut faced a multi-million dollar budget deficit in the early 2000s. Connecticut adopted a stringent welfare reform law during Governor John G. Rowland's tenure, limiting benefits to 21 months. A new death penalty law was passed for the state, as was a law requiring communities to be notified when sex offenders are released from prison. Connecticut in 2005 was looking to attract further business investment to the state.

Foxwoods, a casino run by the Mashantucket Pequots in Ledyard, Connecticut, is a source of much-needed income for the tribe and an attraction for tourists and gamblers.

12 STATE GOVERNMENT

Connecticut has been governed by four basic documents: the Fundamental Orders of 1639; the Charter of the Colony of Connecticut of 1662; the constitution of 1818 (which remained in effect until 1964, when a federal district court, acting on the basis of the US Supreme Court's "one person, one vote" ruling, ordered Connecticut to reapportion and redistrict its legislature); and the constitution of 1965. This last document adjusted representation to conform with population and provided for mandatory reapportionment every 10 years. The 1965 constitution had been amended 29 times by January 2005.

The state legislature is the General Assembly, consisting of a 36-member Senate and 151-member House of Representatives. Regular legislative sessions are held each year, beginning in January in odd-numbered years (when sessions must end no later than in June) and in February in even-numbered years (when sessions must end no later than in May). A majority of legislators may call for special session. Legislators, who must be 18 years old, residents of their districts, and qualified voters in Connecticut, are elected to both houses for two-year terms from single-member districts of substantially equal populations. The legislative salary in 2004 was $28,000.

Elected members of the executive branch are the governor and lieutenant governor (who run jointly and must each be at least 30 years of age), secretary of state, treasurer, comptroller, and attorney general. All are elected for four-year terms and may be reelected. The governor, generally with the advice and consent of the general assembly, selects the heads of state departments, commissions, and offices. As of December 2004, the governor's salary was $150,000.

A bill becomes law when approved by both houses of the General Assembly and signed by the governor. If the governor fails to sign it within five days when the legislature is in session, or within 15 days after it has adjourned, the measure also becomes law. A bill vetoed by the governor may be overridden by a two-thirds vote of the elected members of each house.

A constitutional amendment may be passed in a single legislative session if approved by three-fourths of the total membership of each house. If approved in one session by a majority but by less than three-fourths, the proposed amendments requires approval by majority vote in the next legislative session following a general election. After passage by the legislature, the amendment must be ratified by the voters in the next even-year general election in order to become part of the state constitution.

To vote in state elections, a person must be a US citizen, at least 18 years old, a state resident, and a resident in the town where he or she will vote. Restrictions apply to convicted felons.

13 POLITICAL PARTIES

Connecticut's major political groups during the first half of the 19th century were successively the Federalist Party, the Democratic-Republican coalition, the Democrats, and the Whigs. The political scene also included a number of minor political parties, including the Anti-Masonic, Free Soil, Temperance, and Native American (Know-Nothing) parties, of which the Know-Nothings were the most successful, holding the governorship from 1855 to 1857. The Whig Party collapsed during the controversy over slavery in the 1850s, when the Republican Party emerged as the principal opposition to the Democrats.

From the 1850s to the present, the Democratic and Republican parties have dominated Connecticut politics. The Republicans held power in most of the years between the Civil War and the 1920s. Republican hegemony ended in 1930, when the Democrats elected Wilbur L. Cross as governor. Cross greatly strengthened the Connecticut Democratic Party by supporting organized labor and providing social legislation for the aged and the needy. The success of the increasingly liberal Democrats in the 1930s prodded Connecticut Republicans to become more forward-looking, and the two parties were fairly evenly matched between 1938 and 1954. Connecticut's Democrats have held power in most years since the mid-1950s.

Republican presidential candidates carried Connecticut for five successive elections starting in 1972 and ending with the victory of Democrat Bill Clinton in 1992. In the 1996 election, Clinton again carried the state. In the 2000 presidential election, Democrat Al Gore took the state with 56% of the vote to Republican George W. Bush's 39%. Green Party candidate Ralph Nader won 4% of the vote. In the 2004 presidential election, Democrat John Kerry won 54.3% of the vote to incumbent President George W. Bush's 44.0%. In 2004 there were 1,823,000 registered voters; an estimated 36% were Democratic, 24% Republican, and 40% unaffiliated or members of other parties. The state had seven electoral votes in the 2004 presidential election.

In 2005 Democrats controlled the state Senate, 24–11, and formed a majority in the state House (99 Democrats to 52 Republicans). Following the 2004 elections, Connecticut's delegation of US Representatives consisted of two Democrats and three Republicans (Connecticut lost a congressional seat in 2002). Both of Connecticut's US senators are Democrats: Christopher Dodd, reelected in 2004 for his fifth consecutive term; and Joseph Lieberman, elected to his third term in 2000. Democratic presidential candidate Al Gore chose Lieberman as his running mate in the 2000 presidential election. In 2003, Connecticut ranked eighth among the 50 states in the percentage of women state legislators, at 29.4%.

In 1994 Republican John G. Rowland was elected governor on a platform that included a promise to repeal the state income tax; he was reelected in 1998 and 2002. Rowland resigned in 2004 over a corruption scandal, and on 1 July 2005 Lieutenant Governor M. Jodi Rell succeeded him, becoming the second woman to hold the governorship of the state. US Representative Gary Franks, the first black member of the US House of Representatives from Connecticut and the first black House Republican in 55 years, was unseated in 1996 in his bid for a fourth term. In 1998 he made an unsuccessful run for US Senate, against incumbent (Democrat) Christopher Dodd.

14 LOCAL GOVERNMENT

As of 2005, Connecticut had 8 counties, 30 municipal governments, and 384 special districts. There were 166 school districts. Counties in Connecticut have been geographical subdivisions without governmental functions since county government was abolished in 1960.

Connecticut's cities generally use the council-manager or mayor-council forms of government. The council-manager system provides for an elected council that determines policy, enacts local legislation, and appoints the city manager. The mayor-council system employs an elected chief executive with extensive appointment power and control over administrative agencies.

In most towns, an elected, three-member board of selectmen heads the administrative branch. The town meeting, in which all registered voters may participate, is usually the legislative body. As of 2002, there were 149 townships in the state. Boroughs are generally governed by an elected warden, and borough meetings exercise major legislative functions.

In 2005, local government accounted for about 125,392 full-time (or equivalent) employment positions.

15 STATE SERVICES

To address the continuing threat of terrorism and to work with the federal Department of Homeland Security, homeland security in Connecticut operates under the authority of state statute and executive order; the commissioner for emergency management and homeland security is designated as the state homeland security adviser.

The Department of Education administers special programs for the educationally disadvantaged, the emotionally and physically disabled, and non-English-speaking students. The Department of Transportation operates state-owned airports, oversees bus system operations, and provides for snow removal from state highways and roads. The Department of Social Services has a variety of social programs for state residents, including special services for the physically disabled. The Department of Children and Families investigates cases of child abuse and administers programs dealing with child protection, adoption, juvenile corrections and rehabilitation, and prevention of delinquency.

Among programs sponsored by the Department of Public Health are ones that help people to stop smoking, increase their nutritional awareness, and improve their dental health. The Labor Department provides a full range of services to the unemployed, to job seekers, and to disadvantaged workers. Other departments deal with consumer protection, economic development, environmental protection, housing, mental retardation, information technology, and public safety.

Connecticut Presidential Vote by Political Parties, 1948–2004

YEAR	ELECTORAL VOTE	CONNECTICUT WINNER	DEMOCRAT	REPUBLICAN	PROGRESSIVE	SOCIALIST
1948	8	Dewey (R)	423,297	437,754	13,713	6,964
1952	8	*Eisenhower (R)	481,649	611,012	1,466	2,244
1956	8	*Eisenhower (R)	405,079	711,837	—	—
1960	8	*Kennedy (D)	657,055	565,813	—	—
1964	8	*Johnson (D)	826,269	390,996	—	—
					AMERICAN IND.	
1968	8	Humphrey (D)	621,561	556,721	76,660	—
						AMERICAN
1972	8	*Nixon (R)	555,498	810,763	—	17,239
						US LABOR
1976	8	Ford (R)	647,895	719,261	7,101	1,789
					LIBERTARIAN	CITIZENS
1980	8	*Reagan (R)	541,732	677,210	8,570	6,130
					CONN-ALLIANCE	COMMUNIST
1984	8	*Reagan (R)	569,597	890,877	1,274	4,826
					LIBERTARIAN	NEW ALLIANCE
1988	8	*Bush (R)	676,584	750,241	14,071	2,491
						IND. (Perot)
1992	8	*Clinton (D)	682,318	578,313	5,391	348,771
1996	8	*Clinton (D)	735,740	483,109	5,788	139,523
					GREEN	REFORM
2000	8	Gore (D)	816,015	561,094	64,452	4,731
						PETITIONING CANDIDATE (Nader)
2004	7	Kerry (D)	857,488	693,826	9,564	12,969

*Won US presidential election.

16 JUDICIAL SYSTEM

Connecticut's judicial system has undergone significant streamlining in recent years, with the abolition of municipal courts (1961), the circuit court (1974), the court of common pleas (1978), and the juvenile court (1978), and the creation of an appellate court (1983). Currently, the Connecticut judicial system consists of a supreme court, an appellate court, a superior court, and probate courts.

The Supreme Court comprises the chief justice, five associate justices, and two senior associate justices. The high court hears cases on appeal, primarily from the appellate court but also from the superior court in certain special instances, including the review of a death sentence, reapportionment, election disputes, invalidation of a state statute, or censure of a probate judge. Justices of the Supreme Court, as well as appellate and superior court judges, are nominated by the governor and appointed by the General Assembly for eight-year terms.

The Superior Court, the sole general trial court, has the authority to hear all legal controversies except those over which the probate courts have exclusive jurisdiction. The Superior Court sits in 12 state judicial districts and is divided into trial divisions for civil, criminal, and family cases. As of 1999, there were 167 superior court trial judges.

Connecticut has 132 probate courts. These operate on a fee basis, with judges receiving their compensation from fees paid for services rendered by the court. Each probate district has one probate judge, elected for a four-year term.

As of 31 December 2004, a total of 19,497 prisoners were held in Connecticut's state and federal prisons, a decrease of 1.8% (from 19,846) from the previous year. As of year-end 2004, a total of 1,488 inmates were female, down 3.9% (from 1,548) from the year before. Among sentenced prisoners (one year or more), Connecticut had an incarceration rate of 377 per 100,000 population in 2004.

According to the Federal Bureau of Investigation, Connecticut in 2004 had a violent crime rate (murder/nonnegligent manslaughter; forcible rape; robbery; aggravated assault) of 286.3 reported incidents per 100,000 population, or a total of 10,032 reported incidents. Crimes against property (burglary; larceny/theft; and motor vehicle theft) in that same year totaled 92,046 reported incidents or 2,627.2 reported incidents per 100,000 people. Connecticut has a death penalty, of which lethal injection is the sole method of execution. From 1976 through 5 May 2006, the state has carried out just one execution, which took place in 2005. As of 1 January 2006, there were eight death row inmates.

In 2003, Connecticut spent $158,064,813 on homeland security, an average of $48 per state resident.

17 ARMED FORCES

In 2004, there were 6,759 active-duty military personnel stationed in Connecticut, 1,080 civilian employees and 2,114 Reserve and National Guard. The principal military installation in the state is the US Navy submarine base at Groton. Across the Thames River in New London is the US Coast Guard Academy, one of the nation's four service academies. Founded in 1876 and located at its present site since 1932, this institution offers a four-year curriculum leading to a BS degree and a commission as ensign in the Coast Guard.

In fiscal year 2004, the value of defense contracts was $8.9 billion, and defense payroll, including retired military pay, amounted to $717 million.

There were 268,975 veterans of US military service in Connecticut as of 2003, of whom 49,046 served in World War II; 35,445 in the Korean conflict; 81,636 during the Vietnam era; and 26,660 in the Persian Gulf War. US Veterans Administration spending in Connecticut totaled $563 million in 2004.

As of 31 October 2004, the Connecticut State Police employed 1,213 full-time sworn officers.

18 MIGRATION

Connecticut has experienced four principal migrations: the arrival of European immigrants in the 17th century, the out-migration of many settlers to other states beginning in the 18th century, renewed European immigration in the late 19th century, and the intrastate migration of city dwellers to the suburbs since 1945.

Although the first English settlers found an abundance of fertile farmland in the Connecticut Valley, later newcomers were not so fortunate. It is estimated that in 1800, when Connecticut's population was 250,000, nearly three times that many people had moved away from the state, principally to Vermont, western New York, Ohio, and other Midwestern states.

The influx of European immigrants increased the number of foreign-born in the state from 38,518 in 1850 to about 800,000 by World War I. After World War II, the rush of middle-class whites (many from neighboring states) to Connecticut suburbs, propelled in part by the "baby boom" that followed the war, was accompanied by the flow of minority groups to the cities. All told, Connecticut had a net increase from migration of 561,000 between 1940 and 1970, followed by a net loss of 113,000 from 1970 to 1990. Between 1990 and 1998, the state had a net loss of 217,000 residents in domestic migration, and a net gain of 68,000 in international migration. In 1998, Connecticut admitted 7,780 foreign immigrants. Between 1990 and 1998, the state's overall population decreased by 0.4%. In the period 2000–05, net international migration was 75,991 and net internal migration was -34,273, for a net gain of 41,718 people.

19 INTERGOVERNMENTAL COOPERATION

Among the regional interstate agreements to which Connecticut belongs are the Atlantic States Marine Fisheries Commission, Connecticut River Atlantic Salmon Commission, Connecticut Valley Flood Control Commission, Interstate Compact for Juveniles, Interstate Sanitation Commission (with New York and New Jersey), New England Board of Higher Education, New England Interstate Water Pollution Control Commission, and the Northeastern Forest Fire Protection Compact. Boundary agreements are in effect with Massachusetts, New York, and Rhode Island. In fiscal year 2001, federal grants to Connecticut were almost $4.4 billion. Federal grants declined to $4.064 billion in fiscal year 2005, before gradually increasing to an estimated $4.302 billion in fiscal year 2006 and an estimated $4.368 billion in fiscal year 2007.

²⁰ECONOMY

Connecticut has had a strong economy since the early 19th century, when the state, unable to support its population by farming, turned to a variety of nonagricultural pursuits. Shipbuilding and whaling were major industries in the 1840s and 1850s. New London ranked behind only New Bedford and Nantucket, Massachusetts, among US whaling ports. Connecticut has also been a leader of the insurance industry since the 1790s.

Because defense production has traditionally been important to the state, the economy fluctuates with the rise and fall of international tensions. Connecticut's unemployment rate stood at 8.7% in 1949, dropped to 3.5% in 1951 during the Korean conflict, and rose sharply after the war to 8.3% in 1958. From 1966 to 1968, during the Vietnam War, unemployment averaged between 3.1% and 3.7%, but the rate subsequently rose to 9.5% in 1976. In 1984, in the midst of the Reagan administration's military buildup, Connecticut's unemployment rate dropped below 5%, becoming the lowest in the country. Connecticut lessened its dependence on the defense sector somewhat by attracting nonmilitary domestic and international firms to the state during the 1980s and 1990s. In 1984, more than 250 international companies employed more than 30,000 workers in the state. Connecticut was a leader in the manufacture of aircraft engines and parts, bearings, hardware, submarines, helicopters, typewriters, electronic instrumentation, electrical equipment, guns and ammunition, and optical instruments. Despite its dependence on military contracts, between 1984 and 1991 manufacturing employment declined 22.4%, while nonmanufacturing jobs rose by 11.6%. Nevertheless, the state was hard hit by cuts in military spending in the late 1980s and early 1990s. In 1991, defense-related prime contract awards had dropped 37.7% from the 1990 level. Pratt and Whitney, the jet engine maker, and General Dynamics' Electric Boat division, manufacturer of submarines, announced in 1992 that they would lay off a total of 16,400 workers over the following six years. In 1992, an estimated 70% of manufacturing was defense related, either through direct federal contracts, subcontracts with other companies, or in the manufacturing of basic metals used for weaponry. In 1993, unemployment stood at 7.3%. During the prosperous 1990s, unemployment fell steadily, and had reached 3% by 1999, although the ratio of manufacturing jobs continued to decline (overall, from nearly 50% in 1950 to 20% in 1999). Gross state product (GSP) grew at annual rates of 5.7% in 1998, and 4.4% in 1999, and then soared to 8.7% in 2000. During the national recession of 2001, growth slowed abruptly to 2.6%, as unemployment began to rise again. The downturn continued into 2002, as unemployment rose from 3.5% in June to 4.4% in November 2002.

In 2004, Connecticut's GSP totaled $185.802 billion, of which the real estate sector accounted for $24.370 billion, or 13% of GSP, followed by manufacturing (durable and nondurable goods) at $22.653 billion (12.2% of GSP) and professional and technical services at $13.896 billion (7.4% of GSP). In that same year, there were 322,805 small businesses in the state. Of the 97,311 firms in Connecticut that had employees, a total of 94,723 or 97.3% were small companies. In that same year, a total of 9,064 new businesses were formed in the state, up 6.6% from the previous year. Business terminations that year however, totaled 11,018, a drop of 0.2% from the year before. Business bankruptcies in 2004 totaled 132, down 29.4% from 2003. In 2005, the state's personal bankruptcy (Chapter 7 and Chapter 13) filing rate was 348 filings per 100,000 people, ranking Connecticut 45th in the United States.

²¹INCOME

In 2005, Connecticut had a gross state product (GSP) of $194 billion, which accounted for 1.6% of the nation's gross domestic product and placed the state 23rd among the 50 states and the District of Columbia.

According to the Bureau of Economic Analysis, in 2004 Connecticut had a per capita personal income (PCPI) of $45,318. This ranked second in the United States and was 137% of the national average of $33,050. The 1994–2004 average annual growth rate of PCPI was 4.3%. Connecticut had a total personal income (TPI) of $158,565,559,000, which ranked 23rd in the United States and reflected an increase of 6.5% from 2003. The 1994–2004 average annual growth rate of TPI was 4.9%. Earnings of persons employed in Connecticut increased from $115,256,181,000 in 2003 to $123,120,209,000 in 2004, an increase of 6.8%. The 2003–04 national change was 6.3%.

The US Census Bureau reports that the three-year average median household income for 2002–04 in 2004 dollars was $55,970, compared to a national average of $44,473. During the same period an estimated 8.8% of the population was below the poverty line, as compared to 12.4% nationwide.

²²LABOR

According to the Bureau of Labor Statistics (BLS), in April 2006 the seasonally adjusted civilian labor force in Connecticut numbered 1,830,800, with approximately 71,900 workers unemployed, yielding an unemployment rate of 3.9%, compared to the national average of 4.7% for the same period. Preliminary data for the same period placed nonfarm employment at 1,674,400. Since the beginning of the BLS data series in 1976, the highest unemployment rate recorded in Connecticut was 10% in January 1976. The historical low was 2.1% in November 2000. Preliminary nonfarm employment data by occupation for April 2006 showed that approximately 3.8% of the labor force was employed in construction; 11.5% in manufacturing; 18.6% in trade, transportation, and public utilities; 8.6% in financial activities; 12.1% in professional and business services; 16.4% in education and health services; 7.9% in leisure and hospitality services; and 14.6% in government.

During the early 20th century, Connecticut was consistently antiunion and was one of the leading open-shop states in the northeastern United States. But great strides were made by organized labor in the 1930s with the support of New Deal legislation recognizing union bargaining rights. All workforce services, including recruiting, training, workplace regulation, labor market information, and unemployment insurance, are offered through a statewide partnership of Connecticut's Department of Labor, Regional Workforce Development Boards, and state and community organizations.

The US Department of Labor's Bureau of Labor Statistics reported that in 2005, a total of 247,000 of Connecticut's 1,550,000 employed wage and salary workers were formal members of a union. This represented 15.9% of those so employed, up from 15.3% in 2004, and above the national average of 12%. Overall in 2005, a total of 263,000 workers (17%) in Connecticut were covered by a union or employee association contract, which includes those workers who reported no union affiliation. Connecticut is one of 28 states that does not have a right-to-work law.

As of 1 March 2006, Connecticut had a state-mandated minimum wage rate of $7.40 per hour, which was scheduled to increase to $7.65 per hour on 1 January 2007. In 2004, women in the state accounted for 47.4% of the employed civilian labor force.

23 AGRICULTURE

Agriculture is no longer of much economic importance in Connecticut. The number of farms declined from 22,241 in 1945 to 4,200 in 2004, covering a total of 360,000 acres (145,700 hectares).

Cash receipts from crop sales in 2005 were $358 million. Tobacco production was 3,889,000 lb. (1,768,000 kg) in 2004. Other principal crops are hay, silage, potatoes, sweet corn, tomatoes, apples, and peaches.

24 ANIMAL HUSBANDRY

There were an estimated 56,000 cattle and calves on Connecticut farms in 2005. Their estimated value was $59.9 million. In 2004, there were an estimated 4,200 hogs and pigs, valued at $546,000. During 2003, Connecticut dairy farmers produced an estimated 413 million lb (187.7 million kg) of milk. Also during 2003, poultry farmers produced an estimated 3 million lb. (1.4 million kg) of chicken and received $165,000 for 135,000 lb (46,000 kg) of turkey. Connecticut produced an estimated 795,000 eggs in 2003 at an estimated value of $44.1 million.

25 FISHING

Commercial fishing does not play a major role in the economy. In 2004, the value of commercial landings was $37.8 million for a catch of 21.1 million lb (9.6 million kg). In 2003, the state had only 23 processing and wholesale plants, with a total of about 237 employees. In 2001, the commercial fishing fleet had about 425 boats and vessels.

Several programs have been instituted throughout the years to restore the Atlantic salmon and trout populations on the Connecticut River. Connecticut had 148,125 sport-fishing license holders in 2004.

26 FORESTRY

By the early 20th century, the forests that covered 95% of Connecticut in the 1630s were generally destroyed. Woodland recovery has been stimulated since the 1930s by an energetic reforestation program. Of the state's 1,859,000 acres (752,337 hectares) of forestland in 2004, more than half was wooded with new growth. Lumber production in 2004 totaled 48 million board ft.

State forests covered some 298,000 acres (121,000 hectares) in 2004.

27 MINING

The value of nonfuel mineral production in Connecticut in 2004 was valued by the US Geological Survey at around $131 million. Crushed stone (10 million metric tons, worth $75.7 million) and construction sand and gravel (8.33 million metric tons, valued at $55.6 million), were the state's two leading nonfuel mineral commodities (by value), and accounted for nearly all production (by volume and value). Other commodities produced included common clays and dimension stone. Overall, nonfuel mineral production in 2004 fell 1.5% from 2003.

Demand for virtually all of the state's mineral output is dependent on a healthy construction industry, the main consumer of aggregates.

28 ENERGY AND POWER

As of 2003, Connecticut had 17 electrical power service providers, of which 7 were publicly owned and 3 were investor owned. Five sold only energy but did not provide delivery services, while two provided only delivery services. As of that same year there were 1,559,260 retail customers. Of that total, 1,467,971 received their power from investor-owned service providers, while publicly owned providers had 68,616 customers. There were 22,673 generation-only customers. There was no data on delivery-only customers.

Total net summer generating capability by the state's electrical generating plants in 2003 stood at 7.573 million kW, with total production that same year at 29.545 billion kWh. Of the total amount generated, only 2.8% came from electric utilities, with the remainder, 97.2%, coming from independent producers and combined heat and power service providers. The largest portion of all electric power generated, 16.078 billion kWh (54.4%), came from nuclear plants, with natural gas plants in second place at 5.061 billion kWh (17.1%) and coal-fired plants in third at 4.200 billion kWh (14.2%). Other renewable power sources accounted for 5.3% of all power generated, with petroleum-fired plants at 7%. Hydroelectric plants account for 1.9% of power generated.

As of 2006, Connecticut had one nuclear power generating facility, the Millstone plant in Waterford, which was operated by Dominion Generation.

Two of the four Northeast Heating Oil Reserves established by Congress in 2000 are located in Connecticut; their combined capacities total 850 thousand barrels.

Having no petroleum or gas resources of its own, nor any refineries. Connecticut must rely primarily on imported oil from Saudi Arabia, Venezuela, Nigeria, and other countries. Most of the natural gas used in Connecticut is piped in from Texas and Louisiana.

29 INDUSTRY

Connecticut is one of the most industrialized states, and it has recently diversified toward a broader economic portfolio. Six diverse industry clusters drive the state's economy: aerospace and advanced manufacturing; communications, information, and education; financial services; health and biomedical; business services; and tourism and entertainment.

According to the US Census Bureau's Annual Survey of Manufactures (ASM) for 2004, Connecticut's manufacturing sector covered some 17 product subsectors. The shipment value of all products manufactured in the state that same year was $45.105 billion. Of that total, transportation equipment manufacturing accounted for the largest share at $10.445 billion. It was followed by chemical manufacturing at $7.956 billion; fabricated metal product manufacturing at $5.128 billion; computer and electronic product manufacturing at $3.494 billion; and machinery manufacturing at $3.430 billion.

In 2004, a total of 191,909 people in Connecticut were employed in the state's manufacturing sector, according to the ASM. Of that total, 111,290 were actual production workers. In terms of total employment, the transportation equipment manufacturing industry accounted for the largest portion of all manufacturing employees with 44,885, with 19,894 actual production workers. It was followed by fabricated metal product manufacturing with 33,460 (23,744 actual production workers); machinery manufacturing, with 17,553 (9,040 actual production workers); computer and electronic equipment manufacturing, with 16,722 (7,978 actual production workers); and miscellaneous manufacturing, with 12,877 (7,863 actual production workers).

ASM data for 2004 showed that Connecticut's manufacturing sector paid $9.362 billion in wages. Of that amount, the transportation equipment manufacturing sector accounted for the largest share at $2.786 billion. It was followed by fabricated metal product manufacturing at $1.467 billion; machinery manufacturing at $926.567 million; computer and electronic product manufacturing at $921.795 million; and chemical manufacturing at $665.310 million.

30 COMMERCE

Considering its small size, Connecticut is a busy commercial state. According to the 2002 Census of Wholesale Trade, Connecticut's wholesale trade sector had sales that year totaling $86.9 billion from 4,785 establishments. Wholesalers of durable goods accounted for 2,909 establishments, followed by nondurable goods wholesalers at 1,491 and electronic markets, agents, and brokers accounting for 385 establishments. Sales by durable goods wholesalers in 2002 totaled $24.8 billion, while wholesalers of nondurable goods saw sales of $53.3 billion. Electronic markets, agents, and brokers in the wholesale trade industry had sales of $8.7 billion.

In the 2002 Census of Retail Trade, Connecticut was listed as having 13,861 retail establishments with sales of $41.9 billion. The leading types of retail businesses by number of establishments were: food and beverage stores (2,101); clothing and clothing accessories stores (1,945); miscellaneous store retailers (1,470); and motor vehicle and motor vehicle parts dealers (1,381). In terms of sales, motor vehicle and motor vehicle parts dealers accounted for the largest share of retail sales at $10.1 billion, followed by food and beverage stores at $7.2 billion; general merchandise stores at $4.1 billion; and building material/garden equipment and supplies dealers $3.7 billion. A total of 191,807 people were employed by the retail sector in Connecticut that year.

The estimated value of Connecticut's goods exported abroad was $9.6 billion in 2005. Shipments of transport equipment, non-electrical machinery, electric and electronic equipment, and instruments accounted for most of the state's foreign sales. Tobacco is the major agricultural export. Foreign exports go primarily to Canada and France.

31 CONSUMER PROTECTION

Since 1959, the Connecticut Department of Consumer Protection has been protecting consumers from injury by product use or merchandising deceit. The department conducts regular inspections of wholesale and retail food establishments, drug-related establishments, liquor retailers, bedding and upholstery dealers and manufacturers, and commercial establishments that use weighing and measuring devices. The department conducts investigations into alleged fraudulent activities, provides information and referral services to consumers, and responds to their complaints. It also licenses most professional and occupational trades and registers home improvement contractors. The Lemon Law Arbitration program and consumer guarantee funds in the areas of home improvement, real estate, and health clubs have returned millions of dollars to aggrieved consumers.

The Department of Consumer Protection also works with the state's Office of the Attorney General, which acts as counsel to the Department and represents it through litigation before state and/or federal courts.

When dealing with consumer protection issues, the state's Attorney General's Office can initiate civil and in some cases criminal proceedings; represent the state before state and federal regulatory agencies; become involved in the administration of consumer protection and education programs, and handle consumer complaints. However, the office has limited subpoena powers. In antitrust actions, the attorney general can act on behalf of those consumers who are incapable of acting on their own; initiate damage actions on behalf of the state in state courts; initiate criminal proceedings; and represent counties, cities and other governmental entities in recovering civil damages under state or federal law.

The state's Department of Consumer Protection is located in Hartford. In addition, the city of Middletown also has a Director of Consumer Protection.

32 BANKING

The first banks in Connecticut were established in Hartford, New Haven, Middletown, Bridgeport, Norwich, and New London between 1792 and 1805. By 1850, the state had 54 commercial and 15 savings banks. As of June 2005, the state had 58 insured banks, savings and loans, and saving banks, plus 43 state-chartered and 115 federally chartered credit unions (CUs). Excluding the CUs, the Hartford-West Hartford-East Hartford market area had 30 financial institutions in 2004, followed by the Bridgeport-Stamford-Norwalk area at 26. As of June 2005, CUs accounted for 9.3% of all assets held by all financial institutions in the state, or some $6.542 billion. Banks, savings and loans, and savings banks collectively accounted for the remaining 90.7% or $64.030 billion in assets held.

Banking operations are regulated by the state Department of Banking. The National Graham–Leach–Bliley Financial Modernization Act of 1999, which allowed the conglomeration of banking, securities, and insurance services, was badly received by the Connecticut Banking Commissioner. The over-weighted savings sector in Connecticut discriminates against the movement of capital in securities markets.

Connecticut has a large percentage of thrifts and residential lenders. Two-thirds of insured institutions in the state are savings institutions. Residential real estate loans comprise around half of the average loan portfolio in Connecticut.

33 INSURANCE

Connecticut's preeminence in the insurance field and Hartford's title as "insurance capital" of the nation date from the late 18th century, when state businessmen agreed to bear a portion of a shipowner's financial risks in return for a share of the profits. Marine insurance companies were established in Hartford and major port cities between 1797 and 1805. The state's first insurance company had been formed in Norwich in 1795 to provide fire insurance. The nation's oldest fire insurance firm is Hartford Fire Insurance, active since 1810. Subsequently, Connecticut companies have been leaders in life, accident, casualty, automobile, and multiple-line insurance. The insurance industry is regulated by the state department of insurance.

In 2004 there were 1.8 million individual life insurance policies in force with a total value of $245.9 billion; total value for all categories of life insurance (individual, group, and credit) was $383.9 billion. The average coverage amount is $134,300 per policy holder. Death benefits paid that year totaled $856.5 million.

In 2003, there were 69 property and casualty and 32 life and health insurance companies domiciled in Connecticut. In 2004, direct premiums for property and casualty insurance totaled $6.88 billion. That year, there were 30,291 flood insurance policies in force in the state, with a total value of $5.36 billion. About $675 million of coverage was offered through FAIR (Fair Access to Insurance) plans, which are designed to offer coverage for some natural circumstances, such as wind and hail, in high risk areas.

In 2004, 61% of state residents held employment-based health insurance policies, 3% held individual policies, and 24% were covered under Medicare and Medicaid; 11% of residents were uninsured. In 2003, employee contributions for employment-based health coverage averaged at 22% for single coverage and 23% for family coverage. The state offers a 18-month health benefits expansion program for small-firm employees in connection with the Consolidated Omnibus Budget Reconciliation Act (COBRA, 1986), a health insurance program for those who lose employment-based coverage due to termination or reduction of work hours.

In 2003, there were over 2.3 million auto insurance policies in effect for private passenger cars. Required minimum coverage includes bodily injury liability of up to $20,000 per individual and $40,000 for all persons injured in an accident, as well as property damage liability of $10,000. Uninsured and underinsured motorist coverage are required as well. In 2003, the average expenditure per vehicle for insurance coverage was $982.69, which ranked as the eighth-highest average in the nation.

34 SECURITIES

There are no securities or commodities exchanges in Connecticut. In 2005, there were 1,710 personal financial advisers employed in the state and 5,800 securities, commodities, and financial services sales agents. In 2004, there were over 213 publicly traded companies within the state, with over 60 NASDAQ companies, 63 NYSE listings, and 20 AMEX listings. In 2006, the state had 13 Fortune 500 companies; General Electric (based in Fairfield) ranked first in the state and seventh in the nation with revenues of over $157 billion, followed by Untied Technologies (Hartford), Hartford Financial Services, International Paper (Stamford), and Aetna (Hartford). All five of these companies are traded on the NYSE.

35 PUBLIC FINANCE

The state budget is prepared biennially by the Budget and Financial Management Division of the Office of Policy and Management and submitted by the governor to the General Assembly for consideration. In odd-numbered years, the governor transmits a budget document setting forth his financial program for the ensuing biennium with a separate budget for each of the two fiscal years in the biennium. In the even-numbered years, the governor transmits a report on the status of the budget enacted in the previous year, with recommendations for adjustments and revisions. The budgets are submitted to the legislature in February, and the legislature is supposed to adopt a biennium budget in May or June before the beginning of the fiscal year starting 1 July.

Fiscal year 2006 general funds were estimated at $14.6 billion for resources and $14.0 billion for expenditures. In fiscal year 2004, federal government grants to Connecticut were nearly $5.6 billion.

In the fiscal year 2007 federal budget, Connecticut was slated to receive $2.3 million, out of $100 million, for emergency contingency funding which is targeted for areas with the greatest need.

36 TAXATION

In 2005, Connecticut collected $11,585 million in tax revenues or $3,300 per capita, which placed it fourth among the 50 states in per capita tax burden. The national average was $2,192 per capita. Sales taxes accounted for 28.2% of the total, selective sales taxes 16.1%, individual income taxes 43.4%, corporate income taxes 5.0%, and other taxes 7.3%.

As of 1 January 2006, Connecticut had two individual income tax brackets ranging from 3.0% to 5.0%. The state taxes corporations at a flat rate of 7.5%.

In 2004, local property taxes amounted to $6,801,676,000 or $1,944 per capita. The per capita amount ranks the state behind New Jersey with the second-highest per capita tax burden. Connecticut does not collect property taxes at the state level.

Connecticut taxes retail sales at a rate of 6%. Food purchased for consumption off-premises is tax exempt. The tax on cigarettes is 151 cents per pack, which ranks eighth among the 50 states and the District of Columbia. Connecticut taxes gasoline at 25 cents per gallon. This is in addition to the 18.4 cents per gallon federal tax on gasoline.

According to the Tax Foundation, for every federal tax dollar sent to Washington in 2004, Connecticut citizens received $0.66 in federal spending, which ranks the state second-lowest nationally.

Connecticut—State Government Finances

(Dollar amounts in thousands. Per capita amounts in dollars.)

	AMOUNT	PER CAPITA
Total Revenue	19,518,768	5,578.38
General revenue	17,423,130	4,979.46
Intergovernmental revenue	4,131,625	1,180.80
Taxes	10,291,289	2,941.21
General sales	3,127,221	893.75
Selective sales	1,773,155	506.76
License taxes	385,265	110.11
Individual income tax	4,319,546	1,234.51
Corporate income tax	379,822	108.55
Other taxes	306,280	87.53
Current charges	1,401,387	400.51
Miscellaneous general revenue	1,598,829	456.94
Utility revenue	23,149	6.62
Liquor store revenue	–	–
Insurance trust revenue	2,072,489	592.31
Total expenditure	19,523,465	5,579.73
Intergovernmental expenditure	3,396,810	970.79
Direct expenditure	16,126,655	4,608.93
Current operation	10,880,637	3,109.64
Capital outlay	940,269	268.73
Insurance benefits and repayments	2,620,234	748.85
Assistance and subsidies	437,945	125.16
Interest on debt	1,247,570	356.55
Exhibit: Salaries and wages	4,186,544	1,196.50
Total expenditure	19,523,465	5,579.73
General expenditure	16,669,360	4,764.04
Intergovernmental expenditure	3,396,810	970.79
Direct expenditure	13,272,550	3,793.24
General expenditures, by function:		
Education	4,470,459	1,277.64
Public welfare	4,417,465	1,262.49
Hospitals	1,408,929	402.67
Health	499,702	142.81
Highways	862,082	246.38
Police protection	170,905	48.84
Correction	558,043	159.49
Natural resources	96,389	27.55
Parks and recreation	151,227	43.22
Government administration	977,125	279.26
Interest on general debt	1,247,570	356.55
Other and unallocable	1,809,464	517.14
Utility expenditure	233,871	66.84
Liquor store expenditure	–	–
Insurance trust expenditure	2,620,234	748.85
Debt at end of fiscal year	22,574,585	6,451.72
Cash and security holdings	32,791,485	9,371.67

Abbreviations and symbols: – zero or rounds to zero; (NA) not available; (X) not applicable.

SOURCE: U.S. Census Bureau, Governments Division, 2004 Survey of State Government Finances, January 2006.

37 ECONOMIC POLICY

Connecticut's economic development programs are overseen by its Department of Economic and Community Development (DECD). An important task is administering federal grants made through the Community Development Block Grant (CDBG) program operating since 1974. Connecticut was the first state to establish Enterprise Zones (EZs), starting with six EZ's in 1982 and up to 17 in 2006. EZ's are areas with high rates of unemployment,

poverty and/or public assistance that are granted stimulus packages of tax reductions and exemptions. In 1994, the state established the Community Economic Development Fund (CEDF) to help revitalize distressed neighborhoods by providing greater access to capital for small business and community development organizations. The CEDF provides loans, grants and technical assistance with the aim of supporting job creation and retention and community planning efforts. The state offers low-interest loans and grants for capital expenditures, machinery, land, building, training, and recruiting. Connecticut offers tax credits and abatements for machinery and equipment. Connecticut Innovations is the state's technology development corporation. The Connecticut Economic Resource Center, Inc., coordinates business-to-business marketing and recruitment on behalf of the state. Business recruitment missions have been sent to Europe and Japan to stimulate the state's export program. In 1998, the Governor's Council on Economic Compositeness and Technology was established composed of a collection of CEO's, industry representatives, educators, labor leaders, state commissioners, and legislators. The Governor's Council adopted an Industry Cluster approach to economic development, and has since identified six clusters for particular attention in Connecticut: Tourism (already a separate office), BioScience (since 1998); Aerospace; Software and Information Technology; and Metals Manufacturing (all identified in 1999); and the Maritime Industry (2001). In 2002, Connecticut became the first state to establish an Office of BioScience, located within the DECD. Industry Cluster program, administered by the DECD, is regularly monitored by the Governor's Council to assess progress within the clusters.

In 2006, the DECD's three core responsibilities were: economic development, housing development, and community development. Connecticut's Micro Loan Guarantee Program for Women and Minority Owned Businesses is a special loan guarantee program, offered in conjunction with the CEDF, that helps women- and minority-owned businesses obtain flexible financing. This is for the growth of startup as well as existing businesses. Connecticut also has an Industrial Parks Program, which provides planning and development services, assistance to renovate or demolish vacant industrial buildings, and technical assistance to help municipalities develop industrial parks. In 2006, Connecticut awarded 10 inner city entrepreneurial awards, to highlight and celebrate 10 of the fastest-growing, privately owned companies located in inner cities. In 2006, the US Chamber of Commerce ranked all 50 states on legal fairness towards business. The chamber found Connecticut to be one of five states with the best legal environment for business. The other four were Nebraska, Virginia, Iowa, and Delaware.

38 HEALTH

The infant mortality rate in October 2005 was estimated at 5.4 per 1,000 live births. The birth rate in 2003 was 12.3 per 1,000 population. The abortion rate stood at 21.1 per 1,000 women in 2000. In 2003, about 88.7% of pregnant woman received prenatal care beginning in the first trimester. In 2004, approximately 88% of children received routine immunizations before the age of three.

The crude death rate in 2003 was 8.4 deaths per 1,000 population. As of 2002, the death rates for major causes of death (per

100,000 resident population) were: heart disease, 254.7; cancer, 207; cerebrovascular diseases, 53.8; chronic lower respiratory diseases, 42; and diabetes, 19.5. The mortality rate from HIV infection was 5.4 per 100,000 population. In 2004, the reported AIDS case rate was at about 18.4 per 100,000 population. In 2002, about 51.4% of the population was considered overweight or obese. As of 2004, about 18% of state residents were smokers.

In 2003, Connecticut had 34 community hospitals with about 7,200 beds. There were about 372,000 patient admissions that year and 6.8 million outpatient visits. The average daily inpatient census was about 5,600 patients. The average cost per day for hospital care was $1,684. Also in 2003, there were about 252 certified nursing facilities in the state with 31,248 beds and an overall occupancy rate of about 91.6%. In 2004, it was estimated that about 80.6% of all state residents had received some type of dental care within the year; this was the highest dental care rate in the nation. Connecticut had 369 physicians per 100,000 resident population in 2004 and 972 nurses per 100,000 in 2005. In 2004, there was a total of 2,653 dentists in the state.

Outstanding medical schools are those of Yale University and the University of Connecticut.

About 24% of state residents were enrolled in Medicaid and Medicare programs in 2004. Approximately 11% of the state population was uninsured in 2004. In 2003, state health care expenditures totaled $5.2 million.

³⁹ SOCIAL WELFARE

In 2004, about 128,000 people received unemployment benefits, with the average weekly unemployment benefit at $284. In fiscal year 2005, the estimated average monthly participation in the food stamp program included about 204,146 persons (107,492 households); the average monthly benefit was about $91.11 per person. That year, the total of benefits paid through the state for the food stamp program was about $223 million.

Temporary Assistance for Needy Families (TANF), the system of federal welfare assistance that officially replaced Aid to Families with Dependent Children (AFDC) in 1997, was reauthorized through the Deficit Reduction Act of 2005. TANF is funded through federal block grants that are divided among the states based on an equation involving the number of recipients in each state. Connecticut's TANF program is called JOBS FIRST. In 2004, the state program had 43,000 recipients; state and federal expenditures on this program totaled $162 million in fiscal year 2003.

In December 2004, Social Security benefits were paid to 584,090 Connecticut residents. This number included 406,450 retired workers, 48,820 widows and widowers, 62,320 disabled workers, 24,820 spouses, and 41,680 children. Social Security beneficiaries represented 16.7% of the total state population and 93.6% of the state's population age 65 and older. Retired workers received an average monthly payment of $1,044; widows and widowers, $1,002; disabled workers, $932; and spouses, $537. Payments for children of retired workers averaged $592 per month; children of deceased workers, $721; and children of disabled workers, $282. Federal Supplemental Security Income payments in December 2004 went to 51,536 Connecticut residents, averaging $404 a month.

⁴⁰ HOUSING

In 2004, there were an estimated 1,414,433 housing units in Connecticut, 1,329,950 of which were occupied; 69.7% were owner-occupied. About 59.5% of all units were single-family, detached homes. It was estimated that about 22,730 units were without telephone service, 8,239 lacked complete plumbing facilities, and 6,030 lacked complete kitchen facilities. Most households (47%) relied on fuel oil (such as kerosene) for heating. The average household had 2.55 members.

In 2004, the median value of a single-family detached home was $236,559. The median monthly cost for mortgage owners was $1,603 while the median monthly cost for renters was $811. The state authorized construction of about 11,800 new privately-owned units. In 2006, the state was awarded over $13.6 million in community development block grants from the US Department of Housing and Urban Development (HUD).

⁴¹ EDUCATION

Believing that the Bible was the only true source of God's truths, Connecticut's Puritan founders viewed literacy as a theological necessity. A law code in 1650 required a town of 50 families to hire a schoolmaster to teach reading and writing, and a town of 100 families to operate a school to prepare students for college. Despite such legislation, many communities in colonial Connecticut did not provide sufficient funding to operate first-rate schools. Public education was greatly strengthened in the 19th century by the work of Henry Barnard, who advocated free public schools, state supervision of common schools, and the establishment of schools for teacher training. By the late 1860s and early 1870s, all of Connecticut's public elementary and high schools were tuition free. In 1865, the Board of Education was established.

A characteristic of public-school financing in Connecticut has been high reliance on local support for education. Differences among towns in their wealth bases and taxation were compounded by the mechanism used to distribute a majority of state funds for public education, the flat-grant-per-pupil formula. After the Connecticut Supreme Court, in Horton v. Meskill (1978), declared this funding mechanism to be unconstitutional, the General Assembly in 1979 replaced it with an equity-based model in order to reduce the disparity among towns in expenses per pupil.

In 2004, 88.8% of Connecticut residents age 25 and older were high school graduates. Some 34.5% had obtained a bachelor's degree or higher. As of fall 2002, Connecticut's public schools had a total enrollment of 570,000 students. Of these, 406,000 attended schools from kindergarten through grade eight, and 164,000 attended high school. Approximately 68.3% of the students were white, 13.6% were black, 14.6% were Hispanic, 3.2% were Asian/Pacific Islander, and 0.3% were American Indian/Alaskan Native.

Total enrollment was estimated at 570,000 in fall 2003 and was expected to be 567,000 by fall 2014, a decrease of 0.6% during the period 2002 to 2014. In fall 2003, 74,430 students were enrolled in 361 private schools. Expenditures for public education in 2003/04 were estimated at $6 billion or $10,788 per student, the fifth-highest among the 50 states. Since 1969, the National Assessment of Educational Progress (NAEP) has tested public school students nationwide. The resulting report, *The Nation's Report Card,* stated that in 2005, eighth graders in Connecticut scored 281 out of 500 in mathematics, compared with the national average of 278.

Fall enrollment in college or graduate school was 170,606 in 2002; minority students comprised 21.6% of total postsecondary enrollment. As of 2005, Connecticut had 46 degree-granting institutions. Public institutions of higher education include the University of Connecticut at Storrs; four divisions of the Connecticut State University, at New Britain, New Haven, Danbury, and Willimantic; 12 regional community colleges; and 5 state technical colleges. Connecticut also has 23 private 4-year colleges and universities. Among the oldest institutions are Yale, founded in 1701 and settled in New Haven between 1717 and 1719; Trinity College (1823) in Hartford; and Wesleyan University (1831) in Middletown. Other private institutions include the University of Hartford, University of Bridgeport, Fairfield University, and Connecticut College in New London.

42 ARTS

The Connecticut Commission on the Arts was established in 1965 and was followed in 2003 by the Connecticut Commission on Culture and Tourism (CCT). The CCT includes divisions devoted to arts, films, historic preservation and museums, and tourism. It administers a state art collection and establishes policies for an art bank program. The Commission also partners with the New England Foundation for the Arts. The Connecticut Humanities Council was established in 1974. As of 2006, the Connecticut Humanities Council supported several reading and literacy programs including "Book Voyagers" for young people and "Literature for a Lifetime" for adult readers. In 2005, Connecticut arts organizations received 30 grants totaling $1,207,200 from the National Endowment for the Arts, and 23 grants totaling $1,520,581 through the National Endowment for the Humanities. State funds are also vital to both organizations.

Art museums in Connecticut include the Wadsworth Athenaeum in Hartford, the oldest (1842) free public art museum in the United States; the Yale University Art Gallery and the Yale Center for British Art in New Haven; the Lyman Allyn Museum of Connecticut College in New London, and the New Britain Museum of American Art.

The theater is vibrant in contemporary Connecticut, which has numerous dinner theaters and community theater groups, as well as many college and university theater groups. Professional theaters include the American Shakespeare Festival Theater in Stratford, the Long Wharf Theater and the Yale Repertory Theater in New Haven, the Hartford Stage Company, and the Eugene O'Neill Memorial Theater Center in Waterford.

The state's foremost metropolitan orchestras are the Hartford and New Haven symphonies. Professional opera is presented by the Stanford State Opera and by the Connecticut Opera in Hartford. Prominent dance groups include the Connecticut Dance Company in New Haven, the Hartford Ballet Company, and the Pilobolus Dance Theater in the town of Washington.

The annual International Festival of Arts and Ideas in New Haven has grown steadily since its inception in 1996 and now presents over 300 events throughout the month of June. The Sunken Garden Poetry Festival, presented every summer at the Hill Stead Museum in Farmington, reportedly draws about 1,500 to 3,000 people per reading event.

43 LIBRARIES AND MUSEUMS

In 2001, Connecticut's 194 public library systems had 242 libraries, of which 48 were branches. In that same year, the public library systems held 14,109,000 volumes of books and serial publications, and had a combined circulation of 28,455,000. The system also had 531,000 audio and 519,000 video items, 20,000 electronic format items (CD-ROMs, magnetic tapes, and disks), and seven bookmobiles. The leading public library is the Connecticut State Library (Hartford), which houses about 1,015,463 bound volumes and over 2,451 periodicals, as well as the official state historical museum. Connecticut's most distinguished academic collection is the Yale University library system (over 9 million volumes), headed by the Sterling Memorial Library and the Beinecke Rare Book and Manuscript Library. Special depositories include the Hartford Seminary Foundation's impressive material on Christian-Muslim relations; the Connecticut Historical Society's especially strong collection of materials pertaining to state history and New England genealogy; the Trinity College Library's collection of church documents; the Indian Museum in Old Mystic; the maritime history collections in the Submarine Library at the US Navy submarine base in Groton; and the G. W. Blunt White Library at Mystic Seaport.

Total operating income for the public library system amounted to $146,593,000 in fiscal year 2001, including $272,000 in federal grants and $2,080,000 in state grants. In that same year, operating expenditures totaled $134,538,000, of which 68.2% was spent on staff and 13.6% on the collection.

Connecticut has more than 162 museums, in addition to its historic sites. The Peabody Museum of Natural History at Yale includes an impressive dinosaur hall. Botanical gardens include Harkness Memorial State Park in Waterford, Elizabeth Park in West Hartford, and Hamilton Park Rose Garden in Waterbury. Connecticut's historical sites include the Henry Whitfield House in Guilford (1639), said to be the oldest stone house in the United States; the Webb House in Wethersfield, where George Washington met with the Comte de Rochambeau in 1781 to plan military strategy against the British; Noah Webster's birthplace in West Hartford; and the Jonathan Trumbull House in Lebanon.

44 COMMUNICATIONS

As of 2004, 95.5% of the state's occupied housing units had telephones. Additionally, by June of that same year there were 2,064,204 mobile wireless telephone subscribers. In 2003, 69.2% of Connecticut households had a computer and 62.9% had Internet access. By June 2005, there were 684,597 high-speed lines in Connecticut, 641,329 residential and 43,268 for business.

In 2005, Connecticut had 18 AM and 33 FM major radio stations, and 5 major network television stations. There were educational television stations in Bridgeport, Hartford, and Norwich. In addition, the Hartford and New Haven metropolitan area had the highest cable penetration rate of any urban area, at 88% in 1999. A total of 109,775 domain names were registered in Connecticut by 2000.

[45] PRESS

The *Hartford Courant,* founded in 1764, is generally considered to be the oldest US newspaper in continuous publication. The leading Connecticut dailies in 2005 were the *Hartford Courant,* with an average morning circulation of 204,664 (Sundays, 281,714), and the *New Haven Register,* with an average morning circulation of 92,089 (Sundays, 100,177). Statewide, in 2005 there were 14 morning newspapers, 3 evening newspapers, and 13 Sunday newspapers.

In 2005, there were 83 weekly publications in Connecticut. Of these there are 36 paid weeklies, 41 free weeklies, and 6 combined weeklies. The total circulation of paid weeklies (198,928) and free weeklies (810,901) is 1,009,828.

Leading periodicals are *American Scientist, Greenwich Magazine, Connecticut Magazine, Fine Woodworking, Golf Digest,* and *Tennis.*

[46] ORGANIZATIONS

In 2006, there were over 5,425 nonprofit organizations registered within the state, of which about 3,812 were registered as charitable, educational, or religious organizations.

National organizations with headquarters in Connecticut included the Knights of Columbus (New Haven), the American Institute for Foreign Study (Greenwich), the International Association of Approved Basketball Officials (West Hartford), Keep America Beautiful (Stamford), and Save the Children Federation (Westport). The Academic Council on the United Nations System is housed at Yale University in New Haven.

State arts and educational organizations include the Connecticut Children's Musical Theatre, the Connecticut Educational Media Association, and the Connecticut Historical Commission. The National Theatre of the Deaf is based in West Hartford. The Company of Fifers and Drummers is based in Ivoryton. The International Wheelchair Road Racers Club, the United States Canoe Association, and the National Rowing Association are based in Connecticut.

[47] TOURISM, TRAVEL, AND RECREATION

Tourism has become an increasingly important part of the economy. The government invests over $2.5 million annually to market tourism products. Tourist spending reached $366 million in 2003. Connecticut focuses on metropolitan New York as the largest potential tourist pool. The tourism industry used television advertising to attract more tourists.

Popular tourist attractions include the Mystic Seaport restoration and its aquarium, the Mark Twain House (housing stained glass by Louis Comfort Tiffany) and state capitol in Hartford, the American Clock and Watch Museum in Bristol, the Lock Museum of America in Terryville, and the Yale campus in New Haven. Children of all ages can enjoy the Quassy Amusement Park on Lake Quassapaug. Outstanding events are the Harvard-Yale regatta held each June on the Thames River in New London, and about 50 fairs held in Guilford and other towns between June and October.

[48] SPORTS

The Connecticut Sun became the state's first major league team when it joined the Women's National Basketball Association (WNBA) in 2003. The Sun won the Eastern conference championship in 2004 and 2005, but lost the WNBA Finals both times. (The team was formerly the Orlando Miracle.) Connecticut's only other major league professional team, the Hartford Whalers of the National Hockey League, moved to North Carolina following the 1996–97 season and became the Carolina Hurricanes. The New England Seawolves are members of the Arena Football League. New Haven has a minor league baseball franchise, the Ravens, as do Norwich and New Britain. There are also minor league hockey and basketball teams in the state. Auto racing takes place at Lime Rock Race Track, which is located in Salisbury.

The state licenses off-track betting facilities for horse racing (not actually held in the state) and pari-mutuel operations for greyhound racing and jai alai.

Connecticut schools, colleges, and universities provide amateur athletic competitions, highlighted by Ivy League football games at the Yale Bowl in New Haven. While Yale has won 13 Ivy League football titles, the University of Connecticut has become a force in men's and women's basketball. The Huskies' women's team won the National Collegiate Athletic Association (NCAA) championship in 1995, 2000, back-to-back titles in 2002 and 2003, and in 2004. They have also advanced to two other Final Four tournaments. The men's team won the National Invitational Tournament in 1988 and has made over 30 NCAA Tournament appearances and won the national championship in 1999 and 2004. Other annual sporting events include the US Eastern Ski Jumping Championships in Salisbury in February and the Greater Hartford Open Golf Tournament in Cromwell in June and July.

[49] FAMOUS CONNECTICUTERS

Although Connecticut cannot claim any US president or vice president as a native son, John Moran Bailey (1904–75), chairman of the state Democratic Party (1946–75) and of the national party (1961–68), played a key role in presidential politics as a supporter of John F. Kennedy's successful 1960 campaign.

Two Connecticut natives have served as chief justice of the United States: Oliver Ellsworth (1745–1807) and Morrison R. Waite (1816–88). Associate justices include Henry Baldwin (1780–1844), William Strong (1808–95), and Stephen J. Field (1816–99). Other prominent federal officeholders were Oliver Wolcott (1760–1833), secretary of the treasury; Gideon Welles (1802–78), secretary of the navy; Dean Acheson (1893–1971), secretary of state; and Abraham A. Ribicoff (1910–98), secretary of health, education, and welfare.

An influential US senator was Orville H. Platt (1827–1905), known for his authorship of the Platt Amendment (1901), making Cuba a virtual protectorate of the United States. Also well known are Connecticut senator Abraham A. Ribicoff (served 1963–81) and former governor Lowell P. Weicker Jr. (b.France, 1931 and served 1991–95), the latter first brought to national attention while a US Senator by his work during the Watergate hearings in 1973.

Notable colonial and state governors include John Winthrop Jr. (b.England, 1606–76), Jonathan Trumbull (1710–85), William A. Buckingham (1804–75), Simeon Eben Baldwin (1840–1927),

Marcus Holcomb (1844–1932),Wilbur L. Cross (1862–1948), Chester Bowles (1901–86), Ribicoff, and Ella Tambussi Grasso (1919–81), elected in 1974 and reelected in 1978 but forced to resign for health reasons at the end of 1980 (Grasso was the first woman governor in the United States who did not succeed her husband in the post).

In addition to Winthrop, the founding fathers of Connecticut were Thomas Hooker (b.England, 1586–1647), who was deeply involved in establishing and developing Connecticut Colony, and Theophilus Eaton (b.England, 1590–1658) and John Davenport (b.England, 1597–1670), cofounders and leaders of the strict Puritan colony of New Haven. Other famous historical figures are Israel Putnam (b.Massachusetts, 1718–90), Continental Army major general at the Battle of Bunker Hill, who supposedly admonished his troops not to fire "until you see the whites of their eyes"; diplomat Silas Deane (1737–89); and Benedict Arnold (1741–1801), known for his treasonous activity in the Revolutionary War but also remembered for his courage and skill at Ft. Ticonderoga and Saratoga.

Roger Sherman (b.Massachusetts, 1721–93), a signatory to the Articles of Association, Declaration of Independence (1776), Articles of Confederation (1777), Peace of Paris (1783), and the US Constitution (1787), was the only person to sign all these documents; at the Constitutional Convention, he proposed the "Connecticut Compromise," calling for a dual system of congressional representation. Connecticut's most revered Revolutionary War figure was Nathan Hale (1755–76), the Yale graduate who was executed for spying behind British lines. Radical abolitionist John Brown (1800–1859) was born in Torrington.

Connecticuters prominent in US cultural development include painter John Trumbull (1756–1843), son of Governor Trumbull, known for his canvases commemorating the American Revolution. Joel Barlow (1754–1812) was a poet and diplomat in the early national period. Lexicographer Noah Webster (1758–1843) compiled the *American Dictionary of the English Language* (1828). Frederick Law Olmsted (1822–1903), the first American landscape architect, planned New York City's Central Park. Harriet Beecher Stowe (1811–96) wrote one of the most widely read books in history, *Uncle Tom's Cabin* (1852). Mark Twain (Samuel L. Clemens, b.Missouri, 1835–1910) was living in Hartford when he wrote *The Adventures of Tom Sawyer* (1876), *The Adventures of Huckleberry Finn* (1885), and *A Connecticut Yankee in King Arthur's Court* (1889).

Charles Ives (1874–1954), one of the nation's most distinguished composers, used his successful insurance business to finance his musical career and to help other musicians. Eugene O'Neill (b.New York, 1888–1953), the playwright who won the Nobel Prize for literature in 1936, spent summers in New London during his early years. A seminal voice in modern poetry, Wallace Stevens (b.Pennsylvania, 1879–1955), wrote the great body of his work while employed as a Hartford insurance executive. James Merrill (b.New York, 1926–95), a poet whose works have won the National Book Award (1967), Bollingen Prize (1973), and numerous other honors, lived in Stonington.

Native Connecticuters important in the field of education include Eleazar Wheelock (1711–79), William Samuel Johnson (1727–1819), Emma Willard (1787–1870), and Henry Barnard (1811–1900). Shapers of US history include Jonathan Edwards (1703–58), a Congregationalist minister who sparked the 18th-century religious revival known as the Great Awakening; Samuel Seabury (1729–96), the first Episcopal bishop in the United States; Horace Bushnell (1802–76), said to be the father of the Sunday school; Lyman Beecher (1775–1863), a controversial figure in 19th-century American Protestantism who condemned slavery, intemperance, Roman Catholicism, and religious intolerance with equal fervor; and his son Henry Ward Beecher (1813–87), also a religious leader and abolitionist.

Among the premier inventors born in Connecticut were Abel Buel (1742–1824), who designed the first American submarine; Eli Whitney (1765–1825), inventor of the cotton gin and a pioneer in manufacturing; Charles Goodyear (1800–60), who devised a process for the vulcanization of rubber; Samuel Colt (1814–62), inventor of the six-shooter; Frank Sprague (1857–1934), who designed the first major electric trolley system in the United States; and Edwin H. Land (1909–91), inventor of the Polaroid Land Camera. The Nobel Prize in physiology or medicine was won by three Connecticuters: Edward Kendall (1886–1972) in 1949, John Enders (1897–1985) in 1954, and Barbara McClintock (1902–92) in 1983.

Other prominent Americans born in Connecticut include clock manufacturer Seth Thomas (1785–1859), circus impresario Phineas Taylor "P. T." Barnum (1810–91), jeweler Charles Lewis Tiffany (1812–1902), financier John Pierpont Morgan (1837–1913), pediatrician Benjamin Spock (1903–98), cartoonist Al Capp (1909–79), soprano Eileen Farrell (1920–2002), and consumer advocate Ralph Nader (b.1934). Leading actors and actresses are Ed Begley (1901–70), Katherine Hepburn (1909–2003), Rosalind Russell (1911–76), and Robert Mitchum (1917–97).

Walter Camp (1859–1925), athletic director of Yale University who helped formulate the rules of US football, was a native of Connecticut.

50 BIBLIOGRAPHY

Basker, James G. (ed.). *Early American Abolitionists: A Collection of Anti-Slavery Writings 1760-1820.* New York: Gilder Lehrman Institute of American History, 2005.

Boyle, Joseph Lee. *Fire Cake and Water: The Connecticut Infantry at the Valley Forge Encampment.* Baltimore, Md.: Clearfield, 1999.

Council of State Governments. *The Book of the States, 2006 Edition.* Lexington, Ky.: Council of State Governments, 2006.

Dayton, Cornelia Hughes. *Women before the Bar: Gender, Law, and Society in Connecticut, 1839-1789.* Chapel Hill: University of North Carolina Press, 1995.

Den Ouden, Amy E. *Beyond Conquest: Native Peoples and the Struggle for History in New England.* Lincoln: University of Nebraska Press, 2005.

Dugger, Elizabeth L. *Adventure Guide to Massachusetts and Western Connecticut.* Edison, N.J.: Hunter, 1999.

Hamblen, Charles P. *Connecticut Yankees at Gettysburg.* Kent, Ohio: Kent State University Press, 1993.

Hammerson, Geoffrey A. *Connecticut Wildlife: Biodiversity, Natural History, and Conservation.* Hanover: University Press of New England, 2004.

Menta, John. *The Quinnipiac: Cultural Conflict in Southern New England.* New Haven, Conn.: Peabody Museum of Natural History, 2003.

Rose, Gary L. *Connecticut Politics at the Crossroads.* Lanham, Md.: University Press of America, 1992.

Sletcher, Michael (ed.). *New England.* Vol. 4 in *The Greenwood Encyclopedia of American Regional Cultures.* Westport, Conn.: Greenwood Press, 2004.

Steenburg, Nancy Hathaway. *Children and the Criminal Law in Connecticut, 1635–1855: Changing Perceptions of Childhood.* New York: Routledge, 2005.

US Department of Commerce, Economics and Statistics Administration, US Census Bureau. *Connecticut, 2000. Summary Social, Economic, and Housing Characteristics: 2000 Census of Population and Housing.* Washington, D.C.: US Government Printing Office, 2003.

DECEMBER 7, 1787

DELAWARE

State of Delaware

ORIGIN OF STATE NAME: Named for Thomas West, Baron De La Warr, colonial governor of Virginia; the name was first applied to the bay. **NICKNAME:** The First State; the Diamond State. **CAPITAL:** Dover. **ENTERED UNION:** 7 December 1787 (1st). **SONG:** "Our Delaware." **MOTTO:** Liberty and Independence. **COAT OF ARMS:** A farmer and a rifleman flank a shield that bears symbols of the state's agricultural resources—a sheaf of wheat, an ear of corn, and a cow. Above is a ship in full sail; below, a banner with the state motto. **FLAG:** Colonial blue with the coat of arms on a buff-colored diamond; below the diamond is the date of statehood. **OFFICIAL SEAL:** The coat of arms surrounded by the words "Great Seal of the State of Delaware 1793, 1847, 1907." The three dates represent the years in which the seal was revised. **BIRD:** Blue hen chicken. **FISH:** Sea trout. **FLOWER:** Peach blossom. **TREE:** American holly. **LEGAL HOLIDAYS:** New Year's Day, 1 January; Martin Luther King Jr. Day, 3rd Monday in January; Presidents' Day, 3rd Monday in February; Good Friday, March or April; Memorial Day, last Monday in May; Independence Day, 4 July; Labor Day, 1st Monday in September; Columbus Day, 2nd Monday in October; Veterans' Day, 11 November; Thanksgiving Day, 4th Thursday in November; Day After Thanksgiving; Christmas Day, 25 December. **TIME:** 7 AM EST = noon GMT.

¹LOCATION, SIZE, AND EXTENT

Located on the eastern seaboard of the United States, Delaware ranks 49th in size among the 50 states. The state's total area is 2,044 sq mi (5,295 sq km), of which land takes up 1,932 sq mi (5,005 sq km) and inland water, 112 sq mi (290 sq km). Delaware extends 35 mi (56 km) E–W at its widest; its maximum N–S extension is 96 mi (154 km).

Delaware is bordered on the N by Pennsylvania; on the E by New Jersey (with the line passing through the Delaware River into Delaware Bay) and the Atlantic Ocean; and on the S and W by Maryland.

The boundary length of Delaware, including a general coastline of 28 mi (45 km), totals 200 mi (322 km). The tidal shoreline is 381 mi (613 km). The state's geographic center is in Kent County, 11 mi (18 km) S of Dover.

²TOPOGRAPHY

Delaware lies entirely within the Atlantic Coastal Plain except for its northern tip, above the Christina River, which is part of the Piedmont Plateau. The state's highest elevation is 448 ft (137 m) on Ebright Road, near Centerville, New Castle County. The rolling hills and pastures of the north give way to marshy regions in the south (notably Cypress Swamp), with sandy beaches along the coast. Delaware's mean elevation, 60 ft (18 m), is the lowest in the United States. The lowest point of the state is at sea level at the Atlantic Ocean.

Of all Delaware's rivers, only the Nanticoke, Choptank, and Pocomoke flow westward into Chesapeake Bay. The remainder—including the Christina, Appoquinimink, Leipsic, St. Jones, Murderkill, Mispillion, Broadkill, and Indian—flow into Delaware Bay. There are dozens of inland freshwater lakes and ponds.

³CLIMATE

Delaware's climate is temperate and humid. The normal daily average temperature in Wilmington is 55°F (12°C), ranging from an average low of 24°F (-4°C) in January to and average high of 86°F (30°C) in July. Both the record low and the record high temperatures for the state were established at Millsboro: -17°F (-27°C) on 17 January 1893 and 110°F (43°C) on 21 July 1930. The average annual precipitation (1971–2000) was 42.8 in (108.7 cm) during 1971–2000; about 21 in (53 cm) of snow falls each year. Wilmington's average share of sunshine is 55%—one of the lowest percentages among leading US cities.

⁴FLORA AND FAUNA

Delaware's mixture of northern and southern flora reflects its geographical position. Common trees include black walnut, hickory, sweetgum, and tulip poplar. Shadbush and sassafras are found chiefly in southern Delaware.

Mammals native to the state include the white-tailed deer, red and gray foxes, eastern gray squirrel, muskrat, raccoon, woodcock, and common cottontail. The quail, robin, wood thrush, cardinal, and eastern meadowlark are representative birds, while various waterfowl, especially Canada geese, are common.

The Delaware Bay Estuary, a Ramsar Wetland of International Importance, offers a habitat for over 90% of the North American populations of five species of migratory birds. It has been estimated that over 1 million shorebirds make use of this area. Five species of marine turtle live in the bay and several species of rare and endangered plants occur in surrounding tidal marshes.

In April 2006, a total of 17 species occurring within the state were on the threatened and endangered species list of the US Fish and Wildlife Service. These included 13 animal (vertebrates and invertebrates) and 4 plant species. Among these are the bald eagle, puma, five species of sea turtle, three species of whale, the Delmarva Peninsula fox squirrel, and the small-whorled pogonia.

5 ENVIRONMENTAL PROTECTION

The Coastal Zone Act of 1971 outlaws new industry "incompatible with the protection of the natural environment" of shore areas, but in 1979 the act was amended to permit offshore oil drilling and the construction of coastal oil facilities. The traffic of oil tankers into the Delaware Bay represents an environmental hazard.

In 1982, Delaware enacted a bottle law requiring deposits on most soda and beer bottles; deposits for aluminum cans were made mandatory in 1984. In that year, Delaware became the first state to administer the national hazardous waste program at the state level. The state's municipal governments have constructed three municipal land fills to handle the solid waste produced by the state's 670,000 residents. In 2003, the US Environment Protection Agency (EPA) database listed 64 hazardous waste sites in Delaware, 14 of which were on the National Priorities List as of 2006, including the Dover Air Force Base. In 2005, the EPA spent over $16.5 million through the Superfund program for the cleanup of hazardous waste sites in the state. The same year, federal EPA grants awarded to the state included $6.4 million for a water pollution control revolving fund. In 2003, 13.6 million lb of toxic chemicals were released by the state.

About 17% of the state is covered by wetlands. The Delaware Bay Estuary was designated as a Ramsar Wetland of International Importance in 1992; it is also designated as a Western Hemisphere Shorebird Reserve. Agricultural, industrial, and urban pollution are the main environmental problems for the area, part of which falls under the jurisdiction of the Delaware Department of Natural Resources and Environmental Control. The site, which extends into New Jersey, contains over 70 separate wetlands with ownership in federal, state, county, and private management.

State environmental protection agencies include the Department of natural resources and Environmental Control, Coastal Zone Industrial Control Board, and Council on Soil and Water Conservation.

6 POPULATION

Delaware ranked 45th in population in the United States with an estimated total of 843,524 in 2005, an increase of 7.6% since 2000. Between 1990 and 2000, Delaware's population grew from 666,168 to 783,600, an increase of 17.6%. The population is projected to reach 927,400 by 2015 and 990,694 by 2025.

In 2004, the population density was 425.4 people per square mile. The median age in 2004 was 37.5; 13.1% was age 65 or over, while 23.3% was under 18 years of age.

The largest cities are Wilmington, with an estimated population of 72,664 in 2000, and Dover, the capital, with 138,752 in the metropolitan area in 2004.

7 ETHNIC GROUPS

Black Americans constitute Delaware's largest racial minority, numbering 150,666 in 2000 and comprising about 19.2% of the population. In 2004, 20.4% of the population was black. As of 2000, approximately 37,277 residents, or 4.8% of the total population (up from 16,000, or 2.4% in 1990), was of Hispanic origin. That figure rose to 5.8% in 2004.

Delaware's 44,898 foreign born made up 5.7% of the state's population in 2000 (more than double the total of 22,275, or 3.3%, in 1990). The United Kingdom, Germany, India, Italy, and Canada were the leading places of origin. In 2004, 1.3% of the population reported origin of two or more races.

8 LANGUAGES

English in Delaware is basically North Midland, with Philadelphia features in Wilmington and the northern portion. In the north, one *wants off* a bus, lowers *curtains* rather than blinds, pronounces *wharf* without /h/, and says /noo/ and /doo/ for *new* and *due* and /krik/ for *creek*. In 2000, 662,845 Delawareans—90.5% of the resident population five years of age or older—spoke only English at home.

The following table gives selected statistics from the 2000 Census for language spoken at home by persons five years old and over. The category "African languages" includes Amharic, Ibo, Twi, Yoruba, Bantu, Swahili, and Somali. The category "Other Asian languages" includes Dravidian languages, Malayalam, Telugu, Tamil, and Turkish. The category "Other West Germanic languages" includes Dutch, Pennsylvania Dutch, and Afrikaans.

LANGUAGE	NUMBER	PERCENT
Population 5 years and over	**732,378**	**100.0**
Speak only English	662,845	90.5
Speak a language other than English	69,533	9.5
Speak a language other than English	**69,533**	**9.5**
Spanish or Spanish Creole	34,690	4.7
French (incl. Patois, Cajun)	4,041	0.6
Chinese	3,579	0.5
German	3,420	0.5
Italian	2,860	0.4
Polish	2,036	0.3
Korean	1,598	0.2
African languages	1,289	0.2
Tagalog	1,284	0.2
Other Asian languages	1,280	0.2
Other West Germanic languages	1,245	0.2
French Creole	1,199	0.2
Other Indic languages	1,186	0.2

9 RELIGIONS

The earliest permanent European settlers in Delaware were Swedish and Finnish Lutherans and Dutch Calvinists. English Quakers, Scotch-Irish Presbyterians, and Welsh Baptists arrived in the 18th century, though Anglicization was the predominant trend. The Great Awakening, America's first religious revival, began on 30 October 1739 at Lewes with the arrival of George Whitefield, an Anglican preacher involved in the movement that would later become the Methodist Church. The Methodist Church was the largest denomination in Delaware by the early 19th century. Subsequent immigration brought Lutherans from Germany; Roman Catholics from Ireland, Germany, Italy, and Poland; and Jews from Germany, Poland, and Russia. Most of the Catholic and Jewish immigrants settled in cities, Wilmington in particular.

From 1990 to 2000, the Catholic Church gained 35,399 new members, enough to outnumber the previously dominant mainline Protestants. There were 151,740 Catholics in about 46 congregations in 2000. The United Methodist Church had 59,471 adherents in 162 congregations, Episcopalians numbered 12,993 in 35

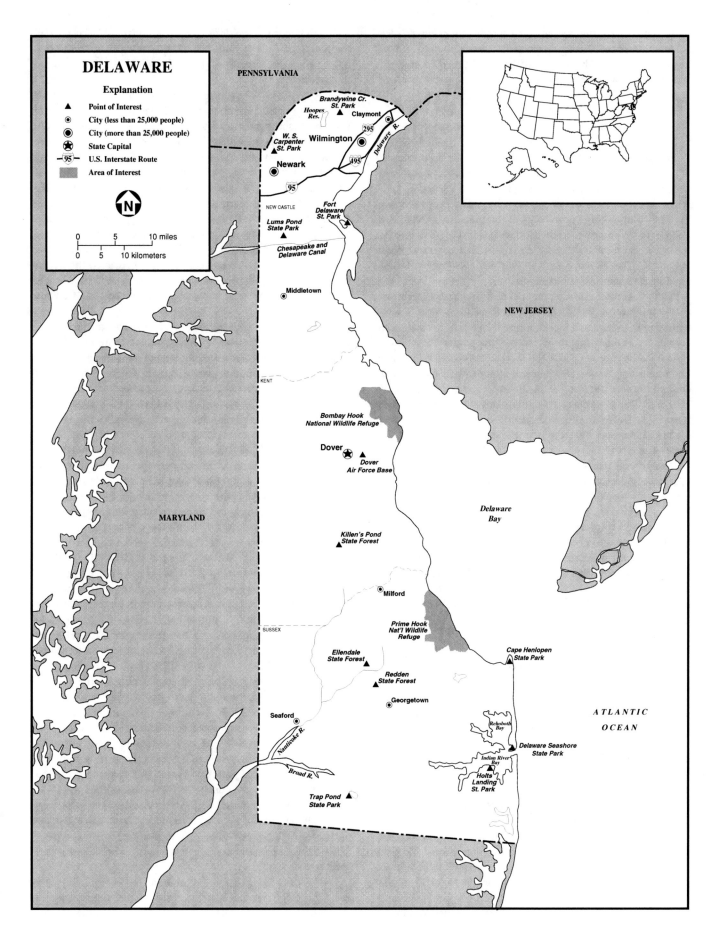

DELAWARE

Explanation

▲ Point of Interest
⊙ City (less than 25,000 people)
◉ City (more than 25,000 people)
★ State Capital
95 U.S. Interstate Route
Area of Interest

0   5   10 miles
0   5   10 kilometers

PENNSYLVANIA

Brandywine Cr.
St. Park
Hoopes
Res.   Claymont
                    295
W. S.
Carpenter   Wilmington
St. Park
                              Delaware R.
        Newark   495

NEW CASTLE
                        Fort
                     Delaware
95   St. Park

Lums Pond
State Park

Chesapeake and
Delaware Canal

Middletown

NEW JERSEY

KENT

Bombay Hook
National Wildlife Refuge

Dover ★ ▲
              Dover
         Air Force Base

MARYLAND

Delaware
Bay

Killen's Pond
State Forest

Milford

Prime Hook
Nat'l Wildlife
Refuge

Ellendale
State Forest   Cape Henlopen
                          State Park
        Redden
        State Forest

              Georgetown   ATLANTIC

                                  OCEAN
Seaford
                          Rehoboth
                          Bay
        Nanticoke R.
                          Delaware Seashore
                          State Park
        Broad R.   Indian River
                          Bay
                          Holts
                          Landing
Trap Pond ▲   St. Park
State Park

congregations, and the Presbyterian Church USA claimed 14,880 adherents in about 37 congregations. There were about 13,500 adherents to Judaism. About 59.4% of the population did not specify affiliation with a religious organization.

10 TRANSPORTATION

The New Castle and Frenchtown Railroad, a portage route, was built in 1832. The state's first passenger line, the Philadelphia, Wilmington, and Baltimore Railroad, opened six years later. As of 2003, there were 247 rail mi (397 km) of track. In that same year, the top commodity originating in the state carried by Delaware's seven railroads was chemicals. Coal was the top commodity shipped by rail that terminated in the state. As of 2006, Amtrak served Wilmington via the Northeast Corridor main line that connected Boston, New York, Philadelphia, Baltimore and Washington DC. The Delaware Authority for Regional Transit (DART) provides state-subsidized bus service.

In 2004, the state had 6,044 mi (9,731 km) of public highways, roads, and streets. In that same year, there were some 716,000 registered vehicles and 533,943 licensed drivers in the state. Delaware's first modern highway, and the first dual highway in the United States, running about 100 mi (160 km) from Wilmington to the southern border, was financed by industrialist T. Coleman du Pont between 1911 and 1924. The twin spans of the Delaware Memorial Bridge connect Delaware highways to those in New Jersey; The Delaware Turnpike section of the John F. Kennedy Memorial Highway links the bridge system with Maryland. The Lewes–Cape May Ferry provides auto and passenger service between southern Delaware and New Jersey.

In 2004, New Castle, Delaware's chief port, handled 8.169 million tons of goods, followed by Wilmington, with 4.998 million tons that same year. The Delaware River is the conduit for much of the oil brought by tanker to the US east coast. In 2004, Delaware had 99 mi (159 km) of navigable inland waterways. In 2003, waterborne shipments totaled 42.081 million tons.

In 2005, Delaware had a total of 49 public and private-use aviation-related facilities. This included 33 airports, 15 heliports, and one seaplane base. Greater Wilmington Airport was the largest and busiest airport in the state.

11 HISTORY

Delaware was inhabited nearly 10,000 years ago, and a succession of various cultures occupied the area until the first European contact. At that time, the Leni-Lenape (Delaware) Indians occupied northern Delaware, while several tribes, including the Nanticoke and Assateague, inhabited southern Delaware. The Dutch in 1631 were the first Europeans to settle in what is now Delaware, but their little colony (at Lewes) was destroyed by Indians. Permanent settlements were made by the Swedes in 1638 (at Wilmington, under the leadership of a Dutchman, Peter Minuit) and by the Dutch in 1651 (at New Castle). The Dutch conquered the Swedes in 1655, and the English conquered the Dutch in 1664. Eighteen years later, the area was ceded by the duke of York (later King James II), its first English proprietor, to William Penn. Penn allowed Delaware an elected assembly in 1704, but the colony was still subject to him and to his deputy governor in Philadelphia; ties to the Penn family and Pennsylvania were not severed until 1776. Boundary quarrels disturbed relations with Maryland until Charles Mason and Jeremiah Dixon surveyed the western boundary of Delaware (and the Maryland-Pennsylvania boundary) during the period 1763–68. By this time, virtually all the Indians had been driven out of the territory.

In September 1777, during the War for Independence, British soldiers marched through northern Delaware, skirmishing with some of Washington's troops at Cooch's Bridge, near Newark, and seizing Wilmington, which they occupied for a month. In later campaigns, Delaware troops with the Continental Army fought so well that they gained the nickname "Blue Hen's Chicken," after a famous breed of fighting gamecocks. On 7 December 1787, Delaware became the first state to ratify the federal Constitution. Although Delaware had not abolished slavery, it remained loyal to the Union during the Civil War. By that time, it was the one slave state in which a clear majority of blacks (about 92%) were already free. However, white Delawareans generally resented the Reconstruction policies adopted by Congress after the Civil War, and by manipulation of registration laws denied blacks the franchise until 1890.

The key event in the state's economic history was the completion of a railroad between Philadelphia and Baltimore through Wilmington in 1838, encouraging the industrialization of northern Delaware. Wilmington grew so rapidly that by 1900 it encompassed 41% of the state's population; by mid-century the city was home to roughly half the state's population. Considerable foreign immigration contributed to this growth, largely from the British Isles (especially Ireland) and Germany in the mid-19th century and from Italy, Poland, and Russia in the early 20th century.

Flour and textile mills, shipyards, carriage factories, iron foundries, and morocco leather plants were Wilmington's leading enterprises for much of the 19th century. By the early 1900s however, E. I. du Pont de Nemours and Co., founded near Wilmington in 1802 as a gunpowder manufacturer, made the city famous as a center for the chemical industry. Du Pont remained the state's largest private employer in the 1990s, but in the 2000s, MBNA, the bank and credit card company, became the state's largest private employer.

During the same period, Delaware's agricultural income rose. Peaches and truck crops flourished in the 19th century, along with corn and wheat; poultry, sorghum, and soybeans became major sources of agricultural income in the 20th century. Sussex County, home to much of the state's farming, had become the fastest-growing county in Delaware by the mid-1990s. The beach areas of rural Sussex attract resort-goers and retirees. Tourism is expected to be aided by the construction of a north–south expressway that will cut travel time to the state's southern beach communities.

During the 1950s, Delaware's population grew by an unprecedented 40%. The growth was greatest around Dover, site of the East Coast's largest air base, and on the outskirts of Wilmington. Wilmington itself lost population after 1945 because of the proliferation of suburban housing developments, offices, and factories, including two automobile assembly plants and an oil refinery. Although many neighborhood schools became racially integrated during the 1950s, massive busing was instituted by court order in 1978 to achieve a racial balance in schools throughout northern Delaware.

The 1980s ushered in a period of dramatic economic improvement. According to state sources, Delaware was one of only two states to improve its financial strength during the recession that plagued the early part of the decade. In 1988, Delaware enjoyed an unemployment rate of 3.3%, the second lowest in the country. The state's revenues grew at an average of 7.7% in the early 1980s, even while it successively cut the personal income tax. Some of Delaware's prosperity came from a 1981 state law that raised usury limits and lowered taxes for large financial institutions. More than 30 banks established themselves in Delaware, including Chase Manhattan Bank and Manufacturers Hanover.

The state also succeeded in using its simplified incorporation procedures to attract both US and foreign companies, bringing in an estimated $1 million in incorporation fees from Asian companies alone in the late 1980s. By the mid-1990s, the state was the registered home of roughly half the Fortune 500 companies and hundreds of thousands of smaller corporations; however, for most, their presence in the state was strictly on paper. The state sustained a low rate of unemployment into the 1990s; in 1999 it was 3.5%, still below the national average. A year earlier the state ranked sixth in the nation for per capita income ($29,932). Per capita income in 2004 was $35,861, ranking ninth in the nation.

While business fared well in Delaware, the state has lagged behind in social welfare indicators. Delaware's rates of teenage pregnancy and infant mortality have been among the highest in the country while its welfare benefits were lower than those of any other mid-Atlantic state with the exception of West Virginia in the 1990s. Other problems include housing shortages, urban sprawl, and pollution.

Ruth Ann Minner, elected Delaware's first woman governor in 2001, was once a receptionist in the governor's office before winning the position herself. In her 2003 State of the State address, she targeted issues such as pollution, industrial cleanups, and toughening campaign finance laws. In 2003, Delaware was launching a prisoner reentry program, designed to help former inmates successfully reenter society instead of committing further crimes and returning to prison. The three-year pilot program was financed with a $2 million federal grant and was to save the state millions of dollars a year and reduce crime. Prior to the 2005–06 winter season, Governor Minner urged Delawareans to conserve energy and protect the environment by changing to efficient compact fluorescent lightbulbs.

12 STATE GOVERNMENT

Delaware has had four state constitutions, adopted in 1776, 1792, 1831, and 1897. Under the 1897 document, as amended (138 times by January 2005), the legislative branch is the General Assembly, consisting of a 21-member Senate and a 41-member House of Representatives. Annual legislative sessions begin in January and must conclude by 30 June. The presiding officers of both houses may issue a joint call for a special session, which is not limited in length. Senators are elected for four years, representatives for two. Members of the House must be at least 24 years old; senators must be 27. All legislators must have been residents of the state for three years and must have lived in their district for one year prior to election. Legislators earned $36,500 annually in 2004.

Delaware's elected executives are the governor and lieutenant governor (separately elected), treasurer, attorney general, and auditor. All serve four-year terms. The governor, who may be reelected twice, must be at least 30 years old and must have been a US citizen for 12 years and a state resident for six years before taking office. As of December 2004, the governor's salary was $132,500. The legislature may override a gubernatorial veto by a three-fifths vote of the elected members of each house. A bill that the governor fails to sign or veto becomes law after 10 days (Sundays excluded) when the legislature is in session. An amendment to the state constitution must be approved by a two-thirds vote in each house of the General Assembly in two successive sessions with an election intervening; Delaware is the only state in which amendments need not be ratified by the voters.

Voters in Delaware must be US citizens, at least 18 years old, and permanent state residents. Restrictions apply to convicted felons and those declared mentally incompetent by the court.

13 POLITICAL PARTIES

The Democrats were firmly entrenched in Delaware for three decades after the Civil War; a subsequent period of Republican dominance lasted until the depression of the 1930s. Since then, the two parties have been relatively evenly matched.

In 2004 there were 554,000 registered voters; an estimated 42% were Democratic, 36% Republican, and 23% unaffiliated or members of other parties. In the 2000 election, Democrat Al Gore won the state with 55% of the vote, to Republican George W. Bush's 42%. Green Party candidate Ralph Nader won 3% of the vote. In 2004, Democrat John Kerry won 53.3% of the vote to incumbent president George W. Bush's 45.8%. The state had three electoral votes in the 2004 presidential election. Democratic senator Joseph Biden was the ranking member of the Senate Foreign Relations Committee in 2003. Democrat Tom Carper was elected Delaware's junior senator in 2000, after having served two terms as state governor, and five terms in the US House of Representatives. Former two-term governor and Republican Michael Castle was reelected Delaware's House Representative in 2004.

Democratic governor Ruth Ann Minner, elected in 2000, was the first woman to serve in a leadership position in Delaware's House of Representatives, the state's first female lieutenant governor, and first female governor. In 2005, Republicans controlled the

Delaware Presidential Vote by Major Political Parties, 1948–2004

YEAR	ELECTORAL VOTE	DELAWARE WINNER	DEMOCRAT	REPUBLICAN
1948	3	Dewey (R)	67,813	69,588
1952	3	*Eisenhower (R)	83,315	90,059
1956	3	*Eisenhower (R)	79,421	98,057
1960	3	*Kennedy (D)	99,590	96,373
1964	3	*Johnson (D)	122,704	78,078
1968	3	*Nixon (R)	89,194	96,714
1972	3	*Nixon (R)	92,283	140,357
1976	3	*Carter (D)	122,596	109,831
1980	3	*Reagan (R)	105,700	111,185
1984	3	*Reagan (R)	101,656	152,190
1988	3	*Bush (R)	108,647	139,639
1992**	3	*Clinton(D)	126,054	102,313
1996**	3	*Clinton(D)	140,355	99,062
2000	3	Gore (D)	180,068	137,288
2004	3	Kerry (D)	200,152	171,660

*Won US presidential election.

**IND. Candidate Ross Perot received 59,213 votes in 1992 and 28,719 votes in 1996.

state House (25–15, with 1 independent member), and Democrats controlled the state Senate (13–8).

14 LOCAL GOVERNMENT

As of 2005, Delaware was divided into three counties. In New Castle, voters elect a county executive and a county council; in Sussex, the members of the elective county council choose a county administrator, who supervises the executive departments of the county government. Kent operates under an elected levy court, which sets tax rates and runs the county according to regulations spelled out by the assembly. Most of Delaware's 57 municipalities elect a mayor and council. In 2005, Delaware had 19 public school districts and 260 special districts. Because of the state's small geographic size, local government in Delaware tends to be weaker than that in other states; here the state operates many programs that elsewhere are found at the local level.

In 2005, local government accounted for about 22,568 full-time (or equivalent) employment positions.

15 STATE SERVICES

To address the continuing threat of terrorism and to work with the federal Department of Homeland Security, homeland security in Delaware operates under the authority of the governor; a homeland security director is appointed to oversee programs related to homeland security.

Public education is supervised by the Department of Education. Highways are the responsibility of the Department of Transportation, while medical care, mental health facilities, drug- and alcohol-abuse programs, and help for the aging fall within the jurisdiction of the Department of Health and Social Services. Public protection services are provided primarily through the Department Safety and Homeland Security and the Department of Correction. The Department of Labor has divisions covering employment services, vocational rehabilitation, unemployment insurance, and equal employment opportunity. The Economic Development Office supports the economic interests of the state. Other services include those of the Department of Services to Children, Youth and Their Families and the Consumer Protection Unit of the Attorney General's Office. The environment is protected by the Department of Natural Resources and Environmental Control.

16 JUDICIAL SYSTEM

Delaware's highest court is the Supreme Court, composed of a chief justice and four associate justices, all appointed by the governor and confirmed by the Senate for 12-year terms, as are all state judges. Other state courts include the court of chancery, comprising a chancellor and two vice-chancellors, and the superior court, which has a president judge and 16 associate judges. There are also judges on the Court of Common Pleas in Wilmington.

Delaware was the last state to abolish the whipping post. During the 1900–42 period, 1,604 prisoners (22% of the state's prison population) were beaten with a cat-o'-nine-tails. The whipping post, nicknamed "Red Hannah," was used for the last time in 1952 but was not formally abolished until 1972.

As of 31 December 2004, a total of 6,927 prisoners were held in Delaware's state and federal prisons, an increase from 6,794 of 2% from the previous year. As of year-end 2004, a total of 557 inmates were female, up by 9.6% from 508 the year before. Among sentenced prisoners (one year or more), Delaware had an incarceration rate of 488 per 100,000 population in 2004.

According to the Federal Bureau of Investigation, Delaware in 2004 had a violent crime rate (murder/nonnegligent manslaughter; forcible rape; robbery; aggravated assault) of 568.4 reported incidents per 100,000 population, or a total of 4,720 reported incidents. Crimes against property (burglary; larceny/theft; and motor vehicle theft) in that same year totaled 26,272 reported incidents or 3,163.9 reported incidents per 100,000 people. Delaware has a death penalty, of which lethal injection is the sole method of execution. Inmates convicted prior to 13 June 1986 were offered hanging as an alternative. However, the state's gallows have since been dismantled. From 1976 through 5 May 2006 the state executed 14 persons, of which the most recent took place in 2005. As of 1 January 2006, there were 18 inmates on death row.

In 2003, Delaware spent $17,771,313 on homeland security, an average of $22 per state resident.

17 ARMED FORCES

Delaware's main defense facility is the military airlift wing at Dover Air Force Base. Active-duty military personnel stationed in Delaware in 2004 totaled 5,915, with 1,228 Guard and National Guard, and 777 civilian employees. Department of Defense contracts awarded the state in 2004 totaled $194 million, and defense payroll, including retired military pay, amounted to $417 million.

There were 80,751 veterans of US military service in Delaware as of 2000, of whom 10,873 served in World War II; 9,071 in the Korean conflict; 23,661 during the Vietnam era; and 11,878 in the Persian Gulf War. US Veterans Administration spending in Delaware in 2004 totaled $167 million.

As of 31 October 2004, the Delaware state police employed 643 full-time sworn officers.

18 MIGRATION

Delaware has attracted immigrants from a variety of foreign countries: Sweden, Finland, and the Netherlands in the early days; England, Scotland, and Ireland during the later colonial period; and Italy, Poland, and Russia, among other countries, during the first 130 years of statehood. The 1960s and 1970s saw the migration of Puerto Ricans to Wilmington. Delaware enjoyed a net gain from migration of 122,000 persons between 1940 and 1970. Between 1970 and 1990, however, there was a net migration of only about 25,000. Net domestic migration between 1990 and 1998 totaled 29,000 while net international migration totaled 8,000. In 1998, Delaware admitted 1,063 foreign immigrants. Between 1990 and 1998, the state's overall population increased 11.6%. In the period 2000–05, net international migration was 11,226 and net internal migration was 27,912, for a net gain of 39,138 people.

19 INTERGOVERNMENTAL COOPERATION

Among the interstate agreements to which Delaware subscribes are the Delaware River and Bay Authority Compact, Delaware River Basin Commission, Atlantic States Marine Fisheries Commission, Interstate Compact for Juveniles, Mid-Atlantic Fishery Management Council, and Southern Regional Education Board. The Delmarva Advisory Council, representing Delaware, Maryland, and Virginia, works with local organizations on the Delmarva Peninsula to develop and implement economic improvement programs. Federal grants to Delaware were $910 million in fiscal year 2005, the second-lowest amount among all the states, behind Wyoming. In fiscal year 2006, federal grants amounted to an estimated $951 million, and in fiscal year 2007, to an estimated $985 million.

20 ECONOMY

Since the 1930s, and particularly since the mid-1970s, Delaware has been one of the nation's most prosperous states. It was one of the few states whose economic growth rate actually increased during the national recession of 2001, accelerating from 4.5% in 1998 to 6.1% in 1999 to 7.3% in 2000, and to 8.75% in 2001. Although manufacturing—preeminently the chemical and automotive industries—has historically been the main contributor to the state's economy, its contribution to gross state product shrunk from 16.5% in 1997 to 12.9% in 2001, compared to a 43% contribution from the finance, insurance and real estate sector and 15.3% from general services (hotels, auto repair, personal, health, legal, educational, recreational, etc). The largest employers in the manufacturing sector, the chemical and automobile manufacturing industries, experienced negative growth coming into the 21st century, output from motor vehicles and equipment manufacturing falling 34% 1999 to 2001, and the output from chemicals and allied products manufacturing showing a net decline of 2.6% 1997 to 2001. By contrast, financial services grew 43% during this period, and general services grew 36.4%. Job creation in manufacturing, which was at a positive 2% year-on-year rate in 1999, turned negative (to net layoffs) by the beginning of 2000 and continued at negative rates throughout 2001 and 2002. Job creation in the finance, insurance and real estate (FIRE) sector continued at year-on-year rates of 2% to 3%, but then turned sharply negative in 2002, reaching -4% by the end of the year. Office space vacancy in Wilmington reached 15% in the fourth quarter 2002, but this was below the national average of 16.5%. Positive factors that augur well for a relatively rapid economic recovery in Delaware are continued moderate housing costs that make Delaware more attractive than neighboring states with higher costs, and a related above-average 17% gain in population 1991 to 2001 (the national average-was 13%) that largely reflected the movement of businesses to Delaware's relatively low-cost business environment.

Delaware's gross state product (GSP) in 2004 was $54.274 billion, of which the real estate sector accounted for $6.290 billion, or 11.5% of GSP, followed by manufacturing at $4.841 billion (8.9% of GSP), and professional and technical services at $3.257 billion (6% of GSP). In that same year, there were 68,495 small businesses operating within the state. Of the state's 25833 firms that had employees that year, 24,006, or 92.9%, were small businesses. In 2004, a total of 3,270 new companies were formed in Delaware, down from the previous year by 4.9%. In that same year, business terminations totaled 3,362, up 6.8% from the previous year. Business bankruptcies in 2004 totaled 276, down 45.3% from 2003. In 2005, the personal bankruptcy (Chapter 7 and Chapter 13) filing rate was 423 filings per 100,000 people, ranking the state 34th in the nation.

21 INCOME

In 2005, Delaware had a gross state product (GSP) of $54 billion which accounted for 0.4% of the nation's gross domestic product

and placed the state at number 40 in highest GSP among the 50 states and the District of Columbia.

According to the Bureau of Economic Analysis, in 2004 Delaware had a per capita personal income (PCPI) of $35,728. This ranked 11th in the United States and was 108% of the national average of $33,050. The 1994–2004 average annual growth rate of PCPI was 4.3%. Delaware had a total personal income (TPI) of $29,656,646,000, which ranked 44th in the United States and reflected an increase of 7.4% from 2003. The 1994–2004 average annual growth rate of TPI was 5.8%. Earnings of persons employed in Delaware increased from $23,845,078,000 in 2003 to $25,377,515,000 in 2004, an increase of 6.4%. The 2003–04 national change was 6.3%.

The US Census Bureau reports that the three-year average median household income for 2002–04 in 2004 dollars was $50,152, compared to a national average of $44,473. During the same period an estimated 8.5% of the population was below the poverty line as compared to 12.4% nationwide.

22 LABOR

According to the Bureau of Labor Statistics (BLS), in April 2006 the seasonally adjusted civilian labor force in Delaware numbered 444,700, with approximately 16,400 workers unemployed, yielding an unemployment rate of 3.7%, compared to the national average of 4.7% for the same period. Preliminary data for the same period placed nonfarm employment at 437,600. Since the beginning of the BLS data series in 1976, the highest unemployment rate recorded in Delaware was 8.2%, in January 1977. The historical low was 2.8%, in October 1988. Preliminary nonfarm employment data by occupation for April 2006 showed that approximately 6.6% of the labor force was employed in construction; 18.8% in trade, transportation, and public utilities; 10.3% in financial activities; 14.3% in professional and business services; 12.5% in education and health services; 9.5% in leisure and hospitality services; and 13.8% in government. Data for manufacturing was unavailable.

The US Department of Labor's Bureau of Labor Statistics reported that in 2005, a total of 46,000 of Delaware's 386,000 employed wage and salary workers were formal members of a union. This represented 11.8% of those so employed, up from 12.4% in 2004, and just below the national average of 12%. Overall in 2005, a total of 50,000 workers (12.9%) in Delaware were covered by a union or employee association contract, which includes those workers who reported no union affiliation. Delaware is one of 28 states without a right-to-work law.

As of 1 March 2006, Delaware had a state-mandated minimum wage rate of $6.15 per hour. In 2004, women in the state accounted for 48.4% of the employed civilian labor force.

23 AGRICULTURE

Though small by national standards, Delaware's agriculture is efficient and productive. In 2005, Delaware's total farm marketings were $895 million, and its income from crops was $172 million.

Tobacco was a leading crop in the early colonial era but was soon succeeded by corn and wheat. Peaches were a mainstay during the mid-19th century, until the orchards were devastated by "the yellows," a tree disease. Today, the major field crops are corn, soybeans, barley, wheat, melons, potatoes, mushrooms, lima beans, and green peas. Production in 2004 included corn for grain, 23,256,000 bushels, valued at $48,838,000; soybeans, 8,736,000 bushels, $45,864,000; wheat, 2,726,000 bushels, $8,314,000; and barley, 2,080,000 bushels, $3,952,000.

24 ANIMAL HUSBANDRY

In 2003 an estimated 8,300 milk cows produced 136 million lb of milk (61.8 million kg). Also during 2003 an estimated 1.5 billion lb (680 million kg) of broilers were produced and valued at an estimated $542.6 million. Broilers accounted for 74% of Delaware's farm receipts in 2004. Delaware had 23,000 cattle and calves valued at around $22.8 million in 2005.

25 FISHING

Fishing, once an important industry in Delaware, has declined in recent decades. The total commercial landings in 2004 brought 4.3 million lb (1.9 million kg), worth $5.4 million. Clams, plentiful until the mid-1970s, are in short supply because of overharvesting. In 2001, the commercial fishing fleet had 184 vessels. Delaware issued 20,544 sport-fishing licenses in 2004.

26 FORESTRY

In 2004, Delaware had approximately 383,000 acres (155,000 hectares) of forestland, of which approximately 92% was classified as private forestland. Nonindustrial private landowners owned 85% of Delaware's forests while approximately 8% was publicly owned, and 7% was owned by the forest industry.

Southern Delaware contains many loblolly pine forests as well as the northernmost stand of bald cypress. Northern Delaware contains more hardwoods, such as oak and yellow poplar. Other common species are gum, maple, and American holly, which is Delaware's state tree. Delaware has approximately 32,000 acres (12,950 hectares) of state forests, which are managed on a multiple-use basis and are open to the public.

27 MINING

The value of nonfuel mineral production in Delaware in 2004 totaled $21.9 million, up more than 22% from 2003, according to data from the US Geological Survey (USGS). However, this figure does not reflect the state's production of magnesium compounds, which are used in chemical and pharmaceutical manufacturing, and were withheld by the USGS to protect company proprietary data. Construction sand and gravel was the leading nonfuel mineral produced in 2004. Output that year was 2.98 million metric tons or $21.9 million. Delaware in 2004 ranked fourth (out of five states) in the production of magnesium compounds (by volume). Magnesium compounds are extracted from seawater close to the mouth of the Delaware Bay near Lewes and, with aluminum hydroxides, are used in the manufacture of antacid products.

28 ENERGY AND POWER

As of 2003, Delaware had 17 electrical power service providers, of which 9 were publicly owned and only one was a cooperative. Of the remainder, one was investor owned, five were energy-only providers and one was a delivery-only provider. As of that same year there were 400,768 retail customers. Of that total, 280,525 received their power from investor-owned service providers.

The state's sole cooperative had 65,407 customers, while publicly owned providers had 54,829 customers.

Total net summer generating capability by the state's electrical generating plants in 2003 stood at 3.393 million kW, with total production that same year at 7.392 billion kWh. Of the total amount generated, only 0.4% came from electric utilities, with the remaining 99.6% coming from independent producers and combined heat and power service providers. The largest portion of all electric power generated, 4.026 billion kWh (54.5%), came from coal-fired plants, with petroleum plants in second place, at 1.716 billion kWh (23.2%) and natural gas plants in third at 1.463 billion kWh (19.8%). Other gas-fueled plants accounted for the remaining 2.5% of all power generated. Delaware has no nuclear power plants.

Delaware has no proven reserves or production of crude oil or natural gas. As of 2005, the state's single refinery had a crude oil distillation capacity of 175,000 barrels per day.

29 INDUSTRY

From its agricultural beginnings, Delaware has developed into an important industrial state. The state's capital, Wilmington, is called the "Chemical Capital of the World," largely because of E. I. du Pont de Nemours and Co., a chemical industry giant originally founded as a powder mill in 1802.

According to the US Census Bureau's Annual Survey of Manufactures (ASM) for 2004, Delaware's manufacturing sector covered some 11 product subsectors. The shipment value of all products manufactured in the state that same year was $17.488 billion. Of that total, chemical manufacturing accounted for the largest share at $6.512 billion. It was followed by transportation equipment manufacturing at $3.299 billion; food manufacturing at $1.782 billion; plastics and rubber product manufacturing at $630.011 million; and paper manufacturing at $5482.594 million.

In 2004, a total of 36,378 people in Delaware were employed in the state's manufacturing sector, according to the ASM. Of that total, 25,669 were actual production workers. In terms of total employment, the food manufacturing industry accounted for the largest portion of all manufacturing employees at 9,202, with 7,874 actual production workers. It was followed by chemical manufacturing with 5,760 employees (3,202 actual production workers); transportation equipment manufacturing at 4,080 (3,505 actual production workers); plastics and rubber products manufacturing at 2,634 employees (1,864 actual production workers); and fabricated metal product manufacturing at 2,220 employees (1,616 actual production workers).

ASM data for 2004 showed that Delaware's manufacturing sector paid $1.623 billion in wages. Of that amount, the chemical manufacturing sector accounted for the largest share at $365.962 million. It was followed by transportation equipment manufacturing at $282.321 million; food manufacturing at $228.561 million; and computer and electronic product manufacturing at $127.029 million.

30 COMMERCE

According to the 2002 Census of Wholesale Trade, Delaware's wholesale trade sector had sales that year totaling $17.2 billion from 997 establishments. Wholesalers of durable goods accounted for 610 establishments, followed by nondurable goods wholesalers at 335 and electronic markets, agents, and brokers accounting for 52 establishments. Sales by nondurable goods wholesalers in 2002 totaled $14.5 billion. Sales data for durable goods wholesalers and electronic markets, agents, and brokers in the wholesale trade industry were not available.

In the 2002 Census of Retail Trade, Delaware was listed as having 3,727 retail establishments with sales of $10.9 billion. The leading types of retail businesses by number of establishments were: food and beverage stores (571); clothing and clothing accessories stores (542); miscellaneous store retailers (449); and motor vehicle and motor vehicle parts dealers (377). In terms of sales, motor vehicle and motor vehicle parts dealers accounted for the largest share of retail sales at $2.7 billion, followed by food and beverage stores at $1.6 billion; general merchandise stores at $1.5 billion; and building material/garden equipment and supplies dealers at $1.01 billion. A total of 51,889 people were employed by the retail sector in Delaware that year.

In 2005, Delaware exported $2.5 billion worth of products to foreign markets.

31 CONSUMER PROTECTION

Consumer protection in Delaware is handled by the Fraud/Consumer Protection Division's Consumer Protection Unit, both of which are under the Office of the Attorney General. Specifically, the Unit is tasked with the responsibility of enforcing the state's consumer protection laws. It investigates consumer complaints; mediates resolution, when appropriate; and takes enforcement, when warranted. It also provides consumer education programs.

When dealing with consumer protection issues, the Attorney General's Office: can initiate civil and criminal proceedings; can represent the state before state and federal regulatory agencies; and has broad subpoena powers. In antitrust actions, the Attorney General's Office: can act on behalf of those consumers who are incapable of acting on their own; can initiate damage actions on behalf of the state in state courts; and can represent counties, cities and other governmental entities in recovering civil damages under state or federal law.

The offices of the Fraud/Consumer Protection Division and Consumer Protection Unit are located in Wilmington.

32 BANKING

As of June 2005, Delaware had 35 insured banks, savings and loans, and saving banks, plus 35 credit unions (CUs), all of them federally chartered. Excluding the CUs, the Philadelphia-Camden-Wilmington market area had 156 financial institutions in 2004, followed by the Dover area at 11. As of June 2005, CUs accounted for only 0.3% of all assets held by all financial institutions in the state, or some $1.377 billion. Banks, savings and loans, and savings banks collectively accounted for the remaining 99.7%, or $457.670 billion in assets held.

At the end of 2002, Delaware was home to six of the nation's leading insured credit card banks, including three of the nation's five largest. These credit card banks managed or held one-third of total credit-card loans nationally. Banking is Delaware's most profitable industry, with 12% of jobs and 36% of the gross state product represented by the finance insurance and real estate (FIRE) sectors. From 2001 to 2003, however, FIRE employment declined steadily.

As of 2004, the state's median past-due/nonaccrual loan rate as a percent of total loans was 1.09%, down from 1.35% in 2003. The median net interest margin (the difference between the lower rates offered to savers and the higher rates charged on loans) stood at 3.90% in 2004, down from 3.97% in 2003. Regulation of state-chartered financial institutions is handled by the Office of the State Bank Commissioner, which is a part of the Delaware Department of State.

33 INSURANCE

In 2004 there were 522,000 individual life insurance policies in force with a total value of over $53 billion; total value for all categories of life insurance (individual, group, and credit) was over $131.3 billion. The average coverage amount is $102,200 per policy holder. Death benefits paid that year totaled $269 million.

As of 2003, there were 83 property and casualty and 46 life and health insurance companies incorporated or organized in the state. In 2004, direct premiums for property and casualty insurance totaled $2 billion. That year, there were 18,490 flood insurance policies in force in the state, with a total value of $3.2 billion. About $218 million of coverage was offered through FAIR plans, which are designed to offer coverage for some natural circumstances, such as wind and hail, in high risk areas.

In 2004, 60% of state residents held employment-based health insurance policies, 3% held individual policies, and 23% were covered under Medicare and Medicaid; 13% of residents were uninsured. In 2003, employee contributions for employment-based health coverage averaged at 18% for single coverage and 21% for family coverage. The state does not offer an expansion program in connection with the Consolidated Omnibus Budget Reconciliation Act (COBRA, 1986), a health insurance program for those who lose employment-based coverage due to termination or reduction of work hours.

In 2003, there were 569,003 auto insurance policies in effect for private passenger cars. Required minimum coverage includes bodily injury liability of up to $15,000 per individual and $30,000 for all persons injured in an accident, as well as property damage liability of $10,000. Personal injury protection is also mandatory. In 2003, the average expenditure per vehicle for insurance coverage was $655.42, which ranked as the ninth-highest average in the nation.

34 SECURITIES

Delaware has no securities exchanges. In 2005, there were 560 personal financial advisers employed in the state. In 2004, there were over 26 publicly traded companies within the state, with over 7 NASDAQ companies, 12 NYSE listings, and 1 AMEX listing. In 2006, the state had one Fortune 500 company; DuPont ranked first in the state and 73rd in the nation, with revenues of over $28.4 billion. Hercules made the Fortune 1,000, at 787th in the nation, with revenues of $2 billion. Both companies are based in Wilmington and traded on the NYSE.

35 PUBLIC FINANCE

The budget director has lead responsibility for preparing Delaware's annual executive budget for submission to the legislature in January, which is expected to adopt a budget by 30 June for the fiscal year, which begins 1 July. There are both constitutional and

Delaware—State Government Finances

(Dollar amounts in thousands. Per capita amounts in dollars.)

	AMOUNT	PER CAPITA
Total Revenue	5,697,849	6,864.88
General revenue	5,144,482	6,198.17
Intergovernmental revenue	1,054,363	1,270.32
Taxes	2,375,482	2,862.03
General sales	–	–
Selective sales	383,383	461.91
License taxes	882,389	1,063.12
Individual income tax	781,212	941.22
Corporate income tax	217,768	262.37
Other taxes	110,730	133.41
Current charges	715,471	862.01
Miscellaneous general revenue	999,166	1,203.81
Utility revenue	9,814	11.82
Liquor store revenue	–	–
Insurance trust revenue	543,553	654.88
Total expenditure	5,387,960	6,491.52
Intergovernmental expenditure	922,710	1,111.70
Direct expenditure	4,465,250	5,379.82
Current operation	3,306,621	3,983.88
Capital outlay	442,787	533.48
Insurance benefits and repayments	401,683	483.96
Assistance and subsidies	86,233	103.90
Interest on debt	227,926	274.61
Exhibit: Salaries and wages	1,796,800	2,164.82
Total expenditure	5,387,960	6,491.52
General expenditure	4,914,614	5,921.22
Intergovernmental expenditure	922,710	1,111.70
Direct expenditure	3,991,904	4,809.52
General expenditures, by function:		
Education	1,701,881	2,050.46
Public welfare	1,022,013	1,231.34
Hospitals	56,802	68.44
Health	289,825	349.19
Highways	392,101	472.41
Police protection	78,262	94.29
Correction	202,782	244.32
Natural resources	82,540	99.45
Parks and recreation	47,294	56.98
Government administration	394,479	475.28
Interest on general debt	227,926	274.61
Other and unallocable	418,709	504.47
Utility expenditure	71,663	86.34
Liquor store expenditure	–	–
Insurance trust expenditure	401,683	483.96
Debt at end of fiscal year	4,158,118	5,009.78
Cash and security holdings	11,244,204	13,547.23

Abbreviations and symbols: – zero or rounds to zero; (NA) not available; (X) not applicable.

SOURCE: *U.S. Census Bureau, Governments Division, 2004 Survey of State Government Finances,* January 2006.

statutory requirements that the governor submit, the legislature adopt, and the governor sign a balanced budget.

Fiscal year 2006 general funds were estimated at $3.8 billion for resources and $3.2 billion for expenditures. In fiscal year 2004, federal government grants to Delaware were nearly $1.2 billion.

In the fiscal year 2007 federal budget, Delaware was slated to receive: $11.2 million in State Children's Health Insurance Program (SCHIP) funds to help Delaware provide health coverage to low-income, uninsured children who do not qualify for Medicaid. This funding was a 23% increase over fiscal year 2006; $5.4 million for the HOME Investment Partnership Program to help Dela-

ware fund a wide range of activities that build, buy, or rehabilitate affordable housing for rent or homeownership, or provide direct rental assistance to low-income people. This funding was an 11% increase over fiscal year 2006.

[36]TAXATION

In 2005, Delaware collected $2,725 million in tax revenues, or $3,229 per capita, which placed it fifth among the 50 states in per capita tax burden. The national average was $2,192 per capita. Selective sales taxes accounted for 14.6% of the total; individual income taxes, 32.4%; corporate income taxes, 9.1%; and other taxes, 43.9%.

As of 1 January 2006, Delaware had six individual income tax brackets ranging from 2.2 to 5.95%. The state taxes corporations at a flat rate of 8.7%.

In 2004, local property taxes amounted to $453,198,00, or $546 per capita. The per capita amount ranks the state 43rd nationally. Delaware has no state level property tax.

Delaware taxes gasoline at 23 cents per gallon. This is in addition to the 18.4 cents per gallon federal tax on gasoline.

According to the Tax Foundation, for every federal tax dollar sent to Washington in 2004, Delaware citizens received $0.79 in federal spending.

[37]ECONOMIC POLICY

Legislation passed in 1899 permits companies to be incorporated and chartered in Delaware even if they do no business in the state and hold their stockholders' meetings elsewhere. Another incentive to chartering in Delaware is the state's court of chancery, which has extensive experience in dealing with corporate problems.

The Delaware Economic Development Office (DEDO) seeks to create jobs by helping existing businesses to grow and by encouraging out-of-state companies to relocate to Delaware. The Development Office offers a variety of financing programs for small businesses, including assistance with land acquisition, loans and tax credits for capital investments, and state grants to match federal awards for research and development. The Delaware Innovation Fund is a private, nonprofit public/private initiative to assist companies with pre-startup seed money, with long-term loans for establishing patents, business plans, and to begin commercialization ($10,000–$150,000). In the year 2000, the Delaware Economic Development Office Director, and several Delaware lawmakers led a trade mission to Taiwan, establishing a Delaware-Taiwan trade office. In 2003, DEDO was one of 70 organizations participating in bioscience "hotbed" campaign, a concerted effort by a group made up of government development agencies, pharmaceutical and bioscience companies, research institutes, universities, and nonprofits to attract capital, personnel and resources to develop a life sciences cluster. Delaware, Maryland, Virginia, and Washington. DC. are recognized as forming a major life sciences hub, dubbed the BioCapital Hub by the industry.

The Delaware Main Street program encourages economic development and revitalization of the state's historic downtowns. The mission of the program supports the Livable Delaware Strategy to promote economic stability, quality of place, and smart growth.

In 2006, the US Chamber of Commerce ranked all 50 states on legal fairness towards business. The chamber found Delaware to be one of five states with the best legal environment for business. The other four were Nebraska, Virginia, Iowa, and Connecticut.

³⁸HEALTH

The infant mortality rate in October 2005 was estimated at 7.4 per 1,000 live births. The birth rate in 2003 was 13.8 per 1,000 population. The abortion rate stood at 31.3 per 1,000 women in 2000. In 2003, about 84.4% of pregnant woman received prenatal care beginning in the first trimester. In 2004, approximately 86% of children received routine immunizations before the age of three.

The crude death rate in 2003 was 8.6 deaths per 1,000 population. As of 2002, the death rates for major causes of death (per 100,000 resident population) were: heart disease, 237.6; cancer, 200.8; cerebrovascular diseases, 50.2; chronic lower respiratory diseases, 43.3; and diabetes, 26.6. The mortality rate from HIV infection was 8.7 per 100,000 population. In 2004, the reported AIDS case rate was at about 18.9 per 100,000 population. In 2002, about 55.6% of the population was considered overweight or obese. As of 2004, about 24.3% of state residents were smokers.

In 2003, Delaware had six community hospitals with about 2,000 beds. There were about 97,000 patient admissions that year and 2 million outpatient visits. The average daily inpatient census was about 1,700 patients. The average cost per day for hospital care was $1,508. Also in 2003, there were about 42 certified nursing facilities in the state, with 4,679 beds and an overall occupancy rate of about 84.7%. In 2004, it was estimated that about 77.2% of all state residents had received some type of dental care within the year. Delaware had 272 physicians per 100,000 resident population in 2004 and 914 nurses per 100,000 in 2005. In 2004, there was a total of 377 dentists in the state.

About 23% of state residents were enrolled in Medicaid and Medicare programs in 2004. Approximately 13% of the state population was uninsured in 2004. In 2003, state health care expenditures totaled $1.3 million.

³⁹SOCIAL WELFARE

In 2004, about 28,000 people received unemployment benefits, with the average weekly unemployment benefit at $247. In fiscal year 2005, the estimated average monthly participation in the food stamp program included about 61,586 persons (26,052 households); the average monthly benefit was about $88.26 per person. That year, the total of benefits paid through the state for the food stamp program was about $65.2 million.

Temporary Assistance for Needy Families (TANF), the system of federal welfare assistance that officially replaced Aid to Families with Dependent Children (AFDC) in 1997, was reauthorized through the Deficit Reduction Act of 2005. TANF is funded through federal block grants that are divided among the states based on an equation involving the number of recipients in each state. Delaware's TANF program is called ABC (A Better Chance). In 2004, the state program had 13,000 recipients; state and federal expenditures on this TANF program totaled $37 million in fiscal year 2003.

In December 2004, Social Security benefits were paid to 148,860 Delaware residents. This number included 96,620 retired workers, 13,290 widows and widowers, 19,880 disabled workers, 6,990 spouses, and 12,080 children. Social Security beneficiaries represented 17.6% of the total state population and 93.8% of the state's population age 65 and older. Retired workers received an average monthly payment of $1,004; widows and widowers, $957; disabled workers, $936; and spouses, $524. Payments for children of retired workers averaged $507 per month; children of deceased workers, $667; and children of disabled workers, $288. Federal Supplemental Security Income payments in December 2004 went to 13,452 Delaware residents, averaging $391 a month.

⁴⁰HOUSING

In 2004, there were approximately 367,448 housing units in Delaware, of which 310,676 were occupied; 72.9% were owner-occupied. About 55.4% of all units were single-family, detached homes. It was estimated that about 6,646 units lacked telephone service, 1,674 lacked complete plumbing facilities, and 2,334 lacked complete kitchen facilities. Most homes are heated by gas or electricity. The average household had 2.59 members.

In 2004, there were 7,900 new privately owned housing units authorized for construction. The median home value was $171,589. The median monthly cost for mortgage owners was $1,191 while renters paid a median of $743 per month. In 2006, the state was awarded over $1.9 million in community development block grants from the US Department of Housing and Urban Development (HUD).

⁴¹EDUCATION

The development of public support and financing for an adequate public educational system was the handiwork of progressive industrialist Pierre S. du Pont, who undertook the project in 1919. Approximately 86.5% of adult Delawareans were high school graduates in 2004; 26.9% had obtained a bachelor's degree or higher.

In fall 2002, 116,000 students were enrolled in public elementary and secondary schools. Of these, 82,000 attended schools from kindergarten through grade eight, and 34,000 attended high school. Approximately 57.3% of the students were white, 31.9% were black, 7.9% were Hispanic, 2.6% were Asian/Pacific Islander, and 0.3% were American Indian/Alaskan Native. Total enrollment was estimated at 116,000 in fall 2003 and expected to be 114,000 in fall 2014, a decrease of 2% during the period 2002 to 2014. There were 25,576 students enrolled in 121 private schools in fall 2003. Expenditures for public education in 2003/04 were estimated at $1.33 billion or $10,228 per student, the seventh-highest among the 50 states. Since 1969, the National Assessment of Educational Progress (NAEP) has tested public school students nationwide. The resulting report, *The Nation's Report Card,* stated that in 2005, eighth graders in Delaware scored 281 out of 500 in mathematics, compared with the national average of 278.

As of fall 2002, there were 49,228 students enrolled in institutions of higher education; minority students comprised 23.7% of total postsecondary enrollment. As of 2005, Delaware had 10 degree-granting institutions. Delaware has two public four-year institutions: the University of Delaware (Newark) and Delaware State College (Dover). Alternatives to these institutions include Widener University and the Delaware Technical and Community College, which has four campuses. There are three independent colleges: Goldey-Beacom College (Wilmington), Wesley College (Dover), and Wilmington College.

42 ARTS

The Delaware Division of the Arts (DDOA) is a branch of the Delaware Department of State, which administers arts-related grants and programs. The Delaware State Arts Council serves as the advisory board for the DDOA. In 2005, Delaware arts organizations received six grants totaling $671,400 from the National Endowment for the Arts. The Delaware Humanities Forum, an independent, nonprofit organization, was established in 1973 to sponsor programs and distribute grants to organizations promoting the understanding and appreciation of the humanities. In 2005, the National Endowment for the Humanities awarded three grants totaling $500,470 for state programs.

Wilmington has a local symphony orchestra, opera society, and drama league. The Playhouse, located in the Du Pont Building in Wilmington, shows first-run Broadway plays. The restored Grand Opera House, part of Delaware's Center for the Performing Arts in Wilmington, is the home of the Delaware Symphony and the Delaware Opera Guild, as well as host to performances of popular music and ballet.

43 LIBRARIES AND MUSEUMS

In 2001, Delaware had 37 public library systems, with a total of 37 libraries and no branches. In that same year, there were 1,468,000 books and serial publications on the system's shelves, and there was a total circulation of 4,543,000. The system also had 60,000 audio and 50,000 video items, and 3,000 electronic format items (CD-ROMs, magnetic tapes, and disks). The University of Delaware's Hugh M. Morris Library, with 2,259,121 volumes, is the largest academic library in the state. Other distinguished libraries include the Eleutherian Mills Historical Library, the Winterthur Library, and the Historical Society of Delaware Library (Wilmington). The Delaware Library Information connects all types of libraries through a statewide computer/telecommunication system. Total public library operating income came to $16,059,000 in fiscal year 2001, including $93,000 from federal grants and $2,906,000 from state grants. For that same year, operating expenditures totaled $14,757,000, of which 61.7% was spent on staff and 15.6% on the collection.

Notable among the state's 27 museums and numerous historical sites are the Hagley Museum and Delaware Art Museum, both in Wilmington, where the Historical Society of Delaware maintains a museum in the Old Town Hall. The Henry Francis du Pont Winterthur Museum features a collection of American antiques and decorative arts. The Brandywine Zoo, adjacent to Rockford Park, is popular with Wilmington's children. The Delaware State Museum is in Dover.

44 COMMUNICATIONS

In 2004, about 96.0% of Delaware's housing units had telephones. Additionally, by June of that same year there were 593,452 mobile wireless telephone subscribers. In 2003, 59.5% of Delaware households had a computer and 53.2% had Internet access. By June 2005, there were 109,468 high-speed lines in Delaware, 100,381 residential and 9,087 for business.

The state had 5 AM and 9 FM major radio stations and one public television station based in Seaford in 2005. Philadelphia and Baltimore commercial television stations are within range. A total of 19,351 Internet domain names were registered in Delaware by 2000.

45 PRESS

The *Wilmington Morning News* and the *Wilmington Evening Journal* merged with the *News Journal* in 1989. The *News Journal* has a daily (afternoon) circulation of 115,641 (139,647 on Sunday), as of 2005. In the state's capital is the *Delaware State News* with a daily circulation of 16,297 and Sunday circulation of 23,964, as of 2005. Statewide, there were two morning, one evening, and two Sunday papers in 2005. Smaller publications include the Newark Post, *Dover Post* and the *Delaware Coast Press.* Wilmington's paid weekly, *Dialog,* ranked fourth in the United States by circulation, 55,700. Magazines include *Delaware Today.*

46 ORGANIZATIONS

In 2006, there were over 1,260 nonprofit organizations registered within the state, of which about 708 were registered as charitable, educational, or religious organizations. Among national organizations headquartered in Delaware are the International Reading Association and the American Philosophical Association. The Ancient and Illustrious Order Knights of Malta is based in Wilmington. State arts and educational organizations include the Delaware Academy of Medicine and the Historical Society of Delaware.

47 TOURISM, TRAVEL, AND RECREATION

Delaware's travel and recreation industry is second only to manufacturing in economic importance. The Delaware Tourism Office is charged with supporting the tourism industry within the state. In 2001, the state launched a campaign entitled, "Delaware: It's Good to be First," which plays upon the state's claim as the first of the original 13 states to ratify the Constitution. In 2001, there were some 12 million visitors to the state. About 36% were day-trip travelers from surrounding states. Shopping (with no sales tax) and the state's beaches are the most popular attractions; outlet shopping malls are a big attraction for tourists. In 2003, Delaware employed 14,800 persons in the tourism industry.

Rehoboth Beach on the Atlantic Coast bills itself as the "Nation's Summer Capital" because of the many federal officials and foreign diplomats who summer there. Nearby Dewey Beach and Bethany Beach are also fast-growing family vacation spots. Events are the Delaware Kite Festival at Cape Henlopen State Park (east of Lewes) every Good Friday, Old Dover Days during the first weekend in May, and Delaware Day ceremonies (7 December, commemorating the day in 1787 when the state ratified the Constitution) throughout the state. Fort Delaware is a popular historic site. Fishing, clamming, crabbing, boating, and swimming are the main recreational attractions. There are 14 state parks. Delaware is also host to thoroughbred horse racing (Delaware Park Racetrack), slot machine gambling, and NASCAR racing. Winterthur, in Brandywine Valley, boasts a Fairy Tale Garden. All three Delaware counties have a merchants' organization, which sponsors demonstrations of arts and crafts.

48 SPORTS

Delaware has two major horse-racing tracks: Harrington, which has harness racing, and Dover Downs, which also has a track for auto racing. The MBNA Platinum 500 stock car race is held in June and the MBNA.com 400 is run in September. Thoroughbred races are held at Delaware Park in Wilmington. Wilmington has a minor league baseball team, the Blue Rocks, in the Carolina League. Additionally, the Fightin' Blue Hens of the University of Delaware field teams in a large number of both men's and women's sports.

⁴⁹FAMOUS DELAWAREANS

Three Delawareans have served as US secretary of state: Louis McLane (1786–1857), John M. Clayton (1796–1856), and Thomas F. Bayard (1828–98). Two Delawareans have been judges on the Permanent Court of International Justice at The Hague: George Gray (1840–1925) and John Bassett Moore (1860–1947). James A. Bayard (b.Pennsylvania, 1767–1815), a US senator from Delaware from 1805 to 1813, was chosen to negotiate peace terms for ending the War of 1812 with the British.

John Dickinson (b.Maryland, 1732–1808), the "Penman of the Revolution," and Caesar Rodney (1728–84), wartime chief executive of Delaware, were notable figures of the Revolutionary era. George Read (b.Maryland, 1733–98) and Thomas McKean (b.Pennsylvania, 1734–1817) were, with Rodney, signers for Delaware of the Declaration of Independence. Naval officers of note include Thomas Macdonough (1783–1825) in the War of 1812 and Samuel F. du Pont (b.New Jersey, 1803–65) in the Civil War.

Morgan Edwards (b.England, 1722–95), Baptist minister and historian, was a founder of Brown University. Richard Allen (b.Pennsylvania, 1760–1831) and Peter Spencer (1779–1843) established separate denominations of African Methodists. Welfare worker Emily P. Bissell (1861–1948) popularized the Christmas seal in the United States, and Florence Bayard Hilles (1865–1954) was president of the National Woman's Party.

Among scientists and engineers were Oliver Evans (1755–1819), inventor of a high-pressure steam engine; Edward Robinson Squibb (1819–1900), physician and pharmaceuticals manufacturer; Wallace H. Carothers (b.Iowa, 1896–1937), developer of nylon at Du Pont; and Daniel Nathans (1928–99), who shared the Nobel Prize in medicine in 1978 for his research on molecular genetics. Eleuthère I. du Pont (b.France, 1771–1834) founded the company that bears his name; Pierre S. du Pont (1870–1954) was architect of its modern growth.

Delaware authors include Robert Montgomery Bird (1806–54), playwright; Hezekiah Niles (b.Pennsylvania, 1777–1839), journalist; Christopher Ward (1868–1944), historian; Henry Seidel Canby (1878–1961), critic; and novelist Anne Parrish (b.Colorado, 1888–1957). Howard Pyle (1853–1911) was known as a writer, teacher, and artist-illustrator.

⁵⁰BIBLIOGRAPHY

Blashfield, Jean F. *Delaware.* New York: Children's Press, 2000.

Colbert, Judy. *Maryland and Delaware: Off the Beaten Path.* Old Saybrook, Conn.: Globe Pequot Press, 1999.

Council of State Governments. *The Book of the States, 2006 Edition.* Lexington, Ky.: Council of State Governments, 2006.

Essah, Patience. *A House Divided: Slavery and Emancipation in Delaware, 1638–1865.* Charlottesville: University Press of Virginia, 1996.

Harper, Steven Craig. *Promised Land: Penn's Holy Experiment, the Walking Purchase, and the Dispossession of Delawares, 1600–1763.* Bethlehem, Pa.: Lehigh University Press, 2006.

Marzec, Robert P. (ed.). *The Mid-Atlantic Region.* Vol. 2 in *The Greenwood Encyclopedia of American Regional Cultures.* Westport, Conn.: Greenwood Press, 2004.

Munroe, John A. *History of Delaware.* 3rd ed. Newark: University of Delaware Press, 1993.

US Department of Commerce, Economics and Statistics Administration, US Census Bureau. *Delaware, 2000. Summary Social, Economic, and Housing Characteristics: 2000 Census of Population and Housing.* Washington, D.C.: US Government Printing Office, 2003.

FLORIDA

State of Florida

ORIGIN OF STATE NAME: Named in 1513 by Juan Ponce de León, who landed during *Pascua Florida,* the Easter festival of flowers. **NICKNAME:** The Sunshine State. **CAPITAL:** Tallahassee. **ENTERED UNION:** 3 March 1845 (27th). **SONG:** "Old Folks at Home" (also known as "The Swanee River"). **MOTTO:** In God We Trust. **FLAG:** The state seal appears in the center of a white field, with four red bars extending from the seal to each corner; the flag is fringed on three sides. **OFFICIAL SEAL:** In the background, the sun's rays shine over a distant highland; in the foreground are a sabal palmetto palm, a steamboat, and an Indian woman scattering flowers on the ground. The words "Great Seal of the State of Florida" and the state motto surround the whole. **BIRD:** Mockingbird. **FISH:** Largemouth bass (freshwater), Atlantic sailfish (saltwater). **FLOWER:** Orange blossom. **TREE:** Sabal palmetto palm. **GEM:** Moonstone. **LEGAL HOLIDAYS:** New Year's Day, 1 January; Martin Luther King Jr. Day, 3rd Monday in January; Memorial Day, last Monday in May; Independence Day, 4 July; Labor Day, 1st Monday in September; Veterans' Day, 11 November; Thanksgiving Days, 4th Thursday and Friday in November; Christmas Day, 25 December. **TIME:** 7 AM EST = noon GMT; 6 AM CST = noon GMT.

¹LOCATION, SIZE, AND EXTENT

Located in the extreme southeastern United States, Florida is the second-largest state (after Georgia) east of the Mississippi River, and ranks 22nd in size among the 50 states.

The total area of Florida is 58,664 sq mi (151,939 sq km), of which land takes up 54,153 sq mi (140,256 sq km) and inland water, 4,511 sq mi (11,683 sq km). Florida extends 361 mi (581 km) E–W; its maximum N–S extension is 447 mi (719 km). The state comprises a peninsula surrounded by ocean on three sides, with a panhandle of land in the NW.

Florida is bordered on the N by Alabama and Georgia (with the line in the NE formed by the St. Mary's River); on the E by the Atlantic Ocean; on the S by the Straits of Florida; and on the W by the Gulf of Mexico and Alabama (separated by the Perdido River).

Offshore islands include the Florida Keys, extending form the state's southern tip into the Gulf of Mexico. The total boundary length of Florida is 1,799 mi (2,895 km). The state's geographic center is in Hernando County, 12 mi (19 km) NNW of Brooksville.

²TOPOGRAPHY

Florida is a huge plateau, much of it barely above sea level. The highest point in the state is believed to be a hilltop in the panhandle, 345 ft (105 m) above sea level, near the city of Lakewood, in Walton County. The lowest point is at sea level at the Atlantic Ocean. The mean elevation is about 100 ft (31 m). No point in the state is more than 70 mi (113 km) from saltwater.

Most of the panhandle region is gently rolling country, much like that of southern Georgia and Alabama, except that large swampy areas cut in from the Gulf coast. Peninsular Florida, which contains extensive swampland, has a relatively elevated central spine of rolling country, dotted with lakes and springs. Its east coast is shielded from the Atlantic by a string of sandbars. The west coast is cut by numerous bays and inlets, and near its southern tip are

the Ten Thousand Islands, a mass of mostly tiny mangrove-covered islets. Southwest of the peninsula lies Key West, which, at 24°33′N, is the southernmost point of the US mainland.

Almost all the southeastern peninsula and the entire southern end are covered by the Everglades, the world's largest sawgrass swamp, with an area of approximately 5,000 sq mi (13,000 sq km). The Everglades is, in a sense, a huge river, in which water flows south–southwest from Lake Okeechobee to Florida Bay. No point in the Everglades is more than 7 ft (2 m) above sea level. Its surface is largely submerged during the rainy season, April to November, and becomes a muddy expanse in the dry months. Slight elevations, known as hammocks, support clumps of cypress and the only remaining stand of mahogany in the continental United States. To the west and north of the Everglades is Big Cypress Swamp, covering about 2,400 sq mi (6,200 sq km), which contains far less surface water.

Lake Okeechobee, in south-central Florida, is the largest of the state's approximately 30,000 lakes, ponds, and sinks. With a surface area of about 700 sq mi (1,800 sq km), it is the fourth-largest natural lake located entirely within the United States. Like all of Florida's lakes, it is extremely shallow, having a maximum depth of 15 ft (5 m), and was formed through the action of groundwater and rainfall in dissolving portions of the thick limestone layer that underlies Florida's sandy soil. The state's numerous underground streams and caverns were created in a similar manner. Because of the high water table, most of the caverns are filled, but some spectacular examples thick with stalactites can be seen in Florida Caverns State Park, near Marianna. More than 200 natural springs send up some 7 billion gallons of groundwater per day through cracks in the limestone. Silver Springs, near Ocala in north-central Florida, has the largest average flow of all inland springs, 823 cu ft (23 cu m) per second.

Florida has more than 1,700 rivers, streams, and creeks. The longest river is the St. Johns, which empties into the Atlantic 19 mi

(42 km) east of Jacksonville: estimates of its length range from 273 to 318 mi (439 to 512 km), an exact figure being elusive because of the swampy nature of the headwaters. Other major rivers are the Suwannee, which flows south from Georgia for 177 mi (285 km) through Florida and empties into the Gulf of Mexico; and the Apalachicola, formed by the Flint and Chattahoochee rivers at the Florida-Georgia border, and flowing southward across the panhandle for 94 mi (151 km) to the Gulf. Jim Woodruff Lock and Dam is located on the Apalachicola about 1,000 ft (300 m) below the confluence of the two feeder rivers. Completed in 1957, the dam created Lake Seminole, most of which is in Georgia.

More than 4,500 islands ring the mainland. Best known are the Florida Keys, of which Key Largo, about 29 mi (47 km) long and less than 2 mi (3 km) wide, is the largest. Key West, less than 4 mi (6 km) long and 2 mi (3 km) wide is a popular resort, and the westernmost.

For much of the geological history of the United States, Florida was under water. During this time, the shells of countless millions of sea animals decayed to form the thick layers of limestone that now blanket the state. The peninsula rose above sea level perhaps 20 million years ago. Even then, the southern portion remained largely submerged, until the buildup of coral and sand around its rim blocked out the sea, leaving dense marine vegetation to decay and form the peaty soil of the present-day Everglades.

3 CLIMATE

A mild, sunny climate is one of Florida's most important natural resources, making it a major tourist center and a retirement home for millions of transplanted northerners. Average annual temperatures range from 65° to 70°F (18° to 21°C) in the north, and from 74° to 77°F (23° to 25°C) in the southern peninsula and on the Keys. At Jacksonville, the average annual temperature is 69°F (20°C); the average low is 58°F (14°C), the average high 79°F (26°C). At Miami, the annual average is 76°F (24°C), with a low of 69°F (21°C) and a high of 83°F (28°C). Key West has the highest annual average temperature in the United States, at 78°F (25°C). The record high temperature, 109°F (43°C), was registered at Monticello on 29 June 1931; the record low, -2°F (-19°C), at Tallahassee on 13 February 1899.

Florida's proximity to the Atlantic and the Gulf of Mexico, and the state's many inland lakes and ponds, together account for the high humidity and generally abundant rainfall, although precipitation can vary greatly from year to year and serious droughts have occurred. At Jacksonville, the average annual precipitation (1971–2000) was 52.3 in (132.8 cm), with an average of 116 days of precipitation a year. At Miami during the same period, precipitation averaged 58.5 in (148.6 cm), with 130 rainy days a year. Rainfall is unevenly distributed throughout the year, more than half generally occurring from June through September; periods of extremely heavy rainfall are common. The highest 24-hour total ever recorded in the United States, 38.7 in (98.3 cm), fell at Yankeetown, west of Ocala on the Gulf coast, on 5–6 September 1950. Despite the high annual precipitation rate, the state also receives abundant sunshine with about 63% of the maximum possible at Jacksonville, and 70% at Miami. Snow is virtually unheard of in southern Florida but does fall on rare occasions in the panhandle and the northern peninsula.

Winds are generally from the east and southeast in the southern peninsula; in northern Florida, winds blow from the north in winter, bringing cold snaps, and from the south in summer. Average wind velocities are 7.9 mph (12.7 km/hr) at Jacksonville and 9.2 mph (14.8 km/hr) at Miami. Florida's long coastline makes it highly vulnerable to hurricanes and tropical storms, which may approach from either the Atlantic or the Gulf coast, bringing winds of up to 150 mph (240 km/hr). On 23–24 August 1992, Hurricane Andrew caused over $10 billion in damage in Florida. The 2005 hurricane season had devastating effects on various regions in Florida. On July 10, Hurricane Dennis made landfill near Pensacola as a Category 3 storm, causing flood damage and power outages for about 400,000 residents. On 26 August 2005, Hurricane Katrina made landfall near Miami as a Category 1 storm, causing extensive damage from wind and flooding and power outages for about 1.3 million. As of early 2006, there were at least 11 related fatalities reported in Florida as a result of this storm. Two months later, Hurricane Wilma made landfall near Naples on October 25 2005 as a Category 3 storm. Wilma caused at least six fatalities in Florida and power outages for another 6 million people, as well as flooding and wind damage. As of early 2006, the estimated cost of damage from all these storms was over $2 billion dollars for the state.

4 FLORA AND FAUNA

Generally, Florida has seven floral zones: flatwoods, scrublands, grassy swamps, savannas, salt marshes, hardwood forests (hammocks), and pinelands. Flatwoods consist of open forests and an abundance of flowers, including more than 60 varieties of orchid. Small sand pines are common in the scrublands; other trees here are the saw palmetto, blackjack, and water oak. The savannas of central Florida support water lettuce, American lotus, and water hyacinth. North Florida's flora includes longleaf and other pines, oaks, and cypresses; one giant Seminole cypress is thought to be 3,500 years old. The state is known for its wide variety of palms, but only 15 are native, and more than 100 have been introduced; common types include royal and coconut. Although pine has the most commercial importance, dense mangrove thickets grow along the lower coastal regions, and northern hardwood forests include varieties of rattan, magnolia, and oak. Numerous rare plants have been introduced, among them bougainvillea and oleander. All species of cacti and orchids are regarded as threatened, as are most types of ferns and palms.

Florida once claimed more than 80 land mammals. The white-tailed deer, wild hog, and gray fox can still be found in the wild; such small mammals as the raccoon, eastern gray and fox squirrels, and cottontail and swamp rabbits remain common. Florida's bird population includes many resident and migratory species. The mockingbird was named the state bird in 1927; among game birds are the bobwhite quail, wild turkey, and at least 30 duck species. Several varieties of heron are found, as well as coastal birds such as gulls, pelicans, and frigates. The Arctic tern stops in Florida during its remarkable annual migration between the North and South poles.

Common Florida reptiles are the diamondback rattler and various water snakes. Turtle species include mud, green, and loggerhead, and various lizards abound. More than 300 native butterflies have been identified. The peninsula is famous for its marine life:

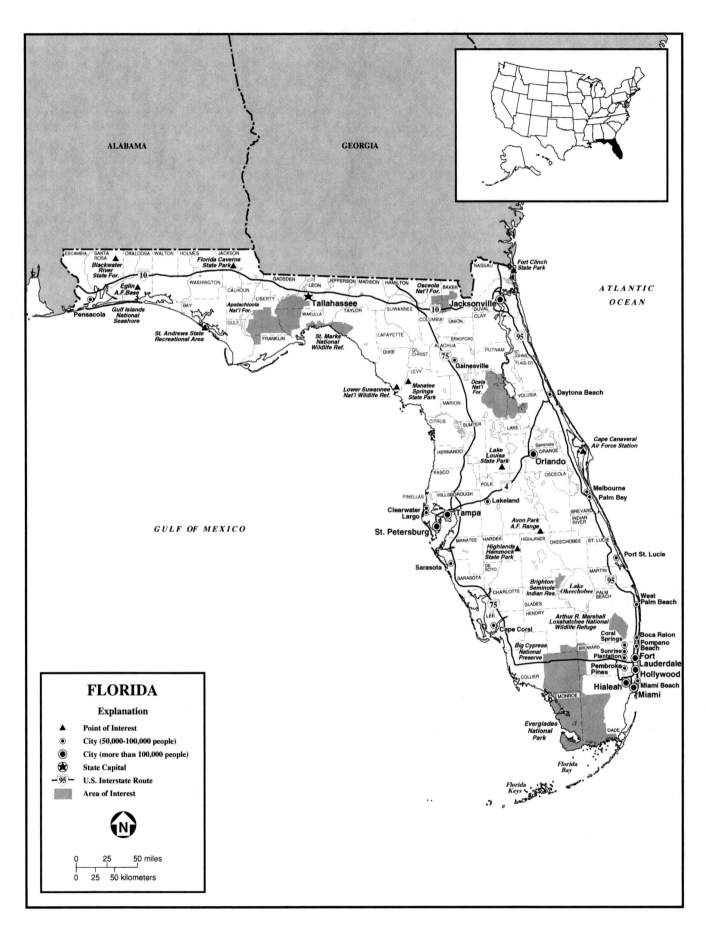

ALABAMA

GEORGIA

ATLANTIC OCEAN

ESCAMBIA SANTA ROSA OKALOOSA WALTON HOLMES JACKSON

Blackwater River State For.

Florida Caverns State Park ▲

Eglin ▲ A.F.Base

Pensacola

WASHINGTON

CALHOUN

Apalachicola Nat'l For.

Gulf Islands National Seashore

St. Andrews State Recreational Area

BAY

GULF

FRANKLIN

LIBERTY

WAKULLA

★ Tallahassee

LEON

GADSDEN

Fort Clinch State Park

NASSAU

JEFFERSON MADISON HAMILTON

Osceola Nat'l For.

BAKER

Jacksonville

DUVAL

10

St. Marks National Wildlife Ref.

TAYLOR

SUWANNEE

COLUMBIA

UNION

CLAY

95

LAFAYETTE

DIXIE

GIL-CHRIST

ST. JOHNS

FLAGLER

BRADFORD

ALACHUA

PUTNAM

75

Gainesville

LEVY

Lower Suwannee Nat'l Wildlife Ref.

▲ Manatee Springs State Park

MARION

Ocala Nat'l For.

VOLUSIA

Daytona Beach

CITRUS

SUMTER

LAKE

HERNANDO

Cape Canaveral Air Force Station

Lake Louisa State Park ▲

Seminole

ORANGE

Orlando

PASCO

OSCEOLA

4

POLK

Melbourne

Palm Bay

PINELLAS

HILLSBOROUGH

Lakeland

BREVARD

Clearwater

Largo

Tampa

Avon Park A.F. Range ▲

INDIAN RIVER

St. Petersburg

MANATEE

HARDEE

HIGHLANDS

OKEECHOBEE

ST. LUCIE

Port St. Lucie

Sarasota

Highlands Hammock State Park ▲

SARASOTA

DE SOTO

Brighton Seminole Indian Res.

Lake Okeechobee

MARTIN

95

CHARLOTTE

GLADES

PALM BEACH

West Palm Beach

LEE

75

HENDRY

Arthur R. Marshall Loxahatchee National Wildlife Refuge

Cape Coral

Coral Springs

Boca Raton

Pompano Beach

Big Cypress National Preserve

BROWARD

Sunrise

Plantation

Fort Lauderdale

Pembroke Pines

Hollywood

COLLIER

Hialeah

Miami Beach

Miami

MONROE

Everglades National Park

DADE

Florida Bay

Florida Keys

GULF OF MEXICO

FLORIDA

Explanation

▲ Point of Interest

◉ City (50,000-100,000 people)

◉ City (more than 100,000 people)

★ State Capital

95 U.S. Interstate Route

Area of Interest

N

| 0 | 25 | 50 miles |
| 0 | 25 | 50 kilometers |

scores of freshwater and saltwater fish, rays, shrimps, live coral reefs, and marine worms.

Everglades National Park hosts a rich array of plant and animal species. including over 300 species of migratory birds, over 1,000 species of seed-bearing plants and over 120 tree species. There have been at least 25 orchid species found in the area. Also noted are 25 species of terrestrial mammals, 4 salamander species, 6 kinds of lizards, 10 land and freshwater turtle species, 12 frog species, and 23 snake species. The Everglades is the only location in the world to serve as home to both the American alligator and the American crocodile. Pelican Island serves as a nesting ground for at least 10 species of birds (about 800 nesting pairs per year) and supports 11 threatened or endangered species, including the manatee. Okefenokee Swamp (which extends into Georgia) supports 233 bird species, 48 mammal species, 66 reptile species, 37 amphibian species, and 36 fish species. One of the largest US populations of the American alligator can be found there as well. All of Florida's lands have been declared sanctuaries for the bald eagle, of which Florida has about 350 pair (second only to Alaska among the 50 states).

In April 2006, a total of 108 species occurring within the state were on the threatened and endangered species list of the US Fish and Wildlife Service. These included 54 animal (vertebrates and invertebrates) and 54 plant species. The state's unusually long list of threatened and endangered wildlife included the American crocodile, shortnose sturgeon, six species of sea turtle, red-cockaded woodpecker, Florida panther, key deer, West Indian (Florida) manatee, six species of mouse, Key Largo woodrat, Everglade snail kite, two species of sparrow, Atlantic salt marsh snake, eastern indigo snake, Okaloosa darter, Stock Island tree snail, and Schaus swallowtail butterfly.

5 ENVIRONMENTAL PROTECTION

Throughout the 20th century, a rapidly growing population, the expansion of agriculture, and the exploitation of such resources as timber and minerals have put severe pressure on Florida's natural environment.

The state agency principally responsible for safeguarding the environment is the Department of Environmental Protection (DEP), created in 1993 by the merger of the Departments of Natural Resources and Environmental Regulation. Its duties include implementing state pollution control laws and improving water-resource management. The department oversees and coordinates the activities of the state's five water-management districts, which have planning and regulatory responsibilities. The department also protects the state's coastal and marine resources. Its Division of State Lands acquires environmentally endangered tracts of land in what has been called the nation's largest environmental land-buying program. More than 1.2 million acres of environmentally important lands have been purchased. The department administers state parks and wilderness lands as well.

The Department of Agriculture and Consumer Services' Division of Forestry manages four state forests plus the Talquin State Lands. The Game and Fresh Water Fish Commission manages nature preserves and regulates hunting and fishing.

Growth, contamination of groundwater, and control of stormwater (nonpoint sources) are the state's most serious environmental problems. Groundwater supplies 90% of the drinking water in the state, as well as 8.2% of industry's needs and 53% of agricultural uses. Groundwater, surface water, and soil contamination have been found across the state. Among the major contaminants were the pesticides ethylene dibromide (2,300 wells statewide) and other chemicals (about 1,000 additional wells). The state's program to clean groundwater contaminated by leaking underground storage tanks is one of the nation's largest and pioneered the pattern followed by many other states. Florida's groundwater quality standards are among the most stringent in the nation.

Contamination of groundwater is not the state's only water problem. The steadily increasing demand for water for both residential and farm use has reduced the subterranean runoff of fresh water into the Atlantic and the Gulf of Mexico. As a result, saltwater from these bodies has begun seeping into the layers of porous limestone that hold Florida's reserves of fresh water. This problem has been aggravated in some areas by the cutting of numerous inlets by developers of coastal property.

The DEP and South Florida Water Management District are undertaking, with various federal agencies, a massive restoration program for the Kissimmee River, Lake Okeechobee, the Everglades, and Florida Bay. This undertaking resulted from the settlement of a lawsuit brought by the federal government. The restoration effort includes: rechannelization of the Kissimmee River canal to restore its floodplains and prevent water pollution from entering Lake Okeechobee; other measures to reduce pollutants in the lake caused by agricultural operations around its edges; creation of large stormwater treatment areas within the Everglades to treat nutrient-rich agricultural waters that are upsetting the ecological balance of the Everglades; and hydrological corrections to improve water delivery to the Everglades and Florida Bay.

In 1960, the only undersea park in the United States, the John Pennekamp Coral Reef State Park, was established in a 75-sq mi (194-sq km) sector off the Atlantic coast of Key Largo, in an effort to protect a portion of the beautiful reefs, rich in tropical fish and other marine life, that adjoin the Keys. Untreated sewage from the Miami area, runoff water polluted by pesticides and other chemicals, dredging associated with coastal development, and the removal of countless pieces of live coral by growing numbers of tourists and souvenir dealers have severely damaged large areas of the reefs. However, most of the Keys is now a National Marine Sanctuary and efforts are being made to improve water quality.

Florida is home to three Ramsar Wetlands of International Importance. The Okefenokee Swamp (which extends into Georgia) was designated in 1986; it is the second largest wetland in the nation. The site is federally owned and managed, in part, under the Okefenokee Wilderness Act of 1974. Everglades National Park was designated in 1987 as an important nesting, staging, and wintering bird habitat. The park was also designated as a UNESCO Man and Biosphere Reserve in 1976 and as a World Heritage Site in 1979. Pelican Island National Wildlife Refuge, located in the Indian River Lagoon along the Atlantic Coast, was designated by Ramsar in 1993. This site has shared ownership between the state and federal government.

In 2003, the US Environment Protection Agency (EPA) database listed 598 hazardous waste sites in Florida, 50 of which were on the National Priorities List as of 2006, including 4 military sites. Florida ranks sixth in the nation for the most National Priority List sites. In 2005, the EPA spent over $8 million through the Superfund program for the cleanup of hazardous waste sites in the state. Also in 2005, federal EPA grants awarded to the state included over $37.9 million for water-quality control and protection projects. A federal research grant of $992,000 was awarded to the Florida Department of Citrus to pursue improved harvesting techniques. In 2003, 126.5 million lb of toxic chemicals were released by the state.

6 POPULATION

Florida, the most populous state in the southeastern United States, is also one of the fastest growing of the 50 states. In 1960, it was the 10th most populous state; by 1980, it ranked 7th with a population of 9,746,324; and by 1990, it ranked 4th, with a population of 12,937,926. Between 1990 and 2000, Florida had the third-largest population gain among the states, surpassed only by California and Texas. In that decade, Florida's population grew from 12,937,926 to 15,982,378, an increase of 23.5% (also one of the largest percentage gains in the country). In 2005, Florida had the fourth-largest population of all 50 states, with an estimated total of 17,789,864, an 11.3% increase since 2000. Florida is expected to have a population of 21.2 million by 2015 and 25.9 million by 2025.

The first US census to include Florida, in 1830, recorded a total population of only 34,730. By 1860, on the eve of the Civil War, the population had more than quadrupled, to 140,424 people; about 80% of them lived in the state's northern rim, where cotton and sugarcane plantations flourished. Newcomers migrating southward in the late 19th century through the early 1920s sharply increased the state's population; the 1930 census was the first in which the state passed the million mark. Migration from other states, especially of retirees, caused a population explosion in the post–World War II period, with much of the increase occurring along the south Atlantic coast. From 1950 to 1960, Florida's population increased 79%, the fastest rate of all the states. From 1960 to 1970, the growth rate was 37%; from 1970 to 1980, 44%; from 1980 to 1990, 33%; and from 1990 to 1998, 15.3%.

In 2004, the average population density was 322.7 per sq mi, the eighth highest in the nation. The median age of the population was 39.3, the fifth-highest median of the 50 states. Nearly 23% of the population was under age 18, while over 16.8% of was 65 years of age or older.

The most populous city in Florida is Jacksonville, the 13th-largest city in the United States in 2004. Its population in that year was estimated at 777,704. Miami is Florida's second-largest city, with an estimated 2004 population of 379,724. The Miami–Ft. Lauderdale–Miami Beach metropolitan area, the state's largest metropolitan region, had an estimated 5,361,723 residents in 2004; the Jacksonville metropolitan area's population was 1,225,381. Florida's second-largest metropolitan area was Tampa-St. Petersburg-Clearwater, with an estimated 2,587,967 residents; the city of Tampa had an estimated 321,772 people, and St. Petersburg had 249,090. Ft. Lauderdale had an estimated population of 164,578. Tallahassee, the state capital, had a population of 156,612.

7 ETHNIC GROUPS

Florida's population consists mainly of whites of northern European stock, blacks, and Hispanics. European immigrants came primarily from Germany and the United Kingdom. Germans were particularly important in the development of the citrus fruit industry. Since World War II, the development of southern Florida as a haven for retired northerners has added new population elements to the state, a trend augmented by the presence of numerous military bases.

Florida's foreign-born population numbered 2,670,828 in 2000, or 16.7% of the state total, the fourth-highest percentage of foreign born in the nation. The largest group of first- and second-generation residents are Cubans, who represented 5.2% of Florida's population in 2000. There were 2,682,715 Hispanics and Latinos in 2000, including 833,120 Cubans (more than 100,000 of whom arrived on Florida shores as refugees in 1980), 482,027 Puerto Ricans, and 363,925 Mexicans. In 2004, 19% of the population was of Hispanic or Latino origin.

The nonwhite population, as reported in 2000, was 3,517,349, or 12% of the total state population. Black-white relations in the 20th century were tense. There were race riots following World War I, and the Ku Klux Klan was openly active until World War II. One of the worst race riots in US history devastated black areas of Miami in the spring of 1980. The black population was estimated at 2,335,505 as of 2000, the fourth-largest in the nation. In 2004, 15.7% of the population was black.

Florida's indigenous inhabitants resisted encroachment from settlers longer and more militantly than tribes in other seaboard states. The leaders in resistance were the Seminole, most of whom by the 1850s had been killed or removed to other states, had fled to the Florida swamplands, or had been assimilated as small farmers. No peace treaty was signed with the Seminole until 1934, following the Indian Reorganization Act that attempted to establish tribal integrity and self-government for Indian nations. In 1939, the Native American population was reported as only 600, but the 2000 census reported a figure of 53,541 Native Americans. The difference is too large to be explained by natural increase, and there is no evidence of marked in-migration; presumably, then, it reflects a growing consciousness of Indian identity. There are seven Indian reservations: five for the Seminole—Big Cypress, Hollywood, Brighton, Immokalee, and Tampa, and two for the Miccosuckee—one on the Tamiami Trail and one north of Alligator Alley near Big Cypress. In 2004, 0.4% of the population was American Indian.

As of 2000 Florida had an Asian population of 266,256 (eighth largest in the nation), or 1.7% of the total state population. That figure had increased to 2% of the population by 2004. The number of Pacific Islanders was estimated at 8,625. In 2004, 0.1% of the population was composed of Pacific Islanders. In 2000 there were 54,310 Filipinos, 46,368 Chinese, 70,740 Asian Indians (up from 22,240 in 1990), 33,190 Vietnamese (up from 14,586 in 1990), 10,897 Japanese, 19,139 Koreans, and 2,131 native Hawaiians. In 2004, 1.2% of the population reported two or more races of origin.

8 LANGUAGES

Spanish and English settlers found what is now Florida inhabited by Indians recently separated from the Muskogean Creeks, who, with the addition of escaped black slaves and remnants of the Apalachee Indians of the panhandle, later became known as the Seminole Indians. Although the bulk of the Seminole were removed to Indian Territory in the 1840s, enough remained to pro-

Florida—Counties, County Seats, and County Areas and Populations

COUNTY	COUNTY SEAT	LAND AREA (SQ MI)	POPULATION (2005 EST.)	COUNTY	COUNTY SEAT	LAND AREA (SQ MI)	POPULATION (2005 EST.)
Alachua	Gainesville	901	223,852	Lake	Tavares	954	277,035
Baker	MacClenny	585	24,569	Lee	Ft. Myers	803	544,758
Bay	Panama City	758	161,558	Leon	Tallahassee	676	245,756
Bradford	Starke	293	28,118	Levy	Bronson	1,100	37,998
Brevard	Titusville	995	531,250	Liberty	Bristol	837	7,773
Broward	Ft. Lauderdale	1,211	1,777,638	Madison	Madison	710	19,092
Calhoun	Blountstown	568	13,290	Manatee	Bradenton	747	306,779
Charlotte	Punta Gorda	690	157,536	Marion	Ocala	1,610	303,442
Citrus	Inverness	629	134,370	Martin	Stuart	555	139,728
Clay	Green Cove Springs	592	171,095	Monroe	Key West	1,034	76,329
Collier	East Naples	1,994	307,242	Nassau	Fernandina Beach	649	64,746
Columbia	Lake City	796	64,040	Okaloosa	Crestview	936	182,172
Miami-Dade	Miami	1,955	2,376,014	Okeechobee	Okeechobee	770	39,836
DeSoto	Arcadia	636	35,406	Orange	Orlando	910	1,023,023
Dixie	Cross City	701	14,647	Osceola	Kissimmee	1,350	231,578
Duval	Jacksonville	776	826,436	Palm Beach	West Palm Beach	1,993	1,268,548
Escambia	Pensacola	660	296,772	Pasco	Dade City	738	429,065
Flagler	Bunnell	491	76,410	Pinellas	Clearwater	280	928,032
Franklin	Apalachicola	545	10,177	Polk	Bartow	1,823	542,912
Gadsden	Quincy	518	46,428	Putnam	Palatka	733	73,568
Gilchrist	Trenton	354	16,402	St. Johns	St. Augustine	617	161,525
Glades	Moore Haven	763	11,252	St. Lucie	Ft. Pierce	581	241,305
Gulf	Port St. Joe	559	13,975	Santa Rosa	Milton	1,024	143,105
Hamilton	Jasper	517	13,983	Sarasota	Sarasota	573	366,256
Hardee	Wauchula	637	28,286	Seminole	Sanford	298	401,619
Hendry	La Belle	1,163	39,561	Sumter	Bushnell	561	64,182
Hernando	Brooksville	478	158,409	Suwannee	Live Oak	690	38,624
Highlands	Sebring	1,029	95,496	Taylor	Perry	1,058	19,622
Hillsborough	Tampa	1,053	1,132,152	Union	Lake Butler	246	14,916
Holmes	Bonifay	488	19,264	Volusia	DeLand	1,113	490,055
Indian River	Vero Beach	497	128,594	Wakulla	Crawfordville	601	28,212
Jackson	Marianna	942	48,985	Walton	De Funiak Springs	1,066	50,324
Jefferson	Monticello	609	14,490	Washington	Chipley	590	22,299
Lafayette	Mayo	545	7,953	**TOTALS**		54,154	17,789,864

vide the basis of the present population. Florida has such Indian place-names as Okeechobee, Apalachicola, Kissimmee, Sarasota, Pensacola, and Hialeah.

The rapid population change that has occurred in Florida since World War II makes accurate statements about the language difficult. Massive migration from the North Central and North Atlantic areas, including a large number of speakers of Yiddish, has materially affected the previously rather uniform Southern speech of much of the state. Borrowing from the Spanish of the expanding number of Cubans and Puerto Ricans in the Miami area has had a further effect.

Representative words in the Southern speech of most native-born Floridians are *light bread* (white bread), *pallet* (temporary bed on the floor), *fairing off* (clearing up), *serenade* (shivaree), *tote* (carry), *snap beans* (green beans); *mosquito hawk* (dragonfly), *crocus sack* (burlap bag), *pullybone* (wishbone), and *comforter* (tied and filled bedcover), especially in south Florida. Largely limited to the northern half of the state are *pinder* (peanut), *croker sack* instead of crocus sack, *fire dogs* (andirons); also, in the Tampa Bay area, *comfort* (tied and filled bedcover), and, in the panhandle, *whirlygig* (merry-go-round). Some north-Florida terms are clearly imported from Georgia: *mutton corn* (green corn), *light-wood* (kindling), and *co-wench!* (a call to cows).

In 2000, 11,569,739 Floridians, representing 76.9% of the resident population five years old and older, spoke only English at home, down from 82.7% in 1990.

The following table gives selected statistics from the 2000 Census for language spoken at home by persons five years old and over. The category "Other Indo-European languages" includes Albanian, Gaelic, Lithuanian, and Rumanian.

LANGUAGE	NUMBER	PERCENT
Population 5 years and over	**15,043,603**	**100.0**
Speak only English	11,569,739	76.9
Speak a language other than English	3,473,864	23.1
Speak a language other than English	**3,473,864**	**23.1**
Spanish or Spanish Creole	2,476,528	16.5
French Creole	208,487	1.4
French (incl. Patois, Cajun)	129,118	0.9
German	89,656	0.6
Italian	67,257	0.4
Portuguese or Portuguese Creole	55,014	0.4
Tagalog	38,442	0.3
Chinese	35,071	0.2
Arabic	32,418	0.2
Vietnamese	30,962	0.2
Polish	24,850	0.2
Greek	23,041	0.2
Russian	19,729	0.1
Other Indo-European languages	18,473	0.1
Yiddish	18,225	0.1
Korean	16,702	0.1
Hebrew	15,360	0.1

[9] RELIGIONS

Dominican and Franciscan friars, intent on converting the Indians, arrived with the Spanish conquistadors and settlers in the

1500s, and for some 200 years Florida's white population was overwhelmingly Catholic. Protestant colonists from Britain arrived in the late 1700s, and significant influx of Protestant settlers from the southern United States followed in the early 1800s. Sephardic Jews from the Carolinas also moved into Florida around this time, although the largest influx of Jews has occurred during the 20th century.

The Roman Catholic Church is the largest religious organization, with 2,316,652 adherents in about 460 parishes in 2004. The next largest group is the Southern Baptist Convention with 1,292,097 adherents in 2,054 congregations in 2000; in 2002 there were 37,234 newly baptized members. Judaism claimed 628,485 adherents in 2000. In 2003, the United Methodist Church reported 477,758 adherents from all of the state's conferences (which include some congregations from Alabama). In 2000, the Assemblies of God had 189,387 members; Presbyterian Church USA, 157,751; and Episcopalians, 152,526. The same year, about 58.9% of the population did not specify affiliation with any religious organization.

Orlando is home to the world headquarters for Campus Crusade For Christ International, an interdenominational Christian evangelical ministry.

10 TRANSPORTATION

Railroad building in the 19th century opened southern Florida to tourism and commerce. During the 20th century, long-distance passenger trains and, more recently, planes and automobiles have brought millions of visitors to the state each year.

The first operating railway in Florida was the St. Joseph Railroad, which inaugurated service on an 8-mi (13-km) track between St. Joseph Bay and Lake Wimico on 14 April 1836, using mules to pull the train. The railroad soon put into operation the state's first steam locomotive on 5 September 1836. By the time the Civil War broke out, railroads connected most of northern Florida's major towns, but the rapid expansion of the state's railroad system, and with it the development of southern Florida, awaited two late-19th-century entrepreneurs: Henry B. Plant; and Henry M. Flagler. Plant's South Florida Railroad extended service to Tampa in 1884. Flagler consolidated a number of small lines in the 1880s into the Florida East Coast Railway with service as far south as Daytona. He then extended service down the Atlantic coast, reaching Palm Beach in 1894, Miami in 1896, and, after construction of an extensive series of bridges, Key West in 1912. The "overseas" railway down the Keys was abandoned in 1935 after a hurricane severely damaged the line.

In 2003, there was a total of 2,956 rail mi (4,759 km) of track in Florida, operated by 14 railroads. In the same year, nonmetallic minerals were the top commodities (by weight) shipped by rail from and to the state. CSX Transportation and Norfolk Southern were the state's operating Class I railroads in 2003, with about 1,896 route mi (3,052 km) of Class I track between them. As of 2006, Amtrak provided passenger rail service to 24 Florida stations.

On 7 June 1979, construction began on a surface rail system for Miami and surrounding areas of Dade County. The first stage of this $1.1 billion mass transit system (known as Metrorail), a 20.5-mi (33-km) line serving Hialeah, Miami International Airport, downtown Miami, and areas to the south, was opened on 20 May 1984.

In 2004, Florida had 119,525 mi (192,435 km) of public roads. The Florida Turnpike's 265-mi (426-km) main section extends from Wildwood in north-central Florida to Ft. Pierce on the Atlantic coast and then south to Miami. A 50-mi (80-km) extension runs between Miramar and Homestead. The Overseas Highway down the Keys, including the famous Seven Mile Bridge (which is actually 35,716 feet, or 10,886 meters—6.8 mi—in length), is part of the state highway system. In 1983, 37 of the 44 bridges connecting the Florida Keys were replaced at a cost of $189 million.

Florida in 2004 had some 15.205 million registered motor vehicles. As of that same year, 13,146,357 people held active Florida drivers' licenses.

Inland waterways in Florida include the southernmost section of the Atlantic Intracoastal Waterway and the easternmost section of the Gulf Intracoastal Waterway, encompassing approximately 1,200 navigable mi (1,931 km) of federally maintained coastal channels for commercial vessels and pleasure craft. Construction began on 27 February 1964 on a barge canal across northern Florida to connect the two intracoastal systems. However, work was ordered stopped by President Richard Nixon on 19 January 1971 because of the threat the canal posed to flora and fauna in the surrounding area.

Florida has several commercially important ports. By far the largest in terms of gross tonnage is Tampa, which handled over 48.289 million tons of cargo in 2004, ranking it the 16th-busiest port in the United States. Other major ports and their 2004 tonnage handled include: Port Everglades in Ft. Lauderdale, 24.899 million tons; Jacksonville, 21.451 million tons; Port Manatee, 4.428 million tons; Miami, 9.754 million tons; Panama City, 2.751 million tons; Port Canaveral, 4.629 million tons; and Palm Beach, 4.146 million tons. In 2004, Florida had 1,540 mi (2,479 km) of navigable waterways. In 2003, waterborne shipments totaled 131.570 million tons.

In 2005, Florida had a total of 832 public and private-use aviation-related facilities. This included 491 airports, 286 heliports, 14 STOLports (Short Take-Off and Landing), and 41 seaplane bases. In addition to civil aviation activity, Florida had more than 20 military airfields. Florida's busiest airport is Orlando International with a total of 15,270,347 enplanements in 2004, making it the 14th-busiest airport in the United States. Other major airports in the state include Miami International with 14,515,591 enplanements in 2004 (15th-busiest in the United States); Tampa International with 8,436,025 enplanements in 2004 (28th-busiest in the United States); Ft. Lauderdale-Hollywood International with 10,040,598 enplanements in 2004 (24th-busiest in the United States); and Fort Myers-Southwest Florida International with 3,320,019 enplanements in 2004 (50th-busiest in the United States).

11 HISTORY

American Indians entered Florida from the north 10,000 to 12,000 years ago, and had reached the end of the peninsula by 1400 BC. As they grew in number, they developed more complex economic and social organization. In northeastern Florida and nearby Georgia, they apparently invented pottery independently about 2000

BC, some 800 years earlier than any other Indian group in North America.

In north Florida, an agricultural and hunting economy organized around village life was typical by this time. South of Tampa Bay and Cape Canaveral, Indians lived mostly along the coast and relied heavily on wild plants and on a large variety of aquatic and land animals for meat. The southern groups did not practice agriculture until about 450 BC, when they began to plant corn in villages around Lake Okeechobee.

As they spread over Florida and adjusted to widely different local conditions, the Indians fell into six main divisions, with numerous subgroups and distinctive cultural traits. When Europeans arrived in the early 16th century, they found nearly 100,000 Indians: 25,000 Apalachee around Tallahassee; 40,000 Timucua in the northeast; on Tampa Bay, 7,000 Tocobaga; on the southwest coast and around Lake Okeechobee, 20,000 Calusa; on the lower southeast coast, 5,000 Tequesta; and in the Jupiter area, 2,000 Ais and Jeaga.

The Spanish who began arriving in the 16th century found the Indians in upper Florida to be relatively tractable, but those in the lower peninsula remained uniformly hostile and resisted to the last. The Spaniards sought to convert the Indians to Christianity and settle them around missions to grow food, to supply labor, and to help defend the province. By 1674, 70 Franciscan friars were working in dozens of missions and stations in a line running west from St. Augustine and north along the sea island coast to Carolina.

The impact of the Europeans on the Indian population was, on the whole, disastrous. Indians died of European-introduced diseases, were killed in wars with whites or with other Indians, or moved away. Raids from South Carolina by the Creeks, abetted by the British, between 1702 and 1708 completely destroyed the missions. When the Spanish departed Florida in 1763, the remaining 300 of the original 100,000 Indians left with them.

As early as 1750, however, small groups of Creek tribes from Georgia and Alabama had begun to move into the north Florida area vacated by the first Indian groups. Called Seminole, the Creek word for runaway or refugee, these Indians did not then constitute a tribe and had no common government or leadership until resistance to white plans to resettle them brought them together. They numbered only 5,000 when Florida became part of the United States.

Pressures on the US president and Congress to remove the Seminole intensified after runaway black slaves began seeking refuge with the Indians. In 1823, the Seminole accepted a reservation north of Lake Okeechobee. Nine years later, an Indian delegation signed a document pledging the Seminole to move within three years to lands in present-day Oklahoma. The Indians' subsequent resistance to removal resulted in the longest and most costly of Indian wars, the Seminole War of 1835–42. The warfare and the Indians' subsequent forced migration left fewer than 300 Seminole in Florida.

The history of the twice-repeated annihilation of Florida Indians is, at the same time, the history of white settlers' rise to power. After Christopher Columbus reached the New World at Hispaniola in 1492, the Caribbean islands became the base for wider searches, one of which brought Juan Ponce de León to Florida. Sailing from Puerto Rico in search of the fabled island of Bimini,

he sighted Florida on 27 March 1513 and reached the coast a week later. Ponce de León claimed the land for Spain and named it La Florida, for Pascua Florida, the Easter festival of flowers; sailing southward around Florida, he may have traveled as far as Apalachicola, on the shore of the panhandle. In 1521, he returned to found a colony at Charlotte Harbor, on the lower Gulf coast, but the Indians fought the settlers. After Ponce de León was seriously wounded, the expedition sailed for Cuba, where he died the same year.

Other Spaniards seeking treasure and lands to govern, followed. Pánfilo de Narváez arrived in 1528, landing near Tampa Bay and marching inland and northward to Tallahassee. Hernando de Soto, a rich and famous associate of Francisco Pizarro in the conquest of Peru, found many men eager to try the same with him in Florida. Appointed governor of Cuba and *adelantado* (loosely, conqueror) of Florida, he followed the route of Narváez to Tallahassee in 1539, finding some food but no promise of wealth. In 1559, Spain sought to establish a settlement on Pensacola Bay, but it was abandoned at the end of two years.

In 1562, Jean Ribault, with a small expedition of French Huguenots, arrived at the St. Johns River, east of present-day Jacksonville, and claimed Florida for France. Another group of French Huguenot settlers built Ft. Caroline, 5 mi (8 km) upriver, two years later. In the summer of 1565, Ribault brought in naval reinforcements, prepared to defend the French claim against the Spaniards, who had sent Pedro Menéndez de Avilés to find and oust the intruders. Menéndez selected St. Augustine as a base, landing on 28 August, and with the aid of a storm withstood the French effort to destroy him. He then marched overland to take Ft. Caroline by surprise, killing most of the occupants and later captured Ribault and his shipwrecked men, most of whom he slaughtered. St. Augustine, the first permanent European settlement in the United States, served primarily, under Spanish rule, as a military outpost, maintained to protect the wealth of New Spain. The Spanish established a settlement at Pensacola in 1698, but it too remained only a small frontier garrison town. In 1763, when Spain ceded Florida to England in exchange for Cuba, about 3,000 Spaniards departed from St. Augusta and 800 from Pensacola, leaving Florida to the Seminole.

British Florida reached from the Atlantic to the Mississippi River and became two colonies, East and West Florida. Settlers established farms and plantations, traded with the Indians, and moved steadily toward economic and political self-sufficiency. These settlers did not join the American Revolution, but Florida was affected by the war nonetheless, as thousands of Loyalists poured into East Florida. In 1781, Spain attacked and captured Pensacola. Two years later, Britain ceded both Floridas back to Spain, whereupon most of the Loyalists left for the West Indies.

The second Spanish era was only nominally Spanish. English influence remained strong, and US penetration increased. Florida west of the Perdido River was taken over by the United States in 1810, as part of the Louisiana Purchase (1803). Meanwhile, renegade whites, runaway slaves, pirates, and political adventures operated almost at will.

Present-day Florida was ceded to the United States in 1821, in settlement of $5 million in claims by US citizens against the Spanish government. At this time, General Andrew Jackson, who three years earlier had led a punitive expedition against the Seminole and their British allies, came back to Florida as military governor. His main tasks were to receive the territory for the United States and to set up a civilian administration, which took office in 1822. William P. DuVal of Kentucky was named territorial governor, and a legislative council was subsequently elected. The new council met first in Pensacola and in St. Augustine, and then, in 1824, in the newly selected capital of Tallahassee, located in the wilderness of north-central Florida, from which the Indians had just been removed. Middle Florida, as it was called, rapidly became an area of slave-owning cotton plantations and was for several decades the fastest-growing part of the territory. The war to remove the Seminole halted the advance of frontier settlement, however, and the Panic of 1837 bankrupted the territorial government and the three banks whose notes it had guaranteed. Floridians drew up a state constitution at St. Joseph in 1838–39 but, being proslavery, had to wait until 1845 to enter the Union paired with the free state of Iowa.

In 1861, Florida, with only 140,000 people, about 40% of them blacks (mostly slaves), only 400 mi (644 km) of railroad, and no manufacturing, seceded from the Union and joined the Confederacy. Some 15,000 whites (one-third of whom died) served in the Confederate army, and 1,200 whites and almost as many blacks joined the Union army. Bitterness and some violence accompanied the Republican Reconstruction government in 1868–76. The conservative Bourbon Democrats then governed for the rest of the century. They encouraged railroad building and other forms of business, and they kept taxes low by limiting government services. Cotton production never recovered to prewar levels, but cattle raising, citrus and vegetable cultivation, forestry, phosphate mining, and, by late in the century, a growing tourist industry took up the slack.

The Spanish-American War in 1898, during which Tampa became the port of embarkation for an expedition to Cuba, stimulated the economy and advertised the state nationwide, not always favorably. Naval activity at Key West and Pensacola became feverish. Lakeland, Miami, Jacksonville, and Fernandina were briefly the sites of training camps.

In 1904, Napoleon Bonaparte Broward was elected governor on a moderately populist platform, which included a program to drain the Everglades lands which the state had received under the Swamp and Overflowed Lands Act of 1850. Drainage did lower water levels, and settlements grew around Lake Okeechobee, developments whose full environmental impact was recognized only much later. By the time Broward took office, Jacksonville had become the state's largest city, with Pensacola and Tampa not far behind, and Key West had dropped from first to fourth. During World War I, more than 42,030 Floridians were in uniform.

Boom, bust, and depression characterized the 1920s. Feverish land speculation brought hundreds of thousands of people to Florida in the first half of the decade. Cresting in 1925, the boom was already over in 1926, when a devastating hurricane struck Miami, burying all hope of recovery. Yet population jumped by more than 50% during the decade, and Miami rose from fourth to second place among Florida cities. Florida's choice of Republican Herbert Hoover over Al Smith in the 1928 presidential election reflected the Protestant and prohibitionist attitudes of most of the state voters at that time.

The 1930s were marked first by economic depression, then by recovery, new enterprise, and rapidly growing government activity. Bank and business failures, as well as defaults on city and county bond issues and on mortgage payments, produced growing economic distress. The state joined the federal government in assuming responsibility for relief and recovery. The legalization of pari-mutuel betting in 1931 created a new industry and a new tax source. The state's first paper mill opened in the same year, revolutionizing the forest industry. Private universities in Miami, Tampa, and Jacksonville were started during the Depression years.

The 1940s opened with recovery and optimism, arising from the stimulus of production for World War II, production that began well before the actual entry of the United States into the war. New army and navy installations and training programs brought business growth. After 1941, Florida seemed to become a vast military training school. The number of army and navy airfield flying schools increased from 5 to 45. Tourist facilities in all major cities became barracks, mess halls, and classrooms, with 70,000 rooms in Miami Beach alone being used to house troops in 1942. Families of thousands of trainees visited the state. Florida was on the eve of another boom.

First discovered but nearly last to be developed, Florida reached a rank of 27th in population only in 1940. Migration brought Florida's ranking to fourth in 1990, increasing its population to more than 12.8 million people. In 1986, Florida absorbed 1,000 arrivals a day. Until the early 1980s, many of those migrants were 65 years of age or over, swelling the proportion of senior citizens in Florida to 50% above the national average. In the mid-1980s, however, the preponderance of newcomers was somewhat younger, 25–44 years old. With an influx of younger residents, of family-rearing age, schools became overcrowded by the 1990s. Nevertheless, Florida is expected to double its 65 and older population between 2000 and 2030, meaning that one in every four residents will be age 65 and older in 2030 in Florida. Approximately 8% of the total US population will live in Florida by that date, which does not include all those holding second homes in Florida.

Newcomers have come in search of opportunities provided by Florida's growing and diversifying economy. Whereas the state once depended on the three industries (tourism, citrus, and construction) for its survival, military spending increased the presence of high-tech, banking, and service industries.

The management of growth in Florida dominated state politics through the second half of the century and promised to remain at the fore at least through the early 2000s. The state's low taxes combined with its rapid population growth to overburden the infrastructure. Roads, water supply, and sewer systems were pushed beyond capacity, posing real environmental threats. Development, both residential and commercial, eroded the state's natural beauty.

Efforts to reapportion Florida's 23 congressional districts and the state legislature's 40 Senate and 120 house seats were complicated by battles between blacks (holding steady at 14% of the population in 1999) and Hispanics over the number and character of minority districts. The absence of black state congressmen or senators, and the paucity of black officials at the state and local levels provoked demands for the creation of "safe districts" for blacks that thereby ensure their representation. Likewise Hispanics, whose numbers grew from 8.8% of the state population in 1980 to 14% by 1999, called for Hispanic districts. However, in the 1990s, Florida's third congressional district, which had a majority of black voters, was declared unconstitutional and ordered redrawn by the US Supreme Court.

Racial and ethnic relations have been another central issue. Tensions between blacks and Hispanics led to violence in 1989 when a Hispanic police officer shot and killed a black motorcyclist who was speeding and driving erratically. Riots broke out in the predominantly black Overton section of Miami and continued for three days.

Miami was again the site of rioting in late April 2000, as some Cuban Americans took to the streets to protest the federal government's handling of the custody case of six-year-old Cuban refugee Elian Gonzalez. The child was the center of an international debacle after he was rescued offshore in November 1999; a fisherman found the boy clinging to a raft after the boat in which he and his mother escaped Cuba had capsized. His mother having died, Miami relatives claimed and cared for the boy while federal officials, including the US attorney general, the Immigration and Naturalization Service, and several courts, grappled with the problem of returning him to his Cuban father. The incident, which ended when the boy arrived back in Havana, remained a point of protest for Miami's Cuban American community, among whom the prevailing sentiment was that, for political reasons, the child should have remained in the states.

The state's crime level received nationwide attention in the early 1990s when a series of incidents claimed the lives of several foreign tourists. For most of the decade Florida held the unwelcome distinction of leading the nation in violent crime. Numbers began to decline, and in 1998, the rate of violent crime per 100,000 residents dropped below 1,000 (to 939), according to the Federal Bureau of Investigation. (That year New Mexico recorded 955 violent crimes per 100,000 residents, making it the most violent state in the nation.)

Tropical storms and hurricanes periodically strike Florida. In August 1992, Hurricane Andrew caused $26.5 billion in damages in south Florida, primarily in and around Homestead. In October 1995, Hurricane Opal wrought an estimated $3 billion in damage in the Panhandle, destroying marinas and shipyards. The 2004 hurricane season devastated Florida: four hurricanes—Charley, Frances, Ivan, and Jeanne—damaged 20% of Florida's homes, and 124 people died. In October 2005, Hurricane Wilma hit southern Florida, and millions of people were left without power.

In December 1998, Floridians mourned the death of Governor Lawton Chiles; the Democrat first rose to prominence in 1970 when he made a 1,000-mi (1,600-km) trek through the state as he successfully campaigned for the US Senate, earning him the nickname "Walkin' Lawton."

Florida became the center of national and international attention in the 7 November 2000 US presidential election. The race between Democratic vice president Al Gore and Republican challenger George W. Bush was extremely close, and on election night, Florida's 25 electoral college votes became the ones that would decide the election. In the early morning hours of 8 November, Gore called Bush to concede the election, but he subsequently retracted his concession when it became apparent that the vote was in question. Because the vote was so close, Florida's election officials began a mandatory recount. In addition to the automatic recount, an investigation was launched into voting irregularities denying rights to minority voters.

Democrats requested hand recounts in four counties, but Bush called for an order banning them. The Florida Supreme Court intervened in the certification process run by the Florida Secretary of State, permitting hand recounts in Broward and Palm Beach counties and blocking certification until an appeal by Gore was heard. The United States 11th Circuit Court of Appeals refused Bush's request that it stop the hand recounts, and Miami-Dade county officials began a manual recount. Bush's lead was gradually reduced from the 537 votes certified on 26 November to 154 by adding votes from partial recounts in Miami-Dade and Palm Beach counties. When the Florida Supreme Court ordered a manual recount of 43,432 "under votes" from as many as 62 counties, the Bush campaign appealed to the United States Supreme Court to stop any vote recounts in Florida. On 9 December 2000, the US Supreme Court, divided 5–4, stepped in to order a stay of the Florida Supreme Court-ordered manual recounts, and on 12 December, it decided, in *Bush v. Gore*, that the Florida Supreme Court had erred in its decision to order manual vote recounts. On 13 December, Gore conceded the election to Bush, who became the nation's 43rd president after the electoral college votes cast on 18 December 2000 were tallied, including Florida's 25 votes.

12 STATE GOVERNMENT

Florida's first constitutional convention, which met from December 1838 to January 1839, drew up the document under which the state entered the Union in 1845. A second constitutional convention, meeting in 1861, adopted the ordinance of secession that joined Florida to the Confederacy. After the war, a new constitution was promulgated in 1865, but not until still another document was drawn up and ratified by the state—the Fourteenth Amendment to the US Constitution—was Florida readmitted to statehood in 1868. A fifth constitution was framed in 1885 and adopted the following year; extensively revised in 1968, this is the document under which the state is now governed. In 1998, Florida voters approved extensive revisions to the constitution; in 2002, voters approved a death penalty amendment, adding the death penalty to the constitution. In addition, in 2002, Florida voters approved several amendments: one requires the state to offer prekindergarten for four-year-olds by 2005; another, to reduce class size in schools by 2010; another animal rights measure protects pregnant pigs from unnecessary confinement; and another prohibits smoking in certain work environments. Overall, the constitution had been amended 104 times by January 2005.

The 1968 constitutional revision instituted annual (rather than biennial) regular sessions of the legislature, which consists of a 40-member Senate and a 120-member House of Representatives. Sessions begin the Tuesday after the first Monday of March and are limited to 60 calendar days. Senators serve four-year terms, with half the Senate being elected every two years; representatives serve two-year terms. All legislators must be at least 21 years old, and must have been residents of Florida the district for two years. The maximum length of a regular legislative session is 60 calendar days, unless it is extended by a three-fifths vote of each house. Special sessions may be called by the governor or by joint action of the presiding officers of the two houses (the president of the Senate and speaker of the House of Representatives). The legislative salary in 2004 was $29,916.

The governor is elected for a four-year term; a two-term limit is in effect. The lieutenant governor is elected on the same ticket as the governor. An amendment adopted by voters in 1998, which took effect in 2002, merged the cabinet offices of treasurer and comptroller into one chief financial office. The other elected cabinet members include the attorney general and agriculture commissioner; the amendment eliminated the offices of secretary of state and education commissioner from the cabinet. State officials must be at least 30 years old, US citizens, and registered voters, and must have been residents of Florida for at least seven years. As of December 2004, the governor's salary was $120,171.

Passage of legislation requires a majority vote of those present and voting in both houses. A bill passed by the legislature becomes law if it is signed by the governor; should the governor take no action on it, it becomes law seven days after receipt if the legislature is still in session, or 15 days after presentation to the governor if the legislature has adjourned. The governor may veto legislation and, in general appropriations bills, may veto individual items. Gubernatorial vetoes may be overridden by a two-thirds vote of the elected legislators in each house.

Amendments to the constitution may originate in three ways: by a joint resolution of the legislature passed by a three-fifths majority of the membership of each house; by action of a constitutional revision commission which, under the constitution, must be periodically convened; or by initiative petition (signed by 8% of the total votes cast in the state in the last election for presidential electors), which may call for a constitutional convention. A proposed amendment becomes part of the constitution if it receives a majority vote in a statewide election. One exception is that under the initiative procedure, an amendment for a new state tax or fee

not in effect as of 7 November 1994 requires a two-thirds majority of voters to become part of the constitution.

To vote in state elections, a person must be at least 18 years old, a US citizen, and a resident in the county of registration. Restrictions apply to convicted felons and those judged by the court as mentally incapacitated.

13 POLITICAL PARTIES

The Democratic and Republican parties are Florida's two principal political organizations. The former is the descendant of one of the state's first two political parties, the Jeffersonian Republican Democrats; this party, along with the Florida Whig Party, was organized shortly before statehood.

Florida's Republican Party was organized after the Civil War and dominated state politics until 1876, when the Democrats won control of the statehouse. Aided from 1889 to 1937 by a poll tax, which effectively disfranchised most of the state's then predominantly Republican black voters, the Democrats won every gubernatorial election but one from 1876 through 1962; the Prohibition Party candidate was victorious in 1916.

By the time Republican Claude R. Kirk Jr. won the governorship in 1966, Florida had already become, for national elections, a two-party state, although Democrats retained a sizable advantage in party registration. Beginning in the 1950s, many registered Democrats became "presidential Republicans," crossing party lines to give the state's electoral votes to Dwight D. Eisenhower in 1952 and 1956 and to Richard M. Nixon in 1960.

A presidential preference primary, in which crossover voting is not permitted, is held on the second Tuesday in March of presidential election years. Because it occurs so early in the campaign season, this primary is closely watched as an indicator of candidates' strength. Primaries to select state and local candidates are held in early September, with crossover voting again prohibited;

Florida Presidential Vote by Political Parties, 1948–2004

YEAR	ELECTORAL VOTE	FLORIDA WINNER	DEMOCRAT	REPUBLICAN	STATES' RIGHTS DEMOCRAT	PROGRESSIVE
1948	8	*Truman (D)	281,988	194,280	89,755	11,620
1952	10	*Eisenhower (R)	444,950	544,036	—	—
1956	10	*Eisenhower (R)	480,371	643,849	—	—
1960	10	Nixon (R)	748,700	795,476	—	—
1964	14	*Johnson (D)	948,540	905,941	—	—
					AMERICAN IND.	
1968	14	*Nixon (R)	676,794	886,804	624,207	—
1972	17	*Nixon (R)	718,117	1,857,759		
					AMERICAN	
1976	17	*Carter (D)	1,636,000	1,469,531	21,325	—
						LIBERTARIAN
1980	17	*Reagan (R)	1,417,637	2,043,006	—	30,457
1984	21	*Reagan (R)	1,448,816	2,730,350	—	744
					NEW ALLIANCE	
1988	21	*Bush (R)	1,656,701	2,618,885	6,665	19,796
					IND. (Perot)	
1992	25	Bush (R)	2,072,798	2,173,310	1,053,067	15,079
1996	25	*Clinton (D)	2,546,870	2,244,536	483,870	23,965
					GREEN	
2000**	25	*Bush, G. W. (R)	2,912,253	2,912,790	97,488	16,415
					REFORM (Nader)	
2004	27	*Bush, G. W. (R)	3,583,544	3,964,522	32,971	11,996

*Won US presidential election.
**REFORM candidate Pat Buchanan received 17,484 votes.

runoff elections are held on the Tuesday five weeks before the general election.

In 2004, there were 10,301,000 registered voters; an estimated 41% were Democratic, 38% Republican, and 21% unaffiliated or members of other parties. In addition to the Democratic and Republican parties, organized groups include the Green, Reform, and Libertarian parties. Minor parties running candidates for statewide office can qualify by obtaining petition signatures from 3% of the state's voters.

In the 1996 presidential election, Florida backed a Democrat for the first time in 20 years, giving 48% of the vote to Bill Clinton; 42% to Republican Bob Dole; and 9% to Independent Ross Perot. In the 2000 presidential election, a mere 275 votes separated Republican candidate George W. Bush from Democrat Al Gore as of 13 December 2000, when the US Supreme Court ruled a controversial hand recount of the Florida vote be stopped. George W. Bush won Florida's 25 electoral votes and became president; in 2004, Bush won 52% of the vote to Democrat John Kerry's 47%.

Former US Senator Lawton Chiles (Democrat) was elected governor in 1990 and reelected in 1994. In 1998, Florida voters elected Republican Jeb Bush to the gubernatorial spot; he was reelected in 2002. Connie Mack, a Republican, was reelected to a second US Senate term in 1994 but decided not to seek a third term in 2000. Democrat Bill Nelson was elected to the Senate in 2000. Democratic Senator Robert Graham was reelected in 1998. Graham mounted a bid for the presidential nomination in 2003, giving up his bid for reelection to the Senate in 2004. Republican Mel Martinez narrowly won the seat formerly held by Graham, with 49.3% of the vote to Democrat Betty Castor's 48.3%.

Florida's US House delegation following the 2004 elections had 18 Republicans and 7 Democrats. The state Senate in 2005 was comprised of 14 Democrats and 26 Republicans, and the state House had 84 Republicans and 36 Democrats.

14 LOCAL GOVERNMENT

In 2005, Florida had 67 counties, 404 municipalities, and 626 special districts. There were 67 school districts.

Generally, legislative authority within each county is vested in a five-member elected board of county commissioners, which also has administrative authority over county departments, except those headed by independently elected officials. In counties without charters, these elected officials usually include a sheriff, tax collector, property appraiser, supervisor of elections, and clerk of the circuit court. County charters may provide for a greater or lesser number of elected officials, and for a professional county administrator (city manager). Before 1968 there was state legislation that restricted county government operations; most of these laws have now been repealed. Counties may generally enact any law not inconsistent with state law. However, the taxing power of county and other local governments is severely limited.

Municipalities are normally incorporated and chartered by an act of the state legislature. Except where a county charter specifies otherwise, municipal ordinances override county laws. Municipal governments may provide a full range of local services. But as populations rapidly expand beyond municipal boundaries, many of these governments have found they lack the jurisdiction to deal adequately with area problems. Annexations of surrounding territory are permissible but difficult under state law. Some municipal governments have reached agreements with county or other local governments for consolidation of overlapping or redundant services or for provision of service by one local government to another on a contract basis. Complete consolidation of a municipal and a county government is authorized by the state constitution, requiring state legislation and voter approval in the area affected. Jacksonville and Duval County succeeded in consolidating by 1985.

The problem of overlapping and uncoordinated service is most serious in the case of the state's 626 special districts. These districts, established by state law and approval of the affected voters, provide a specified service in a defined geographic area. An urban area may have dozens of special districts. State legislation in the 1970s attempted to deal with this problem by permitting counties to set up their own special-purpose districts, whose operations could be coordinated by the county government.

Regional planning councils resulted from the need to cope with problems of greater than local concern. These councils deal with such issues as land management, resource management, and economic development.

In 2005, local government accounted for about 657,329 full-time (or equivalent) employment positions.

15 STATE SERVICES

To address the continuing threat of terrorism and to work with the federal Department of Homeland Security, homeland security in Florida operates under state statute; the public safety commissioner, designated as the state homeland security adviser, oversees programs in training and law enforcement.

A "Sunshine" amendment to the constitution and a statutory code of ethics require financial disclosure by elected officials and top-level public employees; the code prohibits actions by officials and employees that would constitute a conflict of interest. An auditor general appointed by the legislature conducts financial and performance audits of state agencies.

Educational services are provided by the State Department of Education, which sets overall policy and adopts comprehensive objectives for public education, operates the state university and community college systems, and issues bonds (as authorized by the state constitution) to finance capital projects. The Department of Transportation is responsible for developing long-range transportation plans and for construction and maintenance of the state highway system. The Department of Highway Safety and Motor Vehicles licenses drivers, regulates the registration and sale of motor vehicles, and administers the Florida Highway Patrol.

Health services are the responsibility primarily of the Agency for HealthCare Administration. It is also responsible for disease prevention and for assisting localities in performing health services. The Department of Children and Families administers such social welfare programs as Medicaid, food stamps, and foster care and adoption.

The Department of Corrections maintains approximately 60 major correctional institutions. The Corrections Commission reviews the state's correctional efforts, recommends policies, and evaluates the implementation of approved policies. The Department of Law Enforcement is responsible for maintaining public order and enforcing the state criminal code; enforcement activities emphasize combating organized crime, vice, and racketeering.

The state's Army and Air National Guard are under the jurisdiction of the Department of Military Affairs. The Florida Highway Patrol, within the Department of Highway Safety and Motor Vehicles, is the only statewide uniformed police force.

The Florida Division of Housing and Community Development assists the Department of Community Affairs in carrying out its duties related to housing. The Department's Division of Emergency Management is responsible for Florida hazards and disaster prevention.

The Agency for Workforce Innovation is responsible for implementing policy in the areas of workforce development, welfare transition, unemployment compensation, labor market information, early learning and school readiness. The Florida Department of Veterans Affairs is responsible for serving the needs of veterans.

The Department of State manages state historic sites, archives, museums, libraries, and fine arts centers. Enterprise Florida supports new business starts in the state. The Department of Management Services provides administrative support for state agencies and state employees including human resource, insurance, retirement, office facility, purchasing, vehicles/aircraft, property surplus, and information technology services.

16 JUDICIAL SYSTEM

The state's highest court is the Supreme Court, a panel of seven justices that sits in Tallahassee. Every two years, the presiding justices elect one of their number as chief justice. All justices are appointed to six-year terms by the governor upon the recommendation of a judicial nominating commission. They may seek further six-year terms in a yes-no vote in a general election. If the incumbent justice does not receive a majority of "yes" votes, the governor appoints another person to fill the vacancy from the recommended list of qualified candidates.

The Supreme Court has appellate jurisdiction only. The state constitution, as amended, prescribes certain types of cases in which an appeal must be heard, including those in which the death penalty has been ordered and those in which a lower appellate court has invalidated a state law or a provision of the state constitution. The court also hears appeals of state agency decisions on utility rates and may, at its discretion, hear appeals in many other types of cases.

Below the Supreme Court are five district courts of appeal, which sit in Tallahassee, Lakeland, Miami, West Palm Beach, and Daytona Beach. There are 61 district court judges. The method of their selection and retention in office is the same as for supreme court justices. District courts hear appeals of lower court decisions and may review the actions of executive agencies. District court decisions are usually final, since most requests for Supreme Court review are denied.

The state's principal trial courts are its 20 circuit courts, which have original jurisdiction in many types of cases, including civil suits involving more than $5,000, felony cases, and all cases involving juveniles. Circuit courts may also hear appeals from county courts if no constitutional question is involved. Circuit court judges are elected for six-year terms and must have been members of the Florida bar for at least five years before election. There were 468 circuit court judges in 1999.

Each of Florida's 67 counties has a county court with original jurisdiction in misdemeanor cases, civil disputes involving $5,000 or less, and traffic-violation cases. County court judges are elected for four-year terms and must be members of the bar only in counties with populations of 40,000 or more.

As of 31 December 2004, a total of 85,533 prisoners were held in Florida's state and federal prisons, an increase from 82,012, or 4.3% from the previous year. As of year-end 2004, a total of 5,660 inmates were female, up from 5,165, or 9.6%, from the year before. Among sentenced prisoners (one year or more), Florida had an incarceration rate of 486 per 100,000 population in 2004.

According to the Federal Bureau of Investigation, Florida in 2004 had a violent crime rate (murder/nonnegligent manslaughter; forcible rape; robbery; aggravated assault) of 711.3 reported incidents per 100,000 population (the second highest among states, exceeded only by South Carolina), or a total of 123,754 reported incidents. Crimes against property (burglary; larceny/theft; and motor vehicle theft) in that same year totaled 727,141 reported incidents, or 4,179.7 reported incidents per 100,000 people. Florida has a death penalty, which can be carried out by lethal injection or electrocution, depending upon the prisoner's request. From 1976 through 5 May 2006 the state executed 60 persons, of which the most recent execution was in 2005. As of 1 January 2006, there were 388 inmates on death row, the third-highest number in the nation after California and Texas.

In 2003, Florida spent $777,539,269 on homeland security, an average of $48 per state resident.

17 ARMED FORCES

In 2004, there were 71,241 active-duty military personnel in Florida, 20,107 civilian personnel, and 3,068 Reserve and National Guard. Military and civilian personnel were stationed at facilities in Pensacola, Orlando, Jacksonville, and at Eglin AFB. In October 1979, the Key West Naval Air Station was made the headquarters of a new Caribbean Joint Task Force, established to coordinate US military activities in the Caribbean. The state had 29,967 active-duty Air Force personnel in 2004 the largest Air Force bases were Eglin, in Valparaiso; MacDill, near Tampa; and Tyndall, west of Tallahassee. The US Air Force Missile Test Center at Cape Canaveral (called Cape Kennedy from 1963 to 1973) has been the launching site for most US space flights, including all manned flights. US Department of Defense procurement contracts in Florida in 2004 totaled $8.3 billion, seventh-highest in the United States for that year. Defense payroll, including retired military pay, amounted to $9.3 billion. Florida had the highest amount paid to retired military in the United States in 2004.

There were 1,788,496 veterans of US military service in Florida as of 2003, of whom 327,034 served in World War II; 223,057 in the Korean conflict; 457,695 during the Vietnam era; and 246,271 during 1990–2000 (in the Gulf War). US Veterans Administration spending in Florida in 2004 totaled $4.6 billion.

As of 31 October 2004, the Florida Highway Patrol employed 1,671 full-time sworn officers.

18 MIGRATION

Florida is populated mostly by migrants. In 1990, only 30.5% of all state residents were Florida born, compared with 61.8% for the United States as a whole. Only Nevada had a lower proportion of native residents. Migration from other states accounted for more than 85% of Florida's population increase in the 1970s. From 1985 to 1990, net migration gains added another 1,461,550 new residents. Between 1990 and 1998, net domestic migration added 1,035,000 while international migration added 553,000. Florida's overall population increased 15.3% during that same period.

The early European immigrants to Florida—first the Spanish, then the English—never populated the state in significant numbers. Immigration from southern states began even before the United States acquisition of Florida and accelerated thereafter. In the 20th century, US immigrants to Florida came, for the most part, from the Northeast and Midwest, their motivation to escape harsh northern winters. A large proportion of migrants have been retirees and other senior citizens. Between 1970 and 1980, the number of Floridians 65 or over increased by 70%, compared with a 44% increase for the US population as a whole. By 1998, 18.3% of the Florida populace was age 65 or older. In the period 2000–05, net international migration was 528,085 and net internal migration was 1,057,619, for a net gain of 1,585,704 people.

Since the 1960s, Florida has also experienced large-scale migration from the Caribbean and parts of Latin America. Although the state has had a significant Cuban population since the second half of the 19th century, the number of immigrants surged after the Cuban revolution of 1959. From December 1965 to April 1973, an airlift agreed to by the Cuban and US governments landed a quarter of a million Cubans in Miami. Another period of large-scale immigration from Cuba, beginning in April 1980, brought more than 100,000 Cubans into Florida harbors. At the same time, Haitian "boat people" were arriving in Florida in significant numbers, often reaching the southern peninsula packed in barely seaworthy small craft. The number of ethnic Haitians in Florida was reported at 105,495 in 1990. By 1990, a reported 541,011 ethnic Cubans were living in southern Florida, mostly in and around Miami, where the Cuban section had become known as "Little Havana." The US government classified some of them as illegal aliens, fleeing extreme poverty in their native country, but the immigrants claimed to be political refugees and sued to halt deportation proceedings against them. In 1996, a reported 2,186,000 Floridians (15%) were foreign-born. In 1998, 59,965 foreign immigrants were admitted into Florida, the third-highest total of any state, accounting for over 9% of all foreign immigration that year. Of that total, 14,265 were from Cuba; 6,613 from Haiti; and 4,795 from Jamaica. As of 1998, Florida's Hispanic population numbered 2,080,000; those of Hispanic origin numbered 2,243,000.

19 INTERGOVERNMENTAL COOPERATION

In 1953, Florida became a signatory to the Alabama-Florida Boundary Compact. Among the interstate regional compacts in which Florida participates are the Apalachicola–Chattahoochee–Flint River Basin Compact, Southern Regional Education Board, Southern States Energy Board, Southeastern Forest Fire Protection Compact, Atlantic States Marine Fisheries Commission, and Gulf States Marine Fisheries Commission. Federal grants to Florida in fiscal year 2005 totaled $16.266 billion; in fiscal year 2006

federal grants amounted to an estimated $16.176 billion, and were estimated at $17.041 billion for fiscal year 2007.

20 ECONOMY

Farming, lumbering and naval stores industries, all concentrated in northern Florida, were early mainstays of the economy. In the late 19th century, the extension of the railroads down the peninsula opened up an area previously populated only by Indians. Given the favorable climate, central and southern Florida soon became major agricultural areas. Tourism, aggressively promoted by the early railroad builders, became a major industry after World War I and remains so today.

Tourists and winter residents with second homes in Florida contribute billions of dollars annually to the state economy and make retailing and construction particularly important economic sectors. However, this dependence on discretionary spending by visitors and part-time dwellers also makes the economy, and especially the housing industry, highly vulnerable to recession.

The arms buildup during Ronald Reagan's administration helped to expand Florida's aerospace and electronics industries. Even in 1991, after the reduction of the national military budget, Florida ranked seventh nationally in the value of Department of Defense contracts awarded. Florida ranked fourth in the nation in defense electronics manufacturing employment in 1999.

The state's economy, particularly that of the Miami area, has also benefited from an influx of Latin American investment funds. Miami is said to have one of the largest underground economies in the United States, a reference both to the sizable inflow of cash from illicit drug trafficking and to the large numbers of Latin American immigrants working for low, unreported cash wages. Florida's population increased by 16% between 1990 and 1999, due primarily to migration. Strong annual economic growth rates in the late 1990s (averaging 6.6% in 1998–2000) were only moderated to 4.2% in the national recession of 2001. Growth continued damped in 2002, reflecting, particularly, a slowdown in Florida's tourist industry, but remained above the national average. By July 2002, the state was experiencing positive, if small (less than 1%), job growth. As was true in much of the country, the share of manufacturing in Florida's economy decreased in both absolute and relative terms coming into the 21st century. From a peak of $31 billion in 1999, output from the manufacturing sector declined 6.3% by 2001. As a share of the Florida economy, manufacturing declined from 7.7% in 1997 to 5.9% in 2001. By contrast, the financial services and trade sectors (wholesale and retail) each grew by more than 27% 1997 to 2001, and general services (including hotels and tourist services) grew 36.9% during this period.

Florida's gross state product (GSP) in 2004 totaled $599.068 billion, of which the real estate sector accounted for the largest portion at $93.036 billion or 15.5% of GSP, followed by healthcare and social assistance at $44.590 billion (7.4% of GSP) and wholesale trade at $39.285 billion (6.5% of GSP). In that same year, there were an estimated 1,633,574 small businesses in Florida. Of the 449,070 businesses having employees, a total of 444,066 or 98.9% were small companies. An estimated 77,754 new businesses were established in Florida in 2004, up 11.5% from the previous year. Business terminations that same year came to 54,498, down 3.8% from the previous year. Business bankruptcies totaled 1,183 in 2004, down 22.9% from 2003. In 2005, the personal bankruptcy

(Chapter 7 and Chapter 13) filing rate was 556 filings per 100,000 people, ranking Florida as the 25th highest in the nation.

²¹INCOME

In 2005 Florida had a gross state product (GSP) of $674 billion, which accounted for 5.4% of the nation's gross domestic product and placed the state at number four in highest GSP among the 50 states and the District of Columbia.

According to the Bureau of Economic Analysis, in 2004 Florida had a per capita personal income (PCPI) of $31,469. This ranked 25th in the United States and was 95% of the national average of $33,050. The 1994–2004 average annual growth rate of PCPI was 3.8%. Florida had a total personal income (TPI) of $547,107,143,000, which ranked fourth in the United States and reflected an increase of 6.9% from 2003. The 1994–2004 average annual growth rate of TPI was 5.9%. Earnings of persons employed in Florida increased from $346,386,466,000 in 2003 to $375,116,379,000 in 2004, an increase of 8.3%. The 2003–04 national change was 6.3%.

The US Census Bureau reports that the three-year average median household income for 2002–04 in 2004 dollars was $40,171, compared to a national average of $44,473. During the same period an estimated 12.3% of the population was below the poverty line, as compared to 12.4% nationwide.

²²LABOR

According to the Bureau of Labor Statistics (BLS), in April 2006 the seasonally adjusted civilian labor force in Florida numbered 8,903,500, with approximately 265,300 workers unemployed, yielding an unemployment rate of 3%, compared to the national average of 4.7% for the same period. Preliminary data for the same period placed nonfarm employment at 8,013,900. Since the beginning of the BLS data series in 1976, the highest unemployment rate recorded in Florida was 9.7% in March 1976. The historical low was 3% in April 2006. Preliminary nonfarm employment data by occupation for April 2006 showed that approximately 7.7% of the labor force was employed in construction; 4.9% in manufacturing; 19.9% in trade, transportation, and public utilities; 6.7% in financial activities; 17.1% in professional and business services; 11.9% in education and health services; 11.4% in leisure and hospitality services; and 13.6% in government.

The US Department of Labor's Bureau of Labor Statistics reported that in 2005, a total of 401,000 of Florida's 7,389,000 employed wage and salary workers were formal members of a union. This represented 5.4% of those so employed, down from 6% in 2004, and below the national average of 12%. Overall in 2005, a total of 532,000 workers (7.2%) in Florida were covered by a union or employee association contract, which includes those workers who reported no union affiliation. Florida is one of 22 states with a right-to-work law, which is part of the state's constitution.

As of 1 March 2006, Florida had a state-mandated minimum wage rate of $6.40 per hour. In 2004, women in the state accounted for 46.3% of the employed civilian labor force.

²³AGRICULTURE

Florida's most important agricultural products, and the ones for which it is most famous, are its citrus fruits. Florida continues to supply the vast majority of orange juice consumed in the United States. Florida produced 82% of the nation's oranges and 78% of its grapefruits in 2003. It is also an important producer of other fruits, vegetables, and sugarcane.

The total value of Florida's crops in 2005 exceeded $6 billion, fourth highest among the 50 states. Total farm marketings, including livestock marketings and products, exceeded $7.4 billion in 2005 (ninth in the United States). There were about 43,000 farms covering some 10.1 million acres (4.08 million hectares) in 2004; the total represented nearly 30% of the state's entire land area.

The orange was introduced to Florida by Spanish settlers around 1570. Oranges had become an important commercial crop by the early 1800s, when the grapefruit was introduced. In 1886, orange production for the first time exceeded 1 million boxes (1 box equals 90 lb/41 kg). Much of this production came from groves along the northern Atlantic coast and the St. Johns River, which offered easy access to maritime shipping routes north. The expansion of the railroads and severe freezes in the 1890s encouraged the citrus industry to move farther south. Polk, St. Lucie, Indian River, Hendry, and Hardee counties in central Florida are the largest producers of citrus fruits.

The orange crop totaled 242,000,000 boxes each weighing 90-lb (41-kg) in the 2002–03 season. The grapefruit crop was 40,900,000 boxes at 85-lb (39-kg); tangerines, 6,500,000 boxes at 95-lb (43-kg); and tangelos and temple oranges, 2,400,000 boxes at 90-lb (41-kg). There are about 50 processing plants in Florida where citrus fruits are processed into canned or chilled juice, frozen or pasteurized concentrate, or canned fruit sections. Production of frozen concentrate orange juice totaled 195.4 million gallons in 2002. Stock feed made from peel, pulp, and seeds is an important by-product of the citrus-processing industry; annual production is nearly 1 million tons. Other citrus by-products are citrus molasses, D-limonene, alcohol, wines, preserves, and citrus seed oil.

Florida is the country's second leading producer of vegetables. Vegetable farming is concentrated in central and southern Florida, especially in the area south of Lake Okeechobee, where drainage of the Everglades left exceptionally rich soil. In 2004, Florida farmers harvested 15,120,000 hundredweight of tomatoes; they sold 9,246,000 hundredweight of potatoes. Florida's tomato and vegetable growers, who had at one time enjoyed a near-monopoly of the US winter vegetable market, began in the 1990s to face increasing competition from Mexican growers, whose lower-priced produce had captured about half the market by 1995. About two-thirds of all farm laborers are hired hands.

Florida's major field crop is sugarcane (mostly grown near Lake Okeechobee), which enjoyed a sizable production increase in the 1960s and 1970s, following the cutoff of imports from Cuba. In 2004, Florida's sugarcane production was 14,255,000 tons. Florida's second-largest field crop is peanuts (364,000,000 lb/165,400,000 kg in 2004), followed by cotton, hay, corn, tobacco, soybeans, and wheat. Florida leads the nation in the production of watermelons. Greenhouse and nursery products were valued at over $1.6 billion in 2004, 23.8% of farm receipts.

²⁴ANIMAL HUSBANDRY

Florida is an important cattle-raising state. Receipts from cattle and calves in 2004 totaled $443.1 million, or 6.5% of total farm receipts. The Kissimmee Plain, north of Lake Okeechobee, is the largest grazing area. In 2005, Florida had an estimated 1.74 million cattle and calves valued at an estimated $1.4 billion. During 2004, Florida had an estimated 20,000 hogs and pigs valued at around $2.3 million. An estimated 2.8 billion eggs were produced in 2003, worth $145.1 million. Florida had an estimated 142,000 milk cows in 2003 that produced around 2.2 billion lb (1 billion kg) of milk. Also during 2003, Florida poultry farmers produced 511.3 million lb (232.4 million kg) of broilers, valued at $178.9 million.

25 FISHING

In 2004, Florida's total commercial fish catch was 124.5 million lb (56.6 million kg), worth $190.6 million. About 66% of the volume and 76% of the value came from fishing in the Gulf of Mexico. The remainder was from Atlantic waters. The most important commercial species of shellfish are shrimp, spiny lobster, and crabs. Gulf coast shrimp landings totaled 18.2 million lb (8.2 million kg) in 2004. Valuable finfish species include grouper, swordfish, and snapper. Florida's commercial fishing fleet had 4,438 boats and 1,934 vessels in 2002. In 2003, Florida had 376 processing and wholesale plants with an average 4,745 employees.

Florida's extensive shoreline and numerous inland waterways make sport fishing a major recreational activity. Both freshwater and saltwater fishing are important sports. Tarpon, sailfish, and redfish are some of the major saltwater sport species; largemouth bass, panfish, sunfish, catfish, and perch are leading freshwater sport fish. Florida had 1,296,328 sport fishing license holders in 2004.

26 FORESTRY

About 47% of Florida's land area—16,285,000 acres (6,590,000 hectares)—was forested in 2003, when the state had about 2.2% of all forested land in the United States. A total of 4,016,000 acres (1,625,000 hectares) was owned by the forest industry. The most common tree is the pine, which occurs throughout the state but is most abundant in the north.

Florida's logging industry is concentrated in the northern part of the state. The most important forestry product is pulpwood for paper manufacturing. Lumber production in 2004 was 1.07 billion board feet, mostly softwoods, accounting for 2.2% of US production.

Four national forests—Apalachicola, Ocala, Osceola, and Choctawhatchee—covering 1,434,000 acres (580,000 hectares) are located in Florida. State forests covered 1,403,000 acres (568,000 hectares) in 2003. Three of the main activities of state forests are forest management, outdoor recreation, and wildlife management.

Virtually all of Florida's natural forest had been cleared by the mid-20th century; the forests existing today are thus almost entirely the result of reforestation. Since 1928, more than 5.6 billion seedlings have been planted in the state.

27 MINING

According to US Geological Survey data, Florida's total nonfuel mineral production in 2004 was valued at $2.32 billion, up 12.1% from 2003, making the state fourth among the 50 states in the production, by value, of all nonfuel minerals and over 5% of all US output in 2004.

In 2004, Florida led the nation in phosphate rock mining, producing more than six times as much as the next ranking state. By value, the state's top five nonfuel minerals that same year were (in descending value) phosphate rock, crushed stone, cement (portland and masonry) construction sand and gravel, and zirconium concentrates. These five commodities accounted for approximately 94% of all nonfuel mineral output, by value. Florida is also the only state that produces rutile concentrates and staurolite.

Output of crushed stone in 2004 totaled 105 million metric tons and was valued at $675 million, while output of portland cement totaled 5.23 million metric tons and was valued at an estimated $432 million. Construction sand and gravel that same year totaled 29.3 million metric tons and was valued at $146 million.

28 ENERGY AND POWER

As of 2003, Florida had 54 electrical power service providers, of which 32 were publicly owned and 16 were cooperatives. Of the remainder, 5 were investor owned, and 1 was an owner of an independent generator that sold directly to customers. As of that same year there were 8,732,766 retail customers. Of that total, 6,649,226 received their power from investor-owned service providers. Cooperatives accounted for 887,981 customers, while publicly owned providers had 1,195,476 customers. There were 83 independent generator, or "facility" customers.

Total net summer generating capability by the state's electrical generating plants in 2003 stood at 49.418 million kW, with total production that same year at 212.610 billion kWh. Of the total amount generated, 88.4% came from electric utilities, with the remainder coming from independent producers and combined heat and power service providers. The largest portion of all electric power generated, 68.293 billion kWh (32.1%), came from natural gas-fired plants, with coal-fired plants in second place at 67.674 billion kWh (31.8%) and petroleum-fired plants in third at 37.204 billion kWh (17.5%). Other renewable power sources accounted for 2.7% of all power generated, with nuclear plants at 14.6%. Hydroelectric power accounted for only 0.1% of power generated.

As of 2006, Florida had three nuclear power–generating plants: the Crystal River Energy Complex in Citrus County; the St. Lucie plant near Fort Pierce; and the Turkey Point nuclear power station near Miami, in Dade County.

Although Florida produces some oil and natural gas, it is a net importer of energy resources. Its mild climate and abundant sunshine offer great potential for solar energy development, but this potential has not been extensively exploited.

As of 2004, Florida had proven crude oil reserves of 65 million barrels, or less than 1% of all proven US reserves, while output that same year averaged 8,000 barrels per day. Including federal offshore domains, the state that year ranked 16th (15th excluding federal offshore) in proven reserves and 20th (19th excluding federal offshore) in production among the 31 producing states. In 2004, Florida had 70 producing oil wells and accounted for less than 1% of all US production. The state has no refineries.

In 2004, Florida's marketed gas production (all gas produced excluding gas used for repressuring, vented and flared, and nonhydrocarbon gases removed) totaled 3.123 billion cu ft (0.088 billion cu m). As of 31 December 2004, proven reserves of dry or consumer-grade natural gas in 2004 totaled 78 billion cu ft (2.2 billion cu m). There was no data available on the number of producing natural gas and gas condensate wells in the state.

²⁹INDUSTRY

Florida is not a center of heavy industry, and many of its manufacturing activities are related to agriculture and exploitation of natural resources. Leading industries include food processing, electric and electronic equipment, transportation equipment, and chemicals. Nearly 20% of the nation's boat manufacturers are also located in the state. Electric components are primarily manufactured in three east coast counties (Brevard, Palm Beach, and Broward), where about half of the state's electronic component workers reside. Since the perfection of the laser by Martin-Marietta in Orlando in the 1950s, the greater Orlando area has grown to have the third-highest concentration of electro-optics and laser manufacturers in the United States.

The cigar-making industry, traditionally important in Florida, has declined considerably with changes in taste and the cutoff of tobacco imports from Cuba. In the late 1930s, the Tampa area alone had well over 100 cigar factories, employing some 10,000 people. However, by 1997 the number of people employed in the state's cigar-making industry had shrunk to 1,581.

According to the US Census Bureau's Annual Survey of Manufactures (ASM) for 2004, Florida's manufacturing sector covered some 21 product subsectors. The shipment value of all products manufactured in the state that same year was $84.301 billion. Of that total, computer and electronic product manufacturing accounted for the largest share at $13.383 billion. It was followed by food manufacturing at $10.457 billion; chemical manufacturing at $8.520 billion; miscellaneous manufacturing at $6.491 billion; and fabricated metal product manufacturing at $5.994 billion.

In 2004, a total of 354,186 people in Florida were employed in the state's manufacturing sector, according to the ASM. Of that total, 232,136 were actual production workers. In terms of total employment, the computer and electronic product manufacturing industry accounted for the largest portion of all manufacturing employees at 46,769, with 19,562 actual production workers. It was followed by fabricated metal product manufacturing at 40,714 employees (31,091 actual production workers); transportation equipment manufacturing at 31,121 employees (21,016 actual production workers); miscellaneous manufacturing at 30,607 employees (17,028 actual production workers); and food manufacturing with 30,585 employees (21,516 actual production workers).

ASM data for 2004 showed that Florida's manufacturing sector paid $13.967 billion in wages. Of that amount, the computer- and electronic product–manufacturing sector accounted for the largest share at $2.547 billion. It was followed by fabricated metal product manufacturing at $1.382 billion; miscellaneous manufacturing at $1.318 billion; transport equipment manufacturing at $1.180 billion; and food manufacturing at $1.055 billion.

³⁰COMMERCE

According to the 2002 Census of Wholesale Trade, Florida's wholesale trade sector had sales that year totaling $219.4 billion from 31,332 establishments. Wholesalers of durable goods accounted for 19,158 establishments, followed by nondurable goods wholesalers at 10,024 and electronic markets, agents, and brokers accounting for 2,150 establishments. Sales by durable goods wholesalers in 2002 totaled $104.8 billion, while wholesalers of nondurable goods saw sales of $83.9 billion. Electronic markets,

agents, and brokers in the wholesale trade industry had sales of $30.6 billion.

In the 2002 Census of Retail Trade, Florida was listed as having 69,543 retail establishments with sales of $191.8 billion. The leading types of retail businesses by number of establishments were: clothing and clothing accessories stores (11,360); food and beverage stores (8,276); miscellaneous store retailers (8,141); motor vehicle and motor vehicle parts dealers (7,913); and gasoline stations (6,544). In terms of sales, motor vehicle and motor vehicle parts stores accounted for the largest share of retail sales at $54.8 billion, followed by food and beverage stores at $27.6 billion; general merchandise stores at $26.7 billion; and gasoline stations at $13.4 billion. A total of 902,760 people were employed by the retail sector in Florida that year.

The value of all exports sent from Florida was over $33.3 billion in 2005, ranking the state eighth in the nation. Duty-free goods for reshipment abroad pass through Port Everglades, Miami, Orlando, Jacksonville, Tampa, and Panama City, all free-trade zones established to bring international commerce to the state. Imports, including motor vehicles, apparel, aircraft and spacecraft, and machinery came primarily from Japan, Germany, Brazil, Costa Rica, and the Dominican Republic.

³¹CONSUMER PROTECTION

The Division of Consumer Services, a division of the Department of Agriculture and Consumer Services, is the state's clearinghouse for consumer complaints and information and performs the initial review under the Motor Vehicle Warranty Enforcement Act—the so-called Lemon Law. The Division also regulates ballroom dance studios, charitable organizations, health studios, motor vehicle repair shops, pawnshops, sellers of travel, sellers of business opportunities and telemarketers, and maintains the state's No Sales Solicitation Calls list. The Florida Consumers' Council advises the commissioner of agriculture on consumer issues.

The public counsel to the Public Service Commission (PSC), appointed by a joint committee of the legislature, represents the public interest in commission hearings on utility rates and other regulations. The public counsel can also seek judicial review of PSC rulings, and may appear before other state and federal bodies on the public's behalf in utility and transportation matters.

The Department of Business and Professional Regulation oversees pari-mutuel betting; land sales; the operations of condominiums, cooperative apartments, hotels, and restaurants; professions and professional boards; real estate; certified public accounting; and the regulation and licensing of alcoholic beverage and tobacco sales.

In 1983, the state legislature enacted the Motor Vehicle Warranty Enforcement Act, which forces automobile dealers to replace new cars or refund the purchase price if the cars are in constant need of repairs.

Florida's Office of the Attorney General is the enforcement authority for the state's consumer protection activities as per Florida's Deceptive and Unfair Trade Practices Act. Under that law, the state's Attorney General's Office can initiate civil (but not criminal) proceedings; nor can it represent the state before state and federal regulatory agencies. The Office can administer consumer protection and education programs, and the handling of consumer complaints, and does have broad subpoena powers. In antitrust actions, the Attorney General's Office: can act on behalf of those consumers who are incapable of acting on their own; can initiate damage actions on behalf of the state in state courts; can initiate criminal proceedings; and can represent counties, cities and other governmental entities in recovering civil damages under state or federal law.

The Florida Department of Agriculture and Consumer Service, along with the Office of the Attorney General, its Economic Crimes Division and its Multi-State Litigation and Intergovernmental Affairs office are located in Tallahassee. Regional offices are located in Fort Lauderdale, Orlando, Tampa and West Palm Beach. County consumer protection offices are located in Clearwater, Fort Lauderdale, Miami, New Port Richey, Orlando, Tampa and West Palm Beach.

³²BANKING

The Florida Department of Financial Services, Division of Banking, has regulatory and supervisory authority over state-chartered financial institutions in Florida, including commercial banks and nondeposit trust companies, credit unions, savings associations, offices of foreign banks operating in Florida, and money transmitters. The Florida Department of Financial Services also has regulatory and supervisory authority over mortgage brokers and mortgage lenders, consumer finance companies, motor vehicle sales finance companies, commercial and consumer debt collection agencies, cemeteries, and abandoned property.

As of June 2005, Florida had 293 insured banks, savings and loans, and saving banks, plus 97 state-chartered and 125 federally chartered credit unions (CUs). Excluding the CUs, the Miami–Fort Lauderdale–Miami Beach market area had 118 financial institutions in 2004, with $138.101 billion in deposits, followed by the Tampa–St Petersburg–Clearwater area with 65 institutions and $42.620 billion in deposits. As of June 2005, CUs accounted for 22% of all assets held by all financial institutions in the state, or some $37.121 billion. Banks, savings and loans, and savings banks collectively accounted for the remaining 78%, or $131.430 billion in assets held.

International banking grew in Florida during the late 1970s and early 1980s with the establishment of the Edge Act banks in Miami. Located close to Central and South America, with a bilingual population, Florida (especially Miami) has become a Latin American banking center. Many banks in Miami have headquarters outside Florida and engage exclusively in international banking.

In 2004, the median net interest margin (the difference between the lower rates offered to savers and the higher rates charged on loans) of Florida's banks stood at 3.99%, up from 3.97% in 2003. The median percentage of past-due/nonaccrual loans to total loans stood at 0.56%, down from 0.83% in 2003.

³³INSURANCE

In 2004, there were 8 million individual life insurance policies in force with a total value of over $724 billion; total value for all categories of life insurance (individual, group, and credit) was over $1 trillion. The average coverage amount is $90,100 per policy holder. Death benefits paid that year totaled over $3.4 billion.

In 2003, 19 life and health insurance companies and 111 property and casualty insurance companies were domiciled in Florida. In 2004, direct premiums for property and casualty insurance to-taled $32.3 billion. That year, Florida ranked first in the nation in flood insurance, with 1.87 million flood insurance policies in force, with a total value of over $315.7 billion, accounting for about 42% of the national total. About $206 billion of coverage was offered through FAIR plans, which are designed to offer coverage for some natural circumstances, such as wind and hail, in high-risk areas.

In 2004, 47% of state residents held employment-based health insurance policies, 5% held individual policies, and 27% were covered under Medicare and Medicaid; 19% of residents were uninsured. Florida tied with four other states for the fourth-highest percentage of uninsured residents in the nation. In 2003, employee contributions for employment-based health coverage averaged at 21% for single coverage and 30% for family coverage. For family coverage, an average 30% employee-contribution rate is one of the highest in the country. The state offers an 18-month health benefits expansion program for small-firm employees in connection with the Consolidated Omnibus Budget Reconciliation Act (COBRA, 1986), a health insurance program for those who lose employment-based coverage due to termination or reduction of work hours.

In 2003, there were over 10 million auto insurance policies in effect for private passenger cars. Required minimum coverage includes property damage liability of $10,000 and personal injury protection. In 2003, the average expenditure per vehicle for insurance coverage was $1,015.11, the fifth-highest average in the nation.

The insurance industry is regulated by the state's Department of Insurance.

³⁴SECURITIES

No securities exchanges are located in Florida. In 2005, there were 8,870 personal financial advisers employed in the state and 17,740 securities, commodities, and financial services sales agents. In 2004, there were over 576 publicly traded companies within the state, with over 160 NASDAQ companies, 73 NYSE listings, and 35 AMEX listings. In 2006, the state had 14 Fortune 500 companies; Publix Supermarkets (based in Lakeland) ranked first in the state and 104th in the nation with revenues of over $20.7 billion, followed by Tech Data (Clearwater), AutoNation (Fort Lauderdale), Office Depot (Delray Beach), and Lennar (Miami). Tech Data is listed on NASDAQ and the other four companies are listed on the NYSE.

³⁵PUBLIC FINANCE

The Office of Planning and Budget of the governor's office prepares and submits to the legislature the budget for each fiscal year (FY), which runs from 1 July to 30 June. The largest expenditure items are education, health and social concerns, general government, and transportation. By prohibiting borrowing to finance operating expenses, Florida's constitution requires a balanced budget.

The issuance of state bonds is overseen by the State Board of Administration, which consists of the governor, the state treasurer, and the comptroller. Three principal types of bonds are issued. The first consists of bonds backed by the "full faith and credit" of the state and payable from general revenue. Issuance of such bonds generally requires voter approval. The second type consists of revenue bonds, payable from income derived from the capital project financed, for example, from bridge or highway tolls. The third type consists of bonds payable from a constitutionally specified source, for example, higher education bonds backed by the state gross receipts tax, or elementary and secondary education bonds backed by the motor vehicle license tax.

In fiscal year 2006, general funds were estimated at $30.3 billion for resources and $26.8 billion for expenditures. In fiscal year 2004, federal government grants to Florida were nearly $19.6 billion.

In the fiscal year 2007 federal budget, Florida was slated to receive: $233 million, an increase of $12 million over 2006, for activities that will benefit the ecosystem of South Florida including the

Everglades, while supporting future population growth. This includes $48 million to move forward with the Modified Water Delivery project, which will allow more water to pass under Tamiami Trail (US Highway 41) and enter Everglades National Park. Under the Comprehensive Everglades Restoration Plan, Army Corps of Engineers work on seepage control north and south of Tamiami Trail, the Kissimmee River, and aquifer storage and recovery pilot projects will also be a priority; $10 million to replace the air traffic control tower at Palm Beach International Airport in West Palm Beach.

36 TAXATION

In 2005, Florida collected $33,895 million in tax revenues or $1,905 per capita, which placed it 37th among the 50 states in per capita tax burden. The national average was $2,192 per capita. Property taxes accounted for 0.9% of the total: sales taxes, 56.2%; selective sales taxes, 19.0%; corporate income taxes, 5.3%; and other taxes, 18.7%.

As of 1 January 2006, Florida had no state income tax, a distinction it shared with Alaska, Wyoming, Washington, Nevada, Texas, and South Dakota. The state taxes corporations at a flat rate of 5.5%.

In 2004, state and local property taxes amounted to $18,500,291,000 or $1,064 per capita. The per capita amount ranks the state 19th highest nationally. Local governments collected $18,223,505,000 of the total and the state government, $276,786,000.

Florida taxes retail sales at a rate of 6%. In addition to the state tax, local taxes on retail sales can reach as much as 1.50%, making for a potential total tax on retail sales of 7.50%. Food purchased for consumption off-premises is tax exempt. The tax on cigarettes is 33.9 cents per pack, which ranks 44th among the 50 states and the District of Columbia. Florida taxes gasoline at 14.9 cents per gallon. This is in addition to the 18.4 cents per gallon federal tax on gasoline.

According to the Tax Foundation, for every federal tax dollar sent to Washington in 2004, Florida citizens received $1.02 in federal spending.

37 ECONOMIC POLICY

In the late 1990s, Florida intensified its efforts to attract high-tech, high-wage industries such as silicon technologies and aviation/aerospace industries. Florida became the first state in the nation to close its Department of Commerce. All of the state's economic development and international trade strategies are now handled through a partnership of business and government, Enterprise Florida. This new approach calls for collaboration among leaders in government, business, and academia. Enterprise Florida and its regional and local partner organizations provide a statewide network of business assistance resources in the areas of capital acquisition, technology commercialization, manufacturing competitiveness, training, minority and rural business development, incentives, site selection, permitting, and trade development. Through buying blocks of discounting tickets, arranging for bargain airfares, setting up meetings with local business people, and providing a distinctive Florida booth, Enterprise Florida lowers the cost of attending trade shows for Florida exporters. Promoting Florida exports has been a major concern of recent economic

Florida—State Government Finances

(Dollar amounts in thousands. Per capita amounts in dollars.)

	AMOUNT	PER CAPITA
Total Revenue	75,176,415	4,324.21
General revenue	56,671,550	3,259.80
Intergovernmental revenue	16,736,684	962.71
Taxes	30,534,283	1,756.36
General sales	17,128,515	985.25
Selective sales	6,280,891	361.28
License taxes	1,774,881	102.09
Individual income tax	–	–
Corporate income tax	1,441,338	82.91
Other taxes	3,908,658	224.83
Current charges	3,677,747	211.55
Miscellaneous general revenue	5,722,836	329.18
Utility revenue	18,529	1.07
Liquor store revenue	–	–
Insurance trust revenue	18,486,336	1,063.35
Total expenditure	59,943,442	3,448.00
Intergovernmental expenditure	16,473,396	947.56
Direct expenditure	43,470,046	2,500.43
Current operation	30,053,727	1,728.72
Capital outlay	4,999,409	287.57
Insurance benefits and repayments	5,624,775	323.54
Assistance and subsidies	1,665,466	95.80
Interest on debt	1,126,669	64.81
Exhibit: Salaries and wages	7,001,138	402.71
Total expenditure	59,943,442	3,448.00
General expenditure	54,256,955	3,120.91
Intergovernmental expenditure	16,473,396	947.56
Direct expenditure	37,783,559	2,173.34
General expenditures, by function:		
Education	17,737,233	1,020.26
Public welfare	15,415,221	886.70
Hospitals	236,046	13.58
Health	2,829,993	162.78
Highways	5,066,358	291.42
Police protection	403,244	23.19
Correction	2,185,039	125.69
Natural resources	1,472,203	84.68
Parks and recreation	153,633	8.84
Government administration	2,072,853	119.23
Interest on general debt	1,126,669	64.81
Other and unallocable	5,558,463	319.73
Utility expenditure	61,712	3.55
Liquor store expenditure	–	–
Insurance trust expenditure	5,624,775	323.54
Debt at end of fiscal year	23,194,784	1,334.18
Cash and security holdings	177,451,104	10,207.14

Abbreviations and symbols: – zero or rounds to zero; (NA) not available; (X) not applicable.

SOURCE: *U.S. Census Bureau, Governments Division, 2004 Survey of State Government Finances,* January 2006.

policy. The International Trade and Business Development unit of Enterprise Florida is based in Miami with 6 field offices in the state and 14 international offices, including ones in Frankfurt, Germany; London, England; Taipei, Republic of China; Toronto, Canada; Seoul, South Korea; Mexico City, Mexico; Tokyo, Japan; and Sao Paolo, Brazil. Florida has 14 deep-water commercial seaports; 5 barge ports; 9 major shallow-water ports; 4 river ports; and 16 customs ports of entry. As of 2006, 20 Free Trade Zones (FTZs) had been designated, all located at or near seaports and international airports. Value-added in the FTZs is not subject to US customs duties unless processed goods are imported for sale in the domestic market.

[38] HEALTH

Reflecting the age distribution of the state's population, Florida has a relatively low birthrate and a high death rate. The infant mortality rate in October 2005 was estimated at 7.1 per 1,000 live births. The birthrate in 2003 was 12.5 per 1,000 population. The abortion rate stood at 31.9 per 1,000 women in 2000. In 2003, about 85.5% of pregnant woman received prenatal care beginning in the first trimester. In 2004, approximately 89% of children received routine immunizations before the age of three; this represented one of the highest immunization rates in the country.

The crude death rate in 2003 was 9.9 deaths per 1,000 population. As of 2002, the death rates for major causes of death (per 100,000 resident population) were: heart disease, 294.6; cancer, 234.2; cerebrovascular diseases, 61.4; chronic lower respiratory diseases, 54.2; and diabetes, 27.4. The mortality rate from HIV infection was 10.3 per 100,000 population, representing the third-highest rate in the nation (following the District of Columbia and Maryland). In 2004, the reported AIDS case rate was about 33.5 per 100,000 population, representing the third-highest rate in the nation (following the District of Columbia and New York). In 2002, about 53.9% of the population was considered overweight or obese. As of 2004, about 20.1% of state residents were smokers.

In 2003, Florida had 203 community hospitals with about 50,700 beds. There were about 2.2 million patient admissions that year and 22 million outpatient visits. The average daily inpatient census was about 32,800 patients. The average cost per day for hospital care was $1,387. Also in 2003, there were about 693 certified nursing facilities in the state with 82,546 beds and an overall occupancy rate of about 87.2%. In 2004, it was estimated that about 68.2% of all state residents had received some type of dental care within the year. Florida had 258 physicians per 100,000 resident population in 2004 and 780 nurses per 100,000 in 2005. In 2004, there were a total of 9,072 dentists in the state.

In 2004, Florida tied with Pennsylvania and Arkansas for the third-highest percentage of residents on Medicare at 17% (following West Virginia and Maine). Approximately 19% of the state population was uninsured in 2004. In 2003, state health care expenditures totaled $15.3 million.

[39] SOCIAL WELFARE

In 2004, about 300,000 people received unemployment benefits, with the average weekly unemployment benefit at $223. In fiscal year 2005, the estimated average monthly participation in the food stamp program included about 1,381,804 persons (657,576 households); the average monthly benefit was about $96.37 per person. That year, the total of benefits paid through the state for the food stamp program was about $1.59 billion.

Temporary Assistance for Needy Families (TANF), the system of federal welfare assistance that officially replaced Aid to Families with Dependent Children (AFDC) in 1997, was reauthorized through the Deficit Reduction Act of 2005. TANF is funded through federal block grants that are divided among the states based on an equation involving the number of recipients in each state. Florida's TANF program is called the Welfare Transition Program. In 2004, the state program had 116,000 recipients; state and federal expenditures on this TANF program totaled $293 million in fiscal year 2003.

In December 2004, Social Security benefits were paid to 3,381,970 Floridians. This number included 2,294,180 retired workers, 297,870 widows and widowers, 377,030 disabled workers, 178,720 spouses, and 234,170 children. Social Security beneficiaries represented 19.5% of the total state population and 85.6% of the state's population age 65 and older. Retired workers received an average monthly payment of $951; widows and widowers, $924; disabled workers, $895; and spouses, $472. Payments for children of retired workers averaged $453 per month; children of deceased workers, $613; and children of disabled workers, $267. Federal Supplemental Security Income payments in December 2004 went to 412,970 Florida residents, averaging $395 a month. An additional $755,000 of state-administered supplemental payments were distributed to 14,800 residents.

[40] HOUSING

Florida's housing market fluctuated widely in the 1970s and early 1980s. During the mid-1970s recession, home buying dropped off markedly and much newly completed housing could not be sold. By late in the decade, however, the unused housing stock had been depleted and a new building boom was under way. The number of housing units in Florida increased 73.2% between 1970 and 1980, but only by 39.4% between 1980 and 1990. As of 2004, an estimated 29.8% of all housing units had been built in 1990 or later; only 2.5% were built before 1940.

In 2004, there were an estimated 8,009,427 housing units in Florida, ranking the state third in the nation for total number of housing units (after California and Texas). About 6,819,280 of the units were occupied; 70.5% were owner occupied. About 53.3% of all units were single-family, detached homes; 12.3% were in buildings with 20 units or more; and about 10.4% were mobile homes. It was estimated that about 305,291 units were without telephone service, 19,379 lacked complete plumbing facilities, and 26,983 lacked complete kitchen facilities. Over 76% of all units relied on electricity for heating; about 1,845 units were equipped for solar-power heating. The average household had 2.49 members.

In 2004, 255,900 new privately owned housing units were authorized for construction. Multifamily housing ranges from beachfront luxury high rises along the Gold Coast to dilapidated residential hotels in the South Beach section of Miami Beach. The median home value was $149,291. The median monthly cost for mortgage owners was $1,143, while renters paid a median of $766 per month. In September 2005, the state received a grant of $150,000 from the US Department of Housing and Urban Development (HUD) for rural housing and economic development programs. For 2006, HUD allocated to the state over $29.2 million in community development block grants. Also in 2006, HUD offered an additional $82.9 million to the state in emergency funds to rebuild housing that was destroyed by Hurricanes Katrina, Rita, and Wilma in late 2005.

The Division of Florida Land Sales and Condominiums, within the Department of Business Regulation, registers all sellers of subdivided land and oversees the advertising and selling of land, condominiums, and cooperatives. A major controversy involving condominiums in the early 1970s centered on "rec leases." Until the practice was outlawed in mid-decade, condominium developers often retained ownership of such recreational facilities as the swimming pool, clubhouse, and tennis courts, requiring apartment purchasers to pay rent for their use. The rents were generally set quite low at the time of sale, but raised sharply soon after.

41 EDUCATION

In the 1970s, Florida was an innovator in several areas of education, including competency testing, expansion of community colleges, and school finance reform. Further advances were made in 1983 and 1984, when the state increased taxes to help fund education, raised teachers' salaries, initiated the nation's strictest high school graduation requirements, and reformed the curriculum.

Student achievement in reading, writing, and mathematics is measured by national norm-referenced tests selected at the district level, and by the High School Competency Test (HSCT), measuring communication and math skills of 11th grade students. In 2004, 85.9% of Floridians 25 years of age or older were high school graduates; 26% had four or more years of college.

The total enrollment for fall 2002 in Florida's public schools stood at 2,540,000. Of these, 1,809,000 attended schools from kindergarten through grade eight, and 731,000 attended high school. Approximately 51.3% of the students were white, 24.3% were black, 22.1% were Hispanic, 2% were Asian/Pacific Islander, and 0.3% were American Indian/Alaskan Native. Total enrollment was estimated at 2,567,000 in fall 2003 and expected to be 2,790,000 by fall 2014, an increase of 9.9% during the period 2002 to 2014. There were 323,766 students enrolled in 1,803 private schools in fall 2003. Expenditures for public education in 2003/04 were estimated at $2.9 billion or $6,784 per student. Since 1969, the National Assessment of Educational Progress (NAEP) has tested public school students nationwide. The resulting report, *The Nation's Report Card,* stated that in 2005 eighth graders in Florida scored 274 out of 500 in mathematics compared with the national average of 278.

As of fall 2002, there were 776,622 students enrolled in college or graduate school; minority students comprised 37.4% of total postsecondary enrollment. As of 2005, Florida had 169 degree-granting institutions. Of Florida's state universities, the largest is the University of Florida (Gainesville). Also part of the state university system are special university centers, such as the University of Florida's Institute of Food and Agricultural Science, which provide advanced and graduate courses. The State University System also offers instruction at strategic sites away from the regular campuses. In 1972, Florida completed a community college system that put a public two-year college within commuting distance of virtually every resident. Of Florida's 90 private four-year institutions of higher education, by far the largest is the University of Miami (Coral Gables).

The policy-making body for the state university system is the Board of Regents; the chancellor is the system's chief administrative officer. Florida's school finance law, the Florida Education Finance Act of 1973, establishes a funding formula aimed at equalizing both per-pupil spending statewide and the property tax burdens of residents of different school districts.

42 ARTS

The State of Florida's Division of Cultural Affairs (DCA) was established in 1969. The Florida Arts Council (previously the Fine Arts Council of Florida) serves in an advisory capacity to the DCA. The DCA has a partnership with the Southern Arts Federation. The DCA also coordinates a touring program, a public art program that acquires artwork for new state buildings, an arts license plate program, and the Florida Artists Hall of Fame, which includes such luminaries as Zora Neale Hurston, Ernest Hemingway, Ray Charles, Marjorie Kinnan Rawlings, and Robert Rauschenberg. In 2005, Florida arts organizations received 56 grant awards from the National Endowment of the Arts that totaled $1,691,800.

The Florida Humanities Council, established in 1973, sponsors grant programs, a speakers bureau the Florida Center for Teachers, and FORUM, a statewide magazine about Florida culture. In 2005, the National Endowment for the Humanities supported 24 Florida based programs with grants totaling $2,722,345.

Florida is home to a vibrant and diverse cultural community. Florida ranks near the top nationally in state funding for culture and the arts. Cultural organizations thrive in virtually every county and include museums, galleries, symphonies, dance and opera companies, and literary organizations. Offerings range from the Miami Book Fair International at one end of the state, to the widely renowned Jacksonville Jazz Festival, to the National Museum of Naval Aviation in Pensacola at the other end. Key West has long been a gathering place for creative artists, ranging from John James Audubon and Winslow Homer to Ernest Hemingway and Tennessee Williams.

Regional and metropolitan symphony orchestras include the Florida Philharmonic Orchestra (Fort Lauderdale), Florida Orchestra (Tampa), Jacksonville Symphony, and Florida West Coast Symphony (Sarasota). Opera companies include the Florida Grand Opera (Miami) and the Sarasota Opera. The four state theater companies are the Caldwell Theatre Company (Boca Raton), Hippodrome State Theatre (Gainesville), Coconut Grove Playhouse (Miami), and the Asolo Theatre Company (Sarasota). The annual Florida International Festival (FIF), established in 1966, features world-renowned artists in music and dance. The London Symphony Orchestra, which has a summer residency in Daytona Beach, provides an annual concert series for the FIF and the city. In 2005 the London Symphony Orchestra celebrated its 100th anniversary.

Florida is also home to premier museums and performing arts halls, such as the John and Mable Ringling Museum of Art (Sarasota), the Norton Gallery (West Palm Beach), the Miami Art Museum, Orlando Museum of Art, Philharmonic Center for the Arts (Naples), Tampa Bay Performing Arts Center, and the Kravis Center for the Performing Arts (West Palm Beach).

Truly unique cultural institutions also located in Florida include Fairchild Tropical Garden (Miami), the Atlantic Center for the Arts (New Smyrna Beach), and Bok Tower Gardens (Lake

Wales), which as of 2006, still had a working carillon, a set of fixed chromatically tuned bells sounded by hammers and controlled from a keyboard.

43 LIBRARIES AND MUSEUMS

For the fiscal year ending in September 2001, Florida had 72 public library systems, with a total of 473 libraries, of which 417 were branches. In that same year, a total of 29,826,000 volumes of books and serial publications were available, while circulation totaled 81,334,000. The system also had 1,317,000 audio and 1,200,000 video items, 65,000 electronic format items (CD-ROMs, magnetic tapes, and disks), and 32 bookmobiles. The largest public library systems are those of Miami–Dade County (3,886,852 volumes in 1999) and Jacksonville (2,351,104 volumes). The State Library in Tallahassee housed 661,849 volumes. The State Library also distributes federal aid to local libraries and provides other assistance. In fiscal year 2001, total operating income for the public library system was $383,109,000. For that same year, federal aid to Florida's public libraries totaled $2,988,000, while state aid to public libraries was $34,696,000. Operating expenditures that year amounted to $350,251,000, of which 58.9% of spending was on the staff and 17% on the collection. The largest university library in the state is that of the University of Florida, with holdings of more than 3.4 million volumes in 1999. Other major university libraries are those of the University of Miami and Florida State University (2.2 million each).

Florida has about 278 museums, galleries, and historical sites, as well as numerous public gardens. One of the best-known museums is the John and Mabel Ringling Museum of Art (Sarasota), a state owned facility which houses the collection of the late circus entrepreneur, featuring Italian and North European Renaissance paintings. Also in Sarasota are the Ringling Museum of the Circus and the Circus Hall of Fame, and Ca'd'Zan, the Ringling mansion. The estates and homes of a number of prominent former Florida residents are now open as museums. The Villa Vizcaya Museum and Gardens in Miami, originally the estate of International Harvester founder James R. Deering, displays his collection of 15th–18th-century antiques. Railroad developer Henry Morrison Flagler's home in Palm Beach is now a museum in his name. The Society of the Four Arts is also in Palm Beach. On Key West, Ernest Hemingway's home is also a museum. The John James Audubon house in Key West and Thomas Edison's house in Ft. Myers are two of Florida's other great homes.

The Metrozoo-Miami, with an average annual attendance of 650,000, and the Jacksonville Zoological park, 522,000, are among the state's leading zoos. Both Busch Gardens (Tampa) and Sea World of Florida (Orlando) report average annual attendances of over 3,000,000.

The largest historic restoration in Florida is in St. Augustine, where several blocks of the downtown area have been restored to their 18th-century likeness under the auspices of the Historic St. Augustine Preservation Board, a state agency. Castillo de San Marcos, the 17th-century Spanish fort at St. Augustine, is now a national monument under the jurisdiction of the National Park Service and is open to the public. Other Florida cities having historic preservation boards are Pensacola, Tallahassee, and Tampa.

44 COMMUNICATIONS

As of 2004, 93.4% of the state's occupied housing units had telephones. In addition, by June of that same year there were 11,916,615 mobile wireless telephone subscribers. In 2003, 61.0% of Florida households had a computer and 55.6% had Internet access. By June 2005, there were 2,979,706 high-speed lines in Florida, 2,602,957 residential and 376,749 for business.

Florida's first radio station was WFAW (later WQAM) in Miami, which went on the air in 1920. In 2005, the state had 66 major AM stations and 145 major FM radio stations. Miami was also the site of the state's first television station, WTVJ, which began broadcasting on 27 January 1949. Film and television production in Florida is a billion-dollar per year industry with over 5,000 production companies providing more than 100,000 jobs. There were 62 major TV stations in Florida in 2005.

In 1999, the Tampa–St. Petersburg–Sarasota area had 1,485,980 television households, 74% of which had cable. The Orlando–Daytona Beach–Melbourne area had a 77% penetration rate for cable in television-owning households. At West Palm Beach-Fort Pierce, 85% of television households had cable. The Miami–Fort Lauderdale area had 1,441,570 television households, with a 73% penetration rate for cable. A total of 471,645 Internet domain names were registered in Florida by 2000, the fourth-most of any state.

45 PRESS

The *East Florida Gazette*, published in St. Augustine in 1783–84, was Florida's earliest newspaper. The oldest paper still publishing is the *Jacksonville Times-Union* (now *Florida Times-Union),* which first appeared in February 1883.

In 2005, the state had 38 morning papers, 3 evening papers, and 37 Sunday papers.

The leading English-language dailies and their circulations in 2005 were:

AREA	NAME	DAILY	SUNDAY
Ft. Lauderdale	*South Florida Sun-Sentinel* (m,S)	266,889	356,619
Jacksonville	*Florida Times-Union* (m,S)	165,425	227,891
Miami	*Herald* (m,S)	315,988	431,928
Orlando	*Orlando Sentinel* (all day,S)	258,881	374,576
St. Petersburg	*St Petersburg Times* (m,S)	330,091	419,289
Sarasota	*Sarasota Herald-Tribune* (m,S)	110,783	133,970
Tampa	*Tampa Tribune* (m,S)	226,573	304,451
West Palm Beach	*West Palm Beach Post* (m,S)	168,257	204,938

Spanish language newspapers include *Diario Las Americas* and *El Nuevo Herald,* both published in Miami with circulations under 100,000. In 2005, there were 166 weekly publications in Florida. Of these there are 72 paid weeklies, 62 free weeklies, and 32 combined weeklies. The total circulation of paid weeklies (582,448) and free weeklies (1,726,985) is 2,309,433. Two Florida combined weeklies ranked fifth and sixth by circulation in the United States, Melbourne's *Times* (51,300) and East Pasco's *News* (50,725), respectively. Two Florida shopping publications ranked fifth and eighth in the United States, the Miami *Flyer* (1,256,294) and the Tampa *Flyer* (870,656), respectively.

The most widely read periodical published in Florida is the sensationalist *National Enquirer.* There were 11 book publishers in Florida in 2005, including DC Press and University Presses of Florida.

⁴⁶ORGANIZATIONS

In 2006, there were over 12,860 nonprofit organizations registered within the state, of which about 9,430 were registered as charitable, educational, or religious organizations.. Commercial, trade, and professional organizations based in Florida include the American Accounting Association (Sarasota), American Welding Society (Miami), American Electroplaters and Surface Finishers Society (Winter Park), Florida Citrus Mutual (Lakeland), the International Songwriters Guild (Orlando), and Florida Fruit and Vegetable Association (Orlando).

Sports groups include the National Association for Stock Car Auto Racing (NASCAR), USA Waterski, International Game Fish Association, and International Swimming Hall of Fame. The American Association for Nude Recreation is based in Kissimmee.

The Academy of Arts and Sciences of the Americas and the National Foundation for Advancement in the Arts are located in Miami. State and regional organizations for the arts include the Florida Cultural Alliance, the Florida Keys Council of the Arts, and the Jazz Society of Pensacola. State organizations for the environment include the Florida Wildlife Federation and Friends of the Everglades.

The world headquarters of campus Crusade for Christ is located in Orlando.

⁴⁷TOURISM, TRAVEL, AND RECREATION

Tourism is a mainstay of the state's economy. Most of Florida's tourists are from elsewhere in the United States although Miami also attracts large numbers of affluent Latin American travelers, lured at least in part by the Latin flavor the large Cuban community has given the city. In 2005, there were about 85 million visitors to the state.

Supporting the industry is VISIT FLORIDA, a public and private partnership organization established in 1996 in cooperation with the Florida Commission on Tourism. A portion of the funding for the organization comes from the state's $2.05 per day rental car surcharge. Most funding comes from the private sector.

In 2005, over 944,000 Floridians worked directly in tourist- and recreation-related businesses, which generated over $57 billion. The state ranks second in the nation in the number of travel and tourism employees. More than half of all hotels were located in Dade County, where hotels and other tourist accommodations stretch for miles along Collins Avenue in Miami Beach, in the heart of the state's tourist industry.

Florida's biggest tourist attractions are its sun, sand, and surf. According to the state's Department of Commerce, leisure-time activity is the principal reason why more than four-fifths of auto travelers enter the state. Major tourist attractions include Walt Disney World, Universal Orlando, and Sea World Orlando. Other major attractions are the Kennedy Space Center at Cape Canaveral and the St. Augustine historic district.

Nine parks and other facilities in Florida operated by the National Park Service, including Biscayne National Park and Everglades National Park, draw millions of visitors annually. The most popular destination is the Gulf Islands National Seashore, located near Pensacola, followed by the Canaveral National Seashore. Approximately 110 facilities are operated by the Division of Recreation and Parks of the state's Department of Natural Resources.

These facilities include 28 state parks, 28 state recreation areas, and 18 state historical sites. Fishing and boating are major recreational activities at these sites. Florida has more waterparks than anywhere else in the United States: Adventure Island in Tampa; Water Mania in Kissimmee; Disney's Blizzard Beach in Lake Buena Vista; and Wet 'N Wild in Orlando, to name a few.

In the 1970s and early 1980s, the Miami Beach tourist hotels faced increasing competition from Caribbean and Latin American resorts. The city's business community, seeking to boost tourism, strongly backed a 1978 statewide referendum to authorize casino gambling along part of Collins Avenue in Miami Beach and Hollywood; however, the proposal was defeated by a wide margin. In a local advisory referendum in March 1980, Miami Beach voters approved development in South Beach of an $850 million, 250-acre (100-hectare) complex that included hotels and a convention center. Off-track betting, horse racing (four thoroughbred racetracks and one harness racetrack), dog racing (18 greyhound tracks), jai alai (nine frontons), and bingo are all legalized and operative forms of gaming. NASCAR has a huge presence in Florida. The Richard Petty Driving Experience, where courses are offered on a real race course, is located in Walt Disney World Speedway in Orlando. Major League Baseball has spring training in several Florida cities.

⁴⁸SPORTS

Florida has nine major professional sports teams: the Miami Dolphins, Tampa Bay Buccaneers, and Jacksonville Jaguars of the National Football League (NFL); the Miami Heat and the Orlando Magic of the National Basketball Association (NBA); the Tampa Bay Lightning and the Florida Panthers of the National Hockey League; and the Florida Marlins and the Tampa Bay Devil Rays of Major League Baseball. Two Women's National Basketball Association teams and two Major League Soccer teams folded or relocated in 2002. The Miami Heat won the NBA Championship in 2006. Of the football teams, the Dolphins have been by far the most successful, winning the Super Bowl in 1973 (following the NFL's only undefeated season) and 1974, and appearing in three other Super Bowls (in 1972, 1983, and 1985). The Tampa Bay Buccaneers captured a Super Bowl title in 2003, their first ever since joining the NFL in the 1970s. The Florida Marlins won the World Series in 1997 and 2003. Many Major League Baseball teams have their spring training camps in Florida and play exhibition games (in the "Grapefruit League") in the spring.

Several tournaments on both the men's and women's professional golf tours are played in Florida. In auto racing, the Daytona 500 is a top race on the NASCAR Nextel Cup circuit, and the Pennzoil 400 is run at the Homestead-Miami Speedway, while the 24 Hours of Daytona is one of the top sports car races in the world. Three of the major collegiate football bowl games are played in the state: the Orange Bowl in Miami, the Gator Bowl in Jacksonville, and the Florida Citrus Bowl in Orlando.

In collegiate sports, football dominates. The University of Florida, Florida State, and the University of Miami all emerged as nationally ranked powerhouses in the 1980s and 1990s. Miami won the Orange Bowl in 1946, 1984, 1988, 1989, 1992, and 2004, the Sugar Bowl in 1990 and 2001; the Gator Bowl in 2000; and the Cotton Bowl in 1991. The Hurricanes were named national champions in 1983, 1987, 1989, 1991, and 2001. Florida State won the

Orange Bowl in 1993, 1994, and 1996; the Sugar Bowl in 1989, 1998, and 2000; and the Cotton Bowl in 1992. The Seminoles were named national champions in 1993 and 1999. The University of Florida won the Orange Bowl in 1967, 1999, and 2002; the Gator Bowl in 1984 and 1993; the Florida Citrus Bowl in 1998; the Sugar Bowl in 1994; it defeated Florida State in the 1997 Sugar Bowl to win the national championship.

Other annual sporting events include rodeos in Arcadia and Kissimmee and the Pepsi 400 Auto Race in Daytona Beach. Emmitt Smith, Steve Carlton, Chris Evert, and Tracy McGrady were all born in the Sunshine State.

⁴⁹FAMOUS FLORIDIANS

The first Floridian to serve in a presidential cabinet was Alan S. Boyd (b.1922), named the first secretary of transportation (1967–69) by President Lyndon Johnson. Florida also produced one of the major US military figures of World War II, General Joseph Warren Stilwell (1883–1946), dubbed "Vinegar Joe" for his strongly stated opinions. Graduated from West Point in 1904, he served in France during World War I. First posted to China in the 1920s, he became chief of staff to General Chiang Kai-shek and commander of US forces in the China-Burma-India theater during World War II. He was promoted to full general in 1944 but forced to leave China because of his criticism of the Chiang Kai-shek regime. Janet Reno (b.1938), attorney general of the United States in the Clinton administration, was born in Miami.

David Levy Yulee (b.St. Thomas, 1810–86) came to Florida in 1824 and, after serving in the US House of Representatives, was appointed one of the state's first two US senators in 1845, thereby becoming the first Jew to sit in the Senate. He resigned in 1861 to serve in the Confederate Congress. Yulee built the first cross-state railroad, from Fernandina to Cedar Key, in the late 1860s. Ruth Bryan Owen Rohde (b.Illinois, 1885–1954), a longtime Miami resident and member of the US House of Representatives (1929–33), in 1933 became the first woman to head a US diplomatic office abroad when she was named minister to Denmark.

Prominent governors of Florida include Richard Keith Call (b.Virginia, 1792–1862), who came to Florida with General Andrew Jackson in 1821 and remained to become governor of the territory in 1826–39 and 1841–44. In the summer of 1836, Call commanded the US campaign against the Seminole. Although a southerner and a slaveholder, he steadfastly opposed secession. Napoleon Bonaparte Broward (1857–1910) was, before becoming governor, a ship's pilot, and owner of St. Johns River boats. He used one of these, *The Three Friends*, a powerful seagoing tug, to run guns and ammunition to Cuban rebels in 1896. As governor (1905–09), he was noted for a populist program that included railroad regulation, direct elections, state college reorganization and coordination, and drainage of the Everglades under state auspices. As governor in 1955–61, Thomas LeRoy Collins (1909–91) met the desegregation issue by advocating moderation and respect for the law, helping the state avoid violent confrontations. He served as chairman of both the southern and national governors' conferences, and he was named by President Johnson as the first director of the Community Relations Service under the 1964 Civil Rights Act.

Military figures who have played a major role in Florida's history include the Spanish conquistadors Juan Ponce de León (c.1460–1521), the European discoverer of Florida, and Pedro Menéndez de Avilés (1519–74), founder of the first permanent settlement, St. Augustine. Andrew Jackson (b.South Carolina, 1767–1845), a consistent advocate of US seizure of Florida, led military expeditions into the territory in 1814 and 1818 and, after US acquisition, served briefly in 1821 as Florida's military governor before leaving for Tennessee. During the Seminole War of 1835–42, one of the leading military tacticians was Osceola (c.1800–1838), who, although neither born a chief nor elected to that position, rose to the leadership of the badly divided Seminole by force of character and personality. He rallied them to fierce resistance to removal, making skillful use of guerrilla tactics. Captured under a flag of truce in 1837, he was imprisoned; already broken in health, he died in Fort Moultrie in Charleston harbor. During the Civil War, General Edmund Kirby Smith (1824–93), a native of St. Augustine who graduated from West Point in 1845, served as commander (1863–65) of Confederate forces west of the Mississippi River. He surrendered the last of the southern forces at Galveston, Texas, on 26 May 1865.

Among the late-19th-century entrepreneurs who played significant roles in Florida's development, perhaps the most important was Henry Morrison Flagler (b.New York, 1830–1913). Flagler made a fortune in Ohio as an associate of John D. Rockefeller in the Standard Oil Co. and did not even visit Florida until he was in his 50s. However, in the 1880s he began to acquire and build railroads down the length of Florida's east coast and to develop tourist hotels at various points, including St. Augustine, Palm Beach, and Miami, helping to create one of the state's major present-day industries. Henry Bradley Plant (b.Connecticut, 1819–99) did for Florida's west coast what Flagler did for the east. Plant extended railroad service to Tampa in 1884, built a huge tourist hotel there, developed the port facilities, and established steamship lines.

Among Floridians prominent in science was Dr. John F. Gorrie (b.South Carolina, 1802–55), who migrated to Apalachicola in 1833 and became a socially and politically prominent physician, specializing in the treatment of fevers. He blew air over ice brought in by ship from the north to cool the air in sickrooms, and he independently developed a machine to manufacture ice, only to have two others beat him to the patent office by days.

The noted labor and civil rights leader A. Philip Randolph (1889–1979) was a native of Crescent City. Mary McLeod Bethune (b.South Carolina, 1875–1955) was an adviser to President Franklin D. Roosevelt on minority affairs, became the first president (1935) of the National Council of Negro Women, and was a consultant at the 1945 San Francisco Conference that founded the United Nations. A prominent black educator, she opened a school for girls at Daytona Beach in 1904. The school merged with Cookman Institute in 1923 to become Bethune-Cookman College, which she headed until 1942 and again in 1946–47.

Prominent Florida authors include James Weldon Johnson (1871–1938), perhaps best known for his 1912 novel *Autobiography of an Ex-Colored Man*. He was also the first black to be admitted to the Florida bar (1897) and was a founder and secretary of the NAACP. Marjory Stoneman Douglas (b.Minnesota, 1890–1998), who came to Miami in 1915, is the author of several works reflecting her concern for the environment, including *The Everglades: River of Grass* (first published in 1947), *Hurricane* (1958), and *Florida: The Long Frontier* (1967). Marjorie Kinnan Rawlings (b.Washington, DC, 1895–1953) came to Florida in 1928 to do creative writing. After her first novel, *South Moon Under* (1933) came the Pulitzer Prize–winning *The Yearling* (1938), the poignant story of a 12-year-old boy on the Florida frontier in the 1870s. Zora Neale Hurston (1901–60), born in poverty in the all-Negro town of Eatonville and a graduate of Barnard College, spent four years collecting folklore, which she published in *Mules and Men* (1935) and *Tell My Horse* (1938).

Entertainers born in Florida include Sidney Poitier (b.1927), Charles Eugene "Pat" Boone (b.1934), Faye Dunaway (b.1941), and Ben Vereen (b.1946).

Florida's most famous sports figure is Chris Evert Lloyd (Christine Marie Evert, b.1953), who became a dominant force in women's tennis in the mid-1970s. After turning pro in 1973, she won the Wimbledon singles title in 1974, 1976, and 1981 and the US Open from 1975 to 1978 and in 1980 and 1982. She retired from tennis in 1990.

50 BIBLIOGRAPHY

Council of State Governments. *The Book of the States, 2006 Edition.* Lexington, Ky.: Council of State Governments, 2006.

Danese, Tracy E. *Claude Pepper and Ed Ball: Politics, Purpose, and Power.* Gainesville: University Press of Florida, 2000.

Davis, Jack E., and Raymond Arsenault (eds.). *Paradise Lost?: The Environmental History of Florida.* Gainesville: University Press of Florida, 2005.

DeGrove, John Melvin. *Planning Policy and Politics: Smart Growth and the States.* Cambridge, Mass.: Lincoln Institute of Land Policy, 2005.

Faherty, William Barnaby. *Florida's Space Coast: The Impact of NASA on the Sunshine State.* Gainesville: University Press of Florida, 2002.

Gannon, Michael (ed.). *The New History of Florida.* Gainesville, Fla.: University Presses of Florida, 1996.

Groene, Janet, and Gordon Groene. *Florida Guide.* Cold Spring Harbor, N.Y.: Open Road Publishing, 2000.

Jordan, Jeffrey L. *Interstate Water Allocation in Alabama, Florida, and Georgia.* Gainesville: University Press of Florida, 2006.

Lejeune, Jean-François. *The Making of Miami Beach, 1933–1942: The Architecture of Lawrence Murray Dixon.* Miami Beach, Fla.: Bass Museum of Art, 2000.

Mormino, Gary Ross. *Land of Sunshine, State of Dreams: A Social History of Modern Florida.* Gainesville: University Press of Florida, 2005.

Singletary, Wes. *Florida's First Big League Baseball Players: A Narrative History.* Charleston, S.C.: History Press, 2006.

US Department of Commerce, Economics and Statistics Administration, US Census Bureau. *Florida, 2000. Summary Social, Economic, and Housing Characteristics: 2000 Census of Population and Housing.* Washington, D.C.: US Government Printing Office, 2003.

Williams, Horace Randall (ed.). *No Man's Yoke on My Shoulders: Personal Accounts of Slavery in Florida.* Winston-Salem, N.C.: John F. Blair, 2006.

GEORGIA

State of Georgia

ORIGIN OF STATE NAME: Named for King George II of England in 1732. **NICKNAME:** The Empire State of the South; the Peach State. **CAPITAL:** Atlanta. **ENTERED UNION:** 2 January 1788 (4th). **SONG:** "Georgia on My Mind." **MOTTO:** Wisdom, Justice and Moderation. **COAT OF ARMS:** Three columns support an arch inscribed with the word "Constitution;" intertwined among the columns is a banner bearing the state motto. Right of center stands a soldier with a drawn sword, representing the aid of the military in defending the Constitution. Surrounding the whole are the words "State of Georgia 1776." **FLAG:** The Georgia flag has two red stripes and one white stripe. The state coat of arms is on a blue field in the upper left corner. Flag adopted 8 May 2003. **OFFICIAL SEAL:** OBVERSE: same as the coat of arms. REVERSE: a sailing vessel and a smaller boat are offshore; on land, a man and horse plow a field, and sheep graze in the background. The scene is surrounded by the words "Agriculture and Commerce 1776." **BIRD:** Brown thrasher. **FISH:** Largemouth bass. **FLOWER:** Cherokee rose; azalea (wildflower). **TREE:** Live oak. **GEM:** Quartz. **LEGAL HOLIDAYS:** New Year's Day, 1 January; Birthday of Martin Luther King Jr., 3rd Monday in January; Confederate Memorial Day, 26 April; National Memorial Day, last Monday in May; Independence Day, 4 July; Labor Day, 1st Monday in September; Columbus Day, 2nd Monday in October; Veterans' Day, 11 November; Thanksgiving Day, 4th Thursday in November; Robert E. Lee's Birthday, 19 January (observed the day after Thanksgiving); Christmas Day, 25 December. **TIME:** 7 AM EST = noon GMT.

¹LOCATION, SIZE, AND EXTENT

Located in the southeastern United States, Georgia is the largest state east of the Mississippi River, and ranks 21st in size among the 50 states.

The total area of Georgia is 58,910 sq mi (152,576 sq km), of which land comprises 58,056 sq mi (150,365 sq km) and inland water 854 sq mi (2,211 sq km). Georgia extends 254 mi (409 km) E–W; the maximum N–S extension is 320 mi (515 km) E-W.

Georgia is bordered on the N by Tennessee and North Carolina; on the E by South Carolina (with the line formed by the Chattooga, Tugaloo, and Savannah rivers) and by the Atlantic Ocean; on the S by Florida (with the line in the SE defined by the St. Mary's River); and on the W by Alabama (separated in the SW by the Chattahoochee River). The state's geographic center is located in Twiggs County, 18 mi (29 km) SW of Macon.

The Sea Islands extend the length of the Georgia coast. The state's total boundary length is 1,039 mi (1,672 km).

²TOPOGRAPHY

Northern Georgia is mountainous, the central region is characterized by the rolling hills of the Piedmont Plateau, and southern Georgia is a nearly flat coastal plain.

The Blue Ridge Mountains tumble to an end in northern Georgia, where Brasstown Bald, at 4,784 ft (1,459 m), is the highest point in the state. The piedmont slopes slowly to the fall line, descending from about 2,000 ft (610 m) to 300 ft (90 m) above sea level. Stone Mountain, where a Confederate memorial is carved into a mass of solid granite 1,686 ft (514 m) high, is the region's most famous landmark. The mean elevation in the state is approximately 600 ft (183 m).

The piedmont region ends in a ridge of sand hills running across the state from Augusta to Columbus. The residue of an ancient ocean was caught in the vast shallow basin on the Florida border, known as the Okefenokee Swamp, which filled with fresh water over the centuries. The coastal plain, thinly populated except for towns at the mouths of inland rivers, ends in marshlands along the Atlantic Ocean. Sea level at the Atlantic Ocean is the lowest point of the state. Lying offshore are the Sea Islands, called the Golden Isles of Georgia, the most important of which are, from north to south, Tybee, Ossabaw, St. Catherines, Sapelo, St. Simons, Sea Island, Jekyll, and Cumberland.

Two great rivers rise in the northeast: the Savannah, which forms part of the border with South Carolina, and the Chattahoochee, which flows across the state to become the western boundary. The Flint joins the Chattahoochee at the southwestern corner of Georgia to form the Apalachicola, which flows through Florida into the Gulf of Mexico. The two largest rivers of central Georgia, the Ocmulgee and Oconee, flow together to form the Altamaha, which then flows eastward to the Atlantic. Perhaps the best-known Georgia river, though smaller than any of the above, is the Suwannee, flowing southwest through the Okefenokee Swamp, across Florida and into the Gulf of Mexico, and famous for its evocation in the song "Old Folks at Home" by Stephen Foster. Huge lakes created by dams on the Savannah River are Clark Hill Reservoir and Hartwell Lake; artificial lakes on the Chattahoochee River include Lake Seminole, Walter F. George Reservoir, Lake Harding, West Point Reservoir, and Lake Sidney Lanier.

³CLIMATE

The Chattahoochee River divides Georgia into separate climatic regions. The mountain region to the northwest is colder than the rest of Georgia, averaging 39°F (4°C) in January and 78°F (26°C) in July. The state experiences mild winters, ranging from a January average of 44°F (7°C) in the piedmont to 54°F (12°C) on the coast. Summers are hot in the piedmont and on the coast, with July temperatures averaging 80°F (27°C) or above. The record high is 113°F (45°C) at Greenville on 27 May 1978; the record low is -17°F (-27°C), registered in Floyd County on 27 January 1940.

Humidity is high, ranging from 82% in the morning to 56% in the afternoon in Atlanta. Rainfall varies considerably from year to year but averages 50 in (127 cm) annually in the lowlands, increasing to 75 in (191 cm) in the mountains; snow falls occasionally in the interior. Tornadoes are an annual threat in mountain areas, and Georgia beaches are exposed to hurricane tides.

The growing season is approximately 185 days in the mountains and a generous 300 days in southern Georgia.

⁴FLORA AND FAUNA

Georgia has some 250 species of trees, 90% of which are of commercial importance. White and scrub pines, chestnut, northern red oak, and buckeye cover the mountain zone, while loblolly and shortleaf (yellow) pines and whiteback maple are found throughout the piedmont. Pecan trees grow densely in southern Georgia, and white oak and cypress are plentiful in the eastern part of the state. Trees found throughout the state include red cedar, scalybark and white hickories, red maple, sycamore, yellow poplar, sassafras, sweet and black gums, and various dogwoods and magnolias. Common flowering shrubs include yellow jasmine, flowering quince, and mountain laurel. Spanish moss grows abundantly on the coast and around the streams and swamps of the entire coastal plain. Kudzu vines, originally from Asia, are ubiquitous.

Prominent among Georgia fauna is the white-tailed (Virginia) deer, found in some 50 counties. Other common mammals are the black bear, muskrat, raccoon opossum, mink, common cottontail, and three species of squirrel—fox, gray, and flying. No fewer than 160 bird species breed in Georgia, among them the mockingbird, brown thrasher (the state bird), and numerous sparrows; the Okefenokee Swamp is home to the sandhill piper, snowy egret, and white ibis. The bobwhite quail is the most popular game bird. There are 79 species of reptile, including such poisonous snakes as the rattler, copperhead, and cottonmouth moccasin. The state's 63 amphibian species consist mainly of various salamanders, frogs, and toads. The most popular freshwater game fish are trout, bream, bass, and catfish, all but the last of which are produced in state hatcheries for restocking. Dolphins, porpoises, shrimp, oysters, and blue crabs are found off the Georgia coast.

The Okefenokee Swamp (which extends into Georgia) supports 233 bird species, 48 mammal species, 66 reptile species, 37 amphibian species, and 36 fish species. One of the largest US populations of the American alligator can be found there as well.

The state lists 58 protected plants, of which 23—including hairy rattleweed, Alabama leather flower, smooth coneflower, two species of quillwort, pondberry, Canby's dropwort, harperella, fringed campion, and two species of trillium—are endangered. In April 2006, a total of 60 species occurring within the state were on the threatened and endangered species list of the US Fish and Wildlife Service. These included 38 animal (vertebrates and invertebrates) and 22 plant species, such as the bald eagle, eastern indigo snake, West Indian manatee, four species of moccasinshell, five species of turtle, wood stork, three species of whale, red-cockaded woodpecker, and shortnose sturgeon.

⁵ENVIRONMENTAL PROTECTION

In the early 1970s, environmentalists pointed to the fact that the Savannah River had been polluted by industrial waste and that an estimated 58% of Georgia's citizens lived in districts lacking adequate sewage treatment facilities. In 1972, at the prodding of Governor Jimmy Carter, the General Assembly created the Environmental Protection Division (EPD) within the Department of Natural Resources (DNR). This agency administers 21 state environmental laws, most of them passed during the 1970s: the Water Quality Control Act, the Safe Drinking Water Act, the Groundwater Use Act, the Surface Water Allocation Act, the Air Quality Act, the Safe Dams Act, the Asbestos Safety Act, the Vehicle Inspection and Maintenance Act, the Hazardous Site Response Act, the Comprehensive Solid Waste Management Act, the Scrap Tire Amendment, the Underground Storage Tank Act, the Hazardous Waste Management Act, the Sedimentation and Erosion Control Act, the River Basin Management Plans, the Water Well Standards Act, the Oil and Hazardous Materials Spill Act, the Georgia Environmental Policy Act, the Surface Mining Act, and the Oil and Gas and the Deep Drilling Act. The EPD issues all environmental permits, with the exception of those required by the Marshlands Protection and Shore Assistance Acts, which are enforced by the Coastal Resources Division of the DNR.

As of 1997, the state had 7.7 million acres of wetlands. The Okefenokee Swamp (which extends into Florida) was designated in 1986; it is the second largest wetland in the nation. The site is federally owned and managed, in part, under the Okefenokee Wilderness Act of 1974.

Georgia's greatest environmental problems are an increasingly scarce water supply, nonpoint source water pollution, and hazardous waste sites. In 2003, the US US Environment Protection Agency (EPA) (EPA) database listed 408 hazardous waste sites in Georgia, 15 of which were on the National Priorities List as of 2006, including the Robins Air Force Base landfill in Houston County and the Marine Corps Logistics Base in Albany. In 2005, the EPA spent over $9.6 million through the Superfund program for the cleanup of hazardous waste sites in the state. In 2003, 126.7 million lb of toxic chemicals were released in the state. In 2005, federal EPA grants awarded to the state included over $13 million to be offered as loans for water quality and protection projects.

⁶POPULATION

Georgia ranked ninth in population in the United States with an estimated total of 9,072,576 in 2005, an increase of 10.8% since 2000. Between 1990 and 2000, Georgia's population grew from 6,478,453 to 8,186,453, an increase of 26.4% and the fourth-largest population gain among the 50 states for this period. The popu-

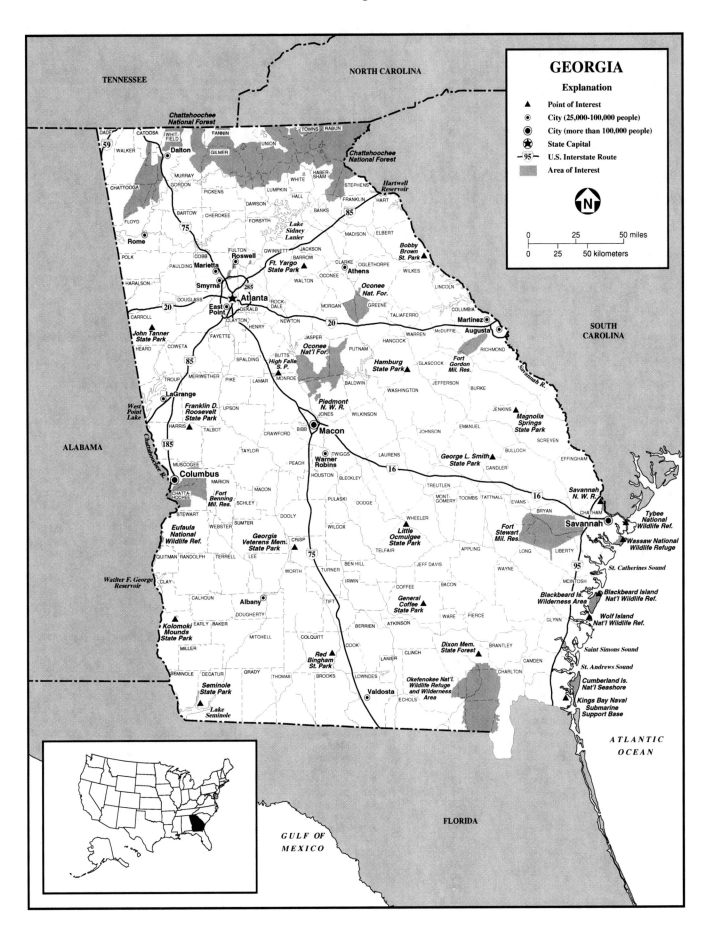

Georgia—Counties, County Seats, and Country Areas and Populations

COUNTY	COUNTY SEAT	LAND AREA (SQ MI)	POPULATION (2005 EST.)	COUNTY	COUNTY SEAT	LAND AREA (SQ MI)	POPULATION (2005 EST.)
Appling	Baxley	510	17,954	Hall	Gainesville	379	165,771
Atkinson	Pearson	344	8,030	Hancock	Sparta	469	9,643
Bacon	Alma	286	10,379	Haralson	Buchanan	283	28,338
Baker	Newton	347	4,154	Harris	Hamilton	464	27,779
Baldwin	Milledgeville	258	45,230	Hart	Hartwell	230	24,036
Banks	Homer	234	16,055	Heard	Franklin	292	11,346
Barrow	Winder	163	59,954	Henry	McDonough	321	167,848
Bartow	Cartersville	456	89,229	Houston	Perry	380	126,163
Ben Hill	Fitzerald	254	17,316	Irwin	Ocilla	362	10,093
Berrien	Nashville	456	16,708	Jackson	Jefferson	342	52,292
Bibb	Macon	253	154,918	Jasper	Monticello	371	13,147
Bleckley	Cochran	219	12,141	Jeff Davis	Hazlehurst	335	13,083
Brantley	Nahunta	444	15,491	Jefferson	Louisville	529	16,926
Brooks	Quitman	491	16,327	Jenkins	Millen	353	8,729
Bryan	Pembroke	441	28,549	Johnson	Wrightsville	307	9,538
Bulloch	Statesboro	678	61,454	Jones	Gray	394	26,836
Burke	Waynesboro	833	23,299	Lamar	Barnesville	186	16,378
Butts	Jackson	187	21,045	Lanier	Lakeland	194	7,553
Calhoun	Morgan	284	5,972	Laurens	Dublin	816	46,896
Camden	Woodbine	649	45,759	Lee	Leesburg	358	31,099
Candler	Metter	248	10,321	Liberty	Hinesville	517	57,544
Carroll	Carrollton	502	105,453	Lincoln	Lincolnton	196	8,207
Catoosa	Ringgold	163	60,813	Long	Ludowici	402	11,083
Charlton	Folkston	780	10,790	Lowndes	Valdosta	507	96,705
Chatham	Savannah	444	238,410	Lumpkin	Dahlonega	287	24,324
Chattahoochee	Cusseta	250	14,679	Macon	Oglethorpe	404	13,745
Chattooga	Summerville	314	26,570	Madison	Danielsville	285	27,289
Cherokee	Canton	424	184,211	Marion	Buena Vista	366	7,244
Clarke	Athens	122	104,439	McDuffie	Thomson	256	21,743
Clay	Ft. Gaines	197	3,242	McIntosh	Darien	425	11,068
Clayton	Jonesboro	148	267,966	Meriwether	Greenville	506	22,919
Clinch	Homerville	821	6,996	Miller	Colquitt	284	6,228
Cobb	Marietta	343	663,818	Mitchell	Camilla	512	23,791
Coffee	Douglas	602	39,674	Monroe	Forsyth	397	23,785
Colquitt	Moultrie	556	43,915	Montgomery	Mt. Vernon	244	8,909
Columbia	Appling	290	103,812	Morgan	Madison	349	17,492
Cook	Adel	232	16,366	Murray	Chatsworth	345	40,812
Coweta	Newman	444	109,903	Muscogee	Columbus	218	185,271
Crawford	Knoxville	328	12,874	Newton	Covington	277	86,713
Crisp	Cordele	275	22,017	Oconee	Watkinsville	186	29,748
Dade	Trenton	176	16,040	Oglethorpe	Lexington	442	13,609
Dawson	Dawsonville	210	19,731	Paulding	Dallas	312	112,411
Decatur	Bainbridge	586	28,618	Peach	Ft. Valley	151	24,794
DeKalb	Decatur	270	677,959	Pickens	Jasper	232	28,442
Dodge	Eastman	504	19,574	Pierce	Blackshear	344	17,119
Dooly	Vienna	397	11,749	Pike	Zebulon	219	16,128
Dougherty	Albany	330	94,882	Polk	Cedartown	312	40,479
Douglas	Douglasville	203	112,760	Pulaski	Hawkinsville	249	9,737
Early	Blakely	516	12,056	Putnam	Eatonton	344	19,829
Echols	Statenville	420	4,253	Quitman	Georgetown	146	2,467
Effingham	Springfield	482	46,924	Rabun	Clayton	370	16,087
Elbert	Elberton	367	20,799	Randolph	Cuthbert	431	7,310
Emanuel	Swainsboro	688	22,108	Richmond	Augusta	326	195,769
Evans	Claxton	186	11,443	Rockdale	Conyers	132	78,545
Fannin	Blue Ridge	384	21,887	Schley	Ellaville	169	4,122
Fayette	Fayetteville	199	104,248	Screven	Sylvania	655	15,430
Floyd	Rome	519	94,198	Seminole	Donalsonville	225	9,226
Forsyth	Cumming	226	140,393	Spalding	Griffin	199	61,289
Franklin	Carnesville	264	21,590	Stephens	Toccoa	177	25,060
Fulton	Atlanta*	534	915,623	Stewart	Lumpkin	452	4,882
Gilmer	Ellijay	427	27,335	Sumter	Americus	488	32,912
Glascock	Gibson	144	2,705	Talbot	Talbotton	395	6,709
Glynn	Brunswick	412	71,874	Taliaferro	Crawfordville	196	1,826
Gordon	Calhoun	355	50,279	Tattnall	Reidsville	484	23,211
Grady	Cairo	459	24,466	Taylor	Butler	382	8,887
Greene	Greensboro	390	15,693	Telfair	MacRae	444	13,205
Gwinnett	Lawrenceville	435	726,273	Terrell	Dawson	337	10,711
Habersham	Clarkesville	278	39,603	Thomas	Thomasville	551	44,692

Georgia—Counties, County Seats, and County Areas and Populations (cont.)

COUNTY	COUNTY SEAT	LAND AREA (SQ MI)	POPULATION (2005 EST.)	COUNTY	COUNTY SEAT	LAND AREA (SQ MI)	POPULATION (2005 EST.)
Tift	Tifton	268	40,793	Warren	Warrenton	286	6,101
Toombs	Lyons	371	27,274	Washington	Sandersville	683	20,118
Towns	Hiawassee	165	10,315	Wayne	Jesup	647	28,390
Treutlen	Soperton	202	6,753	Webster	Perston	210	2,289
Troup	La Grange	415	62,015	Wheeler	Alamo	299	6,706
Turner	Ashburn	289	9,474	White	Cleveland	242	24,055
Twiggs	Jeffersonville	362	10,299	Whitfield	Dalton	291	90,889
Union	Blairsville	320	19,782	Wilcox	Abbeville	382	8,721
Upson	Thomaston	326	27,679	Wilkes	Washington	470	10,457
Walker	La Fayette	446	63,890	Wilkinson	Irwinton	451	10,143
Walton	Monroe	330	75,647	Worth	Sylvester	575	21,996
Ware	Waycross	970	34,492	**TOTALS**		58,123	9,072,576

lation is projected to reach 10.2 million by 2015 and 11.4 million by 2025. The population density was 153.4 per sq mi in 2004.

During the first half of the 18th century, restrictive government policies discouraged settlement. In 1752, when Georgia became a royal colony, the population numbered only 3,500, of whom 500 were blacks. Growth was rapid thereafter, and by 1773, there were 33,000 people, almost half of them black. The American Revolution brought free land and an influx of settlers, so that by 1800 the population had swelled to 162,686. Georgia passed the 1 million mark by 1860, the 2 million mark by 1900, and by 1960, the population had doubled again. Georgia's population increased 19% between 1980 and 1990.

In 2004, the median age was 34. Over 26.4% of the population was under the age of 18, while 9.6% was age 65 or older.

There has always been a strained relationship between rural and urban Georgians, and the state's political system long favored the rural population. Since before the American Revolution, the city people have called country folk "crackers," a term that implies a lack of good manners and may derive from the fact that these pioneers drove their cattle before them with whips.

The state's three largest cities in 2004 were Atlanta, with an estimated population of 419,122; Columbus, 182,850; and Savannah, 129,808. The Atlanta metropolitan area had an estimated population of 4,708,297.

7 ETHNIC GROUPS

Georgia has been fundamentally a white/black state, with minimal ethnic diversity. Most Georgians are of English or Scotch-Irish descent. The number of Georgians who were foreign born rose dramatically between 1990 and 2000, from 173,126 (or 2.6% of the population) to 577,273 (7.1%). The 1990 figure was, in turn, a considerable increase over the 1980 total of 91,480 foreign-born Georgians and the 1970 figure of 33,000.

Between 1970 and 2000, the number of Georgians from Asia or the Pacific Islands increased from 8,838 in 1970 to 24,461 in 1980, to 76,000 in 1990, and to an estimated 177,416 in 2000 (173,170 Asians and 4,246 Pacific Islanders). In 2000, Asian Indians were the largest group, with a population of 46,132, followed by Vietnamese (29,016, up from 6,284 in 1990), Koreans (28,745), and Chinese (27,446). In 2004, 2.6% of the population was Asian and 0.1% was Native Hawaiian or other Pacific Islander.

Georgia's black population declined from a high of 47% of the total population in 1880 to about 26% in 1970, when there were 1,187,149 blacks. Black citizens accounted for 27% of the total population and numbered 1,747,000 in 1990. In 2000, the black population was estimated at 2,349,542, or 28.7% of the state total, the third-largest black population among the 50 states. By 2004, 29.6% of the population was black. Atlanta, which had 255,689 black residents (61.4%) in 2000, has been a significant center for the development of black leadership, especially at Atlanta University. With its long-established black elite, Atlanta has also been a locus for large black-owned business enterprises. There are elected and appointed blacks in the state government, and in 1973, Atlanta elected its first black mayor, Maynard Jackson. By 1984, there were 13 black mayors, including Andrew J. Young of Atlanta.

The American Indian population in Georgia was estimated to be 21,737 in 2000. The great Cherokee Nation and other related tribes had been effectively removed from the state 150 years earlier. In 2004, 0.3% of the population was American Indian. About 5.3% of the population (435,227 people) was of Hispanic or Latino origin as of 2000. That figure had increased to 6.8% by 2004. In 2004, 1% of the population reported origin of two or more races.

8 LANGUAGES

The first Europeans entering what is now Georgia found it occupied almost entirely by Creek Indians of the Muskogean branch of Hokan-Siouan stock. Removed by treaty to Indian Territory after their uprising in 1813, the Creek left behind only such places-names as Chattahoochee, Chattooga, and Okefenokee. Except for the South Midland speech of the extreme northern up-country, Georgia English is typically Southern. Loss of the /r/ after a vowel in the same syllable is common. The diphthong /ai/ as in *right* is so simplified that Northern speakers hear the word as rat. *Can't* rhymes with *paint*, and *borrow, forest, foreign,* and *orange* all have the /ah/ vowel as in *father*. However, a highly unusual variety of regional differences, most of them in long vowels and diphthongs, makes a strong contrast between northern up-country and southern low-country speech. In such words as *care* and *stairs,* for example, many up-country speakers have a vowel like that in *cat,* while many low-country speakers have a vowel like that in *pane*.

In general, northern Georgia *snake doctor* contrasts with southern Georgia *mosquito hawk* (dragonfly), *goobers* with *pinders* (peanuts), *French harp* with *harmonica, plum peach* with *press peach* (both clingstone peaches), *nicker* with *whicker* for a horse's neigh, and *sallet* with *salad.* In Atlanta a big sandwich is a *poorboy;* in Savannah, a peach pit is a *kernel.*

A distinctive variety of black English, called Gullah, is spoken in the islands off the Georgia and South Carolina coast, to which Creole-speaking slaves escaped from the mainland during the 17th and 18th centuries. Characteristic grammatical features include a lack of inflection in the personal pronoun, the invariant form of the *be* verb, and the absence of the final *s* in the third person singular of the present tense. Many of the private personal names stem directly from West African languages.

In 2000, 6,843,038 Georgians—90.1% of the population five years old and older—spoke only English at home, down from 95.2% in 1990.

The following table gives selected statistics from the 2000 Census for language spoken at home by persons five years old and over. The category "African languages" includes Amharic, Ibo, Twi, Yoruba, Bantu, Swahili, and Somali. The category "Other Indic languages" includes Bengali, Marathi, Punjabi, and Romany. The category "Other Asian languages" includes Dravidian languages, Malayalam, Telugu, Tamil, and Turkish.

LANGUAGE	NUMBER	PERCENT
Population 5 years and over	**7,594,476**	**100.0**
Speak only English	6,843,038	90.1
Speak a language other than English	751,438	9.9
Speak a language other than English	**751,438**	**9.9**
Spanish or Spanish Creole	426,115	5.6
French (incl. Patois, Cajun)	43,428	0.6
German	32,777	0.4
Vietnamese	27,671	0.4
Korean	25,814	0.3
African languages	24,752	0.3
Chinese	23,812	0.3
Gujarathi	11,133	0.1
Other Indic languages	9,473	0.1
Other Asian languages	8,673	0.1
Arabic	8,557	0.1
Japanese	8,257	0.1
Hindi	7,596	0.1
Tagalog	7,308	0.1
Russian	7,175	0.1
Urdu	7,109	0.1

[9] RELIGIONS

The Church of England was the established church in colonial Georgia. During this period, European Protestants were encouraged to immigrate and German Lutherans and Moravians took advantage of the opportunity. Roman Catholics were barred and Jews were not welcomed, but persons of both denominations came anyway. In the mid-18th century, George Whitefield, called the Great Itinerant, helped touch off the Great Awakening, the religious revival out of which came the Methodist and Baptist denominations. Daniel Marshall, the first "separate" Baptist in Georgia, established a church near Kiokee Creek in 1772. Some 16 years later, James Asbury formed the first Methodist Conference in Georgia.

The American Revolution resulted in the lessening of the authority of Anglicanism and a great increase in the number of Baptists, Methodists, and Presbyterians. During the 19th century, fundamentalist sects were especially strong among blacks. Roman Catholics from Maryland, Ireland, and Hispaniola formed a numerically small but important element in the cities, and Jewish citizens were active in the leadership of Savannah and Augusta. Catholics and Jews enjoyed general acceptance from the early 1800s until the first two decades of the 20th century, when they became the targets of political demagogues, notably Thomas E. Watson.

In 2000, most of the religious adherents in the state were Evangelical Protestants with the Southern Baptist Convention claiming 1,719,484 adherents in about 3,233 congregations; there were 34,227 newly baptized members in 2002. Mainline Protestants included 476,727 United Methodists (in 2004), 105,774 USA Presbyterians (2000), and 71,950 Episcopalians (2000). Roman Catholic adherents in 2004 numbered about 447,126. Judaism claimed about 93,500 adherents in 2000, and there were about 38,882 Muslims the same year. Only 16 Buddhist and 15 Hindu congregations were reported, without membership numbers. About 55.2% of the population was not counted as part of any religious organization.

[10] TRANSPORTATION

Georgia's location between the Appalachian Mountains and the Atlantic Ocean makes it the link between the eastern seaboard and the Gulf states. In the 18th century, Carolina fur traders crossed the Savannah River at the site of Augusta and followed trails to the Mississippi River. Pioneer farmers soon followed the same trails and used the many river tributaries to send their produce to Savannah, Georgia's first great depot. Beginning in 1816, steamboats plied the inland rivers, but they never replaced the older shallow-drafted Petersburg boats, propelled by poles.

From the 1830s onward, businessmen in the eastern cities of Savannah, Augusta, and Brunswick built railroads west to maintain their commerce. The two principal lines, the Georgia and the Central of Georgia, were required by law to make connection with a state-owned line, the Western and Atlantic, at the new town of Atlanta, which in 1847 became the link between Georgia and the Ohio Valley. By the Civil War, Georgia, with more miles of railroad than any other Deep South state, was a vital link between the eastern and western sectors of the Confederacy. After the war, the railroads contributed to urban growth as towns sprang up along their routes. Trackage increased from 4,532 mi (7,294 km) in 1890 to 7,591 mi (12,217 km) in 1920. But with competition from motor carriers, total trackage declined to 4,848 rail mi (7,805 km) by 2003. In the same year, CSX and Norfolk Southern were the only Class I railroads operating within the state. As of 2006, Amtrak provided east–west service through Atlanta, and north–south service through Savannah. In 1979, Atlanta inaugurated the first mass-transit system in the state, including the South's first subway.

Georgia's old intracoastal waterway carries about 1 million tons of shipping annually and is also used by pleasure craft and fishing vessels. Savannah's modern port facilities handled 28.176 million tons of cargo in 2004, making it the state's main deepwater port and the 28th busiest port in the Unites States. The coastal cities of Brunswick and St. Mary's also have deepwater docks. In 2004, Georgia had 721 mi (1,160 km) of navigable inland waterways. In 2003, waterborne shipments totaled 25.356 million tons.

In the 1920s, Georgia became the gateway to Florida for motorists. Today, I-75 is the main route from Atlanta to Florida, and I-20 is the major east–west highway. Both cross at Atlanta with I-85, which proceeds southeast from South Carolina to Alabama. I-95 stretches along the coast from South Carolina through Savannah to Jacksonville, Florida. During the 1980s, Atlanta invested $1.4 billion in a freeway expansion program that permitted capacity to double. In 2004, Georgia had 116,917 mi (188,236 km) of public roads, some 7.896 million registered motor vehicles, and 5,793,143 licensed drivers.

In 2005, Georgia had a total of 455 public and private-use aviation-related facilities. This included 341 airports, 109 heliports, 4 STOLports (Short Take-Off and Landing), and 1 seaplane base. Hartsfield-Jackson Atlanta International Airport is the air traffic hub in the Southeast and in 2004 was the busiest airport in the United States with 41,123,857 enplanements.

11 HISTORY

The history of what is now Georgia was influenced by two great prehistoric events: first, the upheaval that produced the mountains of the north, and second, the overflow of an ancient ocean that covered and flattened much of the rest of the state. Human beings have inhabited Georgia for at least 12,000 years. The first nomadic hunters were replaced by shellfish eaters who lived along the rivers. Farming communities later grew up at these sites, reaching their height in the Master Farmer culture about AD 800. These Native Americans left impressive mounds at Ocmulgee, near Macon, and at Etowah, north of Atlanta.

During the colonial period, the most important Indian tribes were the Creek, who lived along the central and western rivers, and the Cherokee, who lived in the mountains. By clever diplomacy, the Creek were able to maintain their position as the fulcrum of power between the English on the one hand and the French and Spanish on the other. With the ascendancy of the English and the achievement of statehood, however, the Creek lost their leverage and were expelled from Georgia in 1826. The Cherokee sought to adopt the white man's ways in their effort to avoid expulsion or annihilation. Thanks to their remarkable linguist Sequoyah, they learned to write their own language, later running their own newspaper, the *Cherokee Phoenix,* and their own schools. Some even owned slaves. Unfortunately for the Cherokee, gold was discovered on their lands; the Georgia state legislature confiscated their territory and outlawed the system of self-government the Cherokee had developed during the 1820s. Despite a ruling by the US Supreme Court, handed down by Chief Justice John Marshall, that Georgia had acted illegally, federal and state authorities expelled the Cherokee between 1832 and 1838. Thousands died on the march to Indian Territory (Oklahoma), known ever since as the Trail of Tears.

Georgia's first European explorer was Hernando de Soto of Spain, who in 1540 crossed the region looking for the fabled Seven Cities of Gold. French Huguenots under Jean Ribault claimed the Georgia coast in 1562 but were driven out by the Spanish captain Pedro Menéndez Avilés in 1564, who by 1586 had established the mission of Santa Catalina de Gaule on St. Catherines Island. (The ruins of this mission—the oldest European settlement in Georgia—were discovered by archaeologists in 1982.) By 1700, Jesuit and Franciscan missionaries had established an entire chain of missions along the Sea Islands and on the lower Chattahoochee.

From Charles Town, in the Carolina Colony, the English challenged Spain for control of the region, and by 1702 they had forced the Spaniards back to St. Augustine, Florida. In 1732, after the English had become convinced of the desirability of locating a buffer between the valuable rice-growing colony of Carolina and Indian-held lands to the south and west, King George II granted a charter to a group called the Trustees for Establishing the Colony of Georgia in America. The best known of the trustees was the soldier-politician and philanthropist James Edward Oglethorpe. His original intention was to send debtors from English prisons to Georgia, but Parliament refused to support the idea. Instead, Georgia was to be a place where the industrious poor would produce those things England needed, such as silk and wine, and would guard the frontier. Rum and slavery were expressly prohibited.

Oglethorpe and the first settlers landed at Yamacraw Bluff on 12 February 1733 and were given a friendly reception by a small band of Yamacraw Indians and their chief, Tomochichi. Oglethorpe is best remembered for laying out the town of Savannah in a unique design, featuring numerous plazas that still delight tourists today; however, as a military man, his main interest was defending the colony against the Spanish. After war was declared in 1739, Oglethorpe conducted an unsuccessful siege of St. Augustine. The Spaniards counterattacked at Oglethorpe's fortified town of Frederica on St. Simons Island in July 1742 but were repulsed in a confused encounter known as the Battle of Bloody Marsh, which ended Spanish threats to the British colonies. Soon afterward, Oglethorpe returned permanently to England.

The trustees' restrictions on rum and slavery were gradually removed, and in 1752, control over Georgia reverted to Parliament. Georgia thus became a royal colony, its society, like that of Carolina, shaped by the planting of rice, indigo, and cotton. After the French and Indian War, settlers began to pour into the Georgia backcountry above Augusta. Because these back-country pioneers depended on the royal government for protection against the Indians, they were reluctant to join the protests by Savannah merchants against new British mercantile regulations. When war came, however, the backcountry seized the opportunity to wrest political control of the new state away from Savannah.

Georgians spent the first three years of the Revolutionary War in annual attempts to invade Florida, each of them unsuccessful. The British turned their attention to Georgia late in 1778, reestablishing control of the state as far as Briar Creek, midway between Savannah and Augusta. After a combined French and American force failed to retake Savannah in October 1779, the city was used by the British as a base from which to recapture Charleston, in present-day South Carolina, and to extend their control further inland. For a year, most of Georgia was under British rule, and there was talk of making the restoration permanent in the peace settlement. However, Augusta was retaken in June 1781, and independent government was restored. A year later, the British were forced out of Savannah.

With Augusta as the new capital of Georgia, a period of rapid expansion began. Georgia ratified the US Constitution on 2 January 1788, the fourth state to do so. The invention of the cotton gin by Eli Whitney in 1793 made cotton cultivation profitable in the lands east of the Oconee River, relinquished by the Creek Indians under the Treaty of New York three years earlier. A mania for land speculation climaxed in the mid-1790s with the Yazoo Fraud, in which the state legislature sold 50 million acres (20 million hectares), later the states of Alabama and Mississippi, to land companies of which many of the legislators were members.

Georgia surrendered its lands west of the Chattahoochee River to the federal government in 1802. As the Indians were removed to the west, the lands they had occupied were disposed of by successive lotteries. The settlement of the cotton lands brought prosperity to Georgia, a fact that influenced Georgians to prefer the Union rather than secession during the constitutional crises of 1833 and 1850, when South Carolina was prepared to secede.

After South Carolina did secede in 1860, Georgia also withdrew from the Union and joined the Confederate States of America. Union troops occupied the Sea Islands during 1862. Confederate forces defeated the Union Army's advance into northern Georgia at Chickamauga in 1863, but in 1864, troops under General William Tecumseh Sherman moved relentlessly upon Atlanta, capturing it in September. In November, Sherman began his famous "march to the sea," in which his 60,000 troops cut a swath of destruction 60 mi (97 km) wide. Sherman presented Savannah as a Christmas present to President Abraham Lincoln.

After ratifying the 14th and 15th amendments, Georgia was readmitted to the Union on 15 July 1870. Commercial interests were strong in antebellum Georgia, but their political power was balanced by that of the great planters. After the Democrats recovered control of the state in 1871, business interests dominated politics. Discontented farmers supported an Independent Party in the 1870s and 1880s, and then the Populist Party in the 1890s. Democratic representative Thomas E. Watson, who declared himself a Populist during the early 1890s, was defeated three times in congressional races by the party he had deserted. Watson subsequently fomented antiblack, anti-Jewish, and anti-Catholic sentiment in order to control a bloc of rural votes with which he dominated state politics for 10 years. In 1920, Watson finally was elected to the US Senate, but he died in 1922. Rebecca L. Felton was appointed to succeed him, thus becoming the first woman to serve in the US Senate, although she was replaced after one day.

Franklin D. Roosevelt learned the problems of Georgia farmers firsthand when he made Warm Springs his second home in 1942. However, his efforts to introduce the New Deal to Georgia after he became president in 1933 were blocked by Governor Eugene Talmadge, who advertised himself as a "real dirt farmer." It was not until the administration of Eurith D. Rivers (1937–41) that progressive social legislation was enacted. Governor Ellis Arnall gained national attention for his forward-looking administration (1943–47), which revised the outdated 1877 state constitution and gave the vote to 18-year-olds. Georgia treated the nation to the spectacle of three governors at once when Eugene Talmadge was elected for a fourth time in 1946 but died before assuming office. His son Herman was then elected by the legislature, but the new lieutenant governor, M. E. Thompson, also claimed the office, and Arnall refused to step aside until the issue was resolved. The courts finally decided in favor of Thompson.

The US Supreme Court order to desegregate public schools in 1954 provided Georgia politicians with an emotional issue they exploited to the hilt. A blow was dealt to old-style politics in 1962, however, when the Supreme Court declared the county-unit system unconstitutional. Under this system, state officers and members of Congress had been selected by county units instead of by popular vote since 1911; the new ruling made city voters as important as those in rural areas. During the 1960s, Atlanta was the home base for the civil rights efforts of Martin Luther King Jr., though his campaign to end racial discrimination in Georgia focused most notably on the town of Albany. Federal civil rights legislation in 1964 and 1965 changed the state's political climate by guaranteeing the vote to black citizens. An African American man, Julian Bond, was elected to the state legislature in 1965; in 1973, Maynard Jackson was elected major of Atlanta, thus becoming the first black mayor of a large southern city. For decades, the belief that defense of segregation was a prerequisite for state elective office cost white southerners any chance they might have had for national leadership. Governor Jimmy Carter's unequivocal renunciation of racism in his inaugural speech in 1971 thus marked a turning point in Georgia politics and was a key factor in his election to the presidency in 1976.

Another African American, former US ambassador to the United Nations Andrew Young, succeeded Jackson as mayor of Atlanta in 1981, when that city—and the state—was experiencing an economic boom. The prosperity of Atlanta in the 1970s and 1980s stemmed largely from its service-based economy, which was centered on such industries as the airlines, telecommunications, distribution, and insurance. The decline of service industries in the early 1990s, however, pulled Atlanta and the state of Georgia as a whole into a recession. That decline was epitomized by the 1991 collapse of Eastern Airlines, one of the two airlines that used Atlanta as its hub, which cost Atlanta 10,000 jobs. While Atlanta's economic expansion produced a more mature economy, it also raised the price of labor. Nevertheless, as the decade progressed, the state's economy rebounded, fueled in part by the science and technology sector. Georgia emerged as "a leading light" in the South in building a strong research and technology infrastructure. Both 1996 and 1999 were record years for job growth. The state's unemployment rate was 4% in 1999, slightly lower than the national rate. While the economy boomed, there were changes on the horizon: In 2000, major employers Lockheed Martin, Coca-Cola, and BellSouth announced combined layoffs of more than 15,000 Georgia workers. Still, some analysts predicted the state economy could weather such fluctuations.

In 1996, Atlanta hosted the 26th Summer Olympics, which marked the 100th anniversary of the modern games. The event was marred by the July 27 explosion of a homemade pipe bomb in Centennial Olympic Park, killing one person and injuring dozens of others.

In July 1994, record flooding over a 10-day period caused 31 deaths and millions of dollars in damage in central and southwest Georgia. But in the summer of 2000, Georgians had a decidedly different problem. The state was parched by drought. Some areas had received less rain in the previous 25 months than at any time in recorded weather history. Peanut and cotton farmers in the southern part of the state struggled to irrigate fields. The residents of greater Atlanta, where nearly 100,000 people are added each year, felt the effects as well. Increased demand combined with drought conditions to require authorities to restrict outdoor watering in the 15-county Atlanta region. But the situation promised to reach beyond prevailing weather conditions and preservation measures: Officials estimated that by 2020, the region's demand for water would increase by 50%. Meanwhile Georgia's governor worked with the governors of neighboring Alabama and Florida to reach a voluntary agreement on how to share water from rivers the states share.

Governor Sonny Purdue outlined the problems Georgia faced in his 2003 State of the State address, including a weak economy (following the US recession that had begun in 2001), declining tax revenues, and poor SAT scores. To address the last topic, Purdue stressed the need for higher education standards. In 2003, the Georgia Board of Regents approved raising tuition by as much as 15% at the state's public colleges and universities to compensate for state budget cuts. Georgia's $460 million HOPE Scholarship program, funded by the state lottery, covers all tuition, mandatory fees, and book costs for all Georgia residents attending a state school and maintaining a B average. In 2005, the state still dealt with uninspired economic growth (despite a slightly rising employment rate) created by rising interest rates, dwindling federal fiscal stimulus, and overextended consumers.

12 STATE GOVERNMENT

Georgia's first constitution, adopted in 1777, was considered one of the most democratic in the new nation. Power was concentrated in a unicameral legislature; a Senate was added in 1789. The Civil War period brought a flurry of constitution making in 1861, 1865, and 1868. When the Democrats displaced the Republicans after Reconstruction, they felt obliged to replace the constitution of 1868 with a rigidly restrictive one. This document, adopted in 1877, modified by numerous amendments, and revised in 1945 and 1976, continued to govern the state until July 1983, when a new constitution, ratified in 1982, took effect. There were 63 amendments by January 2005.

The legislature, called the General Assembly, consists of a 56-seat Senate and a 180-seat House of Representatives; all the legislators serve two-year terms. The legislature convenes on the second Monday in January and stays in session for 40 legislative days. Recesses called during a session may considerably extend its length. Special sessions may be called by petition of three-fifths of the members of each house. During the 1960s and 1970s, the legislature engaged in a series of attempts to redistrict itself to provide equal representation based on population; it was finally redistricted in 1981 on the basis of 1980 Census results. House members must be at least 21 years old and senators, at least 25. All legislators must be US citizens, have lived in the state for two years, and have been a resident in their district for at least one year. Legislators received a salary of $16,200 in 2004.

Elected executives include the governor, lieutenant governor, secretary of state, attorney general, comptroller, state school superintendent, commissioner of agriculture, commissioner of labor, and five public service commissioners. Each serves a four-year term. The governor is limited to a maximum of two consecutive terms. To be eligible for office, the governor and lieutenant governor, who are elected separately, must be at least 30 years old and have been US citizens for 15 years and Georgia citizens for six years preceding the election. As of December 2004, the governor's salary was $127,303.

To become law, a bill must be passed by both houses of the legislature and approved by the governor or passed over the executive veto by a two-thirds vote of the elected members of both houses. All revenue measures originate in the House, but the Senate can propose, or concur in, amendments to these bills. Amendments to the constitution may be proposed by a two-thirds vote of the elected members of each chamber and must then be ratified by a majority of the popular vote. If the governor does not sign or veto a bill, it becomes law after six days when the legislature is in session or after 40 days after the legislature has adjourned.

To be eligible to vote in state elections, a person must be at least 18 years old, a US citizen, and a resident in the county of registration. Restrictions apply to convicted felons and those declared mentally incompetent by the court.

13 POLITICAL PARTIES

The first political group to emerge in the state was the Federalist Party, but it was tainted by association with the Yazoo Fraud of

---

Georgia Presidential Vote by Political Parties, 1948–2004

YEAR	ELECTORAL VOTE	GEORGIA WINNER	DEMOCRAT	REPUBLICAN	STATES' RIGHTS DEMOCRAT	PROGRESSIVE	WRITE-IN
1948	12	*Truman (D)	254,646	76,691	85,136	1,636	—
1952	12	Stevenson (D)	456,823	198,961	—	—	—
1956	12	Stevenson (D)	444,6878	222,778	—	—	—
1960	12	*Kennedy (D)	458,638	274,472	—	—	—
1964	12	Goldwater (R)	522,163	616,584	—	—	—
1968	12	Wallace (AI)	334,440	380,111	535,550	—	—
1972	12	*Nixon (R)	289,529	881,490			
1976	12	*Carter (D)	979,409	483,743		1,1681	1,071
					LIBERTARIAN		
1980	12	Carter (D)	890,955	654,168	15,627	—	—
1984	12	*Reagan (R)	706,628	1,068,722	1521	—	—
						NEW ALLIANCE	
1988	12	*Bush (R)	714,792	1,081,331	8,435	5,099	—
						IND. (Perot)	
1992	13	*Clinton (D)	1,008,966	995,252	7,110	309,657	—
1996	13	Dole (R)	1,053,849	1,080,843	17,870	146,337	—
						IND. (Buchanan)	**(Nader)**
2000	13	*Bush, G. W. (R)	1,116,230	1,419,720	36,332	10,926	13,432
						WRITE-IN (Peroutka)	
2004	15	*Bush, G. W. (R)	1,366,149	1,914,254	18,387	580	2,231

*Won US presidential election.

the 1790s. The reform party at this time was the Democratic-Republican Party, headed in Georgia by James Jackson (whose followers included many former Federalists), William Crawford, and George Troup. During the presidency of Andrew Jackson (1829–37), one wing, headed by John Clark, supported the president and called itself the Union Party. The other faction, led by Troup, defended South Carolina's right to nullify laws and called itself the States' Rights Party. Subsequently, the Union Party affiliated with the Democrats, and the States' Rights Party merged with the Whigs. When the national Whig Party collapsed, many Georgia Whigs joined the Native American (Know-Nothing) Party. During Reconstruction, the Republican Party captured the governor's office, but Republican hopes died when federal troops were withdrawn from the state in 1870.

Georgia voted solidly Democratic between 1870 and 1960, despite challenges from the Independent Party in the 1880s and the Populists in the 1890s. Georgia cast its electoral votes for the Democratic presidential candidate in every election until 1964, when Republican Barry Goldwater won the state. Four years later, George C. Wallace of the American Independent Party received Georgia's 12 electoral votes. Republican Richard Nixon carried the state in 1972, as the Republicans also became a viable party at the local level. In 1976, Georgia's native son Jimmy Carter returned the state to the Democratic camp in presidential balloting. Another native Georgian and former Georgia governor, Lester Maddox, was the American Independent candidate in 1976.

Republican George W. Bush won 55% of the vote and Democrat Al Gore won 43% in the 2000 presidential election; in 2004, Bush won 58% to Democrat John Kerry's 41%.

After the 1994 elections, Georgia congressman Newt Gingrich became the first Republican to hold the position of Speaker of the House of Representatives in 40 years. He resigned from Congress in 1999. In 1996, four-term US Democratic senator also Sam Nunn vacated his seat, which was won by Democrat Max Cleland, a Vietnam War veteran and triple amputee who had formerly headed the Veterans Administration. Cleland was defeated for reelection by Republican Saxby Chambliss in 2002.

Georgia's other senator, Republican Paul Coverdell, was elected in a special runoff election in 1992 and reelected in 1998. Coverdell died of a stroke in July 2000; former governor Zell Miller (Democrat) was appointed to succeed him. Miller was elected in November 2000 to serve the remaining four years of the term, but in 2003, he announced he would not run for reelection to the Senate in 2004. His seat was won by Republican Johnny Isakson.

In 1998, Georgians elected Democrat Roy Barnes governor, replacing outgoing (two-term) Democratic governor Zell Miller. Long-time Democrat Sonny Purdue changed party affiliations in 1998 to the Republican Party and won election as governor in 2002. He became the first Republican governor elected since Reconstruction in Georgia. Following the 2004 elections, Georgia's delegation to the House comprised seven Republicans and six Democrats. At the state level, there were 34 Republicans and 22 Democrats in the state Senate and 80 Democrats, 99 Republicans, and 1 independent in the state House in mid-2005. In 2004, there were 4,968,000 registered voters; there is no party registration in the state, which had 15 electoral votes in the presidential election that year.

14 LOCAL GOVERNMENT

The history of county government in Georgia is a long one. In 1758, colonial Georgia was divided into eight parishes, the earliest political districts represented in the Royal Assembly. By the constitution of 1777, the parishes were transformed into counties, and as settlement gradually expanded, the number of counties grew. The Georgia constitution of 1877 granted counties from one to three seats in the House of Representatives, depending on population. This county-unit system was used in counting votes for elected state and congressional offices until 1962, when it was ruled unconstitutional by the US Supreme Court. Originally administered by judges of county courts, today Georgia counties are administered by the commission system. In 1965, the legislature passed a home-rule law permitting local governments to amend their own charters.

The traditional and most common form of municipal government is the mayor-council form. But city managers are employed by some communities, and a few make use of the commission system. During the 1970s, there were efforts to merge some of the larger cities with their counties. However, most county voters showed an unwillingness to be burdened with city problems.

In 2005, Georgia had 159 counties, 531 municipal governments, 581 special districts, and 180 school districts.

In 2005, local government accounted for about 377,938 full-time (or equivalent) employment positions.

15 STATE SERVICES

To address the continuing threat of terrorism and to work with the federal Department of Homeland Security, homeland security in Georgia operates under the authority of executive order; the state homeland security director is appointed.

The State Ethics Commission is charged with providing procedures for public disclosure of all state and local campaign contributions and expenditures.

Educational services are provided by the Board of Education, which exercises jurisdiction over all public schools, including teacher certification and curriculum approval. The superintendent of schools is the board's executive officer. The public colleges are operated by the Board of Regents of the University System of Georgia, whose chief administrator is the chancellor. Air, water, road, and rail services are administered by the Department of Transportation.

The Reorganization Act of 1972 made the Department of Human Resources a catch-all agency for health, rehabilitation, and social-welfare programs. The department offers special services to the mentally ill, drug abusers and alcoholics, neglected and abused children and adults, juvenile offenders, the handicapped, the aged, and the poor.

Public protection services are rendered through the Department of Public Safety. Responsibility for natural-resource protection is lodged with the Department of Natural Resources, into which 33 separate agencies were consolidated in 1972. The Environmental Protection Division is charged with maintaining air, land, and water quality standards; the Wildlife Resources Division manages wildlife resources; and the Parks, Recreation, and Historic Sites Division administers state parks, recreational areas, and historic sites. Labor services are provided by the Department of Labor, which oversees workers' compensation programs.

16 JUDICIAL SYSTEM

Georgia's highest court is the supreme court, created in 1845 and consisting of a chief justice, presiding justice (who exercises the duties of chief justice in his absence), and five associate justices. They are elected by the people to staggered six-year terms in nonpartisan elections.

Georgia's general trial courts are the superior courts, which have exclusive jurisdiction in cases of divorce and land title and in felony cases. As of 1999, there were 175 superior court judges, all of them elected for four-year terms in nonpartisan elections. Cases from local courts can be carried to the court of appeals, consisting of 10 judges elected for staggered six-year terms in nonpartisan elections. Each county has a probate court; there are also separate juvenile courts. Most judges of the county and city courts are appointed by the governor with the consent of the Senate.

As of 31 December 2004, a total of 51,104 prisoners were held in Georgia's state and federal prisons, an increase from 47,208 or 8.3% from the previous year. As of year-end 2004, a total of 3,436 inmates were female, up from 3,145 or 9.3% from the year before. Among sentenced prisoners (one year or more), Georgia had an incarceration rate of 574 per 100,000 population in 2004.

According to the Federal Bureau of Investigation, in 2004 Georgia had a violent crime rate (murder/nonnegligent manslaughter; forcible rape; robbery; aggravated assault) of 455.5 reported incidents per 100,000 population, or a total of 40,217 reported incidents. Crimes against property (burglary; larceny/theft; and motor vehicle theft) in that same year totaled 376,656 reported incidents or 4,265.9 reported incidents per 100,000 people. Georgia has a death penalty, of which lethal injection is the sole method of execution. On 5 October 2001, the Georgia Supreme Court ruled that use of the electric chair was cruel and unusual punishment. From 1976 through 5 May 2006 the state executed 39 persons; three were executed in 2005. As of 1 January 2006, there were 109 inmates on death row.

In 2003, Georgia spent $285,944,298 on homeland security, an average of $34 per state resident.

17 ARMED FORCES

In 2004, there were 88,933 active-duty military personnel stationed in Georgia, 5,076 National Guard and Reserve personnel, and 26,307 civilian employees. Major facilities include Dobbins Air Reserve Base, Ft. Gillem, and Ft. McPherson, all located in the Atlanta area; Ft. Stewart and Hunter Army Airfield near Savannah; Ft. Gordon at Augusta; Moody Air Force Base at Macon; Ft. Benning, a major Army training installation at Columbus; Robins Air Force Base, between Columbus and Macon; and a Navy Supply School in Athens. In 2004, Georgia firms received defense contracts worth $3.9 billion, down from $6.0 billion in 2001. Defense payroll, including retired military pay, amounted to $6.6 billion in 2004.

There were 760,323 veterans of US military service in Georgia as of 2003, of whom 67,200 served in World War II; 63,192 in the Korean conflict; 228,543 during the Vietnam era; and 162,895 in the Persian Gulf War. In all, 77,000 Georgians fought and 1,503 died in World War I, and 320,000 served and 6,754 were killed in World War II. In 2004, federal government expenditures for Georgia veterans amounted to $1.9 billion.

As of 31 October 2004, the Georgia State Police employed 795 full-time sworn officers. The Georgia Bureau of Investigation, part of the Department of Public Safety, operates the Georgia Crime Laboratory, one of the oldest and largest in the United States.

18 MIGRATION

During the colonial period, the chief source of immigrants to Georgia was England; other important national groups were Germans, Scots, and Scotch-Irish. The number of African slaves increased from 1,000 in 1752 to nearly 20,000 in 1776. After the Revolution, a large number of Virginians came to Georgia, as well as lesser numbers of French refugees from Hispaniola and immigrants from Ireland and Germany. Following the Civil War, there was some immigration from Italy, Russia, and Greece. The greatest population shifts during the 20th century have been from country to town and, after World War I, of black Georgians to northern cities. Georgia suffered a net loss through migration of 502,000 from 1940 to 1960 but enjoyed a net gain of 329,000 during 1970–80 and about 500,000 during 1980–90. From 1985 to 1990, Georgia's net gain through migration was greater than that of any other state except California and Florida. There were net gains of 598,000 in domestic migration and 90,000 in international migration between 1990 and 1998. From 1980 to 1990, the share of native-born residents in Georgia fell from 71% to 64.5%. In 1998, Georgia admitted 10,445 immigrants from foreign countries. Between 1990 and 1998, the state's overall population increased 18%. In the period 2000–05, net international migration was 192,844 and net internal migration was 232,666, for a net gain of 425,510 people.

19 INTERGOVERNMENTAL COOPERATION

Multistate agreements in which Georgia participates include the Alabama-Coosa-Tallapoosa River Basin Compact, Appalachian Regional Commission, Atlantic States Marine Fisheries Commission, Historic Chattahoochee Compact, Interstate Rail Passenger Network Compact, Apalachicola-Chattahoochee-Flint River Basin Compact, Southern Regional Education Board, Southeastern Forest Fire Protection Compact, Southern Growth Policies Board, and Southern States Energy Board. In fiscal year 2005, federal aid to Georgia totaled $9.014 billion. For fiscal year 2006, federal grants amounted to an estimated $9.008 billion, and an estimated $9.355 billion in fiscal year 2007.

20 ECONOMY

According to the original plans of Georgia's founders, its people were to be sober spinners of silk. The reality was far different, however. During the period of royally appointed governors, Georgia became a replica of Carolina, a plantation province producing rice, indigo, and cotton. After the Revolution, the invention of the cotton gin established the plantation system even more firmly by making cotton planting profitable in the piedmont. Meanwhile, deerskins and other furs and lumber were produced in the backcountry, while rice remained an important staple along the coast. Turnpikes, canals, and railroads were built, and textile manufacturing became increasingly important, especially in Athens and Augusta.

At the end of the Civil War, the state's economy was in ruins, and tenancy and sharecropping were common. Manufacturing, especially of textiles, was promoted by "New South" spokesmen such as Henry Grady of Atlanta and Patrick Walsh of Augusta. Atlanta, whose nascent industries included production of a thick sweet syrup called Coca-Cola, symbolized the New South idea—then as now. Farmers did not experience the benefits of progress, however. Many of them flocked to the mills, while others joined the Populist Party in an effort to air their grievances. To the planters' relief, cotton prices rose from the turn of the century through World War I. Meanwhile, Georgians lost control of their railroads and industries to northern corporations. During the 1920s, the boll weevil wrecked the cotton crops, and farmers resumed their flight to the cities. Not until the late 1930s did Georgia accept Social Security, unemployment compensation, and other relief measures.

Georgia's economy underwent drastic changes as a result of World War II. Many northern industries moved to Georgia to take advantage of low wages and low taxes, conditions that meant low benefits for Georgians. The raising of poultry and livestock became more important than crop cultivation, and manufacturing replaced agriculture as the chief source of income. In 1997, less than 1% of the employed labor force was working in agriculture; 32% were service workers; 22% retail salespeople; and 19% manufacturers. Georgia is a leader in the making of paper products, tufted textile products, processed chickens, naval stores, lumber, and transportation equipment.

Textile manufacturing, Georgia's oldest industry, remained its single most important industrial source of income until 1999, when output from food processing exceeded it. From 1997 to 2001, annual textile output declined 8.4%, whereas output from food processing increased 12.1%. Other manufacturing sectors were also increasing, so that from 1997 to 2000, there was an overall 16% increase in Georgia's manufacturing output. More than half of the gain was lost, however, in the national recession in 2001, as manufacturing output fell 8.3% in one year, reducing the net gain since 1997 to 6.4%. By contrast, output from general services increased nearly 40% from 1997 to 2001, and from financial services (including insurance and real estate) increased almost 32%. Output from other service areas—wholesale and retail trade, transportation and public utilities, and government—all increased more than 25% from 1997 to 2001. The national recession of 2001, however, affected Georgia's economy worse than most, as its strong annual growth rates at the end of the 20th century (8.2% in 1998, 8.5% in 1999 and 6.7% in 2000) dropped abruptly to 1.5% in 2001. The state lost more than 133,000 jobs from January 2001 to October 2002. Layoffs in the fourth quarter of 2002 amounted to a 2.2% increase over the fourth quarter of 2001, the worst performance in the country.

Georgia's gross state product (GSP) in 2005 was $364 billion, up from $343.125 billion in 2004. Manufacturing (durable and nondurable goods) in 2004 accounted for the biggest portion at $47.677 billion or nearly 13.9% of GSP, followed by real estate at $38.293 billion (11.1% of GSP), and wholesale trade at $25.847 billion (7.5% of GSP). In that same year, there were an estimated 722,089 small businesses in Georgia. Of the 202,979 businesses having employees, a total of 198,271 or 97.7% were small companies. An estimated 29,547 new businesses were established in Georgia in 2004, up 22% from the previous year. Business terminations that same year came to 27,835, up 7.5% from the previous year. Business bankruptcies totaled 2,090 in 2004, up 31.9% from 2003. In 2005, the personal bankruptcy (Chapter 7 and Chapter 13) filing rate was 930 filings per 100,000 people, ranking Georgia as the fifth-highest in the nation.

21 INCOME

In 2005 Georgia had a gross state product (GSP) of $364 billion which accounted for 2.9% of the nation's gross domestic product and placed the state at number 10 in highest GSP among the 50 states and the District of Columbia.

According to the Bureau of Economic Analysis, in 2004, Georgia had a per capita personal income (PCPI) of $29,782. This ranked 36th in the United States and was 90% of the national average of $33,050. The 1994–2004 average annual growth rate of PCPI was 3.7%. Georgia had a total personal income (TPI) of $265,599,116,000, which ranked 12th in the United States and reflected an increase of 5.9% from 2003. The 1994–2004 average annual growth rate of TPI was 6.0%. Earnings of persons employed in Georgia increased from $203,459,898,000 in 2003 to $216,399,592,000 in 2004, an increase of 6.4%. The 2003–04 national change was 6.3%.

The US Census Bureau reports that the three-year average median household income for 2002 to 2004 in 2004 dollars was $43,217 compared to a national average of $44,473. During the same period an estimated 12.0% of the population was below the poverty line as compared to 12.4% nationwide.

22 LABOR

According to the Bureau of Labor Statistics (BLS), in April 2006 the seasonally adjusted civilian labor force in Georgia numbered 4,693,900, with approximately 214,800 workers unemployed, yielding an unemployment rate of 4.6%, compared to the national average of 4.7% for the same period. Preliminary data for the same period placed nonfarm employment at 4,078,100. Since the beginning of the BLS data series in 1976, the highest unemployment rate recorded in Georgia was 8.3% in January 1983. The historical low was 3.4% in December 2000. Preliminary nonfarm employment data by occupation for April 2006 showed that approximately 5.2% of the labor force was employed in construction; 21.4% in trade, transportation, and public utilities; 5.6% in financial activities; 13.4% in professional and business services; 10.6% in education and health services; 9.3% in leisure and hospitality services; and 16.1% in government. Data were unavailable for manufacturing.

The trend during the 1970s, 1980s, and 1990s was toward increased employment in trade and service industries and toward multiple job holding. Employment in agriculture, the leading industry prior to World War II, continued its long-term decline. One indication of declining employment was the decrease in farm population, which went from 515,000 in 1960 to 228,000 in 1970, to 121,000 in 1980, and to 73,647 in 1990. Georgia's farm employment in 1996 totaled about 42,000. The mining, construction, and manufacturing industries registered employment increases but declined in importance relative to such sectors as trade and services.

Georgia is not considered to be a unionized state. Among state laws strictly regulating union activity is a right-to-work law enacted in 1947. In that year, union members in Georgia numbered 256,800.

In 1962, the Georgia legislature denied state employees the right to strike. Strikes in Georgia tend to occur less frequently than in most heavily industrialized states. One of the earliest state labor laws was an 1889 act requiring employers to provide seats for females to use when resting. A child-labor law adopted in 1906 prohibited the employment of children under 10 years of age in manufacturing. A general workers' compensation law was enacted in 1920.

The BLS reported that in 2005, a total of 190,000 of Georgia's 3,765,000 employed wage and salary workers were formal members of a union. This represented 5% of those so employed, down from 6.4% in 2004 and below the national average of 12%. Overall in 2005, a total of 226,000 workers (6%) in Georgia were covered by a union or employee association contract, which includes those workers who reported no union affiliation.

As of 1 March 2006, Georgia had a state-mandated minimum wage rate of $5.15 per hour. In 2004, women in the state accounted for 45.6% of the employed civilian labor force.

23 AGRICULTURE

In 2005, Georgia's farm marketings totaled $5.9 billion (12th in the United States). Georgia ranked first in the production of peanuts and pecans, harvesting 25% of all the pecans grown in the United States in 2004 and 43% of the peanuts.

Cotton, first planted near Savannah in 1734, was the mainstay of Georgia's economy through the early 20th century, and the state's plantations also grew corn, rice, tobacco, wheat, and sweet potatoes. World War I stimulated the cultivation of peanuts along with other crops. By the 1930s, tobacco and peanuts were challenging cotton for agricultural supremacy, and Georgia had also become an important producer of peaches, a product for which the "Peach State" was still widely known in the early 2000s. In 2004, Georgia produced 52,500 tons of peaches.

After 1940, farm mechanization and consolidation were rapid. The number of tractors increased from 10,000 in 1940 to 85,000 by 1955. In 1940, 6 out of 10 farms were tenant operated; by the mid-1960s, this proportion had decreased to fewer than 1 in 6. The number of farms declined from 226,000 in 1945 to 49,000 in 2004, when the average farm size was 218 acres (88 hectares). Georgia's farmland area of 10.7 million acres (4.3 million hectares) represents roughly 30% of its land area.

24 ANIMAL HUSBANDRY

In 2005, Georgia had an estimated 1.21 million cattle and calves valued at around $931.7 million, and in 2004 an estimated 275,000 hogs and pigs valued at around $25.3 million. Cows kept for milk production numbered an estimated 85,000 in 2003, when Georgia dairies produced around 1.4 billion lb (0.64 billion kg) of milk. In the same year, poultry farmers sold an estimated 6.3 billion lb (2.8 billion kg) of broilers, more than any other state, with a value

of $2.14 billion, or about 47% of total farm receipts. The total egg production was 5.05 billion in 2003, valued at $395.8 million.

25 FISHING

In 2004, the total commercial fishing catch in Georgia brought about 6.3 million lb (2.7 million kg) with a value of $11.3 million. Commercial fishing in Georgia involves more shellfish than finfish, the most important of which are caught in the nets of shrimp trawlers. Leading finfish are snappers, groupers, tilefish, and porgy. In 2003, the state had 6 processing and 30 wholesale plants. In 2002, the commercial fleet had about 226 vessels.

In brisk mountain streams and sluggish swamps, anglers catch bass, catfish, jackfish, bluegill, crappie, perch, and trout. In 2005, Georgia had 55 catfish farms covering 1,090 acres (441 hectares), with an inventory of 1.4 million stocker-sized and 6.3 million fingerlings in early 2006. Georgia issued 667,198 sport fishing licenses in 2004.

26 FORESTRY

Georgia, which occupies 1.6% of the total US land area, has nearly 3.3% of the nation's forestland and nearly 5% of the nation's commercial forests. In 2004, Georgia's forest area totaled 24,405,000 acres (9,877,000 hectares), of which 23,802,000 acres (9,633,000 hectares) are commercial forest.

Forests cover about two-thirds of the state's land area. The most densely wooded counties are in the piedmont hills and northern mountains. Ware and Charlton counties in southeastern Georgia, containing the Okefenokee Swamp, are almost entirely forested. About 90% of Georgia's forestland is privately owned.

The chief products of Georgia's timber industry are pine lumber and pine panels for the building industry, hardwood lumber for the furniture industry, and pulp for the paper and box industry. In 2002, Georgia produced nearly 3 billion board feet of lumber (fourth in the United States), of which 87% was softwood (pine). Georgia is the leading softwood producer in the United States.

The chief recreational forest areas are in the Chattahoochee-Oconee National Forest, consisting of two main tracts in the northern and central part of the state. Georgia has 1,856,000 acres (751,123 hectares) of National Forest System lands, 99% of which are within the boundaries of the two major tracts.

27 MINING

According to data from the US Geological Survey, Georgia's output of nonfuel minerals was valued at $1.8 billion, up 3.4% from 2003, making it eighth among the 50 states in the production of nonfuel minerals and accounting for over 4% of the US total.

In 2004, Georgia produced about 24% of all clays in the United States and 2.7 times as much as the next highest state. Kaolin clay was the leading commodity, accounting for over 49% of all nonfuel mineral production, by value, that year and around 86% of all clay output. Crushed stone ranked second and represented over 30%, by value, of all nonfuel mineral output in 2004, followed by fuller's earth (1,4 million metric tons; $142 million), portland masonry cement, and construction sand and gravel.

Production of kaolin clay in 2004 totaled 6.78 million metric tons or $898 million, while output of crushed stone totaled 79.5

million metric tons or $544 million. Fuller's earth production came to 1.4 million metric tons or $142 million.

Georgia was one of two states that produced barite (used by the chemical and industrial filler and pigments industries). Georgia ranked third in the production of mica (out of five states) and in dimension stone; fourth in the output of common clays and crushed stone; fifth in feldspar dimension stone; and eighth in masonry cement. The state is also a producer of blue-gray granite, known as "Elberton granite," which is commonly used for road curbing in the northeastern United States. Overall, Georgia's production of dimension stone totaled 146 million metric tons and was valued at $22.1 million in 2004.

28 ENERGY AND POWER

Georgia is an energy-dependent state that produces only a small proportion of its energy needs, most of it through hydroelectric power. There are no commercially recoverable petroleum or natural gas reserves, and the state's coal deposits are of no more than marginal importance. Georgia does have large amounts of timberland, however, and it has been estimated that 20%–40% of the state's energy demands could be met by using wood that is currently wasted. The state's southern location and favorable weather conditions also make solar power an increasingly attractive energy alternative. Georgia's extensive river system also offers the potential for further hydroelectric development.

As of 2003, Georgia had 98 electrical power service providers, of which 53 were publicly owned and 43 were cooperatives. Of the remaining two, both were investor owned. As of that same year there were 4,156,052 retail customers. Of that total, 2,158,412 received their power from investor-owned service providers. Cooperatives accounted for 1,668,488 customers, while publicly owned providers had 329,152 customers.

Total net summer generating capability by the state's electrical generating plants in 2003 stood at 34.815 million kW, with total production that same year at 124.076 billion kWh. Of the total amount generated, 93.3% came from electric utilities, with the remainder coming from independent producers and combined heat and power service providers. The largest portion of all electric power generated, 78.638 billion kWh (63.3%), came from coal-fired plants, with nuclear fueled plants in second place with 33.256 billion kWh (26.8%). Other renewable power sources, natural gas plants, hydroelectric and petroleum fired plants accounted for the remainder.

As of 2006, Georgia had two operating nuclear power plants: the Edwin I. Hatch power station near Baxley and the Vogtle plant in Burke County, near Augusta.

All utilities are regulated by the Georgia Public Service Commission, which must approve their rates.

Although exploration for oil has taken place off the coast, the state's offshore oil resources are expected to be slight. As of 2004, Georgia had no known proven reserves or production of crude oil or natural gas. The state's only refinery is used to produce asphalt.

29 INDUSTRY

Georgia was primarily an agrarian state before the Civil War, but afterward its cities developed a strong industrial base by taking advantage of abundant waterpower to operate factories. Textiles

have long been dominant, but new industries have also been developed. Charles H. Herty, a chemist at the University of Georgia, discovered a new method of extracting turpentine that worked so well that Georgia led the nation in producing turpentine, tar, rosin, and pitch by 1982. Herty also perfected an economical way of making newsprint from southern pines, which was adopted by Georgia's paper mills. With the onset of World War II, meat-processing plants were built at rail centers, and fertilizer plants and cottonseed mills were expanded.

The state's—and Atlanta's—most famous product was created in 1886 when druggist John S. Pemberton developed a formula that he sold to Asa Griggs Candler, who in 1892 formed the Coca-Cola Co. In 1919, the Candlers sold the company to a syndicate headed by Ernest Woodruff, whose son Robert made "Coke" into the world's most widely known commercial product. The transport equipment, chemical, food-processing, apparel, and forest-products industries today rival textiles in economic importance.

According to the US Census Bureau's Annual Survey of Manufactures (ASM) for 2004, Georgia's manufacturing sector covered some 20 product subsectors. The shipment value of all products manufactured in the state that same year was $131.454 billion. Of that total, food manufacturing accounted for the largest portion at $18.936 billion, followed by transportation equipment manufacturing at $17.266 billion; chemical manufacturing at $12.403 billion; textile product mills at $12.291 billion; paper manufacturing at $9.584 billion; and machinery manufacturing at $7.599 billion.

In 2004, a total of 419,562 people in Georgia were employed in the state's manufacturing sector, according to the ASM. Of that total, 318,415 were actual production workers. In terms of total employment, the food manufacturing industry accounted for the largest portion of all manufacturing employees at 57,116, of which 45,793 were actual production workers, followed by the transportation equipment manufacturing industry at 39,757 (19,562 actual production workers); textile product mills at 34,776 employees (28,756 actual production workers); textile mills at 33,331 employees (29,844 actual production workers); fabricated metal product manufacturing at 28,796 employees (21,670 actual production workers); and plastics and rubber products manufacturing at 28,050 employees (22,499 actual production workers).

ASM data for 2004 showed that Georgia's manufacturing sector paid $15.518 billion in wages. Of that amount, the transportation equipment manufacturing sector accounted for the largest share at $1.921 billion. It was followed by food manufacturing at $1.661 billion; paper manufacturing at $1.058 billion; textile product mills at $1.034 billion; and chemical manufacturing at $1.021 billion.

30 COMMERCE

According to the 2002 Census of Wholesale Trade, Georgia's wholesale trade sector had sales that year totaling $201.09 billion from 13,794 establishments. Wholesalers of durable goods accounted for 8,509 establishments, followed by nondurable goods wholesalers at 4,077 and electronic markets, agents, and brokers, accounting for 1,208 establishments. Sales by durable goods wholesalers in 2002 totaled $112.1 billion, while wholesalers of nondurable goods saw sales of $73.4 billion. Electronic markets, agents, and brokers in the wholesale trade industry had sales of $15.4 billion.

In the 2002 Census of Retail Trade, Georgia was listed as having 34,050 retail establishments with sales of $90.09 billion. The leading types of retail businesses by number of establishments were gasoline stations (4,695); clothing and clothing accessories stores (4,640); food and beverage stores (3,998); motor vehicle and motor vehicle parts dealers (3,949); and miscellaneous store retailers (3,471). In terms of sales, motor vehicle and motor vehicle parts stores accounted for the largest share of retail sales at $24.6 billion, followed by general merchandise stores at $13.5 billion; food and beverage stores at $13.1 billion; gasoline stations at $8.7 billion; and clothing and clothing accessories stores at $5.09 billion. A total of 447,618 people were employed by the retail sector in Georgia that year.

Georgia exported goods worth $20.5 billion in 2005. Savannah is Georgia's most important export center.

[31]CONSUMER PROTECTION

Georgia's basic consumer protection law is the Fair Business Practices Act of 1975, which forbids representing products as having official approval when they do not, outlaws advertising without the intention of supplying a reasonable number of the items advertised, and empowers the administrator of the law to investigate and resolve complaints and seek penalties for unfair practices. The administrator heads the Office of Consumer Affairs, which now also administers laws that regulate charitable solicitation, offers to sell or buy business opportunities, buying services or clubs, and telemarketing.

A comprehensive "Lemon Law" was passed in 1990. In 1997, a number of changes were made in Georgia's basic consumer protection laws. The Consumers' Utility Counsel became a division of the Office of Consumer Affairs. The counsel represents the interests of consumers and small businesses before the Georgia Public Service Commission. Telemarketing, Internet, and home remodeling/home repair fraud became criminal offenses under the jurisdiction of the Office of Consumer Affairs, with maximum sentences of up to 10 years. Multilevel marketing is now covered along with business opportunities. A Consumer Insurance Advocate represents citizens before the Georgia Commissioner of Insurance, the courts, and federal administrative agencies that speak on behalf of consumers with regard to insurance, such as insurance rate increases or the denial of health care services. The Office of Consumer Education attempts to create a more informed marketplace so consumers can protect themselves against fraud.

The state's Attorney General's Office can also become involved in consumer protection. However, these activities are limited to the initiation of civil and criminal proceedings; and the representation of the state before state and federal regulatory agencies. The office has only limited subpoena powers and it has no authority to act in antitrust actions.

The state's Office of Consumer Affairs is located in Atlanta.

[32]BANKING

The state's first bank was a branch of the Bank of the United States, established at Savannah in 1802. Eight years later, the Georgia legislature chartered the Bank of Augusta and the Planters' Bank of Savannah, with the state holding one-sixth of the stock of each bank. The state also subscribed two-thirds of the stock of the Bank of the State of Georgia, which opened branches throughout the region. To furnish small, long-term agricultural loans, in 1828 the state established the Central Bank of Georgia, but this institution collapsed in 1856 because the state kept dipping into its reserves. After the Civil War, the lack of capital and the high cost of credit forced farmers to borrow from merchants under the lien system. By 1900, there were 200 banks in Georgia; with an improvement in cotton prices, their number increased to nearly 800 by World War I. During the agricultural depression of the 1920s, about half these banks failed, and the number has remained relatively stable since 1940. Georgia banking practices came under national scrutiny in 1979, when Bert Lance, President Jimmy Carter's former budget director and the former president of the National Bank of Georgia, was indicted on 33 counts of bank fraud. The federal government dropped its case after Lance was acquitted on nine of the charges, and most of the rest were dismissed.

As of June 2005, Georgia had 346 insured banks, savings and loans, and saving banks, plus 69 state-chartered and 126 federally chartered credit unions (CUs). Excluding the CUs, the Atlanta–Sandy Springs–Marietta market area had 138 financial institutions in 2004, with $94.461 billion in deposits, followed by the Chattanooga area (which includes a portion of Georgia) at 26, with $6.612 billion in deposits. As of June 2005, CUs accounted for 4.6% of all assets held by all financial institutions in the state, or some $12.544 billion. Banks, savings and loans, and savings banks collectively accounted for the remaining 95.4% or $260.170 billion in assets held.

The Georgia Department of Banking and Finance regulates state-chartered banks, CUs, and trust companies. Federally chartered financial institutions are regulated by the US government.

In 2005, Georgia's community banks saw improvements in profitability. Return on assets that year rose to 1.34%, and strong loan growth significantly boosted net interest income. Led by a double-digit growth in construction and development, overall loans increased by 14% in 2005. In 2004, the median net interest margin (the difference between the lower rates offered to savers and the higher rates charged on loans) stood at 4.28%, up from 4.23% in 2003. In addition, commercial real estate (CRE) loans grew from 39.7% of assets ($7.5 billion) in 1996 to 61% of assets ($34.5 billion) in 2005.

[33]INSURANCE

In 2004 there were over 5.6 million individual life insurance policies in force with a total value of over $422.9 billion; total value for all categories of life insurance (individual, group, and credit) was about $684.7 billion. The average coverage amount is $74,600 per policy holder. Death benefits paid that year totaled $1.8 billion.

In 2003 there were 20 life and health insurance companies and 37 property and casualty insurance companies domiciled in Georgia. In 2004, direct premiums for property and casualty insurance totaled $12.6 billion. That year, there were 70,475 flood insurance policies in force in the state, at a total value of $13 billion. About $2.6 billion of coverage was offered through FAIR plans, which are designed to offer coverage for some natural circumstances, such as wind and hail, in high risk areas.

In 2004, 56% of state residents held employment-based health insurance policies, 4% held individual policies, and 23% were covered under Medicare and Medicaid; 17% of residents were uninsured. In 2003, employee contributions for employment-based health coverage averaged at 19% for single coverage and 27% for family coverage. The state offers a three-month health benefits expansion program for small-firm employees in connection with the Consolidated Omnibus Budget Reconciliation Act (COBRA, 1986), a health insurance program for those who lose employment-based coverage due to termination or reduction of work hours.

In 2003, there were over 6 million auto insurance policies in effect for private passenger cars. Required minimum coverage includes bodily injury liability of up to $25,000 per individual and $50,000 for all persons injured in an accident, as well as property damage liability of $25,000. In 2003, the average expenditure per vehicle for insurance coverage was $758.69.

34 SECURITIES

There are no stock or commodity exchanges in Georgia. In 2005, there were 2,770 personal financial advisers employed in the state and 3,950 securities, commodities, and financial services sales agents. In 2004, there were over 231 publicly traded companies within the state, with 91 NASDAQ companies, 58 NYSE listings, and 13 AMEX listings. In 2006, the state had 17 Fortune 500 companies; Home Depot ranked first in the state and 14th in the nation with revenues of over $81.5 billion, followed by United Parcel Service, Coca-Cola, BellSouth, and Coca-Cola Enterprises. All five companies are based in Atlanta and listed on the NYSE.

35 PUBLIC FINANCE

Because the Georgia constitution forbids the state to spend more than it takes in from all sources, the governor attempts to reconcile the budget requests of the state department heads with the revenue predicted by economists for the coming fiscal year. The governor's Office of Planning and Budget prepares the budget, which is then presented to the General Assembly at the beginning of each year's session. The assembly may decide to change the revenue estimate, but it usually goes along with the governor's forecast. The fiscal year begins on 1 July, and the first question for the assembly when it convenes the following January is whether to raise or lower the current year's budget estimate. If the revenues are better than expected, the legislators enact a supplemental budget. If the income is below expectations, cuts can be made.

In fiscal year 2006, general funds were estimated at $19.1 billion for resources and $17.8 billion for expenditures. In fiscal year 2004, federal government grants to Georgia were nearly $11.7 billion.

36 TAXATION

In 2005, Georgia collected $15,676 million in tax revenues or $1,728 per capita, which placed it 42nd among the 50 states in per capita tax burden. The national average was $2,192 per capita. Property taxes accounted for 0.4% of the total, sales taxes 33.9%,

selective sales taxes 10.6%, individual income taxes 46.7%, corporate income taxes 4.5%, and other taxes 3.8%.

As of 1 January 2006, Georgia had six individual income tax brackets ranging from 1.0% to 6.0%. The state taxes corporations at a flat rate of 6.0%.

In 2004, state and local property taxes amounted to $7,844,826,000 or $880 per capita. The per capita amount ranks the state 34th highest nationally. Local governments collected $7,779,708,000 of the total and the state government $65,118,000.

Georgia taxes retail sales at a rate of 4%. In addition to the state tax, local taxes on retail sales can reach as much as 3%, making

Georgia—State Government Finances

(Dollar amounts in thousands. Per capita amounts in dollars.)

	AMOUNT	PER CAPITA
Total Revenue	34,814,306	3,903.82
General revenue	28,204,763	3,162.68
Intergovernmental revenue	9,095,862	1,019.94
Taxes	14,570,573	1,633.84
General sales	4,921,337	551.84
Selective sales	1,547,448	173.52
License taxes	617,663	69.26
Individual income tax	6,830,486	765.92
Corporate income tax	494,701	55.47
Other taxes	158,938	17.82
Current charges	2,388,566	267.84
Miscellaneous general revenue	2,149,762	241.06
Utility revenue	2,353	.26
Liquor store revenue	–	–
Insurance trust revenue	6,607,190	740.88
Total expenditure	34,196,775	3,834.58
Intergovernmental expenditure	9,335,405	1,046.80
Direct expenditure	24,861,370	2,787.77
Current operation	17,587,719	1,972.16
Capital outlay	2,434,332	272.97
Insurance benefits and repayments	3,325,304	372.88
Assistance and subsidies	1,052,824	118.06
Interest on debt	461,191	51.71
Exhibit: Salaries and wages	3,990,821	447.50
Total expenditure	34,196,775	3,834.58
General expenditure	30,869,198	3,461.45
Intergovernmental expenditure	9,335,405	1,046.80
Direct expenditure	21,533,793	2,414.64
General expenditures, by function:		
Education	13,305,305	1,491.96
Public welfare	9,215,633	1,033.37
Hospitals	687,846	77.13
Health	1,003,217	112.49
Highways	1,393,760	156.29
Police protection	241,000	27.02
Correction	1,304,039	146.23
Natural resources	518,165	58.10
Parks and recreation	139,116	15.60
Government administration	758,981	85.11
Interest on general debt	461,191	51.71
Other and unallocable	1,840,945	206.43
Utility expenditure	2,273	.25
Liquor store expenditure	–	–
Insurance trust expenditure	3,325,304	372.88
Debt at end of fiscal year	8,664,363	971.56
Cash and security holdings	64,062,476	7,183.50

Abbreviations and symbols: – zero or rounds to zero; (NA) not available; (X) not applicable.

SOURCE: *U.S. Census Bureau, Governments Division, 2004 Survey of State Government Finances,* January 2006.

for a potential total tax on retail sales of 7%. Food purchased for consumption offpremises is tax exempt. The tax on cigarettes is 37 cents per pack, which ranks 41st among the 50 states and the District of Columbia. Georgia taxes gasoline at 15.3 cents per gallon. This is in addition to the 18.4 cents per gallon federal tax on gasoline.

For every dollar of federal tax collected in 2004, Georgia citizens received $0.96 in federal spending.

37 ECONOMIC POLICY

Since the time of journalist Henry Grady (1851–89), spokesman for the "New South," Georgia has courted industry. Corporate taxes have traditionally been low, wages also low, and unions weak. Georgia's main attractions for new businesses are a favorable location for air, highway, and rail transport, a mild climate, a rapidly expanding economy, tax incentives and competitive wage scales, and an abundance of recreational facilities. During the 1990s, Georgia governors aggressively sought out domestic and foreign investors, and German, Japanese, and South American corporations were lured to the state. The state offers loans to businesses that are unable to obtain conventional financing, provides venture capital to start-up companies, and extends loans to small businesses and to companies in rural areas.

The Georgia Department of Economic Development (GDEcD) is the lead agency for promoting economic development in the state, tasked with recruiting businesses, trade partners, and tourists. The GDEcD was established by law in 1949 as the Department of Commerce (replacing the Agricultural and Industrial Development Board), and later renamed. The GDEcD is overseen by a board of 20 members appointed by the governor. The main operational units are Small Business, International, Innovation and Technology, Existing Industry Support, Tourism, and Film, Video and Music. The state funds city and county development plans, aids recreational projects, promotes research and development, and supports industrial training programs.

38 HEALTH

The infant mortality rate in October 2005 was estimated at 7.8 per 1,000 live births. The birth rate in 2003 was 15.7 per 1,000 population. The abortion rate stood at 16.9 per 1,000 women in 2000. In 2003, about 84% of pregnant woman received prenatal care beginning in the first trimester. In 2004, approximately 85% of children received routine immunizations before the age of three.

The crude death rate in 2003 was 7.7 deaths per 1,000 population. As of 2002, the death rates for major causes of death (per 100,000 resident population) were as follows heart disease, 204.8; cancer, 163.3; cerebrovascular diseases, 49.8; chronic lower respiratory diseases, 36.9; and diabetes, 18.4. The mortality rate from HIV infection was 8.3 per 100,000 population. In 2004, the reported AIDS case rate was at about 18.6 per 100,000 population. In 2002, about 56.1% of the population was considered overweight or obese. As of 2004, about 20.1% of state residents were smokers.

In 2003, Georgia had 146 community hospitals with about 24,600 beds. There were about 926,000 patient admissions that year and 12.8 million outpatient visits. The average daily inpatient census was about 16,500 patients. The average cost per day for hospital care was $1,044. Also in 2003, there were about 360 certified nursing facilities in the state with 39,998 beds and an overall occupancy rate of about 90.9%. In 2004, it was estimated that about 68.2% of all state residents had received some type of dental care within the year. Georgia had 219 physicians per 100,000 resident population in 2004 and 658 nurses per 100,000 in 2005. In 2004, there was a total of 4,024 dentists in the state.

About 23% of state residents were enrolled in Medicaid and Medicare programs in 2004. Approximately 17% of the state population was uninsured in 2004. In 2003, state health care expenditures totaled $10.7 million.

The Medical College of Georgia, established at Augusta in 1828, is one of the oldest medical schools in the United States and the center of medical research in the state. The federal Centers for Disease Control (CDC) were established in Atlanta in 1973; in 1992, the CDC retain its acronym but changed its name to the Centers for Disease and Prevention.

39 SOCIAL WELFARE

As a responsibility of state government, social welfare came late to Georgia. The state waited two years before agreeing to participate in the federal Social Security system in 1937. Eighteen years later, Georgia was distributing only $62 million to the aged, blind, and disabled and to families with dependent children. By 1970, the amount had risen to $150 million, but the state still lagged far behind the national average.

In 2004, about 208,000 people received unemployment benefits, with the average weekly unemployment benefit at $242. In fiscal year 2005, the estimated average monthly participation in the food stamp program included about 921,427 persons (375,739 households); the average monthly benefit was about $94.77 per person. That year, the total of benefits paid through the state for the food stamp program was about $1 billion.

Temporary Assistance for Needy Families (TANF), the system of federal welfare assistance that officially replaced Aid to Families with Dependent Children (AFDC) in 1997, was reauthorized through the Deficit Reduction Act of 2005. TANF is funded through federal block grants that are divided among the states based on an equation involving the number of recipients in each state. In 2004, the state program had 124,000 recipients; state and federal expenditures on this TANF program totaled $203 million in fiscal year 2003.

In December 2004, Social Security benefits were paid to 1,192,050 Georgians. This number included 708,670 retired workers, 118,250 widows and widowers, 187,620 disabled workers, 54,720 spouses, and 122,790 children. Social Security beneficiaries represented 13.5% of the total state population and 91.5% of the state's population age 65 and older. Retired workers received an average monthly payment of $929; widows and widowers, $836; disabled workers, $878; and spouses, $466. Payments for children of retired workers averaged $471 per month; children of deceased workers, $605; and children of disabled workers, $268. Federal Supplemental Security Income payments went to 199,898 Georgia residents in December 2004, averaging $372 a month.

⁴⁰HOUSING

Post–World War II housing developments provided Georgia families with modern, affordable dwellings. The home-loan guarantee programs of the Federal Housing Administration and the Veterans Administration made modest down payments, low interest rates, and long-term financing the norm in Georgia. The result was a vast increase in both the number of houses constructed and the percentage of families owning their own homes.

In 2004, there were an estimated 3,672,677 housing units in Georgia, of which 3,210,006 were occupied; 67.7% were owner occupied. About 65.9% of all units were single-family, detached homes; about 10.9% were mobile homes. It was estimated that about 190,323 units were without telephone service, 7,692 lacked complete plumbing facilities, and 9,071 lacked complete kitchen facilities. Most households relied on gas and electricity for heating. The average household had 2.67 members.

In 2004, 108,400 privately owned housing units were authorized for construction. The median value of a one-family home was about $136,910. The median monthly cost for mortgage owners was $1,126, while renters paid a median of $677 per month. In September 2005, the state received grants of $999,875 from the US Department of Housing and Urban Development (HUD) for rural housing and economic development programs. For 2006, HUD allocated over $40.2 million in community development block grants to the state.

⁴¹EDUCATION

During the colonial period, education was in the hands of private schoolmasters. Georgia's first constitution called for the establishment of a school in each county. The oldest school in the state is Richmond Academy (Augusta), founded in 1788. The nation's oldest chartered public university, the University of Georgia, dates from 1784. Public education was inadequately funded, however, until the inauguration of the sales tax in 1951, then at a 3% rate. By 1960, rural one-teacher schools had disappeared, and children were riding buses to consolidated schools.

Georgia has a comprehensive prekindergarten program, Bright from the Start, for children ages birth to four years old, the HOPE (Helping Outstanding Pupils Educationally) scholarship program, and special programs administered by the Georgia Department of Technical and Adult Education. In 2004, 85.2% of the population age 25 or older had a high school diploma; 27.6% had obtained a bachelor's degree or higher. The Board of Regents of the state university system increased its requirements for students starting college after 1988.

The total enrollment for fall 2002 in Georgia's public schools stood at 1,496,000. Of these, 1,089,000 attended schools from kindergarten through grade eight, and 407,000 attended high school. Approximately 52.1% of the students were white, 38.3% were black, 6.9% were Hispanic, 2.5% were Asian/Pacific Islander, and 0.2% were American Indian/Alaskan Native. Total enrollment was estimated at 1,508,000 in fall 2003 and expected to reach 1,627,000 by fall 2014, an increase of 8.7% during the period 2002–14. In fall 2003, there were 120,697 students enrolled in 665 private schools. Expenditures for public education in 2003/04 were estimated at $13.7 billion. Additionally, instructional services are provided for hearing- and sight-impaired students at three state schools: Atlan-ta Area School for the Deaf, Georgia Academy for the Blind, and Georgia School for the Deaf. Since 1969, the National Assessment of Educational Progress (NAEP) has tested public school students nationwide. The resulting report, *The Nation's Report Card,* stated that in 2005, eighth graders in Georgia scored 272 out of 500 in mathematics compared with the national average of 278.

As of fall 2002, there were 397,604 students enrolled in college or graduate school; minority students comprised 35.6% of total postsecondary enrollment. As of 2005, Georgia had 126 degree-granting institutions. Thirty-five public colleges are components of the University System of Georgia; the largest of these is the University of Georgia (Athens). The largest private university is Emory (Atlanta). A scholarship program was established in 1978 for minority students seeking graduate and professional degrees.

⁴²ARTS

The Georgia Council for the Arts was founded in 1965. Major ongoing programs of the council include the Georgia Folklife Program (est. 1987), the Grassroots Arts Program (est. 1993), and the State Capitol Gallery (est. 1991), which features exhibits from the State Art Collection of over 600 works of art from Georgian artists. In 2005, the National Endowment for the Arts contributed 37 grants totaling $2,788,300 to Georgia's arts programs. Arts organizations in the state receiving federal funding include the Summer Atlanta Jazz Series, the Chamber Music Rural Residencies, the Center for Puppetry Arts, Inc., and the Augusta Opera. The Augusta Opera marked its 40th anniversary in 2006. The Georgia Humanities Council was founded in 1971. In 2005, the National Endowment for the Humanities contributed $1,501,272 to 19 state programs.

During the 20th century, Atlanta replaced Savannah as the major arts center of Georgia, while Athens, the seat of the University of Georgia, continued to share in the cultural life of the university. The state has eight major art museums, as well as numerous private galleries; especially notable is the High Museum of Art in Atlanta, dedicated in 1983—known not just for its expansive collection of artworks but also for its impressive architectural design. The High Museum of Art opened expanded facilities to the public in November 2005 to house its growing needs. The Atlanta Memorial Arts Center was dedicated in 1968 to the 100 members of the association who lost their lives in a plane crash. The Atlanta Art Association was chartered in 1905 and exhibits the work of contemporary Georgia artists.

The theater has enjoyed popular support since the first professional resident theater troupe began performing in Augusta in 1790. Atlanta has a resident theater, and there are community theaters in some 30 cities and counties. Georgia has actively cultivated the filmmaking industry, and in 2004, some 252 productions (including movies) were produced in the state.

Georgia has at least 11 symphony orchestras, ranging from the Atlanta Symphony (est. 1945) to community and college ensembles throughout the state. Atlanta and Augusta have professional ballet touring companies, Augusta has a professional opera company, and choral groups and opera societies perform in all major cities. Macon is home to the Georgia Music Hall of Fame. As of 2006, inductees included Ray Charles (inducted 1979), Otis Redding (inducted 1981), James Brown (inducted 1983), the B-52's (inducted 2000), and Patty Loveless (inducted 2005). The north Georgia mountain communities retain their traditional folk music.

43 LIBRARIES AND MUSEUMS

For the fiscal year ending in June 2001, Georgia had 57 public library systems, with a total of 366 libraries, of which 309 were branches. The holdings of all public libraries that same year totaled 15,143,000 volumes of books and serial publications and had a total combined circulation of 36,229,000. The system also had 401,000 audio and 396,000 video items, 24,000 electronic format items (CD-ROMs, magnetic tapes, and disks), and 28 bookmobiles. The University of Georgia had by far the largest academic collection, including over 3 million books in addition to government documents, microfilms, and periodicals. Emory University, in Atlanta, has the largest private academic library, with about 1,520,921 bound volumes. In 2001, total operating income for the public library system was $155,868,000, including $2,988,000 in federal grants and $34,696,000 in state grants.

Georgia has at least 179 museums, including the Telfair Academy of Arts and Sciences in Savannah, the Georgia State Museum of Science and Industry in Atlanta, the Columbus Museum of Arts and Sciences, and Augusta-Richmond County Museum in Augusta. Atlanta's Cyclorama depicts the 1864 Battle of Atlanta. The Crawford W. Long Medical Museum in Jefferson is a memorial to Dr. Long, a pioneer in the use of anesthetics. A museum devoted to gold mining is located at Dahlonega.

Georgia abounds in historical sites, 100 of which were selected for acquisition in 1972 by the Georgia Heritage Trust Commission. Sites administered by the National Park Service include the Chickamauga and Chattanooga National Military Park, Kennesaw National Battlefield Park, Ft. Pulaski National Monument, and Andersonville National Monument near Americus, all associated with the Civil War, as well as the Ft. Frederica National Monument, an 18th-century English barracks on St. Simons Island. Also of historic interest are Factors Wharf in Savannah, the Hay House in Macon, and Franklin D. Roosevelt's "Little White House" at Warm Springs. The Martin Luther King Jr. National Historic Site was established in Atlanta in 1980. Also in Atlanta are President Jimmy Carter's library, museum, and conference center complex. The state's most important archaeological sites are the Etowah Mounds at Carterville, the Kolomoki Mounds at Blakely, and the Ocmulgee Indian village near Macon.

44 COMMUNICATIONS

Airmail service was introduced to Georgia about 1930, and since then the quantity of mail has increased enormously.

As of 2004, 91.2% of Georgian residences had telephones. Additionally, by June of that same year there were 5,332,517 mobile wireless telephone subscribers. In 2003, 60.6% of Georgia households had a computer and 53.5% had Internet access. By June 2005, there were 1,351,237 high-speed lines in Georgia, 1,142,806 residential and 208,431 for business. In 2005, Georgia had 112 major radio stations, 24 AM and 88 FM. There were 37 major television stations in the same year. Atlanta had 1,774,720 television-owning households in 1999, 70% of which received cable.

On 1 June 1980, Atlanta businessman Ted Turner inaugurated the independent Cable News Network (CNN), which made round-the-clock news coverage available to 4,100 cable television systems throughout the United States. By 1985, CNN was available to 32.3 million households in the United States through 7,731 cable television systems and broadcast to 22 other countries. By the late 1980s, CNN had become well known worldwide. In addition, Turner broadcasts CNN Headline News. A total of 183,093 Internet domain names were registered in Georgia as of 2000.

45 PRESS

Georgia's first newspaper was the *Georgia Gazette,* published by James Johnston from 1763 until 1776. When royal rule was temporarily restored in Savannah, Johnston published the *Royal Georgia Gazette*; when peace came, he changed the name again, this time to the *Gazette of the State of Georgia.* After the state capital was moved to Augusta in 1785, Greensburg Hughes, a Charleston printer, began publishing the *Augusta Gazette.* Today's *Augusta Chronicle* traces its origin to this paper and claims the honor of being the oldest newspaper in the state. In 1817, the *Savannah Gazette* became the state's first daily. After the Indian linguist Sequoyah gave the Cherokee a written language, Elias Boudinot gave them a newspaper, the *Cherokee Phoenix,* in 1828. Georgia authorities suppressed the paper in 1835 and Boudinot joined his tribe's tragic migration westward.

After the Civil War, Henry Grady made the *Atlanta Constitution* the most famous newspaper in the state with his "New South" campaign. Joel Chandler Harris's stories of Uncle Remus appeared in the *Constitution,* as did the weekly letters of humorist Charles Henry Smith, writing under the pseudonym of Bill Arp. In 1958, Ralph E. McGill, editor and later publisher of the *Constitution,* won a Pulitzer Prize for his editorial opposition to racial intolerance. In 2001, the *Constitution* and the Atlanta *Journal* merged to form the *Journal-Constitution,* owned by Cox Newspapers.

As of 2005, Georgia had 30 morning dailies, 4 evening dailies, and 29 Sunday newspapers.

The following table shows the leading daily newspapers with their 2005 estimated circulations:

AREA	NAME	DAILY	SUNDAY
Atlanta	*Journal-Constitution* (m,S)	441,427	606,246
Augusta	*Chronicle* (m,S)	78,069	94,040
Columbus	*Ledger-Enquirer* (m,S)	49,605	57,130
Macon	*Telegraph* (m,S)	69,132	86,004
Savannah	*Morning News* (m,S)	53,825	66,526

Periodicals published in Georgia in 2002 included *Golf World, Atlanta Weekly, Savannah, Industrial Engineering, Robotics World,* and *Southern Accents.* Among the nation's better-known scholarly presses is the University of Georgia Press, which publishes the *Georgia Review.*

46 ORGANIZATIONS

In 2006, there were over 6,580 nonprofit organizations registered within the state, of which about 4,707 were registered as charitable, educational, or religious organizations. National organizations headquartered in Georgia include the National Association of College Deans, Registrars, and Admissions Officers, located in Albany; and the Association of Information and Dissemination

Centers, the American Risk and Insurance Association, and the American Business Law Association, located in Athens.

Many organizations are headquartered in Atlanta, including the Southern Association of Colleges and Schools, the Southern Education Foundation, the Southern Regional Council, the Southern Christian Leadership Conference, the American College of Rheumatology, the Arthritis Foundation, the American Academy of Psychotherapists, and the Federation of Southern Cooperatives.

The Georgia Peanut Commission, Georgia Peanut Producers Association, and the Peanut Advisory Board promote the interests of growers of this popular crop. The Georgia Wildlife Federation addresses issues concerning the environment and conservation.

State and regional organizations that promote the arts, culture, and education include the Blue Ridge Mountains Arts Association, the Georgia Writers Association, Young Georgia Writers, the Institute for the Study of American Cultures, and the National Indian Festival Association. A national Circus Historical Society is located in Alpharetta.

The Carter Center of Emory University in Atlanta was established in 1982 by former president Jimmy Carter and his wife Rosalynn as a peace and human rights advocacy organization. The Martin Luther King Jr. Center for Nonviolent Social Change, the headquarters for the Boys and Girls Clubs of America, and the US office of CARE International are all in Atlanta.

47 TOURISM, TRAVEL, AND RECREATION

In 2005, travelers spent $28.2 billion on visits to Georgia. The Atlanta Metro Region received the most visitor expenditures, about 60%. More than 217,000 jobs are supported by the tourism industry in Georgia. The travel/tourism payroll generated over $1.28 billion in tax revenue.

Major tourist attractions include national forests, national parks, state parks, and historical areas. Other places of interest include the impressive hotels and convention facilities of downtown Atlanta; the Okefenokee Swamp in southern Georgia; Stone Mountain near Atlanta; former President Jimmy Carter's home in Plains; the Jimmy Carter Presidential Library, in Atlanta; the birthplace, church, and gravesite of Martin Luther King Jr., in Atlanta; and the historic squares and riverfront of Savannah. Georgia Aquarium, the world's largest, opened on 23 November 2005.

The varied attractions of the Golden Isles include fashionable Sea Island; primitive Cumberland Island, now a national seashore; and Jekyll Island, owned by the state and leased to motel operators and to private citizens for beach homes. Since 1978, the state, under its Heritage Trust Program, has acquired Ossabaw and Sapelo islands and strictly regulates public access to these wildlife sanctuaries.

Georgia has long been a hunters' paradise. Waynesboro calls itself the "bird-dog capital of the world," and Thomasville in south Georgia is popular with quail hunters.

48 SPORTS

There are four major professional sports teams in Georgia, all in Atlanta. Turner Field and the Georgia Dome, main venues for the 1996 Summer Olympics hosted by the city, serve as the home field for two professional teams: baseball's Atlanta Braves, for whom Henry Aaron hit many of his record 755 home runs, and the At-

lanta Falcons of the National Football League. The Philips Arena houses the Atlanta Hawks of the National Basketball Association and the Atlanta Thrashers of the National Hockey League. The Atlanta Braves won the National League pennant in 1991, 1992, 1995, 1996, and 1999. The Braves went on to win their only World Series championship since moving to Atlanta, defeating the Cleveland Indians in 1995. The Braves lost the series to the Toronto Blue Jays in 1991 and 1992, and to the New York Yankees in 1996 and 1999.

The Golden Corral 500 and the Bass Pro Shops MBNA 500 are two of the NASCAR Nextel Cup auto races held at Atlanta Motor Speedway. The Masters, the most publicized golf tournament in the world, has been played at the Augusta National Golf Club since 1934. The Atlanta Golf Classic is also listed on the professional golfers' tour.

Football and basketball dominate college sports. The University of Georgia Bulldogs, who play in the Southeastern Conference, were named National Champions in football in 1980 and advanced to the Final Four in basketball in 1983. Georgia Tech's Yellow Jackets of the Atlantic Coast Conference are a perennial basketball powerhouse. The Peach Bowl has been an annual postseason football game in Atlanta since 1968.

Professional fishing, sponsored by the Bass Anglers Sportsman's Society, is one of the fastest-growing sports in the state. Another popular summer pastime is rafting. Massive raft races on the Chattahoochee at Atlanta and Columbus, and on the Savannah River at Augusta, draw many spectators and participants.

Atlanta hosted the 1996 Summer Olympic Games at a cost of more than $1 billion.

Jackie Robinson, who broke baseball's color barrier in 1947, and Ty Cobb, nicknamed the "Georgia Peach," were both born in Georgia.

49 FAMOUS GEORGIANS

James Earl "Jimmy" Carter (b.1924), born in Plains, was the first Georgian to serve as president of the United States. He was governor of the state (1971–75) before being elected to the White House in 1976. Georgia has not contributed any US vice presidents; Alexander H. Stephens (1812–83) was vice president of the Confederacy during the Civil War.

Georgians who served on the US Supreme Court include James M. Wayne (1790–1867), John A. Campbell (1811–89), and Joseph R. Lamar (1857–1916). Supreme Court Justice Clarence Thomas, appointed to the court during the George H. W. Bush administration, was born in Savannah on 23 June 1948. Several Georgians have served with distinction at the cabinet level: William H. Crawford (b.Virginia, 1772–1834), Howell Cobb (1815–68), and William G. McAdoo (1863–1941) as secretaries of the treasury; John M. Berrien (b.New Jersey, 1781–1856) as attorney general; John Forsyth (1781–1841) and Dean Rusk (1909–94) as secretaries of state; George Crawford (1798–1872) as secretary of war; and Hoke Smith (b.North Carolina, 1855–1931) as secretary of the interior.

A leader in the US Senate before the Civil War was Robert Toombs (1810–85). Notable US senators in recent years were Walter F. George (1878–1957), Richard B. Russell (1897–1971), Herman Talmadge (1913–2002), and Sam Nunn (b.1938). Carl Vinson (1883–1981) was chairman of the House Armed Services Committee.

Many Georgians found fame in the ranks of the military. Confederate General Joseph Wheeler (1836–1906) became a major general in the US Army during the Spanish-American War. Other Civil War generals included W. H. T. Walker (1816–64); Thomas R. R. Cobb (1823–62), who also codified Georgia's laws; and John B. Gordon (1832–1904), later a US senator and governor of the state. Gordon, Alfred Colquitt (1824–94), and wartime governor Joseph E. Brown (b.South Carolina, 1821–94) were known as the "Bourbon triumvirate" for their domination of the state's Democratic Party from 1870 to 1890. Generals Courtney H. Hodge (1887–1966) and Lucius D. Clay (1897–1978) played important roles in Europe during and after World War II.

Sir James Wright (b.South Carolina 1714–85) was Georgia's most important colonial governor. Signers of the Declaration of Independence for Georgia were George Walton (b.Virginia, 1741–1804), Button Gwinnett (b.England, 1735–77), and Lyman Hall (b.Connecticut, 1724–90). Signers of the US Constitution were William Few (b.Maryland, 1748–1828) and Abraham Baldwin (b.Connecticut, 1754–1807). Revolutionary War hero James Jackson (b.England, 1757–1806) organized the Democratic-Republican Party (today's Democratic Party) in Georgia.

The first Georgians, the Indians, produced many heroes. Tomochichi (c.1664–1739) was the Yamacraw chief who welcomed James Edward Oglethorpe and the first Georgians. Alexander McGillivray (c.1759–93), a Creek chief who was the son of a Scottish fur trader, signed a treaty with George Washington in a further attempt to protect the Creek lands. Osceola (1800–1838) led his Seminole into the Florida swamps rather than move west. Sequoyah (b.Tennessee, 1773–1843) framed an alphabet for the Cherokee, and John Ross (Coowescoowe, b.Tennessee, 1790–1866) was the first president of the Cherokee Republic.

Among influential Georgian educators were Josiah Meigs (b.Connecticut, 1757–1822), the first president of the University of Georgia, and Milton Antony (1784–1839), who established the Medical College of Georgia in Augusta in 1828. Crawford W. Long (1815–78) was one of the first doctors to use ether successfully in surgical operations. Paul F. Eve (1806–77) was a leading teacher of surgery in the South, and Joseph Jones (1833–96) pioneered in the study of the causes of malaria.

Distinguished black Georgians include churchmen Henry M. Turner (b.South Carolina, 1834–1915) and Charles T. Walker (1858–1921), educators Lucy Laney (1854–1933) and John Hope (1868–1936), and civil rights activists William Edward Burghardt (W.E.B.) DuBois (b.Massachusetts, 1968–1963) and Walter F. White (1893–1955). One of the best-known Georgians was Martin Luther King Jr. (1929–68), born in Atlanta, leader of the March on Washington in 1963 and winner of the Nobel Peace Prize in 1964 for his leadership in the campaign for civil rights; he was assassinated in Memphis, Tennessee, while organizing support for striking sanitation workers. Black Muslim leader Elijah Muhammad (Elijah Poole, 1897–1975) was also a Georgian. Other prominent black leaders include Atlanta mayor and former United Nations ambassador Andrew Young (b.Louisiana, 1932), former Atlanta mayor Maynard Jackson (b.Texas, 1938–2003), and Georgia senator Julian Bond (b.Tennessee, 1940).

Famous Georgia authors include Sidney Lanier (1842–81), Joel Chandler Harris (1848–1908), Lillian Smith (1857–1966), Conrad Aiken (1889–1973), Erskine Caldwell (1902–87), Caroline Miller (1903–92), Frank Yerby (1916–91), Carson McCullers (1917–67), James Dickey (1923–97), and Flannery O'Connor (1925–64). Also notable is Margaret Mitchell (1900–49), whose Pulitzer Prize–winning *Gone with the Wind* (1936) typifies Georgia to many readers.

Entertainment celebrities include songwriter Johnny Mercer (1909–76); actors Charles Coburn (1877–1961) and Oliver Hardy (1877–1961); singers and musicians Harry James (1916–83), Ray Charles (Ray Charles Robinson, 1930–2004), James Brown (b.1933), Little Richard (Richard Penniman, b.1935), Jerry Reed (b.1937), Gladys Knight (b.1944), and Brenda Lee (b.1944); and actors Melvyn Douglas (1901–81), Sterling Holloway (1905–92), Ossie Davis (1917–2005), Barbara Cook (b.1927), Jane Withers (b.1927), Joanne Woodward (b.1930), and Burt Reynolds (b.1936).

Major sports figures include baseball's "Georgia Peach," Tyrus Raymond "Ty" Cobb (1886–1961); Jack Roosevelt "Jackie" Robinson (1919–72), the first black to be inducted into the Baseball Hall of Fame; and Robert Tyre "Bobby" Jones (1902–71), winner of the "grand slam" of four major golf tournaments in 1930.

Robert E. "Ted" Turner (b.Ohio, 1939), an Atlanta businessman-broadcaster, owns the Atlanta Hawks and the Atlanta Braves and skippered the *Courageous* to victory in the America's Cup yacht races in 1977. Architect John C. Portman Jr. (b.South Carolina, 1924), was the developer of Atlanta's Peachtree Center.

⁵⁰BIBLIOGRAPHY

Carter, Jimmy. *An Hour before Daylight: Memories of a Rural Boyhood.* New York: Simon & Schuster, 2001.

Coastal Southeast 2005: Georgia, North Carolina, South Carolina. Park Ridge, Ill.: ExxonMobil Travel Publications, 2005.

Coleman, Kenneth, et al. *A History of Georgia.* 2nd ed. Athens: University of Georgia Press, 1991.

Council of State Governments. *The Book of the States, 2006 Edition.* Lexington, Ky.: Council of State Governments, 2006.

DeGrove, John Melvin. *Planning Policy and Politics: Smart Growth and the States.* Cambridge, Mass.: Lincoln Institute of Land Policy, 2005.

Doak, Robin S. *Voices from Colonial America. Georgia, 1521–1776.* Washington, D.C.: National Geographic Society, 2006.

Grant, L. Donald. *The Way It Was in the South: The Black Experience in Georgia.* Secaucus, N.J.: Carol Publishing Group, 1993.

Inscoe, John C. (ed.). *Georgia in Black and White: Explorations in the Race Relations of a Southern State, 1865–1950.* Athens: University of Georgia Press, 1994.

Jordan, Jeffrey L. *Interstate Water Allocation in Alabama, Florida, and Georgia.* Gainesville: University Press of Florida, 2006.

King, Coretta Scott. *My Life with Martin Luther King.* Rev. ed. New York: H. Holt, 1993.

Lane, Mills. *The People of Georgia: An Illustrated History.* 2nd ed. Savannah: Library of Georgia, 1992.

Lepa, Jack H. *Breaking the Confederacy: The Georgia and Tennessee Campaigns of 1864.* Jefferson, N.C.: McFarland, 2005.

McAuliffe, Emily. *Georgia Facts and Symbols.* Mankato, Minn.: Hilltop Books, 1999.

Norman, Corrie E., and Don S. Armentrout. (eds.) *Religion in the Contemporary South: Changes, Continuities, and Contexts.* Knoxville: University of Tennessee Press, 2005.

Olmstead, Marty. *Hidden Georgia.* Berkeley, Calif.: Ulysses Press, 2000.

Reidy, Joseph P. *From Slavery to Agrarian Capitalism in the Cotton Plantation South: Central Georgia, 1800–1880.* Chapel Hill: University of North Carolina Press, 1992.

US Department of Commerce, Economics and Statistics Administration, US Census Bureau. *Georgia, 2000. Summary Social, Economic, and Housing Characteristics: 2000 Census of Population and Housing.* Washington, D.C.: US Government Printing Office, 2003.

Warren, Mervyn A. *King Came Preaching: The Pulpit Power of Dr. Martin Luther King, Jr.* Downers Grove, Ill.: InterVarsity Press, 2001.

HAWAII

State of Hawaii

ORIGIN OF STATE NAME: Unknown. The name may stem from Hawaii Loa, traditional discoverer of the islands, or from Hawaiki, the traditional Polynesian homeland. **NICKNAME:** The Aloha State. **CAPITAL:** Honolulu. **ENTERED UNION:** 21 August 1959 (50th). **SONG:** "Hawaii Ponoi." **MOTTO:** *Ua mau ke ea o ka aina i ka pono* (The life of the land is perpetuated in righteousness). **COAT OF ARMS:** The heraldic shield of the Hawaiian kingdom is flanked by the figures of Kamehameha I, who united the islands, and Liberty, holding the Hawaiian flag. Below the shield is a phoenix surrounded by taro leaves, banana foliage, and sprays of maidenhair fern. **FLAG:** Eight horizontal stripes, alternately white, red, and blue, represent the major islands, with the British Union Jack (reflecting the years that the islands were under British protection) in the upper left-hand corner. **OFFICIAL SEAL:** Same as coat of arms, with the words "State of Hawaii 1959" above and the state motto below. **BIRD:** Nene (Hawaiian goose). **FLOWER:** Pua aloalo (yellow hibiscus). **TREE:** Kukui (candlenut tree). **LEGAL HOLIDAYS:** New Year's Day, 1 January; Birthday of Martin Luther King Jr., 3rd Monday in January; Presidents' Day, 3rd Monday in February; Kuhio Day, 26 March; Good Friday and Easter, March or April; Memorial Day, last Monday in May; Kamehameha Day, 11 June; Independence Day, 4 July; Statehood Day, 3rd Friday in August; Labor Day, 1st Monday in September; Election Day, 1st Tuesday after 1st Monday in November; Veterans' Day, 11 November; Thanksgiving Day, 4th Thursday in November; Christmas Day, 25 December. **TIME:** 2 AM Hawaii-Aleutian Standard Time = noon GMT.

¹LOCATION, SIZE, AND EXTENT

The state of Hawaii is an island group situated in the northern Pacific Ocean, about 2,400 mi (3,900 km) wsw of San Francisco. The smallest of the five Pacific states, Hawaii ranks 47th in size among the 50 states.

The 132 Hawaiian Islands have a total area of 6,470 sq mi (16,758 sq km), including 6,425 sq mi (16,641 sq km) of land and only 45 sq mi (117 sq km) of inland water. The island chain extends over 1,576 mi (2,536 km) N–S and 1,425 mi (2,293 km) E–W. The largest island, Hawaii (known locally as the "Big Island"), extends 76 mi (122 km) E–W and 93 mi (150 km) N–S; Oahu, the most populous island, extends 44 mi (71 km) E–W and 30 mi (48 km) N–S.

The eight largest islands of the Hawaiian group are Hawaii (4,035 sq mi/10,451 sq km), Maui (734 sq mi/1,901 sq km), Oahu (617 sq mi/1,598 sq km), Kauai (558 sq mi/1,445 sq km), Molokai (264 sq mi/684 sq km), Lanai (141 sq mi/365 sq km), Niihau (73 sq mi/189 sq km), and Kahoolawe (45 sq mi/117 sq km). The general coastline of the island chain is 750 mi (1,207 km); the tidal shoreline totals 1,052 mi (1,693 km). The state's geographic center is off Maui, at 20°15′ N, 156°20′ w.

²TOPOGRAPHY

The 8 major and 124 minor islands that make up the state of Hawaii were formed by volcanic eruptions. Mauna Loa, on the island of Hawaii, is the world's largest active volcano, at a height of 13,675 ft (4,168 m). Kilauea, on the eastern slope of Mauna Loa, is the world's largest active volcanic crater: Beginning on 24 May 1969, it spewed forth 242 million cu yd (185 million cu m) of lava, spreading over an area of 19.3 sq mi (50 sq km). The longest volcanic eruption in Hawaii lasted 867 days. Further indications of Ha-

waii's continuing geological activity are the 14 earthquakes, each with a magnitude of 5 or more on the Richter scale, that shook the islands from 1969 to 1979; one quake, at Puna, on Hawaii in 1975, reached a magnitude of 7.2.

Hawaii, Maui, Kauai, and Molokai are the most mountainous islands. The highest peak in the state is Puu Wekiu (13,796 ft/4,208 m), on Hawaii; the largest natural lake, Halulu (182 acres/74 hectares), Niihau; the largest artificial lake, Waiia Reservoir (422 acres/171 hectares), Kauai; and the longest rivers, Kaukonahua Stream (33 mi/53 km) in the north on Oahu and Wailuku River (32 mi/51 km) on Hawaii. While much of the Pacific Ocean surrounding the state is up to 20,000 ft (6,100 m) deep, Oahu, Molokai, Lanai, and Maui stand on a submarine bank at a depth of less than 2,400 ft (730 m). The lowest point of the state is sea level at the Pacific Ocean. The mean elevation is approximately 3,030 ft (924 m).

³CLIMATE

Hawaii has a tropical climate cooled by trade winds. Normal daily temperatures in Honolulu average 73°F (22°C) in February and 81°F (27°C) in August; the average wind speed is a breezy 11.3 mph (18.2 km/h). The record high for the state is 100°F (38°C), set at Pahala on 27 April 1931, and the record low is 12°F (-11°C), set at Mauna Kea Observatory on 17 May 1979.

Rainfall is extremely variable, with far more precipitation on the windward (northeastern) than on the leeward side of the islands. Mt. Waialeale, Kauai, is reputedly the rainiest place on earth, with a mean annual total of 486 in (1,234 cm). Kukui, Maui, holds the US record for the most precipitation in one year—739 in (1,878 cm) in 1982. Average annual precipitation in Honolulu (1971–

2000) was 18.3 in (46.5 cm). In the driest areas—on upper mountain slopes and in island interiors, as in central Maui—the average annual rainfall is less than 10 in (25 cm). Snow falls at the summits of Mauna Loa, Mauna Kea, and Haleakala—the highest mountains. The highest tidal wave (tsunami) in the state's history reached 56 ft (17 m).

⁴FLORA AND FAUNA

Formed over many centuries by volcanic activity, Hawaii's topography—and therefore its flora and fauna—have been subject to constant and rapid change. Relatively few indigenous trees remain; most of the exotic trees and fruit plants have been introduced since the early 19th century. Of the 2,200 species and subspecies of flora, more than half are endangered, threatened, or extinct.

The only land mammal native to the islands is the Hawaiian hoary bat, now endangered; there are no indigenous snakes. In April 2006, a total of 317 species occurring within the state were on the threatened and endangered species list of the US Fish and Wildlife Service. These included 44 animal (vertebrates and invertebrates) and 273 plant species. The endangered humpback whale migrates to Hawaiian waters in winter; other marine animals abound. Four species of sea turtle are also endangered. Among threatened birds are several varieties of honeycreeper, short-tailed albatross, Hawaiian coot, and the Hawaiian goose (nene). The nene (the state bird), once close to extinction, now numbers in the hundreds and is on the increase. The Kawainui and Hamakua Marsh Complex, a Ramsar Wetland of International Importance, provides a habitat for at least four of the states endangered bird species, including the nene.

Animals considered endangered by the state but not on the federal list include the Hawaiian storm petrel, Hawaiian owl, Maui 'amakihi (*Loxops virens wilsoni*), and 'I'iwi (*Vestiaria coccinea*).

⁵ENVIRONMENTAL PROTECTION

Environmental protection responsibilities are vested in the Department of Land and Natural Resources, and in the Environmental Management Division of the Department of Health. The Hawaii Environmental Policy Act of 1974 established environmental policies and guidelines for state agencies. Also enacted in 1974 was the Environmental Impact Statement Law, which mandated environmental assessments for all state and county projects and some private projects. Noise pollution requirements for the state are among the strictest in the United States, and air and water purity levels are well within federal standards.

Since much of Hawaii's natural wetlands have been filled in for use as agricultural lands or for urban expansion projects, wetlands now cover less than 3% of the state. The Kawainui and Hamakua Marsh Complex was designated as a Ramsar Wetland of International Importance in February 2005. Besides serving as a habitat for at least four species of endangered birds, the site is considered to be a cultural and archeological resource, one that is sacred to some native Hawaiians. In January 2006, the Hawaii Department of Land and Natural Resources received a federal Coastal Wetlands Conservation grant of $646,250 for restoration projects in marsh. In 2005, federal Environmental Protection Agency (EPA) grants awarded to the state included $323,930 for a beach water quality monitoring and public notification program.

The EPA banned the use of ethylene dibromide (EDB), a pesticide used in the state's pineapple fields, after high levels of the chemical were found in wells on the island of Oahu in 1983. In 2003, 3.1 million lb of toxic chemicals were released in the state. In 2003, the US EPA's database listed 87 hazardous waste sites in Hawaii, three of which were on the National Priorities List as of 2006, including the Del Monte Corp. Oahu Plantation, the Naval Computer and Telecommunications Area, and the Pearl Harbor Naval Complex. In 2005, the EPA spent over $41,000 through the Superfund program for the cleanup of hazardous waste sites in the state.

⁶POPULATION

Hawaii ranked 42nd in population in the United States with an estimated total of 1,275,194 in 2005, an increase of 5.3% since 2000. Between 1990 and 2000, Hawaii's population grew from 1,108,229 to 1,211,537, an increase of 9.3%. The population is projected to reach 1.38 million by 2015 and 1.43 million by 2025. Almost four-fifths of the population lives on Oahu, primarily in the Greater Honolulu metropolitan area. Population density was 196.6 people per sq mi in 2004.

In 2004, the median age was 38. Persons under 18 years old accounted for 23.7% of the population, while 13.6% of the population was age 65 or older.

By far the largest city is Honolulu, with an estimated 2004 population of 377,260. The Greater Honolulu metropolitan area had an estimated 899,593 residents in 1999. The city of Honolulu is coextensive with Honolulu County.

⁷ETHNIC GROUPS

Hawaii has the nation's highest percentage of Asian residents—41.6% in 2000, when its Asian population numbered 503,868. In 2004, 41.8% of the population was Asian. In 2000, Pacific Islanders numbered 113,539 (including 80,137 native Hawaiians), 22,003 were black, and 3,535 were American Indians or Alaska Natives. About 87,699, or 7.2% of the total population, were Hispanic or Latino in 2000. Foreign-born residents numbered 212,229 in 2000, or 17.5% of the total state population—the fifth-highest percentage of foreign born among the 50 states. In 2004, 9.1% of the population was Native Hawaiian or other Pacific Islander, 2.2% was black, 0.3% was American Indian or Alaska Native, and 7.9% was of Hispanic or Latino origin. A full 20.1% of the population reported origin of two or more races.

Of Hawaii's Asian residents in 2000, 201,764 were Japanese, 170,635 were Filipino, 56,600 were Chinese, and 23,637 were Korean. The earliest Asian immigrants, the Chinese, were superseded in number in 1900 by the Japanese, who have since become a significant factor in state politics. The influx of Filipinos and other Pacific Island peoples was largely a 20th-century phenomenon. In recent decades, ethnic Hawaiians have been increasingly intent on preserving their cultural identity.

⁸LANGUAGES

Although massive immigration from Asia and the US mainland since the mid-19th century has effectively diluted the native population, the Hawaiian lexical legacy in English is conspicuous. Newcomers soon add to their vocabulary the words *aloha* (love, good-bye), *haole* (white foreigner), *malihini* (newcomer), *lanai*

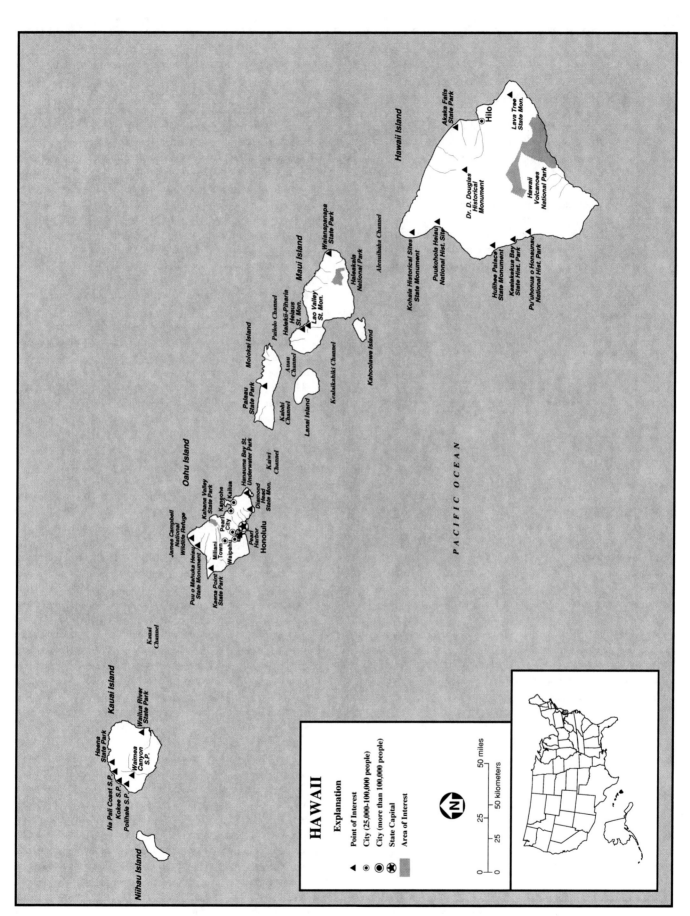

Hawaii Island

Akaka Falls
State Park

Hilo

Lava Tree
State Mon.

Dr. D. Douglas
Historical
Monument

Hawaii
Volcanoes
National Park

Kohala Historical Sites
State Monument

Puukohola Heiau
National Hist. Site

Hulihee Palace
State Monument

Kealakekua Bay
State Hist. Park

Pu'uhonua o Honaunau
National Hist. Park

Waianapanapa
State Park

Maui Island

Haleakala
National Park

Alenuihaha Channel

Iao Valley
St. Mon.

Halekii-Piihana
Heiau
St. Mon.

Pailolo Channel

Molokai Island

Palaau
State Park

Auau
Channel

Kalohi
Channel

Lanai Island

Kealaikahiki Channel

Kahoolawe Island

PACIFIC OCEAN

Oahu Island

James Campbell
National
Wildlife Refuge

Kahana Valley
State Park

Kaneohe

Kailua

Hanauma Bay St.
Underwater Park

Diamond
Head
State Mon.

Puu o Mahuka Heiau
State Monument

Mililani
Town

Waipahu

Pearl
City

Pearl
Harbor

Honolulu

Keana Point
State Park

Kaiwi
Channel

Kauai Channel

Kauai Island

Wailua River
State Park

Haena
State Park

Na Pali Coast S.P.

Kokee S.P.

Polihale S.P.

Waimea
Canyon
S.P.

Niihau Island

HAWAII

Explanation

Point of Interest ▲

City (25,000–100,000 people) ◉

City (more than 100,000 people) ◉

State Capital ✪

Area of Interest ▨

N

0   25   50 miles

0   25   50 kilometers

(porch), *tapa* (bark cloth), *mahimahi* (a kind of fish), *ukulele*, *muumuu*, and the common directional terms *mauka* (toward the mountains) and *makai* (toward the sea), customarily used instead of "north," "east," "west," and "south." Native place-names are numerous—Waikiki, Hawaii, Honolulu, Mauna Kea, and Molokai, for example.

Most native-born residents of Hawaiian ancestry speak one of several varieties of Hawaiian pidgin, a lingua franca incorporating elements of Hawaiian, English, and other Asian and Pacific languages. In 2000, 73.4% (down from 75.2% in 1990) of Hawaiians five years old or older spoke only English at home.

The following table gives selected statistics from the 2000 Census for language spoken at home by persons five years old and over. The category "Other Pacific Island languages" includes Chamorro, Hawaiian, Ilocano, Indonesian, and Samoan. The category "Other Indo-European languages" includes Albanian, Gaelic, Lithuanian, and Rumanian.

LANGUAGE	NUMBER	PERCENT
Population 5 years and over	**1,134,351**	**100.0**
Speak only English	832,226	73.4
Speak a language other than English	302,125	26.6
Speak a language other than English	**302,125**	**26.6**
Other Pacific Island languages	90,111	7.9
Tagalog	60,967	5.4
Japanese	56,225	5.0
Chinese	29,363	2.6
Spanish or Spanish Creole	18,820	1.7
Korean	18,337	1.6
Vietnamese	8,270	0.7
German	3,986	0.4
French (incl. Patois, Cajun)	3,310	0.3
Laotian	1,920	0.2
Thai	1,496	0.1
Other Indo-European languages	1,288	0.1
Portuguese or Portuguese Creole	1,238	0.1

⁹RELIGIONS

Congregationalist missionaries arrived in 1820 and Roman Catholics in 1827. Subsequent migration brought Mormons and Methodists. Anglican representatives were invited by King Kamehameha IV in 1862. Confucianism, Taoism, and Buddhism arrived with the Chinese during the 1850s; by the turn of the century, Shinto and five forms of Mahayana Buddhism were being practiced by Japanese immigrants.

The largest religious group is the Roman Catholic Church, with 234,588 adherents in 66 parishes as of 2004. The Latter-Day Saints (Mormons) reported a membership of 64,608 in 127 congregations for 2006, an increase from 2000, when 42,758 adherents in 112 congregations were reported. There are two Mormon temples in the state: Laie, Oahu (est. 1919) and Kona (est. 1999). Other major groups (with 2000 data) include the Assemblies of God, 21,754 members, and the Southern Baptist Convention, 20,901 members. The Southern Baptist Convention reported 636 newly baptized members in 2002. The United Church of Christ had 17, 362 adherents in 2005. In 2000, the Jewish population was at about 7,000. There were 73 Buddhist, 1 Muslim, and 8 Hindu congregations reported that year without specific membership numbers. About 63.8% of the population did not specify a religious affiliation.

Aloha International, founded in 1973, is a nondenominational organization based in Kapaa that promotes a system of spiritual healing known as *Huna*. The organization reports a membership of about 14,000. There are several local chapters of Young Life, a Christian youth organization, and Soka Gakkai International, a Buddhist organization.

¹⁰TRANSPORTATION

Hawaii has only two railroads: the nonprofit Hawaiian Railway Society, with 6.5 mi (10.5 km) of track on Oahu; and the commercial-recreational Lahaina, Kaanapali and Pacific on Maui, with 6 mi (10 km) of track. The islands of Oahu, Hawaii, Maui, and Kauai have public bus systems. In 2004, Hawaii's 843,876 licensed drivers traversed 4,318 mi (6,951 km) of roads and streets. There were some 532,000 passenger cars registered in 2004, along with approximately 394,000 trucks of all types and around 4,000 buses.

Hawaii's busiest port is Honolulu, with 19.085 million tons of cargo handled in 2004, making it the 39th-busiest port in the United States. Other major Hawaiian ports and their 2004 tonnage handled include Barbers Point, Oahu, 6.086 million tons; Hilo, 1.850 million tons; and Kahului, Maui, 3.9 million tons. In 2003, waterborne shipments totaled 23.642 million tons.

Most scheduled interisland passenger traffic and most transpacific travel is by air. In 2005, Hawaii had a total of 48 public and private-use aviation-related facilities. This included 31 airports and 17 heliports. The state's busiest air terminal is Honolulu International Airport, which had a total of 9,579,076 enplanements in 2004 , making it the 25th-busiest airport in the United States.

¹¹HISTORY

Hawaii's earliest inhabitants were Polynesians who came to the islands in double-hulled canoes between 1,000 and 1,400 years ago, either from Southeast Asia or from the Marquesas in the South Pacific. The Western world learned of the islands in 1778, when an English navigator, Captain James Cook, sighted Oahu; he named the entire archipelago the Sandwich Islands after his patron, John Montagu, Fourth Earl of Sandwich. At that time, each island was ruled by a hereditary chief under a caste system called *kapu*. Subsequent contact with European sailors and traders exposed the Polynesians to smallpox, venereal disease, liquor, firearms, and Western technology—and fatally weakened the kapu system. Within 40 years of Cook's arrival, one of the island chiefs, Kamehameha (whose birth date, designated as 11 June, is still celebrated as a state holiday), had consolidated his power on Hawaii, conquered Maui and Oahu, and established a royal dynasty in what became known as the Kingdom of Hawaii.

The death of Kamehameha I in 1819 preceded the arrival of Protestant missionaries by a year. One of the first to come was the Reverend Hiram Bingham, who, as pastor in Honolulu, was instrumental in converting Hawaiians to Christianity. Even before Bingham arrived, however, Liholiho, successor to the throne under the title of Kamehameha II, had begun to do away with the kapu system. After the king's death from measles while on a state trip to England in 1824, another son of Kamehameha I, Kauikeaouli, was proclaimed King Kamehameha III. His reign saw the establishment of public schools, the first newspapers, the first sugar plantation, a bicameral legislature, and the establishment of Honolulu as the kingdom's capital city. Hawaii's first written constitution was promulgated in 1840, and in 1848 a land reform called the Great Mahele abolished the feudal land system and legitimized private landholdings, in the process fostering the expansion of sugar plantations. The power behind the throne during this period was Dr. Gerrit P. Judd, a medical missionary who served as finance minister and interpreter for Kamehameha III.

Diplomatic maneuverings during the 1840s and 1850s secured recognition of the kingdom from the United States, Britain, and France. As the American presence on the islands increased, however, so did pressure for US annexation—a movement opposed by Alexander Liholiho, who ruled as Kamehameha IV after his father's death in 1854. His brief reign and that of his brother Lot (Kamehameha V) witnessed the arrival of Chinese contract laborers and the first Japanese immigrants, along with the continued growth of Hawaii as an international port of call (especially for whalers) and the increasing influence of American sugar planters. Lot's death in 1872 left no direct descendant of Kamehameha, and the legislature elected a new king, whose death only a year later required yet another election. The consequent crowning of Kalakaua, known as the Merry Monarch, inaugurated a stormy decade during which his imperial schemes clashed with the power of the legislature and the interests of the planters. The most significant event of Kalakaua's unstable reign was the signing of a treaty with the United States in 1876, guaranteeing Hawaii an American sugar market. The treaty was renewed in 1887 with a clause leasing Pearl Harbor to the United States.

Kalakaua died during a visit to San Francisco in 1891 and was succeeded by his sister, Liliuokalani, the last Hawaiian monarch. Two years later, after further political wrangling, she was deposed in an American-led revolution that produced a provisional government under the leadership of Sanford B. Dole. The new regime immediately requested annexation by the United States, but the treaty providing for it bogged down in the Senate and died after the inauguration of President Grover Cleveland, an opponent of expansionism. The provisional government then drafted a new constitution and on 4 July 1894 proclaimed the Republic of Hawaii, with Dole as president. The Spanish-American War, which fanned expansionist feelings in the United States and pointed up the nation's strategic interests in the Pacific, gave proponents of annexation the opportunity they had been seeking. The formal transfer of sovereignty took place on 12 August 1898, and Dole became Hawaii's first territorial governor when the act authorizing the annexation became effective in June 1900.

Notable in the territorial period were a steady US military buildup, the creation of a pineapple canning industry by James D. Dole (the governor's cousin), the growth of tourism (spurred in 1936 by the inauguration of commercial air service), and a rising desire for statehood, especially after passage of the Sugar Act of 1934, which lowered the quota on sugar imports from Hawaii. The Japanese attack on Pearl Harbor on 7 December 1941, crippling the US Pacific fleet and causing some 4,000 casualties, quickly turned Hawaii into an armed camp under martial law. The record of bravery compiled by Nisei of the 442d Regiment on the European front did much, on the other hand, to allay the mistrust that some mainlanders felt about the loyalties of Hawaiians of Japanese ancestry. Hawaii also bore a disproportionate burden during the Korean conflict, suffering more casualties per capita than any of the 48 states.

Hawaiians pressed for statehood after World War II, but Congress was reluctant, partly because of racial antipathy and partly because of fears that Hawaii's powerful International Longshoremen's and Warehousemen's Union was Communist controlled. The House of Representatives passed a statehood bill in 1947, but the Senate refused. Not until 1959, after Alaska became the 49th state, did Congress vote to let Hawaii enter the Union. President Dwight D. Eisenhower signed the bill on 18 March, and the question was then put to the Hawaiian electorate, who voted for statehood on 27 June 1959 by a margin of about 17 to 1. Hawaii became the 50th state on 21 August 1959.

Defense, tourism, and food processing have been the mainstays of Hawaii's economy, with the state playing an increasingly important role as an economic, educational, and cultural bridge between the United States and the nations of Asia and the Pacific. Hawaiians have faced the challenge of preserving the natural beauty of their environment while accommodating a growing population (especially on Oahu) and a thriving tourist industry. In May 2000, President Bill Clinton issued orders to federal agencies to expand their coastline protection programs, including those protecting Hawaii's coral reefs.

A prominent political issue in recent years has been the achievement of some form of sovereignty by native Hawaiians. Control of an estimated 2 million acres of land is also at stake. In 1996 a majority of the islands' roughly 200,000 descendants of indigenous Hawaiians (in 2005, roughly 400,000) voted to establish some form of self-government. In August 1998, the 100th anniversary of the US annexation of Hawaii, protesters marched in Washington, DC, demanding their full sovereignty from the US government. In July 2000, the movement got some backing in a rights bill introduced in Congress by Hawaiian senator Daniel Akaka. The bill asked that Native Hawaiians be allowed to form their own government and have status similar to that of American Indians. In 2005, the Akaka Bill (amended many times) was opposed by certain Native Hawaiian groups because it would allow the US Department of the Interior too much administrative power over their affairs.

Hawaii's tourism industry was negatively affected by the 2001 recession, the 11 September 2001 terrorist attacks on the United States, and the 2003 Iraq War. Hawaii's tourism business declined by about one-third in one month after the start of the Iraq War on 19 March 2003. That year, the Hawaii legislature passed a nonbinding resolution condemning portions of the 2001 USA Patriot Act and the 2002 Homeland Security Act (which include sweeping federal powers to combat terrorism) and called on state and local officials to avoid any actions that threatened the civil rights of any of Hawaii's residents. Hawaii was the first state to go on record against the Patriot and Homeland Security acts.

12 STATE GOVERNMENT

The constitution of the state of Hawaii was written by the constitutional convention of 1950, ratified by the people of the territory of Hawaii that year, and then amended by the 1959 plebiscite on the statehood question. By January 2005, it had been amended 104 times.

There is a bicameral legislature of 25 senators elected from eight senatorial districts for four-year terms, and 51 representatives elected for two-year terms. The legislature meets annually on the third Wednesday in January; the session is limited to 60 legislative days, but a two-thirds petition by the membership secures an extension (limited to 15 days). Special sessions may be called by petition of two-thirds of the members of each house. To be eligible to serve as a legislator, a person must have attained the age of majority (18), be an American citizen, have been a resident of the state for at least three years, and be a qualified voter of his district. The legislative salary in 2004 was $32,000, unchanged from 1999.

The governor and lieutenant governor are jointly elected for concurrent four-year terms and must be of the same political party. They are the only elected officers of the executive branch, except for the 13 members of the Board of Education, who also serve four-year terms. The governor, who may be reelected only once, must be at least 30 years old, a qualified voter, and must have resided in the state for five years. As of December 2004, the governor's salary was $94,780, unchanged from 1999.

The legislature can override the governor's veto by a two-thirds vote of the elected members of both houses. If the governor neither signs nor vetoes a bill, it becomes law after 10 days (excepting Saturdays, Sundays, and holidays) when the legislature is in session or after 45 days (excepting Saturdays, Sundays, and holidays) after the legislature has adjourned.

A constitutional amendment may be proposed by the legislature with a two-thirds vote in each house in one session or a majority vote in each house in two sessions. It must then be approved by a majority of the voters during elections.

Voters in Hawaii must be US citizens, state residents, and at least 18 years old. Restrictions apply to convicted felons and those declared mentally incompetent by the court.

13 POLITICAL PARTIES

Both Republicans and Democrats established party organizations early in the 20th century, when Hawaii was still a territory. Before statehood, the Republican Party dominated the political scene; since the 1960s, however, Hawaii has been solidly Democratic.

Democrat Al Gore won 56% of the vote in the presidential election in 2000, while Republican George W. Bush garnered 38%, and Green Party candidate Ralph Nader took 6%. Four years later, Democrat John Kerry won 54% of the vote to Republican incumbent George W. Bush's 45%. Democrat Daniel K. Inouye first won election to the US Senate in 1962; he was reelected in 1968, 1974, 1980, 1986, 1992, 1998, and 2004. Democratic senator Dan-

iel K. Akaka, first appointed in 1990 and elected to a full term in 1994, was reelected in 2000. Both of Hawaii's representatives to the House were Democrats in 2005. A Republican, Linda Lingle, was elected governor in 2002. In 2005, Democrats held 20 of the seats in the state Senate, while Republicans held just 5. In the state House, Democrats held 41 seats to the Republican's 10. In 2004, there were 647,000 registered voters; there is no party registration in the state. The state had four electoral votes in the 2004 presidential election.

14 LOCAL GOVERNMENT

The state is divided into five principal counties: Hawaii, including the island of Hawaii; Maui, embracing the islands of Maui, Kahoolawe, Lanai, and Molokai; Honolulu, coextensive with the city of Honolulu and covering all of Oahu and the northwestern Hawaiian Islands, from Nihoa to Kure Atoll; Kauai, including the islands of Kauai and Niihau; and Kalawao on Molokai. Kalawao is represented in the state legislature as part of Maui County.

Because there are no further forms of local government, the counties provide some services that are traditionally performed in other states by cities, towns, and villages, notably fire and police protection, refuse collection, and street maintenance and lighting. On the other hand, the state government provides many functions that are normally performed by counties on the mainland. Each principal county has an elected council and a mayor.

In 2005, the state had 15 special districts and one public school system.

In 2005, local government accounted for about 14,344 full-time (or equivalent) employment positions.

15 STATE SERVICES

To address the continuing threat of terrorism and to work with the federal Department of Homeland Security, homeland security in Hawaii operates under the authority of the governor; the adjutant general is designated as the state homeland security adviser.

Hawaii's first ombudsman, empowered to investigate complaints by the public about any officer or employee of state or county government, took office in 1969. The State Ethics Commission, a legislative agency, implements requirements for financial disclosure by state officials and investigates alleged conflicts of interest and other breaches of ethics.

The Department of Education is headed by an elected Board of Education. It operates hundreds of schools in the state, including several for the physically and mentally disabled. It also regulates private schools and certifies teachers. The Board of Regents of the University of Hawaii oversees the state's higher educational institutions. The State Public Library system provides Hawaii's residents with access to education, information, programs and services. Highways, airports, harbors, and other facilities are the concern of the Department of Transportation.

The Department of Health operates public hospitals and various programs for the mentally ill, the developmentally disabled, and alcoholics. Civil defense and the Air and Army National Guards are under the jurisdiction of the Department of Defense. The Department of Land and Natural Resources focuses on the environment.

The Corrections Division of the Department of Public Safety operates the state prison system, along with programs for juve-

Hawaii Presidential Vote by Major Political Parties, 1960–2004

YEAR	ELECTORAL VOTE	HAWAII WINNER	DEMOCRAT	REPUBLICAN
1960	3	*Kennedy (D)	92,410	92,295
1964	4	*Johnson (D)	163,249	44,022
1968	4	Humphrey (D)	141,324	91,425
1972	4	*Nixon (R)	101,433	168,933
1976	4	*Carter (D)	147,375	140,003
1980	4	Carter (D)	135,879	130,112
1984	4	*Reagan (R)	147,154	185,050
1988	4	Dukakis (D)	192,364	158,625
1992**	4	*Clinton (D)	179,310	136,822
1996**	4	*Clinton (D)	205,012	113,943
2000***	4	Gore (D)	205,286	137,845
2004	4	Kerry (D)	231,708	194,191

*Won US presidential election.
**IND. candidate Ross Perot received 53,003 votes in 1992 and 27,358 votes in l996.
***GREEN Party candidate Ralph Nader received 21,623 votes in 2000.

nile offenders. The Department of Human Services is responsible for social services, housing, health care, child welfare, disabilities, and programs for the aged, women, and fathers. Unemployment insurance, occupational safety and health laws, and workers' compensation programs are run by the Department of Labor and Industrial Relations.

16 JUDICIAL SYSTEM

The supreme court, the highest in the state, consists of a chief justice and four associate justices, all of them appointed by the governor with the advice and consent of the Senate. All serve 10-year terms, up to the mandatory retirement age of 70.

The state is divided into four judicial circuits with 27 circuit court judges and four intermediate appellate court judges, also appointed by the governor with the advice and consent of the Senate to 10-year terms. Circuit courts are the main trial courts, having jurisdiction in most civil and criminal cases. District courts, whose judges are appointed by the chief justice with the advice and consent of the Senate to six-year terms, function as inferior courts within each judicial circuit; district court judges may also preside over family court proceedings. Hawaii also has a land court and a tax appeal court.

As of 31 December 2004, a total of 5,960 prisoners were held in Hawaii's state and federal prisons, an increase from 5,828 or 2.3% from the previous year. As of year-end 2004, a total of 699 inmates were female, up from 685 or 2% from the year before. Among sentenced prisoners (one year or more), Hawaii had an incarceration rate of 329 per 100,000 population in 2004.

According to the Federal Bureau of Investigation, in 2004 Hawaii had a violent crime rate (murder/nonnegligent manslaughter; forcible rape; robbery; aggravated assault) of 254.4 reported incidents per 100,000 population, or a total of 3,213 reported incidents. Crimes against property (burglary; larceny/theft; and motor vehicle theft) in that same year totaled 60,525 reported incidents or 4,792.8 reported incidents per 100,000 people. Hawaii does not have a death penalty.

In 2003, Hawaii spent $120,409,439 on homeland security, an average of $57 per state resident.

17 ARMED FORCES

Hawaii is the nerve center of US defense activities in the Pacific. CINCPAC (Commander-in-Chief Pacific), headquartered at Camp H. M. Smith in Honolulu, directs the US Pacific Command, largest of the six US Unified Commands, and is responsible for all US military forces in the Pacific and Indian oceans and southern Asia. Effective 24 October 2002, the title Commander in Chief, US Pacific Command was changed to Commander, US Pacific Command (CDRUSPACOM). Military prime contract awards in the fiscal year 2004 totaled $1.7 billion, and defense payroll, including retired military pay, amounted to $3.3 billion.

As of 2004, Hawaii was home base for 65,302 Department of Defense military and civilian personnel. The US Navy and Marines accounted for 24,440 personnel; the Army, 19,408; and the Air Force, 6,801. Pearl Harbor is home port for 40 ships. The major Army bases, all on Oahu, are Schofield Barracks, Ft. Shafter, and Ft. DeRussy; Air Force bases include Hickam and Wheeler. Military reservations occupy nearly one-fourth of Oahu's land area.

There were 107,310 veterans of US military service in Hawaii as of 2003, of whom 13,644 served in World War II; 11,093 in the Korean conflict; 33,858 during the Vietnam era; and 17,058 in the Gulf War. Expenditures for veterans totaled $311 million in fiscal year 2004.

18 MIGRATION

The US mainland and Asia have been the main sources of immigrants to Hawaii since the early 19th century. Immigration remains a major source of population growth: Between 1950 and 1980, Hawaii's net gain from migration was 91,000, and between 1980 and 1983, 15,000. In the 1980s, migration accounted for 23% of the net increase in population.

Since the early 1970s, about 40,000 mainland Americans have come each year to live in Hawaii. More than half are military personnel and their dependents, on temporary residence during their term of military service. From 1985 to 1990, Hawaii suffered a net loss from migration within the United States but experienced an overall net gain in migration due to immigration from abroad. Between 1990 and 1998, the net loss from domestic migration was 80,000. During the same period there was a net gain of 51,000 from international migration. In 1998, 5,465 foreign immigrants arrived in Hawaii. Between 1990 and 1998, the state's overall population increased 7.6%. In the period 2000–05, net international migration was 30,068 and net internal migration was –13,112, for a net gain of 16,956 people.

19 INTERGOVERNMENTAL COOPERATION

Among the interstate accords in which Hawaii participates are the Western Interstate Corrections Compact and the Western Interstate Commission for Higher Education. Federal grants were estimated at $1.5 billion in fiscal year 2001. Following a national trend, federal grants dropped to $1.387 billion in fiscal year 2005. In fiscal year 2006, they stood at an estimated $1.415 billion, and an estimated $1.422 billion in fiscal year 2007.

20 ECONOMY

Tourism remains Hawaii's leading employer, revenue producer, and growth sector. However, agricultural diversification (including the cultivation of flowers and nursery products, papaya, and macadamia nuts), aquaculture, manganese nodule mining, and film and television production have broadened the state's economic base. Economic growth was relatively sluggish in Hawaii at the end of the 20th century, accelerating from only 2.2% in 1998 to 3.3% in 1999 to 4.6% in 2000. The national recession of 2001 and the aftereffects of the 11 September 2001 terrorist attacks on the United States helped reduce the annual growth rate to 2.8% in 2001, mainly through the impact on tourism. By the third quarter of 2002, however, hotel revenue in Hawaii was showing an increase over 2001, in contrast to hotel revenues in other parts of the country. Payroll employment, after declining sharply in 2001, was also showing increases.

Hawaii's gross state product (GSP) in 2005 totaled $54 billion; in 2004 real estate was the largest sector at 16.5% of GSP, followed by lodging and food service at 8.4%, and health care and social services at 6.8%. In that same year, there were an estimated 105,242 small businesses in Hawaii. Of the 29,791 businesses having employees, a total of 28,844 or 96.8% were small companies.

An estimated 3,698 new businesses were established in the state in 2004, up 1.1% from the previous year. Business terminations that same year came to 3,754, down 6.4% from 2003. Business bankruptcies totaled 47 in 2004, down 34.7% from the year before. In 2005, the personal bankruptcy (Chapter 7 and Chapter 13) filing rate was 299 filings per 100,000 people, ranking Hawaii as the 48th highest in the nation.

21 INCOME

In 2005, Hawaii had a gross state product (GSP) of $54 billion, which accounted for 0.4% of the nation's gross domestic product and placed the state at number 42 in highest GSP among the 50 states and the District of Columbia.

According to the Bureau of Economic Analysis, in 2004, Hawaii had a per capita personal income (PCPI) of $32,625. This ranked 20th in the United States and was 99% of the national average of $33,050. The 1994–2004 average annual growth rate of PCPI was 2.8%. Hawaii had a total personal income (TPI) of $41,176,427,000, which ranked 40th in the United States and reflected an increase of 8.0% from 2003. The 1994–2004 average annual growth rate of TPI was 3.4%. Earnings of persons employed in Hawaii increased from $30,504,321,000 in 2003 to $33,021,075,000 in 2004, an increase of 8.3%. The 2003–04 national change was 6.3%.

The US Census Bureau reports that the three-year average median household income for 2002–04 in 2004 dollars was $53,123 compared to a national average of $44,473. During the same period, an estimated 9.7% of the population was below the poverty line, as compared to 12.4% nationwide.

22 LABOR

According to the Bureau of Labor Statistics (BLS), in April 2006, the seasonally adjusted civilian labor force in Hawaii numbered 645,600. Approximately 18,000 workers were unemployed, yielding an unemployment rate of 4.6%, compared to the national average of 4.7% for the same period. Preliminary data for the same period placed nonfarm employment at 615,400. Since the beginning of the BLS data series in 1976, the highest unemployment rate recorded in Hawaii was 10.2% in March 1976. The historical low was 2.2% in November 1989. Preliminary nonfarm employment data by occupation for April 2006 showed that approximately 5.7% of the labor force was employed in construction; 2.4% in manufacturing; 19.8% in trade, transportation, and public utilities; 11.5% in education and health services; 17.5% in leisure and hospitality services; and 19.5% in government. Data were unavailable for financial activities and services.

Unionization was slow to develop in Hawaii. After World War II, however, the International Longshoremen's and Warehousemen's Union organized workers in the sugar and pineapple industries and then on the docks. The International Brotherhood of Teamsters is also well established.

The BLS reported that in 2005, a total of 141,000 of Hawaii's 545,000 employed wage and salary workers were formal members of a union. This represented 25.8% of those so employed, up from 23.7% in 2004, well above the national average of 12%. Overall in 2005, a total of 145,000 workers (26.7%) in Hawaii were covered by a union or employee association contract, which includes those workers who reported no union affiliation. Hawaii does not have a right-to-work law.

As of 1 March 2006, Hawaii had a state-mandated minimum wage of $6.75 per hour, which will increase to $7.25 per hour on 1 January 2007. In 2004, women in the state accounted for 48.5% of the employed civilian labor force. Hawaii is one of only five states where union membership is higher than 20% of the labor force.

23 AGRICULTURE

Export crops—especially sugar cane and pineapple—dominate Hawaiian agriculture, which had farm receipts exceeding $553 million in 2005.

The islands of Hawaii (Maui, Molokai, Oahu, and Kauai) are the only places in the United States where coffee is grown commercially; production in 2004–05 totaled 7.1 million lb (3.2 million kg). Another tropical product, pineapple, has also become a substantial export crop, with 215,000 tons produced in 2004, valued at $79.9 million, as well as macadamia nuts and tropical flowers. Taro (coco yam), used for making poi, is also grown; production in 2004 was 5.2 million lb (2.8 million kg), valued at $2,808,000. Banana production in 2003 was 22.5 million lb (10.2 million kg), valued at $9.2 million, and ginger root, 6 million lb (2.7 million kg), valued at $5.4 million.

24 ANIMAL HUSBANDRY

Hawaii had an estimated 155,000 cattle and calves worth $97.6 million in 2005. In 2004, the estimated number of hogs and pigs was 22,000, worth $3.5 million. Poultry farms produced an estimated 117.2 million eggs in 2003, worth $9.4 million. Most of the eggs were for domestic consumption, making eggs one of the very few farm commodities in which the state is close to self-sufficient. Most of the state's cattle farms are in Hawaii and Maui counties.

25 FISHING

Although it is expanding, Hawaii's commercial catch remains surprisingly small. In 2004, Hawaii landings brought in 24.2 million lb (11 million kg) with a value of $57.2 million. Though the port of Honolulu ranked eighth in the nation that year in catch value ($44.6 million), it was 42d in quantity (18.2 million lb/8.3 million kg). The most valuable commercial species are swordfish and bigeye tuna. In 2001, the state had 2,814 commercial fishing boats and vessels. Sport fishing is extremely popular, with bass, bluegill, tuna, and marlin among the most sought-after varieties. In 2004, the state had 5,796 sport fishing license holders.

26 FORESTRY

As of 2003, Hawaii had 1,748,000 acres (707,940 hectares) of forestland and water reserves, with 700,000 acres (283,500 hectares) classified as commercial timberland, most of it located on the island of Hawaii. The majority of the locally grown wood is used in the manufacture of furniture, flooring, and craft items. As the sugar industry downsizes, there is an initiative to expand the forest industry by planting trees on lands formerly planted in sugarcane. Hawaii has the eighth-largest state-owned forest and natural area reserve system in the United States. Some 57% of forests are within the State Conservation District.

27 MINING

As of 2003, mining in Hawaii, mostly involved the extraction of sand and gravel from open pits and the quarrying of stone for crushed stone, mainly for use by the state's construction industry. According to preliminary data from the US Geological Survey, the value of Hawaii's nonfuel mineral production in 2003 (the latest year for which data was available) was estimated to be around $74 million (up about 2% from 2002).

In 2003, preliminary data showed that the output of construction grade sand and gravel totaled 600,000 metric tons or $6.9 million, while the production of crushed stone totaled 6.5 million metric tons or $66.6 million.

28 ENERGY AND POWER

Devoid of indigenous fossil fuels and nuclear installations, Hawaii depends on imported petroleum for about 78% of its energy needs. Coal, hydroelectric power, natural gas, windmills, geothermal energy, and sugarcane wastes contribute the rest.

As of 2003, Hawaii had seven electrical power service providers, of which three were investor owned and three were owners of independent generators that sold directly to customers. The remaining service provider was a cooperative. As of that same year, there were 447,584 retail customers. Of that total, 415,208 received their power from investor-owned service providers. The state's sole cooperatives accounted for 32,361 customers, while there were 15 independent generator or "facility" customers.

Total net summer generating capability by the state's electrical generating plants in 2003 stood at 2.268 million kW, with total production that same year at 10.976 billion kWh. Of the total amount generated, 59.2% came from electric utilities, with the remainder coming from independent producers and combined heat and power service providers. The largest portion of all electric power generated, 8.502 billion kWh (77.5%), came from petroleum-fired plants, with coal-fired plants in second place at 1.644 billion kWh (15%) and other renewable power sources in third place at 696.766 million kWh (6.3%). Hydroelectric and other gas-fueled plants accounted for the remainder. All of Hawaii's electric power plants are privately owned.

As of 2004, Hawaii had no known proven reserves or production of crude oil or natural gas. As of 2005, the state's two refineries had a combined crude oil distillation capacity of 147,000 barrels per day.

29 INDUSTRY

As of 2004, food and food products accounted for slightly more than 23% of the shipment value of all manufactured goods produced in Hawaii, including sugar and pineapples. Other major industries are clothing; stone, clay, and glass products; fabricated metals; and shipbuilding.

According to the US Census Bureau's Annual Survey of Manufactures (ASM) for 2004, Hawaii's manufacturing sector covered some five product subsectors. The shipment value of all products manufactured in the state that same year was $4.560 billion. Of that total, food manufacturing accounted for the largest share at $1.066 billion. It was followed by nonmetallic mineral product manufacturing at $206.697 million; printing and related support activities at $176.659 million; miscellaneous manufacturing at $106.213 million; and apparel manufacturing at $88.540 million.

In 2004, a total of 14,035 people in Hawaii were employed in the state's manufacturing sector, according to the ASM. Of that total,

8,901 were actual production workers. In terms of total employment, the food manufacturing industry accounted for the largest portion of all manufacturing employees at 4,773 with 3,253 actual production workers. It was followed by printing and related support activities at 1,569 employees (875 actual production workers); apparel manufacturing at 1,456 employees (934 actual production workers); miscellaneous manufacturing at 1,364 employees (639 actual production workers); and nonmetallic mineral product manufacturing with 1,046 employees (654 actual production workers).

ASM data for 2004 showed that Hawaii's manufacturing sector paid $522.317 million in wages. Of that amount, the food manufacturing sector accounted for the largest share at $193.384 million. It was followed by printing and related support services at $51.311 million; nonmetallic mineral product manufacturing at $46.481 million; miscellaneous manufacturing at $42.363 million; and apparel manufacturing at $27.977 million.

30 COMMERCE

According to the 2002 Census of Wholesale Trade, Hawaii's wholesale trade sector had sales that year totaling $9.9 billion from 1,876 establishments. Wholesalers of durable goods accounted for 861 establishments, while the number of nondurable goods wholesalers totaled 919, with electronic markets, agents, and brokers accounting for 96 establishments. Sales by nondurable goods wholesalers in 2002 totaled $5.9 billion. Sales data for wholesalers of durable goods and for electronic markets, agents, and brokers in the wholesale trade industry was not available.

In the 2002 Census of Retail Trade, Hawaii was listed as having 4,924 retail establishments with sales of $13 billion. The leading types of retail businesses by number of establishments were clothing and clothing accessories stores (1,239); miscellaneous store retailers (809); food and beverage stores (722); and motor vehicle and motor vehicle parts dealers (336). In terms of sales, general merchandise stores accounted for the largest share of retail sales at $2.56 billion, followed by motor vehicle and motor vehicle parts dealers at $2.55 billion and food and beverage stores at $2.2 billion. A total of 63,794 people were employed by the retail sector in Hawaii that year.

Hawaii's central position in the Pacific ensures a sizable flow of goods through the Honolulu Customs District. Exports in 2005 totaled $1.02 billion. Hawaii's major trading partners are Japan for exports and Japan, Singapore and Indonesia for imports.

31 CONSUMER PROTECTION

Hawaii's Office of Consumer Protection, a division of the Department of Commerce and Consumer Affairs, enforces the state's consumer protection laws and provides information regarding landlord–tenant matters. It was created in 1969 to protect the interests of consumers and legitimate businesses by investigating consumer complaints alleging unfair or deceptive trade practices in a broad range of areas, including advertising, refunds, motor vehicle rentals, door-to-door sales, and credit practices.

In support of the state's Office of Consumer Protection, the state's attorney general can initiate civil and criminal proceedings; administer consumer protection and education programs; and handle consumer complaints. However, the Attorney General's Office has only limited subpoena powers and cannot represent the state before other state or federal regulatory agencies. In antitrust actions, the Attorney General's Office can act on behalf of those consumers who are incapable of acting on their own; initiate damage actions on behalf of the state in state courts; initiate criminal proceedings; and represent counties, cities, and other governmental entities in recovering civil damages under state or federal law.

The Office of Consumer Protection has offices in the cities of Hilo, Honolulu, and Wailuku.

32BANKING

As of June 2005, Hawaii had seven insured banks, savings and loans, and saving banks, plus three state-chartered and 96 federally chartered credit unions (CUs). Excluding the CUs, the Honolulu market area had 10 financial institutions in 2004. As of June 2005, CUs accounted for 16.1% of all assets held by all financial institutions in the state, or some $6.750 billion. Banks, savings and loans, and savings banks collectively accounted for the remaining 83.9% or $35.090 billion of assets held. The regulation of Hawaii's financial institutions is handled by the Department of Commerce and Consumer Affairs Division of Financial Institutions.

In 2004, the median net interest margin (the difference between the lower rates offered to savers and the higher rates charged on loans) stood at 4.24%, down from 4.50% in 2003. As of fourth quarter 2005, the median percentage of past due/nonaccrual loans to total loans stood at 0.22%, down from 0.57% in 2004 and 0.86% in 2003.

33INSURANCE

In 2004 there were 577,000 individual life insurance policies in force with a total value of $58.5 billion; total value for all categories of life insurance (individual, group, and credit) was $91.4 billion. The average coverage amount was $101,500 per policy holder. Death benefits paid that year totaled over $234 million.

In 2003, there were three life and health insurance and 17 property and casualty insurance companies were domiciled in the state. In 2004, direct premiums for property and casualty insurance totaled $2 billion. That year, there were 49,379 flood insurance policies in force in the state, with a total value of $6.5 billion.

In 2004, 60% of state residents held employment-based health insurance policies, 3% held individual policies, and 24% were covered under Medicare and Medicaid; 10% of residents were uninsured. In 2003, employee contributions for employment-based family health coverage averaged about 26%. The average employee contribution for single coverage was 8%, the lowest in the nation. The state does not offer a health benefits expansion program in connection with the Consolidated Omnibus Budget Reconciliation Act (COBRA, 1986), a health insurance program for those who lose employment-based coverage due to termination or reduction of work hours.

In 2003, there were 730,946 auto insurance policies in effect for private passenger cars. Required minimum coverage includes bodily injury liability of up to $20,000 per individual and $40,000 for all persons injured in an accident, as well as property damage liability of $10,000. Personal injury protection is also required. In 2003, the average expenditure per vehicle for insurance coverage was $774.39.

34SECURITIES

The Honolulu Stock Exchange, established in 1898, discontinued trading on 30 December 1977. In 2005, there were 430 personal financial advisers employed in the state and 320 securities, commodities, and financial services sales agents. In 2004, there were 18 publicly traded companies within the state, with five NASDAQ companies, three NYSE listings, and three AMEX listings. In 2006, the state had two Fortune 1,000 companies; Hawaiian Electric Industries (NYSE) ranked first in the state and 755 in the nation with revenues of over $2.2 billion, followed by Alexander and Baldwin (NASDAQ).

35PUBLIC FINANCE

Development and implementation of Hawaii's biennial budget are the responsibilities of the Department of Budget and Finance. The fiscal year (FY) runs from 1 July through 30 June.

Beginning in fiscal year 2000, reductions in state taxes were scheduled through fiscal year 2006, including cuts in the general excise tax, a cut in the services tax for out-of-state end usage, and incentives for high-technology business in Hawaii. From 1995 to 2000, the number of high-technology companies in Hawaii more than doubled, from 300 to 629.

In fiscal year 2006, general funds were estimated at $5.2 billion for resources and $4.6 billion for expenditures. In fiscal year 2004, federal government grants to Hawaii were nearly $2.1 billion.

In the fiscal year 2007 federal budget, Hawaii was slated to receive $15.3 million in State Children's Health Insurance Program (SCHIP) funds to help the state provide health coverage to low-income, uninsured children who do not qualify for Medicaid. This funding is a 23% increase over fiscal year 2006. It is also scheduled to receive $8.3 million for the HOME Investment Partnership Program to help Hawaii fund a wide range of activities that build, buy, or rehabilitate affordable housing for rent or homeownership, or provide direct rental assistance to low-income people. This funding is a 12% increase over fiscal year 2006.

36TAXATION

In 2005, Hawaii collected $4,434 million in tax revenues or $3,478 per capita, which placed it second among the 50 states in per capita tax burden. The national average was $2,192 per capita. Sales taxes accounted for 48.2% of the total, selective sales taxes 13.8%, individual income taxes 31.2%, corporate income taxes 2.8%, and other taxes 4.1%.

As of 1 January 2006, Hawaii had nine individual income tax brackets ranging from 1.4 to 8.25%. The state taxes corporations at rates ranging from 4.4 to 6.4% depending on tax bracket.

In 2004, local property taxes amounted to $720,798,000 or $571 per capita. The per capita amount ranks the state 42nd highest nationally. Hawaii does not collect property taxes at the state level.

Hawaii taxes retail sales at a rate of 4%. Food purchased for consumption off premises is taxable; however, an income tax credit is allowed to offset sales tax on food. The tax on cigarettes is 140 cents per pack, which ranks 11th among the 50 states and the District of Columbia. Hawaii taxes gasoline at 16 cents per gallon. This is in addition to the 18.4 cents per gallon federal tax on gasoline.

According to the Tax Foundation, for every federal tax dollar sent to Washington in 2004, Hawaii citizens received $1.60 in federal spending.

37 ECONOMIC POLICY

Business activity in Hawaii is limited by physical factors: Land for development is scarce, living costs are relatively high, heavy industry is environmentally inappropriate, and there are few land-based mineral operations. On the other hand, Hawaii is well placed as a trading and communications center, and Hawaii's role as a defense outpost and tourist haven remains vital. The Department of

Business, Economic Development and Tourism (DBEDT) is the lead agency for economic development and planning. The Office of Planning, a separate agency attached to the DBEDT, has specific responsibility for the continuous process of long-range strategic planning. Ongoing projects in the Office of Planning include facilitating a task force on "Recapturing the Magic of Waikiki," a case study in keeping resort areas vital and attractive; implementing the Environmental Protection Agency-funded Brownfields Cleanup Revolving Loan Fund program; mapping the islands' agricultural subdivisions; and implementing a state Smart Growth strategy, including conducting stakeholder and public information meetings to increase awareness of Smart Growth principles and practices. The Aloha Tower Development Corporation (ATDC), formed in 1981 to develop the area around the historic landmark in downtown Honolulu, is another separate agency attached to the DBEDT. The Aloha Tower Marketplace, completed in 1994, was its first major project. The ATDC seeks to attract private investors to both strengthen the international economic base of the community and to enhance the beautification of the waterfront. The area has been included in an Enterprise Zone (EZ), making business tenants eligible for tax incentives. In 2006, Hawaii had 19 designated EZs, which are areas with high rates of unemployment, poverty, and/or public assistance. Another separate agency attached to the DBEDT is the High Technology Development Corporation (HTDC), established in 1982. Other separate agencies coordinated by the DBEDT include the Hawaii Tourist Authority, the Natural Energy of Hawaii Authority, the Hawaii Community Development Authority, the Land Use Commission, and the Housing and Community Development Corporation. The DBEDT administers the state's Foreign Trade Zone (FTZ) program, established under a grant issued to Hawaii by the federal Foreign-Trade Zones Board in 1965. As of 2006, 13 sites on the islands of Oahu, Maui, and Hawaii had received FTZ designations, and, of these, three general-purpose and four special-purpose zones were active. Other divisions within the DBEDT include the Business Development and Marketing Division; the Research and Economic Analysis Division; and the Energy, Resources and Technology Division.

38 HEALTH

The infant mortality rate in October 2005 was estimated at 5.6 per 1,000 live births. The birth rate in 2003 was 14.4 per 1,000 population. In 2000, the abortion rate stood at 22.1 per 1,000 women, a figure that was above the national average of 21.3 per 1,000 for the same year but substantially lower than the 1992 rate of 46 per 1,000. In 2003, about 82.4% of pregnant woman received prenatal care beginning in the first trimester. In 2004, approximately 81% of children received routine immunizations before the age of three.

The crude death rate in 2003 was 7.1 deaths per 1,000 population. As of 2002, the death rates for major causes of death (per 100,000 resident population) were as follows: heart disease, 201.8; cancer, 156.2; cerebrovascular diseases, 65.2; chronic lower respiratory diseases, 21.3; and diabetes, 16.4. The mortality rate from HIV infection was 2.1 per 100,000 population. In 2004, the reported AIDS case rate was at about 10.8 per 100,000 population. In 2002, about 51.6% of the population was considered overweight or obese. As of 2000, about 19.7% of state residents were smokers.

Hawaii—State Government Finances

(Dollar amounts in thousands. Per capita amounts in dollars.)

	AMOUNT	PER CAPITA
Total Revenue	8,229,259	6,520.81
General revenue	6,675,478	5,289.60
Intergovernmental revenue	1,639,868	1,299.42
Taxes	3,849,135	3,050.03
General sales	1,900,377	1,505.85
Selective sales	569,922	451.60
License taxes	123,257	97.67
Individual income tax	1,169,205	926.47
Corporate income tax	58,119	46.05
Other taxes	28,255	22.39
Current charges	882,232	699.07
Miscellaneous general revenue	304,243	241.08
Utility revenue	–	–
Liquor store revenue	–	–
Insurance trust revenue	1,553,781	1,231.21
Total expenditure	7,856,134	6,225.15
Intergovernmental expenditure	134,452	106.54
Direct expenditure	7,721,682	6,118.61
Current operation	5,999,477	4,753.94
Capital outlay	466,569	369.71
Insurance benefits and repayments	775,163	614.23
Assistance and subsidies	124,136	98.36
Interest on debt	356,337	282.36
Exhibit: Salaries and wages	2,021,447	1,601.78
Total expenditure	7,856,134	6,225.15
General expenditure	7,080,971	5,610.91
Intergovernmental expenditure	134,452	106.54
Direct expenditure	6,946,519	5,504.37
General expenditures, by function:		
Education	2,487,630	1,971.18
Public welfare	1,346,566	1,067.01
Hospitals	244,076	193.40
Health	416,241	329.83
Highways	214,046	169.61
Police protection	13,779	10.92
Correction	158,029	125.22
Natural resources	109,514	86.78
Parks and recreation	57,703	45.72
Government administration	442,979	351.01
Interest on general debt	356,337	282.36
Other and unallocable	1,234,071	977.87
Utility expenditure	–	–
Liquor store expenditure	–	–
Insurance trust expenditure	775,163	614.23
Debt at end of fiscal year	5,746,194	4,553.24
Cash and security holdings	13,195,390	10,455.94

Abbreviations and symbols: – zero or rounds to zero; (NA) not available; (X) not applicable.

SOURCE: U.S. Census Bureau, Governments Division, 2004 Survey of State Government Finances, January 2006.

In 2003, Hawaii had 24 community hospitals with about 3,100 beds. There were about 112,000 patient admissions that year and 1.9 million outpatient visits. The average daily inpatient census was about 2,200 patients. The average cost per day for hospital care was $1,350. Also in 2003, there were about 45 certified nursing facilities in the state with 4,059 beds and an overall occupancy rate of about 93.8%. Hawaii had 302 physicians per 100,000 resident population in 2004 and 725 nurses per 100,000 in 2005. In 2004, there was a total of 997 dentists in the state.

Hawaii comes the closest of any state to providing universal health care coverage as a result of a 1974 law that requires employers to provide health insurance for full-time workers and a state insurance plan for low-income, part-time workers and Medicaid recipients. About 24% of state residents were enrolled in Medicaid and Medicare programs in 2004. Approximately 10% of the state population was uninsured in 2004. In 2003, state health care expenditures totaled $2.1 million.

39 SOCIAL WELFARE

In 2004, about 24,000 people received unemployment benefits, with the average weekly unemployment benefit at $323. In fiscal year 2005, the estimated average monthly participation in the food stamp program included about 93,584 persons (47,309 households); the average monthly benefit was about $138.88 per person, which was the highest average in the nation. That year, the total of benefits paid through the state for the food stamp program was about $155.8 million.

Temporary Assistance for Needy Families (TANF), the system of federal welfare assistance that officially replaced Aid to Families with Dependent Children (AFDC) in 1997, was reauthorized through the Deficit Reduction Act of 2005. TANF is funded through federal block grants that are divided among the states based on an equation involving the number of recipients in each state. In 2004, the state program had 23,000 recipients; state and federal expenditures on this TANF program totaled $91 million in fiscal year 2003.

In December 2004, Social Security benefits were paid to 199,240 Hawaiians. This number included 141,990 retired workers, 16,210 widows and widowers, 18,050 disabled workers, 9,480 spouses, and 13,510 children. Social Security beneficiaries represented 15.6% of the total state population and 87.5% of the state's population age 65 and older. Retired workers received an average monthly payment of $945; widows and widowers, $879; disabled workers, $915; and spouses, $444. Payments for children of retired workers averaged $464 per month; children of deceased workers, $627; and children of disabled workers, $282. Federal Supplemental Security Income payments went to 22,251 Hawaii residents in December 2004 , averaging $437 a month.

40 HOUSING

In 2004, there were an estimated 482,873 housing units, 427,673 of which were occupied. Only 58.9% were owner occupied, ranking the state at 48th out of 51 (the 50 states and the District of Columbia) in the number of homeowners. About 51.4% of all units were single-family, detached homes. About 22% of all housing units were within buildings of 20 or more units, which ranks as the second-highest percentage of this category of housing in the nation (after the District of Columbia). Most units relied on electricity for heating, but about 5,476 units were equipped for solar power. It was estimated that 20,719 units were lacking telephone service, 4,972 lacked complete plumbing facilities, and 8,549 lacked complete kitchen facilities. The average household had 2.87 members.

In 2004, 9,000 privately owned housing units were authorized for construction. Median home value was $364,840, the second highest in the nation. The median monthly cost for mortgage owners was $1,648 while renters paid a median of $871 per month; both figures represented the third-highest monthly median costs in the nation. In September 2005, the state received a grant of $400,000 from the US Department of Housing and Urban Development (HUD) for rural housing and economic development programs. For 2006, HUD allocated over $5.2 million in community development block grants to the state.

41 EDUCATION

Education has developed rapidly in Hawaii: In 2004, 88% of all state residents 25 years of age or older had completed high school; 26.6% had completed four or more years of college.

Hawaii is the only state to have a single, unified public school system. It was founded in 1840. Total enrollment for fall 2002 stood at 184,000. Of these, 131,000 attended schools from kindergarten through grade eight, and 53,000 attended high school. Approximately 20.2% of the students were white, 2.4% were black, 4.5% were Hispanic, 72.4% were Asian/Pacific Islander, and 0.5% were American Indian/Alaska Native. Total enrollment was estimated at 183,000 in fall 2003 and is expected to be 193,000 by fall 2014, an increase of 5% during the period 2002–14. In fall 2003, there were 37,228 students enrolled in 133 private schools. Expenditures for public education in 2003–04 were estimated at $1.7 billion. Since 1969, the National Assessment of Educational Progress (NAEP) has tested public school students nationwide. The resulting report, *The Nation's Report Card,* stated that in 2005, eighth graders in Hawaii scored 266 out of 500 in mathematics compared with the national average of 278.

As of fall 2002, there were 65,368 students enrolled in college or graduate school; minority students composed 65.4% of total postsecondary enrollment. As of 2005, Hawaii had 20 degree-granting institutions. The University of Hawaii maintains three campuses—Manoa (by far the largest), Hilo, and West Oahu. Private colleges include Brigham Young University–Hawaii Campus, Chaminade University of Honolulu, and Hawaii Pacific College. There are seven community colleges.

42 ARTS

The Hawaii State Foundation on Culture and the Arts (HSFCA) was founded in 1965. Ongoing programs include the Folk Arts Program (est. 1983) and the Hawaii State Art Museum, which opened in 2002 to feature artworks from the State Art Collection of the HSFCA. In 2005, Hawaiian arts organizations received 17 grants totaling $934,900 from the National Endowment for the Arts. The Hawaii Council for the Humanities was established in 1972 and has since granted over $4 million for over 500 projects in the state. In 2005, the state received eight grants totaling $1,207,532 from the National Endowment for the Humanities. The HSFCA was scheduled to host an International Cultural Summit in 2006, celebrating the foundation's 40th anniversary. The mission of the summit was to bring together artists, educators, and civic leaders from the state and around the world in order to discuss contemporary issues concerning culture and art in local and global communities.

The Neal Blaisdell Center in Honolulu has a 2,158-seat theater and concert hall, an 8,800-seat arena, and display rooms. Other performance facilities in Honolulu are the John F. Kennedy Theatre at the University of Hawaii, the Waikiki Shell for outdoor concerts, and the Hawaii Opera Theater, which presents three operas each season. The opera's 2007 season included *Samson and Dalila, Don Giovanni,* and *Madama Butterfly.* The Honolulu Symphony Orchestra performs both on Oahu and on the neighboring islands. Founded in 1900, the Honolulu Symphony holds claim to being the oldest American orchestra west of the Rocky Mountains. Other Oahu cultural institutions are the Honolulu Community Theater, Honolulu Theater for Youth, Windward Theater Guild, and Polynesian Cultural Center.

The annual Cherry Blossom Festival includes a number of Japanese cultural events presented from January through March, mostly on Oahu. The Honolulu Festival, established in 1994 as a forum to encourage cultural cooperation and understanding, presents a number of art exhibits and musical performances. Though fairly new, the Honolulu Festival has grown rapidly, drawing approximately 5,000 participants from Japan alone in 2005. The Aloha Festivals, which began in 1946, now consist of over 300 events taking place on six islands throughout the months of August and September to celebrate the music, dance, and history of the various cultures represented in the state; it is Hawaii's largest festival and the only statewide celebration held in the United States. In 2006, the Aloha Festivals marked its 60th anniversary with the theme *Nā Paniolo Nui O Hawa'ii—The Great Cowboys of Hawaii.*

43 LIBRARIES AND MUSEUMS

For the fiscal year ending in June 2001, the Hawaii State Public Library System (HSPLS) was the state's sole public library system, operating a total of 50 libraries, of which 49 were branches. The system had a combined book and serial publication collection in that same year of 3,195,000 volumes and a total circulation of 6,747,000. The system also had 185,000 audio and 58,000 video items, 3,000 electronic format items (CD-ROMs, magnetic tapes, and disks), and four bookmobiles. In 2000, the University of Hawaii library system in Honolulu had approximately 3 million volumes. In fiscal year 2001, total operating income of the HSPLS came to $23,876,000, including $895,000 in federal grants and $21,504,000 in state grants.

Hawaii has 42 major museums and cultural attractions. Among the most popular sites are the National Memorial Cemetery of the Pacific, USS *Arizona* Memorial at Pearl Harbor, Polynesian Cultural Center, Sea Life Park, Bernice P. Bishop Museum (specializing in Polynesian ethnology and natural history), and Honolulu Academy of Arts. Outside Oahu, the Kilauea Visitor Center (Hawaii Volcanoes National Park) and Kokee Natural History Museum (Kauai) attract the most visitors.

44 COMMUNICATIONS

Commercial interisland wireless service began in 1901, and radiotelephone service to the mainland was established in 1931. In 2004, 95.4% of Hawaii's occupied housing units had telephones. In addition, by June of that same year, there were 819,262 mobile

wireless telephone subscribers. In 2003, 63.3% of Hawaii households had a computer and 55.0% had Internet access. Hawaii had 12 major AM radio stations and 21 major FM stations as of 2003, as well as 10 major television stations. A total of 27,025 internet domain names were registered in Hawaii as of 2000.

45 PRESS

In 2005, Hawaii had eight daily newspapers (six morning and two evening) and six Sunday newspapers: the *Honolulu Advertiser* (141,341 daily, 161,325 Sundays), *Honolulu Star-Bulletin* (64,305 daily, 64,344 Sunday), *Hawaii Tribune-Herald* (18,806 daily, 22,150 Sundays), *Maui News* (21,478 daily, 25,938 Sundays), *West Hawaii Today* (12,397 daily, 15,916 Sundays), and the *Garden Island* (8,677 daily, 9,130 Sundays).

46 ORGANIZATIONS

In 2006, there were over 1,035 nonprofit organizations registered within the state, of which about 758 were registered as charitable, educational, or religious organizations. The leading organization headquartered in Honolulu is the East–West Center, a vehicle of scientific and cultural exchange. Other educational organizations of national and international interest include the International Tsunami Information Center, the Pacific Whale Foundation, and the Meteoritical Society.

State organizations promoting local and regional arts and culture include the Historic Hawaii Foundation, the Hawaiian Historical Society, the Native Hawaiian Culture and Arts Program, the Honolulu Academy of the Arts, and the Polynesian Cultural Center. State environmental concerns are supported through the Conservation Council for Hawaii and the Hawaii Agriculture Research Center, which focuses on the local sugarcane industry.

47 TOURISM, TRAVEL, AND RECREATION

In 2004, there were 7 million visitor arrivals to the islands, an increase of 8% over 2003. Travel expenditures by visitors who arrived by air reached $10.8 billion. In 2003, Hawaii employed 153,600 people in the travel and tourism industry. An estimated 42% of visitors are from other US states. The largest international market (1.5 million visitors) is Japan.

Visitors come for scuba diving, snorkeling, swimming, fishing, whale watching, and sailing; for the hula, luau, lei, and other distinctive island pleasures; for the tropical climate and magnificent scenic beauty; and for a remarkable variety of recreational facilities, including 7 national parks and historic sites, 74 state parks, 626 county parks, 17 public golf courses, and 1,600 recognized surfing sites. Major visitor attractions include the Volcano National Park (Hawaii); USS *Arizona* Memorial (Oahu); Waimea Canyon (Kawai); Diamondhead Beach and Honolulu (Oahu); and Polynesian Cultural Center (Oahu). Visitors can tour coffee and pineapple plantations. The Hawaiian Islands are a popular vacation spot for honeymooners.

48 SPORTS

Hawaii has no major professional sports teams. Since 1982, the Aloha Bowl, a major college football postseason game played on Christmas Day, has been played in Aloha Stadium in Honolulu, as is the Hula Bowl, a postseason all-star game in January for college players. The Pro Bowl (the National Football League's all-star game) is also played in Honolulu on the weekend following the Super Bowl. Surfing is an extremely popular sport in Hawaii, as it is the home of the Banzai Pipeline, north of Oahu. Here, the yearly Duke Kahanamoku and Makaha surfing meets take place. Hawaii is also the site of an annual Professional Golfers' Association tournament and the world-famous Ironman Triathlon competition. The Transpac Yacht Race is held biennially from California to Honolulu. Kona is the site of the International Billfish Tournament, and the Hawaii Big Game Fishing Club holds statewide tournaments each year. Football, baseball, and basketball are the leading collegiate sports. The University of Hawaii Rainbow Warriors produce the most well-known collegiate teams.

49 FAMOUS HAWAIIANS

Hawaii's best-known federal officeholder is Daniel K. Inouye (b.1924), a US senator since 1962 and the first person of Japanese ancestry ever elected to Congress. Inouye, who lost an arm in World War II, came to national prominence during the Senate Watergate investigation of 1973, when he was a member of the Select Committee on Presidential Campaign Activities. George R. Ariyoshi (b.1926), who was elected governor of Hawaii in 1974, was the first Japanese American to serve as chief executive of a state.

Commanding figures in Hawaiian history were King Kamehameha I (1758?–1819), who unified the islands through conquest, and Kamehameha III (Kauikeaouli, 1813–54), who transformed Hawaii into a constitutional monarchy. Two missionaries who shaped Hawaiian life and politics were Hiram Bingham (b.Vermont, 1789–1869) and Gerrit Parmele Judd (b.New York, 1803–73). Sanford B. Dole (1844–1926) and Lorrin Andrews Thurston (1858–1931) were leaders of the revolutionary movement that overthrew Queen Liliuokalani (1838–1917), established a republic, and secured annexation by the United States. Dole was the republic's first president and the territory's first governor. Another prominent historical figure was Bernice Pauahi Bishop (1831–88), of the Kamehameha line, who married an American banker and left her fortune to endow the Kamehameha Schools in Honolulu; the Bishop Museum was founded by her husband in her memory. Honolulu-born Luther Halsey Gulick (1865–1918), along with his wife, Charlotte Vetter Gulick (b.Ohio, 1865–1928), founded the Camp Fire Girls.

Don Ho (b.1930) is a prominent Hawaiian-born entertainer; singer-actress Bette Midler (b.1945) was also born in Hawaii. Duke Kahanamoku (1889–1968) held the Olympic 100-meter free-style swimming record for almost 20 years.

50 BIBLIOGRAPHY

Chambers, John H. *Hawaii.* Northampton, Mass.: Interlink Books, 2005.

Coffman, Tom. *Nation Within: The Story of America's Annexation of the Nation of Hawai'i.* Kane'ohe, Hawaii: Tom Coffman/EPI-Center, 1998.

Council of State Governments. *The Book of the States, 2006 Edition.* Lexington, Ky.: Council of State Governments, 2006.

Haas, Michael (ed.). *Multicultural Hawaii: the Fabric of a Multiethnic Society.* New York: Garland Publications, 1998.

Odo, Franklin. *No Sword to Bury: Japanese Americans in Hawai'i during World War II.* Philadelphia: Temple University Press, 2004.

Pratt, Richard C., and Zachary A. Smith (eds.). *Politics and Public Policy in Hawaii.* Albany: State University of New York Press, 1992.

Richardson, K. D. *Reflections of Pearl Harbor: An Oral History of December 7, 1941.* Westport, Conn.: Praeger Publishers, 2005.

Trask, Haunani-Kay. *From a Native Daughter: Colonialism and Sovereignty in Hawaii.* Monroe, Maine: Common Courage, 1993.

US Department of Commerce, Economics and Statistics Administration, US Census Bureau. *Hawaii, 2000. Summary Social, Economic, and Housing Characteristics: 2000 Census of Population and Housing.* Washington, D.C.: US Government Printing Office, 2003.

Wooden, Wayne S. *Return to Paradise: Continuity and Change in Hawaii.* Lanham, Md.: University Press of America, 1995.

IDAHO

State of Idaho

ORIGIN OF STATE NAME: Apparently coined by a lobbyist-politician, George M. Willing, who claimed the word came from an Indian term meaning "gem of the mountains." **NICKNAME:** The Gem State. **CAPITAL:** Boise. **ENTERED UNION:** 3 July 1890 (43rd). **SONG:** "Here We Have Idaho." **MOTTO:** *Esto perpetua* (Let it be perpetual). **FLAG:** On a blue field with gilt fringe, the state seal appears in the center with the words "State of Idaho" on a red band below. **OFFICIAL SEAL:** With cornucopias at their feet, a female figure (holding the scales of justice in one hand and a pike supporting a liberty cap in the other) and a miner (with pick and shovel) stand on either side of a shield depicting mountains, rivers, forests, and a farm; the shield rests on a sheaf of grain and is surmounted by the head of a stag above whose antlers is a scroll with the state motto. The words "Great Seal of the State of Idaho" surround the whole. **BIRD:** Mountain bluebird. **FLOWER:** Syringa. **TREE:** Western white pine. **GEM:** Star garnet. **LEGAL HOLIDAYS:** New Year's Day, 1 January; Birthday of Martin Luther King Jr. and Idaho Human Rights Day, 3rd Monday in January; Presidents' Day, 3rd Monday in February; Memorial Day, last Monday in May; Independence Day, 4 July; Labor Day, 1st Monday in September; Columbus Day, 2nd Monday in October; Veterans' Day, 11 November; Thanksgiving Day, 4th Thursday in November; Christmas Day, 25 December. **TIME:** 5 AM MST = noon GMT; 4 AM PST = noon GMT.

¹LOCATION, SIZE, AND EXTENT

Situated in the northwestern United States, Idaho is the smallest of the eight Rocky Mountain states and 13th in size among the 50 states.

The total area of Idaho is 83,564 sq mi (216,431 sq km), of which land composes 82,412 sq mi (213,447 sq km) and inland water 1,152 sq mi (2,984 sq km). With a shape described variously as a hatchet, a snub-nosed pistol, and a pork chop, Idaho extends a maximum of 305 mi (491 km) E–W and 479 mi (771 km) N–S.

Idaho is bordered on the N by the Canadian province of British Columbia; on the NE by Montana; on the E by Wyoming; on the S by Utah and Nevada; and on the W by Oregon and Washington (with part of the line formed by the Snake River). The total boundary length of Idaho is 1,787 mi (2,876 km). The state's geographic center is in Custer County, sw of Challis.

²TOPOGRAPHY

Idaho is extremely mountainous. Its northern two-thirds consists of a mountain massif broken only by valleys carved by rivers and streams, and by two prairies: the Big Camas Prairie around Grangeville and the Palouse Country around Moscow. The Snake River Plain extends E–W across Idaho from Yellowstone National Park to the Boise area, curving around the southern end of the mountain mass. A verdant high-mountain area encroaches into the southeastern corner; the rest of Idaho's southern edge consists mostly of low, dry mountains. Among the most important ranges are the Bitterroot (forming the border with Montana), Clearwater (the largest range), Salmon River, Sawtooth, Lost River, and Lemhi mountains. More than 40 peaks rise above 10,000 ft (3,000 m), of which the highest is Mt. Borah, at 12,662 ft (3,862 m), in the Lost River range. Idaho's lowest point is 710 ft (217 m) near Lewiston, where the Snake River leaves the Idaho border and en-

ters Washington. The mean elevation of the state is approximately 5,000 ft (1,525 m).

The largest lakes are Pend Oreille (180 sq mi/466 sq km), Coeur d'Alene, and Priest in the panhandle, and Bear on the Utah border. The Snake River—one of the longest in the United States, extending 1,038 mi (1,671 km) across Wyoming, Idaho, and Washington—dominates the southern part of the state. The Salmon River—the "River of No Return," a salmon-spawning stream that flows through wilderness of extraordinary beauty—separates northern from southern Idaho. The Clearwater, Kootenai, Bear, Boise, and Payette are other major rivers. There are ice caves near Shoshone and American Falls, and a large scenic cave near Montpelier. Near Arco is an expanse of lava, craters, and caves called the Craters of the Moon, another scenic attraction. At Hell's Canyon in the northernmost part of Adams County, the Snake River cuts the deepest gorge in North America, 7,913 ft (2,412 m) deep.

³CLIMATE

The four seasons are distinct in Idaho, but not all parts simultaneous. Spring comes earlier and winter later to Boise and Lewiston, which are protected from severe weather by nearby mountains and call themselves "banana belts." Eastern Idaho has a more continental climate, with more extreme temperatures; climatic conditions there and elsewhere vary with the elevation. Average temperatures in Boise range from 29°F (-2°C) in January to 74°F (23°C) in July. The record low, -60°F (-51°C), was set at Island Park Dam on 16 January 1943; the record high, 118°F (48°C), at Orofino on 28 July 1934. The corresponding extremes for Boise are -25°F (-31°C) and 111°F (44°C).

Humidity is low throughout the state. Precipitation in southern Idaho averages 13 in (33 cm) per year; in the north, over 30 in (76 cm). Average annual precipitation at Boise is about 11.8 in (29 cm), with more than 20 in (53 cm) of snow. Much greater accumulations of snow are experienced in the mountains.

⁴FLORA AND FAUNA

With 10 life zones extending from prairie to mountaintop, Idaho has some 3,000 native plants. Characteristic evergreens are Douglas fir and western white pine (the state tree); oak/mountain mahogany, juniper/piñon, ponderosa pine, and spruce/fir constitute the other main forest types. Syringa is the state flower. MacFarlanes four-o'clock, water howellia, Spalding's catchfly, and Ute ladies-tresses were the state's four threatened plant species as of April 2006.

Classified as game mammals are the elk, moose, white-tailed and mule deer, pronghorn antelope, bighorn sheep, mountain goat, black bear, mountain lion, cottontail, and pigmy rabbit. Several varieties of pheasant, partridge, quail, and grouse are the main game birds, and there are numerous trout, salmon, bass, and whitefish species in Idaho's lakes and streams. Rare animal species include the wolverine, kit fox, and pika. The grizzly bear and bald eagle are listed as threatened, while the woodland caribou, gray (timber) wolf, American peregrine falcon, and whooping crane are endangered. A total of 17 animal species occurring within the state were listed as threatened or endangered as of April 2006, including the woodland caribou, whooping crane, and three species of salmon.

⁵ENVIRONMENTAL PROTECTION

The environmental protection movement in Idaho dates from 1897, when President Grover Cleveland established the Bitterroot Forest Preserve, encompassing much of the northern region. In the early 1930s, the US Forest Service set aside some 3 million acres (1.2 million hectares) of Idaho's roadless forestland as primitive areas. The Taylor Grazing Act of 1934 regulated grazing on public lands, providing for the first time some relief from the overgrazing that had transformed much of Idaho's grassland into sagebrush desert. Thirty years later, Idaho senator Frank Church was floor sponsor for the bill creating the National Wilderness System, which now contains most of the primitive areas set aside earlier. Many miles of Idaho streams are now in the Wild and Scenic Rivers System, another congressional accomplishment in which Senator Church played a leading role. In 1970, Governor Cecil Andrus (later, US secretary of the interior) was elected, partly on a platform of environmental protection. On 17 January 2001, the site near Jerome of a World War II camp where Japanese Americans were interned became Minidoka Internment National Monument; the National Park Service began planning for visitor facilities there in 2002.

The Department of Health and Welfare's Division of Environment is responsible for enforcing environmental standards. Air quality improved greatly between 1978 and 1997, following the passage of federal regulations strengthening the Clean Air Act. Vehicle emissions were responsible for high carbon monoxide levels in the Boise area in the late 1970s and 1980s. Emissions have dropped to the point that no carbon monoxide violations have occurred for several years. In 2003, 61.3 million lb of toxic chemicals were released in the state.

Water quality is generally good. Most of the existing problems stem from runoff from agricultural lands. Water quality is rated as only fair in the Upper Snake River Basin and in the Southwest Basin around Boise, and as poor in the Bear River Basin, partly be-cause of municipal effluents from Soda Springs and Preston. The state has 386,000 acres of wetlands. The Idaho Department of Fish and Game has implemented plans to acquire privately owned wetlands deemed to be in danger. The plan runs from 1991 to 2005.

Since 1953, nuclear waste has been buried at the Idaho National Engineering Laboratory west of Idaho Falls or discharged in liquid form into the underground aquifer; some isotopes are migrating toward the boundaries of the site. Tailings from a former uranium-ore milling operation near Lowman are a potential health hazard. A top-priority site for hazardous-waste cleanup is Bunker Hill Mining at Smelterville; two sites in Pocatello are also considered candidates for cleanup. In 2003, the US Environment Protection Agency (EPA) database listed 87 hazardous waste sites in Idaho, six of which were on the National Priorities List as of 2006. Three sites were deleted from the National Priority List in 2006, but another three sites were also proposed, including Blackbird Mine, St. Maries Creosote, and the Stibnite Yellow Pine Mining Area. In 2005, the EPA spent over $17.8 million through the Superfund program for the cleanup of hazardous waste sites in the state. Also in 2005, federal EPA grants awarded to the state included $5.2 million for a clean water state revolving fund, as well as a $2.5 million grant for a drinking water state revolving fund. A $32,000 grant was offered to assist school districts in the adoption of indoor air quality programs.

⁶POPULATION

Idaho ranked 39th in population in the United States with an estimated total of 1,429,096 in 2005, an increase of 10.4% since 2000. Between 1990 and 2000, Idaho's population grew from 1,006,749 to 1,293,953, an increase of 28.5%—the fifth-largest percentage gain among the 50 states for this period. The population is projected to reach 1.6 million by 2015 and 1.8 million by 2025. Population density in 2004 was 16.8 persons per sq mi. The median age was 34.3 in 2004. Nearly 26.7% of the population was under age 18, while 11.4% was age 65 or older.

Although no part of Idaho except Boise is genuinely urban, even Boise does not have a large central city. Boise's estimated population in 2004 was 190,122; The Boise–Nampa metropolitan area had an estimated population of 524,884. Other major cities with large populations include Pocatello (83,155), Idaho Falls (110,435), and Lewiston (58,654).

⁷ETHNIC GROUPS

The 2000 Census included 17,645 American Indians. There are five reservations; the most extensive is that of the Nez Perce in northern Idaho, with a total population of 17,959 in 2000. In 2004, 1.4% of the population was American Indian.

There is a very small population of black Americans (5,456 in 2000) and a larger number of Asians (11,889 in 2000), 2,642 of them Japanese. In 2004, 0.6% of the population was black and 1% Asian. In 2000, there were 101,690 persons of Hispanic origin. In 2004, 8.9% of the population was of Hispanic or Latino origin. In 2004, 1.3% of the population reported origin of two or more races. There is a very visible Basque community in the Boise area, with an organization devoted to preserving their language and culture.

The foreign born (64,080) accounted for about 5% of Idaho's population in 2000, up from 28,905 (2.8%) in 1990.

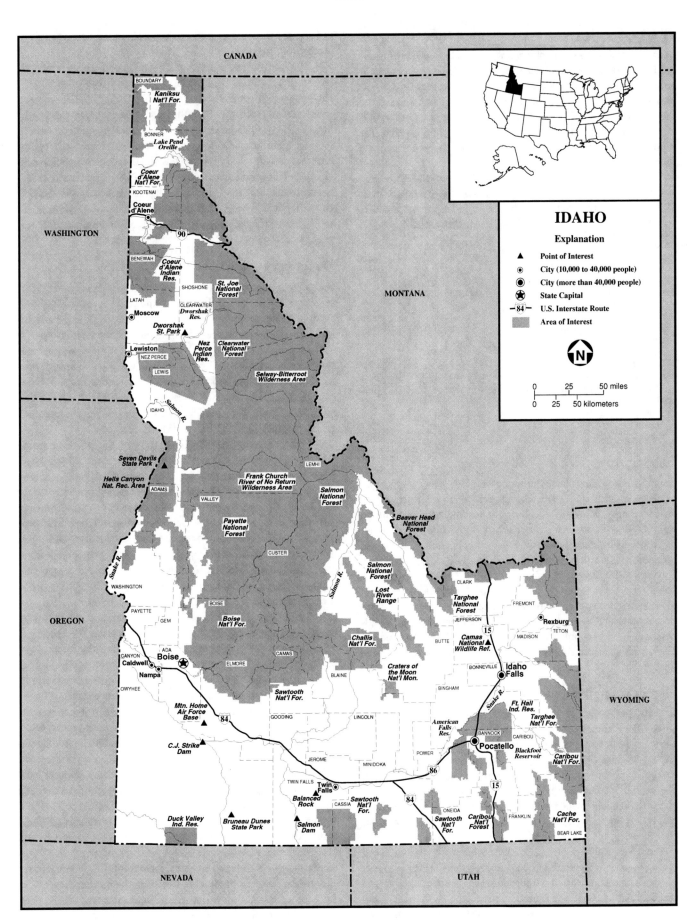

CANADA

BOUNDARY

Kaniksu Nat'l For.

BONNER

Lake Pend Oreille

WASHINGTON

Coeur d'Alene Nat'l For.

KOOTENAI

Coeur d'Alene

90

BENEWAH

Coeur d'Alene Indian Res.

SHOSHONE

St. Joe National Forest

MONTANA

LATAH

Moscow

CLEARWATER
Dworshak Res.

Dworshak St. Park

Nez Perce Indian Res.

Clearwater National Forest

Lewiston

NEZ PERCE

LEWIS

Selway-Bitterroot Wilderness Area

IDAHO

Salmon R.

Seven Devils State Park

Hells Canyon Nat. Rec. Area

ADAMS

LEMHI

Frank Church River of No Return Wilderness Area

Salmon National Forest

Beaver Head National Forest

VALLEY

Payette National Forest

Snake R.

WASHINGTON

CUSTER

Salmon R.

Salmon National Forest

Lost River Range

CLARK

Targhee National Forest

FREMONT

OREGON

PAYETTE

GEM

BOISE

Boise Nat'l For.

JEFFERSON

MADISON

TETON

Rexburg

15

CANYON

ADA

Boise

Challis Nat'l For.

BUTTE

Camas National Wildlife Ref.

BONNEVILLE

Idaho Falls

Caldwell

Nampa

ELMORE

CAMAS

Craters of the Moon Nat'l Mon.

BLAINE

Snake R.

Ft. Hall Ind. Res.

Targhee Nat'l For.

WYOMING

OWYHEE

Mtn. Home Air Force Base

Sawtooth Nat'l For.

BINGHAM

American Falls Res.

BANNOCK

Pocatello

Blackfoot Reservoir

C.J. Strike Dam

84

GOODING

LINCOLN

CARIBOU

Caribou Nat'l For.

JEROME

POWER

86

MINIDOKA

TWIN FALLS

Twin Falls

15

Balanced Rock

CASSIA

Sawtooth Nat'l For.

Duck Valley Ind. Res.

Bruneau Dunes State Park

Salmon Dam

84

ONEIDA

Sawtooth Nat'l Forest

Caribou Nat'l Forest

FRANKLIN

Cache Nat'l For.

BEAR LAKE

NEVADA   UTAH

IDAHO

Explanation

▲   Point of Interest

⊙   City (10,000 to 40,000 people)

◉   City (more than 40,000 people)

★   State Capital

—84—   U.S. Interstate Route

▨   Area of Interest

N

0	25	50 miles
0	25	50 kilometers

[8] LANGUAGES

In the general word stock, only a few place-names, such as Nampa, Pocatello, and Benewah, reflect the presence of Idaho Indians. In Idaho, English reflects a merger of Northern and North Midland features, with certain Northern pronunciations marking the panhandle. In 2000, 90.7% of the people five years old or older spoke only English in the home, down from 93% in 1990. The number of persons speaking other languages at home included the following:

The following table gives selected statistics from the 2000 Census for language spoken at home by persons five years old and over. The category "Other Native North American languages" includes Apache, Cherokee, Choctaw, Dakota, Keres, Pima, and Yupik.

LANGUAGE	NUMBER	PERCENT
Population 5 years and over	**1,196,793**	**100.0**
Speak only English	1,084,914	90.7
Speak a language other than English	111,879	9.3
Speak a language other than English	**111,879**	**9.3**
Spanish or Spanish Creole	80,241	6.7
German	5,666	0.5
French (incl. Patois, Cajun)	3,345	0.3
Other Native North American languages	2,020	0.2
Serbo-Croatian	1,694	0.1
Japanese	1,651	0.1
Chinese	1,456	0.1
Portuguese or Portuguese Creole	1,374	0.1
Vietnamese	1,213	0.1
Tagalog	1,119	0.1
Russian	1,113	0.1
Italian	1,106	0.1

[9] RELIGIONS

Roman Catholic and Presbyterian missionaries first came to Idaho between 1820 and 1840. The Church of Jesus Christ of Latter-Day Saints (Mormon) has been the leading religion in Idaho since 1860; with about a quarter of the population, the number of Mormons in Idaho is second only to that in Utah. Catholicism predominates north of Boise.

In 2006, the Church of Jesus Christ of Latter-Day Saints (Mormon) reported a statewide membership of 376,661 members in 937 congregations; there were two temples in the state with a third under construction as of 2006. As of 2000, there were 18,745 adherents in the Assemblies of God and 17,683 United Methodists. There were also 130,847 Roman Catholics and an estimated 1,050 Jews.

[10] TRANSPORTATION

In 2004, Idaho had 47,101 mi (75,832 km) of public roads and streets, the vast majority of them rural. The major east–west highways are I-90, I-84 (formerly I-80N), and US 12; US 95, Idaho 55, US 93, and I-15 are among the most traveled north–south routes. Idaho had some 1.370 million registered vehicles, including around 569,000 automobiles, 751,000 trucks of all types, and about 1,000 buses in 2004, when there were 942,983 licensed drivers. Boise, Pocatello, and Idaho Falls have mass transit systems (bus lines).

There were 1,678 rail mi (2,701 km) used by the nine railroads operating within the state in 2003. Among the state's two Class I railroads, the Union Pacific Railroad serves southern Idaho, and the Burlington Northern Santa Fe crosses the panhandle. As of 2006, Amtrak provided east–west passenger service to Idaho via its Empire Builder train connection at Sandpoint to Chicago or Seattle/Portland.

In 2005, Idaho had a total of 255 public and private-use aviation-related facilities. This included 204 airports, 44 heliports, 2 STOLports (Short Take-Off and Landing), and 5 seaplane bases. The modern airport at Boise is the state's busiest. In 2004, Boise Air Terminal/Gowen Field had 1,451,728 passenger enplanements.

Other transport facilities are 6,100 mi (9,800 km) of pipeline, carrying virtually all the natural gas and most of the gasoline consumed in Idaho, and a Snake River port at Lewiston that links Idaho, Montana, and the Dakotas with the Pacific via 464 mi (747 km) of navigable waterways in Washington State. Idaho had 111 mi (178 km) of navigable inland waterways in 2004 . In 2003 waterborne shipments totaled 1.061 million tons.

[11] HISTORY

Human beings came to the land now known as Idaho about 15,000 years ago. Until 1805, only Indians and their ancestors had ever lived in the area, eking out a bare living from seeds and roots, insects, small animals, and what fishing and big-game hunting they could manage. At the time of white penetration, Shoshone and Northern Paiute Indians lived in the south, as did two linked tribal families, the Salishan and Shapwailutan (including the Nez Perce, who greeted the Lewis and Clark expedition when it entered Idaho in 1805; it was their food and canoes that helped these explorers reach the Columbia River and the Pacific).

Fur trappers—notably David Thompson, Andrew Henry, and Donald Mackenzie—followed within a few years. Missionaries came later; Henry Harmon Spalding founded a mission among the Nez Perce in 1836. The Oregon Trail opened in 1842, but for two decades, people merely crossed Idaho over it; virtually no one settled. In 1860, 14 years after Idaho had officially become US land through the Oregon Treaty with the United Kingdom, Mormons from Utah established Franklin, Idaho's first permanent settlement, and began farming. Gold was discovered that summer in northern Idaho; a gold rush, lasting several years, led directly to the organizing of the Idaho Territory on 10 July 1863.

Boise became the capital of Idaho in 1864, and the following decade saw the inauguration of telegraph service, the linking of Franklin with the transcontinental railway, and the birth of the territory's first daily newspaper. Idaho's population nearly doubled between 1870 and 1880, and the pressure of white settlement impinging on Indian hunting and fishing grounds touched off a series of wars in the late 1870s. The most famous of those was the Nez Perce War, culminating in Chief Joseph's surrender in Montana on 5 October 1877 and the subsequent confinement of Idaho Indians to reservations.

Lead and silver were discovered in south-central Idaho in 1880 and in the panhandle in 1884, touching off yet another stampede of would-be miners. With a population of 88,548 in 1890, Idaho was eligible to enter the Union, becoming the 43rd state on 3 July. Statehood came to Idaho at a time of turmoil, when Mormons and non-Mormons were contending for political influence, the Populist Party was challenging the established political organizations, and violent labor disputes were sweeping the mining districts. In 1907, in a case that grew out of the labor conflict, William "Big Bill" Haywood (defended by Clarence Darrow) was acquitted on charges that he conspired to assassinate former Idaho governor Frank Steunenberg, who was murdered on 30 December 1905.

From 1895 onward, federal land and irrigation projects fostered rapid economic growth. The modern timber industry began in 1906 with the completion of one of the nation's largest sawmills at Potlatch. By World War I, agriculture had become a leading enterprise; however, a farm depression in the 1920s lasted up to the Great Depression of the 1930s and ended only with the onset of World War II. After the war, an agro-industrial base was established, with fertilizers and potato processing leading the way. Idaho has also developed a thriving tourist industry, with large numbers of vacationers visiting the Sun Valley ski resort and the state's other scenic areas. Population expansion and the push for economic growth have collided with a new interest in the environment, creating controversies over land-use planning, mineral development, and water supply and dam construction. In April 2000, the National Wildlife Federation urged President Bill Clinton to designate the Owyhee Canyonlands, a 1.8-million acre scenic area in southwest Idaho, a national monument. The efforts to persuade Clinton failed, and environmentalists, ranchers, and off-road vehicle riders came together to agree on a conservation plan suitable to all. In 2004, they came up with the Owyhee Initiative, which will protect nearly 400 miles of river corridors and 500,000 acres of wild lands as wilderness, including the canyons themselves. Livestock grazing in wilderness areas will be gradually retired. Public lands in Owyhee County will be closed to cross-country all-terrain vehicles during preparation of a recreation plan that will manage motorized recreation on a designated system of roads and trails.

Idaho celebrated its 100th year of statehood in 1990, at the same time ushering in a decade in which the major environmental issue was nuclear waste contamination. The matter was highlighted by wildfires that raged in western states during the summer of 2000. One blaze charred the grounds of the Idaho National Engineering and Environmental Lab, a nuclear research and waste storage facility. Thirty thousand acres were burned before the fire was brought under control. But environmentalists, concerned citizens, and many Idaho lawmakers remained concerned that such storage facilities are vulnerable to natural disaster and pose a serious threat. In the early 2000s, wildfires broke out in the West once again, including Idaho. In the summer of 2002, wildfires burned over 7.1 million acres of public and private land in the United States, most of it in the West.

12 STATE GOVERNMENT

Idaho's 1889 constitution, amended 117 times as of January 2005, continues to govern the state today. The bicameral legislature, consisting of a 35-seat Senate and a 70-member House of Representatives, meets annually beginning the Monday closest to 9 January. There is no constitutional limit on the length of the session. Special sessions may only be summoned by the governor and are limited to 20 days. Legislators must be US citizens, at least 18 years old, qualified voters, and residents of their district for at least a year. All legislators serve two-year terms. In 2004, the legislative salary was $15,646.

The executive branch is headed by seven elected officials: the governor and lieutenant governor (who run separately), secretary of state, attorney general, comptroller, treasurer, and superinten-

dent of public instruction. All serve four-year terms. The governor, who must be a US citizen, at least 30 years old, and a state resident for at least two years prior to election, can sign or veto a bill. Vetoes may be overridden by a two-thirds vote of the elected members in each house. If the governor neither signs nor vetoes a bill, it becomes law after five days when the legislature is in session and after 10 days when the legislature has adjourned. As of December 2004, the governor's salary was $98,500.

The state constitution may be amended with the consent of two-thirds of each house and a majority of the voters at the next general election. Provisions for initiative, referendum, and recall were added by amendment to the state constitution in 1912 but not implemented by the legislature until 1933. The initiative procedure was employed in 1974 to pass the Sunshine Act, mandating registration by lobbyists and campaign financing disclosures by candidates for public office. An Idaho voter must be at least 18 years old, a US citizen, and a resident of the county and state for at least 30 days prior to election day. Restrictions apply to convicted felons.

13 POLITICAL PARTIES

Idahoans have usually voted Republican in presidential elections but sometimes have elected Democrats to Congress or the statehouse. The state has become increasingly Republican in the 21st century, however. The dominant Republican in the 20th century was US senator William E. Borah, an isolationist-progressive who opposed US entry into the League of Nations but advocated world disarmament and supported prohibition, the graduated income tax, and some New Deal reforms; as chairman of the Senate Foreign Relations Committee from 1924 to 1940, he was one of the most influential legislators in the nation.

One measure of the conservatism of Idaho voters in the 1960s and 1970s was the showing by George Wallace's American Independent Party in 1968 (12.6% of the total vote) and his American Party in 1972 (9.3%, the highest of any state). In 2000, Republican George W. Bush received 69% of the vote, while Democrat Al Gore won 28% and Reform Party candidate Patrick Buchanan captured

Idaho Presidential Vote by Major Political Parties, 1948–2004

YEAR	ELECTORAL VOTE	IDAHO WINNER	DEMOCRAT	REPUBLICAN
1948	4	*Truman (D)	107,370	101,514
1952	4	*Eisenhower (R)	395,081	180,707
1956	4	*Eisenhower (R)	105,868	166,979
1960	4	Nixon (R)	138,853	161,597
1964	4	*Johnson (D)	148,920	143,557
1968	4	*Nixon (R)	389,273	165,369
1972	4	*Nixon (R)	380,826	199,384
1976	4	Ford (R)	126,549	204,151
1980	4	*Reagan (R)	110,192	290,699
1984	4	*Reagan (R)	108,510	297,523
1988	4	*Bush (R)	147,272	253,881
1992**	4	Bush (R)	137,013	202,645
1996**	4	Dole (R)	165,443	256,595
2000	4	*Bush, G. W. (R)	138,637	336,937
2004	4	*Bush, G. W. (R)	181,098	409,235

*Won US presidential election.

**IND. candidate Ross Perot received 130,395 votes in 1992 and 62,518 votes in 1996.

2%. In 2004, Bush won 68.5% to Democratic challenger John Kerry's 30.4%. In 2004, there were 798,000 registered voters; there is no party registration in the state. The state had four electoral votes in the 2004 presidential election.

A Democrat, Cecil Andrus, served four terms as governor, retiring in 1994. In winning the governor's office in November 1994, Republican Phil Batt ended 24 years of Democratic control of that office. He was succeeded by another Republican, Dirk Kempthorne, following the 1998 election; Kempthorne was reelected in 2002. In mid-2005, the state legislature had 28 Republicans and 7 Democrats in the state Senate and 57 Republicans and 13 Democrats in the state House. In the 2004 elections, Idaho voters again elected two Republicans to represent them in the US House. Its US senators, Larry Craig, reelected in 2002, and Mike Crapo, reelected in 2004, are also Republicans.

14 LOCAL GOVERNMENT

As of 2005, Idaho had 44 counties, 200 municipal governments, 115 public school districts, and 798 special districts or authorities. Most counties elect three commissioners and other officers, usually including an assessor, treasurer, coroner, and sheriff. Nearly all cities have an elected mayor and council of four to six members. School districts have elected board members.

In 2005, local government accounted for about 54,268 full-time (or equivalent) employment positions.

15 STATE SERVICES

To address the continuing threat of terrorism and to work with the federal Department of Homeland Security, homeland security in Idaho operates under the authority of state statue and executive order; the emergency management director is designated as the state homeland security adviser.

The executive agencies concerned with education are the State Board of Education and the Department of Education. Under the heading of human resources are the Departments of Health and Welfare, Employment, and Correction and the Idaho State Police. Under the general rubric of natural resources come the Departments of Lands, Water Resources, Fish and Game, and Parks and Recreation. Self-governing agencies and the Departments of Agriculture, Finance, Insurance, Commerce and Labor, and Transportation oversee economic development and regulation. Within the Executive Office of the Governor are a number of funds, divisions, boards, commissions, and other bodies. The Information Technology Resource Management Council supports high-tech endeavors in the state.

16 JUDICIAL SYSTEM

Idaho's highest court, the supreme court, consists of five justices, each elected at large on a nonpartisan ballot to a six-year term. The justice with the shortest remaining term automatically becomes chief justice. There is a three-member court of appeals. The district court, with 37 judges in 1999, is the main trial court in civil and criminal matters, while magistrates' courts handle traffic, misdemeanor, and minor civil cases and preliminary hearings in felony cases. As with the state's supreme court justices, appeals court justices and district court judges are elected by nonpartisan ballot for six years and four years, respectively. Magistrates are appointed by a commission and run for four-year terms in the first general election succeeding the 18-month period following appointment.

As of 31 December 2004, a total of 6,375 prisoners were held in Idaho's state and federal prisons, an increase from 5,737 or 11.1% from the previous year. As of year-end 2004, a total of 647 inmates were female, up from 591 or 5% from the year before. Among sentenced prisoners (one year or more), Idaho had an incarceration rate of 454 per 100,000 population in 2004.

According to the Federal Bureau of Investigation, in 2004 Idaho had a violent crime rate (murder/nonnegligent manslaughter; forcible rape; robbery; aggravated assault) of 244.9 reported incidents per 100,000 population, or a total of 3,412 reported incidents. Crimes against property (burglary; larceny/theft; and motor vehicle theft) in that same year totaled 38,933 reported incidents or 2,794.4 reported incidents per 100,000 people. Idaho has a death penalty, which can be carried out by lethal injection or firing squad, of which the latter is to be used only if lethal injection is impractical. From 1976 through 5 May 2006, the state executed only one person, which was carried out in January 1994. As of 1 January 2006, there were 20 inmates on death row.

In 2003, Idaho spent $41,282,044 on homeland security, an average of $28 per state resident.

17 ARMED FORCES

Mountain Home Air Force Base, located about 50 mi (80 km) southeast of Boise, has 4,516 active-duty military personnel. In 2004, 5,640 active-duty military personnel, 489 civilian personnel, and 1,455 Guard and National Guard personnel were stationed in Idaho. Defense contract awards to Idaho firms totaled $186 million in fiscal year 2004. Another $535 million in defense payroll spending came to the state.

Idaho casualties in US wars included 1,419 in World War II, 132 in Korea, and 187 in Vietnam. There were 133,183 veterans of US military service in Idaho as of 2003, of whom 16,712 served in World War II; 13,095 in the Korean conflict; 39,565 during the Vietnam era; and 26,264 in the Persian Gulf War. Total expenditures for Idaho veterans were $363 million in fiscal year 2004.

As of 31 October 2004, the Idaho State Police employed 242 full-time sworn officers.

18 MIGRATION

Idaho's first white immigrants came from Utah, California, and Oregon in the early 1860s. By the end of the Civil War, the chief sources of immigrants were the southern and border states. Homesteaders from the Midwest, Utah, and Scandinavia arrived at the end of the 19th century.

Since 1960, immigrants have come largely from California. Idaho suffered a net loss from migration of 109,000 persons between 1940 and 1970 but had a net gain of 110,000 persons in the 1970s. During the 1980s, Idaho had a net loss of 28,000 persons from migration. Between 1990 and 1998, the state had net gains of 129,000 in domestic migration and 15,000 in international migration. In 1998, 1,504 immigrants from foreign countries arrived in Idaho. The state's overall population increased 22% between 1990 and 1998, making it one of the fastest-growing states in the United States, superseded only by Nevada and Arizona during the same time period. In the period 2000–05, net international migration was 14,522 and net internal migration was 61,273, for a net gain of 75,795 people.

19 INTERGOVERNMENTAL COOPERATION

Idaho cooperates with Utah and Wyoming in the Bear River Compact; with Oregon, Washington, and Alaska in the Pacific States Marine Fisheries Commission; with Wyoming in the Snake River Compact; with Washington, Oregon, and Montana in the Northwest Power and Conservation Council; and in the Western Interstate Commission for Higher Education, Western Interstate Energy Council, Western States Water Council, and numerous other interstate compacts. Federal grants amounted to $1.465 billion in fiscal year 2005, $1.54 billion in fiscal year 2006, and $1.729 billion in fiscal year 2007.

20 ECONOMY

Fur trapping was Idaho's earliest industry. Agriculture and mining began around 1860, with agriculture dominating since the 1870s. Timber became important after 1900, and tourism and manufacturing—especially food processing and forest products—after 1945. Currently, agriculture, mining, forest products, and food processing are Idaho's largest industries.

The Idaho economy prospered in the 1970s. Machinery and transportation equipment manufacturing grew 20% between 1970 and 1980, and services expanded 7.5%. The early 1980s, in contrast, brought a national recession in which Idaho lost 8% of its employment base. Recovery required a restructuring of Idaho's mining, forest products, and agricultural industries that resulted in the laying off of large numbers of employees. Other industries posted significant gains in employment in the 1980s. Chemical manufacturing employment grew 36% in the early and mid-1980s, and jobs in the paper industry increased 30%. Travel and tourism employment rose 35% between 1982 and 1991, and high-tech jobs increased 50% between 1986 and 1990. Disputes with the federal government over the management of federal lands remained central to the discussion of Idaho's economic policy, as the federal government owns 60% of Idaho's public land. The disputes center on such matters as grazing fees, costs of water from government projects, species protection, and mining regulations. The electronics industry continued to grow during the 1990s, as evidenced by expansions announced by Hewlett-Packard, Micron, and Zilog. Construction employment also increased. Other manufacturing sectors were also increasing, so that from 1997 to 2000, there was an overall 37% increase in Idaho's manufacturing output and an increase in its relative share of total state output, from 20.2% to 22.1%. More than half of the gain was lost, however, in the national recession in 2001, as manufacturing output fell 19.4% in one year, reducing the net gain since 1997 to 10.3% and manufacturing's share in the state economy to a new low of 17.8%. The recession and continued slowdown severely impacted Idaho's economy, as strong annual growth rates at the end of the 20th century—5.6% in 1998, 11.4% in 1999, and 6.3% in 2000—abruptly fell to 0.4% in 2001. The highest rate of job loss was in the construction sector, where employment fell 11% from December 2001 to December 2002. Over the same period, employment in manufacturing fell 4% and about 4,500 high-paid, high-tech jobs were lost. Idaho's economy was also afflicted in 2002 by drought conditions that reduced grazing land and threatened the state's potato crop.

Idaho farmers were also hurt by historically low milk prices in 2002 and into 2003.

In 2004, Idaho's gross state product (GSP) totaled $43.571 billion, of which manufacturing (durable and nondurable goods) was the largest sector at $6.231 billion or 14.3% of GSP, followed by real estate at $5.191 billion (11.9% of GSP), and health care and social services at $2.914 billion (6.6% of GSP). In that same year, there were an estimated 131,663 small businesses in Idaho. Of the 43,675 businesses having employees, a total of 42,384 or 97% were small companies. An estimated 7,814 new businesses were established in the state in 2004, up 30.3% from the year before. Business terminations that same year came to 5,716, down 15.2% from 2003. There were 160 business bankruptcies in 2004, down 28.9% from the previous year. In 2005, the personal bankruptcy (Chapter 7 and Chapter 13) filing rate was 704 filings per 100,000 people, ranking Idaho as the 12th highest in the nation.

21 INCOME

In 2005, Idaho had a gross state product (GSP) of $47 billion, which accounted for 0.4% of the nation's gross domestic product and placed the state at number 43 in highest GSP among the 50 states and the District of Columbia.

According to the Bureau of Economic Analysis, in 2004, Idaho had a per capita personal income (PCPI) of $26,877. This ranked 46th in the United States and was 81% of the national average of $33,050. The 1994–2004 average annual growth rate of PCPI was 3.7%. Idaho had a total personal income (TPI) of $37,497,434,000, which ranked 42nd in the United States and reflected an increase of 8.2% from 2003. The 1994–2004 average annual growth rate of TPI was 5.8%. Earnings of persons employed in Idaho increased from $25,779,208,000 in 2003 to $28,215,416,000 in 2004, an increase of 9.5%. The 2003–04 national change was 6.3%.

The US Census Bureau reports that the three-year average median household income for 2002–04 in 2004 dollars was $42,519 compared to a national average of $44,473. During the same period an estimated 10.5% of the population was below the poverty line, as compared to 12.4% nationwide.

22 LABOR

According to the Bureau of Labor Statistics (BLS), in April 2006, the seasonally adjusted civilian labor force in Idaho numbered 761,200. Approximately 25,600 workers were unemployed, yielding an unemployment rate of 3.4%, compared to the national average of 4.7% for the same period. Preliminary data for the same period placed nonfarm employment at 638,100. Since the beginning of the BLS data series in 1976, the highest unemployment rate recorded in Idaho was 9.4% in February 1983. The historical low was 3.2% in March 2006. Preliminary nonfarm employment data by occupation for April 2006 showed that approximately 8.1% of the labor force was employed in construction; 10% in manufacturing; 19.9% in trade, transportation, and public utilities; 4.9% in financial activities; 12.6% in professional and business services; 10.8% in education and health services; 9.7% in leisure and hospitality services; and 18.1% in government.

Idaho was a pioneer in establishing the eight-hour workday and in outlawing yellow-dog contracts. In 1958, Idaho voters rejected right-to-work legislation. Governor John Evans vetoed similar legislation in 1982. However, in 1986, Idaho became one of 22 states with a right-to-work law when voters approved the law.

The BLS reported that in 2005, a total of 31,000 of Idaho's 606,000 employed wage and salary workers were formal members of a union. This represented 5.2% of those so employed, down from 5.8% in 2004 and well under the national average of 12%. Overall in 2005, a total of 38,000 workers (6.3%) in Idaho were covered by a union or employee association contract, which includes those workers who reported no union affiliation.

As of 1 March 2006, Idaho had a state-mandated minimum wage of $5.15 per hour. In 2004, women in the state accounted for 45.8% of the employed civilian labor force.

23 AGRICULTURE

Receipts from farm marketings totaled $4.5 billion in 2005 (21st in the United States); farm industry income was about $1.9 billion. As of 2004, Idaho led the United States in potato production; was second in sugar beets and barley; third in hops, peppermint oil; and fourth in spearmint oil.

Development of the russet potato in the 1920s gave Idaho its most famous crop. In 2004, the state produced 131,970,000 hundredweight of potatoes (29% of the US total); some 90% was grown on about 110,000 acres (45,000 hectares) of irrigated land on the Snake River plain. About three-fourths of the crop is processed into frozen french fries, instant mashed potatoes, and other products. Other leading crops were hay, 5,350,000 tons, valued at $556,690,000; wheat, 101,710,000 bushels, $357,427,000; barley, 59,800,000 bushels (second in the United States), $176,410,000; and sugar beets, 5,491,000 tons, $216,980,000.

As of 2004, Idaho had 11.8 million acres (5.4 million hectares) in farms, roughly 22% of the state's land area; its estimated 25,000 farms, (including ranches) averaged about 472 acres (191 hectares). Almost 3.5 million acres (1.4 hectares) of land were irrigated.

24 ANIMAL HUSBANDRY

In 2005, there were an estimated 2 million cattle and calves worth around $2.2 billion. In 2004, Idaho had an estimated 21,000 hogs and pigs worth around $2.1 million. Idaho had an estimated 404,000 dairy cows, which produced 8.8 billion lb (3.4 million kg) of milk in 2003. In the same year, Idaho produced an estimated 2.3 million lb (1 million kg) of chicken, and the state produced an estimated 243 million eggs worth $14.5 million. Also during 2003, the state produced an estimated 24.7 million lb of sheep and lambs, which grossed $20.8 million for Idaho farmers. Shorn wool production in 2004 totaled an estimated 2.1 million lb (0.95 million kg).

25 FISHING

In 2004, there were some 403,741 licensed sport fishermen catching trout along with salmon, steelhead, bass, and 32 other gamefish species. Idaho is a leading producer of farm-raised trout: Its 55 trout farms had $32.6 million in sales in 2004, more than any other state and 47% of the US total. There are about 19 state hatcheries and three national fish hatcheries located within the state.

The Idaho Fish Health Center in Orofino is a federally sponsored research facility.

26 FORESTRY

As of 2004, Idaho forests covered 23.5 million acres (9.5 million hectares), or about 40% of the state's land area, with 16,824,000 acres (6,809,000 hectares) classified as commercial timberland. Of the total forest area in 2003, the federal government controlled 79%; state government, 5%; and private owners, 16%. National Forest System lands in Idaho totaled 21,575,000 acres (8,731,000 hectares) in 2005. Idaho forests are used increasingly for ski areas, hunting, and other recreation, as well as for timber and pulp. Total lumber production was 1.7 billion board feet (10th in the United States) in 2004, almost all softwoods.

27 MINING

Idaho's estimated value of nonfuel mineral production in 2004 was $446 million, up almost 66% from 2003, according to preliminary data from the US Geological Survey (USGS). The data placed Idaho 34th in the production, by value, of nonfuel minerals in 2004, accounting for 1% of the US total.

In descending order, phosphate rock, construction sand and gravel, molybdenum concentrates, silver, portland cement, and crushed stone were the top minerals produced that year, accounting for around 91%, by value, of all nonfuel mineral output by the state.

According to USGS estimates (by volume) for 2004, Idaho ranked second nationally in the production of phosphate rock and industrial garnets (out of two states) and was third in the output of silver and lead, fourth in molybdenum concentrates and zeolites, fifth in pumice and zinc, and sixth in gemstones. Idaho is also a producer of gold, copper, and lime.

In 2004, preliminary data showed crushed stone production at 3.2 million metric tons or $16.2 million, with output of sand and gravel for construction at 18.2 million metric tons or $66.8 million.

28 ENERGY AND POWER

As of 2003, Idaho had 32 electrical power service providers, of which 11 were publicly owned and 16 were cooperatives. Of the remainder, four were investor owned and one was an owner of an independent generator that sold directly to customers. As of that same year, there were 687,334 retail customers. Of that total, 577,986 received their power from investor-owned service providers. Cooperatives accounted for 69,850 customers, while publicly owned providers had 39,497 customers. There was only one independent generator or "facility" customer.

Total net summer generating capability by the state's electrical generating plants in 2003 stood at 3.002 million kW, with total production that same year at 10.422 billion kWh. Of the total amount generated, 74.2% came from electric utilities, with the remainder coming from independent producers and combined heat and power service providers. The largest portion of all electric power generated, 8.354 billion kWh (80.1%), came from hydroelectric plants, with natural gas–fired plants in second place at 1.374 billion kWh (13.2%). Other renewable power sources accounted for 5.2% of all power generated, with coal and "other" types of generating facilities accounting for the remainder.

Idaho's large size, widespread and relatively rural population, and lack of public transportation foster reliance on motor vehicles and imported petroleum products. Natural gas is also imported. Hot water from thermal springs is used to heat buildings in Boise.

As of 2004, Idaho had no known proven reserves or production of crude oil or natural gas. There are no refineries located within the state.

29 INDUSTRY

Although resource industries such as food processing, chemical manufacturing, and lumber production continue to be important manufacturing sectors in Idaho's economy, computer and electronic product manufacturing accounted for the state's primary manufacturing sector as of 2004.

According to the US Census Bureau's Annual Survey of Manufactures (ASM) for 2004, Idaho's manufacturing sector covered some 13 product subsectors. The shipment value of all products manufactured in the state that same year was $16.583 billion. Of that total, computer and electronic product manufacturing accounted for the largest share at $6.076 billion. It was followed by food manufacturing at $4.455 billion; wood product manufacturing at $1.853 billion; chemical manufacturing at $802.844 million; and paper manufacturing at $734.884 million.

In 2004, a total of 56,479 people in Idaho were employed in the state's manufacturing sector, according to the ASM. Of that total, 36,632 were actual production workers. In terms of total employment, the computer and electronic product manufacturing industry accounted for the largest portion of all manufacturing employees at 15,552, with 4,054 actual production workers. It was followed by food manufacturing at 13,238 employees (11,451 actual production workers); wood product manufacturing at 7,019 employees (6,025 actual production workers); fabricated metal product manufacturing at 3,456 employees (2,667 actual production workers); and furniture and related product manufacturing with 2,051 employees (1,667 actual production workers).

ASM data for 2004 showed that Idaho's manufacturing sector paid $2.107 billion in wages. Of that amount, the computer and electronic product manufacturing sector accounted for the largest share at $739.972 million. It was followed by food manufacturing at $391.014 million; wood product manufacturing at $223.840 million; fabricated metal product manufacturing at $119.999 million; and paper manufacturing at $100.246 million.

Ore-Ida Foods is a leading potato processor, and J. R. Simplot engages in food processing and fertilizer production. Boise Cascade (with headquarters at Boise), Potlatch, and Louisiana-Pacific dominate the wood-products industry. Morrison-Knudsen, a diversified engineering and construction company that also has forest-products interests, has its headquarters in Boise.

30 COMMERCE

According to the 2002 Census of Wholesale Trade, Idaho's wholesale trade sector had sales that year totaling $11.4 billion from 1,989 establishments. Wholesalers of durable goods accounted for 1,168 establishments, followed by nondurable goods wholesalers at 735 and electronic markets, agents, and brokers accounting for 86 establishments. Sales by durable goods wholesalers in 2002 totaled $5.8 billion, while wholesalers of nondurable goods saw

sales of $4.7 billion. Electronic markets, agents, and brokers in the wholesale trade industry had sales of $926.2 million.

In the 2002 Census of Retail Trade, Idaho was listed as having 5,874 retail establishments with sales of $13.5 billion. The leading types of retail businesses by number of establishments were motor vehicle and motor vehicle parts dealers (868); miscellaneous store retailers (674); gasoline stations (663); building material/garden equipment and supplies dealers (661); and food and beverage stores (549). In terms of sales, motor vehicle and motor vehicle parts dealers accounted for the largest share of retail sales at $3.7 billion, followed by general merchandise stores at $2.3 billion; food and beverage stores at $1.8 billion; and building material/garden equipment and supplies at $1.4 billion. A total of 69,641 people were employed by the retail sector in Idaho that year.

Foreign exports of goods from Idaho were valued at $3.2 billion in 2005 (38th in the United States).

31 CONSUMER PROTECTION

The Idaho Office of the Attorney General is responsible for investigating consumer complaints and enforcing most consumer laws through its Consumer Protection Unit. However, Idaho's Credit Code is administered through the Department of Finance, which also resolves consumer credit complaints under that law. The legislature has enacted the state's Consumer Protection, Telephone Solicitation, and Pay-Per-Telephone Call acts for purposes of protecting both consumers and businesses against unfair or deceptive acts in trade and commerce, and providing efficient and economical procedures to secure such protection. The Idaho Consumer Protection Unit seeks to fulfill this charge through education, mediation, and enforcement efforts. In 1990, the Idaho Consumer Protection Act was modernized, and in 1992 the Telephone Solicitation and Pay-Per-Telephone Call Acts were passed, as well as the Charitable Solicitation Act in 1993.

In support of its Consumer Protection Unit, the Idaho Office of the Attorney General has broad subpoena powers; can initiate civil (but not criminal) proceedings; and can represent the state before state and federal regulatory agencies, as well as support the administration of consumer protection and education programs and handle formal consumer complaints. In antitrust actions, the Office of the Attorney General can act on behalf of those consumers who are incapable of acting on their own; initiate damage actions on behalf of the state in state courts; and represent counties, cities, and other governmental entities in recovering civil damages under state or federal law.

The Consumer Protection Unit of the Idaho Attorney General's Office is located in Boise.

32 BANKING

As of June 2005, Idaho had 17 insured banks, savings and loans, and saving banks, plus 42 state-chartered and 24 federally chartered credit unions (CUs). Excluding the CUs, the Boise City-Nampa market area had 21 financial institutions in 2004 with $6.171 billion in deposits, followed by Coeur d'Alene with 14 institutions and $1.472 billion in deposits. As of June 2005, CUs accounted for 31.1% of all assets held by all financial institutions in the state, or some $2.739 billion. Banks, savings and loans, and savings banks collectively accounted for the remaining 68.9% or $6.060 billion in assets held.

The 1997 Idaho Savings Bank Act permitted state-chartered savings banks in Idaho, repealing the Savings and Loan Act. The Idaho Department of Finance's Financial Institutions Bureau regulates and supervises Idaho's state-chartered commercial banks, savings banks, credit unions, trust companies, and bank holding companies. Idaho's insured institutions increased their profitability in 2004 as the median return on average assets ratio (the measure of earnings in relation to all resources) rose from 0.98% in 2003 to 0.99%. The median net interest margin (the difference between the lower rates offered savers and the higher rates charged on loans) was 5.34% in the fourth quarter of 2005, up from 4.69% in 2004 and 4.65% in 2003.

33 INSURANCE

In 2004, there were 498,000 individual life insurance policies in force with a total value of over $49.4 billion; total value for all categories of life insurance (individual, group, and credit) was over $84 billion. The average coverage amount was $99,200 per policy holder. Death benefits paid that year totaled $204 million.

In 2003, 12 property and casualty and six life and health insurance companies were domiciled in the state. In 2004, direct premiums for property and casualty insurance totaled $1.68 billion. That year, there were 5,651 flood insurance policies in force in the state, with a total value of $960 million.

In 2004, 53% of state residents held employment-based health insurance policies, 7% held individual policies, and 22% were covered under Medicare and Medicaid; 17% of residents were uninsured. In 2003, employee contributions for employment-based health coverage averaged at 16% for single coverage and 28% for family coverage. The state does not offer a health benefits expansion program in connection with the Consolidated Omnibus Budget Reconciliation Act (COBRA, 1986), a health insurance program for those who lose employment-based coverage due to termination or reduction of work hours.

In 2003, there were over 1 million auto insurance policies in effect for private passenger cars. Required minimum coverage includes bodily injury liability of up to $25,000 per individual and $50,000 for all persons injured in an accident, as well as property damage liability of $15,000. In 2003, the average expenditure per vehicle for insurance coverage was $585.34, one of the lowest averages in the nation.

34 SECURITIES

Idaho has no stock exchanges. In 2005, there were 540 personal financial advisers employed in the state and 630 securities, commodities, and financial services sales agents. In 2004, there were over 34 publicly traded companies within the state, with four NASDAQ companies, six NYSE listings, and one AMEX listing. In 2006, the state had two Fortune 500 companies; Albertson's (food and drug stores) ranked first in the state and 47th in the nation with revenues of over $40.3 billion, followed by Micron Technology. Washington Group Intl. made the Fortune 1,000 list at 586th in the nation. Albertson's and Micron Technology are listed on the NYSE; Washington Group Intl. is an OTC listing.

35 PUBLIC FINANCE

Idaho's annual budget, prepared by the Division of Financial Management, is submitted by the governor to the legislature for amendment and approval. The fiscal year (FY) runs from 1 July to 30 June. The state constitution requires that the legislature pass a balanced budget, and the governor, as the chief budget officer, ensures that expenditures do not exceed revenues.

In fiscal year 2006, general funds were estimated at $2.3 billion for resources and $2.2 billion for expenditures. In fiscal year 2004, federal government grants to Idaho were nearly $2.0 billion.

Idaho—State Government Finances

(Dollar amounts in thousands. Per capita amounts in dollars.)

	AMOUNT	PER CAPITA
Total Revenue	7,112,364	5,098.47
General revenue	5,309,905	3,806.38
Intergovernmental revenue	1,741,394	1,248.31
Taxes	2,647,790	1,898.06
General sales	1,036,924	743.31
Selective sales	366,231	262.53
License taxes	220,800	158.28
Individual income tax	907,795	650.75
Corporate income tax	103,784	74.40
Other taxes	12,256	8.79
Current charges	470,037	336.94
Miscellaneous general revenue	450,684	323.07
Utility revenue	–	–
Liquor store revenue	76,766	55.03
Insurance trust revenue	1,725,693	1,237.06
Total expenditure	5,762,624	4,130.91
Intergovernmental expenditure	1,496,785	1,072.96
Direct expenditure	4,265,839	3,057.95
Current operation	2,848,421	2,041.88
Capital outlay	539,447	386.70
Insurance benefits and repayments	611,969	438.69
Assistance and subsidies	132,212	94.78
Interest on debt	133,790	95.91
Exhibit: Salaries and wages	817,284	585.87
Total expenditure	5,762,624	4,130.91
General expenditure	5,093,039	3,650.92
Intergovernmental expenditure	1,496,785	1,072.96
Direct expenditure	3,596,254	2,577.96
General expenditures, by function:		
Education	2,013,929	1,443.68
Public welfare	1,197,420	858.37
Hospitals	39,186	28.09
Health	112,441	80.60
Highways	524,242	375.80
Police protection	43,206	30.97
Correction	170,981	122.57
Natural resources	178,812	128.18
Parks and recreation	26,054	18.68
Government administration	268,481	192.46
Interest on general debt	133,790	95.91
Other and unallocable	384,497	275.63
Utility expenditure	–	–
Liquor store expenditure	57,616	41.30
Insurance trust expenditure	611,969	438.69
Debt at end of fiscal year	2,383,841	1,708.85
Cash and security holdings	11,735,412	8,412.48

Abbreviations and symbols: – zero or rounds to zero; (NA) not available; (X) not applicable.

SOURCE: *U.S. Census Bureau, Governments Division, 2004 Survey of State Government Finances,* January 2006.

In the fiscal year 2007 federal budget, Idaho was slated to receive $25.4 million in State Children's Health Insurance Program (SCHIP) funds to provide health coverage to low-income, uninsured children who do not qualify for Medicaid. This funding is a 23% increase over fiscal year 2006. The state is also scheduled to receive $7.3 million for the HOME Investment Partnership Program to help Idaho fund a wide range of activities that build, buy, or rehabilitate affordable housing for rent or homeownership or provide direct rental assistance to low-income people. This funding is a 12% increase over fiscal year 2006.

36 TAXATION

In 2005, Idaho collected $2,934 million in tax revenues or $2,054 per capita, which placed it 30th among the 50 states in per capita tax burden. The national average was $2,192 per capita. Sales taxes accounted for 38.5% of the total, selective sales taxes 12.7%, individual income taxes 35.5%, corporate income taxes 4.8%, and other taxes 8.6%.

As of 1 January 2006, Idaho had eight individual income tax brackets ranging from 1.6 to 7.8%. The state taxes corporations at a flat rate of 7.6%.

In 2004, local property taxes amounted to $1,084,470,000 or $777 per capita. The per capita amount ranks the state 36th highest nationally. Idaho does not collect property taxes at the state level.

Idaho taxes retail sales at a rate of 6%. In addition to the state tax, local taxes on retail sales can reach as much as 3%, making for a potential total tax on retail sales of 9%. Food purchased for consumption off premises is taxable; however, an income tax credit is allowed to offset sales tax on food. The tax on cigarettes is 57 cents per pack, which ranks 33rd among the 50 states and the District of Columbia. Idaho taxes gasoline at 25 cents per gallon. This is in addition to the 18.4 cents per gallon federal tax on gasoline.

According to the Tax Foundation, for every federal tax dollar sent to Washington in 2004, Idaho citizens received $1.28 in federal spending.

37 ECONOMIC POLICY

The Idaho Department of Commerce and Labor coordinates economic development initiatives in the state, which are carried out by various departments and executive councils. The International Business Division of the Department of Commerce and Labor has as its mission the identification of opportunities for Idaho products in international markets and helping Idaho companies capitalize on these. In 2005, key export markets for Idaho's goods were in China, Canada, Singapore, the United Kingdom, Taiwan, and Japan. The Division of Economic and Community Affairs, within the office of the governor, seeks to widen markets for Idaho products and goods and services, encourage film production in the state, attract new business and industry to Idaho, expand and enhance existing enterprises, and promote the state travel industry. Incentives for investment include conservative state fiscal policies and a probusiness regulatory climate. Idaho offers industrial revenue bonds to assist companies with the financing of land, buildings, and equipment used in manufacturing. The state extends loans to businesses seeking to start up or expand and for energy conservation improvements. To help distressed areas, there are matching grants for economic development as well as train-

ing in strategic planning and economic diversification techniques. Cities and counties may also apply for community development block grants.

38 HEALTH

The infant mortality rate in October 2005 was estimated at 6.3 per 1,000 live births. The birth rate in 2003 was 16 per 1,000 population. The abortion rate stood at 7 per 1,000 women in 2000. In 2003, about 81.4% of pregnant woman received prenatal care beginning in the first trimester. In 2004, approximately 81% of children received routine immunizations before the age of three.

The crude death rate in 2003 was 7.6 deaths per 1,000 population. As of 2002, the death rates for major causes of death (per 100,000 resident population) were as follows: heart disease, 188.8; cancer, 159.4; cerebrovascular diseases, 54.9; chronic lower respiratory diseases, 44.4; and diabetes, 23.9. The mortality rate from HIV infection was unavailable. In 2004, the reported AIDS case rate was at about 1.6 per 100,000 population, the third lowest in the nation that year. In 2002, about 55% of the population was considered overweight or obese. As of 2004, about 17.4% of state residents were smokers, one of the lowest percentages in the nation.

In 2003, Idaho had 39 community hospitals with about 3,400 beds. There were about 136,000 patient admissions that year and 2.8 million outpatient visits. The average daily inpatient census was about 1,900 patients. The average cost per day for hospital care was $1,235. Also in 2003, there were about 80 certified nursing facilities in the state with 6,258 beds and an overall occupancy rate of about 76%. In 2004, it was estimated that about 67.7% of all state residents had received some type of dental care within the year. Idaho had 175 physicians per 100,000 resident population in 2004 and 657 nurses per 100,000 in 2005. In 2004, there was a total of 824 dentists in the state.

About 22% of state residents were enrolled in Medicaid and Medicare programs in 2004. Approximately 17% of the state population was uninsured in 2004. In 2003, state health care expenditures totaled $1.1 million.

39 SOCIAL WELFARE

In 2004, about 50,000 people received unemployment benefits, with the average weekly unemployment benefit at $229. In fiscal year 2005, the estimated average monthly participation in the food stamp program included about 93,441 persons (37,151 households); the average monthly benefit was about $91.83 per person. That year, the total of benefits paid through the state for the food stamp program was about $102 million.

Temporary Assistance for Needy Families (TANF), the system of federal welfare assistance that officially replaced Aid to Families with Dependent Children (AFDC) in 1997, was reauthorized through the Deficit Reduction Act of 2005. TANF is funded through federal block grants that are divided among the states based on an equation involving the number of recipients in each state. Idaho's TANF program is called Temporary Assistance for Families in Idaho. In 2004, the state program had 3,000 recipients; state and federal expenditures on this TANF program totaled $7 million in fiscal year 2003.

In December 2004, Social Security benefits were paid to 219,250 Idaho residents. This number included 140,330 retired workers, 19,940 widows and widowers, 27,430 disabled workers, 14,130 spouses, and 17,420 children. Social Security beneficiaries represented 15.7% of the total state population and 96.8% of the state's population age 65 and older. Retired workers received an average monthly payment of $931; widows and widowers, $914; disabled workers, $879; and spouses, $469. Payments for children of retired workers averaged $499 per month; children of deceased workers, $613; and children of disabled workers, $234. Federal Supplemental Security Income payments went to 20,993 Idaho residents in December 2004, averaging $383 a month. An additional $686,000 in state-administered supplemental payments were distributed to 12,398 residents.

40 HOUSING

In 2004, there were an estimated 578,774 housing units within the state, 515,252 of which were occupied. About 72.4% of all units were owner occupied. About 71.1% of all units were single-family, detached homes; 10.8% were mobile homes. Most units relied on utility gas and electricity for heating. It was estimated that 22,347 units were without telephone service, 2,419 lacked complete plumbing facilities, and 3,220 lacked complete kitchen facilities. The average household had 2.64 members.

In 2004, 18,100 privately owned housing units were authorized for construction. Median home value was at $120,825. The median monthly cost for mortgage owners was about $953 while renters paid a median of $566 per month. In 2006, the state received over $9.1 million in community development block grants from the US Department of Housing and Urban Development (HUD).

41 EDUCATION

As of 2004, 87.9% of Idahoans over the age of 25 were high school graduates and 23.8% had obtained a bachelor's degree or higher.

The total enrollment in Idaho's public schools for fall 2002 stood at 249,000. Of these, 173,000 attended schools from kindergarten through grade eight, and 75,000 attended high school. Approximately 84.1% of the students were white, 0.9% were black, 12% were Hispanic, 1.5% were Asian/Pacific Islander, and 1.6% were American Indian/Alaska Native. Total enrollment was estimated at 250,000 in fall 2003 and is expected to be 283,000 by fall 2014, an increase of 13.8% during the period 2002–14. There were 10,994 students enrolled in 107 private schools in fall 2003. Expenditures for public education in 2003–04 were estimated at $1.7 billion or $6,028 per student, the second lowest among the 50 states. Since 1969, the National Assessment of Educational Progress (NAEP) has tested public school students nationwide. The resulting report, *The Nation's Report Card,* stated that in 2005, eighth graders in Idaho scored 281 out of 500 in mathematics compared with the national average of 278.

As of fall 2002, there were 72,072 students enrolled in college or graduate school; minority students composed 7.6% of total postsecondary enrollment. As of 2005, Idaho had 14 degree-granting institutions. The leading public higher educational institutions are the University of Idaho at Moscow; Idaho State University (Pocatello); Boise State University; and Lewis-Clark State College in Lewiston. The State Board of Education offers scholarships to graduates of accredited Idaho high schools.

42 ARTS

The Idaho Commission on the Arts, founded in 1966, offers grants to support both creative and performing artists. In 2005, the commission hosted the National Association of State Arts Agencies annual meeting, bringing together some 385 arts administrators in Boise. Also in 2005, the Idaho Commission on the Arts and other Idaho arts organizations received nine grants totaling $699,100 from the National Endowment for the Arts. The commission is a partner with the regional Western States Arts Federation. The Idaho Humanities Council was established in 1973. In 2004, the council provided nearly $100,000 in grants and 292 speakers bureau programs supporting the humanities. In 2005, the state received $530,730 in the form of six grants from the National Endowment for the Humanities.

The Boise Philharmonic is Idaho's leading professional orchestra; other symphony orchestras are in Coeur d'Alene, Moscow, Pocatello, and Twin Falls. Boise and Moscow have seasonal theaters. The Boise Philharmonic is notable for its long history—it can trace its roots to around 1885 and the formation of the Boise City Orchestra. As of 2006, this orchestra performed for 14,000 students annually with their Children's Concerts. The annual summer Idaho Shakespeare Festival, in Boise, presents a series of plays in its outdoor Festival Amphitheater and Reserve. Boise is also home to Ballet Idaho, the state's professional ballet company. In 2005, the company performed in the mainstage productions of *Giselle* and *The Princess and the Pea,* as well as toured the state in December performing *The Nutcracker.*

The Boise Art Museum began in 1931 and is the only American Association of Museums (AAM) accredited art museum in the state. The museum's permanent collection emphasizes 20th-century American art, particularly art from the Pacific Northwest and American Realism. The 2006 exhibitions included *Native Perspectives on the Trail: A Contemporary American Indian Art Portfolio* and *Frank Lloyd Wright and the House Beautiful*—over 100 original objects designed by Wright were showcased.

43 LIBRARIES AND MUSEUMS

For the fiscal year ending in September 2001, Idaho had 106 public library systems, with a total of 143 libraries, of which 39 were branches. In that same year, the systems had a combined book and serial publications stock of 3,577,000 volumes and a total circulation of more than 8,723,000. The systems also had 126,000 audio and 103,000 video items, 3,000 electronic format items (CD-ROMs, magnetic tapes, and disks), and seven bookmobiles. The largest public library system was the Boise Public Library and Information Center, with about 340,800 volumes. The state's leading academic library was at the University of Idaho (Moscow); it had 1,064,707 volumes, as of 2000. In fiscal year 2001, total operating income for the public library system was $25,787,000, which included $177,000 in federal grants and $$737,000 in state grants.

The state also has 31 museums, notably the Boise Art Museum, Idaho State Historical Museum (Boise), and the Idaho Museum of Natural History (Pocatello). The University of Idaho Arboretum is at Moscow, and there is a zoo at Boise and an animal park in Idaho Falls. Major historical sites include Cataldo Mission near Kellogg, Spalding Mission near Lapwai, and Nez Perce National Historical Park in north-central Idaho.

44 COMMUNICATIONS

As of 2004, 94.8% of Idaho's occupied housing units had telephones. Additionally, by June of that same year, there were 653,779 mobile wireless telephone subscribers. In 2003, 69.2% of Idaho households had a computer and 56.4% had Internet access. By June 2005, there were 148,964 high-speed lines in Idaho, 134,698 residential and 14,266 for business.

Idaho's first radio station, built by a Boise high school teacher and his students, began transmitting in 1921, was licensed in 1922, and six years later was sold and given the initials KIDO—the same call letters later assigned to Idaho's first permanent television station, which began broadcasting in 1953 and subsequently became KTVB. As of 2005, the state had 43 major operating radio stations (8 AM, 35 FM) and 13 major television stations. Several large cable systems serviced the state in 2005. In 2000, a total of 21,563 internet domain names were registered in the state.

45 PRESS

Idaho, site of the first printing press in the Northwest, had 12 daily newspapers in 2005 (10 morning and 2 evening) and 8 Sunday papers. The most widely read newspaper was the *Idaho Statesman,* published in Boise, with a circulation of 63,023 daily and 83,857on Sundays in 2005. Caxton Printers, founded in 1902, is the state's leading publishing house. Leading magazines from the state are *Idaho* magazine and the industry trade magazines *Spudman* and *Sugar.*

46 ORGANIZATIONS

In 2006, there were over 1,170 nonprofit organizations registered within the state, of which about 797 were registered as charitable, educational, or religious organizations.

The Appaloosa Horse Club is among the few national organizations with headquarters in Idaho. One of the largest state business associations is the Idaho Potato Commission, a department of the state dedicated to research and promotion of the potato growers industry.

Educational organizations on the national level include the National Center for Constitutional Studies. State educational and cultural organizations include the Idaho Falls Arts Council, the Idaho State Historical Society, and the Idaho Humanities Council, as well as a number of county historical societies. There is an Indian Heritage Council in McCall.

47 TOURISM, TRAVEL, AND RECREATION

In 2004, Idaho supported over 50,000 jobs and earned $2.97 billion. Total revenues for the summer of 2005 were up 10.5%. Tourists come to Idaho primarily for outdoor recreation—river trips, skiing, camping, hunting, fishing, fly-fishing, kayaking and hiking. There are 19 ski resorts; by far the most famous is Sun Valley, which opened in 1936. Boise is the most popular destination within the state.

Tourist attractions include two national parks, the Craters of the Moon National Monument, the Nez Perce National Historical Park, and the Hell's Canyon and Sawtooth national recreational areas. A sliver of Yellowstone National Park is in Idaho. Portions of the Lewis and Clark Trail and the Oregon Trail lie within the state as well. The Snake River area is a national conservation area for birds of prey, as is the Kootenai National Wildlife Refuge. Silverwood Theme Park caters to those who want to visit amusement parks (Coeur d'Alene). Visitors can also travel parts of the Oregon Trail.

48 SPORTS

Idaho has no major professional teams. Idaho had a team, the Steelheads, in the West Coast Hockey League until 2003. In college sports, the Idaho State Bengals and the University of Idaho Vandals play Division I basketball and Division I-A football in the Big Sky and Big West conferences, respectively. Boise State University is the largest university in the Big West Conference, with a football team in Division I. Most county seats hold pari-mutuel quarter-horse racing a few days a year, and Boise's racing season (including thoroughbreds) runs three days a week for five months. World chariot racing championships have been held at Pocatello, as are the National Circuit Rodeo Finals. Polo was one of Boise's leading sports from 1910 through the 1940s. Idaho cowboys have won numerous riding, roping, and steer-wrestling championships. Skiing is very popular throughout the state, and there is a world-class resort at Sun Valley. Golf is also quite popular. Harmon Killebrew, a Hall of Fame baseball player, and Picabo Street, an Olympic gold medalist, were born in Idaho.

49 FAMOUS IDAHOANS

Leading federal officeholders born in Idaho include Ezra Taft Benson (1899–1994), US secretary of agriculture from 1953 to 1961 and president of the Church of Jesus Christ of Latter-Day Saints; and Cecil D. Andrus (b.Oregon, 1931), governor of Idaho from 1971 to 1977 and 1987 to 1995, and US secretary of the interior from 1977 to 1981. Maverick Republican William E. Borah (b.Illinois, 1865–1940) served in the US Senate from 1907 until his death. Frank Church (1924–84) entered the US Senate in 1957 and became chairman of the Senate Foreign Relations Committee in 1979; he was defeated in his bid for a fifth term in 1980. Important state officeholders were the nation's first Jewish governor, Moses Alexander (b.Germany, 1853–1932) and New Deal governor C. Ben Ross (1876–1946).

Author Vardis Fisher (1895–1968) was born and spent most of his life in Idaho, which was also the birthplace of poet Ezra Pound (1885–1972). Nobel Prize–winning novelist Ernest Hemingway (b.Illinois, 1899–1961) is buried at Ketchum. Gutzon Borglum (1871–1941), the sculptor who carved the Mt. Rushmore National Memorial in South Dakota, was an Idaho native. Idaho is the only state in the United States with an official seal designed by a woman, Emma Edwards Green (b.California, 1856–1942).

Baseball slugger Harmon Killebrew (b.1936) and football star Jerry Kramer (b.1936) are Idaho's leading sports personalities.

50 BIBLIOGRAPHY

Arrington, Leonard J. *History of Idaho.* Moscow: University of Idaho Press, 1994.

Council of State Governments. *The Book of the States, 2006 Edition.* Lexington, Ky.: Council of State Governments, 2006.

Domitz, Gary, and Leonard Hitchcock, (eds.). *Idaho History: A Bibliography.* Centennial ed. Pocatello: Idaho State University Press, 1991.

Johnston, Terry C. *Lay the Mountains Low: the Flight of the Nez Perce from Idaho and the Battle of the Big Hole, August 9–10, 1877.* New York: St. Martin's Press, 2000.

Mann, John W. W. *Sacajawea's People: The Lemhi Shoshones and the Salmon River Country.* Lincoln: University of Nebraska Press, 2004.

Preston, Thomas. *Intermountain West: Idaho, Nevada, Utah, and Arizona.* Vol. 2, *The Double Eagle Guide to 1,000 Great Western Recreation Destinations.* 2nd ed. Billings, Mont.: Discovery Publications, 2003.

Ritter, Sharon A. *Lewis and Clark's Mountain Wilds: A Site Guide to the Plants and Animals They Encountered in the Bitterroots.* Moscow: University of Idaho Press, 2002.

Spence, Clark C. *For Wood River or Bust: Idaho's Silver Boom of the 1880s.* Moscow: University of Idaho Press; Boise: Idaho State Historical Society, 1999.

US Department of Commerce, Economics and Statistics Administration, US Census Bureau. *Idaho, 2000. Summary Social, Economic, and Housing Characteristics: 2000 Census of Population and Housing.* Washington, D.C.: US Government Printing Office, 2003.

ILLINOIS

ILLINOIS

State of Illinois

ORIGIN OF STATE NAME: French derivative of *Iliniwek*, meaning "tribe of superior men," a Native American group formerly in the region. **NICKNAME:** The Prairie State; Land of Lincoln (slogan). **CAPITAL:** Springfield. **ENTERED UNION:** 3 December 1818 (21st). **SONG:** "Illinois." **MOTTO:** State Sovereignty–National Union. **FLAG:** The inner portion of the state seal and the word "Illinois" on a white field. **OFFICIAL SEAL:** An American eagle perched on a boulder holds in its beak a banner bearing the state motto; below the eagle is a shield resting on an olive branch. Also depicted are the prairie, the sun rising over a distant eastern horizon, and on the boulder, the dates 1818 and 1868, the years of the seal's introduction and revision, respectively. The words "Seal of the State of Illinois Aug. 26th 1818" surround the whole. **BIRD:** Cardinal. **FISH:** Bluegill. **FLOWER:** Native violet. **TREE:** White oak. **LEGAL HOLIDAYS:** New Year's Day, 1 January; Birthday of Martin Luther King Jr., 3rd Monday in January; Lincoln's Birthday, 12 February; George Washington's Birthday, 3rd Monday in February; Memorial Day, last Monday in May; Independence Day, 4 July; Labor Day, 1st Monday in September; Columbus Day, 2nd Monday in October; Election Day, 1st Tuesday after the 1st Monday in November in even-numbered years; Veterans' Day, 11 November; Thanksgiving Day, 4th Thursday in November; Christmas Day, 25 December. **TIME:** 6 AM CST = noon GMT.

¹LOCATION, SIZE, AND EXTENT

Situated in the eastern north-central United States, Illinois ranks 24th in size among the 50 states. Its area totals 56,345 sq mi (145,934 sq km), of which land comprises 55,645 sq mi (144,120 sq km) and inland water 700 sq mi (1,814 sq km). Illinois extends 211 mi (340 km) E–W; its maximum N–S extension is 381 mi (613 km).

Illinois is bounded on the N by Wisconsin; on the E by Lake Michigan and Indiana (with the line in the SE defined by the Wabash River); on the extreme SE and S by Kentucky (with the line passing through the Ohio River); and on the W by Missouri and Iowa (with the entire boundary formed by the Mississippi River).

The state's boundaries total 1,297 mi (2,088 km). The geographic center of Illinois is in Logan County, 28 mi (45 km) NE of Springfield.

²TOPOGRAPHY

Illinois is flat. Lying wholly within the Central Plains, the state exhibits a natural topographic monotony relieved mainly by hills in the northwest (an extension of Wisconsin's Driftless Area) and throughout the southern third of the state, on the fringes of the Ozark Plateau. The highest natural point, Charles Mound, tucked into the far northwest corner, is only 1,235 ft (377 m) above sea level—far lower than Chicago's towering skyscrapers. The low point, at the extreme southern tip along the Mississippi River, is 279 ft (85 m) above sea level. The mean elevation is about 600 ft (183 m).

Although some 2,000 rivers and streams totaling 9,000 mi (14,500 km) crisscross the land, pioneers in central Illinois confronted very poor drainage. The installation of elaborate and expensive networks of ditches and tiled drains was necessary before commercial agriculture became feasible. Most of the 2,000 lakes of 6 acres (2.4 hectares) or more were created by dams. The most

important rivers are the Wabash and the Ohio, forming the southeastern and southern border; the Mississippi, forming the western border; and the Illinois, flowing northeast–southwest across the central region and meeting the Mississippi at Grafton, just northwest of the junction between the Mississippi and the Missouri rivers. The artificial Lake Carlyle (41 sq mi/106 sq km) is the largest body of inland water. Illinois also has jurisdiction over 1,526 sq mi (3,952 sq km) of Lake Michigan.

³CLIMATE

Illinois has a temperate climate, with cold, snowy winters and hot, wet summers—ideal weather for corn and hogs. The seasons are sharply differentiated: Mean winter temperatures are 22°F (-6°C) in the north and 37°F (3°C) in the south; mean summer temperatures are 70°F (21°C) in the north and 77°F (25°C) in the south. The record high, 117°F (47°C), was set at East St. Louis on 14 July 1954; the record low, -36°F (-37.8°C), was registered at Congerville on 5 January 1999.

The average farm sees rain one day in three, for a total of 36 in (91 cm) of precipitation a year. An annual snowfall of 37 in (94 cm) is normal for northern Illinois, decreasing to 24 in (61 cm) or less in the central and southern regions. Chicago's record 90 in (229 cm) of snow in the winter of 1978–79 created monumental transportation problems, enormous personal hardship, and even a small political upheaval when incumbent Mayor Michael Bilandic lost a primary election to Jane Byrne in February 1979, partly because of his administration's slowness in snow removal.

Chicago is nicknamed the "Windy City" because in the 1800s, New York journalists labeled Chicagoans "the windy citizenry out west" and called some Chicago leaders "loudmouth and windy"— not because of fierce winds. In fact, the average wind speed, 10.4 mph (16.7 km/h), is lower than that of Boston, Honolulu, Cleveland, and 16 other major US cities. The flat plains of Illinois are favorable to tornado activity.

⁴FLORA AND FAUNA

Urbanization and commercial development have taken their toll on the plant and animal resources of Illinois. Northern and central Illinois once supported typical prairie flora, but nearly all the land has been given over to crops, roads, and suburban lawns. About 90% of the oak and hickory forests that once were common in the north have been cut down for fuel and lumber. In the forests that do remain, mostly in the south, typical trees are black oak, sugar maple, box elder, slippery elm, beech, shagbark hickory, white ash, sycamore, black walnut, sweet gum, cottonwood, black willow, and jack pine. Characteristic wildflowers are the Chase aster, French's shooting star, lupine, primrose violet, purple trillium, small fringed gentian, and yellow fringed orchid.

Before 1800, wildlife was abundant on the prairies, but the bison, elk, bear, and wolves that once roamed freely have long since vanished. The white-tailed deer (the state animal) disappeared in 1910 but was successfully reintroduced in 1933 by the Department of Conservation. Among the state's fur-bearing mammals are opossum, raccoon, mink, red and gray foxes, and muskrat. More than 350 birds have been identified, with such game birds as ruffed grouse, wild turkey, and bobwhite quail especially prized. Other indigenous birds are the cardinal (the state bird), horned lark, blue jay, purple martin, black-capped chickadee, tufted titmouse, bluebird, cedar waxwing, great crested flycatcher, and yellow-shafted flicker. Mallard and black ducks are common, and several subspecies of Canada goose are also found. The state claims 17 types of native turtle, 46 kinds of snake, 19 varieties of salamander, and 21 types of frog and toad. Heavy industrial and sewage pollution have eliminated most native fish, except for the durable carp and catfish. Coho salmon were introduced into Lake Michigan in the 1960s, thus reviving sport fishing.

The Cache River–Cypress Creek Wetlands area in southern Illinois is home to 138 species of trees and shrubs, 11 species of ferns, 87 types of fish, 25 species of snail, 19 mussels, 181 bird species, 47 different mammals, and 54 reptile and amphibian species. Swamp woodlands host the oldest living stand of trees east of the Mississippi. The water locust and green hawthorn found here are considered to be the largest trees of their species in the United States. Seventy-nine of the plant and animal species found on the state list of threatened or endangered species can be found in the wetland. The area also serves as a winter habitat for over 260,000 migratory birds each year.

In 1973, the state Department of Conservation established an endangered and threatened species protection program. In April 2006, a total of 25 species occurring within the state were on the threatened and endangered species list of the US Fish and Wildlife Service. These included 16 animal (vertebrates and invertebrates) and 9 plant species. Included among the threatened animals are the bald eagle and gray wolf. Endangered species include the piping plover, pallid sturgeon, Hine's emerald dragonfly, Higgins' eye pearly mussel, and the least tern. The leafy prairie-clover was listed; small-whorled pogonia, lakeside daisy, prairie bush-clover, and eastern prairie fringed orchid are among the other threatened plant species.

⁵ENVIRONMENTAL PROTECTION

The history of conservation efforts in Illinois can be categorized into three stages. From 1850 to the 1930s, city and state parks were established and the beauty of Chicago's lakefront was successfully preserved. During the next stage, in the 1930s, federal intervention through the Civilian Conservation Corps and other agencies focused on upgrading park facilities and, most important, on reversing the severe erosion of soils, particularly in the hilly southern areas. Soil conservation laws took effect in 1937, and within a year the first soil conservation district was formed. By 1970, 98 districts, covering 44% of the state's farmland, promoted conservation cropping systems, contour plowing, and drainage.

The third stage of environmentalism began in the late 1960s, when Attorney General William J. Scott assumed the leadership of an antipollution campaign; he won suits against steel mills, sanitary districts, and utility companies and secured the passage of clean air and water legislation. The Illinois Environmental Protection Act of 1970 created the Pollution Control Board to set standards and conduct enforcement proceedings, and the Environmental Protection Agency (EPA) to establish a comprehensive program for protecting environmental quality. In 1980, the Department of Nuclear Safety was established. The federal EPA has also helped upgrade water and air quality in Illinois.

The years since the enactment of specific environmental laws and regulations have seen a noticeable improvement in environmental quality. Dirty air has become less prevalent. The Illinois EPA maintains more than 200 air-monitoring stations to measure different types of pollutants. Many of these stations are in the Chicago area. The agency also conducts about 2,500 facility inspections each year to verify compliance with air regulations. Because Illinois formerly produced about 6 million tons of hazardous wastes annually, the state agency tried to pinpoint and clean up abandoned hazardous waste sites. In 1984, Illinois began a three-year, $20 million program to eliminate the 22 worst sites and to evaluate nearly 1,000 other potential hazardous waste sites. Thanks to that program, over 60 sites were cleaned up by the mid-1990s. Progress has been made toward the voluntary cleanup of contaminated sites. In 1997, the Illinois General Assembly enacted a law developing a state underground storage tank program, and since May of that year over 14,800 releases from underground storage tanks have been reported, 5,800 of which have completed remediation under the new initiative. In 2003, the US EPA database listed 455 hazardous waste sites in Illinois, 41 of which were on the National Priorities List as of 2006, including 4 military sites. Illinois ranks seventh in the nation for the most sites on the National Priorities List. In 2005, the EPA spent over $4 million through the Superfund program for the cleanup of hazardous waste sites in the state. Also in 2005, federal EPA grants awarded to the state included $50.7 million for wastewater treatment work projects and $31.9 million to assist public water systems in compliance with the Safe Drinking Water Act. In 2003, 132.4 million lb of toxic chemicals were released in the state.

About 3.5% of the state is wetland, most of which is governed under the state-imposed Interagency Wetland Policy Act of 1989. The Cache River–Cypress Creek Wetlands area in southern Illinois was designated as a Ramsar Wetland of International Importance in 1994. The site consists of several separate conservation areas that are jointly management through the US Fish and Wild-

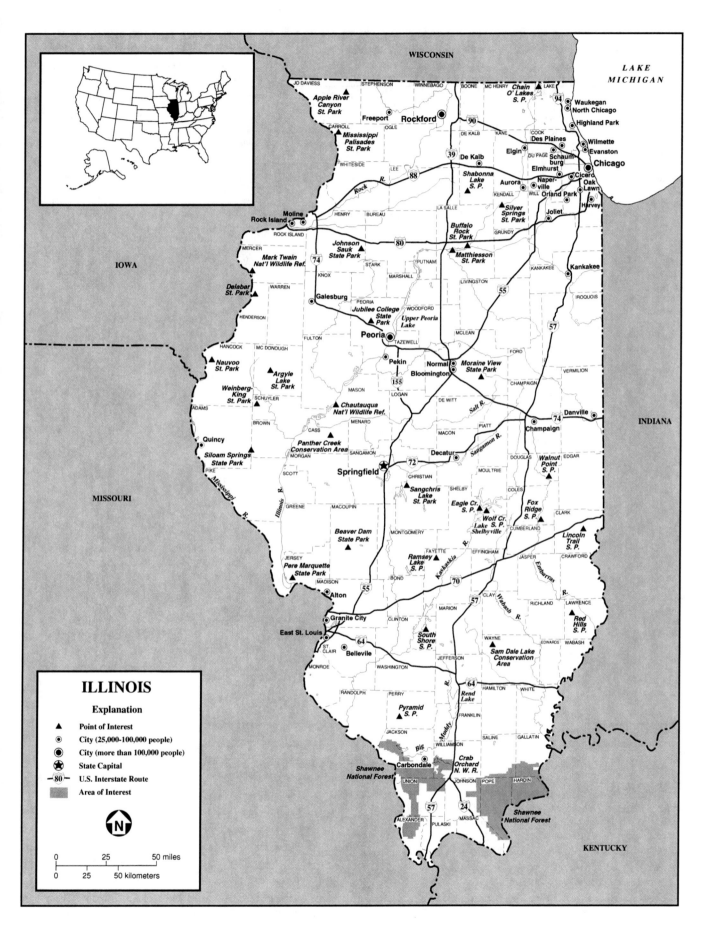

Illinois—Counties, County Seats, and County Areas and Populations

COUNTY	COUNTY SEAT	LAND AREA (SQ MI)	POPULATION (2005 EST.)	COUNTY	COUNTY SEAT	LAND AREA (SQ MI)	POPULATION (2005 EST.)
Adams	Quincy	852	67,040	Livingston	Pontiac	1,046	39,186
Alexander	Cairo	236	8,927	Logan	Lincoln	619	30,603
Bond	Greenville	377	18,027	Macon	Decatur	581	110,167
Boone	Belvidere	282	50,483	Macoupin	Carlinville	865	49,111
Brown	Mt. Sterling	306	6,835	Madison	Edwardsville	728	264,309
Bureau	Princeton	869	35,330	Marion	Salem	573	40,144
Calhoun	Hardin	250	5,163	Marshall	Lacon	388	13,217
Carroll	Mt. Carroll	444	16,086	Mason	Havana	536	15,741
Cass	Virginia	374	13,898	Massac	Metropolis	241	15,348
Champaign	Urbana	998	184,905	McDonough	Macomb	590	31,966
Christian	Taylorville	710	35,176	McHenry	Woodstock	606	303,990
Clark	Marshall	506	16,976	McLean	Bloomington	1,185	159,013
Clay	Louisville	469	14,122	Menard	Petersburg	315	12,738
Clinton	Carlyle	472	36,095	Mercer	Aledo	559	16,912
Coles	Charleston	509	51,065	Monroe	Waterloo	388	31,040
Cook	Chicago	958	5,303,683	Montgomery	Hillsboro	705	30,396
Crawford	Robinson	446	19,898	Morgan	Jacksonville	568	35,722
Cumberland	Toledo	346	10,973	Moultrie	Sullivan	325	14,510
DeKalb	Sycamore	634	97,665	Ogle	Oregon	759	54,290
De Witt	Clinton	397	16,617	Peoria	Peoria	621	182,328
Douglas	Tuscola	417	19,950	Perry	Pinckneyville	443	22,815
DuPage	Wheaton	337	929,113	Piatt	Monticello	439	16,680
Edgar	Paris	623	19,157	Pike	Pittsfield	830	17,099
Edwards	Albion	223	6,784	Pope	Golconda	374	4,211
Effingham	Effingham	478	34,581	Pulaski	Mound City	203	6,794
Fayette	Vandalia	709	21,713	Putnam	Hennepin	160	6,094
Ford	Paxton	486	14,157	Randolph	Chester	583	33,122
Franklin	Benton	414	39,723	Richland	Olney	360	15,798
Fulton	Lewistown	871	37,708	Rock Island	Rock Island	423	147,808
Gallatin	Shawneetown	325	6,152	Saline	Harrisburg	385	26,072
Greene	Carrollton	543	14,581	Sangamon	Springfield	866	192,789
Grundy	Morris	423	43,838	Schuyler	Rushville	436	7,073
Hamilton	McLeansboro	436	8,301	Scott	Winchester	251	5,412
Hancock	Carthage	796	19,153	Shelby	Shelbyville	747	22,322
Hardin	Elizabethtown	181	4,718	Stark	Toulon	288	6,169
Henderson	Oquawka	373	7,972	St. Clair	Belleville	672	260,067
Henry	Cambridge	824	50,591	Stephenson	Freeport	564	47,965
Iroquois	Watseka	1,118	30,677	Tazewell	Pekin	650	129,999
Jackson	Murphysboro	590	57,954	Union	Jonesboro	414	18,202
Jasper	Newton	496	10,020	Vermilion	Danville	900	82,344
Jefferson	Mt. Vernon	570	40,434	Wabash	Mt. Carmel	224	12,570
Jersey	Jerseyville	373	22,456	Warren	Monmouth	543	17,558
Jo Daviess	Galena	603	22,580	Washington	Nashville	563	14,922
Johnson	Vienna	346	13,169	Wayne	Fairfield	715	16,796
Kane	Geneva	524	482,113	White	Carmi	497	15,284
Kankakee	Kankakee	679	107,972	Whiteside	Morrison	682	59,863
Kendall	Yorkville	322	79,514	Will	Joliet	844	642,813
Knox	Galesburg	720	53,309	Williamson	Marion	427	63,617
Lake	Waukegan	454	702,682	Winnebago	Rockford	516	288,695
LaSalle	Ottawa	1,139	112,604	Woodford	Eureka	527	37,448
Lawrence	Lawrenceville	374	15,930	**TOTALS**		55,651	12,763,371
Lee	Dixon	725	35,669				

life Service, Ducks Unlimited, the Nature Conservancy, and the Illinois Department of Conservation.

⁶POPULATION

Illinois ranked fifth in population in the United States with an estimated total of 12,763,371 in 2005, an increase of 2.8% since 2000. Between 1990 and 2000, Illinois's population grew from 11,430,602 to 12,419,293, an increase of 8.6%. The population is projected to reach 13 million by 2015 and 13.3 million by 2025. Illinois ceded its third-place ranking to California by 1950 and fourth place to Texas during the 1960s. In 2004, population density was 228.8 per sq mi.

The population of Illinois was only 12,282 in 1810. Ten years later, the new state had 55,211 residents. The most rapid period of growth came in the mid-19th century, when heavy immigration made Illinois one of the fastest-growing areas in the world. Between 1820 and 1860, the state's population doubled every 10 years. The rate of increase slowed somewhat after 1900, especially during the 1930s, although the population more than doubled between 1900 and 1960. Population growth was very slow in the 1970s, about 0.3% a year; the rate of growth from 1980 to 1990 was a tiny 0.04%. However, a rebound occurred in the 1990s. The age distribution of the state's population in 2004 closely mirrored the national pattern, with 25.5% under age 18 and 12% aged 65 or older. The median age in 2004 was 35.4.

The rapid rise of Chicago as a metropolitan area meant that a large proportion of the state's population was concentrated in cities from a relatively early date. Thus, by 1895, 50% of Illinoisans lived in urban areas, whereas the entire country reached that point only in 1920. By 1990, 83% of the population lived in metropolitan areas, compared with 75.2% nationally. With an estimated population of 9,391,515 in 2004, Greater Chicago was the third-largest metropolitan area in the nation. The state's other major metropolitan areas, with their estimated 2004 populations, were Peoria, 367,860, and Rockford, 335,278. The largest city in 2004 was Chicago, with an estimated 2,862,244 residents, followed by Aurora, 166,614; Rockford, 152,452; Naperville, 140,106; Joliet, 129,519; Peoria, 112,720; and Springfield, 114,738.

⁷ETHNIC GROUPS

The American Indian population of Illinois disappeared by 1832 as a result of warfare and emigration. By 2000, however, Indian migration from Wisconsin, Minnesota, and elsewhere brought the Native American population to 31,006, concentrated in Chicago. In 2004, 0.3% of the population was American Indian.

French settlers brought in black slaves from the Caribbean in the mid-18th century; in 1752, one-third of the small non-Indian population was black. Slavery was slowly abolished in the early 19th century. For decades, however, few blacks entered the state, except to flee slavery in neighboring Kentucky and Missouri. Freed slaves did come to Illinois during the Civil War, concentrating in the state's southern tip and in Chicago. By 1900, 109,000 blacks lived in Illinois. Most held menial jobs in the cities or eked out a precarious existence on small farms in the far south. Large-scale black migration, mainly to Chicago, began during World War I. By 1940, Illinois had a black population of 387,000; extensive wartime and postwar migration brought the total in 2000 to 1,876,875, of whom more than half lived within the city of Chicago, which was close to 40% black. Smaller numbers of black Illinoisans lived in Peoria, Rockford, and certain Chicago suburbs. In 2004, 15.1% of the state's population was black.

The Hispanic population did not become significant until the 1960s. In 2000, the number Hispanics and Latinos was 1,530,262, living chiefly in Chicago. There were 1,144,390 persons of Mexican origin (up from 557,536 in 1990), 157,851 Puerto Ricans, and 18,438 Cubans; most of the remainder came from other Caribbean and Latin American countries. The Hispanic or Latino population represented 12.3% of the total state population. That figure had risen to 14% by 2004.

In 2000, there were 76,725 Chinese in Illinois, 20,379 Japanese, 86,298 Filipinos, 51,453 Koreans, and 19,101 Vietnamese (up from 8,550 in 1990). The total Asian population was estimated at 423,603, placing Illinois sixth among the 50 states in number of Asian residents. Pacific Islanders numbered 4,610. In 2004, 4% of the population was Asian, and 0.1% was of Pacific Island origin. In 2004, 1.1% of the population reported origin of two or more races.

Members of non-British European ethnic groups are prevalent in all the state's major cities and in many farming areas. In 2000, 1,529,058 persons were foreign born (12.3% of the total population), including 389,928 Europeans, 359,812 Asians, 731,397 from Latin American countries, 26,158 Africans, and 2,553 from Oceanic countries. The most common ancestries of Illinois residents are German, Irish, Polish, English, and Italian.

There are also significant numbers of Scandinavians, Irish, Lithuanians, Serbs, Eastern European Jews, Ukrainians, Slovaks, Hungarians, Czechs, Greeks, and Dutch. Except for the widely dispersed Germans, most of these ethnic groups live in and around Chicago.

Most ethnic groups in Illinois maintain their own newspapers, clubs, festivals, and houses of worship. These reminders of their cultural heritage are now largely symbolic for the European ethnics, who have become highly assimilated into a "melting pot" society. Such was not always the case, however. In 1889, the legislature attempted to curtail foreign-language schools, causing a sharp political reaction among German Lutherans, German Catholics, and some Scandinavians. The upshot was the election of a German-born Democrat, John Peter Altgeld, as governor in 1892. During World War I, anti-German sentiment was intense in the state despite the manifest American loyalty of the large German element, then about 25% of the state's population. The Germans responded by rapidly abandoning the use of their language and dissolving most of their newspapers and clubs. At about the same time, the US government, educators, social workers, and business firms sponsored extensive "Americanization" programs directed at the large numbers of recent arrivals from Poland, Italy, and elsewhere. The public schools especially played a major role in the assimilation process, as did the Catholic parochial schools, which sought to protect the immigrants' religious, but not their ethnic, identities.

⁸LANGUAGES

A number of place-names—Illinois itself, Chicago, Peoria, Kankakee, and Ottawa—attest to the early presence of various Algonkian-speaking tribes, such as the Kickapoo, Sauk, and Fox, and particularly those of the Illinois Federation, the remnants of which moved west of the Mississippi River after the Black Hawk War of 1832.

Nineteenth-century western migration patterns determined the rather complex distribution of regional language features. Excepting the Chicago metropolitan area and the extreme northwestern corner of Illinois, the northern quarter of the state is dominated by Northern speech. An even greater frequency of Northern features appears in the northeastern quadrant; in this region, speakers get *sick to the stomach, catch cold* (take cold), use *dove* as the past tense of dive, pronounce *hog, fog, frog, crop,* and *college* with the vowel /ah/, and sound a clear /h/ in *whine, wheel,* and *wheat.*

Settlement from Pennsylvania and Ohio led to a mix of Northern and North Midland speech in central Illinois, with such dominating Northern features as *white bread, pail, greasy* with an /s/ sound, and *creek* rhyming with *stick.* Here appear Midland *fishworm* (earthworm), *firebug* (firefly), *wait on* (wait for), *dived* as the past tense of dive, *quarter til four* (3:45), and *sick at one's stomach* (but sick on the stomach in German communities near East St. Louis).

Migration from South Midland areas in Indiana and Kentucky affected basic speech in the southern third of Illinois, known as Egypt. Here especially occur South Midland and Southern *pullybone* (wishbone), *dog irons* (andirons), *light bread* (white bread), and in extreme southern countries, *loaf bread, snakedoctor* (dragonfly), *redworm* (earthworm), *ground squirrel* (chipmunk), *plum peach* (clingstone peach), *to have a crow to pick* (to have a bone to pick) with someone, and the pronunciations of *coop* with the vowel of *put* and of *greasy* with a /z/ sound. Such speech is found also in the northwestern corner around Galena, where Kentucky miners who came to work in the lead mines brought such pronunciations as bulge with the vowel of *put, soot* with the vowel of *but,* and /yelk/ for *yolk.*

Metropolitan Chicago has experienced such complex in-migration that, although it still has a basic Northern/Midland mix, elements of almost all varieties of English appear somewhere. The influx since World War II of speakers of black English, a Southern dialect, and of nonstandard Appalachian English has aggravated language problems in the schools. Foreign-language schools were common in the 1880s and 1890s, but by 1920, all instruction was in English. The policy of monolingual education came into question in the 1970s, when the state legislature mandated bilingual classes for immigrant children, especially Spanish speakers.

In Chicago, rough-and-tumble politics have created a new meaning for *clout; prairie* means a vacant lot, *porch* includes the meaning of *stoop,* and *cornbread* has been generalized to include the meanings of *corn pone* and *hush puppies.* A fuel and food stop on the Illinois tollway system is an *oasis.*

In 2000, English was spoken at home by 80.8% of all state residents five years of age and older, down from 85.8% in 1990.

The following table gives selected statistics from the 2000 Census for language spoken at home by persons five years old and over. The category "Other Indo-European languages" includes Albanian, Gaelic, Lithuanian, and Rumanian. The category "Other Slavic languages" includes Czech, Slovak, and Ukrainian. The category "Other Asian languages" includes Dravidian languages, Malayalam, Telugu, Tamil, and Turkish. The category "Other Indic languages" includes Bengali, Marathi, Punjabi, and Romany.

LANGUAGE	NUMBER	PERCENT
Population 5 years and over	**11,547,505**	**100.0**
Speak only English	9,326,786	80.8
Speak a language other than English	2,220,719	19.2
Speak a language other than English	**2,220,719**	**19.2**
Spanish or Spanish Creole	1,253,676	10.9
Polish	185,749	1.6
Chinese	65,251	0.6
German	63,366	0.5
Tagalog	63,366	0.5
Italian	51,975	0.5
Korean	43,712	0.4
French (incl. Patois, Cajun)	40,812	0.4
Greek	40,581	0.4
Russian	38,053	0.3
Arabic	35,397	0.3
Other Indo-European languages	32,806	0.3
Urdu	32,420	0.3
Serbo-Croatian	29,631	0.3
Gujarathi	28,725	0.2
Other Slavic languages	27,772	0.2
Other Asian languages	26,745	0.2
Hindi	18,734	0.2
Other Indic languages	17,632	0.2
Vietnamese	16,487	0.1
Other and unspecified languages	15,885	0.1
Japanese	15,481	0.1
African languages	15,379	0.1

⁹RELIGIONS

Before 1830, little religion of any sort was practiced on the Illinois frontier. Energetic Protestant missionaries set out to evangelize this un-Christian population, and they largely succeeded. By 1890, 36% of the adults in Illinois were affiliated with evangelical denominations—chiefly Methodist, Disciples of Christ, Baptist, Congregationalist, and Presbyterian—while 35%, mostly immigrants, belonged to liturgical denominations (chiefly Roman Catholic, Lutheran, and Episcopal). The remaining adults acknowledged no particular denomination.

Illinois has had episodes of religious bigotry: At Carthage in 1844, the Mormon founder Joseph Smith was killed by a mob, and strong but brief waves of anti-Catholicism developed in the 1850s (the "Know-Nothing" movement) and 1920s (the Ku Klux Klan). Robert Green Ingersoll, a self-proclaimed agnostic, was appointed attorney general of Illinois in 1867–69, but his identity as an agnostic prevented him from ever being elected into politics. Nevertheless, tolerance of religious diversity has been the norm for most of the state's history.

Beginning about 1830, a group of Latter-Day Saints (Mormons) moved into Nauvoo and formed a fairly strong religious community there. By 1846, persecution from citizens of neighboring cities inspired the massive migration to Utah over the Mormon Trail. Because many of the Saints passed through the territory on their way to Utah, the group continued to maintain some missionary presence in the state. In 1962, the church began restoration projects of historical sites at Nauvoo. An annual pageant is held in Nauvoo and a rebuilt Nauvoo temple was dedicated in 2002. There is also a temple in Chicago (est. 1985). As of 2006, the church reported a statewide membership of 52,500.

The largest religious institution is the Roman Catholic Church, which had 3,948,768 adherents in 2004; about 2,442,000 members belonged to the archdiocese of Chicago in that year. The largest Protestant denomination is the United Methodist Church, with 365,182 adherents (in 2000), followed by the Southern Baptist Convention with 305,838 adherents (2000). The Southern Baptist Convention reported 6,522 newly baptized members in the state in 2002. Other major Protestant groups (with 2000 data) include the Evangelical Lutheran Church in America with 279,724 adherents and the Lutheran Church–Missouri Synod with 278,008 adherents. In 2005, the United Church of Christ reported a statewide membership of about 121,371. The Jewish population was estimated at 270,000 in 2000 and the Muslim community had about 125,203 adherents. There are over 11,000 Mennonites throughout the state. About 44.7% of the population did not specify a religious affiliation.

The Moody Bible Institute in Chicago is a nondenominational, conservative Christian seminary that also sponsors well-known publishing and broadcasting services. In 2006, it was listed among America's best colleges by *U.S. News & World Report.* The American Conference of Cantors, a Jewish organization, and the International Conference of Christians and Jews are based in Chicago. AMF International (formerly known as the American Messianic Fellowship) was founded in Chicago in 1887 and maintains headquarters in Lansing, Illinois. Awana Clubs International, a Christian organization of children and youth clubs, was also founded in Chicago and currently has its international headquarters in Streamwood. The Evangelical Church Alliance International is based in Bradley. The National Spiritual Assembly of the Baha'is of the United States is located in Evanston.

¹⁰TRANSPORTATION

The fact that Illinois is intersected by several long-distance transportation routes has been of central importance in the state's economic development for a century and a half. Eastern access by way of the major rivers and the Great Lakes system facilitated extensive migration to Illinois even before the coming of the railroads in the 1850s. Most of the nation's rail lines converge on Illinois, and Chicago and St. Louis (especially East St. Louis) have been the two main US railroad centers since the late 19th century. Interstate highways, notably the main east–west routes, also cross the state, and Chicago's central location in the United States has made it a major transfer point for airline connections.

After several false starts in the 1830s and 1840s, the state's railroad system was begun in the 1850s. The Illinois Central was aided by the first land grant (state sponsored), which opened up downstate lands in the years before the Civil War. By 1890, about 10,000 mi (16,000 km) of track crisscrossed the state, placing 90% of all Illinois farms no more than 5 mi (8 km) from a rail line. The railroads stimulated not only farming but also coal mining, and in the process created tens of thousands of jobs in track and bridge construction, maintenance, traffic operations, and the manufacture of cars, rails, and other railroad equipment.

However, the rise of automobile and truck traffic (starting in the 1920s and 1930s) and later competition from airlines dealt the railroads a serious blow. In the 1970s, their unprofitable passenger business (except for important commuter lines around Chicago that were taken over by public agencies) was shed, while the railroads concentrated on long-distance freight traffic. The bankruptcy of the Penn Central, Rock Island, and Milwaukee Road systems during the 1970s also impelled some companies, notably the Illinois Central Gulf and the Chicago and North Western, to shift their attention to real estate and manufacturing. Abandoned railroad tracks and right-of-ways reverted to the private sector in the 1990s or were developed into public bicycle trails, walking paths, and greenways to take advantage of the scenic beauty of the state. As of 2003, there were 39 railroad companies in Illinois operating 9,757 route mi (15,708 km) of track within the state. Of that total in that year, seven were deemed Class I railroads. As of 2006, Chicago was the hub of Amtrak's passenger service, which operated 12 named trains, connecting a total of 14 cities in Illinois.

Mass transit is of special importance to Chicago, where subways, buses, and commuter railroads are essential to daily movement. The transit systems were built privately but eventually were acquired by the city and regional transportation authorities. Ridership declines every year, as fewer people work in the central city and as more people choose the privacy and convenience of travel by automobile. Federal aid to mass transit, beginning in 1964, and state aid, initiated in 1971, have only partly stemmed the decline. Outside Chicago, transit service is available in some of the older, larger cities.

The road system of Illinois was inadequate until the 1920s, when an elaborate program to build local and trunk highways first received heavy state aid. In 2004, there were 138,624 mi (223,184 km) of public roadway serving some 9.417 million registered vehicles, including around 5.580 million automobiles and 3.547 million trucks of all types, operated by 8,057,683 licensed drivers. The main east–west routes are I-90, I-88, I-80, I-74, I-72, I-70, and I-64. I-94 links Chicago with Milwaukee to the north and Indiana to the east, while I-57 and I-55 connect Chicago with the south and southwest (St. Louis), respectively.

Barge traffic along the Mississippi, Ohio, and Illinois rivers remains important, especially for the shipment of grain. The port of Chicago no longer harbors the sailing ships that brought lumber, merchandise, and people to a fast-growing city. However, the port is still the largest on the Great Lakes, handling 24.602 million tons of cargo in 2004, mostly grain and iron ore, and the 35th busiest port in the United States. For that same year, Illinois had 1,095 mi (1,762 km) of navigable inland waterways. In 2003, waterborne shipments totaled 113.314 million tons.

Midway International Airport in Chicago became the world's busiest after World War II but was superseded by O'Hare International Airport, which opened in the late 1950s. O'Hare lost its title as busiest airport in the world in March 2000 when it was superseded by Atlanta's Hartsfield International. In 2005, Illinois had a total of 860 public and private-use aviation-related facilities. This included 586 airports, 265 heliports, two STOLports (Short Take-Off and Landing), and seven seaplane bases. O'Hare International Airport had 36,100,147 enplanements in 2004, making it the second-busiest airport in the United States. In that same year, Chicago Midway International had 9,238,592 enplanements, making it the 26th-busiest airport in the United States.

¹¹HISTORY

Different tribes of Paleo-Indians lived in Illinois as long ago as 8000 BC. By 2000 BC, the cultivation of plants and use of ceramics were known to village dwellers; the first pottery appeared during the Woodland phase, a millennium later. Between 500 BC and AD 500, skilled Hopewellian craftsmen practiced a limited agriculture, developed an elaborate social structure, and constructed burial mounds. Huge mounds, which still exist, were built along the major rivers by the Middle Mississippian culture, about AD 900.

It is not known why the early native civilizations died out, but by the time white explorers arrived in the 17th century, the state was inhabited by seminomadic Algonkian-speaking tribes. The Kickapoo, Sauk, and Fox lived in the north, while the shores of Lake Michigan were populated by the Potawatomi, Ottawa, and Ojibwa. The Kaskaskia, Illinois (Iliniwek), and Peoria tribes roamed across the central prairies, and the Cahokia and Tamoroa lived in the south. Constant warfare with tribes from neighboring areas, plus disease and alcohol introduced by white fur traders and settlers, combined to decimate the Native American population. Warfare with the whites led to a series of treaties, the last in 1832, that removed all of the Indians to lands across the Mississippi.

French missionaries and fur traders from Quebec explored the rivers of Illinois in the late 17th century. Father Jacques Marquette and trader Louis Jolliet were the first to reach the area now known as the state of Illinois in 1673, when they descended the Mississippi as far as the Arkansas River and then returned by way of the Illinois River. The first permanent settlement was a mission built by French priests at Cahokia, near present-day St. Louis, in 1699. It was followed by more southerly settlements at Kaskaskia in 1703 and Ft. Chartres in 1719. In 1765, pursuant to the Treaty of Paris

(1763), which ended the French and Indian War, the British took control of the Illinois country, but they established no settlements of their own. Most of the French settlers were Loyalists during the American Revolution. However, they put up no resistance when Virginia troops, led by George Rogers Clark, captured the small British forts at Cahokia and Kaskaskia in 1778. Virginia governed its new territory in desultory fashion, and most of the French villagers fled to Missouri. In 1784, Virginia relinquished its claim to Illinois, which three years later became part of the newly organized Northwest Territory. In 1800, Illinois was included in the Indiana Territory. Nine years later, the Illinois Territory, including the present state of Wisconsin, was created; Kaskaskia became the territorial capital, and Ninian Edwards was appointed territorial governor by President James Madison. A territorial legislature was formed in 1812. During the War of 1812, British and Indian forces combined in a last attempt to push back American expansion into the Illinois country, and much fighting took place in the area. On 3 December 1818, Illinois was formally admitted to the Union as the 21st state. The capital was moved to Vandalia in 1820 and to Springfield in 1839.

Apart from a few thousand nomadic Indians and the remaining French settlers and their slaves, Illinois was largely uninhabited before 1815; two years after statehood, the population barely exceeded 55,000. The withdrawal of British influence after the War of 1812 and the final defeat of the Indian tribes in the Black Hawk War of 1832 opened the fertile prairies to settlers from the south, especially Kentucky. The federal government owned most of the land, and its land offices did a fast business on easy terms. Before the 1830s, most of the pioneers were concerned with acquiring land titles and pursuing subsistence agriculture, supplemented by hunting and fishing. An effort in 1824 to call a constitutional convention to legalize slavery failed because of a widespread fear that rich slaveholders would seize the best land, squeezing out the poor yeoman farmers. Ambitious efforts to promote rapid economic development in the 1830s led to fiscal disaster. Three state banks failed; a lavish program of building roads, canals, and railroads totally collapsed, leaving a heavy state debt that was not paid off until 1880. Despite these setbacks, the steady influx of land-hungry poor people and the arrival after 1840 of energetic Yankee entrepreneurs, all attracted by the rich soil and excellent water routes, guaranteed rapid growth.

Although Illinois gradually eliminated French slavery and even served as a conduit to Canada for slaves escaping from the South, the state was deeply divided over the slavery issue and remained unfriendly territory for blacks and their defenders. The abolitionist leader Elijah P. Lovejoy was killed in Alton in 1837, and as late as 1853, the state passed legislation providing that free blacks entering Illinois could be sold into slavery. In 1856, however, the new Republican Party nominated and Illinois voters elected a governor, William H. Bissell, on a reform program that included support for school construction, commercial and industrial expansion, and the abolition of slavery. During the Civil War, Illinois sent half its young men to the battlefield and supplied the Union armies with huge amounts of food, feed, and horses. The strong-handed wartime administration of Republican governor Richard Yates guaranteed full support for the policies of Abraham Lincoln, who had been prominent in Illinois political life since the 1840s and had been nominated for the presidency in 1860 at a Republi-

can convention held in Chicago. Democratic dissenters were suppressed, sometimes by force, leaving a legacy of bitter feuds that troubled the "Egypt" section (the southern third of the state) for decades thereafter.

Economic and population growth quickened after 1865, exemplified by the phenomenal rise of Chicago, which became the principal city of the Midwest. Responding to opportunities presented by the coming of the railroads, boosters in hundreds of small towns and cities built banks, grain elevators, retail shops, small factories, ornate courthouses, and plain schools in an abundance of civic pride. The Democrats sought the support of the working class and small farmers, assuming an attitude of hostility toward banks, high railroad freight rates, protective tariffs, and antiunion employers, but they failed to impose any significant restraints on business expansion. They were more successful, however, in opposing Prohibition and other paternalistic methods of social control demanded by reformers such as Frances Willard, a leader in the Women's Christian Temperance Union and the Prohibition Party. In Chicago and other cities, the Democrats were less concerned with social reform than with building lucrative political machines on the backs of the poor Irish, Polish, and Czech Catholic immigrants, who kept arriving in large numbers. Statewide, Illinois retained a highly competitive two-party system, even as the excitement and high voter turnouts characteristic of 19th-century elections faded rapidly in the early 20th century.

During the second half of the 19th century, Illinois became the center of the American labor movement. Workers joined the Knights of Labor in the 1870s and 1880s and fought for child-labor laws and the eight-hour workday. Union organizing led to several spectacular incidents, including the Haymarket riot in 1886 and the violent Pullman strike in 1894, which was suppressed by federal troops at the behest of President Grover Cleveland. A coalition of Germans, labor, and small farmers elected John Peter Altgeld to the governorship in 1892. After 1900, Illinois became a center of the Progressive movement, led by Jane Addams and Republican governor Frank Lowden. Lowden reorganized the state government in 1917 by placing experts in powerful positions in state and municipal administrations.

After the Great Fire of 1871 destroyed Chicago's downtown section (but not its main residential or industrial areas), the city's wealthy elite dedicated itself to rebuilding Chicago and making it one of the great metropolises of the world. Immense steel mills, meat-packing plants, and factories sprang up, and growth was spectacular in the merchandising, banking, and transportation fields. Their fortunes made, Chicago's business leaders began building cultural institutions in the 1890s that were designed to rival the best in the world: the Chicago Symphony, the Art Institute of Chicago, and the Field Museum of Natural History. The World's Columbian Exposition of 1893 was a significant international exhibition of the nation's technological achievements, and it focused worldwide attention on what was by then the second-largest American city. A literary renaissance, stimulated by the new realism that characterized Chicago's newspapers, flourished for a decade or two before World War I, but the city was recognized chiefly for its contributions in science, architecture, and (in the 1920s) jazz.

The first three decades of the 20th century witnessed almost unbroken prosperity in all sections except Egypt, the downstate region where poor soil and the decline of the coal industry produced widespread poverty. The slums of Chicago were poor, too, because most of the hundreds of thousands of new immigrants had arrived virtually penniless. After 1920, however, large-scale immigration ended, and the immigrants' steady upward mobility, based on savings and education, became apparent. During the Prohibition era, a vast organized crime empire rose to prominence, giving Chicago and Joliet a reputation for gangsterism, violence, and corruption; the most notorious gangster was Al Capone. Money, whether legally or illegally acquired, mesmerized Illinois in the 1920s as never before—and never since.

The Great Depression of the 1930s affected the state unevenly, with agriculture hit first and recovering first. Industries began shutting down in 1930 and did not fully recover until massive military contracts during World War II restored full prosperity. The very fact of massive depression brought discredit to the probusiness Republican regime that had run the state with few exceptions since 1856. Blacks, white ethnics, factory workers, and the undereducated, all of whom suffered heavily during the early years of the Depression, responded enthusiastically to President Franklin D. Roosevelt's New Deal. They elected Henry Horner, a Democrat, to the governorship in 1932, reelected him in 1936, and flocked to the new industrial unions of the Congress of Industrial Organizations, founded in 1938.

World War II and its aftermath brought prosperity, as well as new anxiety about national security in a nuclear age. The chilling events of the 1960s and 1970s—assassinations, the Vietnam War, the race riots, and the violence that accompanied the 1968 Democratic National Convention in Chicago—helped reshape many people's attitudes in Illinois. The problems attendant on heavy industrialization, particularly air and water pollution and urban decay, began to be addressed for the first time. This transformation was perhaps best exemplified in Chicago, where voters elected Jane Byrne as the city's first woman mayor in 1979 and chose Harold Washington as its first black mayor in 1983.

The economy of Illinois, like those of other Rust Belt states, suffered a severe recession in the early 1980s. By the end of the decade, the economy had begun to rebound, but many industrial jobs were permanently lost, as industries sought to improve efficiency and productivity through automation. In 1990, the unemployment rate in Illinois was 7.2%, in contrast to the national average of 5.2%. Into the 1990s, industrial losses slowed while the service industries and the newer high-tech industries, which had gained a foothold in the Greater Chicago area, became dominant. By 1998, as the United States experienced the longest sustained economic boom in its history, many in Illinois felt the prosperity. The state ranked eighth in the nation for per capita income, and by 1999 unemployment in the state had fallen to 4.3%, in line with the national average. The poverty rate also fell during the decade, from 11.9% in 1989 to 10.1% a decade later.

Chicago's infrastructure has suffered several problems. In 1992 there was a rupture in the 60-mi (96-km) maze of tunnels that lies beneath downtown. Water from the Chicago River flooded basements and sub-basements in the city's central Loop district with as much as 30 ft (9 m) of water, forcing the temporary closure of many downtown buildings and businesses, including the Chicago Board of Trade, City Hall, and Marshall Fields department store. In August 1999, the downtown area was without power when a

substation failed. About 2,300 Commonwealth Edison (ComEd) customers in the Loop, including skyscrapers, numerous businesses, and university buildings, were without electricity. Again buildings were forced to close, sending thousands of workers home early. Later that month ComEd suffered another high-profile outage when power was lost at the city's popular Field Museum, forcing its closure. In 2000, barge and other commercial boat operators on the Chicago River complained that the increase in recreational boater traffic on the waterway posed a serious danger to safety.

In June 2000, a panel of experts convening for a legislative history roundtable in Springfield concluded that the state's 1980 cutback amendment, which reduced the size of the Illinois General Assembly by one-third, had been a detriment to state government for two decades. The 1980 amendment ended the state's system of three-member house districts; experts argued that the old system had encouraged Republicans and Democrats to work together and that the new, one-member house district system resulted in "a higher degree of partisanship and bitterness."

Meanwhile, the state was embroiled in a bribe-for-licenses scandal involving Governor George Ryan. It was alleged that truck driver's licenses were issued in exchange for campaign contributions (from trucking companies) when Ryan was secretary of state. Indictments were handed down to some state officials, but the governor insisted he knew nothing about the contributions and said if the accusations proved to be true, the money would be contributed to charities. Ryan left after one term in office due to the scandal, succeeded by Rod Blagojevich.

In 2003, the state had a $5 billion budget deficit and was experiencing the worst recession in two decades. In 2002, Illinois lost 23,000 manufacturing jobs. In his State of the State address, Governor Blagojevich targeted four areas in need of attention: jobs, schools, health care, and crime. In June 2003, the Illinois legislature passed a $10 billion budget allowing for increased school spending. The budget also called for increasing casino taxes and eliminating tax exemptions for trucking, chemical, insurance, and other industries.

In 2004, Governor Blagojevich announced a plan to make Illinois the first state in the nation to provide consumers with access to prescription drugs from Canada, Ireland, and the United Kingdom. The I-SaveRx prescription drug importation program began in October 2004. In October 2005, Governor Blagojevich praised the Illinois General Assembly for passing his All Kids health insurance proposal and reaffirmed his commitment to signing it. The plan would make Illinois the first state in the nation to provide affordable, comprehensive health insurance for every child in the state. Earlier in the year, Blagojevich committed himself to expanding, improving, and promoting access to health care for Illinois families. Also in 2005, Blagojevich promoted his Higher Standards, Better Schools Initiative—a comprehensive proposal to increase education funding and better prepare students to compete and succeed in the economy of the 21st century. Blagojevich's budget plan for fiscal year 2006 was $43.56 billion.

12 STATE GOVERNMENT

Illinois has had four constitutions. The first, written in 1818, was a short document modeled on those of New York, Kentucky, and Ohio. An attempt to rewrite the charter to allow slavery failed in a bitterly contested referendum in 1824. A new constitution in 1848 democratized government by providing for the popular election of judges. A third constitution, enacted in 1870, lasted a century; its unique feature was a voting system for the lower house of the state legislature that virtually guaranteed minority party representation in each electoral district. Important amendments in 1884 and 1904, gave the governor an item veto over appropriation bills and provided a measure of home rule for Chicago, respectively. In 1970, a fourth constitution streamlined state offices, improved accounting procedures, reformed the state tax system, and gave the state rather than local governments the major responsibility for financing education. The state bill of rights was expanded to include provisions banning discrimination in housing and employment and recognizing women's rights. An elected judiciary and the state's unique representational system were retained.

Under the 1970 constitution, amended 11 times as of January 2005, the upper house of the General Assembly consists of a Senate of 59 members, who are elected on a two-year cycle to four-year terms. Until 1980, the lower house, the House of Representatives, consisted of 177 members, with three representatives elected for two-year terms from each district. Each voter was empowered to cast three ballots for representatives, giving one vote to each of three candidates, one and a half votes to each of two, or all three to one candidate; each party never nominated more than two candidates in any single district. In November 1980, however, Illinois voters chose to reduce the size of House membership to 118 (2 representatives from each district) and to eliminate the proportional system. Annual legislative sessions, which are not limited in length, begin in January. A joint call by the presiding officers in both houses may secure a special session, also of unlimited duration. Legislators must be US citizens, at least 21 years old, and residents of their district for at least two years prior to election. The legislative salary was $55,788 in 2004.

The executive officers elected statewide are the governor and lieutenant governor (who run jointly), secretary of state, treasurer, comptroller, and attorney general. Each serves a four-year term and is eligible for reelection. An important revision of appointive offices in 1917 made most agency heads responsible to the governor. In the 1970s, the governor's office expanded its control over the budget and the higher education complex, further augmenting an already strong executive position. The governor must be a US citizen, at least 25 years old, a qualified voter, and a state resident for three years prior to election. As of December 2004, the governor's salary was $150,691.

Bills passed by both houses of the legislature become law if signed by the governor, if left unsigned for 60 days (whether or not the legislature is in session), or if vetoed by the governor but passed again by three-fifths of the elected members of each house. Constitutional amendments require a three-fifths vote by the legislature for placement on the ballot. Amendments may also be initiated by a petition of 8% of the total votes cast in the prior gubernatorial election. Either a simple majority of those voting in the election or three-fifths of those voting on the amendment is sufficient for ratification.

Qualified voters must be US citizens, at least 18 years old, and unable to claim the right to vote elsewhere. There is a 30-day precinct residency requirement. Jailed felons may not vote.

13 POLITICAL PARTIES

The Republican and Democratic parties have been the only major political groups in Illinois since the 1850s. Illinois is a closely balanced state, with a slight Republican predominance from 1860 to 1930 giving way in seesaw fashion to a highly competitive situation statewide. In Chicago and Cook County, an equally balanced

Illinois Presidential Vote by Political Parties, 1948–2004

YEAR	ELECTORAL VOTE	ILLINOIS WINNER	DEMOCRAT	REPUBLICAN	SOCIALIST LABOR	PROHIBITION	COMMUNIST	SOCIALIST
1948	28	*Truman (D)	1,994,715	1,961,103	3,118	11,959	—	11,522
1952	27	*Eisenhower (R)	2,013,920	2,457,327	9,363	—	—	—
1956	27	*Eisenhower (R)	1,775,682	2,623,327	8,342	—	—	—
1960	27	*Kennedy (D)	2,377,846	2,368,988	10,560	—	—	—
1964	26	*Johnson (D)	2,796,833	1,905,946	—	—	—	—
						AMERICAN IND.		
1968	26	*Nixon (R)	2,039,814	2,174,774	13,878	390,958	—	—
						AMERICAN		
1972	26	*Nixon (R)	1,913,472	2,788,179	12,344	2,471	4,541	—
						LIBERTARIAN		SOC. WORKERS
1976	26	Ford (R)	2,271,295	2,364,269	2,422	8,057	9,250	3,615
						CITIZENS		
1980	26	*Reagan (R)	1,981,413	2,358,094	10,692	38,939	9,711	1,302
1984	24	*Reagan (R)	2,086,499	2,707,103	2,716	10,086	—	—
1988	24	*Bush (R)	2,215,940	2,310,939	10,276	14,944	—	—
						NEW ALLIANCE	IND. (Perot)	POPULIST
1992	22	*Clinton (D)	2,453,350	1,734,096	5,267	9,218	840,515	3,577
1996	22	*Clinton (D)	2,341,744	1,587,021	—	22,548	346,408	—
						GREEN	(Buchanan)	
2000	22	Gore (D)	2,589,026	2,019,421	103,759	11,623	16,106	—
						WRITE-IN (Nader)		WRITE-IN (Peroutka)	WRITE-IN (Cobb)
2004	21	Kerry (D)	2,891,550	2,345,946	3,571	32,442	440	241

*Won US presidential election.

division before 1930 gave way to heavy Democratic predominance forged during the New Deal.

The Democrats, organized by patronage-hungry followers of President Andrew Jackson in the 1830s, dominated state politics to the mid-1850s. They appealed to subsistence farmers, former Southerners, and poor Catholic immigrants. Though they advocated minimal government intervention, Democratic officials were eager for the patronage and inside deals available in the fast-growing state. Their outstanding leader, Stephen Douglas, became a major national figure in the 1850s but never lost touch with his base of support. After Douglas died in 1861, many Illinois Democrats began to oppose the conduct of the Civil War and became stigmatized as "Copperheads." The success of the Republican war policies left the Democrats in confusion in the late 1860s and early 1870s. Negative attitudes toward blacks, banks, railroads, and Prohibition kept a large minority of Illinoisans in the Democratic fold, while the influx of Catholic immigrants replenished the party's voter base. However, the administration of Governor John Peter Altgeld (1893–97), coinciding with a deep depression and labor unrest, split the party, and only one other Democrat held the governorship between 1852 and 1932. The intraparty balance between Chicago and downstate changed with the rise of the powerful Cook County Democratic organization in the 1930s. Built by Mayor Anton Cermak and continued from 1955 to 1976 by six-term Mayor Richard J. Daley, the Chicago Democratic machine totally controlled the city, dominated the state party, and exerted enormous power at the national level. However, the machine lost its clout with the election in 1979 of independent Democrat Jane Byrne as Chicago's first woman mayor and again in 1983, when Harold Washington became its first black mayor. Although Richard Daley's son, also named Richard Daley, won the mayoralty in 1989, the machine has never recovered the power it once enjoyed. Richard Daley was elected to his fifth consecutive term as mayor of Chicago in 2003.

The Republican Party, born amid the political chaos of the 1850s, brought together most former Whigs and some Democrats who favored industrialization and opposed slavery. Abraham Lincoln, aided by many talented lieutenants, forged a coalition of commercial farmers, businessmen, evangelical Protestants, skilled craftsmen, professionals, and later, patronage holders and army veterans. Ridiculing the Democrats' alleged parochialism, the Republican Party called for vigorous prosecution of the Civil War and Reconstruction and for an active policy of promoting economic growth by encouraging railroads and raising tariffs. However, such moralistic crusades as the fight for Prohibition frequently alienated large voting blocs (especially the Germans) from the Republicans.

In the early 20th century, Republican politicians built their own ward machines in Chicago and succumbed to corruption. William "Big Bill" Thompson, Chicago's Republican mayor in the 1910s and 1920s, openly allied himself with the gangster Al Capone. Moralistic Republicans, who were strongest in the smaller towns, struggled to regain control of their party. They succeeded in the 1930s, when the Republican political machines in Chicago collapsed or switched their allegiance to the Democrats.

Since then, the Republicans have become uniformly a party of the middle and upper-middle classes, hostile to machine politics, welfare, and high taxes but favorable to business, education, and environmental protection. Although the Republican Party has a stronger formal organization in Illinois than in most other states, its leading candidates have exuded an aura of independence. Republican James R. Thompson, elected to the governorship in 1976 and reelected in 1978 and 1982, served in that office longer than any other. Thompson was followed by Republican Jim Edgar in 1990. In November 1998, Illinois voters elected Republican George H. Ryan for governor, but his administration was dogged by controversy surrounding the licensing of truck drivers when Ryan served as secretary of state, and he served only one term. Democrat Rod R. Blagojevich was elected governor in 2002.

The Whigs ran a close second to the Democrats from 1832 to 1852. Taken over in the 1840s by a group of professional organizers under Lincoln's leadership, the Whigs simply vanished after their crushing defeat in 1852. Notable among the smaller parties was the Native American ("Know-Nothing") Party, which controlled Chicago briefly in the 1850s. The Prohibitionists, Greenbackers, Union Labor, and Populist parties were weak forces in late-19th-century Illinois. The Socialist Party, strongest among coal miners and central European immigrants, grew to a minor force in the early 20th century and elected the mayor of Rockford for many years.

Illinois provided two important leaders of the national Republican Party in the 1860s—Abraham Lincoln and Ulysses S. Grant. The only major-party presidential nominee from the state between 1872 and 1976, however, was Governor Adlai Stevenson, the unsuccessful Democratic candidate in 1952 and 1956. In 1980, three native-born Illinoisans pursued the Republican Party nomination. The first, US representative Philip Crane, was the earliest to declare his candidacy but failed in the primaries. The second, US representative John Anderson, dropped out of the Republican primaries to pursue an independent candidacy, ultimately winning more than 6% of the popular vote nationally and in Illinois, but no electoral votes. The third, Ronald Reagan, a native of Tampico, won both the Republican nomination and the November election, becoming the 40th president of the United States; he was elected by a heavy majority of Illinois voters in 1980 and reelected in 1984.

In the 2000 presidential election, Democrat Al Gore won 55% of the vote, Republican George W. Bush received 43%, and Green Party candidate Ralph Nader garnered 2%. In 2004, Bush won 50% in his successful bid for reelection to Democrat John Kerry's 49%. In 2004 there were 8,594,000 registered voters; there is no party registration. The state had 21 electoral votes in the 2004 presidential election, a loss of 1 vote over 2000.

In 1996, Democratic senator Richard J. Durbin won the race to succeed retiring US senator Paul Simon; Durbin was reelected in 2002. Illinois elected its first black female senator, Carol Moseley Braun, in 1992; she was defeated by Republican Peter G. Fitzgerald in 1998. Fitzgerald did not run for a second term; the seat he left vacant was won in 2004 by Democrat Barack Obama. In the 1994 elections, the once-powerful chairman of the US House Ways and Means Committee, Dan Rostenkowski, was defeated by a relative unknown, Michael P. Flanagan. Rostenkowski, an 18-term Chicago Democrat, had been indicted on corruption charges, a fact that did not go unnoticed by an electorate that was already in an anti-incumbent mood. In the 2004 elections, Illinois voters sent nine Republicans and ten Democrats to the US House of Representatives. In mid-2005, there were 32 Republicans, 26 Democrats, and 1 independent in the state Senate and 65 Democrats and 53 Republicans in the state House.

14 LOCAL GOVERNMENT

Illinois has more units of local government (most with property-taxing power) than any other state. In 2005, there were 102 counties, 1,291 municipalities, 934 public school districts, and 3,145 special districts. In 2002, there were 1,431 townships.

County government in Illinois dates from 1778, when Virginia, claiming authority over the territory, established the earliest counties. Today, the major county offices are elective: county board chairman, county clerk (chief administrative officer), clerk of the circuit court, sheriff, state's attorney, treasurer, coroner, and superintendent of schools. Cook County, which encompasses all of Chicago and many of its suburbs, controls hospital and welfare programs in Chicago, thus spreading the cost over both the city's own tax base and that of the more affluent suburbs. The New England township system was made optional by the state's 1848 constitution, and eventually 85 counties, including Cook County, adopted the idea. Townships, which elect administrators and local judges, also handle tax collection.

Chicago is governed by an elected mayor, clerk, treasurer, and city council composed of 50 aldermen. The mayor's power has been closely tied with the city's Democratic Party organization. Independent candidates are elected to the city council from time to time, but the Democratic machine generally staffs the city with its members.

Larger municipalities are administered by an elected mayor and council members; most smaller communities are administered by nonpartisan city managers, though some have elected mayors.

In 2005, local government accounted for about 504,379 full-time (or equivalent) employment positions.

15 STATE SERVICES

To address the continuing threat of terrorism and to work with the federal Department of Homeland Security, homeland security in Illinois operates under the authority of the governor; a special assistant to the governor coordinates homeland security activities in the state.

Officials responsible to the governor of Illinois and the members of Congress, as well as to the mayor of Chicago, actively provide ombudsman service, although there is no state office by that name. Illinois has a board of ethics, but the US attorney's office in Chicago has far more potent weapons at its disposal: Many top political leaders were indicted and convicted in the 1970s, including federal judge and former Governor Otto Kerner and, in 1980, Attorney General William Scott.

Educational services provided by the Illinois Board of Education include teacher certification and placement, curriculum development, educational assessment and evaluation, and programs for the disadvantaged, gifted, handicapped, and ethnic and racial minorities. The Board of Higher Education and the Illinois Community College Board oversee postsecondary education. The Department of Transportation handles highways, traffic safety, and airports.

State agencies offering health and welfare services include the Department of Children and Family Services, which focus-

es on foster care, the deaf, the blind, and the handicapped, and the Department of Human Services, which supervises Medicaid, food stamps, and Temporary Assistance for Needy Families (TANF). The Illinois Council on Developmental Disabilities operates homes and outpatient centers for the developmentally disabled and the mentally ill. Established in 1973, the Department on Aging provides nutritional and field services. The Department of Veterans Affairs administers bonus and scholarship programs and maintains four veterans' homes with nursing facilities, including one with an Alzheimer's unit, and at least three with 300 or more beds.

State responsibility for public protection is divided among several agencies: the Office of the Attorney General, Department of Corrections, Prisoner Review Board, Law Enforcement Training and Standards Board, and Military Affairs Department. Resource protection is supervised by the Department of Natural Resources, which oversees fish hatcheries, state parks, nature reserves, game preserves, and forest fire protection. The Department of Labor mediates disputes and handles unemployment compensation. The Department of Human Rights, founded in 1980, seeks to ensure equal employment, housing, and credit opportunities.

16 JUDICIAL SYSTEM

The state's highest court is the Illinois Supreme Court, which consists of seven justices elected by judicial districts for 10-year terms. The justices elect one of their number as chief justice for three years. The Illinois Supreme Court has appellate jurisdiction generally but has original jurisdiction in cases relating to revenue, mandamus, and habeas corpus. The chief justice, assisted by an administrative director, has administrative and supervisory authority over all other courts. The appellate court is divided into five districts; appellate judges, also elected for 10-year terms, hear appeals from the 22 circuit courts, which handle civil and criminal cases. Circuit judges are elected for six-year terms. Repeated efforts to remove the state's judgeships from partisan politics have failed in the face of strong party opposition.

The penal system, under the general supervision of the Department of Corrections (established in 1970), includes large prisons at Joliet (1860), Pontiac (1871), Menard (1878), and Stateville (1919), near Joliet, plus juvenile facilities and an active parole division. The Cook County House of Corrections is highly active, as are federal facilities in Chicago and Marion.

As of 31 December 2004, a total of 44,054 prisoners were held in Illinois' state and federal prisons, an increase (from 43,418) of 1.5% from the previous year. As of year-end 2004, a total of 2,750 inmates were female, up from 2,700 or 1.9% from the year before. Among sentenced prisoners (includes some sentenced to one year or less), Illinois had an incarceration rate of 346 per 100,000 population in 2004.

According to the Federal Bureau of Investigation, in 2004 Illinois had a violent crime rate (murder/nonnegligent manslaughter; forcible rape; robbery; aggravated assault) of 542.9 reported incidents per 100,000 population, or a total of 69,026 reported incidents. Crimes against property (burglary; larceny/theft; and motor vehicle theft) in that same year totaled 405,070 reported incidents or 3,186.1 reported incidents per 100,000 people. Illinois has a death penalty, of which lethal injection is the sole method. However, the state has authorized electrocution should lethal injection be ruled unconstitutional. From 1976 through 5 May 2006, the state executed 12 persons, all of whom were executed prior to 2005. As of 1 January 2006, there were 10 death row inmates.

In 2003, Illinois spent $225,709,514 on homeland security, an average of $18 per state resident.

17 ARMED FORCES

The most important military installations in Illinois are the Great Lakes Naval Training Center near Chicago, with 5,317 active-duty military personnel, and Scott Air Force Base near Belleville with 7,678 active-duty military personnel. Great Lakes Naval Training Sites are the Navy's largest technical training operation, with up to 4,500 students at any time, training approximately 15,000 students annually. Total active-duty military personnel in Illinois numbered 20,812 in 2004, with 9,045 civilian personnel. Illinois firms received defense contract awards amounting to $3.0 billion in 2004. In addition, another $3.02 billion in defense payroll spending came to the state.

About 1 million Illinoisans served in World War II, of whom 30,000 were killed. There were 896,640 veterans of US military service in Illinois as of 2003, of whom 141,968 served in World War II; 109,644 in the Korean conflict; 270,629 during the Vietnam era; and 126,068 in the Persian Gulf War. Expenditures for veterans reached $1.9 billion in 2004.

As of 31 October 2004, the Illinois State Police employed 2,008 full-time officers.

18 MIGRATION

Apart from the small French settlements along the Mississippi River that were formed in the 18th century, most early white migration into Illinois came from the South, as poor young farm families trekked overland to southern Illinois from Kentucky, Tennessee, and the Carolinas between 1800 and 1840. After 1830, migration from Indiana, Ohio, and Pennsylvania filled the central portion of the state, while New Englanders and New Yorkers came to the northern portion.

Immigration from Europe became significant in the 1840s and continued in a heavy stream for about 80 years. Before 1890, most of the new arrivals came from Germany, Ireland, Britain, and Scandinavia. These groups continued to arrive after 1890, but they were soon outnumbered by heavy immigration from southern and eastern Europe. The opening of prairie farms, the burgeoning of towns and small cities, and the explosive growth of Chicago created a continuous demand for unskilled and semiskilled labor. Concern for the welfare of these newcomers led to the establishment of Hull House (1889) by Jane Addams in Chicago. Hull House served as a social center, shelter, and advocate for immigrants. Launching the settlement movement in America, its activities helped popularize the concept of cultural pluralism. The University of Chicago was one of the first major universities to concern itself with urban ecology and with the tendency to "ghettoize" culturally and economically disadvantaged populations.

The outbreak of World War I interrupted the flow of European immigrants but also increased the economy's demand for unskilled labor. The migration of blacks from states south of Illinois—especially from Arkansas, Tennessee, Louisiana, Mississippi, and Alabama—played an important role in meeting the demand for labor during both world wars. After World War II, the further collapse of the cotton labor market drove hundreds of thousands more blacks to Chicago and other northern cities.

In contrast to the pattern of foreign and black migration to Illinois was the continued westward search by native-born whites for new farmland, a phenomenon that produced a net outflow among this group from 1870 to 1920. After World War II, native whites again left the state in large numbers, with Southern California as a favorite destination. After 1970, for the first time, more blacks began leaving than entering Illinois.

The major intrastate migration pattern has been from farms to towns. Apart from blacks, who migrated considerable distances from farms in the South, most ex-farmers moved only 10–30 mi (16–48 km) to the nearest town or city.

During the 1970s, the state lost 649,000 persons in net migration, for an annual rate of 0.5%. From 1980 to 1983, the net loss from migration totaled 212,000, or 0.6% annually. From 1985 to 1990, the net loss from migration came to 139,360. Between 1990 and 1998, there was a net loss of 516,000 persons from domestic migration and a net gain of 337,000 from international migration. In 1998, 33,163 immigrants from foreign countries arrived in Illinois, the sixth-highest number for any state and over 5% of all foreign immigration to the United States for that year. The greatest number of foreign-born residents that year came from Mexico, totaling 10,127. In 1998, the Illinois Hispanic population numbered 1,145,000, while those of Hispanic origin numbered 1,224,000. Between 1990 and 1998, the state's overall population increased 5.4%. In the period 2000–05, net international migration was 328,020 and net internal migration was -391,031, for a net loss of 63,011 people.

19 INTERGOVERNMENTAL COOPERATION

Illinois participates in many interstate compacts, including such regional accords and commissions as the Bi-State Development Agency Compact (with Missouri), Great Lakes Commission, Wabash Valley Compact, Ohio River Basin Commission, and Ohio River Valley Water Sanitation Commission. In 1985, Illinois and seven other states formed the Great Lakes Charter to protect the lakes' water supply. Federal grants to Illinois totaled $12.902 billion in fiscal year 2005, an estimated $12.699 billion in fiscal year 2006, and an estimated $13.205 billion in fiscal year 2007.

20 ECONOMY

The economic development of Illinois falls into four periods: the frontier economy, up to 1860; the industrial transition, 1860–1900; industrial maturity, 1900–1950; and the transition to a service economy, 1950 to the present.

In the first phase, subsistence agriculture was dominant; the cost of transportation was high, cities were small and few, and cash markets for farm products hardly existed. The main activity was settling and clearing the land. A rudimentary market economy developed at the end of the period, with real estate and land speculation emerging as the most lucrative activities.

The industrial transition began about 1860, stimulated by the construction of the railroad network, which opened up distant markets for farm products and rural markets for manufactured items. The Civil War stimulated the rapid growth of cash farming, commercial and financial institutions, and the first important factories. The last quarter of the 19th century saw the closing of the agricultural frontier in Illinois and the rapid growth of commercial towns and industrial cities, especially Chicago.

Industrial maturity was reached in the early 20th century. Large factories grew, and small ones proliferated. Chicago's steel industry, actually centered in Gary, Indiana, became second in size only to Pittsburgh's, while the state took a commanding lead in food production, agricultural implement manufacture, and agricultural finance. The Depression of the 1930s stifled growth in the state and severely damaged the coal industry, but with the heavy industrial and food demands created by World War II, the state recovered its economic health.

Since 1950, the importance of manufacturing has declined, but a very strong shift into services—government, medicine, education, law, finance, and business—has underpinned the state's economic vigor.

Severe competition from Japan wreaked havoc in the state's steel, television, and automotive industries during the 1980s, while Illinois's high-wage, high-cost business climate encouraged the migration of factories to the southern states. Meat-packing, once the most famous industry in Illinois, dwindled after the closing of the Chicago stockyards in 1972. Chicago remained the nation's chief merchandising center during the early 1980s, and an influx of huge international banks boosted the city's financial strength.

In the 1990s, Illinois's major industries included primary and secondary metals; industrial and farm equipment; electric equipment and appliances; electronic components; food processing; and printing equipment. Output from the state's manufacturing sector continued to grow in absolute terms until 1999; a small 0.5% contraction in 2000 (more than compensated for by annual overall growth rates averaging over 5.2% 1998 to 2000) was followed by sharp 5% contraction during the national recession of 2001. As a percentage of total output, manufacturing fell from 17.8% in 1997 to 14.4% in 2001. By contrast, financial services increased 31.5% and general services almost 28% over this time period. In the period 2001–02, the state's diverse economy closely mirrored national trends. The biggest job losses were in manufacturing, totaling approximately 64,000 in the two-year period, compared to 35,700 jobs lost in general services, 24,700 in trade, and 12,700 in transportation and utilities. The annual decline in jobs had moderated to 1.3% by September 2002 (from 1.6% in December 2001).

In 2004, the gross state product (GSP) in Illinois totaled $521.900 billion, of which manufacturing (durable and nondurable goods) made up the largest portion at $71.028 billion or 13.6% of GSP, followed by real estate at $64.434 billion (12.3% of GSP) and professional and technical services at $42.671 billion (8.1% of GSP). In that same year, there were an estimated 1,001,185 small businesses in Illinois. Of the 285,208 businesses having employees, a total of 280,373 or 98.3% were small companies. An estimated 28,453 new businesses were established in the state in 2004, down 1.7% from the year before. Business terminations that same year came to 33,472, down 18.6% from 2003. There were 912 business bankruptcies in 2004, down 8% from the previous year. In 2005, the state's personal bankruptcy (Chapter 7 and Chapter 13) filing rate was 671 filings per 100,000 people, ranking Illinois as the 14th highest in the nation.

²¹INCOME

In 2005 Illinois had a gross state product (GSP) of $560 billion, which accounted for 4.5% of the nation's gross domestic product and placed the state fifth in GSP among the 50 states and the District of Columbia.

According to the Bureau of Economic Analysis, in 2004, Illinois had a per capita personal income (PCPI) of $34,721. This ranked 14th in the United States and was 105% of the national average of $33,050. The 1994–2004 average annual growth rate of PCPI was 3.8%. Illinois had a total personal income (TPI) of $441,372,577,000, which ranked fifth in the United States and reflected an increase of 3.4% from 2003. The 1994–2004 average annual growth rate of TPI was 4.5%. Earnings of persons employed in Illinois increased from $339,209,331,000 in 2003 to $351,081,708,000 in 2004, an increase of 3.5%. The 2003–04 national change was 6.3%.

The US Census Bureau reports that the three-year average median household income for 2002–04 in 2004 dollars was $45,787 compared to a national average of $44,473. During the same period, 12.5% of the population was below the poverty line, compared to 12.4% nationwide.

²²LABOR

According to the Bureau of Labor Statistics (BLS), in April 2006, the seasonally adjusted civilian labor force in Illinois numbered 6,525,100. Approximately 332,500 workers were unemployed, yielding an unemployment rate of 5.1%, compared to the national average of 4.7% for the same period. Preliminary data for the same period placed nonfarm employment at 5,919,700. Since the beginning of the BLS data series in 1976, the highest unemployment rate recorded in Illinois was 12.9% in February 1983. The historical low was 4.1% in March 1999. Preliminary nonfarm employment data by occupation for April 2006 showed that approximately 4.6% of the labor force was employed in construction; 11.5% in manufacturing; 20.1% in trade, transportation, and public utilities; 6.9% in financial activities; 14.3% in professional and business services; 12.7% in education and health services; 8.9% in leisure and hospitality services; and 14.2% in government.

The first labor organizations sprang up among German tailors, Teamsters, and carpenters in Chicago in the 1850s and among British and German coal miners after the Civil War. The period of industrialization after the Civil War saw many strikes, especially in coal mining and construction, many of them spontaneous rather than union related. The Knights of Labor organized extensively in Chicago, Peoria, and Springfield in the 1870s and 1880s, reaching a membership of 52,000 by 1886. However, in the aftermath of the Haymarket riot—during which a dynamite blast at a labor rally killed seven policemen and four civilians—the Knights faded rapidly. More durable was the Chicago Federation of Labor, formed in 1877 and eventually absorbed by the American Federation of Labor (AFL). Strongest in the highly skilled construction, transportation, mining, and printing industries, the federation stood aside from the 1894 Pullman strike, led by industrial union organizer Eugene V. Debs, a bitter struggle broken by federal troops over the protest of Governor John Peter Altgeld.

Labor unions are powerful in Chicago but relatively weak downstate. The major unions are the International Brotherhood of

Teamsters, the United Steelworkers of America, the International Association of Machinists, the United Automobile Workers, the United Brotherhood of Carpenters, and the American Federation of State, County, and Municipal Employees. The Illinois Education Association, though not strictly a labor union, has become one of the state's most militant employee organizations, often calling strikes and constituting the most active lobby in the state. In 1983, a new law granted all public employees except police and firemen the right to strike.

The BLS reported that in 2005, a total of 927,000 of the state's 5,473,000 employed wage and salary workers were formal members of a union. This represented 16.9% of those so employed, up from 16.8% in 2004 and above the national average of 12%. Overall in 2005, a total of 965,000 workers (17.6%) in Illinois were covered by a union or employee association contract, which includes those workers who reported no union affiliation. Illinois is one of 28 states that does not have a right-to-work law.

As of 1 March 2006, Illinois had a state-mandated minimum wage of $6.50 per hour. In 2004, women in the state accounted for 46.5% of the employed civilian labor force.

23 AGRICULTURE

Total agricultural income in 2005 reached $8.7 billion in Illinois, ranking the state seventh in the nation. Crops accounted for nearly 79% of the value of farm marketings, with corn and soybeans as the leading cash commodities.

Prior to 1860, agriculture was the dominant occupation, and food for home consumption was the leading product. Enormous effort was devoted to breaking the thick prairie soil in the northern two-thirds of the state. Fences and barns were erected, and in the 1870s and 1880s, the drainage of low-lying areas in central Illinois was a major concern. Commercial agriculture was made possible by the extension of the railroad network in the 1860s and 1870s. Corn, wheat, hogs, cattle, and horses were the state's main products in the 19th century. Since then, wheat and poultry have declined greatly in significance, while soybeans and, to a lesser extent, dairy products and vegetables have played an increasingly important role. The mechanization and electrification of agriculture, beginning about 1910, proceeded at an unmatched pace in Illinois. Strong interest in scientific farming, including the use of hybrid corn, sophisticated animal-breeding techniques, and chemical fertilizers, has also fostered a steady, remarkable growth in agricultural productivity.

The number of farms reached a peak of 264,000 in 1900 and began declining rapidly after World War II, down to 73,000 in 2004. Total acreage in farming was 27.5 million acres (11.1 million hectares) in 2004, down from 32.8 million acres (13.3 million hectares) in 1990. The average farm size more than doubled from 124 acres (50 hectares) in 1900 to 377 acres (152 hectares) in 2004. The farm population, which averaged 1.2 million persons from 1880 to 1900, declined to 314,000 in 1980; by then, about half the people who lived on farms commuted to work in stores, shops, and offices.

The major agricultural region is the Corn Belt, covering all of central and about half of northern Illinois. Among the 50 states, Illinois ranked second only to Iowa in the production of corn and soybeans during 2000–04.

Agriculture is big business in the state, though very few farms are owned by corporations (except "family corporations," a tax device). The financial investment in agriculture is enormous, largely because of the accelerating cost of land. The value of land quadrupled during the 1970s to an average of $2,013 per acre in 1980, fell to $1,536 per acre by 1992, but rose to $2,210 by 1997 and $2,610 by 2004.

24 ANIMAL HUSBANDRY

Livestock is raised almost everywhere in Illinois, but production is concentrated especially in the west-central region. In 2005, Illinois farms had an estimated 1.38 million cattle and calves worth around $1.1 billion. Illinois farms had an estimated 4 million hogs and pigs in 2004, worth around $400 million. The Dairy Belt covers part of northern Illinois. Milk production in 2003 totaled an estimated 2 billion lb (0.9 billion kg). During 2003, Illinois poultry farmers sold an estimated 7.1 million lb (3.2 million kg) of chicken. An estimated 973 million eggs were produced in 2003, worth around $51 million.

25 FISHING

Commercial fishing is relatively insignificant in Illinois. Sport fishing is of modest importance in southern Illinois and around Lake Michigan. Some 450 lakes and ponds and 200 streams and rivers are open to the public. In 2004, there were 713,120 sport anglers licensed in Illinois. The state Division of Fisheries operates four fish hatcheries, producing more than 50 million fish of 18 species for stocking Illinois waters. In 2004, Illinois had 18 catfish farms covering 320 acres (130 hectares).

26 FORESTRY

Forestland covering 4,331,000 acres (1,753,000 hectares) makes up about 12% of the state's land area. Forests in the northern two-thirds of the state are predominately located in the northwestern part of the state and along major rivers and streams. The majority of Illinois's forests are located in the southern one-third of the state. Some 4,087,000 acres (1,654,000 hectares) are classified as commercial forests and 89% privately owned. As of 2005, Illinois had two national forests, with a total National Forest System acreage of 857,000 acres (347,000 hectares). In 2004, lumber production totaled 123 million board feet.

27 MINING

According to preliminary data from the US Geological Survey (USGS), the estimated value of Illinois nonfuel mineral production in 2003 was $911 million, a decrease from 2002 of about 1%. The USGS data ranked Illinois 16th among the 50 states by the total value of its nonfuel mineral production, accounting for around 2.5% of total US output.

All of the state's nonfuel mineral output in 2003 was accounted for by industrial minerals, of which crushed stone was the leading item produced, accounting for around 46% of all production by value. Portland cement ranked second at around 23%, while construction sand and gravel stood at nearly 17% and industrial sand and gravel at 8%. Lime, fuller's earth, and tripoli accounted for most of the remainder.

For 2003, preliminary data showed that Illinois produced 72.6 million metric tons of crushed stone, valued at $421 million; construction sand and gravel output totaled 33.2 million metric tons, or $153 million; and industrial sand and gravel production totaling 4.51 million metric tons, or $72.9 million. Portland cement production that same year came to 2.8 million metric tons, or an estimated $207 million.

Until 1997, Illinois was the only state with reported fluorspar production. A combination of increased competition from foreign imports and a decrease in the use of chlorofluorocarbons (because of environmental concerns) was mostly responsible for the decline in domestic production. Fluorspar had been mined commercially in Hardin County since 1870, and in 1996, the last two operating fluorspar mines in the United States were closed (making it difficult to obtain fluorite, the state mineral).

28 ENERGY AND POWER

Illinois is one of the nation's leading energy producers and consumers. As of 2003, Illinois had 92 electrical power service providers, of which 41 were publicly owned and 27 were cooperatives. Of the remainder, nine were investor owned, 11 were generation-only suppliers, 3 were delivery-only suppliers, and 1 was an owner of an independent generator that sold directly to customers. As of that same year, there were 5,457,799 retail customers. Of that total, 4,931,955 received their power from investor-owned service providers. Cooperatives accounted for 258,814 customers, while publicly owned providers had 254,387 customers. There were 12,642 generation-only customers and only one independent generator or "facility" customer. There were no data on the number of delivery-only customers.

Total net summer generating capability by the state's electrical generating plants in 2003 stood at 45.541 million kW, with total production that same year at 189.055 billion kWh. Of the total amount generated, 94.9% came from electric utilities, with the remainder coming from independent producers and combined heat and power service providers. The largest portion of all electric power generated, 94.733 billion kWh (50.1%), came from nuclear power plants, with coal-fired plants in second place at 87.981 billion kWh (46.5%) and natural gas-fired plants in third place at 3.902 billion kWh (2.1%). Other renewable power sources, petroleum, hydroelectric, and plants using other types of gases accounted for the remaining facilities.

As of 2006, Illinois had six nuclear power generating facilities: the Braidwood Station in Will County; the Byron plant in Ogle County; the Clinton Power Station near Clinton; the Dresden plant in Grundy County; the La Salle County plant; and the Quad Cities plant near the cities of Davenport, Rock Island, Moline, and East Moline.

As of 2004, Illinois had proven crude oil reserves of 92 million barrels, or less than 1% of all proven US reserves, while output that same year averaged 30,000 barrels per day. Including federal offshore domains, the state that year ranked 15th (14th excluding federal offshore) in proven reserves and 15th (14th excluding federal offshore) in production among the 31 producing states. In 2004, Illinois had 16,859 producing oil wells, accounting for 1% of all US production. The state's four refineries had a combined crude oil distillation capacity of 896,000 barrels per day.

In 2004, Illinois had 251 producing natural gas and gas condensate wells. In that same year, marketed gas production (all gas produced excluding gas used for repressuring, vented and flared,

and nonhydrocarbon gases removed) totaled 174 million cu ft (4.9 million cu m).

Coal is abundant throughout Illinois, with the largest mines in the south and central regions. Coal mining reached its peak in the 1920s but suffered thereafter from high pricing policies, the Depression of the 1930s, and environmental restrictions against burning high-sulfur coal in the 1970s. In 2004, Illinois had 19 producing coal mines, seven of which were surface mines and 12 were underground. Coal production that year totaled 31,853,000 short tons, up from 31,640,000 short tons in 2003. Of the total produced in 2004, underground mines accounted for 26,907,000 short tons. Recoverable coal reserves in 2004 totaled 796 million tons. One short ton equals 2,000 lb (0.907 metric tons).

29 INDUSTRY

Manufacturing in Illinois, concentrated in but not limited to Chicago, has always been diverse. Before 1860s, small gristmills, bakeries, and blacksmith shops handled what little manufacturing was done. Industry tripled in size in the 1860s, doubled in the 1870s, and doubled again in the 1880s, until manufacturing employment leveled off at 10%–12% of the population. Value added by manufacture grew at a compound annual rate of 8.1% between 1860 and 1900 and at a rate of 6.3% until 1929.

According to the US Census Bureau's Annual Survey of Manufactures (ASM) for 2004, Illinois' manufacturing sector covered some 20 product subsectors. The shipment value of all products manufactured in the state that same year was $210.042 billion. Of that total, food manufacturing accounted for the largest share at $32.669 billion. It was followed by chemical manufacturing at $28.221 billion; machinery manufacturing at $26.085 billion; fabricated metal product manufacturing at $18.620 billion; petroleum and coal products manufacturing at $18.109 billion; and plastics and rubber products manufacturing at $12.759 billion.

In 2004, a total of 676,061 people in Illinois were employed in the state's manufacturing sector, according to the ASM. Of that total, 466,252 were actual production workers. In terms of total employment, the fabricated metal product manufacturing industry accounted for the largest portion of all manufacturing employees at 103,818, with 76,955 actual production workers. It was followed by machinery manufacturing at 84,390 employees (52,647 actual production workers); food manufacturing at 80,454 employees (59,980 actual production workers); plastics and rubber products manufacturing at 55,183 employees (42,305 actual production workers); and chemical manufacturing with 49,396 employees (25,740 actual production workers).

ASM data for 2004 showed that the state's manufacturing sector paid $29.166 billion in wages. Of that amount, the fabricated metal product manufacturing sector accounted for the largest share at $4.243 billion. It was followed by machinery manufacturing at $3.915 billion; chemical manufacturing at $2.951 billion; food manufacturing at $2.851 billion; and transportation equipment manufacturing at $2.211 billion.

By far the leading industrial center is Chicago, followed by Rockford, the East St. Louis area, Rock Island and Moline in the Quad Cities region, and Peoria.

³⁰COMMERCE

Chicago is the leading wholesaling center of the Midwest. According to the 2002 Census of Wholesale Trade, the wholesale trade sector had sales that year totaling $317.4 billion from 20,520 establishments. Wholesalers of durable goods accounted for 11,911 establishments, followed by nondurable goods wholesalers at 6,670 and electronic markets, agents, and brokers accounting for 1,939 establishments. Sales by durable goods wholesalers in 2002 totaled $155.7 billion, while wholesalers of nondurable goods saw sales of $135.7 billion. Electronic markets, agents, and brokers in the wholesale trade industry had sales of $25.9 billion.

In the 2002 Census of Retail Trade, Illinois was listed as having 43,022 retail establishments with sales of $131.4 billion. The leading types of retail businesses (by number of establishments) were food and beverage stores (6,114); clothing and clothing accessories stores (6,078); miscellaneous store retailers (4,965); motor vehicle and motor vehicle parts dealers (4,375); and gasoline stations (4,153). In terms of sales, motor vehicle and motor vehicle parts stores accounted for the largest share of retail sales at $32.6 billion, followed by food and beverage stores at $18.7 billion; general merchandise stores at $18.4 billion; nonstore retailers at $13.05 billion; and building material/garden equipment and supplies dealers at $10.9 billion. A total of 601,465 people were employed by the retail sector in Illinois that year.

Illinois ranked sixth among the states in exports with estimated exports of $35.8 billion in 2005.

³¹CONSUMER PROTECTION

The Office of the Attorney General is the most active protector of Illinois consumers with its Consumer Protection Division, which handles around 28,000 complaints a year. Within the Consumer Protection Division are the Franchise Bureau, Health Care Bureau, Charitable Trusts Bureau, and Consumer Fraud Bureau. The Department of Insurance also has a Consumer Division. The Department of Human Rights was established in 1979 to protect individuals in regard to employment, public accommodations, and other areas. Nearly half of all claims involve motor vehicle or home repair fraud in the state of Illinois.

The Illinois Office of the Attorney General can initiate civil, and, in antitrust actions, criminal proceedings; it can also represent the state before state and federal regulatory agencies; and is responsible for the administration of consumer protection and education programs; and the handling of consumer complaints. However, the office has only limited subpoena powers. In antitrust actions, the Attorney General's Office can act on behalf of those consumers who are incapable of acting on their own and can initiate damage actions on behalf of the state in state courts. However, the office cannot represent counties, cities, and other governmental entities in recovering civil damages under state or federal law.

The state's Consumer Fraud Bureau has offices in Carbondale, Chicago, and Springfield. The Governor's Office of Citizens Assistance is located in Springfield. The cities of Chicago and Des Plaines also have offices devoted to consumer protection.

³²BANKING

Banking was highly controversial in 19th-century Illinois. Modernizers stressed the need for adequate venture capital and money supplies, but traditionalist farmers feared they would be impoverished by an artificial "money monster." Efforts to create a state bank floundered in confusion, while the dubious character of most private banknotes inspired the state to ban private banks altogether. The major breakthrough came during the Civil War, when federal laws encouraged the establishment of strong national banks in all the larger cities, and Chicago quickly became the financial center of the Midwest. Apart from the 1920s and early 1930s, when numerous neighborhood and small-town banks folded, the banking system has flourished. The Bureau of Banks and Trust Companies at the Office of Banks and Real Estate regulates state-chartered banks and trust companies.

As of June 2005, Illinois had 718 insured banks, savings and loans, and saving banks, plus 366 state-chartered and 117 federally chartered credit unions (CUs). Illinois had the highest number of banks of any state (Texas was second with 677) in 2005, due in large part to past state regulations that restricted branch banking. From 1870 through 1970, even the state's largest banks were limited to just one office. However, by 1993, branch banking without limitation had become available. Excluding the CUs, the Chicago–Naperville–Joliet market area accounted for the vast bulk of the state's financial institutions and deposits in 2004, with 309 institutions and $239.618 billion in deposits. The Bloomington–Normal area was second in terms of deposits with $9.549 billion, while the Davenport–Moline–Rock Island area (which includes portions of Iowa and Illinois) was tied with Peoria for second place in the number of financial institutions at 46 each. As of June 2005, CUs accounted for 5.8% of all assets held by all financial institutions in the state, or some $22.192 billion. Banks, savings and loans, and savings banks collectively accounted for the remaining 94.2% or $357.480 billion in assets held.

As of fourth quarter 2005, the median net interest margin (the difference between the lower rates offered to savers and the higher rates charged on loans) stood at 3.70%, down from 3.71% in 2004, but up from 3.67% in 2003. The median percentage of pastdue/nonaccrual loans to total loans for the same time periods stood at 1.59%, 1.63%, and 1.78%, respectively.

³³INSURANCE

Illinois is a major center of the insurance industry. In 2004, there were 8 million individual life insurance policies in force with a total value of over $636 billion; total value for all categories of life insurance (individual, group, and credit) was over $1 trillion. The average coverage amount was $79,100 per policy holder. Death benefits paid that year totaled $2.66 billion.

In 2003, 71 life and health insurance and 186 property and casualty insurance companies were domiciled in Illinois. In 2004, direct premiums for property and casualty insurance totaled $21.2 billion. That year, there were 44,444 flood insurance policies in force in the state, with a total value of $5.4 billion. About $1.1 billion of coverage was offered through FAIR (Fair Access to Insurance) Plans, which are designed to offer coverage for some natural circumstances, such as wind and hail, in high-risk areas.

Illinois fire and casualty companies are among the US leaders. State Farm is based in Bloomington, and Allstate, a subsidiary of Sears, Roebuck, is in Chicago. Blue Cross–Blue Shield, the nation's largest hospital and medical insurance program, is headquartered in Chicago.

In 2004, 58% of state residents held employment-based health insurance policies, 5% held individual policies, and 21% were covered under Medicare and Medicaid; 14% of residents were uninsured. In 2003, employee contributions for employment-based health coverage averaged 17% for single coverage and 23% for family coverage. The state offers a nine-month health benefits expansion program for small-firm employees in connection with the Consolidated Omnibus Budget Reconciliation Act (COBRA, 1986), a health insurance program for those who lose employment-based coverage due to termination or reduction of work hours.

In 2003, there were over 7.3 million auto insurance policies in effect for private passenger cars. Required minimum coverage includes bodily injury liability of up to $20,000 per individual and $40,000 for all persons injured in an accident, as well as property damage liability of $15,000. Uninsured motorist coverage is also mandatory. In 2003, the average expenditure per vehicle for insurance coverage was $760.98.

³⁴ SECURITIES

The Chicago Stock Exchange (CHX) is the third most active stock exchange in the United States by volume. It was founded in 1882. After a 1949 merger with the St. Louis, Cleveland, and Minneapolis/St. Paul stock exchanges, the organization was known as the Midwest Stock Exchange. The New Orleans Stock Exchange was added to the group in 1959. The name reverted back to Chicago Stock Exchange in 1993. As of 2006, the CHX trades over 3,500 NYSE, AMEX, NASDAQ, and CHX-exclusive issues.

The most intensive trading in Chicago takes place on the three major commodity exchanges. The Chicago Board of Trade has set agricultural prices for the world since 1848, especially in soybeans, corn, and wheat. The Chicago Mercantile Exchange specializes in pork bellies (bacon), live cattle, potatoes, and eggs; since 1972, it has also provided a market for world currency futures. The Mid-America Commodity Exchange, the smallest of the three, has a colorful ancestry dating from 1868. It features small-lot futures contracts on soybeans, silver, corn, wheat, and live hogs.

In 2005, there were 3,540 personal financial advisers employed in the state and 14,940 securities, commodities, and financial services sales agents. In 2004, there were over 449 publicly traded companies within the state, with over 120 NASDAQ companies, 195 NYSE listings, and 53 AMEX listings. In 2006, the state had 32 Fortune 500 companies; State Farm Insurance Companies (with mutual funds listed on NASDAQ) ranked first in the state and 22nd in the nation with revenues of over $59.2 million, followed by the NYSE listed Boeing, Sears Holdings, Walgreens, and Motorola.

³⁵ PUBLIC FINANCE

Among the larger states, Illinois is known for its low taxes and conservative fiscal policy. The Bureau of the Budget, under the governor's control, has major responsibility for the state's overall fiscal program, negotiating annually with key legislators, cabinet officers, and outside pressure groups. The governor then submits the budget to the legislature for amendment and approval. The fiscal year (FY) runs from 1 July to 30 June.

Fiscal year 2006 general funds were estimated at $27.5 billion for resources and $27.0 billion for expenditures. In fiscal year 2004, federal government grants to Illinois were nearly $16.5 billion.

In the federal budget for the 2007 fiscal year, Illinois was slated to receive $233.1 million for major cities throughout the state to fund buses, railcars, and maintenance facilities essential to sustaining public transportation systems that serve their communities; $96.6 million for the renovation of the Dirksen US Courthouse in Chicago, including the modernization of building systems and the

Illinois—State Government Finances

(Dollar amounts in thousands. Per capita amounts in dollars.)

	AMOUNT	PER CAPITA
Total Revenue	61,255,138	4,818.69
General revenue	46,518,645	3,659.43
Intergovernmental revenue	14,172,550	1,114.90
Taxes	25,490,593	2,005.24
General sales	6,922,587	544.57
Selective sales	5,603,955	440.84
License taxes	2,385,596	187.66
Individual income tax	8,139,558	640.31
Corporate income tax	2,068,574	162.73
Other taxes	370,323	29.13
Current charges	3,211,635	252.65
Miscellaneous general revenue	3,643,867	286.65
Utility revenue	–	–
Liquor store revenue	–	–
Insurance trust revenue	14,736,493	1,159.26
Total expenditure	53,429,176	4,203.05
Intergovernmental expenditure	13,303,609	1,046.54
Direct expenditure	40,125,567	3,156.51
Current operation	26,072,092	2,050.98
Capital outlay	2,467,325	194.09
Insurance benefits and repayments	7,620,381	599.46
Assistance and subsidies	1,280,524	100.73
Interest on debt	2,685,245	211.24
Exhibit: Salaries and wages	5,974,189	469.96
Total expenditure	53,429,176	4,203.05
General expenditure	45,808,795	3,603.59
Intergovernmental expenditure	13,303,609	1,046.54
Direct expenditure	32,505,186	2,557.05
General expenditures, by function:		
Education	15,272,814	1,201.45
Public welfare	12,694,089	998.59
Hospitals	994,622	78.24
Health	2,696,902	212.15
Highways	3,096,955	243.62
Police protection	399,085	31.39
Correction	1,284,453	101.04
Natural resources	395,095	31.08
Parks and recreation	373,134	29.35
Government administration	1,395,966	109.81
Interest on general debt	2,685,245	211.24
Other and unallocable	4,520,435	355.60
Utility expenditure	–	–
Liquor store expenditure	–	–
Insurance trust expenditure	7,620,381	599.46
Debt at end of fiscal year	48,726,054	3,833.08
Cash and security holdings	104,783,007	8,242.84

Abbreviations and symbols: – zero or rounds to zero; (NA) not available; (X) not applicable.

SOURCE: *U.S. Census Bureau, Governments Division, 2004 Survey of State Government Finances,* January 2006.

renovation of interior space; $42.8 million to continue the construction and rehabilitation of transit rail systems in Chicago; $38 million in incremental funding for a $152 million project for the construction of a US I-80 to I-88 north–south connector in Illinois; $37.5 million in incremental funding for a $150 million project for the Mississippi River Bridge in Illinois; $13.5 million to improve public transportation in Illinois for the elderly, persons with disabilities, and persons with lower-incomes providing access to job and health care facilities; and $12.4 million to provide transportation in rural areas statewide meeting the needs of individuals that may have no other means of transportation.

36 TAXATION

In 2005, Illinois collected $26,412 million in tax revenues or $2,069 per capita, which placed it 29th among the 50 states in per capita tax burden. The national average was $2,192 per capita. Property taxes accounted for 0.2% of the total, sales taxes 27.2%, selective sales taxes 23.3%, individual income taxes 30.1%, corporate income taxes 8.3%, and other taxes 10.9%.

As of 1 January 2006, Illinois had one individual income tax bracket of 3.0%. The state taxes corporations at a flat rate of 7.3%.

In 2004, state and local property taxes amounted to $17,888,828,000 or $1,407 per capita. The per capita amount ranks the state ninth nationally. Local governments collected $17,831,744,000 of the total and the state government $57,084,000.

Illinois taxes retail sales at a rate of 6.25%. In addition to the state tax, local taxes on retail sales can reach as much as 3%, making for a potential total tax on retail sales of 9.25%. Food purchased for consumption off premises is taxable although at a lower rate. The tax on cigarettes is 98 cents per pack, which ranks 21st among the 50 states and the District of Columbia. Illinois taxes gasoline at 20.1 cents per gallon. This is in addition to the 18.4 cents per gallon federal tax on gasoline.

According to the Tax Foundation, for every federal tax dollar sent to Washington in 2004, Illinois citizens received $0.73 in federal spending.

37 ECONOMIC POLICY

The state's policy toward economic development has engendered political controversy since the 1830s. Before the Civil War, the Democrats in power usually tried to slow, though not reverse, the tide of rapid industrial and commercial growth. The Republican ascendancy between the 1850s and the 1930s (with a few brief interruptions) produced a generally favorable business climate, which in turn fostered rapid economic growth. The manufacturing sector eroded slowly in the 1960s and 1970s, as incentives and tax credits for new industry were kept at a modest level. In 1989, however, the state began to aggressively encourage companies undergoing modernization or commercializing new technologies by enacting the Technology Advancement and Development Act, which invests in companies developing advanced technologies for commercial purposes.

In 2006, the lead government agency coordinating economic development programs was the Department of Commerce and Economic Opportunity (DCEO), previously called the Department of Commerce and Community Affairs. The name change indicated a shift in emphasis toward inclusion ("no community left behind") in the economic downturn that followed the prosperous 1990s—a shift, for instance, from primary emphasis on keeping up with the latest digital technology (as in the government's Science and Technology Initiative of 2000 that included "technology challenge" business and educational grants, and research funding) to a concern with bridging the "digital divide." The Illinois Department of Human Services (DHS) was given managerial control of the Team Illinois initiative, which featured the pooling of resources of virtually every state agency, including the DCEO, to address the needs of the state's poorest communities. The goal of Team Illinois was to work with residents, elected officials, local business leaders, and community stakeholders to help build needed infrastructure. The creation of public-private partnerships and the empowerment of community stakeholders were to be central parts of the approach. Hopkins Park in Pembroke Township, a rural community in Kankakee County, was the first of four communities scheduled to receive Team Illinois assistance. Infrastructural improvements under way included road repair, a new Technology Learning Center, public-private partnerships to build affordable housing, the removal and cleanup of tire dumps (by the Illinois EPA), and health screenings and immunizations (by the Department of Public Health). Internationally, the DCEO's role is that of the "sales department for Illinois." It maintains trade and investment offices in Toronto, Mexico City, Tokyo, Warsaw, Johannesburg, Brussels, Shanghai, and Hong Kong. The promotion of jobs, tourism, minority-owned enterprises, and foreign markets for Illinois products is the department's major responsibility. The assistance by the DCEO includes equity capital and low interest loans for small businesses; low-interest financing to communities undergoing infrastructure improvements which help create or retain jobs; tax-exempt bonds for companies expanding or renovating their physical plant; and grants for employee training and retraining.

38 HEALTH

The infant mortality rate in October 2005 was estimated at 7.6 per 1,000 live births. The birth rate in 2003 was 14.4 per 1,000 population. The abortion rate stood at 23.2 per 1,000 women in 2000. In 2003, about 85.4% of pregnant woman received prenatal care beginning in the first trimester. In 2004, approximately 83% of children received routine immunizations before the age of three.

The crude death rate in 2002 was 8.5 deaths per 1,000 population. The same year, the death rates for major causes of death (per 100,000 resident population) were as follows: heart disease, 244.6; cancer, 196.3; cerebrovascular diseases, 57; chronic lower respiratory diseases, 38.3; and diabetes, 23.9. The mortality rate from HIV infection was 3.9 per 100,000 population. In 2004, the reported AIDS case rate was at about 13.2 per 100,000 population. In 2002, about 55.8% of the populations was considered overweight or obese. As of 2004, about 22.2% of state residents were smokers.

Hospitals abound in Illinois, with Chicago serving as a diagnostic and treatment center for patients throughout the Midwest. In 2003, Illinois had 192 community hospitals with about 35,000 beds. There were about 1.5 million patient admissions that year and 27 million outpatient visits. The average daily inpatient census was about 22,400 patients. The average cost per day for hospital care was $1,497. Also in 2003, there were about 827 certified nursing facilities in the state with 106,734 beds and an overall occupancy rate of about 74.8%. In 2004, it was estimated that about 72.6% of all state residents had received some type of dental care within the year. Illinois had 284 physicians per 100,000 resident population in 2004 and 803 nurses per 100,000 in 2005. In 2004, there was a total of 7,958 dentists in the state.

In 2005, University of Chicago Hospitals ranked 14th on the Honor Roll of Best Hospitals 2005 by *U.S. News & World Report.* In the same report, the hospital ranked seventh in the nation for best care in cancer. Children's Memorial Hospital, Chicago, ranked within the top 25 hospitals for best reputation in pediatric care.

About 21% of state residents were enrolled in Medicaid and Medicare programs in 2004. Approximately 14% of the state population was uninsured in 2004. In 2003, state health care expenditures totaled $13.2 million.

39 SOCIAL WELFARE

Prior to the 1930s, social welfare programs were the province of county government and private agencies. Asylums, particularly poor farms, were built in most counties following the Civil War; they provided custodial care for orphans, the very old, the helpless, sick, and itinerant "tramps." Most people who needed help, however, turned to relatives, neighbors, or church agencies. The local and private agencies were overwhelmed by the severe Depression of the 1930s, forcing first the state and then the federal government to intervene. Social welfare programs are implemented by county agencies but funded by local and state taxes and federal aid.

In 2004, about 392,000 people received unemployment benefits, with the average weekly unemployment benefit at $279. In fiscal year 2005, the estimated average monthly participation in the food stamp program included about 1,158,271 persons (520,350 households); the average monthly benefit was about $100.73 per person. That year, the total of benefits paid through the state for the food stamp program was about $1.4 billion.

Temporary Assistance for Needy Families (TANF), the system of federal welfare assistance that officially replaced Aid to Families with Dependent Children (AFDC) in 1997, was reauthorized through the Deficit Reduction Act of 2005. TANF is funded through federal block grants that are divided among the states based on an equation involving the number of recipients in each state. In 2004, the state TANF program had 89,000 recipients; state and federal expenditures on this TANF program totaled $132 million in fiscal year 2003.

In December 2004, Social Security benefits were paid to 1,883,750 Illinois residents. This number included 1,221,330 retired workers, 195,560 widows and widowers, 210,030 disabled workers, 100,520 spouses, and 156,300 children. Social Security beneficiaries represented 14.8% of the total state population and 90.2% of the state's population age 65 and older. Retired workers received an average monthly payment of $993; widows and widowers, $960; disabled workers, $924; and spouses, $498. Payments for children of retired workers averaged $492 per month; children of deceased workers, $652; and children of disabled workers, $277. Federal Supplemental Security Income payments went to 255,624 Illinois residents in December 2004, averaging $427 a month. An additional $2.3 million of state-administered supplemental payments were distributed to 30,501 residents.

40 HOUSING

Flimsy cabins and shacks provided rude shelter for many Illinoisans in pioneer days. Later, the balloon-frame house, much cheaper to build than traditional structures, became a trademark of the Prairie State. After a third of Chicago's wooden houses burned in 1871, the city moved to enforce more stringent building codes. The city's predominant dwelling then became the three- or five-story brick apartment house. Great mansions were built in elite areas of Chicago (first Prairie Avenue, later the Gold Coast), and high-rise lakefront luxury apartments first became popular in the 1920s. In the 1970s, Chicago pioneered the conversion of luxury apartment buildings to condominiums.

In 2004, there were an estimated 5,094,186 housing units in Illinois, of which 4,659,791 were occupied; 69.2% were owner occupied. About 58.9% of all units were single-family, detached homes. Most units rely on utility gas for heating. It was estimated that 247,234 units were without telephone service, 15,492 lacked complete plumbing facilities, and 16,789 lacked complete kitchen facilities. The average household had 2.66 members.

In 2004, 59,800 new privately owned units were authorized for construction. The median home value was $167,711. The median monthly cost for mortgage owners was $1,370, while renters paid a median of $698 per month. In 2006, the state received over $32.4 million in community development block grants from the US Department of Housing and Urban Development (HUD). The city of Chicago received similar grants of over $85 million.

41 EDUCATION

In 1854, Ninian Edwards became the first superintendent of public education. His first and most difficult task was to convince pioneer parents that a formal education was a necessary part of the lives of their children. By the mid-1870s, education in Illinois had become a going enterprise. Edwards helped create an outstanding public school system, although the city of Chicago was hard-pressed to construct enough school buildings to serve the growing numbers of students until foreign immigration subsided in the 1920s. The dedication of these educators continued to improve the quality of education, but it was not until the development of a good highway system and state funding for the transporting of students that rural Illinois would see the demise of one-room schoolhouses. In one decade, 1944–54, state-mandated school consolidation/reorganization reduced the number of school districts from 11,955 to 2,607.

In 2004, 86.8% of the Illinois population 25 years and over held high school diplomas, with 27.4% continuing their education and earning a bachelor's degree or higher.

Total public school enrollment for fall 2002 stood at 2,084,000. Of these, 1,488,00 attended schools from kindergarten through grade eight, and 597,000 attended high school. Approximately 57.4% of the students were white, 21.1% were black, 17.7% were Hispanic, 3.6% were Asian/Pacific Islander, and 0.2% were American Indian/Alaskan Native. Total enrollment was estimated at 2,086,000 in fall 2003 and expected to be 2,118,000 by fall 2014, an increase of 1.6% during the period 2002–14. Expenditures for public education in 2003/04 were estimated at $21 billion. Non-public schools, dominated by Chicago's extensive Roman Catholic school system, have shown a slight decrease since the early

1980s. In fall 2003, 270,490 students were enrolled in 1,346 private schools. Since 1969, the National Assessment of Educational Progress (NAEP) has tested public school students nationwide. The resulting report, *The Nation's Report Card,* stated that in 2005, eighth graders in Illinois scored 278 out of 500 in mathematics, the same as the national average.

As of fall 2002, there were 776,622 students enrolled in college or graduate school; minority students comprised 31% of total postsecondary enrollment. As of 2005, Illinois had 173 degree-granting institutions. The University of Illinois system has both the largest and smallest public university campuses. The University of Illinois at Springfield was formerly Sangamon State University. Champaign–Urbana is the state's most populous campus. Nearly half of all Illinois college students attend one of the state's 48 public community colleges.

⁴²ARTS

The Illinois Arts Council was founded in 1965. In 2005, state organizations received 92 grants totaling $2,903,600 from the National Endowment for the Arts. The Illinois Humanities Council, founded in 1974, offers programs that include a lecture/presentation series program called the Heartland Chautauqua and the Odyssey Project, as of 2006 an ongoing opportunity, which offers free college-level courses in the humanities to individuals with incomes below the poverty level. In 2005, the National Endowment for the Humanities sponsored 49 grants for state programs, with a total contribution of $5,957,480. A humanities fellowship of $210,000 was awarded to the American Institute of Indian Studies in Chicago in 2003.

Chicago emerged in the late 19th century as the leading arts center of the Midwest, and as of 2005, it continued to hold this premier position. The major downstate facilities include the Krannert Center at the University of Illinois (Champaign–Urbana), founded in 1969—having served more than 350,000 people annually.

Architecture is the outstanding art form in Illinois. Chicago—where the first skyscrapers were built in the 1880s—has been a mecca for modern commercial and residential architects ever since the fire of 1871. The Art Institute of Chicago, incorporated in 1879, is the leading art museum in the state. Although its holdings, largely donated by wealthy Chicagoans, cover all the major periods, its French Impressionist collection is especially noteworthy. In 2005, the Art Institute of Chicago revealed the master plans for a new building—the last addition to the museum was made in 1988. The museum commissioned architect Renzo Piano to design the $200 million project; the new building was scheduled to open to the public in 2009. Another example of bold contemporary architecture is the $172-million State of Illinois Center in Chicago, which opened in 1985.

Theater groups abound—there were 116 theatrical producers in 1982—notably in Chicago, where the Second City comedy troupe and the Steppenwolf Theatre are located; the city's best playwrights and performers, however, often gravitate to Broadway in New York or Hollywood. Film production was an important industry in Illinois before 1920, when operations shifted to the sunnier climate and more opulent production facilities of southern California. By the early 1980s, however, the Illinois Film Office had staged an impressive comeback, and television films and motion pictures were being routinely shot in the state. In 2004, films

shot in Illinois included *Spiderman 2, I Robot, Oceans 12,* and *Batman Begins.*

The Chicago Symphony Orchestra, organized by Theodore Thomas in 1891, quickly acquired world stature; its permanent conductors have included Frederick Stock, Fritz Reiner, Sir George Solti, who regularly took the symphony on triumphant European tours, and Daniel Barenboim (since 1991). German immigrants founded many musical societies in Chicago in the late 19th century, when the city also became a major center of musical education. Opera flourished in Chicago in the early 20th century, collapsed during the early 1930s, but was reborn through the founding of the Lyric Opera in 1954. Chicago's most original musical contribution was jazz, imported from the South by black musicians in the 1920s. Such jazz greats as King Oliver, Louis Armstrong, Jelly Roll Morton, Benny Goodman, and Gene Krupa all worked or learned their craft in the speakeasies and jazz houses of the city's South Side. More recently, Chicago became the center of an urban blues movement, using electric rather than acoustic guitars and influenced by jazz. The Jazz Institute of Chicago was founded in 1969 and provides such programs as the Jazz Fair, also known as, the Winter Delights Jazz Fair and the JazzCity Series.

The seamy side of Chicago has fascinated writers throughout the 20th century. Well-known American novels set in Chicago include two muckraking works, Frank Norris's *The Pit* (1903) and Upton Sinclair's *The Jungle* (1906), as well as James T. Farrell's *Studs Lonigan* (1935) and Saul Bellow's *The Adventures of Augie March* (1953). Famous American plays associated with Chicago are *The Front Page* (1928), by Ben Hecht and Charles MacArthur, and *A Raisin in the Sun* (1959), by Lorraine Hansberry.

⁴³LIBRARIES AND MUSEUMS

For the fiscal year ending in June 2001, Illinois had 629 public library systems, with a total of 786 libraries, of which 157 were branches. Libraries and library science are particularly strong in Illinois. In that same year, the state's public library systems had a combined book and serial publications stock of 41,620,000 volumes and a total circulation of 83,703,000. The system also had 1,991,000 audio and 1,309,000 video items, 412,000 electronic format items (CD-ROMs, magnetic tapes, and disks), and 25 bookmobiles. The facilities in Peoria, Oak Park, Evanston, Rockford, and Quincy are noteworthy; the Chicago Public Library system (with 6,490,452 volumes) operates 89 branch libraries and the Illinois Regional Library for the Blind and Physically Handicapped. The outstanding libraries of the University of Illinois (Champaign–Urbana) and the University of Chicago (with over 8,000,000 and 6,419,936 volumes respectively) constitute the state's leading research facilities, and the University of Illinois has a famous library school. Principal historical collections are located at the Newberry Library in Chicago, the Illinois State Historical Society in Springfield, and the Chicago Historical Society. In fiscal year 2001, operating income for the public library system totaled $512,341,000, which included $2,850,000 in federal grants and $37,445,000 in state grants.

Illinois has 277 museums and historical sites. Chicago's Field Museum of Natural History, with an annual attendance of over 1.2 million, has sponsored numerous worldwide expeditions in the course of acquiring some 13 million anthropological, zoological, botanical, and geological specimens. The Museum of Science and Industry, near the University of Chicago, attracts two million visitors a year, mostly children, to see its exhibits of industrial technology. Also noteworthy are the Adler Planetarium, Shedd Aquarium, and the Oriental Institute Museum of the University of Chicago. The Brookfield Zoo, near Chicago, opened in 1934; smaller zoos can be found in Chicago's Lincoln Park and in Peoria, Elgin, and other cities.

Just about every town has one or more historic sites authenticated by the state. The most popular is New Salem, near Springfield, where Abraham Lincoln lived from 1831 to 1837. Its reconstruction, begun by press magnate William Randolph Hearst in 1906, includes one original cabin and numerous replicas. The most important archaeological sites are the Dixon Mounds, 40 mi (64 km) south of Peoria, and the Koster Excavation in Calhoun County, north of St. Louis, Missouri.

44 COMMUNICATIONS

Illinois has an extensive communications system. The state's households with telephones numbered about 90.1% of all households in 2004. In addition, by June of that same year there were 7,529,966 mobile wireless telephone subscribers. In 2003, 60.0% of Illinois households had a computer and 51.1% had Internet access. By June 2005, there were 1,854,004 high-speed lines in Illinois, 1,658,639 residential and 195,365 for business.

Illinois had 36 major AM and 130 major FM commercial radio stations in 2005, when 31 major television stations served the state. In 1999, the Chicago area had the third-largest number of television households of all metropolitan areas (3,204,710), with cable in 65%.

In 1979, WGN-TV in Chicago became a "superstation," with sports programs, movies, and advertising. Although the three major networks own stations in Chicago, they originate very little programming from the city. However, as a major advertising center, Chicago produces many commercials and industrial films. Most educational broadcasting in Illinois comes from state universities and the Chicago public and Catholic school systems.

A total of 259,713 Internet domain names were registered in the state in the year 2000.

45 PRESS

The state's first newspaper, the *Illinois Herald*, was begun in Kaskaskia in 1814. From the 1830s through the end of the 19th century, small-town weeklies exerted powerful political influence. After 1900, however, publishers discovered that they needed large circulations to appeal to advertisers, so they toned down their partisanship and began adding a broad range of features to attract a wider audience.

The most popular magazines published in Chicago are *Playboy* and *Ebony*. Many specialized trade and membership magazines, such as the *Lion* and the *Rotarian*, are published in Chicago, which is also the printing and circulation center for many magazines edited in New York. The popular *Cricket Magazine* for children is published in LaSalle-Peru.

As of 2005, Illinois had 26 morning newspapers (including all-day papers), 41 evening dailies, and 32 Sunday papers. The Illinois editions of St. Louis newspapers are also widely read. The Chicago *Tribune* was the eighth-largest daily and fourth-largest Sunday newspaper nationwide in 2005, based on circulation figures.

The following table shows the state's leading dailies with their 2005 estimated circulations:

AREA	NAME	DAILY	SUNDAY
Chicago	*Sun-Times* (m,S)	481,980	377,640
	Tribune (m,S)	600,988	963,927
Peoria	*Journal Star* (m,S)	76,879	87,188
Rockford	*Register Star* (m,S)	64,518	77,183
Springfield	*State Journal–Register* (m,S)	55,334	64,548

In 2005, there were 459 weekly publications in Illinois. Of these there are 310 paid weeklies, 64 free weeklies, and 85 combined weeklies. The total circulation of paid weeklies (1,420,940) and free weeklies (1,459,988) is 2,880,938. The Chicago paid weekly, *Southwest News-Herald*, ranked fifth in the United States based on its circulation of 54,000, and the Des Plaines, *Mount Prospect Journal*, ranked second in the United States based on circulation for combined weeklies, 90,996. Two Illinois shopping publications—the Chicago *Local Values* (1,672,500) and the Tinley Park *Penny Saver* (456,953)—ranked second and twelfth in the United States, respectively.

46 ORGANIZATIONS

Before the Civil War, Yankee-dominated towns and cities in northern Illinois sponsored lyceums, debating circles, women's clubs, temperance groups, and antislavery societies. During the 20th century, Chicago's size and central location attracted the headquarters of numerous national organizations, though far fewer than New York or, more recently, Washington, D.C.

In 2006, there were over 15,985 nonprofit organizations registered within the state, of which about 10,432 were registered as charitable, educational, or religious organizations. Major national service and fraternal bodies with headquarters in Chicago or nearby suburbs include the Benevolent and Protective Order of Elks of the USA, Lions Clubs International, Loyal Order of Moose, and Rotary International.

Chicago has long been a center for professional organizations, among them the most powerful single US medical group, the American Medical Association, founded in 1847, and the American Hospital Association, begun in 1898. Other major groups include associations of surgeons, dentists, veterinarians, osteopaths, and dietitians, as well as the Blue Cross and Blue Shield Association and the National Easter Seal Society. The national offices of the Alzheimer's Association are in Chicago.

The American Bar Association has its headquarters in Chicago, as do several smaller legal groups, including the American Judicature Society and the Commercial Law League of America. Librarians also have a base in Chicago; the American Library Association, the Society of American Archivists, and the associations of law and medical librarians are all headquartered in the city. The National Parent–Teacher Association is the only major national educational group. The Illinois State Historical Society promotes the study of state history.

A variety of trade organizations, such as the American Marketing Association, are based in Chicago, though many have moved to Washington, D.C. The American Farm Bureau Federation operates out of Park Ridge. The National Dairy Council is also based in the state. State agricultural organizations include the Illinois Corn Marketing Board, the Illinois Christmas Tree Association, and the Illinois Soybean Association. The National Women's Christian

Temperance Union, one of the most important of all US pressure groups in the 19th century, has its headquarters in Evanston. The World Bocce Association is based in Elmhurst.

47 TOURISM, TRAVEL, AND RECREATION

The tourist industry is of special importance to Chicago, which has become the nation's leading convention center. Business travel accounts for 36% of all state travel in 2004, when tourism and travel expenditures contributed some $24 billion to the state economy. Over 300,000 people were employed in the industry. In 2004, Illinois generated $764 billion in tourism payroll.

Chicago's chief tourist attractions are its museums, restaurants, and shops. Chicago also boasts the world's tallest building, the Sears Tower, which is 110 stories and 1,454 feet (443 meters) high. Chicago entertains visitors with museums (Shedd Aquarium, Field Museum, Museum of Science and Industry, and Art Institute), shopping (Magnificent Mile along Michigan Avenue), and the Brookfield Zoo. There are 42 state parks, 4 state forests, 36,659 campsites, and 25 state recreation places. Downtown Chicago is home to many public beaches and recreation areas on Lake Michigan. The Lincoln Home National Historic Site in Springfield was one of the state's most popular tourist attractions; the Abraham Lincoln Presidential Library and Museum opened to the public on 14 October 2004 (library) and 16–19 April 2005 (museum). Galesburg, Illinois is the home of poet Carl Sandburg. In Nauvoo, visitors can see a re-creation of the original Mormon Temple. Spoon River Drive, in Fulton County, will take tourists past places mentioned in Edgar Lee Masters' *Spoon River Anthology*. Hartford, Illinois, has a Lewis and Clark Interpretive Center. The Ronald Reagan home and visitor center is located in Dixon, Illinois. Swimming, bicycling, hiking, camping, horseback riding, fishing, and motorboating are the most popular recreational activities. Even more popular than hunting is wildlife observation, an activity that engages millions of Illinoisans annually.

48 SPORTS

Illinois has six major professional sports teams, all of which play in Chicago: the Cubs and the White Sox of Major League Baseball, the Bears of the National Football League, the Bulls of the National Basketball Association, the Fire of Major League Soccer, and the Blackhawks of the National Hockey League.

The Cubs last won a World Series in 1908, the White Sox in 1917. The Bears won the Super Bowl in 1985. The Bulls established a remarkable basketball dynasty fueled by the play of Michael Jordan, perhaps the best athlete in the history of basketball, winning National Basketaball Association (NBA) championships in 1991, 1992, 1993, 1996, 1997, and 1998. They were the first basketball team to win three consecutive championships since the Boston Celtics set the probably unbreakable record of eight consecutive titles from 1959 to 1966. The Bulls' string of titles ended, however, as Jordan retired in 1999 and the title-winning team was dismantled. The Blackhawks won the Stanley Cup in 1934, 1938, and 1961. The state also has minor league baseball, basketball, and hockey teams.

The White Sox built a new ballpark, Comiskey Park, which opened in 1993. The Cubs play their home games at Wrigley Field, perhaps one of the most venerable parks because of its ivy-covered outfield walls. Horse racing is very popular in the state, with pari-mutuel betting allowed. The Golden Glove Boxing Tournament is held annually in February in Chicago.

In collegiate sports, the emphasis is on basketball and football. The University of Illinois and Northwestern University compete in the Big Ten Conference. Illinois won the Rose Bowl in 1947, 1952, and 1964 and was named National Champion in 1923. In a remarkable revival of its football program, Northwestern won its first Big Ten title in 46 years in 1995. The Northwestern Wildcats played in the Rose Bowl for the first time since 1949, when they recorded their only victory in the New Year's Day game. Southern Illinois won the National Invitational Tournament in basketball in 1967. The DePaul Blue Demons of Conference USA consistently rank high among college basketball teams.

49 FAMOUS ILLINOISANS

Abraham Lincoln (b.Kentucky, 1809–65), 16th president of the United States, is the outstanding figure in Illinois history, having lived and built his political career in the state between 1830 and 1861. The only Illinois native to be elected president is Ronald Reagan (1911–2004), who left the state after graduating from Eureka College to pursue his film and political careers in California. Ulysses S. Grant (b.Ohio, 1822–85), the nation's 18th president, lived in Galena on the eve of the Civil War. Adlai E. Stevenson (b.Kentucky, 1835–1914), founder of a political dynasty, served as US vice president from 1893 to 1897, but was defeated for the same office in 1900. His grandson, also named Adlai E. Stevenson (b.California, 1900–65), served as governor of Illinois from 1949 to 1953, was the Democratic presidential nominee in 1952 and 1956, and ended his career as US ambassador to the United Nations. Charles Gates Dawes (b.Ohio, 1865–1951), a Chicago financier, served as vice president from 1925 to 1929 and shared the 1925 Nobel Peace Prize for the Dawes Plan to reorganize German finances. William Jennings Bryan (1860–1925), a leader of the free-silver and Populist movements, was the Democratic presidential nominee in 1896, 1900, and 1908.

US Supreme Court justices associated with Illinois include David Davis (b.Maryland, 1815–86); John M. Harlan (1899–1971); Chicago-born Arthur Goldberg (1908–90), who also served as US secretary of labor and succeeded Stevenson as UN ambassador; Harry A. Blackmun (1908–97); and John Paul Stevens (b.1920). Melville Fuller (b.Maine, 1833–1910) served as chief justice from 1888 to 1910.

Many other politicians who played important roles on the national scene drew their support form the people of Illinois. They include Stephen Douglas (b.Vermont, 1813–61), senator from 1847 to 1861, Democratic Party leader and 1860 presidential candidate, but equally famous as Lincoln's opponent in a series of debates on slavery in 1858; Lyman Trumbull (b.Connecticut, 1813–96), senator from 1855 to 1873 who helped secure passage of the 13th and 14th amendments to the US Constitution; Joseph "Uncle Joe" Cannon (b.North Carolina, 1836–1926), Republican congressman from Danville for half a century and autocratic Speaker of the House from 1903 to 1911; Henry Rainey (1860–1934), Democratic Speaker of the House during 1933–34; Everett McKinley Dirksen (1896–1969), senator and colorful Republican leader during the 1950s and 1960s; Charles H. Percy (b.Florida, 1919), Republican senator from 1967 to 1985; John B. Anderson (b.1922), Republican congressman for 20 years and an independent presidential candidate in 1980; and Robert H. Michel (b.1923), House Republican leader in the 1980s.

Noteworthy governors of the state, in addition to Stevenson, were Richard Yates (b.Kentucky, 1815–73), who maintained Illinois's loyalty to the Union during the Civil War and Richard J. Daley (1902–76) was the Democratic boss and mayor of Chicago from 1955 to 1976.

Phyllis Schlafly (b.Missouri, 1924) of Alton became nationally known as an antifeminist conservative crusader during the 1970s. An outstanding Illinoisan was Jane Addams (1860–1935), founder of Hull House (1889), author, reformer, prohibitionist, feminist, and tireless worker for world peace; in 1931, she shared the Nobel Peace Prize. A Nobel award in literature went to Saul Bellow (b.Canada, 1915–2005), and the economics prize was given to Milton Friedman (b.New York, 1912), leader of the so-called Chicago School of economists, and to Theodore Schultz (b.South Dakota, 1902–98) in 1979.

Some of the most influential Illinoisans have been religious leaders; many of them also exercised social and political influence. Notable are Methodist circuit rider Peter Cartwright (b.Virginia, 1785–1872); Dwight Moody (b.Massachusetts, 1837–99), leading force in the National Women's Christian Temperance Union and the feminist cause; Mother Frances Xavier Cabrini (b.Italy, 1850–1917), the first American to be canonized; Bishop Fulton J. Sheen (1895–1979), influential spokesman for the Roman Catholic Church; Elijah Muhammad (Elijah Poole, b.Georgia, 1897–1975), leader of the Black Muslim movement; and Jesse Jackson (b.North Carolina, 1941), civil rights leader and one of the most prominent black spokesmen of the 1980s and 1990s.

Outstanding business and professional leaders who lived in Illinois include John Deere (b.Vermont, 1804–86), industrialist and inventor of the steel plow; Cyrus Hall McCormick (b.Virginia, 1809–84), inventor of the reaping machine; Nathan Davis (1817–1904), the "father of the American Medical Association"; railroad car inventor George Pullman (b.New York 1831–97); meatpacker Philip Armour (b.New York, 1832–1901); merchant Marshall Field (b.Massachusetts, 1834–1906); merchant Aaron Montgomery Ward (b.New Jersey, 1843–1913); sporting-goods manufacturer Albert G. Spalding (1850–1915); breakfast-food manufacturer Charles W. Post (1854–1911); William Rainey Harper (b.Ohio, 1856–1906), first president of the University of Chicago; and lawyer Clarence Darrow (b.Ohio, 1857–1938).

Artists who worked for significant periods in Illinois (usually in Chicago) include architects William Le Baron Jenney (b.Massachusetts, 1832–1907), Dankmar Adler (b.Germany, 1844–1900), Daniel H. Burnham (b.New York, 1846–1912), John Wellborn Root (b.Georgia, 1850–91), Louis Sullivan (b.Massachusetts, 1856–1924), Frank Lloyd Wright (b.Wisconsin, 1869–1959), and Ludwig Mies van der Rohe (b.Germany, 1886–1969).

Important writers include humorist Finley Peter Dunne (1867–1936), creator of the fictional saloonkeeper-philosopher Mr. Dooley, and novelists Hamlin Garland (b.Wisconsin, 1860–1940), Edgar Rice Burroughs (1875–1950), John Dos Passos (1896–1970), Ernest Hemingway (1899–1961), and James Farrell (1904–79).

Performing artists connected with the state include opera stars Mary Garden (b.Scotland, 1877–1967) and Sherrill Milnes (b.1935); clarinetist Benny Goodman (1909–86); pop singers Mel Torme (1925–99) and Grace Slick (b.1939); jazz musician Miles Davis (b.1926–91); showmen Gower Champion (1921–80) and Robert Louis "Bob" Fosse (b.1927–87); comedians Jack Benny (Benjamin Kubelsky, 1894–1974), Harvey Korman (b.1927), Bob Newhart (b.1929), and Richard Pryor (1940–2005); and a long list of stage and screen stars, including Gloria Swanson (1899–1983), Ralph Bellamy (b.1904–91), Robert Young (1907–98), Karl Malden (Malden Sekulovich, b.1913), William Holden (1918–81), Jason Robards Jr. (1922–2000), Charlton Heston (b.1922), Rock Hudson (Roy Fitzgerald, 1925–85), Donald O'Connor (1925–2003), Bruce Dern (b.1936), and Raquel Welch (Raquel Tejeda, b.1942).

Dominant figures in the Illinois sports world include Ernest "Ernie" Banks (b.Texas, 1931) of the Chicago Cubs; Robert "Bobby" Hull (b.Canada, 1939) of the Chicago Black Hawks; owner George Halas (1895–83); and running backs Harold Edward "Red" Grange (b.Pennsylvania, 1903–91), Gale Sayers (b.Kansas, 1943), and Walter Payton (b.Mississippi, 1954–99) of the Chicago Bears; and collegiate football coach Amos Alonzo Stagg (b.New Jersey, 1862–1965).

⁵⁰BIBLIOGRAPHY

Best, Wallace D. *Passionately Human, No Less Divine: Religion and Culture in Black Chicago, 1915–1952.* Princeton, N.J.: Princeton University Press, 2005.

Biles, Roger. *Illinois: A History of the Land and Its People.* De Kalb: Northern Illinois University Press, 2005.

Carrier, Lois. *Illinois: Crossroads of a Continent.* Urbana: University of Illinois Press, 1993.

Council of State Governments. *The Book of the States, 2006 Edition.* Lexington, Ky.: Council of State Governments, 2006.

Hendricks, Wanda A. *Gender, Race, and Politics in the Midwest: Black Club Women in Illinois.* Bloomington: Indiana University Press, 1998.

Gove, Samuel Kimball. *Illinois Politics and Government: The Expanding Metropolitan Frontier.* Lincoln: University of Nebraska Press, 1996.

Illinois, State of. Department of Commerce and Community Affairs. *Illinois Data Book,* Springfield: Illinois Department of Commerce and Community Affairs. 1994.

Petterchak, Janice A. (ed.). *Illinois History: An Annotated Bibliography.* Westport, Conn.: Greenwood, 1995.

Simeone, James. *Democracy and Slavery in Frontier Illinois: The Bottomland Republic.* De Kalb: Northern Illinois University Press, 2000.

Striner, Richard. *Father Abraham: Lincoln's Relentless Struggle to End Slavery.* New York: Oxford University Press, 2006.

US Department of Commerce, Economics and Statistics Administration, US Census Bureau. *Illinois, 2000. Summary Social, Economic, and Housing Characteristics: 2000 Census of Population and Housing.* Washington, D.C.: US Government Printing Office, 2003.

INDIANA

State of Indiana

ORIGIN OF STATE NAME: Named "land of Indians" for the many Indian tribes that formerly lived in the state. **NICKNAME:** The Hoosier State. **CAPITAL:** Indianapolis. **ENTERED UNION:** 11 December 1816 (19th). **SONG:** "On the Banks of the Wabash, Far Away." **MOTTO:** The Crossroads of America. **FLAG:** A flaming torch representing liberty is surrounded by 19 gold stars against a blue background. The word "Indiana" is above the flame. **OFFICIAL SEAL:** In a pioneer setting, a farmer fells a tree while a buffalo flees from the forest and across the prairie; in the background, the sun sets over distant hills. The words "Seal of the State of Indiana 1816" surround the scene. **BIRD:** Cardinal. **FLOWER:** Peony. **TREE:** Tulip poplar. **LEGAL HOLIDAYS:** New Year's Day, 1 January; Birthday of Martin Luther King Jr., 3rd Monday in January; Good Friday, Friday before Easter, March or April; Primary Election Day, 1st Tuesday after 1st Monday in May in even-numbered years; Memorial Day, last Monday in May; Independence Day, 4 July; Labor Day, 1st Monday in September; Columbus Day, 2nd Monday in October; Election Day, 1st Tuesday after 1st Monday in November in even-numbered years; Veterans' Day, 11 November; Thanksgiving Day, 4th Thursday in November; Lincoln's Birthday, 12 February (observed the day after Thanksgiving); Christmas Day, 25 December; Washington's Birthday, 3rd Monday in February (observed the day after Christmas). **TIME:** 7 AM EST = noon GMT; 6 AM CST = noon GMT.

¹LOCATION, SIZE, AND EXTENT

Situated in the eastern north-central United States, Indiana is the smallest of the 12 midwestern states and ranks 38th in size among the 50 states.

Indiana's total area is 36,185 sq mi (93,720 sq km), of which land takes up 35,932 sq mi (93,064 sq km) and water the remaining 253 sq mi (656 sq km). Shaped somewhat like a vertical quadrangle, with irregular borders on the s and w, the state extends about 160 mi (257 km) E–W and about 280 mi (451 km) N–S.

Indiana is bordered on the N by Michigan (with part of the line passing through Lake Michigan); on the E by Ohio; on the SE and s by Kentucky (the entire line formed by the north bank of the Ohio River); and on the w by Illinois (with the line in the sw demarcated by the Wabash River). The total boundary length of Indiana is 1,696 mi (2,729 km).

Indiana's geographic center is located in Boone County, 14 mi (23 km) NNW of Indianapolis.

²TOPOGRAPHY

Indiana has two principal types of terrain: slightly rolling land in the northern half of the state and rugged hills in the southern half, extending to the Ohio River. The highest point in the state, a hill in Franklin Township (Wayne County), is 1,257 ft (383 m) above sea level; the lowest point, on the Ohio River, is 320 ft (98 m). The mean elevation is approximately 700 ft (214 m). The richest soil is in the north-central region, where the retreating glacier during the last Ice Age enriched the soil, scooped out lakes, and cut passageways for rivers.

Four-fifths of the state's land is drained by the Wabash River, which flows westward across the north-central region and turns southward to empty into the Ohio, and by its tributaries, the White, Eel, Mississinewa, and Tippecanoe rivers. The northern region is drained by the Maumee River, which flows into Lake Erie at Toledo, Ohio, and by the Kankakee River, which joins the Illinois River in Illinois. In the southwest, the two White River forks empty into the Wabash, and in the southeast, the Whitewater River flows into the Ohio.

In addition to Lake Michigan on the northwestern border, there are more than 400 lakes in the northern part of the state. The largest lakes include the Wawasee, Maxinkuckee, Freeman, and Shafer. There are mineral springs at French Lick and West Baden in Orange County and two large caves at Wyandotte and Marengo in adjoining Crawford County.

The underlying rock strata found in Indiana were formed from sediments deposited during the Paleozoic Era, when the land was submerged. About 400 million years ago, the first uplift of land, the Cincinnati arch, divided the Indiana region into two basins, a small one in the north and a large one in the southwest. The land was steadily elevated and at one time formed a lush swamp, which dried up some 200 million years ago when the climate cooled. During the Ice Ages, about five-sixths of the land lay under ice some 2,000 ft (600 m) thick. The retreat of the glacier more than 10,000 years ago left excellent topsoil and drainage conditions in Indiana.

³CLIMATE

Temperatures vary from the extreme north to the extreme south of the state; the annual mean temperature is 49°F–58°F (9°c–12°c) in the north and 57°F (14°c) in the south. The annual average for Indianapolis is 53°F (11°c). Although Indiana sometimes has temperatures below 0°F (-18°c) during the winter, the average temperatures in January range between 17°F (-8°c) and 35°F (2°c). Average temperatures during July vary from 63°F (17°c) to 88°F

(31°C). The record high for the state was 116°F (47°C) set on 14 July 1936 at Collegeville, and the record low was -36°F (-38°C) on 19 January 1994 at New Whiteland.

The growing season averages 155 days in the north and 185 days in the south. Rainfall is distributed fairly evenly throughout the year, although drought sometimes occurs in the southern region. The average annual precipitation in the state is 40 in (102 cm), ranging from about 35 in (89 cm) near Lake Michigan to 45 in (114 cm) along the Ohio River; during 1971–2000, Indianapolis had an average of 41 in (104 cm) per year. The annual snowfall in Indiana averages less than 22 in (56 cm). Average wind speed in the state is 8 mph (13 km/h), but gales sometimes occur along the shores of Lake Michigan, and there are occasional tornadoes in the interior.

Parts of Indiana are prone to severe thunderstorms and tornados. On 6 November 2005, a tornado that swept through Evansville left 23 people dead.

4 FLORA AND FAUNA

Because the state has a relatively uniform climate, plant species are distributed fairly generally throughout Indiana. There are 124 native tree species, including 17 varieties of oak, as well as black walnut, sycamore, and tulip tree (yellow poplar), the state tree. Fruit trees—apple, cherry, peach, and pear—are common. Local indigenous species—now reduced because of industrialization and urbanization—include the persimmon, black gum, and southern cypress along the Ohio River; tamarack and bog willow in the northern marsh; and white pine, sassafras, and pawpaw near Lake Michigan. American elderberry and bittersweet are common shrubs, while various jack-in-the-pulpits and spring beauties are among the indigenous wild flowers. The peony is the state flower. As of April 2006, Mead's milkweed and Pitcher's thistle were considered threatened and running buffalo clover was considered endangered.

Although the presence of wolves and coyotes has been reported occasionally, the red fox is Indiana's only common carnivorous mammal. Other native mammals are the common cottontail, muskrat, raccoon, opossum, and several types of squirrel. Many waterfowl and marsh birds, including the black duck and great blue heron, inhabit northern Indiana, while the field sparrow, yellow warbler, and red-headed woodpecker nest in central Indiana. Various catfish, pike, bass, and sunfish are native to state waters.

The US Fish and Wildlife Service listed 21 Indiana animal species (vertebrates and invertebrates) as threatened or endangered as of April 2006. Among these are the bald eagle, Indiana and gray bats, gray wolf, piping plover, and two species of butterfly.

5 ENVIRONMENTAL PROTECTION

During the 19th century, early settlers cut down much of Indiana's forests for farms, leaving the land vulnerable to soil erosion and flood damage, particularly in the southern part of the state. In 1919, the legislature created the State Department of Conservation (which in 1965 became the Department of Natural Resources) to reclaim worn-out soil, prevent further erosion, and control the pollution of rivers and streams. In 1986, the Indiana Department of Environmental Management was initiated as a watchdog over the environmental laws and regulations designed to preserve the environmental well-being of the state. Still, almost 85% of Indiana's original wetlands have been lost and, in 1997, it was estimated that the state continues to lose 1–3% of its remaining wetlands per year.

The Department of Natural Resources regulates the use of Indiana's lands, waters, forests, and wildlife resources. Specifically, the department manages land subject to flooding, preserves natural rivers and streams, grants mining permits and regulates stripmining, plugs and repairs faulty/abandoned oil and gas wells, administers existing state parks and preserves and buys land for new ones, regulates hunting and fishing, and examines any damage to fish and wildlife by investigating industrial accidents. Also, the department is responsible for preventing soil erosion and flood damage and for conserving and disposing of water in the state's watersheds.

The Indiana Department of Environmental Management (IDEM) seeks to protect public health through the implementation and management of environmental programs. The focus of the environmental programs is to protect Indiana's air, land, and water resources, as the proper management of these resources contribute to the health and well-being of the citizens of Indiana. Prior to April 1986, these environmental programs were under the auspices of the State Board of Health (ISBH).

In addition to the IDEM and the Department of Natural Resources, the following boards exist to aid in environmental involvement: Air Pollution Control Board, Water Pollution Control Board, Pollution Prevention Control Board, and Solid Waste Management Board.

In 1990, Indiana lawmakers passed landmark legislation that created an Office of Pollution Prevention and Technical Assistance within IDEM. OPPTA's long-term goal is to ensure that all Indiana industries use pollution prevention techniques as the preferred method for reducing waste and protecting the environment. This policy, along with programs that encourage reuse and recycling and discourage landfilling and incineration, will help conserve natural resources.

In March 1990, Indiana's Water Pollution Control Board adopted some of the strictest water quality standards in the nation. The standards set criteria for more than 90 chemicals and designated almost all water bodies for protection of aquatic life and recreational use. These standards will help improve and protect the quality of water in Indiana's lakes, rivers, and streams.

The IDEM devotes much attention to identifying, cleaning up, and remediating all forms of toxic contamination. On 31 January 1986, the agency gained federal delegation for the Resource Conservation and Recovery Act (RCRA), which governs the generation, storage, treatment, transport, and disposal of all hazardous waste. Beyond the RCRA, the IDEM encourages companies to examine their production cycles and to adopt processes that won't create hazardous waste. The Department of Environmental Management offers technical assistance for the installation of pollution prevention equipment and encourages consumers to rethink their use and disposal of hazardous household goods and chemicals. When that waste is not properly handled and disposed of, expensive remediation is often required. In 2003, 234.8 million lb of toxic chemicals were released in the state. In 2003, the US Environment Protection Agency's (EPA) database listed 210 hazardous waste sites in Indiana, 29 of which were on the National Priorities List as of 2006. In 2005, the EPA spent over $8.8 million through

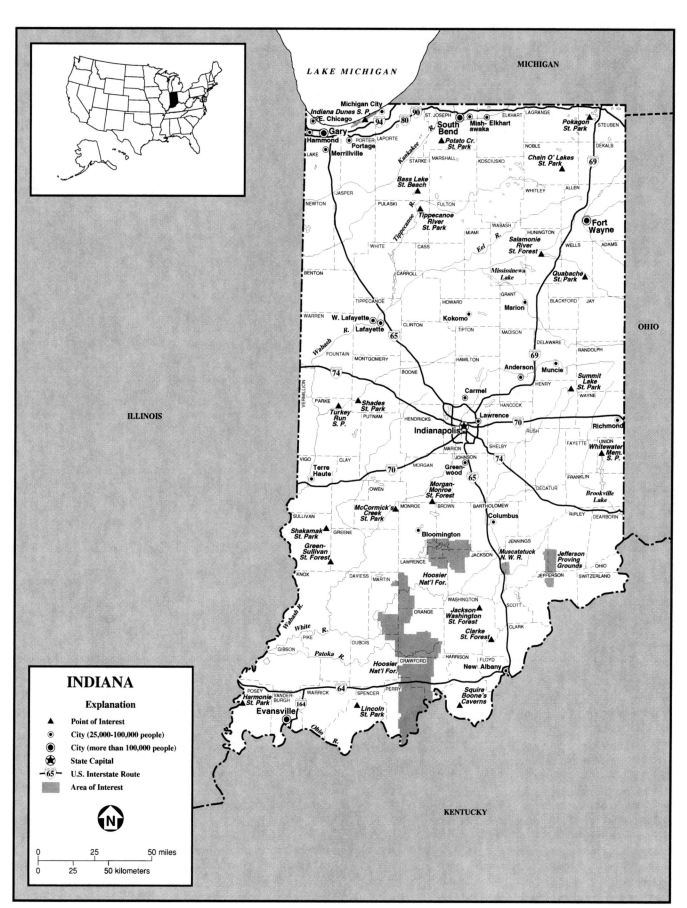

LAKE MICHIGAN

MICHIGAN

Michigan City
Indiana Dunes S. P.
E. Chicago
Gary
Hammond
Portage
Merrillville

ST. JOSEPH
South Bend
Mish- Elkhart
awaka

LAGRANGE

STEUBEN

Pokagon
St. Park

DEKALB

Chain O' Lakes
St. Park

Potato Cr.
St. Park

Kankakee

STARKE
MARSHALL
KOSCIUSKO

NOBLE

69

Bass Lake
St. Beach

PULASKI
FULTON

WHITLEY

ALLEN

Tippecanoe
River
St. Park

MIAMI
WABASH

Fort
Wayne

Salamonie
River
St. Forest

HUNINGTON
WELLS
ADAMS

WHITE
CASS

Eel

Mississinewa
Lake

Quabache
St. Park

CARROLL

GRANT

BLACKFORD
JAY

BENTON

TIPPECANOE

HOWARD

Kokomo

TIPTON

W. Lafayette
Lafayette

CLINTON

MADISON

DELAWARE

RANDOLPH

WARREN

65

FOUNTAIN

BOONE

HAMILTON

Anderson
Muncie

69

Summit
Lake
St. Park

WAYNE

MONTGOMERY

Carmel

HENRY

74

PARKE

Shades
St. Park

HENDRICKS

Lawrence

70

Richmond

Turkey
Run
S. P.

PUTNAM

Indianapolis

HANCOCK

RUSH

FAYETTE
UNION

Whitewater
Mem.
S. P.

VERMILLION

MARION

SHELBY

VIGO
CLAY

70

MORGAN

Greenwood

JOHNSON

74

FRANKLIN

DECATUR

Brookville
Lake

Terre
Haute

65

OWEN

Morgan-
Monroe
St. Forest

BROWN

BARTHOLOMEW

McCormick's
Creek
St. Park

MONROE

Columbus

RIPLEY
DEARBORN

SULLIVAN

Shakamak
St. Park

GREENE

Bloomington

JENNINGS

Green-
Sullivan
St. Forest

Muscatatuck
N. W. R.

Jefferson
Proving
Grounds

KNOX

DAVIESS
MARTIN

Hoosier
Nat'l For.

JACKSON

OHIO

JEFFERSON
SWITZERLAND

Wabash R.

White

R.

PIKE

DUBOIS

LAWRENCE

WASHINGTON

Jackson
Washington
St. Forest

Clarke
St. Forest

SCOTT

CLARK

GIBSON

Patoka

R.

Hoosier
Nat'l For.

CRAWFORD

HARRISON

FLOYD

New Albany

POSEY
VANDER-
BURGH

WARRICK

64

SPENCER

PERRY

Squire
Boone's
Caverns

Harmonie
St. Park

164

Evansville

Lincoln
St. Park

Ohio

R.

KENTUCKY

ILLINOIS

OHIO

INDIANA

Explanation

▲ Point of Interest

◉ City (25,000-100,000 people)

◎ City (more than 100,000 people)

★ State Capital

—65— U.S. Interstate Route

▨ Area of Interest

N

| 0 | 25 | 50 miles |

| 0 | 25 | 50 kilometers |

Indiana—Counties, County Seats, and County Areas and Populations

COUNTY	COUNTY SEAT	LAND AREA (SQ MI)	POPULATION (2005 EST.)	COUNTY	COUNTY SEAT	LAND AREA (SQ MI)	POPULATION (2005 EST.)
Adams	Decatur	340	33,849	Madison	Anderson	453	130,412
Allen	Fort Wayne	659	344,006	Marion	Indianapolis	396	863,133
Bartholomew	Columbus	409	73,540	Marshall	Plymouth	444	46,945
Benton	Fowler	407	9,039	Martin	Shoals	339	10,386
Blackford	Hardford City	166	13,849	Miami	Peru	369	35,620
Boone	Lebanon	424	52,061	Monroe	Bloomington	385	121,407
Brown	Nashville	312	15,154	Montgomery	Crawfordsville	505	38,239
Carroll	Delphi	372	20,426	Morgan	Martinsville	409	69,778
Cass	Logansport	414	40,130	Newton	Kentland	401	14,456
Clark	Jeffersonville	376	101,592	Noble	Albion	413	47,448
Clay	Brazil	360	27,142	Ohio	Rising Sun	87	5,874
Clinton	Frankfort	405	34,091	Orange	Paoli	408	19,770
Crawford	English	307	11,216	Owen	Spencer	386	22,823
Daviess	Washington	432	30,466	Parke	Rockville	444	17,362
Dearborn	Lawrenceburg	307	49,082	Perry	Cannelton	481	19,032
Decatur	Greensburg	373	25,184	Pike	Petersburg	341	12,766
Dekalb	Auburn	364	41,659	Porter	Valparaiso	419	157,772
Delaware	Muncie	392	116,362	Posey	Mt.vernon	410	26,852
Dubois	Jasper	429	40,858	Pulaski	Winamac	435	13,783
Elkhart	Goshen	466	195,362	Putnam	Greencastle	482	36,957
Fayette	Connersville	215	24,885	Randolph	Winchester	454	26,684
Floyd	New Albany	150	71,997	Ripley	Versailles	447	27,710
Fountain	Covington	398	17,462	Rush	Rushville	408	17,823
Franklin	Brookville	385	23,085	St. Joseph	South Bend	459	266,160
Fulton	Rochester	369	20,665	Scott	Scottsburg	192	23,820
Gibson	Princeton	490	33,408	Shelby	Shelbyville	412	43,766
Grant	Marion	415	70,557	Spencer	Rockport	400	20,528
Greene	Bloomfield	546	33,479	Starke	Knox	309	22,933
Hamilton	Noblesville	398	240,685	Steuben	Angola	308	33,773
Hancock	Greenfield	307	63,138	Sullivan	Sullivan	452	21,763
Harrison	Corydon	486	36,827	Switzerland	Vevay	224	9,718
Hendricks	Danville	409	127,483	Tippecanoe	Lafayette	502	153,875
Henry	New Castle	395	47,244	Tipton	Tipton	261	16,385
Howard	Kokomo	293	84,977	Union	Liberty	163	7,208
Huntington	Huntington	366	38,236	Vanderburgh	Evansville	236	173,187
Jackson	Brownstown	514	42,237	Vermillion	Newport	260	16,562
Jasper	Rensselaer	561	31,876	Vigo	Terre Haute	405	102,592
Jay	Portland	384	21,606	Wabash	Wabash	398	33,843
Jefferson	Madison	363	32,430	Warren	Williamsport	366	8,785
Jennings	Vernon	378	28,427	Warrick	Boonville	391	56,362
Johnson	Franklin	321	128,436	Washington	Salem	516	27,885
Knox	Vincennes	520	38,366	Wayne	Richmond	404	69,192
Kosciusko	Warsaw	540	76,072	Wells	Bluffton	370	28,085
Lagrange	Lagrange	380	36,875	White	Monticello	506	24,463
Lake	Crown Point	501	493,297	Whitley	Columbia City	336	32,323
Laporte	Laporte	600	110,512	**TOTALS**		36,036	6,271,973
Lawrence	Bedford	452	46,403				

the Superfund program for the cleanup of hazardous waste sites in the state. Also in 2005, federal EPA grants awarded to the state included $25.9 million for a wastewater revolving loan program and $11.2 million for a drinking water revolving fund.

Since the IDEM was established in 1986, enforcement activity has increased fivefold. This is due, in part, to its unified Office of Enforcement, which consolidated enforcement staff who had been working separately in offices for air, solid waste, hazardous waste, and water. A key strategy in enforcement actions is to encourage violators to adopt pollution-prevention practices or restore environmental damage as part of their penalty.

Some of the state's most serious environmental challenges lie in Lake and Porter counties in northwest Indiana. A century of spills, emissions, and discharges to the environment there require comprehensive, regionally coordinated programs. In 1991, the IDEM opened a regional office in Gary to act as a liaison with local officials, concerned citizens, and industry. This office is helping drive the development of a comprehensive remediation plan, including the involvement of concerned citizens through the Citizen's Advisory for the Remediation of the Environment (CARE) committee. The Northwest Indiana Remedial Action Plan (RAP) is a threephased program designed especially for the Grand Calumet River and the Indiana Harbor Ship Canal. Both waterways are heavily contaminated and, if left in their current state, would certainly degrade the waters of Lake Michigan, the primary source of drinking water for the northwest Indiana area. The RAP is a direct result of treaties of the International Joint Commission, a coalition formed to protect the waters between the United States and Canada.

The IDEM now offers expertise and approval for voluntary cleanup plans. When a voluntary cleanup is completed properly, the IDEM will issue a certificate of completion, and the governor will provide a covenant not to sue for further action involving the damage revealed to the IDEM. This innovative program has led to many cleanups at virtually no cost to Indiana citizens.

6 POPULATION

Indiana ranked 15th in population in the United States with an estimated total of 6,271,973 in 2005, an increase of 3.1% since 2000. Between 1990 and 2000, Indiana's population grew from 5,544,159 to 6,080,485, an increase of 9.7%. The population is projected to reach 6.5 million by 2015 and 6.7 million by 2025. The population density in 2004 was 173.9 persons per sq mi. In 2004, the median age was 35.7. Persons under 18 years old accounted for 25.7% of the population, while 12.4% was age 65 or older.

Although the French founded the first European settlement in Indiana in 1717, the census population was no more than 5,641 in 1800, when the Indiana Territory was established. Settlers flocked to the state during the territorial period, and the population rose to 24,520 by 1810. After Indiana became a state in 1816, its population grew even more rapidly, reaching 147,178 in 1820 and 988,416 in 1850. At the outbreak of the Civil War, Indiana had 1,350,428 inhabitants and ranked fifth in population among the states.

Indiana was relatively untouched by the great waves of European immigration that swept the United States from 1860 to 1880. In 1880, when the state's population was 1,978,301, Indiana had fewer foreign-born residents (about 7% of its population) than any other northern state. Indiana had doubled its population to 5,193,669 by the time of the 1970 Census.

Indianapolis, the capital and largest city, expanded its boundaries in 1970 to coincide with those of Marion County, thereby increasing its area to 388 sq mi (1,005 sq km) and its population by some 50% (the city and county limits also include four self-governing communities). The estimated population was 784,242 in 2004; the Indianapolis metropolitan area had an estimated population of 1,621,613. Other cities with 2004 populations estimated at more than 100,000 were Fort Wayne, 219,351; Evansville, 117,156; and South Bend, 105,494. All of these cities suffered population declines in the 1970s, 1980s, and 1990s.

7 ETHNIC GROUPS

Originally an agricultural state, Indiana was settled by Native Americans moving west, by a small group of French Creoles, and by European immigrant farmers. Although railroad building and industrialization attracted other immigrant groups—notably the Irish, Hungarians, Italians, Poles, Croats, Slovaks, and Syrians—foreign immigration to Indiana declined sharply in the 20th century, although there was a rebound in the final decade. As of 2000, foreign-born Hoosiers numbered 186,534 (3% of the total state population), nearly double the figure of 94,263 in 1990.

Restrictions on foreign immigration and the availability of jobs spurred the migration of black Americans to Indiana after World War I; by 2000, the state had 510,034 blacks, representing about 8.4% of the total population. Approximately one-fifth of all Indiana blacks live in the industrial city of Gary. In 2004, 8.8% of the population was black.

In 2000, approximately 3.5% (214,536) of Indiana's population was of Hispanic or Latino origin, up sharply from 1.8% (99,000) in 1990. Hispanics and Latinos accounted for 4.3% of the population in 2004. The Asian population was estimated at 59,126 in 2000,

including 14,685 Asian Indians (up from 6,093 in 1990), 12,531 Chinese (6,128 in 1990), 6,674 Filipinos, 7,502 Koreans, 5,065 Japanese, and 4,843 Vietnamese (2,420 in 1990). Pacific Islanders numbered 2,005. In 2004, 1.2% of the population was Asian, and the Pacific Islander population was negligible.

The natives of early-19th-century Indiana came from a variety of Algonkian-speaking tribes, including Delaware, Shawnee, and Potawatomi. By 1846, however, all Indian lands in the state had been seized or ceded, and most Native Americans had been removed. In 2000, there were 15,815 Native Americans. In 2004, 0.3% of the population was composed of Native Americans.

8 LANGUAGES

Several Algonkian Indian tribes, including some from the east, met the white settlers who arrived in Indiana in the early 1800s. The heritage of the Delaware, Potawatomi, Miami, and other groups survives in many place-names, from Kokomo to Nappanee, Muncie, and Shipshewana.

In 2000, 93.5% of all Hoosiers five years old and older spoke only English at home, down from 95.2% in 1990.

The following table gives selected statistics from the 2000 Census for language spoken at home by persons five years old and over. The category "Other West Germanic languages" includes Dutch, Pennsylvania Dutch, and Afrikaans. The category "Other Slavic languages" includes Czech, Slovak, and Ukrainian.

LANGUAGE	NUMBER	PERCENT
Population 5 years and over	**5,657,818**	**100.0**
Speak only English	5,295,736	93.6
Speak a language other than English	362,082	6.4
Speak a language other than English	**362,082**	**6.4**
Spanish or Spanish Creole	185,576	3.3
German	44,142	0.8
French (incl. Patois, Cajun)	18,065	0.3
Other West Germanic languages	15,706	0.3
Chinese	9,912	0.2
Polish	7,831	0.1
Serbo-Croatian	5,843	0.1
Japanese	5,339	0.1
Arabic	5,338	0.1
Other Slavic languages	5,129	0.1
Korean	5,032	0.1
Italian	4,798	0.1
Vietnamese	4,746	0.1
Greek	4,233	0.1
Tagalog	4,016	0.1

Except for the dialect mixture in the industrial northwest corner and the Northern-dialect fringe of counties along the Michigan border, Indiana speech is essentially that of the South Midland pioneers from south of the Ohio River, with a transition zone toward North Midland, north of Indianapolis. Between the Ohio River and Indianapolis, South Midland speakers use evening for late afternoon, eat *clabber cheese* instead of cottage cheese, are wary of *frogstools* rather than toadstools, once held that *toadfrogs* and not plain toads caused warts, eat *goobers* instead of peanuts at a ball game, and may therefore be *sick at the stomach*. In the same region, some Hoosiers use a few Midland words that also occur north of Indianapolis, such as *rock fence* (stone wall), *French harp* (harmonica), *mud dauber* (wasp), *shucks* (leaves on an ear of corn), and perhaps even some expanding North Midland words, such as *run* (a small stream), *teetertotter* (seesaw), and *fishworm*. North of Indianapolis, speakers with a Midland Pennsylvania background wish on the *pullybone* of a chicken, may use a *trestle* (sawhorse), and are likely to get their hands *greezy* rather than *greasy*. Such was the Hoosier talk of James Whitcomb Riley.

⁹RELIGIONS

The first branch of Christianity to gain a foothold in Indiana was Roman Catholicism, introduced by the French settlers in the early 18th century. The first Protestant church was founded near Charlestown by Baptists from Kentucky in 1798. Three years later, a Methodist church was organized at Springville; in 1806, Presbyterians established a church near Vincennes; and the following year, Quakers built their first meetinghouse at Richmond. The Disciples of Christ, Lutherans, the United Brethren, Mennonites, and Jews were among the later 19th-century arrivals.

A dissident religious sect, the Shakers, established a short-lived community in Sullivan County in 1808. In 1815, some German separatists led by George Rapp founded a community called the Harmonie Society, which flourished briefly. Rapp moved his followers to Pennsylvania and sold the town to a Scottish social reformer, Robert Owen, in 1825. Owen renamed the town New Harmony and tried to establish a nonreligious utopia there, but the experiment failed after three years. A group of religious dissidents founded the Pentecostal Church of God at Beaver Dam in 1881; the world headquarters of the church, which had 101,921 adherents nationwide in 2000, is now at Anderson. The Youth for Christ movement started in Indianapolis in 1943.

The Roman Catholic Church is the largest single denomination, with about 765,699 adherents in 2004. One of the largest Protestant denominations is the United Methodist Church, which had about 212,667 members in 2004. Others (with 2000 membership data) include the Church of Christ (205,408 adherents), the Southern Baptist Convention (124,452), the American Baptist Church (115,101), and the Lutheran Church–Missouri Synod (111,522). The Southern Baptist Convention reported 3,769 newly baptized members in the state in 2002. The estimated Jewish population of the state in 2000 was 18,000, down from 20,314 members in 1990. The Muslim community had about 11,000 members in 2000. There were also over 17,000 Mennonites and over 19,000 members of Amish communities statewide. About 57% of the population (over 3.4 million people) was not counted as part of any religious organization.

Indianapolis services as a home base for several religious organizations, including the Christian Fellowship International, the international headquarters of the Pentecostal Assemblies of the World, Inc., and the Office of the General Minister and President of the Christian Church (Disciples of Christ), as well as several other offices of this denomination.

¹⁰TRANSPORTATION

Indiana's central location in the United States and its position between Lake Michigan to the north and the Ohio River to the south gave the state its motto, "The Crossroads of America." Historically, the state took advantage of its strategic location by digging canals to connect Indiana rivers and by building roads and railroads to provide farmers access to national markets.

The success of the state's first railroad, completed in 1847 between Madison and Indianapolis, led to a tenfold increase in track mileage during the 1850s, and more railroad expansion took place after the Civil War. In 2003, there were 37 railroads operating on 5,136 rail mi (8,269 km) of track, of which the state's five Class I railroads operated 3,828 route mi (6,163 km) of track. As of 2006, regularly scheduled Amtrak passenger trains served Indianapolis, Hammond/Whiting, South Bend, and seven other stations in the state. Indianapolis and other major cities have public transit systems that are subsidized heavily by the state and federal governments. The South Shore commuter railroad connects South Bend, Gary, and East Chicago with Chicago, Illinois.

The east–west National Road (US 40) reached Indiana in 1827, and the north–south Michigan Road (US 421) was built in the late 1830s. In 2003, there were 94,597 mi (152,301 km) of public roads of all types in the state. In 2004, motor vehicle registrations totaled around 5.587 million, including 3.043 million passenger cars and 2.382 million trucks of all types. Several of the nation's largest moving companies have their headquarters in Indiana.

Water transportation has been important from the earliest years of European settlement. The Wabash and Erie Canal, constructed in the 1830s from Fort Wayne east to Toledo, Ohio, and southwest to Lafayette, was vital to the state's market economy. In 1836, the state legislature earmarked $10 million for an ambitious network of canals, but excessive construction costs and the financial panic of 1837 caused the state to go virtually bankrupt and default on its bonds. Nevertheless, the Wabash Canal was extended to Terre Haute and Evansville by the early 1850s.

The transport of freight via Lake Michigan and the Ohio River helped to spark Indiana's industrial development. A deepwater port on Lake Michigan, which became operational in 1970, provided access to world markets via the St. Lawrence Seaway. Indiana Harbor handled 18.228 million tons of goods in 2004, making it the 40th-busiest port in the United States, while the tonnage at the port of Gary totaled 8.531 million tons that same year. In 2004, Indiana had 353 mi (586 km) of navigable inland waterways. In 2003, waterborne shipments totaled 68.059 million tons.

In 2005, Indiana had a total of 629 public and private-use aviation-related facilities. This included 492 airports, 121 heliports, 3 STOLports (Short Take-Off and Landing), and 13 seaplane bases. Indianapolis International Airport is the state's main airport. In 2004, it handled 3,992,097 enplanements, making it the 45th-busiest airport in the United States.

¹¹HISTORY

When the first human beings inhabited Indiana is not known. Hundreds of sites used by primitive hunters, fishermen, and food gatherers before 1000 BC have been found in Indiana. Burial mounds of the Woodland culture (1000 BC to AD 900), when the bow and arrow appeared, have been located across the state. The next culture, called Mississippian and dating about AD 900 to 1500, is marked by gardens, ceramics, tools, weapons, trade, and social organization. It is well illustrated by remains of an extensive village on the north side of the Ohio River near Newburgh. The unidentified inhabitants are believed to have come up from the south about 1300, for reasons not known, and to have migrated back before 1500, again for unknown reasons.

The next Indian invaders, and the first to be seen by white men, were the Miami and Potawatomi tribes that drifted down the west side of Lake Michigan and turned across the northern sector of what is now Indiana after the middle of the 17th century. The

Kickapoo and Wea tribes pushed into upper Indiana from northern Illinois. The southern two-thirds of the present state was a vast hunting ground, without villages.

The first European penetration was made in the 1670s by the French explorers Father Jacques Marquette and René-Robert Cavelier, Sieur de la Salle. After the founding of Detroit in 1701, the Maumee-Wabash river route to the lower Ohio was discovered. At the portage between the two rivers, Jean Baptiste Bissot, Sieur de Vincennes, lived at Kekionga, the principal village of the Miami and the present site of Fort Wayne. The first French fort was built farther down the Wabash among the Wea, near modern Lafayette, in 1717. Three years later, Fort Miami was erected. Vincennes's son constructed another fort on the Wabash in 1732, at the site of the town later named for him.

English traders venturing down the Ohio River disputed the French trade monopoly, and as a result of the French and Indian War, French Canada was given up to the British in 1760. Indians under Chief Pontiac captured the two forts in northern Indiana, and the area was not securely in English hands until 1765. The prerevolutionary turbulence in the Atlantic seaboard colonies was hardly felt in Indiana, although the region did not escape the Revolutionary War itself. Colonel George Rogers Clark, acting for Virginia, captured Vincennes from a British garrison early in 1779 after a heroic march. Two years later, a detachment of 108 Pennsylvanians, passing down the Ohio to reinforce Clark, was surprised by a force of French Canadians and Indians under Mohawk Captain Joseph Brant; most of the Pennsylvanians were killed during the battle or after capture.

Following the Revolutionary War, the area northwest of the Ohio River was granted to the new nation; known as the Northwest Territory, it included present-day Indiana, Ohio, Illinois, Michigan, Wisconsin, and part of Minnesota. The first US settlement in Indiana was made in 1784 on land opposite Louisville, Kentucky. granted to Clark's veterans by Virginia. (The new town, called Clarksville, still exists.) Americans also moved into Vincennes. Government was established by the Continental Congress under the Northwest Ordinance of 1787. Again, Indiana unrest endangered all settlements north of the Ohio, and the small US Army, with headquarters at Cincinnati, met defeat at what is now Fort Wayne in 1790 and disaster in neighboring Ohio in 1791. General Anthony Wayne was put in command of an enlarged army and defeated the Indians in 1794 at Fallen Timbers (near Toledo, Ohio). British meddling was ended by Jay's Treaty later the same year. Wayne then built a new fort—named for him—among the Miami.

In 1800, as Ohio prepared to enter the Union, the rest of the Northwest Territory was set off and called the Indiana Territory, with its capital at Vincennes. There, Elihu Stout established a newspaper, the *Indiana Gazette,* in 1804. After the Michigan Territory was detached in 1805 and the Illinois Territory in 1809, Indiana assumed its present boundaries. The federal census counted 24,520 people in Indiana in 1810, including a new Swiss colony on the Ohio, where settlers planted vineyards and made wine.

William Henry Harrison was appointed the first governor and, with a secretary and three appointed judges, constituted the government of the Indiana Territory. Under the Northwest Ordinance, when the population reached 5,000 adult males, it was allowed to elect an assembly and nominate candidates for an upper house. When the population totaled 60,000—as it did in 1815—the voters were allowed to write a state constitution and apply for admission to the Union. A short constitution excluding slavery and recommending public schools was adopted, and Indiana became the 19th state on 11 December 1816.

Meanwhile, Indiana had seen Governor Harrison lead US troops up the Wabash in 1811 and beat off an Indian attack at Tippecanoe. The War of 1812 took Harrison away from Indiana, and battles were fought in other theaters. Hoosiers suffered Indian raids, and two forts were besieged for a few days. After the war, new settlers began pouring into the state from the upper South and in fewer numbers from Ohio, Pennsylvania, New York, and New England. A group of German Pietists led by George Rapp settled Harmonie on the lower Wabash in 1815 and stayed 10 years before selling out to Robert Owen, a visionary with utopian dreams that failed at the village he renamed New Harmony. In 1816, Tom Lincoln brought his family from Kentucky, and his son Abe grew up in southern Indiana from age 7 to 21.

Unlike most other states, Indiana was settled from south to north. The inhabitants were called Hoosiers; the origin of the word is obscure, but the term may have come from an Anglo-Saxon word for hill dwellers. Central and northern Indiana were opened up as land was purchased from the Indians. The Potawatomi were forced to go west in 1838, and the Miami left in 1846. Commerce flowed south to the Ohio River in the form of corn, hogs, whiskey, and timber. Indianapolis was laid out as a planned city and centrally located capital in 1820, but 30 years passed before its population caught up to the size of Madison and New Albany on the Ohio.

An overambitious program of internal improvements (canals and roads) in the 1830s plunged the state into debts it could not pay. Railroads, privately financed, began to tie Indiana commercially with the east. The Irish came to dig canals and lay the rails, and Germans, many of them Catholics, came to do woodworking and farming. Levi Coffin, a Quaker who moved to Fountain City in 1826, opened a different kind of road, the Underground Railroad, to help escaping slaves from the South.

A new constitution in 1851 showed Jacksonian preferences for more elective offices, shorter terms, a one-term governorship, limited biennial legislative sessions, county government, obligatory common schools, and severe limits on state debt. But this constitution also prohibited blacks from entering the state.

Hoosiers showed considerable sympathy with the South in the 1850s, and there was considerable "copperhead" activity in the early 1860s. Nevertheless, Indiana remained staunchly in the Union under Governor Oliver P. Morton, sending some 200,000 soldiers to the Civil War. The state suffered no battles, but General John Hunt Morgan's Confederate cavalry raided the southeastern sector of Indiana in July 1863.

After the Civil War, small local industries expanded rapidly. The first nonfarm enterprises were gristmills, sawmills, meat-packing plants, distilleries and breweries, leatherworking shops, furniture factories, and steamboat and carriage makers. Wagons made by Studebaker in South Bend won fame during the war, as did Van Camp's canned pork and beans from Indianapolis. Discovery of natural gas in several northeastern counties in 1886, and the resultant low fuel prices, spurred the growth of glass factories. Elwood Haynes of Kokomo designed a one-cylinder horseless carriage in

1894 and drove it. As America became infatuated with the new autos, 375 Indiana factories started turning them out. A racetrack for testing cars was built outside Indianapolis in 1908, and the famous 500-mi (805-km) race on Memorial Day weekend began in 1911. Five years earlier, US Steel had constructed a steel plant at the south end of Lake Michigan. The town built by the company to house the workers was called Gary, and it grew rapidly with the help of the company and the onset of World War I. Oil refineries were developed in the same area, known as the Calumet region.

Of the millions of immigrants who flocked to the United States from 1870 to 1914, very few settled in Indiana. The percentage of foreign-born residents declined from 9% in 1860 to 7% in 1880, all of them from northern Europe and over half from Germany. By 1920, the percentage was down to 5%, although some workers from southern and eastern Europe had gravitated to the industries of the Calumet.

Although many Hoosiers of German and Irish descent favored neutrality when World War I began, Indiana industries eventually boomed with war orders, and public sympathy swung heavily toward the Allies. Indiana furnished 118,000 men and women to the armed forces and suffered the loss of 3,370—a much smaller participation than during the Civil War, from a population more than twice the size.

After 1920, only about a dozen makes of cars were still being manufactured in Indiana, and those factories steadily lost out to the Big Three car makers in Detroit. The exception was Studebaker in South Bend, which grew to more than 23,000 employees during World War II. The company finally closed its doors in 1965. Auto parts continued to be a big business, however, along with steel-making and oil refining in the Calumet region. Elsewhere, there was manufacturing of machinery, farm implements, railway cars, furniture, and pharmaceuticals. Meat packing, coal mining, and limestone quarrying continued to be important. With increasing industrialization, cities grew, particularly in the northern half of the state, and the number of farms diminished. The balance of rural and urban population, about even in 1920, tilted in favor of urban dwellers.

World War II had a greater impact on Indiana than did World War I. Most factories converted to production of war materials; 300 held defense orders in 1942. Du Pont built a huge powder plant near Charlestown. The slack in employment was taken up, women went into factories, more rural families moved to cities, and military training facilities were created. The enormous Jefferson Proving Ground tested ammunition and parachutes.

After the war, many small local industries were taken over by national corporations, and their plants were expanded. By 1984, the largest employer in Indiana was General Motors, with 47,800 employees in six cities. Inland Steel, with 18,500 workers, was second, followed by US Steel with 13,800 workers. Although the state's population in the mid-1980s was about two-thirds urban and one-third rural, agriculture retained much of its importance.

Nostalgia for an older, simpler, rural way of life has pervaded much Hoosier thinking. The shoreline area of industrial Gary notwithstanding (although it, too, was the subject of cleanups during the 1990s), Indiana stands high in conservation, owing to the vision of Richard Lieber, a state official who from 1933 to 1944 promoted the preservation of land for state parks and recreational areas, as well as for state and federal forests.

The percentage of registered voters in Indiana who participate in elections has generally exceeded the national average by a wide margin. The evenness of strength between the two major political parties during much of its history made Indiana a swing state, eagerly courted by Democrats and Republicans alike. However, by the 21st century, Indiana had become one of the safest Republican states in the nation, seen as one of the most conservative states outside of the Deep South. In 1967, Democrat Richard Hatcher became one of the nation's first African Americans to serve as head of a major city when he was elected mayor of Gary. In 1988, Indiana native son J. Danforth Quayle, then a US senator, was elected vice president of the United States on the Republican ticket with George H. W. Bush.

The state legislature was dominated by rural interests until reapportionment in 1966 gave urban counties more representation. Biennial sessions were then changed to annual, although they are still limited in duration. The direct primary for nomination of governor, lieutenant governor, and US senator was mandated in 1975.

In the early 1980s, Indiana, along with other manufacturing-intensive states, suffered a recession that was compounded by declining farm prices and high operating costs for farmers. Later in the decade, the state's economy improved with the expansion of service industries, which continued through the 1990s. While the state's unemployment rate of 3% in 1999 was below the national average, median income and per capita income levels ranked in the mid-ranges nationally, owing in part to the state's agricultural and manufacturing character. Indiana's business leaders remained concerned in 2000 that Indiana had not attracted enough high-tech companies and that the state's economy was too reliant on the "old economy" manufacturing sector, causing many to worry about the consequences of a downturn. At the same time, the Indianapolis area lost several high-profile corporate headquarters.

In October 1999, for the first time in its 183-year history, the state named an African American, Justice Robert D. Rucker, to the Indiana Supreme Court. Governor Frank O'Bannon's appointment won praises from the legal community.

In 2002, the US Supreme Court let stand a 2001 federal appeals court ruling (*Indiana Civil Liberties Union v. O'Bannon*) that a proposed 7-ft stone monument of the Ten Commandments, Bill of Rights, and preamble to the 1851 Indiana constitution on state capitol grounds violated the establishment clause of the First Amendment.

As of January 2003, Indiana had a $300 million budget deficit—like more than half of the 50 states that year that had budget shortfalls. In the struggle to come up with a two-year budget, Republican legislators squared off against Democratic governor O'Bannon on issues such as funding Medicaid and education. However, on 8 September 2003, Governor O'Bannon suffered a massive stroke while attending a conference in Chicago; he died on 13 September. He was succeeded by Lieutenant Governor Joe Kernan. In November 2004, Kernan lost the governorship to Republican Mitch Daniels Jr., who had been President George W. Bush's director of the Office of Management and Budget (OMB). Upon coming to office in 2005, Daniels, who is a first generation Arab American, called for strict controls on all state spending increases as a way to improve the state's fiscal situation—the budget being some $700 million out of balance. Daniels also called for a one-time, one-year tax increase of 1% on all Hoosiers making more than $100,000 per year. The measure was seen to be out of character for a conservative who had kept a tight rein on spending while at the OMB.

12 STATE GOVERNMENT

The first state constitution took effect when Indiana became a state in 1816. Reportedly written by convention delegates beneath a huge elm tree in Corydon, the first state capital, the brief document prohibited slavery and recommended a free public school system, including a state university.

This constitution did not allow for amendment, however, and a new constitution that did so was adopted in 1851. The second constitution authorized more elective state officials, gave greater responsibility to county governments, and prohibited the state from going into debt (except under rare circumstances). It also established biennial rather than annual sessions of the state legislature, a provision that was not repealed until 1971. With amendments (46 as of January 2005), the second constitution is still in effect today.

The Indiana General Assembly consists of a 50-member Senate elected to four-year terms, with half the senators elected every two years, and a 100-member House of Representatives elected to two-year terms. Legislators now meet in annual sessions, beginning the second Monday of January and lasting no longer than 61 legislative days during odd-numbered years (or not past April 30) and no longer than 30 legislative days in even-numbered years (or not past March 15). Members of the General Assembly must be US citizens and have been a resident of Indiana for at least two years and a resident of their district for at least one year. A senator must be at least 25 years old, a representative at least 21 years old. Senators and representatives are paid the same base salary and allowances; legislative leaders receive additional compensation. The legislative salary was $11,600 in 2004, unchanged from 1999.

The state's chief executive is the governor, elected to a four-year term and eligible for reelection, although ineligible to serve more than eight years in a twelve-year period. The governor must be at least 30 years old, a US citizen for at least five years, and a state resident for five years prior to election. Only the governor may call special sessions of the legislature (limited to 30 legislative days or 40 calendar days). The governor may veto bills passed by the legislature, but his or her veto can be overridden by a majority vote of the elected members in each house. If a bill is left unsigned for seven days (whether or not the legislature is in session), it becomes law. As of December 2004, the governor's salary was $95,000.

Indiana's other top elected officials are the lieutenant governor, secretary of state, treasurer, comptroller, attorney general, and superintendent of public instruction. Each is elected to a four-year term. The lieutenant governor, elected jointly with the governor, is constitutionally empowered to preside over the state Senate and to act as governor if the office should become vacant or the incumbent is unable to discharge his or her duties.

Legislation may be introduced in either house of the General Assembly, although bills for raising revenue must originate in the House of Representatives. A bill approved by both houses goes to the governor for signing into law; if the governor declines to sign it within seven days, the bill becomes law, but if the governor vetoes it, majorities of at least 26 votes in the Senate and 51 votes in the House are required to override the veto. Should the governor veto a bill after the end of a legislative session, it must be returned to the legislature when that body reconvenes.

A proposed amendment to the state constitution must be approved by a majority vote in two successive legislative sessions and be submitted to the voters for approval or rejection at the next general election.

In order to vote in Indiana, a person must be a US citizen, at least 18 years old, and a resident of the voting precinct for 30 days before the next election. Those jailed for criminal convictions may not vote.

13 POLITICAL PARTIES

The Democratic Party has been one of the two major political parties since Indiana became a state in 1816, as has the Republican Party since its inception in 1854. In that year, Hoosiers voted for Democrat James Buchanan for president, but in 1860, the voters supported Republican Abraham Lincoln. After voting Republican in four successive presidential elections, Indiana voted Democratic in 1876 and became a swing state. More recently, a Republican trend has been evident: The state voted Republican in 15 out of 16 presidential elections between 1940 and 2000.

Third-party movements have rarely succeeded in Indiana. Native son Eugene V. Debs, the Socialist Party leader who was personally popular in Indiana, received only 36,931 votes in the state in 1912 while garnering more than 900,000 votes nationally. Even in 1932, during the Great Depression, Socialist candidate Norman Thomas won only 21,388 votes in Indiana. The most successful third-party movement in recent decades was George Wallace's American Independent Party, which took 243,108 votes (11.5% of the Indiana total) in 1968. In each of the four presidential elections of the 1970s and early 1980s, minority party candidates together received only 1.1% or less of the votes cast.

In 2000, Indiana gave 57% of the vote to Republican George W. Bush and 41% to Democrat Al Gore. In 2004, Bush increased his margin to 60% of the vote over Democrat John Kerry, who won 39%. In 1996, Democrat Frank L. O'Bannon was voted in to succeed two-term Democratic governor Evan Bayh; O'Bannon was reelected in 2000. However, O'Bannon suffered a massive stroke in September 2003, and Lieutenant Governor Joseph E. Kernan became governor when O'Bannon died. Kernan was defeated by Republican Mitch Daniels in 2004. Republican Richard Lugar won election to his fifth term in the US Senate in 2000. The other Senate seat, which again went to the Republicans in the 1992 election, was surrendered to the Democrats in 1998 when Bayh was voted in; he won reelection in 2004.

Indiana's delegation to the US House of Representatives following the 2004 elections included two Democrats and seven Republicans. In mid-2005, the state Senate had 33 Republicans and 17 Democrats. The state House had 52 Republicans and 48 Democrats. In 2004, there were 4,009,000 registered voters; there is no party registration in the state. The state had 11 electoral votes in the 2004 presidential election, a loss of 1 vote over the 2000 election.

¹⁴LOCAL GOVERNMENT

In 1816, when Indians controlled central and northern Indiana, the state had only 15 counties. By 1824, the number of counties had grown to 49. As of 2005, there were 92 counties.

Counties in Indiana have traditionally provided law enforcement in rural areas, operated county courts and institutions, maintained county roads, administered public welfare programs, and collected taxes. Under a home-rule law enacted by the state in 1980, they also have "all the power they need for the effective operation of government as to local affairs" or, in effect, all powers not specifically reserved by the state. In 1984, counties were given the power to impose local income taxes.

The county's business is conducted by a board of county commissioners, consisting of three members elected to four-year terms. Nine officials who are also elected to four-year terms exercise executive functions: the county auditor, treasurer, recorder, clerk, surveyor, sheriff, prosecuting attorney, coroner, and assessor. The county's appointed officials include the county superintendent of schools, highway supervisor, highway engineer, extension agent, attorney, and physician. An elected seven-member county council exercises taxing power and acts as a check on the board of county commissioners. The major exception to this general pattern is Marion County, which in 1970 was consolidated with the city of Indianapolis and is governed by an elected mayor and council.

Townships (1,008 in 2002) provide assistance for the poor and assess taxable property. Each township is administered by a trustee who is elected to a four-year term. In a few townships, the trustee oversees township schools, but most public schools are run by community school corporations.

Indiana's municipal governments (567 in 2005) are governed by elected city councils. City officials, including the mayor and city clerk, are generally elected for four-year terms. Indianapolis and Marion County were consolidated in 1969.

In 2005, Indiana had 295 public school districts and 1,125 special districts.

In 2005, local government accounted for about 239,827 full-time (or equivalent) employment positions.

¹⁵STATE SERVICES

To address the continuing threat of terrorism and to work with the federal Department of Homeland Security, homeland security in Indiana operates under state statute; the homeland security director oversees homeland security in the state.

In 1974, Indiana's state legislature created the State Ethics and Conflicts of Interest Commission to formulate and regulate a code of ethics for state officials. The state ethics commissioner investigates reported cases of misconduct or violations of the code of ethics by any state official or employee. After holding hearings, the commission reports violations to the governor and makes its findings public. Top-level state officials and heads of state departments must provide statements of their financial interests to the commission.

In 1977, the state established an interdepartmental board for the coordination of human service programs. Members include the chief administrative officers of state agencies for senior citizens and community services, mental health, health, corrections, and public welfare. The Family and Social Services Administration provides assistance to persons and families requiring help from one of these agencies and monitors federal service programs in the state.

Indiana Presidential Vote by Political Parties, 1948–2004

YEAR	ELECTORAL VOTES	INDIANA WINNER	DEMOCRAT	REPUBLICAN	PROGRESSIVE	PROHIBITION
1948	13	Dewey (R)	807,833	821,079	9,649	14,711
1952	13	*Eisenhower (R)	801,530	1,136,259	1,222	15,335
1956	13	*Eisenhower (R)	783,908	1,182,811	—	6,554
1960	13	*Nixon (R)	952,358	1,175,120	—	6,746
1964	13	*Johnson (D)	1,170,848	911,118		8,266
					AMERICAN IND.	
1968	13	*Nixon (R)	806,659	1,067,885	243,108	4,616
					PEOPLE'S	SOC. WORKERS
1972	13	*Nixon (R)	708,568	1,405,154	4,544	5,575
					AMERICAN	
1976	13	Ford (R)	1,014,714	1,185,958	14,048	5,695
					CITIZENS	LIBERTARIAN
1980	13	*Reagan (R)	844,197	1,255,656	4,852	19,627
1984	12	*Reagan (R)	841,481	1,377,230	—	6,741
					NEW ALLIANCE	
1988	12	*Bush (R)	860,643	1,297,763	10,215	—
					IND. (Perot)	
1992	12	Bush (R)	848,420	989,375	455,934	7,936
1996	12	Dole (R)	887,424	1,006,693	224,299	15,632
					(Buchanan)	
2000**	12	*Bush, G. W. (R)	901,980	1,245,836	16,959	15,530
					WRITE-IN (Nader)	
2004	11	*Bush, G. W. (R)	969,011	1,479,438	1,328	18,058

*Won US presidential election.
**WRITE-IN candidate Ralph Nader received 18,531 votes in 2000.

Educational services are provided by the Department of Education and the Commission on Proprietary Education, which accredits private vocational, technical, and trade schools in the state. Health services are supplied by the Department of Health and emergency medical services commission. Disabled citizens are assisted by the Governor's Planning Council for People with Disabilities. The Civil Rights Commission enforces state antidiscrimination laws. The Department of Transportation is responsible for transportation services, and the Department of Veteran Affairs caters to the needs of veterans.

16JUDICIAL SYSTEM

The Indiana Supreme Court consists of five justices who are appointed by the governor from names submitted by a nonpartisan judicial nominating committee. To qualify for selection, a nominee must have practiced law in the state for at least 10 years or have served as judge of a lower court for at least five years. A justice serves for two years and then is subject to approval by referendum in the general election. If approved by the voters, the justice serves a 10-year term before again being subject to referendum. The chief justice of the Indiana Supreme Court is chosen by the nominating commission and serves a five-year term.

The Indiana State Court of Appeals consists of 15 justices who serve 10-year terms. The court exercises appellate jurisdiction under rules set by the Indiana Supreme Court. Both the clerk and the reporter for the state's high courts are chosen in statewide elections for four-year terms.

Superior courts, probate courts, and circuit courts all function as general trial courts and are presided over by 279 judges who serve terms of six years. When the justice of the peace system in the counties was abolished by the state legislature in 1976, small-claims dockets (civil cases involving up to $1,500) were added to circuit and county courts.

As of 31 December 2004, a total of 24,008 prisoners were held in Indiana's state and federal prisons, an increase from 23,069 or 4.1% from the previous year. As of year-end 2004, a total of 1,892 inmates were female, up from 1,758 or 7.6% from the year before. Among sentenced prisoners (one year or more), Indiana had an incarceration rate of 383 per 100,000 population in 2004.

According to the Federal Bureau of Investigation, in 2004 Indiana had a violent crime rate (murder/nonnegligent manslaughter; forcible rape; robbery; aggravated assault) of 325.4 reported incidents per 100,000 population, or a total of 20,294 reported incidents. Crimes against property (burglary; larceny/theft; and motor vehicle theft) in that same year totaled 211,929 reported incidents or 3,397.6 reported incidents per 100,000 people. Indiana has a death penalty, of which lethal injection is the sole method of execution. From 1976 through 5 May 2006, the state executed 17 persons, of which five were executed in 2005 and one in 2006 (as of 5 May). As of 1 January 2006, Indiana had 26 inmates on death row.

In 2003, Indiana spent $110,288,354 on homeland security, an average of $18 per state resident.

17ARMED FORCES

US defense installations in Indiana had 1,131 active duty military personnel, 9,877 Reserve and National Guard personnel, and 4,169 civilian personnel in 2004. Army installations include the Jeffer-

son Proving Ground. Grissom Air Force Base, which had been the state's only Air Force base, was closed in 1994. The Navy operates a weapons support center at Crane. Within the state $3.1 billion in prime defense contracts were awarded in fiscal year 2004, and there was another $1.2 billion in defense payroll spending.

Indiana supported the Union during the Civil War; about 200,000 Hoosiers served in Northern armies, and some 24,400 died while in service. During World War I, a Hoosier reportedly was the first American soldier to fire a shot, and the first American soldier killed was from Indiana; in all, about 118,000 Indiana citizens served and 3,370 lost their lives. In World War II, about 338,000 Hoosiers served in the armed forces, and some 10,000 died in line of duty. There were 550,871 veterans of US military service in Indiana as of 2003, of whom 74,109 served in World War II; 62,481 in the Korean conflict; 169,679 during the Vietnam era; and 79,307 in the Gulf War. After World War II, the state paid a bonus to veterans for the first time; in fiscal year 2004, veterans' expenditures in Indiana totaled $1.0 billion.

As of 31 October 2004, the Indiana State Police employed 1,155 full-time sworn officers.

18MIGRATION

Indiana's early settlers were predominantly northern Europeans who migrated from eastern and southern states. The influx of immigrants to the United States in the late 19th and early 20th centuries had little impact on Indiana. In 1860, only 9% of the state's population was foreignborn, mostly Germans and Irish. The percentage was only 5.6% in 1900 and further declined to 5.2% by 1920 and to just 1.7% by 1990. The principal migratory pattern since 1920 has been within the state, from the farms to the cities.

In 1860, more than 91% of the population lived in rural areas; the percentage fell to 67% in 1900, 50% in 1920, and 40% in 1960. In 1990, 65% of the population was urban and only 35% was rural.

Since World War II, Indiana has lost population through a growing migratory movement to other states, mostly to Florida and the Southwest. From 1960 to 1970, Indiana suffered a net loss of about 16,000 persons through migration, and from 1970 to 1983, a net total of 340,000 left the state. From 1985 to 1990, however, there was a net gain in migration of over 35,000, 90% of whom came from abroad. Between 1990 and 1998, the state had a net gain of 76,000 persons through domestic migration and a net gain of 25,000 in international migration. In 1998, 3,981 foreign immigrants arrived in Indiana. Between 1990 and 1998, the state's overall population increased 6.4%. In the period 2000–05, net international migration was 55,656 and net internal migration was -17,000, for a net gain of 38,656 people.

19INTERGOVERNMENTAL COOPERATION

Indiana's Commission on Interstate Cooperation promotes cooperation with other states and with the federal government. It acts largely through the Council of State Governments. Indiana is a member of such interstate regulatory bodies as the Great Lakes Commission, the Interstate Mining Compact Commission, the Midwest Interstate Low-Level Radioactive Waste Compact Commission, the Ohio River Basin Commission, and the Ohio River Valley Water Sanitation Commission.

The Indiana-Kentucky Boundary Compact was signed by Indiana in 1943 and received congressional approval the same year. In 1985, Indiana joined seven other states in signing a Great Lakes Charter, aimed at further protecting the lakes' resources. Federal grants to Indiana totaled $6.476 billion in fiscal year 2005, an estimated $6.913 billion in fiscal year 2006, and an estimated $7.318 billion in fiscal year 2007.

20ECONOMY

Indiana is both a leading agricultural and industrial state. The economy was almost entirely agricultural until after the Civil War. By 1900, rapid industrial development had tripled the number of factories in the state to 18,000, employing a total of 156,000 workers. During that period, the mechanization of agriculture doubled of the number of farms to a peak of 220,000 in 1900.

Metals and other manufacturing industries surged during and after World War I, lagged during the Great Depression of the 1930s, then surged again during and after World War II. Between 1940 and 1950, the number of wage earners in the state nearly doubled. Job opportunities brought in many workers from other states and encouraged the growth of labor unions.

The state's industrial development in Indianapolis, Gary, and other cities has been based on its plentiful natural resources—coal, natural gas, timber, stone, and clay—and on good transportation facilities. The northwestern corner of the state is the site of one of the world's greatest concentrations of heavy industry, especially steel. Indiana produced 24% of the nation's steel in 1999, the most of any state. Until the end of the 20th century, the manufacturing sector continued to grow in absolute terms (15% between 1997 and 2000) and continued to account for about 30% of the Indiana's total output. In the national recession of 2001, however, manufacturing output fell 9.2%, and manufacturing fell to 27.2% of total output. The Indiana economy experienced 8.1% growth in 1998, which moderated to 2.9% in 1999 and 4.7% in 2000, and then plunged to 0.1% in 2001. Job creation, which had averaged over 2% a quarter since 1993, became negative (layoffs exceeding job creation) by the second half of 2001 and remained negative throughout 2002. Although the unemployment rate remained below the national average, Indiana had the highest foreclosure rate on conventional family mortgages among the states in 2002.

In 2004, Indiana's gross state product (GSP) totaled $227.569 billion, of which manufacturing accounted for $63.477 billion or 27.8% of GSP, followed by real estate at $22.197 billion (9.7% of GSP) and health care and social services $16.035 billion (7% of GSP). In that same year, there were an estimated 451,437 small businesses in Indiana. Of the 125,746 businesses having employees, a total of 122,716 or 97.6% were small companies. An estimated 13,906 new businesses were established in the state in 2004, up 3.4% from the year before. Business terminations that same year came to 15,282, up 1% from 2003. There were 524 business bankruptcies in 2004, down 18.1% from the previous year. In 2005, the personal bankruptcy (Chapter 7 and Chapter 13) filing rate was 896 filings per 100,000 people, ranking Indiana as the sixth-highest in the nation.

21INCOME

In 2005, Indiana had a gross state product (GSP) of $239 billion, which accounted for 1.9% of the nation's gross domestic product and placed the state at number 16 in highest GSP among the 50 states and the District of Columbia.

According to the Bureau of Economic Analysis, in 2004, Indiana had a per capita personal income (PCPI) of $30,204. This ranked 33rd in the United States and was 91% of the national average of $33,050. The 1994–2004 average annual growth rate of PCPI was 3.8%. Indiana had a total personal income (TPI) of $188,064,673,000, which ranked 16th in the United States and reflected an increase of 5.1% from 2003. The 1994–2004 average annual growth rate of TPI was 4.6%. Earnings of persons employed in Indiana increased from $137,378,109,000 in 2003 to $144,552,055,000 in 2004, an increase of 5.2%. The 2003–04 national change was 6.3%.

The US Census Bureau reports that the three-year average median household income for 2002–04 in 2004 dollars was $43,003 compared to a national average of $44,473. During the same period, 10.2% of the population was below the poverty line, as compared to 12.4% nationwide.

22LABOR

According to the Bureau of Labor Statistics (BLS), in April 2006 the seasonally adjusted civilian labor force in Indiana numbered 3,252,000. Approximately 159,500 workers were unemployed, yielding an unemployment rate of 4.9%, compared to the national average of 4.7% for the same period. Preliminary data for the same period placed nonfarm employment at 2,972,000. Since the beginning of the BLS data series in 1976, the highest unemployment rate recorded in Indiana was 12.8% in November 1982. The historical low was 2.6% in April 1999. Preliminary nonfarm employment data by occupation for April 2006 showed that approximately 5.1% of the labor force was employed in construction; 19.2% in manufacturing; 19.6% in trade, transportation, and public utilities; 4.7% in financial activities; 9.2% in professional and business services; 12.8% in education and health services; 9.4% in leisure and hospitality services; and 14.3% in government.

Most industrial workers live in Indianapolis and the Calumet area of northwestern Indiana. The American Federation of Labor first attempted to organize workers at the US Steel Company's plant in Gary in 1919, but a strike to get union recognition failed. Other strikes by Indiana coal miners and railway workers in 1922 had limited success. By 1936, however, the Congress of Industrial Organizations had won bargaining rights and the 40-hour workweek from US Steel, and union organization spread to other industries throughout the state.

The BLS reported that in 2005, a total of 346,000 of Indiana's 2,789,000 employed wage and salary workers were formal members of a union. This represented 12.4% of those so employed, up from 11.4% in 2004 and just above the national average of 12%. Overall in 2005, a total of 368,000 workers (13.2%) in Indiana were covered by a union or employee association contract, which includes those workers who reported no union affiliation. Although Indiana is one of 22 states with a right-to-work law, the law is applicable only to school system employees.

As of 1 March 2006, Indiana had a state-mandated minimum wage of $5.15 per hour. In 2004, women in the state accounted for 47% of the employed civilian labor force.

23 AGRICULTURE

Agriculture in Indiana is a large and diverse industry that plays a vital role in the state's economic stability, with 59,300 farms containing 15,000,000 acres (6,800,000 hectares) of farmland. In 2005, cash receipts from the sale of all commodities (crops and livestock) reached $5.4 billion. In the same year, Indiana ranked 16th in the United States in cash receipts from the sale of all commodities; crop sales amounted to $3.5 billion, and livestock sales totaled $1.9 billion.

Over 80% of Indiana's farm operators live on the farm, while more than 55% of farmers have a principal occupation other than farming. The average age for Indiana farmers is 54 years old, and the average farm size is 250 acres (101 hectares).

Corn and soybeans are Indiana's two main crops. In 2004 the state produced 929,040,000 bushels of corn for grain, ranking fifth in the United States. Indiana also grew 287,040,000 bushels of soybeans, the third most in the nation. Other principal field crops, based upon 2004 crop statistics, include spearmint, 64,000 lb; peppermint 594,000 lb; and cantaloupes 500,000 cwt.

24 ANIMAL HUSBANDRY

Indiana dairy farmers produced an estimated 2.9 billion lb (1.3 billion kg) of milk from 149,000 milk cows in 2003. The state's poultry farmers sold an estimated 24.8 million lb (11.3 million kg) of chicken and an estimated 396.8 million lb of turkey during 2003.

Indiana had an estimated 850,000 cattle and calves worth around $799 million in 2005.

25 FISHING

Fishing is not of commercial importance in Indiana. Fishing for bass, pike, perch, catfish, and trout is a popular sport with Indiana anglers. In 2004, there were 522,389 sport fishing licenses issued by the state. There are eight state fish hatcheries.

26 FORESTRY

About 20% of Indiana's total land area was forested in 2004. Indiana has 4,501,000 acres (1,822,000 hectares) of forestland, of which 96% or 4,342,000 acres (1,757,000 hectares) is considered commercial timberland. Some 75% of the commercial forestland is located in the southern half of Indiana, where oak, hickory, beech, maple, yellow poplar, and ash predominate in the uplands. Soft maple, sweetgum, pin oak, cottonwood, sycamore, and river birch are the most common species found in wetlands and drainage corridors.

Indiana's wood-using industries manufacture everything from the "crinkle" center lining in cardboard boxes to the finest furniture in the world. Other wood products include pallets, desks, fancy face veneer, millwork, flooring, mobile homes, and recreational vehicle components. In 2004, Indiana produced 333 million board feet of lumber, 99% hardwood. Indiana has always been noted for the quality of its hardwood forests and the trees it produces.

27 MINING

According to data from the US Geological Survey (USGS), the value of Indiana's nonfuel mineral production in 2004 was $764 million, an increase from 2003 of almost 7%. The USGS data ranked Indiana 22nd among the 50 states by the total value of its nonfuel mineral production, accounting for around 1.7% of total US output.

In 2004, the state's leading nonfuel mineral by value was cement (portland and masonry), followed by crushed stone, construction sand and gravel, and lime, altogether which accounted for almost 92% of all nonfuel mineral output by the state.

The state's top two mineral commodities were crushed stone (estimated 2001 output 56 million metric tons, valued at $264 million) and cement (portland cement production was an estimated 2.86 million metric tons, valued at $195 million).

A total of 3,564 people were employed by Indiana's nonfuel minerals sector in 2004, up 1% from the previous year.

28 ENERGY AND POWER

Indiana is largely dependent on fossil fuels for its energy supplies. Petroleum has become an important power source for automobiles, home heating, and electricity. Nevertheless, coal has continued to be the state's major source of power, meeting about half of Indiana's energy needs.

As of 2003, Indiana had 119 electrical power service providers, of which 72 were publicly owned and 41 were cooperatives. The remaining six were investor owned. As of that same year, there were 2,966,062 retail customers. Of that total, 2,215,877 received their power from investor-owned service providers. Cooperatives accounted for 494,708 customers, while publicly owned providers had 255,477 customers.

Total net summer generating capability by the state's electrical generating plants in 2003 stood at 25.640 million kW, with total production that same year at 124.888 billion kWh. Of the total amount generated, 90% came from electric utilities, with the remainder coming from independent producers and combined heat and power service providers. The largest portion of all electric power generated, 117.756 billion kWh (94.3%), came from coal-fired plants, with natural gas plants in second place at 3.049 billion kWh (2.4%) and plants using other gases in third place at 2.952 billion kWh (2.1%). Other renewable power sources, hydroelectric, petroleum, and "other" types of generating facilities accounted for the remainder.

The state has no nuclear power plants. In 1984, construction of the planned Marble Hill nuclear power plant on the Ohio River near Madison was permanently suspended by the Public Service Co. of Indiana because of escalating construction costs; total cost estimates had risen from $1.4 billion during the planning stage in 1973 to more than $7 billion.

As of 2004, Indiana had proven crude oil reserves of 11 million barrels, or less than 1% of all proven US reserves, while output that same year averaged 5,000 barrels per day. Including federal offshore domains, the state that year ranked 24th (23rd excluding federal offshore) in proven reserves and 24th (23rd excluding Federal Offshore) in production among the 31 producing states. In 2004, Indiana had 4,788 producing oil wells. The state's two refineries had a combined crude oil distillation capacity of 433,000 barrels per day.

In 2004, Indiana had 2,386 producing natural gas and gas condensate wells. In that same year, marketed gas production (all gas produced excluding gas used for repressuring, vented and flared, and nonhydrocarbon gases removed) totaled 1.464 billion cu ft (0.041 billion cu m). There was no data available on the state's proven reserves of natural gas.

In 2004, Indiana had 29 producing coal mines, 22 of which were surface mines and 7 were underground. Coal production that year totaled 35,110,000 short tons, down from 35,355,000 short tons in 2003. Of the total produced in 2004, surface mines accounted for 25,018,000 short tons. Recoverable coal reserves in 2004 totaled 398 million short tons. One short ton equals 2,000 lb (0.907 metric tons).

29 INDUSTRY

The industrialization of Indiana that began during the Civil War era was spurred by technological advances in processing agricultural products, manufacturing farm equipment, and improving transportation facilities. Meat-packing plants, textile mills, furniture factories, and wagon works—including Studebaker wagons—were soon followed by metal foundries, machine shops, farm implement plants, and a myriad of other durable goods plants.

New industries included a pharmaceutical house started in Indianapolis in 1876 by a druggist named Eli Lilly, and several automobile manufacturing shops established in South Bend and other cities by 1900. In 1906, the US Steel Co. laid out the new town of Gary for steelworkers and their families.

Indiana is a leading producer of compact discs, elevators, recreational vehicles, mobile homes, refrigerators and freezers, storage batteries, small motors and generators, mobile homes, household furniture, burial caskets, and musical instruments. Most manufacturing plants are located in and around Indianapolis and in the Calumet region.

According to the US Census Bureau's Annual Survey of Manufactures (ASM) for 2004, Indiana's manufacturing sector covered some 18 product subsectors. The shipment value of all products manufactured in the state that same year was $183.563 billion. Of that total, transportation equipment manufacturing accounted for the largest share at $57.766 billion. It was followed by primary metal manufacturing at $24.151 billion; chemical manufacturing at $17.522 billion; food manufacturing at $13.611 billion; and fabricated metal product manufacturing at $12.523 billion.

In 2004, a total of 534,942 people in Indiana were employed in the state's manufacturing sector, according to the ASM. Of that total, 403,781 were actual production workers. In terms of total employment, the transportation equipment manufacturing sector accounted for the largest portion of all manufacturing employees at 139,699, with 106,870 actual production workers. It was followed by the fabricated metal product manufacturing industry at 58,816 (44,879 actual production workers); plastics and rubber products manufacturing at 45,581 employees (36,807 actual production workers); primary metal manufacturing at 45,220 employees (36,123 actual production workers); machinery manufacturing at 38,362 employees (27,185 actual production workers); and food manufacturing with 31,693 employees (23,238 actual production workers).

ASM data for 2004 showed that Indiana's manufacturing sector paid $23.343 billion in wages. Of that amount, the transportation equipment manufacturing sector accounted for the largest share at $7.129 billion. It was followed by primary metal manufacturing at $2.610 billion; fabricated metal product manufacturing at $2.288 billion; machinery manufacturing at $1.655 billion; and plastics and rubber products manufacturing at $1.577 billion.

30 COMMERCE

According to the 2002 Census of Wholesale Trade, Indiana's wholesale trade sector had sales that year totaling $79.8 billion from 8,213 establishments. Wholesalers of durable goods accounted for 5,080 establishments, followed by nondurable goods wholesalers at 2,415 and electronic markets, agents, and brokers accounting for 718 establishments. Sales by durable goods wholesalers in 2002 totaled $31.2 billion, while wholesalers of nondurable goods saw sales of $39.8 billion. Electronic markets, agents, and brokers in the wholesale trade industry had sales of $8.7 billion.

In the 2002 Census of Retail Trade, Indiana was listed as having 24,322 retail establishments with sales of $67.2 billion. The leading types of retail businesses by number of establishments were: motor vehicle and motor vehicle parts dealers (3,199); miscellaneous store retailers (2,963); gasoline stations (2,904); and clothing and clothing accessories stores, tied with food and beverage stores (2,633 each). In terms of sales, motor vehicle and motor vehicle parts stores accounted for the largest share of retail sales at $17.3 billion, followed by general merchandise stores at $11.7 billion; food and beverage stores at $7.5 billion; gasoline stations at $7.03 billion; and building material/garden equipment and supplies dealers $5.8 billion. A total of 343,551 people were employed by the retail sector in Indiana that year.

Indiana ranked 11th among the 50 states in exports during 2005, when its goods shipped abroad were valued at $21.4 billion. Major farm exports are soybeans; feed grains; wheat; meat (including poultry) and meat products; fats, oils, and greases; and hides and skins. Principal nonfarm exports include transportation equipment, electric and electronic equipment, nonelectric machinery, primary metals products, chemicals and allied products, food and kindred products, and fabricated metal products.

31 CONSUMER PROTECTION

The Division of Consumer Protection of the Office of the Attorney General was created in 1971 and is empowered to investigate consumer complaints, initiate and prosecute civil actions, and warn consumers about deceptive sales practices. There is also a Utility Regulatory Commission that regulates the business of public utilities, including rates and environmental compliance plans.

The Consumer Protection Division consists of three sections. The General Consumer Complaint Investigation and Mediation Section attempts to mediate consumer complaints against businesses that are not regulated as licensed professionals by either the federal of state government. If a pattern of deceptive practices is determined, litigation may follow. The Licensed Professional Section handles complaints against most professionals licensed by the state of Indiana, except medical professionals, which come under the Medical Licensing Section.

When dealing with consumer protection issues, the state's Attorney General's Office can initiate civil but not criminal proceedings; represent the state before state and federal regulatory agencies; administer consumer protection and education programs; handle formal consumer complaints; and exercise broad subpoena powers. However, the Attorney General's Office cannot represent individual residents or consumers. In antitrust actions, the Attorney General's Office can act on behalf of those consumers who are incapable of acting on their own and can initiate damage actions on behalf of the state in state courts. However, the office cannot represent counties, cities, and other governmental entities in recovering civil damages under state or federal law.

Indiana's Consumer Protection Division has offices in Indianapolis.

³²BANKING

The large-scale mechanization of agriculture in Indiana after 1850 encouraged the growth of banks to lend money to farmers to buy farm machinery, using their land as collateral. The financial panic of 1893 caused most banks in the state to suspend operations, and the Depression of the 1930s caused banks to foreclose many farm mortgages and dozens of banks to fail. The nation's subsequent economic recovery, together with the federal reorganization of the banking system, helped Indiana banks to share in the state's prosperity during and after World War II.

As of June 2005, Indiana had 193 insured banks, savings and loans, and saving banks, plus 49 state-chartered and 180 federally chartered credit unions (CUs). Excluding the CUs, the Indianapolis market area accounted for the majority of the state's financial institutions and deposits in 2004, with 56 institutions and $24.898 billion in deposits. As of June 2005, CUs accounted for 12.6% of all assets held by all financial institutions in the state, or some $14.845 billion. Banks, savings and loans, and savings banks collectively accounted for the remaining 87.4% or $103.420 billion in assets held.

As of fourth quarter 2005, past due/nonaccrual loans accounted for 1.98% of all loans, down from 2.23% in 2004. The median net interest margin (the difference between the lower rates offered to savers and the higher rates charged on loans) in fourth quarter 2005 stood at 3.79%, up from 3.66% in 2004.

The Department of Financial Institutions regulates the operations of Indiana's state-chartered banks, savings and loan associations, and credit unions and monitors their observance of the state's Uniform Consumer Credit Code. The department is headed by a seven-member board; each board member serves a four-year term, and no more than four members may be of the same political party. A full-time director, also appointed by the governor to a four-year term, is the department's chief executive and administrative officer.

³³INSURANCE

In 2004, there were 3.8 million individual life insurance policies in force with a total value of over $235.7 billion; total value for all categories of life insurance (individual, group, and credit) was $380.5 billion. The average coverage amount was $61,800 per policy holder. Death benefits paid that year totaled at over $1.1 billion.

As of 2003, there were 77 property and casualty and 40 life and health insurance companies domiciled in the state. In 2004, direct premiums for property and casualty insurance totaled $10.1 billion. That year, there were 28,854 flood insurance policies in force in the state, with a total value of $2.89 billion. About $526 million of coverage was offered through FAIR (Fair Access to Insurance) Plans, which are designed to offer coverage for some natural circumstances, such as wind and hail, in high-risk areas.

In 2004, 59% of state residents held employment-based health insurance policies, 4% held individual policies, and 23% were covered under Medicare and Medicaid; 14% of residents were uninsured. In 2003, employee contributions for employment-based health coverage averaged 21% for single coverage and 25% for family coverage. The state does not offer a health benefits expansion program in connection with the Consolidated Omnibus Budget Reconciliation Act (COBRA, 1986), a health insurance program for those who lose employment-based coverage due to termination or reduction of work hours.

In 2003, there were over 4.1 million auto insurance policies in effect for private passenger cars. Required minimum coverage includes bodily injury liability of up to $25,000 per individual and $50,000 for all persons injured in an accident, as well as property damage liability of $10,000. In 2003, the average expenditure per vehicle for insurance coverage was $670.39.

The Department of Insurance licenses insurance carriers and agents in Indiana, and it enforces regulations governing the issuance of policies.

³⁴SECURITIES

There are no securities exchanges in Indiana. In 2005, there were 1,220 personal financial advisers employed. In 2004, there were over 116 publicly traded companies within the state, with over 67 NASDAQ companies, 22 NYSE listings, and 2 AMEX listings. In 2006, the state had five Fortune 500 companies; Wellpoint (based in Indianapolis) ranked first in the state and 38th in the nation with revenues of over $45.1 billion, followed by Eli Lilly (Indianapolis), Cummins (Columbus), NiSource (Merrillville), and Conseco (Carmel). All five companies are listed on the NYSE.

³⁵PUBLIC FINANCE

The State Budget Agency acts as watchdog over state financial affairs. The agency prepares the budget for the governor and presents it to the General Assembly. The budget director, appointed by the governor, serves with four legislators (two from each house) on the state budget committee, which helps to prepare the budget. The state budget agency receives appropriations requests from the heads of state offices, estimates anticipated revenues for the biennium, and administers the budget. The fiscal year (FY) runs from 1 July to 30 June of the following year. Budgets are prepared for the biennium beginning and ending in odd-numbered years.

In fiscal year 2006, general funds were estimated at $12.2 billion for resources and $11.9 billion for expenditures. In fiscal year 2004, federal government grants to Indiana were nearly $7.4 billion.

³⁶TAXATION

In 2005, Indiana collected $12,854 million in tax revenues or $2,049 per capita, which placed it 31st among the 50 states in per capita tax burden. The national average was $2,192 per capita. Property taxes accounted for 0.1% of the total, sales taxes 38.9%,

Indiana—State Government Finances

(Dollar amounts in thousands. Per capita amounts in dollars.)

	AMOUNT	PER CAPITA
Total Revenue	26,917,365	4,322.69
General revenue	23,464,893	3,768.25
Intergovernmental revenue	7,057,449	1,133.36
Taxes	11,957,470	1,920.26
General sales	4,759,445	764.32
Selective sales	2,147,509	344.87
License taxes	448,387	72.01
Individual income tax	3,807,861	611.51
Corporate income tax	644,787	103.55
Other taxes	149,481	24.01
Current charges	2,673,197	429.29
Miscellaneous general revenue	1,776,777	285.33
Utility revenue	–	–
Liquor store revenue	–	–
Insurance trust revenue	3,452,472	554.44
Total expenditure	25,373,330	4,074.73
Intergovernmental expenditure	7,963,397	1,278.85
Direct expenditure	17,409,933	2,795.88
Current operation	13,014,329	2,089.98
Capital outlay	1,700,913	273.15
Insurance benefits and repayments	1,791,377	287.68
Assistance and subsidies	455,884	73.21
Interest on debt	447,430	71.85
Exhibit: Salaries and wages	3,461,530	555.89
Total expenditure	25,373,330	4,074.73
General expenditure	23,542,970	3,780.79
Intergovernmental expenditure	7,963,397	1,278.85
Direct expenditure	15,579,573	2,501.94
General expenditures, by function:		
Education	9,041,115	1,451.92
Public welfare	5,675,769	911.48
Hospitals	284,348	45.66
Health	590,479	94.83
Highways	1,920,891	308.48
Police protection	226,051	36.30
Correction	675,194	108.43
Natural resources	269,222	43.23
Parks and recreation	63,291	10.16
Government administration	600,690	96.47
Interest on general debt	447,430	71.85
Other and unallocable	3,748,490	601.97
Utility expenditure	38,983	6.26
Liquor store expenditure	–	–
Insurance trust expenditure	1,791,377	287.68
Debt at end of fiscal year	13,079,818	2,100.50
Cash and security holdings	36,948,023	5,933.52

Abbreviations and symbols: – zero or rounds to zero; (NA) not available; (X) not applicable.

SOURCE: *U.S. Census Bureau, Governments Division, 2004 Survey of State Government Finances,* January 2006.

selective sales taxes 17.1%, individual income taxes 32.8%, corporate income taxes 6.4%, and other taxes 4.8%.

As of 1 January 2006, Indiana had one individual income tax bracket of 3.4%. The state taxes corporations at a flat rate of 8.5%.

In 2004, state and local property taxes amounted to $6,073,538,000 or $975 per capita. The per capita amount ranks the state 26th highest nationally. Local governments collected $6,064,615,000 of the total and the state government $8,923,000.

Indiana taxes retail sales at a rate of 6%. Food purchased for consumption off premises is tax exempt. The tax on cigarettes is 55.5 cents per pack, which ranks 34th among the 50 states and the District of Columbia. Indiana taxes gasoline at 18 cents per gallon. This is in addition to the 18.4 cents per gallon federal tax on gasoline.

For every dollar of federal tax collected in 2004, Indiana citizens received $0.97 in federal spending.

37 ECONOMIC POLICY

The state's early economic policy was to provide farmers with access to markets by improving transportation facilities. During the Civil War era, Indiana encouraged industrial growth. In modern times, the state has financed extensive highway construction, developed deepwater ports on Lake Michigan and the Ohio River, and worked to foster industrial growth and develop its tourist industry. Tax incentives to business included a phaseout, by 1994, of the "intangibles" tax on stocks, bonds, and notes.

In the 1990s, the state government focused on a series of economic development initiatives. These included programs offering job training and retraining, the promotion of new businesses and tourism, the development of infrastructure, and the provision of investment capital for start-up companies—as well as programs providing additional tax incentives. The Indiana Economic Development Corporation (IEDC—prior to 2005, the Department of Commerce), which has sole responsibility for economic development, solicits new businesses to locate in Indiana, promotes sales of exports abroad, plans the development of energy resources, continues to foster the expansion of agriculture, and helps minority-group owners of small businesses. In the 2000 budget, the General Assembly provided $50 million for Governor Frank O'Bannon's 21st Century Research and Technology Fund to stimulate high-technology development. In 2006, the IEDC operated 10 international offices in strategic locations around the world: Sydney, Toronto, São Paulo, Beijing, Jerusalem, Amsterdam, Tokyo, Seoul, Mexico City, and Taipei.

38 HEALTH

The infant mortality rate in October 2005 was estimated at 7.9 per 1,000 live births. The birth rate in 2003 was 14 per 1,000 population. The abortion rate stood at 9.4 per 1,000 women in 2000. In 2003, about 81.5% of pregnant woman received prenatal care beginning in the first trimester. In 2004, approximately 79% of children received routine immunizations before the age of three.

The crude death rate in 2003 was 9.1 deaths per 1,000 population. As of 2002, the death rates for major causes of death (per 100,000 resident population) were as follows: heart disease, 248.8; cancer, 208.9; cerebrovascular diseases, 60.4; chronic lower respiratory diseases, 50.9; and diabetes, 27.4. The mortality rate from HIV infection was 1.9 per 100,000 population. In 2004, the reported AIDS case rate was at about 6.3 per 100,000 population. In 2002, about 58.7% of the population was considered overweight or obese. As of 2004, about 24.8% of state residents were smokers.

In 2003, Indiana had 112 community hospitals with about 18,900 beds. There were about 712,000 patient admissions that year and 15 million outpatient visits. The average daily inpatient census was about 11,000 patients. The average cost per day for hospital care was $1,352. Also in 2003, there were about 527 certified nursing facilities in the state with 55,475 beds and an overall occupancy rate of about 73.2%. In 2004, it was estimated that about 66.6% of all state residents had received some type of dental care within the year. Indiana had 222 physicians per 100,000 resident population in 2004 and 834 nurses per 100,000 in 2005. In 2004, there was a total of 2,939 dentists in the state.

About 23% of state residents were enrolled in Medicaid and Medicare programs in 2004. Approximately 14% of the state was uninsured in 2004. In 2003, state health care expenditures totaled $5.4 million.

³⁹SOCIAL WELFARE

In 2004, about 187,000 people received unemployment benefits, with the average weekly unemployment benefit at $267. In fiscal year 2005, the estimated average monthly participation in the food stamp program included about 556,285 persons (240,045 households); the average monthly benefit was about $93.87 per person. That year, the total of benefits paid through the state for the food stamp program was about $626.6 million.

Temporary Assistance for Needy Families (TANF), the system of federal welfare assistance that officially replaced Aid to Families with Dependent Children (AFDC) in 1997, was reauthorized through the Deficit Reduction Act of 2005. TANF is funded through federal block grants that are divided among the states based on an equation involving the number of recipients in each state. The employment services section of Indiana's TANF program is called IMPACT (Indiana Manpower Placement and Comprehensive Training). In 2004, the state program had 131,000 recipients; state and federal expenditures on this TANF program totaled $125 million in fiscal year 2003.

In December 2004, Social Security benefits were paid to 1,038,130 Indiana residents. This number included 657,840 retired workers, 105,260 widows and widowers, 134,020 disabled workers, 54,400 spouses, and 86,610 children. Social Security beneficiaries represented 16.8% of the total state population and 95.2% of the state's population age 65 and older. Retired workers received an average monthly payment of $1,003; widows and widowers, $955; disabled workers, $899; and spouses, $507. Payments for children of retired workers averaged $526 per month; children of deceased workers, $660; and children of disabled workers, $259. Federal Supplemental Security Income payments went to 96,191 Indiana residents in December 2004, averaging $398 a month. An additional $297,000 of state-administered supplemental payments were distributed to 1,140 residents.

⁴⁰HOUSING

In 2004, the state had an estimated 2,690,619 housing units, 2,412,885 of which were occupied; 71.8% were owner occupied. About 21% of all units were built before 1939. About 71.5% of all units are single-family, detached homes. Most units relied on utility gas and electricity for heating, but about 1,030 units were equipped for solar power. It was estimated that 158,051 units lacked telephone service, 10,304 lacked complete plumbing facilities, and 12,973 lacked complete kitchen facilities. The average household had 2.51 members.

In 2004, 39,200 privately owned housing units were authorized for construction. The median home value was $110,020. The median monthly cost for mortgage owners was $963. Renters paid a median of $589 per month. In 2006, the state received over $31.5 million in community development block grants from the US Department of Housing and Urban Development (HUD).

⁴¹EDUCATION

Although the 1816 constitution recommended the establishment of public schools, the state legislature did not provide funds for education. The constitution of 1851 more specifically outlined the state's responsibility to support a system of free public schools. Development was rapid following passage of this document; more than 2,700 schoolhouses were built in the state from 1852 to 1857, and an adult literacy rate of nearly 90% was achieved by 1860. The illiteracy rate was reduced to 5.2% for the adult population in 1900, to 1.7% in 1950, and to only 0.7% in 1970, when Indiana ranked 14th among the 50 states. In 2004, 87.2% of those aged 25 years and over were high school graduates, and 21.1% had completed four or more years of college.

The total enrollment for fall 2002 in Indiana's public schools stood at 1,004,000. Of these, 714,000 attended schools from kindergarten through grade eight, and 290,000 attended high school. Approximately 81.5% of the students were white, 12.4% were black, 4.8% were Hispanic, 1.1% were Asian/Pacific Islander, and 0.2% were American Indian/Alaska Native. Total enrollment was estimated at 1,009,000 in fall 2003 and was expected to be 1,029,000 by fall 2014, a 2.5% increase during the period 2002–14. Expenditures for public education in 2003–04 were estimated at $10 billion or $8,280 per student, closest to the $8,287 United States average. There were 109,101 students enrolled in 784 private schools in fall 2003. Since 1969, the National Assessment of Educational Progress (NAEP) has tested public school students nationwide. The resulting report, *The Nation's Report Card,* stated that in 2005, eighth graders in Indiana scored 282 out of 500 in mathematics, compared with the national average of 278.

As of fall 2002, there were 342,064 students enrolled in college or graduate school; minority students comprised 12.6% of total postsecondary enrollment. In 2005, Indiana had 101 degree-granting institutions. Indiana University, the state's largest institution of higher education, was founded in 1820. It is one of the largest state universities in the United States, with a total of eight campuses. The Bloomington campus has a nationally recognized music program. Other major state universities include Purdue University (Lafayette), Ball State University (Muncie), and Indiana State University (Terre Haute). Well-known private universities in the state include Notre Dame (at South Bend) and Butler (Indianapolis). Small private colleges and universities include DePauw (Greencastle), Earlham (Richmond), Hanover (Hanover), and Wabash (Crawfordsville).

⁴²ARTS

The earliest center for artists in Indiana was the Art Association of Indianapolis, founded in 1883. It managed the John Herron Art Institute, consisting of a museum and art school (1906–08). Around 1900, art colonies sprang up in Richmond, Muncie, South Bend, and Nashville. Indianapolis remains the state's cultural center, especially since the opening in the late 1960s of the Lilly Pavilion of the Decorative Arts; the Krannert Pavilion, which houses the paintings originally in the Herron Museum; the Clowes Art Pavilion; and the Grace Showalter Pavilion of the Performing Arts (all collectively known as the Indianapolis Museum of Art). Since 1969, the Indiana Arts Commission has taken art—and artists— into many Indiana communities; the commission also sponsors biennial awards to artists in the state. In 2004, the Indiana Arts Commission awarded 86 artists up to $1,000 per grant as part of the Individual Artist Project—461 grants were awarded overall for that year, aiding artists in 85 of Indiana's 92 counties.

The state's first resident theater company established itself in Indianapolis in 1840, and the first theater building, the Metropolitan, was opened there in 1858. Ten years later, the Academy of Music was founded as the center for dramatic activities in Indianapolis. In 1875, the Grand Opera House opened there, and the following year it was joined by the English Opera House, where touring performers such as Sarah Bernhardt, Edwin Booth, and Ethel Barrymore held the stage. Amateur theater has been popular since the founding in 1915 of the nation's oldest amateur drama group, the Little Theater Society, which later became the Civic Theater of Indianapolis. The Civic Theater's 2005–06 season included performances of *Annie Get Your Gun, Disney's Beauty and the Beast,* and *Brighton Beach Memoirs.*

Music has flourished in Indiana. Connersville reportedly was the first American city to establish a high school band, while Richmond claims the first high school symphony orchestra. The Indianapolis Symphony Orchestra was founded in 1930. There are 23 other symphony orchestras in the state. The Indianapolis Opera was founded in 1975. The Arthur Jordan College of Music is part of Butler University in Indianapolis, and the music program at Indiana University's Bloomington campus has a national reputation, especially its string department, which has attracted some of the world's most renowned musicians to its faculty. The annual Indiana Fiddlers' Gathering, founded in 1973, is a three-day festival featuring the bluegrass, swing fiddle, string band, and Celtic and other ethnic music.

In 2005, the Indiana Arts Commission and other Indiana arts organizations received 19 grants totaling $935,700 from the National Endowment for the Arts. The Indiana Humanities Council sponsors programs that include Habits of the Heart, a youth volunteer leadership development program, and History Alive!—an educational program featuring live portrayals of famous historical figures. In 2005, the National Endowment for the Humanities supported 28 programs in the state with grants totaling $2,599,475.

43 LIBRARIES AND MUSEUMS

For the calendar year 2001, Indiana had 239 public library systems with a total of 430 libraries, of which 191 were branches. The state constitution of 1816 provided for the establishment of public libraries. A majority of Indiana cities opened such libraries but neglected to provide adequate financing. Semiprivate libraries did better: Workingmen's libraries were set up by a bequest at New Harmony and 14 other towns. After the state legislature provided for township school libraries in 1852, more than two-thirds of the townships established them, and the public library system has thrived ever since. In 2001, operating income for the state's public library system totaled $245,243,000, including $784,000 from federal grants and $19,947,000 from state grants. The largest book collections are at public libraries in Indianapolis, Fort Wayne, Gary, Evansville, Merrillville, and Hammond. The total book stock of all Indiana public libraries in 2001 was 22,145,000 volumes of books and serial publications, and a total circulation of 62,744,000. The system also had 1,146,000 audio and 1,068,000

video items, 72,000 electronic format items (CD-ROMs, magnetic tapes, and disks), and 38 bookmobiles.

The Indiana State Library has a strong collection of documents about Indiana's history and a large genealogical collection. The Indiana University Library has special collections on American literature and history and an extensive collection of rare books; the University of Notre Dame has a noteworthy collection on medieval history; and the Purdue University Libraries contain outstanding industrial and agricultural collections, as well as voluminous materials on Indiana history.

Private libraries and museums include those maintained by historical societies in Indianapolis, Fort Wayne, and South Bend. Also of note are the General Lew Wallace Study Museum in Crawfordsville and the Elwood Haynes Museum of early technology in Kokomo. In all, Indiana had 179 museums in 2000 registered with the American Association of Museums. Many county historical societies maintain smaller museums, such as the Wayne County Historical Museum.

Indiana's historical sites of most interest to visitors are the Lincoln Boyhood National Memorial near Gentryville, the Levi Coffin Home (one of the Underground Railroad stops) in Fountain City, the Benjamin Harrison Memorial Home and the James Whitcomb Riley Home in Indianapolis, and the Grouseland Home of William Henry Harrison in Vincennes. Among several archaeological sites are two large mound groups: one at Mounds State Park near Anderson, which dates from about AD 800–900, and a reconstructed village site at Angel Mounds, Newburgh, which dates from 1300–1500.

44 COMMUNICATIONS

About 91.8% of all households had telephone service in 2004. Additionally, by June of that same year there were 2,844,568 mobile wireless telephone subscribers. In 2003, 59.6% of Indiana households had a computer and 51.0% had Internet access. By June 2005, there were 745,511 high-speed lines in Indiana, 678,417 residential and 67,094 for business. The state's first radio station was licensed in 1922 at Purdue University, Lafayette. Indiana had 20 major AM, 102 major FM radio stations, and 30 television stations as of 2005. Powerful radio and television transmissions from Chicago and Cincinnati also blanket the state. In 1999, the Indianapolis area had 963,320 television households, 65% of which received cable. A total of 73,696 internet domain names were registered in the state in 2000.

45 PRESS

The first newspaper was published in Indiana at Vincennes in 1804 and a second pioneer weekly appeared at Madison nine years later. By 1830, newspapers were also being published in Terre Haute, Indianapolis, and 11 other towns; the following year, the state's oldest surviving newspaper, the *Richmond Palladium,* began publication. Most pioneer newspapers were highly political and engaged in acrimonious feuds; in 1836, for example, the *Indianapolis Journal* referred to the editors of the rival *Democrat* as "the Lying, Hireling Scoundrels." By the time of the Civil War, Indiana had 154 weeklies and 13 dailies.

The last third of the 19th century brought a sharp increase in both the number and the quality of newspapers. Two newspapers that later became the state's largest in circulation, the *Indianapo-*

lis News and the *Star,* began publishing in 1869 and 1903, respectively. In 1941, there were 294 weekly and 98 daily newspapers in Indiana; the number declined after World War II because of fierce competition for readers and advertising dollars, rising operating costs, and other financial difficulties.

In 2005, the state had 24 morning dailies and 44 evening dailies; Sunday papers numbered 25. In 2005, the Indianapolis morning *Star* had a daily circulation of 252,021 (Sunday circulation, 358,261) and the Gary *Post-Tribune's* circulation averaged 65,621 daily and 73,795 on Sundays.

A number of magazines are published in Indiana, including *Children's Digest* and the *Saturday Evening Post.*

Indiana is noted for its literary productivity. The list of authors claimed by Indiana up to 1966 showed a total of 3,600. Examination of the 10 best-selling novels each year from 1900 to 1940 (allowing 10 points to the top best-seller, down to 1 point for the 10th best-selling book) showed Indiana with a score of 213 points, exceeded only by New York's 218.

Many Hoosier authors were first published by Indiana's major book publisher, Bobbs-Merrill. Indiana University Press is an important publisher of scholarly books.

46 ORGANIZATIONS

In 2006, there were over 8,895 nonprofit organizations registered within the state, of which about 5,099 were registered as charitable, educational, or religious organizations. National organizations with headquarters in the state include the American Camping Association, located in Martinsville, and the Amateur Athletic Union of the United States, the American Legion, the US Gymnastics Federation, and Kiwanis International and Circle K International, all in Indianapolis. National sports and hobby associations based in Indiana include the Academy of Model Aeronautics, the United States Auto Club, the United States Rowing Association, USA Track and Field (which sponsors a Hall of Fame), and USA Gymnastics.

There are several fraternities with national offices in the state, including Delta Psi Omega, Alpha Chi Omega, Alpha Gamma Delta, Kappa Delta Pi, and Lambda Chi Alpha. Professional and educational organizations include the American College of Sports Medicine, American Theatre Critics Association, and Bands of America.

Philanthropic foundations headquartered in Indiana include the Eugene V. Debs Foundation (Terre Haute) and the Irwin Sweeny-Miller Foundation (Columbus). The international headquarters of the Pentecostal Assemblies of the World is located in Indianapolis. The Indiana Arts Commission is the primary state organization for promoting study and appreciation for the arts. There are numerous local arts organizations and many county historical societies. The Quilters Hall of Fame is located in Marion.

47 TOURISM, TRAVEL, AND RECREATION

Tourism is of moderate economic importance to Indiana; in 2004, the industry declined slightly. That year, some 57.7 million visitors to the state spent $6.5 billion, down from $6.7 billion in 2003. The industry supported some 94,000 full-time jobs. Tourism payroll is $1.7 billion.

About 70% of visitors participate in outdoor activities. Summer resorts are located in the north along Lake Michigan and in

Steuben and Kosciusko counties, where there are nearly 200 lakes. Popular tourist sites include the reconstructed village of New Harmony, site of the famous communal living experiments of the early 19th century; the Indianapolis Motor Speedway and Museum (home of the Indianapolis 500 auto race); and the George Rogers Clark National Historic Park at Vincennes. The city of Huntington has a museum dedicated to US vice presidents and Fort Wayne has a Lincoln Museum. The city of Fremont has the Wild Winds Buffalo Preserve, and the College Football Hall of Fame is in South Bend, also home to the University of Notre Dame.

Indiana has 23 state parks comprising 59,292 acres (21,800 hectares). The largest state park is Brown County (15,543 acres/6,290 hectares), near Nashville. There are 15 state fish and wildlife preserves, totaling about 75,200 acres (30,400 hectares). The largest are Pigeon River, near Howe, and Willow Slough, at Morocco. Game animals during the hunting season include deer, squirrel, and rabbit; ruffed grouse, quail, ducks, geese, and partridge are the main game birds.

In addition to the Indiana State Museum, there are 15 state memorials, including the Wilbur Wright State Memorial at his birthplace near Millville, the Ernie Pyle birthplace near Dana, and the old state capitol at Corydon. Among the natural attractions are the Indiana Dunes National Lakeshore on Lake Michigan (12,534 acres/5,072 hectares); the state's largest waterfall, Cataract Falls, near Cloverdale; and the largest underground cavern, at Wyandotte.

48 SPORTS

Indiana is represented in professional sports by the Indiana Pacers of the National Basketball Association, the Indiana Fever of the Women's National Basketball Association, and the National Football League's Colts, which moved to Indianapolis from Baltimore in 1984. There are also several minor league baseball, basketball, and hockey teams in the state.

The state's biggest annual sports event is the Indianapolis 500, which has been held at the Indianapolis Motor Speedway on Memorial Day or the Sunday before every year since 1911 (except for the war years 1917 and 1942–45). The race is now part of a three-day festival held over Memorial Day weekend that attracts crowds of over 300,000 spectators, the largest crowd for any sporting event anywhere in the world.

The state's most popular amateur sport is basketball. The high school boys' basketball tournament culminates on the last Saturday in March, when the four finalists play afternoon and evening games to determine the winner. A tournament for girls' basketball teams began in 1976. Basketball is also popular at the college level: Indiana University won the National Collegiate Athletic Association (NCAA) Division I basketball championship in 1940, 1953, 1976, 1981, and 1987 and the National Invitational Tournament (NIT) in 1979; Purdue University won the NIT title in 1974; and Indiana State, led by state basketball legend Larry Bird, advanced to the NCAA finals in 1979. Evansville College won the NCAA Division II championships in 1959–60, 1964–65, and 1971.

Collegiate football in Indiana has a colorful tradition stretching back to at least 1913, when Knute Rockne of Notre Dame unleashed the forward pass as a potent football weapon. Notre Dame, which competes as an independent, was recognized as National Champion in 1946–47, 1949, 1966, 1973 (with Alabama),

1977, and 1988. The Notre Dame Fighting Irish won the following string of bowl games: the Orange Bowl in 1975 and 1990; the Cotton Bowl in 1971, 1978, 1979, 1993, and 1994; the Sugar Bowl in 1973 and 1992; and the Fiesta Bowl in 1989. Indiana and Purdue compete in the Big Ten Conference. Purdue won the Rose Bowl in 1967. Indiana State is part of the Missouri Valley Conference.

The Little 500, a 50-mi (80-km) bicycle race, is held each spring at Indiana University's Bloomington campus. The RCA Championships are held annually in Indianapolis.

Other annual sporting events include the National Muzzle-Loading Rifle Association Championship Shoot, which is held in Friendship in September, and the Sugar Creek canoe race, which is held in Crawfordsville in April.

⁴⁹ FAMOUS INDIANANS

Indiana has contributed one US president and four vice presidents to the nation. Benjamin Harrison (b.Ohio, 1833–1901), the 23rd president, was a Republican who served one term (1889–93) and then returned to Indianapolis, where his home is now a national historic landmark. Three vice presidents were Indiana residents: Thomas Hendricks (b.Ohio, 1819–85), who served only eight months under President Grover Cleveland and died in office; Schuyler Colfax (b.New York, 1823–85), who served under President Ulysses S. Grant; and Charles Fairbanks (b.Ohio, 1852–1918), who served under President Theodore Roosevelt. Two vice presidents were native sons: Thomas Marshall (1854–1925), who served two four-year terms with President Woodrow Wilson, and James Danforth Quayle of Indianapolis (b.1947), President George H. W. Bush's running mate in the 1988 presidential election. Marshall, remembered for his wit, originated the remark, "What this country needs is a good five-cent cigar."

Other Indiana-born political figures include Eugene V. Debs (1855–1926), Socialist Party candidate for president five times, and Wendell L. Willkie (1892–1944), the Republican candidate in 1940.

A dozen native and adoptive Hoosiers have held cabinet posts. Hugh McCulloch (b.Maine, 1808–95) was twice US secretary of the treasury, in 1865–69 and 1884–85. Walter Q. Gresham (b.England, 1832–95) was successively postmaster general, secretary of the treasury, and secretary of state. John W. Foster (1836–1917) was an editor and diplomat before service as secretary of state under President Benjamin Harrison. Two other postmasters general came from Indiana: Harry S. New (1858–1937) and Will H. Hays (1879–1954). Hays resigned to become president of the Motion Picture Producers and Distributors (1922–45) and enforced its moral code in Hollywood films through what became widely known as the Hays Office. Two Hoosiers served as US secretary of the interior: Caleb B. Smith (b.Massachusetts, 1808–64) and John P. Usher (b.New York, 1816–89). Richard W. Thompson (b.Virginia, 1809–1900) was secretary of the Navy. William H. H. Miller (b.New York, 1840–1917) was attorney general. Two native sons and Purdue University alumni have been secretaries of agriculture: Claude R. Wickard (1873–1967) and Earl Butz (b.1909). Paul V. McNutt (1891–1955) was a governor of Indiana, high commissioner to the Philippines, and director of the Federal Security Administration.

Only one Hoosier, Sherman Minton (1890–1965), has served on the US Supreme Court. Ambrose Burnside (1824–81) and Lew Wallace (1827–1905) were Union generals during the Civil War; Wallace later wrote popular historical novels. Oliver P. Morton (1823–77) was a strong and meddlesome governor during the war and a leader of the Radical Republicans during the postwar Reconstruction. Colonel Richard Owen (b.England, 1810–90) commanded Camp Morton (Indianapolis) for Confederate prisoners; after the war, some of his grateful prisoners contributed to place a bust of Owen in the Indiana statehouse. Rear Admiral Norman Scott (1889–1942) distinguished himself at Guadalcanal during World War II. Nearly 70 Hoosiers have won the Medal of Honor.

Dr. Hermann J. Muller (b.New York, 1890–1967) of Indiana University won the Nobel Prize in physiology or medicine in 1946 for proving that radiation can produce mutation in genes. Harold C. Urey (1893–1981) won the Nobel Prize in chemistry in 1934, and Wendell Stanley (1904–71) won it in 1946. The Nobel Prize in economics was awarded to Paul Samuelson (b.1915) in 1970. The Pulitzer Prize in biography was awarded in 1920 to Albert J. Beveridge (b.Ohio, 1862–1927) for his *Life of John Marshall*. Beveridge also served in the US Senate. Booth Tarkington (1869–1946) won the Pulitzer Prize for fiction in 1918 and 1921. A. B. Guthrie (1901–91) won it for fiction in 1950. The Pulitzer Prize in history went to R. C. Buley (1893–1968) in 1951 for *The Old Northwest*.

Aviation pioneer Wilbur Wright (1867–1912) was born in Millville. Other figures in the public eye were chemist Harvey W. Wiley (1844–1930), who was responsible for the Food and Drug Act of 1906; Emil Schram (1893–1897), president of the New York Stock Exchange from 1931 to 1951; and Alfred C. Kinsey (b.New Jersey, 1894–1956), who investigated human sexual behavior and issued the two famous "Kinsey reports" in 1948 and 1953.

Indiana claims such humorists as George Ade (1866–1944), Frank McKinney "Kin" Hubbard (b.Ohio, 1868–1930), and Don Herold (1889–1966). Historians Charles (1874–1948) and Mary (1876–1958) Beard, Claude Bowers (1878–1958), and Glenn Tucker (1892–1976) were Hoosiers. Maurice Thompson (1844–1901) and George Barr McCutcheon (1866–1928) excelled in historical romances. The best-known poets were James Whitcomb Riley (1849–1916) and William Vaughn Moody (1869–1910). Juvenile writer Annie Fellows Johnston (1863–1931) produced the "Little Colonel" series.

Other Indiana novelists include Edward Eggleston (1837–1902), Meredith Nicholson (1866–1947), David Graham Phillips (1868–1911), Gene Stratton Porter (1868–1924), Theodore Dreiser (1871–1945), Lloyd C. Douglas (1877–1951), Rex Stout (1886–1975), William E. Wilson (1906–88), Jessamyn West (1907–84), and Kurt Vonnegut (b.1922). Well-known journalists were news analyst Elmer Davis (1890–1958), war correspondent Ernie Pyle (1900–45), and columnist Janet Flanner "Genet" (1892–1978) of *The New Yorker*.

Among the few noted painters Indiana has produced are Theodore C. Steele (1847–1928), William M. Chase (1851–1927), J. Ottis Adams (1851–1927), Otto Stark (1859–1926), Wayman Adams (1883–1959), Clifton Wheeler (1883–1953), Marie Goth (1887–1975), C. Curry Bohm (1894–1971), and Floyd Hopper (1909–84).

Composers of Indiana origin have worked mainly in popular music: Paul Dresser (1857–1906), Cole Porter (1893–1964), and Howard Hoagland "Hoagy" Carmichael (1899–1981). Howard

Hawks (1896–1977) was a renowned film director. Entertainers from Indiana include actor and dancer Clifton Webb (Webb Hollenbeck, 1896–1966); orchestra leader Phil Harris (1904–95); comedians Ole Olsen (1892–1963), Richard "Red" Skelton (1913–97), and Herb Shriner (b.Ohio, 1918–70); actresses Marjorie Main (1890–1975) and Carole Lombard (Jane Peters, 1908–42); and singer Michael Jackson (b.1958).

Hoosier sports heroes include Knute Rockne (b.Norway, 1888–1931), famed as a football player and coach at Notre Dame. Star professionals who played high school basketball in Indiana include Oscar Robertson (b.Tennessee, 1938) and Larry Bird (b.1956), who was honored at Indiana State University in 1978–79 as college basketball's player of the year.

50 BIBLIOGRAPHY

Blakey, George T. *Creating a Hoosier Self-Portrait: The Federal Writers' Project in Indiana, 1935–1942.* Bloomington: Indiana University Press, 2005.

Boomhower, Ray E. *Jacob Piatt Dunn, Jr.: A Life in History and Politics, 1855-1924.* Indianapolis: Indiana Historical Society, 1997.

Cayton, Andrew R. L. *Frontier Indiana.* Bloomington: Indiana University Press, 1996.

Council of State Governments. *The Book of the States, 2006 Edition.* Lexington, Ky.: Council of State Governments, 2006.

Ferrucci, Kate. *Limestone Lives: Voices from the Indiana Stone Belt.* Bloomington, Ind.: Quarry Books, 2004.

Gisler, Margaret. *Fun with the Family in Indiana: Hundreds of Ideas for Day Trips with the Kids.* Guilford, Conn.: Globe Pequot Press, 2000.

McAuliffe, Bill. *Indiana Facts and Symbols.* New York: Hilltop Books, 1999.

Nation, Richard Franklin. *At Home in the Hoosier Hills: Agriculture, Politics, and Religion in Southern Indiana, 1810–1870.* Bloomington: Indiana University Press, 2005.

US Department of Commerce, Economics and Statistics Administration, US Census Bureau. *Indiana, 2000. Summary Social, Economic, and Housing Characteristics: 2000 Census of Population and Housing.* Washington, D.C.: US Government Printing Office, 2003.

IOWA

State of Iowa

ORIGIN OF STATE NAME: Named for Iowa Indians of the Siouan family. **NICKNAME:** The Hawkeye State. **CAPITAL:** Des Moines. **ENTERED UNION:** 28 December 1846 (29th). **SONG:** "The Song of Iowa." **MOTTO:** Our Liberties We Prize and Our Rights We Will Maintain. **FLAG:** There are three vertical stripes of blue, white, and red; in the center a spreading eagle holds in its beak a blue ribbon with the state motto. **OFFICIAL SEAL:** A sheaf and field of standing wheat and farm utensils represent agriculture; a lead furnace and a pile of pig lead are to the right. In the center stands a citizen-soldier holding a US flag with a liberty cap atop the staff in one hand and a rifle in the other. Behind him is the Mississippi River with the steamer *Iowa* and mountains; above him an eagle holds the state motto. Surrounding this scene are the words "The Great Seal of the State of Iowa" against a gold background. **BIRD:** Eastern goldfinch. **FLOWER:** Wild rose. **TREE:** Oak. **LEGAL HOLIDAYS:** New Year's Day, 1 January; Birthday of Martin Luther King Jr., 3rd Monday in January; Memorial Day, last Monday in May; Independence Day, 4 July; Labor Day, 1st Monday in September; Veterans' Day, 11 November; Thanksgiving Day, 4th Thursday in November; Christmas Day, 25 December. **TIME:** 6 AM CST = noon GMT.

¹LOCATION, SIZE, AND EXTENT

Located in the western north-central United States, Iowa is the smallest of the midwestern states situated w of the Mississippi River and ranks 25th in size among the 50 states.

The total area of Iowa is 56,275 sq mi (145,752 sq km), of which land takes up 55,965 sq mi (144,949 sq km) and inland water 310 sq mi (803 sq km). The state extends 324 mi (521 km) E–W; its maximum extension N–S is 210 mi (338 km).

Iowa is bordered on the N by Minnesota; on the E by Wisconsin and Illinois (with the line formed by the Mississippi River); on the s by Missouri (with the extreme southeastern line defined by the Des Moines River); and on the w by Nebraska and South Dakota (with the line demarcated by the Missouri River and a tributary, the Big Sioux).

The total boundary length of Iowa is 1,151 mi (1,853 km). The state's geographic center is in Story County near Ames.

²TOPOGRAPHY

The topography of Iowa consists of a gently rolling plain that slopes from the highest point of 1,670 ft (509 m) in the northwest (Osceola County) to the lowest point of 480 ft (146 m) in the southeast at the mouth of the Des Moines River. About two-thirds of the state lies between 800 ft (244 m) and 1,400 ft (427 m) above sea level; the mean elevation of land is 1,100 ft (336 m).

Supremely well suited for agriculture, Iowa has the richest and deepest topsoil in the United States and an excellent watershed. Approximately two-thirds of the state's area is drained by the Mississippi River, which forms the entire eastern boundary, and its tributaries. The western part of the state is drained by the Missouri River and its tributaries. Iowa has 13 natural lakes. The largest are Spirit Lake (9 mi/14 km long) and West Okoboji Lake (6 mi/10 km long), both near the state's northwest border.

The Iowa glacial plain was formed by five different glaciers. The last glacier, which covered about one-fifth of the state's area, re-

treated from the north-central region some 10,000 years ago, leaving the topsoil as its legacy. Glacial drift formed the small lakes in the north. The oldest rock outcropping, located in the state's northwest corner, is about 1 billion years old.

³CLIMATE

Iowa lies in the humid continental zone and generally has hot summers, cold winters, and wet springs.

Temperatures vary widely during the year, with an annual average of 49°F (9°C). The state averages 166 days of full sunshine and 199 cloudy or partly cloudy days. Des Moines, in the central part of the state, has an average maximum temperature of 86°F (30°C) in July and an average minimum of 11°F (-4°C) in January. The record low temperature for the state is -47°F (-44°C), established at Washta on 12 January 1912 and recorded again on Elkader on 3 February 1996; the record high is 118°F (48°C), registered at Keokuk on 20 July 1934. Annual precipitation averages 32.4 in (82 cm) at Des Moines; statewide, snowfall averages 33.2 in (84 cm) annually and relative humidity averages 72%.

⁴FLORA AND FAUNA

Although most of Iowa is under cultivation, such unusual wild specimens as bunchberry and bearberry can be found in the northeast, where the loess soil supports tumblegrass, western beard-tongue, and prickly pear cactus. Other notable plants are pink lady's slipper and twinleaf in the eastern woodlands, arrowgrass in the northwest, and erect dryflower and royal and cinnamon ferns in sandy regions. More than 80 native plants can no longer be found, and at least 35 others are confined to a single location. The federal government classified five plant species as threatened as of April 2006. Among these are the northern wild monkshood and the eastern and western prairie fringed orchids.

Common Iowa mammals include red and gray foxes, raccoon, opossum, woodchuck, muskrat, common cottontail, gray fox, and flying squirrel. The bobolink and purple martin have flyways over the state; the cardinal, rose-breasted grosbeak, and eastern goldfinch (the state bird) nest there. Game fish include rainbow trout, smallmouth bass, and walleye; in all, Iowa has 140 native fish species.

Rare animals include the pygmy shrew, ermine, black-billed cuckoo, and crystal darter. Listed as threatened or endangered by the federal government in April 2006 were eight species of animal, including the Indiana bat, bald eagle, Higgins' eye pearlymussel, piping plover, Topeka Shiner, Iowa Pleistocene snail, pallid sturgeon, and the least tern.

5 ENVIRONMENTAL PROTECTION

Because this traditionally agricultural state's most valuable resource has been its topsoil, Iowa's conservation measures beginning in the 1930s were directed toward preventing soil erosion and preserving watershed runoff. In the 1980s and 1990s, Iowans were particularly concerned with improving air quality, preventing chemical pollution, and preserving water supplies. While wetlands once covered about 11% of the state, as of 1997, that percentage had dwindled down to about 1.2%. The Wetlands Reserve Program of the 1990 Food, Agriculture, Conservation and Trade Act was created to reclaim some of the state's lost wetlands.

On 1 July 1983, the Department of Water, Air and Waste Management came into operation, with responsibility for environmental functions formerly exercised by separate state agencies. Functions of the new department include regulating operation of the state's 2,900 public water supply systems, overseeing nearly 1,200 municipal and industrial wastewater treatment plants, inspecting dams, and establishing chemical and bacterial standards to protect the quality of lakes. The department also enforces laws prohibiting open dumping of solid wastes, regulates the construction and operation of 140 solid waste disposal projects, and monitors the handling of hazardous wastes. It also establishes standards for air quality and regulates the emission of air pollutants from more than 600 industries and utilities.

In 2003, 37.4 million lb of toxic chemicals were released in the state. In 2003, Iowa had 172 hazardous waste sites listed in the US Environment Protection Agency (EPA) database, 11 of which were on the National Priorities List as of 2006, including the Iowa Ammunition Plant and the John Deere Ottumwa works landfill. In 2005, federal EPA grants awarded to the state included $17.9 million for a clean water revolving fund.

6 POPULATION

Iowa ranked 30th in population in the United States with an estimated total of 2,966,934 in 2005, an increase of 1.4% since 2000. Between 1990 and 2000, Iowa's population grew from 2,776,755 to 2,926,324, an increase of 5.4%. The population is projected to reach 2,993,222 million by 2025. The population density in 2004 was 52.9 persons per sq mi.

Iowa's population growth was rapid during the early years of settlement. When the first pioneers arrived in the early 19th century, an estimated 8,000 Indians were living within the state's present boundaries. From 1832 to 1840, the number of white settlers increased from fewer than 50 to 43,112. The population had almost doubled to more than 80,000 by the time Iowa became a state in 1846. The great influx of European immigrants who came via other states during the 1840s and 1850s caused the new state's

population to soar to 674,913 at the 1860 Census. By the end of the next decade, the population had reached nearly 1,200,000; by 1900, it had surpassed 2,200,000. The state's population growth leveled off in the 20th century.

In 2004, the median age in Iowa was 38. About 23% of the populace was under age 18, while 14.7% was age 65 or older.

In 2004, the largest cities with populations of 100,000 or more were Des Moines, 194,311, and Cedar Rapids, 122,206. Other large cities include Davenport, Sioux City, Waterloo, Dubuque, and Iowa City. In 2004, the Des Moines metropolitan area had 511,878 residents; the Davenport metropolitan area had 375,437 residents that year.

7 ETHNIC GROUPS

In 2000, there were 61,853 black Americans, 8,989 American Indians, and 82,473 Hispanics and Latinos living in Iowa. In 2004, blacks made up 2.3% of the population, Hispanics and Latinos 3.5%, Asians 1.4%, and American Indians 0.3%. That year, 0.9% of the population reported origin of two or more races.

In 2000, among Iowans of European descent, there were 1,046,153 Germans (35.7% of the state total); 395,905 Irish (13.5%); and 277,487 English (9.5%). The foreign-born population numbered 91,085 (3.1%), more than double the total of 43,316 in 1990. Primary countries of origin included Germany, Mexico, Laos, Canada, Korea, and Vietnam.

8 LANGUAGES

A few Indian place-names are the legacy of the early Siouan Iowa Indians and the westward-moving Algonkian Sauk and Fox tribes who pushed them out: Iowa, Ottumwa, Keokuk, Sioux City, Oskaloosa, Decorah.

The following table gives selected statistics from the 2000 Census for language spoken at home by persons five years old and over. The category "Other West Germanic languages" includes Dutch, Pennsylvania Dutch, and Afrikaans. The category "African languages" includes Amharic, Ibo, Twi, Yoruba, Bantu, Swahili, and Somali. The category "Scandinavian languages" includes Danish, Norwegian, and Swedish.

LANGUAGE	NUMBER	PERCENT
Population 5 years and over	**2,738,499**	**100.0**
Speak only English	2,578,477	94.2
Speak a language other than English	160,022	5.8
Speak a language other than English	**160,022**	**5.8**
Spanish or Spanish Creole	79,491	2.9
German	17,262	0.6
French (incl. Patois, Cajun)	7,476	0.3
Serbo-Croatian	6,452	0.2
Vietnamese	6,182	0.2
Chinese	5,191	0.2
Laotian	3,939	0.1
Other West Germanic languages	3,552	0.1
Korean	2,493	0.1
Scandinavian languages	2,385	0.1
Russian	2,233	0.1
African languages	2,137	0.1
Arabic	2,053	0.1

In 2000, 94.2% of all Iowans aged five or more spoke only English at home, down from 96.1% in 1990.

Iowa English reflects the three major migration streams: Northern in that half of the state above Des Moines and North Midland

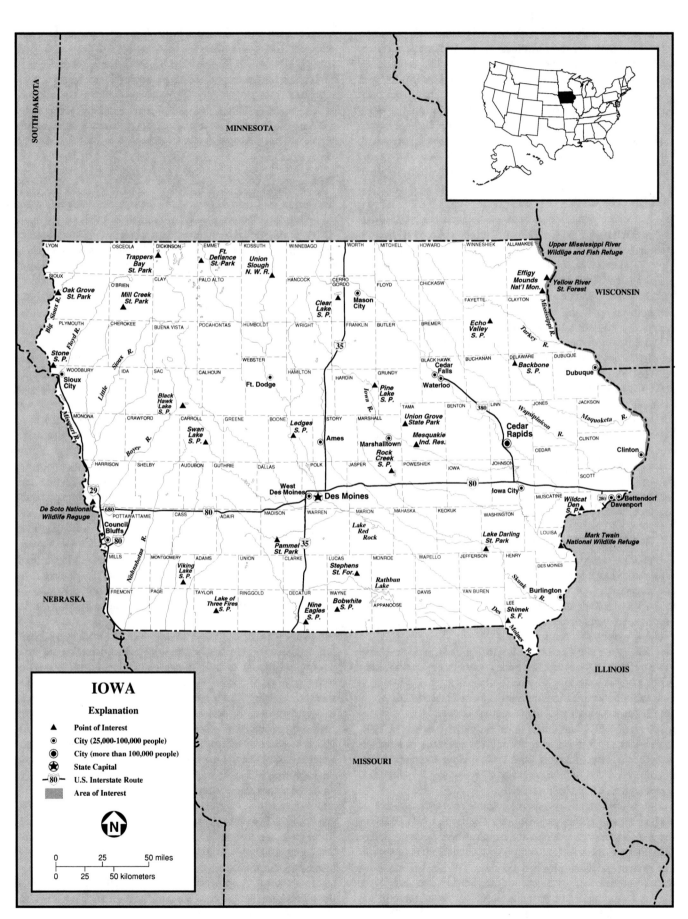

in the southern half, with a slight South Midland trace in the extreme southeastern corner. Although some Midland features extend into upper Iowa, rather sharp contrasts exist between the two halves. In pronunciation, Northern features contrast directly with Midland: /hyumor/ with /yumor/, /ah/ in *on* and *fog* with /aw/, the vowel of *but* in *bulge* with the vowel of *put*, and /too/ with /tyoo/ for *two*. Northern words also contrast with Midland words: *crab* with *crawdad*, *corn on the cob* with *roasting ears*, *quarter to* with *quarter till*, *barnyard* with *barn lot*, and *gopher* with *ground squirrel*.

9RELIGIONS

The first church building in Iowa was constructed by Methodists in Dubuque in 1834; a Roman Catholic church was built in Dubuque the following year. By 1860, the largest religious sects were the Methodists, Presbyterians, Catholics, Baptists, and Congregationalists. Other religious groups who came to Iowa during the 19th century included Lutherans, Dutch Reformers, Quakers, Mennonites, Jews, and the Community of True Inspiration, or Amana Society, which founded seven communal villages.

Mainline Protestantism is predominant in the state, even though the largest single Protestant denomination is the Evangelical Free Church of America, which had about 268,211 members in 2000. Other major Protestant denominations include the United Methodist Church (with 195,024 adherents in 2004), the Lutheran Church–Missouri Synod (120,075 adherents in 2000), the Presbyterian Church USA (69,974 adherents in 2000), and the United Church of Christ (36,326 adherents in 2005). Roman Catholic Church membership was about 506,698 in 2004. The Jewish community had about 6,400 members in 2000. The same year, Muslims numbered about 4,717. Nearly 41.5% (over 1.2 million) of the state population did not specify a religious affiliation.

10TRANSPORTATION

Early settlers came to Iowa by way of the Ohio and Mississippi rivers and the Great Lakes, then traveled overland on trails via wagon and stagecoach. The need of Iowa farmers to haul their products to market over long distances prompted the development of the railroads, particularly during the 1880s. River traffic still plays a vital role in the state's transport.

In 2003, Iowa had 4,248 mi (6,839 km) of track, including 2,849 route miles (4,587 km) of Class I track operated by four railroads. Amtrak operates the long-distance California Zephyr (Chicago to Oakland, California) and Southwest Chief (Chicago to Los Angeles, California), serving six major stations in Iowa.

Iowa had 113,377 mi (182,536 km) of public roadway in 2004. In that same year, there were about 3.461 million registered vehicles in the state, including some 1.872 million automobiles, approximately 1.448 million trucks of all types, and around 1,000 buses, with 2,003,723 licensed drivers.

Iowa is bordered by two great navigable rivers, the Mississippi and the Missouri. They provided excellent transport facilities for the early settlers via keelboats and paddle-wheel steamers. Today, rivers remain an important part of Iowa's intermodal transportation system. In 2004, Iowa had 492 miles (792 km) of navigable inland waterways. In 2003, waterborne shipments totaled 14.471 million tons. Important terminal ports on the Mississippi are Dubuque and Davenport, and on the Missouri, Sioux City and Council Bluffs. These rivers provide shippers a gateway to an extensive inland waterway system that has access to ports in St. Paul, Chicago, Pittsburgh, Houston, and New Orleans. Most docks in Iowa are privately owned, and all are privately operated.

In 2005, Iowa had a total of 322 public and private-use aviation-related facilities. This included 233 airports, 87 heliports, and 2 STOLports (Short Take-Off and Landing). Iowa's busiest airfield is Des Moines International Airport, which in 2004 had 975,859 enplanements.

11HISTORY

The fertile land now known as the state of Iowa was first visited by primitive hunting bands of the Paleo-Indian period some 12,000 years ago. The first permanent settlers of the land were the Woodland Indians, who built villages in the forested areas along the Mississippi River, introduced agriculture, and left behind only their animal-shaped burial mounds.

Not until June 1673 did the first known white men come to the territory. When Louis Jolliet, accompanied by five French voyageurs and a Jesuit priest, Jacques Marquette, stopped briefly in Iowa on his voyage down the Mississippi, the region was uninhabited except for the Sioux in the west and a few outposts of Illinois and Iowa Indians in the east. Iowa was part of the vast, vaguely defined Louisiana Territory that extended from the Gulf of Mexico to the Canadian border and was ruled by the French until title was transferred to Spain in 1762. Napoleon took the territory back in 1800 and then promptly sold all of the Louisiana Territory to the amazed American envoys who had come to Paris seeking only the purchase of New Orleans and the mouth of the Mississippi. After Iowa thus came under US control in 1803, the Lewis and Clark expedition worked its way up the Missouri River to explore the land that President Thomas Jefferson had purchased so cheaply. Iowa looked as empty as it had to Jolliet 130 years earlier. The only white man who had come to explore its riches before the American annexation was an enterprising former French trapper, Julien Dubuque. Soon after the American Revolution, he obtained from the Fox Indians the sole right to work the lead mines west of the Mississippi, and for 20 years Dubuque was the only white settler in Iowa.

The first wave of migrants into Iowa were the Winnebago, Sauk, and Fox, driven there by the US Army, which was clearing Wisconsin and Illinois of their Indian populations to make way for white farmers. Although President Andrew Jackson had intended that the Louisiana Territory lying north of Missouri should forever be Indian land, the occupation of Iowa by the Indians was brief. Following an abortive attempt by an aging Sauk chieftain, Black Hawk, to win his lands in Illinois, the Sauk and Fox were driven westward in 1832 and forced to cede their lands in eastern Iowa to the incoming white settlers.

Placed under the territorial jurisdiction of Michigan in 1834, and then two years later under the newly created territory of Wisconsin, Iowa became a separate territory in 1838. The first territorial governor, Robert Lucas, extended county boundaries and local government westward, planned for a new capital city to be located on the Iowa River, resisted Missouri's attempt to encroach on Iowa territory, and began planning for statehood by drawing boundary lines that included not only the present state of Iowa but also southern Minnesota up to present-day Minneapolis.

Because a new state seeking admission to the Union at that time could expect favorable action from Congress only if accompanied by a slave state, Iowa was designed to come into the Union with Florida as its slaveholding counterpart. A serious dispute over how large the state would be delayed Iowa's admission into the Union until 28 December 1846, but by the delay the people of Iowa got what they wanted—all the land between the Mississippi and Missouri rivers—even though they had to abandon Lucas's northern claim.

The settlement of Iowa was rapidly accomplished. With one-fourth of the nation's fertile topsoil located within its borders, Iowa was a powerful magnet that drew farmers by the thousands from Indiana, Ohio, and Tennessee, and even from faraway Virginia, the Carolinas, New York, and New England. Except for German and Irish immigrants along the eastern border and later Scandinavian immigrants during the 1870s and 1880s, Iowa was settled primarily by Anglo-American stock. The settlers were overwhelmingly Protestant in religion and remarkably homogeneous in ethnic and cultural backgrounds. Although New Englanders made up only 5% of Iowa's early population, they had a cultural influence that far exceeded their numbers. Many small Iowa towns—with their large frame houses, elm-lined streets, and Congregational churches—looked like New England villages faithfully replicated on the prairie.

Fiercely proud of its claim to be the first free state created out of the Louisiana Purchase, Iowa was an important center of abolitionist sentiment throughout the 1850s. The Underground Railroad for fugitive slaves from the South ran across the southern portion of Iowa to the Mississippi River. Radical abolitionist John Brown spent the winters of 1857 and 1859 in the small Quaker village of Springdale, preparing for his attack on the US arsenal at Harpers Ferry, in western Virginia.

Although the Democrats had a slight edge over their Whig opposition in the early years of statehood, a majority of Iowa voters in 1856 supported the new Republican Party and, for the most part, did so in succeeding years. A Republican legislative majority in 1857 scrapped the state's first constitution, which had been written by Jacksonian Democrats 12 years earlier. The new document moved the state capital from Iowa City westward to Des Moines, but it provided that the state university would remain forever in Iowa City.

When the Civil War came, Iowa overwhelmingly supported the Union cause. Iowans fought not only for their ideals, the abolition of slavery, and the preservation of the Union but also for the very practical objective of keeping open the Mississippi River, the main artery for transport of agricultural products.

In the decades following the Civil War, Iowans on the national scene, most notably US senators James Harlan and his successor William B. Allison, belonged to the conservative Republican camp, but they frequently faced liberal Republican and Populist opposition inside the state. The railroad had been lavishly welcomed by Iowans in the 1850s; by the 1870s, Iowa farmers were desperately trying to free themselves from the stranglehold of the rail lines. The National Grange was powerful enough in Iowa to put through the legislature the so-called Granger laws to regulate the railroads. At the turn of the century, as the aging Allison's hold on the state weakened, Iowa became a center for Republican progressivism.

Following World War I, the conservatives regained control of the Republican Party. They remained in control until, during the 1960s, new liberal leadership was forced on the party because of the debacle of Barry Goldwater's 1964 presidential campaign, controversy over US involvement in Vietnam, and effective opposition from a revitalized Democratic Party led by Harold Hughes. After Hughes gave up the governorship in 1969 to become a US senator, Republicans once more dominated the executive branch, but Democrats gained control of the state legislature and made strong inroads at the top levels of state government.

Iowa's economy suffered in the 1980s from a combination of high debt, high interest rates, numerous droughts, and low crop prices. Businesses left the state or automated, shrinking their workforces. The population dropped by 7.9%. By the 1990s, the companies that had survived were in a much stronger position, and diversification efforts in both the agricultural and manufacturing sectors had ushered in a period of prosperity. The number of jobs in the service sector grew by 10%, and the state's unemployment rate in 1992 was 4.7%, substantially lower than the national average. By 1999, it had dropped to 2.5%, the lowest rate in the nation. In Iowa, as elsewhere in the Midwest, high-tech and service industries continued to pull workers away from farming—and away from the state, causing many to worry about a disappearing way of life. While the governor worked with state officials to entice young Iowans who had fled the state to return home, farming promised to be a hard sell for even the best marketers, as many of the state's agricultural producers eked by. By 2003, the US economy was slowly recovering from its 2001 recession, and Iowa was also feeling the effects.

A debilitating drought hit Iowa in 1988, reducing corn and soybean harvests to their lowest levels in 14 years and prompting Governor Terry Branstad to declare a statewide emergency. In 1993, unusually heavy spring and summer rains produced record floods along the Mississippi River by mid-July. Countless levees, or earthen berms designed to raise the height of river banks, collapsed or were overrun. The entire state of Iowa was declared a disaster area. Altogether, it was estimated that 40 million acres of farmland had been severely damaged and 500,000 acres permanently ruined. Agricultural woes continued to plague the state later in the decade. In 1999, Governor Tom Vilsack declared that Iowa was in a farm crisis, warning that problems plaguing the state's agricultural economy would soon affect urban and suburban areas. With the state's farmers getting record low prices for corn, soybeans, cattle, and hogs, producers were struggling to pay their loans.

In 1999, Governor Vilsack proposed one of the most dramatic increases in environmental spending in the state's recent history, asking for $10.5 million in new spending to improve the quality of Iowa's rivers and streams. He said the money was necessary to clean the state's waterways and boost recreation.

In 2001, the state took steps to allow refugees from other countries, including Afghanistan, to locate in small Iowa towns. During the early 2000s Governor Vilsack established a record for promoting education, signing into law over $200 million in new bills aimed at reducing class sizes. In 2003, he aimed to further improve education, health care, and the environment. Iowa House and Senate Republican leaders created an "Iowa Values Fund," a $503 economic development program, also supported by Vilsack. In 2005, the state was pursuing a comprehensive economic growth strategy focusing on renewable energy, life sciences, financial services, advanced manufacturing, and improving cultural and recreational opportunities. The governor made Iowa's energy independence a goal, and to that effect, the state from 2000 to 2005 nearly tripled its ethanol production and by 2006 was projected to be the nation's leading producer of ethanol.

12 STATE GOVERNMENT

Iowa has had two state constitutions. The constitution of 1857 replaced the original constitution of 1846 and, with 52 amendments as of January 2005 (three of which were later nullified by the state supreme court), is still in effect.

The state legislature, or General Assembly, consists of a 50-member Senate and a 100-member House of Representatives. Senators serve four-year terms, with half the members elected every two years. Representatives are elected to two-year terms. The legislature convenes each year on the second Monday in January. Length of the session is 110 calendar days in odd years, and 100 calendar days in even years. Special sessions may only be called by the governor and length is not limited. Each house may introduce or amend legislation, with a simple majority vote required for passage. Proposed amendments must be approved by a majority vote in two sessions of the legislature before they are sent to voters for ratification. The governor's veto of a bill may be overridden by a two-thirds vote of the elected members in both houses. Unless vetoed, a bill becomes law after three days when the legislature is in session. Legislators must be US citizens and must have resided in the state for a year and in the district for at least 60 days prior to election; a representative must be at least 21 years old, and a senator 25. The legislative salary was $21,380.54 in 2004.

The state's elected executives are the governor, lieutenant governor, secretary of state, treasurer, attorney general, auditor, and secretary of agriculture, all serving four-year terms. The governor and lieutenant governor, elected jointly, must be US citizens for at least two years, at least 30 years old, and residents of the state for at least two years. As of December 2004, the governor's salary was $107,482.

To vote in Iowa, a person must be a US citizen, at least 18 years old, a state resident, and not able to claim the right to vote elsewhere. Restrictions apply to those convicted of certain crimes and to those judged by the court to be mentally incompetent to vote.

13 POLITICAL PARTIES

For 70 years following the Civil War, a majority of Iowa voters supported the Republicans over the Democrats in nearly all state and national elections. During the Great Depression of the 1930s, Iowa briefly turned to the Democrats, supporting Franklin D. Roosevelt in two presidential elections. But from 1940 through 1984, the majority of Iowans voted Republican in 10 of 12 presidential elections. Republicans won 35 of the 45 gubernatorial elections from 1900 through 2002 and controlled both houses of the state legislature for 112 of the 130 years from 1855 to 1984.

In the 1960s, Iowa showed signs of a Democratic upsurge. Harold Hughes, a liberal Democrat, revitalized the party in Iowa and was elected governor for three two-year terms before moving on to the US Senate. During the post-Watergate period of the mid-1970s, Democrats captured both US Senate seats, five of the six congressional seats, and both houses of the Iowa legislature.

By the 1990s, a balance had reasserted itself. In 2000, Iowa gave Democrat Al Gore 49% of the vote, while Republican George W. Bush received 48%, and Green Party candidate Ralph Nader picked

Iowa Presidential Vote by Political Parties, 1948–2004

YEAR	ELECTORAL VOTE	IOWA WINNER	DEMOCRAT	REPUBLICAN	PROGRESSIVE	PROHIBITION	SOCIALIST LABOR
1948	10	*Truman (D)	522,380	494,018	12,125	3,382	4,274
1952	10	*Eisenhower (R)	451,513	808,906	5,085	2,882	—
							CONSTITUTION
1956	10	*Eisenhower (R)	501,858	729,187	—	—	3,202
1960	10	Nixon (R)	550,565	722,381	—	—	—
1964	9	*Johnson (D)	733,030	449,148	—	1,902	—
					SOC. WORKERS	**AMERICAN IND.**	
1968	9	*Nixon (R)	476,699	619,106	3,377	66,422	—
						AMERICAN	**PEACE AND FREEDOM**
1972	8	*Nixon (R)	496,206	706,207	—	22,056	1,332
							LIBERTARIAN
1976	8	Ford (R)	619,931	632,863	—	3,040	1,452
					CITIZENS		
1980	8	*Reagan (R)	508,672	676,026	2,191	NA	12,324
1984	8	*Reagan (R)	605,620	703,088	—	—	—
1988	8	Dukakis (D)	670,557	545,355	755	540	2,494
					IND. (Perot)		
1992	7	*Clinton (D)	586,353	504,891	253,468	3,079	1,177
1996	7	*Clinton (D)	620,258	492,644	105,159	—	2,315
					REFORM	**GREEN**	
2000	7	Gore (D)	638,517	634,373	5,731	29,374	3,209
					CONSTITUTION (Peroutka)	**NOMINATED BY PETITION** (Nader)	
2004	7	*Bush, G. W. (R)	741,898	751,957	1,304	5,973	2,992

*Won US presidential election.

up 2%. In 2004, Bush increased his support to 50% to Democrat John Kerry's 49%. In 2004, there were 2,107,000 registered voters. In 1998, 32% of registered voters were Democratic, 33% Republican, and 35% unaffiliated or members of other parties. The state had seven electoral votes in the 2004 presidential election.

Republican Terry Branstad won election to a fifth term as governor in 1994. But in the 1998 election, he was succeeded by Democrat Tom Vilsack, who won reelection in 2002. As of 2005, a Democrat and a Republican both served in the US Senate—Republican Charles Grassley, who won election to a fourth term in 1998, and Democrat Tom Harkin, who won reelection in 2002. In the 2004 elections, Iowans sent four Republicans and one Democrat to represent them in the US House. In mid-2005, in the state Senate was evenly split, with 25 Democrats and 25 Republicans. The state House was narrowly controlled by the Republicans, with 51 to the Democrats 49.

Iowa's presidential caucuses are held in January of presidential campaign years (ahead of New Hampshire, which also has a primary in January). This is earlier than any other state, thus giving Iowans a degree of influence in national politics.

14 LOCAL GOVERNMENT

The state's 99 counties are governed by boards of supervisors. In general, county officials, including the auditor, treasurer, recorder, and sheriff, are elected to four-year terms. They enforce state laws, collect taxes, supervise welfare activities, and manage roads and bridges.

Local government was exercised by 948 municipal units in 2005. The mayor-council system functioned in the great majority of these municipalities, though some of the larger cities employ the council-manager or commission system. Iowa's towns and cities derive their local powers from the state constitution, but the power to tax is authorized by the state General Assembly. In 2005, there were 374 public school districts and 542 special districts.

In 2005, local government accounted for about 132,928 full-time (or equivalent) employment positions.

15 STATE SERVICES

To address the continuing threat of terrorism and to work with the federal Department of Homeland Security, homeland security in Iowa operates under gubernatorial authority and state statute; the emergency management director is designated as the state homeland security adviser.

The Department of Education is responsible for educational services in Iowa. It assists local school boards in supplying special educational programs and administers local education agencies.

Transportation services are directed by the Department of Transportation, which is responsible for the safe and efficient operation of highways, motor vehicles, airports, railroads, public transit, and river transportation. The department's Motor Vehicle Division licenses drivers, road vehicles, and car dealers. Other departments include those for corrections, cultural affairs, economic development, human services, justice, and revenue. Iowa 2010 and IowAccess provide internet gateways to the state.

Health and welfare services are provided by the Department of Human Services. Public protection is the responsibility of the Departments of Public Defense and of Public Safety.

16 JUDICIAL SYSTEM

The Iowa Supreme Court consists of seven justices who are appointed by the governor and confirmed to eight-year terms by judicial elections held after they have served on the bench for at least one year. Judges may stand for reelection before their terms expire. The justices select one of their number as chief justice. The court exercises appellate jurisdiction in civil and criminal cases, supervises the trial courts, and prescribes rules of civil and appellate procedure. The Iowa Supreme Court transfers certain cases to the court of appeals, a six-member appellate court that began reviewing civil and criminal cases in 1977, and may review its decisions. Judges on the court of appeals are appointed and confirmed to six-year terms in the same manner as supreme court justices; they elect one of their members as chief judge.

The state is divided into eight judicial districts, each with a chief judge appointed to a two-year term by the chief justice of the supreme court. District court judges are appointed to six-year terms by the governor from nominations submitted by district nominating commissions. Appointees must stand for election after they have served as judges for at least one year.

As of 31 December 2004, a total of 8,525 prisoners were held in Iowa's state and federal prisons, a decrease from 8,546 or 0.2% from the previous year. As of year-end 2004, a total of 757 inmates were female, up from 716 or 5.7% from the year before. Among sentenced prisoners (one year or more), Iowa had an incarceration rate of 288 per 100,000 population in 2004.

According to the Federal Bureau of Investigation, Iowa in 2004, had a violent crime rate (murder/nonnegligent manslaughter; forcible rape; robbery; aggravated assault) of 270.9 reported incidents per 100,000 population, or a total of 8,003 reported incidents. Crimes against property (burglary; larceny/theft; and motor vehicle theft) in that same year totaled 85,836 reported incidents or 2,905.3 reported incidents per 100,000 people. Iowa does not have a death penalty.

In 2003, Iowa spent $52,308,231 on homeland security, an average of $18 per state resident.

17 ARMED FORCES

In 2004, 2,772 active-duty military personnel were stationed in Iowa: Reserves and National Guard personnel numbered 5,008. Iowa firms received defense contract awards amounting to $733 million in 2004, and another $480 million in defense payroll spending was paid in the state.

There were 265,960 veterans of US military service in Iowa as of 2003, of whom 41,922 served in World War II; 35,402 in the Korean conflict; 84,106 during the Vietnam era; and 34,411 in Persian Gulf War. The federal government expended $586 million for veterans in Iowa during fiscal year 2004.

As of 31 October 2004, the Iowa Department of Public Safety employed 559 full-time sworn officers.

18 MIGRATION

Iowa was opened, organized, and settled by a generation of native migrants from other states. According to the first federal census of Iowa in 1850, 31% of the total population of 192,214 came from nearby midwestern states (Illinois, Wisconsin, Indiana, Michigan, and Ohio), 14% from the five southern border states, and 13% from the Middle Atlantic states.

Another 10% of the state's 1850 population consisted of immigrants from northern Europe. The largest group were Germans who had fled military conscription; the next largest group had sought to escape the hardships of potato famine in Ireland or agricultural and technological displacement in Scotland, England, and Wales. They were joined in the 1850s by Dutch immigrants seeking religious liberty, and in the 1860s and 1870s by Norwegians and Swedes. During and immediately after the Civil War, some former slaves fled the South for Iowa, and more blacks settled in Iowa cities after 1900.

But many of the migrants who came to Iowa did not stay long. Some Iowans left to join the gold rush, and others settled lands in the West. Migration out of the state has continued to this day as retired Iowans seeking warmer climates have moved to California and other southwestern states; from 1970 through 1990, Iowa's net loss through migration amounted to over 266,000.

An important migratory trend within the state has been from the farm to the city. Although Iowa has remained a major agricultural state, the urban population surpassed the rural population by 1960 and increased to over 60.6% of the total population by 1990. Between 1990 and 1998, Iowa had a net loss of 13,000 in domestic migration and a net gain of 19,000 in international migration. In 1998, 1,655 foreign immigrants arrived in the state. Between 1990 and 1998, Iowa's overall population increased by 3.1%. In the period 2000–05, net international migration was 29,386 and net internal migration was -41,140, for a net loss of 11,754 people.

[19] INTERGOVERNMENTAL COOPERATION

Iowa is a signatory to the Midwest Interstate Low-Level Radioactive Waste Compact Commission, the Iowa-Missouri and Iowa-Nebraska boundary compacts, and a number of other major interstate compacts and agreements. Federal grants to the Iowa state government amounted to $2.951 billion in fiscal year 2005, an estimated $3.056 billion in fiscal year 2006, and an estimated $3.119 billion in fiscal year 2007.

[20] ECONOMY

Iowa's economy is based on agriculture. Although the value of the state's manufactures exceeds the value of its farm production, manufacturing is basically farm centered. The major industries are food processing and the manufacture of agriculture-related products, such as farm machinery.

Periodic recessions—and especially the Great Depression of the 1930s—have afflicted Iowa farmers and adversely affected the state's entire economy. But technological progress in agriculture and the proliferation of manufacturing industries have enabled Iowans to enjoy general prosperity since World War II. Because the state's population is scattered, the growth of light manufacturing has extended to hundreds of towns and cities.

In the late 1970s, the state's major economic problem was inflation, which boosted the cost of farm equipment and fertilizers. In the early 1980s, high interest rates and falling land prices created serious economic difficulties for farmers and contributed to the continuing decline of the farm population. By 1992, the state had recovered, but annual growth rates remained comparatively low. At the end of the 20th century, growth rates accelerated

somewhat (from 1.7% in 1998 to 3% in 1999 to 4.8% in 2000), but then fell to 1.4% in the national recession of 2001. The recession's impact on Iowa's unemployment rate was relatively mild, as the increase peaked at 4.4% in January 2002, and then fell to 3.9% by the end of the year. From 1997 to 2001, manufacturing output decreased almost every year in both absolute and relative terms, declining 5.7% in absolute terms across these five years, and, as a share of total state output, from about 25% in 1997 to 21% of the total in 2001. During the same period, output from general services increased 28.6%; from financial services, 24.4%; from the transportation and utilities sector, 23.7%; and from the government sector, 21.6%. Performance in Iowa's agricultural sector was positive in 2002, largely because Iowa escaped the drought that was hampering output in other states and the prices received by Iowa farmers.

In 2001, Iowa's gross state product (GSP) totaled $111.114 billion, of which manufacturing contributed $22.859 billion or 20.5% of GSP, followed by real estate at $9.834 billion (8.8% of GSP) and health care and social services at $7.475 billion (6.7% of GSP). In that same year, there were an estimated 243,932 small businesses in Iowa. Of the 69,354 businesses having employees, an estimated 67,648 or 97.5% were small companies. An estimated 5,954 new businesses were established in the state in 2004, up 7.6% from the year before. Business terminations that same year came to 7,391, up 0.2% from 2003. There were 360 business bankruptcies in 2004, up 11.5% from the previous year. In 2005, the personal bankruptcy (Chapter 7 and Chapter 13) filing rate was 417 filings per 100,000 people, ranking Iowa as the 36th highest in the nation.

[21] INCOME

In 2005, Iowa had a gross state product (GSP) of $114 billion, which accounted for 0.9% of the nation's gross domestic product and placed the state at number 30 in highest GSP among the 50 states and the District of Columbia.

According to the Bureau of Economic Analysis, in 2004 Iowa had a per capita personal income (PCPI) of $31,058. This ranked 28th in the United States and was 94% of the national average of $33,050. The 1994–2004 average annual growth rate of PCPI was 4.3%. Iowa had a total personal income (TPI) of $91,712,120,000, which ranked 30th in the United States and reflected an increase of 9.1% from 2003. The 1994–2004 average annual growth rate of TPI was 4.7%. Earnings of persons employed in Iowa increased from $62,520,383,000 in 2003 to $69,573,490,000 in 2004, an increase of 11.3%. The 2003–04 national change was 6.3%.

The US Census Bureau reports that the three-year average median household income for 2002–04 in 2004 dollars was $43,042 compared to a national average of $44,473. During the same period, 9.7% of the population was below the poverty line, as compared to 12.4% nationwide.

[22] LABOR

According to the Bureau of Labor Statistics (BLS), in April 2006, the seasonally adjusted civilian labor force in Iowa numbered 1,674,200. Approximately 59,800 workers were unemployed, yielding an unemployment rate of 3.6%, compared to the national average of 4.7% for the same period. Preliminary data for the same period placed nonfarm employment at 1,502,600. Since the beginning of the BLS data series in 1976, the highest unemployment rate recorded in Iowa was 8.5% in May 1983. The historical low was 2.6% in January 2000. Preliminary nonfarm employment data by occupation for April 2006 showed that approximately 5% of the labor force was employed in construction; 15.5% in manufacturing; 20.5% in trade, transportation, and public utilities; 6.6% in financial activities; 7.6% in professional and business services; 13.2% in education and health services; 8.7% in leisure and hospitality services; and 16.4% in government.

The labor movement generally has not been strong in Iowa, and labor unions have had little success in organizing farm laborers. The Knights of Labor, consisting mostly of miners and railroad workers, was organized in Iowa in 1876 and enrolled 25,000 members by 1885. But the Knights practically disappeared after 1893, when the American Federation of Labor (AFL) established itself in the state among miners and other workers. The Congress of Industrial Organizations (CIO) succeeded in organizing workers in public utilities, meat packing, and light industries in 1937. After 1955, when the AFL and CIO merged, the power and influence of labor unions increased in the state.

Iowa did not forbid the employment of women in dangerous occupations or prohibit the employment of children under 14 years of age in factories, shops, or mines until the early 1900s.

The BLS reported that in 2005, a total of 157,000 of Iowa's 1,369,000 employed wage and salary workers were formal members of a union. This represented 11.5% of those so employed, up from 10.5% in 2004 but still below the national average of 12%. Overall in 2005, a total of 185,000 workers (13.5%) in Iowa were covered by a union or employee association contract, which includes those workers who reported no union affiliation. Iowa is one of 22 states with a right-to-work law.

As of 1 March 2006, Iowa had a state-mandated minimum wage of $5.15 per hour. In 2004, women in the state accounted for 47.6% of the employed civilian labor force.

23 AGRICULTURE

Iowa recorded a (realized) gross farm income of $14.2 billion in 2005, the third-highest in the United States. Nearly half of all cash receipts from marketing came from the sale of livestock and meat products; about one-fifth derived from the sale of feed grains. During 2000–04, Iowa ranked first in output of corn for grain and soybeans and fifth for oats.

The early settlers planted wheat. Iowa ranked second in wheat production by 1870, but as the Wheat Belt moved farther west, the state's farmers turned to raising corn to feed their cattle and hogs. Two important 20th-century developments were the introduction in the 1920s of hybrid corn and the utilization of soybeans as a feed grain on a massive scale during World War II. Significant postwar trends included the rapid mechanization of farming and the decline of the farm population.

In 2004, Iowa had 89,700 farms, with an average size of 353 acres (143 hectares) per farm. This total represents a decrease of 50,000 farms since 1970, although the amount of land being farmed has only declined 1% to 31,700,000 acres (14,400,000 hectares) over the same period.

Nearly all of Iowa's land is tillable, and about nine-tenths of it is given to farmland. Corn is grown practically everywhere; wheat is raised in the southern half of the state and in counties bordering the Mississippi and Missouri rivers.

In 2004, production of corn for grain totaled 2.24 billion bushels, valued at $4.26 billion; soybeans, 497.4 million bushels, $2.51 billion; oats, 10.1 million bushels; and hay, 6.24 million tons.

24 ANIMAL HUSBANDRY

Iowa had an estimated 3.6 million cattle and calves in 2005, worth around $3.2 billion. In 2004, Iowa was ranked first among the 50 states in the number of hogs and pigs with 16.1 million, worth around $1.77 billion.

Pigs, calves, lambs, and chickens are raised throughout the state, particularly in the Mississippi and Missouri river valleys, where good pasture and water are plentiful. Iowa farmers are leaders in applying modern livestock breeding methods to produce lean hogs, tender corn-fed cattle, and larger-breasted chickens and turkeys.

In 2003, Iowa farmers produced an estimated 30.7 million lb (14 million kg) of sheep and lambs, which grossed a total of around $31.6 million. Also during 2003, Iowa farmers produced 267.7 million lb (121.6 million kg) of turkeys, worth $96.4 million. In the same year an estimated 10.4 billion eggs were produced (first in the United States), worth around $460.5 million.

Iowa dairy farmers produced 3.8 billion lb (1.7 million kg) of milk from 201,000 dairy cows in 2003.

25 FISHING

Fishing has very little commercial importance in Iowa. Game fishing in the rivers and lakes, however, is a popular sport. In 2004, there were 429,689 sport fishermen licensed in the state.

26 FORESTRY

Lumber and woodworking were important to the early settlers, but the industry has since declined in commercial importance. In 2004, Iowa had 2.7 million acres (1.1 million hectares) of forestland, which represents 7.5% of the state's land area, up from 1.6 million acres (650,000 hectares) in 1974. The state's lumber industry produced 78 million board feet of lumber in 2004.

27 MINING

According to preliminary data from the US Geological Survey (USGS), the value of Iowa's nonfuel mineral production in 2003 (the latest year for which data was available) was $478 million, a decrease from 2002 of about 2%. The USGS data ranked Iowa as 29th among the 50 states by the total value of its nonfuel mineral production, accounting for over 1% of total US output.

In descending order, the data showed cement (portland and masonry), crushed stone, construction sand and gravel, and gypsum as the state's leading nonfuel minerals produced in 2003, which collectively accounted for 97% of total output by value.

The preliminary data for 2003 showed crushed stone output by Iowa as totaling 34.7 million metric tons, with a value of $187 million, while construction grade sand and gravel production stood at 13 million metric tons or $60.2 million. That same year Iowa was also shown to be a producer of common clays with output at 256,000 metric tons, and with a value of $763,000.

28ENERGY AND POWER

Although Iowa's fossil fuel resources are extremely limited, the state's energy supply has been adequate.

As of 2003, Iowa had 186 electrical power service providers, of which 138 were publicly owned and 44 were cooperatives. Of the remainder, three were investor owned, and one was an owner of an independent generator that sold directly to customers. As of that same year, there were 1,477,518 retail customers. Of that total, 1,068,855 received their power from investor-owned service providers. Cooperatives accounted for 205,658 customers, while publicly owned providers had 202,844 customers. There were 161 independent generator or "facility" customers.

Total net summer generating capability by the state's electrical generating plants in 2003 stood at 10.074 million kW, with total production that same year at 42.116 billion kWh. Of the total amount generated, 93.8% came from electric utilities, with the remainder coming from independent producers and combined heat and power service providers. The largest portion of all electric power generated, 35.819 billion kWh (85%), came from coal-fired plants, with nuclear plants in second place at 3.987 billion kWh (9.5%). Other renewable power sources accounted for 2.6% of all power generated, with hydroelectric, petroleum, and natural gas–fueled generating plants accounting for the remainder.

As of 2006, Iowa had one nuclear power generating plant, the single-reactor Duane Arnold plant in the town of Palo.

Extensive coalfields in southeastern Iowa were first mined in 1840. The boomtown of Buxton, in Monroe County, mined sufficient coal in 1901 to support a population of 6,000 people, of whom 5,500 were transplanted southern blacks, but the mines closed in 1918 and Buxton became a ghost town. The state's annual bituminous coal production reached nearly 9 million tons in 1917–18. Coal output in 1994 was only 46,000 tons; recoverable coal reserves totaled 1.1 billion tons in 2001.

As of 2004, Iowa had no known proven reserves nor any production of crude oil or natural gas. However, the state did have a single rotary rig in operation. There were no refineries in Iowa.

29INDUSTRY

Because Iowa was primarily a farm state, the first industries were food processing and the manufacture of farm implements. These industries have retained a key role in the economy, with over 100,000 farms operating in the state in 2000. Iowa has also added a variety of other manufactures—including pens, washing machines, and even mobile homes.

According to the US Census Bureau's Annual Survey of Manufactures (ASM) for 2004, Iowa's manufacturing sector covered some 18 product subsectors. The shipment value of all products manufactured in the state that same year was $79.469 billion. Of that total, food manufacturing accounted for the largest share at $28.137 billion. It was followed by machinery manufacturing at $13.726 billion; chemical manufacturing at $9.244 billion; transportation equipment manufacturing at $3.770 billion; and fabricated metal product manufacturing at $3.541 billion.

In 2004, a total of 217,229 people in Iowa were employed in the state's manufacturing sector, according to the ASM. Of that total, 157,675 were actual production workers. In terms of total employment, the food manufacturing industry accounted for the largest portion of all manufacturing employees at 49,239, with 39,085 actual production workers. It was followed by machinery manufacturing at 31,014 employees (20,233 actual production workers); transportation equipment manufacturing at 16,410 employees (13,196 actual production workers); fabricated metal product manufacturing at 19,804 employees (15,355 actual production workers); plastics and rubber products manufacturing at 15,004 employees (12,168 actual production workers); and electrical equipment, appliance, and component manufacturing at 10,704 employees (7,806 actual production workers).

ASM data for 2004 showed that Iowa's manufacturing sector paid $8.496 billion in wages. Of that amount, the food manufacturing sector accounted for the largest share at $1.742 billion. It was followed by machinery manufacturing at $1.432 billion; fabricated metal product manufacturing at $752.822 million; and transport equipment manufacturing at $597.232 million.

30COMMERCE

According to the 2002 Census of Wholesale Trade, Iowa's wholesale trade sector had sales that year totaling $33.5 billion from 4,926 establishments. Wholesalers of durable goods accounted for 2,635 establishments, followed by nondurable goods wholesalers at 2,018 and electronic markets, agents, and brokers accounting for 273 establishments. Sales by durable goods wholesalers in 2002 totaled $11.3 billion, while wholesalers of nondurable goods saw sales of $18.8 billion. Electronic markets, agents, and brokers in the wholesale trade industry had sales of $3.2 billion.

In the 2002 Census of Retail Trade, Iowa was listed as having 13,859 retail establishments with sales of $31.1 billion. The leading types of retail businesses by number of establishments were gasoline stations stores (1,997); motor vehicle and motor vehicle parts dealers (1,879); building material/garden equipment and supplies dealers (1,705); and miscellaneous store retailers (1,590). In terms of sales, motor vehicle and motor vehicle parts dealers accounted for the largest share of retail sales at $7.9 billion, followed by general merchandise stores at $4.9 billion; food and beverage stores $4.2 billion; and building material/garden equipment and supplies dealers $3.7 billion. A total of 176,251 people were employed by the retail sector in Iowa that year.

The leading export commodities are feed grains and products, soybeans and soybean products, and meats and meat products. Diversity has been rising with the addition of industrial machinery, instruments and measurement devices, electronics, specialized transportation equipment, and chemicals and pharmaceuticals. Exports of goods from Iowa in 2005 were valued at $7.3 billion.

31CONSUMER PROTECTION

Iowa has laws prohibiting fraud and misrepresentation in sales and advertising and harassment in debt collecting, in addition to other consumer protection laws. There is a cooling-off period of three days for door-to-door purchases, and there is also a defective motor vehicle or "Lemon Law" statute. The Iowa attorney general's Consumer Protection Division deals with consumer fraud complaints, educates the public about such schemes, and litigates cases of consumer fraud. The Iowa Consumer Fraud Act is the primary piece of legislation enforced by the Consumer Protection Division.

When dealing with consumer protection issues, the state's Attorney General's Office (through its Consumer Protection Division) can initiate civil and criminal proceedings; represent the state before state and federal regulatory agencies; administer consumer protection and education programs; handle formal consumer complaints; and exercise broad subpoena powers. In antitrust actions, the Attorney General's Office cannot act on behalf of those consumers who are incapable of acting on their own but can initiate damage actions on behalf of the state in state courts and initiate criminal proceedings. However, the office has no authority to represent counties, cities, and other governmental entities in recovering civil damages under state or federal law.

The Iowa attorney general's Consumer Protection Division is located in Des Moines.

32 BANKING

As of June 2005, Iowa had 413 insured banks, savings and loans, and saving banks, plus 155 state-chartered and only two federally chartered credit unions (CUs). Excluding the CUs, the Omaha–Council Bluffs market area (which includes portions of Nebraska and Iowa) had the bulk of the state's financial institutions and deposits in 2004 at 74 and $14.442 billion, respectively. The Des Moines area was second with 49 institutions and $9.845 billion in deposits for that same year. As of June 2005, CUs accounted for 9.3% of all assets held by all financial institutions in the state, or some $5.275 billion. Banks, savings and loans, and savings banks collectively accounted for the remaining 90.7% or $51.740 billion in assets held.

The Division of Banking supervises and regulates the state's chartered banks, loan companies, and mortgage bankers/brokers. As of fourth quarter 2005, the net interest margin (the difference between the lower rates offered to savers and the higher rates charged on loans) stood at 3.73%, down from 3.80% in 2004 and 3.79% in 2003, which has resulted in an earnings decline for 2005.

33 INSURANCE

In 2004, there were 2.1 million individual life insurance policies in force with a total value of over $145 billion; total value for all categories of life insurance (individual, group, and credit) was over $213 billion. The average coverage amount was $68,600 per policy holder. Death benefits paid that year totaled at over $651 million.

In 2003, Iowa had 26 life and health and 55 property and casualty insurance companies domiciled in the state. In 2004, direct premiums for property and casualty insurance totaled $4.4 billion. That year, there were 9,746 flood insurance policies in force in the state, with a total value of $1 billion. About $119 million of coverage was offered through FAIR (Fair Access to Insurance) Plans, which are designed to offer coverage for some natural circumstances, such as wind and hail, in high-risk areas.

In 2004, 59% of state residents held employment-based health insurance policies, 7% held individual policies, and 23% were covered under Medicare and Medicaid; 10% of residents were uninsured. In 2003, employee contributions for employment-based health coverage averaged 21% for single coverage and 26% for family coverage. The state offers a nine-month health benefits ex-

pansion program for small-firm employees in connection with the Consolidated Omnibus Budget Reconciliation Act (COBRA, 1986), a health insurance program for those who lose employment-based coverage due to termination or reduction of work hours.

In 2003, there were over 2.2 million auto insurance policies in effect for private passenger cars. Required minimum coverage includes bodily injury liability of up to $20,000 per individual and $40,000 for all persons injured in an accident, as well as property damage liability of $15,000. In 2003, the average expenditure per vehicle for insurance coverage was $580.15, the third-lowest average in the nation (above South Dakota and North Dakota).

The commissioner of insurance, appointed by the governor, supervises all insurance business transacted in the state.

34 SECURITIES

There are no securities exchanges in Iowa. In 2005, there were 780 personal financial advisers employed in the state and 2,120 securities, commodities, and financial services sales agents. In 2004, there were over 49 publicly traded companies within the state, with over 18 NASDAQ companies and 15 NYSE listings. In 2006, the state had two Fortune 500 companies; Principal Financial Group ranked first in the state and 261st in the nation with revenues of over $9 billion, followed by Maytag. Rockwell Collins ranked 550th in the Fortune 1,000 listing. All three companies are listed on the NYSE.

35 PUBLIC FINANCE

The state budget is prepared by the Department of Management with the governor's approval and is adopted or revised by the General Assembly. Each budget is prepared for the biennium of the upcoming fiscal year (FY) and the one following. The fiscal year runs from 1 July to 30 June.

In fiscal year 2006, general funds were estimated at $5.2 billion for resources and $4.9 billion for expenditures. In fiscal year 2004, federal government grants to Iowa were nearly $4.0 billion.

36 TAXATION

In 2005, Iowa collected $5,751 million in tax revenues or $1,939 per capita, which placed it 33rd among the 50 states in per capita tax burden. The national average was $2,192 per capita. Sales taxes accounted for 29.9% of the total, selective sales taxes 15.7%, individual income taxes 39.2%, corporate income taxes 3.2%, and other taxes 11.9%.

As of 1 January 2006, Iowa had nine individual income tax brackets ranging from 0.36 to 8.98%. The state taxes corporations at rates ranging from 6.0 to 12.0% depending on tax bracket.

In 2004, local property taxes amounted to $3,188,869,000 or $1,080 per capita. The per capita amount ranks the state 18th nationally. Iowa does not collect property taxes at the state level.

Iowa taxes retail sales at a rate of 5%. In addition to the state tax, local taxes on retail sales can reach as much as 2%, making for a potential total tax on retail sales of 7%. Food purchased for consumption off premises is tax exempt. The tax on cigarettes is 36 cents per pack, which ranks 42nd among the 50 states and the District of Columbia. Iowa taxes gasoline at 20.7 cents per gallon. This is in addition to the 18.4 cents per gallon federal tax on gasoline.

Iowa—State Government Finances

(Dollar amounts in thousands. Per capita amounts in dollars.)

	AMOUNT	PER CAPITA
Total Revenue	15,291,539	5,178.31
General revenue	11,845,227	4,011.25
Intergovernmental revenue	4,038,220	1,367.50
Taxes	5,143,126	1,741.66
General sales	1,617,505	547.75
Selective sales	819,818	277.62
License taxes	575,515	194.89
Individual income tax	1,958,697	663.29
Corporate income tax	89,826	30.42
Other taxes	81,765	27.69
Current charges	1,776,175	601.48
Miscellaneous general revenue	887,706	300.61
Utility revenue	410	.14
Liquor store revenue	135,957	46.04
Insurance trust revenue	3,309,945	1,120.88
Total expenditure	13,424,350	4,546.00
Intergovernmental expenditure	3,529,971	1,195.38
Direct expenditure	9,894,379	3,350.62
Current operation	7,063,915	2,392.11
Capital outlay	1,103,983	373.85
Insurance benefits and repayments	1,299,364	440.01
Assistance and subsidies	265,644	89.96
Interest on debt	161,473	54.68
Exhibit: Salaries and wages	2,299,205	778.60
Total expenditure	13,424,350	4,546.00
General expenditure	12,031,051	4,074.18
Intergovernmental expenditure	3,529,971	1,195.38
Direct expenditure	8,501,080	2,878.79
General expenditures, by function:		
Education	4,670,535	1,581.62
Public welfare	3,112,742	1,054.09
Hospitals	898,849	304.39
Health	195,740	66.29
Highways	1,365,758	462.50
Police protection	71,393	24.18
Correction	219,859	74.45
Natural resources	224,415	76.00
Parks and recreation	20,330	6.88
Government administration	470,965	159.49
Interest on general debt	161,473	54.68
Other and unallocable	618,992	209.61
Utility expenditure	855	.29
Liquor store expenditure	93,080	31.52
Insurance trust expenditure	1,299,364	440.01
Debt at end of fiscal year	4,857,614	1,644.98
Cash and security holdings	27,063,116	9,164.62

Abbreviations and symbols: – zero or rounds to zero; (NA) not available; (X) not applicable.

SOURCE: *U.S. Census Bureau, Governments Division, 2004 Survey of State Government Finances,* January 2006.

According to the Tax Foundation, for every federal tax dollar sent to Washington in 2004, Iowa citizens received $1.11 in federal spending.

37 ECONOMIC POLICY

Since World War II, the state government has attracted new manufacturing industries to Iowa by granting tax incentives and by encouraging a favorable business climate. The Iowa Department of Economic Development (IDED) coordinates economic development activity in the state. It helps local communities diversify their economies, assists companies already in the state, and helps exporters to sell their products abroad. In the 1990s, the Iowa state government stressed such development goals as agricultural diversification, increased small business support, creation of high-tech jobs, and expansion of tourism. The Iowa Values Fund (IVF) is a 10-year economic development program designed to transform Iowa's economy by creating high-quality jobs through business development and expansion across Iowa. With a $35 million annual appropriation for business development and marketing, the IVF assists Iowa companies to expand, as well as attract new businesses to the state. The Venture Network of Iowa is a statewide forum operated by the Iowa Communications Network where Iowa entrepreneurs, investors, and business advisers interact, network, and find financial and intellectual capital. Iowa combines community development block grant and HOME funding from the US Department of Housing and Urban Development (HUD) to fund housing activities, including rehabilitation, new construction, assistance to homebuyers, assistance to tenants, administrative costs, and lead-safe housing. The state also offers financial assistance programs to businesses for programs to retain or create jobs, capital investment, to utilize agricultural commodities, to establish or expand minority and women-owned enterprises, to support low income and disabled entrepreneurs, to build or improve a community's infrastructure (railroads, roads, etc.), and to foster construction of new industrial facilities. In 2006, the US Chamber of Commerce ranked all 50 states on legal fairness toward business. The chamber found Iowa to be one of five states with the best legal environment for business. The other four were Nebraska, Virginia, Connecticut, and Delaware.

38 HEALTH

The infant mortality rate in October 2005 was estimated at 5.2 per 1,000 live births. The birth rate in 2003 was 13 per 1,000 population. The abortion rate stood at 9.8 per 1,000 women in 2000. In 2003, about 88.9% of pregnant woman received prenatal care beginning in the first trimester. In 2004, approximately 86% of children received routine immunizations before the age of three.

The crude death rate in 2003 was 9.5 deaths per 1,000 population. As of 2002, the death rates for major causes of death (per 100,000 resident population) were as follows: heart disease, 278.6; cancer, 220.4; cerebrovascular diseases, 75.8; chronic lower respiratory diseases, 53.8; and diabetes, 25. Iowa has the second-highest rate in the nation for cerebrovascular disease, following Arizona. The mortality rate from HIV infection was 1 per 100,000 population, the lowest in the nation. In 2004, the reported AIDS case rate was at about 2.2 per 100,000 population. In 2002, about 58.8% of the population was considered overweight or obese. As of 2004, about 20.8% of state residents were smokers.

In 2003, Iowa had 116 community hospitals with about 11,000 beds. There were about 363,000 patient admissions that year and 9.7 million outpatient visits. The average daily inpatient census was about 6,500 patients. The average cost per day for hospital care was $952. Also in 2003, there were about 454 certified nursing facilities in the state with 35,428 beds and an overall occupancy rate of about 78.5%. In 2004, it was estimated that about 75.1% of all state residents had received some type of dental care within the year. Iowa had 218 physicians per 100,000 resident population in 2004 and 1,009 nurses per 100,000 in 2005. In 2004, there was a total of 1,546 dentists in the state.

About 23% of state residents were enrolled in Medicaid and Medicare programs in 2004. Approximately 10% of the state was uninsured in 2004. In 2003, state health care expenditures totaled $2.7 million.

39 SOCIAL WELFARE

In 2004, about 89,000 people received unemployment benefits, with the average weekly unemployment benefit at $261. In fiscal year 2005, the estimated average monthly participation in the food stamp program included about 206,696 persons (89,655 households); the average monthly benefit was about $88.60 per person. That year, the total of benefits paid through the state for the food stamp program was about $219.7 million.

Temporary Assistance for Needy Families (TANF), the system of federal welfare assistance that officially replaced Aid to Families with Dependent Children (AFDC) in 1997, was reauthorized through the Deficit Reduction Act of 2005. TANF is funded through federal block grants that are divided among the states based on an equation involving the number of recipients in each state. Iowa's TANF program is called the Family Investment Program (FIP). In 2004, the state program had 45,000 recipients; state and federal expenditures on this TANF program totaled $60 million in fiscal year 2003.

In December 2004, Social Security benefits were paid to 545,990 Iowa residents. This number included 358,340 retired workers, 60,150 widows and widowers, 58,310 disabled workers, 34,490 spouses, and 34,700 children. Social Security beneficiaries represented 18.6% of the total state population and 96.1% of the state's population age 65 and older. Retired workers received an average monthly payment of $952; widows and widowers, $925; disabled workers, $857; and spouses, $480. Payments for children of retired workers averaged $517 per month; children of deceased workers, $644; and children of disabled workers, $266. Federal Supplemental Security Income payments went to 42,618 Iowa residents in December 2004, averaging $370 a month. An additional $1.4 million of state-administered supplemental payments were distributed to 4,448 residents.

40 HOUSING

In 2004, there were 1,292,976 housing units in Iowa, of which 1,175,771 were occupied; 73.8% were owner occupied, placing the state fourth in the nation in the percentage of homeownership. About 74.7% of all units were single-family, detached homes. About 31.5% of all units were built in 1939 or earlier. Most households relied on utility gas and electricity for heating. It was estimated that 52,215 lacked telephone service, 4,728 lacked complete plumbing facilities, and 5,037 lacked complete kitchen facilities. The average household had 2.42 members.

In 2004, 16,300 privately owned housing units were authorized for construction. Median home value was $95,901. The median monthly cost for mortgage owners was $942. Renters paid a median of $533 per month. In 2006, the state received over $26.4 million in community development block grants from the US Department of Housing and Urban Development (HUD).

41 EDUCATION

In 2004, 89.8% of Iowans age 25 and older were high school graduates, compared to the national average of 84%. Some 24.3% had obtained a bachelor's degree or higher.

The total enrollment for fall 2002 in Iowa's public schools stood at 482,000. Of these, 326,000 attended schools from kindergarten through grade eight, and 156,000 attended high school. Approximately 88.2% of the students were white, 4.5% were black, 4.9% were Hispanic, 1.8% were Asian/Pacific Islander, and 0.6% were American Indian/Alaska Native. Total enrollment was estimated at 476,000 in fall 2003 and was expected to be 452,000 by fall 2014, a decline of 6.3% during the period 2002–14. There were 45,309 students enrolled in 266 private schools in fall 2003. Expenditures for public education in 2003–04 were estimated at $4.28 billion. Since 1969, the National Assessment of Educational Progress (NAEP) has tested public school students nationwide. The resulting report, *The Nation's Report Card*, stated that in 2005 eighth graders in Iowa scored 284 out of 500 in mathematics compared with the national average of 278.

As of fall 2002, there were 202,546 students enrolled in institutions of higher education; minority students comprised 8.2% of total postsecondary enrollment. As of 2005, Iowa had 63 degree-granting institutions. Iowa has three state universities and 35 private four-year colleges. Since the public community college system began offering vocational and technical training in 1960, total enrollment has increased rapidly, and the number of different career programs has grown. Iowa's small liberal arts colleges and universities include Briar Cliff College, Sioux City; Coe College, Cedar Rapids; Cornell College, Mt. Vernon; Drake University, Des Moines; Grinnell College, Grinnell; Iowa Wesleyan College, Mt. Pleasant; Loras College, Dubuque; and Luther College, Decorah.

42 ARTS

Beginning with the public lecture movement in the late 19th century and the Chautauqua shows in the early 20th century, cultural activities have gradually spread throughout the state. There is now an opera company in Des Moines and art galleries, little theater groups, symphony orchestras, and ballet companies in other major cities and college towns. The University of Iowa receives funding from the National Endowment for the Arts to support the development of its music and theater activities.

The Des Moines Arts Center is a leading exhibition gallery for native painters and sculptors. The Des Moines Arts Festival, established in 1998, draws an attendance of nearly 800,000 people each year. There are regional theater groups in Des Moines, Davenport, and Sioux City. The Writers' Workshop at the University of Iowa has an international reputation and was the first creative writing degree program in the United States. In 2003, the National Endowment for the Humanities awarded a National Humanities Medal to the workshop—the first medal awarded to the university and only the second medal given to an institution rather than an individual.

The Iowa Arts Council (IAC) was established as a state agency in 1967. In 1986, the IAC became a division of the Department of Cultural Affairs, which also includes the State Historical Society of Iowa. In 2005, state organizations received 16 grants totaling $776,700 from the National Endowment for the Arts. Humanities

Iowa, founded in 1971, sponsors over $1.5 million of programs each year. In 2005, the National Endowment for the Humanities sponsored 11 programs with grants totaling $906,482. The state also contributes to the efforts of the Arts Council and Humanities Iowa, and private sources provide additional funding.

43 LIBRARIES AND MUSEUMS

Iowa's first tax-supported public library was founded in Independence in 1873. Since then, the system has continued to expand. For the fiscal year ending in June 2001, the state had 537 public library systems, with a total of 561 libraries, of which 24 were branches. In that same year, Iowa's public library system had total book and serial publication holdings of 11,450,000 volumes, and a total circulation of 25,498,000. The system also had 446,000 audio and 402,000 video items, 15,000 electronic format items (CD-ROMs, magnetic tapes, and disks), and six bookmobiles. Among the principal libraries in Iowa are the State Library in Des Moines, the State Historical Society Library in Iowa City, the libraries of the University of Iowa (also in Iowa City), and the Iowa State University Library in Ames. In fiscal year 2001, operating income for the state's public library system was $73,270,000, which included $582,000 from federal grants and $2,236,000 from the state.

Iowa had 134 museums and zoological parks in 2000. The Herbert Hoover National Historic Site, in West Branch, houses the birthplace and grave of the 31st US president and a library and museum with papers and memorabilia. Other historical sites include the grave of French explorer Julien Dubuque, near the city named for him; the girlhood home of suffragist Carrie Chapman Cat at Charles Cityt; and the seven communal villages of the Amana colonies.

44 COMMUNICATIONS

The first post office in Iowa was established at Augusta in 1836. Mail service developed slowly with the spread of population, and rural free delivery of mail did not begin until 1897.

The first telegraph line was built between Burlington and Bloomington (now Muscatine) in 1848. Telegraph service throughout the state is provided by Western Union. In 2004, about 95.4% of all occupied housing units had telephones. In addition, by June of that same year there were 1,445,711 mobile wireless telephone subscribers. In 2003, 64.7% of Iowa households had a computer and 57.1% had Internet access. By June 2005, there were 325,711 high-speed lines in Iowa, 293,824 residential and 31,887 for business.

Among the first educational radio broadcasting stations in the United States was one established in 1919 at the State University in Iowa City and another in 1921 at Iowa State University in Ames. The first commercial radio station west of the Mississippi, WDC at Davenport, began broadcasting in 1921. In 2005, there were 110 major radio stations, including 37 AM stations and 73 FM stations. In the same year, Iowa had a total of 21 network television stations.

A total of 34,789 internet domain names were registered in the state in 2000.

45 PRESS

Iowa's first newspaper, the *Dubuque Visitor*, was founded in 1836 but lasted only a year. The following year, the *Fort Madison Patriot* and the *Burlington Territorial Gazette* were established; the latter

paper, now the *Hawk Eye*, is the oldest newspaper in the state. In 1860, the *Iowa State Register* was founded. As the *Des Moines Register and Tribune*, it grew to be the state's largest newspaper. The *Tribune* ceased publication in 1982; the *Register* remains preeminent, with a morning circulation of 152,800 and a Sunday circulation of 243,302 as of 2005.

Major newspapers and their estimated circulations at 2001–02 are listed as follows:

AREA	NAME	DAILY	SUNDAY
Cedar Rapids	*Gazette* (m,S)	63,493	76,828
Des Moines	*Register* (m,S)	152,800	243,302
Dubuque	*Telegraph Herald* (m,S)	28,621	34,195
Sioux City	*Journal* (m,S)	41,182	42,268
Waterloo	*Courier* (e,S)	42,679	51,836

Overall, Iowa had 37 dailies (21 evening, 16 morning) and 12 Sunday papers in 2005. Also published in Iowa were over 100 periodicals, among them *Better Homes and Gardens* and *Successful Farming, Midwest Today,* and *The Iowan.*

46 ORGANIZATIONS

In 2006, there were over 5,085 nonprofit organizations registered within the state, of which about 3,031 were registered as charitable, educational, or religious organizations. Among the organizations headquartered in Iowa are the National Farmers Organization (Corning), the American College Testing Program (Iowa City), the National Meals on Wheels Foundation (Iowa City), the National Collegiate Honors Council (Ames), and the Antique Airplane Association (Ottumwa). State educational and cultural organizations include the Iowa Arts Council, the Iowa Historic Preservation Alliance, and the State Historical Society of Iowa. There is a Czech Heritage Foundation in Cedar Rapids and a Danish American Heritage Society in Ames. Special interest associations with offices in Iowa include the Balloon Federation of America and the Bohemia Ragtime Society.

47 TOURISM, TRAVEL, AND RECREATION

The Mississippi and Missouri rivers offer popular water sports facilities for both out-of-state visitors and resident vacationers. Iowa's "Little Switzerland" region in the northeast, with its high bluffs of woodlands overlooking the Mississippi, is popular for hiking and camping. Notable tourist attractions in the area include the Effigy Mounds National Monument (near Marquette), which has hundreds of prehistoric Indian mounds and village sites, and the Buffalo Ranch (at Fayette), with its herd of live buffalo. Tourist sites in the central part of the state include the state capitol and the Herbert Hoover National Historic Site, with its Presidential Library and Museum. Tourists can also visit the Amana colonies, a reconstructed site of an experimental living community. Arnolds Park is the home of the Iowa Rock and Roll Museum. The city of Le Mars is known as the ice cream capital of the world and the home of Well Dairy. Sioux City hosts the Lewis and Clark Interpretive Center. The city of Boone is the birthplace of Mamie Doud Eisenhower, wife of President Dwight D. Eisenhower.

Iowa has about 85,000 acres (34,400 hectares) of lakes and reservoirs and 19,000 mi (30,600 km) of fishing streams. There are 52 state parks covering 33,811 acres and seven state forests, covering

25,000 acres (10,000 hectares); these and other state recreational areas attract numerous visitors every year.

In 2005, there were some 30.5 million visitors to the state. This showed an increase from 17.1 million in 2001. Travel generated expenditures of $4.3 billion in 2002 and increased to $5.0 billion. In 2005, there were over 62,290 travel-related jobs in the state in 2005, generating a $969 million payroll. Travel and tourism is fast becoming one of the major sources of income in Iowa.

48 SPORTS

Iowa has no major professional sports teams, but the state is proud of its Iowa Barnstormers in the Arena Football League. The team has advanced to two Arena Bowls in the league's short existence. Minor league baseball and basketball teams make their home in Des Moines, Cedar Rapids, Clinton, Sioux City, Burlington, and the Quad Cities. High school and college basketball and football teams draw thousands of spectators, particularly to the state high school basketball tournament at Des Moines in March. Large crowds also fill stadiums and fieldhouses for the University of Iowa games in Iowa City and Iowa State University games in Ames. In intercollegiate competition, the University of Iowa Hawkeyes belong to the Big Ten Conference. They have a legendary wrestling program that has won the National Collegiate Athletic Association (NCAA) Championship 20 times. Iowa went to the Rose Bowl in 1957, 1959, 1982, 1986, and 1991, winning in 1957 and 1959. The Iowa State University Cyclones are in the Big Twelve Conference. A popular track-and-field meet for college athletes is the Drake Relays, held every April in Des Moines. Horse racing is popular at state and county fairgrounds, as is stock car racing at small-town tracks. The Register's Annual Great Bicycle Ride across Iowa is held each July. There are rodeos in Sidney and Fort Madison, and the National Balloon Classic is held in Indianola.

49 FAMOUS IOWANS

Iowa was the birthplace of Herbert Clark Hoover (1874–1964), the first US president born west of the Mississippi. Although he was orphaned and left the state for Oregon at the age of 10, he always claimed Iowa as his home. His long and distinguished career included various relief missions in Europe, service as US secretary of commerce (1921–29), and one term in the White House (1929–33). Hoover was buried in West Branch, the town of his birth. Iowa also produced one US vice president, Henry A. Wallace (1888–1965), who served in that office during Franklin D. Roosevelt's third term (1941–45). Wallace was also secretary of agriculture (1933–41) and commerce (1945–47); he ran unsuccessfully as the Progressive Party's presidential candidate in 1948.

Two Kentucky-born members of the US Supreme Court were residents of Iowa prior to their appointments: Samuel F. Miller (1816–90) and Wiley B. Rutledge (1894–1949). Iowans who served in presidential cabinets as secretary of the interior were James Harlan (b.Illinois, 1820–99), Samuel J. Kirkwood (b.Maryland, 1813–94), Richard Ballinger (1858–1922), and Ray Lyman Wilbur (1875–1949). Ray Wilbur's brother Curtis (1867–1954) was secretary of the Navy, and James W. Good (1866–1929) was secretary of war. Appropriately enough, Iowans have dominated the post of secretary of agriculture in this century. They included, in addition to Wallace, James "Tama Jim" Wilson (b.Scotland, 1835–1920), who served in that post for 16 years and set a record for longevity in a single cabinet office; Henry C. Wallace (b.Illinois, 1866–1924), the father of the vice president; and Edwin T. Meredith (1876–1928). Harry L. Hopkins (1890–1946) was Franklin D. Roosevelt's closest adviser in all policy matters, foreign and domestic, and served in a variety of key New Deal posts. Prominent US senators from Iowa have included James W. Grimes (b.New Hampshire, 1816–72), whose vote, given from a hospital stretcher, saved President Andrew Johnson from being convicted of impeachment charges in 1868; earlier, Grimes had been governor of the state when its 1857 constitution was adopted. William Boyd Allison (b.Ohio, 1829–1908) was the powerful chairman of the Senate Appropriations Committee for nearly 30 years.

Among Iowa's most influential governors were the first territorial governor, Robert Lucas (b.Virginia, 1781–1853); Cyrus C. Carpenter (b.Pennsylvania, 1829–98); William Larrabee (b.Connecticut, 1832–1912); Horace Boies (b.New York, 1827–1923); and, in recent times, Harold Hughes (1922–96) and Robert D. Ray (b.1928).

Iowa has been home to a large number of radical dissenters and social reformers. Abolitionists, strong in Iowa before the Civil War, included James W. Grimes, Josiah B. Grinnell (b.Vermont, 1821–91), and Asa Turner (b.Massachusetts, 1799–1885). George D. Herron (b.Indiana, 1862–1925) made Iowa a center of the Social Gospel movement before helping to found the Socialist Party. William "Billy" Sunday (1862–1935) was an evangelist with a large following among rural Americans. James B. Weaver (b.Ohio, 1833–1912) ran for the presidency on the Greenback-Labor ticket in 1880 and as a Populist in 1892. John L. Lewis (1880–1969), head of the United Mine Workers, founded the Congress of Industrial Organizations (CIO).

Iowa can claim two winners of the Nobel Peace Prize: religious leader John R. Mott (b.New York, 1865–1955) and agronomist and plant geneticist Norman E. Borlaug (b.1914). Three other distinguished scientists who lived in Iowa were George Washington Carver (b.Missouri 1864–1943), Lee De Forest (1873–1961), and James Van Allen (b.1914). George H. Gallup (1904–84), a public-opinion analyst, originated the Gallup Polls.

Iowa writers of note include Hamlin Garland (b.Wisconsin, 1860–1940), Octave Thanet (Alice French, b.Massachusetts, 1850–1934), Bess Streeter Aldrich (1881–1954), Carl Van Vechten (1880–1964), James Norman Hall (1887–1951), Thomas Beer (1889–1940), Ruth Suckow (1892–1960), Phillip D. Strong (1899–1957), MacKinlay Kantor (1904–77), Wallace Stegner (1909–93), and Richard P. Bissell (1913–77). Iowa's poets include Paul H. Engle (1908–91), who directed the University of Iowa's famed Writers' Workshop, and James S. Hearst (1900–83). Two Iowa playwrights, Susan Glaspell (1882–1948) and her husband, George Cram Cook (1873–1924), were instrumental in founding influential theater groups.

Iowans who have contributed to America's musical heritage include popular composer Meredith Willson (1902–84), jazz musician Leon "Bix" Beiderbecke (1903–31), and bandleader Glenn Miller (1904–44). Iowa's artists of note include Grant Wood (1892–1942), whose *American Gothic* is one of America's best-known paintings, and printmaker Mauricio Lasansky (b.Argentina, 1914).

Iowa's contributions to the field of popular entertainment include William F. "Buffalo Bill" Cody (1846–1917); circus impresario Charles Ringling (1863–1926) and his four brothers; the reigning American beauty of the late 19th century, Lillian Russell (Helen Louise Leonard, 1860–1922); and one of America's best-loved movie actors John Wayne (Marion Michael Morrison, 1907–79). Johnny Carson (1925–2005), host of the *Tonight Show* for many years, was born in Corning. Iowa sports figures of note are baseball Hall of Famers Adrian C. "Cap" Anson (1851–1922) and Robert "Bob" Feller (b.1918) and football All-American Nile Kinnick (1918–44).

50 BIBLIOGRAPHY

Council of State Governments. *The Book of the States, 2006 Edition.* Lexington, Ky.: Council of State Governments, 2006.

Friedricks, William B. *Covering Iowa: The History of the Des Moines Register and Tribune Company, 1849-1985.* Ames: Iowa State University Press, 2000.

Landau, Diana. *Iowa: the Spirit of America.* New York: Harry N. Abrams, 1998.

Maharidge, Dale. *Denison, Iowa: Searching for the Soul of America through the Secrets of a Midwest Town.* New York: Free Press, 2005.

Mobil Travel Guide. Great Plains 2006: Iowa, Kansas, Missouri, Nebraska, Oklahoma. Lincolnwood, Ill.: ExxonMobil Travel Publications, 2006.

Morain, Thomas J. (ed.). *Family Reunion: Essays on Iowa.* Ames: Iowa State University Press, 1995.

Offenburger, Chuck. *Ah, You Iowans!: At Home, At Work, At Play, At War.* Ames: Iowa State University Press, 1992.

Riley, Glenda, (ed.). *Prairie Voices: Iowa's Pioneering Women.* Ames: Iowa State University Press, 1996.

US Department of Commerce, Economics and Statistics Administration, US Census Bureau. *Iowa, 2000. Summary Social, Economic, and Housing Characteristics: 2000 Census of Population and Housing.* Washington, D.C.: US Government Printing Office, 2003.

Winebrenner, Hugh. *Iowa Precinct Caucuses: the Making of a Media Event.* Ames: Iowa State University Press, 1998.

KANSAS

KANSAS

State of Kansas

ORIGIN OF STATE NAME: Named for the Kansa (or Kaw) Indians, the "people of the south wind." **NICKNAME:** The Sunflower State; the Jayhawker State. **CAPITAL:** Topeka. **ENTERED UNION:** 29 January 1861 (34th). **SONG:** "Home on the Range;" "The Kansas March." (march). **MOTTO:** *Ad astra per aspera* (To the stars through difficulties). **FLAG:** The flag consists of a dark blue field with the state seal in the center; a sunflower on a bar of twisted gold and blue is above the seal; the word "Kansas" is below it. **OFFICIAL SEAL:** A sun rising over mountains in the background symbolizes the east; commerce is represented by a river and a steamboat. In the foreground, agriculture, the basis of the state's prosperity, is represented by a settler's cabin and a man plowing a field. Beyond this is a wagon train heading west and a herd of buffalo fleeing from two Indians. Around the top is the state motto above a cluster of 34 stars; the circle is surrounded by the words "Great Seal of the State of Kansas, January 29, 1861." **BIRD:** Western meadowlark. **FLOWER:** Wild native sunflower. **TREE:** Cottonwood. **LEGAL HOLIDAYS:** New Year's Day, 1 January; Birthday of Martin Luther King Jr., 3rd Monday in January; Memorial Day, last Monday in May; Independence Day, 4 July; Labor Day, 1st Monday in September; Columbus Day, 2nd Monday in October; Veterans' Day, 11 November; Thanksgiving Day, 4th Thursday in November; Christmas Day, 25 December. **TIME:** 6 AM CST = noon GMT; 5 AM MST = noon GMT.

¹LOCATION, SIZE, AND EXTENT

Located in the western north-central United States, Kansas is the second-largest Midwestern state (following Minnesota) and ranks 14th among the 50 states.

The total area of Kansas is 82,277 sq mi (213,097 sq km), of which 81,778 sq mi (211,805 sq km) are land, and the remaining 499 sq mi (1,292 sq km) inland water. Shaped like a rectangle except for an irregular corner in the NE, the state has a maximum extension E–W of about 411 mi (661 km) and an extreme N–S distance of about 208 mi (335 km).

Kansas is bounded on the N by Nebraska, on the E by Missouri (with the line in the NE following the Missouri River), on the S by Oklahoma, and on the W by Colorado, with a total boundary length of 1,219 mi (1,962 km). The geographic center of Kansas is in Barton County, 15 mi (24 km) NE of Great Bend.

²TOPOGRAPHY

Although the popular image of the state is one of unending flatlands, Kansas has a diverse topography. Three main land regions define the state. The eastern third consists of the Osage Plains, Flint Hills, Dissected Till Plains, and Arkansas River Lowlands. The central third comprises the Smoky Hills (which include the Dakota sandstone formations, Greenhorn limestone formations, and chalk deposits) to the north and several lowland regions to the south. To the west are the Great Plains proper, divided into the Dissected High Plains and the High Plains. Kansas generally slopes eastward from a maximum elevation of 4,039 ft (1,232 m) at Mt. Sunflower (a mountain in name only) on the Colorado border to 679 ft (207 m) by the Verdigris River at the Oklahoma border. The mean elevation of the state is approximately 2,000 ft (610 m). More than 50,000 streams run through the state, and there

are hundreds of artificial lakes. Major rivers include the Missouri, which defines the state's northeastern boundary; the Arkansas, which runs through Wichita; and the Kansas (Kaw), which runs through Topeka and joins the Missouri at Kansas City.

The geographic center of the 48 contiguous states is located in Smith County, in north-central Kansas, at 39°50′N and 98°35′W. Forty miles (64 km) south of this point, in Osborne County at 39°13′27″N and 98°32′31″W, is the North American geodetic datum, the controlling point for all land surveys in the United States, Canada, and Mexico. Extensive beds of prehistoric ocean fossils lie in the chalk beds of two western counties, Logan and Gove.

³CLIMATE

Kansas's continental climate is highly changeable. The average mean temperature is 55°F (13°C). The record high is 121°F (49°C), recorded near Alton on 24 July 1936, and the record low, -40°F (-40°C), was registered at Lebanon on 13 February 1905. The normal annual precipitation ranges from slightly more than 40 in (101.6 cm) in the southeast to as little as 16 in (40.6 cm) in the west; in Wichita, average annual precipitation (1971–2000) was 30.4 in (77.2 cm). The overall annual precipitation for the state averages 27 in (68.6 cm), although years of drought have not been uncommon. About 70%–77% of the precipitation falls between 1 April and 30 September. The annual mean snowfall ranges from about 36 in (91.4 cm) in the extreme northwest to less than 11 in (27.9 cm) in the far southeast. Tornadoes are a regular fact of life in Kansas. Dodge City is said to be the windiest city in the United States, with an average wind speed of 14 mph (23 km/h).

⁴FLORA AND FAUNA

Native grasses, consisting of 60 different groups subdivided into 194 species, cover one-third of Kansas, which is much overgrazed.

Bluestem—both big and little—which grows in most parts of the state, has the greatest forage value. Other grasses include buffalo grass, blue and hairy gramas, and alkali sacaton. One native conifer, eastern red cedar, is found generally throughout the state. Hackberry, black walnut, and sycamore grow in the east while box elder and cottonwood predominate in western Kansas. There are no native pines. The wild native sunflower, the state flower, is found throughout the state. Other characteristic wildflowers include wild daisy, ivy-leaved morning glory, and smallflower verbena. The western prairie fringed orchid and Mead's milkweed, listed as threatened species by the US Fish and Wildlife Service in April 2006, are protected under federal statutes.

Kansas's indigenous mammals include the common cottontail, black-tailed jackrabbit, black-tailed prairie dog, muskrat, opossum, and raccoon; the white-tailed deer is the state's only big-game animal. There are 12 native species of bat, 2 varieties of shrew and mole, and 3 types of pocket gopher. The western meadowlark is the state bird. Kansas has the largest flock of prairie chickens remaining on the North American continent. The US Fish and Wildlife Service named 12 animal species occurring in the state as threatened or endangered in April 2006. Among these are the Indiana and gray bats, bald eagle, Eskimo curlew, Topeka Shiner, and black-footed ferret.

Cheyenne Bottoms, a Ramsar Wetland of International Importance, serves as a habitat for the endangered whooping crane and is also considered to be an important site for over 800,000 migratory birds each year. Nearly 45% of all migratory shorebirds that nest in North America use Cheyenne Bottoms as a staging area. The salt marshes of the Quivira National Wildlife Refuge (also a Ramsar site) serve as a nesting, migration, and winter habitat for over 311 species of bird, including the endangered peregrine falcon and bald eagle.

5ENVIRONMENTAL PROTECTION

No environmental problem is more crucial for Kansas than water quality, and its protection remains a primary focus of the state's environmental efforts, which include active regulatory and remedial programs for both surface and groundwater sources. Maintenance of air quality is also a primary effort, and the state works actively with the business community to promote pollution prevention.

Strip-mining for coal is decreasing in southeast Kansas, and the restoration of resources damaged by previous activities is ongoing.

Kansas is home to two Ramsar Wetlands of International Importance. Cheyenne Bottoms, located in Barton County, was designated in 1988. The site includes a state wildlife area, managed by the Kansas Department of Wildlife and Parks, and the Cheyenne Bottoms Preserve, managed by the Nature Conservancy. The site is also considered to be part of the Western Hemisphere Shorebird Reserve Network. The Quivira National Wildlife Refuge was designated by Ramsar in 2002. It includes freshwater and inland salt marshes. This site has been a National Wildlife Refuge since 1955.

In 2003, 28.9 million lb of toxic chemicals were released in the state. The state has sufficient capacity for handling solid waste, although the total number of solid waste facilities has decreased in recent years. In 2003, Kansas had 307 hazardous waste sites listed in the US Environment Protection Agency (EPA) database,

10 of which were on the National Priorities List as of 2006. Five sites were deleted from the National Priority List in 2006, but another two, the Sunflower Army Ammunition Plant and the Tri-County Public Airport, were proposed. In 2005, the EPA spent over $512,000 through the Superfund program for the cleanup of hazardous waste sites in the state. The same year, federal EPA grants awarded to the state included $9.7 million for a wastewater state revolving fund and $4.2 million for additional water quality projects.

6POPULATION

Kansas ranked 33rd in population in the United States with an estimated total of 2,744,687 in 2005, an increase of 2.1% since 2000. Between 1990 and 2000, Kansas's population grew from 2,477,574 to 2,688,418, an increase of 8.5%. The population is projected to reach 2.85 million by 2015 and 2.91 million by 2025. The population density in 2004 was 33.4 persons per sq mi.

When it was admitted to the Union in 1861, Kansas's population was 107,206. During the decade that followed, the population grew by 240%, more than 10 times the US growth rate. Steady growth continued through the 1930s, but in the 1940s, the population declined by 4%. Since then, the population has risen, though at a slower pace than the national average.

In 2004, the median age for Kansans was 36.1; 25% of the population was below the age of 18 while 13% was 65 or older.

Whereas the populations of Wichita and Topeka grew 8.6% and 1.0% respectively, the population of Kansas City dropped 7.1% during the 1980s. Estimates for 2004 showed about 353,823 residents for Wichita, 162,728 for Overland Park, and 145,004 for Kansas City. The Wichita metropolitan area had an estimated 584,671 residents.

7ETHNIC GROUPS

White settlers began to pour into Kansas in 1854, dispersing the 36 Indian tribes living there and precipitating a struggle over the legal status of slavery. Remnants of six of the original tribes still make their homes in the state. Some Indians live on three reservations covering 30,000 acres (12,140 hectares); others live and work elsewhere, returning to the reservations several times a year for celebrations and observances. There were 24,936 Indians in Kansas as of 2000. In 2004, American Indians made up 1% of the population.

Black Americans in Kansas numbered 154,198, or 5.7% of the population, in 2000, when the state also had 188,252 Hispanics and Latinos. In 2004, 5.9% of the population was black and 8.1% of Hispanic or Latino origin. The 2000 Census recorded 46,806 Asian residents, the largest group being 11,623 Vietnamese (up from 6,001 in 1990), followed by 8,153 Asian Indians and 7,624 Chinese. There were also sizable communities of Laotians and Cambodians. In 2004, 2.1% of the population was Asian, and 0.1% was of Pacific Island origin. That year, 1.6% of the population reported origin of two or more races.

The foreign born numbered 80,271 (2% of the population) in 2000, the most common lands of origin being Mexico, Germany, and Vietnam. Among persons who reported descent from a single ancestry group, the leading nationalities were German (914,955), English (391,542), and Irish (424,133).

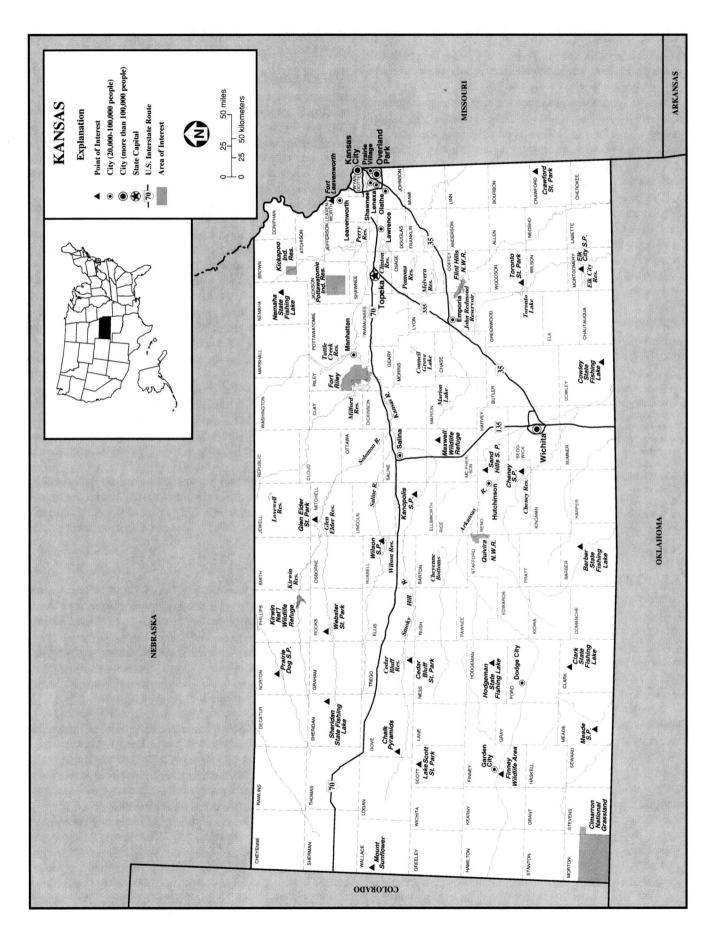

8 LANGUAGES

Plains Indians of the Macro-Siouan group originally populated what is now Kansas; their speech echoes in such place-names as Kansas, Wichita, Topeka, Chetopa, and Ogallah.

Regional features of Kansas speech are almost entirely those of the Northern and North Midland dialects, reflecting the migration into Kansas in the 1850s of settlers from the East. Kansans typically use *fish(ing) worms* as bait, play as children on a *teetertotter*, see a *snakefeeder* (dragonfly) over a /krik/ (creek), make *white bread* sandwiches, carry water in a *pail,* and may designate the time 2:45 as a *quarter to,* or *of, or till* three.

The migration by southerners in the mid-19th century is evidenced in southeastern Kansas by such South Midland terms as *pullybone* (wishbone) and *light bread* (white bread); the expression *wait on* (wait for) extends farther westward.

In 2000, 2,281,705 Kansans—91.3% of the residents five years old or older (down from 94.3% in 1990)—spoke only English at home.

The following table gives selected statistics from the 2000 Census for language spoken at home by persons five years old and over.

LANGUAGE	NUMBER	PERCENT
Population 5 years and over	**2,500,360**	**100.0**
Speak only English	2,281,705	91.3
Speak a language other than English	218,655	8.7
Speak a language other than English	**218,655**	**8.7**
Spanish or Spanish Creole	137,247	5.5
German	16,821	0.7
Vietnamese	10,393	0.4
French (incl. Patois, Cajun)	6,591	0.3
Chinese	6,473	0.3
Korean	3,666	0.1
Laotian	3,147	0.1
Arabic	2,834	0.1
Tagalog	2,237	0.1
Russian	1,994	0.1

9 RELIGIONS

Protestant missions played an important role in early Kansas history. Isaac McCoy, a Baptist minister, was instrumental in founding the Shawnee Baptist Mission in Johnson County in 1831. Later, Baptist, Methodist, Quaker, Presbyterian, and Jesuit missions became popular stopover points for pioneers traveling along the Oregon and Santa Fe trails. Mennonites were drawn to the state by a law passed in 1874 allowing exemption from military service on religious grounds. Religious freedom is specifically granted in the Kansas constitution, and a wide variety of religious groups are represented in the state.

Roman Catholics constitute the single largest religious group in the state, with 409,906 adherents in 2004. One of the leading Protestant denominations is the United Methodist Church, with 162,202 members in 2004. Others (with 2000 membership data) include the Southern Baptist Convention with 101,696 adherents; the American Baptist Church, 64,312; the Lutheran Church–Missouri Synod, 62,712; and the Christian Church (Disciples of Christ), 56,908. The estimated Jewish population in 2000 was 14,500, which represents an increase of over 5,000 adherents since 1990. There were over 18,000 Mennonites throughout the state and about 3,470 Muslims. About 50.6% of the population (or over 1.3 million people) did not report affiliation with a religious organization.

10 TRANSPORTATION

In the heartland of the nation, Kansas is at the crossroads of US road and railway systems. In 2001, Kansas had 25,638 bridges (third in the nation behind Texas and Ohio). In 2004, the state had 135,017 mi (217,377 km) of public roads. In that same year, there were some 845,000 automobiles, around 1.71 million trucks of all types, and some 1,000 buses registered in Kansas. In 2004, Kansas had 1,979,746 licensed drivers.

In the late 1800s, the two major railroads, the Kansas Pacific (now the Union Pacific) and the Santa Fe (now the Burlington Northern-Santa Fe) acquired more than 10 million acres (4 million hectares) of land in the state and then advertised for immigrants to come and buy it. By 1872, the railroads stretched across the state, creating in their path the towns of Ellsworth, Newton, Caldwell, Wichita, and Dodge City. One of the first "cow towns" was Abilene, the terminal point for all cattle shipped to the East.

In 2003, the state had 6,269 route mi (10,093 km) of railroad track. As of 2006, Amtrak's Southwest Chief passenger train crosses Kansas, serving six stations in the state en route from Chicago to Los Angeles.

In 2005, Kansas had a total of 409 public and private-use aviation-related facilities. This included 370 airports, 38 heliports, and 1 STOLport (Short Take-Off and Landing). The state's busiest airport is Kansas City International. In 2004, the airport had 5,040,595 enplanements, making it the 39th busiest airport in the United States.

River barges move bulk commodities along the Missouri River. The chief river ports are Atchison, Leavenworth, Lansing, and Kansas City. In 2004, Kansas had 120 mi (193 km) of navigable inland waterways. In 2003, waterborne shipments totaled 1.694 million tons.

11 HISTORY

Present-day Kansas was first inhabited by Paleo-Indians approximately 10,000 years ago. They were followed by several prehistoric cultures, forerunners of the Plains tribes—the Wichita, Pawnee, Kansa, and Osage—that were living or hunting in Kansas when the earliest Europeans arrived. These tribes were buffalo hunters who also farmed and lived in small permanent communities. Around 1800, they were joined on the Central Plains by the nomadic Cheyenne, Arapaho, Comanche, and Kiowa.

The first European, explorer Francisco Coronado, entered Kansas in 1541, searching for riches in the fabled land of Quivira. He found no gold but was impressed by the land's fertility. A second Spanish expedition to the Plains was led by Juan de Onate in 1601. Between 1682 and 1739, French explorers established trading contacts with the Indians. France ceded its claims to the area to Spain in 1762 but received it back from Spain in 1800.

Most of Kansas was sold to the United States by France as part of the Louisiana Purchase of 1803. (The extreme southwestern corner was gained after the Mexican War.) Lewis and Clark examined the country along the Missouri River in 1804, and expeditions under the command of Zebulon Pike (1806) and Stephen Long (1819) traversed the land from east to west. Pike and Long were not impressed with the territory's dry soil, the latter calling the area "unfit for civilization, and of course uninhabitable by a people depending on agriculture for their subsistence."

Largely because of these negative reports, early settlement of Kansas was sparse, limited to a few thousand eastern Indians who were removed from their lands and relocated in what is now eastern Kansas. Included were such once-powerful tribes as the Shawnee, Delaware, Ojibwa, Wyandot, Ottawa, and Potawatomi. They were joined by a number of Christian missionaries seeking to transform the Indians into Christian farmers.

William Becknell opened the Santa Fe Trail to wagon traffic in 1822, and for 50 years that route, two-thirds of which lay in Kansas, was of commercial importance to the West. During the 1840s and 1850s, thousands of migrants crossed northeastern Kansas on the California-Oregon Trail. In 1827, Ft. Leavenworth was established, followed by Ft. Scott (1842) and Ft. Riley (1853). Today, Ft. Leavenworth and Ft. Riley are the two largest military installations in the state.

The Kansas Territory was created by the Kansas-Nebraska Act (30 May 1854), with its western boundary set at the Rocky Mountains. Almost immediately, disputes arose as to whether Kansas would enter the Union as a free or slave state. Both free-staters and proslavery settlers were brought in, and a succession of governors tried to bring order out of the chaos arising from the two groups' differences. Free-staters established an extralegal government at Topeka following the establishment of a territorial capital at Lecompton.

Because of several violent incidents, the territory became known as "Bleeding Kansas." One of the most memorable attacks came in May 1856, when the town of Lawrence was sacked by proslavery forces. John Brown, an abolitionist who had recently arrived from upstate New York, retaliated by murdering five proslavery settlers. Guerrilla skirmishes continued for the next few years along the Kansas–Missouri border. The final act of violence was the Marais des Cygnes massacre in 1858, which resulted in the death of several free-staters. In all, about 50 people were killed in the territorial period—not an extraordinary number for a frontier community.

After several attempts to write a constitution acceptable to both anti- and proslavery groups, the final document was drafted in 1859. Kansas entered the Union on 29 January 1861 as a free state. Topeka was named the capital, and the western boundary was moved to its present location.

Although Kansas lay west of the major Civil War action, more than two-thirds of its adult males served in the Union Army, giving it the highest military death rate among the northern states. Kansas units saw action in the South and West, most notably at Wilson's Creek, Cane Hill, Prairie Grove, and Chickamauga. The only full-scale battle fought in Kansas was at Mine Creek in 1864, at the end of General Sterling Price's unsuccessful Confederate campaign in the West. The most tragic incident on Kansas soil came on 21 August 1863, when Confederate guerrilla William C. Quantrill raided Lawrence, killing at least 150 persons and burning the town.

Following the Civil War, settlement expanded in Kansas, particularly in the central part of the state. White settlers encroached on the hunting grounds of the Plains tribes, and the Indians retaliated with attacks on white settlements. Treaty councils were held, the largest at Medicine Lodge in 1867, but not until 1878 did conflict cease between Indians and whites. Most of the Indians were even-

tually removed to the Indian Territory in what is now Oklahoma. Also during this period, buffalo, slaughtered for food and hides, all but disappeared from the state.

By 1872, both the Union Pacific and the Santa Fe railroads crossed Kansas, and other lines were under construction. Rail expansion brought more settlers, who established new communities. It also led to the great Texas cattle drives that meant prosperity to a number of Kansas towns—including Abilene, Ellsworth, Wichita, Caldwell, and Dodge City—from 1867 to 1885. This was when Bat Masterson, Wyatt Earp, Doc Holliday, and Wild Bill Hickok reigned in Dodge City and Abilene—the now romantic era of the Old West.

A strain of hard winter wheat that proved particularly well suited to the state's soil was brought to Kansas in the 1870s by Russian Mennonites fleeing czarist rule, and Plains agriculture was thereby transformed. There were also political changes: The state adopted limited female suffrage in 1887. Prohibition, made part of the state constitution in 1880, was a source of controversy until its repeal in 1948.

Significant changes in agriculture, industry, transportation, and communications came after 1900. Mechanization became commonplace in farming, and vast areas were opened to wheat production, particularly during World War I. Some automobile manufacturing took place, and the movement for "good roads" began. The so-called agrarian revolt of the late 19th century, characterized politically by populism, evolved into the Progressive movement of the early 1900s, which focused attention on control of monopolies, public health, labor legislation, and more representative politics. Much of the Progressive leadership came from Kansas; Kansan newspaper editor and national Progressive leader William Allen White devoted considerable energy to Theodore Roosevelt's Bull Moose campaign in 1912.

Kansas suffered through the Great Depression of the 1930s. The state's western region, part of the Dust Bowl, was hardest hit. Improved weather conditions and the demands of World War II revived Kansas agriculture in the 1940s. The World War II era also saw the development of industry, especially in transportation. Wichita had been a major center of the aircraft industry in the 1920s and 1930s, and its plants became vital to the US war effort. Other heavy industry grew, and mineral production—oil, natural gas, salt, coal, and gypsum—expanded greatly. In 1952, a native Kansan, Dwight D. Eisenhower, was elected to the first of two terms as president of the United States. Two years later, Topeka became the focal point of a landmark in US history—the US Supreme Court ruling in the *Brown v. Board of Education* case that banned racial segregation in the nation's schools.

After World War II, Kansas grew increasingly urban. Agriculture became highly commercialized and the state became home to dozens of large companies that process and market farm products and supply materials to crop producers. Livestock production, especially in closely controlled feedlots, is a major enterprise. Kansas farmers were hit hard by the recession of the 1980s. Agricultural banks failed and many farms were lost, their owners forced into bankruptcy. As part of a solution, the state government worked to expand international exports of Kansas products, securing, for example, a trade agreement with the St. Petersburg region of Russia in 1993. The late 1980s and early 1990s also saw dramatic extremes of weather. Kansas received less than 25% of its normal average rainfall in 1988. Topsoil erosion damaged 865,000 acres (354,650 hectares) and drought drove up commodity prices and depleted grain stocks. From April through September of 1993, Kansas experienced the worst floods of the century. Some 13,500 people evacuated their homes, and the floods caused $574 million worth of damage.

In the 1990s, in response to the economic problems created by severe weather and a slowdown in industrial growth, the state government implemented a number of measures, including block grants to cities, to bolster economic development. Amid the sustained economic boom of the late 1990s, Kansas generally prospered. Unemployment dropped to just 3%, more than 1 percentage point below the national average, in 1999. The state's poverty rate declined in the period between 1989 (when it was 11.5%) and 1998, when it was 9.6%. But with farmers and ranchers still struggling in 1999, a bipartisan group of rural legislators came together to introduce a plan to address what was by then perceived as a crisis in the state's agricultural economy. Their nine-point plan aimed to shore up the farming sector by restraining the anticompetitive market forces they believed threatened family farmers.

In 1996, native son and US Senate majority leader Robert Dole won the Republican presidential nomination but was defeated by Democratic incumbent Bill Clinton, although Dole carried his home state with 54% of the vote to Clinton's 36%.

In 1999, the Kansas Board of Education voted 6–4 to adopt standards that downplayed the importance of evolution and omitted the Big Bang theory of the universe's origin from the curriculum. Though the standards were not mandatory, they drew national attention, with critics decrying the standards as "backward looking." The decision was later reversed. In 2005, Kansas adopted a constitutional amendment to ban same-sex marriage, and the Kansas Board of Education resumed hearings to determine whether evolution should once again be eliminated from state science standards.

The Kansas economy was improving in 2003, after the 2001 US recession. Unemployment in Kansas stood at 5% in July 2003.

The national unemployment rate in July 2003 was 6.2%. In 2003, Kansas had a $230 million budget deficit for 2004, and Governor Kathleen Sebelius in April called for bond sales, expanded gambling, and more rapid tax collection to cover the shortfall. Her plans were met with opposition from the Republican-controlled legislature, however. In 2003, Sebelius focused on education, health care, transportation, and the economy. She also set forth plans to streamline state government and encourage citizen involvement in local communities. Sebelius in 2005 continued to stress goals of improving education, health care, and creating jobs. From 2003 to 2005, Wichita's aircraft industry was shored up, business development in small Kansas towns was increasing, and heavy investments were made in bioscience research at universities and medical centers.

¹²STATE GOVERNMENT

The form of Kansas's constitution was a matter of great national concern, for the question of whether Kansas would be a free or slave state was in doubt throughout the 1850s. After three draft constitutions failed to win popular support or congressional approval, a fourth version, banning slavery, was drafted in July 1859 and ratified by Kansas voters that October. Signed by President James Buchanan on 29 January 1861, this constitution (with 92 subsequent amendments as of 2005, one of which was subsequently nullified by the state supreme court) governs Kansas to the present day.

The Kansas legislature consists of a 40-member Senate and a 125-member House of Representatives. Senators serve four-year terms and House members serve for two years; elections are held in even-numbered years. Legislative sessions, which begin the second Monday of January each year, are limited to 90 calendar days in even-numbered years but are unlimited in odd-numbered years. Legislators may call a special session by petition to the governor of two-thirds the membership of each house. Length of special sessions is not limited. Legislators must be at least 18 years old, state citizens, residents of their districts, and qualified voters.

Kansas Presidential Vote by Political Parties, 1948–2004

YEAR	ELECTORAL VOTE	KANSAS WINNER	DEMOCRAT	REPUBLICAN	PROGRESSIVE	SOCIALIST	PROHIBITION
1948	8	Dewey (R)	351,902	423,039	4,603	2,807	6,468
1952	8	*Eisenhower (R)	273,296	616,302	6,038	530	6,038
1956	8	*Eisenhower (R)	296,317	566,878	—	—	3,048
1960	8	Nixon (R)	363,213	561,474	—	—	4,138
1964	7	*Johnson (D)	464,028	386,579	—	1,901	5,393
					AMERICAN IND.		
1968	7	*Nixon (R)	302,996	478,674	88,921	—	2,192
1972	7	*Nixon (R)	270,287	619,812	21,808	—	4,188
						LIBERTARIAN	
1976	7	Ford (R)	430,421	502,752	4,724	3,242	1,403
1980	7	*Reagan (R)	326,150	566,812	7,555	14,470	—
1984	7	*Reagan (R)	333,149	677,296	—	3,329	—
1988	7	*Bush (R)	422,636	554,049	3,806	12,553	—
					IND. (Perot)		
1992	6	Bush (R)	390,434	449,951	312,358	4,314	—
1996	6	Dole (R)	387,659	583,245	92,639	4,557	—
					(Nader)		REFORM
2000	6	*Bush, G. W. (R)	399,276	622,332	36,086	4,525	7,370
					REFORM (Nader)		INDEPENDENT
2004	6	*Bush, G. W. (R)	434,993	736,456	9,348	4,013	2,899

*Won US presidential election.

In 2004, legislators received a per diem salary of $78.75 during regular sessions.

Constitutional amendments are proposed by the legislature, where they must be approved by two-thirds of the members before being sent to the voters for ratification. A maximum of five proposed amendments may be submitted to the state's voters at any one time.

Officials elected statewide are the governor and lieutenant governor (elected jointly), secretary of state, attorney general, treasurer, and commissioner of insurance. Members of the state Board of Education are elected by districts. All elected state officials serve four-year terms. The governor cannot serve more than two consecutive terms. Every office in the executive branch is controlled by either the governor or another elected official. There are no formal age, citizenship, or residency provisions for a gubernatorial candidate's qualifications for office. As of December 2004, the governor's salary was $98,331.

A bill becomes law when it has been approved by 21 senators and 63 representatives and signed by the governor. A veto can be overridden by two-thirds of the elected members of both houses. If the governor neither vetoes nor signs a bill, it becomes law after 10 days (whether or not the legislature is in session).

To vote in the state, a person must be a US citizen, 18 years old at the time of the election, a resident of Kansas, and not able to claim the right to vote elsewhere. Restrictions apply to those convicted of certain crimes and to those judged by the court to be mentally incompetent to vote.

13 POLITICAL PARTIES

Kansas was dominated by the Republican Party for the first three decades of statehood (1860s–1880s). Although the Republicans remain the dominant force in state politics, the Democrats controlled the governorship in the early 2000s.

The Republican Party of early Kansas espoused the abolitionist ideals of the New England settlers who sought to ban slavery from the state. After the Civil War, the railroads played a major role in Republican politics and won favorable tax advantages from the elected officials. The party's ranks swelled with the arrival of immigrants from Scandinavia and Germany, who tended to side with the party's strongly conservative beliefs.

The Republicans' hold over state life was shaken by the Populist revolt toward the end of the 19th century. The high point of Populist Party power came in 1892, when the insurgents won all statewide elective offices and also took control of the Senate. When electoral irregularities denied them control of the House, they temporarily seized the House chambers. The two parties then set up separate houses of representatives, the Populists meeting one day and the Republicans the next. This continued for six weeks, until the Kansas Supreme Court ruled that the Republicans constituted the rightful legal body. After a Republican sweep in 1894, the Populists returned to office in 1896, but the party declined rapidly thereafter.

The Democrats rose to power in the state as a result of a split between the conservative and progressive wings of the Republican Party in 1912. Nevertheless, the Democrats were very much a minority party until after World War II. Democratic Kathleen Sebelius was elected governor in 2002. Republicans have regularly controlled the legislature. In 2004, there were 1,694,000 registered voters. In 1998, 29% of registered voters were Democratic, 45% Republican, and 26% unaffiliated or members of other parties.

In 1988 and 1992, Kansans voted for George H. W. Bush in the presidential elections. In the 1996 election, native Kansan Bob Dole won 54% of the vote; Bill Clinton received 36%; and Independent Ross Perot garnered 9%. In the 2000 and 2004 elections, Republican George W. Bush won 58% and 62% of the vote, respectively, to Democrat Al Gore's 37% (in 2000) and Democrat John Kerry's 36% (in 2004). The state had six electoral votes in the 2004 presidential election.

Bob Dole, first elected to the US Senate in 1968 and elected Senate majority leader in 1984, reclaimed the post of majority leader when the Republicans gained control of the Senate in the elections of 1994. In a surprise move in May 1996, Dole announced his retirement from the Senate to concentrate on his presidential campaign. In November, the race to fill his remaining term was won by Republican Sam Brownback. Completing the term, Brownback won his first full term in November 1998; he was reelected in 2004. Kansas's other Republican senator, Nancy Landon Kassebaum, also vacated her seat in 1996; it was won by Republican congressman Pat Roberts, who was reelected in 2002. In the 2004 elections, Kansas voters sent three Republicans and one Democrat to the US House. In the state legislature in mid-2005, there were 30 Republicans and 10 Democrats in the state Senate and 83 Republicans and 42 Democrats in the state House.

14 LOCAL GOVERNMENT

As of 2005, Kansas had 105 counties, 627 municipal governments, 304 public school districts, and 1,533 special districts. As of 2002, there were 1,299 townships.

By law, no county can be less than 432 sq mi (1,119 sq km). Each county government is headed by elected county commissioners. Other county officials include the county clerk, treasurer, register of deeds, attorney, sheriff, clerk of district court, and appraiser. Most cities are run by mayor-council systems.

In 2005, local government accounted for about 137,278 full-time (or equivalent) employment positions.

15 STATE SERVICES

To address the continuing threat of terrorism and to work with the federal Department of Homeland Security, homeland security in Kansas operates under the authority of the governor; the adjutant general is designated as the state homeland security adviser.

All education services, including community colleges, are handled by the state Board of Education; the state university system lies within the jurisdiction of the Board of Regents. The Department of Human Resources administers employment and worker benefit programs. The Kansas Housing Resources Corporation creates housing opportunities for Kansans. Social, vocational, and children's and youth programs are run by the Department of Social and Rehabilitation Services. The Department of Health and Environment supervises health, environment, and laboratory services. Other departments focus on agriculture, corrections, revenue, transportation, wildlife and parks, aging, and information systems and communication.

A "Sunset Law" automatically abolishes specified state agencies at certain times unless they receive renewed statutory authority.

16 JUDICIAL SYSTEM

The Kansas Supreme Court, the highest court in the state, is composed of a chief justice and six other justices. All justices are appointed by the governor but after one year must run for election in the next general election. They are then elected for six-year terms. In case of rejection by the voters, the vacancy is filled by appointment. An intermediate-level court of appeals consists of a chief judge and six other judges appointed by the governor; like supreme court justices, they must be elected to full terms, in this case for four years.

In January 1977, probate, juvenile, and county courts, as well as magistrate courts of countywide jurisdiction, were replaced by district courts. The 31 district courts are presided over by 156 district and associate district judges and 69 district magistrate judges.

As of 31 December 2004, a total of 8,966 prisoners were held in state and federal prisons in Kansas, a decrease (from 9,132) of 1.8% from the previous year. As of year-end 2004, a total of 620 inmates were female, down from 629 or 1.4% from the year before. Among sentenced prisoners (includes some sentenced to one year or less), Kansas had an incarceration rate of 327 per 100,000 population in 2004.

According to the Federal Bureau of Investigation, Kansas in 2004, had a violent crime rate (murder/nonnegligent manslaughter; forcible rape; robbery; aggravated assault) of 374.5 reported incidents per 100,000 population, or a total of 10,245 reported incidents. Crimes against property (burglary; larceny/theft; and motor vehicle theft) in that same year totaled 108,694 reported incidents or 3,973.5 reported incidents per 100,000 people. Kansas had a death penalty until 17 December 2004 when the state's death penalty statutes were declared unconstitutional. However, as of 1 January 2006, eight inmates remained on death row.

In 2003, Kansas spent $56,896,421 on homeland security, an average of $21 per state resident.

17 ARMED FORCES

The US Army's First Infantry Division, known as the Big Red One, was located at Ft. Riley in Junction City until 1996, when the colors of the First Infantry Division moved to Würzburg, Germany. Founded in 1827, Ft. Leavenworth is the oldest continuously active military fort west of the Mississippi. The Army's Combined Arms Center Command (CAC) and General Staff College is housed there. McConnell Air Force Base is located in Wichita. A total of 20,039 active-duty federal military personnel, along with 3,762 civilian personnel, were stationed in Kansas in 2004. In 2004, $1.4 billion in defense contracts was awarded to state firms, up from $762 million in 1995–96 and down from $2.4 billion in 1983–84. In addition, another $1.5 billion in defense payroll spending, including retired military pay, came to the state.

There were 246,359 veterans of US military service in Kansas as of 2003, of whom 36,042 served in World War II; 26,804 in the Korean conflict; 76,710 during the Vietnam era; and 38,422 in the Gulf War. During fiscal year 2004, expenditures on veterans were $592 million.

As of 31 October 2004, the Kansas Highway Patrol employed 535 full-time sworn officers.

18 MIGRATION

By the 1770s, Kansas was inhabited by a few thousand Indians, mainly from five tribes: the Kansa (Kaw) and the Osage, both of whom had migrated from the East, the Pawnee from the North, and the Wichita and Comanche, who had come from the Southwest. In 1825, the US government signed a treaty with the Kansa and Osage that allowed eastern Indians to settle in the state.

The first wave of white migration came during the 1850s with the arrival of New England abolitionists who settled in Lawrence, Topeka, and Manhattan. They were followed by a much larger wave of emigrants from the eastern Missouri and the upper Mississippi Valley, drawn by the lure of wide-open spaces and abundant economic opportunity.

The population swelled as a result of the Homestead Act of 1862, which offered land to anyone who would improve it and live on it for five years. The railroads promoted the virtues of Kansas overseas and helped sponsor immigrant settlers. By 1870, 11% of the population was European. More than 30,000 blacks, mostly from the South, arrived during 1878–80. Crop failures caused by drought in the late 1890s led to extensive out-migration from the western half of the state. Another period of out-migration occurred in the early 1930s, when massive dust storms drove people off the land. Steady migration from farms to cities has been a feature of Kansas since the early 20th century, with urban population surpassing farm population after World War II. From 1980 to 1990, the urban population increased from 66.7% to 69.1% of the state's total. Also from 1980 to 1990, Kansas had a net loss of 63,411 from migration. Only 10 of Kansas's 105 counties recorded a net gain from migration in the 1980s. Between 1990 and 1998, the state had a net loss of 13,000 in domestic migration and a gain of 24,000 in international migration. In 1998, 3,184 foreign immigrants arrived in the state. Between 1990 and 1998, Kansas's overall population increased 6.1%. In the period 2000–05, net international migration was 38,222 and net internal migration was -57,763, for a net loss of 19,541 people.

19 INTERGOVERNMENTAL COOPERATION

Kansas is a member of the Arkansas River Compact of 1949, Arkansas River Compact of 1965, Central Interstate Low-Level Radioactive Waste Compact, Kansas-Nebraska Big Blue River Compact, Kansas City Area Transportation Authority, Kansas-Missouri Boundary Compact and Culture District Compact, Missouri River Toll Bridge Compact, Republican River Compact, and other interstate bodies. The Interstate Cooperation Commission assists state officials and employees in maintaining contact with governmental units in other states. In fiscal year 2001, Kansas received over $2.7 billion in federal grants. Following a national trend, that amount dropped to $2.561 billion in fiscal year 2005, before gradually recovering to an estimated $2.663 billion in fiscal year 2006 and an estimated $2.755 billion in fiscal year 2007.

20 ECONOMY

Although wheat production has long been the mainstay of the Kansas economy, efforts to bring other industries into the state began as early as the 1870s, when the railroads linked Kansas to eastern markets. By 2000, agricultural products and meat-packing industries were rivaled by the large aircraft industry centered in

Wichita. Four Kansas companies, all located in Wichita, manufacture 70% of the world's general aviation aircraft. The Kansas City metropolitan area is a center of automobile production and printing. Metal fabrication, printing, and mineral products industries predominate in the nine southeastern counties. Kansas continues to lead all states in wheat production. The national recession of 2001 had a relatively mild impact on the Kansas economy. The annual economic growth rate, which had averaged 5% from 1998 to 2000, dipped to 3.2% in 2001. Net job creation, though sharply slowed by layoffs in 2001 and 2002, including several rounds of layoffs in the Wichita aircraft manufacturing industry, remained positive, in contrast to the nation as whole, in which job creation turned to net layoffs in the second half of 2001 and stayed negative throughout 2002. In December 2002, however, unemployment in Kansas was at the relatively high level of 4.6%. The farm sector was also afflicted by drought conditions, which persisted into the winter of 2002–03. In 2002, on a year-by-year basis, wheat production was down 19%, corn production down 26%, and soybean production down 29%. Kansas's rural population continues its long-term decline as people migrate to urban areas seeking better employment opportunities. Since 1970, 67 of the state's 105 counties have lost population, and in 19 of these, the rate of decrease accelerated during the 1990s. From 1997 to 2001, Kansas farm output experienced a net decrease of 34.5%, from $2.7 billion to $1.8 billion.

The state's gross state product (GSP) in 2004 totaled $98.946 billion, of which manufacturing (durable and nondurable goods) accounted for the largest portion at $14.897 billion or 15% of GSP, followed by real estate at $8.790 billion (8.8% of GSP) and health care and social services at $6.930 billion (7% of GSP). In that same year, there were an estimated 229,776 small businesses in Kansas. Of the 69,241 businesses that had employees, a total of 67,120 or 96.9% were small companies. An estimated 6,742 new businesses were established in the state in 2004, down 11.6% from the year before. Business terminations that same year came to 7,250, down 13.6% from 2003. There were 268 business bankruptcies in 2004, down 11.6% from the previous year. In 2005, the state's personal bankruptcy (Chapter 7 and Chapter 13) filing rate was 585 filings per 100,000 people, ranking Kansas as the 21st highest in the nation.

21 INCOME

In 2005, Kansas had a gross state product (GSP) of $105 billion, which accounted for 0.9% of the nation's gross domestic product and placed the state at number 32 in highest GSP among the 50 states and the District of Columbia.

According to the Bureau of Economic Analysis, in 2004, Kansas had a per capita personal income (PCPI) of $31,078. This ranked 27th in the United States and was 94% of the national average of $33,050. The 1994–2004 average annual growth rate of PCPI was 4.0%. Kansas had a total personal income (TPI) of $84,957,195,000, which ranked 31st in the United States and reflected an increase of 5.0% from 2003. The 1994–2004 average annual growth rate of TPI was 4.6%. Earnings of persons employed in Kansas increased from $61,785,883,000 in 2003 to $65,176,017,000 in 2004, an increase of 5.5%. The 2003–04 national change was 6.3%.

The US Census Bureau reports that the three-year average median household income for 2002–04 in 2004 dollars was $43,725 compared to a national average of $44,473. During the same period, 10.7% of the population was below the poverty line, compared to 12.4% nationwide.

22 LABOR

According to the Bureau of Labor Statistics (BLS), in April 2006, the seasonally adjusted civilian labor force in Kansas numbered 1,481,300. Approximately 67,400 workers were unemployed, yielding an unemployment rate of 4.6%, compared to the national average of 4.7% for the same period. Preliminary data for the same period placed nonfarm employment at 1,345,900. Since the beginning of the BLS data series in 1976, the highest unemployment rate recorded in Kansas was 7.4% in September 1982. The historical low was 2.9% in October 1978. Preliminary nonfarm employment data by occupation for April 2006 showed that approximately 4.9% of the labor force was employed in construction; 19.3% in manufacturing; 19.3% in trade, transportation, and public utilities; 9.8% in professional and business services; 12.4% in education and health services; 8.4% in leisure and hospitality services; and 18.9% in government. Data were unavailable for financial services.

The BLS reported that in 2005, a total of 85,000 of Kansas's 1,210,000 employed wage and salary workers were formal members of a union. This represented 7% of those so employed, down from 8.4% in 2004 and below the national average of 12%. Overall in 2005, a total of 115,000 workers (9.5%) in Kansas were covered by a union or employee association contract, which includes those workers who reported no union affiliation. Kansas is one of 22 states with a right-to-work law, which is a part of the state's constitution.

As of 1 March 2006, Kansas had a state-mandated minimum wage rate of $2.65 per hour. However, that rate does not apply to employment covered by the Federal Fair Labor Standards Act. In 2004, women in the state accounted for 46% of the employed civilian labor force.

23 AGRICULTURE

Known as the Wheat State and the breadbasket of the nation, Kansas typically produces more wheat than any other state. It ranked fifth in total farm income in 2005, with cash receipts of $9.7 billion.

Because of fluctuating prices, Kansas farmers have always risked economic disaster. During the 1920s, depressed farm prices forced many new farmers out of business. By World War II, Kansas farmers were prospering again, as record prices coincided with record yields. Since then, improved technology has favored corporate farms at the expense of small landholders. Between 1940 and 2002, the number of farms declined from 159,000 to 64,500, while the average size of farms more than doubled (to 732 acres/296 hectares). Income from crops in 2005 totaled $3.1 billion.

Other leading crops are alfalfa, hay, oats, barley, popcorn, rye, dry edible beans, corn and sorghums for silage, wild hay, red clover, and sugar beets.

24 ANIMAL HUSBANDRY

In 2001, Kansas dairy farmers had an estimated 111,000 milk cows that produced 2.11 billion lb (0.96 billion kg) of milk.

In 2005, Kansas farmers had an estimated 6.65 million cattle and calves (second in the United States) worth $5.51 billion. Kansas farmers had an estimated 1.72 million hogs and pigs worth around $160 million in 2004. An estimated 6.9 million lb (3.1 million kg) of sheep and lambs were produced by Kansas farmers in 2003 and sold for $6.1 million. The wool clip in 2004 totaled 485,000 lb (220,000 kg).

25 FISHING

There is little commercial fishing in Kansas. Sport fishermen can find bass, crappie, catfish, perch, and pike in the state's reservoirs and artificial lakes. In 2004, there were 265,238 fishing licenses issued by the state. The Kansas Department of Wildlife and Parks' objectives for fisheries include provision of 11.7 million angler trips annually on Kansas reservoirs, lakes, streams, and private waters, while maintaining the quantity and quality of the catch. There are four state hatcheries.

26 FORESTRY

Kansas was at one time so barren of trees that early settlers were offered 160 acres (65 hectares) free if they would plant trees on their land. This program was rarely implemented, however, and today much of Kansas is still treeless.

Kansas has 1,545,000 acres (625,000 hectares) of forestland, 2.9% of the total state area. There are 1,491,000 acres (491,000 hectares) of commercial timberland, of which 96% are privately owned.

27 MINING

According to data from the US Geological Survey (USGS), the value of nonfuel mineral production by Kansas in 2004 was $754 million, an increase from 2003 of 8.3%. The USGS data ranked Kansas as 23rd among the 50 states by the total value of its nonfuel mineral production, accounting for almost 1.7% of total US output.

Portland cement, Grade-A helium, salt, and crushed stone were the leading nonfuel mineral commodities produced by the state, accounting for around 28%, 25%, 17%, and 14%, respectively, of all nonfuel mineral production by value in 2004 and about 84% of all output collectively. Nationally, Kansas continued to rank first out of only two states in the production of Grade-A and crude helium. In addition, the state was fifth in the production of salt and eighth in the production of gypsum.

Portland cement production in 2004 totaled 2.69 million metric tons and was valued at an estimated $212 million. Grade-A helium output that same year totaled 82 million cu m and was valued at $189 million, while salt production totaled 2.89 million metric tons, with a value of $127 million. The production of crushed stone totaled 19.8 million metric tons and was valued at $109 million. Kansas was also a producer of common clays and dimension stone in 2004.

A total of 7,041 people were employed in Kansas in all aspects of mining during 2004.

28 ENERGY AND POWER

As of 2003, Kansas had 154 electrical power service providers, of which 119 were publicly owned and 29 were cooperatives. The remaining, six were investor owned. As of that same year, there were 1,400,945 retail customers. Of that total, 952,229 received their power from investor-owned service providers. Cooperatives ac-

counted for 212,001 customers, while publicly owned providers had 236,715 customers.

Total net summer generating capability by the state's electrical generating plants in 2003 stood at 10.887 million kW, with total production that same year at 46.567 billion kWh. Of the total amount generated, 99.1% came from electric utilities, with the remainder coming from independent producers and combined heat and power service providers. The largest portion of all electric power generated, 35.109 billion kWh (75.4%), came from coal-fired plants, with nuclear plants in second place at 8.889 billion kWh (19.1%). Other renewable power sources accounted for 0.8%% of all power generated, with petroleum and natural gas–fired plants at 2.1% and 2.6%, respectively.

As of 2006, Kansas had one single-unit nuclear plant, the Wolf Creek plant in Burlington.

As of 2004, Kansas had proven crude oil reserves of 245 million barrels, or 1% of all proven US reserves, while output that same year averaged 92,000 barrels per day. Including federal offshore domains, the state that year ranked 11th (10th excluding federal offshore) in proven reserves and ninth (eighth excluding federal offshore) in production among the 31 producing states. In 2004, Kansas had 40,474 producing oil wells. As of 2005, the state's three refineries had a combined crude oil distillation capacity of 296,200 barrels per day.

In 2004, Kansas had 18,120 producing natural gas and gas condensate wells. In that same year, marketed gas production (all gas produced excluding gas used for repressuring, vented and flared, and nonhydrocarbon gases removed) totaled 397.121 billion cu ft (11.2 billion cu m). As of 31 December 2004, proven reserves of dry or consumer-grade natural gas totaled 4,652 billion cu ft (132.1 billion cu m).

Kansas in 2004, had only one producing coal mine, a surface operation. Coal production that year totaled 71,000 short tons, down from 154,000 short tons in 2003. One short ton equals 2,000 lb (0.907 metric tons).

29 INDUSTRY

Kansas is a world leader in aviation, claiming a large share of both US and world production and sales of commercial aircraft. Wichita is a manufacturing center for Boeing, Cessna, Learjet, and Raytheon, which combined manufacture approximately 70% of the world's general aviation aircraft.

According to the US Census Bureau's Annual Survey of Manufactures (ASM) for 2004, Kansas's manufacturing sector covered some 17 product subsectors. The shipment value of all products manufactured in the state that same year was $56.464 billion. Of that total, transportation equipment manufacturing accounted for the largest share at $15.553 billion. It was followed by food manufacturing at $14.704 billion; machinery manufacturing at $4.413 billion; petroleum and coal products manufacturing at $4.286 billion; and chemical manufacturing at $3.654 billion.

In 2004, a total of 167,982 people in Kansas were employed in the state's manufacturing sector, according to the ASM. Of that total, 117,307 were actual production workers. In terms of total employment, the transportation equipment manufacturing industry accounted for the largest portion of all manufacturing employees at 40,982 with 24,250 actual production workers. It was followed by food manufacturing at 30,574 employees (24,828 actual production workers); machinery manufacturing at 17,677 employees (11,786 actual production workers); fabricated metal product manufacturing at 13,598 employees (9,941 actual production workers); and plastics and rubber products manufacturing with 11,632 employees (9,782 actual production workers).

ASM data for 2004 showed that Kansas's manufacturing sector paid $6.937 billion in wages. Of that amount, the transportation equipment manufacturing sector accounted for the largest share at $2.239 billion. It was followed by food manufacturing at $918.509 million; machinery manufacturing at $710.873 billion; fabricated metal product manufacturing at $483.794 million; and plastics and rubber products manufacturing at $435.765 million.

30 COMMERCE

Domestically, Kansas is not a major commercial state. According to the 2002 Census of Wholesale Trade, Kansas's wholesale trade sector had sales that year totaling $44.1 billion from 4,705 establishments. Wholesalers of durable goods accounted for 2,535 establishments, followed by nondurable goods wholesalers at 1,741 and electronic markets, agents, and brokers accounting for 429 establishments. Sales by durable goods wholesalers in 2002 totaled $18.1 billion, while wholesalers of nondurable goods saw sales of $21.9 billion. Electronic markets, agents, and brokers in the wholesale trade industry had sales of $4.03 billion.

In the 2002 Census of Retail Trade, Kansas was listed as having 11,890 retail establishments with sales of $26.5 billion. The leading types of retail businesses by number of establishments were motor vehicle and motor vehicle parts dealers (1,612); gasoline stations (1,464); miscellaneous store retailers (1,382); and food and beverage stores (1,379). In terms of sales, motor vehicle and motor vehicle parts dealers accounted for the largest share of retail sales at $6.8 billion, followed by general merchandise stores $4.7 billion; food and beverage stores at $3.8 billion; gasoline stations $2.6 billion; and building material/garden equipment and supplies dealers $2.3 billion. A total of 144,874 people were employed by the retail sector in Kansas that year.

Exporters located in Kansas exported $6.7 billion in merchandise during 2005.

31 CONSUMER PROTECTION

The attorney general's Consumer Protection and Antitrust Division enforces the Kansas Consumer Protection Act, which protects consumers against fraud and false advertising. The consumer credit commissioner is responsible for administering the state's investment and common credit codes.

When dealing with consumer protection issues, the state's Attorney General's Office (through its Consumer Protection Division) can initiate civil and criminal proceedings; represent the state before state and federal regulatory agencies; administer consumer protection and education programs; handle formal consumer complaints; and exercise broad subpoena powers. In antitrust actions, the Attorney General's Office can act on behalf of those consumers who are incapable of acting on their own and can initiate damage actions on behalf of the state in state courts. However, the office cannot commence criminal proceedings, nor can it represent counties, cities, and other governmental entities in recovering civil damages under state or federal law.

The attorney general's Consumer Protection and Antitrust Division is located in Topeka. County government-based consumer protection offices are located in the cities of Olathe and Wichita.

32 BANKING

As of June 2005, Kansas had 371 insured banks, savings and loans, and saving banks, plus 94 state-chartered and 26 federally chartered credit unions (CUs). Excluding the CUs, the Kansas City (Missouri and Kansas) market area had the most financial institutions in the state with 152 and deposits at $32.593 billion, followed by Wichita at 58 and $8.453 billion, respectively. As of June 2005, CUs accounted for 5% of all assets held by all financial institutions in the state, or some $3.082 billion. Banks, savings and loans, and savings banks collectively accounted for the remaining 95% or $58.460 billion in assets held.

Regulation of Kansas's state-chartered financial institutions is handled by the Kansas Office of the State Bank Commissioner. In 1993, the state savings and loan commissioner's office was merged into the state bank commissioner's office.

In 2005, the state's insured financial institutions reported a median return on assets (ROA) of 1.02%, up slightly from 2004, which stood at 1%. The improvement in ROA resulted from lower loan losses and improved net interest margins.

33 INSURANCE

In 2004 there were over 1.6 million individual life insurance policies in force with a total value of over $129 billion; total value for all categories of life insurance (individual, group, and credit) was about $195 billion. The average coverage amount was $76,800 per policy holder. Death benefits paid that year totaled $570 million.

In 2003, 12 life and health and 27 property and casualty insurance companies were domiciled in Kansas. In 2004, direct premiums for property and casualty insurance totaled $4.4 billion. That year, there were 9,933 flood insurance policies in force in the state, with a total value of $1 billion. About $290 million of coverage was offered through FAIR (Fair Access to Insurance) Plans, which are designed to offer coverage for some natural circumstances, such as wind and hail, in high risk areas.

In 2004, 59% of state residents held employment-based health insurance policies, 6% held individual policies, and 21% were covered under Medicare and Medicaid; 11% of residents were uninsured. In 2003, employee contributions for employment-based health coverage averaged at 23% for single coverage and 29% for family coverage. The state offers a six-month health benefits expansion program for small-firm employees in connection with the Consolidated Omnibus Budget Reconciliation Act (COBRA, 1986), a health insurance program for those who lose employment-based coverage due to termination or reduction of work hours.

In 2003, there were over 2.2 million auto insurance policies in effect for private passenger cars. Required minimum coverage includes bodily injury liability of up to $25,000 per individual and $50,000 for all persons injured in an accident, as well as property damage liability of $10,000. Personal injury protection and uninsured motorist coverage are also required. In 2003, the average expenditure per vehicle for insurance coverage was $610.29.

34 SECURITIES

There are no stock exchanges in Kansas. In 2005, there were 800 personal financial advisers employed in the state and 1,480 securities, commodities, and financial services sales agents. In 2004, there were over 46 publicly traded companies within the state, with over 26 NASDAQ companies, 4 NYSE listings, and 2 AMEX listings. In 2006, the state had one Fortune 500 company; YRC Worldwide (on NASDAQ) ranked 263rd in the nation with revenues of over $8.7 million. Seaboard (AMEX), Payless Shoesource (NYSE), Ferrellgas Partners (NYSE), and Westar Energy (NYSE) all made the Fortune 1,000 list.

35 PUBLIC FINANCE

The state budget is prepared by the Division of the Budget and submitted by the governor to the legislature for approval. The fiscal year (FY) runs from 1 July to 30 June. Generally, according to state law, no Kansas governmental unit may issue revenue bonds to finance current activities. These must operate on a cash basis. Bonds may be issued for such capital improvements as roads and buildings.

In fiscal year 2006, general funds were estimated at $5.6 billion for resources and $5.1 billion for expenditures. In fiscal year 2004, federal government grants to Kansas were $3.4 billion.

In the fiscal year 2007 federal budget, Kansas was slated to receive $33.9 million in State Children's Health Insurance Program (SCHIP) funds to help the state provide health coverage to low-income, uninsured children who do not qualify for Medicaid. This funding is a 23% increase over fiscal year 2006. The state was also scheduled to receive $14.5 million for the HOME Investment Partnership Program to help Kansas fund a wide range of activities that build, buy, or rehabilitate affordable housing for rent or homeownership, or provide direct rental assistance to low-income people. This funding is a 13% increase over fiscal year 2006.

36 TAXATION

In 2005, Kansas collected $5,599 million in tax revenues or $2,040 per capita, which placed it 32nd among the 50 states in per capita tax burden. The national average was $2,192 per capita. Property taxes accounted for 1.1% of the total, sales taxes 35.6%, selective sales taxes 14.1%, individual income taxes 36.6%, corporate income taxes 4.4%, and other taxes 8.2%.

As of 1 January 2006, Kansas had three individual income tax brackets ranging from 3.5% to 6.45%. The state taxes corporations at a flat rate of 4.0%.

In 2004, state and local property taxes amounted to $3,246,616,000 or $1,187 per capita. The per capita amount ranks the state 14th nationally. Local governments collected $3,189,062,000 of the total and the state government $57,554,000.

Kansas taxes retail sales at a rate of 5.30%. In addition to the state tax, local taxes on retail sales can reach as much as 3%, making for a potential total tax on retail sales of 8.30%. Food purchased for consumption off premises is taxable, although an income tax credit is allowed to offset sales tax on food. The tax on cigarettes is 79 cents per pack, which ranks 27th among the 50 states and the District of Columbia. Kansas taxes gasoline at 24 cents per gallon. This is in addition to the 18.4 cents per gallon federal tax on gasoline.

According to the Tax Foundation, for every federal tax dollar sent to Washington in 2004, Kansas citizens received $1.12 in federal spending.

37 ECONOMIC POLICY

The first state commission to promote industrial development was formed in 1939. In 1986, this commission was reorganized into the Kansas Department of Commerce, and in 1992 it became the Department of Commerce and Housing. The department later renamed itself the Department of Commerce (KDOC) once again. The department in 2006 consisted of five divisions: Agriculture

Kansas—State Government Finances

(Dollar amounts in thousands. Per capita amounts in dollars.)

	AMOUNT	PER CAPITA
Total Revenue	11,044,146	4,039.56
General revenue	9,868,956	3,609.71
Intergovernmental revenue	3,000,037	1,097.31
Taxes	5,283,676	1,932.58
General sales	1,932,927	707.00
Selective sales	790,225	289.04
License taxes	274,619	100.45
Individual income tax	1,915,530	700.63
Corporate income tax	166,609	60.94
Other taxes	203,766	74.53
Current charges	897,814	328.39
Miscellaneous general revenue	687,429	251.44
Utility revenue	–	–
Liquor store revenue	–	–
Insurance trust revenue	1,175,190	429.84
Total expenditure	11,207,121	4,099.17
Intergovernmental expenditure	2,878,801	1,052.96
Direct expenditure	8,328,320	3,046.20
Current operation	5,736,524	2,098.22
Capital outlay	1,032,362	377.60
Insurance benefits and repayments	1,104,320	403.92
Assistance and subsidies	288,708	105.60
Interest on debt	166,406	60.87
Exhibit: Salaries and wages	1,639,641	599.72
Total expenditure	11,207,121	4,099.17
General expenditure	10,102,801	3,695.25
Intergovernmental expenditure	2,878,801	1,052.96
Direct expenditure	7,224,000	2,642.28
General expenditures, by function:		
Education	4,444,689	1,625.71
Public welfare	2,475,046	905.28
Hospitals	107,780	39.42
Health	287,430	105.13
Highways	1,225,504	448.25
Police protection	74,193	27.14
Correction	316,669	115.83
Natural resources	185,658	67.91
Parks and recreation	7,466	2.73
Government administration	420,302	153.73
Interest on general debt	166,406	60.87
Other and unallocable	391,658	143.25
Utility expenditure	–	–
Liquor store expenditure	–	–
Insurance trust expenditure	1,104,320	403.92
Debt at end of fiscal year	4,571,408	1,672.06
Cash and security holdings	14,077,579	5,149.08

Abbreviations and symbols: – zero or rounds to zero; (NA) not available; (X) not applicable.

SOURCE: *U.S. Census Bureau, Governments Division, 2004 Survey of State Government Finances,* January 2006.

Marketing Development; Community Development; Travel and Tourism; Business Development; and Trade Development. In the 21st century, the KDOC has recommended investments in the fields of aviation, plastics, value-added agriculture, call centers, administrative service centers, and wholesale, packaging, and distribution. Events sponsored by the KDOC include training in downtown revitalization, conferences on finding new markets though international trade and, for leaders, facilitating international business, and workshops on applying for community development block grants (CDBGs).

Kansas provides tax-exempt bonds to help finance business and industry. Specific tax incentives include job expansion and investment tax credits; tax exemptions or moratoriums on land, capital improvements, and specific machinery; and certain corporate income tax exemptions.

38 HEALTH

The infant mortality rate in October 2005 was estimated at 6.3 per 1,000 live births. The birth rate in 2003 was 14.5 per 1,000 population. The abortion rate stood at 21.4 per 1,000 women in 2000. In 2003, about 87.8% of pregnant woman received prenatal care beginning in the first trimester. In 2004, approximately 78% of children received routine immunizations before the age of three.

The crude death rate in 2003 was 9 deaths per 1,000 population. As of 2002, the death rates for major causes of death (per 100,000 resident population) were as follows: heart disease, 246; cancer, 197.4; cerebrovascular diseases, 67.9; chronic lower respiratory diseases, 50.3; and diabetes, 28.2. The mortality rate from HIV infection was 1.4 per 100,000 population. In 2004, the reported AIDS case rate was at about 4.2 per 100,000 population. In 2002, about 57.5% of the population was considered overweight or obese. As of 2004, about 19.8% of state residents were smokers.

In 2003, Kansas had 134 community hospitals with about 10,600 beds. There were about 331,000 patient admissions that year and 6 million outpatient visits. The average daily inpatient census was about 5,900 patients. The average cost per day for hospital care was $952. Also in 2003, there were about 374 certified nursing facilities in the state with 27,045 beds and an overall occupancy rate of about 78%. In 2004, it was estimated that about 74.5% of all state residents had received some type of dental care within the year. Kansas had 235 physicians per 100,000 resident population in 2004 and 923 nurses per 100,000 in 2005. In 2004, there was a total of 1,360 dentists in the state.

About 21% of state residents were enrolled in Medicaid and Medicare programs in 2004. Approximately 11% of the state population was uninsured in 2004. In 2003, state health care expenditures totaled $2.7 million.

The University of Kansas has the state's only medical and pharmacology schools. The university's Mid-America Cancer Center and Radiation Therapy Center are the major cancer research and treatment facilities in the state. The Menninger Foundation has a research and treatment center for mental health.

39 SOCIAL WELFARE

Public assistance and social programs are coordinated through the Department of Human Resources and the Department of Social and Rehabilitation Services. In 2004, about 68,000 people received unemployment benefits, with the average weekly unemployment benefit at $272. In fiscal year 2005, the estimated average monthly participation in the food stamp program included about 177,782 persons (78,165 households); the average monthly benefit was about $84.37 per person. That year, the total of benefits paid through the state for the food stamp program was about $179.9 million.

Temporary Assistance for Needy Families (TANF), the system of federal welfare assistance that officially replaced Aid to Families with Dependent Children (AFDC) in 1997, was reauthorized through the Deficit Reduction Act of 2005. TANF is funded through federal block grants that are divided among the states based on an equation involving the number of recipients in each state. Kansas's TANF program is called Kansas Works. In 2004, the state program had 44,000 recipients; state and federal expenditures on this TANF program totaled $83 million fiscal year 2003.

In December 2004, Social Security benefits were paid to 447,140 Kansas residents. This number included 291,570 retired workers, 45,770 widows and widowers, 51,520 disabled workers, 24,660 spouses, and 33,620 children. Social Security beneficiaries represented 16.4% of the total state population and 93.7% of the state's population age 65 and older. Retired workers received an average monthly payment of $979; widows and widowers, $956; disabled workers, $866; and spouses, $497. Payments for children of retired workers averaged $497 per month; children of deceased workers, $628; and children of disabled workers, $253. Federal Supplemental Security Income payments went to 38,476 Kansas residents in December 2004, averaging $384 a month.

40 HOUSING

Kansas has relatively old housing stock. According to a 2004 survey, about 20% of all housing units were built in 1939 or earlier and 49.6% were built between 1940 and 1979. The overwhelming majority (73.8%) were one-unit, detached structures and 69.5% were owner occupied. The total number of housing units in 2004 was estimated at 1,185,114, of which 1,076,366 were occupied. Most units relied on utility gas and electricity for heating. It was estimated that 46,269 units lacked telephone service, 3,554 lacked complete plumbing facilities, and 5,093 lacked complete kitchen facilities. The average household had 2.47 members.

In 2004, 13,300 privately owned units were authorized for construction. The median home value was $102,458. The median monthly cost for mortgage owners was $1,013. Renters paid a median of $567 per month. In 2006, the state received over $17.2 million in community development block grants from the US Department of Housing and Urban Development (HUD).

41 EDUCATION

In 2004, 89.6% of those age 25 and older were high school graduates, compared to the national average of 84%. Some 30% had obtained a bachelor's degree or higher.

In 1954, Kansas was the focal point of a US Supreme Court decision that had enormous implications for US public education. The court ruled in *Brown v. Board of Education of Topeka* that Topeka's "separate but equal" elementary schools for black and white students were inherently unequal, and it ordered the school system to integrate.

Total public school enrollment for fall 2002 stood at 471,000. Of these, 322,000 attended schools from kindergarten through grade eight, and 149,000 attended high school. Approximately 76.4% of the students were white, 8.9% were black, 11% were Hispanic, 2.3% were Asian/Pacific Islander, and 1.4% were American Indian/Alaskan Native. Total enrollment was estimated at 465,000 in fall 2003 and was estimated to be 471,000 by fall 2014, an increase of 0.1% during the period 2002–14. Expenditures for public education in 2003/04 were estimated at $3.96 billion. There were 41,762 students enrolled in 229 private schools in fall 2003. Since 1969, the National Assessment of Educational Progress (NAEP) has tested public school students nationwide. The resulting report, *The Nation's Report Card,* stated that in 2005, eighth graders in Kansas scored 284 out of 500 in mathematics compared with the national average of 278.

As of fall 2002, there were 188,049 students enrolled in institutions of higher education; minority students comprised 13.3% of total postsecondary enrollment. In 2005 Kansas had 63 degree-granting institutions. There are 9 four-year public institutions, 27 public two-year schools, and 21 private nonprofit four-year institutions. In addition, Kansas has a state technical institute, a municipal university (Washburn University, Topeka), and an American Indian university. Kansas State University was the nation's first land-grant university. Washburn University and the University of Kansas have the state's two law schools. The oldest higher-education institution in Kansas is Highland Community College, which was chartered in 1857. The oldest four-year institution is Baker University, a United Methodist institution, which received its charter just three days after Highland's was issued. The Kansas Board of Regents offers scholarships and tuition grants to Kansas students in need.

42 ARTS

The Kansas Arts Commission is a state arts agency governed by a 12-member panel of commissioners appointed for four-year rotating terms by the governor. The commission's annual budget is made up of funds appropriated by the Kansas legislature and grants awarded to the agency by the National Endowment for the Arts. In 2005, the Kansas Arts Commission and other Kansas arts organizations received 12 grants totaling $767,470 from the National Endowment for the Arts. The Arts Commission is also in partnership with the regional Mid-America Arts Alliance. The Kansas Humanities Council, founded in 1972, sponsors programs involving over 500,000 people each year. In 2005, the state received $864,264 in the form of 13 grants from the National Endowment for the Humanities.

The largest and most active arts organization in the state is the Wichita Symphony Orchestra; established in 1944, it is one of the oldest arts organizations in the state. The Koch Industries Twilight Pops Concert has become the largest event of the annual Wichita River Festival. Attracting some 100,000 people, the Wichita Symphony performs a wide range of music at this outdoor concert, including favorite patriotic pieces and rock choices. The Topeka Performing Arts Center presents concerts and shows of a variety of music. Topeka also hosts the Topeka Symphony, established in 1946. The 2005/06 season marked the Topeka Symphony's 60th Anniversary Diamond Jubilee celebration.

The Wichita Art Museum, established in 1915, is noted for its emphasis on American art and American artistic heritage. Its per-manent Roland P. Murdock Collection boasts works by Mary Cassatt, Winslow Homer, and Edward Hopper.

43 LIBRARIES AND MUSEUMS

In 2001, Kansas had 321 public library systems, with a total of 373 libraries, of which 53 were branches. In that same year, the state's public library system had 10,438,000 volumes of books and serial publications on its shelves and a total circulation of 21,488,000. The system also had 339,000 audio and 411,000 video items, 21,000 electronic format items (CD-ROMs, magnetic tapes, and disks), and five bookmobiles. The Dwight D. Eisenhower Library in Abilene houses a collection of papers and memorabilia from the 34th president. There is also a museum. The Menninger Foundation Museum and Archives in Topeka maintains various collections pertaining to psychiatry. The Kansas State Historical Society Library (Topeka) contains the state's archives. Volumes of books and documents on the Old West are found in the Cultural Heritage and Arts Center Library in Dodge City. with 10,207,000 volumes and a circulation of 20,808,000. In 2001, operating income for the state's public library system totaled $770,029,000, which included $607,000 in federal grants and $1,870,000 in state grants.

Almost 188 museums, historical societies, and art galleries were scattered across the state in 2000. The Dyche Museum of Natural History at the University of Kansas, Lawrence, draws many visitors. The Kansas State Historical Society maintains an extensive collection of ethnological and archaeological materials in Topeka.

Among the art museums are the Mulvane Art Center in Topeka, the Helen Foresman Spencer Museum of Art at the University of Kansas, and the Wichita Art Museum. The Dalton Museum in Coffeyville displays memorabilia from the famed Dalton family of desperadoes. La Crosse is the home of the Barbed Wire Museum, displaying more than 500 varieties of barbed wire. The Emmett Kelly Historical Museum in Sedan honors the world-famous clown born there. The US Cavalry Museum is on the grounds of Ft. Riley. The Sedgwick County Zoo in Wichita and the Topeka Zoo are the largest of seven zoological gardens in Kansas.

The entire town of Nicodemus, where many blacks settled after the Civil War, was made a national historic landmark in 1975. The chalk formations of Monument Rocks in western Kansas constitute the state's only national natural landmark. Ft. Scott and Ft. Larned are national historic parks.

44 COMMUNICATIONS

About 94.8% of all households had telephone service in 2004. Additionally, by June of that same year, there were 1,345,160 mobile wireless telephone subscribers. In 2003, 63.8% of Kansas households had a computer and 54.3% had Internet access. By June 2005, there were 419,938 high-speed lines in Kansas, 385,369 residential and 34,569 for business.

The state had 15 major AM and 54 major FM radio stations, 14 major commercial television stations, and 4 public television stations in 2005. In 2000, Kansas had registered a total of 42,009 Internet domain names.

45 PRESS

Starting with the *Shawnee Sun,* a Shawnee-language newspaper founded by missionary Jotham Meeker in 1833, the press has played an important role in Kansas history. The most famous Kansas newspaperman was William Allen White, whose *Emporia Gazette* was a leading voice of Progressive Republicanism around the turn of the century. Earlier, John J. Ingalls launched his political career by editing the *Atchison Freedom's Champion*. Captain Henry King came from Illinois to found the *State Record* and *Daily Capital* in Topeka.

In 2005, Kansas had 43 daily newspapers (9 morning and 34 evening) and 14 Sunday papers.

Leading newspapers and their circulations in 2005 were as follows:

AREA	NAME	DAILY	SUNDAY
Topeka	*Capital-Journal* (m,S)	89,469	64,585
Wichita	*Eagle* (m,S)	96,506	146,727

The *Kansas City* (Missouri) *Star* (275,747 daily; 388,425 Sundays) is widely read in the Kansas as well as in the Missouri part of the metropolitan area.

46 ORGANIZATIONS

In 2006, there were over 3,790 nonprofit organizations registered within the state, of which about 2,440 were registered as charitable, educational, or religious organizations. Among the national organizations headquartered in Kansas are the American Association for Public Opinion Research, American Institute of Baking, American Medical Society for Sports Medicine, International Association for Jazz Education, and Lefthanders International.

State and regional cultural and educational organizations include the Association of Community Arts Agencies of Kansas and the Kansas State Historical Society, as well as a number of county historical societies and regional arts groups. The national offices of Mennonite Women USA and Mennonite Voluntary services are in Newton.

47 TOURISM, TRAVEL, AND RECREATION

Kansas has 23 state parks, 2 national historic sites, 24 federal reservoirs, 48 state fishing lakes, more than 100 privately owned campsites, and more than 304,000 acres (123,000 hectares) of public hunting and game management lands. The two major national historic sites are Ft. Larned and Ft. Scott, both 19th-century Army bases on the Indian frontier. In 2002, the top five parks (based on number of visitors) were Hillsdale State Park (1.6 million), El Dorado State Park (1 million), Clinton Lake, Perry Lake, and Tuttle Creek Lake.

The most popular tourist attraction, with over 2.4 million visitors in 2002, is Cabela's (Kansas City), a 190,000 square-foot showroom and shopping center featuring a mule deer museum, a 65,000 gallon aquarium, a gun library, and Yukon base camp grill. The next-ranking visitor sites in 2002 were Harrah's Prairie Band Casino (Mayetta), the Kansas City Speedway, Sedgwick County Zoo (Wichita), Woodlands Race Tracks (Kansas City), New Theatre Restaurant (Overland Park), Exploration Place (Wichita) and the Kansas Cosmosphere and Space Center (Hutchinson).

Topeka features a number of tourist attractions, including the state capitol, state historical museum, and Menninger Foundation. Dodge City offers a reproduction of Old Front Street as it was when the town was the "cowboy capital of the world." Historic Wichita Cowtown is another frontier-town reproduction. In

Hanover stands the only remaining original and unaltered Pony Express station. A recreated "Little House on the Prairie," near the childhood home of Laura Ingalls Wilder, is 13 mi (21 km) southwest of Independence. The Eisenhower Center in Abilene contains the 34th president's family home, library, and museum. The state fair is held in Hutchinson.

Kansas has six national parks including the site of the famous school desgregation lawsuit *Brown v. the Board of Education* (in Shawnee County). Carrie Nation (of Medicine Lodge) founded the Temperance Movement leading to the Prohibition Act, which outlawed the sale and consumption of alcohol. The University of Kansas (at Lawrence) is home to the Dole Institute of Politics, founded by former vice president Robert Dole. Famous aviator Amelia Earhart hails from Abilene, as does President Dwight D. Eisenhower. Each April, the city of Flint Hills hosts the Prairie Fire Festival, when there is a controlled burn of dead prairie material.

48 SPORTS

There are no major professional sports teams in Kansas. The minor league Wichita Wranglers play in the Double-A Texas League and the Kansas City T-Bones play in the Northern League. There is also a minor league hockey team in Wichita. During spring, summer, and early fall, horses are raced at Eureka Downs. The national Greyhound Association Meet is held in Abilene.

The University of Kansas and Kansas State both play collegiate football in the Big Twelve Conference. Kansas went to the Orange Bowl in 1948 and 1969, losing both times. The Jayhawks won the Aloha Bowl in 1992 and 1995. Kansas State played in the Cotton Bowl in 1996 and 1997, winning in 1996, and they won the Fiesta Bowl in 1998. In basketball, Kansas won the National Collegiate Athletic Association (NCAA) Championship in 1952 and 1988 and has appeared in 12 Final Four Tournaments. The National Junior College Basketball Tournament is held in Hutchinson each March. The Kansas Relays take place at Lawrence in April. The Flint Hills Rodeo in Strong City is one of many rodeos held statewide. The Kansas Speedway hosts the NASCAR Nextel Cup and Busch series event.

A US sporting event unique to Kansas is the International Pancake Race, held in Liberal each Shrove Tuesday. Women wearing housedresses, aprons, and scarves run along an S-shaped course carrying skillets and flipping pancakes as they go.

Hall of Fame pitcher Walter Johnson was born in Humboldt, NFL great Barry Sanders in Wichita, and basketball legend Adolph Rupp in Halstead.

49 FAMOUS KANSANS

Kansas claims only one US president and one US vice president. Dwight D. Eisenhower (b.Texas, 1890–1969) as elected the 34th president in 1952 and reelected in 1956; he had served as the Supreme Commander of Allied Forces in World War II. He is buried in Abilene, his boyhood home. Charles Curtis (1860–1936) was vice president during the Herbert Hoover administration.

Two Kansans have been associate justices of the US Supreme Court: David J. Brewer (1837–1910) and Charles E. Whittaker (1901–73). Other federal officeholders from Kansas include William Jardine (1879–1955), secretary of agriculture; Harry Woodring (1890–1967), secretary of war; and Georgia Neese Clark Gray (1900–95), treasurer of the Unites States. Prominent US senators include Edmund G. Ross (1826–1907), who cast a crucial acquittal vote at the impeachment trial of Andrew Johnson; John J. Ingalls (1833–1900), who was also a noted literary figure; Joseph L. Bristow (1861–1944), a leader in the Progressive movement; Arthur Caper (1865–1951), a former publisher and governor; Robert Dole (b.1923), who was the Republican candidate for vice president in 1976, twice served as Senate majority leader, and was his party's presidential candidate in 1996; and Nancy Landon Kassebaum (b.1932), elected to the US Senate in 1978. Among the state's important US representatives were Jeremiah Simpson (1842–1905), a leading Populist, and Clifford R. Hope (1893–1970), important in the farm bloc. Gary Hart, a senator and a presidential candidate in 1984 and 1988, was born in Ottowa, Kansas, on 28 November 1936.

Notable Kansas governors include George W. Glick (1827–1911); Walter R. Stubbs (1858–1929); Alfred M. Landon (1887–1984), who ran for US president on the Republican ticket in 1936; and Frank Carlson (1893–1984). Other prominent political figures were David L. Payne (1836–84), who helped open Oklahoma to settlement; Carry Nation (1846–1911), the colorful prohibitionist; and Frederick Funston (1865–1917), hero of the Philippine campaign of 1898 and a leader of San Francisco's recovery after the 1906 earthquake and fire.

Earl Sutherland (1915–74) won the Nobel Prize in 1971 for physiology or medicine. Other leaders in medicine and science include Samuel J. Crumbine (1862–1954), a public health pioneer; the doctors Menninger—C. F. (1862–1953), William (1899–1966), and Karl (1893–1990)—who established the Menninger Foundation, a leading center for mental health; Arthur Hertzler (1870–1946), a surgeon and author; and Clyde Tombaugh (1906–97), who discovered the planet Pluto.

Kansas also had several pioneers in aviation, including Clyde Cessna (1880–1954), Glenn Martin (1886–1955), Walter Beech (1891–1950), Amelia Earhart (1898–1937), and Lloyd Stearman (1898–1975). Cyrus K. Holliday (1826–1900) founded the Santa Fe Railroad; William Coleman (1870–1957) was an innovator in lighting; and Walter Chrysler (1875–1940) was a prominent automotive developer.

Most famous of Kansas writers was William Allen White (1868–1944), whose son, William L. White (1900–73), also had a distinguished literary career; Damon Runyon (1884–1946) was a popular journalist and storyteller. Novelists include Edgar Watson Howe (1853–1937), Margaret Hill McCarter (1860–1938), Dorothy Canfield Fisher (1879–1958), Paul Wellman (1898–1966), and Frederic Wakeman (b.1909). Gordon Parks (1912–2006) has made his mark in literature, photography, and music. William Inge (1913–73) was a prize-winning playwright who contributed to the Broadway stage. Notable painters are Sven Birger Sandzen (1871–1954), John Noble (1874–1934), and John Steuart Curry (1897–1946). Sculptors include Robert M. Gage (1892–1981), Bruce Moore (1905–80), and Bernard Frazier (1906–76). Among

composers and conductors are Thurlow Lieurance (b.Iowa 1878–1963), Joseph Maddy (1891–1966), and Kirke L. Mechem (b.1926). Jazz great Charlie "Bird" Parker (Charles Christopher Parker Jr., 1920–55) was born in Kansas City.

Stage and screen notables include Fred Stone (1873–1959), Joseph "Buster" Keaton (1895–1966), Milburn Stone (1904–80), Charles "Buddy" Rogers (1904–99), Vivian Vance (1912–79), Edward Asner (b.1929), and Shirley Knight (b.1937). The clown Emmett Kelly (1898–1979) was a Kansan. Operatic performers include Marion Talley (1906–83) and Kathleen Kersting (1909–65).

Glenn Cunningham (1909–88) and Jim Ryun (b.1947) both set running records for the mile. Also prominent in sports history were James Naismith (1861–1939), the inventor of basketball; baseball pitcher Walter Johnson (1887–1946); and Gale Sayers (b.1943), a football running back.

⁵⁰BIBLIOGRAPHY

Bair, Julene. *One Degree West: Reflections of a Plainsdaughter.* Minneapolis, Minn.: Mid-List Press, 2000.

Council of State Governments. *The Book of the States, 2006 Edition.* Lexington, Ky.: Council of State Governments, 2006.

Dean, Virgil W. (ed.). *John Brown to Bob Dole: Movers and Shakers in Kansas History.* Lawrence: University Press of Kansas, 2006.

Everhart, Michael J. *Oceans of Kansas: A Natural History of the Western Interior Sea.* Bloomington: Indiana University Press, 2005.

Frederickson, H. George (ed.). *Public Policy and the Two States of Kansas.* Lawrence: University Press of Kansas, 1992.

Hoard, Robert J., and William E. Banks (eds.). *Kansas Archaeology.* Lawrence: University Press of Kansas in Association with the Kansas State Historical Society, 2006.

Mobil Travel Guide. Great Plains 2006: Iowa, Kansas, Missouri, Nebraska, Oklahoma. Lincolnwood, Ill.: ExxonMobil Travel Publications, 2006.

Preston, Thomas. *Great Plains: North Dakota, South Dakota, Nebraska, Kansas, Oklahoma, and Texas.* Vol. 4, *The Double Eagle Guide to 1,000 Great Western Recreation Destinations.* Billings, Mont.: Discovery Publications, 2003.

Richmond, Robert W. *Kansas, a Land of Contrasts.* Wheeling, Ill.: Harland Davidson, 1999.

Shortridge, James R. *Peopling the Plains: Who Settled Where in Frontier Kansas.* Lawrence: University Press of Kansas, 1995.

Socolofsky, Homer, and Virgil W. Dean. *Kansas History: An Annotated Bibliography.* New York: Greenwood, 1992.

US Department of Commerce, Economics and Statistics Administration, US Census Bureau. *Kansas, 2000. Summary Social, Economic, and Housing Characteristics: 2000 Census of Population and Housing.* Washington, D.C.: US Government Printing Office, 2003.

KENTUCKY

Commonwealth of Kentucky

ORIGIN OF STATE NAME: Possibly derived from the Wyandot Indian word *Kah-ten-tah-teh* (land of tomorrow). **NICKNAME:** The Bluegrass State. **CAPITAL:** Frankfort. **ENTERED UNION:** 1 June 1792 (15th). **SONG:** "My Old Kentucky Home." **MOTTO:** United We Stand, Divided We Fall. **FLAG:** A simplified version of the state seal on a blue field. **OFFICIAL SEAL:** In the center are two men exchanging greetings; above and below them is the state motto. On the periphery are two sprigs of goldenrod and the words "Commonwealth of Kentucky." **BIRD:** Cardinal. **FISH:** Bass. **FLOWER:** Goldenrod. **TREE:** Tulip poplar. **LEGAL HOLIDAYS:** New Year's Day, 1 January, plus one extra day; Birthday of Martin Luther King Jr., 3rd Monday in January; Washington's Birthday, 3rd Monday in February; Good Friday, March or April, half-day holiday; Memorial Day, last Monday in May; Independence Day, 4 July; Labor Day, 1st Monday in September; Veterans' Day, 11 November; Thanksgiving Day, 4th Thursday in November, plus one extra day; Christmas Day, 25 December, plus one extra day. **TIME:** 7 AM EST = noon GMT; 6 AM CST = noon GMT.

¹LOCATION, SIZE, AND EXTENT

Located in the eastern south-central United States, the Commonwealth of Kentucky is the smallest of the eight south-central states and ranks 37th in size among the 50 states.

The total area of Kentucky is 40,409 sq mi (104,659 sq km), of which land makes up 39,669 sq mi (102,743 sq km) and inland water 740 sq mi (1,917 sq km). Kentucky extends about 350 mi (563 km) E–W; its maximum N–S extension is about 175 mi (282 km).

Kentucky is bordered on the N by Illinois, Indiana, and Ohio (with the line roughly following the north bank of the Ohio River); on the NE by West Virginia (with the line formed by the Big Sandy and Tug Fork rivers); on the SE by Virginia; on the S by Tennessee; and on the W by Missouri (separated by the Mississippi River). Because of a double bend in the Mississippi River, about 10 sq mi (26 sq km) of SW Kentucky is separated from the rest of the state by a narrow strip of Missouri.

After 15 years of litigation, Kentucky in 1981 accepted a US Supreme Court decision giving Ohio and Indiana control of at least 100 feet (30 meters) of the Ohio River from the northern shore. This in effect returned Kentucky's border to what it was in 1792, when Kentucky entered the Union.

The total boundary length of Kentucky is 1,290 mi (2,076 km). The state's geographic center is in Marion County, 3 mi (5 km) NW of Lebanon.

²TOPOGRAPHY

The eastern quarter of the state is dominated by the Cumberland Plateau, on the western border of the Appalachians. At its western edge, the plateau meets the uplands of the Lexington Plain (known as the Bluegrass region) to the north and the hilly Pennyroyal to the south. These two regions, which together make up nearly half

the state's area, are separated by a narrow curving plain known as the Knobs because of the shapes of its eroded hills. The most level area of the state consists of the western coalfields bounded by the Pennyroyal to the east and the Ohio River to the north. In the far west are the coastal plains of the Mississippi River; this region is commonly known as the Purchase, having been purchased from the Chickasaw Indians.

The highest point in Kentucky is Black Mountain on the southeastern boundary in Harlan County, at 4,139 ft (2,162 m). The lowest point is 257 ft (78 m), along the Mississippi River in Fulton County. The state's mean altitude is 750 ft (229 m).

The only large lakes in Kentucky are artificial. The biggest is Cumberland Lake (79 sq mi/205 sq km); Kentucky Lake, Lake Barkley, and Dale Hollow Lake straddle the border with Tennessee.

Including the Ohio and Mississippi rivers on its borders and the tributaries of the Ohio, Kentucky claims at least 3,000 mi (4,800 km) of navigable rivers—sometimes said to have more water than any other state except Alaska. Among the most important of Kentucky's rivers are the Kentucky, 259 mi (417 km); the Cumberland, partly in Tennessee; the Tennessee, also in Tennessee and Alabama; and the Big Sandy, Green, Licking, and Tradewater rivers. All, except for a portion of the Cumberland, flow northwest into the Ohio and thence to the Mississippi. Completion in 1985 of the Tennessee–Tombigbee Waterway, linking the Tennessee and Tombigbee rivers in Alabama, gave Kentucky's Appalachian coalfields direct water access to the Gulf of Mexico for the first time.

Drainage through porous limestone rock has honeycombed much of the Pennyroyal with underground passages, the best known of which is Mammoth Cave, now a national park. The Cumberland Falls, 92 ft (28 m) high and 100 ft (30 m) wide, are located in Whitely County.

³CLIMATE

Kentucky has a moderate, relatively humid climate, with abundant rainfall.

The southern and lowland regions are slightly warmer than the uplands. In Louisville, the normal monthly average temperature ranges from 33°F (1°C) in January to 78°F (25°C) in July. The record high for the state was 114°F (46°C), registered in Greensburg on 28 July 1930; the record low, -37°F (-40°C), in Shelbyville on 19 January 1994.

Average daily relative humidity in Louisville ranges from 58% to 81%. The average annual precipitation at Louisville is about 43.6 in (110 cm); snowfall totals about 16 in (41 cm) a year.

⁴FLORA AND FAUNA

Kentucky's forests are mostly of the oak/hickory variety, with some beech/maple stands. Four species of magnolia are found, and the tulip poplar, eastern hemlock, and eastern white pine are also common; the distinctive "knees" of the cypress may be seen along riverbanks. Kentucky's famed bluegrass is said to be actually blue only in May when dwarf iris and wild columbine are in bloom. Rare plants include the swamp loosestrife and showy gentian. In April 2006, the US Fish and Wildlife Service listed eight Kentucky plant species as threatened or endangered, including Braun's rockcress, Cumberland sandwort, running buffalo clover, and Short's goldenrod.

Game mammals include the raccoon, muskrat, opossum, mink, gray and red foxes, and beaver; the eastern chipmunk and flying squirrel are common small mammals. At least 300 bird species have been recorded, of which 200 are common. Blackbirds are a serious pest, with some roosts numbering 5–6 million; more desirable avian natives include the cardinal (the state bird), robin, and brown thrasher, while eagles are winter visitors. More than 100 types of fish have been identified.

Rare animal species include the swamp rabbit, black bear, raven (Corvus corax), and mud darter. In April 2006, a total of 31 animal species occurring within the state (vertebrates and invertebrates) were on the threatened and endangered species list of the US Fish and Wildlife Service. These included three species of bat (Indiana, Virginia big-eared, and gray), the bald eagle, puma, piping plover, Kentucky cave shrimp, and three species of pearly mussel.

⁵ENVIRONMENTAL PROTECTION

The National Resources and Environmental Protection Cabinet, with broad responsibility, includes the departments of Natural Resources, Environmental Protection, and Surface Mining Reclamation and Enforcement, as well as the Kentucky Nature Preserves Commission. The Environmental Quality Commission, created in 1972 to serve as a watchdog over environmental concerns, is a citizen's group of seven members appointed by the governor.

The most serious environmental concern in Kentucky is repairing and minimizing damage to land and water from strip-mining. Efforts to deal with such damage are relatively recent. The state has had a strip-mining law since 1966, but the first comprehensive attempts at control did not begin until the passage in 1977 of the Federal Surface Mining Control and Reclamation Act.

Also active in environmental matters is the Department of Environmental Protection, consisting of four divisions. The Division of Water administers the state's Safe Drinking Water and Clean Water acts and regulation of sewage disposal. The Division of Waste Management oversees solid waste disposal systems in the state. The Air Pollution Control Division monitors industrial discharges into the air and other forms of air pollution. Most air pollution has declined since the 1970s, with lead air concentrations down by 97% since 1970. A special division is concerned with Maxey Flats, a closed nuclear waste disposal facility in Fleming County, where leakage of radioactive materials was discovered.

There are 15 major dams in Kentucky, and more than 900 other dams. Flooding is a chronic problem in southeastern Kentucky, where strip-mining has exacerbated soil erosion.

In 2003, Kentucky had 149 hazardous waste sites listed in the US Environment Protection Agency (EPA) database, 14 of which were on the National Priorities List as of 2006, including Maxey Flats Nuclear Disposal in Hillsboro. In 2005, the EPA spent over $1.8 million through the Superfund program for the cleanup of hazardous waste sites in the state. The same year, federal EPA grants awarded to the state included $16.8 million for the state clean water revolving fund program and $3.4 million for implementation of nonpoint source management programs. In 2003, 90.6 million lb of toxic chemicals were released in the state.

⁶POPULATION

Kentucky ranked 26th in population in the United States with an estimated total of 4,173,405 in 2005, an increase of 3.2% since 2000. Between 1990 and 2000, Kentucky's population grew from 3,685,296 to 4,041,769, an increase of 9.7%. The population was projected to reach 4.35 million by 2015 and 4.48 million by 2025. The population density in 2004 was 104.7 persons per sq mi.

In 2004 the median age was 37.3. Persons under 18 years old accounted for 23.6% of the population while 12.5% was age 65 or older.

During the early decades of settlement, population grew rapidly, from a few hundred in 1780 to 564,317 in 1820, by which time Kentucky was the sixth most populous state. By 1900, however, when the population was 2,147,174, growth had slowed considerably. For most of the 20th century, Kentucky's growth rate was significantly slower than the national average.

As of 2004, Louisville–Jefferson County had an estimated population of about 556,332. Lexington–Fayette had an estimated population of 266,358. The population of the Louisville (Kentucky–Indiana) metropolitan area was estimated at 1,200,847; the Lexington metropolitan area had 424,661.

⁷ETHNIC GROUPS

Though a slave state, Kentucky never depended on a plantation economy. In 1830, almost 25% of the population was black. After the Civil War, a lack of jobs and migration to the industrial cities of the Midwest in the 1890s may have accounted for a dwindling black population. In 2000 the black population of Kentucky was relatively low at 295,994 (7.3%). In 2004, 7.5% of the population was black. Kentucky was a center of the American (or Know-Nothing) Party, a pre–Civil War movement whose majority were staunchly anti-immigration and anti-Catholic. With relatively little opportunity for industrial employment, Kentucky attracted small numbers of foreign immigrants in the 19th and 20th cen-

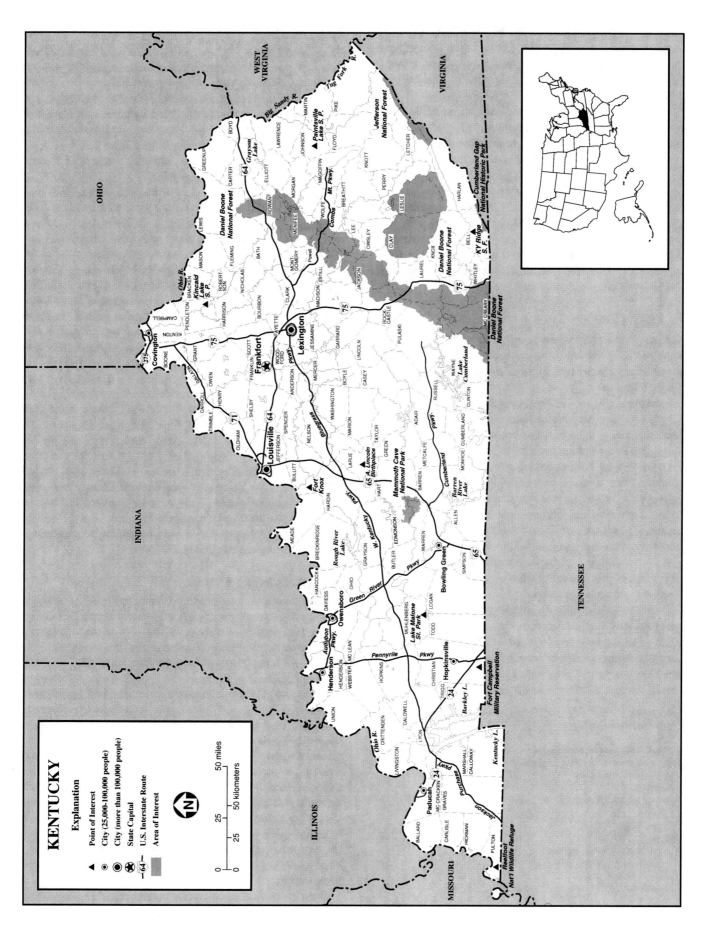

KENTUCKY

Explanation

▲ Point of Interest

⊙ City (25,000–100,000 people)

⊙ City (more than 100,000 people)

✪ State Capital

64 U.S. Interstate Route

▨ Area of Interest

50 miles

50 kilometers

turies. The state had 80,271 foreign-born residents in 2000 (2% of the total population), up from 34,119 in 1990. Among persons reporting a single ancestry in the 2000 census, a total of 391,542 claimed English descent, 514,955 German, 424,133 Irish, and 66,147 French.

In 2000, the Asian population was estimated at 29,744, and the American Indian population was estimated at 8,616. The 2000 census reported 3,818 Koreans, 6,771 Asian Indians (up from 2,367 in 1990), 3,683 Japanese, 3,596 Vietnamese (up from 1,340 in 1990), and 5,397 Chinese (up from 3,137). In 2004, 0.9% of the population was Asian, and American Indians accounted for 0.2% of the population. In 2000, a total of 59,939 (1.5%) state residents were Hispanic or Latino, up from 33,000 (0.8%) in 1990, with 31,385 reporting Mexican ancestry and 6,469 Puerto Rican ancestry. In 2004, 1.9% of the population was of Hispanic or Latino origin. Pacific Islanders numbered 1,460 in 2000. In 2004, 1% of the population reported origin of two or more races.

8 LANGUAGES

Kentucky was a fought-over hunting ground for Ohio Shawnee, Carolina Cherokee, and Mississippi Chickawaw Indians. Place-names from this heritage include Etowah (Cherokee) and Paducah (Chickasaw).

Speech patterns in the state generally reflect the first settlers' Virginia and Kentucky backgrounds. South Midland features are best preserved in the mountains, but some common to Midland and Southern are widespread.

Other regional features are typically both South Midland and Southern. After a vowel, the /r/ may be weak or missing. *Coop* has the vowel of *put*, but *root* rhymes with *boot*. In southern Kentucky, earthworms are *redworms,* a burlap bag a *tow sack* or the Southern *grass sack,* and green beans *snap beans.* A young man may *carry,* not escort, his girlfriend to a party. Subregional terms appear in abundance. In the east, kindling is *pine,* a seesaw is a *ridyhorse,* and the freestone peach is an *openstone peach.* In central Kentucky, a moth is a *candlefly.*

In 2000, 96.1% of all residents five years old and older spoke only English at home, down from 97.5% in 1990.

The following table gives selected statistics from the 2000 Census for language spoken at home by persons five years old and over. The category "Other West Germanic languages" includes Dutch, Pennsylvania Dutch, and Afrikaans.

LANGUAGE	NUMBER	PERCENT
Population 5 years and over	**3,776,230**	**100.0**
Speak only English	3,627,757	96.1
Speak a language other than English	148,473	3.9
Speak a language other than English	**148,473**	**3.9**
Spanish or Spanish Creole	70,061	1.9
German	17,898	0.5
French (incl. Patois, Cajun)	12,499	0.3
Chinese	4,608	0.1
Japanese	3,777	0.1
Korean	3,730	0.1
Other West Germanic languages	3,616	0.1
Arabic	3,165	0.1
Serbo-Croatian	3,070	0.1
Vietnamese	3,018	0.1
Russian	2,162	0.1
Tagalog	2,070	0.1

9 RELIGIONS

Throughout its history, Kentucky has been predominantly Protestant. A group of New Light Baptists who, in conflict with established churches in Virginia, immigrated to Kentucky under the leadership of Lewis Craig and built the first church in the state in 1781, near Lancaster. The first Methodist Church was established near Danville in 1783; within a year, Roman Catholics had also built a church, and a presbytery of 12 churches had been organized. There were 42 churches in Kentucky by the time of statehood, with a total membership of 3,095.

Beginning in the last few years of the 18th century, the Great Revival sparked a new religious fervor among Kentuckians, a development that brought the Baptists and Methodists many new members. The revival, which had begun among the Presbyterians, led to a schism in that sect. Presbyterian minister Barton W. Stone organized what turned out to be the era's largest frontier revival meeting, at Cane Ridge (near Paris), in August 1801. Differences over doctrine led Stone and his followers to withdraw from the Synod of Kentucky in 1803, and they formed their own church, called simply "Christian." The group later formed an alliance with the sect now known as the Christian Church (Disciples of Christ).

As of 2000, Evangelical Protestantism was predominant with the single largest denomination within the state being the Southern Baptist Convention with 979,994 adherents; there were 17,528 new baptized members in 2002. The next largest Protestant denomination is the United Methodist Church, which had 208,720 adherents in 2000, but reported only 152,727 members in 2003. The Christian Churches and Churches of Christ had 106,638 adherents in 2000 and the Roman Catholic Church had about 382,042 members in 2004. There were an estimated 11,350 Jews in Kentucky in 2000 and about 4,696 Muslims. Over 1.8 million people (46.6% of the population) were not counted as members of any religious organization in the 2000 survey.

10 TRANSPORTATION

Statewide transportation developed slowly in Kentucky. Although freight and passengers were carried by river and later by rail during the 19th century, mountains and lack of good roads made land travel in eastern Kentucky so arduous that the region was for a long time effectively isolated from the rest of the state.

The first railroad in Kentucky, the Lexington and Ohio, opened on 15 August 1832 with a 26-mi (42-km) route from Lexington to Frankfort. Not until 1851 did the railroad reach the Ohio River. In November 1859, Louisville was connected with Nashville, Tennessee, by the Louisville and Nashville Railroad; heavily used by the Union, it was well maintained during the Civil War. Railroad construction increased greatly after the conflict ended. By 1900, Kentucky had three times the track mileage it had in 1870. As of 2003, Kentucky had 2,823 rail mi (4,545 km), of which 2,299 miles were Class I track. In that same year, there were five Class I railroads operating in the state. Coal was the top commodity originating in the state shipped by the railroads. Rail service to the state, nearly all of which was freight, was provided by 15 railroads. As of 2006, there were four Amtrak stations in Kentucky.

The trails of Indians and buffalo became the first roads in Kentucky. Throughout the 19th century, counties called on their citizens to maintain some roads although maintenance was haphazard. The best roads were the toll roads. This system came to an end as a result of the "tollgate war" of the late 19th and early 20th centuries—a rebellion in which masked Kentuckians, demanding free roads, raided tollgates and assaulted their keepers. Not until 1909, however, was a constitutional prohibition against the spending of state funds on highways abolished. In 1912, a state highway commission was created, and by 1920, roads had improved considerably. In 2004, Kentucky had 77,366 mi (124,559 km) of public roads and 2.8 million licensed drivers. In that same year, there were some 1.855 million automobiles, about 1.415 million trucks of all types, and around 2,000 buses registered in the state.

Until displaced by the railroads in the late 1800s, the Ohio River and its tributaries, along with the Mississippi, were Kentucky's primary commercial routes for trade with the South and the West. The Kentucky Port and River Development Commission was created by the legislature in 1966 to promote river transportation. Louisville, on the Ohio River, is the chief port. In 2004, traffic through the port totaled 7.799 million tons. Paducah is the outlet port for traffic on the Tennessee River. In that same year, Kentucky had 1,591 mi (2,561 km) of navigable inland waterways. In 2003, waterborne shipments totaled 99.332 million tons.

In 2005, Kentucky had a total of 208 public and private-use aviation-related facilities. This included 149 airports, 58 heliports, and 1 STOLport (Short Take-Off and Landing). The largest of these was Cincinnati/Northern Kentucky International Airport, with 10,864,547 enplanements in 2004, making it the 22nd-busiest airport in the United States.

11 HISTORY

Six distinctive Indian cultures inhabited the region now known as Kentucky. The earliest nomadic hunters occupied the land for several thousand years, and were followed by the seminomadic Woodland and Adena cultures (1000 BC–AD 1000). Remains of the Mississippian and Fort Ancient peoples (AD 1000–1650) indicate that they were farmers and hunters who often dwelled in stockaded villages, subsisting on plentiful game and fish supplemented by crops of beans, corn, and squash.

No Indian nations resided in central and eastern Kentucky when these areas were first explored by British-American surveyors Thomas Walker and Christopher Gist in 1750 and 1751. The dominant Shawnee and Cherokee tribes utilized the region as a hunting ground, returning to homes in the neighboring territories of Ohio and Tennessee. Early descriptions of Kentucky generated considerable excitement about the fertile land and abundant wildlife. The elimination of French influence after the French and Indian War intensified pressures to open the region to American settlement—pressures that were initially thwarted by Britain's Proclamation of 1763, barring such western migration until Native American interests could be protected. This artificial barrier proved impossible to maintain, however, and the first permanent white settlement in Kentucky was finally established at Harrodstown (now Harrodsburg) in 1774 by a group of settlers from Virginia and Pennsylvania.

The most ambitious settlement scheme involved the Transylvania Land Company, a creation of North Carolina speculator Richard Henderson, assisted by the famed woodsman Daniel Boone. Henderson purchased a huge tract of land in central Kentucky from the Cherokee and established Fort Boonesborough. The first political meeting by whites in Kentucky, held at Fort Boonesborough on 23 May 1775, provided for rule by the Transylvania proprietors and a representative assembly. Henderson then sought approval for creation of a 14th colony, but the plan was blocked by Virginians determined to claim Kentucky as a possession of the Old Dominion. On 1 December 1776, the new state of Virginia incorporated its new County of Kentucky.

Kentucky's image soon changed from "western Eden" to "dark and bloody ground," as it became the scene of frequent clashes between Ohio-based Indians and the growing number of white settlements dotting the central Bluegrass region. Nevertheless, immigrants continued to come westward, down the Ohio River and through the Cumberland Gap. Kentucky became the principal conduit for migration into the Mississippi Valley. By the late 1780s, settlements were gaining in population, wealth, and maturity, and it was obvious that Kentucky could not long remain under the proprietorship of distant Virginia. Virginia yielded permission for the drafting of a Kentucky state constitution, and in June 1792, Kentucky entered the Union as the 15th state.

Over the next several decades, Kentucky prospered because of its diverse agricultural and processing industries. Although there were 225,483 slaves in the state in 1860, Kentucky was spared the evils of one-crop plantation agriculture. Nevertheless, its economy was tightly linked to the lower South's, a tie facilitated by the completion in 1829 of a canal around the Ohio River falls at Louisville. Hemp was one such connection; the plant was the principal source of rope and bagging used to bind cotton bales. Kentucky was also a major supplier of hogs, mules, workhorses, prepared meats, salt, flour, and corn for the plantation markets of the South. The state became a center for breeding and racing fine thoroughbred horses, an industry that thrives today on Bluegrass horse farms as virtually the state symbol. More important was the growing and processing of tobacco, an enterprise accounting for half the agricultural income of Kentucky farmers by 1860. Finally, whiskey began to be produced in vast quantities by the 1820s, culminating in the standardization of a fine, aged amber-red brew known throughout the world as bourbon, after Bourbon County.

Despite this economic development, several social and cultural problems disturbed the state. Much of the agricultural productivity came from farms employing slave labor, while the less affluent majority of white families often dwelled on less fertile upland farms. Efforts were repeatedly made to consider the slavery question. Leaders such as Henry Clay, Reverend Robert J. Breckinridge, and the fiery antislavery advocate Cassius Marcellus Clay urged an end to the "peculiar institution." Because of racial phobias and hostility to "Yankee meddling," the appeal was rejected. During the Civil War, Kentuckians were forced to choose sides between the Union, led in the north by Kentucky native Abraham Lincoln, and the Confederacy, led in the South by Kentucky native Jefferson Davis.

Although the state legislature finally opted for the Union side, approximately 30,000 men went south to Confederate service, while up to 100,000—including nearly 24,000 black soldiers—served in the Union army. For four years the state was torn with conflict over the collapse of slavery and wracked with guerrilla warfare and partisan feuds. Vigilantism and abuse of black people continued into the turbulent Reconstruction period, until legislative changes in the early 1870s began to restrain Ku Klux Klan violence and bring increased civil rights to black people.

The decades to 1900 saw other progress. Aided by liberal tax exemptions, railroad construction increased threefold, and development of timber and coal reserves began in eastern Kentucky. Industrial employment and productivity increased by more than 200%, drawing rural folk into the growing cities of Louisville and Lexington. In 1900, Kentucky ranked first among Southern states in per capita income.

An economic and political crisis was developing, however, that would send shock waves across the state. Farmers, especially western Kentucky "dark leaf" tobacco farmers, were feeling the brunt of a prolonged price depression. The major national farm protest movements—the Grange, the Farmers' Alliance, and the Populist Party—all found support here, for by 1900 a third of all Kentucky farmers were landless tenants, and the size of the average family farm had fallen below 10 acres (4 hectares). Calls for currency inflation, reform of corporate monopolies, and improved rights for industrial workers reached a climax in the gubernatorial election of 1899. Republican William S. Taylor narrowly defeated the more reform-minded Democrat William Goebel and was sworn into office. Democrats, claiming electoral fraud, instituted a recount. On 30 January 1900, Goebel, a state senator, was shot while approaching the capitol; as he lingered near death, the legislature, controlled by Democrats, declared him governor. Goebel died immediately thereafter, and his lieutenant governor, J. C. W. Beckham, was administered the oath of office. Further bloodshed was averted, the courts upheld the Goebel–Beckham election, and "Governor" Taylor fled the state.

Goebel's assassination weighed heavily, however. The state was polarized, outside investment plummeted, and Kentucky fell into a prolonged economic and moral depression. By 1940, the state ranked last among the 48 states in per capita income and was burdened by an image of clan feuding and homicide, poverty, and provincial courthouse politics. The Great Depression hit the state hard, though an end to Prohibition revived the dormant whiskey industry.

Kentucky changed greatly after World War II. Between 1945 and 1980, the farm population decreased by 76% and the number of farms by 53%. In later decades, after tobacco was revealed to be a public health hazard, many farmers turned to raising other crops. Although Kentucky remained relatively poor, positive change was evident even in rural communities—the result of better roads, education, and government programs. The state's poverty rate fell steadily over the decades, from 22.9% in 1969 to 13.5% in 1998, when it ranked as the 18th-poorest state in the nation (a great improvement from earlier in the century). However, in 2003–04, the state's poverty rate had increased to 16%, up from 14.3% in 2002–03. The national poverty rate in 2003–04 was 12.6%.

In response to lawsuits by a coalition of school districts, Kentucky's supreme court ruled in 1990 that the state's public education system was unconstitutional and ordered the legislature to design a new system of school funding and administration. In response, the Kentucky Education Reform Act was passed that year and implemented over the next five years. But more questions regarding the constitutionality of school programs, or prospective programs, lay ahead. By 2000 legislators were considering a proposal that would allow the Ten Commandments to be displayed in classrooms, alongside other historical documents. The proposal was part of a larger movement that urged officials to allow public schools to teach the role of religion in American history and culture. At the same time, many Kentuckians supported the return of prayer to schools. By 2003, federal judges had ordered the Ten Commandments be removed from school classrooms and court-

Kentucky Presidential Vote by Political Parties, 1948–2004

YEAR	ELECTORAL VOTE	KENTUCKY WINNER	DEMOCRAT	REPUBLICAN	STATES' RIGHTS DEMOCRAT	PROHIBITION	PROGRESSIVE	SOCIALIST
1948	11	*Truman (D)	466,756	341,210	10,411	1,245	1,567	1,284
1952	10	Stevenson (D)	495,729	495,029	—	1,161	—	—
1956	10	*Eisenhower (R)	476,453	572,192	—	2,145	—	—
1960	10	Nixon (R)	521,855	602,607	—	—	—	—
					STATES' RIGHTS			
1964	9	*Johnson (D)	669,659	372,977	3,469	—	—	—
					AMERICAN IND.			SOC. WORKERS
1968	9	*Nixon (R)	397,541	462,411	193,098	—	—	2,843
						AMERICAN	PEOPLE'S	
1972	9	*Nixon (R)	371,159	676,446	—	17,627	1,118	—
1976	9	*Carter (D)	615,717	531,852	2,328	8,308	—	—
							LIBERTARIAN	CITIZENS
1980	9	*Reagan (R)	617,417	635,274	—	—	5,531	1,304
1984	9	*Reagan (R)	539,539	821,702	—	—	1,776	599
1988	9	*Bush (R)	580,368	734,281	4,994	1,256	2,118	—
					IND. (Perot)			
1992	8	*Clinton (D)	665,104	617,178	203,944	430	4,513	989
1996	8	*Clinton (D)	636,614	623,283	120,396	—	4,009	—
						REFORM		GREEN
2000	8	*Bush, G. W. (R)	638,898	872,492	—	4,173	2,896	23,192
					WRITE-IN (Brown)	CONSTITUTION (Peroutka)		INDEPENDENT (Nader)
2004	8	*Bush, G. W. (R)	712,733	1,069,439	13	2,213	2,619	8,856

*Won US presidential election.

houses in several Kentucky counties, ruling that the postings of the commandments had violated the separation between church and state.

The Paducah Gaseous Diffusion Plant was a point of concern for state environmentalists in 2000. Senior Kentucky environmental officials complained that the US Department of Energy (DOE) had used security clearances to prevent state environmental inspectors from getting full access to the plant, which enriches uranium for nuclear-reactor fuel. The plant was also the site of a massive cleanup effort in 2000, as DOE officials crushed drums that once contained uranium. Critics charged that the drums had been left in the open for decades and rain water had washed radioactivity into the environment.

Republican Ernie Fletcher was elected governor in 2003. By 2005 he had set about to make Kentucky more business-friendly, to create a flexible tax code, encourage healthy lifestyles (the governor is a physician), provide for quality education for Kentucky's children, and improve the transportation infrastructure. He reorganized the state government, eliminating some cabinet positions, and worked to make sure state resources were being used efficiently.

12 STATE GOVERNMENT

Kentucky's current and fourth constitution was adopted on 28 September 1891. By January 2005, it had been amended 41 times. Earlier constitutions were adopted in 1792, 1799, and 1850.

The state legislature, called the General Assembly, consists of the House of Representatives, which has 100 members elected for two-year terms, and the Senate, with 38 members elected for staggered four-year terms. A constitutional amendment approved by the voters in November 1979 provided for the election of legislators in even-numbered years, a change scheduled for completion by November 1988. The assembly meets in regular sessions of no more than 60 legislative days, beginning Tuesday after the first Monday in January of each even-numbered year. Only the governor may call special sessions, which are not limited in length. Except for revenue-raising measures, which must be introduced in the House of Representatives, either chamber may introduce or amend a bill. Most bills may be passed by voting majorities equal to at least two-fifths of the membership of each house. Measures requiring an absolute majority in each house include those that appropriate money or create a debt or enact emergency measures to take effect immediately. Proposed amendments to the constitution require a three-fifths vote of each house. A majority of the members of each house is required to override the governor's veto. If the governor neither vetoes nor signs a bill, it becomes law after 10 days when the legislature is in session, and 90 days after the adjournment of the legislature when it is not in session.

A member of the Senate must have been a citizen of Kentucky for six years preceding election, a representative for two. A senator must be at least 30 years old and a representative at least 24 years old. Legislators must have been residents in their districts for at least one year prior to election. The constitutional limit of $12,000 for salaries of public officials, which is thought to apply to legislators, has been interpreted by the courts in terms of 1949 dollars and thus may be increased considerably—and has been. In 2004 most legislators in Kentucky probably received less than $14,000 per year based on per diem in-session salaries of $166.34.

The elected executive officers of Kentucky are the governor and lieutenant governor (elected jointly), secretary of state, attorney general, treasurer, auditor of public accounts, and commissioner of agriculture. All serve four-year terms; a constitutional amendment allows a second term for those offices. The governor and lieutenant governor must be at least 30 years old, US citizens, and citizens and residents of Kentucky for six years. As of December 2004, the governor's salary was $127,146.

A three-fifths majority of each house plus a voting majority of the electorate must approve any proposed constitutional amendment. Before a constitutional convention may be called, two regular sessions of the General Assembly must approve it, and the call must be ratified at the polls by a majority voting on the proposal and equal to at last one-fourth the number of voters who cast ballots in the last general election.

To vote in Kentucky, one must be a US citizen, be at least 18 years old, have been a resident in the county for at least 28 days prior to election day, and not able to claim the right to vote elsewhere. Restrictions apply to convicted felons and those declared mentally incompetent by the court.

13 POLITICAL PARTIES

A rift was created in Kentucky politics by the presidential election of 1824, which had to be determined in the US House of Representatives because neither John Quincy Adams nor Andrew Jackson won a majority of the Electoral College. Representative Henry Clay voted for Adams, despite orders by the Kentucky General Assembly to support Jackson, thereby splitting the state into two factions: supporters of Clay, who became Whigs, and supporters of Jackson, who became Democrats. The Whigs dominated Kentucky politics until Clay's death in 1852, after which, as the Whigs divided over slavery, most Kentuckians turned first to the Native American (or Know-Nothing) Party and then to the Democrats. Regional divisions in party affiliation during the Civil War era, according to sympathy with the South and slavery (Democrats) or with the Union and abolition (Republicans), have persisted in the state's voting patterns. In general, the poorer mountain areas tend to vote Republican, while the more affluent lowlanders in the Bluegrass and Pennyroyal tend to vote Democratic.

Republican presidential candidate George W. Bush won the state by large margins in both 2000 and 2004—57% to Democrat Al Gore's 41% (2000) and 59.5% to Democrat John Kerry's 39.7% (2004). In 2004 there were 2,819,000 registered voters. In 1998, 61% of registered voters were Democratic, 32% Republican, and 7% unaffiliated or members of other parties. The state had eight electoral votes in the 2004 presidential election.

In 1983, Martha Layne Collins, a Democrat, defeated Republican candidate Jim Bunning to become Kentucky's first woman governor. Republican Ernie Fletcher was elected governor in 2003. In mid-2005, Republicans held 21 seats in the state Senate, Democrats held 15; and an Independent held 1. The Democrats dominated the House of Representatives, with 57 seats to the Republicans' 43. At the national level, Kentucky was represented by Republican Senator Mitch McConnell, reelected in 2002; and Republican Senator Jim Bunning, first elected in 1998 and reelected in 2004. As of 2004, Kentucky voters had elected five Republicans and one Democrat to the US House.

¹⁴LOCAL GOVERNMENT

The form of Kentucky's county government is of English origin. The chief governing body is the fiscal court, consisting of the county judge and district magistrates or commissioners. Other elected officials are the sheriff, jailer, attorney, and court clerk. All are elected for four-year terms. As of 2005, the state had 120 counties.

In 2005, Kentucky had 424 municipalities. Cities are assigned by the state's General Assembly to six classes, based on population. The two largest cities, categorized as first-class, are Louisville and Lexington. The mayor or other chief executive officer in the top three classes must be elected; in the bottom classes, the executive may be either elected by the people or appointed by a city council or commission. Mayors serve four-year terms; members of city legislative boards, also provided for in the state constitution, are generally elected for terms of two years.

Other units of local government in Kentucky include special districts (720 in 2005), such as districts for sewer and flood control and area-development districts for regional planning. The state had 176 public school districts in 2005.

In 2005, local government accounted for about 159,190 full-time (or equivalent) employment positions.

¹⁵STATE SERVICES

To address the continuing threat of terrorism and to work with the federal Department of Homeland Security, homeland security in Kentucky operates under executive order; the homeland security director is designated as the state homeland security advisor.

Educational services are provided through the Department of Education. The Council on Postsecondary Education oversees the state-supported colleges, universities, and technical schools. The Human Rights Commission and the Commission on Women are administered by the governor's office. Transportation services are administered by the Transportation Cabinet. Health, welfare, and other human services are provided primarily by the Health and Family Services Cabinet. Among the agencies that provide public protection services are the Department of Military Affairs, the Public Protection Department, and the Consumer Protection and Education Division. Corrections and parole were transferred in 1981 from the Department of Justice to the Corrections Department. The Department of State Police is part of the Justice and Public Safety Cabinet.

Housing rights for members of minority groups are provided by the Commission on Human Rights. The Cabinet for Economic Development oversees industrial and community development programs. Also assisting in community development are programs within the Office of Local Government, which was organized as an independent agency of the office of the governor in 1982.

Natural resource protection services are provided by the separate departments of Natural Resources and Environmental Protection, and by the Division of Mine Reclamation and Enforcement. The Commerce Cabinet deals with Kentucky's parks, tourism, cultural heritage, and arts.

Labor services are administered by the Labor Department; its areas of concern include labor-management relations, occupational safety and health, and occupational injury and disease compensation. Other cabinets include those for finance and administration and personnel.

¹⁶JUDICIAL SYSTEM

In accordance with a constitutional amendment approved in 1975 and fully implemented in 1978, judicial power in Kentucky is vested in a unified court of justice. The highest court is the Kentucky Supreme Court, consisting of a chief justice and six associate justices. It has appellate jurisdiction and also bears responsibility for the budget and administration of the entire system. Justices are elected from seven supreme court districts for terms of eight years; they elect one of their number to serve for the remaining term as chief justice.

The Court of Appeals consists of 14 judges, 2 elected from each supreme court district. The court divides itself into panels of at least 3 judges that may sit anywhere in the state. The judges also serve eight-year terms and elect one of their number to serve a four-year term as chief judge.

Circuit courts, with original and appellate jurisdiction, are held in each county. There are 56 judicial circuits. Circuit court judges are elected for terms of eight years. In 1999, there were 108 circuit court judges. In circuits with more than one judge, the judges elect one of their number as chief judge for a two-year term. Under the revised judicial system, district courts, which have limited and original jurisdiction, replaced various local and county courts. There is no mandatory retirement age.

As of 31 December 2004, a total of 17,814 prisoners were held in Kentucky's state and federal prisons, an increase from 16,622 of 7.2% from the previous year. As of year-end 2004, a total of 1,560 inmates were female, up from 1,411 or 10.6% from the year before. Among sentenced prisoners (one year or more), Kentucky had an incarceration rate of 412 per 100,000 population in 2004.

According to the Federal Bureau of Investigation, Kentucky in 2004, had a violent crime rate (murder/nonnegligent manslaughter; forcible rape; robbery; aggravated assault) of 244.9 reported incidents per 100,000 population, or a total of 10,152 reported incidents. Crimes against property (burglary; larceny/theft; and motor vehicle theft) in that same year totaled 105,209 reported incidents or 2,537.7 reported incidents per 100,000 people. Kentucky has a death penalty, of which lethal injection is the sole method of execution for those sentenced after 31 March 1998. Inmates sentenced prior to that date may select lethal injection or electrocution. From 1976 through 5 May 2006, the state has executed only two persons. There were no executions in 2005 or 2006 (as of 5 May). As of 1 January 2006, Kentucky had 37 inmates on death row.

In the past, Kentucky had a reputation for lawlessness. In 1890, more homicides were reported in Kentucky than in any other state except New York. Blood feuds among Kentucky families were notorious throughout the country. However, crime rates have diminished to a comparatively low level.

In 2003, Kentucky spent $144,012,593 on homeland security, an average of $35 per state resident.

¹⁷ARMED FORCES

The US Department of Defense had 22,861 personnel in Kentucky in 2004, including 17,039 active-duty military and 3,762 civilians.

US Army installations in the state include Ft. Knox (site of the US gold depository) near Louisville, and Ft. Campbell (partly in Tennessee). Kentucky received $4.1 billion in prime federal defense contracts in 2004, and $2.4 billion in defense payroll spending.

There were 359,845 veterans of US military service in Kentucky as of 2003, of whom 46,266 served in World War II; 40,025 in the Korean conflict; 111,844 during the Vietnam era; and 57,006 during the Gulf War. Expenditures on Kentucky veterans amounted to more than $1.0 billion in 2004.

As of 31 October 2004, the Kentucky State Police employed 943 full-time sworn officers.

[18] MIGRATION

During the frontier period, Kentucky first attracted settlers from eastern states, especially Virginia and North Carolina. Prominent among early foreign immigrants were people of English and Scotch-Irish ancestry, who tended to settle in the Kentucky highlands, which resembled their Old World homelands.

Kentucky's black population increased rapidly during the first 40 years of statehood. By the 1830s, however, slavery had become less profitable in the state, and many Kentucky owners either moved to the Deep South or sold their slaves to new owners in that region. During the 1850s, nearly 16% of Kentucky's slave population—more than 43,000 blacks—were sold or moved from the state. A tiny percentage of Kentucky's blacks, probably fewer than 200, emigrated to Liberia under the auspices of the Kentucky Colonization Society.

The waves of European immigration that inundated many states during the late 19th century left Kentucky virtually untouched. In 1890, Kentucky's population was nearly 98% native-born. At that time, there were more than 284,000 blacks in the state—a number that was to fall precipitously until the 1950s because of migration to industrial cities in the Midwest.

Until the early 1970s there was a considerable out-migration of whites, especially from eastern Kentucky to industrial areas of Ohio, Indiana, and other nearby states. The state's net loss to migration from 1960 to 1970 totaled 153,000 persons. This tide of out-migration was temporarily reversed during the 1970s, with Kentucky recording a net migration gain of 131,000 persons. From 1980 to 1990, net loss to migration totaled about 22,000. Between 1990 and 1998, Kentucky had net gains of 90,000 in domestic migration and 14,000 in international migration. In 1998, 2,017 foreign immigrants arrived in the state. Between 1990 and 1998, Kentucky's overall population increased 6.8%. In the period 2000–05, net international migration was 27,435 and net internal migration was 32,169, for a net gain of 59,604 people.

[19] INTERGOVERNMENTAL COOPERATION

Among the many interstate regional commissions in which Kentucky participates are the Breaks Interstate Park Compact with Virginia, Appalachian Regional Commission, Interstate Mining Compact Commission, Interstate Oil and Gas Compact, Southern Growth Policies Board, Ohio River Basin Commission, Ohio River Valley Water Sanitation Commission, Southeastern Forest Fire Protection Compact, Southern Regional Energy Board, Southern States Energy Board, and Tennessee–Tombigbee Waterway Development Authority. Kentucky also participates in the Tennessee

Valley Authority. The Council of State Governments, founded in 1925 to foster interstate cooperation, has its headquarters in Lexington. Kentucky received $5.251 billion in federal grants in fiscal year 2005, an estimated $5.555 billion in fiscal year 2006, and an estimated $5.647 billion in federal grants in fiscal year 2007.

[20] ECONOMY

Between statehood and the Civil War, Kentucky was one of the preeminent agricultural states, partly because of good access to river transportation down the Ohio and the Mississippi to southern markets. Coal mining had become an important part of the economy by the late 19th century. Although agriculture is still important in Kentucky, manufacturing has grown rapidly since World War II and was, by the mid-1980s, the most important sector of the economy as a source of both employment and personal income. Kentucky leads the nation in the production of bituminous coal and whiskey, and ranks second in tobacco output.

In contrast to the generally prosperous Bluegrass area and the growing industrial cities, eastern Kentucky, highly dependent on coal mining, has long been one of the poorest regions in the United States. Beginning in the early 1960s, both the state and federal governments undertook programs to combat poverty in Appalachian Kentucky. Personal income is much lower, and unemployment higher, than in the rest of the state. In 1997, 38 of the 49 Appalachian counties received Local Government Economic Development Fund (LGEDF) aid from the coal severance tax. The Kentucky Rural Development Act, covering all 49 Appalachian counties, gives liberal tax incentives to new manufacturing start-ups in those areas that have had higher unemployment rates than the state during the previous five years, or a have current rate that is at least twice the state average. During the 1990s, declines in Kentucky's traditional sectors—tobacco, textiles, apparel, and coal mining—was compensated for by job growth in motor vehicle manufacturing, fabricated metals, appliances, and other durable goods. The establishment of a major UPS hub in Kentucky plus growth in agricultural research and commercialization activity helped further the state's economic transformation. Manufactures reached more than 27.5% of gross state product by 1998, when overall growth reached 6%. Growth in 1999 and 2000 averaged 4.35%, and then dropped to 2.6% in 2001 in the context of the national recession. Manufacturing output, which had grown 10.6% from 1997 to 2000, fell 1.9% in 2001, and to 25.2% as a percent of total state output. In 2002, job losses in manufacturing slowed while employment in service-producing sectors strengthened. Kentucky was one of only five states where employment grew more than 1% in 2002.

Kentucky's gross state product (GSP) in 2004 totaled $136.446 billion, of which manufacturing contributed the largest portion at $28.708 billion (21% of GSP), followed by real estate at $12.306 billion (9% of GSP), and health care and social services at $10.484 billion (7.6% of GSP). In that same year, there were an estimated 317,115 small businesses in Kentucky. Of the 83,046 businesses that had employees, a total of 80,595 or 97% were small companies. An estimated 8,807 new businesses were established in the state in 2004, up 8% from the year before. Business terminations that same year came to 8,597, down 20.4% from 2003. There were 319 business bankruptcies in 2004, down 2.4% from the previous year. In 2005, the state's personal bankruptcy (Chapter 7 and

Chapter 13) filing rate was 722 filings per 100,000 people, ranking Kentucky 11th in the nation.

21INCOME

In 2005 Kentucky had a gross state product (GSP) of $140 billion which accounted for 1.1% of the nation's gross domestic product and placed the state at number 27 in highest GSP among the 50 states and the District of Columbia.

According to the Bureau of Economic Analysis, in 2004 Kentucky had a per capita personal income (PCPI) of $27,265. This ranked 44th in the United States and was 82% of the national average of $33,050. The 1994–2004 average annual growth rate of PCPI was 4.1%. Kentucky had a total personal income (TPI) of $112,925,244,000, which ranked 27th in the United States and reflected an increase of 5.7% from 2003. The 1994–2004 average annual growth rate of TPI was 4.9%. Earnings of persons employed in Kentucky increased from $81,381,470,000 in 2003 to $85,767,091,000 in 2004, an increase of 5.4%. The 2003–04 national change was 6.3%.

The US Census Bureau reports that the three-year average median household income for 2002–04 in 2004 dollars was $37,396, compared to a national average of $44,473. During the same period an estimated 15.4% of the population was below the poverty line as compared to 12.4% nationwide.

22LABOR

According to the Bureau of Labor Statistics (BLS), in April 2006 the seasonally adjusted civilian labor force in Kentucky numbered 2,022,000, with approximately 123,600 workers unemployed, yielding an unemployment rate of 6.1%, compared to the national average of 4.7% for the same period. Preliminary data for the same period placed nonfarm employment at 1,843,500. Since the beginning of the BLS data series in 1976, the highest unemployment rate recorded in Kentucky was 12.1% in December 1982. The historical low was 4% in March 2000. Preliminary nonfarm employment data by occupation for April 2006 showed that approximately 4.7% of the labor force was employed in construction; 14.1% in manufacturing; 20.7% in trade, transportation, and public utilities; 4.8% in financial activities; 9.4% in professional and business services; 12.9% in education and health services; 9.2% in leisure and hospitality services; and 17% in government.

Although a small number of trade unions existed in Kentucky before the 1850s, it was not until after the Civil War that substantial unionization took place. During the 1930s, there were long, violent struggles between the United Mine Workers (UMW) and the mine owners of eastern Kentucky. The UMW won bargaining rights in 1938, but after World War II, the displacement of workers because of mechanization, a drastic drop in the demand for coal, and evidence of mismanagement and corruption within the UMW served to undercut the union's position. Following the announcement by the UMW in 1962 that its five hospitals would be sold or closed, unemployed mine workers began protracted picketing of nonunion mines. Episodes of violence accompanied the movement, which succeeded in closing the mines but not in keeping them closed. The protests dissipated when public works jobs were provided for unemployed fathers among the miners, beginning in late 1973. Increased demand for coal in the 1970s led to a substantial increase in jobs for miners, and the UMW, under different leaders, began a new drive to organize the Cumberland Plateau.

The US Department of Labor's Bureau of Labor Statistics reported that in 2005, a total of 164,000 of Kentucky's 1,696,000 employed wage and salary workers were formal members of a union. This represented 9.7% of those so employed, up from 9.6% in 2004, but still below the national average of 12%. Overall in 2005, a total of 184,000 workers (10.8%) in Kentucky were covered by a union or employee association contract, which includes those workers who reported no union affiliation. Kentucky is one of 28 states that do not have a right-to-work law.

As of 1 March 2006, Kentucky had a state-mandated minimum wage rate of $5.15 per hour. In 2004, women in the state accounted for 45.1% of the employed civilian labor force.

23AGRICULTURE

With cash receipts totaling $3.9 billion—$1.2 million from crops and $2.7 billion from livestock—Kentucky ranked 24th among the 50 states in farm marketings in 2005.

Kentucky tobacco, first marketed in New Orleans in 1787, quickly became the state's most important crop. Kentucky ranked first among tobacco-producing states until it gave way to North Carolina in 1929. Corn has long been one of the state's most important crops, not only for livestock feed but also as a major ingredient in the distilling of whiskey. Although hemp is no longer an important crop in Kentucky, its early significance to Kentucky farmers, as articulated in Congress by Henry Clay, was partly responsible for the establishment by the United States of a protective tariff system. From 1849 to 1870, the state produced nearly all the hemp grown in the United States.

In 2004 there were approximately 85,000 farms in Kentucky, with an average size of 162 acres (66 hectares). In 2005, 43% of Kentucky's population was considered rural, and 18% of the state's population owed its living to agriculture. In 2004 Kentucky farms produced some 234,500,000 lb of tobacco, the second most in the nation. Leading field crops (in bushels) in 2004 included corn for grain, 173,280,000; soybeans, 57,200,000; wheat, 20,520,000; sorghum, 1,040,000; and barley, 616,000. Farmers also harvested 5,928,000 tons of hay, including 888,000 tons of alfalfa.

24ANIMAL HUSBANDRY

Since early settlement days, livestock raising has been an important part of Kentucky's economy. The Bluegrass region, which offers excellent pasturage and drinking water, has become renowned as a center for horse breeding, including thoroughbreds, quarter horses, American saddle horses, Arabians, and standardbreds. In 2004, sales of horses accounted for 23% of Kentucky's farm receipts.

In 2005, Kentucky had an estimated 2.25 million cattle and calves worth $1.82 billion. In 2004, Kentucky farmers had an estimated 350,000 hogs and pigs, worth around $27.6 million. Kentucky produced an estimated 1.46 billion lb (0.66 billion kg) of milk from 116,000 dairy cows in 2003.

[25] FISHING

Fishing is of little commercial importance in Kentucky. In 2004, Kentucky had 580,917 fishing license holders. In 2005 there were 60 catfish farms covering 600 acres (243 hectares), with an inventory of 800,000 fingerlings in early 2006. The Wolf Creek National Fish Hatchery in Jamestown raises rainbow and brown trout and stocks 90 different areas within the state.

[26] FORESTRY

In 2004 there were 11,391,000 acres (4,828,000 hectares) of forested land in Kentucky—47% of the state's land area. Over 90% of the forestland is classified as commercially viable for timber production.

The most heavily forested areas are in the river valleys of eastern Kentucky, in the Appalachians. In 2004, Kentucky produced 662 million board feet of lumber, nearly all of it in hardwoods. The Division of Forestry of the Department of Natural Resources manages approximately 30,000 acres (12,300 hectares) of state-owned forestland and operates two forest tree nurseries producing 7–9 million seedling trees a year.

There are two national forests—the Daniel Boone and the Jefferson on Kentucky's eastern border—enclosing two national wilderness areas. These two national forests had a combined area of 1,415,744 acres (572,952 hectares) in 2005. Gross acreage of all Kentucky lands in the National Forest System was 2,212,000 acres (895,000 hectares) in 2003. National parks in the state include the Mammoth Cave National Park and the Cumberland Gap National Historical Park on Kentucky's eastern border.

[27] MINING

According to preliminary data from the US Geological Survey (USGS), the estimated value of nonfuel mineral production by Kentucky in 2003 was $559 million, an increase from 2002 of 3%. The USGS data ranked Kentucky as 24th among the 50 states by the total value of its nonfuel mineral production, accounting for about 1.5% of total US output.

According to preliminary figures, crushed stone was the state's leading nonfuel mineral commodity, accounting for around 57% (51.9 million metric tons; $317 million) of Kentucky's nonfuel mineral production by value in 2003. It was followed (in descending order) by lime, cement (portland and masonry), and construction sand and gravel. Collectively, these four commodities accounted for about 98% of the state's nonfuel mineral output by value. Nationally, the state ranked third in ball clays and in lime, and 10th in common clay. According to preliminary USGS data for 2003, the state produced 8.8 million metric tons of construction sand and gravel, with a value of $35.2 million.

[28] ENERGY AND POWER

As of 2003, Kentucky had 62 electrical power service providers, of which 30 were publicly owned and 24 were cooperatives. Of the remainder, six were investor owned, one was federally operated, and one was an owner of an independent generator that sold directly to customers. As of that same year there were 2,117,138 retail customers. Of that total, 1,170,276 received their power from investor-owned service providers. Cooperatives accounted for 744,263 customers, while publicly owned providers had 202,575 customers. There were 22 federal customers and two were independent generator or "facility" customers.

Total net summer generating capability by the state's electrical generating plants in 2003 stood at 19.068 million kW, with total production that same year at 91.718 billion kWh. Of the total amount generated, 88% came from electric utilities, with the remainder coming from independent producers and combined heat and power service providers. The largest portion of all electric power generated, 84.060 billion kWh (91.6%), came from coal-fired plants, with hydroelectric plants in second place at 3.948 billion kWh (4.3%) and petroleum fueled plants in third at 2.944 billion kWh (3.2%). Other renewable power sources and natural gas fueled plants accounted for 0.3% and 0.5%, respectively.

Southern Kentucky shares in the power produced by the Tennessee Valley Authority, which supports a coal-fired steam electric plant in Kentucky at Paducah.

Most of Kentucky's coal came from the western fields of the interior coal basin until late in the 19th century, when the lower-sulfur Cumberland Plateau coal reserves of the Appalachian region were discovered. In 2004, eastern Kentucky produced 90,871,000 short tons of coal, and western Kentucky 23,373,000 short tons. Overall, Kentucky in 2004, had 419 producing coal mines, 196 of which were surface mines and 223 were underground. Total coal output that year totaled 114,244,000 short tons, up from 112,806,000 short tons in 2003. Of the total produced in 2004, surface mines accounted for 42,487,000 short tons. Recoverable coal reserves in 2004 totaled 1.129 billion short tons. One short ton equals 2,000 lb (0.907 metric tons).

As of 2004, Kentucky had proven crude oil reserves of 27 million barrels, or less than 1% of all proven US reserves, while output that same year averaged 7,000 barrels per day. Including federal offshore domains, the state that year ranked 21st (20th excluding federal offshore) in proven reserves and 21st (20th excluding federal offshore) in production among the 31 producing states. In 2004 Kentucky had 18,075 producing oil wells. As of 2005, the state's two refineries had a combined crude oil distillation capacity of 227,500 barrels per day.

Oil shale is found in a band stretching from Lawrence County in the northeast through Madison and Washington counties in central Kentucky to Jefferson County in the north-central region.

In 2004, Kentucky had 13,920 producing natural gas and gas condensate wells. In 2003 (the latest year for which data was available), marketed gas production (all gas produced excluding gas used for repressuring, vented and flared, and nonhydrocarbon gases removed) totaled 87.608 billion cu ft (2.49 billion cu m). As of 31 December 2004, proven reserves of dry or consumer-grade natural gas totaled 1.880 billion cu ft (0.157 billion cu m).

[29] INDUSTRY

Although primarily an agricultural state during the 19th century, Kentucky was a leading supplier of manufactures to the South before the Civil War. Manufacturing activities are largely concentrated in Louisville and Jefferson County and other cities bordering the Ohio River. Kentucky is the leading producer of American whiskey. It also is one of the nation's largest producers of trucks in assembly plants at Louisville as well as for automobiles at Bowling Green and Georgetown.

According to the US Census Bureau's Annual Survey of Manufactures (ASM) for 2004, Kentucky's manufacturing sector covered some 20 product subsectors. The shipment value of all products manufactured in the state that same year was $97.253 billion. Of that total, transportation equipment manufacturing accounted for the largest share at $34.220 billion. It was followed by primary metal manufacturing at $9.178 billion; chemical manufacturing at $7.984 billion; food manufacturing at $7.646 billion; and paper manufacturing at $4.418 billion.

In 2004, a total of 246,749 people in Kentucky were employed in the state's manufacturing sector, according to the ASM. Of that total, 187,621 were actual production workers. In terms of total employment, the transportation equipment manufacturing industry accounted for the largest portion of all manufacturing employees at 50,032, with 41,325 actual production workers. It was followed by food manufacturing at 22,863 employees (17,400 actual production workers); fabricated metal product manufacturing at 21,442 employees (15,783 actual production workers); plastics and rubber products manufacturing at 18,858 employees (15,068 actual production workers); and machinery manufacturing with 17,535 employees (11,982 actual production workers).

ASM data for 2004 showed that Kentucky's manufacturing sector paid $10.344 billion in wages. Of that amount, the transportation equipment manufacturing sector accounted for the largest share at $2.626 billion. It was followed by fabricated metal product manufacturing at $794.193 million; chemical manufacturing at $739.002 million; food manufacturing at $730.046 million; machinery manufacturing at $710.472 billion; and primary metal manufacturing at $634.640 billion.

30 COMMERCE

According to the 2002 Census of Wholesale Trade, Kentucky's wholesale trade sector had sales that year totaling $51.8 billion from 4,630 establishments. Wholesalers of durable goods accounted for 2,827 establishments, followed by nondurable goods wholesalers at 1,447 and electronic markets, agents, and brokers accounting for 356 establishments. Sales by durable goods wholesalers in 2002 totaled $20.5 billion, while wholesalers of nondurable goods saw sales of $27.1 billion. Electronic markets, agents, and brokers in the wholesale trade industry had sales of $4.08 billion.

In the 2002 Census of Retail Trade, Kentucky was listed as having 16,847 retail establishments with sales of $40.06 billion. The leading types of retail businesses by number of establishments were: gasoline stations (2,443); motor vehicle and motor vehicle parts dealers (2,171); miscellaneous store retailers (1,978); and food and beverage stores (1,961). In terms of sales, motor vehicle and motor vehicle parts stores accounted for the largest share of retail sales at $9.5 billion, followed by general merchandise stores at $7.6 billion; food and beverage stores at $5.5 billion; gasoline stations at $4.5 billion; and building material/garden equipment and supplies dealers at $3.6 billion. A total of 214,192 people were employed by the retail sector in Kentucky that year.

Exporters located in Kentucky exported $14.8 billion in merchandise during 2005.

31 CONSUMER PROTECTION

Consumer protection is primarily the responsibility of the Office of Consumer Protection, which is a part of the state Attorney General's Office. Created in 1972, the office assists consumers with disputes in the marketplace through the mediation of consumer complaints; the litigation of violators of the Consumer Protection Act; and the education of consumers. The mediation branch handles consumer complaints.

However, other state agencies also operate consumer protection divisions that are specific to the particular agency. The Office of Insurance, which regulates insurance companies and agents within the state, has a Division of Consumer Protection and Education. The state's Department of Agriculture has a Division of Regulation and Inspection under its Office for Consumer and Environmental Services. The Division's responsibilities include the inspection of gas pumps, amusement park rides, weight and measurement devices, tobacco warehouses, and eggs. The state's Public Service Commission, which regulates utilities operating within the state, has a Division of Consumer Services.

When dealing with consumer protection issues, the state's Attorney General's Office can initiate civil and criminal proceedings; represent the state before state and federal regulatory agencies; administer consumer protection and education programs; and exercise broad subpoena powers. In antitrust actions, the Attorney General's Office can act on behalf of those consumers who are incapable of acting on their own; initiate damage actions on behalf of the state in state courts; initiate criminal proceedings; and represent counties, cities and other governmental entities in recovering civil damages under state or federal law.

The Consumer Protection Division has offices in the cities of Louisville and Frankfort.

32 BANKING

As of June 2005, Kentucky had 230 insured banks, savings and loans, and saving banks, plus 33 state-chartered and 75 federally chartered credit unions (CUs). Excluding the CUs, the Louisville market area had the most number of financial institutions with 53, as well as the largest portion of deposits at $19.289 billion in 2004, followed by the Lexington–Fayette area at 21 and $6.683 billion, respectively. As of June 2005, CUs accounted for 7.7% of all assets held by all financial institutions in the state, or some $4.378 billion. Banks, savings and loans, and savings banks collectively accounted for the remaining 92.3% or $52.280 billion in assets held.

Eighty-one percent of the state's insured banks have less than $250 million in assets. The median return on assets (ROA) ratio (the measure of earnings in relation to all resources) and net interest margin (the difference between the lower rates offered to savers and the higher rates charged on loans) increased in 2004 for Kentucky's banks. For that year, ROA stood at 1.10%, up from 1.05% in 2003, while NIM in 2004 stood at 4.01%, up from 3.95% in the previous year.

Regulation of Kentucky's state-chartered financial institutions is carried out by the state's Office of Financial Institutions.

33 INSURANCE

In 2004, Kentuckians held some 2.6 million life insurance policies, with a total value of over $139 billion; total value for all categories of life insurance (individual, group, and credit) was over $213 billion. The average coverage amount is $52,500 per policy holder. Death benefits paid that year totaled at about $679.3 million.

As of 2003, there were 8 property and casualty and 10 life and health insurance companies domiciled in the state. In 2004, direct premiums for property and casualty insurance totaled $5.75 billion. The same year, there were 20,921 flood insurance policies in force in the state, with a total value of $2 billion. About $150 million of coverage was held through FAIR plans, which are designed to offer coverage for some natural circumstances, such as wind and hail, in high risk areas.

In 2004, 52% of state residents held employment-based health insurance policies, 4% held individual policies, and 28% were covered under Medicare and Medicaid; 14% of residents were uninsured. In 2003, employee contributions for employment-based health coverage averaged at 20% for single coverage and 25% for family coverage. The state offers an 18-month health benefits expansion program for small-firm employees in connection with the Consolidated Omnibus Budget Reconciliation Act (COBRA, 1986), a health insurance program for those who lose employment-based coverage due to termination or reduction of work hours.

In 2003, there were over 2.8 million auto insurance policies in effect for private passenger cars. Required minimum coverage includes bodily injury liability of up to $25,000 per individual and $50,000 for all persons injured in an accident, as well as property damage liability of $10,000. Personal injury protection is also required. In 2003, the average expenditure per vehicle for insurance coverage was $737.46.

³⁴SECURITIES

There are no securities exchanges in Kentucky. In 2005, there were 480 personal financial advisers employed in the state and 2,350 securities, commodities, and financial services sales agents. In 2004, there were over 64 publicly traded companies within the state, with over 30 NASDAQ companies, 13 NYSE listings, and 3 AMEX listings. In 2006, the state had six Fortune 500 companies; Humana (in Louisville) ranked first in the state and 150th in the nation with revenues of over $14.4 million, followed by Ashland, Inc. (Covington), Yum Brands (Louisville), Omnicare (Covington), Lexmark International (Lexington), and Kindred Healthcare all of which are listed on the NYSE.

³⁵PUBLIC FINANCE

The Kentucky biennial state budget is prepared by the Governor's Office for Policy and Management late in each odd-numbered year and submitted by the governor to the General Assembly for approval. The fiscal year (FY) runs from 1 July to 30 June.

Fiscal year 2006 general funds were estimated at $9.1 billion for resources and $8.4 billion for expenditures. In fiscal year 2004, federal government grants to Kentucky were $6.7 billion.

³⁶TAXATION

In 2005, Kentucky collected $9.1 billion in tax revenues, or $2,179 per capita, which placed it 23rd among the 50 states in per capita tax burden. The national average was $2,192 per capita. Property taxes accounted for 5.2% of the total; sales taxes, 28.5%; selective

sales taxes, 18.2%; individual income taxes, 33.4%; corporate income taxes, 5.3%; and other taxes, 9.3%.

As of 1 January 2006, Kentucky had six individual income tax brackets ranging from 2.0% to 6.0%. The state taxes corporations at rates ranging from 4.0% to 7.0% depending on tax bracket.

In 2004, state and local property taxes amounted to $2.14 billion, or $516 per capita. The per capita amount ranks the state 45th highest nationally. Local governments collected $1,680,995,000 of the total and the state government $455,460,000.

Kentucky taxes retail sales at a rate of 6%. Food purchased for consumption off-premises is tax exempt. The tax on cigarettes is

Kentucky—State Government Finances

(Dollar amounts in thousands. Per capita amounts in dollars.)

	AMOUNT	PER CAPITA
Total Revenue	20,180,416	4,872.14
General revenue	17,382,099	4,196.55
Intergovernmental revenue	5,795,618	1,399.23
Taxes	8,463,400	2,043.31
General sales	2,466,033	595.37
Selective sales	1,540,274	371.87
License taxes	542,480	130.97
Individual income tax	2,819,393	680.68
Corporate income tax	381,538	92.11
Other taxes	713,682	172.30
Current charges	1,895,335	457.59
Miscellaneous general revenue	1,227,746	296.41
Utility revenue	–	–
Liquor store revenue	–	–
Insurance trust revenue	2,798,317	675.60
Total expenditure	20,072,526	4,846.10
Intergovernmental expenditure	3,967,334	957.83
Direct expenditure	16,105,192	3,888.26
Current operation	11,108,836	2,682.00
Capital outlay	1,604,185	387.30
Insurance benefits and repayments	2,430,915	586.89
Assistance and subsidies	533,329	128.76
Interest on debt	427,927	103.31
Exhibit: Salaries and wages	3,067,912	740.68
Total expenditure	20,072,526	4,846.10
General expenditure	17,641,550	4,259.19
Intergovernmental expenditure	3,967,334	957.83
Direct expenditure	13,674,216	3,301.36
General expenditures, by function:		
Education	6,392,502	1,543.34
Public welfare	5,274,909	1,273.52
Hospitals	682,476	164.77
Health	535,507	129.29
Highways	1,730,937	417.90
Police protection	155,292	37.49
Correction	452,482	109.24
Natural resources	345,119	83.32
Parks and recreation	134,567	32.49
Government administration	667,476	161.15
Interest on general debt	427,927	103.31
Other and unallocable	842,356	203.37
Utility expenditure	61	.01
Liquor store expenditure	–	–
Insurance trust expenditure	2,430,915	586.89
Debt at end of fiscal year	8,116,460	1,959.55
Cash and security holdings	33,990,295	8,206.25

Abbreviations and symbols: – zero or rounds to zero; (NA) not available; (X) not applicable.

SOURCE: *U.S. Census Bureau, Governments Division, 2004 Survey of State Government Finances*, January 2006.

30 cents per pack, which ranks 45th among the 50 states and the District of Columbia. Kentucky taxes gasoline at 18.5 cents per gallon. This is in addition to the 18.4 cents per gallon federal tax on gasoline.

According to the Tax Foundation, for every federal tax dollar sent to Washington in 2004, Kentucky citizens received $1.45 in federal spending.

37 ECONOMIC POLICY

The Kentucky Cabinet for Economic Development seeks to encourage businesses to locate in Kentucky and to expand through its job creation program. Various available programs offer companies tax credits totaling as much as 100% of their investment. Low interest loans and bonds also are available. Additional incentives are available to qualified businesses for locating in one of Kentucky's enterprise zones, Appalachian counties, or in Kentucky's federal empowerment zone. Incentives also are available for tourist attractions that locate in Kentucky. Regional industrial parks are currently being developed to provide available, accessible, and marketable land in areas where an abundant labor force is available. The Kentucky Economic Development Finance Authority (KEDFA) was established within the Cabinet for Economic Development to further the state's economic goals through financial assistance and tax credit programs. Tax credit programs offered include those under the Bluegrass State Skills Corporation Skills Training Investment Act; the Kentucky Rural Economic Development Act (to support manufacturing enterprises in rural areas); the Kentucky Jobs Act (for the expansion of service and technology related projects); the Kentucky Industrial Development Act (for new and expanding manufacturing projects); the Kentucky Economic Opportunity Zone Program (for certified Opportunity Zones); and the Kentucky Investment Fund Act (for approved venture capital investments). Other incentives are offered under programs for Enterprise Zones, Industrial Revenue Bonds, the Commonwealth Small Business Development Corporation, the Kentucky Tourism Development Act, and the Local Government Economic Development Fund.

38 HEALTH

The infant mortality rate in October 2005 was estimated at 6.6 per 1,000 live births. The birth rate in 2003 was 13.4 per 1,000 population. The abortion rate stood at 5.3 per 1,000 women in 2000. In 2003, about 87% of pregnant woman received prenatal care beginning in the first trimester. In 2004, approximately 79% of children received routine immunizations before the age of three.

The crude death rate in 2003 was 9.8 deaths per 1,000 population. As of 2002, the death rates for major causes of death (per 100,000 resident population) were: heart disease, 285.8; cancer, 230.6; cerebrovascular diseases, 62.4; chronic lower respiratory diseases, 58.7; and diabetes, 30.9. The mortality rate from HIV infection was 2.4 per 100,000 population. In 2004, the reported AIDS case rate was at about 6.1 per 100,000 population. In 2002, about 59.4% of the population was considered overweight or obese. As of 2004, Kentucky hosted the highest percentage of resident smokers, with about 27.4%.

In 2003, Kentucky had 103 community hospitals with about 14,900 beds. There were about 600,000 patient admissions that year and 8.5 million outpatient visits. The average daily inpatient census was about 9,300 patients. The average cost per day for hospital care was $1,106. Also in 2003, there were about 296 certified nursing facilities in the state with 25,629 beds and an overall occupancy rate of about 89%. In 2004, it was estimated that about 71.3% of all state residents had received some type of dental care within the year. Kentucky had 233 physicians per 100,000 resident population in 2004 and 904 nurses per 100,000 in 2005. In 2004, there were a total of 2,325 dentists in the state.

About 28% of state residents were enrolled in Medicaid and Medicare programs in 2004. Approximately 14% of the state population uninsured in 2004. In 2003, state health care expenditures totaled $5 million.

39 SOCIAL WELFARE

In 2004, about 121,000 people received unemployment benefits, with the average weekly unemployment benefit at $257. In fiscal year 2005, the estimated average monthly participation in the food stamp program included about 570,277 persons (245,707 households); the average monthly benefit was about $89.36 per person. That year, the total of benefits paid through the state for the food stamp program was about $611.4 million.

Temporary Assistance for Needy Families (TANF), the system of federal welfare assistance that officially replaced Aid to Families with Dependent Children (AFDC) in 1997, was reauthorized through the Deficit Reduction Act of 2005. TANF is funded through federal block grants that are divided among the states based on an equation involving the number of recipients in each state. Kentucky's TANF program is called the Kentucky Transition Assistance Program (K-TAP). In 2004, the state program had 78,000 recipients; state and federal expenditures on this TANF program totaled $119 million in fiscal year 2003.

In December 2004, Social Security benefits were paid to 784,910 Kentucky residents. This number included 408,110 retired workers, 92,390 widows and widowers, 152,410 disabled workers, 50,400 spouses, and 81,590 children. Social Security beneficiaries represented 18.9% of the total state population and 92.9% of the state's population age 65 and older. Retired workers received an average monthly payment of $903; widows and widowers, $814; disabled workers, $879; and spouses, $425. Payments for children of retired workers averaged $441 per month; children of deceased workers, $596; and children of disabled workers, $261. Federal Supplemental Security Income payments in December 2004 went to 179,438 Kentucky residents, averaging $392 a month. An additional $1.4 million of state-administered supplemental payments were distributed to 4,406 residents.

40 HOUSING

In 2004, Kentucky had 1,842,971 housing units, 1,647,464 of which were occupied. About 70.1% were owner-occupied. About 67% of all units were single-family, detached homes; 13.9% were mobile homes. Though most units relied on utility gas or electricity for heating, about 11,533 units used coke or coal and 37,785 relied on wood. It was estimated that 109,895 units lacked telephone service,

13,677 lacked complete plumbing facilities, and 9,421 lacked complete kitchen facilities. The average household had 2.45 members.

In 2004, 22,600 privately owned units were authorized for construction. The median home value was $98,438. The median monthly cost for mortgage owners was $888. Renters paid a median of $503 per month. In September 2005, the state received grants of $2.15 million from the US Department of Housing and Urban Development (HUD) for rural housing and economic development programs. For 2006, HUD allocated to the state over $27.3 million in community development block grants.

⁴¹EDUCATION

Kentucky was relatively slow to establish and support its public education system and has consistently ranked below the national average in the educational attainments of its citizens. In 2004, 81.8% of all adults had completed four years of high school, below the national average of 84%; 21% had completed four or more years of college, below the national average of 26%.

The total enrollment for fall 2002 in Kentucky's public schools stood at 661,000. Of these, 477,000 attended schools from kindergarten through grade eight, and 184,000 attended high school. Approximately 87% of the students were white, 10.4% were black, 1.5% were Hispanic, 0.8% were Asian/Pacific Islander, and 0.2% were American Indian/Alaskan Native. Total enrollment was estimated at 650,000 in fall 2003 but was expected to be 618,000 by fall 2014, a decline of 6.5% during the period 2002 to 2014. Expenditures for public education in 2003/04 were estimated at $5.24 billion. There were 71,067 students enrolled in 368 private schools in fall 2003. Since 1969, the National Assessment of Educational Progress (NAEP) has tested public school students nationwide. The resulting report, *The Nation's Report Card,* stated that in 2005, eighth graders in Kentucky scored 274 out of 500 in mathematics compared with the national average of 278.

As of fall 2002, there were 225,489 students enrolled in institutions of higher education; minority students comprised 10.8% of total postsecondary enrollment. As of 2005, Kentucky had 77 degree-granting institutions. Kentucky's higher education facilities include 8 public 4-year institutions, 26 public 2-year schools, and 26 private 4-year nonprofit institutions. The University of Kentucky, established in 1865 at Lexington, is the state's largest public institution. The University of Louisville (1798) is also state supported. Loans and grants to Kentucky students are provided by the Kentucky Higher Education Assistance Authority.

In 1990 the Kentucky Education Reform Act established SEEK (Support Education Excellence in Kentucky). SEEK is a program that balances the available education dollars among poor and wealthy counties.

⁴²ARTS

The Kentucky Arts Council (KAC) was formed in 1965. The council is a division of the Kentucky Department of the Arts within the Commerce Cabinet and is authorized to promote the arts through such programs as Arts in Education and the State Arts Resources Program. Other ongoing programs include the Craft Marketing Program, which promotes the state's craft industry, and the Folklife Program, a partnership with the Kentucky Historical Society. The Arts Kentucky is a statewide membership organization for artists, performers, craftspeople, and community arts groups.

The Kentucky Center for the Arts in Louisville, dedicated in 1983, serves as home to the Louisville Orchestra (est. 1937) and the Kentucky Opera the twelfth-oldest opera company in the United States. The Louisville Ballet (est. 1952) also resides in the Kentucky Center for the Arts. Over the years, the Louisville Orchestra has recorded numerous works by contemporary composers. As of 2006, the Louisville Ballet entertained more than 75,000 people each year and reached over 15,000 children annually, through their education programs.

Bluegrass, a form of country music performed on fiddle and banjo and played at a rapid tempo is named after the style pioneered by Kentuckian Bill Monroe and his Blue Grass Boys. The Actors Theater of Louisville holds the annual Humana Festival of New American Plays; in 2006 the festival celebrated its 30th anniversary.

In 2005, the KAC and other arts organizations received 22 grants totaling $1,020,800 from the National Endowment for the Arts. KAC also receives funding from the state to develop its arts education programs. Kentucky Chautauqua, an ongoing program of the Kentucky Humanities Council, sponsors impersonations of historical characters from Kentucky's past that travel across the state for presentations. In 2005, the state received nine grants totaling $1,576,792 from the National Endowment for the Humanities.

⁴³LIBRARIES AND MUSEUMS

For the fiscal year ending in June 2001, Kentucky had 116 public library systems, with a total of 189 libraries, of which 73 were branches. In that same year, the systems had a combined total of 7,891,000 volumes of books and serial publications on their shelves, and a total circulation of 20,807,000. The system also had 269,000 audio and 225,000 video items, 12,000 electronic format items (CD-ROMs, magnetic tapes, and disks), and 94 bookmobiles. The regional library system included university libraries and the state library at Frankfort, as well as city and county libraries. The Kentucky Historical Society in Frankfort also maintains a research library of more than 85,000 volumes. In fiscal year 2001, operating income for the state's public library system totaled $79,874,000, including $458,000 in federal grants and $5,033,000 in state funding. For that same year, operating expenditures totaled $70,421,000, of which 56.4% was spent on staff members, and 16.4% on the collection.

The state has more than 107 museums. Art museums include the University of Kentucky Art Museum and the Headley-Whitney Museum in Lexington, the Allen R. Hite Art Institute at the University of Louisville, and the J. B. Speed Art Museum, also in Louisville. Among Kentucky's equine museums are the International Museum of the Horse and the American Horse Museum, both in Lexington, and the Kentucky Derby Museum in Louisville. The John James Audubon Museum is located in Audubon State Park at Henderson.

Leading historical sites include Abraham Lincoln's birthplace at Hodgenville and the Mary Todd Lincoln and Henry Clay homes in Lexington. The Kentucky Historical Society in Frankfort operates three museums, supports a mobile museum system that brings exhibits about Kentucky history to schools, parks, and local gatherings, and aids over 400 local historical organizations.

44 COMMUNICATIONS

Only 91.4% of all occupied housing units in the state had a telephone in 2004. In addition, by June of that same year there were 2,000,459 mobile wireless telephone subscribers. In 2003, 58.1% of Kentucky households had a computer and 49.6% had Internet access. By June 2005, there were 370,337 high-speed lines in Kentucky, 330,957 residential and 39,362 for business.

In 1922, Kentucky's first radio broadcasting station, WHAS, was established. By 2005, there were 73 major radio stations, 15 AM and 58 FM. That year there were 29 major television broadcasting stations, including 17 public broadcasting stations. There were 576,850 television households, 65% of which received cable in 1999. By 2000, Kentucky had registered a total of 39,264 Internet domain names.

45 PRESS

In 2005, Kentucky had 23 daily newspapers (10 morning, 13 evening), and 14 Sunday papers.

The following table shows the leading Kentucky newspapers with their approximate 2005 circulations:

AREA	NAME	DAILY	SUNDAY
Lexington	*Herald-Leader* (m,S)	114,234	145,500
Louisville	*Courier-Journal* (m,S)	207,655	273,891

Magazines include *Kentucky Living* and *Kentucky Monthly*.

46 ORGANIZATIONS

In 2006, there were over 3,895 nonprofit organizations registered within the state, of which about 2,524 were registered as charitable, educational, or religious organizations. Notable organizations with headquarters in Kentucky include the Thoroughbred Club of America, the United States Polo Association, the Jockeys' Guild, and the Burley Tobacco Growers Cooperative Association (all in Lexington); the Burley Auction Warehouse Association (Mt. Sterling); the National Softball Association in Nicholasville, and Sons of the American Revolution and the American Saddlebred Horse Association (all in Louisville).

The Council of State Governments in Lexington is a co-sponsor of the National Crime Prevention Institute and the National Emergency Management Association (both are also in Lexington). The National Police Officers Association of America is based in Louisville.

The American Quilter's Society is located in Paducah. State organizations for local arts and culture include the Filson Club, the Kentucky Guild of Artists and Craftsmen, and the Ohio Valley Art League. Special interest organizations in the state include the American Checker Federation and the Corvette Club of America.

47 TOURISM, TRAVEL, AND RECREATION

The economic impact of tourism within the state approached $10 billion and supported of over 164,000 travel-related jobs. The strength of this sector of the economy was attributed, in part, to the impact of the Kentucky Tourism Development Act of 1996, which provides incentives for new or expanding tourist-related businesses. As of 2003, total private investment in tourism reached $500 million.

One of the state's top tourist attractions is Mammoth Cave National Park, which contains an estimated 150 mi (241 km) of underground passages. Other units of the national park system in Kentucky include a re-creation of Abraham Lincoln's birthplace in Hodgenville and Cumberland Gap National Historical Park, which extends into Tennessee and Virginia.

The state operates 15 resort parks (13 of them year round). The state also operates 15 recreational parks and 9 shrines. Breaks Interstate Park, on the Kentucky-Virginia border, is noted for the Russell Fork River Canyon, which is 1,600 feet (488 meters) deep; the park is supported equally by the two states.

In 1979, the Kentucky Horse Park opened in Lexington. The Kentucky State Fair is held every August at Louisville. The Kentucky Derby (horse racing) is the first leg of the prestigious Triple Crown held in May in Lexington. Cave City is home to Dinosaur World.

48 SPORTS

There are no major league professional sports teams in Kentucky. There is a minor league baseball team in Louisville that plays in the Triple-A International League. There are also two minor league hockey teams in Kentucky that play in the American Hockey League.

The first known horse race in Kentucky was held in 1783. The annual Kentucky Derby, first run on 17 May 1875, has become the single most famous event in US thoroughbred racing. Held on the first Saturday in May at Churchill Downs in Louisville, the Derby is one of three races for three-year-olds constituting the Triple Crown. Keeneland Race Course in Lexington is the site of the Blue Grass Stakes and other major thoroughbred races. The Kentucky Futurity, an annual highlight of the harness racing season, is usually held on the first Friday in October at the Red Mile in Lexington.

Rivaling horse racing as a spectator sport is collegiate basketball. The University of Kentucky Wildcats, who play in the Southeastern Conference, won National Collegiate Athletic Association (NCAA) Division I basketball championships in 1948–49, 1951, 1958, 1978, 1996, and 1998, and the National Invitation Tournament (NIT) in 1946 and 1976. The University of Louisville Cardinals, who play in Conference USA, captured the NCAA crown in 1980 and 1986, and won an NIT title in 1956. Kentucky Wesleyan, at Owensboro, was the NCAA Division II titleholder in 1966, 1968–69, 1973, 1987, 1990, 1999, and 2001.

49 FAMOUS KENTUCKIANS

Kentucky has been the birthplace of one US president, four US vice presidents, the only president of the Confederacy, and several important jurists, statesmen, writers, artists, and sports figures.

Abraham Lincoln (1809–65) the 16th president of the United States, was born in Hodgenville, Hardin (now Larue) County, and spent his developing years in Indiana and Illinois. Elected as the first Republican president in 1860 and reelected in 1864, Lincoln reflected his Kentucky roots in his opposition to secession and the expansion of slavery, and in his conciliatory attitude toward the defeated southern states. His wife, Mary Todd Lincoln (1818–82), was a native of Lexington.

Kentucky-born US vice presidents have all been Democrats. Richard M. Johnson (1780–1850) was elected by the Senate after a deadlock in the Electoral College; John C. Breckinridge (1821–75) in 1857 became the youngest man ever to hold the office; Adlai E. Stevenson (1835–1914) served in Grover Cleveland's second administration. The best-known vice president was Alben W. Barkley (1877–1956), who, before his election with President Harry S Truman in 1948, was a US senator and longtime Senate majority leader.

Frederick M. Vinson (1890–1953) was the only Kentuckian to serve as chief justice of the United States. Noteworthy associate justices were John Marshall Harlan (1833–1911), famous for his dissent from the segregationist *Plessy v. Ferguson* decision (1896), and Louis B. Brandeis (1856–1941), the first Jew to serve on the Supreme Court and a champion of social reform.

Henry Clay (b.Virginia, 1777–1852) came to Lexington in 1797 and went on to serve as speaker of the US House of Representatives, secretary of state, and US senator; he was also a three-time presidential candidate. Other important federal officeholders from Kentucky include attorneys general John Breckinridge (b.Virginia, 1760–1806) and John J. Crittenden (1787–1863), who also served with distinction as US senator; treasury secretaries Benjamin H. Bristow (1830–96) and John G. Carlisle (1835–1910); and US senator John Sherman Cooper (1901–91). Zachary Taylor (1784–1850), 12th US president, spent much of his adult life in Kentucky and is buried there.

Among noteworthy state officeholders, Isaac Shelby (b.Maryland 1750–1826) was a leader in the movement for statehood and the first governor of Kentucky. William Goebel (1856–1900) was the only US governor assassinated in office. Albert B. ("Happy") Chandler (1898–1991), twice governor, also served as US senator and as commissioner of baseball.

A figure prominently associated with frontier Kentucky is the explorer and surveyor Daniel Boone (b.Pennsylvania, 1734–1820). Other frontiersmen include Kit Carson (1809–68) and Roy Bean (1825?–1903). During the Civil War, Lincoln's principal adversary was another native Kentuckian, Jefferson Davis (1808–89). Davis moved south as a boy to a Mississippi plantation home, subsequently serving as US senator from Mississippi, US secretary of war, and president of the Confederate States of America.

Other personalities of significance include James G. Birney (1792–1857) and Cassius Marcellus Clay (1810–1903), both major antislavery spokesmen. Clay's daughter Laura (1849–1941) and Madeline Breckinridge (1872–1920) were important contributors to the women's suffrage movement. Henry Watterson (1840–1921) founded and edited the *Louisville Courier-Journal* and was a major adviser to the Democratic Party. Carry Nation (1846–1911) was a leader of the temperance movement. During the 1920s, Kentuckian John T. Scopes (1900–70) gained fame as the defendant in the "monkey trial" in Dayton, Tenn.; Scopes was prosecuted for teaching Darwin's theory of evolution. Whitney M.

Young (1921–71), a prominent black leader, served as head of the National Urban League.

Thomas Hunt Morgan (1866–1945), honored for his work in heredity and genetics, was a Nobel Prize winner. Journalists born in Kentucky include Irvin S. Cobb (1876–1944), who was also a humorist and playwright, and Arthur Krock (1887–1974), a winner of four Pulitzer Prizes. Notable businessmen include Harland Sanders (b.Indiana, 1890–1980), founder of Kentucky Fried Chicken restaurants.

Kentucky has produced several distinguished creative artists. These include painters Matthew Jouett (1787–1827), Frank Duveneck (1848–1919), and Paul Sawyer (1865–1917); folk song collector John Jacob Niles (1891–1980); and novelists Harriette Arnow (1908–86) and Wendell Berry (b.1934). Robert Penn Warren (1905–89), a novelist, poet, and critic, won the Pulitzer Prize three times and was the first author to win the award in both the fiction and poetry categories.

Among Kentuckians well recognized in the performing arts are film innovator D. W. Griffith (David Lewelyn Wark Griffith, 1875–1948), Academy Award–winning actress Patricia Neal (b.1926), and country music singer Loretta Lynn (b.1932). Kentucky's sports figures include basketball coach Adolph Rupp (b.Kansas, 1901–77), shortstop Harold ("Pee Wee") Reese (1919–99), football great Paul Hornung (b.1935), and world heavyweight boxing champions Jimmy Ellis (b.1940) and Muhammad Ali (Cassius Clay, b.1942).

50 BIBLIOGRAPHY

Alvey, R. Gerald. *Kentucky Bluegrass Country.* Jackson: University Press of Mississippi, 1992.

Bryant, Ron D. *Kentucky History: An Annotated Bibliography.* Westport, Conn.: Greenwood Press, 2000.

Burns, David M. *Gateway: Dr. Thomas Walker and the Opening of Kentucky.* Middlesboro, Ky.: Bell County Historical Society, 2000.

Clark, Thomas Dionysius. *The Kentucky.* Lexington: University Press of Kentucky, 1992.

Council of State Governments. *The Book of the States, 2006 Edition.* Lexington, Ky.: Council of State Governments, 2006.

Friend, Craig Thompson. *Along the Maysville Road: The Early American Republic in the Trans-Appalachian West.* Knoxville: University of Tennessee Press, 2005.

Harrison, Lowell Hayes, and James C. Klotter. *A New History of Kentucky.* Lexington: University Press of Kentucky, 1997.

Jones, K. Randell. *In the Footsteps of Daniel Boone.* Winston-Salem, N.C.: John F. Blair, 2005.

Klass, Raymond. *Mammoth Cave National Park: Reflections.* Lexington: University Press of Kentucky, 2005.

Kozar, Richard. *Daniel Boone and the Exploration of the Frontier.* Philadelphia: Chelsea House Publishers, 1999.

Kentucky Cabinet for Economic Development. Division of Research. *1997 Kentucky Deskbook of Economic Statistics.* Frankfort, 1997.

Kleber, John E. (ed.). *The Kentucky Encyclopedia.* Lexington: University Press of Kentucky, 1992.

Lucas, Marion Brunson. *A History of Blacks in Kentucky: From Slavery to Segregation, 1760–1891.* 2nd ed. Frankfort: Kentucky Historical Society, 2003.

Miller, Penny M. *Kentucky Politics & Government: Do We Stand United?* Lincoln: University of Nebraska Press, 1994.

US Department of Commerce, Economics and Statistics Administration, US Census Bureau. *Kentucky, 2000. Summary Social, Economic, and Housing Characteristics: 2000 Census of Population and Housing.* Washington, D.C.: US Government Printing Office, 2003.

Williams, Rob (comp.). *A Citizen's Guide to the Kentucky Constitution.* Rev. ed. Frankfort: Legislative Research Commission, 1995.

LOUISIANA

State of Louisiana

ORIGIN OF STATE NAME: Named in 1682 for France's King Louis XIV. **NICKNAME:** The Pelican State. **CAPITAL:** Baton Rouge. **ENTERED UNION:** 30 April 1812 (18th). **SONG:** "Give Me Louisiana;" "You are My Sunshine;" "State March Song." **MOTTO:** Union, Justice, and Confidence. **FLAG:** On a blue field, fringed on three sides, a white pelican feeds her three young, symbolizing the state providing for its citizens; the state motto is inscribed on a white ribbon. **OFFICIAL SEAL:** In the center, a pelican and its young are as depicted on the flag; the state motto encircles the scene, and the words "State of Louisiana" surround the whole. **BIRD:** Eastern brown pelican. **FISH:** Crustacean: Crawfish. **FLOWER:** Magnolia; Louisiana iris (wildflower). **TREE:** Bald cypress. **GEM:** Agate. **LEGAL HOLIDAYS:** New Year's Day, 1 January; Birthday of Martin Luther King Jr., 3rd Monday in January; Mardi Gras Day, Tuesday before Ash Wednesday, February; Good Friday, Friday before Easter, March or April; Independence Day, 4 July; Huey Long's Birthday, 30 August, by proclamation of the governor; Labor Day, 1st Monday in September; Election Day, 1st Tuesday in November in even-numbered years; Veterans' Day, 11 November; Thanksgiving Day, 4th Thursday in November; Christmas Day, 25 December. Legal holidays in Baton Rouge parish also include Inauguration Day, once every four years in January. **TIME:** 6 AM CST = noon GMT.

¹LOCATION, SIZE, AND EXTENT

Situated in the western south-central United States, Louisiana ranks 31st in size among the 50 states. The total area of Louisiana is 47,751 sq mi (123,675 sq km), including 44,521 sq mi (115,309 sq km) of land and 3,230 sq mi (8,366 sq km) of inland water. The state extends 237 mi (381 km) E–W; its maximum N–S extension is 236 mi (380 km). Louisiana is shaped roughly like a boot, with the heel in the SW corner and the toe at the extreme SE.

Louisiana is bordered on the N by Arkansas; on the E by Mississippi (with part of the line formed by the Mississippi River and part, in the extreme SE, by the Pearl River); on the S by the Gulf of Mexico; and on the W by Texas (with part of the line passing through the Sabine River and Toledo Bend Reservoir). The state's geographic center is in Avoyelles Parish, 3 mi (5 km) SE of Marksville. The total boundary length of Louisiana is 1,486 mi (2,391 km). Louisiana's total tidal shoreline is 7,721 mi (12,426 km).

²TOPOGRAPHY

Louisiana lies wholly within the Gulf Coastal Plain. Alluvial lands, chiefly of the Red and Mississippi rivers, occupy the north-central third of the state. East and west of this alluvial plain are the upland districts, characterized by rolling hills sloping gently toward the coast. The coastal-delta section, in the southernmost portion of the state, consists of the Mississippi Delta and the coastal lowlands. The highest elevation in the state is Driskill Mountain at 535 ft (163 m), in Bienville Parish; the lowest, 8 ft (2 m) below sea level, in New Orleans. The mean elevation of the state is approximately 100 ft (31 m).

Louisiana has the most wetlands of all the states, about 11,000 sq mi (28,000 sq km) of floodplains and 7,800 sq mi (20,200 sq km) of coastal swamps, marshes, and estuarine waters. The largest lake, actually a coastal lagoon, is Lake Pontchartrain, with an area of more than 620 sq mi (1,600 sq km). Toledo Bend Reservoir, an

artificial lake along the Louisiana–Texas border, has an area of 284 sq mi (736 sq km). The most important rivers are the Mississippi, Red, Pearl, Atchafalaya, and Sabine. Most drainage takes place through swamps between the bayous, which serve as outlets for overflowing rivers and streams. Louisiana has nearly 2,500 coastal islands covering some 2,000 sq mi (5,000 sq km).

³CLIMATE

Louisiana has a relatively constant semitropical climate. Rainfall and humidity decrease, and daily temperature variations increase, with distance from the Gulf of Mexico. The normal daily temperature in New Orleans is 69°F (20°C), ranging from 53°F (11°C) in January to 82°F (27°C) in July. The all-time high temperature is 114°F (46°C), recorded at Plain Dealing on 10 August 1936; the all-time low, -16°F (-27°C), was set at Minden on 13 February 1899. New Orleans has sunshine 58% of the time, and the average annual rainfall is about 61.6 in (156 cm). Snow falls occasionally in the north, but rarely in the south.

Prevailing winds are from the south or southeast. During the summer and fall, tropical storms and hurricanes frequently batter the state, especially along the coast. The 2005 hurricane season devastated much of the Gulf region, primarily through Hurricane Katrina. Katrina made landfall at Buras on 29 August 2005 as a Category 4 storm. The combination of high winds and flooding led to levee damage around New Orleans, allowing flood waters to cover about 80% of the city, with depths as high as 20 ft (6.3 m). One month later, Hurricane Rita made landfall near Johnson's Bayou as a Category 3 storm. Initial reports from Hurricane Rita alone included 119 deaths and $8 billion in damage. As of early 2006, damage assessments for Hurricane Katrina were still underway. Over 1,300 deaths had been reported, well over 1 million people were displaced, and the cost of rebuilding was estimated at over $150 billion.

4FLORA AND FAUNA

Forests in Louisiana consist of four major types: shortleaf pine uplands, slash and longleaf pine flats and hills, hardwood forests in alluvial basins, and cypress and tupelo swamps. Important commercial trees also include beech, eastern red cedar, and black walnut. Among the state's wildflowers are the ground orchid and several hyacinths; two species (Louisiana quillwort and American chaffseed) were listed as endangered in April 2006. Spanish moss (actually a member of the pineapple family) grows profusely in the southern regions but is rare in the north.

Louisiana's varied habitats—tidal marshes, swamps woodlands, and prairies—offer a diversity of fauna. Deer, squirrel, rabbit, and bear are hunted as game, while muskrat, nutria, mink, opossum, bobcat, and skunk are commercially significant furbearers. Prized game birds include quail, turkey, woodcock, and various waterfowl, of which the mottled duck and wood duck are native. Coastal beaches are inhabited by sea turtles, and whales may be seen offshore. Freshwater fish include bass, crappie, and bream; red and white crawfishes are the leading commercial crustaceans. Threatened animal species include five species (green, hawksbill, Kemp's ridley, leatherback, and loggerhead) of sea turtle. In April 2006, a total of 23 species occurring within the state were on the threatened and endangered species list of the US Fish and Wildlife Service. These included 20 animal (vertebrates and invertebrates) and 3 plant species. Among those listed were the Louisiana black bear, bald eagle, Alabama heelsplitter, and red-cockaded woodpecker.

5ENVIRONMENTAL PROTECTION

Louisiana's earliest and most pressing environmental problem was the chronic danger of flooding by the Mississippi River. In April and May 1927, one of the worst floods in the state's history inundated more than 1,300,000 acres (526,000 hectares) of agricultural land, left 300,000 people homeless, and would have swept away much of New Orleans had levees below the city not been dynamited. The following year, the US Congress funded construction of a system of floodways and spillways to divert water from the Mississippi when necessary. These flood control measures and dredging for oil and gas exploration created another environmental problem—the slowing of the natural flow of silt into the wetlands. As a result, salt water from the Gulf of Mexico has seeped into the wetlands.

The city of New Orleans suffered a major environmental disaster under Hurricane Katrina, which swept through the area in September 2005. High winds and flooding eventually led to a breach in the levees around New Orleans, allowing flood waters to cover about 80% of the city, with depths as high as 20 ft (6.3 m). Hundreds of homes, industries, and other public buildings were destroyed releasing a myriad of contaminants into the air, water, and soil. As of early 2006, environmental cleanup and damage assessments were still underway.

In 1984, Louisiana consolidated much of its environmental protection efforts into a new state agency—The Department of Environmental Quality (DEQ). Among its responsibilities are maintenance of air and water quality, solid-waste management, hazardous waste disposal, and control of radioactive materials. According to the Louisiana Environmental Action Plan (LEAP to 2000 Project), toxic air pollution, industrial and municipal waste-water discharges, and coastal wetland loss head the list of state residents' environmental concerns. Louisiana's problem in protecting its wetlands differs from that of most other states in that its wetlands are more than wildlife refuges—they are central to the state's agriculture and fishing industries. Assessment of the environmental impact of various industries on the wetlands has been conducted under the Coastal Zone Management Plan of the Department of Natural Resources.

The two largest wildlife refuges in the state are the Rockefeller Wildlife Refuge, comprising 84,000 acres (34,000 hectares) in Cameron and Vermilion parishes, and the Marsh Island Refuge, 82,000 acres (33,000 hectares) of marshland in Iberia Parish. Both are managed by the Department of Wildlife and Fisheries. Louisiana's coastal marshes represent almost 40% of such lands in the country. Catahoula Lake, located in LaSalle and Rapides parishes, was designated as a Ramsar Wetland of International Importance in 1991, primarily for its role as a habitat for migratory birds. The site is managed jointly by the US Fish and Wildlife Service, the US Army Corps of Engineers, and the Louisiana Department of Wildlife and Fisheries. In 1996, wetlands, which once covered more than half the state, accounted for about one-third of Louisiana's land.

With approximately 100 major chemical and petrochemical manufacturing and refining facilities located in Louisiana, many DEQ programs deal with the regulation of hazardous waste generation, management and disposal, and chemical releases to the air and water. Trends in air monitoring have, for example, continued to show decreases in criteria pollutants. In 1993, Louisiana became one of the first states in the nation to receive federal approval for stringent new solid waste landfill regulations, and the department has developed a Statewide Solid Waste Management Plan which encourages waste reduction. In 2003, Louisiana had 155 hazardous waste sites included in the US Environment Protection Agency (EPA) database, 11 of which were included on the National Priorities List as of 2006, including the Louisiana Army Ammunition Plant in Doyline. Nine sites were deleted from the National Priority List in 2006, but three new sites were proposed. In 2005, federal EPA grants awarded to the state included $14.8 million for the state revolving loan program (in support of water quality projects) and $2.4 million for water pollution control projects in urban and agricultural settings.

In 2003, 126.8 million lb of toxic chemicals were released in the state. Of the total river miles in the state impacted by pollution, 69% of the pollution is due to nonpoint sources such as agricultural and urban runoff. Efforts by DEQ to curb nonpoint source pollution have included the support and cooperation of the agricultural community and other state and federal agencies.

Among the most active citizen's groups on environmental issues are the League of Women Voters, the Sierra Club (Delta Chapter), and the Louisiana Environmental Action Network (LEAN). Curbside recycling programs exist in 28 parishes.

6POPULATION

Louisiana ranked 24th in population in the United States with an estimated total of 4,523,628 in 2005, an increase of 1.2% since 2000. Between 1990 and 2000, Louisiana's population grew from

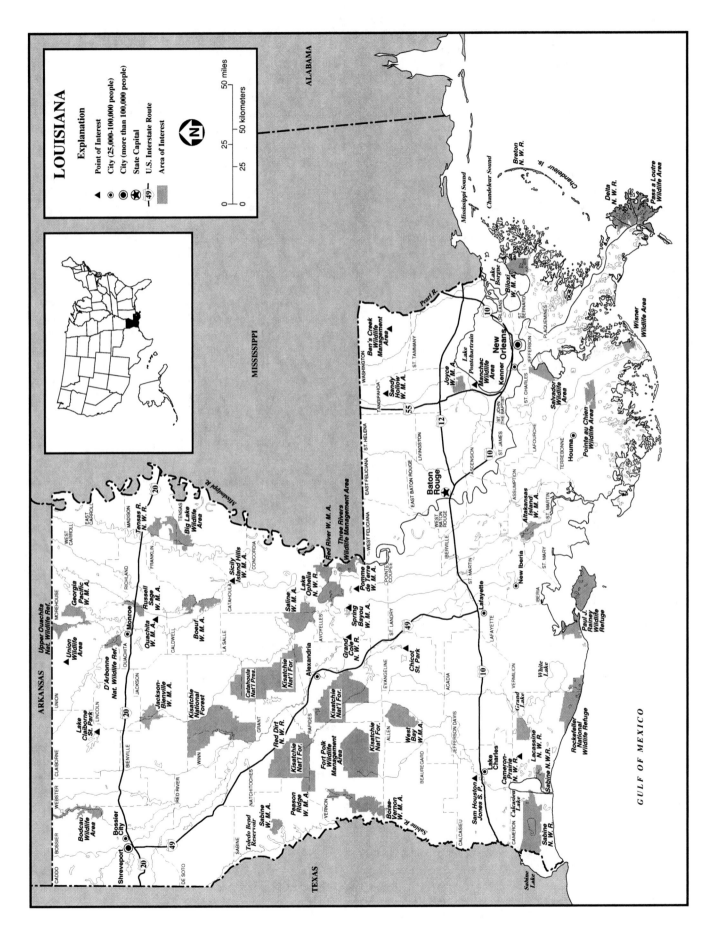

4,219,973 to 4,468,976, an increase of 5.9%. The population is projected to reach 4.67 million by 2015 and 4.76 million by 2025.

At the time of the 1980 census, Louisiana ranked 19th among the 50 states, with a population of 4,203,972, representing an increase of more than 15% since 1970. However, by 1990 the population was 4,219,973, representing only a 0.3% gain, and ranking had slipped to 21st. The population density in 2004 was 104.2 persons per sq mi.

In 2004 the median age was 35.2. Persons under 18 years old accounted for 25.8% of the population while 11.7% was age 65 or older.

New Orleans is the largest city, with an estimated 2004 population of 462,269, followed by Baton Rouge, 224,097; and Shreveport, 198,675. Baton Rouge, the capital, had grown with exceptional speed since 1940, when its population was 34,719; however, since 1980, the population has been decreasing. Among the state's largest metropolitan areas are New Orleans, with an estimated 1,319,589, and Baton Rouge, with 728,731.

[7] ETHNIC GROUPS

Louisiana, most notably the Delta region, is an enclave of ethnic heterogeneity in the South. At the end of World War II, the established population of the Delta, according to descent, included blacks, French, Spanish (among them Central and South Americans and Islenos, Spanish-speaking migrants from the Canary Islands), Filipinos, Italians, Chinese, American Indians, and numerous other groups.

Blacks made up about 32.5% of the population in 2000 (the second-highest percentage among the 50 states), and were estimated to number 1,451,944. They include descendants of "free people of color," some of whom were craftsmen and rural property owners before the Civil War (a few were slaveholding plantation owners). Many of these, of mixed blood, are referred to locally as "colored Creoles" and have constituted a black elite in both urban and rural Louisiana. The black population of New Orleans constituted 67.3% of the city's residents in 2000; New Orleans elected its first black mayor, Ernest N. "Dutch" Morial, in 1977. In 2004, 33% of the state's population was black.

Two groups that have been highly identified with the culture of Louisiana are Creoles and Acadians (also called Cajuns). Both descend primarily from early French immigrants to the state, but the Cajuns trace their origins from the mainly rural people exiled from Acadia (Nova Scotia) in the 1740s, while the Creoles tend to be city people from France and, to a lesser extent, from Nova Scotia or Hispaniola. (The term "Creole" also applies to the relatively few early Spanish settlers and their descendants.) Although Acadians have intermingled with Spaniards and Germans, they still speak a French patois and retain a distinctive culture and cuisine. In 2000, 179,739 residents claimed Acadian/Cajun ancestry. In 2000, 107,738, or 2.4% of the population, were Hispanic or Latino. That figure had risen to 2.8% of the population by 2004.

At the time of the 2000 census, 115,885 Louisianians (2.6% of the population) were foreign born. France, Germany, Ireland, and the United Kingdom provided Louisiana with the largest ancestry groups. As of 2000, there were 25,477 American Indians in Louisiana, along with 54,758 and Asians, including 24,358 Vietnamese. Pacific Islanders numbered 1,240. In 2004, 0.6% of the population was American Indian, 1.4% Asian, and 0.8% of the population claimed origin of two or more races.

[8] LANGUAGES

White settlers in Louisiana found several Indian tribes of the Caddoan confederacy, from at least five different language groups. In 1990, about 495 Louisiana residents spoke an American Indian language at home. Place-names from this heritage include Coushatta, Natchitoches, and Ouachita.

Louisiana English is predominantly Southern. Notable features of the state's speech patterns are *pen* and *pin* as sound-alikes and, in New Orleans, the so-called Brooklyn pronunciation of *bird* as /boyd/. A pecan sugar candy is well known as *praline*.

In 2000, 3,771,003 Louisiana residents—90.8% of the population five years old and older (up from 89.9% in 1990)—spoke only English at home.

Unique to Louisiana is a large enclave, west of New Orleans, where a variety of French called Acadian (Cajun) is the first language. From it, and from early colonial French, English has taken such words as *pirogue* (dugout canoe), *armoire* (wardrobe), *boudin* (blood sausage), and *lagniappe* (extra gift).

The following table gives selected statistics from the 2000 Census for language spoken at home by persons five years old and over. The category "African languages" includes Amharic, Ibo, Twi, Yoruba, Bantu, Swahili, and Somali.

LANGUAGE	NUMBER	PERCENT
Population 5 years and over	**4,153,367**	**100.0**
Speak only English	3,771,003	90.8
Speak a language other than English	382,364	9.2
Speak a language other than English	**382,364**	**9.2**
French (incl. Patois, Cajun)	194,314	4.7
Spanish or Spanish Creole	105,189	2.5
Vietnamese	23,326	0.6
German	8,047	0.2
Chinese	5,731	0.1
Arabic	5,489	0.1
French Creole	4,470	0.1
Italian	3,730	0.1
Tagalog	3,335	0.1
Korean	2,402	0.1
African languages	2,278	0.1

[9] RELIGIONS

Spanish missionaries brought Roman Catholicism to Louisiana in the early 16th century, and many of them were killed in their attempts to convert the Indians. During the early days, the most active religious orders were the Jesuits, Capuchins, and Ursuline nuns. Until the Louisiana Purchase, the public practice of any but the Catholic religion was prohibited, and Jews were entirely banned.

Joseph Willis, a mulatto preacher who conducted prayer meetings at what is now Lafayette in 1804, organized the first Baptist church west of the Mississippi, at Bayou Chicot in 1812. In the Opelousas region, in 1806, the first Methodist church in the state was organized. The first Episcopal church was established in New Orleans in 1805, a Methodist church in 1813, a Presbyterian church in 1817, a synagogue in 1828, and a Baptist church in 1834. After the Civil War, blacks withdrew from white-dominated churches to form their own religious groups, mainly Baptist and Methodist.

The Roman Catholic Church is the largest Christian denomination, with 1,312,237 church members statewide in 2004; the archdiocese of New Orleans had 488,004 members that year. One of the leading Protestant denominations is the Southern Baptist Convention, with 768,587 members in 2000 and 13,391 newly baptized members reported in 2002. The United Methodist Church had about 127,059 members statewide in 2004. Other Protestant denominations (with 2000 membership data) include Assemblies of God, 49,041, and the Episcopal Church, 33,653. There were about 16,500 Jews residing in Louisiana in 2000, a majority of them in New Orleans. The Muslim community had about 13,050 members. Voodoo, in some cases blended with Christian ritual, is more widespread in Louisiana than anywhere else in the United States, although the present number of practitioners is impossible to ascertain. Over 1.8 million people (about 41.2% of the population) did not claim any religious affiliation in the 2000 survey.

¹⁰TRANSPORTATION

New Orleans is a major center of domestic and international freight traffic. In volume of domestic and foreign cargo handled, however, the Port of South Louisiana, which stretches 54 miles along the Mississippi River, is the largest tonnage port in the Western Hemisphere and third in the world. Although Louisiana's roads remained poor until the 1930s, the state was one of the nation's major rail centers by the end of the 19th century, and New Orleans was one of the first cities to develop a mass transit system.

Several short-run railroads were built in Louisiana during the 1830s. The first of these, and the first rail line west of the Alleghenies, was the Pontchartrain Railroad, which opened, using horse-drawn vehicles, on 23 April 1831. New Orleans was connected with New York before the Civil War, with Chicago by 1873, and with California in 1883 via a line that subsequently became part of the Southern Pacific. Railroads soon rivaled the Mississippi River in the movement of goods to and from New Orleans. There were six Class I line-haul railroads in Louisiana in 2003. Total railroad mileage was 3,426 route mi (5,515 km), of which 2,788 miles (4,488 km) was Class I right-of-way. Chemicals that same year, were the top commodity originating in the state that were transported by rail. As of 2006, Amtrak provided connecting passenger service to Los Angeles, Chicago, and New York, carrying passengers from seven stations through the state. The New Orleans and Carrollton Railroads, a horse-drawn trolley system, began service in 1835. Fifty-nine years later, electric trolleys came into use.

Louisiana's first road-building boom began after Huey Long entered the statehouse. When Long took office in 1928, the state had no more than 300 mi (480 km) of paved roads. By 1931 there were 1,583 mi (2,548 km). At the end of 2004, Louisiana had a total of 60,941 mi (98,115 km) of public roads, most of them rural. Also that year, there were 1.926 million automobiles and 1.747 million trucks registered in the state, with 3,169,627 drivers' licenses in force.

Early in the nation's history, the Mississippi River emerged as the principal route for north–south traffic, and New Orleans soon became the South's main port. The advent of the steamboat in 1812 solved the problem of upstream navigation, which previously had required three or four months for a distance that could be covered downstream in 15 days. (Barges moved by towboats eventually supplanted steamboats as cargo carriers.) An important breakthrough in international transportation was the deepening of the channel at the mouth of the Mississippi by means of jetties, the first of which were completed in 1879. The port of New Orleans is served by more than 100 steamship lines, 20 common carrier lines, and about 100 contract carrier barge lines. The Louisiana Offshore Oil Port (LOOP), the first deepwater oil port in the United States, was opened in 1981. Located south of New Orleans in the Gulf of Mexico, the supertanker facility has a designed capacity of 1,400,000 barrels of oil a day. Large ports include Baton Rouge, with a tonnage of 57.082 million tons in 2004 (tenth-busiest port in the United States); New Orleans, with 78.085 million tons (seventh-busiest in the United States); and the Port of Plaquemines, with 54.404 million tons (13th busiest). The Port of South Louisiana in that same year handled 224.187 million tons was the busiest port in the United States. Louisiana in 2004 had 2,823 mile (4,545 km) of navigable inland waterways. In 2003, waterborne shipments totaled 469.461 million tons.

In 2005, Louisiana had a total of 495 public and private-use aviation-related facilities. This included 242 airports, 237 heliports, and 16 seaplane bases. The state's busiest airport was the Louis Armstrong New Orleans International Airport. In 2004, the airport had 4,839,400 enplanements, making it the 40th-busiest airport in the United States.

¹¹HISTORY

The region now known as Louisiana is largely the creation of the Mississippi River; the process of land building still goes on in the Atchafalaya Basin and below New Orleans on the Mississippi Delta. Louisiana was never densely inhabited in prehistoric times, and at no time, probably, did as many as 15,000 Indians live inside the present boundaries of the state. The main relic of prehistoric inhabitants is the great earthwork at Poverty Point, near Marksville, but other Indian mounds are to be found in alluvial and coastal regions.

When white exploration and settlement of North America began, various tribes of Caddo Indians inhabited northwestern Louisiana, and small Tunican-speaking groups lived in the northeast. In the southwest were a number of rather primitive people of the Atakapa group; in south-central Louisiana, the Chitimacha ranged through the marshes and lowlands. Various small Muskogean tribes, related to the Choctaw, lived east of the Mississippi in the "Florida parishes," so called because they were once part of Spanish West Florida. The Natchez Indians, whose main villages were in present-day Mississippi near the city that still bears their name, fought with the French settlers in Louisiana's early history but were exterminated in the process.

Several Spanish explorers sailed along the coast of Louisiana, but Hernando de Soto was probably the first to penetrate the state's present boundaries, in 1541. Almost a century and a half passed before Robert Cavelier, Sieur de la Salle, departing from Canada, reached the mouth of the Mississippi on 9 April 1682, named the land there Louisiana in honor of King Louis XIV, and claimed it for France. La Salle's later attempt at a permanent settlement failed, but in 1699 an expedition headed by Pierre le Moyne, Sieur d'Iberville, made a settlement on Biloxi Bay. In 1714, Louis Juchereau de St. Denis established Natchitoches, the first permanent European settlement in Louisiana; Iberville's brother, the Sieur de Bienville, established New Orleans four years later.

Louisiana did not thrive economically under French rule, either as a royal colony or, from 1712 to 1731, under the proprietorship first of Antoine Crozat and then of John Law's Company of the Indies. On the other hand, French culture was firmly implanted there, and non-French settlers, especially Germans from Switzerland and the Rhineland, were quickly Gallicized. In 1762, on the verge of losing the rest of its North American empire to Great Britain in the French and Indian War, France ceded Louisiana to Spain. Governed by Spaniards, the colony was much more prosperous, although it was a burden on the Spanish treasury. New settlers—Americans, Spaniards, Canary Islanders, and, above all, Acadian refugees from Nova Scotia—added to the population. By 1800 there were about 50,000 inhabitants, a considerable number of them black slaves imported from Africa and the West Indies. The availability of slave labor, Eli Whitney's invention of the cotton gin, and Étienne de Boré's development of a granulation process for making cane sugar set the stage for future prosperity, though not under Spanish auspices. In 1800, by the secret Treaty of San Ildefonso, Napoleon forced the feeble Spanish government to return Louisiana to France. Three years later, having failed to reestablish French rule and slavery in Haiti, Napoleon sold Louisiana to the United States to keep it from falling into the hands of Great Britain.

President Thomas Jefferson concluded what was probably the best real estate deal in history, purchasing 800,000 sq mi (2,100,000 sq km) for $15,000,000 and thus more than doubling the size of the United States at a cost of about 3 cents per acre. He made William C. C. Claiborne the governor of the huge new acquisition. The next year, that part of the purchase south of 33°N was separated from the remainder and designated the Territory of Orleans. The people of the territory then began the process of learning self-government, something with which they had had no experience under France and Spain. After the census of 1810 showed that the population had risen to 76,556, the people were authorized by Congress to draw up a state constitution. The constitutional convention met under the presidency of Julian Poydras in a coffeehouse in New Orleans and adopted, with a few changes, the constitution then in effect in Kentucky. In the meantime, in 1810, a revolt against Spain had taken place in West Florida. When the proposed Louisiana constitution reached Washington, Congress added that part of West Florida between the Mississippi and Pearl rivers to the new state, which entered the Union on 30 April 1812.

The key event in the Americanization of Louisiana was the campaign for New Orleans in December 1814 and January 1815, actually fought after the War of 1812 had ended. A force of British veterans under General Sir Edward Pakenham sailed into Lake Borgne and established itself below New Orleans at Chalmette. There they were met by detachments of Creoles, Acadians, blacks, and even Jean Lafitte's pirates, all from Louisiana, as well as Tennesseans, Kentuckians, and Choctaw Indians, with the whole army under the command of Andrew Jackson. After several preliminary battles, the British were bloodily defeated when they launched an all-out assault on Jackson's line.

From 1815 to 1861, Louisiana was one of the most prosperous states in the South, producing sugar and cotton on its rich alluvial lands and grazing hogs and cattle in the wooded hills of the north and on the prairies of the southwest. Yeoman farmers and New Orleans workers far outnumbered the wealthy planters but the planters, whose slaves made up almost half the population, dominated Louisiana politically and economically. When the secession crisis came in 1861, the planters led Louisiana into the Confederacy and, after four bloody years, to total defeat. The state suffered crippling economic losses during the Civil War, but the greatest loss was the lives of tens of thousands of young white men who died in defense of the South, and of thousands of blacks who died seeking and fighting for freedom. Louisiana did not fully recover from this disaster until the mid-20th century.

After the Civil War, radical Republican governments elected by black voters ruled the state, but declining support from the North and fierce resistance from Louisiana whites brought the Reconstruction period to an end. Black people and their few white allies lost control of state government, and most of the former slaves became laborers on sugar plantations or sharecroppers in the cotton fields. There, as the years passed, they were joined by more and more landless whites. In 1898, blacks were disfranchised almost entirely by a new state constitution drawn up primarily for that purpose. This constitution also significantly reduced the number of poorer whites who voted in Louisiana elections.

The vast majority of Louisiana whites—whether hill farmers, Cajuns along the southern rivers and bayous, lumbermen in the yellow pine forests, or workers in New Orleans—were little better off than the black or white sharecroppers. Many economic changes had taken place: rice had become a staple crop on the southwestern prairies, and an oil boom had begun after the turn of the century. But just as before the Civil War, large landowners—combined with New Orleans bankers, businessmen, and politicians—dominated state government, effectively blocking political and social reform. The Populist movement, which succeeded in effecting some change in other southern states, was crushed in Louisiana.

Not until 1928, with the election of Huey P. Long as governor, did the winds of change strike Louisiana; having been so long delayed, they blew with gale force. The years from 1928 through 1960 could well be called the Long Era: three Longs—Huey, who was assassinated in 1935; his brother Earl, who served as governor three times; and Huey's son Russell, who became a powerful US senator—dominated state politics for most of the period. From a backward agricultural state, Louisiana evolved into one of the world's major petrochemical-manufacturing centers. Offshore drilling sent clusters of oil wells 60 mi (97 km) out into the Gulf. The pine lands were reforested, and soybeans provided a new source of income. What had been one of the most parsimonious states became one of the most liberal in welfare spending, care for the aged, highway building, and education. The state could afford these expanding programs because of ever-increasing revenues from oil and gas.

In the mid-1980s, a drop in world oil prices rocked Louisiana's economy, hurting the oil exploration and service industries and raising the state's unemployment rate in 1986 to 13%, the highest in the nation. For most of the 1990s, in spite of an increase in service-sector and high-tech jobs, Louisiana had more people living in poverty than any other state. Louisiana had for decades been among the nation's poorest; the percentage of residents living in poverty in 1998 was 19.1%, making it the second-poorest state in the nation. In 1999 it was reported that Louisiana also ranked second-lowest in the nation for its care of children; the report took into account such factors as infant mortality rates, teen pregnancy rates, and children who lived in poverty or lacked health care. Other problems confronting the state at the turn of the century included racial tensions, disposing of toxic wastes from the petrochemical industry, depletion of oil and gas resources, and the ongoing struggle to institute good government.

The announcement in February 1985 by Russell B. Long, senator since 1948, that he would not seek reelection, and the indictment of former Governor Edwin W. Edwards by a federal grand jury on conspiracy charges during the same month, caused turmoil in Louisiana's political arena. Edwards was defeated in 1987 by Buddy Roemer, a young, well-educated Republican who promised to clean up government. In 1989, racial tensions surfaced when white supremacist David Duke, running as a Republican, narrowly won a seat in the Louisiana state legislature. Duke later ran unsuccessfully for the US Senate and for governor, but his runs for office had raised concerns about the level of frustration of many white voters. In 1995 gubernatorial candidate Murphy "Mike" Foster, Republican, promised more Roemer-like reforms. As he faced reelection four years later, some analysts said the Bayou State had made progress in building a trustworthy and responsive government. Nevertheless, Foster was criticized for favoring the oil industry and being soft on big gambling. He still managed to win another term, claiming 64% of the vote, becoming the first Republican governor in Louisiana history to be reelected. He offered the New Orleans Saints professional football team $186.5 million in subsidies in 2002 to keep the team from moving out of the state. Foster maintained the football team had a salutary effect on Louisiana's economy.

On 29 August 2005, Hurricane Katrina landed on the state, in what was one of the worst natural disasters in US history. New Orleans had been evacuated, but some 150,000 people were unable to leave before the storm hit. A day after the storm appeared to have bypassed the city's center, levees were breached by the storm surge and water submerged the metropolis. Those unable to leave the city were sheltered in the Louisiana Superdome and New Orleans Convention Center; air conditioning, electricity, and running water failed, making for unsanitary and uncomfortable conditions. They were later transferred to other shelters, including the Houston Astrodome. The costs of the hurricane and flooding were exceedingly high in terms of both loss of life and economic damage: more than 1,000 people died and damages were estimated to reach $150 billion. Katrina had global economic consequences, as imports, exports, and oil supplies—including production, importation, and refining—were disrupted. The Federal Emergency Management Agency (FEMA) of the Department of Homeland Security, and President George W. Bush were criticized in varying degrees for their lack of adequate response to the disaster. Race and class issues also came to the fore, as the majority of New Orleans residents unable to evacuate the city and affected by the catastrophe were poor and black.

12 STATE GOVERNMENT

Louisiana has had 11 constitutions (more than any other state), the latest, as of 2006, was enacted in 1974. By January 2005 it had been amended 129 times. The state legislature consists of a 39-member Senate and a 105-member House of Representatives. The legislature meets annually, beginning the last Monday in March

in even-numbered years and on the last Monday in April in odd-numbered years. The even-numbered year session is limited to 60 legislative days in 85 calendar days; the odd-numbered year session is limited to 45 legislative days in 60 calendar days. Special sessions may be called by a majority petition of each house, with length limited to 30 calendar days. All legislators are elected for concurrent four-year terms; they must be at least 18 years old, qualified voters, and have resided in the state for two years and in their districts for at least one year preceding election. The legislative salary in 2004 was $16,800.

Statewide elected executive officials include the governor and lieutenant governor (separately elected), secretary of state, attorney general, treasurer, commissioner of agriculture, commissioner of insurance, and commissioner of elections. All are elected for four-year terms. The governor must be a qualified elector, be at least 25 years old, and a US and Louisiana citizen for five years preceding election; after two full consecutive terms, a governor may not run for reelection. The same eligibility requirements apply to the lieutenant governor, except that there is no limit on succession to the latter office. As of December 2004, the governor's salary was $94,532. Other executive agencies are the State Board of Elementary and Secondary Education, whose eight elected members and three appointed members serve four-year terms, and the Public Service Commission, whose five members serve for six years.

To become law, a bill must receive majority votes in both the Senate and the House and be signed by the governor, be left unsigned (for 10 days when the legislature is in session or for 20 days following the legislature's adjournment) but not vetoed by the governor, or be passed again by two-thirds votes of elected members of both houses over the governor's veto. Appropriation bills must originate in the House but may be amended by the Senate. The governor has an item veto on appropriation bills. Constitutional amendments require approval by two-thirds of the elected members of each house and ratification by a majority of the people voting on it at the next general election.

Voters in Louisiana must be US citizens, 18 years old, and state residents. Restrictions apply to convicted felons and those declared mentally incompetent by the court.

13 POLITICAL PARTIES

The major political organizations are the Democratic Party and the Republican Party, each affiliated with the national party. However, differences in culture and economic interests have made Louisiana's politics extremely complex. Immediately following statehood, the primary political alignment was according to ethnic background, Anglo or Latin. By the 1830s, however, Louisiana politics reflected the national division of Jacksonian Democrats and National Republicans, who were by mid-decade replaced by the Whigs. By and large, the Whigs were favored by the Anglo-Americans while the Democrats were favored by those of French and Spanish descent. When the Whig Party fell apart over slavery, many former Whigs supported the Native American (Know-Nothing) Party.

Louisiana was one of the three southern states whose disputed electoral votes put Republican Rutherford B. Hayes in the White House in 1877, in return for his agreement to withdraw federal troops from the South, thus putting an end to Reconstruction. The ensuing period of Bourbon Democratic dominance in Louisiana, a time of reaction and racism in politics (though a few blacks continued to hold office), lasted until the early 1890s, when worsening economic conditions inspired Populists and Republicans to challenge Democratic rule. The attempt failed largely because Democratic landowners were able to control the ballots of their black sharecroppers and "vote" them Democrats. The recognition that it was the black vote, however well-controlled, that held the balance in Louisiana politics impelled the Democrats to seek its elimination as an electoral factor. The constitution of 1898 imposed a poll tax, a property requirement, a literacy test, and other measures that succeeded in reducing the number of registered black voters from 130,000 at the beginning of 1897 to 5,320 in March 1900 and 1,342 by 1904. White registration also declined, from 164,000 in 1897 to 92,000 in 1904, because the new constitutional requirements tended to disfranchise poor whites as well as blacks.

Between 1900 and 1920, the New Orleans Ring, or Choctaw Club, was the dominant power in state politics. Growing political discontent led 5,261 Louisianians (6.6% of those voting) to cast their ballots for the Socialist presidential candidate in 1912. A few Socialists won local office that year in Winn Parish, a center of Populist activity in the 1890s and the birthplace of Huey Long in 1893.

During his relatively brief career as a member of the Railroad Commission, governor, and US senator, Long committed government resources to public service to an extent without precedent in the state. He also succeeded in substituting for the traditional Democratic Party organization a state machine geared primarily toward loyalty to himself and, after his assassination in 1935, to the Long family name, which kept its hold on the voters despite a series of scandals that publicized the corruption of his associates. When blacks began voting in increasing numbers during the

1940s, they tended to favor Democratic candidates from the Long camp. The Longs repaid their loyalty: when race became a bitterly divisive issue in the late 1940s and 1950s—Louisiana gave its presidential vote to the States' Rights "Dixiecrat" candidate in 1948— the Longs supported the national Democratic ticket.

The 1960s and 1970s saw a resurgence of the Republican Party and the election in 1979 of David C. Treen, the state's first Republican governor since Reconstruction. Treen was succeeded by Democrat Edwin Edwards in 1983, Democrat Charles Roemer in 1987, and Edwin Edwards again in 1991. In 1995, Louisiana elected another Republican governor—Murphy J. "Mike" Foster, who was reelected in 1999. Foster was unable to run for reelection in November 2003, due to term limits. In 2003, Democrat Kathleen Babineaux Blanco won the governor's election, and became Louisiana's first female governor. In 2004 there were 2,806,000 registered voters. In 1998, 62% of registered voters were Democratic, 21% Republican, and 16% unaffiliated or members of other parties.

In 2005, US senators from Louisiana were Republican David Vitter (elected in 2004) and Democrat Mary L. Landrieu (elected 1996 to replaced retiring Senator J. Bennett Johnston Jr. and reelected in 2002). Landrieu is the daughter of former New Orleans mayor Moon Landrieu. Following the 2004 elections Louisiana's delegation of US representatives consisted of two Democrats and five Republicans. In mid-2005, 24 of the state senators were Democrats and 15 were Republicans; 67 of the state representatives were Democrats and 37 were Republicans.

In 2000 and 2004, Louisianians gave Republican George W. Bush 53% and 56% of the vote, respectively in the presidential elections, while Democrat Al Gore received 45% (2000) and Dem-

Louisiana Presidential Vote by Political Parties, 1948–2004

YEAR	ELECTORAL VOTE	LOUISIANA WINNER	DEMOCRAT	REPUBLICAN	STATES' RIGHTS DEMOCRAT	PROGRESSIVE	AMERICAN IND.
1948	10	Thurmond (SRD)	136,344	72,657	204,290	3,035	—
1952	10	Stevenson (D)	345,027	306,925	—	—	—
					UNPLEDGED		
1956	10	*Eisenhower (R)	243,977	329,047	44,520	—	—
					NAT'L STATES' RIGHTS		
1960	10	*Kennedy (D)	407,339	230,980	169,572	—	—
1964	10	Goldwater (R)	387,068	509,225	—	—	—
1968	10	Wallace (AI)	309,615	257,535	—	—	530,300
					AMERICAN	SOC. WORKERS	
1972	10	*Nixon (R)	298,142	686,852	44,127	12,169	—
					LIBERTARIAN	COMMUNIST	
1976	10	*Carter (D)	661,365	587,446	3,325	7,417	10,058
						CITIZENS	
1980	10	*Reagan (R)	708,453	792,853	8,240	1,584	10,333
1984	10	*Reagan (R)	651,586	1,037,299	1,876	9,502	—
						POPULIST	NEW ALLIANCE
1988	10	*Bush (R)	717,460	883,702	4,115	18,612	2,355
						IND. (Perot)	AMERICA FIRST
1992	9	*Clinton (D)	815,971	733,386	3,155	211,478	18,545
1996	9	*Clinton (D)	927,837	712,586	7,499	123,293	—
						GREEN	REFORM
2000	9	*Bush, G. W. (R)	792,344	927,871	2,951	20,473	14,356
					THE BETTER LIFE (Nader)		CONSTITUTION (Peroutka)
2004	9	*Bush, G. W. (R)	820,299	1,102,169	2,781	7,032	5,203

*Won US presidential election.

ocrat John Kerry received 42% (2004). The state had nine electoral votes in the 2004 presidential election.

¹⁴LOCAL GOVERNMENT

The ecclesiastical districts, called parishes, into which Louisiana was divided in the late 17th century remain the primary political divisions in the state, serving functions similar to those of counties in other states.

In 2005, there were 64 parishes, most of them governed by police jury (governing board). Juries range from 3 to 15 elected members. Other parish officials are the sheriff, clerk of court, assessor, and coroner. Each parish elects a school board whose members generally serve six-year terms; all other officers serve four-year terms. In 2005, there were 78 public school districts in the state.

As of 2005, Louisiana also had 302 municipal governments. Municipalities are classed by the state (based on population) as village, town, or city. Municipal officials include the mayor, chief of police, and council or board of aldermen. In 2005, Louisiana had 45 special districts established by the legislature.

In 2005, local government accounted for about 192,400 full-time (or equivalent) employment positions.

¹⁵STATE SERVICES

To address the continuing threat of terrorism and to work with the federal Department of Homeland Security, homeland security in Louisiana operates under the authority of state statute and executive order; the adjutant general is designated as the state homeland security advisor.

Louisiana's ethics laws are administered by the Board of Ethics under the Department of Civil Service. Departments focus on labor, natural resources, revenue, environmental quality, social services, state civil service, wildlife and fisheries, and youth services.

Educational services are provided through the Department of Education, which has jurisdiction over elementary, secondary, higher, and vocational-technical instruction, as well as the state schools for the visually impaired, hearing-impaired, and other handicapped children. Highways, waterways, airports, and mass transit are the province of the Department of Transportation and Development. Environmental affairs, conservation, forestry, and mineral resources are the responsibility of the Department of Natural Resources. The Motor Vehicle Office, Fire Protection Office, Emergency Preparedness Office, and Alcoholic Beverage Control Office are all within the Department of Public Safety.

Health services are administered mainly through the Department of Health and Hospitals (DHH), including Medicare, Medicaid, mental health services, services for citizens with developmental disabilities, and public health services. Such programs as supplemental food stamps, child welfare services, and services for the disabled, blind, and deaf, are administered by the Department of Social Services.

¹⁶JUDICIAL SYSTEM

Louisiana's legal system is the only one in the United States to be based on civil or Roman law, specifically the Code Napoléon of France. Under Louisiana state law, cases may be decided by judicial interpretation of the statutes, without reference to prior court cases, whereas in other states and in the federal courts the common law prevails, and decisions are generally based on previous judicial interpretations and findings. In actual practice, Louisiana laws no longer differ radically from US common law, and most Louisiana lawyers and judges now cite previous cases in their arguments and rulings.

The highest court in Louisiana is the Supreme Court, with appellate jurisdiction. It consists of a chief justice who is chosen by seniority of service, and seven associate justices, all of them elected from six supreme court districts (the first district has two judges) for staggered 10-year terms. There are five appellate circuits in the state, each divided into three districts; the five circuits are served by 54 judges, all of them elected for overlapping 10-year terms. Each of the state's district courts serves at least one parish and has at least one district judge, elected for a six-year term; there are 222 district judges. District courts have original jurisdiction in criminal and civil cases. City courts are the principal courts of limited jurisdiction.

Louisiana may have been the first state to institute a system of leasing convict labor. Large numbers of convicts were leased, especially after the Civil War, until the practice was discontinued in the early 1900s. The abuses entailed in this system may be suggested by the fact that, of 700 convicts leased in 1882, 149 died in service.

As of 31 December 2004, a total of 36,939 prisoners were held in Louisiana's state and federal prisons, an increase from 36,047 of 2.5% from the previous year. As of year-end 2004, a total of 2,386 inmates were female, down from 2,405 or 0.8% from the year before. Among sentenced prisoners (one year or more), Louisiana had an incarceration rate of 816 people per 100,000 population in 2004, the highest in the United States.

According to the Federal Bureau of Investigation, Louisiana in 2004, had a violent crime rate (murder/nonnegligent manslaughter; forcible rape; robbery; aggravated assault) of 638.7 reported incidents per 100,000 population, or a total of 28,844 reported incidents. Crimes against property (burglary; larceny/theft; and motor vehicle theft) in that same year totaled 199,153 reported incidents or 4,410.2 reported incidents per 100,000 people. Louisiana has a death penalty, of which lethal injection is the sole method of execution. From 1976 through 5 May 2006, the state has executed 27 persons, although there were no executions in 2005, or in 2006 (as of 5 May). As of 1 January 2006, Louisiana had 85 inmates on death row.

Judges may also impose sentences of hard labor.

In 2003, Louisiana spent $530,079,419 on homeland security, an average of $117 per state resident.

¹⁷ARMED FORCES

In 2004, the US Department of Defense had 33,000 personnel in Louisiana including 22,254 active-duty military and 3,315 civilians. There was one major army installation in the state, Ft. Polk at Leesville; an Air Force base at Barksdale near Bossier City; and a naval air station and support station in the vicinity of New Orleans. During fiscal year 2004, Louisiana firms received defense contracts totaling $2.5 billion. In addition, $1.8 billion in defense payroll, including retired military pay, was paid in the state.

There were 366,957 veterans of US military service in Louisiana as of 2003, of whom 48,602 served in World War II; 37,321 in the Korean conflict; 109,441 during the Vietnam era; and 66,646 during the Persian Gulf War. Expenditures on veterans during fiscal year 2004 amounted to $1.1 billion.

As of 31 October 2004, the Louisiana State Police employed 1,199 full-time sworn officers.

[18] MIGRATION

Louisiana was settled by an unusually diverse assortment of immigrants. The Company of the Indies, which administered Louisiana from 1717 until 1731, at first began importing French convicts, vagrants, and prostitutes because of the difficulty of finding willing colonists. Next the company turned to struggling farmers in Germany and Switzerland, who proved to be more suitable and productive settlers. The importation of slaves from Africa and the West Indies began early in the 18th century.

Attracted by generous land grants, perhaps 10,000 Acadians, or Cajuns—people of French descent who had been exiled from Nova Scotia (Acadia) during the 1740s—migrated to Louisiana after the French and Indian War. They settled in the area of Lafayette and Breaux Bridge and along Bayou Lafourche and the Mississippi River. Probably the second-largest group to migrate in the late 18th century came from the British colonies and, after the Revolution, from the United States. Between 1800 and 1870, Americans settled the area north of the Red River. Small groups of Canary Islanders and Spaniards from Malaga also settled in the south, and in 1791, a number of French people fled to Louisiana during the slave insurrection on Hispaniola.

During the 1840s and 1850s, masses of Irish and German immigrants came to New Orleans. In the late 1880s, a large number of Midwestern farmers migrated to the prairies of southwestern Louisiana to become rice farmers. Louisiana did not immediately begin losing much of its black population after the Civil War. In fact, the number of blacks who migrated to Louisiana from the poorer southeastern states during the postwar years may have equaled the number of blacks who migrated before the war or were brought into the state as slaves. In 1879, however, "Kansas fever" struck blacks from the cotton country of Louisiana and Mississippi, and many of them migrated to the Wheat State; however, many later returned to their home states.

Beginning in World War II, large numbers of both black and white farm workers left Louisiana and migrated north and west. During the 1960s, the state had a net out-migration of 15% of its black population, but the trend had slowed somewhat by 1975.

Recent migration within the state has been from north to south, and from rural to urban areas, especially to Shreveport, Baton Rouge, and the suburbs of New Orleans. From 1980 to 1990, however, the state's urban population fell from 68.6% to 68.1% Overall, Louisiana suffered a net loss from migration of about 368,000 from 1940 to 1990. Between 1990 and 1998, the state had a net loss of 117,000 in domestic migration and a net gain of 25,000 in international migration. In 1998, 2,193 foreign immigrants arrived in Louisiana. Between 1990 and 1998, the state's overall population increased 3.5%. In the period 2000–05, net international migration was 20,174 and net internal migration was -89,547, for a net loss of 69,373 people.

[19] INTERGOVERNMENTAL COOPERATION

Among the interstate and regional efforts in which Louisiana participates are the Central Interstate Low-Level Radioactive Waste Compact, Interstate Oil and Gas Compact, Interstate Compact for Juveniles, Gulf States Marine Fisheries Commission, Red River Compact, Sabine River Compact, Tangipahoa River Waterway Compact, South Central Interstate Forest Fire Protection Compact, Southern Growth Policies Board, Southern Dairy Compact, Southern Rapid Rail Transit Compact, Southern States Energy Board, and Southern Regional Education Board. Federal grants to Louisiana during fiscal year 2005 amounted to $6.6 billion; that figure rose to an estimated $6.897 billion in fiscal year 2006 and an estimated $6.949 billion in fiscal year 2007.

[20] ECONOMY

Before the Civil War, when Louisiana was one of the most prosperous of southern states, its economy depended primarily on two then-profitable crops—cotton and sugar—and on its position as the anchor of the nation's principal north–south trade route. But the upheaval and destruction wrought by the war, combined with severe flood damage to cotton crops, falling cotton prices, and the removal of the federal bounty on sugar, left the economy stagnant through the end of the 19th century, although New Orleans retained its commercial importance as an exporter of cotton and grain.

With the addition of two major crops, rice and soybeans, the rebirth of the timber industry as a result of reforestation, the demand for pine for paper pulp, and most dramatically, the rise of the petrochemical industry, Louisiana's economy has regained much of its former vitality. Today, Louisiana ranks second only to Texas in the value of its mineral products.

Louisiana is primarily an industrial state, but its industries are to a large degree based on its natural resources, principally oil, natural gas, water, and timber. This reliance on a natural resource-based industrial sector has come at a price. These industries, and the state's economy, are subject to sharp commodity price swings, leading to a boom and bust cycle, particularly in the oil and natural gas sectors, as well as in those industries that are heavily reliant upon the price of oil and natural gas. A booming oil industry in the 1970s fueled an expansion in Louisiana's economy, but that expansion ended in the early 1980s, when the price of oil dropped from $37 a barrel in 1981 to $15 a barrel in 1986. Employment in oil and gas extraction consequently dropped from 100,000 to 55,000. In addition, energy-related industries such as barge building, machinery manufacturing, and rig/platform production also suffered. At the same time that oil prices dropped, natural gas prices rose, forcing a contraction in the chemical industry which uses large quantities of natural gas. Chemicals were also hurt by a leap in the exchange value of the dollar in the mid-1980s, as Louisiana exports a large part of its chemical production. A subsequent drop in the dollar's exchange value in the late 1980s and early 1990s enabled the chemical industry not only to rebound, but to expand. A higher dollar in the late 1990s once again reversed the chemical industry's growth. In an attempt to offset losses in employment, Louisiana built several riverboat casinos and a land-based casino in 1995 which added about 7,000 jobs. The oil and gas extraction sector, however, continued to grow in both absolute and relative terms. While Louisiana has also seen growth in the state's various service sectors, output from manufacturing as a percent of gross state product has decreased from 16.8% in 1997 to 7.5% in 2004. During the national recession in 2001, employment gains continued in health services, lodging establishments, state services, and in the transportation and public utilities sector. In August 2005, the state, along with the city and port of New Orleans, and the oil and natural gas industries were severely affected by Hurricane Katrina, and it was expected to take years for the state to recover from the damage inflicted.

Louisiana's gross state product (GSP) in 2004 totaled $152.944 billion, of which mining (about 99% is oil and gas production) contributed $19.669 billion or 12.8% of GSP, followed by real estate at $15.354 billion (10% of GSP), and manufacturing (durable and nondurable goods) at $11.522 billion (7.5% of GSP). In that same year, there were an estimated 347,436 small businesses in Louisiana. Of the 96,084 businesses that had employees, a total of 93,742 or 97.6% were small companies. An estimated 9,875 new businesses were established in the state in 2004, up 6.2% from the year before. Business terminations that same year came to 9,668, down 20.6% from 2003. There were 622 business bankruptcies in 2004, up 24.6% from the previous year. In 2005, the state's personal bankruptcy (Chapter 7 and Chapter 13) filing rate was 649 filings per 100,000 people, ranking Louisiana as the 17th-highest in the nation.

21 INCOME

In 2005 Louisiana had a gross state product (GSP) of $166 billion which accounted for 1.3% of the nation's gross domestic product and placed the state at number 24 in highest GSP among the 50 states and the District of Columbia.

According to the Bureau of Economic Analysis, in 2004 Louisiana had a per capita personal income (PCPI) of $27,297. This ranked 43rd in the United States and was 83% of the national average of $33,050. The 1994–2004 average annual growth rate of PCPI was 4.0%. Louisiana had a total personal income (TPI) of $123.0 billion, which ranked 25th in the United States and reflected an increase of 5.9% from 2003. The 1994–2004 average annual growth rate of TPI was 4.4%. Earnings of persons employed in Louisiana increased from $86.9 billion in 2003 to $91.3 billion in 2004, an increase of 5.1%. The 2003–04 national change was 6.3%.

The US Census Bureau reports that the three-year average median household income for 2002 to 2004 in 2004 dollars was $35,523 compared to a national average of $44,473. During the same period an estimated 17.0% of the population was below the poverty line as compared to 12.4% nationwide.

22 LABOR

According to the Bureau of Labor Statistics (BLS), in April 2006 the seasonally adjusted civilian labor force in Louisiana was 1,872,700, with approximately 90,100 workers unemployed, yielding an unemployment rate of 4.8%, compared to the national average of 4.7% for the same period. Preliminary data for the same period placed nonfarm employment at 1,759,500. Since the beginning of the BLS data series in 1976, the highest unemployment rate recorded in Louisiana was 12.9% in September 1986. The historical low was 4.3% in February 2006. Preliminary nonfarm employment data by occupation for April 2006 showed that approximately 6% of the labor force was employed in construction; 8.1% in manufacturing; 20.5% in trade, transportation, and public utilities; 5.3% in financial activities; 9.6% in professional and business

services; 11.9% in education and health services; 9.6% in leisure and hospitality services; and 21% in government.

During the antebellum period, Louisiana had both the largest slave market in the United States—New Orleans—and the largest slave revolt in the nation's history, in St. Charles and St. John the Baptist parishes in January 1811. New Orleans also had a relatively large free black population, and many of the slaves in the city were skilled workers, some of whom were able to earn their freedom by outside employment. Major efforts to organize Louisiana workers began after the Civil War. There were strikes in the cane fields in the early 1880s, and in the mid-1880s, the Knights of Labor began to organize the cane workers. The strike they called in 1886 was ended by hired strikebreakers, who killed at least 30 blacks. Back in New Orleans, the Knights of Labor led a general strike in 1892. The Brotherhood of Timber Workers began organizing in 1910 but had little to show for their efforts except the scars of violent conflict with the lumber-mill owners.

A right-to-work law was passed in 1976, partly as a result of violent conflict between an AFL-CIO building trades union and an independent union over whose workers would build a petrochemical plant near Lake Charles. In 1979, a police strike began in New Orleans on the eve of Mardi Gras, causing the cancellation of most of the parades, but it collapsed the following month.

The BLS reported that in 2005, a total of 114,000 of Louisiana's 1,778,000 employed wage and salary workers were formal members of a union. This represented 6.4% of those so employed, down from 7.6% in 2004, and below the national average of 12%. Overall in 2005, a total of 132,000 workers (7.4%) in Louisiana were covered by a union or employee association contract, which includes those workers who reported no union affiliation. Louisiana is one of 22 states with a right-to-work law.

As of 1 March 2006, Louisiana did not have a state-mandated minimum wage law. Employees in that state however, were covered under federal minimum wage statutes. In 2004, women in the state accounted for 47.8% of the employed civilian labor force.

23 AGRICULTURE

With a farm income of $2.1 billion in 2005—57% from crops—Louisiana ranked 34th among the 50 states. Nearly every crop grown in North America can be raised somewhere in Louisiana. In the south are strawberries, oranges, sweet potatoes, and truck crops; in the southeast, sugarcane; and in the southwest, rice and soybeans. Soybeans—which were introduced into Louisiana after World War I—are also raised in the cotton-growing area of the northeast and in a diagonal belt running east-northwest along the Red River. Oats, alfalfa, corn, potatoes, and peaches are among the other crops grown in the north.

As of 2004, there were an estimated 27,200 farms covering 7.85 million acres (3.18 million hectares) with an average farm size of 290 acres (117 hectares). Louisiana ranked second in the United States in sugar cane production. Cash receipts for the sugar crop in 2003 amounted to $304.2 million 10,320,000 tons. Louisiana ranked third in the value of its rice production in 2004, $223.9 million for 28,522,000 hundredweight (a unit of measure equal to 100 lb); and eighth for upland cotton in 2004, $200.5 million for 885,000 bales.

[24] ANIMAL HUSBANDRY

In the mid-19th century, before rice production began there, southwestern Louisiana was a major cattle-raising area. Today, cattle are raised mainly in the southeast (between the Mississippi and Pearl rivers), in the north-central region, and in the west.

In 2005, there were an estimated 860,000 cattle and calves worth $670.8 million. In 2004, Louisiana had an estimated 16,000 hogs and pigs worth around $1.7 million. Dairy farmers had an estimated 43,000 milk cows, which produced 519 million lb (236 million kg) of milk in 2003. Also during 2003, poultry farmers produced an estimated 7.5 million lb (3.4 million kg) of chicken, which sold for $631,000, and an estimated 487 million eggs worth around $35.9 million.

[25] FISHING

In 2004, Louisiana was second behind only Alaska in the size and value of its commercial landings, with nearly 1.1 billion lb (500 million kg) valued at $274.4 million. Leading ports in volume were Empire-Venice (379 million lb/172 million kg, third in the nation), Intracoastal City (301.8 million lb/137.2 million kg, fifth in the nation), and Cameron (243.1 million lb/110.5 million kg, sixth in the nation). In value, Empire-Venice was sixth in the nation with $60.2 million and Dulac-Chauvin was 11th with $42.8 million.

The most important species caught in Louisiana are shrimp, hard blue crab, and oysters. In 2004, shrimp landings in Louisiana amounted to 134.3 million lb/61 million kg), the highest in the nation. Hard blue crab landings in the state accounted for 26% of the national total. In 2002, the state commercial fleet had 8,874 boats and 2,084 vessels. In 2003, there were 90 processing and 114 wholesale plants in the state.

Louisiana produces most of the US crawfish harvest. With demand far exceeding the natural supply, crawfish farming began about 1959. In 2004, 1,126 crawfish farms covered some 118,250 acres (47,856 hectares), producing 69.5 million lb (28.1 million kg). Spring water levels of the state's Atchafalaya Basin cause the wild crawfish harvest to vary from year to year. Catfish are also cultivated in Louisiana, on 38 farms covering some 7,600 acres (3,075 hectares) in 2005, with a 2006 inventory of about 18.4 million fingerlings and 12.2 million stocker-sized catfish. Cash receipts from sales of catfish were $14.3 million in 2004.

The Natchitoches National Fish Hatchery focuses on paddlefish, striped bass, and pallid sturgeon, but also raises largemouth bass, bluegill, and catfish in limited quantities.

Louisiana had 639,139 sport fishing license holders in 2004.

[26] FORESTRY

As of 2004, there were 14,017,000 acres (5,673,000 hectares) of forestland in Louisiana, representing over half the state's land area and 2% of all US forests. The principal forest types are loblolly and shortleaf pine in the northwest, longleaf and slash pine in the south, and hardwood in a wide area along the Mississippi River. More than 99% of Louisiana's forests are commercial timberland, over 90% of it privately owned. Lumber production totaled 1.52 billion board feet in 2004.

Louisiana has one national forest, Kisatchie, with a gross area of 1,022,373 acres (413,754 hectares) within its boundaries; gross acreage of National Forest System lands in the state was 2,049,000 acres (829,000 hectares) in 2005. Near the boundaries of Kisatchie's Evangeline Unit is the Alexander State Forest, established in 1923.

[27] MINING

According to preliminary data from the US Geological Survey (USGS), the estimated value of nonfuel mineral production by Louisiana in 2003 was $331 million, an increase from 2002 of about 6%. The USGS data ranked Louisiana as 34th among the 50 states by the total value of its nonfuel mineral production, accounting for around 1% of total US output.

Salt was the state's leading nonfuel mineral commodity in 2003, accounting for about 41% of all nonfuel mineral production (by value) that year. It was followed by construction sand and gravel, which accounted for 32% of all nonfuel mineral output (by value), crushed stone, industrial sand and gravel (about 4% of output by value), and lime. According to preliminary data, the production of salt in 2003 totaled 12.1 million metric tons and was valued at $135 million, while the output of construction sand and gravel totaled 19.7 million metric tons, with a value of $107 million. Industrial sand and gravel output in 2003 totaled 529,000 metric tons and was valued at $11.8 million, according to the preliminary data. Louisiana in 2003 was the largest salt producing state in the United States.

[28] ENERGY AND POWER

As of 2003, Louisiana had 43 electrical power service providers, of which 22 were publicly owned and 13 were cooperatives. Of the remainder, five were investor owned, and three were owners of independent generators that sold directly to customers. As of that same year there were 2,131,340 retail customers. Of that total, 1,611,090 received their power from investor-owned service providers. Cooperatives accounted for 366,208 customers, while publicly owned providers had 153,740 customers. There were 302 independent generator or "facility" customers.

Total net summer generating capability by the state's electrical generating plants in 2003 stood at 25.748 million kW, with total production that same year at 94.885 billion kWh. Of the total amount generated, 45.8% came from electric utilities, with the remainder (54.2%) coming from independent producers and combined heat and power service providers. The largest portion of all electric power generated, 45.434 billion kWh (47.9%), came from natural gas fired plants, with coal-fired plants in second place at 22.888 billion kWh (24.1%) and nuclear fueled plants in third at 16.126 billion kWh (17%). Other renewable power sources accounted for 3.3%% of all power generated, with petroleum fired plants at 3.1%, plants using other types of gases at 2.8%, hydroelectric at 0.9% and "other" types of generating facilities at 0.8%.

As of 2006, Louisiana had two nuclear power plants: the River Bend plant in West Feliciana, near Baton Rouge; and the Waterford plant near Taft, in St. Charles Parish.

Oil and gas production has expanded greatly since World War II, but production reached its peak in the early 1970s and proven reserves are declining. As of 2004, Louisiana had proven crude oil reserves of 427 million barrels, or 2% of all proven US reserves, while output that same year averaged 228,000 barrels per day. Including federal offshore domains, the state that year ranked eighth (seventh excluding federal offshore) in proven reserves and fifth (fourth excluding federal offshore) in production among the 31 producing states. In 2004 Louisiana had 19,970 producing oil wells and accounted for 4% of all US production. As of 2005, the state's 17 refineries had a combined crude oil distillation capacity of 2,772,723 barrels per day.

In 2004, Louisiana had 20,734 producing natural gas and gas condensate wells. In that same year, marketed gas production (all gas produced excluding gas used for repressuring, vented and flared, and nonhydrocarbon gases removed) totaled 1,357.366 billion cu ft (38.5 billion cu m). As of 31 December 2004, proven reserves of dry or consumer-grade natural gas totaled 9,588 billion cu ft (272.2 billion cu m).

Louisiana in 2004, had two producing coal mines, both of which were surface operations. Coal production that year totaled 3,805,000 short tons, down from 4,028,000 short tons in 2003. One short ton equals 2,000 lb (0.907 metric tons).

29INDUSTRY

According to the US Census Bureau's Annual Survey of Manufactures (ASM) for 2004, Louisiana's manufacturing sector covered some 19 product subsectors. The shipment value of all products manufactured in the state that same year was $124.304 billion. Of that total, petroleum and coal products manufacturing accounted for the largest share at $53.365 billion. It was followed by chemical manufacturing at $39.911 billion; transportation equipment manufacturing at $7.369 billion; food manufacturing at $6.601 billion; and paper manufacturing at $4.456 billion.

In 2004, a total of 140,985 people in Louisiana were employed in the state's manufacturing sector, according to the ASM. Of that total, 103,159 were actual production workers. In terms of total employment, the chemical manufacturing industry accounted for the largest portion of all manufacturing employees at 22,903 with 14,458 actual production workers. It was followed by fabricated metal product manufacturing at 19,992 employees (15,284 actual production workers); transportation equipment manufacturing at 19,184 employees (14,788 actual production workers); food manufacturing at 17,607 employees (12,995 actual production workers); and paper manufacturing with 8,680 employees (6,964 actual production workers).

ASM data for 2004 showed that Louisiana's manufacturing sector paid $6.704 billion in wages. Of that amount, the chemical manufacturing sector accounted for the largest share at $1.630 billion. It was followed by transportation equipment manufacturing at $940.776 million; fabricated metal product manufacturing at $793.515 million; petroleum and coal products manufacturing at $774.905 million; and food manufacturing at $517.504 million.

The Standard Oil Refinery (now owned by Exxon) that is today the largest in North America began operations in Louisiana in 1909, the same year construction started on the state's first long-distance oil pipeline. Since then, a huge and still-growing petrochemical industry has become a dominant force in the state's economy. Other expanding industries are wood products and, especially since World War II, shipbuilding.

The principal industrial regions extend along the Mississippi River from north of Baton Rouge to New Orleans, and also include the Monroe, Shreveport, Morgan City, and Lake Charles areas.

30COMMERCE

According to the 2002 Census of Wholesale Trade, Louisiana's wholesale trade sector had sales that year totaling $47.1 billion from 5,904 establishments. Wholesalers of durable goods accounted for 3,672 establishments, followed by nondurable goods wholesalers at 1,987 and electronic markets, agents, and brokers accounting for 245 establishments. Sales by durable goods wholesalers in 2002 totaled $15.2 billion, while wholesalers of nondurable goods saw sales of $28.9 billion. Electronic markets, agents, and brokers in the wholesale trade industry had sales of $3.01 billion.

In the 2002 Census of Retail Trade, Louisiana was listed as having 17,613 retail establishments with sales of $41.8 billion. The leading types of retail businesses by number of establishments were: gasoline stations (2,545); food and beverage stores (2,336); clothing and clothing accessories stores (2,299); and motor vehicle and motor vehicle parts dealers (1,998). In terms of sales, motor vehicle and motor vehicle parts stores accounted for the largest share of retail sales at $11 billion, followed by general merchandise stores at $7.8 billion; food and beverage stores at $5.4 billion; gasoline stations at $4.3 billion; and building material/garden equipment and supplies dealers at $3.3 billion. A total of 228,290 people were employed by the retail sector in Louisiana that year.

Exporters located in Louisiana exported $19.2 billion in merchandise during 2005.

31CONSUMER PROTECTION

Consumer protection is the responsibility of the Consumer Protection Section, which is under the state's Office of the Attorney General. The section investigates and mediates consumer complaints, takes action against companies allegedly engaging in unfair business practices, distributes consumer publications, and registers multi-level marketing, telemarketing, and charitable organizations, as authorized by the state's Unfair and Deceptive Trade Practices Act. However, the section does not handle the areas of insurance, banking, or utilities.

When dealing with consumer protection issues, the state's Attorney General's Office can initiate civil and criminal proceedings; represent the state before state and federal regulatory agencies; administer consumer protection and education programs; handle formal consumer complaints; and exercise broad subpoena powers. However, the Attorney General's office cannot represent individual consumers. In antitrust actions, the Attorney General's Office can act on behalf of those consumers who are incapable of acting on their own; initiate damage actions on behalf of the state in state courts; and represent counties, cities, and other governmental entities in recovering civil damages under state or federal law. However, the Office cannot file for criminal proceedings for antitrust actions.

The offices of the Consumer Protection Section of the Attorney General's Office is located in Baton Rouge. A county government office is also located in the city of Gretna.

32BANKING

As of June 2005, Louisiana had 164 insured banks, savings and loans, and saving banks, plus 53 state-chartered and 201 federally chartered credit unions (CUs). Excluding the CUs, the New Orleans-Metairie-Kenner market area accounted for the largest portion of the state's financial institutions and deposits in 2004, with 42 institutions and $20.066 billion in deposits. As of June 2005, CUs accounted for 8.9% of all assets held by all financial institutions in the state, or some $5.986 billion. Banks, savings and loans, and savings banks collectively accounted for the remaining 91.1% or $61.010 billion in assets held.

Louisiana state-chartered banks are regulated by the Office of Financial Institutions under the Department of Economic Development. Federally chartered banks are regulated by the Office of the Comptroller of the Currency.

As of fourth quarter 2005, the median net interest margin (the difference between the lower rates offered to savers and the higher rates charged on loans), was 4.59%, up from 4.42% in 2004 and 4.40% in 2003. Prior to Hurricanes Katrina and Rita, 2005 was on track to be a record year for earnings by the financial institutions based in Louisiana. However, those insured institutions located in the most heavily impacted parishes, as of early 2006 continued to report significant decreases in profits. In fourth quarter 2005, median return on assets for those parishes was 0.46%.

33 INSURANCE

In 2004 there were over 4.6 million individual life insurance policies in force with a total value of over $179 billion; total value for all categories of life insurance (individual, group, and credit) was over $267 billion. The average coverage amount is $38,500 per policy holder. Death benefits paid that year totaled at about $910.6 million.

There were 58 life and health and 33 property and casualty insurance companies domiciled in the state at the end of 2003. In 2004, direct premiums for property and casualty insurance totaled $7.4 billion. That year, there were 380,192 flood insurance policies in force in the state, with a total value of $53.9 billion. About $1.2 billion of coverage was held in Beach and Windstorm plans and another $22.7 billion of coverage was held through FAIR plans, which are designed to offer coverage for some natural circumstances, such as wind and hail, in high risk areas.

In 2004, 48% of state residents held employment-based health insurance policies, 5% held individual policies, and 28% were covered under Medicare and Medicaid; 19% of residents were uninsured. Louisiana tied with four other states as having the fourth-highest percentage of uninsured residents in the nation. In 2003, employee contributions for employment-based health coverage averaged at 19% for single coverage. The average employee contribution for family coverage was one of the highest in the nation at 30%. The state offers a 12-month health benefits expansion program for small-firm employees in connection with the Consolidated Omnibus Budget Reconciliation Act (COBRA, 1986), a health insurance program for those who lose employment-based coverage due to termination or reduction of work hours.

In 2003, there were over 2.6 million auto insurance policies in effect for private passenger cars. Required minimum coverage includes bodily injury liability of up to $10,000 per individual and $20,000 for all persons injured in an accident, as well as property damage liability of $10,000. In 2003, the average expenditure per vehicle for insurance coverage was $1,013.93, the sixth-highest average in the nation.

The Department of Insurance administers Louisiana's laws governing the industry.

34 SECURITIES

There are no securities or commodities exchanges in Louisiana. In 2005, there were 670 personal financial advisers employed in the state and 1,340 securities, commodities, and financial services sales agents. In 2004, there were over 73 publicly traded companies within the state, with over 18 NASDAQ companies, 17 NYSE listings, and 5 AMEX listings. In 2006, the state had two Fortune 500 companies; Entergy (based in New Orleans) ranked first in the state and 218th in the nation with revenues of over $10.7 billion, followed by Freeport-McMoRan Copper and Gold, Inc. (New Orleans) at 480th in the nation. Shaw Group (Baton Rouge), CenturyTel (Monroe), and SCP Pool (Covington) were listed in the Fortune 1,000. SCP Pool is listed on NASDAQ and the others are listed with the NYSE.

35 PUBLIC FINANCE

The budget is prepared by the state executive budget director and submitted annually by the governor to the legislature for amendment and approval. The fiscal year (FY) runs from 1 July through 30 June.

Fiscal year 2006 general funds were estimated at $7.1 billion for resources and $6.7 billion for expenditures. In fiscal year 2004, federal government grants to Louisiana were $7.7 billion.

In the fiscal year 2007 federal budget, Louisiana was slated to receive: $37.5 million in incremental funding for a $150 million project for the construction of the 36-mile segment of I-49 between the Arkansas State line and I-220 in Shreveport; $25 million for planning, design, and science-related efforts to restore the Louisiana coastal wetlands and barrier island ecosystem.

36 TAXATION

In 2005, Louisiana collected $8,639 million in tax revenues or $1,910 per capita, which placed it 36th among the 50 states in per capita tax burden. The national average was $2,192 per capita. Property taxes accounted for 0.5% of the total, sales taxes 33.1%, selective sales taxes 20.0%, individual income taxes 27.7%, corporate income taxes 4.1%, and other taxes 14.6%.

As of 1 January 2006, Louisiana had three individual income tax brackets ranging from 2% to 6%. The state taxes corporations at rates ranging from 4% to 8% depending on tax bracket.

In 2004, state and local property taxes amounted to $2.5 billion or $502 per capita. The per capita amount ranks the state fifth-lowest nationally. Local governments collected $2.2 billion of the total and the state government $39.7 million.

Louisiana taxes retail sales at a rate of 4%. In addition to the state tax, local taxes on retail sales can reach as much as 6.25%, making for a potential total tax on retail sales of 10.25%. Food purchased for consumption off-premises is exempt from state tax, but subject to local taxes. The tax on cigarettes is 36 cents per pack, which ranks 42nd among the 50 states and the District of Columbia. Louisiana taxes gasoline at 20 cents per gallon. This is in addition to the 18.4 cents per gallon federal tax on gasoline.

According to the Tax Foundation, for every federal tax dollar sent to Washington in 2004, Louisiana citizens received $1.45 in federal spending.

Louisiana—State Government Finances

(Dollar amounts in thousands. Per capita amounts in dollars.)

	AMOUNT	PER CAPITA
Total Revenue	23,730,239	5,265.20
General revenue	19,156,139	4,250.31
Intergovernmental revenue	6,995,885	1,552.23
Taxes	8,030,495	1,781.78
General sales	2,680,716	594.79
Selective sales	1,929,796	428.18
License taxes	429,068	95.20
Individual income tax	2,192,038	486.36
Corporate income tax	236,745	52.53
Other taxes	562,132	124.72
Current charges	2,390,841	530.47
Miscellaneous general revenue	1,738,918	385.83
Utility revenue	4,870	1.08
Liquor store revenue	–	–
Insurance trust revenue	4,569,230	1,013.81
Total expenditure	20,471,959	4,542.26
Intergovernmental expenditure	4,410,251	978.53
Direct expenditure	16,061,708	3,563.72
Current operation	11,117,933	2,466.81
Capital outlay	1,303,178	289.15
Insurance benefits and repayments	2,459,609	545.73
Assistance and subsidies	501,576	111.29
Interest on debt	679,412	150.75
Exhibit: Salaries and wages	3,754,815	833.11
Total expenditure	20,471,959	4,542.26
General expenditure	18,007,725	3,995.50
Intergovernmental expenditure	4,410,251	978.53
Direct expenditure	13,597,474	3,016.97
General expenditures, by function:		
Education	6,433,899	1,427.53
Public welfare	4,122,416	914.67
Hospitals	1,648,253	365.71
Health	471,892	104.70
Highways	1,138,233	252.55
Police protection	259,125	57.49
Correction	608,725	135.06
Natural resources	396,585	87.99
Parks and recreation	214,417	47.57
Government administration	672,278	149.16
Interest on general debt	679,412	150.75
Other and unallocable	1,362,490	302.31
Utility expenditure	4,625	1.03
Liquor store expenditure	–	–
Insurance trust expenditure	2,459,609	545.73
Debt at end of fiscal year	10,182,940	2,259.36
Cash and security holdings	43,125,998	9,568.67

Abbreviations and symbols: – zero or rounds to zero; (NA) not available; (X) not applicable.

SOURCE: *U.S. Census Bureau, Governments Division, 2004 Survey of State Government Finances,* January 2006.

37 ECONOMIC POLICY

The Office of Commerce and Industry in the Department of Economic Development seeks to encourage investment and create jobs in the state and to expand the markets for Louisiana products. Financial assistance services for industrial development include state and local tax incentives and state "Enterprise Zone" legislation. The Louisiana Small Business Equity Corporation and the Louisiana Minority Business Development Authority offer financial assistance. Beginning in 1999, the Louisiana Economic Development Council prepared annual reports and action plans with a view to the implementation of the state's Master Plan for Economic Development dubbed Vision 2020. The three main goals of Vision 2020 were to, by 2020, recreate Louisiana as a place where all citizens are engaged in the pursuit of knowledge; create an economy driven by technology-intensive industries, and rank among the top 10 states in standard of living indicators. Successes in 2002 were reported in providing economic development incentives, and developing infrastructure for biosciences, information technology, research and development, and education.

With the devastation wrought by Hurricane Katrina and the breaching of the levees in New Orleans in 2005, Louisiana was faced with an entirely new economic development scenario. In September 2005, President George W. Bush announced he would create a Gulf Opportunity Zone for Louisiana, Mississippi, and Alabama. Businesses would be able to double to $200,000 the amount they could deduct from their taxes for investments in new equipment. It would also provide a 50% bonus depreciation and make loan guarantees available. Congress passed the Gulf Opportunity Zone Act in December 2005, which provides a number of tax incentives to encourage the rebuilding of areas ravaged by Hurricanes Katrina, Rita, and Wilma.

38 HEALTH

The infant mortality rate in October 2005 was estimated at 9.5 per 1,000 live births, representing the third-highest rate in the country (following the District of Columbia and Mississippi). The birth rate in 2003 was 14.5 per 1,000 population. The abortion rate stood at 13 per 1,000 women in 2000. In 2003, about 84.1% of pregnant woman received prenatal care beginning in the first trimester. In 2004, approximately 75% of children received routine immunizations before the age of three.

The crude death rate in 2003 was 9.5 deaths per 1,000 population. As of 2002, the death rates for major causes of death (per 100,000 resident population) were: heart disease, 249.5; cancer, 210.6; cerebrovascular diseases, 57.9; chronic lower respiratory diseases, 37.8; and diabetes, 39.6. Louisiana had the second-highest diabetes death rate in the nation, following West Virginia. The state also had the second-highest homicide death rate at 13.5 per 100,000 population (following the District of Columbia at 40.1 per 100,000); the national average death rate by homicide is 6.1 per 100,000. The mortality rate from HIV infection was 8.1 per 100,000 population. In 2004, the reported AIDS case rate was at about 22.4 per 100,000 population, the fifth-highest rate in the nation. In 2002, about 58.4% of the population was considered overweight or obese. As of 2004, about 23.4% of state residents were smokers.

In 2003, Louisiana had 127 community hospitals with about 17,800 beds. There were about 690,000 patient admissions that year and 10.8 million outpatient visits. The average daily inpatient census was about 10,600 patients. The average cost per day for hospital care was $1,177. Also in 2003, there were about 314 certified nursing facilities in the state with 38,397 beds and an overall occupancy rate of about 75.9%. In 2004, it was estimated that about 68.2% of all state residents had received some type of dental care within the year. Louisiana had 262 physicians per 100,000 resident population in 2004 and 873 nurses per 100,000 in 2005. In 2004, there were a total of 2,040 dentists in the state.

About 28% of state residents were enrolled in Medicaid and Medicare programs in 2004. Approximately 19% of the state population was uninsured in 2004. In 2003, state health care expenditures totaled $6.3 million.

39 SOCIAL WELFARE

In 2004, about 90,000 people received unemployment benefits, with the average weekly unemployment benefit at $195. In fiscal year 2005, the estimated average monthly participation in the food stamp program included about 807,896 persons (318,126 households); the average monthly benefit was about $100.96 per person. That year, the total of benefits paid through the state for the food stamp program was about $978.7 million.

Temporary Assistance for Needy Families (TANF), the system of federal welfare assistance that officially replaced Aid to Families with Dependent Children (AFDC) in 1997, was reauthorized through the Deficit Reduction Act of 2005. TANF is funded through federal block grants that are divided among the states based on an equation involving the number of recipients in each state. Louisiana's TANF cash assistance program is called the Family Independent Temporary Assistance Program (FITAP), and the work program is called FIND Work (Family Independence Work Program). In 2004, the state program had 46,000 recipients; state and federal expenditures on this TANF program totaled $73 million fiscal year 2003.

In December 2004, Social Security benefits were paid to 739,180 Louisiana residents. This number included 377,770 retired workers, 104,640 widows and widowers, 109,910 disabled workers, 57,750 spouses, and 89,110 children. Social Security beneficiaries represented 16.4% of the total state population and 90.3% of the state's population age 65 and older. Retired workers received an average monthly payment of $888; widows and widowers, $826; disabled workers, $887; and spouses, $438. Payments for children of retired workers averaged $420 per month; children of deceased workers, $563; and children of disabled workers, $253. Federal Supplemental Security Income payments in December 2004 went to 169,549 Louisiana residents, averaging $391 a month. An additional $38,000 of state-administered supplemental payments were distributed to 4,797 residents.

40 HOUSING

The Indians of Louisiana built huts with walls made of clay kneaded with Spanish moss and covered with cypress bark or palmetto leaves. The earliest European settlers used split cypress boards filled with clay and moss; a few early 18th-century houses with clay and moss walls remain in the Natchitoches area. Examples of later architectural styles also survive, including buildings constructed of bricks between heavy cypress posts, covered with plaster; houses in the raised cottage style, supported by brick piers and usually including a wide gallery and colonettes; the Creole dwellings of the Vieux Carre in New Orleans, built of brick and characterized by balconies and French windows; and urban and plantation houses from the Greek Revival period of antebellum Louisiana.

In 2004, Louisiana had an estimated 1,919,859 housing units, of which 1,713,680 were occupied. About 66.2% were owner-occupied. An estimated 65.7% of all units were single-family, detached homes. Nearly 39% of all housing units were built between 1970 and 1989. Most units relied on utility gas or electricity for heating. It was estimated that 121,505 units lacked telephone service, 7,424 lacked complete plumbing facilities, and 8,581 lacked complete kitchen facilities. The average household had 2.56 members.

In 2004, 23,000 privately owned units were authorized for construction. The median home value was $95,910. The median monthly cost for mortgage owners was $902. Renters paid a median of $540 per month. In September 2005, the state received a grant of $300,000 from the US Department of Housing and Urban Development (HUD) for rural housing and economic development programs. For 2006, HUD allocated to the state over $29.3 million in community development block grants (CDGB). New Orleans received over $15.4 million in CDBG grants the same year. Also in 2006, HUD offered an additional $6.2 billion to the state in emergency funds to rebuild housing that was destroyed by Hurricanes Katrina, Rita, and Wilma in late 2005.

41 EDUCATION

Most education in Louisiana was provided through private (often parochial) schools until Reconstruction. Not until Huey Long's administration, when spending for education increased greatly and free textbooks were supplied, did education become a high priority of the state. As of 2004, 78.7% of Louisianians 25 years and older had completed high school, well below the national average of 84%. Some 22.4% had completed four or more years of college, below the national average of 26%.

Integration of New Orleans public schools began in 1960; two years later, the archbishop of New Orleans required that all Catholic schools under his jurisdiction be desegregated. However, it took a federal court order in 1966 to bring about integration in public schools throughout the state. By 1980, 36% of minority students in Louisiana were in schools with less than 50% minority enrollment, and 25% were in schools with 99–100% minority enrollment.

The total enrollment for fall 2002 in Louisiana's public schools stood at 730,000. Of these, 537,000 attended schools from kindergarten through grade eight, and 194,000 attended high school. Approximately 48.5% of the students were white, 47.7% were black, 1.8% were Hispanic, 1.3% were Asian/Pacific Islander, and 0.7% were American Indian/Alaskan Native. Total enrollment was estimated at 709,000 in fall 2003 and was expected to be 707,000 by fall 2014, a decline of 3.3% during the period 2002 to 2014. Expenditures for public education in 2003–04 were estimated at $5.7 billion. In fall 2003, there were 140,492 students enrolled in 440 private schools. Since 1969, the National Assessment of Educational Progress (NAEP) has tested public school students nationwide. The resulting report, The Nation's Report Card, stated that in 2005 eighth graders in Louisiana scored 268 out of 500 in mathematics compared with the national average of 278.

As of fall 2002, there were 232,140 students enrolled in college or graduate school; minority students comprised 34.7% of total postsecondary enrollment. As of 2005, Louisiana had 90 degree-granting institutions. There are 16 public four-year schools, 46 public two-year institutions, and 10 private four-year nonprofit institutions. The center of the state university system is Louisiana State University (LSU), founded at Baton Rouge; LSU also has campuses at Alexandria, Eunice, and Shreveport, and includes the University of New Orleans. Tulane University, founded in New

Orleans in 1834, is one of the most distinguished private universities in the South, as is Loyola University, also in New Orleans. Southern University Agricultural and Mechanical System at Baton Rouge (1881) is one of the largest predominantly black universities in the country; other campuses are in New Orleans and Shreveport. Another mainly black institution is Grambling State University (1901).

The Louisiana Student Financial Assistance Commission and the Louisiana Tuition Trust Authority administer state loan, grant, and scholarship programs managed by the Louisiana Office of Student Financial Assistance. The state Council for the Development of French in Louisiana (CODOFIL) organizes student exchanges with Quebec, Belgium, and France and aids Louisianians studying French abroad.

⁴²ARTS

The Louisiana Division of the Arts (LDOA; est. 1977), the largest arts grantmaker in the state, is an agency of the state Office of Cultural Development, Department of Culture, Recreation and Tourism. In the aftermath of Hurricanes Katrina and Rita of 2005, the LDOA worked with the Louisiana Partnership for the Arts to assess the impact these disasters had on the art communities. Arts projects are funded in every parish (county) in the state through the LDOA Decentralized Arts Funding Program. In 2005, Louisiana arts organizations received 24 grants totaling $1,150,100 from the National Endowment for the Arts.

The Louisiana Endowment for the Humanities was established in 1971. As of 2006, ongoing programs included "Relic: Readings in Literature and Culture" and "Prime Time Family Reading Time." In 2005, the National Endowment for the Humanities awarded 17 grants totaling $2,037,337 to state organizations.

New Orleans has long been one of the most important centers of artistic activity in the South. The earliest theaters were French, and the first of these was started by refugees from Hispaniola, who put on the city's first professional theatrical performance in 1791. The American Theater, which opened in 1824, attracted many of the finest actors in America, as did the nationally famous St. Charles. Showboats traveled the Mississippi and other waterways, bringing dramas, musicals, and minstrel shows to river towns and plantations as early as the 1840s, with their heyday being the 1870s and 1880s.

Principal theaters included the New Orleans Theater of the Performing Arts, the Saenger Theater in New Orleans (one of the "grand old theaters"), the Tulane Theater, and Le Petit Theatre du Vieux Carre. Le Petit Theatre was established in 1916 and has been recognized as one of the leading community theaters in the nation. During the 2004–05 season Le Petit Theatre began a construction project on the main stage providing a complete orchestra pit, a new stage, and a fly loft—the stage had been unchanged since 1922. Junebug Productions is a black touring company based in New Orleans. Louisiana State University (LSU) at Baton Rouge has theaters for both opera and drama. Baton Rouge, Shreveport, Monroe, Lake Charles, and Hammond are among the cities with little theaters, and Baton Rouge, Lafayette, and Lake Charles have ballet companies. There are symphony orchestras in most of the larger cities, the Louisiana Philharmonic Orchestra (LPO) being the best known. Although Hurricane Katrina battered the state, devastating New Orleans in 2005, the LPO returned to New Orleans with a spring concert season during March, April, and May 2006.

It is probably in music that Louisiana has made its most distinctive contributions to culture. Jazz was born in New Orleans around 1900; among its sources was the music played by brass bands at carnivals and at Negro funerals, and its immediate precursor was the highly syncopated music known as ragtime. Early jazz in the New Orleans style is called Dixieland; Louis Armstrong pioneered the transformation of jazz from the Dixieland ensemble style to a medium for solo improvisation. Traditional Dixieland has been played by performers associated with the Preservation Hall, Dixieland Hall, and the New Orleans Jazz Club. In 2005, many of the buildings that housed these organizations and clubs were either severely damaged or destroyed by the forces of Hurricane Katrina. Despite having to close buildings, groups like the Hall Jazz Band of the Preservation Hall continued touring; the Preservation Hall celebrated its 45th anniversary on tour in 2006. Equally distinctive is Cajun music, dominated by the sound of the fiddle and accordion.

Visual arts in the state flourish, especially in New Orleans, home to the Ogden Museum of Southern Art. Prompted by the devastation of Hurricane Katrina the museum showcased several special exhibits including, *Come Hell and High Water: Portraits of Hurricane Katrina Survivors, New Housing Prototypes for New Orleans,* and *Louisiana Story: A Photographic Journey.*

⁴³LIBRARIES AND MUSEUMS

For the calendar year 2001, Louisiana's 64 parishes were served by 65 public library systems, with a total of 329 libraries, of which 264 were branches. In that same year, the public library system had 10,850,000 volumes of books and serial publications on its shelves, and had a total circulation of 18,376,000. The system also had 230,000 audio and 309,000 video items, 13,000 electronic format items (CD-ROMs, magnetic tapes, and disks), and 30 bookmobiles. The New Orleans Public Library, with 14 branches and 739,473 books, features a special collection on jazz and folk music, and the Tulane University Library (1,765,000 volumes) has special collections on jazz and Louisiana history. Among the libraries with special black-studies collections are those of Grambling State University, Southern University Agricultural and Mechanical System at Baton Rouge, Xavier University of Louisiana at New Orleans, and the Amistad Collection at Tulane University. The library of Northwestern State University at Natchitoches has special collections on Louisiana history, folklore, Indians, botany, and oral history. In 2001, operating income for the state's public library system was $112,068,000, which included $107,000 in federal funds and $6,817,000 in state funds.

As of 2000, Louisiana had 89 museums and historic sites, as well as more than 27 art collections. Leading art museums are the New Orleans Museum of Art, the Lampe Gallery in New Orleans, and the R. W. Norton Art Gallery at Shreveport. The art museum of the Louisiana Arts and Science Center at Baton Rouge is located in the renovated Old Illinois Central Railroad Station. The oldest and largest museum in the state is the Louisiana State Museum, an eight-building historic complex in the Vieux Carre. There is a military museum in Beauregard House at Chalmette National Historical Park, on the site of the Battle of New Orleans, and a Confederate Museum in New Orleans. The Bayou Folk Museum at Cloutierville is in the restored home of author Kate Chopin; the Longfellow-Evangeline State Commemorative Area has a historical museum on its site. Among the state's scientific museums are the Lafayette Natural History Museum, Planetarium, and Nature Station, and the Museum of Natural Science in Baton Rouge. Audubon Park and Zoological Gardens are in New Orleans. The "Louisiana and Lower Mississippi Valley Collection" at LSU is an extensive collection of Louisiana history, photographs, and manuscripts.

44 COMMUNICATIONS

The second rural free delivery route in the United States, and the first in Louisiana, was established on 1 November 1896 at Thibodaux. As of 2004, 90.9% of Louisiana's occupied housing units had telephones. Additionally, by June of that same year there were 2,547,153 mobile wireless telephone subscribers. In 2003, 52.3% of Louisiana households had a computer and 44.1% had Internet access. By June 2005, there were 536,339 high-speed lines in Louisiana, 475,284 residential and 610,055 for business.

In 2005, the state had 77 major radio broadcasting stations (15 AM and 62 FM) as well as 32 television stations. In 1999, New Orleans had 629,820 television households, 76% of which had cable TV.

As of 2000, a total of 46,786 Internet domain names had been registered in Louisiana.

45 PRESS

At one time, New Orleans had as many as nine daily newspapers (four English, three French, one Italian, and one German), but by 1997 there was only one, the *Times-Picayune*. In 2005, Louisiana had a total of 15 morning dailies, 11 evening dailies, and 21 Sunday papers.

The following table shows the principal dailies with their approximate 2005 circulations:

AREA	NAME	DAILY	SUNDAY
Baton Rouge	*Advocate* (m,S)	87,026	115,442
New Orleans	*Times-Picayune* (m,S)	252,799	281,374
Shreveport	*Times* (m,S)	62,551	77,090

Two influential literary magazines originated in the state. The *Southern Review* was founded at Louisiana State University in the 1930s by Robert Penn Warren and Cleanth Brooks. The *Tulane Drama Review*, founded in 1955, moved to New York University in 1967 but is still known by its original acronym, *TDR*.

46 ORGANIZATIONS

In 2006, there were over 3,076 nonprofit organizations registered within the state, of which about 2,085 were registered as charitable, educational, or religious organizations. Among business or professional organizations with headquarters in Louisiana are the American Shrimp Processors Association and the Southern Pine Council. Blue Key, a national honor society, has its headquarters in Metairie. The American Bone Marrow Donor Registry is based in Mandeville.

State and local organization for the arts include the Acadiana Arts Council, the Louisiana Division of the Arts, the Louisiana Historical Association, the Louisiana Preservation Alliance, the New Orleans Jazz Club, the North Central Louisiana Arts Council, and the Northeast Louisiana Arts Council.

Civil rights groups represented in the state include the National Association for the Advancement of Colored People (NAACP) and the Urban League. Especially active during the 1970s were the local branches of the American Civil Liberties Union, the Louisiana Coalition on Jails and Prisons, and its legal arm, the Southern Prisoners Defense Council, and the Fishermen's and Concerned Citizens Association of Plaquemines Parish, which organized a campaign against the continued domination of the parish by the descendants of Leander Perez, a racist judge who wielded power there for 50 years until his death in 1969.

The Invisible Empire, Knights of the Ku Klux Klan, is headquartered in Denham Springs.

47 TOURISM, TRAVEL, AND RECREATION

In 2000, there were 15.4 million visitors to the state of Louisiana. Initial reports for 2001 estimated a total travel-related economic impact of $9 billion, including support for 124,200 jobs. The two most popular activities for tourists were shopping and gambling. However, in 2005 Hurricane Katrina devastated New Orleans and surrounding areas, and tourism was virtually eliminated. Because two-thirds of New Orleans was submerged, a majority of the population was forced to relocate, either temporarily or permanently. Tulane and Loyola universities were forced to cancel at least one semester of classes. Many of those students did not return. As of 2006, only the French Quarter of New Orleans was able to support some tourism. A Mardi Gras celebration was held, but it was shortened from its usual month to a week.

New Orleans is one of the major tourist attractions in the United States. Known for its fine restaurants, serving such distinctive fare as gumbo, jambalaya, crawfish, and beignets, along with an elaborate French-inspired haute cuisine, New Orleans also offers jazz clubs, the graceful buildings of the French Quarter, and a lavish carnival called Mardi Gras ("Fat Tuesday"). Beginning on the Wednesday before Shrove Tuesday, parades and balls staged by private organizations called krewes are held almost nightly. In other towns, people celebrate Mardi Gras in their own, no less uproarious, manner. Probably the greatest attraction of Louisiana is its French heritage. Everything from French law, to the division of the state into parishes instead of counties, to the French cuisine, and to the use of the Creole language, is a major attraction to tourists.

Among the many other annual events that attract visitors to the state are the blessing of the shrimp fleet at the Louisiana Shrimp and Petroleum Festival in Morgan City on Labor Day weekend and the blessing of the cane fields during the Louisiana Sugar Cane Festival at New Iberia in September. October offers the International Rice Festival (including the Frog Derby) at Crowley, Louisiana Cotton Festival at Ville Platte (with a medieval jousting tournament), the Louisiana Yambilee Festival at Opelousas, and the Louisiana State Fair at Shreveport. Attractions of the Natchitoches Christmas Festival include 170,000 Christmas lights and spectacular fireworks displays. There are tours of plantations starting in St. Francisville. Monroe is the home of the first Coca-Cola bottler, Joseph Biedenhorn. Jean Lafitte National Historical Park has 10 miles of raised boardwalks through the Louisiana swamps and marshes from which tourists can view wildlife (especially alligators).

Louisiana's 34 state parks and recreation sites total 39,000 acres (15,800 hectares).

⁴⁸SPORTS

Louisiana has two major professional sports teams: the Saints of the National Football League and the Hornets of the National Basketball Association. The Hornets were formerly located in Charlotte. Both the Saints and Hornets are located in New Orleans, however, due to Hurricane Katrina, both teams were forced to play in San Antonio and Oklahoma City, respectively. The Super Bowl has been held in New Orleans six times: in 1978, 1981, 1986, 1990, 1997, and 2002. It has been played in the Louisiana Superdome, the largest indoor arena in the United States.

New Orleans also has a minor league baseball team, the Zephyrs, of the Triple-A Pacific Coast League. In Shreveport, the Captains compete in the Double-A Texas League. There are several other minor league baseball and hockey teams scattered throughout the state.

During the 1850s, New Orleans was the horse-racing center of the United States, and racing is still popular in the state. The principal tracks are the Louisiana Jockey Club at the Fair Grounds in New Orleans, and Evangeline Downs at Lafayette. Gambling has long been widespread in Louisiana, particularly in the steamboat days, when races along the Mississippi drew huge wagers.

From the 1880s to World War I, New Orleans was the nation's boxing capital, and in 1893, the city was the site of the longest bout in boxing history, between Andy Bowen and Jack Burke, lasting 7 hours and 19 minutes—110 rounds—and ending in a draw. The TPC of Louisiana at Fairfield is a newly constructed championship-level golf course that became the home of the PGA's HP Classic in 2005.

In 1935, Tulane University inaugurated the Sugar Bowl (which they won that year for the first and only time), an annual New Year's Day event and one of the most prestigious bowl games in college football. Louisiana State University (LSU) won the Sugar Bowl in 1959, 1965, and 1968. They were named National Champions in 1958 and co-champions with USC in 2003. The LSU Tigers baseball team won the College World Series in 1991, 1993, 1996, and 1997. The LSU Tigers appeared in the National Collegiate Athletic Association (NCAA) Final Four in 1953, 1981, 1986, and 2006, and have had a number of famous basketball alumni, including "Pistol" Pete Maravich and Shaquille O'Neal.

Professional sports heroes Terry Bradshaw, Bill Russell, and Marshall Faulk all were born within the state's borders.

⁴⁹FAMOUS LOUISIANIANS

Zachary Taylor (b.Virginia, 1784–1850) is the only US president to whom Louisiana can lay claim. Taylor, a professional soldier who made his reputation as an Indian fighter and in the Mexican War, owned a large plantation north of Baton Rouge, which was his residence before his election to the presidency in 1848. Edward Douglass White (1845–1921) served first as associate justice of the US Supreme Court and then as chief justice.

Most other Louisianians who have held national office won more fame as state or confederate officials. John Slidell (b.New York, 1793–1871), an antebellum political leader, also played an important role in Confederate diplomacy. Judah P. Benjamin (b.West Indies, 1811–84), of Jewish lineage, was a US senator before the Civil War; during the conflict he held three posts in the Confederate cabinet, after which he went to England and became a leading barrister. Henry Watkins Allen (b.Virginia, 1820–66) was elected governor of Confederate Louisiana in 1864, after he had been maimed in battle; perhaps the best administrator in the South, he installed a system of near-socialism in Louisiana as the fortunes of the Confederacy waned. During and after the Civil War, many Louisianians won prominence as military leaders. Leonidas Polk (b.North Carolina, 1806–64), the state's first Episcopal bishop, became a lieutenant general in the Confederate Army and died in the Atlanta campaign. Zachary Taylor's son Richard (b.Kentucky, 1826–79), a sugar planter who also became a Confederate lieutenant general, is noted for his defeat of Nathaniel P. Bank's Union forces in the Red River campaign of 1864. Pierre Gustave Toutant Beauregard (1818–93) attained the rank of full general in the Confederate Army and later served as director of the Louisiana state lottery, one of the state's major sources of revenue at that time. In the modern era, General Claire Chennault (b.Texas, 1893–1958) commanded the famous "Flying Tigers" and then the US 14th Air Force in China during World War II.

Throughout the 20th century, the Longs have been the first family of Louisiana politics. Without question, the most important state officeholder in Louisiana history was Huey P. Long (1893–1935), a latter-day Populist who was elected to the governorship in 1928 and inaugurated a period of social and economic reform. In the process, he made himself very nearly an absolute dictator within Louisiana. After his election to the US Senate, the "King Fish" became a national figure, challenging Franklin D. Roosevelt's New Deal with his "Share the Wealth" plan and flamboyant oratory. Huey's brother Earl K. Long (1895–1960) served three times as governor. Huey's son, US Senator Russell B. Long (1918–2003), was chairman of the Finance Committee—and, consequently, one of the most powerful men in Congress—from 1965 to 1980.

Also prominent in Louisiana history were Robert Cavelier, Sieur de la Salle (b.France, 1643–87), who was the first to claim the region for the French crown; Pierre le Moyne, Sieur d'Iberville (b.Canada, 1661–1706), who commanded the expedition that first established permanent settlements in the lands La Salle had claimed; his brother, Jean Baptiste le Moyne, Sieur de Bienville (b.Canada, 1680–1768), governor of the struggling colony and founder of New Orleans; and Bernardo de Galvez (b.Spain, 1746–86), who, as governor of Spanish Louisiana during the last years of the American Revolution, conquered British-held Florida in a series of brilliant campaigns. William Charles Coles Claiborne (b.Virginia, 1775–1817) was the last territorial and first state governor of Louisiana. The state's first Republican governor, Henry Clay Warmoth (b.Illinois, 1842–1932), came there as a Union officer before the end of the Civil War and was sworn in at age 26. Jean Étienne de Boré (b.France, 1741–1820) laid the foundation of the Louisiana sugar industry by developing a process for granulating sugar from cane; Norbert Rillieux (birthplace unknown, 1806–94), a free black man, developed the much more efficient vacuum pan process of refining sugar.

Andrew Victor Schally (b.Poland, 1926), a biochemist on the faculty of the Tulane University School of Medicine, shared the Nobel Prize for medicine in 1977 for his research on hormones.

Among other distinguished Louisiana professionals have been historian T. Harry Williams (1909–79), who won the Pulitzer Prize for his biography of Huey Long; architect Henry Hobson Richardson (1838–86); and four doctors of medicine: public health pioneer Joseph Jones (b.Georgia, 1833–96), surgical innovator Rudolph Matas (1860–1957), surgeon and medical editor Alton V. Ochsner (b.South Dakota, 1896–1981), and heart specialist Michael De Bakey (b.1908).

Louisiana's important writers include George Washington Cable (1844–1925), an early advocate of racial justice; Kate O'Flaherty Chopin (b.Missouri, 1851–1904); playwright and memoirist Lillian Hellman (1905–84); and novelists Walker Percy (b.Alabama, 1916–1990); Truman Capote (1924–84); Ernest Gaines (b.1933), author of *The Autobiography of Miss Jane Pittman*; Shirley Ann Grau (b.1929); and John Kennedy Toole (1937–69), the last two being winners of the Pulitzer Prize.

Louisiana has produced two important composers, Ernest Guiraud (1837–92) and Louis Gottschalk (1829–69). Jelly Roll Morton (Ferdinand Joseph La Menthe, 1885–1941), Pete Fountain (b.1930), and Sidney Bechet (1897–1959) were important jazz musicians, and Louis "Satchmo" Armstrong (1900–1971) was one of the most prolific jazz innovators and popular performers in the nation. The distinctive rhythms of pianist and singer Professor Longhair (Henry Byrd, 1918–80) were an important influence on popular music. Other prominent Louisianians in music are gospel singer Mahalia Jackson (1911–72), pianist-singer-songwriter Antoine "Fats" Domino (b.1928), and pop singer Jerry Lee Lewis (b.1935).

Louisiana baseball heroes include Hall of Famer Melvin Thomas "Mel" Ott (1909–58) and pitcher Ron Guidry (b.1950). Terry Bradshaw (b.1948), a native of Shreveport, quarterbacked the Super Bowl champion Pittsburgh Steelers during the 1970s. Player-coach William F. "Bill" Russell (b.1934) led the Boston Celtics to 10 National Basketball Association championships between 1956 and 1969. Chess master Paul Morphy (1837–84) was born in New Orleans.

50 BIBLIOGRAPHY

Abrahams, Roger D. *Blues for New Orleans: Mardi Gras and America's Creole Soul.* Philadelphia: University of Pennsylvania Press, 2006.

Bell, Caryn Cossé. *Revolution, Romanticism, and the Afro-Creole Protest Tradition in Louisiana, 1718–1868.* Baton Rouge: Louisiana State University Press, 1997.

Brinkley, Douglas. *The Great Deluge: Hurricane Katrina, New Orleans, and the Mississippi Gulf Coast.* New York: Morrow, 2006.

Calhoun, Milburn. *Louisiana Almanac, 2006–07.* Gretna, La.: Pelican Publishing Co., 2006.

Council of State Governments. *The Book of the States, 2006 Edition.* Lexington, Ky.: Council of State Governments, 2006.

Fairclough, Adam. *Race & Democracy: The Civil Rights Struggle in Louisiana, 1915–1972.* Athens: University of Georgia Press, 1995.

Ferris, William (ed.). *The South.* Vol. 7 in *The Greenwood Encyclopedia of American Regional Cultures.* Westport, Conn.: Greenwood Press, 2004.

Hogue, James Keith. *Uncivil War: Five New Orleans Street Battles and the Rise and Fall of Radical Reconstruction.* Baton Rouge: Louisiana State University Press, 2006.

Jobb, Dean. *The Cajuns: A People's Story of Exile and Triumph.* New York: John Wiley & Sons, 2005.

Levinson, Sanford, and Bartholomew Sparrow (eds.). *The Louisiana Purchase and American Expansion, 1803–1898.* Lanham, Md.: Rowman & Littlefield Publishers, 2005.

McAuliffe, Emily. *Louisiana Facts and Symbols.* Mankato, Minn.: Hilltop Books, 1999.

Norman, Corrie E., and Don S. Armentrout (eds.). *Religion in the Contemporary South: Changes, Continuities, and Contexts.* Knoxville: University of Tennessee Press, 2005.

Tregle, Joseph George. *Louisiana in the Age of Jackson: A Clash of Cultures and Personalities.* Baton Rouge: Louisiana State University Press, 1999.

US Department of Commerce, Economics and Statistics Administration, US Census Bureau. *Louisiana, 2000. Summary Social, Economic, and Housing Characteristics: 2000 Census of Population and Housing.* Washington, D.C.: US Government Printing Office, 2003.

Worth, Richard. *Voices from Colonial America. Louisiana, 1682–1803.* Washington, D.C.: National Geographic Society, 2005.

MAINE

State of Maine

ORIGIN OF STATE NAME: Derived either from the French for a historical district of France, or from the early use of "main" to distinguish coast from islands. **NICKNAME:** The Pine Tree State. **CAPITAL:** Augusta. **ENTERED UNION:** 15 March 1820 (23rd). **SONG:** "State of Maine Song." **MOTTO:** *Dirigo* ("I direct" or "I lead"). **COAT OF ARMS:** A farmer and sailor support a shield on which are depicted a pine tree, a moose, and water. Under the shield is the name of the state; above it are the state motto and the North Star. **FLAG:** The coat of arms is on a blue field, with a yellow fringed border surrounding three sides. **OFFICIAL SEAL:** Same as the coat of arms. **BIRD:** Chickadee. **FISH:** Landlocked salmon. **FLOWER:** White pine cone, tassel; wintergreen (herb). **TREE:** White pine. **LEGAL HOLIDAYS:** New Year's Day, 1 January; Birthday of Martin Luther King Jr., 3rd Monday in January; Washington's Birthday, 3rd Monday in February; Patriots' Day, 3rd Monday in April; Memorial Day, last Monday in May; Independence Day, 4 July; Labor Day, 1st Monday in September; Columbus Day, 2nd Monday in October; Veterans Day, 11 November; Thanksgiving Day, 4th Thursday in November and day following; Christmas Day, 25 December. **TIME:** 7 AM EST = noon GMT.

¹LOCATION, SIZE, AND EXTENT

Situated in the extreme northeastern corner of the United States, Maine is the nation's most easterly state, the largest in New England, and 39th in size among the 50 states.

The total area of Maine is 33,265 sq mi (86,156 sq km), including 30,995 sq mi (80,277 sq km) of land and 2,270 sq mi (5,879 sq km) of inland water. Maine extends 207 mi (333 km) E–W; the maximum N–S extension is 322 mi (518 km).

Maine is bordered on the N by the Canadian provinces of Quebec (with the line passing through the St. Francis River) and New Brunswick (with the boundary formed by the St. John River); on the E by New Brunswick (with the lower eastern boundary formed by the Chiputneticook Lakes and the St. Croix River); on the SE and S by the Atlantic Ocean; and on the W by New Hampshire (with the line passing through the Piscataqua and Salmon Falls rivers in the SW) and Quebec.

Hundreds of islands dot Maine's coast. The largest is Mt. Desert Island; others include Deer Isle, Vinalhaven, and Isle au Haut. The total boundary length of Maine is 883 mi (1,421 km).

The state's geographic center is in Piscataquis County, 18 mi (29 km) N of Dover-Foxcroft. The easternmost point of the United States is West Quoddy Head, at 66°57′W.

²TOPOGRAPHY

Maine is divided into four main regions: coastal lowlands, piedmont, mountains, and uplands.

The narrow coastal lowlands extend, on average, 10–20 mi (16–32 km) inland from the irregular coastline, but occasionally disappear altogether, as at Mt. Desert Island and on the western shore of Penobscot Bay. Mt. Cadillac on Mt. Desert Island rises abruptly to 1,532 ft (467 m), the highest elevation on the Atlantic coast north of Rio de Janeiro, Brazil. The transitional hilly belt, or piedmont,

broadens from about 30 mi (48 km) wide in the southwestern part of the state to about 80 mi (129 km) in the northeast.

Maine's mountain region, the Longfellow range, is at the northeastern end of the Appalachian Mountain system. This zone, extending into Maine from the western border for about 150 mi (250 km) and averaging about 50 mi (80 km) wide, contains nine peaks over 4,000 ft (1,200 m), including Mt. Katahdin, which at 5,267 ft (1,606 m) is the highest point in the state. The summit of Katahdin marks the northern terminus of the 2,000-mi (3,200-km) Appalachian Trail. Maine's uplands form a high, relatively flat plateau extending northward beyond the mountains and sloping downward toward the north and east. The mean elevation of the state is approximately 600 ft (183 m). The eastern part of this zone is the Aroostook potato-farming region; the western part is heavily forested.

Of Maine's more than 2,200 lakes and ponds, the largest are Moosehead Lake, 117 sq mi (303 sq km), and Sebago Lake, 13 mi (21 km) by 10 mi (16 km). Of the more than 5,000 rivers and streams, the Penobscot, Androscoggin, Kennebec, and Saco rivers drain historically and commercially important valleys. The longest river in Maine is the St. John, but it runs for most of its length in the Canadian province of New Brunswick. The lowest point of the state is at sea level at the Atlantic Ocean.

³CLIMATE

Maine has three climatic regions: the northern interior zone, comprising roughly the northern half of the state, between Quebec and New Brunswick; the southern interior zone; and the coastal zone. The northern zone is both drier and cooler in all four seasons than either of the other zones, while the coastal zone is more moderate in temperature year-round than the other two.

The annual mean temperature in the northern zone is about 40°F (5°C); in the southern interior zone, 44°F (7°C); and in the coastal zone, 46°F (8°C). Record temperatures for the state are

-48°F (-44°C), registered at Van Buren on 19 January 1925, and 105°F (41°C) at North Bridgton on 10 July 1911. The mean annual precipitation increases from 40.2 in (102 cm) in the north to 41.5 in (105 cm) in the southern interior and 45.7 in (116 cm) on the coast. Average annual precipitation at Portland is about 43.6 in (110 cm); average annual snowfall is 70.5 in (179 cm).

⁴FLORA AND FAUNA

Maine's forests are largely softwoods, chiefly red and white spruces, balsam fir (Abies balsamea), eastern hemlock, and white and red pine. Important hardwoods include beech, yellow and white birches, sugar and red maples, white oak, black willow, black and white ashes, and American elm, which has fallen victim in recent years to Dutch elm disease. Maine is home to most of the flowers and shrubs common to the north temperate zone, including an important commercial resource, the low-bush blueberry. Maine has seventeen rare orchid species. Two species, the small whorled pogonia and the eastern prairie fringed orchid, were classified by the US Fish and Wildlife Service as threatened as of April 2006; the furbish lousewart was classified as endangered that year.

About 30,000 white-tailed deer are killed by hunters in Maine each year, but the herd does not appear to diminish. Moose hunting was banned in Maine in 1935; however, in 1980, 700 moose-hunting permits were issued for a six-day season, and moose hunting has continued despite attempts by some residents to ban the practice. Other common forest animals include the bobcat, beaver, muskrat, river otter, mink, fisher, raccoon, red fox, and snow-shoe hare. The woodchuck is a conspicuous inhabitant of pastures, meadows, cornfields, and vegetable gardens. Seals, porpoises, and occasionally finback whales are found in coastal waters, along with virtually every variety of North Atlantic fish and shellfish, including the famous Maine lobster. Coastal waterfowl include the osprey, herring and great black-backed gulls, great and double-crested cormorants, and various duck species. Matinicus Rock, a small uninhabited island about 20 mi (32 km) off the coast near the entrance to Penobscot Bay, is the only known North American nesting site of the common puffin, or sea parrot.

Eleven Maine animal species (vertebrates and invertebrates) were classified as threatened or endangered by the US Fish and Wildlife Service in 2006, including the bald eagle, piping plover, Atlantic Gulf of Maine salmon, two species of whale, and leather-back sea turtle.

⁵ENVIRONMENTAL PROTECTION

The Department of Environmental Protection administers laws regulating the development of large residential, commercial, and industrial sites; the protection and improvement of air and water quality; the prevention and cleanup of oil spills; the control of hazardous wastes; the licensing of oil terminals; the protection of state-significant natural resources (including wetlands, rivers, streams and brooks, and fragile mountain areas); and mining. The Land Use Regulation Commission, established in 1969, extends the principles of town planning and zoning to Maine's 411 unorganized townships, 313 "plantations," and numerous coastal islands that have no local government and might otherwise be subject to ecologically unsound development. About 25% of the state

contains wetlands; these generally owned by private landowners, timber companies, or other individuals.

In 2003, 9.3 million lb of toxic chemicals were released in the state. Also in 2003, Maine had 59 hazardous waste sites listed in the US Environment Protection Agency (EPA) database, 12 of which were on the National Priorities List as of 2006, including Brunswick Naval Station, Loring Air Force Base, and Portsmouth Naval Shipyard. In 2005, the EPA spent over $1.7 million through the Superfund program for the cleanup of hazardous waste sites in the state. The same year, the state received about $2 million in other federal EPA grants.

⁶POPULATION

Maine ranked 40th in population in the United States with an estimated total of 1,321,505 in 2005, an increase of 3.7% since 2000. Between 1990 and 2000, Maine's population grew from 1,227,928 to 1,274,923, an increase of 3.8%. The population is projected to reach 1.38 million by 2015 and 1.41 million by 2025. The population density in 2004 was 42.7 persons per sq mi.

In 2004 the median age was 40.7, the highest median in the nation. Persons under 18 years old accounted for 21.4% of the population while 14.4% was age 65 or older.

The area that now comprises the state of Maine was sparsely settled throughout the colonial period. At statehood, Maine had 298,335 residents. The population doubled by 1860, but then grew slowly until the 1970s, when its growth rate went above the national average.

More than half the population lives on less than one-seventh of the land, within 25 mi (40 km) of the Atlantic coast, and almost half of the state is virtually uninhabited. Although almost half of Maine's population is classified as urban; much of the urban population lives in towns and small cities. The state's major cities, all with populations under 100,000, are Portland, Bangor, and Lewiston-Auburn. The Portland metropolitan area had an estimated population of 510,791 in 2004. The Bangor metropolitan area had an estimated 148,196 people and the Lewiston-Auburn area had 107,022.

⁷ETHNIC GROUPS

Maine's population is primarily Yankee, both in its English and Scotch-Irish origins and in its retention of many of the values and folkways of rural New England. The largest minority group consists of French-Canadians. Among those reporting at least one specific ancestry group in 2000, 274,423 claimed English ancestry; 181,663 French (not counting 110,344 who claimed Canadian or French-Canadian); and 192,901 Irish. There were 36,691 foreign-born residents. The population of Hispanics and Latinos in 2000 was 9,360, less than 1% of the state total. In 2004, 0.9% of the population was or Hispanic or Latino origin.

The most notable ethnic issue in Maine during the 1970s was the legal battle of the Penobscot and Passamaquoddy Indians—living on two reservations covering 27,546 acres (11,148 hectares)—to recover 12,500,000 acres (5,059,000 hectares) of treaty lands. A compromise settlement in 1980 awarded them $81.5 million, two-thirds of which went into a fund enabling the Indians to purchase 300,000 acres (121,000 hectares) of timberland. In 1995, Maine's American Indian population included the following groups living on or near reservations (with population estimates): the Penob-

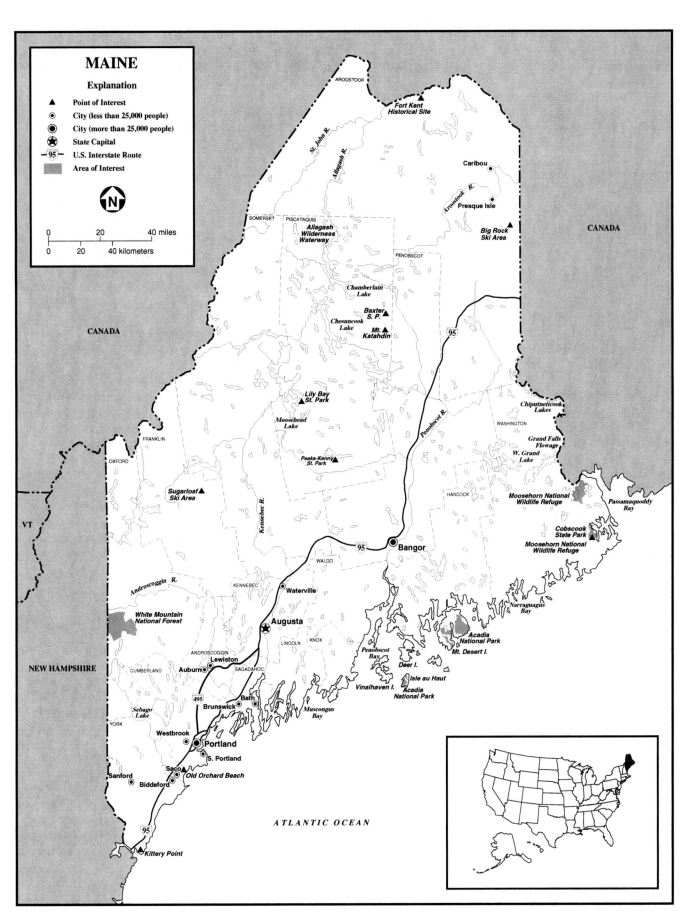

MAINE

Explanation

▲ Point of Interest
⊙ City (less than 25,000 people)
◉ City (more than 25,000 people)
✪ State Capital
—95— U.S. Interstate Route
▨ Area of Interest

N

0   20   40 miles
0   20   40 kilometers

CANADA

CANADA

AROOSTOOK

St. John R.

Allagash R.

Fort Kent
Historical Site

Caribou

Aroostook R.

Presque Isle

Big Rock
Ski Area

SOMERSET PISCATAQUIS

Allagash
Wilderness
Waterway

PENOBSCOT

Chamberlain
Lake

Baxter
S. P.

Chesuncook
Lake

Mt.
Katahdin

95

Lily Bay
St. Park

Moosehead
Lake

FRANKLIN

OXFORD

Peaks-Kenny
St. Park

Sugarloaf
Ski Area

Kennebec R.

Penobscot R.

Chiputneticook
Lakes

WASHINGTON

Grand Falls
Flowage

W. Grand
Lake

HANCOCK

Moosehorn National
Wildlife Refuge

Passamaquoddy
Bay

Cobscook
State Park

Moosehorn National
Wildlife Refuge

VT

White Mountain
National Forest

Androscoggin R.

KENNEBEC

Waterville

WALDO

Bangor

Narraguagus
Bay

Augusta

LINCOLN KNOX

Penobscot
Bay

Deer I.

Acadia
National Park

Mt. Desert I.

ANDROSCOGGIN

Lewiston

SAGADAHOC

Isle au Haut

Vinalhaven I.

Acadia
National Park

NEW HAMPSHIRE

CUMBERLAND

Auburn

495

Bath

Sebago
Lake

Brunswick

Muscongus
Bay

YORK

Westbrook

Portland

S. Portland

Sanford

Saco

Old Orchard Beach

Biddeford

ATLANTIC OCEAN

95

Kittery Point

scot Tribe (1,206); the Aristook Band of Micmac (1,155); Pleasant Point (878); the Passamaquoddy (722); and the Houlton Band of Maliseets (331). The Indian population as a whole was reported as 7,098 in 2000. In 2004, 0.6% of the population was composed of American Indians.

As of 2000, Maine had 6,760 black residents and 9,111 Asians, including 2,034 Chinese, 1,159 Filipinos, and 1,021 Asian Indians. Pacific Islanders numbered 382. In 2004, 0.7% of the population was black and 0.8% Asian. That year, 0.9% of the population reported origin of two or more races.

8 LANGUAGES

Descendants of the Passamaquoddy and Penobscot Indians of the Algonkian family who inhabited Maine at the time that European settlers arrived still lived there in the mid-1980s. Algonkian place-names abound: Saco, Millinocket, Wiscasset, Kennebec, Skowhegan.

Maine English is celebrated as typical Yankee speech. Final /r/ is absent, a vowel sound between /ah/ and the /a/ in *cat* appears in *car* and *garden, aunt* and *calf. Coat* and *home* have a vowel that to outsiders sounds like the vowel in *cut.* Maple syrup comes from *rock* or *sugar maple* trees in a *sap* or *sugar orchard*; cottage cheese is *curd cheese*; and pancakes are *fritters*.

In 2000, 92.2% of Maine residents five years old or older reported speaking only English in the home, up from 90.8% in 1990.

The decline of parochial schools and a great increase in the number of young persons attending college have begun to erode the linguistic and cultural separateness that marks the history of the Franco-American experience in Maine.

The following table gives selected statistics from the 2000 Census for language spoken at home by persons five years old and over. The category "Other Native North American languages" includes Apache, Cherokee, Choctaw, Dakota, Keres, Pima, and Yupik. The category "Other Indo-European languages" includes Albanian, Gaelic, Lithuanian, and Rumanian. The category "Scandinavian languages" includes Danish, Norwegian, and Swedish.

LANGUAGE	NUMBER	PERCENT
Population 5 years and over	**1,204,164**	**100.0**
Speak only English	1,110,198	92.2
Speak a language other than English	93,966	7.8
Speak a language other than English	**93,966**	**7.8**
French (incl. Patois, Cajun)	63,640	5.3
Spanish or Spanish Creole	9,611	0.8
German	4,006	0.3
Italian	1,476	0.1
Chinese	1,259	0.1
Other Native North American languages	1,182	0.1
Mon-Khmer, Cambodian	1,084	0.1
Vietnamese	911	0.1
Russian	896	0.1
Other Indo-European languages	785	0.1
Scandinavian languages	779	0.1
Tagalog	771	0.1
Greek	767	0.1
Polish	763	0.1

9 RELIGIONS

Maine had about 217,676 Roman Catholics in 2004 and an estimated 8,290 Jews in 2000. The leading Protestant denominations are the United Methodist Church, with 31,689 adherents (in 2000); the American Baptists USA, 26,259 (in 2000); and the

United Church of Christ, 23,086 (in 2005). The Muslim community had about 800 members. Over 800,000 people (about 63.6% of the population) were not counted as members of any religious organization.

10 TRANSPORTATION

Railroad development in Maine, which reached its peak in 1924, has declined rapidly since World War II (1939–45), and passenger service has been dropped altogether. Although Maine had no Class I railroads in 2003, seven regional and local railroads operated on 1,148 rail mi (1,848 km) of track. As of 2006, Amtrak provided service to four stations in Maine via its north–south Downeaster train from Portland to Boston.

About three-quarters of all communities and about half the population depend entirely on highway trucking for the overland transportation of freight. In 2004, Maine had 22,748 mi (36,624 km) of public roads. In that same year, there were 1.086 million registered motor vehicles and 984,829 licensed drivers in the state. The Maine Turnpike and I-95, which coincide between Portland and Kittery, are the state's major highways.

River traffic has been central to the lumber industry. Only since World War II has trucking replaced seasonal log drives downstream from timberlands to the mills, a practice that is now outlawed for environmental reasons. Maine has 10 established seaports, with Portland and Searsport being the main depots for overseas shipping. In 2004, Portland harbor handled 29.709 million tons, and Searsport handled 1.832 million tons. Crude oil, fuel oil, and gasoline were the chief commodities. In 2004, Maine had 73 mi (117 km) of navigable inland waterways. In 2003, waterborne shipments totaled 31.698 million tons.

In 2005, Maine had a total of 153 public and private-use aviation-related facilities. This included 103 airports, 13 heliports, and 37 seaplane bases. Portland International Jetport is the largest and most active airport in Maine. In 2004, Portland International had 687,344 passengers enplaned.

11 HISTORY

The first inhabitants of Maine—dating from 3000 to 1000 BC—are known to archaeologists as the Red Paint People because of the red ocher that has been found in their graves. This Paleolithic group had evidently disappeared long before the arrival of the Algonkian-speaking Abnaki (meaning "living at the sunrise"), or Wabanaki. Just at the time of European settlement, an intertribal war and a disastrous epidemic of smallpox swept away many of the Abnaki, some of whom had begun peaceful contacts with the English. After that, most Indian contacts with Europeans were with the French.

The first documented visit by a European to the Maine coast was that of Giovanni da Verrazano during his voyage of 1524, but one may infer from the record that the Abnaki he met there had encountered white men before. Sometime around 1600, English expeditions began fishing the Gulf of Maine regularly. The first recorded attempts to found permanent colonies, by the French on an island in the St. Croix River in 1604 and by the English at Sagadahoc in 1607, both failed. By 1630, however, there were permanent English settlements on several islands and at nearly a dozen spots along the coast.

The first grant of Maine lands was to Sir Ferdinando Gorges from the Council from New England, a joint-stock company that received and made royal grants of New England territory and which Gorges himself dominated. He and Captain John Mason received the territory between the Merrimack River (in present-day New Hampshire and Massachusetts) and the Kennebec River in 1622. Seven years later, the two grantees divided their land at the Piscataqua River, and Gorges became sole proprietor of the "Province of Maine." The source of the name is not quite clear. It seems likely that some connection with the historical French province of the same name was intended, but the name was also used to distinguish the mainland from the islands.

Sir Ferdinando's various schemes for governing the territory and promoting a feudal-style settlement never worked. A few years after his death in 1647, the government of the Massachusetts Bay Colony began absorbing the small Maine settlements. Massachusetts purchased the title to Maine from the Gorges heirs in 1677, and Maine became a district of Massachusetts with the issuance of a new royal charter in 1691. During the first hundred years of settlement, Maine's economy was based entirely on fishing, trading, and exploitation of the forests. The origin of the Maine shipbuilding industry, the early settlement of the interior parts of southern Maine, and the beginning of subsistence farming all date from about the time that New England's supply center of white-pine masts for the Royal Navy moved from Portsmouth, N.H., to Falmouth (now the city of Portland).

The first naval encounter of the Revolutionary War occurred in Machias Bay, when, on 12 June 1775, angry colonials captured the British armed schooner Margaretta. On 8 October 1775, a British naval squadron shelled and set fire to Falmouth. Wartime Maine was the scene of two anti-British campaigns, both of which ended in failure: an expedition through the Maine woods in the fall of 1775 intended to drive the British out of Quebec, and a disastrous 1779 expedition in which a Massachusetts amphibious force, failing to dislodge British troops at Castine, scuttled many of its own ships near the mouth of the Penobscot River.

The idea of separation from Massachusetts began surfacing as early as 1785, but popular pressure for such a movement did not mount until the War of 1812. The overwhelming vote for statehood in an 1819 referendum was a victory for William King, who would become the first governor, and his fellow Jeffersonian Democratic-Republicans. Admission of Maine as a free state was joined with the admission of Missouri as a slave state in the Missouri Compromise of 1820.

Textile mills and shoe factories came to Maine between 1830 and 1860 as part of the industrialization of Massachusetts. After the Civil War, the revolution in papermaking that substituted wood pulp for rags brought a vigorous new industry to Maine. By 1900, Maine was one of the leading papermaking states in the United States, and the industry continues to dominate the state as of 2005. Shipbuilding joined paper manufacturing as a leading employer in the state, enjoying a boom in government contracts in the 1980s.

In 1972, the Penobscot and Passamaquoddy Indians filed a land claims suit against the federal government for property that amounted to the northern two-thirds of Maine, claiming that a 1794 treaty, under which the Passamaquoddy handed over most of its land while receiving nothing in exchange, had not been rat-

ified by Congress, and therefore violated the Indian Non-Intercourse Act of 1790. The government settled the suit in 1980 by paying the tribes $81.5 million, which was allocated to purchase commercial and industrial properties in Maine.

The rise of tourism and the often conflicting concerns for economic development and environmental protection have been key issues in the state since the 1940s. Tourism grew substantially in the 1980s, 1990s, and into the 2000s, especially in coastal areas, where an influx of residents changed the character of many seaside towns. Former seasonal resorts were converted to year-round communities, posing new challenges for growth management. The state's environmental concerns included sewage treatment, deforestation, overfishing, and hazardous waste disposal.

Maine's economy turned in its best performance in more than a decade in 1999, with strong job growth, continued increases in retail sales, and significant improvement in nearly all other indicators. The state's income growth topped the national average from 1998 to 1999, finishing among the five fastest growing states. According to government figures, income growth in Maine, which still had the lowest per capita income in New England, was fueled by higher wages in services, construction, finance, insurance, and real estate. At the same time, there were concerns that the gain in income was the result of Maine workers holding down more than one job in order to make ends meet. Analysts also warned that the hot state economy could be threatened by a shortage of workers, since the state's population was not growing at a commensurate rate.

Maine's economy suffered with that of the nation's in the early 2000s, coming on the back of a recession in 2001. By 2003, Maine had a $24 million budget deficit. Governor John Baldacci had plans to implement a large-scale healthcare program for state employees, open it to private employers, and pay for it without increased taxes. This plan, Dirigo Health, was signed into law in June 2003. A citizen initiative set for referendum in November 2003 was to mandate a large increase in state assistance to local school systems. It was rejected.

In 2005, the state was making plans for the closing of military bases, including the Brunswick Naval Air Station. Governor Baldacci created a Maine Office of Redevelopment and Re-employment with an Advisory Council to coordinate local and statewide interests with regard to the closures.

12 STATE GOVERNMENT

The Maine constitution, based on that of Massachusetts but incorporating a number of more democratic features, was adopted in 1819 and amended 169 times by January 2005. (This figure does not include one amendment approved by the voters in 1967 that is inoperative until implemented by legislation.) The state constitution may be amended by a two-thirds vote of the legislature and a majority vote at the next general election.

The bicameral legislature, consisting of a 35-member Senate and a 151-member House of Representatives, convenes biennially (in even-numbered years) in joint session to elect the secretary of state, attorney general, and state treasurer. Legislative sessions begin in December of the general election year and run into June of the following (odd-numbered year); the second session begins in January of the next even-numbered year, runs into April, and is limited to consideration of budgetary matters, legislation in the governor's call, emergency legislation, and legislation referred to committees for study. The presiding officers of each house may jointly call for a special session as long as they have the support of a majority of members of each political party in each house. All legislators, who serve two-year terms, must have been US citizens for at least five years, residents of the state for at least one year, and have lived in their district at least three months prior to election. The minimum age for representatives is 21, for senators it is 25. The legislative salary in 2004 was $11,384 for the first year and $8,302 for the second.

The governor, who serves a four-year term and is limited to two consecutive terms, is the only official elected statewide. (Rules of succession dictate that should the governor become incapacitated, he or she would be succeeded by the president of the state Senate.) A gubernatorial veto may be overridden by a two-thirds vote of members present and voting in each legislative chamber. An unsigned bill that is not vetoed becomes law after 10 days whether the legislature is in session or not. The governor must be at least 30 years old, a citizen of the United States for at least 15 years, and a state resident for 5 years. As of December 2004, the governor's salary was $70,000, unchanged from 1999.

To vote in Maine, one must be a US citizen, a resident of the state and municipality, and at least 18 years old. Those under guardianship because of mental illness may not vote.

13 POLITICAL PARTIES

Maine's two major political parties are the Democratic and the Republican, each affiliated with the national party. An independent candidate, James B. Longley, beat the candidates of both major parties in the gubernatorial election of 1974.

During the early decades of statehood, Jeffersonian and Jacksonian Democrats remained in power quite consistently. In 1854, however, reformers rallied around the new Republican Party, which dominated Maine politics for the next hundred years. Maine's strong Republican tradition continued into the middle and late 1950s, when Margaret Chase Smith distinguished herself in the US Senate as a leader of national importance. The rise of

Democrat Edmund S. Muskie, elected governor in 1954 and 1956 and to the first of four terms in the US Senate in 1960, signaled a change in Maine's political complexion. Muskie appealed personally to many traditionally Republican voters, but his party's resurgence was also the result of demographic changes, especially an increase in the proportion of French-Canadian voters.

In the November 1994 elections, Independent Angus King was voted into the executive office, and Maine became the only state in the nation with an Independent governor. King was reelected in 1998. In 2002, Democrat John Baldacci was elected governor. In 1994 Republican Olympia Snowe won the US Senate seat vacated by retiring Democrat George J. Mitchell (she was reelected in 2000); in 1996 Republican Susan E. Collins won the seat left vacant by retiring three-term senator William S. Cohen, also a Republican (Collins was reelected in 2002). In the 2000 presidential elections Democrat Al Gore won 49% of the presidential vote, Republican George W. Bush received 44%, and Green Party candidate Ralph Nader won 6%. In 2004, Democrat John Kerry won 53.4% in his challenge to incumbent President Bush, who garnered 44.6%. In 2004 elections, Maine Democrats retained control of both US House seats. Also in 2002 there were 957,000 registered voters. In 1998, 32% of registered voters were Democratic, 29% Republican, and 39% unaffiliated or members of other parties. In mid-2005, the state House of Representatives had 76 Democrats, 73 Republicans, and 2 independents, while the state Senate had 19 Democrats and 16 Republicans. The state had four electoral votes in the 2004 presidential election.

14 LOCAL GOVERNMENT

The principal units of local government in 2005 included 16 counties, 22 municipal governments, 282 public school districts and 222 special districts. Maine's counties function primarily as judicial districts. As is customary in New England, the basic instrument of town government is the annual town meeting, with an elective board of selectmen supervising town affairs between meetings; some of the larger towns employ full-time town managers. In 2002, there were 467 townships in the state.

In 2005, local government accounted for about 54,868 full-time (or equivalent) employment positions.

15 STATE SERVICES

To address the continuing threat of terrorism and to work with the federal Department of Homeland Security, homeland security in Maine operates under the authority of the governor; the emergency management director is designated as the state homeland security advisor.

The State Board of Education and Department of Educational and Cultural Services supervise the public education system. The Department of Transportation, established in 1972, includes divisions responsible for aviation and railroads, a bureau to maintain highways and bridges, the Maine Port Authority, the State Ferry Advisory Board, and the Maine Aeronautical Advisory Board.

Various agencies responsible for health and social welfare were combined into the Department of Human Services in 1975 (now the Department of Health and Human Services). The Maine State Housing Authority, established in 1969, provides construction loans and technical assistance and conducts surveys of the state's housing needs. The Commission on Governmental Ethics and

Maine Presidential Vote by Major Political Parties, 1948–2004

YEAR	ELECTORAL VOTE	MAINE WINNER	DEMOCRAT	REPUBLICAN
1948	5	Dewey (R)	111,916	150,234
1952	5	*Eisenhower (R)	118,806	232,353
1956	5	*Eisenhower (R)	102,468	249,238
1960	5	*Eisenhower (R)	102,468	249,238
1960	5	Nixon (R)	181,159	240,608
1964	4	*Johnson (D)	262,264	118,701
1968	4	Humphrey (D)	217,312	169,254
1972	4	*Nixon (R)	160,584	256,458
1976	4	Ford (R)	232,279	236,320
1980	4	*Reagan (R)	220,974	238,522
1984	4	*Reagan (R)	214,515	336,500
1988	4	*Bush (R)	243,569	307,131
1992**	4	*Clinton (D)	263,420	206,504
1996**	4	*Clinton (D)	312,788	186,378
2000	4	Gore (D)	319,951	286,616
2004	4	Kerry (D)	396,842	330,201

*Won US presidential election.
**IND. candidate Ross Perot received 206,820 votes in 1992 and 85,970 votes in 1996.

Election Practices, an advisory and investigative body, was created in 1975 to serve as a watchdog over the legislature. Other organizations include the departments of agriculture, corrections, professional and financial legislation, and labor; and the bureaus of motor vehicles and parks and lands.

16 JUDICIAL SYSTEM

The highest state court in Maine is the Supreme Judicial Court, with a chief justice and six associate justices appointed by the governor (with the consent of the legislature) for seven-year terms (as are all other state judges). The Supreme Judicial Court has statewide appellate jurisdiction in all civil and criminal matters. The 16-member superior court, which has original jurisdiction in cases involving trial by jury and also hears some appeals, holds court sessions in all 16 counties. The district courts hear non-felony criminal cases and small claims and juvenile cases, and have concurrent jurisdiction with the superior court in divorce and civil cases involving less than $30,000. A probate court judge is elected in each county.

As of 31 December 2004, a total of 2,024 prisoners were held in Maine's state and federal prisons, an increase from 2,013 of 0.5% from the previous year. As of year-end 2004, a total of 125 inmates were female, up from 124 or 0.8% from the year before. Among sentenced prisoners (one year or more), Maine had an incarceration rate of 148 per 100,000 population in 2004, the lowest in the United States.

According to the Federal Bureau of Investigation, Maine in 2004, had a violent crime rate (murder/nonnegligent manslaughter; forcible rape; robbery; aggravated assault) of 103.5 reported incidents per 100,000 population (the second-lowest in the United States after North Dakota), or a total of 1,364 reported incidents. Crimes against property (burglary; larceny/theft; and motor vehicle theft) in that same year totaled 31,740 reported incidents or 2,409.6 reported incidents per 100,000 people. Maine has not had a death penalty since 1887. The state does provide for life without parole.

In 2003, Maine spent $78,866,791 on homeland security, an average of $61 per state resident.

17 ARMED FORCES

The largest US military installation in Maine is the Naval Air Station at Brunswick, home of a wing of anti-submarine patrol squadrons. Defense Department personnel in Maine totaled 11,051, including 4,535 active military and 5,216 civilians in 2004. State firms received over $1.5 billion in defense contracts in 2004. General Dynamics, a major defense contractor, is one of the state's largest private employers. Its Bath Iron Works division designs and builds complex, technologically advanced naval ships; another division, the Saco Operations, produces armament systems and is a leading producer of small and medium caliber machine guns, and cannon barrels, as well as, a test facility. In addition, another $805 million in defense payroll spending, including retired military pay, was paid out.

There were 143,726 veterans of US military service in Maine as of 2003, of whom 19,904 served in World War II; 16,954 in the Korean conflict; 45,061 during the Vietnam era; and 17,991 during the Gulf War. Expenditures on veterans amounted to some $503 million during 2004.

As of 31 October 2004, the Maine State Police employed 311 full-time sworn officers.

18 MIGRATION

Throughout the 1600s, 1700s, and early 1800s, Maine's population grew primarily by immigration from elsewhere in New England. About 1830, after agriculture in the state had passed its peak, Maine farmers and woodsmen began moving west. Europeans and French Canadians came to the state, but not in sufficient numbers to offset this steady emigration.

Net losses from migration have continued through most of this century. Between 1940 and 1970, for example, the net loss was 163,000. However, there was a net gain of about 80,000 from 1970 to 1990. From 1980 to 1990, Maine's urban population declined from 47.5% to 44.6% of the state's total. Between 1990 and 1998, the state had a net loss of 15,000 in domestic migration and a net gain of 3,000 in international migration. In 1998, Maine admitted 709 foreign immigrants. Between 1990 and 1998, the State's overall population increased 1.3%. In the period 2000–05, net international migration was 5,004 and net internal migration was 36,804, for a net gain of 41,808 people.

19 INTERGOVERNMENTAL COOPERATION

Regional agreements in which Maine participates include the Maine-New Hampshire School Compact, which authorizes interstate public school districts. Maine also takes part in the Atlantic States Marine Fisheries Commission, Interstate Compact for Juveniles, Northeastern Forest Fire Protection Compact; and the New England Interstate Water Pollution Control, Corrections Control, Board of Higher Education, and Radiological Health Protection compacts. In fiscal year 2005, Maine received $2.197 billion in federal grants; that figure fell to an estimated $2.125 billion in fiscal year 2006, before rising to an estimated $2.245 billion in fiscal year 2007.

20 ECONOMY

Maine's greatest economic strengths, as they have been since the beginning of European settlement, are its forests and waters, yielding wood products, water power, fisheries, and ocean commerce. As of 2005, paper manufacturing, for which both forests and water power are essential, was among the largest industries. However, since the 1980s manufacturing employment has dropped; and especially since 1992, services sector and trading sector employment has risen.

Maine's greatest current economic weakness is its limited access to the national transportation network that links major production and manufacturing centers with large metropolitan markets. On the other hand, this relative isolation, combined with the state's traditional natural assets, has contributed to Maine's attractiveness as a place for tourism and recreation. It also meant that the national recession in 2001 largely bypassed Maine's economy because of its limited involvement in the growth fields of information technology and equity venture capitalism. Annual growth in Maine's gross state product, which at 5.9% in both 1998 and 1999, and rising to 6.4% in 2000, did moderate to 3.2% in 2001, but employment had returned to peak levels reached before the recession by mid-2002. Tax revenue shortfalls were also less than other New

England states, all more affected by the abrupt decline in capital gains income.

Maine's gross state product in 2004 totaled $43.336 billion, of which real estate was the largest component at $5.821 billion or 13.4% of GSP, followed by manufacturing (durable and nondurable goods) at $5.177 billion (11.9% of GSP), and healthcare and social assistance at $4.554 billion (10.5% of GSP). In that same year, there were an estimated 141,936 small businesses in Maine. Of the 40,304 businesses that had employees, an estimated total of 39,288 or 97.5% were small companies. An estimated 4,300 new businesses were established in the state in 2004, up 6.6% from the year before. Business terminations that same year came to 4,987, up 5.8% from 2003. There were 138 business bankruptcies in 2004, up 31.4% from the previous year. In 2005, the state's personal bankruptcy (Chapter 7 and Chapter 13) filing rate was 352 filings per 100,000 people, ranking Maine as the 44th highest in the nation.

21 INCOME

In 2005 Maine had a gross state product (GSP) of $45 billion which accounted for 0.4% of the nation's gross domestic product and placed the state at number 44 in highest GSP among the 50 states and the District of Columbia.

According to the Bureau of Economic Analysis, in 2004 Maine had a per capita personal income (PCPI) of $30,046. This ranked 34th in the United States and was 91% of the national average of $33,050. The 1994–2004 average annual growth rate of PCPI was 4.5%. Maine had a total personal income (TPI) of $39,510,398,000, which ranked 41st in the United States and reflected an increase of 6.0% from 2003. The 1994–2004 average annual growth rate of TPI was 5.1%. Earnings of persons employed in Maine increased from $26,649,983,000 in 2003 to $28,240,580,000 in 2004, an increase of 6.0%. The 2003–04 national change was 6.3%.

The US Census Bureau reports that the three-year average median household income for 2002 to 2004 in 2004 dollars was $39,395 compared to a national average of $44,473. During the same period an estimated 12.2% of the population was below the poverty line as compared to 12.4% nationwide.

22 LABOR

According to the Bureau of Labor Statistics (BLS), in April 2006 the seasonally adjusted civilian labor force in Maine numbered 716,300, with approximately 30,000 workers unemployed, yielding an unemployment rate of 4.2%, compared to the national average of 4.7% for the same period. Preliminary data for the same period placed nonfarm employment at 613,300. Since the beginning of the BLS data series in 1976, the highest unemployment rate recorded in Maine was 9% in March 1977. The historical low was 3% in January 2001. Preliminary nonfarm employment data by occupation for April 2006 showed that approximately 5% of the labor force was employed in construction; 9.7% in manufacturing; 20.4% in trade, transportation, and public utilities; 5.5% in financial activities; 8.3% in professional and business services; 18.4% in education and health services; 9.7% in leisure and hospitality services; and 17.1% in government.

The US Department of Labor's Bureau of Labor Statistics reported that in 2005, a total of 69,000 of Maine's 582,000 employed wage and salary workers were formal members of a union. This represented 11.9% of those so employed, up from 11.3% in 2004, but still below the national average of 12%. Overall in 2005, a total of 79,000 workers (13.6%) in Maine were covered by a union or employee association contract, which includes those workers who reported no union affiliation. Maine is one of 28 states that does not have a right-to-work law.

As of 1 March 2006, Maine had a state-mandated minimum wage rate of $6.50 per hour. In 2004, women in the state accounted for 48.1% of the employed civilian labor force.

23 AGRICULTURE

Maine's gross farm income in 2005 was $546 million (43rd in the United States). There were 7,200 farms in 2004, with an estimated 1,370,000 acres (554,000 hectares) of land.

Maine's agriculture and food processing industries contribute over $1 billion annually to the state's economy. Maine produces more food crops for human consumption than any other New England state. Maine ranks first in the world in the production of blueberries, producing over 25% of the total blueberry crop and over 50% of the world's wild blueberries. Maine is also home to the largest bio-agricultural firm in the world, which produces breeding stock for the broiler industry worldwide. In New England, Maine ranks first in potato production and second in the production of milk and apples. Nationally, Maine ranks third in maple syrup and seventh in potatoes with 19,220,000 hundredweight. The greenhouse/nursery and wild blueberry sectors have also shown steady growth in total sales since 1990.

24 ANIMAL HUSBANDRY

In 2005, Maine had an estimated 92,000 cattle and calves worth around $101.2 million. Dairy farmers had an estimated 35,000 milk cows, which produced 624 million lb (283.6 million kg) of milk in 2003. Poultry farmers sold an estimated 10.2 million lb (4.6 million kg) of chickens in the same year. South-central Maine is the leading poultry region.

25 FISHING

Fishing has been important to the economy of Maine since its settlement. In 2004, Maine landings brought a total of 208.4 million lb (84.3 million kg) with a value of $315.8 million (the third highest value in the nation). Rockland and Portland were main ports.

The most valuable Maine fishery product is the lobster. In 2004, Maine led the nation in landings of American lobster for the 23rd consecutive year, with 58.5 million lb (26.6 million kg), valued at $238.5 million. Flounder, halibut, scallops, and shrimp are also caught. Maine also was the leading state in soft clams catch, with 2.4 million lb of meats (1.1 million kg) in 2004. In 2003, there were 35 processing and 176 wholesale plants in the state, with a total of about 1,780 employees. The state commercial fleet in 2001 had 5,836 boats and 1,656 vessels.

In 2004, Maine had 15 trout farms, with sales of $363,000. Maine has nine inland fish hatcheries and hosts two national fish hatcheries. In 2004, there were 270,698 licensed sports fishing participants in the state.

26 FORESTRY

Maine's 17.7 million acres (7.2 million hectares) of forest in 2003 contained over 3.6 billion trees and covered 90% of the state's land area, the largest percentage for any state in the United States. About 16,952,000 acres (6,860,000 hectares) are classified as commercial timberland, over 96% of it privately owned, and half of that by a dozen large paper companies and land managing corporations. Principal commercial hardwood include ash, hard maple, white and yellow birch, beech, and oak; commercially significant softwoods include white pine, hemlock, cedar, spruce, and fir. Total lumber production in 2004 was 964 million board feet, of which 86% was softwood.

27 MINING

According to preliminary data from the US Geological Survey (USGS), the estimated value of nonfuel mineral production by Maine in 2003 was $100 million, only a marginal increase from 2002.

Construction minerals and materials accounted for the bulk of the state's nonfuel mineral output, by value, in 2003. According to the USGS, construction sand and gravel, and crushed stone collectively accounted for around 65% of the state's nonfuel mineral output, by value that year. According to the preliminary data, Maine produced 9.3 million metric tons of construction sand and gravel, with a value of $39.1 million, while crushed stone output stood at 4.4 million metric tons and was valued at $26 million. Portland cement and dimension granite were also important nonfuel mineral commodities produced in Maine that same year.

In 2003, Maine was ranked 12th among the 50 states in the production of gemstones by value ($262,000), according to the USGS data.

28 ENERGY AND POWER

As of 2003, Maine had 29 electrical power service providers, of which 4 were publicly owned and 3 were cooperatives. Of the remainder, one was investor owned, two were owners of independent generators that sold directly to customers, fourteen were generation-only suppliers and five were delivery-only providers. As of that same year there were 760,859 retail customers. Of that total, energy only suppliers had 748,446 customers, while only 33 received their power from investor-owned service providers. Cooperatives accounted for 2,402 customers, and publicly owned providers had 9,976 customers. There were only two independent generator or "facility" customers. There was no customer data on delivery-only service providers.

Total net summer generating capability by the state's electrical generating plants in 2003 stood at 4.285 million kW, with total production that same year at 18.971 billion kWh. Of the total amount generated, all of it (100%) came from independent producers and combined heat and power service providers. The largest portion of all electric power generated, 9.438 billion kWh (49.8%), came from natural gas fired plants, with plants using other renewable sources in second place with 3.909 billion kWh (20.6%) and hydroelectric plants in third place at 3.172 billion kWh (16.7%). Petroleum and coal fueled power plants accounted for 10.1% and 2% of all power generated, respectively, while "other" types of generating facilities accounted for0.8%.

Maine no longer generates electricity through nuclear power. Citing economic and regulatory concerns, the owners of Maine's only nuclear power plant, the Maine Yankee Atomic Power Com-

pany plant in Wicasset, was shut down in 1997, and as of 2003 it was being dismantled and the site restored for other uses.

With no proven reserves or production of crude oil, coal or natural gas, all these products, must be imported into the state from either abroad or from other states. Natural gas is piped into the southwest corner of the state, and is available in Portland and the Lewiston-Auburn area.

29 INDUSTRY

Manufacturing in Maine has always been dependent upon the forests. During the 18th and 19th centuries, the staples of Maine industry were shipbuilding and lumber; as of 2005, papermaking and wood products, footwear, textiles and apparel, shipbuilding, and electronic components and accessories are all important industries.

Maine has the largest paper-production capacity of any state in the nation. There are large paper mills and pulp mills in more than a dozen towns and cities. As of 2004, wood-related industries—paper, lumber, wood products—accounted for about 25% of the value of all manufactured product shipments by value.

According to the US Census Bureau's Annual Survey of Manufactures (ASM) for 2004, Maine's manufacturing sector covered some 16 product subsectors. The shipment value of all products manufactured in the state that same year was $13.656 billion. Of that total, paper manufacturing accounted for the largest share at $3.601 billion. It was followed by transportation equipment manufacturing at $2.019 billion; food manufacturing at $1.623 billion; wood and paper product manufacturing at $1.240 billion; computer and electronic product manufacturing at $760.719 million; and fabricated metal product manufacturing at $710.573 million.

In 2004, a total of 57,901 people in Maine were employed in the state's manufacturing sector, according to the ASM. Of that total, 42,472 were actual production workers. In terms of total employment, the transportation equipment manufacturing industry accounted for the largest portion of all manufacturing employees at 9,005, with 6,618 actual production workers. It was followed by paper manufacturing at 8,454 employees (6,800 actual production workers); food manufacturing at 7,708 employees (5,206 actual production workers); wood product manufacturing at 5,700 employees (4,452 actual production workers); and fabricated metal product manufacturing with 3,996 employees (2,978 actual production workers).

ASM data for 2004 showed that Maine's manufacturing sector paid $2.316 billion in wages. Of that amount, the paper manufacturing sector accounted for the largest share at $489.690 million. It was followed by transportation equipment manufacturing at $373.078 million; food manufacturing at $251.645 million; wood product manufacturing at $183.615 million; and computer and electronic product manufacturing at $167.160 million.

30 COMMERCE

According to the 2002 Census of Wholesale Trade, Maine's wholesale trade sector had sales that year totaling $10.3 billion from 1,669 establishments. Wholesalers of durable goods accounted for 927 establishments, followed by nondurable goods wholesalers at 662 and electronic markets, agents, and brokers accounting for 80 establishments. Sales by durable goods wholesalers in 2002 totaled $3 billion, while wholesalers of nondurable goods saw sales of $6.7

billion. Electronic markets, agents, and brokers in the wholesale trade industry had sales of $584.3 million.

In the 2002 Census of Retail Trade, Maine was listed as having 7,050 retail establishments with sales of $16.05 billion. The leading types of retail businesses by number of establishments were: miscellaneous store retailers (943); food and beverage stores (940); gasoline stations (893); clothing and clothing accessories stores (636); and building materials/garden equipment and supplies dealers (635). In terms of sales, motor vehicle and motor vehicle parts dealers accounted for the largest share of retail sales at $3.7 billion, followed by food and beverage stores at $2.7 billion; general merchandise stores at $1.9 billion; gasoline stations at $1.49 billion; and building material/garden equipment and supplies dealers at $1.40 billion. A total of 80,251 people were employed by the retail sector in Maine that year.

Maine has shipping facilities located in Portland, Searsport, and Eastport. Exports from Maine totaled $2.3 billion in 2005. Maine's largest trading partners are Canada, Singapore, Malaysia, Japan, and the UK.

31 CONSUMER PROTECTION

Consumer protection issues in Maine are handled by the state's Attorney General's Office and the Bureau of Financial Institutions. Under the Attorney General's Office are the Consumer Protection Division and the Office of Credit Regulation. The Consumer Protection Division is responsible for the protection of consumers through enforcement of a wide variety of laws including Maine's Unfair Trade Practices Act, and the state's merger statute, the Mini-Sherman Act. The Division also provides a consumer mediation service under its Consumer Mediation Program, which uses volunteer mediators to resolve disputes between businesses and consumers.

The second department is the Office of Consumer Credit Regulation which was established in 1974 to protect state residents from unjust and misleading consumer credit practices, particularly in relation to the federal Truth-in-Lending Act. The agency also administers state laws regulating collection agencies, credit reporting agencies, mortgage companies, loan brokers, rent-to-own companies, pawn brokers, money order issuers, check cashers, and money transmitters.

However, consumer complaints regarding credit cards and banks are the responsibility of the Bureau of Financial Institution's Consumer Outreach Program.

When dealing with consumer protection issues, the state's Attorney General's Office can initiate civil and criminal proceedings; represent the state before state and federal regulatory agencies; administer consumer protection and education programs; and exercise broad subpoena powers. In antitrust actions, the Attorney General's Office can act on behalf of those consumers who are incapable of acting on their own; initiate damage actions on behalf of the state in state courts; and initiate criminal proceedings. However, the Attorney General cannot represent counties, cities and other governmental entities in recovering civil damages under state or federal law.

The Office of Consumer Credit Regulation and the Consumer Protection Division are both located in Augusta.

32 BANKING

As of June 2005, Maine had 37 insured banks, savings and loans, and saving banks, plus 12 state-chartered and 63 federally chartered credit unions (CUs). Excluding the CUs, the Portland-South Portland-Biddeford market area accounted for the largest portion of the state's financial institutions and deposits in 2004, with 22 institutions and $8.021 billion in deposits. As of June 2005, CUs accounted for 7.9% of all assets held by all financial institutions in the state, or some $3.974 billion. Banks, savings and loans, and savings banks collectively accounted for the remaining 92.1% or $46.590 billion in assets held.

Regulation of Maine's state-chartered banks is the responsibility of the Department of Professional and Financial Regulation's Bureau of Banking.

33 INSURANCE

In 2004 there were 583,000 individual life insurance policies in force with a total value of about $43.8 billion; total value for all categories of life insurance (individual, group, and credit) was about $81 billion. The average coverage amount is $75,200 per policy holder. Death benefits paid that year totaled at about $197.4 million.

In 2003, there were 2 life and health and 23 property and casualty insurance companies were domiciled in the state. In 2004, direct premiums for property and casualty insurance totaled $1.89 billion. That year, there were 7,064 flood insurance policies in force in the state, with a total value of 1 billion.

In 2004, 51% of state residents held employment-based health insurance policies, 4% held individual policies, and 10% of residents were uninsured. In 2003, employee contributions for employment-based health coverage averaged at 18% for single coverage and 28% for family coverage. The state offers a 12-month health benefits expansion program for small-firm employees in connection with the Consolidated Omnibus Budget Reconciliation Act (COBRA, 1986), a health insurance program for those who lose employment-based coverage due to termination or reduction of work hours.

In 2003, there were 979.487 auto insurance policies in effect for private passenger cars. Required minimum coverage includes bodily injury liability of up to $50,000 per individual and $100,000 for all persons injured in an accident, as well as property damage liability of $25,000. Uninsured and underinsured motorist insurance are also mandatory. In 2003, the average expenditure per vehicle for insurance coverage was $630.79.

34 SECURITIES

There are no securities or commodities exchanges in Maine. In 2005, there were 300 personal financial advisers employed in the state and 850 securities, commodities, and financial services sales agents. In 2004, there were at least sixteen publicly traded companies within the state, with seven NASDAQ companies, two NYSE listings, and four AMEX listings. In 2006, the state had one Fortune 500 company, Energy East, locate in New Gloucester. Listed on the NYSE, Energy East was 405 on the list of 500 largest companies in the nation, with revenues in excess of $5.2 billion.

35 PUBLIC FINANCE

Maine's biennial budget is prepared by the Bureau of the Budget, within the Department of Administrative and Financial Services, and submitted by the governor to the Legislature for consideration. The fiscal year (FY) extends from 1 July to 30 June.

Fiscal year 2006 general funds were estimated at $2.8 billion for resources and $2.8 billion for expenditures. In fiscal year 2004, federal government grants to Maine were $2.7 billion.

Maine—State Government Finances

(Dollar amounts in thousands. Per capita amounts in dollars.)

	AMOUNT	PER CAPITA
Total Revenue	8,309,930	6,319.34
General revenue	6,795,343	5,167.56
Intergovernmental revenue	2,573,528	1,957.06
Taxes	2,896,759	2,202.86
General sales	917,248	697.53
Selective sales	442,904	336.81
License taxes	158,199	120.30
Individual income tax	1,160,028	882.15
Corporate income tax	111,616	84.88
Other taxes	106,764	81.19
Current charges	537,145	408.48
Miscellaneous general revenue	787,911	599.17
Utility revenue	–	–
Liquor store revenue	90,996	69.20
Insurance trust revenue	1,423,591	1,082.58
Total expenditure	7,322,061	5,568.11
Intergovernmental expenditure	1,049,160	797.84
Direct expenditure	6,272,901	4,770.27
Current operation	4,809,684	3,657.55
Capital outlay	412,412	313.62
Insurance benefits and repayments	588,977	447.89
Assistance and subsidies	209,796	159.54
Interest on debt	252,032	191.66
Exhibit: Salaries and wages	667,051	507.26
Total expenditure	7,322,061	5,568.11
General expenditure	6,671,149	5,073.12
Intergovernmental expenditure	1,049,160	797.84
Direct expenditure	5,621,989	4,275.28
General expenditures, by function:		
Education	1,653,605	1,257.49
Public welfare	2,286,375	1,738.69
Hospitals	54,515	41.46
Health	437,145	332.43
Highways	536,777	408.20
Police protection	61,840	47.03
Correction	112,083	85.23
Natural resources	186,889	142.12
Parks and recreation	11,225	8.54
Government administration	256,764	195.26
Interest on general debt	252,032	191.66
Other and unallocable	821,899	625.02
Utility expenditure	–	–
Liquor store expenditure	61,935	47.10
Insurance trust expenditure	588,977	447.89
Debt at end of fiscal year	4,643,988	3,531.55
Cash and security holdings	13,952,432	10,610.21

Abbreviations and symbols: – zero or rounds to zero; (NA) not available; (X) not applicable.

SOURCE: *U.S. Census Bureau, Governments Division, 2004 Survey of State Government Finances,* January 2006.

On 5 January 2006 the federal government released $100 million in emergency contingency funds targeted to the areas with the greatest need, including $1.6 million for Maine.

36 TAXATION

In 2005, Maine collected $3,071 million in tax revenues or $2,323 per capita, which placed it 19th among the 50 states in per capita tax burden. The national average was $2,192 per capita. Property taxes accounted for 1.4% of the total, sales taxes 30.4%, selective sales taxes 13.9%, individual income taxes 42.3%, corporate income taxes 4.4%, and other taxes 7.5%.

As of 1 January 2006, Maine had four individual income tax brackets ranging from 2.0 to 8.5%. The state taxes corporations at rates ranging from 3.5 to 8.93% depending on tax bracket.

In 2004, state and local property taxes amounted to $2,099,394,000 or $1,596 per capita. The per capita amount ranks the state sixth-highest nationally. Local governments collected $2,054,086,000 of the total and the state government $45,308,000.

Maine taxes retail sales at a rate of 5%. Food purchased for consumption off-premises is tax exempt. The tax on cigarettes is 200 cents per pack, which ranks fourth among the 50 states and the District of Columbia. Maine taxes gasoline at 25.9 cents per gallon. This is in addition to the 18.4 cents per gallon federal tax on gasoline.

According to the Tax Foundation, for every federal tax dollar sent to Washington in 2004, Maine citizens received $1.40 in federal spending.

37 ECONOMIC POLICY

The Finance Authority of Maine (FAME) encourages industrial and recreational projects by insuring mortgage loans, selling tax-exempt bonds to aid industrial development and natural-resource enterprises, authorizing municipalities to issue such revenue bonds, and guaranteeing loans to small businesses, veterans, and natural-resource enterprises. The Department of Economic and Community Development (DECD), created in 1987, provides technical, financial, training, and marketing assistance for existing Maine businesses and companies interested in establishing operations in the state. The DECD offers programs in the areas of business development, international trade, tourism, film, and community development. Pine Tree Development Zone (PTDZ) legislation was enacted in 2003 and amended in 2005. The initiative supports new "qualified business activity" in Maine by offering manufacturers, financial service businesses, and targeted technology companies the chance to greatly reduce, or in some cases, virtually eliminate state taxes for up to 10 years.

38 HEALTH

The infant mortality rate in October 2005 was estimated at 6.1 per 1,000 live births. The birth rate in 2003 was 10.6 per 1,000 population, the lowest rate in the country for that year. The abortion rate stood at 9.9 per 1,000 women in 2000. In 2003, about 87.5% of pregnant woman received prenatal care beginning in the first trimester. In 2004, approximately 82% of children received routine immunizations before the age of three.

The crude death rate in 2003 was 9.6 deaths per 1,000 population. As of 2002, the death rates for major causes of death (per 100,000 resident population) were: heart disease, 244.9; cancer,

247.7; cerebrovascular diseases, 63.6; chronic lower respiratory diseases, 61.1; and diabetes, 31.2. Maine had the second-highest cancer death rate in the nation, following West Virginia. The mortality rate from HIV infection was not available. In 2004, the reported AIDS case rate was at about 4.6 per 100,000 population. In 2002, about 55.9% of the population was considered overweight or obese. As of 2004, about 20.9% of state residents were smokers.

In 2003, Maine had 37 community hospitals with about 3,700 beds. There were about 149,000 patient admissions that year and 6.5 million outpatient visits. The average daily inpatient census was about 2,200 patients. The average cost per day for hospital care was $1,416. Also in 2003, there were about 119 certified nursing facilities in the state with 7,552 beds and an overall occupancy rate of about 92.1%. In 2004, it was estimated that about 69.6% of all state residents had received some type of dental care within the year. Maine had 302 physicians per 100,000 resident population in 2004 and 1,009 nurses per 100,000 in 2005. In 2004, there were a total of 629 dentists in the state.

In 2003, Maine ranked first in the nation for the highest percentage of residents on Medicaid at 29%. In 2004, the state had the second-highest percentage of residents on Medicare at 18%. Approximately 10% of the state population was uninsured in 2004. In 2003, state health care expenditures totaled $2.1 million.

39 SOCIAL WELFARE

In 2004, about 33,000 people received unemployment benefits, with the average weekly unemployment benefit at $235. In fiscal year 2005, the estimated average monthly participation in the food stamp program included about 152,910 persons (78,170 households); the average monthly benefit was about $88.40 per person. That year, the total of benefits paid through the state for the food stamp program was about $162.2 million.

Temporary Assistance for Needy Families (TANF), the system of federal welfare assistance that officially replaced Aid to Families with Dependent Children (AFDC) in 1997, was reauthorized through the Deficit Reduction Act of 2005. TANF is funded through federal block grants that are divided among the states based on an equation involving the number of recipients in each state. Maine's TANF work program is called Additional Support for People in Retraining and Employment (ASPIRE). In 2004, the state program had 27,000 recipients; state and federal expenditures on this TANF program totaled $87 million in fiscal year 2003.

Despite Maine's relatively low personal income and large proportion of residents below the poverty level, welfare payments per capita generally fall short of the national norms. In December 2004, Social Security benefits were paid to 265,470 Maine residents. This number included 160,320 retired workers, 25,390 widows and widowers, 43,580 disabled workers, 13,590 spouses, and 22,590 children. Social Security beneficiaries represented 20.2% of the total state population and 95.3% of the state's population age 65 and older. Retired workers received an average monthly payment of $882; widows and widowers, $856; disabled workers, $819; and spouses, $444. Payments for children of retired workers averaged $451 per month; children of deceased workers, $630; and children of disabled workers, $231. Federal Supplemental Security Income payments in December 2004 went to 31,641 Maine residents, averaging $364 a month. An additional $615,000 of state-administered supplemental payments were distributed to 32,557 residents.

40 HOUSING

Housing for Maine families has improved substantially since 1960, when the federal census categorized 57,000 of Maine's 364,650 housing units as deteriorated or dilapidated. Between 1970 and 1989, over 200,000 new units were built. However, as of 2004, about 31.7% of the entire housing stock was built in 1939 or earlier.

There were an estimated 676,667 housing units in Maine in 2004. Approximately 534,412 of the total units were occupied, with 72.9% being owner-occupied. About 68.9% of all units are single-family, detached homes. Fuel oils and kerosene are the primary heating fuel for most units. It was estimated that 12,214 units lacked telephone service, 3,771 lacked complete plumbing facilities, and 3,336 lacked complete kitchen facilities. The average household had 2.39 members.

In 2004, 8,800 privately owned units were authorized for construction. The median home value is $143,182. The median monthly cost for mortgage owners was $1,020. Renters paid a median of $582 per month. In September 2005, the state received grants of $548,824 from the US Department of Housing and Urban Development (HUD) for rural housing and economic development programs. For 2006, HUD allocated to the state over $14 million in community development block grants.

41 EDUCATION

In 2004, 87.1% of Maine residents age 25 and older were high school graduates; 24.2% had obtained a bachelor's degree or higher.

The total enrollment for fall 2002 in Maine's public schools stood at 204,000. Of these, 142,000 attended schools from kindergarten through grade eight, and 63,000 attended high school. Approximately 95.8% of the students were white, 1.7% were black, 0.8% were Hispanic, 1.2% were Asian/Pacific Islander, and 0.5% were American Indian/Alaskan Native. Total enrollment was estimated at 200,000 in fall 2003 and expected to be 178,000 by fall 2014, a decline of 12.8% during the period 2002 to 2014. In fall 2003 there were 20,696 students enrolled in 151 private schools. Expenditures for public education in 2003/04 were estimated at $2.2 billion or $9,534 per student. Since 1969, the National Assessment of Educational Progress (NAEP) has tested public school students nationwide. The resulting report, *The Nation's Report Card,* stated that in 2005 eighth graders in Maine scored 281 out of 500 in mathematics compared with the national average of 278.

As of fall 2002, there were 63,308 students enrolled in institutions of higher education; minority students comprised 4.9% of total postsecondary enrollment. As of 2005 Maine had 30 degree-granting institutions. Since 1968, the state's public colleges and universities have been incorporated into a single University of Maine System. The original land grant campus is at Orono; the other major campus in the system is the University of Southern Maine at Portland and Gorham. The state also operates the Maine Maritime Academy at Castine and the Maine Technical College System, comprised of seven technical colleges. Of the state's private colleges and professional schools, Bowdoin College in Brunswick, Colby College in Waterville, and Bates College in Lewiston are the best known.

⁴²ARTS

Maine has long held an attraction for painters and artists, Winslow Homer and Andrew Wyeth among them. The state abounds in summer theaters, the oldest and most famous of which is at Ogunquit. The Ogunquit Playhouse is one of the nation's leading summer theaters and in 2006 it celebrated its 74th anniversary. The Portland Symphony (est. 1923) is Maine's leading orchestra and is recognized as one of the nation's top orchestras of its size. Augusta and Bangor also host symphonies. The Maine State Ballet Company is based in Westbrook. The Portland Ballet is also well known in the state. The Bossov Ballet Theatre in Pittsfield is part of a boarding school for high school students looking for rigorous preprofessional training in dance. In 2001, the Maine Grand Opera Company gave its first performances, at the Camden Opera House. There are many local theater groups.

The Arcady Summer Music Festival (est. 1980) specializes in chamber music performances. The annual Bowdoin Summer Music Festival (est. 1964), presented at Bowdoin College in Brunswick, provides programs for over 200 students—ranging from high school to graduate studies—annually.

In 1979, Maine became the first state to allow inheritance taxes to be paid with qualified artworks. The Maine Arts Commission is an independent state agency funded in part by the Maine State Legislature and the National Endowment for the Arts. The state Department of Educational and Cultural Services has an Arts and Humanities Bureau that provides funds to artists in residence, Maine touring artists, and community arts councils. In 2005, the Maine Arts Commission and other Maine arts organizations received 20 grants totaling $956,826 from the National Endowment for the Arts. Additional funds are provided from the state and other private sources.

The Maine Humanities Council (MHC), founded in 1975, provides support to approximately 100 nonprofit art organizations each year. In 2004, MHC awarded 87 grants to 81 organizations throughout the state. Several ongoing reading programs sponsored in part by MHC include "Born to Read," for children and youth; "New Books, New Readers," for adult learners; and "Let's Talk About It," for adult readers. In 2005, the state received 10 grants totaling $1,021,426 from the National Endowment for the Humanities.

⁴³LIBRARIES AND MUSEUMS

For the calendar year 2001, Maine had 273 public library systems, with a total of 280 libraries, of which there were seven branches. In that same year, the system had 5,891,000 volumes of books and serial publications, and a combined total circulation of 8,155,000. The system also had 126,000 audio and 135,000 video items, and 2,000 electronic format items (CD-ROMs, magnetic tapes, and disks). Leading libraries and their book holdings in 1998 included the Maine State Library at Augusta (150,000 volumes), Bowdoin College at Brunswick (901,589), and the University of Maine School of Law (300,000). In 2001, operating income for the state's public library system was $27,985,000, which included $$1,000 in federal grants and $174,000 in state grants.

Maine has at least 121 museums and historic sites. The Maine State Museum in Augusta houses collections in history, natural history, anthropology, marine studies, mineralogy, science, and technology. The privately supported Maine Historical Society in Portland maintains a research library and the Wadsworth Longfellow House, the boyhood home of Henry Wadsworth Longfellow. The largest of several maritime museums is in Bath.

⁴⁴COMMUNICATIONS

In 2004, 96.6% of occupied housing units had telephones. In addition, by June of that same year there were 610,533 mobile wireless telephone subscribers. In 2003, 67.8% of Maine households had a computer and 57.9% had Internet access. By June 2005, there were 176,816 high-speed lines in Maine, 165,428 residential and 11,388 for business.

Maine had 33 major commercial radio stations (5 AM, 28 FM) in 2005, along with 11 major television stations. Educational television stations broadcast from Bangor, Calais, Lewiston, Portland, and Presque Isle. By 2000, a total of 25,583 Internet domain names had been registered in Maine.

⁴⁵PRESS

Maine had seven daily newspapers in 2005 and four papers with Sunday editions.

The most widely read newspapers with approximate 2005 circulation numbers are as follows:

AREA	NAME	DAILY	SUNDAY
Augusta	*Kennebec Journal* (m,S)	15,167	14,422
Bangor	*Daily News* (m,S)	62,462	74,754 (wknd)
Portland	*Press Herald/Sunday Telegram*	77,788	125,858

Regional interest magazines include *Maine Times* and *Down East*.

⁴⁶ORGANIZATIONS

In 2006, there were over 2,300 nonprofit organizations registered within the state, of which about 1,660 were registered as charitable, educational, or religious organizations. Among the organizations with headquarters in Maine are the Maine Potato Council (Presque Isle), the Maine Lobstermen's Association (Stonington), the Wild Blueberry Association of North America (Bar Harbor), and the Potato Association of America (Orono).

State and local organizations for arts and education include the Bluegrass Music Association of Maine, Maine Arts Commission, the Maine Folklife Center, the Maine Historical Society, the Maine Humanities Council, Maine Preservation, and the National Poetry Foundation, based at the University of Maine. There are a number of smaller local arts organizations and municipal and regional historical societies as well.

⁴⁷TOURISM, TRAVEL, AND RECREATION

In 2004, the state of Maine hosted 43 million travelers who spent $13.6 billion. About 34 million travelers were on day trips throughout the state, with nearly 71% of tourist activity involved out-of-state travelers. There were 8.9 million overnight trips. Tourism generated 176,600 jobs and created $3.8 billion in revenue.

Though Maine is a year-round resort destination, 59% of travelers arrive during the months of July, August, and September. Sightseeing and outdoor activities are the primary tourist attractions.

In the summer, the southern coast offers sandy beaches, icy surf, and several small harbors for sailing and saltwater fishing. Northeastward, the scenery becomes more rugged and spectacular, and sailing and hiking are the primary activities. Hundreds of lakes, ponds, rivers, and streams offer opportunities for freshwater bathing, boating, and fishing. Whitewater canoeing lures the adventurous along the Allagash Wilderness Waterway in northern Maine. Maine has always attracted hunters, especially during the fall deer season. Wintertime recreation facilities include nearly 60 ski areas and countless opportunities for cross-country skiing.

There are 12 state parks and beaches. Baxter State Park in central Maine includes Mount Katahdin. Acadia National Park is a popular attraction, along with other wildlife areas, refuges, and forests. Aroostook, Maine's largest and northernmost county, has five state parks. The state fair is held at Bangor. The Acadia area features Acadia National Park and the site of Campobello, Franklin Delano Roosevelt's summer home. The area containing the Kennebec and Moose rivers and Lake George has three state parks. Kennebunkport on the southern coast is the site of the family home of President George H. W. Bush. Route 1, between Kittery and Fort Kent, has the largest three-dimensional model of the solar system in the world.

48 SPORTS

Maine has no major professional sports teams. The Portland Pirates (a minor league hockey team) of the American Hockey League play on their home ice at the Cumberland County Civic Center in Portland. Minor league baseball's Sea Dogs of the Double-A Eastern League play their games at Hadlock Field, which opened in 1994. Harness racing is held at Scarborough Downs and other tracks and fairgrounds throughout the state. Sailing is a popular participant sport with a Windsummer Festival held each July at Boothbay Harbor and a Retired Skippers Race at Castine in August. Joan Benoit-Samuelson, famous distance runner during the 1980s, was born in Cape Elizabeth.

49 FAMOUS MAINERS

The highest federal officeholders born in Maine were Hannibal Hamlin (1809–91), the nation's first Republican vice president, under Abraham Lincoln, and Nelson A. Rockefeller (1908–79), governor of New York State from 1959 to 1973 and US vice president under Gerald Ford. James G. Blaine (b.Pennsylvania, 1830–93), a lawyer and politician, served 13 years as a US representative from Maine and a term in the Senate; on his third try, he won the Republican presidential nomination in 1884 but lost to Grover Cleveland, later serving as secretary of state (1889–92) under Benjamin Harrison. Edmund S. Muskie (1914–96), leader of the Democratic revival in Maine in the 1950s, followed two successful terms as governor with 21 years in the Senate until appointed secretary of state by President Jimmy Carter in 1980.

Other conspicuous state and national officeholders have included Rufus King (1755–1827), a member of the Continental Congress and Constitutional Convention and US minister to Great Britain; William King (1768–1852), leader of the movement for Maine statehood and the state's first governor; Joshua Lawrence

Chamberlain, (1828–1914), Civil War hero and four-term governor who established the college that eventually became the University of Maine; Thomas Bracket Reed (1839–1902), longtime speaker of the US House of Representatives; and Margaret Chase Smith (1897–1995), who served longer in the US Senate—24 years—than any other woman.

Names prominent in Maine's colonial history include those of Sir Ferdinando Gorges (b.England, 1566–1647), the founder and proprietor of the colony; Sir William Phips (1651–95), who became the first American knight for his recovery of a Spanish treasure, later serving as royal governor of Massachusetts; and Sir William Pepperrell (1696–1759), who led the successful New England expedition against Louisburg in 1745, for which he became the first American-born baronet.

Maine claims a large number of well-known reformers and humanitarians: Dorothea Lynde Dix (1802–87), who led the movement for hospitals for the insane; Elijah Parish Lovejoy (1802–37), an abolitionist killed while defending his printing press from a proslavery mob in St. Louis, Missouri; Neal Dow (1804–97), who drafted and secured passage of the Maine prohibition laws of 1846 and 1851, later served as a Civil War general, and ran for president on the Prohibition Party ticket in 1880; and Harriet Beecher Stowe (b.Connecticut, 1811–96), whose *Uncle Tom's Cabin* (1852) was written in Maine.

Other important writers include poet Henry Wadsworth Longfellow (1807–82), born in Portland while Maine was still part of Massachusetts; humorist Artemus Ward (Charles Farrar Browne, 1834–67); Sarah Orne Jewett (1849–1909), novelist and short-story writer; Kate Douglas Wiggin (1856–1923), author of *Rebecca of Sunnybrook Farm;* Kenneth Roberts (1885–1957), historical novelist; and Robert Peter Tristram Coffin (1892–1955), poet, essayist, and novelist. Edwin Arlington Robinson (1869–1935) and Edna St. Vincent Millay (1892–1950) were both Pulitzer Prize-winning poets, and novelist Marguerite Yourcenar (b.Belgium, 1903–87), a resident of Mt. Desert Island, became in 1980 the first woman ever elected to the Académie Française. Winslow Homer (b.Massachusetts, 1836–1910) had a summer home at Prouts Neck, where he painted many of his seascapes.

50 BIBLIOGRAPHY

Alampi, Gary (ed.). *Gale State Rankings Reporter.* Detroit: Gale Research, Inc., 1994.

Beem, Edgar Allen. *Maine: the Spirit of America.* New York: Harry N. Abrams, 2000.

Goulka, Jeremiah E. (ed.). *The Grand Old Man of Maine: Selected Letters of Joshua Lawrence Chamberlain, 1865-1914.* Chapel Hill: University of North Carolina Press, 2004.

Churchill, Edwin A., Joel W. Eastman, and Richard W. Judd (eds.). *Maine: The Pine Tree State from Prehistory to the Present.* Orono: University of Maine Press, 1995.

Cities of the United States. 5th ed. Farmington Hills: Thomson Gale, 2005.

Council of State Governments. *The Book of the States, 2006 Edition.* Lexington, Ky.: Council of State Governments, 2006.

FDIC, Division of Research and Statistics. *Statistics on Banking: A Statistical Profile of the United States Banking Industry.* Washington, D.C.: Federal Deposit Insurance Corporation, 1993.

McAuliffe, Emily. *Maine Facts and Symbols*. New York: Hilltop Books, 2000.

Palmer, Kenneth T. *Maine Politics & Government*. Lincoln: University of Nebraska Press, 1992.

Parker, Carol Mason. *Maine*. Uhrichsville, Ohio: Barbour Publishing, 2005.

Potholm, Christian P. *This Splendid Game: Maine Campaigns and Elections, 1940–2002*. Lanham, Md.: Lexington Books, 2003.

Smith, David C. *Studies in the Land: The Northeast Corner*. New York: Routledge, 2002.

US Department of Commerce, Economics and Statistics Administration, US Census Bureau. *Maine, 2000. Summary Social, Economic, and Housing Characteristics: 2000 Census of Population and Housing*. Washington, D.C.: US Government Printing Office, 2003.

US Department of Education, National Center for Education Statistics. Office of Educational Research and Improvement. *Digest of Education Statistics, 1993*. Washington, D.C.: US Government Printing Office, 1993.

US Department of the Interior, US Fish and Wildlife Service. *Endangered and Threatened Species Recovery Program*. Washington, D.C.: US Government Printing Office, 1990.

MARYLAND

State of Maryland

ORIGIN OF STATE NAME: Named for Henrietta Maria, queen consort of King Charles I of England. **NICK-NAME:** The Old Line State and the Free State. **CAPITAL:** Annapolis. **ENTERED UNION:** 28 April 1788 (7th). **SONG:** "Maryland, My Maryland." **MOTTO:** *Fatti maschii, parole femine* (Manly deeds, womanly words). **FLAG:** Bears the quartered arms of the Calvert and Crossland families (the paternal and maternal families of the founders of Maryland). **OFFICIAL SEAL:** REVERSE: A shield bearing the arms of the Calverts and Crosslands is surmounted by an earl's coronet and a helmet and supported by a farmer and fisherman. The state motto (originally that of the Calverts) appears on a scroll below. The circle is surrounded by the Latin legend *Scuto bonæ voluntatis tuæ; coronasti nos,* meaning "With the shield of thy favor hast thou compassed us"; and "1632," the date of Maryland's first charter. OBVERSE: Lord Baltimore is seen as a knight in armor on a charger. The surrounding inscription, in Latin, means "Cecilius, Absolute Lord of Maryland and Avalon New Foundland, Baron of Baltimore." **BIRD:** Baltimore oriole. **FISH:** Rockfish. **FLOWER:** Black-eyed Susan. **TREE:** White oak. **LEGAL HOLIDAYS:** New Year's Day, 1 January; Birthday of Martin Luther King Jr., 3rd Monday in January; Presidents' day, 3rd Monday in February; Memorial Day, last Monday in May; Independence Day, 4 July; Labor Day, 1st Monday in September; Columbus Day, 12 October; Veterans' Day, 11 November; Thanksgiving Day, 4th Thursday in November plus one day; Christmas Day, 25 December. **TIME:** 7 AM EST = noon GMT.

¹LOCATION, SIZE, AND EXTENT

Located on the eastern seaboard of the United States in the South Atlantic region, Maryland ranks 42d in size among the 50 states.

Maryland's total area—10,460 sq mi (27,092 sq km)—comprises 9,837 sq mi (25,478 sq km) of land and 623 sq mi (1,614 sq km) of inland water. The state extends 199 mi (320 km) E–W and 126 mi (203 km) N–S.

Maryland is bordered on the N by Pennsylvania; on the E by Delaware and the Atlantic Ocean; on the S and SW by Virginia, the District of Columbia, and West Virginia (with the line passing through the Chesapeake Bay and Potomac River); and on the extreme W by West Virginia. Important islands in Chesapeake Bay, off Maryland's Eastern Shore (the Maryland sector of the Delmarva Peninsula), include Kent, Bloodsworth, South Marsh, and Smith.

The total boundary length of Maryland is 842 mi (1,355 km), including a general coastline of 31 mi (50 km); the total tidal shoreline extends 3,190 mi (5,134 km). The state's geographic center is in Prince George's County, 4.5 mi (7.2 km) NW of Davidsonville.

²TOPOGRAPHY

Three distinct regions characterize Maryland's topography. The first and major area, falling within the Atlantic Coastal Plain, is nearly bisected by the Chesapeake Bay, dividing Maryland into the Eastern Shore and the Western Shore. The Piedmont Plateau, west of the coastal lowlands, is broad, rolling upland with several deep gorges cut by rivers. Further west, from the Catoctin Mountains in Frederick County to the West Virginia border, is the Appalachian Mountain region, containing the state's highest hills. Backbone Mountain, in Garrett County in westernmost Mary-

land, is the state's highest point, at 3,360 ft (1,025 m). The mean elevation of the state is approximately 350 ft (107 m).

A few small islands lie in the Chesapeake Bay, Maryland's dominant waterway. Extending 195 mi (314 km) inland from the Atlantic and varying in width from 3 to 20 mi (5–32 km), the bay comprises 3,237 sq mi (8,384 sq km), of which 1,726 sq km (4,470 sq km) are under Maryland's jurisdiction. Principal rivers include the Potomac, forming much of the southern and western border; the Patapsco, which runs through Baltimore; the Patuxent, draining the Western Shore; and the Susquehanna, crossing the Pennsylvania border and emptying into the Chesapeake Bay in northeastern Maryland. The state has 23 rivers and other bays, as well as many lakes and creeks, none of any great size. The lowest point of the state is at sea level at the Atlantic Ocean.

³CLIMATE

Despite its small size, Maryland exhibits considerable climatic diversity. Temperatures vary from an annual average of 48°F (9°C) in the extreme western uplands to 59°F (15°C) in the southeast, where the climate is moderated by the Chesapeake Bay and the Atlantic Ocean. The annual average temperature for Baltimore is 56°F (13°C), ranging from 33°F (1°C) in January to 78°F (25°C) in July. The record high temperature for the state is 109°F (43°C), set on 10 July 1936 in Cumberland and Frederick counties; the record low, -40°F (-40°C), occurred on 13 January 1912 at Oakland in Garrett County.

Precipitation averages about 49 in (124 cm) annually in the southeast, but only 36 in (91 cm) in the Cumberland area west of the Appalachians; Baltimore averaged 41.9 in (106 cm) annually 1971–2000. As much as 100 in (254 cm) of snow falls in western

Garrett County, while 8–10 in (20–25 cm) is average for the Eastern Shore; and Baltimore receives about 20.8 in (52 cm).

⁴FLORA AND FAUNA

Maryland's three life zones—coastal plain, piedmont, and Appalachian—mingle wildlife characteristic of both North and South. Most of the state lies within a hardwood belt in which red and white oaks, yellow poplar, beech, blackgum, hickory, and white ash are represented; shortleaf and loblolly pines are the leading softwoods. Honeysuckle, Virginia creeper, wild grape, and wild raspberry are also common. Wooded hillsides are rich with such wild flowers as Carolina cranesbill, trailing arbutus, Mayapple, early blue violet, wild rose, and goldenrod. Seven plant species were listed by the US Fish and Wildlife Service as threatened or endangered in April 2006, including Canby's dropwort, sandplain gerardia, northeastern bulrush, and harperella.

The white-tailed (Virginia) deer, eastern cottontail, raccoon, and red and gray foxes are indigenous to Maryland, although urbanization has sharply reduced their habitat. Common small mammals are the woodchuck, eastern chipmunk, and gray squirrel. The brown-headed nuthatch has been observed in the extreme south, the cardinal and tufted titmouse are common in the piedmont, and the chestnut-sided warbler and rose-breasted grosbeak are native to the Appalachians. Among saltwater species, shellfish—especially oysters, clams, and crabs—have the greatest economic importance. Eighteen Maryland animal species (vertebrates and invertebrates) were listed as threatened or endangered in 2006, including the Indiana bat, Maryland darter, bald eagle, Delmarva Peninsula fox squirrel, three species of whale, and five species of turtle.

⁵ENVIRONMENTAL PROTECTION

Maryland's Department of Natural Resources manages water allocation, fish and wildlife, state parks and forests, land reclamation and open space. The Maryland Department of the Environment (MDE) serves as the state's primary environmental protection agency. MDE protects and restores the quality of Maryland's land, air, and water by assessing, preventing and controlling sources of pollution for the benefit of public health, the environment and future generations. MDE regulations control the storage, transportation, and disposal of hazardous wastes and ensure long-term, environmentally sound solid waste recycling and disposal capabilities. In 2003, 45.5 million lb of toxic chemicals were released in the state. Also in 2003, Maryland had 168 hazardous waste sites listed in the US Environment Protection Agency (EPA) database, 17 of which were on the National Priorities List as of 2006, including Andrews Air Force Base, Curtis Bay Coast Guard Yard, and Patuxent River Naval Air Station. In 2005, the EPA spent over $962,000 through the Superfund program for the cleanup of hazardous waste sites in the state. The same year, federal EPA grants awarded to the state included $2.3 million to support various Chesapeake Bay ecosystem protection projects.

MDE has broad regulatory, planning, and management responsibility for water quality, air quality, solid and hazardous waste management, stormwater management, sediment control, wetlands and waterways management, and water allocation. MDE also plays a pivotal role in Maryland's initiatives to protect and restore the Chesapeake Bay and has divided the state into 10 major tributary watershed basins, each of which have specific nutrient reduction strategies designed to give the Bay added protection from the effects of stormwater run-off, airborne pollutants, and direct discharges. The Chesapeake Bay Estuarine Complex was designated as a Ramsar Wetland of International Importance in 1987. In total, Maryland has about 591,000 acres (239,169 hectares) of wetlands.

MDE operates an innovative infrastructure financing program that leverages federal, state, and local funds to upgrade wastewater treatment plants, connect residents to public sewer systems, and improve water supply facilities. In addition, the Maryland Environmental Service, a quasi-public agency, contracts with local governments to design, construct, finance, and operate wastewater treatment plants, water supply systems, and recycling facilities.

The Maryland Department of Natural Resources (DNR) is responsible for the management, enhancement, and preservation of the state's living and natural resources. Utilizing an ecosystem approach to land, waterway, and species management, DNR programs and services support the health of the Chesapeake Bay and its tributaries, sustainable populations of fishery and wildlife species, and an integrated network of public lands and open space.

The Maryland Office of Planning's mission is to plan for the most effective development of the state and all of its resources. The Office assists state agencies and local governments to more effectively achieve environmental, agricultural, and natural resource objectives by integrating them with comprehensive planning and land use management. The state has recently embarked on a Neighborhood Conservation and Smart Growth initiative to encourage population and economic growth in priority funding areas, and to use a Rural Legacy Program to preserve agricultural, forest, and other rural lands from development.

⁶POPULATION

Maryland ranked 19th in population in the United States with an estimated total of 5,600,388 in 2005, an increase of 5.7% since 2000. Between 1990 and 2000, Maryland's population grew from 4,781,468 to 5,296,486, an increase of 10.8%. The population is projected to reach 6.2 million by 2015 and 6.7 million by 2025. In 2004 the median age was 36.8. Persons under 18 years old accounted for 25.1% of the population while 11.4% was age 65 or older.

The state's population doubled between 1940 and 1970 and increased 7.5% between 1970 and 1980. The enormous expansion of the federal government and exodus of people from Washington, DC, to the surrounding suburbs contributed to the rapid growth that made Maryland the 17th most populous state in 1980, with 4,216,446 residents. There was an increase of 13.4% between 1980 and 1990, when Maryland held the 19th ranking, with 4,781,468 people. The population density in 2004 was 572.3 persons per sq mi, the fifth-highest among the 50 states.

Almost all the growth since World War II has occurred in the four suburban counties around Washington, DC, and Baltimore. Metropolitan Baltimore, embracing Carroll, Howard, Hartford, Anne Arundel, and Baltimore counties, expanded from 2,244,700 to 2,491,254 between 1984 and 2000; the city of Baltimore, on the other hand, declined from 763,570 to 736,000 during the same period, and to an estimated 638,614 in 2002. Baltimore is the state's only major city; the estimated population in 2004 for the city prop-

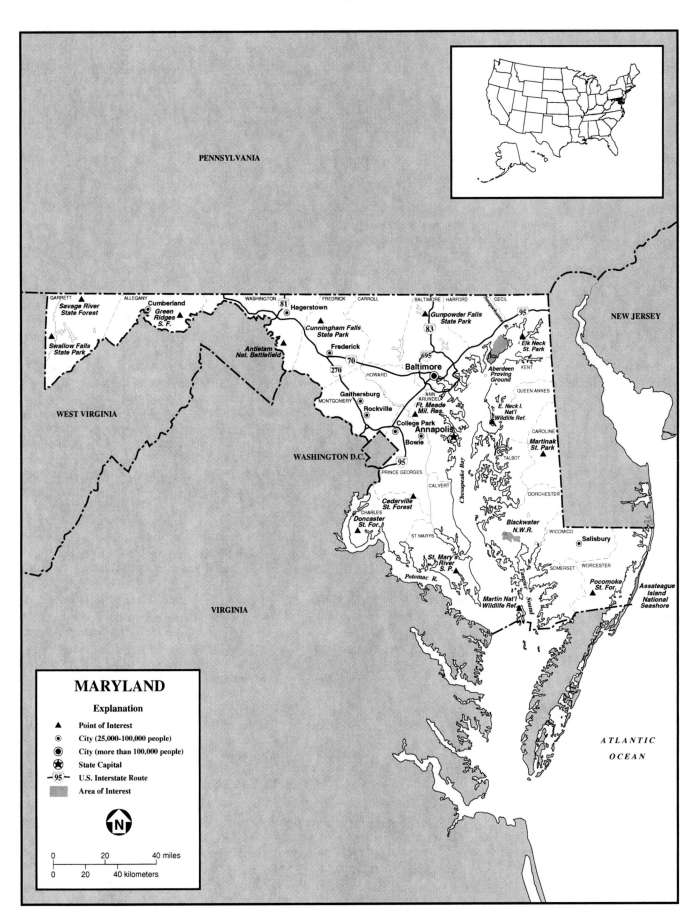

PENNSYLVANIA

NEW JERSEY

WEST VIRGINIA

GARRETT

Savage River
State Forest

ALLEGANY   Cumberland
           Green
           Ridges
           S. F.

Swallow Falls
State Park

WASHINGTON

Hagerstown

Cunningham Falls
State Park

Frederick

Antietam
Nat. Battlefield

FREDRICK   CARROLL

BALTIMORE   HARFORD

CECIL

Gunpowder Falls
State Park

Susquehanna R.

Elk Neck
St. Park

KENT

Aberdeen
Proving
Ground

QUEEN ANNES

Baltimore

HOWARD

Gaithersburg

MONTGOMERY

Rockville

College Park

Bowie

ANN
ARUNDEL

Ft. Meade
Mil. Res.

Annapolis

WASHINGTON D.C.

PRINCE GEORGES

Cedarville
St. Forest

CHARLES

Doncaster
St. For.

CALVERT

ST MARYS

St. Marys
River
S.P.

Potomac R.

Martin Nat'l
Wildlife Ref.

E. Neck I.
Nat'l
Wildlife Ref.

CAROLINE

Martinak
St. Park

TALBOT

DORCHESTER

Blackwater
N.W.R.

WICOMICO   Salisbury

Chesapeake Bay

Tangier Sound

SOMERSET   WORCESTER

Pocomoke
St. For.

Assateague
Island
National
Seashore

VIRGINIA

ATLANTIC

OCEAN

MARYLAND

Explanation

▲ Point of Interest
◉ City (25,000-100,000 people)
◎ City (more than 100,000 people)
✪ State Capital
─95─ U.S. Interstate Route
▨ Area of Interest

N

0   20   40 miles
0   20   40 kilometers

er was 636,251. The Baltimore metropolitan area has an estimated population of 2,639,213 in 2004. Several west-central counties belong to the Washington metropolitan area, and Cecil County, in the northeast, is part of metropolitan Wilmington, Delaware.

7 ETHNIC GROUPS

Blacks, numbering 1,477,411 in 2000, constitute the largest racial minority in Maryland. About one-third of Maryland's black population lives in the city of Baltimore. In 2004, 29.1% of the population was black.

Hispanics and Latinos, mostly from Puerto Rico and Central America, numbered 227,000 in 2000 (4.3% of the total population), up from 125,000. In 2004, 5.4% of the population was of Hispanic or Latino origin. In 2000, the Asian population was relatively large: 39,155 Koreans, 49,400 Chinese (nearly double the 1990 total of 26,479), 26,608 Filipinos, 6,620 Japanese, and 16,744 Vietnamese (up from 7,809 in 1990); the total Asian population was estimated at 210,929 in 2000. In 2004, 4.6% of the population was Asian. Pacific Islanders numbered 2,303 in 2000. In 2004, 0.1% of the population was of Pacific Island origin.

Foreign-born residents numbered 518,315, or 9.8% of the total population, in 2000, up from 313,494, or 6.5%, in 1990. Many immigrated to Maryland in the 1970s. A significant proportion of the state's German, Polish, and Russian immigrants were Jewish refugees arriving just before and after World War II. In 2000, the combined Native American population (including Eskimos and Aleuts) was estimated at 15,423. In 2004, 0.3% of the population was of American Indian or Native Alaskan origin.

8 LANGUAGES

Several Algonkian tribes originally inhabited what is now Maryland. There are some Indian place-names, such as Potomac, Susquehanna, and Allegheny.

The state's diverse topography has contributed to unusual diversity in its basic speech. Geographical isolation of the Delmarva Peninsula, proximity to the Virginia piedmont population, and access to southeastern and central Pennsylvania helped to yield a language mixture that now is dominantly Midland and yet reflects earlier ties to Southern English.

Regional features occur as well. In the northeast are found eastern Pennsylvania *pavement* (sidewalk) and *baby coach* (baby carriage). In the north and west are *poke* (bag), *quarter till, sick on the stomach, openseed peach* (freestone peach), and Pennsylvania German *ponhaws* (scrapple). In the southern portion are found *light bread* (white bread), *curtain* (shade), *carry* (escort), *crop* as /krap/, and *bulge* with the vowel of *put*. East of Chesapeake Bay are *mosquito hawk* (dragonfly), *paled fence* (picket fence), *poor* (rhyming with *mower*), and *Mary* with the vowel of *mate*. In central Maryland, an earthworm is a *baitworm*.

In 2000, some 4,322,329 residents, or 87% of the population five years old or older (down from 91.1% in 1990) spoke only English at home.

The following table gives selected statistics from the 2000 Census for language spoken at home by persons five years old and over. The category "African languages" includes Amharic, Ibo, Twi, Yoruba, Bantu, Swahili, and Somali. The category "Other Asian languages" includes Dravidian languages, Malayalam, Telugu, Tamil,

and Turkish. The category "Other Indic languages" includes Bengali, Marathi, Punjabi, and Romany.

LANGUAGE	NUMBER	PERCENT
Population 5 years and over	**4,945,043**	**100.0**
Speak only English	4,322,329	87.4
Speak a language other than English	622,714	12.6
Speak a language other than English	**622,714**	**12.6**
Spanish or Spanish Creole	230,829	4.7
French (incl. Patois, Cajun)	42,838	0.9
Chinese	41,883	0.8
African languages	36,967	0.7
Korean	32,937	0.7
German	23,796	0.5
Tagalog	18,495	0.4
Russian	17,584	0.4
Vietnamese	14,891	0.3
Italian	13,798	0.3
Other Asian languages	12,405	0.3
Persian	11,951	0.2
Hindi	11,389	0.2
Other Indic languages	11,345	0.2
Greek	10,717	0.2
Arabic	10,458	0.2

9 RELIGIONS

Maryland was founded as a haven for Roman Catholics, who still make up the largest single religious group in the states although their political supremacy ended in 1692, when Anglicanism (now the Episcopal Church) became the established religion. Laws against "popery" were enacted by 1704 and Roman Catholic priests were harassed; the state constitution of 1776, however, placed all Christian faiths on an equal footing. The state's first Lutheran church was built in 1729, the first Baptist church in 1742, and the earliest Methodist church in 1760. Jews settled in Baltimore in the early 1800s, with a much larger wave of Jewish immigration in the late 19th century.

As of 2000, there were 952,389 Roman Catholics in Maryland; the Archdiocese of Baltimore reported 517,679 Catholics in 2005. Adherents of the major Protestant denominations (with 2000 data) include United Methodists, 297,729 members; Southern Baptists, 142,401 members; Evangelical Lutherans,103,644 members; and Episcopalians, 81,061 members. In 2000, there were an estimated 216,000 Jews and about 52,867 Muslims. Though membership numbers were unavailable, reports indicate there were about 32 Buddhist congregations and 26 Hindu congregations in 2000. Over 3 million people (about 56.7% of the population) were not counted as members of any religious organization.

The Lutheran World Relief organization is based in Baltimore as is World Relief, an affiliate of the National Association of Evangelicals. The Adventist Community Services relief program is based in Silver Springs.

10 TRANSPORTATION

Some of the nation's earliest efforts toward the development of a reliable transportation system began in Maryland. In 1695, a public postal road was opened from the Potomac River through Annapolis and the Eastern Shore to Philadelphia. Construction on the National Road (now US 40) began at Cumberland in 1811; within seven years, the road was a conduit for settlers in Ohio. The first commercial steamboat service from Baltimore started in 1813, and steamboats were active all along the Chesapeake during the 1800s. The Delaware and Chesapeake Canal, linking Chesapeake Bay and the Delaware River, opened in 1829.

Maryland's first railroad, the Baltimore and Ohio (B&O), was started in 1828. In 1835, it provided the first passenger train service to Washington, DC, and Harpers Ferry, Virginia (now West Virginia). By 1857, the line was extended to St. Louis, and its freight capacity helped build Baltimore into a major center of commerce. In the 1850s, the Pennsylvania Railroad began to buy up small Maryland lines and provide direct service to northern cities.

CSX Transportation and Norfolk Southern are the Class I railroads operating in the state, along with one regional, five local, and two switching and terminal railroads. As of 2003, total rail miles in Maryland amounted to 1,153 mi (1,856 km), including about 835 mi (1,343 km) of Class I track. The Maryland Transportation Department's Railroad Administration subsidizes four commuter lines, as well as freight lines in western Maryland and on the Eastern Shore. As of 2006, Amtrak operated four stations in Maryland, providing east–west service from Washington DC to Chicago and north–south service on the Northeast Corridor main line.

The Maryland Mass Transit Administration inaugurated Baltimore's first subway line on 21 November 1983. The combined underground-elevated line ran for 8 mi (13 km) from downtown Baltimore to Reisterstown Plaza. Later, the Baltimore Metro was extended for 6 mi (10 km) to Owings Mills, just outside the city limits. The Metro cost nearly $1 billion to build. In 1984, the Washington, DC, mass transit system was extended to the Maryland suburbs, including Bethesda and Rockville.

About half of Maryland's roads serve metropolitan Baltimore and Washington. As of 2004, there were 30,809 mi (49,602 km) of public roadway. The major toll road is the John F. Kennedy Memorial Highway (I-95), linking Baltimore with Wilmington, Delaware, and the New Jersey Turnpike. There were 3,594,251 licensed drivers and 4.150 million motor vehicles of all types registered in Maryland as of 2004.

The Port of Baltimore handled 47.399 million tons of cargo in 2004, making it the 17th busiest port in the United States. Of that total, 24.950 million tons were imports that year. For that same year, Maryland had 532 mi (856 km) of navigable inland waterways. In 2003, waterborne shipments totaled 47.533 million tons.

In 2005, Maryland had a total of 221 public and private-use aviation-related facilities. This included 145 airports, 69 heliports, 1 STOLport (Short Take-Off and Landing), and 6 seaplane bases. Baltimore-Washington International (BWI) Airport is the state's main air terminal and also serves the Washington DC, area. In 2004, Baltimore–Washington had 10,103,563 enplanements, making it the 23rd-busiest airport in the United States.

11 HISTORY

The Indian tribes living in the region that was to become Maryland were Algonkian-speakers: the Accomac, Nanticoke, and Wicomico on the Eastern Shore, and the Susquehannock, Yacomico, and Piscataway on the Western Shore. The Susquehannock, the most powerful tribe at the time of English colonization, claimed all the land lying between the Susquehanna and Potomac rivers. Although the Algonkian Indians hunted for much of their food, many tribes (including the Susquehannock) also had permanent settlements where they cultivated corn (maize), vegetables, tobac-

co, and other crops. George Alsop, in his *Character of the Province of Maryland* (1666), noted that Susquehannock women "are the Butchers, Cooks, and Tillers of the ground but the men think it below the honour of a Masculine to stoop to any thing but that which their Gun, or Bow and Arrows can Command." European penetration of the Chesapeake region began early in the 16th century, with the expeditions of Giovanni da Verrazano, a Florentine navigator, and the Spaniard Lucas Vázquez de Ayllón. Captain John Smith, leader of the English settlement at Jamestown, Virginia, was the first English explorer of Chesapeake Bay (1608) and produced a map of the area that was used for years.

The founding of Maryland is intimately tied to the career of another Englishman, George Calvert. A favorite of King James I, Calvert left the Church of England in 1624 to become a Roman Catholic. He announced his conversion in 1625 and—because Catholics were not allowed to hold public office in England at that time—then resigned his post as secretary of state and, against the king's wishes, retired from the royal court. As a reward for Calvert's service, the king bestowed upon him large Irish estates and a peerage with the title of Baron of Baltimore. Two years later, Calvert sailed for the New World, landing in Newfoundland, to which he had received title in 1621. After a severe winter, however, Calvert decided to seek his fortunes where the weather was warmer—in Virginia. Not well-received there because of his religion, Calvert returned to England and asked King Charles I (James's successor) for land south of Virginia; instead he received a grant north of the Potomac. Virginia's agents in England contested Calvert's right to this land strenuously but unsuccessfully, and when he died in 1632, the title passed to his son Cecilius Calvert, 2nd Baron Baltimore (usually called Lord Baltimore), who named the region Maryland after the queen consort of Charles I, Henrietta Maria. At this time, the land grant embraced not only present-day Maryland but also the present State of Delaware, a large part of Pennsylvania, and the valley between the north and south branches of the Potomac River. Not until the 1760s was the final boundary between Pennsylvania and Maryland (as surveyed by Charles Mason and Jeremiah Dixon) established by royal decree, and nearly a century passed before Maryland conceded to Virginia the land between the north and south branches of the Potomac.

The government of provincial Maryland was absolute, embodying the most extensive grant of royal powers to a colonial settlement. Lord Baltimore's main source of income as lord proprietary was the quitrents settlers paid for their land; in return for his authority, Calvert had to give the king only two Indian arrows yearly. Lord Baltimore assigned to his half-brother, Leonard Calvert, the task of organizing the settlement of the colony. On 22 November 1633, Calvert and approximately 250 settlers, including many Roman Catholics and two Jesuit priests, set sail for America on two ships, the Ark and the Dove. They landed at St. Clements Island on 25 March 1634. Two days later, Calvert purchased a site from the Indians, named it St. Marys (the first capital of Maryland), and assumed the governorship of the colony.

The early days of settlement were tumultuous. The refusal by a Virginia colonist, William Claiborne of Kent Island, to acknowledge Lord Baltimore's charter led to a small war that ended in 1638 with a temporary victory for Governor Calvert. The conflict in England during the 1640s found an echo in the struggle between Puritans and Roman Catholics in Maryland, a conflict that saw the two-year exile of Governor Calvert to Virginia, the assumption of power by English representatives (including Claiborne and one of the Puritan leaders) in 1652, a subsequent civil war, and finally the recognition of Lord Baltimore's charter by Oliver Cromwell in 1657.

Cecilius Calvert died in 1675. His successor was Charles Calvert, 3rd Baron Baltimore and the next lord proprietary. His tenure, which lasted until 1715, saw a decisive change in the character of the province. In 1689, with Protestants ascendant in both England and Maryland, the British crown assumed direct control over the province, and in 1692, the Church of England became Maryland's established religion. When Charles Calvert died, his successor, Benedict Leonard Calvert, 4th Baron Baltimore, was granted full proprietary rights—but only because he had embraced the Protestant faith. Proprietary rule continued through his legitimate heirs until the eve of the American Revolution.

Throughout this period, the upper and lower houses of the colonial assembly—consisting, respectively, of the governor and his council and of delegates elected from the counties—quarreled over taxation and the extension of English statutes to free Marylanders. Having already secured most rights from the proprietor, the lower house was somewhat reluctant to vote for independence from the British crown, on whose authority the proprietary government now rested. After its initial hesitancy, however, Maryland cast its lot with the Revolution and sent approximately 20,000 soldiers to fight in the war. The Continental Congress met in Baltimore from December 1776 to March 1777 and in Annapolis from November 1783 to June 1784. These cities were thus among the eight that served as US capitals before the designation of a permanent seat of government in Washington, DC.

Maryland was one of the last states to sign the Articles of Confederation, not ratifying them until other states dropped their claims to what later became the Northwest Territory. On 28 April 1788, Maryland became the seventh state to ratify the federal constitution. The state constitution, drawn up in 1776, was weighted heavily in favor of property holders and the rural counties, at the expense of the propertyless and the city of Baltimore; the legislature removed the property qualifications in 1810.

Maryland's prosperity during the colonial and early federal period waxed and waned according to the world price of tobacco, the staple crop of tidewater and southern Maryland. Planters increasingly employed slave labor on farms and plantations, and the black population grew rapidly in the 18th century. German immigrants began moving into western Maryland, where wheat became the primary crop. The cultivation of wheat also helped make Baltimore's fortune. Founded in 1729 and incorporated in 1796, the city of Baltimore was blessed with a harbor well suited to the export and import trade. As commerce developed, shipbuilding emerged as a major economic activity. By the early 19th century, Baltimore was already the state's major center of commerce and industry.

The city and harbor were the site of extensive naval and military operations during the War of 1812. It was during the bombardment of Ft. McHenry in 1814 that Francis Scott Key, detained on the British frigate, composed "The Star-Spangled Banner," which became the US national anthem in March 1931.

After the War of 1812, Maryland history was marked by the continued growth of Baltimore and increasing division over im-

migration, slavery, and secession. The chartering in 1827 of the Baltimore and Ohio (B and O) Railroad, which eventually linked Maryland with the markets of the Ohio Valley and the West, added to the city's economic vitality. But distrust of the thousands of newcomers—especially of Irish immigrants and their Roman Catholicism—and fear of the economic threat they supposedly represented spurred the rise of nativist political groups, such as the Know-Nothings, who persecuted the immigrants and dominated Maryland politics in the 1850s.

Although not many Marylanders were in favor of secession, they were hostile to the idea of using force against the secessionist states. On 19 April 1861, as the 6th Massachusetts Regiment passed through Baltimore, it was attacked by a mob of southern sympathizers in a riot that left 4 soldiers and 12 civilians dead. Ten days later, the Maryland house of delegates, following the lead of Governor Thomas Hicks, rejected a bill of secession. Throughout the Civil War, Maryland was largely occupied by Union troops because of its strategic location and the importance for the northern cause of the B and O Railroad. Marylanders fought on both sides during the war, and one major battle took place on Maryland soil—the Battle of Antietam (1862), during which a Union army thwarted a Confederate thrust toward the north, but at an enormous cost to both sides. Confederate armies invaded the state on two other occasions, when General Robert E. Lee brought his troops through the state on the way to Gettysburg in 1863 and when Lieutenant general Jubal Early ravaged the Hagerstown area and threatened Baltimore in 1864. The Maryland legislature, almost totally pro-Union by 1864, passed a new constitution, which among other things abolished slavery.

The state's economic activity increased during Reconstruction, as Maryland, and especially Baltimore, played a major role in rebuilding the South. Maryland's economic base gradually shifted from agriculture to industry, with shipbuilding, steelmaking, and the manufacture of clothing and shoes leading the way. The decades between the Civil War and World War I were also notable for the philanthropic activities of such wealthy businessmen as John Hopkins, George Peabody, and Enoch Pratt, who endowed some of the state's most prestigious cultural and educational institutions. The years after World War I saw the emergence of a political figure without equal in Maryland's more recent history: Albert C. Ritchie, a Democrat who won election to the governorship in 1919 and served in that office until 1935, just one year before his death. Stressing local issues, states' rights, and opposition to prohibition, Ritchie remained in power until Harry W. Nice, a Republican but an advocate of New Deal reforms, defeated him in 1934.

The decades after World War II were marked by significant population growth. From 1980 to 1990 alone, Maryland grew by 13.4%, well above the national rate of 9.8%. Baltimore, which, though still the hub of the state's economy, had fallen into decay and became the focus of a redevelopment project. Much of the downtown area and harbor facilities were revitalized by urban projects, begun in the late 1970s and continued into the 21st century. These featured the Charles Center development, the waterfront renovation of the Inner Harbor, Oriole Park at Camden Yards, and a $150-million convention center at the Inner Harbor.

Although Maryland's economy declined less than those of other states during the recession of the late 1980s, the state suffered from the contraction of defense industry. Nevertheless, service industry employment, primarily in the Baltimore-Washington corridor, gave Maryland the fifth-highest state income in the country as of the mid-1990s—a ranking it maintained as of 1998. Federal government and high-tech employment accounted for many of these jobs. As of 2004, Maryland had the third-highest median household income among the states, at $57,424, which is 29% higher than the national median. Maryland in 2004 ranked fourth among the states in per capita personal income ($39,247). Maryland had the sixth-lowest poverty rate in the nation in 2004, at 8.8%, compared with 13.1% for the nation as a whole.

Maryland's 370-year history of tobacco farming appeared to be drawing to a close in 2000. Nearly 90% of the state's tobacco farmers indicated they would accept a government buyout later that year. The crop that had settled the Chesapeake had become risky, with the tobacco industry under attack for the health hazards of its products. The state by 2003 had implemented a tobacco buyout program, whereby the state agreed to pay farmers $1 per pound of tobacco that they would sell for the following 10 years based on the average amount of tobacco they sold between 1996 and 1998. Farmers agree to plant alternative crops instead of tobacco. As of January 2004, 785 growers were to participate in the buyout program, representing 80% of eligible growers and 7.3 million lb of tobacco.

The environmental cleanup of Chesapeake Bay, begun in the mid-1980s, continued into the 21st century. In an effort to further protect the bay's ecosystem, in 1999 Maryland Governor Parris Glendening announced a plan to protect 60,000 forested acres on the Eastern Shore from development. Nevertheless, the bay faced more immediate threats such as the April 2000 oil spill into the Patuxent River, which flows into the Chesapeake. Federal officials faulted Maryland Power Company for its efforts to clean up the spill, the worst in the company's 104-year history. Governor Rob-

ert L. Ehrlich Jr., elected in 2002, was continuing the cleanup of the Chesapeake Bay.

In 2005, Governor Ehrlich announced conservation of 828 acres near Antietam Battlefield. The plan supported Maryland's $9.3 billion tourism industry, and provides environmental benefits for the state. Annually, 11 million visitors take advantage of Maryland's parks and natural, historic, and cultural resources.

12 STATE GOVERNMENT

Maryland's first state constitution was enacted in 1776. Subsequent constitutions were ratified in 1851, 1864, and 1867. By January 2005, it had 218 amendments.

Under the 1867 constitution, as amended, the General Assembly, Maryland's legislative body, consists of two branches: a 47-member Senate and a 141-member house of delegates. Legislative sessions begin the second Wednesday of January of each year and are limited to 90 calendar days. Special sessions, which are limited to 30 calendar days, may be called by a petition of the majority in each house. All legislators serve four-year terms and must have been citizens of the state for at least a year and of their district for at least six months prior to election. Senators must be at least 25 years old, delegates 21. The legislative salary was $31,509 in 2004.

Executives elected statewide are the governor and lieutenant governor (who run jointly), the comptroller of the treasury, and the attorney general; all serve four-year terms. The state treasurer is elected by joint ballot of the General Assembly, while the secretary of state is appointed by the governor. The governor, who may serve no more than two four-year terms in succession, also appoints other members of the executive council (cabinet) and the heads of major boards and commissions. The chief executive must be a US citizen at least 30 years old, must have been a resident of Maryland for five years before election, and must have been a reg-

Maryland Presidential Vote by Political Parties, 1948–2004

YEAR	ELECTORAL VOTE	MARYLAND WINNER	DEMOCRAT	REPUBLICAN	PROGRESSIVE	STATES' RIGHTS DEMOCRAT	SOCIALIST
1948	8	Dewey (R)	286,521	294,814	9,983	2,467	2,941
1952	9	*Eisenhower (R)	395,337	499,424	7,313	—	—
1956	9	*Eisenhower (R)	372,613	559,738	—	—	—
1960	9	*Kennedy (D)	565,808	489,538	—	—	—
1964	10	*Johnson (D)	730,912	385,495	—	—	—
					AMERICAN IND.		
1968	10	Humphrey (D)	538,310	517,995	178,734	—	—
					AMERICAN		
1972	10	*Nixon (R)	505,781	829,305	18,726	—	—
1976	10	*Carter (D)	759,612	672,661	—	—	—
						LIBERTARIAN	
1980	10	Carter (D)	726,161	680,606	—	14,192	—
1984	10	*Reagan (R)	787,935	879,918	—	5,721	—
1988	10	*Bush (R)	826,304	876,167	5,115	6,748	—
							IND. (Perot)
1992	10	*Clinton (D)	988,571	707,094	2,786	4,715	281,414
1996	10	*Clinton (D)	966,207	681,530	—	8,765	115,812
					GREEN		**REFORM**
2000	10	Gore (D)	1,145,782	813,797	53,768	5,310	4,248
							POPULIST
							(Nader)
2004	10	Kerry (D)	1,334,493	1,024,703	3,632	6,094	11,854

*Won US presidential election.

istered voter in the state for five years. As of December 2004, the governor's salary was $135,000.

Bills passed by majority vote of both houses of the assembly become law when signed by the governor or if left unsigned for six days while the legislature is in session or 30 days if the legislature has adjourned. The only exception is the budget bill, which becomes effective immediately upon legislative passage. Gubernatorial vetoes may be overridden by three-fifths votes of the elected members in both houses. Proposed constitutional amendments also require approval by three-fifths of both houses of the legislature before submission to the voters at the next general election.

Eligible voters are US citizens who are at least 18 years old and are residents of the Maryland county in which they will vote. Restrictions apply to convicted felons and those declared mentally incompetent by the court.

13 POLITICAL PARTIES

The Republican and Democratic parties are the dominant political groups in Maryland. Before the Civil War, the Democrats drew much of their strength from the slaveholding Eastern Shore, while their opponents, the Whigs, were popular in Baltimore and other centers of antislavery activity. The collapse of the Whigs on both the national and local levels corresponded with the rise in Maryland of the Native American ("Know-Nothing") Party, whose anti-immigrant and anti-Catholic attitudes appealed to Marylanders who saw their livelihood threatened by Roman Catholic immigrants. The Know-Nothings swept Baltimore in 1855 and won the governorship in 1857; Maryland was the only state to cast its electoral votes for the Know-Nothing presidential candidate, Millard Fillmore, in 1856. The Native American Party declined rapidly, however, and by 1860, Maryland was back in the Democratic column, voting for the secessionist John Breckinridge.

Revelations of influence peddling and corruption afflicted both major parties during the 1970s. In 1973, Republican Spiro T. Agnew, then vice president of the United States, was accused of taking payments from people who had done business with the state government while he was Baltimore County executive and then governor of Maryland until 1969. Agnew pleaded nolo contendere to a federal charge of income tax evasion and resigned from the vice-presidency on 10 October 1973. His gubernatorial successor, Democrat Marvin Mandel, was convicted of mail fraud and racketeering in 1977; he served 20 months of a 36-month prison sentence before receiving a presidential pardon in 1981.

Maryland was one of the few states carried by President Jimmy Carter in the November 1980 presidential election, but four years later the state went for President Ronald Reagan in the national Republican landslide. In 2000, Maryland gave 57% of its vote to Democrat Al Gore, 40% to Republican George W. Bush, and 3% to Green Party candidate Ralph Nader. In 2004, Democratic challenger John Kerry won 55.7% of the vote to incumbent Bush's 44.6%.

In the 1994 governor's race, one of the closest in Maryland history, Democrat Parris N. Glendening won; he was reelected in 1998. Republican Robert L. Ehrlich Jr. was elected governor in 2002. The two senators from Maryland, Paul S. Sarbanes and Barbara Mikulski, both Democrats, were reelected in 2000 and 2004, respectively. In 2004 there were 3,105,000 registered voters. In

1998, 58% of registered voters were Democratic, 20% Republican, and 12% unaffiliated or members of other parties.

Following the November 2004 elections, Maryland's US congressional delegation consisted of six Democrats and two Republicans. In mid-2005 there were 33 Democrats and 14 Republicans in the state Senate, and 98 Democrats and 43 Republicans in the state House. The state had 10 electoral votes in the 2000 presidential election.

14 LOCAL GOVERNMENT

As of 2005, there were 24 counties, 157 municipal governments, and 85 special districts in Maryland. Most counties have charter governments, in which voters elect a county executive and council members. The other counties, which tend to be rural, are governed by boards of county commissioners. County government is highly developed in Maryland, and there are numerous appointed county officials with responsibilities ranging from civil defense to liquor licensing.

The city of Baltimore is the only one in Maryland not contained within a county. It provides the same services as a county, and shares in state aid according to the same allocation formulas. The city (not to be confused with Baltimore County, which surrounds the city of Baltimore but has its county seat at Towson) is governed by an elected mayor and city council. Other cities and towns are each governed by a mayor, with or without a council, depending on the local charter. In 2005, Maryland had 25 public school systems.

In 2005, local government accounted for about 187,955 full-time (or equivalent) employment positions.

15 STATE SERVICES

To address the continuing threat of terrorism and to work with the federal Department of Homeland Security, homeland security in Maryland operates under the authority of executive order; the homeland security director is designated as the state homeland security advisor.

The State Ethics Commission, established in 1979, monitors compliance by state officeholders and employees with the Maryland public ethics law in order to avoid conflicts of interest; the Joint Committee on Legislative Ethics, created in 1972, has similar responsibilities with respect to General Assembly members. The Fair Campaign Financing Commission provides for the public financing of elections and sets campaign spending limits.

The State Board of Education is an independent policymaking body whose 12 members are appointed by the governor; its responsibilities include selection of a superintendent of schools to run the Education Department. The growth and development of postsecondary institutions are the responsibility of the Maryland Higher Education Commission. The Department of Transportation oversees air, road, rail, bridge, and mass transit. The Department of Health and Mental Hygiene coordinates public health programs, regulates in-state medical care, and supervises the 24 local health departments. Social services and public assistance programs as well as employment security lie within the jurisdiction of the Department of Human Resources. The Department of Housing and Community Development assures the provision of low-cost housing. The Department of Business and Economic Development advances job opportunities and works to bring new businesses into the state. It also serves in a public relations capacity at home and abroad to stimulate international trade and tourism, and also invests in the arts and promotes sports events.

Maryland's Department of Public Safety and Correctional Services has statewide responsibility for the supervision and rehabilitation of adjudicated individuals, while the Department of Labor, Licensing, and Regulation supervises employment training, job match services, unemployment insurance, and many of the state's licensing and regulatory boards for businesses and trades. The Department of State Police enforces state motor vehicle and criminal laws, preserves public peace, maintains safe traffic on public streets and highways, enforces laws relating to narcotics, and incorporates the office of the State Fire Marshal. Other organizations include the departments of agriculture, assessments and taxation, natural resources, personnel, and rehabilitation services (for those with disabilities).

16JUDICIAL SYSTEM

The Court of Appeals is Maryland's highest court. It is comprised of a chief judge and six associate judges. Each is appointed to the court by the governor, but must be confirmed by the voters within two years of appointment. Most criminal appeals are decided by the court of special appeals, consisting of a chief judge and 12 associate judges, selected in the same manner as judges of the high court. Each case must be heard by a panel of at least three judges of the high court. All state judges serve 10-year terms.

In 1971, 12 district courts took the place of all justices of the peace, county trial judges, magistrates, people's courts, and the municipal court of Baltimore. District courts handle all criminal, civil, and traffic cases, with appeals being taken to one of eight circuit courts. Circuit court judges are appointed by the governor and stand for election to 15-year terms. District court judges are appointed by the governor and confirmed by the Senate to 10-year terms. The city of Baltimore and all counties except Montgomery and Hartford have orphans' courts composed of two judges and one chief judge, all of them elected to four-year terms.

As of 31 December 2004, a total of 23,285 prisoners were held in Maryland's state and federal prisons, a decrease from 23,791 of 2.1% from the previous year. As of year-end 2004, a total of 1,180 inmates were female, down from 1,248 or 5.4% from the year before. Among sentenced prisoners (one year or more), Maryland had an incarceration rate of 406 per 100,000 population in 2004.

According to the Federal Bureau of Investigation, Maryland in 2004, had a violent crime rate (murder/nonnegligent manslaughter; forcible rape; robbery; aggravated assault) of 700.5 reported incidents per 100,000 population (third-highest among the states in the United States after Florida and South Carolina), or a total of 38,932 reported incidents. Crimes against property (burglary; larceny/theft; and motor vehicle theft) in that same year totaled 202,326 reported incidents or 3,640.2 reported incidents per 100,000 people. Maryland has a death penalty, of which lethal injection or lethal gas are the methods of execution. However, the latter method is open only to those inmates convicted of capital offenses that were committed on or after 25 March 1994. From 1976 through 5 May 2006, the state executed five persons, including one execution in 2005. As of 1 January 2006, Maryland had eight inmates on death row.

In 2003, Maryland spent $495,455,173 on homeland security, an average of $91 per state resident.

17ARMED FORCES

As of 2004, there were 35,531 active US military personnel in Maryland, 2,593 National Guard and Reserve, and 25,417 civilian personnel. Ft. Meade is located in Baltimore, and the Aberdeen Proving Ground is in Harford County. Perhaps Maryland's best-known defense installation is Andrews Air Force Base in Camp Springs, a military airlift center. Annapolis is the home of the US Naval Academy. Total military personnel at all naval facilities, including the National Naval Medical Center at Bethesda, was 7,335 in 2004. Federal defense contract awards to Maryland firms were approximately $9.2 billion in 2004, fourth-highest in the United States for that year. In addition, there was another $4.9 billion in defense payroll spending, including retired military pay.

There were 486,298 veterans of US military service in Maryland as of 2003, of whom 57,970 served in World War II; 46,740 in the Korean conflict; 142,266 during the Vietnam era; and 86,225 in the Gulf War. In 2004, expenditures on veterans exceeded $1.1 billion.

As of 31 October 2004, the Maryland State Police employed 1,575 full-time sworn officers.

18MIGRATION

Maryland's earliest white settlers were English; many of them farmed lands on the Eastern Shore. As tobacco crops wore out the soil, these early immigrants moved on to the fertile Western Shore and piedmont. During the 19th century, Baltimore ranked second only to New York as a port of entry for European immigrants. First to come were the Germans, followed by the Irish, Poles, East European Jews, and Italians; a significant number of Czechs settled in Cecil County during the 1860s. After the Civil War, many blacks migrated to Baltimore, both from rural Maryland and from southern states.

Since World War II, intrastate migration has followed the familiar urban/suburban pattern: both the Baltimore metropolitan area and the Maryland part of the metropolitan Washington, DC, area have experienced rapid growth while the inner cities have lost population. Overall, Maryland experienced a net loss from migration of about 36,000 between 1970 and 1980, much of it to Pennsylvania, Virginia, and Florida; the out-migration stopped during the 1980s, however, with a net gain of over 200,000 from 1980 to 1990. Between 1990 and 1998, Maryland had a net loss of 49,000 in domestic migration and a net gain of 118,000 in international migration. Maryland's foreign-born population totaled 412,000, or 8% of the total population, in 1996. In 1998, 15,561 foreign immigrants arrived in the state—the 10th-highest total of any state for that year. Between 1990 and 1998, the state's overall population increased 7.4%. In the period 2000–05, net international migration was 108,972 and net internal migration was 9,752, for a net gain of 118,724 people.

19INTERGOVERNMENTAL COOPERATION

Maryland is active in several regional organizations, including the Southern Regional Education Board, Atlantic States Marine Fisheries Commission, Mid-Atlantic Fishery Management Council, Interstate Mining Compact Commission, Appalachian Regional

Commission, Susquehanna River Basin Commission (with Pennsylvania and New York), and the Potomac River Fisheries Commission (with Virginia). Representatives of Maryland, Virginia, and the District of Columbia form the Washington Metropolitan Area Transit Authority, which coordinates regional mass transit. Other cooperation focuses on the Chesapeake Bay, and on the creation of the Woodrow Wilson Bridge and Tunnel. The Delmarva Advisory Council, representing Delaware, Maryland, and Virginia, works with local organizations on the Delmarva Peninsula to develop and implement economic improvement programs. In fiscal year 2005, federal grants to Maryland totaled $8.589 billion, an estimated $8.892 billion in fiscal year 2006, before falling to an estimated $8.217 billion in fiscal year 2007.

20 ECONOMY

Throughout the colonial period, Maryland's economy was based on one crop—tobacco. Not only slaves but also indentured servants worked the fields, and when they earned their freedom, they too secured plots of land and grew tobacco for the European market. By 1820, however, industry was rivaling agriculture for economic preeminence. Shipbuilding, metalworking, and commerce transformed Baltimore into a major city. Within 60 years, it was a leading manufacturer of men's clothing and had the largest steel making plant in the United States.

Although manufacturing output continues to rise, the biggest growth areas in Maryland's economy are government, construction, trade, and services. Maryland employees are the best educated in the nation, with more than one-third of those over age 25 possessing a bachelor's degree in 2000. With the expansion of federal employment in the Washington metropolitan area by 40% from 1961 to 1980, many US government workers settled in suburban Maryland, primarily Prince George's and Montgomery counties. Construction and services in those areas expanded accordingly. The growth of state government boosted employment in Anne Arundel and Baltimore counties. Also of importance to the economy are fishing and agriculture (primarily dairy and poultry farming) on the Eastern Shore and coal mining in Garrett and Allegheny counties. Manufacturing has shifted toward high technology, information, and health-related products. While manufacturing output (durable and nondurable goods) has continued to grow, its relative weight in the gross state product has fallen from 8.5% in 1997 to 6.1% in 2004. Annual growth rates averaged 6.2% 1998 to 2000, and only fell to 5.4% in the national recession and slowdown of 2001. Increased federal government spending, particularly in defense-related industries, is expected to assure Maryland's economic recovery in 2002, and into 2003.

Maryland's gross state product (GSP) was $227.991 billion in 2004, of which the real estate sector accounted for the largest portion at $34.763 billion or 15.2% of GSP, followed by professional and technical services at $22.780 billion (9.9% of GSP), and health-care and social services at $16.815 billion (7.3% of GSP). In that same year, there were an estimated 477,233 small businesses in Maryland. Of the 137,338 businesses that had employees, a total of 134,095 or 97.6% were small companies. An estimated 21,751 new businesses were established in the state in 2004, up 5,1% from the year before. Business terminations that same year came to 20,636, down 4.9% from 2003. There were 417 business bankruptcies in 2004, down 20.3% from the previous year. In 2005, the state's personal bankruptcy (Chapter 7 and Chapter 13) filing rate was 618 filings per 100,000 people, ranking Maryland as the 19th highest in the nation.

21 INCOME

In 2005 Maryland had a gross state product (GSP) of $245 billion which accounted for 2.0% of the nation's gross domestic product and placed the state at number 15 in highest GSP among the 50 states and the District of Columbia.

According to the Bureau of Economic Analysis, in 2004 Maryland had a per capita personal income (PCPI) of $39,631. This ranked fifth in the United States and was 120% of the national average of $33,050. The 1994–2004 average annual growth rate of PCPI was 4.5%. Maryland had a total personal income (TPI) of $220,402,185,000, which ranked 14th in the United States and reflected an increase of 6.8% from 2003. The 1994–2004 average annual growth rate of TPI was 5.5%. Earnings of persons employed in Maryland increased from $145,140,178,000 in 2003 to $155,190,491,000 in 2004, an increase of 6.9%. The 2003–04 national change was 6.3%.

The US Census Bureau reports that the three-year average median household income for 2002 to 2004 in 2004 dollars was $56,763 compared to a national average of $44,473. During the same period an estimated 8.6% of the population was below the poverty line as compared to 12.4% nationwide.

22 LABOR

According to the Bureau of Labor Statistics (BLS), in April 2006 the seasonally adjusted civilian labor force in Maryland numbered 2,997,700, with approximately 105,700 workers unemployed, yielding an unemployment rate of 3.5%, compared to the national average of 4.7% for the same period. Preliminary data for the same period placed nonfarm employment at 2,580,100. Since the beginning of the BLS data series in 1976, the highest unemployment rate recorded in Maryland was 8.3% in August 1982. The historical low was 3.3% in March 2000. Preliminary nonfarm employment data by occupation for April 2006 showed that approximately 7.3% of the labor force was employed in construction; 5.3% in manufacturing; 18.4% in trade, transportation, and public utilities; 6.2% in financial activities; 15% in professional and business services; 14% in education and health services; 9% in leisure and hospitality services; and 18.2% in government.

Baltimore was a leading trade union center by the early 1830s although union activity subsided after the Panic of 1837. The Baltimore Federation of Labor was formed in 1889, and by 1900, the coal mines had been organized by the United Mine Workers. In 1902, Maryland passed the first workers' compensation law in the United States. It was declared unconstitutional in 1904 but was subsequently revived.

The US Department of Labor's Bureau of Labor Statistics reported that in 2005, a total of 337,000 of Maryland's 2,530,000 employed wage and salary workers were formal members of a union. This represented 13.3% of those so employed, up from 10.9% in 2004, and above the national average of 12%. Overall in 2005, a total of 379,000 workers (15%) in Maryland were covered by a union or employee association contract, which includes those workers who reported no union affiliation. Maryland is one of 28 states that do not have a right-to-work law.

As of 1 March 2006, Maryland had a state-mandated minimum wage rate of $6.15 per hour. In 2004, women in the state accounted for 48.1% of the employed civilian labor force.

23 AGRICULTURE

Maryland ranked 36th among the 50 states in agricultural income in 2005, with estimated receipts of $1,666 million, about 41% of that in crops.

Until the Revolutionary War, tobacco was the state's only cash crop; in 2004, Maryland produced an estimated 1,870,000 lb of tobacco. Corn and cereal grains are grown mainly in southern Maryland. Production in 2004 included 65,025,000 bushels of corn for grain; 21,285,000 bushels of soybeans, $112,811,000; 8,555,000 bushels of wheat, $26,093,000, and 2,847,000 bushels of barley, $5,409,000. Commercial vegetables, cultivated primarily on the Eastern Shore, were valued at $36.6 million in 2004. Fruits are also cultivated.

Maryland had some 12,100 farms covering 2,050,000 acres (830,000 hectares) in 2004.

24 ANIMAL HUSBANDRY

The Eastern Shore is an important dairy and poultry region; cattle are raised in north-central and western Maryland, while the central region is notable for horse breeding. In 2003, poultry farmers produced an estimated 6.4 million lb (2.9 million kg) of chickens and 1.37 billion lb (0.63 billion kg) of broilers for around $494.7 million. Also in 2003, Maryland farmers produced an estimated 813 million eggs worth around $46.2 million.

An estimated 1.2 billion lb (0.6 billion kg) of milk was produced in 2003 from 78,000 dairy cows. Maryland farms and ranches had an estimated 235,000 cattle and calves worth around $237 million in 2005. In 2004, there were an estimated 26,000 hogs and pigs, worth $2.6 million.

25 FISHING

In 2004, Maryland had a total commercial catch of 49.5 million lb (22.5 million kg), valued at $49.2 million. Maryland is a leading source of oysters, clams, and crabs. About 19% of the nation's supply of hard blue crabs comes from Maryland. Ocean City is the state's leading fishing port.

In 2003, the state had 17 processing and 58 wholesale plants with a total of about 1,417 employees. In 2001, the commercial fleet had at least 32 vessels.

The Fisheries Administration of the Department of Natural Resources monitors fish populations and breeds and implants oysters. It also stocks inland waterways with finfish. The state has five cold water and four warm water hatcheries. Maryland had 362,181 licensed sport anglers in 2004.

26 FORESTRY

Maryland's 2,566,000 acres (1,139,000 hectares) of forestland covers about 40% of the state's land area. More than 90% of that (2,372,000 acres/961,570 hectares) was classified as commercial forest, 90% of it privately owned. Hardwoods predominate, with red and white oaks and yellow poplar among the leading hardwood varieties. Lumber production in 2004 was 272 million board feet.

Forest management and improvement lie within the jurisdiction of the Maryland Department of Natural Resources Forest Service.

27 MINING

According to preliminary data from the US Geological Survey (USGS), the estimated value of nonfuel mineral production by Maryland in 2003 was $382 million, a decrease from 2002 of about 4.5%. The USGS data ranked Maryland as 33rd among the 50 states by the total value of its nonfuel mineral production, accounting for 1% of total US output.

Portland cement, crushed stone, and construction sand and gravel were the state's leading nonfuel minerals, by value, in 2003. Collectively, these three commodities (with crushed marble, shell and taprock) accounted for over 95% of the state's output of nonfuel minerals, by value.

According to preliminary figures from the USGS for 2003, the production of portland cement in Maryland totaled 1.9 million metric tons, and was valued at $143 million. Crushed stone output that same year stood at 21.8 million metric tons, and had a value of $138 million, while construction sand and gravel production totaled 11.4 million metric tons and was valued at $78.1 million). Maryland in 2003 was also a producer of dimension stone and common clays.

28 ENERGY AND POWER

As of 2003, Maryland had 24 electrical power service providers, of which 5 were publicly owned and 3 were cooperatives. Of the remainder, four were investor owned, one was an owner of an independent generator that sold directly to customers, while six were generation only suppliers and five were delivery only service providers. As of that same year there were 2,295,305 retail customers. Of that total, 2,010,338 received their power from investor-owned service providers. Cooperatives accounted for 174,291 customers, while publicly owned providers had 32,111 customers. There was only one independent generator or "facility" customer. Generation-only suppliers had 78,564 customers. There was no data on the number of customers using delivery-only providers.

Total net summer generating capability by the state's electrical generating plants in 2003 stood at 12.472 million kW, with total production that same year at 52.244 billion kWh. Of the total amount generated, only 0.1% came from electric utilities, with the remaining 99.9% coming from independent producers and combined heat and power service providers. The largest portion of all electric power generated, 29.939 billion kWh (57.3%), came from coal-fired plants, with nuclear plants in second place at 13.690 billion kWh (18.9%) and petroleum fueled plants in third at 3.572 billion kWh (6.8%). Other renewable power sources accounted for 1.7% of all power generated, with hydroelectric accounting for 5.1%, natural gas fueled plants at 2.3%, plants using other types of gases at 0.6%.

As of 2006, Maryland had one nuclear power generating facility, the Calvert Cliffs plant.

Coal, Maryland's lone fossil fuel resource, is mined in Allegheny and Garrett counties, along the Pennsylvania border. In 2004, Maryland had 19 producing coal mines, 16 of which were surface mines and 3 were underground. Coal production that year totaled 5,225,000 short tons, up from 5,056,000 short tons in 2003. Of the total produced in 2004, the state's three underground mines accounted for the bulk at 3,339,000 short tons. Recoverable coal reserves in 2001 totaled 17 million short tons. One short ton equals 2,000 lb (0.907 metric tons).

As of 2004, Maryland had no crude oil refineries, nor any proven reserves, or production.

In 2004, Maryland had seven producing natural gas and gas condensate wells. In 2003 (the latest year for which data was available), marketed gas production (all gas produced excluding gas used for repressuring, vented and flared, and nonhydrocarbon gases removed) totaled 48 million cu ft (1.36 million cu m). There was no data available on the state's proven reserves of natural gas.

29 INDUSTRY

During the early 1800s, Maryland's first industries centered around the Baltimore shipyards. Small ironworks cast parts for sailing vessels, and many laborers worked as shipbuilders. By the 1850s, Baltimore was also producing weather-measuring instruments and fertilizers, and by the 1930s, it was a major center of metal refining. The city remains an important manufacturer of automobiles and parts, steel, and instruments. Manufacturing is led by the printing and publishing industry, the food industry, the machinery industry, and the chemical industry.

According to the US Census Bureau's Annual Survey of Manufactures (ASM) for 2004, Maryland's manufacturing sector covered some 19 product subsectors. The shipment value of all products manufactured in the state that same year was $36.489 billion. Of that total, computer and electronic product manufacturing accounted for the largest share at $5.839 billion. It was followed by food manufacturing at $5.477 billion; chemical manufacturing at $4.990 billion; transport equipment manufacturing at $2.394 billion; and fabricated metal product manufacturing at $2.175 billion.

In 2004, a total of 135,773 people in Maryland were employed in the state's manufacturing sector, according to the ASM. Of that total, 85,668 were actual production workers. In terms of total employment, the computer and electronic product manufacturing industry accounted for the largest portion of all manufacturing employees at 23,880, with 6,897 actual production workers. It was followed by printing and related support activities at 15,332 employees (11,195 actual production workers); food manufacturing at 14147 employees (10,187 actual production workers); fabricated metal product manufacturing at 12,297 employees (8,699 actual production workers); chemical manufacturing at 9,626 employees (5,694 actual production workers); machinery manufacturing at 8,224 employees (5,003 actual production workers); and plastics and rubber products manufacturing with 6,851 employees (5,189 actual production workers).

ASM data for 2004 showed that Maryland's manufacturing sector paid $6.309 billion in wages. Of that amount, the computer and electronic product manufacturing sector accounted for the largest share at $1.653 billion. It was followed by printing and related support activities at $556.758 million; chemical manufacturing at $528.906 million; fabricated metal product manufacturing at $490.015 million; and food manufacturing at $471.262 million.

30 COMMERCE

According to the 2002 Census of Wholesale Trade, Maryland's wholesale trade sector had sales that year totaling $60.6 billion from 6,104 establishments. Wholesalers of durable goods accounted for 3,764 establishments, followed by nondurable goods wholesalers at 1,813 and electronic markets, agents, and brokers accounting for 527 establishments. Sales by durable goods wholesalers in 2002 totaled $30.8 billion, while wholesalers of nondurable goods saw sales of $22.8 billion. Electronic markets, agents, and brokers in the wholesale trade industry had sales of $6.9 billion.

In the 2002 Census of Retail Trade, Maryland was listed as having 19,394 retail establishments with sales of $60.06 billion. The leading types of retail businesses by number of establishments were: food and beverage stores (3,332); clothing and clothing accessories stores (2,918); miscellaneous store retailers (2,075); and motor vehicle and motor vehicle parts dealers (1,746). In terms of sales, motor vehicle and motor vehicle parts dealers accounted for the largest share of retail sales at $16.3 billion, followed by food and beverage stores at $10.5 billion; general merchandise stores at $7.7 billion; building material/garden equipment and supplies dealers at $4.8 billion; and gasoline stations at $4.1 billion. A total of 285,561 people were employed by the retail sector in Maryland that year.

Most of Maryland's retail facilities are located in the Baltimore metropolitan area and Montgomery and Prince George's counties surrounding Washington, DC. These counties are home to about 90% of Maryland's 5 million residents. The Washington-Baltimore Consolidated Metropolitan Statistical Area is among the nation's top 10 retail markets.

Exports by Maryland companies totaled $7.1 billion in 2005. While export activities in established markets such as Europe and Canada are still predominant, strong inroads have been made in targeted trade areas of Asia and Latin America.

31 CONSUMER PROTECTION

The state agency generally responsible for controlling unfair and deceptive trade practices is the Division of Consumer Protection within the Attorney General's Office. However, consumer complaints involving state-chartered financial institutions are the responsibility of the Office of Financial Regulation, while the state's automotive "Lemon Law" is the responsibility of the Motor Vehicle Administration, which is part of the Department of Transportation, although any litigation is handled by the Attorney General's Office.

When dealing with consumer protection issues, the state's Attorney General's Office can initiate civil and criminal proceedings (the latter must be done in conjunction with the local district attorney); administer consumer protection and education programs; handle formal consumer complaints; and exercise broad subpoena powers. However, the Attorney General cannot represent the state before state and federal regulatory agencies. In antitrust actions, the Attorney General's Office cannot act on behalf of those consumers who are incapable of acting on their own, but can initiate damage actions on behalf of the state in state courts; file criminal proceedings; and represent counties, cities and other governmental entities in recovering civil damages under state or federal law.

The Consumer Protection Division's main office is located in Baltimore, but it also has regional offices in Cumberland, Frederick, Hagerstown, Hughesville and Salisbury. County government consumer protection offices are located in Columbia and Rockville.

32 BANKING

As of June 2005, Maryland had 113 insured banks, savings and loans, and saving banks, plus 11 state-chartered and 109 federally chartered credit unions (CUs). Excluding the CUs, the Washington DC-Arlington-Alexandria market area, the Baltimore-Towson -Alexandria market area accounted for the largest portion of the state's financial institutions and deposits in 2004, at 90 and $43.864 billion, respectively. As of June 2005, CUs accounted for 21.5% of all assets held by all financial institutions in the state, or some $13.558 billion. Banks, savings and loans, and savings banks collectively accounted for the remaining 78.5% or $49.420 billion in assets held.

All state-chartered banks, savings and loan associations and trusts are regulated by the state's Commissioner of Financial Regulation, within the Department of Labor, Licensing and Regulation.

In 2004, the median percentage of past-due and nonaccrual loans to total loans was 0.93%, down from 1.14% in 2003. As of fourth quarter 2005 that same rate had fallen further to 0.89%.

33 INSURANCE

In 2004 there were over 3.47 million individual life insurance policies in force with a total value of about $275 billion; total value for all categories of life insurance (individual, group, and credit) was over $433 billion. The average coverage amount is $79,200 per policy holder. Death benefits paid that year totaled at over $1.17 billion.

As of 2003, there were 46 property and casualty and 10 life and health insurance companies domiciled in the state. In 2004, direct premiums for property and casualty insurance totaled $8.28 billion. That year, there were 54,882 flood insurance policies in force in the state, with a total value of $8 billion.

The Maryland Automobile Insurance Fund, a quasi-independent agency created in 1972, pays claims against uninsured motorists (i.e., hit-and-run drivers, out-of-state uninsured motorists, and state residents driving in violation of Maryland's compulsory automobile insurance law), and sells policies to Maryland drivers unable to obtain insurance from private companies.

In 2004, 61% of state residents held employment-based health insurance policies, 4% held individual policies, and 19% were covered under Medicare and Medicaid; 14% of residents were uninsured. In 2003, employee contributions for employment-based health coverage averaged at 23% for single coverage and 29% for family coverage. The state offers an 18-month health benefits expansion program for small-firm employees in connection with the Consolidated Omnibus Budget Reconciliation Act (COBRA, 1986), a health insurance program for those who lose employment-based coverage due to termination or reduction of work hours.

In 2003, there were over 3.7 million auto insurance policies in effect for private passenger cars. Required minimum coverage includes bodily injury liability of up to $20,000 per individual and $40,000 for all persons injured in an accident, as well as property damage liability of $15,000. Personal injury protection and uninsured motorist coverage are also mandatory. In 2003, the average expenditure per vehicle for insurance coverage was $890.86.

The State Insurance Division of the Department of Licensing and Regulation licenses all state insurance companies, agents, and brokers, and must approve all policies for sale in the state.

34 SECURITIES

There are no securities or commodities exchanges in Maryland. In 2005, there were 2,450 personal financial advisers employed in the state and 3,600 securities, commodities, and financial services sales agents. In 2004, there were over 175 publicly traded companies within the state, with over 67 NASDAQ companies, 37 NYSE listings, and 13 AMEX listings. In 2006, the state had five Fortune 500 companies; Lockheed Martin (in Bethesda) ranked first in the state and 52nd in the nation with revenues of over $37.2 billion, followed by Constellation Energy (Baltimore), Marriott International (Bethesda), Coventry Health Care (Bethesda), and Black and Decker (Towson). All five companies are listed on the NYSE.

35 PUBLIC FINANCE

The state budget, prepared by the Department of Budget and Management, is submitted annually by the governor to the General Assembly for amendment and approval. The fiscal year (FY) runs from 1 July to 30 June.

Fiscal year 2006 general funds were estimated at $13.5 billion for resources and $12.3 billion for expenditures. In fiscal year 2004, federal government grants to Maryland were $8.8 billion.

In the fiscal year 2007 federal budget, Maryland was slated to receive: $178.5 million for the continued consolidation of Food and Drug Administration facilities at White Oak. The request includes funding for the Building One renovation and for construction of the Office of the Commissioner and Office of Regulatory Affairs office building, and for other infrastructure needs; $6 million for improvements at the Center for Veterinary Medicine in Laurel. These funds will support the replacement of the underground water distribution systems for a central utility plant and 13 laboratory buildings with a modern, high efficiency, high quality, and low maintenance system; $5.8 million for improvements at the Center for Devices and Radiological Health's (CDRH) White Oak site in Silver Spring. These funds will allow for the upgrade of the major mechanical systems of an old laboratory and convert it into a machine fabrication shop and a photo science laboratory for the CDRH.

36 TAXATION

In 2005, Maryland collected $13,497 million in tax revenues or $2,410 per capita, which placed it 14th among the 50 states in per capita tax burden. The national average was $2,192 per capita. Property taxes accounted for 3.9% of the total, sales taxes 21.4%,

Maryland—State Government Finances

(Dollar amounts in thousands. Per capita amounts in dollars.)

	AMOUNT	PER CAPITA
Total Revenue	28,395,564	5,106.20
General revenue	22,841,717	4,107.48
Intergovernmental revenue	6,456,870	1,161.10
Taxes	12,314,799	2,214.49
General sales	2,945,060	529.59
Selective sales	2,267,364	407.73
License taxes	511,559	91.99
Individual income tax	5,277,844	949.08
Corporate income tax	447,487	80.47
Other taxes	865,485	155.63
Current charges	2,304,963	414.49
Miscellaneous general revenue	1,765,085	317.40
Utility revenue	107,076	19.25
Liquor store revenue	–	–
Insurance trust revenue	5,446,771	979.46
Total expenditure	25,343,680	4,557.40
Intergovernmental expenditure	5,632,520	1,012.86
Direct expenditure	19,711,160	3,544.54
Current operation	14,025,013	2,522.03
Capital outlay	1,624,740	292.17
Insurance benefits and repayments	2,493,018	448.30
Assistance and subsidies	697,114	125.36
Interest on debt	871,275	156.68
Exhibit: Salaries and wages	4,011,309	721.33
Total expenditure	25,343,680	4,557.40
General expenditure	22,299,005	4,009.89
Intergovernmental expenditure	5,632,520	1,012.86
Direct expenditure	16,666,485	2,997.03
General expenditures, by function:		
Education	7,366,076	1,324.60
Public welfare	5,490,400	987.30
Hospitals	405,108	72.85
Health	1,524,186	274.08
Highways	1,655,814	297.75
Police protection	418,856	75.32
Correction	1,064,123	191.35
Natural resources	484,135	87.06
Parks and recreation	255,796	46.00
Government administration	785,901	141.32
Interest on general debt	871,275	156.68
Other and unallocable	1,977,335	355.57
Utility expenditure	551,657	99.20
Liquor store expenditure	–	–
Insurance trust expenditure	2,493,018	448.30
Debt at end of fiscal year	13,600,741	2,445.74
Cash and security holdings	44,014,692	7,914.89

Abbreviations and symbols: – zero or rounds to zero; (NA) not available; (X) not applicable.

SOURCE: *U.S. Census Bureau, Governments Division, 2004 Survey of State Government Finances,* January 2006.

selective sales taxes 17.7%, individual income taxes 41.9%, corporate income taxes 6.0%, and other taxes 9.0%.

As of 1 January 2006, Maryland had four individual income tax brackets ranging from 2.0 to 4.75%. The state taxes corporations at a flat rate of 7.0%.

In 2004, state and local property taxes amounted to about $6 billion or $1,082 per capita. The per capita amount ranks the state 17th highest nationally. Local governments collected $5,539,833,000 of the total and the state government $478,796,000.

Maryland taxes retail sales at a rate of 5%. Food purchased for consumption off-premises is tax exempt. The tax on cigarettes is 100 cents per pack, which ranks 19th among the 50 states and the District of Columbia. Maryland taxes gasoline at 23.5 cents per gallon. This is in addition to the 18.4 cents per gallon federal tax on gasoline.

According to the Tax Foundation, for every federal tax dollar sent to Washington in 2004, Maryland citizens received $1.44 in federal spending.

37 ECONOMIC POLICY

The Department of Business and Economic Development (DBED), created in 1995, encourages new firms to locate in Maryland and established firms to expand their in-state facilities, promotes the tourist industry, and disseminates information about the state's history and attractions. The department helps secure industrial mortgage loans for businesses that create new jobs, and also provides small-business loans, low-interest construction loads, assistance in plant location and expansion; and supports the Division of Business Development to allow companies to maximize their use of state services. In addition, the department assists local governments in attracting federal funds for economic development and maintains programs to encourage minority businesses, the marketing of seafood, and the use of Ocean City Convention Hall. In 2006, the DBED maintained international offices in Mexico City, Monterrey (Mexico), Beijing, Shanghai, Taipei, Singapore, Bangalore (India), Shorashim (Israel), and Paris. The Department of State Planning oversees state and regional development programs and helps local governments develop planning goals.

During the 1930s, Maryland pioneered in urban design with the new town of Greenbelt, in Prince George's County. A wholly planned community, Columbia, was built in Howard County during the 1960s. More recently, redevelopment of Baltimore's decaying inner city has been aggressively promoted. Harborplace, a waterside pavilion featuring hundreds of shops and restaurants, formally opened in 1980, and an industrial park was developed in a high-unemployment section of northwest Baltimore during the early 1980s. Not far from Harborplace are the 33-story World Trade Center and the National Aquarium. Urban restoration has also been encouraged by urban homesteading: a Baltimorean willing to make a commitment to live in an old brick building and fix it up can submit a closed bid to buy it. An analogous "shopsteading" program to attract merchants has also been encouraged.

In 1982, Maryland initiated a program of state enterprise zones to encourage economic growth by focusing state and local resources on designated areas requiring economic stimulus. Five of these enterprise zones were located in western Maryland, four in the central part of the state, and one on the Eastern Shore. There were 29 state enterprise zones in 2006. With Delaware, Virginia, and Washington DC, Maryland has been recognized as part of an international life sciences hub, dubbed the BioCapital hub. Maryland companies and agencies participate in bioscience "hotbed" campaigns, concerted efforts by groups made up of government development agencies, pharmaceutical and bioscience companies, research institutes, universities, and nonprofits to attract capital, personnel and resources to develop a life sciences cluster. Over 500 foreign-based businesses have been established in Maryland, creating over 75,000 jobs. The Office of International Business (OIB) within the DBED, offers assistance to foreign companies for location, relocation, and expansion, in addition to providing assistance to Maryland exporters.

38 HEALTH

The infant mortality rate in October 2005 was estimated at 8.2 per 1,000 live births. The birth rate in 2003 was 13.6 per 1,000 population. The abortion rate stood at 29 per 1,000 women in 2000. In 2003, about 83.7% of pregnant woman received prenatal care beginning in the first trimester. In 2004, approximately 80% of children received routine immunizations before the age of three.

The crude death rate in 2003 was 8.1 deaths per 1,000 population. As of 2002, the death rates for major causes of death (per 100,000 resident population) were: heart disease, 220; cancer, 190.4; cerebrovascular diseases, 51.5; chronic lower respiratory diseases, 35.6; and diabetes, 27.8. The mortality rate from HIV infection was 11.2 per 100,000 population, representing the second-highest rate in the country (following the District of Columbia at 40.8 per 100,000); the national HIV death rate was 4.9 per 100,000. In 2004, the reported AIDS case rate was at about 26.1 per 100,000 population, the fourth-highest rate in the country. In 2002, about 55.2% of the population was considered overweight or obese. As of 2004, about 19.5% of state residents were smokers.

In 2003, Maryland had 51 community hospitals with about 11,600 beds. There were about 645,000 patient admissions that year and 6.5 million outpatient visits. The average daily inpatient census was about 8,700 patients. The average cost per day for hospital care was $1,571. Also in 2003, there were about 243 certified nursing facilities in the state with 29,362 beds and an overall occupancy rate of about 86.1%. In 2004, it was estimated that about 75.8% of all state residents had received some type of dental care within the year. Maryland had 389 physicians per 100,000 resident population in 2004 and 875 nurses per 100,000 in 2005. In 2004, there were a total of 4,169 dentists in the state.

About 19% of state residents were enrolled in Medicaid and Medicare programs in 2004. Approximately 14% of the state population was uninsured in 2004. In 2003, state health care expenditures totaled $6.8 million.

Maryland's two medical schools are at Johns Hopkins University, which operates in connection with the Johns Hopkins Hospital and has superbly equipped research facilities, and at the University of Maryland—both located in Baltimore. Johns Hopkins Hospital ranked first on the Honor Roll of Best Hospitals 2005 by *U.S. News & World Report*; in the same report, it ranked third for best pediatric hospitals and best care for cancer and heart disease. Federal health centers located in Bethesda include the National Institutes of Health and the National Naval Medical Center.

39 SOCIAL WELFARE

In 2004, about 109,000 people received unemployment benefits, with the average weekly unemployment benefit at $254. In fiscal year 2005, the estimated average monthly participation in the food stamp program included about 288,943 persons (131,556 households); the average monthly benefit was about $92.33 per person. That year, the total of benefits paid through the state for the food stamp program was about $320.1 million.

Temporary Assistance for Needy Families (TANF), the system of federal welfare assistance that officially replaced Aid to Families with Dependent Children (AFDC) in 1997, was reautho-

rized through the Deficit Reduction Act of 2005. TANF is funded through federal block grants that are divided among the states based on an equation involving the number of recipients in each state. Maryland's TANF program is called the Family Investment Program (FIP). In 2004, the state program had 59,000 recipients; state and federal expenditures on this TANF program totaled $32 million in fiscal year 2003.

In December 2004, Social Security benefits were paid to 761,160 Maryland residents. This number included 499,620 retired workers, 75,210 widows and widowers, 86,860 disabled workers, 35,200 spouses, and 64,270 children. Social Security beneficiaries represented 13.7% of the total state population and 87.4% of the state's population age 65 and older. Retired workers received an average monthly payment of $962; widows and widowers, $923; disabled workers, $926; and spouses, $493. Payments for children of retired workers averaged $511 per month; children of deceased workers, $639; and children of disabled workers, $287. Federal Supplemental Security Income payments in December 2004 went to 92,776 Marylanders, averaging $408 a month. An additional $641,000 of state-administered supplemental payments were distributed to 2,973 residents.

40 HOUSING

Maryland has sought to preserve many of its historic houses. Block upon block of two-story brick row houses, often with white stoops, fill the older parts of Baltimore, and stone cottages built to withstand rough winters are still found in the western counties. Greenbelt and Columbia exemplify changing modern concepts of community planning.

There were an estimated 2,250,339 housing units in Maryland in 2004, of which 2,077,900 were occupied; 69.5% were owner-occupied. About 51.9% of all units are single-family, detached homes. Most units rely on utility gas and electricity for heating. It was estimated that 61,901 units lacked telephone service, 6,034 lacked complete plumbing facilities, and 5,885 lacked complete kitchen facilities. The average household had 2.61 members.

In 2004, 27,400 privately owned units were authorized for construction. The median home value was $216,529. The median monthly cost for mortgage owners was $1,406. Renters paid a median of $837 per month. In 2006, the state received over $8 million in community development block grants from the US Department of Housing and Urban Development (HUD). The city of Baltimore received over $23.9 million in community development block grants.

The Department of Housing and Community Development, formed in 1987, oversees all housing and cultural resource areas, providing neighborhood rehabilitation and revitalization, development financing, historical and cultural programs, and information technology. The Maryland Housing Fund of the Department insures qualified lending institutions against losses on home mortgage loans.

41 EDUCATION

As of 2004, 87.4% of Marylanders 25 years and older had completed high school compared the national average of 84%. Some 35.2% had at least four years of college, far surpassing the national average of 26%. Maryland students must pass state High School Assessments (HSA) in order to graduate from high school.

The total enrollment for fall 2002 in Maryland's public schools stood at 867,000. Of these, 610,000 attended schools from kindergarten through grade eight, and 256,000 attended high school. Approximately 50.4% of the students were white, 37.9% were black, 6.4% were Hispanic, 4.9% were Asian/Pacific Islander, and 0.4% were American Indian/Alaskan Native. Total enrollment was estimated at 863,000 in fall 2003 and was expected to be 858,000 by fall 2014, a decline of 1% during the period 2002 to 2014. There were 149,253 students enrolled in 727 private schools. Expenditures for public education in 2003/04 were estimated at $8.7 billion. Since 1969, the National Assessment of Educational Progress (NAEP) has tested public school students nationwide. The resulting report, *The Nation's Report Card,* stated that in 2005 eighth graders in Maryland scored 278 out of 500 in mathematics, matching the national average.

As of fall 2002, there were 300,269 students enrolled in college or graduate school; minority students comprised 36% of total postsecondary enrollment. In 2005 Maryland had 63 degree-granting institutions. The institutions of higher education in Maryland are organized as follows: (1) the public four-year colleges and universities, (2) the community colleges, (3) the independent colleges and universities, and (4) the private career schools.

The state's public four-year institutions include the University of Maryland System, Morgan State University, and St. Mary's College of Maryland. The University of Maryland System is comprised of 13 separate degree-granting institutions located throughout the state. Included, there are two research and public service institutions reporting to the System—the Center for Environmental and Estuarine Studies and the University of Maryland Biotechnology Institute. These institutions are governed by a single board of regents and a system administration. Morgan State University, the designated public urban teaching university, is governed by a single board of regents. Morgan is one of Maryland's four historically black institutions. St. Mary's College of Maryland, the State's public honors college, is the state's only "state-related" institution. As such, the college has more operational autonomy than the other public four-year institutions, particularly concerning procurement, budget, and personnel administration.

The 16 community colleges are two-year, open-admission institutions with courses and programs leading to certificates and associate degrees, as well as career-oriented and continuing education/community service programs. They receive their funding from three sources: 1) state funding through a funding formula; 2) local funding through a negotiated budget process; and 3) students' tuition and fees. Baltimore City Community College became a state institution in 1990/91 and receives the majority of its funding from the state. The state provides funding to independent colleges and universities in Maryland under a statutory formula. Eligible independent institutions must meet certain standards concerning the date of establishment, type of degrees conferred, accreditation, and affirmative action programs. St. John's College in Annapolis is known for its unique program that includes study of the ancient Greek and Latin classics in their original languages.

The Maryland Higher Education Commission serves as the state's agency that provides, as part of its primary mission, coordination, regulatory oversight, and program approval for Maryland's postsecondary education system. The State Scholarship Administration oversees state scholarship programs.

[42] ARTS

Although close to the arts centers of Washington, DC, Maryland has its own cultural attractions. Baltimore, a major theatrical center in the 1800s, still has many legitimate theaters. Center Stage in Baltimore is the designated state theater of Maryland, and the Olney Theatre in Montgomery County is the official state summer theater. Arts organizations are aided by the Maryland State Arts Council, established in 1967 and led by a body of 17 appointed citizens.

The state's leading orchestra is the Baltimore Symphony; it began in 1916 and is the only major American orchestra that started as an established branch of the municipal government. In early February 2005, the Baltimore Symphony began performing in the new Music Center at Strathmore. Baltimore is also the home of the Baltimore Opera Company, and its jazz clubs were the launching pads for such musical notables as Eubie Blake, Ella Fitzgerald, and Cab Calloway. Annapolis hosts a symphony, an opera company, and the Ballet Theatre of Maryland. The National Ballet (est. 1948) is the oldest professional ballet company in the state. One of the newest additions to the arts community is the Maryland Symphony Orchestra in Hagerstown, established in 1982. The Peabody Institute of Johns Hopkins University in Baltimore is one of the nation's most distinguished music schools. As of 2006, the Peabody Institute's conservatory offered 26 major fields including opera, chamber music, composition, computer music, recording arts, and music education. Both the Maryland Ballet Company and Maryland Dance Theater are nationally known.

In 2005, the Maryland State Arts Council and other arts organizations received grants totaling 36 grants totaling $2,507,890 from the National Endowment for the Arts (NEA). The Maryland Humanities Council (MHC) was founded in 1973. The MHC reached approximately 900,000 Marylanders through their programs in 2004. As of 2006, MHC provided programs such as "Maryland Center for the Book" and the first annual Youth Film JAM in May 2006—a festival providing free screenings of award-winning films followed by discussions with film critics and the festival advisory committee. In 2005, the state received 26 grants, totaling $2,645,201, from the National Endowment for the Humanities.

[43] LIBRARIES AND MUSEUMS

For the fiscal year ending June 2001, Maryland's 24 public library systems had 175 libraries, of which 158 were branches. In that same year, the system also operated 19 bookmobiles, had 15,323,000 volumes of books and serial publications on its shelves, and had a combined total circulation of 46,595,000. The system also had 774,000 audio and 443,000 video items, and 5,000 electronic format items (CD-ROMs, magnetic tapes, and disks). The center of the state library network is the Enoch Pratt Free Library in the city of Baltimore. Founded in 1886, it had 28 branches, over 2.8 million volumes, and a circulation of over 1.5 million in 1999. Each county also has its own library system. The largest academic libraries are those of Johns Hopkins University (2,507,232 volumes in 1999) and the University of Maryland at College Park (2.2 million). The Maryland Historical Society Library specializes in genealogy, heraldry, and state history. The Maryland State Archives houses government records, private manuscripts, maps, and photographs. Maryland is also the site of several federal libraries, including the National Agricultural Library at Beltsville, with over 2 million volumes; the National Library of Medicine at Bethesda, 2,200,000; and the National Oceanic and Atmospheric Administration Library at Rockville, with about 1 million volumes in 1999. In 2001, operating income for the state's public library system was $182,940,000, including $1,854,000 in federal grants and $24,406,000 in state grants.

Of the approximately 147 museums and historic sites in the state, the major institutions are the US Naval Academy Museum in Annapolis and Baltimore's Museum of Art, National Aquarium Seaport and Maritime Museum, Maryland Academy of Sciences, the Maryland Historical Society Museum, and Peale Museum, the oldest museum building in the United States. Important historic sites include Ft. McHenry National Monument and Shrine in Baltimore (inspiration for "The Star-Spangled Banner") and Antietam National Battlefield Site near Sharpsburg.

[44] COMMUNICATIONS

In 2004, 93.4% of Maryland's occupied housing units had telephones. Additionally, by June of that same year there were 3,575,747 mobile wireless telephone subscribers. In 2003, 66.0% of Maryland households had a computer and 59.2% had Internet access. By June 2005, there were 913,068 high-speed lines in Maryland, 822,436 residential and 90,632 for business.

The state had 12 major AM and 35 major FM radio stations in 2005. Maryland has 13 major television stations, including public broadcasting stations in Annapolis, Baltimore, Frederick, Hagerstown, Oakland, and Salisbury. Maryland also receives the signals of many Washington, DC. broadcast stations. The Baltimore area had almost 1 million television households, 68% of which received cable in 1999.

[45] PRESS

The *Maryland Gazette,* established at Annapolis in 1727, was the state's first newspaper. It wasn't until 1773 that Baltimore got its first paper, the *Maryland Journal and Baltimore Advertiser,* but by 1820 there were five highly partisan papers in the city. The *Baltimore Sun,* founded in 1837, reached its heyday after 1906, when H. L. Mencken became a staff writer. Mencken, who was also an important editor and critic, helped found the *American Mercury* magazine in 1924.

As of 2005, Maryland had 10 morning and 3 afternoon dailies, as well as 9 Sunday papers. The most influential newspaper published in Baltimore is the *Sun* (daily, 280,717; Sunday, 454,045). The *Washington Post* (707,690 daily; 1,007,487 Sundays) is also widely read in Maryland.

[46] ORGANIZATIONS

In 2006, there were over 6,690 nonprofit organizations registered within the state, of which about 4,804 were registered as charitable, educational, or religious organizations. National medically oriented organizations with headquarters in Maryland include the National Federation of the Blind, the American Urological Association, the American Occupational Therapy Association, National Foundation for Cancer Research, the American Speech-Language-Hearing Association, the Cystic Fibrosis Foundation, the National Association of the Deaf, and the American Music Therapy Association.

Leading commercial, professional, and trade groups include the Aircraft Owners and Pilots Association, the American Fisheries Society, the International Association of Chiefs of Police, and the Retailer's Bakery of America.

Lacrosse, a major sport in the state, is represented by the Lacrosse Foundation in Baltimore and the US Intercollegiate Lacrosse Association in Chestertown. The National Amateur Baseball Federation, the American Tennis Association, and the National 4-H Council are also based in the state.

A number of military organizations are based in Maryland, including the Air Force Historical Foundation, the American Military Society, AMVETS (American Veterans of World War II, Korea, and Vietnam), the Black Military History Institute of America, the Vietnam Veterans of America, and the Blue Star Mothers of America. The National Flag Day Foundation is based in Baltimore.

Historical and cultural organizations include the Baltimore and Ohio Railroad Historical Society, the Edgar Allan Poe Society of Baltimore, and the Folk Alliance. There are also a number of county and regional historical societies. Education and research associations on the national level include the Jane Goodall Institute for Wildlife Research, Education, and Conservation, and the Wildlife Society.

Social action and civil rights organizations based in Maryland include the National Association for the Advancement of Colored People, Catholic Relief Services, and Goodwill Industries International.

[47] TOURISM, TRAVEL, AND RECREATION

In 2004, the state hosted over 21 million travelers. About 80% of all travelers were residents of one of the following states: Maryland, Pennsylvania, Virginia, New York, New Jersey, Florida, North Carolina, California, Ohio, Delaware, and West Virginia.

Attractions include parks, historical sites, and national seashore (Assateague Island). Annapolis, the state capital, is the site of the US Naval Academy. On Baltimore's waterfront are monuments to Francis Scott Key and Edgar Allan Poe, historic Ft. McHenry, and many restaurants serving the city's famed crab cakes and other seafood specialties. Ocean City is the state's major seaside resort, and there are many resort towns along Chesapeake Bay. Camp David, in Thurmont, is the home of presidential retreat. The Richard M. Nixon Presidential Library is in College Park. The state's office of tourism developed a "Star Spangled Banner Tour"—a 100-mi (160-km) scenic driving tour ending at Fort McHenry, where the national anthem was composed. Near Camden Yard (home of the Baltimore Orioles) is the childhood home of Babe Ruth, who played for the New York Yankees. Baltimore also features the National Aquarium. The Preakness Race (thoroughbred racing) is the second leg of the Triple Crown and is run at the State Fairgrounds in Baltimore. There are 19 state parks with camping facilities and 10 recreation areas. The Civil War battlefield at Antietam and other Civil War trails are located in Maryland.

[48] SPORTS

Maryland has two major professional sports teams: the Baltimore Orioles of Major League Baseball and the Baltimore Ravens of the National Football League. The Ravens (formerly the Browns) moved from Cleveland after the 1995 season, and play in a downtown stadium, built in 1998, near Oriole Park at Camden Yards. The NFL's Washington Redskins play in a new stadium, Jack Kent Cooke Stadium, in Landover, but are still considered a team of the District of Columbia. The Orioles won the World Series in 1966, 1970, and 1983, and American League titles in 1969, 1971, 1979, and 1983.

There are several minor league baseball teams in the state, including teams in Bowie, Frederick, Delmarva, Aberdeen, and Hagerstown.

Ever since 1750, when the first Arabian thoroughbred horse was imported by a Maryland breeder, horse racing has been a popular state pastime. The major tracks are Pimlico (Baltimore), Bowie, and Laurel. Pimlico is the site of the Preakness Stakes, the second leg of racing's Triple Crown. Harness racing is held at Ocean Downs in Ocean City; quarter-horse racing takes place at several tracks throughout the state; and several steeplechase events, including the prestigious Maryland Hunt Cup, are held annually.

In men's collegiate basketball, the University of Maryland won the National Collegiate Athletic Association (NCAA) Championship in 2002, the ACC Tournament title in 2004, and the National Invitation Tournament in 1972. The Maryland women's basketball team won the National Championship in 2006. Morgan State took the NCAA Division II title in 1974. Another major sport is lacrosse; Johns Hopkins, the Naval Academy, and the University of Maryland all have performed well in intercollegiate competition. In fact, Johns Hopkins has won the NCAA National Championship eight times, most recently in 2005.

Every weekend from April to October, Marylanders compete in jousting tournaments held in four classes throughout the state. In modern jousting, designated as the official state sport, horseback riders attempt to pick up small rings with long, lance-like poles. The state championship is held in October.

Babe Ruth, perhaps the greatest baseball player to ever play the game, was one of many star athletes to be born in the state.

49 FAMOUS MARYLANDERS

Politicians

Maryland's lone US vice president was Spiro Theodore Agnew (1918–96), who served as governor of Maryland before being elected as Richard Nixon's running mate in 1968. Reelected with Nixon in 1972, Agnew resigned the vice-presidency in October 1973 after a federal indictment had been filed against him. Roger Brooke Taney (1777–1864) served as attorney general and secretary of the treasury in Andrew Jackson's cabinet before being confirmed as US chief justice in 1836; his most historically significant case was the *Dred Scott* decision in 1856, in which the Supreme Court ruled that Congress could not exclude slavery from any territory.

Three associate justices of the US Supreme Court were also born in Maryland. Thomas Johnson (1732–1819), a signer of the Declaration of Independence, served as the first governor of the State of Maryland before his appointment to the Court in 1791. Samuel Chase (1741–1811) was a Revolutionary leader, another signer of the Declaration of Independence, and a local judicial and political leader before being appointed to the high court in

1797; impeached in 1804 because of his alleged hostility to the Jeffersonians, he was acquitted by the Senate the following year. As counsel for the National Association for the Advancement of Colored People, Thurgood Marshall (1908–93), argued the landmark *Brown v. Board of Education* school desegregation case before the Supreme Court in 1954; President Lyndon Johnson appointed him to the Court 13 years later.

Other major federal officeholders born in Maryland include John Hanson (1721–83), a member of the Continental Congress and first president to serve under the Articles of confederation (1781–82); Charles Carroll of Carrollton (1737–1832), a signer of the Declaration of Independence and US senator from 1789 to 1792; John Pendleton Kennedy (1795–1870), secretary of the Navy under Millard Fillmore and a popular novelist known by the pseudonym Mark Littleton; Reverdy Johnson (1796–1876), attorney general under Zachary Taylor; Charles Joseph Bonaparte (1851–1921) secretary of the Navy and attorney general in Theodore Roosevelt's cabinet; and Benjamin Civiletti (b.New York, 1935), attorney general under Jimmy Carter. Among the many important state officeholders are William Paca (1740–99), a signer of the Declaration of Independence and later governor; Luther Martin (b.New Jersey, 1748–1826), Maryland's attorney general from 1778 to 1805 and from 1818 to 1822, as well as defense counsel in the impeachment trial of Chase and in the treason trial of Aaron Burr; John Eager Howard (1752–1827), Revolutionary soldier, governor, and US senator; and Albert C. Ritchie (1876–1936), governor from 1919 to 1935. William D. Schaefer (b.1921) was mayor of Baltimore from 1971–87; he was elected governor in 1987.

Lawyer and poet Francis Scott Key (1779–1843) wrote "The Star-Spangled Banner"—now the national anthem—in 1814. The prominent abolitionists Frederick Douglass (Frederick Augustus Washington Bailey, 1817?–95) and Harriet Tubman (1820?–1913) were born in Maryland, as was John Carroll (1735–1815), the first Roman Catholic bishop in the United States and founder of Georgetown University. Elizabeth Ann Bayley Seton (b.New York, 1774–1821), canonized by the Roman Catholic Church in 1975, was the first native-born American saint. Stephen Decatur (1779–1820), a prominent naval officer, has been credited with the toast "Our country, right or wrong!"

Business Leaders

Prominent Maryland business leaders include Alexander Brown (b.Ireland, 1764–1834), a Scotch-Irish immigrant who built the firm that is now the second-oldest private investment banking house in the United States; George Peabody (b.Massachusetts, 1795–1869), founder of the world-famous Peabody Conservatory of Music (now the Peabody Institute of Johns Hopkins University); and Enoch Pratt (b.Massachusetts, (1808–96) who endowed the Enoch Pratt Free Library in Baltimore. Benjamin Banneker (1731–1806), a free black, assisted in surveying the new District of Columbia and published almanacs from 1792 to 1797. Ottmar Mergenthaler (b.Germany, 1854–99), who made his home in Baltimore, invented the linotype machine.

Educators and Physicians

Financier-philanthropist Johns Hopkins (1795–1873) was a Marylander, and educators Daniel Coit Gilman (b.Connecticut, 1831–1908) and William Osler (b.Canada, 1849–1919, also a famed physician), were prominent in the establishment of the university and medical school named in Hopkins' honor. Peyton Rous (1879–1970) won the 1966 Nobel Prize for physiology or medicine.

Writers

Maryland's best-known modern writer was H(enry) L(ouis) Mencken (1880–1956), a Baltimore newspaper reporter who was also a gifted social commentator, political wit, and student of the American language. Edgar Allan Poe (b.Massachusetts, 1809–49), known for his poems and eerie short stories, died in Baltimore, and novelist-reformer Upton Sinclair (1878–1968) was born there. Other writers associated with Maryland include James M. Cain (1892–1976), Leon Uris (1924–2003), John Barth (b.1930), and Russell Baker (b.1925). Painters John Hesselius (b.Pennsylvania, 1728–78) and Charles Willson Peale (1741–1827) are also linked with the state.

Actors and Musicians

Most notable among Maryland actors are Edwin Booth (1833–93) and his brother John Wilkes Booth (1838–65), notorious as the assassin of President Abraham Lincoln. Maryland was the birthplace of several jazz musicians, including James Hubert "Eubie" Blake (1883–1983), William Henry "Chick" Webb (1907–39), and Billie Holiday (1915–59).

Sports Figures

Probably the greatest baseball player of all time, George Herman "Babe" Ruth (1895–1948) was born in Baltimore. Other prominent ballplayers include Robert Moses "Lefty" Grove (1900–75), James Emory "Jimmy" Foxx (1907–67), and Al Kaline (b.1934). Former lightweight boxing champion Joe Gans (1874–1910) was a Maryland native.

50 BIBLIOGRAPHY

Alampi, Gary, (ed.). *Gale State Rankings Reporter.* Detroit: Gale Research, Inc., 1994.

Cities of the United States. 5th ed. Farmington Hills: Thomson Gale, 2005.

Council of State Governments. *The Book of the States, 2006 Edition.* Lexington, Ky.: Council of State Governments, 2006.

Coursey, Denise Hawkins, and Matthew Coursey. *Frommer's Maryland & Delaware.* Foster City, CA: IDG Books Worldwide, 2000.

DeGrove, John Melvin. *Planning Policy and Politics: Smart Growth and the States.* Cambridge, Mass.: Lincoln Institute of Land Policy, 2005.

FDIC, Division of Research and Statistics. *Statistics on Banking: A Statistical Profile of the United States Banking Industry.* Washington, D.C.: Federal Deposit Insurance Corporation, 1993.

Fuke, Richard Paul. *Imperfect Equality: African Americans and the Confines of White Racial Attitudes in Post-Emancipation Maryland.* New York: Fordham University Press, 1999.

Harp, David W. *The Great Marsh: An Intimate Journey into a Chesapeake Wetland.* Baltimore, Md.: Johns Hopkins University Press, 2002.

Leone, Mark P. *The Archaeology of Liberty in an American Capital: Excavations in Annapolis.* Berkeley: University of California Press, 2005.

Maryland, State of. Department of Economic and Community Development. *Maryland Statistical Abstract 1993–94.* Annapolis: State of Maryland, 1995.

Marzec, Robert P. (ed.). *The Mid-Atlantic Region.* Vol. 2 in *The Greenwood Encyclopedia of American Regional Cultures.* Westport, Conn.: Greenwood Press, 2004.

Riordan, Timothy B. *The Plundering Time: Maryland and the English Civil War, 1645–1646.* Baltimore, Md.: Maryland Historical Society, 2004.

US Department of Commerce, Economics and Statistics Administration, US Census Bureau. *Maryland, 2000. Summary Social, Economic, and Housing Characteristics: 2000 Census of Population and Housing.* Washington, D.C.: US Government Printing Office, 2003.

US Department of Education, National Center for Education Statistics. Office of Educational Research and Improvement. *Digest of Education Statistics, 1993.* Washington, D.C.: US Government Printing Office, 1993.

US Department of the Interior, US Fish and Wildlife Service. *Endangered and Threatened Species Recovery Program.* Washington, DC: US Government Printing Office, 1990.

MASSACHUSETTS

Commonwealth of Massachusetts

ORIGIN OF STATE NAME: Derived from the name of the Massachusett Native American tribe that lived on Massachusetts Bay; the name is thought to mean "at or about the Great Hill." **NICKNAME:** The Bay State. **CAPITAL:** Boston. **ENTERED UNION:** 6 February 1788 (6th). **SONG:** "All Hail to Massachusetts;" "Massachusetts" (folksong). **MOTTO:** *Ense petit placidam sub libertate quietem* (By the sword we seek peace, but peace only under liberty). **COAT OF ARMS:** On a blue shield, a Native American depicted in gold holds in his right hand a bow, in his left an arrow pointing downward. Above the bow is a five-pointed silver star. The crest shows a bent right arm holding a broadsword. Around the shield beneath the crest is a banner with the state motto in green. **FLAG:** The coat of arms on a white field. **OFFICIAL SEAL:** Same as the coat of arms, with the inscription *Sigillum Reipublicæ Massachusettensis* (Seal of the Republic of Massachusetts). **BIRD:** Chickadee. **FISH:** Cod. **FLOWER:** Mayflower (ground laurel). **TREE:** American elm. **GEM:** Rhodonite. **LEGAL HOLIDAYS:** New Year's Day, 1 January; Birthday of Martin Luther King Jr., 3rd Monday in January; Washington's Birthday, 3rd Monday in February; Patriots' Day, 3rd Monday in April; Memorial Day, last Monday in May; Independence Day, 4 July; Labor Day, 1st Monday in September; Columbus Day, 2nd Monday in October; Veterans Day, 11 November; Thanksgiving Day, appointed by the governor, customarily the 4th Thursday in November; Christmas Day, 25 December. Legal holidays in Suffolk County include Evacuation Day, 17 March; and Bunker Hill Day, 17 June. **TIME:** 7 AM EST = noon GMT.

¹LOCATION, SIZE, AND EXTENT

Located in the northeastern United States, Massachusetts is the fourth-largest of the six New England states and ranks 45th in size among the 50 states.

The total area of Massachusetts is 8,284 sq mi (21,456 sq km), of which land comprises 7,824 sq mi (20,265 sq km) and inland water occupies 460 sq mi (1,191 sq km). Massachusetts extends about 190 mi (306 k) E–W; the maximum N–S extension is about 110 mi (177 km). Massachusetts is bordered on the N by Vermont and New Hampshire; on the E by the Atlantic Ocean; on the S by the Atlantic Ocean and by Rhode Island and Connecticut; and on the W by New York.

Two important islands lie south of the state's fishhook-shaped Cape Cod peninsula: Martha's Vineyard (108 sq mi or 280 sq km) and Nantucket (57 sq mi or 148 sq km). The Elizabeth Islands, SW of Cape Cod and NW of Martha's Vineyard, consist of 16 small islands separating Buzzards Bay from Vineyard Sound. The total boundary length of Massachusetts is 515 mi (829 km), including a general coastline of 192 mi (309 km); the tidal shoreline, encompassing numerous inlets and islands, is 1,519 mi (2,444 km). The state's geographic center is located in Worcester County, in the northern section of the city of Worcester.

²TOPOGRAPHY

Massachusetts is divided into four topographical regions: coastal lowlands, interior lowlands, dissected uplands, and residuals of ancient mountains. The coastal lowlands, located on the state's eastern edge, extend from the Atlantic Ocean 30–50 mi (48–80 km) inland and include Cape Cod and the offshore islands. The northern shoreline of the state is characterized by rugged high slopes, but at the southern end, along Cape Cod, the ground is flatter and covered with grassy heaths.

The Connecticut River Valley, characterized by red sandstone, curved ridges, meadows, and good soil, is the main feature of west-central Massachusetts. The Berkshire Valley to the west is filled with streams in its northern end, including the two streams that join below Pittsfield to form the Housatonic River.

East of the Connecticut River Valley are the eastern uplands, an extension of the White Mountains of New Hampshire. From elevations of 1,100 ft (335 m) in midstate, this ridge of heavily forested hills slopes down gradually toward the rocky northern coast.

In western Massachusetts, the Taconic Range and Berkshire Hills (which extend southward from the Green Mountains of Vermont) are characterized by numerous hills and valleys. Mt. Greylock, close to the New York border, is the highest point in the state, at 3,487 ft (1,064 m). Northeast of the Berkshires is the Hoosac Range, an area of plateau land. Its high point is Spruce Hill, at 1,974 ft (602 m). The mean elevation of the state is approximately 500 ft (153 m). The lowest point is at sea level on the Atlantic Ocean.

There are more than 4,230 mi (6,808 km) of rivers in the state. The Connecticut River, the longest, runs southward through west-central Massachusetts; the Deerfield, Westfield, Chicopee, and Millers rivers flow into it. Other rivers of note include the Charles and the Mystic, which flow into Boston harbor; the Taunton, which empties into Mount Hope Bay at Fall River; the Blackstone, passing through Worcester on its way to Rhode Island; the Housatonic, winding through the Berkshires; and the Merrimack, flowing from New Hampshire to the Atlantic Ocean via the state's northeast corner. Over 1,100 lakes dot the state; the largest, the artificial Quabbin Reservoir in central Massachusetts, covers 24,704 acres

(9,997 hectares). The largest natural lake is Assawompset Pond in southern Massachusetts, occupying 2,656 acres (1,075 hectares).

Hilly Martha's Vineyard is roughly triangular in shape, as is Nantucket Island to the east. The Elizabeth Islands are characterized by broad, grassy plains.

Millions of years ago, three mountainous masses of granite rock extended northeastward across the state. The creation of the Appalachian Mountains transformed limestone into marble, mud, and gravel into slate and schist, and sandstone into quartzite. The new surfaces were worn down several times. Then, during the last Ice Age, retreating glaciers left behind the shape of Cape Cod as well as a layer of soil, rock, and boulders.

3 CLIMATE

Although Massachusetts is a relatively small state, there are significant climatic differences between its eastern and western sections. The entire state has cold winters and moderately warm summers, but the Berkshires in the west have both the coldest winters and the coolest summers. The normal January temperature in Pittsfield in the Berkshires is 21°F (-5°C), while the normal July temperature is 67°F (19°C). The interior lowlands are several degrees warmer in both winter and summer; the normal July temperature is 71°F (22°C). The coastal sections are the warmest areas of the state; the normal January temperature for Boston is 30°F (-1°C), and the normal July temperature is 74°F (23°C). The record high temperature in the state is 107°F (42°C), established at Chester and New Bedford on 2 August 1975; the record low is -35°F (-37°C), registered at Chester on 12 January 1981.

Precipitation ranges from 39 to 46 in (99 to 117 cm) annually, with an average for Boston of 42.9 in (108 cm). The average snowfall for Boston is 40.9 in (103 cm), with the range in the Berkshires considerably higher. Boston's average wind speed is 13 mph (21 km/hr).

4 FLORA AND FAUNA

Maple, birch, beech, oak, pine, hemlock, and larch cover the Massachusetts uplands. Common shrubs include rhodora, mountain laurel, and shadbush. Various ferns, maidenhair and osmund among them, grow throughout the state. Typical wildflowers include the Maryland meadow beauty and false loosestrife, as well as several varieties of orchid, lily, goldenrod, and aster. In April 2006, the US Fish and Wildlife Service listed the northeastern bulrush, sandplain gerardia, and small whorled pogonia as threatened and endangered plant species within the state.

As many as 76 species of mammals, 74 of them native species, have been counted in Massachusetts. Common native mammals include the white-tailed deer, bobcat, river otter, striped skunk, mink, ermine, fisher, raccoon, black bear, gray fox, muskrat, porcupine, beaver, red and gray squirrels, snowshoe hare, little brown bat, and masked shrew. Among the Bay State's 336 resident bird species are the mallard, ruffed grouse, bobwhite quail, ring-necked pheasant, herring gull, great horned and screech owls, downy woodpecker, blue jay, mockingbird, cardinal, and song sparrow. Native inland fish include brook trout, chain pickerel, brown bullhead, and yellow perch; brown trout, carp, and smallmouth and largemouth bass have been introduced. Native amphibians include the Jefferson salamander, red-spotted newt, eastern American toad, gray tree frog, and bullfrog. Common reptiles are the snapping turtle, stinkpot, spotted turtle, northern water snake, and northern black racer. The venomous timber rattlesnake and northern copperhead are found mainly in Norfolk, Hampshire, and Hampden counties. The Cape Cod coasts are rich in a variety of shellfish, including clams, mussels, shrimps, and oysters. Twenty Massachusetts animal species (vertebrates and invertebrates) were classified as threatened or endangered in 2006. Among them were the American burying beetle, the bald eagle, puma, shortnose sturgeon, five species of whale, and four species of turtle.

5 ENVIRONMENTAL PROTECTION

All environmentally related programs are administered by the Executive Office of Environmental Affairs (EOEA) and its five agencies: the Department of Environmental Management (DEM); the Department of Environmental Protection (DEP); the Department of Fisheries, Wildlife and Environmental Law Enforcement (DFWELE); the Department of Food and Agriculture (DFA); and the Metropolitan District Commission (MDC).

EOEA agencies protect the state's more than 3,100 lakes and ponds covering about 150,000 acres (61,000 hectares); some 2,000 rivers and streams flowing 10,700 mi (17,200 km); 810,000 acres (about 328,000 hectares) of medium- and high-yield aquifers underlying about a sixth of the state; over a half-million acres (about 200,000 hectares) of wetlands covering about a 12% of the state; and 1,500 mi (2,400 km) of coastal capes, coves, and estuaries.

With disposal of treated sewage sludge in Boston Harbor halted in 1991 and with improved sewage treatment, the harbor as of 2005 was markedly cleaner. In 1988, 10% of the flounder caught in Boston Harbor had liver tumors caused by toxic chemicals; as of 1993, no flounder tested had tumors. In 1994, the state opened a new primary water treatment plant, and in 1996, a second new treatment facility also began operation.

Between 1978 and 1985, Massachusetts averaged 24 air pollution (i.e., ozone) violation days per year; between 1985 and 1993, the average dropped to 14. Since 1990, the state has averaged 7 violation days per year. With the adoption of Massachusetts acid rain legislation in 1985, sulfur dioxide output from Massachusetts sources has been cut by 17%. Additional decreases, particularly from out-of-state power plants, are expected to further cut sulfur dioxide emissions in half by 2000. In response to the Massachusetts Toxic Use Reduction Program and certain federal requirements, toxic air emissions were reduced by about a third between 1989 and 1996. In 2003, 9 million lb of toxic chemicals were released in the state.

The state's solid waste recycling and composting rate stood at 28% in 1994; its goal for 2000 was 46%. In the mid-1990s, 341 of the state's 351 communities had some type of recycling program, and about 49% of solid waste was incinerated. In 2003, Massachusetts had 411 hazardous waste sites listed in the US Environment Protection Agency (EPA) database, 31 of which were on the National Priorities List as of 2006, including Materials Technology Laboratory (US Army), Otis Air National Guard Base, and South Weymouth Naval Air Station. In 2005, the EPA spent over $47.5 million through the Superfund program for the cleanup of hazardous waste sites in the state. The same year, federal EPA grants awarded to the state included $29.6 million for the drinking water state revolving fund program. A $771,279 grant was awarded to implement coastal beach monitoring projects and a $74,000 grant

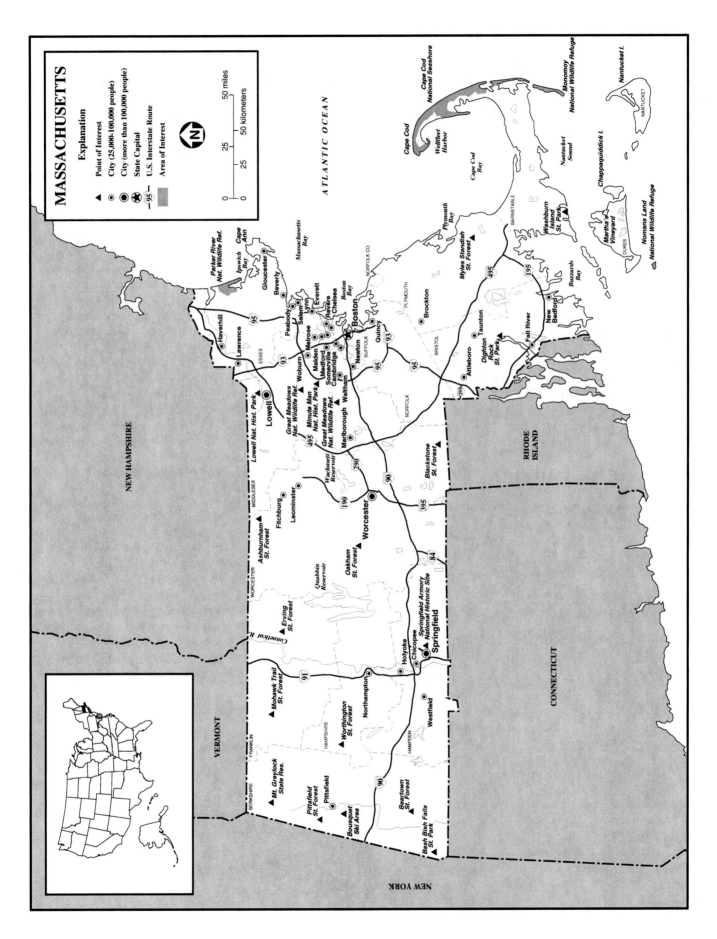

MASSACHUSETTS

Explanation

▲ Point of Interest
⊙ City (25,000-100,000 people)
◉ City (more than 100,000 people)
✪ State Capital
—95— U.S. Interstate Route
▨ Area of Interest

50 miles
50 kilometers
0   25   50
0   25

ATLANTIC OCEAN

NEW HAMPSHIRE

VERMONT

NEW YORK

CONNECTICUT

RHODE ISLAND

Cape Cod National Seashore
Monomoy National Wildlife Refuge
Nantucket I.
Cape Cod
Wellfleet Harbor
NANTUCKET
Cape Cod Bay
BARNSTABLE
Washburn Island St. Park
Buzzards Bay
Martha's Vineyard
Chappaquiddick I.
DUKES
Nomans Land National Wildlife Refuge
Nantucket Sound
Plymouth Bay
Myles Standish St. Forest
495
195
Massachusetts Bay
Parker River Nat. Wildlife Ref.
Ipswich Bay
Cape Ann
Gloucester
Beverly
Salem
Peabody
Lynn
Everett
Revere
Chelsea
Boston Bay
Boston
Quincy
Brockton
Taunton
New Bedford
Fall River
Attleboro
Dighton Rock St. Park
BRISTOL
PLYMOUTH
NORFOLK CO
Melrose
Woburn
Malden
Medford
Somerville
Cambridge
Waltham
Newton
Haverhill
Lawrence
ESSEX
Lowell
Lowell Nat. Hist. Park
Great Meadows Nat. Wildlife Ref.
Minute Man Nat. Hist. Park
Great Meadows Nat. Wildlife Ref.
Marlborough
SUFFOLK
NORFOLK
Blackstone St. Forest
295
195
95
93
90
290
190
395
MIDDLESEX
Fitchburg
Leominster
Ashburnham St. Forest
Wachusett Reservoir
Worcester
WORCESTER
Oakham St. Forest
Quabbin Reservoir
Erving St. Forest
84
Springfield Armory National Historic Site
Springfield
Chicopee
Holyoke
Northampton
HAMPSHIRE
Westfield
HAMPDEN
91
90
Mohawk Trail St. Forest
Worthington St. Forest
FRANKLIN
Connecticut R.
BERKSHIRE
Mt. Greylock State Res.
Pittsfield St. Forest
Pittsfield
Bousquet Ski Area
Beartown St. Forest
Bash Bish Falls St. Park

was awarded for a project to encourage food waste composting in the supermarket industry.

Since about 1900, the Commonwealth has protected 528,400 acres (208,730 hectares) through acquisitions or restrictions, an area equal to 10% of the total land mass of the state. In 1993/94, the state added 8,930 acres (3,614 hectares) to its stock of protected land, expending $41 million in the effort. Federal, county, local, and private nonprofit agencies and organizations provide another 375,680 acres (152,038 hectares) of open space.

6 POPULATION

As New England's most populous state, Massachusetts has seen its population grow steadily since colonial times. However, since the early 1800s, its growth rate has often lagged behind that of the rest of the nation. Massachusetts's population, according to the 1990 federal census, was 6,016,425 (13th in the nation), an increase of 4.9% over 1980, and much better than the 0.8% growth rate of the 1970s. Reasons behind the population lag include a birthrate well below the US average, and a net out-migration of 301,000 people between 1970 and 1983, the largest drop of all New England states.

Massachusetts ranked 13th in population in the United States with an estimated total of 6,398,743 in 2005, an increase of 0.8% since 2000. Between 1990 and 2000, Massachusetts's population grew from 6,016,425 to 6,349,097, an increase of 5.5%. The population is projected to reach 6.7 million by 2015 and 6.9 million by 2025. The population density in 2004 was 818.2 persons per sq mi, the third highest in the nation. In 2004 the median age was 38.1. Persons under 18 years old accounted for 22.8% of the population while 13.3% was age 65 or older.

The state's biggest city is Boston, which ranked 24th among the largest US cities with a population of 569,165 in 2004, up from an estimated 547,725 in 1994. Other large cities (with their 2004 estimated populations) are Worcester, 175,966, and Springfield, 152,091. The Greater Boston area had an estimated metropolitan population of 4,424,649.

7 ETHNIC GROUPS

Early industrialization helped make Massachusetts a mecca for many European migrants, particularly the Irish. As late as 1990 more than half of the population identified with at least one single ancestry group. As of 2000 the largest were the Irish (22.5% of the population), Italian (13.5%), English (11.4%), French (8%), Polish (5.1%), and Portuguese (4.4%). In that year, the foreign born numbered 772,983, or 12.2% of the state's population.

Massachusetts has always had a black population, and has contributed such distinguished figures as poet Phillis Wheatley and NAACP founder W.E.B. DuBois (the first black Ph.D. from Harvard) to US cultural and public life. A sizable class of black professionals has developed, and the 20th century has seen an influx of working-class blacks from southern states. In 2000 there were 343,454 black Americans in Massachusetts, 5.4% of the population. Blacks constituted more than 25% of Boston's population. In 2004, 6.8% of Massachusetts' population was black. The state also had 428,729 Hispanics and Latinos in 2000, predominantly Puerto Rican and Dominican. In 2004, 7.7% of the population was of Hispanic or Latino origin.

Greater Boston has a small, well-organized Chinatown; in the suburbs reside many Chinese professionals and businesspeople, as well as those connected with the region's numerous educational institutions. Statewide, there were 84,392 Chinese in 2000 (up from 47,245 in 1990), 33,962 Vietnamese (up from 13,101 in 1990), 19,696 Cambodians, 17,369 Koreans, and 10,539 Japanese. In 2000, the total Asian population was estimated at 238,124, and the Native American population (including Eskimos and Aleuts) totaled an estimated 15,015. Pacific Islanders numbered 2,489. In 2004, 4.6% of the population was Asian, 0.3% American Indian or Alaskan Native, and 0.1% of Pacific Island origin. That year, 1.3% of the population reported origin of two or more races. Cape Cod has settlements of Portuguese fishermen, as has New Bedford.

8 LANGUAGES

Some general Algonkian loanwords and a few place-names—such as Massachusetts itself, Chicopee, Quebbin, and Naukeag—are the language echoes of the Massachuset, Pennacook, and Mahican Indians so historically important in the founding of Massachusetts Bay Colony and Old Colony, now Plymouth.

On the whole, Massachusetts English is classed as Northern, but early migration up the Connecticut River left that waterway a sometimes sharp, sometimes vague boundary, setting off special variations within the eastern half of the state. Two conspicuous but now receding features long held prestige because of the cultural eminence of Boston: the absence of /r/ after a vowel, as in *fear* and *port*, and the use of a vowel halfway between the short /a/ of *cat* and /ah/ in *half* and *past* as well as in *car* and *park*. Eastern Massachusetts speakers are likely to have /ah/ in *orange* and to pronounce *on* and *fog* with the same vowel as in *form*. In the east, a sycamore is a *buttonwood*, a tied and filled quilt is a *comforter*, a *creek* is a saltwater inlet, and pancakes may be called *fritters*.

Around Boston are heard the intrusive /r/ as in "the lawr of the land," the /oo/ vowel in *butcher, tonic* for soft drink, *submarine* for a large sandwich, and *milkshake* for a concoction lacking ice cream. West of the Connecticut River are heard the /aw/ sound in *orange*, / ah/ in *on* and *fog*, and the short /a/ of *cat* in *half* and *bass; buttonball* is a sycamore, and *comfortable* is a tied quilt.

In 2000, 81.3% of the population five years of age or older (down from 84.8% in 1990) spoke only English at home.

The following table gives selected statistics from the 2000 Census for language spoken at home by persons five years old and over.

LANGUAGE	NUMBER	PERCENT
Population 5 years and over	**5,954,249**	**100.0**
Speak only English	4,838,679	81.3
Speak a language other than English	1,115,570	18.7
Speak a language other than English	**1,115,570**	**18.7**
Spanish or Spanish Creole	370,011	6.2
Portuguese or Portuguese Creole	159,809	2.7
French (incl. Patois, Cajun)	84,484	1.4
Chinese	71,412	1.2
Italian	59,811	1.0
French Creole	43,519	0.7
Russian	32,580	0.5
Vietnamese	30,400	0.5
Greek	28,819	0.5
Polish	27,631	0.5
Mon-Khmer, Cambodian	21,549	0.4
German	20,029	0.3
Arabic	18,742	0.3

9RELIGIONS

While Protestant sects have contributed greatly to the state's history and development, more than half the state's population is Roman Catholic, a fact that has had a profound effect on Massachusetts politics and policies.

Both the Pilgrims, who landed on Plymouth Rock in 1620, and the Puritans, who formed the Massachusetts Bay Company in 1629, came to the land to escape harassment by the Church of England. These early communities were based on strict religious principles and forbade the practice of differing religions. Religious tolerance was included in the Charter of 1692, to protect the Baptists, Anglicans, and Catholics who had by then arrived in the colony.

The major influx of Roman Catholics came in the 1840s with the arrival of the Irish in Boston. By the 1850s, they had migrated to other towns and cities and formed the backbone of the state's industrial workforce. Later migration by Italian Catholics, German Catholics, and Eastern European Jews turned the state, by 1900, into a melting pot of religions and nationalities, although many of these minorities did not win substantial acceptance from the Protestant elite until the World War II era.

As of 2004, there were 3,033,367 Roman Catholics in Massachusetts, representing nearly half of the total population; the archdiocese of Boston held 2,077,487 members that year. The largest Protestant denominations in 2000 were: the Episcopal Church, 98,963; the United Methodist Church, 64,028; and the American Baptists (USA), 52,716. In 2005, the United Church of Christ reported a statewide membership of 89,264. The second largest religious affiliation is Judaism, with about 275,000 adherents in 2000. The Muslim population the same year was about 41,497 people. Though membership numbers were not available, reports noted that there were about 57 Buddhist congregations and 20 Hindu congregations throughout the state. About 35% of the population did not specify a religious affiliation.

Although small, the Church of Christ, Scientist, is significant to Massachusetts's history. Its first house of worship was founded in 1879 in Boston by Mary Baker Eddy, who four years earlier had published the Christian Science textbook *Science and Health with Key to the Scriptures*. In Boston, the church continues to publish an influential newspaper, the *Christian Science Monitor*. Membership numbers are not published, but the church claims about 2,000 branch churches and societies in over 80 countries. Administrative and special group offices for the Unitarian Universalist Association are also located in Boston.

10TRANSPORTATION

The first rail line in the United States, a 3-mi (5-km) stretch from the Neponset River to the granite quarries in Quincy, was built in 1826. The first steam railroad in New England, connecting Boston and Lowell, was completed seven years later. By the late 1830s, tracks were laid from Boston to Worcester and to Providence, Rhode Island, and during the next two decades, additional railroad lines opened up new cities for industrial expansion.

As of 2003, 10 railroads transported freight through Massachusetts: CSX Transportation, the state's sole Class I railroad; the Providence & Worcester and Guilford Rail, the state's regional railroads; and seven other local and switching and terminal railroads.

In that same year, the state had 1,255 rail mi (2,020 km) of railroad. As of 2006, Boston was the northern terminus of Amtrak's Northeast Corridor route, linking New England with Washington, DC, via New York City and Philadelphia. East-west service from Boston to Chicago was also provided by Amtrak.

Commuter service is coordinated by the Massachusetts Bay Transportation Authority (MBTA), formed in 1964 to consolidate bus, commuter rail, high-speed trolley, and subway services to the 79 cities and towns in the Greater Boston area. The Boston subway, which began operation in 1897, is the oldest subway system in the United States. Boston also is one of the few cities in the United States with an operating trolley system. About 40% of all Bostonians commute to work by public transportation, the second-highest percentage in the nation, following New York City.

In 2004, there were 35,783 mi (57,610 km) of public roadways crisscrossing the state. The major highways, which extend from and through Boston like the spokes of a wheel, include I-95, which runs north–south; the Massachusetts Turnpike (I-90), which runs west to the New York State border; I-93, which leads north to New Hampshire; State Highway 3 to Cape Cod; and State Highway 24 to Fall River. The other major road in the state is I-91, which runs north–south through the Connecticut River Valley. More than $3 billion was spent by all units of government for highways in 1997. In 2004, some 5.532 million motor vehicles registered in the state, of which about 3.486 were automobiles, approximately 1.898 million were trucks of all types, and around 11,000 were buses. There were also around 137,000 motorcycles registered with the state in that same year. There were 4,645,857 licensed driver's licenses in the state for 2004.

Because it is the major American city closest to Europe, Boston is an important shipping center for both domestic and foreign cargo. In 2004, a total of 25.796 million tons of cargo passed through the Port of Boston. All port activity is under the jurisdiction of the Massachusetts Port Authority, which also operates Logan International Airport and Hanscom Field in Bedford. Fall River was another important port with a cargo total of 3.161 million tons that same year. In 2004, Massachusetts had 90 mi (144 km) of navigable inland waterways. In 2003, waterborne shipments totaled 30.655 million tons.

In 2005, Massachusetts had a total of 232 public and private-use aviation-related facilities. This included 76 airports, 137 heliports, 1 STOLport (Short Take-Off and Landing), and 18 seaplane bases. Logan International, near Boston, is the busiest airport in the state. In 2004, the airport had 12,758,020 enplanements, making it the 18th-busiest airport in the United States.

11HISTORY

Some 15,000 years ago, when the last of the glaciers receded form the land we call Massachusetts, what remained was a rocky surface scoured of most of its topsoil. In time, however, forests grew to support a rich variety of wildlife. When the first Indians arrived from the south, game abounded and fish were plentiful in streams and along the coast. These first Indians were hunter-gatherers; their successors not only foraged for food but also cleared fields for planting corn (maize) and squash. Periodically they burned away the woodland underbrush, a technique of forest management that stimulated the vegetation that supported game. When English settlers arrived, they encountered five main Algonkian tribes: the Nauset, a fishing people on Cape Cod; the Wampanoag in the southeast; the Massachusetts in the northeast; the Nipmuc in the central hills; and the Pocumtuc in the west.

The earliest European explorers—including the Norsemen, who may have reached Cape Cod—made no apparent impact on these Algonkian groups, but in the wake of John and Sebastian Cabot's voyages (1497 and following), fishermen from England, France, Portugal, and Spain began fishing off the Massachusetts coast. By the mid-16th century, they were regularly going ashore to process and pack their catch. Within 50 years, fur trading with the Indians was established.

Permanent English settlement, which would ultimately destroy the Algonkian peoples, began in 1620 when a small band of Puritans left their haven at Leiden in the Netherlands to start a colony in the northern part of Virginia lands, near the Hudson River. Their ship, the Mayflower, was blown off course by an Atlantic storm, and they landed on Cape Cod before settling in an abandoned Wampanoag village they called Plymouth. Ten years later, a much larger Puritan group settled the Massachusetts Bay Colony, some miles to the north in Salem. Between 1630 and 1640, about 20,000 English people, chiefly Puritans, settled in Massachusetts with offshoots moving to Connecticut and Rhode Island.

The leaders of the Massachusetts settlement, most notably John Winthrop, a country gentleman with some legal training, intended to make their colony an exemplary Christian society. Though church and state were legally separate, they were mutually reinforcing agencies; thus, when Roger Williams and Anne Hutchinson were separately found guilty of heresy in the 1630s, they were banished by the state. All male church members had a voice in both church and state leadership, though both institutions were led by college-educated men. In order to provide for future leaders, Harvard College (now Harvard University) was founded in 1636.

After the beginning of the English revolution in 1640, migration to Massachusetts declined abruptly. Farming soon overtook fishing and fur trading in economic importance; after the trade in beaver skins was exhausted, the remaining Indian tribes were decimated in King Philip's War (1675–76). Shipbuilding and Atlantic commerce also brought prosperity to the Massachusetts Bay Colony, which was granted a new charter by King William and Queen Mary in 1692, merging Massachusetts and the colony of Plymouth. In that year, 19 people were executed for witchcraft on the gallows at Salem before Massachusetts authorities put a stop to the proceedings.

During the 18th century, settlement spread across the entire colony. Boston, the capital, had attained a population of 15,000 by 1730; it was an urbane community of brick as well as wooden buildings, with nearly a dozen church spires distinguishing its skyline by the 1750s. Religious revivals, also occurring elsewhere in America, swept Massachusetts in the 1730s and 1740s, rekindling piety and dividing the inhabitants into competing camps. Although the conflicts had ebbed by the 1750s, Massachusetts did not achieve unity again until the resistance to British imperial actions during the next two decades.

Up to this time, imperial government had rested lightly on Massachusetts, providing more advantages than drawbacks for commerce. The colony had actively supported British expeditions against French Canada, and supply contracts during the French and Indian War had enriched the economy. But the postwar recession after 1763 was accompanied by a new imperial policy that put pressure on Massachusetts as well as other colonies. None of the crown's three objectives—tight regulation of trade, the raising of revenue, and elimination of key areas of colonial political autonomy—were popular among the merchants, tradespeople, and farmers of Massachusetts. From 1765, when Bostonians violently protested the Stamp Act, Massachusetts was in the vanguard of the resistance.

At first, opposition was largely confined to Boston and surrounding towns, although the legislature, representing the entire colony, was active in opposing British measures. By December 1773, when East India Company tea was dumped into Boston harbor to prevent its taxation, most of the colony was committed to resistance. Newspaper polemics composed by Samuel Adams and his cousin John, among others, combined with the persuasive activities of the Boston Committee of Correspondence, helped convince a majority of Massachusetts residents that the slogan "no taxation without representation" stood for the preservation of their communities. When Parliament retaliated for the Tea Party by closing the port of Boston in 1774, rescinding the colony's 1692 charter, and remaking the government to put it under London's control, Massachusetts was ready to rebel. Military preparations began immediately on both sides. After almost a year of confrontation, battle began at Lexington and Concord on 19 April 1775. By this time, Massachusetts had the backing of the Continental Congress.

For Massachusetts, the battlefield experience of the Revolution was largely confined to 1775, the climaxes being the Battle of Bunker Hill and the British evacuation of Boston the following year. Thereafter, Massachusetts soldiers were active throughout the colonies, but the theater of action shifted southward. A new republican constitution, adopted in 1780, was the first state constitution to be submitted to the electorate for ratification.

Social and economic conditions in post-Revolutionary Massachusetts were much like those of the colonial era. Although the Shays Rebellion, an uprising of central and western farmers led by Daniel Shays in 1786–87, challenged the political hegemony of commercially oriented eastern leaders, the latter succeeded in maintaining their hold on the state. Massachusetts, which entered the Union on 6 February 1788, was the center of Federalism from 1790 until the mid-1820s. Although Jeffersonian Republicans and Jacksonian Democrats achieved substantial followings, Federalist policies, embodied in the Whigs in the 1830s and the Republicans from the late 1850s, were dominant. This political continuity was based on the importance of national commercial and industrial development to the state.

Even before 1800, it was clear that Massachusetts could not sustain growth in agriculture. Its soil had never been excellent, and the best lands were tired, having been worked for generations with little regard for conservation. Much of the state's population departed for New York, Ohio, and beyond during the first decades of the 19th century. Those who stayed maintained productive agriculture, concentrating more and more on fruits and dairying, but they also developed commerce and industry. At Waltham, Lowell, and Lawrence the first large-scale factories in the United States were erected, and smaller textile mills throughout the state helped to make Massachusetts a leader in the cloth industry. At Springfield and Watertown, US armories led the way in metalworking, while shoes and leather goods brought prosperity to Lynn, and whale products and shipbuilding to New Bedford. By the 1850s, steam engines and clipper ships were both Bay State products.

The industrial development of Massachusetts was accompanied by a literary and intellectual flowering that was partly in reaction to the materialism and worldliness associated with urban and industrial growth. Concord, the home of Ralph Waldo Emerson, Henry David Thoreau, and a cluster of others, became the center of the transcendentalist movement in philosophy. Social reform also represented an assertion of moral values, whether in the field of education, health care, temperance, or penology. Abolitionism, the greatest of the moral reform efforts, found some of its chief leaders in Massachusetts, among them William Lloyd Garrison and Wendell Phillips, as well as a host of supporters.

In the years following the Civil War, Massachusetts emerged as an urban industrial state. Its population, fed by immigrants from England, Scotland, Germany, and especially Ireland, grew rapidly in the middle decades of the century. Later, between 1880 and 1920, another wave of immigrants came from French Canada, Italy, Russia, Poland, Scandinavia, Portugal, Greece, and Syria. Still later, between 1950 and 1970, black southerners and Puerto Ricans settled in the cities.

From the election of Lincoln in 1860 through the 1920s, Massachusetts was led by Protestant Yankee Republicans; most Democrats were Catholics. Class, ethnic, and religious tensions were endemic, occasionally erupting into open conflict. Three such episodes gained national attention. In 1912, immigrant textile workers in Lawrence were pitted against Yankee capitalists. A highly publicized strike of 1919 had the largely Irish-American police force rebelling against Yankees in city and state government, and brought Governor Calvin Coolidge—who suppressed the strike and refused to reinstate the striking policemen—to national prominence. In 1921, Nicola Sacco and Bartolomeo Vanzetti, Italian immigrant anarchists, were convicted for a payroll robbery and murder, though there was bitter controversy regarding the quality of the evidence against them. Before they were executed in 1927, their case and the issues it raised polarized political opinion throughout the United States. Subsequently, electoral competition between Democrats and Republicans emerged as a less divisive outlet for class and ethnic tensions. Since 1959, the Democrats have enjoyed ascendance statewide, and Republicans have won only when their candidates stood close to the Democrats on the issues. Party loyalties as such have waned, however.

The Massachusetts economy, relatively stagnant between 1920 and 1950, revived in the second half of the 20th century through a combination of an educated and skilled workforce, capital resources, and political clout. As the old industries and the mill cities declined, new high-technology manufacturing developed in Boston's suburban perimeter, centering on start-up manufacturing firms along Route 128 outside Boston. Electronics, computers, and defense-oriented industries led the way, stimulating a general prosperity in which service activities such as banking, insurance, health care, and higher education were especially prominent. As a result, white-collar employment and middle-class suburbs flourished, though run-down mill towns and Yankee dairy farms and orchards still dotted the landscape.

In this respect, as in its politics, Massachusetts resembled many other areas of the Northeast. It was a multiracial state in which the general welfare was defined by shifting coalitions of ethnic groups and special interests. From a national perspective, Massachusetts voters appeared liberal; the Bay State was the only one to choose Democrat George McGovern over President Richard M. Nixon in 1972, and, since the 1970s, has been a perennially secure base for Senator Edward M. Kennedy. Yet Boston was also the site of some of the most extreme anti-integration tension during the same era; Massachusetts was simultaneously a center of efforts in favor of the Equal Rights Amendment and against abortion.

Massachusetts's defiance of political categories continued into the 1990s. In 1990, blaming the current governor, Democrat Michael Dukakis, for the economy's decline, Massachusetts voters elected a Republican, William Weld, as governor. Yet Weld in fact espoused a blend of liberal and conservative positions. A fiscal conservative who called for cutting taxes and reducing programs such as Medicaid and state employee pension plans, Weld took a liberal stance on social issues, supporting gay rights, abortion rights, and strict protection of the environment. In August 1997, Weld resigned as governor to pursue an appointment as ambassador to Mexico.

Beginning in 1989, the Massachusetts economy declined dramatically, losing 14% of its total jobs in three years. Like other parts of New England, Massachusetts was hit hard by the recession of the early 1990s, and the state's economic woes were aggravated by the collapse in the late 1980s of speculative real estate ventures. The saturation of the real estate market forced retrenchments not only of that industry but of construction as well. By 1992, a number of indications suggested that a recovery had begun to take hold, aided in part by the privatization of highway maintenance, prison health care, and some other state-run operations.

By the mid-1990s, the Massachusetts economy was in the midst of a vigorous upturn, credited largely to the strength of its leading local industries, including software and mutual funds, and the health of the US economy as a whole. In 1996 the state's unemployment level fell to 4%, the lowest it had been since 1989. By 1999 the unemployment rate had dropped further, to 3.2%. Its 1998 per capita income of $32,902 was the third highest in the nation and had grown at the second-fastest rate (second only to that of Wyoming). Massachusetts' per capital personal income was $41,801 in 2004, second highest in the nation, behind Connecticut.

Despite that record, the thriving economy came to an abrupt halt in 2001, as the United States entered a recession marked by a large increase in job losses. In 2003, Massachusetts had a $3 billion budget deficit. Issues facing the legislature that year included Medicaid spending and a prescription drug program for senior citizens. The state Senate had approved a measure calling for a ban on smoking in the workplace, which was being considered by the House of Representatives. (This ban on smoking in the workplace, including in bars and restaurants—private clubs and cigar bars excepted—came into effect in July 2004.) In addition, the state was considering the legality of same-sex marriages. Republican governor Mitt Romney, a business executive and fiscal conservative elected in 2002, took a liberal stand on some social issues, such as supporting abortion choice and gay rights, but he also advocated reinstatement of the death penalty. Romney recommended a 0.3%

reduction in the personal income tax for his 2006 budget, from 5.3% to 5.0%.

Balancing development with environmental conservation was among the issues the state grappled with at the dawn of the 21st century. In 2000 the legislature approved a statewide initiative to preserve open space through local land-acquisition funds. The funds were to come from a $20 surcharge on all transactions at the Registry of Deeds and Land Court; communities would also be given the option to allow voters to approve a property tax increase of up to 3% to support the measure.

The state was the setting of a national controversy in April 2000: in a report condemning lax oversight of the largest public works project in US history, a federal task force charged that managers of Boston's multibillion-dollar highway project intentionally concealed cost overruns. Known as "Big Dig," the massive project includes building a 10-lane expressway under Boston and extending the Massachusetts Turnpike beneath Boston Harbor to Logan International Airport. State officials had revealed in February that the project, which began in 1991, was $1.4 billion over its $10.8 billion budget, making it more expensive than the Boston Harbor cleanup. The project to restore the harbor, considered the nation's filthiest in 1990, was drawing to a successful close in 2000, in spite of cost overruns. Portions of the highway project, including the extension of I-90 through the Ted Williams Tunnel to Logan Airport were completed in January 2003. During 2004, the old elevated Central Artery (formerly I-93) came down, creating 27 acres for a new tree-lined boulevard and cross streets, sidewalks, parks, and other refurbished open space. As of October 2005, 97% of the construction on the Big Dig project was complete.

Massachusetts was at the center of the sexual abuse scandals plaguing the Catholic Church in the early 2000s. Cardinal Bernard F. Law stepped down as Archbishop of Boston in December 2002 after widespread criticism of his handling of charges that priests sexually abused children, and of allegations of cover-ups. The Vatican replaced Law with Sean Patrick O'Malley as Archbishop of Boston in 2003.

In November 2003, the Massachusetts Supreme Court became the first state supreme court in the nation to rule that same-sex marriages were legal. The court ruled that denying individuals from the "protections, benefits, and obligations of civil marriage solely because that person would marry a person of the same sex violates the Massachusetts constitution." Massachusetts became the first state to legally allow gay marriages to take place on 17 May 2004. In September 2005, the Massachusetts state legislature rejected a proposed state constitutional amendment that would have banned gay marriage but allowed civil unions.

12 STATE GOVERNMENT

The first state constitution, drawn up soon after the signing of the Declaration of Independence, was rejected by the electorate. A revised draft was not approved by the state voters until 15 June 1780, following two constitutional conventions. This constitution, as amended (120 times by January 2005), governs Massachusetts and is, according to the state, the oldest written constitution in the world still in effect.

The legislature of Massachusetts, known as the General Court, is composed of a 40-member Senate and 160-member House of Representatives, all of whom are elected every two years in even-numbered years. Annual legislative sessions begin the first Wednesday in January and must conclude by November 15 one year and by July 31 the following year. Additionally, legislators may petition to convene special sessions. Members of the Senate must have resided in Massachusetts for at least five years and must be residents of their districts; representatives must have lived in their districts for at least one year prior to election. The minimum age for all legislators is 18, and they must be qualified voters. The legislative salary was $53,379.93 in 2004.

The governor and lieutenant governor are elected jointly every four years. The governor appoints all state and local judges, as well as the heads of the executive offices. Both the governor and lieutenant governor must have resided in the state for at least seven years; there is no minimum age specified for the offices. As of December 2004, the governor's salary was $135,000 (Gov. Mitt Romney waives his salary). Other elected officials include the attorney general, secretary of the commonwealth, treasurer and receiver-general, and auditor of the commonwealth. All serve four-year terms.

Any Massachusetts citizen may file a bill through a state legislator, or a bill may be filed directly by a legislator or by the governor. To win passage, a bill must gain a majority vote of both houses of the legislature. After a bill is passed, the governor has 10 days in which to sign it, return it for reconsideration (usually with amendments), veto it, or hold onto it until after the legislature adjourns ("pocket veto"). A veto may be overridden by a two-thirds vote of the members present in both houses.

An amendment to the constitution may be introduced by any house or Senate member (legislative amendment); if it is approved by two successive sessions of the legislature, the amendment is then submitted to the voters at the next general election. An amendment may also be introduced by a petition signed by 3% of the total votes cast for governor in the last state election, which must be at least 25,000 qualified voters, and that is presented in a joint session of the General Court. No more than one-fourth of the signatures may come from any one county. The majority vote on the amendment must be 30% of the total ballots cast at the election.

To vote in a Massachusetts district, a person must be a US citizen, at least 18 years old, and a state resident. Convicted felons and those declared mentally incompetent by the court may not vote.

13 POLITICAL PARTIES

The Federalist Party, represented nationally by John Adams, dominated Massachusetts in the late 18th and early 19th centuries. The state turned to the Whig Party in the second quarter of the 19th century. Predominantly Yankee in character, the Whigs supported business growth, promoted protective tariffs, and favored such enterprises as railroads and factories. The new Republican Party, to which most Massachusetts Whigs gravitated when their party split in the 1850s, was a prime mover of abolitionism and played an important role in the election of Abraham Lincoln as president in 1860. Republicans held most of the major state elective offices, as well as most US congressional seats, until the early 1900s.

The Democratic Party's rise starting in the 1870s was tied directly to massive Irish immigration. Other immigrant groups also gravitated toward the Democrats, and in 1876, the state's first Democratic congressman was elected. In 1928, the state voted for Democratic presidential candidate Alfred E. Smith, a Roman Catholic, the first time the Democrats won a majority in a Massachusetts presidential election. Democrats have subsequently, for the most part, dominated state politics. In 1960, John F. Kennedy, who had been a popular US senator from Massachusetts, became the first Roman Catholic president in US history. Since then the state has voted for all Democratic presidential candidates except Republican Ronald Reagan in 1980 and 1984; in 1972, it was the only state carried by Democrat George McGovern. Massachusetts chose its native son, Democratic governor Michael Dukakis, for president in 1988 and voted again for a Democrat in the next three elections, giving Al Gore 60% of the vote, Republican George W. Bush 33%, and Green Party candidate Ralph Nader 6% in 2000. In 2004, state voters gave native son, Democrat John Kerry, 53.4% of the vote to incumbent George W. Bush's 44.6%. In 2004 there were 3,973,000 registered voters. In 1998, 37% of registered voters were Democratic, 13% Republican, and 50% unaffiliated or members of other parties. The state had 12 electoral votes in the 2004 presidential election.

From 1990 to 1997, the governorship was held by a Republican, William Weld. Weld resigned in 1997 to pursue an appointment as ambassador to Mexico, at which time he was succeeded by lieutenant governor and fellow Republican Argeo Paul Cellucci. Cellucci was elected in his own right in November 1998. In 2002, Republican Mitt Romney was elected governor. Following the 2004 election, the US Senate seats for Massachusetts were held by Democrats Edward Kennedy (last elected in 2000) and John Kerry (last elected in 2002). In 2003, Kerry launched an unsuccessful campaign for the presidency. The 10-member US House delegation following the 2004 elections again consisted entirely of Democrats. In December 2005 the Massachusetts state Senate had 34 Democrats and 6 Republicans, while the state House of Representatives, known as the General Court, had 139 Democrats, 20 Republicans, with 1 Independent.

14 LOCAL GOVERNMENT

As of 2005, Massachusetts had 14 counties, 45 municipal governments, 349 school districts, and 403 special districts. In 2002 there were also 306 townships.

In most counties, which mostly serve judicial purposes, executive authority is vested in commissioners elected to four-year terms. Other county officials include the register of probate and family court, sheriff, clerk of courts, county treasurer, and register of deeds.

All Massachusetts cities are governed by mayors and city councils. Towns are governed by selectmen, who are usually elected to either one- or two-year terms. Town meetings—a carryover from the colonial period, when every taxpayer had an equal voice in town government—still take place. By state law, to be designated as a city, a place must have at least 12,000 residents. Towns with more than 6,000 inhabitants may hold representative town meetings limited to elected officials.

In 2005, local government accounted for about 233,729 full-time (or equivalent) employment positions.

15 STATE SERVICES

To address the continuing threat of terrorism and to work with the federal Department of Homeland Security, homeland security in Massachusetts operates under the authority of state statute; activities are overseen by the public safety director.

State services are provided through the 14 executive offices and major departments that constitute the governor's cabinet. The heads of these departments are appointed by the governor. The Ethics in Massachusetts State Government organization distributes information on state government scandals.

Educational services are administered by the Department of Education. Included under its jurisdiction are the State Board of Education and Board of Higher Education, the Massachusetts community college and state college systems, the University of

Massachusetts Presidential Vote by Political Party, 1948–2004

YEAR	ELECTORAL VOTE	MASSACHUSETTS WINNER	DEMOCRAT	REPUBLICAN	SOCIALIST LABOR	PROGRESSIVE
1948	16	*Truman (D)	1,151,788	909,370	5,535	38,157
1952	16	*Eisenhower (R)	1,083,525	1,292,325	1,957	4,636
1956	16	*Eisenhower (R)	948,190	1,393,197	5,573	—
1960	16	*Kennedy (D)	1,487,174	976,750	3,892	—
1964	14	*Johnson (D)	1,786,422	549,727	4,755	—
						AMERICAN IND.
1968	14	Humphrey (D)	1,469,218	766,844	6,180	87,088
					SOC. WORKERS	AMERICAN
1972	14	McGovern (D)	1,332,540	1,112,078	10,600	2,877
1976	14	*Carter (D)	1,429,475	1,030,276	8,138	7,555
					LIBERTARIAN	
1980	14	*Reagan (R)	1,048,562	1,054,213	21,311	—
1984	13	*Reagan (R)	1,239,600	1,310,936	—	—
						NEW ALLIANCE
1988	13	Dukakis (D)	1,401,415	1,194,635	24,251	9,561
						IND. (Perot)
1992	12	*Clinton (D)	1,318,639	805,039	9,021	630,731
1996	12	*Clinton (D)	1,571,763	718,107	20,426	227,217
						GREEN
2000	12	Gore (D)	1,616,487	878,502	16,366	173,564
2004	12	Kerry (D)	1,803,800	1,071,109	15,022	10,623

*Won US presidential election.

Massachusetts, the Council of the Arts and Humanities, and the State Library.

The Executive Office of Transportation supervises the Department of Public Works and has responsibility for the planning and development of transportation systems within the state, including the Massachusetts Port Authority, the Massachusetts Highway Department, the Massachusetts Turnpike Authority, the Massachusetts Bay Transportation Authority, the Registry of Motor Vehicles, and the Massachusetts Aeronautics Commission.

All public health, mental health, youth, and veterans' programs are administered by the Executive Office of Health and Human Services. Also under its jurisdiction is the Department of Public Health. The Executive Office of Public Safety includes the Department of Correction, Emergency Management Agency, National Guard, and State Police.

The Executive Office of Consumer Affairs and Business Regulation regulates state standards and registers professional workers. The departments of telecommunications and energy are also part of this office, as are the divisions regulating banks and insurance. Housing services are provided through the Department of Housing and Community Development.

The Executive Office of Environmental Affairs protects the state's marine and wildlife, and monitors the quality of its air, water, and food. Labor and industrial relations are monitored through the Department of Labor, which administers the minimum wage law, occupational safety laws, and child labor laws, among others. The Executive Office of Economic Development helps to improve the economic climate in the state and promotes exports and tourism.

16 JUDICIAL SYSTEM

All statewide judicial offices are filled by the governor, with the advice and consent of the executive council.

The Supreme Judicial Court, composed of a chief justice and six other justices, is the highest court in the state. It has appellate jurisdiction in matters of law and also advises the governor and legislature on legal questions. The superior courts, actually the highest level of trial court, have a chief justice and 79 other justices; these courts hear law, equity, civil, and criminal cases, and make the final determination in matters of fact. The appeals court, consisting of a chief justice and 13 other justices, hears appeals of decisions by district and municipal courts. There are also district and municipal courts and trial court judges. Other court systems in the state include the land court, probate and family court, housing court (with divisions in Boston and Hampden counties), and juvenile court (with divisions in Boston, Springfield, Worcester, and Bristol counties).

As of 31 December 2004, a total of 10,144 prisoners were held in Massachusetts' state and federal prisons, a decrease from 10,232 of 0.9% from the previous year. As of year-end 2004, a total of 741 inmates were female, up from 708 or 4.7% from the year before. Among sentenced prisoners (one year or more), Massachusetts had an incarceration rate of 232 per 100,000 population in 2004.

According to the Federal Bureau of Investigation, Massachusetts in 2004, had a violent crime rate (murder/nonnegligent manslaughter; forcible rape; robbery; aggravated assault) of 458.8 reported incidents per 100,000 population, or a total of 29,437 reported incidents. Crimes against property (burglary; larceny/theft; and motor vehicle theft) in that same year totaled 157,825

reported incidents or 2,459.7 reported incidents per 100,000 people. Massachusetts has no death penalty.

Under Massachusetts' gun control laws, all guns must be registered, and there is a mandatory one-year jail sentence for possession without a permit.

In 2003, Massachusetts spent $299,944,420 on homeland security, an average of $48 per state resident.

17 ARMED FORCES

The military installations located in Massachusetts in 2004 had 4,382 active-duty military personnel, 7,315 National Guard and Reserve, and 3,049 civilian personnel. The largest installation in the state is the Laurence G. Hanscom Air Force Base in Bedford. Other installations include the Army reserve and development center at Natick, Westover Air Reserve Base, one of 11 Air Force Reserve host bases, home to the 439th Airlift Wing, and, the Navy's South Weymouth Naval Air Station closed in 1997 and redeveloped for multiple uses including parks and recreation. Defense contracts awarded in 2004 totaled $6.96 billion, eighth-highest in the United States for that year. In addition, Massachusetts received another $1.1 billion in defense payroll spending, including retired military pay.

There were 490,882 military veterans living in the state in 2003, of which 90,933 served in World War II; 65,672 during the Korean conflict; 142,892 during the Vietnam era; and 51,292 during the Persian Gulf War. In 2004, expenditures on veterans exceeded $1.3 billion.

As of 31 October 2004, the Massachusetts State Police employed 2,199 full-time sworn officers.

18 MIGRATION

Massachusetts was founded by the migration of English religious groups to its shores, and for over a century their descendants dominated all activity in the state. The first non-English to enter Massachusetts in significant numbers were the Irish, who migrated in vast numbers during the 1840s and 1850s. By 1860, one-third of Boston's population was Irish, while nearly one-fourth of Middlesex and Norfolk counties and one-fifth of the inhabitants of Berkshire, Bristol, Essex, and Hampden counties were Irish-born. Other ethnic groups—such as the Scottish, Welsh, Germans, and Poles—were also entering the state at this time, but their numbers were small by comparison. During the late 1880s and 1890s, another wave of immigrants—from Portugal, Spain, Italy, Russia, and Greece—arrived. Irish and Italians continued to enter the state during the 20th century.

A slow but steady migration from Massachusetts farm communities began during the mid-1700s and continued well into the 1800s. The first wave of farmers resettled in northern Connecticut, Vermont, New Hampshire, and Maine. Later farmers moved to New York's Mohawk Valley, Ohio, and points farther west. Out-migration has continued into recent times: from 1970 to 1990, Massachusetts lost nearly 400,000 residents in net migration to other states but experienced an overall net increase from migration of 59,000 due to migration from abroad. Between 1990 and 1998, the state had a net loss of 237,000 in domestic migration and a net gain of 135,000 in international migration. In 1996, Massachusetts's foreign-born population numbered 591,000, or nearly 10% of the state's total population. In 1998, 15,869 foreign immigrants arrived in Massachusetts, the 8th-highest total of any state for that year. Between 1990 and 1998, the state's overall population increased 2.2%. In the period 2000–05, net international migration was 162,674 and net internal migration was -236,415, for a net loss of 73,741 people.

The only significant migration from other areas of the United States to Massachusetts has been the influx of southern blacks since World War II. According to census estimates, Massachusetts gained 84,000 blacks between 1940 and 1975; between 1990 and 1998, the black population grew from 300,000 to 395,000 persons, mostly in the Boston area.

19 INTERGOVERNMENTAL COOPERATION

Massachusetts participates in numerous regional agreements, including the New England Interstate Corrections, Police, Board of Higher Education, Radiological Health Protection, and Interstate Water Pollution Control compacts. The state is also a party to the Atlantic States Marine Fisheries Commission, the Northeastern Forest Fire Protection Compact, the Connecticut River Valley Flood Control Compact, the Bay State-Ocean State Compact with Rhode Island, the Merrimack River Basin Flood Control Compact, the Thames River Flood Control Compact, and the Connecticut River Atlantic Salmon Compact.

Border agreements include the Connecticut-Massachusetts Boundary Compact (ratified by Massachusetts in 1908), the Massachusetts-New York Compact of 1853, and the Massachusetts-Rhode Island Compact of 1859. During fiscal year 2001, the state received over $9.7 billion in federal grants. Following a national trend, that amount was decreased significantly to $8.589 billion in fiscal year 2005, an estimated $8.892 billion in fiscal year 2006, and an estimated $8.217 billion in fiscal year 2007.

20 ECONOMY

From its beginnings as a farming and seafaring colony, Massachusetts became one of the most industrialized states in the country in the late 19th century and, more recently, a leader in the manufacture of high-technology products.

During the colonial and early national periods, the towns of Salem, Gloucester, Marblehead, and Boston, among others, gave the state strong fishing and shipbuilding industries. Boston was also an important commercial port and a leading center of foreign commerce. Agriculture was important, but productivity of the rocky soil was limited, and by the mid-1800s, farming could not sustain the expanding population. The opening of the Erie Canal, and subsequent competition with cheaper produce grown in the West, hastened agriculture's decline in the Bay State.

Massachusetts's rise as a center of manufacturing began in the early 1800s, when cottage industries developed in small farming communities. Large factories were then built in towns with water power. The country's first "company town," Lowell, was built in the early 1820s to accommodate the state's growing textile industry. Throughout the rest of the 19th century, the state supplied the nation with most of its shoes and woven goods.

Underbid by cheap labor in the south and in other countries, the shoe and textile industries died a slow and painful death. Manufacturing remained central to Massachusetts's economy, however. Fueled in part by a dramatic increase in the Pentagon's budget during the Reagan administration which focused on high-tech-nology weaponry, as well as by significant advances in information technology, high-tech companies sprung up around the periphery of Boston in the 1970s and early 1980s. Wholesale and retail trade, transportation and public utilities also prospered. In the late 1980s, the boom ended. The minicomputer industry failed to innovate at the same pace as its competitors elsewhere at the same time that the market became increasingly crowded, and defense contractors suffered from cuts in military spending. Between 1988 and 1991, jobs in both high-tech and non–high tech manufacturing declined by 17%. The early 1980s also saw the rise of speculative real estate ventures which collapsed at the end of the decade when the market became saturated. Employment in construction dropped 44% between 1988 and 1991, and real estate jobs declined 23.8%. Wholesale and retail trade lost 100,000 jobs. Hurt by unsound loans, banks were forced to retrench. Unemployment rose to 9% in 1991.

The economy recovered in the 1990s, as evidenced by several banks' announcement of new lending programs as well as a reduction in the unemployment rate to 4% by 1997. Annual growth rates soared to 7.8% in 1998, 6.8% in 1999 and 9.8% in 2000 as Massachusetts benefited from information technology (IT) and stock market booms of the late 1990s. However, in the collapse of the dot.com bubble in the national recession of 2001, Massachusetts was the hardest hit among the New England economies, as growth abruptly plummeted to 1.7% in 2001. Continued weakness in national business investment and in equity markets continued to impede economic growth in Massachusetts in 2002.

Massachusetts's gross state product (GSP) in 2004 totaled $317.798 billion, of which real estate accounted for the largest portion at $43.439 billion or 13.6% of GSP, followed by manufacturing (durable and nondurable goods) at $34.912 billion (10.9% of GSP), and healthcare and social assistance at $26.353 billion (8.2% of GSP). In that same year, there were an estimated 599,389 small businesses in Massachusetts. Of the 178,752 businesses that had employees, a total of 175,217 or 98% were small companies. An estimated 18,822 new businesses were established in the state in 2004, down 0.9% from the year before. Business terminations that same year came to 20,270, down 7.3% from 2003. There were 315 business bankruptcies in 2004, down 20.5% from the previous year. In 2005, the state's personal bankruptcy (Chapter 7 and Chapter 13) filing rate was 278 filings per 100,000 people, ranking Massachusetts as the 50th highest in the nation.

21 INCOME

In 2005 Massachusetts had a gross state product (GSP) of $329 billion which accounted for 2.6% of the nation's gross domestic product and placed the state at number 13 in highest GSP among the 50 states and the District of Columbia.

According to the Bureau of Economic Analysis, in 2004 Massachusetts had a per capita personal income (PCPI) of $42,176. This ranked third in the United States and was 128% of the national average of $33,050. The 1994–2004 average annual growth rate of PCPI was 4.8%. Massachusetts had a total personal income (TPI) of $270,235,901,000, which ranked 11th in the United States and reflected an increase of 5.8% from 2003. The 1994–2004 average annual growth rate of TPI was 5.4%. Earnings of persons employed in Massachusetts increased from $204,746,728,000 in 2003 to $218,451,912,000 in 2004, an increase of 6.7%. The 2003–04 national change was 6.3%.

The US Census Bureau reports that the three-year average median household income for 2002 to 2004 in 2004 dollars was $52,354 compared to a national average of $44,473. During the same period an estimated 9.8% of the population was below the poverty line as compared to 12.4% nationwide.

22 LABOR

According to the Bureau of Labor Statistics (BLS), in April 2006 the seasonally adjusted civilian labor force in Massachusetts numbered 3,338,600, with approximately 163,900 workers unemployed, yielding an unemployment rate of 4.9%, compared to the national average of 4.7% for the same period. Preliminary data for the same period placed nonfarm employment at 3,218,000. Since the beginning of the BLS data series in 1976, the highest unemployment rate recorded in Massachusetts was 10.9% in January 1976. The historical low was 2.7% in December 2000. Preliminary nonfarm employment data by occupation for April 2006 showed that approximately 4.4% of the labor force was employed in construction; 9.4% in manufacturing; 17.7% in trade, transportation, and public utilities; 6.9% in financial activities; 14.5% in professional and business services; 18.4% in education and health services; 9.1% in leisure and hospitality services; and 12.7% in government.

Some of the earliest unionization efforts took place in Massachusetts in the early 1880s, particularly in the shipbuilding and construction trades. However, the most important trade unions to evolve were those in the state's textile and shoe industries. The workers had numerous grievances: shoebinders' salaries of $1.60–$2.40 a week during the 1840s, workdays of 14 to 17 hours, wages paid in scrip that could be cashed only at company stores (which charged exorbitantly high prices), and children working at dangerous machinery. In 1867, a seven-week-long shoemakers' strike at Lynn, the center of the shoe business, was at that time the longest strike in US history.

After the turn of the century, the state suffered a severe decline in manufacturing, and employers sought to cut wages to make up for lost profits. This resulted in a number of strikes by both the United Textile Workers and the Boot and Shoe Workers Union. The largest strike of the era was at Lawrence in 1912, when textile workers (led by a radical labor group, the Industrial Workers of the World) closed the mills, and the mayor called in troops in an attempt to reopen them. Although the textile and shoe businesses are no longer major employers in the state, the United Shoe Workers of America, the Brotherhood of Shoe and Allied Craftsmen, the United Textile Workers, and the Leather Workers International Union of America have their headquarters in Massachusetts.

Massachusetts was one of the first states to enact child labor laws. In 1842, it established the 10-hour day for children under 12. In 1867, it forbade employment for children under 10. The nation's first Uniform Child Labor Law, establishing an 8-hour day for children ages 14 to 16, was enacted by Massachusetts in 1913. Massachusetts was also the first state to enact minimum wage guidelines (1912).

The US Department of Labor's Bureau of Labor Statistics reported that in 2005, a total of 402,000 of Massachusetts' 2,886,000 employed wage and salary workers were formal members of a union. This represented 13.9% of those so employed, up from 13.5% in

2004, and above the national average of 12%. Overall in 2005, a total of 431,000 workers (14.9%) in Massachusetts were covered by a union or employee association contract, which includes those workers who reported no union affiliation. Massachusetts is one of 28 states that does not have a right-to-work law.

As of 1 March 2006, Massachusetts had a state-mandated minimum wage rate of $6.75 per hour. In 2004, women in the state accounted for 48.3% of the employed civilian labor force.

23 AGRICULTURE

As of 2004, there were 6,100 farms in Massachusetts, covering 520,000 acres (210,000 hectares). Farming was mostly limited to the western Massachusetts counties of Hampshire, Franklin, and Berkshire, and southern Bristol County. Total agricultural income for 2005 was estimated at $390 million (47th of the 50 states), of which crops provided 76%. Although the state is not a major farming area, it is the second-largest producer of cranberries in the United States; production for 2004 was 180,400,000 lb, about 28% of the US total. Output totals for other crops in 2004 were as follows: corn for silage, 374,000 tons; hay, 181,000 tons; and tobacco, 989,000 lb. While of local economic importance, these figures are tiny fractions of US totals.

24 ANIMAL HUSBANDRY

Massachusetts is not a major producer of livestock. The state had 48,000 cattle and calves worth around $52.8 million in 2005, and an estimated 12,000 hogs and pigs worth $1.3 million in 2004. Also during 2003, poultry farmers sold 863,000 lb (392,000 kg) of chickens, and the state produced an estimated 73 million eggs, worth around $4.8 million. An estimated 19,000 milk cows produced 332 million lb (151 million kg) of milk in 2003. During 2003, the state produced around 1.8 million lb (0.8 million kg) of turkeys worth $2.7 million.

25 FISHING

The early settlers earned much of their income from the sea. The first shipyard in Massachusetts opened at Salem Neck in 1637 and, during the years before independence, the towns of Salem, Newburyport, Plymouth, and Boston were among the colonies' leading ports. By 1807, Massachusetts's fishing fleet made up 88% of the US total. For much of the 19th century, Nantucket and, later, New Bedford were the leading US whaling centers. But with the decline of the whaling industry came a sharp drop in the importance of fishing to the livelihood of the state. By 1978, the fishing industry ranked 13th in importance of the 15 industries monitored by the state. However, the fishing ports of New Bedford and Gloucester were still among the busiest in the United States in 2004. New Bedford ranked first in the nation in catch value at $206.5 million and seventh in the nation for catch volume at 175.1 million lb (79.6 million kg). Gloucester was 12th in the nation in catch value ($42.7 million) and tenth in volume (113.3 million lb/51.5 million kg).

In 2004, Massachusetts ranked second in the nation for total commercial catch value at $326.1 million. The total catch volume that year was 336.9 million lb (153.1 million kg). The quahog catch of 14.1 million lb (6.4 million kg) was the second largest in the nation. The lobster catch was also the second largest with 11.3 million lb (5.1 million kg) valued at $51.5 million. Massachusetts was the leading producer of sea scallops with 28.1 million lb (12.8 million kg). In 2003, there were 232 fish processing and wholesale plants with an annual average of 4,504 employees in the state. The commercial fleet in 2001 had about 5,235 boats and vessels.

The state's long shoreline and many rivers make sport fishing a popular pastime for both deepsea and freshwater fishermen. The fishing season runs from mid-April through late October, with the season extended through February for bass, pickerel, panfish, and trout. In 2004, there were 203,139 fishing license holders.

26 FORESTRY

Forestry is a minor industry in the state. Forested lands cover about 3,126,000 acres (1,265,000 hectares), 76% of which are private lands. Wooded areas lost to urbanization in recent years have been offset by the conversion of inactive agricultural areas into forests. Red oak and white ash are found in the west; specialty products include maple syrup and Christmas trees. The wood and paper products industries require more pulp than the state currently produces. Lumber production in 2004 totaled 60 million board ft, 60% hardwood.

Massachusetts has the sixth-largest state park system in the nation, with 38 state parks and 74 state forests totaling some 273,000 acres (110,000 hectares). There are no national forests in Massachusetts.

27 MINING

According to preliminary data from the US Geological Survey (USGS), the estimated value of nonfuel mineral production by Massachusetts in 2003 was $186 million, a decrease from 2002 of about 4%.

By value, crushed stone, construction sand and gravel, and lime were the state's top three nonfuel mineral commodities in 2003, according to USGS data. Collectively, these commodities accounted for around 94% of the state's nonfuel mineral output, by value. According to preliminary figures for 2003, a total of 13.2 million metric tons of crushed stone, valued at $104 million, were produced, while 11.4 million metric tons of sand and gravel, worth $70.7 million, were produced. Massachusetts in 2003 was also a producer of dimension stone and common clays. Dimension stone output that year totaled 81,000 metric tons and was valued at $10.5 million, while output of common clays totaled 36,000 metric tons and was valued at $321,000, according to the preliminary data. Nationally, the state ranked fifth in dimension stone in 2003.

28 ENERGY AND POWER

As of 2003, Massachusetts had 69 electrical power service providers, of which 41 were publicly owned, 7 were investor owned, 4 were owners of independent generators that sold directly to customers, 9 were generation-only suppliers, and 8 were delivery-only providers. As of that same year there were 2,927,308 retail customers. Of that total, 2,456,890 received their power from investor-owned service providers. Publically owned providers had 382,808 customers, while 132 were independent generator or "facility" customers. Generation-only suppliers had 87,478 customers. There was no data on the number of delivery-only service customers.

Total net summer generating capability by the state's electrical generating plants in 2003 stood at 13.877 million kW, with to-

tal production that same year at 48.385 billion kWh. Of the total amount generated, only 4.2% came from electric utilities, with the remaining 95.8% coming from independent producers and combined heat and power service providers. The largest portion of all electric power generated, 22.423 billion kWh (46.3%), came from natural gas fired plants, with coal-fired plants in second place at 10.896 billion kWh (22.5%) and petroleum fueled plants in third at 7.459 billion kWh (15.4%). Nuclear power accounted for 10.3% of all power generated followed by other renewable power sources and hydroelectric sources.

In 2006, the Pilgrim power plant in Plymouth was Massachusetts' only operating nuclear power plant.

Boston Edison supplies electricity to the city of Boston; the rest of the state is served by 13 other companies, although a few municipalities do generate their own power. Power companies are regulated by the Department of Public Utilities, which establishes rates and monitors complaints from customers.

As of 2004, Massachusetts had no proven reserves of crude oil or coal, although oil exploration off the coast of Cape Cod did take place 1979 following a lengthy court battle. Environmentalists and fishermen had sought to prevent development of an oil industry in the region, which is one of the richest fishing grounds in the country. The state has no refineries.

The state consumes but does not produce natural gas. In 2004 about 373 billion cu ft (10.5 billion cu m) of natural gas were delivered. Slightly more than 30% of the gas sold was for residential use, 54% for industries and electricity generation, and 15% for commercial use.

The state encourages energy conservation and the development of alternative energy systems by granting tax credits to qualifying industries. Private researchers and the state have established demonstration projects for solar energy systems and other alternatives to fossil fuels.

29 INDUSTRY

Massachusetts was the nation's first major industrial state, and during the later part of the 19th century, it was the US leader in shoemaking and textile production. By 1860, the state was a major producer of machinery and milled nearly one-fourth of the country's paper.

Massachusetts remains an important manufacturing center. Nearly all the major manufacturing sectors had plants in Massachusetts's eastern counties. Significant concentrations of industrial machinery employment are in Attleboro, Wilmington, Worcester, and the Springfield area. Much of the manufacturing industry is located along Route 128, a superhighway that circles Boston from Gloucester in the north to Quincy in the south and is unique in its concentration of high-technology enterprises. Massachusetts's future as a manufacturing center depends on its continued preeminence in the production of computers, optical equipment, and other sophisticated instruments.

According to the US Census Bureau's Annual Survey of Manufactures (ASM) for 2004, Massachusetts' manufacturing sector covered some 20 product subsectors. The shipment value of all products manufactured in the state that same year was $76.538 billion. Of that total, computer and electronic product manufacturing accounted for the largest share at $20.757 billion. It was followed by chemical manufacturing at $9.254 billion; miscellaneous manufacturing at $6.437 billion; food manufacturing at $6.053 billion; and fabricated metal product manufacturing at $5.823 billion.

In 2004, a total of 302,263 people in Massachusetts were employed in the state's manufacturing sector, according to the ASM. Of that total, 179,747 were actual production workers. In terms of total employment, the computer and electronic product manufacturing industry accounted for the largest portion of all manufacturing employees at 58,806, with 25,353 actual production workers. It was followed by fabricated metal product manufacturing at 34,054 employees (24,028 actual production workers); miscellaneous manufacturing at 31,425 employees (19,006 actual production workers); machinery manufacturing at 23,887 employees (13,294 actual production workers); chemical manufacturing at 23,305 employees (10,354 actual production workers); and food manufacturing with 21,120 employees (13,743 actual production workers).

ASM data for 2004 showed that Massachusetts' manufacturing sector paid $14.895 billion in wages. Of that amount, the computer and electronic product manufacturing sector accounted for the largest share at $3.766 billion. It was followed by fabricated metal product manufacturing at $1.528 billion; chemical manufacturing at $1.501 billion; miscellaneous manufacturing at $1.354 billion; and machinery manufacturing at $1.327 billion.

30 COMMERCE

Massachusetts's machinery and electrical goods industries are important components of the state's wholesale trade, along with motor vehicle and automotive equipment, and paper and paper products. According to the 2002 Census of Wholesale Trade, Massachusetts' wholesale trade sector had sales that year totaling $127.1 billion from 9,333 establishments. Wholesalers of durable goods accounted for 5,546 establishments, followed by nondurable goods wholesalers at 2,826 and electronic markets, agents, and brokers accounting for 961 establishments. Sales by durable goods wholesalers in 2002 totaled $52.1 billion, while wholesalers of nondurable goods saw sales of $55.1 billion. Electronic markets, agents, and brokers in the wholesale trade industry had sales of $19.8 billion.

In the 2002 Census of Retail Trade, Massachusetts was listed as having 25,761 retail establishments with sales of $73.9 billion. The leading types of retail businesses by number of establishments were: food and beverage stores (4,529); clothing and clothing accessories stores (3,764); miscellaneous store retailers (2,979); and gasoline stations (2,333). In terms of sales, motor vehicle and motor vehicle parts dealers accounted for the largest share of retail sales at $17.6 billion, followed by food and beverage stores at $13.7 billion; general merchandise stores at $7.1 billion; and building material/garden equipment and supplies dealers $6.1 billion. A total of 359,149 people were employed by the retail sector in Massachusetts that year.

Exporters located in Massachusetts exported $22.04 billion in merchandise during 2005, ranking 10th in the nation.

31 CONSUMER PROTECTION

Consumer protection in Massachusetts is handled by two state entities: the Executive Office of Consumer Affairs and Business Regulation, which serves as an information and referral center for consumer complaints and oversees the activities of many of the state's regulatory agencies; and the Office of the Attorney General which has a Consumer Protection and Antitrust Division that handles consumer complaints either through litigation or nine face-to-face mediation programs. The Massachusetts Consumer Council also advises the governor and legislature and there are many local consumer councils.

When dealing with consumer protection issues, the state's Attorney General's Office can initiate civil and criminal proceedings; represent the state before state and federal regulatory agencies; administer consumer protection and education programs; handle formal consumer complaints; and exercise broad subpoena powers. In antitrust actions, the Attorney General's office can act on behalf of those consumers who are incapable of acting on their own; initiate damage actions on behalf of the state in state courts; initiate criminal proceedings; and represent counties, cities and other governmental entities in recovering civil damages under state or federal law.

The Executive Office of Consumer Affairs and Business Regulation and the Attorney General Office's Consumer Protection and Antitrust Division are both located in Boston. The Attorney General's Office also has regional offices in New Bedford, Springfield and Worcester. County government consumer affairs offices are located in Greenfield, Northampton, Pittsfield, Quincy, Worcester, Boston, Cambridge, Fall River, Haverhill, Hyannis, Lawrence, Lowell, Medford, Natick, Newton, North Weymouth, Plymouth, Revere, Springfield and Waltham.

32 BANKING

By the mid-1800s, Boston had developed into a major banking center whose capital financed the state's burgeoning industries. As of 2005 banking remained an important sector of the state's economy.

As of June 2005, Massachusetts had 195 insured banks, savings and loans, and saving banks, plus 103 state-chartered and 149 federally chartered credit unions (CUs). Excluding the CUs, the Boston-Cambridge-Quincy market area accounted for the largest portion of the state's financial institutions and deposits in 2004, with 154 institutions and $141.035 billion in deposits. As of June 2005, CUs accounted for 8.8% of all assets held by all financial institutions in the state, or some $22.128 billion. Banks, savings and loans, and savings banks collectively accounted for the remaining 91.2% or $230.670 billion in assets held.

State chartered savings banks, trust companies, co-operative banks, credit unions, and other financial service providers, including mortgage lenders and brokers, debt collection agencies, foreign transmittal agencies, check cashers, and credit grantors, are regulated by the state's Division of Banks, within the Office of Consumer Affairs and Business Regulation. The division administers the state's banking laws and oversees bank and financial institution practices and policies.

In 2004, the median percentage of past-due/nonaccrual loans to total loans stood at 0.60%, down from 0.70% in 2003. In that same year, the median net interest margin (the difference between the lower rates offered to savers and the higher rates charged on loans) for the state's insured institutions stood at 3.50%, down from 3.54% in 2003. Around 82% of insured institutions headquartered in Massachusetts are savings institutions, and residential real estate loans make up some 65% of the average loan portfolio.

33 INSURANCE

Insurance is an important business in Massachusetts, and some of the largest life and property and casualty insurance companies in the nation have their headquarters in Boston.

In 2004 there were over 3.1 million individual life insurance policies in force with a total value of over $349 billion; total value for all categories of life insurance (individual, group, and credit) was about $571 billion. The average coverage amount is $111,700 per policy holder. Death benefits paid that year totaled at over $1.2 billion.

As of 2003, there were 55 property and casualty and 19 life and health insurance companies domiciled in the state. In 2004, direct premiums for property and casualty insurance totaled $11.8 billion. That year, there were 40,473 flood insurance policies in force in the state, with a total value of $7.1 billion. About $39 billion of coverage was held through FAIR plans, which are designed to offer coverage for some natural circumstances, such as wind and hail, in high risk areas.

On 4 April 2006, the Massachusetts legislature approved a bill designed to make the purchase of health insurance a requirement for all state residents by 1 July 2007. The governor accepted most of the bill into law on 13 April. Under the terms of the bill, government subsidies will be available to assist low-income residents and employers with 11 employees or more may be required to either provide coverage for their workers or to pay an annual per employee fee to the government. Beginning in January 2008, residents could be required to report information concerning their health insurance policy on their state income tax return. Those who do not provide such proof of coverage may lose their personal state tax exemption and face penalties of up to half the cost of the lowest priced insurance policy. This bill, the first such legislation in the United States, is designed to address the issue of paying for the health care for over 500,000 of uninsured and underinsured residents.

In 2004, 60% of state residents held employment-based health insurance policies, 4% held individual policies, and 25% were covered under Medicare and Medicaid; 11% of residents were uninsured. In 2003, employee contributions for employment-based health coverage averaged at 20% for single coverage and 24% for family coverage. The state offers an 18-month health benefits expansion program for small-firm employees in connection with the Consolidated Omnibus Budget Reconciliation Act (COBRA, 1986), a health insurance program for those who lose employment-based coverage due to termination or reduction of work hours.

In 2003, there were over 4.1 million auto insurance policies in effect for private passenger cars. Required minimum coverage includes bodily injury liability of up to $20,000 per individual and $40,000 for all persons injured in an accident, as well as property damage liability of $5,000. Personal injury protection and uninsured motorist coverage are also mandatory. In 2003, the average expenditure per vehicle for insurance coverage was $1,051.60, which ranked as the fourth-highest average in the nation (after New Jersey, New York, and the District of Columbia).

New England Mutual Life Insurance Co. of Boston was the first mutual company to be chartered in the United States and remains one of the largest firms in the business. John Hancock Mutual Life, also of Boston, is one of the largest life insurance companies in the United States.

All aspects of the insurance business in Massachusetts, including the licensing of agents, and brokers and the examination of all insurance companies doing business in the state, are controlled by the Division of Insurance, under the Executive Office of Consumer Affairs and Business Regulation.

34 SECURITIES

The Boston Stock Exchange, founded in 1834, is the only stock exchange in Massachusetts. The BSE has approximately 200 members, handles over 2,000 stocks, and is the fastest-growing stock exchange in the United States (increasing trade volume tenfold during the 1990s). In 2005, there were 7,070 securities, commodities, and financial services sales agents employed in the state. In 2004, there were over 468 publicly traded companies within the state, with over 235 NASDAQ companies, 101 NYSE listings, and 64 AMEX listings. In 2006, the state had nine Fortune 500 companies; Massachusetts Mutual Life Insurance (based in Springfield) ranked first in the state and 92nd in the nation with revenues of over $22.7 billion, followed by Raytheon (Waltham), Liberty Mutual Insurance Group (Boston), Staples (Framingham), and TJX Companies (Framingham). Staples is listed on NASDAQ while the other four companies are on the NYSE.

The Securities Division of the Office of the Secretary of the Commonwealth is responsible for licensing and monitoring all brokerage firms in the state.

35 PUBLIC FINANCE

The Massachusetts budget is prepared by the Executive Office of Administration and Finance and is presented by the governor to the legislature for revision and approval. The fiscal year (FY) runs from 1 July to 30 June.

Fiscal year 2006 general funds were estimated at $28.1 billion for resources and $25.5 billion for expenditures. In fiscal year 2004, federal government grants to Massachusetts were $13.8 billion.

In 5 January 2006 the Bush administration released $100 million in emergency contingency funds targeted to the areas with the greatest need, including $4.7 million for Massachusetts.

36 TAXATION

In 2005, Massachusetts collected $18,015 million in tax revenues or $2,815 per capita, which placed it seventh among the 50 states in per capita tax burden. The national average was $2,192 per capita. Sales taxes accounted for 21.6% of the total, selective sales taxes 10.5%, individual income taxes 53.8%, corporate income taxes 7.4%, and other taxes 6.7%.

As of 1 January 2006, Massachusetts had a single individual income tax bracket of 5.3%. The state taxes corporations at a flat rate of 9.5%.

In 2004, state and local property taxes amounted to $9,814,315,000 or $1,532 per capita. The per capita amount ranks the state seventh-highest nationally. Local governments collected $9,814,264,000 of the total and the state government $51,000.

Massachusetts taxes retail sales at a rate of 5%. Food purchased for consumption off-premises is tax exempt. The tax on cigarettes is 151 cents per pack, which ranks eighth among the 50 states and the District of Columbia. Massachusetts taxes gasoline at 21 cents per gallon. This is in addition to the 18.4 cents per gallon federal tax on gasoline.

According to the Tax Foundation, for every federal tax dollar sent to Washington in 2004, Massachusetts citizens received $0.77 in federal spending.

37 ECONOMIC POLICY

The Executive Office of Economic Development is responsible for setting economic policy, promoting Massachusetts as a place to do business, increasing the job base, and generating economic activity in the Commonwealth.

The following agencies are within the Executive Office of Economic Development: Department of Business and Technology; Office of Consumer Affairs and Business Regulation; Department of Labor; and Department of Workforce Development. Other agencies addressing issues of economic development are: the Massachusetts Development Finance Agency (Mass Development); the Massachusetts Alliance for Economic Development; the Workforce Training Fund; the Massachusetts Office of International Trade and Investment; the Massachusetts Technology Collaborative, the Massachusetts Technology Development Corp., and the Department of Housing and Community Development.

Throughout most of the 1990's and up to 2002, the state economic development plan was guided by the 1993 report entitled "Choosing to Compete: A Statewide Strategy for Economic Growth and Job Creation." The Massachusetts Economic Development Incentive Program (EDIP), launched in 1993, was a series of initiatives geared to stimulate job creation, attract new businesses, and help firms expand. There were 34 Economic Target Areas (ETAs) throughout the state. Cities and towns, in partnership with the Commonwealth and private enterprises, also developed economic programs to attract new business. In 2002, building on what was seen as the success of the Choosing to Compete campaign, the former Department of Economic Development issued a new framework entitled "Toward a New Prosperity: Building Regional Competitiveness Across the Commonwealth." The approach divides the state economy into seven regional clusters, each with unique developmental needs and potentials. Six overall goals were stated: to improve the business climate for all business clusters; to support entrepreneurship and innovation; to prepare the workforce for the future; to build an information infrastructure for the 21st century; to ensure that economic growth is compatible with communities and the environment, and to the improve the outcome from government actions.

38 HEALTH

The infant mortality rate in October 2005 was estimated at 5 per 1,000 live births. The birth rate in 2003 was 12.5 per 1,000 population. The abortion rate stood at 21.4 per 1,000 women in 2000. In 2003, about 90% of pregnant woman received prenatal care beginning in the first trimester. In 2004, approximately 89% of children received routine immunizations before the age of three.

The crude death rate in 2003 was 8.8 deaths per 1,000 population. As of 2002, the death rates for major causes of death (per

Massachusetts—State Government Finances

(Dollar amounts in thousands. Per capita amounts in dollars.)

	AMOUNT	PER CAPITA
Total Revenue	41,615,765	6,495.36
General revenue	32,979,924	5,147.48
Intergovernmental revenue	8,997,317	1,404.29
Taxes	16,839,243	2,628.26
General sales	3,743,204	584.24
Selective sales	1,859,410	290.22
License taxes	664,556	103.72
Individual income tax	8,830,334	1,378.23
Corporate income tax	1,301,076	203.07
Other taxes	440,663	68.78
Current charges	2,594,314	404.92
Miscellaneous general revenue	4,549,050	710.01
Utility revenue	130,376	20.35
Liquor store revenue	–	–
Insurance trust revenue	8,505,465	1,327.53
Total expenditure	38,405,514	5,994.31
Intergovernmental expenditure	6,202,583	968.09
Direct expenditure	32,202,931	5,026.21
Current operation	20,238,600	3,158.83
Capital outlay	4,317,975	673.95
Insurance benefits and repayments	4,318,252	673.99
Assistance and subsidies	702,842	109.70
Interest on debt	2,625,262	409.75
Exhibit: Salaries and wages	4,117,062	642.59
Total expenditure	38,405,514	5,994.31
General expenditure	33,646,572	5,251.53
Intergovernmental expenditure	6,202,583	968.09
Direct expenditure	27,443,989	4,283.44
General expenditures, by function:		
Education	7,580,759	1,183.20
Public welfare	10,552,819	1,647.08
Hospitals	414,685	64.72
Health	686,758	107.19
Highways	3,015,459	470.65
Police protection	407,951	63.67
Correction	972,276	151.75
Natural resources	272,138	42.48
Parks and recreation	305,471	47.68
Government administration	1,389,776	216.92
Interest on general debt	2,566,137	400.52
Other and unallocable	5,482,343	855.68
Utility expenditure	440,690	68.78
Liquor store expenditure	–	–
Insurance trust expenditure	4,318,252	673.99
Debt at end of fiscal year	50,981,152	7,957.10
Cash and security holdings	65,110,609	10,162.42

Abbreviations and symbols: – zero or rounds to zero; (NA) not available; (X) not applicable.

SOURCE: *U.S. Census Bureau, Governments Division, 2004 Survey of State Government Finances,* January 2006.

100,000 resident population) were: heart disease, 229.3; cancer, 216.5; cerebrovascular diseases, 55.4; chronic lower respiratory diseases, 42.7; and diabetes, 22.1. The mortality rate from HIV infection was 3.6 per 100,000 population. In 2004, the reported AIDS case rate was at about 8.8 per 100,000 population. In 2002, about 51.3% of the population was considered overweight or obese, representing the lowest percentage among the 50 states. As of 2004, about 18.4% of state residents were smokers.

Programs for treatment and rehabilitation of alcoholics are administered by the Division of Alcoholism of the Department of

Health, under the Executive Office of Human Services. The Division of Communicable Disease Control operates venereal disease clinics throughout the state and provides educational material to schools and other groups. The Division of Drug Rehabilitation administers drug treatment from a statewide network of hospital agencies and self-help groups. The state also runs a lead-poisoning prevention program. In Massachusetts, all health-care facilities are registered by the Department of Public Health. The Division of Health Care Quality inspects and licenses hospitals, clinics, school infirmaries, and blood banks every two years. Licensing of nursing homes is also under its control.

In 2003, Massachusetts had 79 community hospitals with about 16,000 beds. There were about 785,000 patient admissions that year and 19.6 million outpatient visits. The average daily inpatient census was about 11,900 patients. The average cost per day for hospital care was $1,631. Also in 2003, there were about 478 certified nursing facilities in the state with 52,323 beds and an overall occupancy rate of about 89.8%. In 2004, it was estimated that about 79.5% of all state residents had received some type of dental care within the year; this was the third-highest dental care percentage in country (after Connecticut and Minnesota). Massachusetts had 451 physicians per 100,000 resident population in 2004 and 1,201 nurses per 100,000 in 2005; these rates some of the highest health-care worker–population rates in the nation. In 2004, there were a total of 5,143 dentists in the state.

Four prominent medical schools are located in the state: Harvard Medical School, Tufts University School of Medicine, Boston University School of Medicine, and the University of Massachusetts School of Medicine. In 2005, Massachusetts General Hospital in Boston ranked third on the Honor Roll of Best Hospitals 2005 by *U.S. News & World Report.* In the same report, it ranked fifth in the nation for care of heart disease and heart surgery and twelfth for care of cancer. Brigham and Women's Hospital, Boston ranked twelfth on the Honor Roll and sixth for best care in heart disease and heart surgery. The Children's Hospital Boston was ranked as second in the nation for best pediatric care. The Dana-Farber Cancer Institute in Boston was ranked fourth in the nation for cancer care.

About 25% of state residents were enrolled in Medicaid and Medicare programs in 2004. Approximately 11% of the state population was uninsured in 2004. In 2003, state health care expenditures totaled $7.7 million.

³⁹SOCIAL WELFARE

In 2004, about 239,000 people received unemployment benefits, with the average weekly unemployment benefit at $351. In fiscal year 2005, the estimated average monthly participation in the food stamp program included about 368,122 persons (176,121 households); the average monthly benefit was about $82.18 per person. That year, the total of benefits paid through the state for the food stamp program was about $363 million.

Temporary Assistance for Needy Families (TANF), the system of federal welfare assistance that officially replaced Aid to Families with Dependent Children (AFDC) in 1997, was reauthorized through the Deficit Reduction Act of 2005. TANF is funded through federal block grants that are divided among the states based on an equation involving the number of recipients in each state. The Massachusetts TANF cash assistance program is called Transitional Aid to Families with Dependent Children (TAFDC), and the work program is called the Employment Services Program (ESP). In 2004, the state program had 108,000 recipients; state and federal expenditures on this TANF program totaled $355 million in fiscal year 2003.

In December 2004, Social Security benefits were paid to 1,066,620 Massachusetts residents. This number included 692,260 retired workers, 96,030 widows and widowers, 146,990 disabled workers, 47,430 spouses, and 83,910 children. Social Security beneficiaries represented 16.6% of the total state population and 90.7% of the state's population age 65 and older. Retired workers received an average monthly payment of $961; widows and widowers, $933; disabled workers, $883; and spouses, $483. Payments for children of retired workers averaged $480 per month; children of deceased workers, $677; and children of disabled workers, $266. Federal Supplemental Security Income payments in December 2004 went to 169,205 Massachusetts residents, averaging $438 a month.

⁴⁰HOUSING

Massachusetts's housing stock, much older than the US average, reflects the state's colonial heritage and its ties to English architectural traditions. Two major styles are common: colonial, typified by a wood frame, two stories, center hall entry, and center chimney; and Cape Cod, one-story houses built by fishermen, typified by shallow basements, shingled roofs, clapboard fronts, and unpainted shingled sides weathered gray by the salt air. Many new houses are also built in these styles.

As of 2004, there were an estimated 2,672,061 housing units in the state, of which 2,435,421 were occupied; 64.6% were owner-occupied. About 52.5% of all housing units were single-family, detached homes. About 37.1% of all units were built before or during 1939. Nearly 42% of all units rely on utility gas for heating and 33.6% use fuel oil or kerosene. It was estimated that 50,724 units lacked telephone service, 7,775 lacked complete plumbing facilities, and 10,402 lacked complete kitchen facilities. The average household had 2.55 members.

In 2004, 22,500 new housing units were authorized for construction. The median home value was $331,200, the fourth highest in the United States. The median monthly cost for mortgage owners was $1,645. Renters paid a median of $852 per month. In 2006, the state received over $34.3 million in community development block grants from the US Department of Housing and Urban Development (HUD). The city of Boston received over $20.9 million in community development block grants.

The Executive Office of Communities and Development administers federal housing programs for the state. The Massachusetts Housing Finance Agency finances the construction and rehabilitation of housing by private and community groups.

⁴¹EDUCATION

Massachusetts has a long history of support for education. The Boston Latin School opened in 1635 as the first public school in the colonies. Harvard College—the first college in the United States—was founded the following year. In 1647, for the first time, towns with more than 50 people were required by law to establish tax-supported school systems. More firsts followed: the country's first board of education, compulsory school attendance law, training school for teachers, state school for the retarded, and school for the blind. The drive for quality public education in the state was intensified through the efforts of educator Horace Mann, who during the 1830s and 1840s was also a leading force for the improvement of school systems throughout the United States.

In 2004, 86.9% of state residents age 25 or older were high school graduates, and 36.7% had completed four or more years of college. Total public school enrollment for fall 2002 stood at 983,000. Of these, 701,000 attended schools from kindergarten through grade eight, and 282,000 attended high school. Approximately 74.6% of the students were white, 8.8% were black, 11.5% were Hispanic, 4.7% were Asian/Pacific Islander, and 0.3% were American Indian/Alaskan Native. Total enrollment was estimated at 978,000 in fall 2003 and was expected to be 919,000 by fall 2014, a decline of 6.5% during the period 2002 to 2014. Expenditures for public education in 2003/04 were estimated at $11.7 billion or $10,693 per student, the sixth-highest among the 50 states. Since 1969, the National Assessment of Educational Progress (NAEP) has tested public school students nationwide. The resulting report, *The Nation's Report Card,* stated that in 2005 eighth graders in Massachusetts scored 292 out of 500 in mathematics compared with the national average of 278.

The early years of statehood saw the development of private academies, where the students could learn more than the basic reading and writing skills that were taught in the town schools at the time. Some of these private preparatory schools remain, including such prestigious institutions as Andover, Deerfield, and Groton. In fall 2003 there were 134,708 students enrolled in 688 private schools.

As of fall 2002, there were 431,224 students enrolled in college or graduate school; minority students comprised 20.4% of total postsecondary enrollment. In 2005 Massachusetts had 122 degree-granting institutions. The major public university system is the University of Massachusetts, with campuses at Amherst, Boston, Dartmouth, and Lowell, and a medical school at Worcester. The Amherst campus was established in 1863, and the Boston campus in 1965. The state has a total of 15 public colleges and universities, while the Massachusetts Board of Regional Community Colleges has 16 campuses.

Harvard University, which was established in Cambridge originally as a college for clergymen and magistrates, has grown to become one of the country's premier institutions. Also located in Cambridge are Radcliffe College (whose enrollment is included in Harvard's), founded in 1879, and the Massachusetts Institute of Technology, or MIT (1861). Mount Holyoke College, the first US college for women, was founded in 1837. Other prominent private schools and their dates of origin are Amherst College (1821); Boston College (1863); Boston University (1869); Brandeis University (1947); Clark University (1887); Hampshire College (1965); the New England Conservatory of Music (1867); Northeastern University (1898); Smith College (1871); Tufts University (1852); Wellesley College (1875); and Williams College (1793).

Among the tuition assistance programs available to state residents are the Massachusetts General Scholarships, awarded to thousands of college students annually, and Massachusetts Honor Scholarships, for outstanding performance on the Scholastic Aptitude Test (SAT). The State Board of Education establishes standards and policies for the public schools throughout the state;

its programs are administered by the Department of Education. Higher education planning and programs are under the control of the Higher Education Coordinating Council.

The landmark Education Reform Act of 1993 established new systems of financial support for public elementary and secondary schools and instituted major reforms in governance, professional development, student educational goals, curricula, and assessments.

42 ARTS

Boston is the center of artistic activity in Massachusetts, and Cape Cod and the Berkshires are areas of significant seasonal artistic activity. In 1979, Massachusetts became the first state to establish a lottery solely for funding the arts. Boston is the home of several small theaters, some of which offer previews of shows bound for Broadway. Well-known local theater companies include the American Repertory Theatre and the Huntington Theatre. The 2006/07 season marked the Huntington Theatre's 25th anniversary; productions that season included the pre-Broadway, *Radio Golf* and the world premiere, *Mauritius.* Of the regional theaters scattered throughout the state, the Williamstown Theater in the Berkshires and the Provincetown Theater on Cape Cod are especially noteworthy.

The Boston Symphony, one of the major orchestras in the United States, was founded in 1881, and its principal conductors have included Serge Koussevitzky, Charles Munch, Erich Leinsdorf, and Seiji Ozawa. Emmanuel Church in Boston's Back Bay is known for its early music concerts, and chamber music by first-rate local and internationally known performers is presented at the New England Conservatory's Jordan Hall and other venues throughout the city. During the summer, the Boston Symphony is the main attraction of the Berkshire Music Festival at Tanglewood in Lenox. An offshoot of the Boston Symphony, the Boston Pops Orchestra, gained fame under the conductorship of Arthur Fiedler. Its mixture of popular, jazz, and light symphonic music continued under the direction of Fiedler's successors, John Williams and Keith Lockhart. As of the 2006, Lockhart still presided over the Boston Pops as director and opened the season with a performance featuring Elvis Costello. Boston is also the headquarters of the Boston Lyric Opera. Prominent in the world of dance are the Boston Ballet Company and the Jacob's Pillow Dance Festival in the Berkshires. *Ploughshares,* a literary journal published through Emerson College in Boston, has become well known nationally as a showplace for new writers.

The Massachusetts Cultural Council provides grants and services to support public programs in the arts, sciences, and the humanities. Grants are made to organizations, schools, communities and artists. In 2005, the Massachusetts Cultural Council and other arts organizations received 87 grants totaling $4,587,600 from the National Endowment for the Arts (NEA). The Massachusetts Foundation for the Humanities was founded in 1974. The foundation offers unique traveling seminars; the 2005 "Saudades de Portugal" seminar provided the opportunity to travel to Portugal. In 2005, the National Endowment for the Humanities contributed $7,502,287 to 79 state programs.

43 LIBRARIES AND MUSEUMS

The first public library in the United States was established in Boston in 1653. Massachusetts has one of the most important university libraries in the country, and numerous museums and historical sites commemorate the state's rich colonial history. For the fiscal year ending in June 2001, Massachusetts had 371 public library systems, with a total of 490 libraries, of which 119 were branches. The system served 351 towns and cities, and had 30,465,000 volumes of books and serial publications on its shelves, with a total circulation of 45,803,000 in that same year. The system also had 858,000 audio and 742,000 video items, 39,000 electronic format items (CD-ROMs, magnetic tapes, and disks), and 10 bookmobiles. The major city libraries are in Boston, Worcester, and Springfield. In fiscal year 2001, operating income for the state's public libraries was $220,510,000 including $1,107,000 in federal grants and $20,725,000 in state grants.

The Boston Athenaeum, with 650,000 volumes, is the most noteworthy private library in the state. The American Antiquarian Society in Worcester has a 690,000-volume research library of original source material dating from colonial times to 1876.

Harvard University's library system is one of the largest in the world, with 14,311,152 volumes in 1999. Other major academic libraries are those of Boston University, the University of Massachusetts (Amherst), Smith College, and Boston College.

Boston houses a number of important museums, among them the Museum of Fine Arts with vast holdings of artwork including extensive Far East and French impressionists collections and American art and furniture, the Isabella Stewart Gardner Museum, the Museum of Science, the Massachusetts Historical Society, and the Children's Museum. Harvard University's museums include the Fogg Art Museum, the Peabody Museum of Archaeology and Ethnology, the Museum of Comparative Zoology, and the Botanical Museum. Other museums of note are the Whaling Museum in New Bedford, the Essex Institute in Salem, the Worcester Art Museum, the Clark Art Institute in Williamstown, the Bunker Hill Museum near Boston, and the National Basketball Hall of Fame in Springfield. In addition, many towns have their own historical societies and museums, including Historic Deerfield, Framingham Historical and Natural History Society, Ipswich Historical Society, Lexington Historical Society, and Marblehead Historical Society. Plymouth Plantation in Plymouth is a re-creation of life in the 17th century, and Old Sturbridge Village, a working historical farm, displays 18th- and 19th-century artifacts. The state had over 344 museums in 2000.

44 COMMUNICATIONS

The first American post office was established in Boston in 1639. Alexander Graham Bell first demonstrated the telephone in 1876 in Boston. As of 2004, 93.4% of the state's occupied housing units had telephones. In addition, by June of that same year there were 3,919,139 mobile wireless telephone subscribers. In 2003, 64.1% of Massachusetts households had a computer and 58.1% had Internet access. By June 2005, there were 1,235,672 high-speed lines in Massachusetts, 1,123,606 residential and 112,066 for business.

The state had 32 major AM stations and 64 major FM stations in 2005, when 10 major television stations were also in operation. In Boston, WGBH is a major producer of programming for the Public Broadcasting Service. In 1999, the Boston metropolitan area had 2,210,580 television-owning households, 80% of which received cable (the second-highest penetration rate for any city).

In 2000, Massachusetts had 239,358 Internet domain name registrations, ranking seventh among all the states.

45 PRESS

Milestones in US publishing history that occurred in the state include the first book printed in the English colonies (Cambridge, 1640), the first regularly issued American newspaper, the *Boston News-Letter* (1704), and the first published American novel, William Hill Brown's *The Power of Sympathy* (Worcester, 1789). During the mid-1840s, two noted literary publications made their debut, the *North American Review* and the *Dial,* the latter under the editorial direction of Ralph Waldo Emerson and Margaret Fuller. The *Atlantic,* which began publishing in 1857, *Harvard Law Review, Harvard Business Review,* and *New England Journal of Medicine* are other influential publications.

As of 2005 there were 32 daily newspapers in the state (including 14 morning, 18 evening) and 16 papers with Sunday editions. The *Boston Globe,* the most widely read newspaper in the state, has won numerous awards for journalistic excellence on the local and national levels. The *Christian Science Monitor* is highly respected for its coverage of national and international news.

Major daily newspapers and their average circulations in 2005 were:

AREA	NAME	DAILY	SUNDAY
Boston	*Christian Science Monitor* (m)	60,723	
	Globe (m,S)	451,471	707,813
	Herald (m,S)	240,759	152,813
Hyannis	*Cape Cod Times* (m,S)	50,896	60,004
Worcester	*Telegram & Gazette* (m,S)	103,113	121,437

Massachusetts is also a center of book publishing, with more than 100 publishing houses. Among them are Little, Brown and Co.; Houghton Mifflin; Merriam-Webster; and Harvard University Press.

46 ORGANIZATIONS

In 2006, there were over 10,485 nonprofit organizations registered within the state, of which about 7,701 were registered as charitable, educational, or religious organizations.

Headquartered in Massachusetts are the National Association of Independent Schools, the National Commission for Cooperative Education, both in Boston, and the National Bureau of Economic Research in Cambridge. The Union of Concerned Scientists in Cambridge and the International Physicians for the Prevention of Nuclear War in Boston—recipient of the 1985 Nobel Peace Prize—are major public affairs associations based in the state.

Academic and scientific organizations headquartered in Boston include the American Meteorological Society, American Society of Law and Medicine, American Surgical Association, the Visiting Nurse Associations of America and Optometric Research Institute. The American Academy of Arts and Sciences is located in Cambridge. Other education and research organizations with national scope and membership include the Albert Einstein Institution, the Albert Schweitzer Fellowship, the Bostonian Society, the Plymouth Rock Foundation, the Thoreau Society, and the Titanic Historical Society. There are numerous municipal and regional historical, preservations, and arts organizations.

Among the many professional, business, and consumer organizations based in Massachusetts are the American Institute of Management and the International Brotherhood of Police Officers in Quincy; the Wood Products Manufacturers Association in Gardner; and the National Consumer Law Center, Northern Textile Association, and Wool Manufacturers Council in Boston.

The national Organic Trade Association is based in Greenfield and the Cranberry Institute is in East Wareham. Local environmental groups include the Association to Preserve Cape Cod, the Boston Harbor Association, the Nantucket Conservation Foundation, a few chapters of Trout Unlimited.

Oxfam-America, the US affiliate of the international humanitarian relief agency, is located in Boston. Students Against Destructive Decisions/Students Against Drunk Driving (SADD) is based in Marlborough. The Christian Science Publishing Society, which publishes the *Christian Science Monitor,* is located in Boston. The Unitarian Universalist Association of Congregations, a major body of the Unitarian Church, is also based in Boston.

Major sports associations in the state are the Eastern College Athletic Conference in Centerville and the American Hockey League in Springfield.

47TOURISM, TRAVEL, AND RECREATION

In 2004, there were over 31.2 million travelers to and within the state. There were 1.4 million international visitors to the state, with Canada and the United Kingdom being the largest markets. About 20% of all tourist activity involves residents traveling within the state. The travel industry supports over 125,300 jobs with a payroll of $3.2 billion.

A trip to Boston might include visits to such old landmarks as the Old North Church, the USS *Constitution,* and Paul Revere's House, and such newer attractions as the John Hancock Observatory, the skywalk above the Prudential Tower, Quincy Market, Faneuil Hall, and Copley Place. Boston Common, one of the oldest public parks in the country, is the most noteworthy municipal park. The well-marked Freedom Trail takes visitors on a walking and driving tour of historical sites, including the cities of Lexington and Concord.

About 19% of all trips are made to Cape Cod (Barnstable County). Among its many attractions are beaches, fishing, good dining spots, several artists' colonies with arts and crafts fairs, antique shops, and summer theaters. Beaches, fishing, and quaint villages are also the charms of Nantucket Island and Martha's Vineyard.

The Berkshires are the summer home of the Berkshire Music Festival at Tanglewood and the Jacob's Pillow Dance Festival in Lee, and during the winter also provide recreation for cross-country and downhill skiers. Essex County on the North Shore of Massachusetts Bay offers many seaside towns and the art colony of Rockport. Its main city, Salem, contains the Witch House and Museum as well as Nathaniel Hawthorne's House of Seven Gables. Middlesex County, to the west of Boston, holds the university city of Cambridge as well as the battlegrounds of Lexington and Concord. In Concord are the homes of Henry David Thoreau, Ralph Waldo Emerson, and Louisa May Alcott. Norfolk County, south of Boston, has the homes of three US presidents: John Adams and John Quincy Adams in Quincy and John F. Kennedy in Brookline.

The seaport town and former whaling center of New Bedford and the industrial town of Fall River are in Bristol County. Plymouth County offers Plymouth Rock, Plymouth Plantation, and a steam-train ride through some cranberry bogs. The town of Springfield, birthplace of basketball, hosts the Basketball Hall of Fame; in June 1985 it opened in its present location, which welcomed its one-millionth visitor in July 1988. Springfield also has the Dr. Seuss National Memorial Sculpture Garden and the Eric Carle Museum of Picture Book Arts. Plum Island has a nature preserve and a natural barrier reef. Many visitors visit Massachusetts in the fall to travel the Mohawk Trail to view the fall foliage. The John Fitzgerald Kennedy Presidential Library is in Boston.

Massachusetts has 79 operational state parks.

48SPORTS

There are five major professional sports teams in Massachusetts: the Boston Red Sox of Major League Baseball, the New England Patriots of the National Football League, the Boston Celtics of the National Basketball Association, the Boston Bruins of the National Hockey League, and the New England Revolution of Major League Soccer.

The Red Sox won the World Series in 2005 by defeating their rivals, the New York Yankees. The Patriots have won nine division championships, five conference championships, and the Super Bowl in 2001, 2003, and 2004. The Celtics are the winningest team in NBA history; they have won the championship 16 times, including the seemingly unbeatable record of 8 consecutive titles from 1959 to 1966. They last won an NBA championship in 1986. The Bruins won the Stanley Cup in 1929, 1939, 1941, 1970, and 1972. Additionally, there are minor league hockey teams in Springfield, Worcester, and Lowell.

Suffolk Downs in East Boston features thoroughbred horse racing and harness racing takes place at the New England Harness Raceway in Foxboro. Dog racing can be seen at Raynham Park in Raynham, Taunton Dog Track in North Dighton, and Wonderland Park in Revere.

Probably the most famous amateur athletic event in the state is the Boston Marathon, a race of more than 26 mi (42 km) held every Patriots' Day (third Monday in April). It attracts many of the world's top long-distance runners. During the summer, a number of boat races are held. Rowing is also popular. Each October the traditional sport is celebrated at the Head of the Charles, a regatta held on the Charles River between collegiate rowing teams.

In collegiate sports, the University of Massachusetts has become a nationally ranked basketball powerhouse, reaching the Final Four in 1996; Boston College has appeared in 12 bowl games, highlighted by a victory in the Cotton Bowl in 1985; and the annual Harvard–Yale football game is one of the traditional rites of autumn.

49FAMOUS BAY STATERS

Massachusetts has produced an extraordinary collection of public figures. Its four US presidents were John Adams (1735–1826), a signer of the Declaration of Independence; his son John Quincy Adams (1767–1848); John Fitzgerald Kennedy (1917–63), and George Herbert Walker Bush (b.Milton, 12 June 1924). All four served in Congress. John Adams was also the first US vice president; John Quincy Adams served as secretary of state under James

Monroe, Calvin Coolidge (b.Vermont, 1872–1933) was governor of Massachusetts before his election to the vice-presidency in 1920 and his elevation to the presidency in 1923. George Bush was elected vice president on the Republican ticket in 1980 and reelected in 1984. Bush was elected president in 1988. Two others who held the office of vice president were another signer of the Declaration of Independence, Elbridge Gerry (1744–1814), for whom the political practice of gerrymandering is named, and Henry Wilson (b.New Hampshire, 1812–75), a US senator from Massachusetts before his election with Ulysses S. Grant.

Massachusetts's great jurists include US Supreme Court Justices Joseph Story (1779–1845), Oliver Wendell Holmes Jr. (1841–1935), Louis D. Brandeis (b.Kentucky, 1856–1941), and Felix Frankfurter (b.Austria, 1882–1965). David Souter (b.1939), a Supreme Court justice appointed during the Bush administration, was born in Melrose. Stephen Breyer (b.California, 1939), another Supreme Court justice, was a Circuit Court of Appeals judge in Boston before his appointment. Important federal officeholders at the cabinet level were Henry Knox (1750–1806), the first secretary of war; Timothy Pickering (1745–1820), the first postmaster general and later secretary of war and secretary of state under George Washington and John Adams; Levi Lincoln (1749–1820), attorney general under Jefferson; William Eustis (1753–1825), secretary of war under Madison; Jacob Crowninshield (1770–1808), secretary of the navy under Jefferson, and his brother Benjamin (1772–1851), who held the same office under Madison; Daniel Webster (b.New Hampshire, 1782–1852), US senator from Massachusetts who served as secretary of state under William Henry Harrison, John Tyler, and Millard Fillmore; Edward Everett (1794–1865), a governor and ambassador who served as secretary of state under Fillmore; George Bancroft (1800–91), a historian who became secretary of the Navy under James K. Polk; Caleb Cushing (1800–79), attorney general under Franklin Pierce; Charles Devens (1820–91), attorney general under Rutherford B. Hayes; Christian Herter (1895–1966), secretary of state under Dwight Eisenhower; Elliot L. Richardson (1920–99), secretary of health, education and welfare, secretary of defense, and attorney general under Richard Nixon; Henry Kissinger (b.Germany, 1923), secretary of state under Nixon and Gerald Ford and a Nobel Peace Prize winner in 1973; and Robert F. Kennedy (1925–68), attorney general under his brother John and later US senator from New York.

Other federal officeholders include some of the most important figures in American politics. Samuel Adams (1722–1803), the Boston Revolutionary leader, served extensively in the Continental Congress and was later governor of the Bay State. John Hancock (1737–93), a Boston merchant and Revolutionary, was the Continental Congress's first president and later became the first elected governor of the state. In the 19th century, Massachusetts sent abolitionist Charles Sumner (1811–74) to the Senate. As ambassador to England during the Civil War, John Quincy Adams's son Charles Francis Adams (1807–86) played a key role in preserving US-British amity. At the end of the century, Henry Cabot Lodge (1850–1924) emerged as a leading Republican in the US Senate, where he supported regulatory legislation, protectionist tariffs, and restrictive immigration laws, and opposed women's suffrage and the League of Nations; his grandson, also Henry Cabot Lodge (1902–85), was an internationalist who held numerous federal posts and was a US senator. Massachusetts has provided two US

House speakers: John W. McCormack (1891–1980) and Thomas P. "Tip" O'Neill Jr. (1912–94). Other well-known legislators include Edward W. Brooke (b.1919), the first black US senator since Reconstruction, and Edward M. Kennedy (b.1932), President Kennedy's youngest brother and a leading Senate liberal. Paul Tsongas (1941–97), a senator and presidential candidate during the 1992 election, was born in Lowell, Massachusetts. Michael S. Dukakis (b.1933), a former governor of the state and the 1988 Democratic nominee for president, was born in Brookline.

Among other historic colonial and state leaders were John Winthrop (b.England, 1588–1649), a founder of Massachusetts and longtime governor; William Bradford (b.England, 1590–1657), a founder of Plymouth, its governor, and author of its classic history; Thomas Hutchinson (1711–80), colonial lieutenant governor and governor during the 1760s and 1770s; and Paul Revere (1735–1818), the Patriot silversmith-courier, who was later an industrial pioneer.

Literary genius has flourished in Massachusetts. In the 17th century, the colony was the home of poets Anne Bradstreet (1612–72) and Edward Taylor (1645–1729) and of the prolific historian, scientist, theologian, and essayist Cotton Mather (1663–1728). Notables of the 18th century include the theologian Jonathan Edwards (b.Connecticut, 1703–58), poet Phillis Wheatley (b.Senegal, 1753–84), and numerous political essayists and historians. During the 1800s, Massachusetts was the home of novelists Nathaniel Hawthorne (1804–64), Louisa May Alcott (b.Pennsylvania, 1832–88), Horatio Alger (1832–99), and Henry James (b.New York, 1843–1916); essayists Ralph Waldo Emerson (1803–82) and Henry David Thoreau (1817–62); and such poets as Henry Wadsworth Longfellow (b.Maine, 1807–82), John Greenleaf Whittier (1807–92), Oliver Wendell Holmes Sr. (1809–94), James Russell Lowell (1819–91), and Emily Dickinson (1830–86). Classic historical writings include the works of George Bancroft, William Hickling Prescott (1796–1859), John Lothrop Motley (1814–77), Francis Parkman (1823–93), and Henry B. Adams (1838–1918). Among 20th-century notables are novelists John P. Marquand (b.Delaware, 1893–1960) and John Cheever (1912–82); poets Elizabeth Bishop (1911–79), Robert Lowell (1917–77), Anne Sexton (1928–74), and Sylvia Plath (1932–63); and historian Samuel Eliot Morison (1887–1976). In philosophy, Charles Sanders Peirce (1839–1914) was one of the founders of pragmatism; Henry James's elder brother, William (b.New York, 1842–1910), was a pioneer in the field of psychology; and George Santayana (b.Spain, 1863–1952), philosopher and author, grew up in Boston. Mary Baker Eddy (b.New Hampshire, 1821–1910) founded the Church of Christ, Scientist, during the 1870s.

Reformers have abounded in Massachusetts, especially in the 19th century. William Lloyd Garrison (1805–79), Wendell Phillips (1811–84), and Lydia Maria Child (1802–80) were outstanding abolitionists. Lucretia Coffin Mott (1793–1880), Lucy Stone (1818–93), Abigail Kelley Foster (1810–87), Margaret Fuller (1810–50), and Susan Brownell Anthony (1820–1906) were leading advocates of women's rights. Horace Mann (1796–1859), the state secretary of education, led the fight for public education; and Mary Lyon (1797–1849) founded Mount Holyoke, the first women's college.

Efforts to improve the care and treatment of the sick, wounded, and handicapped were led by Samuel Gridley Howe (1801–76), Dorothea Lynde Dix (1802–87), and Clara Barton (1821–1912), founder of the American Red Cross. The 20th-century reformer and NAACP leader William Edward Burghardt Du Bois (1868–1963) was born in Great Barrington.

Leonard Bernstein (1918–90) was a composer and conductor of worldwide fame. Arthur Fiedler (1894–79) was the celebrated conductor of the Boston Pops Orchestra. Composers include William Billings (1746–1800), Carl Ruggles (1876–1971), and Alan Hovhaness (1911–2000). Charles Bulfinch (1763–1844), Henry H. Richardson (b.Louisiana, 1838–86), and Louis Henri Sullivan (1856–1924) have been among the nation's important architects. Painters include John Singleton Copley (1738–1815), James Whistler (1834–1903), Winslow Homer (1836–1910), and Frank Stella (b.1936); Horatio Greenough (1805–52) was a prominent sculptor.

Among the notable scientists associated with Massachusetts are Nathaniel Bowditch (1773–1838), a mathematician and navigator; Samuel F. B. Morse (1791–1872), inventor of the telegraph; and Robert Hutchins Goddard (1882–1945), a physicist and rocketry pioneer.

Two professors at the Massachusetts Institute of Technology, in Cambridge, have won the Nobel Prize in economics—Paul A. Samuelson (b.Indiana, 1915), in 1970, and Franco Modigliani (b.Italy, 1918–2003), in 1985. Other winners of the Nobel Prize include: Merton Miller (1923–2000), in economics; William Sharpe (b.1934), in economics; Douglass C. North (b.1920), 1993 co-recipient in economics; Elias James Carey (b.1928); Henry Kendall (1926–99), 1990 co-recipient in physics; and Joseph E. Murray (b.1919), the 1990 winner in medicine or physiology.

Massachusetts's most famous journalist has been Isaiah Thomas (1750–1831). Its great industrialists include textile entrepreneurs Francis Lowell (1775–1817) and Abbott Lawrence (1792–1855). Elias Howe (1819–67) invented the sewing machine.

Massachusetts was the birthplace of television journalists Mike Wallace (b.1918) and Barbara Walters (b.1931). Massachusetts-born show business luminaries include director Cecil B. DeMille (1881–1959); actors Walter Brennan (1894–1974), Jack Haley (1901–79), Ray Bolger (1904–84), Bette Davis (1908–84), and Jack Lemmon (1925–2001); and singers Donna Summer (b.1948) and

James Taylor (b.1948). Outstanding among Massachusetts-born athletes was world heavyweight boxing champion Rocky Marciano (Rocco Francis Marchegiano, 1925–69), who retired undefeated in 1956.

[50] BIBLIOGRAPHY

Bedford, Henry F. (ed.). *Their Lives and Numbers: The Condition of Working People in Massachusetts, 1870–1900.* Ithaca: Cornell University Press, 1995.

Burgan, Michael. *Massachusetts.* Washington, D.C.: National Geographic, 2005.

Council of State Governments. *The Book of the States, 2006 Edition.* Lexington, Ky.: Council of State Governments, 2006.

Mandell, Daniel R. *Behind the Frontier: Indians in Eighteenth-Century Eastern Massachusetts.* Lincoln: University of Nebraska Press, 1996.

Pletcher, Larry. *It Happened in Massachusetts.* Helena, Mont.: TwoDot, 1999.

Pollak, Vivian R. (ed.). *A Historical Guide to Emily Dickinson.* New York: Oxford University Press, 2004.

Porter, Susan L. (ed.). *Women of the Commonwealth: Work, Family, and Social Change in Nineteenth-Century Massachusetts.* Amherst: University of Massachusetts Press, 1996.

Rothenberg, Winifred Barr. *From Market-Places to a Market Economy: The Transformation of Rural Massachusetts.* Chicago: University of Chicago Press, 1992.

Taymor, Betty. *Running Against the Wind: the Struggle of Women in Massachusetts Politics.* Boston: Northeastern University Press, 2000.

Tree, Christina. *Massachusetts, An Explorer's Guide: Beyond Boston and Cape Cod.* Woodstock, Vt.: Countryman Press, 1998.

US Department of Commerce, Economics and Statistics Administration, US Census Bureau. *Massachusetts, 2000. Summary Social, Economic, and Housing Characteristics: 2000 Census of Population and Housing.* Washington, D.C.: US Government Printing Office, 2003.

MICHIGAN

State of Michigan

ORIGIN OF STATE NAME: Possibly derived from the Fox Indian word *mesikami,* meaning "large lake." **NICKNAME:** The Wolverine State. **CAPITAL:** Lansing. **ENTERED UNION:** 26 January 1837 (26th). **SONG:** "Michigan, My Michigan" (unofficial). **MOTTO:** *Si quaeris peninsulam amoenam circumspice* (If you seek a pleasant peninsula, look about you). **COAT OF ARMS:** In the center, a shield depicts a peninsula on which a man stands, at sunrise, holding a rifle. At the top of the shield is the word "Tuebor" (I will defend), beneath it the state motto. Supporting the shield are an elk on the left and a moose on the right. Over the whole, on a crest, is an American eagle beneath the US motto, *E pluribus unum.* **FLAG:** The coat of arms centered on a dark blue field, fringed on three sides. **OFFICIAL SEAL:** The coat of arms surrounded by the words "The Great Seal of the State of Michigan" and the date "A.D. MDCCCXXXV." (1835, the year the state constitution was adopted). **BIRD:** Robin. **FISH:** Trout. **FLOWER:** Apple blossom. **TREE:** White pine. **GEM:** Chlorastrolite (Isle Royale Greenstone). **LEGAL HOLIDAYS:** New Year's Day, 1 January; Birthday of Martin Luther King Jr., 3rd Monday in January; Presidents' Day, 3rd Monday in February; Memorial Day, last Monday in May; Independence Day, 4 July; Labor Day, 1st Monday in September; Election Day, 1st Tuesday after the first Monday in November in even-numbered years; Veterans' Day, 11 November; Thanksgiving Day, 4th Thursday in November plus one day; Christmas Day, 25 December. **TIME:** 7 AM EST = noon GMT; 6 AM CST = noon GMT.

¹LOCATION, SIZE, AND EXTENT

Located in the eastern north-central United States, Michigan is the third-largest state E of the Mississippi River and ranks 23rd in size among the 50 states.

The total area of Michigan (excluding Great Lakes waters) is 58,527 sq mi (151,585 sq km), of which land takes up 56,954 sq mi (147,511 sq km) and inland water 1,573 sq mi (4,074 sq km). The state consists of the upper peninsula adjoining three of the Great Lakes—Superior, Huron, and Michigan—and the lower peninsula, projecting northward between Lakes Michigan, Erie, and Huron. The upper peninsula extends 334 mi (538 km) E–W and 215 mi (346 km) N–S; the lower peninsula's maximum E–W extension is 220 mi (354 km), and its greatest N–S length is 286 mi (460 km).

Michigan's upper peninsula is bordered on the N and E by the Canadian province of Ontario (with the line passing through Lake Superior, the St. Mary's River, and Lake Huron); on the s by Lake Huron, the Straits of Mackinac separating the two peninsulas, and Lake Michigan; and on the sw and w by Wisconsin (with the line passing through the Menominee, Brule, and Montreal rivers). The lower peninsula is bordered on the N by Lake Michigan, the Straits of Mackinac, and Lake Huron; on the E by Ontario (with the line passing through Lake Huron, the St. Clair River, Lake St. Clair, and the Detroit River); on the SE by Ontario and Ohio (with the line passing through Lake Erie); on the s by Ohio and Indiana; and on the w by Illinois and Wisconsin (with the line passing through Lake Michigan and Green Bay). The state's geographic center is in Wexford County, 5 mi (8 km) NNW of Cadillac.

Among the most important islands are Isle Royale in Lake Superior; Sugar, Neebish, and Drummond islands in the St. Mary's River; Bois Blanc, Mackinac, and Les Cheneaux islands in Lake Huron; Beaver Island in Lake Michigan; and Belle Isle and Grosse Ile in the Detroit River.

The state's total boundary length is 1,673 mi (2,692 km). The total freshwater shoreline is 3,121 mi (5,023 km).

²TOPOGRAPHY

Michigan's two peninsulas are generally level land masses. Flat lowlands predominate in the eastern portion of both peninsulas and in scattered areas elsewhere. The state's lowest point, 571 ft (174 m), is found in southeastern Michigan along Lake Erie. Higher land is found in the western area of the lower peninsula, where elevations rise to as much as 1,600 ft (500 m); the hilly uplands of the upper peninsula attain elevations of 1,800 ft (550 m). The state's highest point, at 1,979 ft (603 m), is Mt. Arvon, in Baraga County. The mean elevation is approximately 900 ft (275 m).

Michigan's political boundaries extend into four of the five Great Lakes, giving Michigan jurisdiction over 16,231 sq mi (42,038 sq km) of Lake Superior, 13,037 sq mi (33,766 sq km) of Lake Michigan, 8,975 sq mi (23,245 sq km) of Lake Huron, and 216 sq mi (559 sq km) of Lake Erie, for a total of 38,459 sq mi (99,608 sq km). In addition, Michigan has about 35,000 inland lakes and ponds, the largest of which is Houghton Lake, on the lower peninsula, with an area of 31 sq mi (80 sq km).

The state's leading river is the Grand, about 260 mi (420 km) long, flowing through the lower peninsula into Lake Michigan. Other major rivers that flow into Lake Michigan include the St. Joseph, Kalamazoo, Muskegon, Pere Marquette, and Manistee. On the eastern side of the peninsula, the Saginaw River and its tributaries drain an area of some 6,000 sq mi (15,500 sq km), forming the state's largest watershed. Other important rivers that flow into Lake Huron include the Au Sable, Thunder Bay, and Cheboygan.

In the southeast, the Huron and Raisin rivers flow into Lake Erie. Most major rivers in the upper peninsula (including the longest, the Menominee) flow southward into Lake Michigan and its various bays. Tahquamenon Falls, in the eastern part of the upper peninsula, is the largest of the state's more than 150 waterfalls. Wetlands account for about 15% of the total land area of the state.

Most of the many islands belonging to Michigan are located in northern Lake Michigan and in Lake Huron, although the largest, Isle Royale, about 44 mi (71 km) long by 8 mi (13 km) wide, is found in northern Lake Superior. In northern Lake Michigan, Beaver Island is the largest, while Drummond Island, off the eastern tip of the upper peninsula, is the largest island in the northern Lake Huron area.

Michigan's geological development resulted from its location in what was once a basin south of the Laurentian Shield, a landmass covering most of eastern and central Canada and extending southward into the upper peninsula. Successive glaciers that swept down from the north dumped soil from the shield into the basin and eroded the basin's soft sandstone, limestone, and shale. With the retreat of the last glacier from the area about 6000 BC, the two peninsulas, the Great Lakes, and the islands in these lakes began to emerge, assuming their present shapes about 2,500 years ago.

³CLIMATE

Michigan has a temperate climate with well-defined seasons. The warmest temperatures and longest frost-free period are found most generally in the southern part of the lower peninsula; Detroit has an average temperature of 49°F (9°C), ranging from 24°F (-4°C) in January to 73°F (22°C) in July. Colder temperatures and a shorter growing season prevail in the more northerly regions; Sault Ste. Marie has an average of 40°F (4°C), ranging from 14°F (-10°C) in January to 64°F (17°C) in July. The coldest temperature ever recorded in the state is -51°F (-46°C), registered at Vanderbilt on 9 February 1934; the all-time high of 112°F (44°C) was recorded at Mio on 13 July 1936. Both sites are located in the interior of the lower peninsula, away from the moderating influence of the Great Lakes.

Detroit had an average annual precipitation of 32.3 in (82 cm). The greatest snowfall is found in the extreme northern areas, where cloud cover created by cold air blowing over the warmer Lake Superior waters causes frequent heavy snow along the northern coast; Houghton and Calumet, on the Keweenaw Peninsula, average 183 in (465 cm) of snow a year, more than any other area in the state. Similarly, Lake Michigan's water temperatures create a snow belt along the west coast of the lower peninsula.

Cloudy days are more common in Michigan than in most states, in part because of the condensation of water vapor from the Great Lakes. Detroit has sunshine, on average, only 35% of the days in December and January, and 53% year-round. The annual average relative humidity at Detroit is 81% at 7 AM, dropping to 60% at 1 PM; at Sault Ste. Marie, the comparable percentages are 85% and 67%, respectively. The southern half of the lower peninsula is an area of heavy thunderstorm activity. Late spring and early summer are the height of the tornado season.

⁴FLORA AND FAUNA

Maple, birch, hemlock, aspen, spruce, and fir predominate in the upper peninsula; maple, birch, aspen, pine, and beech in the lower.

Once common in the state, elms have largely disappeared because of the ravages of disease, while the white pine (the state tree) and red pine, which dominated northern Michigan forests and were prime objects of logging operations, have been replaced in cutover lands by aspen and birch. The area south of a line from about Muskegon to Saginaw Bay formerly held the only significant patches of open prairie land (found chiefly in southwestern Michigan) and areas of widely scattered trees, called oak openings. Intensive agricultural development, followed by urban industrial growth, leveled much of this region's forests, although significant wooded acreage remains, especially in the less populated western regions.

Strawberries, raspberries, gooseberries, blueberries, and cranberries are among the fruit-bearing plants and shrubs that grow wild in many areas of the state, as do mushrooms and wild asparagus. The state flower, the apple blossom, calls to mind the importance of fruit-bearing trees and shrubs in Michigan, but wild flowers also abound, with as many as 400 varieties found in a single county. Eight Michigan plant species were listed by the US Fish and Wildlife Service as threatened or endangered as of April 2006, including the American hart's -tongue fern, dwarf lake iris, Michigan Monkey-flower, and Eastern prairie fringed orchid.

Michigan's fauna, like its flora, has been greatly affected by settlement and, in a few cases, by intensive hunting and fishing. Moose are now confined to Isle Royale, as are nearly all the remaining wolves, which once roamed throughout the state. The caribou and passenger pigeon have been extirpated, but the elk and turkey have been successfully reintroduced in the 20th century. There is no evidence that the state's namesake, the wolverine, was ever found in Michigan, at least in historic times. Despite intensive hunting, the deer population remains high. Other game animals include the common cottontail, snowshoe hare, raccoon, and various squirrels. In addition to the raccoon, important native furbearers are the river otter and the beaver, once virtually exterminated but now making a strong comeback.

More than 300 types of birds have been observed. Aside from the robin (the state bird), the most notable bird is Kirtland's warbler, which nests only in a 60-sq-mi (155-sq-km) section of jack-pine forest in north-central Michigan. Ruffed grouse, bobwhite quail, American woodcock, and various ducks and geese are hunted extensively. Populations of ring-necked pheasant, introduced in 1895, have dropped at an alarming rate in recent decades. Reptiles include the painted turtle and the massasauga, the state's only poisonous snake.

Whitefish, perch, and lake trout (the state fish) are native to the Great Lakes while perch, bass, and pike are indigenous to inland waters. In 1877, the carp was introduced, with such success that it has since become a nuisance. Rainbow and brown trout have also been planted, and in the late 1960s, the state enjoyed its most spectacular success with the introduction of several species of salmon.

The first Michigan list of threatened or endangered animals in 1976 included 64 species, 15 endangered and 49 threatened. In 2006, the US Fish and Wildlife Service listed 13 Michigan animals as threatened or endangered. These included the Indiana bat, two species of beetle, two species of butterfly, gray wolf, bald eagle, piping plover, and Kirtland's warbler.

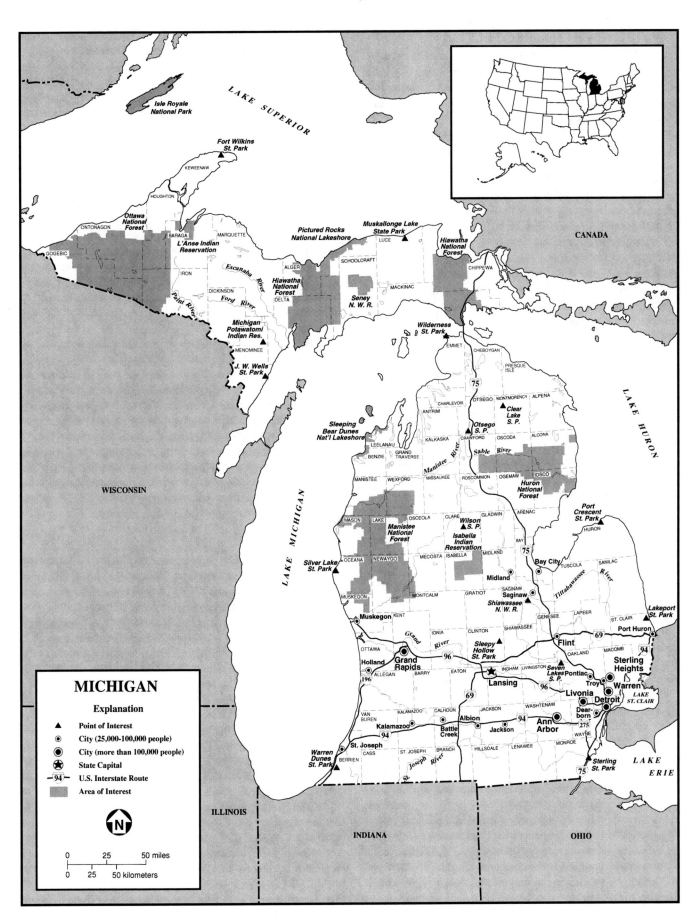

LAKE SUPERIOR

Isle Royale
National Park

CANADA

Fort Wilkins
St. Park

KEWEENAW

HOUGHTON

Ottawa
National
Forest

ONTONAGON

BARAGA

MARQUETTE

L'Anse Indian
Reservation

Pictured Rocks
National Lakeshore

Muskallonge Lake
State Park

LUCE

Hiawatha
National
Forest

GOGEBIC

Escanaba River

ALGER

SCHOOLCRAFT

CHIPPEWA

IRON

DICKINSON

Ford River

Hiawatha
National
Forest

DELTA

Seney
N. W. R.

MACKINAC

Paint River

Michigan
Potawatomi
Indian Res.

MENOMINEE

J. W. Wells
St. Park

Wilderness
St. Park

EMMET

CHEBOYGAN

PRESQUE
ISLE

Sleeping
Bear Dunes
Nat'l Lakeshore

CHARLEVOIX

OTSEGO

MONTMORENCY

ALPENA

Clear
Lake
S. P.

ANTRIM

Otsego
S. P.

WISCONSIN

LEELANAU

BENZIE

GRAND
TRAVERSE

KALKASKA

CRAWFORD

OSCODA

ALCONA

Manistee River

Sable River

MANISTEE

WEXFORD

MISSAUKEE

ROSCOMMON

OGEMAW

IOSCO

Huron
National
Forest

LAKE MICHIGAN

MASON

LAKE

OSCEOLA

CLARE

GLADWIN

ARENAC

Wilson
S. P.

Manistee
National
Forest

Isabella
Indian
Reservation

BAY

Port
Crescent
St. Park

HURON

Silver Lake
St. Park

OCEANA

NEWAYGO

MECOSTA

ISABELLA

MIDLAND

Bay City

TUSCOLA

SANILAC

Midland

MUSKEGON

MONTCALM

GRATIOT

SAGINAW

Saginaw

Tittabawassee River

Lakeport
St. Park

Muskegon

KENT

IONIA

Grand River

CLINTON

SHIAWASSEE

Shiawassee
N. W. R.

GENESEE

LAPEER

ST. CLAIR

Port Huron

Holland

Grand
Rapids

OTTAWA

ALLEGAN

BARRY

EATON

Sleepy
Hollow
St. Park

Lansing

INGHAM

LIVINGSTON

Flint

OAKLAND

Seven
Lakes
S. P.

Pontiac

Troy

MACOMB

Sterling
Heights

Warren

Livonia

Detroit

Dear-
born

LAKE
ST. CLAIR

Kalamazoo

VAN
BUREN

KALAMAZOO

CALHOUN

Albion

JACKSON

WASHTENAW

Ann
Arbor

WAYNE

St. Joseph

Battle
Creek

Jackson

Warren
Dunes
St. Park

BERRIEN

CASS

ST. JOSEPH

BRANCH

HILLSDALE

LENAWEE

MONROE

Sterling
St. Park

LAKE
ERIE

St. Joseph River

LAKE HURON

75

75

96

196

69

94

94

96

69

275

75

69

MICHIGAN

Explanation

▲ Point of Interest

⊙ City (25,000-100,000 people)

◉ City (more than 100,000 people)

★ State Capital

—94— U.S. Interstate Route

▓ Area of Interest

Ⓝ

| 0 | 25 | 50 miles |

| 0 | 25 | 50 kilometers |

ILLINOIS

INDIANA

OHIO

5ENVIRONMENTAL PROTECTION

The Michigan Department of Natural Resources (DNR) is the state's 4th-largest department employing approximately 3,700 persons. It is responsible for the administration of hundreds of programs affecting every aspect of the environment. These programs are based on state and federal laws calling for the protection and management of natural resources, including: air, water, fish, wildlife, recreational activities, wetlands, forests, minerals, oil, and gas. The regulatory programs operated by the DNR conserve and manage natural resources by controlling access or limiting their use and removal. Most of these programs rely on permit or license systems such as hunting or fishing licenses, forest use permits, and air/wastewater discharge permits.

Responding to citizens' concerns and new federal legislation, Michigan enacted programs to address water and air pollution as well as waste problems. At least 10 major environmental programs were established under Michigan law during the 1970s and 1980s, directing the DNR to assume new responsibilities and authorities. These included the Wetland Protection Act of 1980, Inland Lakes and Streams Act, the Resource Recovery Act, the Solid Waste Management Act, and the Hazardous Waste Management Act. In addition, changes in administrative rules and amendments to existing statutes greatly expanded the scope of some programs such as air and water pollution control (Air Pollution Control Act and Water Resources Commission Act). These legislated changes, coupled with reorganization measures enacted by executive order, greatly expanded the state's role in environmental protection matters and substantially increased the scope of DNR's mission.

Governor William Milliken decided Michigan would be better served if all environmental programs were under one roof. Executive Order 1973-2 transferred three programs from the Department of Public Health to the DNR, including sewage system maintenance and certification; solid waste disposal; and licensing of septic tank cleaners. Further transfers were accomplished under Executive Order 1973-2a, which changed the status of the Water Resources Commission (WRC), making it subordinate to the Natural Resources Commission (NRC). Additionally, Executive Order 1973-2a transferred the Air Pollution Control Commission to the DNR under the jurisdiction of the NRC. The Executive Order divided the DNR for the first time into two branches: the natural resources branch, and the environmental protection branch. The Executive Orders of 1973 clearly consolidated and defined the DNR's environmental protection responsibilities.

As the 1970s drew to a close, Michigan enacted two major pollution control laws: the Solid Waste Management Act and the Hazardous Waste Management Act. These acts provide the legal basis for the separate management of hazardous wastes under a detailed regulatory program. The two waste management laws substantially increased the DNR's enforcement and administrative responsibilities. In addition to these two acts, several other laws were enacted or amended by the legislature in the late 1970s and 1980s which had a major impact on the Department. For example, the Environmental Response Act provides for the identification of sites of environmental contamination throughout the state and an appropriation procedure to support the cleanup of contamination sites in the state. Other programs created by statute included the Clean Michigan Fund and the Leaking Underground Storage

Tanks Act. Each of these statutes required the DNR to assume new program responsibilities and authorities in the 1980s.

As the policy body over the DNR, the NRC consists of seven members appointed by the governor, with the advice of the Senate. The NRC sets the overall direction of the department and hires the director to carry out its policies. The department is organized both programmatically and geographically. The three program areas, each headed by a deputy director, include: resource management; environmental protection; and policy, budget, and administration. The three geographical regions split the state into the north, central, and south zones, each headed by a deputy director. The deputy directors report to the director of the DNR.

The mission of the department is to conserve and develop the state's natural resources and to protect and enhance the state's environmental quality in order to provide clean air, clean water, productive land, and healthy life. Additionally, the department seeks to provide quality recreational opportunities to the people of Michigan through the effective management of state recreational lands and parks, boating facilities, and population of fish and wildlife.

In 2003, 101.6 million pounds of toxic chemicals were released in the state. In 2003, Michigan had 343 hazardous waste sites listed in the US Environment Protection Agency (EPA) database, 66 of which were on the National Priorities List as of 2006, including Shiawassee River, the Clare City Water Supply, and the Sturgis Municipal Wells. In 2006, Michigan ranked at fifth in the nation for the highest number of sites on the National Priority List. In 2005, the EPA spent over $21.5 million through the Superfund program for the cleanup of hazardous waste sites in the state. The same year, federal EPA grants awarded to the state included $46.3 million for the state clean water revolving fund and $33.9 million for the drinking water revolving fund.

6POPULATION

Michigan ranked eighth in population in the United States with an estimated total of 10,120,860 in 2005, an increase of 1.8% since 2000. Between 1990 and 2000, Michigan's population grew from 9,295,297 to 9,938,444, an increase of 6.9%. The population is projected to reach 10.59 million by 2015 and 10.71 million by 2025. The population density in 2004 was 178.5 persons per sq mi.

Michigan was never inhabited by more than a few thousand Indians. As late as 1810, the non-Indian population of Michigan Territory was only 4,762. The late 1820s marked the start of steady, often spectacular, growth. The population increased from 31,639 people in 1830 to 212,267 in 1840 and 397,654 in 1850. Subsequently, the state's population grew by about 400,000 each decade until 1910, when its population of 2,810,173 ranked eighth among the 46 states. Industrial development sparked a sharp rise in population to 4,842,325 by 1930, pushing Michigan ahead of Massachusetts into seventh place.

In 2004, the median age of Michigan's population was 36.6. In the same year, 25.1% of the on under age 18 while 12.3% was age 65 or older. Approximately half of the state's population is concentrated in the Detroit metropolitan area.

Detroit has always been Michigan's largest city since its founding in 1701, but its growth, like the state's, was slow until well into the 19th century. The city's population grew from 21,019 in 1850 to 285,704 in 1900, when it ranked as the 13th-largest city

Michigan—Counties, County Seats, and County Areas and Populations

COUNTY	COUNTY SEAT	LAND AREA (SQ MI)	POPULATION (2005 EST.)	COUNTY	COUNTY SEAT	LAND AREA (SQ MI)	POPULATION (2005 EST.)
Alcona	Harrisville	679	11,653	Lake	Balwin	568	12,069
Alger	Munising	912	9,662	Lapeer	Lapeer	658	93,361
Allegan	Allegan	832	113,174	Leelanau	Leland	341	22,157
Alpena	Alpena	568	30,428	Lenawee	Adrian	753	102,033
Antrim	Bellaire	480	24,422	Livingston	Howell	575	181,517
Arenac	Standish	368	17,154	Luce	Newberry	905	6,789
Baraga	L'Anse	901	8,746	Mackinac	St. Ignace	1,025	11,331
Barry	Hastings	560	59,892	Macomb	Mt. Clemens	483	829,453
Bay	Bay City	447	109,029	Manistee	Manistee	543	25,226
Benzie	Beulah	322	17,644	Marquette	Marquette	1,822	64,760
Berrien	St. Joseph	576	162,611	Mason	Ludington	495	28,986
Branch	Coldwater	508	46,460	Mecosta	Big Rapids	560	42,391
Calhoun	Marshall	712	139,191	Menominee	Menominee	1,045	24,996
Cass	Cassopolis	496	51,996	Midland	Midland	525	84,064
Charlevoix	Charlevoix	421	26,722	Missaukee	Lake City	565	15,299
Cheboygan	Cheboygan	720	27,463	Monroe	Monroe	557	153,935
Chippewa	Sault Ste. Marie	1,590	38,780	Montcalm	Stanton	713	63,893
Clare	Harrison	570	31,653	Montmorency	Atlanta	550	10,445
Clinton	St. Johns	573	69,329	Muskegon	Muskegon	507	175,554
Crawford	Grayling	559	15,074	Newaygo	White Cloud	847	50,019
Delta	Escanaba	1,173	38,347	Oakland	Pontiac	875	1,214,361
Dickinson	Iron Mt.	770	28,032	Oceana	Hart	541	28,473
Eaton	Charlotte	579	107,394	Ogemaw	West Branch	569	21,905
Emmet	Petoskey	468	33,580	Ontonagon	Ontonagon	1,311	7,363
Genesee	Flint	642	443,883	Osceola	Reed City	569	23,750
Gladwin	Gladwin	505	27,209	Oscoda	Mio	568	9,298
Gogebic	Bessemer	1,105	16,861	Otsego	Gaylord	516	24,665
Grand Traverse	Traverse City	466	83,971	Ottawa	Grand Haven	567	255,406
Gratiot	Ithaca	570	42,345	Presque Isle	Rogers City	656	14,330
Hillsdale	Hillsdale	603	47,066	Roscommon	Roscommon	528	26,079
Houghton	Houghton	1,014	35,705	Saginaw	Saginaw	815	208,356
Huron	Bad Axe	830	34,640	St. Clair	Port Huron	734	171,426
Ingham	Mason	560	278,592	St. Joseph	Centreville	503	62,984
Ionia	Ionia	577	64,608	Sanilac	Sandusky	964	44,752
Iosco	Tawas City	546	26,992	Schoolcraft	Manistique	1,173	8,819
Iron	Crystal Falls	1,163	12,299	Shiawassee	Corunna	541	72,945
Isabella	Mt. Pleasant	576	65,618	Tuscola	Caro	812	58,428
Jackson	Mackson	705	163,629	Van Buren	Paw Paw	612	78,812
Kalamazoo	Kalamazoo	562	240,536	Washtenaw	Ann Arbor	710	341,847
Kalkaska	Kalkaska	563	17,239	Wayne	Detroit	615	1,998,217
Kent	Grand Rapids	862	596,666	Wexford	Cadillac	566	31,876
Keweenaw	Eagle River	544	2,195	**TOTALS**		56,959	10,120,860

in the country. Within the next 30 years, the booming automobile industry pushed the city up into fourth place, with a population of 1,568,662 in 1930. Since 1950, when the total reached 1,849,568, Detroit has lost population, dropping to 1,514,063 in 1970, 1,203,369 in 1980 and to 1,028,000 in 1990, when it held seventh place among US cities. The 2004 population was estimated at 900,198, putting Detroit in 11th place. As Detroit lost population, however, many of its suburban areas grew at an even greater rate. The Detroit metropolitan area totaled an estimated 4,493,165 in 2004, up from 4,320,203 in 1995 and 3,950,000 in 1960.

Other Michigan cities with estimated 2004 populations in excess of 100,000 include Grand Rapids with a population of 195,115; Warren, 136,118; Sterling Heights, 127,476; Flint, 119,716; Lansing (the capital), 116,941; and Ann Arbor, 113,567.

[7] ETHNIC GROUPS

The 2000 census counted about 58,479 American Indians, including Eskimos and Aleuts. Most were scattered across the state, with a small number concentrated on the four federal reservations, comprising 16,635 acres (6,732 hectares). In the 1990s the Ottawa, Ojibwa, and Potawatomi were the principal groups with active tribal organizations. In 2004, 0.6% of the population was American Indian.

In 2000, the black population of Michigan totaled an estimated 1,412,742. In 1980, nearly two-thirds lived in Detroit, where they made up 75.7% of the population, the highest percentage in any US city of 1 million or more. Detroit, which experienced severe race riots in 1943 and 1967, has had a black mayor since 1974. In 2004, 14.3% of the state's residents were black.

The 2000 census found that 523,589 state residents (5.3%) were foreign born, up from 355,393 (3.8%) in 1990. There were 323,877 Hispanics and Latinos living in the state in 2000, of which 220,769 were of Mexican descent. In 2004, 3.7% of the state's population was of Hispanic or Latino origin. The state's Asian population has been increasing: as of 2000, the total number of Asians was 176,510. The census reported 54,631 Asian Indians (up from 18,100 in 1990), 17,377 Filipinos, 33,189 Chinese (up from 17,100 in 1990), 20,886 Koreans, 11,288 Japanese, and 13,673 Vietnamese (up from 5,229 in 1990). In 2004, 2.2% of the population was Asian. Pacific Islanders numbered 2,692 in 2000. In 2004, 1.4% of the population reported origin of two or more races.

Although state residents of first- or second-generation European descent are, almost without exception, decreasing in number and proportion, their influence remains great. Detroit continues to have numerous well-defined ethnic neighborhoods, and Hamtramck, a city surrounded by Detroit, is still dominated by its Polish population. Elsewhere in Michigan, Frankenmuth is the site of an annual German festival, and the city of Holland has an annual tulip festival that attracts about 400,000 people each spring. In the upper peninsula, the Finnish culture dominates in rural areas; in the iron and copper mining regions, descendants of immigrants from Cornwall in England, the original mining work force, and persons of Scandinavian background predominate.

8 LANGUAGES

Before white settlement, Algonkian-language tribes occupied what is now Michigan, with the Menomini and Ojibwa in the upper peninsula and Ottawa on both sides of the Straits of Mackinac. Numerous place-names recall their presence: Michigan itself, Mackinaw City, Petoskey, Kalamazoo, Muskegon, Cheboygan, and Dowagiac.

Except for the huge industrial area in southeastern Michigan, English in the state is remarkably homogeneous in its retention of the major Northern dialect features of upper New York and western New England. Common are such Northern forms as *pail, wishbone, darning needle* (dragonfly), *mouth organ* (harmonica), *sick to the stomach, quarter to four* (3:45), and *dove* as past tense of *dive.* Common also are such pronunciations as the /ah/ vowel in *fog, frog,* and *on;* the /aw/ vowel in *horrid, forest,* and *orange; creek* as /krik/; *root* and *roof* with the vowel of *put;* and *greasy* with an /s/ sound. *Swale* (a marsh emptying into a stream) and *clock shelf* (mantel) are dying Northern words not carried west of Michigan. *Pank* (to pack down, as of snow) is confined to the upper peninsula, and *pasty* (meat-filled pastry) is borrowed from Cornish miners and heard in the upper peninsula and a few other areas. A minister is a *dominie* in the Dutch area around Holland and Zeeland.

Southern blacks have introduced into the southeastern automotive manufacturing areas a regional variety of English that, because it has class connotations in the North, has become a controversial educational concern. Three of its features are perhaps more widely accepted than others: the coalescence of /e/ and /i/ before a nasal consonant, so that *pen* and *pin* sound alike; the loss of /r/ after a vowel, so that *cart* and *cot* also sound alike; and the lengthening of the first part of the diphthong /ai/, so that *time* and *Tom* sound alike, as do *ride* and *rod.*

In 2000, 91.6% of the state's population five years old or older spoke only English at home, down from 93.4% in 1990.

The following table gives selected statistics from the 2000 Census for language spoken at home by persons five years old and over. The category "Other Indo-European languages" includes Albanian, Gaelic, Lithuanian, and Rumanian. The category "Other Slavic languages" includes Czech, Slovak, and Ukrainian. The category "Other Asian languages" includes Dravidian languages, Malayalam, Telugu, Tamil, and Turkish. The category "Other Indic languages" includes Bengali, Marathi, Punjabi, and Romany.

LANGUAGE	NUMBER	PERCENT
Population 5 years and over	**9,268,782**	**100.0**
Speak only English	8,487,401	91.6
Speak a language other than English	781,381	8.4
Speak a language other than English	**781,381**	**8.4**
Spanish or Spanish Creole	246,688	2.7
Arabic	75,412	0.8
German	52,366	0.6
Polish	40,372	0.4
French (incl. Patois, Cajun)	38,914	0.4
Other and unspecified languages	32,189	0.3
Italian	30,052	0.3
Other Indo-European languages	27,241	0.3
Chinese	26,955	0.3
Other Slavic languages	14,682	0.2
Other Asian languages	14,611	0.2
Other Indic languages	14,140	0.2
Korean	13,314	0.1
Serbo-Croatian	11,950	0.1
Tagalog	11,917	0.1
Vietnamese	11,776	0.1
Russian	11,701	0.1
Japanese	11,480	0.1
Greek	11,167	0.1

9 RELIGIONS

The Roman Catholic Church was the only organized religion in Michigan until the 19th century. Detroit's St. Anne's parish, established in 1701, is the second-oldest Catholic parish in the country. In 1810, a Methodist society was organized near Detroit. After the War of 1812, as settlers poured in from the east, Presbyterian, Congregational, Baptist, Episcopal, and Quaker churches were founded. The original French Catholics, reduced to a small minority by the influx of American Protestants, were soon reinforced by the arrival of Catholic immigrants from Germany, Ireland, and, later, from eastern and southern Europe. The Lutheran religion was introduced by German and Scandinavian immigrants; Dutch settlers were affiliated with the Reformed Church in America. The first Jewish congregations were organized in Detroit by German Jews, with a much greater number of eastern European Jews arriving toward the end of the 1800s. The Orthodox Christian Church and the Islamic religion have been introduced by immigrants from the Near East during the 20th century.

Michigan had 2,265,286 Roman Catholics in 2004; with 1,481,866 in the archdiocese of Detroit. Among Protestant denominations, the largest groups are the Missouri Synod Lutherans, with about 244,231 adherents (in 2000), and the United Methodists, with about 171,916 adherents (in 2004). Evangelical Lutherans numbered about 160,836 adherents in 2000. The Christian Reformed Church had about 112,711 members that year and the Presbyterian Church USA had 104,471. The Seventh Day Adventists, who had their world headquarters in Battle Creek from 1855 to 1903, numbered 37,712 in 2000. The Jewish community had about 110,000 members. Over 5.7 million people (about 58% of the population) were not counted as members of any religious organization.

10 TRANSPORTATION

Because of Michigan's location, its inhabitants have always depended heavily on the Great Lakes for transportation. Not until the 1820s did land transportation systems begin to be developed. Although extensive networks of railroads and highways now reach into all parts of the state, the Great Lakes remain major avenues of commerce.

The first railroad company in the Midwest was chartered in Michigan in 1830, and six years later the Erie and Kalamazoo, operating between Toledo, Ohio, and Adrian, became the first railroad in service west of the Appalachians. Between 1837 and 1845, the state government sought to build three lines across southern Michigan, before abandoning the project and selling the two lines it had partially completed to private companies. The pace of railroad construction lagged behind that in other Midwestern states until after the Civil War. Only then did the combination of federal and state aid, and Michigan's booming economy lead to an enormous expansion in trackage, from fewer than 800 mi (1,300 km) in 1860 to a peak of 9,021 mi (14,518 km) in 1910. With the economic decline of northern Michigan and the resulting drop in railroad revenues, Class I trackage declined to 2,752 rail mi (4,430 km) by 2003, out of a total of 4,495 rail mi (7,236 km) in that year. A total of 23 railroads provided freight service in the state as of 2003, of which four were Class I railroads. The Michigan state government, through the Department of Transportation, has helped to revive the railroad system through its Rail Program. Most railroad passenger service is provided by Amtrak, which as of 2006, provided service to 23 stations in the state, connecting them to Chicago.

Railroads have been used only to a limited degree in the Detroit area as commuter carriers, although efforts have been made to improve this service. In the early 1900s, more than 1,000 mi (1,600 km) of inter-urban rail lines provided rapid transit service in southern Michigan, but automobiles and buses drove them out of business, and the last line shut down in 1934. Street railway service began in a number of cities in the 1860s, with Detroit taking over its street railways in 1922. Use of these public transportation systems declined sharply after World War II. By the 1950s, streetcars had been replaced by buses, but by 1960 many small communities had abandoned city bus service altogether. During the 1970s, with massive government aid, bus service was restored to many cities and was improved in others, and the number of riders generally increased.

As of 2004, the state had 122,382 mi (197,035 km) of roads. Major expressways included I-94 (Detroit to Chicago), I-96 (Detroit to Grand Rapids), and I-75 (from the Ohio border to Sault Ste. Marie). In 2004, there were some 4.632 million registered passenger cars, about 3.613 million trucks of all types, around 10,000 buses, and some 227,000 motorcycles. Licensed drivers numbered 7,103,404 during that same year.

The completion in 1957 of the Mackinac Bridge, the fourth-longest suspension span in the world, eliminated the major barrier to easy movement between the state's two peninsulas. The International Bridge at Sault Ste. Marie, the Blue-Water Bridge at Port Huron, the Ambassador Bridge at Detroit, and the Detroit–Windsor Tunnel link Michigan with Canada.

The opening of the St. Lawrence Seaway in 1959 made it possible for a large number of oceangoing vessels to dock at Michigan ports. In 2004, the port of Detroit handled 16.858 million tons of cargo making it the 42nd-busiest port in the United States. Other major ports in Michigan that same year were Presque Isle, which handled, 10.134 million tons, while Escanaba handled 6.620 million tons, and the limestone-shipping port of Calcite handled

8.949 million tons. In 2003, waterborne shipments totaled 66.387 million tons.

Michigan was a pioneer in developing air transportation service. The Ford Airport at Dearborn in the 1920s had one of the first air passenger facilities and was the base for some of the first regular airmail service. In 2005, Michigan had a total of 485 public and private-use aviation-related facilities. This included 381 airports, 95 heliports, 2 STOLports (Short Take-Off and Landing), and 7 seaplane bases. The state's major airport is Detroit Metropolitan Wayne County Airport. In 2004, the airport had 17,046,176 enplaned passengers, making it the 11th-busiest airport in the United States.

[11] HISTORY

Indian hunters and fishermen inhabited the region now known as Michigan as early as 9000 BC; these peoples were making use of copper found in the upper peninsula—the first known use of a metal by peoples anywhere in the western hemisphere. Around 1000 BC, their descendants introduced agriculture into southwestern Michigan. In the latter part of the prehistoric era, the Indians appear to have declined in population.

In the early 17th century, when European penetration began, Michigan's lower peninsula was inhabited by tribes of Native Americans who may have moved west of Lake Michigan for temporary periods during periods of war. In the upper peninsula there were small bands of Ojibwa along the St. Marys River and the Lake Michigan shore; in the west, Menomini Indians lived along the present Michigan-Wisconsin border. Both tribes were of Algonkian linguistic stock, as were most Indians who later settled in the area, except for the Winnebago of the Siouan group in the Green Bay region of Lake Michigan, and the Huron of Iroquoian stock in the Georgian Bay area of Canada. In the 1640s, the Huron were nearly wiped out by other Iroquois tribes from New York, and the survivors fled westward with their neighbors to the north, the Ottawa Indians. Eventually, both tribes settled at the Straits of Mackinac before moving to the Detroit area early in the 18th century. During the same period, the Potawatomi and Miami Indians moved from Wisconsin into southern Michigan.

For two centuries after the first Europeans came to Michigan, the Indians remained a vital force in the area's development. They were the source of the furs that the whites traded for, and they also were highly respected as potential allies when war threatened between the rival colonial powers in North America. However, after the War of 1812, when the fur trade declined and the possibility of war receded, the value of the Indians to the white settlers diminished. Between 1795 and 1842, Indian lands in Michigan were ceded to the federal government, and the Huron, Miami, and many Potawatomi were removed from the area. Some Potawatomi were allowed to remain on lands reserved for them, along with most of the Ojibwa and Ottawa Indians in the north.

The first European explorer known to have reached Michigan was a Frenchman, Etienne Brulé, who explored the Sault Ste. Marie area around 1620. Fourteen years later, Jean Nicolet explored the Straits of Mackinac and the southern shore of the upper peninsula en route to Green Bay. Missionary and fur trading posts, to which were later added military forts, were established at Sault Ste. Marie by Father Jacques Marquette in 1668, and then at St. Ignace in 1671. By the 1860s, several temporary posts had been established in the lower peninsula. In 1701, Antoine Laumet de la Mothe Cadillac founded a permanent settlement at the site of present-day Detroit.

Detroit and Michigan grew little at first, however, because the rulers of the French colony of New France were obsessed with the fur trade, which did not attract large numbers of settlers. After France's defeat in the French and Indian War, fears that the British would turn the area over to English farmers from the coastal colonies, with the consequent destruction of the Indian way of life, led the Indians at Detroit to rebel in May 1763, under the leadership of the Ottawa chief Pontiac. Other uprisings resulting from similar grievances soon spread throughout the west but ended in failure for the Indians. Pontiac gave up his siege of Detroit after six months, and by 1764 the British were in firm control. Nevertheless, the British authorities did not attempt to settle the area. The need to protect the fur trade placed the people of Michigan solidly on the British side during the American Revolution, since a rebel triumph would likely mean the migration of American farmers into the west, converting the wilderness to cropland. The British occupied Michigan and other western areas for 13 years after the Treaty of Paris in 1783 had assigned these territories to the new United States. The US finally got possession of Michigan in the summer of 1796.

Michigan became a center of action in the War of 1812. The capture of Detroit by the British on 16 August 1812 was a crushing defeat for the Americans. Although Detroit was recaptured by the Americans in September 1813, continued British occupation of the fort on Mackinac Island, which they had captured in 1812, enabled them to control most of Michigan. The territory was finally returned to American authority under the terms of the Treaty of Ghent at the end of 1814. With the opening in 1825 of the Erie Canal, which provided a cheap, all-water link between Michigan and New York City, American pioneers turned their attention to these northern areas, and during the 1820s settlers for the first time pushed into the interior of southern Michigan.

Originally part of the Northwest Territory, Michigan had been set aside in 1805 as a separate territory, but with boundaries considerably different from those of the subsequent state. On the south, the territory's boundary was a line set due east from the southernmost point of Lake Michigan; on the north, only the eastern tip of the upper peninsula was included. In 1818 and 1834, areas as far west as Iowa and the Dakotas were added to the territory for administrative purposes. By 1833, Michigan had attained a population of 60,000, qualifying it for statehood. The territorial government's request in 1834 that Michigan be admitted to the Union was rejected by Congress, however, because of a dispute over Michigan's southern boundary. When Indiana became a state in 1816, it had been given a 10-mi (16-km) strip of land in southwestern Michigan, and Michigan now refused to accede to Ohio's claim that it should be awarded lands in southeastern Michigan, including the present site of Toledo. In 1835, Michigan militia defeated the efforts of Ohio authorities to take over the disputed area during the so-called Toledo War, in which no one was killed. Nevertheless, Ohio's superior political power in Congress ultimately forced Michigan to agree to relinquish the Toledo Strip. In return, Congress approved the state government that the people of Michigan had set up in 1835. As part of the compromise that finally brought Michigan into the Union on 26 January 1837, the new state was given land in the upper peninsula west of St. Ignace as compensation for the loss of Toledo.

Youthful Stevens T. Mason, who had led the drive for statehood, became Michigan's first elected governor, but he and the Democratic Party fell out of grace when the new state was plunged into financial difficulties during the depression of the late 1830s. The party soon returned to power and controlled the state until the mid-1850s. In Michigan, as elsewhere, it was the slavery issue that ended Democratic dominance. In July 1854, antislavery Democrats joined with members of the Whig and Free-Soil parties at a convention in Jackson to organize the Republican Party. In the elections of 1854, the Republicans swept into office in Michigan, controlling the state, with rare exceptions, until the 1930s.

Abraham Lincoln was not the first choice of Michigan Republicans for president in 1860, but when he was nominated, they gave him a solid margin of victory that fall and again in 1864. Approximately 90,000 Michigan men served in the Union army, taking part in all major actions of the Civil War. Michigan's Zachariah Chandler was one of the leaders of the Radical Republicans in the US Senate who fought for a harsh policy toward the South during Reconstruction.

Michigan grew rapidly in economic importance. Agriculture sparked the initial growth of the new state and was responsible for its rapid increase in population. By 1850, the southern half of the lower peninsula was filling up, with probably 85% of the state's population dependent in some way on agriculture for a living. Less than two decades later, exploitation of vast pine forests in northern Michigan had made the state the top lumber producer in the United States. Settlers were also attracted to the same area by the discovery of rich mineral deposits, which made Michigan for a time the nation's leading source of iron ore, copper, and salt.

Toward the end of the 19th century, as timber resources were being exhausted and as farming and mining reached their peak stages of development, new opportunities in manufacturing opened up. Such well-known Michigan companies as Kellogg, Dow Chemical, and Upjohn had their origins during this period. The furniture industry in Grand Rapids, the paper industry in Kalamazoo, and numerous other industries were in themselves sufficient to ensure the state's increasing industrial importance. But the sudden popularity of Ransom E. Olds's Oldsmobile runabout, manufactured first in Lansing, inspired a host of Michiganians to produce similar practical, relatively inexpensive automobiles. By 1904, the most successful of the new models, Detroit's Cadillac and the first Fords, together with the Oldsmobile, had made Michigan the leading automobile producer in the country—and, later, in the world. The key developments in Michigan's auto industry were the creation of General Motors by William C. Durant in 1908; Henry Ford's development of the Model T in 1908, followed by his institution of the moving assembly line in 1913–14; and Walter P. Chrysler's 1925 formation of the automobile corporation named after him.

Industrialization brought with it urbanization; the census of 1920 for the first time showed a majority of Michiganians living in towns and cities. Nearly all industrial development was concentrated in the southern third of the state, particularly the southeastern area, around Detroit. The northern two-thirds of the state, where nothing took up the slack left by the decline in lumber and mining output, steadily lost population and became increasingly troubled economically. Meanwhile, the Republican Party, under such progressive governors as Fred Warner and Chase Osborn—and, in the 1920s, under a brilliant administrator, Alexander Groesbeck—showed itself far better able than the Democratic opposition to adjust to the complexities of a booming industrial economy.

The onset of the depression of the 1930s had devastating effects in Michigan. The market for automobiles collapsed; by 1932, half of Michigan's industrial workers were unemployed. The ineffectiveness of the Republican state and federal governments during the crisis led to a landslide victory for the Democrats. In traditionally Republican areas of rural Michigan, the defection to the Democratic Party in 1932 was only temporary, but in the urban industrial areas, the faith of the factory workers in the Republican Party was, for the great majority, permanently shaken. These workers, driven by the desire for greater job security, joined the recruiting campaign launched by the new Congress of Industrial Organizations (CIO). By 1941, with the capitulation of Ford Motor, the United Automobile Workers (UAW) had organized the entire auto industry, and Michigan had been converted to a strongly pro-union state.

Eventually, the liberal leadership of the UAW and of other CIO unions in the state allied itself with the Democratic Party to provide the funds and organization the party needed to mobilize worker support. The coalition elected G. Mennen Williams governor in 1948 and reelected him for five successive two-year terms. By the mid-1950s, the Democrats controlled virtually all statewide elective offices. Because legislative apportionment still reflected an earlier distribution of population, however, the Republicans maintained their control of the legislature and frustrated the efforts of the Williams administration to institute social reforms. In the 1960s, as a result of US Supreme Court rulings, the legislature was reapportioned on a strictly equal-population basis. This shifted a majority of legislative seats into urban areas, enabling the Democrats generally to control the legislature at that time.

In the meantime, Republican moderates, led by George Romney, gained control of their party's organization. Romney was elected governor in 1962 and served until 1969, when he was succeeded by William G. Milliken, who held the governorship for 14 years. When Milliken chose not to run in the 1982 election, the statehouse was captured by the Democrats, ending 20 years of Republican rule. The new governor, James J. Blanchard, faced the immediate tasks of saving Michigan from bankruptcy and reducing the unemployment rate, which had averaged more than 15% in 1982 (60% above the US average).

The nationwide recession of the early 1980s hit Michigan harder than most other states because of its effect on the auto industry, which had already suffered heavy losses primarily as a result of its own inability to foresee the demise of the big luxury cars and because of the increasing share of the American auto market captured by foreign, mostly Japanese, manufacturers. In 1979, Chrysler had been forced to obtain $1.2 billion in federally guaranteed loans to stave off bankruptcy, and during the late 1970s and the first two years of the 1980s, US automakers were forced to lay off hundreds of thousands of workers, tens of thousands of whom left the state. Many smaller businesses, dependent on the auto industry, closed their doors, adding to the unemployment problem and to the state's fiscal problem; as the tax base shrank, state revenues plummeted, creating a budget deficit of nearly $1 billion. Two

months after he took office in January 1983, Governor Blanchard was forced to institute budget cuts totaling $225 million and lay off thousands of government workers; at his urging, the state legislature increased Michigan's income tax by 38%.

As the recession eased in 1983, Michigan's economy showed some signs of improvement. The automakers became profitable, and Chrysler was even able to repay its $1.2 billion in loans seven years before it was due, rehire 100,000 workers, and make plans to build a $500-million technological center in the northern Detroit suburb of Auburn Hills. By May 1984, Michigan's unemployment rate had begun to drop, but the state faced the difficult task of restructuring its economy to lessen its dependence on the auto industry.

By the late 1980s, there were signs that Michigan had succeeded in diversifying its economy. Fewer than one in four wage earners worked in factories in 1988, a drop from 30% in 1978. Despite continued layoffs and plant closings by auto manufacturers between 1982 and 1988, Michigan added half a million more jobs than it lost. Many of the new jobs were in small engineering and applied technology companies, which found opportunities in the big manufacturers' efforts to automate. The state established a $100-million job retraining program to upgrade the skills of displaced factory workers, and contributed $5 million to a joint job training program created by General Motors and the United Automobile Workers. In the mid-1990s, the manufacture of transportation equipment was still Michigan's most important industry, with 28% of domestic automobiles produced in the state. Employment, wages, exports, and housing starts were all on the rise.

In the late 1990s prosperity across the nation had boosted Americans' appetite for new automobiles, including gas-guzzling sports utility vehicles. Combined with sales of other light trucks, SUVs bolstered the Big Three, now leaner and more competitive than in the pre-recession era. In 1998 Chrysler Corporation merged with German-based Daimler-Benz to form DaimlerChrysler, with headquarters in Michigan and Germany. Construction in the state was boosted by numerous road improvement projects during the late 1990s, a new Northwest Airlines terminal at Detroit Metropolitan Airport, voter-approved casinos in Detroit, and demand for new housing. In 1999, the robust economy had resulted in a low unemployment rate of 3.8%. In 2000 the state led the nation in home ownership, exceeding the national average by as much as 10%.

Republican governor John Engler, first elected in 1990 and winning his third term in 1998, aggressively courted business during his administration. He was criticized by some for doing so at the expense of the state's environment. Engler had also, early on, garnered intense opposition to his plan to cut the state's welfare role. Nevertheless, he continued to be reelected. Among the state's challenges in 2000 were education reform (and the question of school vouchers), preserving farmlands in the face of development and urban sprawl, and, in conjunction with neighboring states and Canada, further cleanup and conservation of the Great Lakes system.

In 2002, Jennifer Granholm was elected Michigan's first female governor and the first Democrat to win the office since John Engler took office. In 2003, Granholm pledged to balance the state's budget (the state had a $1.8 billion deficit for fiscal year 2003/04), planned to create a corridor to attract technology companies to

Michigan (particularly in the biotech and pharmaceutical sectors), to support education, and to purchase prescription drugs in bulk. In 2005, Granholm announced a plan (the MI Opportunity Partnership) to fill 90,000 job vacancies. The plan allows for job training to place out-of-work citizens in such needed positions as health care and the skilled trades.

Michigan was one of the states affected by the 14 August 2003 massive power blackout in Canada, the Northeast, and Midwestern states. The largest electrical outage in US history affected 9,300 square miles and a population of over 50 million.

12 STATE GOVERNMENT

Michigan has had four constitutions. The first, adopted in 1835 when Michigan was applying for statehood, was followed by constitutions adopted in 1850, 1908, and 1963. By January 2005, there were 25 amendments.

The legislature consists of a Senate of 38 members, elected for terms of four years, and a House of Representatives of 110 members, elected for two-year terms. The legislature meets annually, beginning the second Wednesday of January, for a session of indeterminate length. Special sessions may only be called by the governor. Legislation may be adopted by a majority of each house, but to override a governor's veto a two-thirds vote of the elected and serving members of each house is required. A legislator must be at least 21 years old, a US citizen, and a qualified voter of the district in which he or she resides. The legislative salary was $79,650 in 2004.

Elected executive officials include the governor and lieutenant governor (who run jointly), secretary of state, and attorney general, all serving four-year terms. Elections are held in even-numbered years between US presidential elections. The governor and lieutenant governor must be at least 30 years old and must have been registered voters in the state for at least four years prior to election. As of December 2004, the governor's salary was $177,000. The governor, who is limited to serving two consecutive terms, appoints the members of the governing boards and/or directors of executive departments, with the exception of the Department of Education, whose head is appointed by the elected State Board of Education. The trustees of Michigan State University, the University of Michigan, and Wayne State University are also elected by the state's voters. Trustees serve eight-year terms.

Legislative action is completed when a bill has been passed by both houses of the legislature and signed by the governor. A bill also becomes law if not signed by the governor after a 14-day period when the legislature is in session. The governor may stop passage of a bill by vetoing it or, if the legislature adjourns before the 14-day period expires, by refusing to sign it.

The constitution may be amended by a two-thirds vote of both houses of the legislature and a majority vote at the next general election. An amendment also may be proposed by registered voters through petition and submission to the general electorate; the petition must be signed by 10% of total voters for all candidates at the last gubernatorial election. Every 16 years, the question of calling a convention to revise the constitution must be submitted to the voters; the question was first put on the ballot in 1978 and was rejected.

A voter in Michigan must be a US citizen, at least 18 years old, and must have been a resident of the state and city or township for 30 days prior to election day. Those confined to jail after conviction and sentencing are ineligible to vote, but convicted felons may vote after completing their entire sentence, including parole and probation.

Michigan Presidential Vote by Political Parties, 1948–2004

YEAR	ELECTORAL VOTE	MICHIGAN WINNER	DEMOCRAT	REPUBLICAN	PROGRESSIVE	SOCIALIST	PROHIBITION
1948	19	Dewey (R)	1,003,448	1,038,595	46,515	6,063	13,052
						SOC. WORKERS	
1952	20	*Eisenhower (R)	1,230,657	1,551,529	3,922	655	10,331
1956	20	*Eisenhower (R)	1,359,898	1,713,647	—	—	6,923
					SOC. LABOR		
1960	20	*Kennedy (D)	1,687,269	1,620,428	1,718	4,347	2,029
1964	21	*Johnson (D)	2,136,615	1,060,152	1,704	3,817	—
							AMERICAN IND.
1968	21	Humphrey (D)	1,593,082	1,370,665	1,762	4,099	331,968
							AMERICAN
1972	21	*Nixon (R)	1,459,435	1,961,721	2,437	1,603	63,321
					PEOPLE'S		LIBERTARIAN
1976	21	Ford (R)	1,696,714	1,893,742	3,504	1,804	5,406
					CITIZENS	COMMUNIST	
1980	21	*Reagan (R)	1,661,532	1,915,225	11,930	3,262	41,597
1984	20	*Reagan (R)	1,529,638	2,251,571	1,191	—	10,055
					NEW ALLIANCE	WORKERS LEAGUE	
1988	20	*Bush (R)	1,675,783	1,965,486	2,513	1,958	18,336
					IND. (Perot)	TISCH IND. CITIZENS	
1992	18	*Clinton (D)	1,871,182	1,554,940	824,813	8,263	10,175
1996	18	*Clinton (D)	1,989,653	1,481,212	336,670	—	27,670
						GREEN	
2000	18	Gore (D)	2,170,418	1,953,139	—	84,165	16,711
					IND. (Nader)		
2004	17	Kerry (D)	2,479,183	2,313,746	24,035	5,325	10,552

*Won US presidential election

13 POLITICAL PARTIES

From its birth in 1854 through 1932, the Republican Party dominated state politics, rarely losing statewide elections and developing strong support in all parts of the state, both rural and urban. The problems caused by the economic depression of the 1930s revitalized the Democratic Party and made Michigan a strong two-party state. Democratic strength was concentrated in metropolitan Detroit, while Republicans maintained their greatest strength in "outstate" areas, except for the mining regions of the upper peninsula, where the working class, hit hard by the depression, supported the Democrats.

Most labor organizations, led by the powerful United Automobile Workers union, have generally supported the Democratic Party since the 1930s. But in recent years, moderate Republicans have had considerable success in attracting support among previously Democratic voters.

Among minor parties, only Theodore Roosevelt's Progressive Party, which captured the state's electoral vote in 1912, has succeeded in winning a statewide contest. George Wallace captured 10% of the total vote cast for president in 1968; Ross Perot almost doubled that showing in 1992 with 19% of the vote.

Between 1948 and 1992, the Republican candidate for president carried Michigan in nine out of 13 elections, but Michiganians gave Democrat Bill Clinton 44% of the vote in 1992 and 52% in 1996. In 2000, Democrat Al Gore received 51% of the presidential vote to Republican George W. Bush's 47%. Green Party candidate Ralph Nader won 2%. In 2004, Democratic challenger John Kerry won 51% of the vote to Bush's 48%. The state had 17 electoral votes in the 2004 presidential election, a decrease of 1 over 2000.

Republican governor John Engler served three terms as governor, ending in January 2003. (Michigan limits its governors to serving two consecutive terms, but the law became effective after Engler's election, so he was grandfathered.) In November 2002, Democrat Jennifer Granholm became Michigan's first female governor. In 2004 there were 7,164,000 registered voters; there is no party registration in the state.

Four-term Democratic Senator Carl Levin was reelected in 2002. Republican Spencer Abraham was elected to the Senate in 1994, replacing retiring Democrat Donald Riegel. Abraham sought a second term in 2000, but failed to win reelection. He was named President George W. Bush's Secretary of Energy in 2001. Democrat Debbie Stabenow, Michigan's first female US senator, defeated Abraham in 2000 for the Senate seat. After the 2004 elections, the state's 15-member US House delegation consisted of six Democrats and nine Republicans. On the state level, in mid-2005 there were 22 Republicans and 16 Democrats in the state Senate, and 58 Republicans and 52 Democrats in the House.

14 LOCAL GOVERNMENT

In 2005, local government included 83 counties, 533 municipal governments, 734 public school districts, and 366 special districts. In 2002, there were also 1,242 townships. Each county is administered by a county board of commissioners whose members, ranging in number from 3 to 35 according to population, are elected for two-year terms. Executive authority is vested in officers (the sheriff, prosecuting attorney, treasurer, clerk, and register of deeds), who are generally elected for four-year terms. Some counties place overall administrative responsibility in the hands of a county manager or administrator.

Most cities are governed by home-rule legislation, adopted in 1909, enabling them to establish their own form of government under an adopted charter. Some charters provide for the election of a mayor, who usually functions as the chief executive officer of the city. Other cities have chosen the council-manager system, with a council appointing the manager to serve as chief executive and the office of mayor being largely ceremonial. Many villages are incorporated under home-rule legislation in order to provide services such as police and fire protection.

Township government, its powers strictly limited by state law, consists of a supervisor, clerk, treasurer, and up to four trustees, all elected for four-year terms and together forming the township board.

In 2005, local government accounted for about 363,776 full-time (or equivalent) employment positions.

15 STATE SERVICES

To address the continuing threat of terrorism and to work with the federal Department of Homeland Security, homeland security in Michigan operates under the authority of the executive order; the state emergency management director is designated as the state homeland security advisor.

Educational services are handled in part by the Department of Education, which distributes state school-aid funds, certifies teachers, and operates the Schools for the Deaf and Blind at Flint. The state-supported colleges and universities are independent of the department's control, each being governed by an elected or appointed board. Although most of the funds administered by the Department of Transportation go for highway construction and maintenance, some allocations support improvements of railroad, bus, ferry, air, and port services.

Health and welfare services are provided by the Department of Community Health and the Department of Civil Rights, as well as through programs administered by the Department of Labor and Economic Growth, the Office of Services to the Aging, the Department of Environmental Quality, the Michigan Women's Commission, the Spanish-Speaking Affairs Commission, and the Veterans Trust Fund. The state's Army and Air National Guard units are maintained by the Department of Military and Veterans Affairs. Civil defense is part of the Department of State Police, and state prisons and other correctional facilities are maintained by the Department of Corrections.

Housing services are provided by the State Housing Development Authority. The Department of Labor and Economic Growth establishes and enforces rules and standards relating to safety, wages, licenses, fees, and conditions of employment. The Employment Security Commission administers unemployment benefits and assists job seekers.

16 JUDICIAL SYSTEM

Michigan's highest court is the state supreme court, consisting of seven justices elected for eight-year terms. The chief justice is elected by the members of the court. The court hears cases on appeal from lower state courts and also administers the state's entire court system. The 1963 constitution provided for an 18-member court of appeals to handle most of the cases that previously had clogged the high court's calendar. Unless the supreme court agrees to review a court of appeals ruling, the latter's decision is final. As of 1999, 28 appeals court justices are elected from each of four districts for six-year terms. The supreme court appoints a chief judge of the appeals court.

The major trial courts in the state as of 1999 were the circuit courts, encompassing 210 judicial seats, with the judges elected for six-year terms. The circuit courts have original jurisdiction in all felony criminal cases, civil cases involving sums of more than $10,000, and divorces. As of January 1998, the circuit courts have a "family" division to better serve families and individuals. The circuit courts also hear appeals from lower courts and state administrative agencies. Probate courts have original jurisdiction in cases involving juveniles and dependents, and also handle wills and estates, adoptions, and commitments of the mentally ill. The 1963 constitution provided for the abolition of justice-of-the-peace courts and nearly all municipal courts, although the Detroit "Recorders Court" was not abolished until 1996 in a controversial move supported by the Republican governor and legislative majority but opposed by most Democratic leaders. To replace them, 101 district courts, some consisting of two or more divisions, have been established. These courts handle civil cases involving sums of less than $10,000, minor criminal violations, and preliminary examinations in all felony cases.

As of 31 December 2004, a total of 48,883 prisoners were held in Michigan's state and federal prisons, a decrease from 49,358 of 1% from the previous year. As of year-end 2004, a total of 2,113 inmates were female, up from 2,198 or 1.5% from the year before. Among sentenced prisoners (one year or more), Michigan had an incarceration rate of 483 per 100,000 population in 2004.

According to the Federal Bureau of Investigation, Michigan in 2004, had a violent crime rate (murder/nonnegligent manslaughter; forcible rape; robbery; aggravated assault) of 490.2 reported incidents per 100,000 population, or a total of 49,577 reported incidents. Crimes against property (burglary; larceny/theft; and motor vehicle theft) in that same year totaled 309,208 reported incidents or 3,057.6 reported incidents per 100,000 people. Michigan has had no death penalty on its law books since 1846, when it became the first state in the United States to abolish capital punishment. Although there have been efforts to restore the death penalty, none of these attempts had been successful as of 2006.

In 2003, Michigan spent $226,349,928 on homeland security, an average of $23 per state resident.

17 ARMED FORCES

In 2004, there 4,419 active-duty military personnel, 11,373 Guard, National Guard, and Reserve, and 3,572 civilian personnel in Michigan. The Detroit Arsenal at Warren is the state's largest center for civilians, 3,009. In 2004 Michigan firms received over $2.6 billion in defense contracts, and $1.2 billion in defense payroll, including retired military pay.

As of 2003, there were 836,950 veterans of US military service living in Michigan. Of these, 124,006 served in World War II; 98,681 served in the Korean conflict; 264,267 served during the Vietnam era, and 110,061 served in the Gulf War. Expenditures on veterans exceeded $1.4 billion in 2004.

As of 31 October 2004, the Michigan State Police employed 1,591 full-time sworn officers.

18 MIGRATION

The earliest European immigrants were the French and English. The successive opening of interior lands for farming, lumbering, mining, and manufacturing proved an irresistible attraction for hundreds of thousands of immigrants after the War of 1812, principally Germans, Canadians, English, Irish, and Dutch. During the second half of the 19th century, lumbering and mining opportunities in northern Michigan attracted large numbers of Cornishmen, Norwegians, Swedes, and Finns. The growth of manufacturing in southern Michigan at the end of the century brought many Poles, Italians, Russians, Belgians, and Greeks to the state. After World War II, many more Europeans immigrated to Michigan, plus smaller groups of Mexicans, other Spanish-speaking peoples from Latin America, and large numbers of Arabic-speaking peoples, particularly in Detroit, who by the late 1970s were more numerous there than in any other US city.

The first large domestic migration into Michigan came in the early 19th century after the War of 1812. Heavy immigration took place in the 1920s and 1930s, especially from northeastern states, particularly New York and Pennsylvania, and from Ohio. Beginning in 1916, the demand for labor in Michigan's factories started the second major domestic migration to Michigan, this time by southern blacks who settled mainly in Detroit, Flint, Pontiac, Grand Rapids, and Saginaw. During World War II, many southern whites migrated to the same industrial areas. Between 1940 and 1970, a net total of 518,000 migrants were drawn to Michigan. The economic problems of the auto industry in the 1970s and 1980s caused a significant reversal of this trend, with the state suffering a net loss of 496,000 by out-migration in the 1970s and over 460,000 in the 1980s. Between 1990 and 1998, Michigan had a net loss of 190,000 in domestic migration and a net gain of 87,000 in international migration. In 1996, Michigan's foreign-born population totaled 491,000, or 5% of its total population. In 1998, 13,943 foreign immigrants entered the state, the 11th-highest total for any state that year. Michigan's overall population increased 5.6% between 1990 and 1998. In the period 2000–05, net international migration was 122,901 and net internal migration was -165,084, for a net loss of 42,183 people.

Intrastate migration has been characterized since the late 19th century by a steady movement from rural to urban areas. Most parts of northern Michigan have suffered a loss of population since the early years of this century although a back-to-the-land movement, together with the growth of rural Michigan as a retirement area, appeared to reverse this trend beginning in the 1970s. Since 1950, the central cities have experienced a steady loss of population to the suburbs, in part caused by the migration of whites from areas that were becoming increasingly black. By 1998, Michigan's black population numbered 1,405,000, of whom over 1,100,000 lived in the Detroit–Ann Arbor–Flint metropolitan area.

19 INTERGOVERNMENTAL COOPERATION

The Commission on Intergovernmental Cooperation of the Michigan legislature represents the state in dealings with the Council of State Governments and its allied organizations. Since 1935, the state has joined more than 20 interstate compacts, dealing mainly with such subjects as gas and oil problems, law enforcement, pest control, civil defense, tax reciprocity, and water resources. Compacts include the Boundary Compact Between Minnesota, Wisconsin, and Michigan; Interstate Compact for Juveniles, and the Great Lakes Commission. In 1985, Michigan, seven other Great Lakes states, and the Canadian provinces of Quebec and Ontario signed the Great Lakes Charter, designed to protect the lakes' water resources.

The International Bridge Authority, consisting of members from Michigan and Canada, operates a toll bridge connecting Sault Ste. Marie, Mich., and Sault Ste. Marie, Ontario. Federal grants to Michigan totaled $10.355 billion in fiscal year 2005, an estimated $10.078 billion in fiscal year 2006, and an estimated $10.210 billion in fiscal year 2007.

20ECONOMY

On the whole, Michigan benefited from its position as the center of the auto industry during the first half of the 20th century when Detroit and other south Michigan cities were the fastest-growing industrial areas in the United States. But the state's dependence on automobile production has caused grave and persistent economic problems since the 1950s. Michigan's unemployment rates in times of recession have far exceeded the national average, since auto sales are among the hardest hit in such periods. Even in times of general prosperity, the auto industry's emphasis on labor-saving techniques and its shifting of operation from the state have reduced the number of jobs available to Michigan workers. Although the state was relatively prosperous during the record automotive production years of the 1960s and 1970s, the high cost of gasoline and the encroachment of imports on domestic car sales had disastrous effects by 1980, when it became apparent that the state's future economic health required greater diversification of industry. Agriculture, still dominant in the rural areas of southern Michigan, remains an important element in the state's economy, and in northern Michigan, forestry and mining continue but generally at levels far below earlier boom periods. Output from manufactures peaked in 1999 at close to $84 billion, about 27% of gross state product, but in 2001, after an 11.85% fall from 2000 levels, manufacturing output accounted for only 23.1% of gross state product. By contrast, services of various sorts accounted for over 70% of total output in 2001. In 2002, Michigan lagged the national economy, and was not expected to recover in the short-term, while it manufacturing sector goes through restructuring.

Michigan's gross state product (GSP) in 2004 totaled $372.169 billion, of which manufacturing (durable and nondurable goods) accounted for the largest portion at $76.261 billion or 20.4% of GSP, followed by the real estate sector at $42.930 (11.5% of GSP), and professional and technical services at $28.977 billion (7.7% of GSP). In that same year, there were an estimated 765,487 small businesses in Michigan. Of the 213,104 businesses that had employees, an estimated total of 209,751 or 98.4% were small companies. An estimated 24,625 new businesses were established in the state in 2004, up 11.8% from the year before. Business terminations that same year came to 24,584, down 0.7% from 2003. There were 681 business bankruptcies in 2004, down 0.4% from the previous year. In 2005, the state's personal bankruptcy (Chapter 7 and Chapter 13) filing rate was 618 filings per 100,000 people, ranking Michigan as the 18th highest in the nation.

21INCOME

In 2005 Michigan had a gross state product (GSP) of $378 billion which accounted for 3.0% of the nation's gross domestic product and placed the state at number 9 in highest GSP among the 50 states and the District of Columbia.

According to the Bureau of Economic Analysis, in 2004 Michigan had a per capita personal income (PCPI) of $32,079. This ranked 23rd in the United States and was 97% of the national average of $33,050. The 1994–2004 average annual growth rate of PCPI was 3.5%. Michigan had a total personal income (TPI) of $324,134,088,000, which ranked ninth in the United States and reflected an increase of 1.8% from 2003. The 1994–2004 average annual growth rate of TPI was 4.1%. Earnings of persons employed in Michigan increased from $251,820,728,000 in 2003 to $254,041,008,000 in 2004, an increase of 0.9%. The 2003–04 national change was 6.3%.

The US Census Bureau reports that the three-year average median household income for 2002 to 2004 in 2004 dollars was $44,476 compared to a national average of $44,473. During the same period an estimated 12.1% of the population was below the poverty line as compared to 12.4% nationwide.

22LABOR

According to the Bureau of Labor Statistics (BLS), in April 2006 the seasonally adjusted civilian labor force in Michigan numbered 5,157,600, with approximately 369,500 workers unemployed, yielding an unemployment rate of 7.2%, compared to the national average of 4.7% for the same period. Preliminary data for the same period placed nonfarm employment at 4,387,200. Since the beginning of the BLS data series in 1976, the highest unemployment rate recorded in Michigan was 16.9% in November 1982. The historical low was 3.2% in March 2000. Preliminary nonfarm employment data by occupation for April 2006 showed that approximately 4.3% of the labor force was employed in construction; 15% in manufacturing; 18.1% in trade, transportation, and public utilities; 5% in financial activities; 13.6% in professional and business services; 13% in education and health services; 9.4% in leisure and hospitality services; and 15.3% in government.

Michigan's most powerful and influential industrial union since the 1930s has been the United Automobile Workers (UAW); its national headquarters is in Detroit. Under its long-time president Walter Reuther and his successors, Leonard Woodcock, Douglas Fraser, Owen Bieber, and Stephen Yokich, the union has been a dominant force in the state Democratic Party. In recent years, as government employees and teachers have been organized, unions and associations representing these groups have become increasingly influential. Under the Michigan Public Employment Relations Act of 1965, public employees have the right to organize and to engage in collective bargaining, but are prohibited from striking. However, strikes of teachers, college faculty members, and government employees have been common since the 1960s, and little or no effort was made to enforce the law.

Certain crafts and trades were organized in Michigan in the 19th century, with one national labor union, the Brotherhood of Locomotive Engineers, having been founded at meetings in Michigan in 1863, but efforts to organize workers in the lumber and mining industries were generally unsuccessful. Michigan acquired a reputation as an open-shop state, and factory workers showed little interest in unions at a time when wages were high. But the catastrophic impact of the depression of the 1930s completely changed these attitudes. With the support of sympathetic state and federal government officials, Michigan workers were in the forefront of the greatest labor-organizing drive in American history. The successful sit-down strike by the United Automobile Workers against General Motors in 1936–37 marked the first major victory of the new Congress of Industrial Organizations. Since then, a strong labor movement has provided manufacturing workers in Michigan with some of the most favorable working conditions in the country.

The US Department of Labor's Bureau of Labor Statistics reported that in 2005, a total of 880,000 of Michigan's 4,288,000 employed wage and salary workers were formal members of a union. This represented 20.5% of those so employed, down from 21.6% in 2004, but well above the national average of 12%. Overall in 2005, a total of 916,000 workers (21.4%) in Michigan were covered by a union or employee association contract, which includes those workers who reported no union affiliation. Michigan is one of only five states whose union membership rate is over 20% and is one of 28 states that does not have a right-to-work law.

As of 1 March 2006, Michigan had a state-mandated minimum wage rate of $5.15 per hour. In 2004, women in the state accounted for 47% of the employed civilian labor force.

23 AGRICULTURE

In 2005, Michigan's agricultural income was estimated at over $3.9 billion, placing Michigan 22nd among the 50 states. About 60% came from crops and the rest from livestock and livestock products; dairy products, nursery products, cattle, corn, and soybeans were the principal commodities. The state in 2004 ranked second in output of tart cherries, third in apples, and fourth in prunes and plums.

The growing of corn and other crops indigenous to North America was introduced in Michigan by the Indians around 100 BC, and early French settlers tried to develop European-style agriculture during the colonial era. But little progress was made until well into the 19th century, when farmers from New York and New England poured into the interior of southern Michigan. By mid-century, 34,000 farms had been established, and the number increased to a peak of about 207,000 in 1910. The major cash crop at first was wheat, until soil exhaustion, insect infestations, bad winters, and competition from huge wheat farms to the west forced a de-emphasis on wheat and a move toward agricultural diversity. Both the number of farms and the amount of farm acreage had declined by 2004 to 53,200 farms and 10,100,000 acres (4,088,000 hectares).

The southern half of the lower peninsula is the principal agricultural region, and the area along Lake Michigan is a leader in fruit growing. Potatoes are profitable in northern Michigan, while eastern Michigan (the "Thumb" area near Lake Huron) is a leading bean producer. The Saginaw Valley leads the state in sugar beets. The south-central and southeastern counties are major centers of soybean production. Leading field crops in 2004 included 257,280,000 bushels of corn for grain, valued at $463,104,000; 75,240,000 bushels of soybeans, worth $379,962,000; and 40,960,000 bushels of wheat, worth $122,880,000. Output of commercial apples totaled 720,000,000 lb (327,000,000 kg).

24 ANIMAL HUSBANDRY

The same areas of southern Michigan that lead in crop production also lead in livestock and livestock products, except that the northern counties are more favorable for dairying than for crop production.

In 2005, there were an estimated 1,010,000 cattle and calves, valued at $1.07 billion. The state had an estimated 940,000 hogs and pigs in 2004, valued at $103.4 million.

In 2003, dairy farmers had an estimated 302,000 milk cows which produced around 6.36 million lb (2.89 million kg) of milk. Poultry farmers produced 1.89 billion eggs, valued at around $93.7 million, in 2003.

25 FISHING

Commercial fishing, once an important factor in the state's economy, was relatively minor by the early 2000s. In 2004, the commercial catch was 8.4 million lb (3.8 million kg) valued at $6.2 million. Principal species landed are silver salmon and alewives.

Sport fishing continues to flourish and is one of the state's major tourist attractions. A state salmon-planting program, begun in the mid-1960s, has made salmon the most popular game fish for Great Lakes sport fishermen. The state has also sought, through breeding and stocking programs, to bring back the trout, which was devastated by an invasion of lamprey. In 2004, the state issued 1,171,742 sport fishing licenses.

A bitter dispute raged during the 1970s between state officials and Ottawa and Ojibwa commercial fishermen, who claimed that Indian treaties with the federal government exempted them from state fishing regulations. The state contended that without such regulations, Indian commercial fishing would have a devastating impact on the northern Great Lakes' fish population. A federal court in 1979 upheld the Indians' contention; but in 1985, the state secured federal court approval of a compromise settlement intended to satisfy both Indian and non-Indian groups.

There are three national fisheries in Michigan. In 2005/06, $9.5 million of federal funds were allocated for sport fish restoration projects in Michigan.

26 FORESTRY

In 2004, Michigan's forestland totaled 19.3 million acres (7.8 million hectares), or more than half the state's total land area. Approximately 96% of it is classified as timberland, about two-thirds of it privately owned. The major forested regions are in the northern two-thirds of the state, where great pine forests enabled Michigan to become the leading lumber-producing state in the last four decades of the 19th century. These cutover lands regenerated naturally or were reforested in the 20th century. Lumber production was 844 million board feet in 2004.

State and national forests covered 6.9 million acres (2.8 million hectares), or about one-fifth of the state's land area.

27 MINING

According to preliminary data from the US Geological Survey (USGS), the estimated value of nonfuel mineral production by Michigan in 2003 was $1.35 billion, a decrease from 2002 of about 9%. The USGS data ranked Michigan as seventh among the 50 states by the total value of its nonfuel mineral production, accounting for around 3.5% of total US output.

Although Michigan in 2003 was the second-largest iron ore producing state in the United States, portland cement was the state's top nonfuel mineral, by value, which was followed by iron ore, construction sand and gravel, crushed stone, salt and magnesium compounds. Collectively, these six commodities accounted for about 91% of all nonfuel mineral output in the state, by value.

Michigan was first nationally in magnesium chloride produced, and ranked second in the production of peat, industrial sand and gravel, bromine and of course, iron ore (after Minnesota). Michigan ranked third in construction sand and gravel, and potash, fourth in portland cement, seventh in salt and eighth in masonry cement.

According to preliminary figures for 2003, Michigan's production of construction sand and gravel totaled 70 million metric tons, which was valued at $245 million, while output of crushed stone, that year totaled 41.2 million metric tons, and was valued at $173 million. Salt output in 2003, according to the preliminary data totaled 1.53 million metric tons and was valued at $105 million.

Michigan also produced small quantities of copper, silver and other mineral specimens for sale to collectors and museums.

28 ENERGY AND POWER

As of 2003, Michigan had 79 electrical power service providers, of which 41 were publicly owned and 10 were cooperatives. Of the remainder, nine were investor owned, five were owners of independent generators that sold directly to customers, twelve were generation-only suppliers, and two were delivery-only providers. As of that same year there were 4,713,966 retail customers. Of that total, 4,136,049 received their power from investor-owned service providers. Cooperatives accounted for 277,906 customers, while publicly owned providers had 299,378 customers. Generation-only suppliers had 628 customers and 5 were independent generator or "facility" customers. There was no data on the number of delivery-only customers.

Total net summer generating capability by the state's electrical generating plants in 2003 stood at 30.450 million kW, with total production that same year at 111.347 billion kWh. Of the total amount generated, 86.8% came from electric utilities, with the remainder coming from independent producers and combined heat and power service providers. The largest portion of all electric power generated, 67.777 billion kWh (60.9%), came from coal-fired plants, with nuclear power plants in second place with 27.953 billion kWh (25.1%, and natural gas fueled plants in third place at 11.374 billion kWh (10.2%). Other renewable power sources accounted for 2.5% of all power generated. Petroleum fired plants, and hydroelectric generating facilities accounted for the remainder.

The two major electric utilities are Detroit Edison, serving the Detroit area and portions of the eastern part of the lower peninsula, and Consumers Power, serving most of the remainder of the lower peninsula. Rates of the utility companies are set by the Public Service Commission.

As of 2006, Michigan had three operating nuclear power plants; the Donald C Cook plant in Berrien County; the Enrico Fermi plant near Detroit; and the Palisades plant near South Haven.

Michigan is dependent on outside sources for most of its fuel needs. As of 2004, Michigan had proven crude oil reserves of 53 million barrels, or less than 1% of all proven US reserves, while output that same year averaged 18,000 barrels per day. Including federal offshore domains, the state that year ranked 17th (16th excluding federal offshore) in proven reserves and 18th (17th excluding federal offshore) in production among the 31 producing states. In 2004 Michigan had 3,675 producing oil wells. As of 2005, the state's single refinery had a combined crude oil distillation capacity of 74,000 barrels per day.

In 2004, Michigan had 8,500 producing natural gas and gas condensate wells. In that same year, marketed gas production (all gas produced excluding gas used for repressuring, vented and flared, and nonhydrocarbon gases removed) totaled 259.681 billion cu ft (7.37 billion cu m). As of 31 December 2004, proven reserves of dry or consumer-grade natural gas totaled 3,091 billion cu ft (87.8 billion cu m).

Bituminous coal reserves (estimated at 127.7 million tons) remain in southern Michigan, but production is negligible. There was no recorded coal production in 2004.

29 INDUSTRY

Manufacturing, a minor element in Michigan's economy in the mid-19th century, grew rapidly in importance until, by 1900, an estimated 25% of the state's jobholders were factory workers. The rise of the auto industry in the early 20th century completed the transformation of Michigan into one of the most important manufacturing areas in the world.

Motor vehicles and equipment dominate the state's economy, representing almost 40% of the state's manufacturing payroll, while the value of shipments by these manufacturers was slightly more than half of the total. Production of nonelectrical machinery, primary and fabricated metal products, and metal forgings and stampings was directly related to automobile production.

The Detroit metropolitan area is the major industrial region: this area includes not only the heavy concentration of auto-related plants in Wayne, Oakland, and Macomb counties, but also major steel, chemical, and pharmaceutical industries, among others. Flint, Grand Rapids, Saginaw, Ann Arbor, Lansing, and Kalamazoo are other major industrial centers.

The auto industry's preponderance in Michigan manufacturing has come to be viewed in recent years as more of a liability than an asset. When times are good, as they were in the 1960s and early 1970s, automobile sales soar to record levels and Michigan's economy prospers. But when the national economy slumps, these sales plummet, pushing the state into a far deeper recession than is felt by the nation as a whole.

According to the US Census Bureau's Annual Survey of Manufactures (ASM) for 2004, Michigan's manufacturing sector covered some 19 product subsectors. The shipment value of all products manufactured in the state that same year was $220.454 billion. Of that total, transportation equipment manufacturing accounted for the largest share at $111.568 billion. It was followed by machinery manufacturing at $17.549 billion; fabricated metal product manufacturing at $14.024 billion; chemical manufacturing at $11.823 billion; and food manufacturing at $11.659 billion.

In 2004, a total of 651,947 people in Michigan were employed in the state's manufacturing sector, according to the ASM. Of that total, 478,466 were actual production workers. In terms of total employment, the transportation equipment manufacturing industry accounted for the largest portion of all manufacturing employees at 202,998, with 167,690 actual production workers. It was followed by fabricated metal product manufacturing at 82,746 employees (60,331 actual production workers); machinery manufacturing at 75,818 employees (47,854 actual production workers); plastics and rubber products manufacturing at 60,688 employees (45,689 actual production workers); and furniture and related product manufacturing with 29,664 employees (19,086 actual production workers).

ASM data for 2004 showed that Michigan's manufacturing sector paid $32.547 billion in wages. Of that amount, the transportation equipment manufacturing sector accounted for the largest share at $12.753 billion. It was followed by machinery manufacturing at $4.039 billion; fabricated metal product manufacturing at $3.335 billion; plastics and rubber products manufacturing at $2.119 billion; chemical manufacturing at $1.745 billion; and primary metal manufacturing at $1.442 billion.

30 COMMERCE

According to the 2002 Census of Wholesale Trade, Michigan's wholesale trade sector had sales that year totaling $165.9 billion from 12,876 establishments. Wholesalers of durable goods accounted for 8,102 establishments, followed by nondurable goods wholesalers at 3,370 and electronic markets, agents, and brokers accounting for 1,404 establishments. Sales by durable goods wholesalers in 2002 totaled $92.9 billion. Sales data was unavailable for nondurable goods and for electronic markets, agents, and brokers in the wholesale trade industry.

In the 2002 Census of Retail Trade, Michigan was listed as having 38,876 retail establishments with sales of $109.3 billion. The leading types of retail businesses by number of establishments were: food and beverage stores (5,973); clothing and clothing accessories stores (4,792); miscellaneous store retailers (4,486); and motor vehicle and motor vehicle parts dealers (4,234). In terms of sales, motor vehicle and motor vehicle parts stores accounted for the largest share of retail sales at $31.7 billion, followed by food and beverage stores at $13.1 billion; building material/garden equipment and supplies dealers at $9.4 billion; gasoline stations at $8.7 billion; and health and personal care stores $6.6 billion. A total of 520,958 people were employed by the retail sector in Michigan that year.

With its ports open to oceangoing vessels through the St. Lawrence Seaway, Michigan is a major exporting and importing state for foreign as well as domestic markets. Exports of Michigan's manufactured goods totaled $37.5 billion in 2005, ranking the state fifth in the United States.

31 CONSUMER PROTECTION

Michigan's Office of the Attorney General is responsible for the enforcement of most of the state's consumer protection laws through its Consumer Protection Division. However, other departments, such as the Department of Consumer and Industry Services which has the responsibility of regulating professions,

corporations and nursing homes, may also have their own consumer protection sections.

Under the state's Consumer Protection Act of 1976, a range of specific misrepresentations in advertising and commerce are prohibited. In addition, the law also regulates down payment returns, the signing of service contracts and other agreements and mandates that sellers of business opportunities must file with the state Attorney General. The state also has an item pricing law and regulations covering the volume and availability of advertised items. Michigan also has laws that regulate motor vehicle services and repairs, as well as a so-called "Lemon Law" that is applicable to the sale of new motor vehicles.

A number of local governments have instituted consumer affairs offices, with Detroit's being especially active.

When dealing with consumer protection issues, the state's Attorney General's Office can initiate civil and criminal proceedings; represent the state before state and federal regulatory agencies; administer consumer protection and education programs; handle formal consumer complaints; and exercise broad subpoena powers. In antitrust actions, the Attorney General's Office can act on behalf of those consumers who are incapable of acting on their own; initiate damage actions on behalf of the state in state courts; and initiate criminal proceedings. However the Attorney General's Office cannot represent counties, cities or other governmental entities in recovering civil damages under state or federal law.

The state's Consumer Protection Division is located in Lansing. County and city government consumer protection offices are respectively located in Mt Clemens and Detroit.

32 BANKING

Michigan's banks in the territorial and early statehood years were generally wildcat speculative ventures. More restrained banking activities date from the 1840s when the state's oldest bank, the Detroit Bank and Trust, was founded. A crisis that developed in the early 1930s forced Governor William Comstock to close all banks in February 1933 in order to prevent collapse of the entire banking system. Federal and state authorities supervised a reorganization and reform of the state's banks that has succeeded in preventing any major problems from arising since that time.

As of June 2005, Michigan had 173 insured banks, savings and loans, and saving banks, plus 251 state-chartered and 152 federally chartered credit unions (CUs). Excluding the CUs, the Detroit-Warren-Livonia market area accounted for the largest portion of the state's financial institutions and deposits in 2004, with 58 institutions and $77.033 billion in deposits. As of June 2005, CUs accounted for 12.8% of all assets held by all financial institutions in the state, or some $31.221 billion. Banks, savings and loans, and savings banks collectively accounted for the remaining 87.2% or $211.930 billion in assets held.

In 2004, banks with less than $1 billion in assets ("community banks") accounted for about 92.5% of the state's insured institutions, but larger banks held most of the state's assets. In that same year, the median net interest margin (NIMs) (the difference between the lower rates offered to savers and the higher rates charged on loans), stood at 4.08%, down from 4.12% in 2003. The median percentage of past-due/nonaccrual loans to total loans in 2004 was 1.82%, down from 2.15% in 2003.

33 INSURANCE

In 2004 there were over 4.9 million individual life insurance policies in force with a total value of about $362 billion; total value for all categories of life insurance (individual, group, and credit) was over $629.7 billion. The average coverage amount is $72,800 per policy holder. Death benefits paid that year totaled $1.9 billion.

As of 2003, there were 65 property and casualty and 19 life and health insurance companies domiciled in the state. In 2004, direct premiums for property and casualty insurance totaled $16 billion. That year, there were 25,447 flood insurance policies in force in

Michigan—State Government Finances

(Dollar amounts in thousands. Per capita amounts in dollars.)

	AMOUNT	PER CAPITA
Total Revenue	57,461,347	5,686.99
General revenue	46,780,063	4,629.86
Intergovernmental revenue	13,749,908	1,360.84
Taxes	24,061,065	2,381.34
General sales	7,894,458	781.32
Selective sales	2,949,792	291.94
License taxes	1,545,457	152.95
Individual income tax	6,576,065	650.84
Corporate income tax	1,841,010	182.21
Other taxes	3,254,283	322.08
Current charges	5,385,255	532.98
Miscellaneous general revenue	3,583,835	354.69
Utility revenue	–	–
Liquor store revenue	675,747	66.88
Insurance trust revenue	10,005,537	990.26
Total expenditure	52,684,622	5,214.23
Intergovernmental expenditure	19,035,055	1,883.91
Direct expenditure	33,649,567	3,330.32
Current operation	23,462,732	2,322.12
Capital outlay	2,452,289	242.70
Insurance benefits and repayments	5,627,428	556.95
Assistance and subsidies	1,010,175	99.98
Interest on debt	1,096,943	108.57
Exhibit: Salaries and wages	6,741,508	667.21
Total expenditure	52,684,622	5,214.23
General expenditure	46,507,284	4,602.86
Intergovernmental expenditure	19,035,055	1,883.91
Direct expenditure	27,472,229	2,718.95
General expenditures, by function:		
Education	20,341,302	2,013.19
Public welfare	9,950,158	984.77
Hospitals	1,812,750	179.41
Health	3,350,239	331.58
Highways	3,259,528	322.60
Police protection	295,537	29.25
Correction	1,637,305	162.05
Natural resources	453,032	44.84
Parks and recreation	125,377	12.41
Government administration	930,080	92.05
Interest on general debt	1,096,943	108.57
Other and unallocable	3,255,033	322.15
Utility expenditure	–	–
Liquor store expenditure	549,910	54.42
Insurance trust expenditure	5,627,428	556.95
Debt at end of fiscal year	20,959,946	2,074.42
Cash and security holdings	70,891,515	7,016.18

Abbreviations and symbols: – zero or rounds to zero; (NA) not available; (X) not applicable.

SOURCE: U.S. Census Bureau, Governments Division, 2004 Survey of State Government Finances, January 2006.

the state, with a total value of $3.1 billion. About $15.3 billion of coverage was held through FAIR plans, which are designed to offer coverage for some natural circumstances, such as wind and hail, in high risk areas.

In 2004, 59% of state residents held employment-based health insurance policies, 4% held individual policies, and 26% were covered under Medicare and Medicaid; 11% of residents were uninsured. In 2003, employee contributions for employment-based health coverage averaged at 15% for single coverage and 18% for family coverage. The state does not offer a health benefits expansion program in connection with the Consolidated Omnibus Budget Reconciliation Act (COBRA, 1986), a health insurance program for those who lose employment-based coverage due to termination or reduction of work hours.

In 2003, there were over 6.4 million auto insurance policies in effect for private passenger cars. Required minimum coverage includes bodily injury liability of up to $20,000 per individual and $40,000 for all persons injured in an accident, as well as property damage liability of $10,000. Personal injury protection is also mandatory. In 2003, the average expenditure per vehicle for insurance coverage was $931.14.

34 SECURITIES

There are no securities or commodity exchanges in Michigan. In 2005, there were 2,410 personal financial advisers employed in the state and 6,040 securities, commodities, and financial services sales agents. In 2004, there were over 166 publicly traded companies within the state, with over 65 NASDAQ companies, 43 NYSE listings, and 5 AMEX listings. In 2006, the state had 21 Fortune 500 companies; General Motors (based in Detroit) ranked first in the state and third in the nation with revenues of over $192.6 billion, followed by Ford Motor (Dearborn), Dow Chemical (Midland, Delphi (Troy), and Lear (Southfield). All five companies were listed on the NYSE. Ford Motor was ranked at fifth in the nation on the Fortune 500 list with revenues of over $177.2 billion.

35 PUBLIC FINANCE

The state constitution requires the governor to submit a budget proposal to the legislature each year. This executive budget, prepared by the Department of Management and Budget, is reviewed, revised, and passed by the legislature. During the fiscal year (FY), which extends from 1 October to 30 September, if actual revenues drop below anticipated levels, the governor, in consultation with the legislative appropriations committees, must reduce expenditures to meet the constitutional requirement that the state budget be kept in balance.

In 1977, the legislature created a budget stabilization fund. A portion of tax revenues collected in good times is held in reserve to be used during periods of recession, when the funding of essential state services is threatened. In 1978, a tax limitation amendment put a lid on government spending by establishing a fixed ratio of state revenues to personal income in the state. Further efforts to limit taxes were rejected by the voters in 1980 and 1984.

F2006 general funds were estimated at $9.0 billion for resources and $9.0 billion for expenditures. In fiscal year 2004, federal government grants to Michigan were $13.2 billion.

In the fiscal year 2007 federal budget, Michigan was slated to receive: $16.9 million to develop a national cemetery in Great Lakes.

36 TAXATION

In 2005, Michigan collected $24,340 million in tax revenues or $2,405 per capita, which placed it 15th among the 50 states in per capita tax burden. The national average was $2,192 per capita. Property taxes accounted for 8.8% of the total, sales taxes 33.2%, selective sales taxes 14.2%, individual income taxes 28.4%, corporate income taxes 7.8%, and other taxes 7.5%.

As of 1 January 2006, Michigan had one individual income tax bracket of 3.9%.

In 2004, state and local property taxes amounted to $11,978,654,000 or $1,186 per capita, which ranks the state 15th nationally in per capita taxation. Local governments collected $9,886,721,000 of the total and the state government $2,091,933,000.

Michigan taxes retail sales at a rate of 6%. Food purchased for consumption off-premises is tax exempt. The tax on cigarettes is 200 cents per pack, which ranks fourth among the 50 states and the District of Columbia. Michigan taxes gasoline at 19 cents per gallon. This is in addition to the 18.4 cents per gallon federal tax on gasoline.

According to the Tax Foundation, for every federal tax dollar sent to Washington in 2004, Michigan citizens received $0.85 in federal spending.

37 ECONOMIC POLICY

The Michigan Economic Development Corporation (MEDC) has a long tradition of promoting economic development. Through the Michigan CareerSite web page, economic development and job training programs are outlined. The mission of MEDC is to work with businesses, state government, and local communities to make Michigan more business-friendly. MEDC is a corporation, not a traditional government agency.

Michigan is part of the so-called Rust Belt, the region of the country dominated by steel-based industries from the 1940s to the 1980s. To focus economic development on new industries, Michigan has taken a number of steps, including cutting taxes for individuals and businesses. In the 1990s, Michigan taxpayers, both individuals and businesses, benefited from 21 tax cuts. The result has been the 13th-lowest tax burden in the country for 2000 and a robust economy with unemployment levels lower than the national average since 1995.

Michigan's Economic Growth Authority offers generous tax breaks to firms that locate a facility in Michigan, and offers substantial employment opportunities to Michigan workers. The state's Renaissance Zone program exempts companies and individuals within designated areas throughout the state from all state and local taxes as an incentive to rebuild and revitalize specific areas. Renaissance Zones include urban, rural, and former military installation sites. In 2006, Michigan also had 11 designated Smart Zones, which are collaborations between universities, industry, research organizations, government, and other community institutions to stimulate growth of technology-based businesses, particularly those focused on commercializing ideas and patents that result from R&D efforts.

38 HEALTH

The infant mortality rate in October 2005 was estimated at 7.7 per 1,000 live births. The birth rate in 2003 was 13 per 1,000 population. The abortion rate stood at 21.6 per 1,000 women in 2000. In 2003, about 86.1% of pregnant woman received prenatal care beginning in the first trimester. In 2004, approximately 81% of children received routine immunizations before the age of three.

The crude death rate in 2003 was 8.6 deaths per 1,000 population. As of 2002, the death rates for major causes of death (per 100,000 resident population) were: heart disease, 265.3; cancer, 198.8; cerebrovascular diseases, 57.8; chronic lower respiratory diseases, 44.1; and diabetes, 27.7. The mortality rate from HIV infection was 2.4 per 100,000 population. In 2004, the reported AIDS case rate was at about 6.5 per 100,000 population. In 2002, about 60.2% of the resident population was considered overweight or obese, representing the fourth-highest rate in the country for this category. As of 2004, about 23.2% of state residents were smokers.

In 2003, Michigan had 144 community hospitals with about 25,800 beds. There were about 1.1 million patient admissions that year and 27 million outpatient visits. The average daily inpatient census was about 17,100 patients. The average cost per day for hospital care was $1,382. Also in 2003, there were about 431 certified nursing facilities in the state with 49,225 beds and an overall occupancy rate of about 84.4%. In 2004, it was estimated that about 76.9% of all state residents had received some type of dental care within the year. Michigan had 289 physicians per 100,000 resident population in 2004 and 804 nurses per 100,000 in 2005. In 2004, there were a total of 6,039 dentists in the state.

In 2005, the University of Michigan Medical Center in Ann Arbor ranked eleventh on the Honor Roll of Best Hospitals 2005 by *U.S. News & World Report*. In the same report, the hospital ranked ninth in the nation for best care in cancer.

About 26% of state residents were enrolled in Medicaid and Medicare programs in 2004. Approximately 11% of the state population was uninsured in 2004. In 2003, state health care expenditures totaled $11.5 million.

39 SOCIAL WELFARE

Until the 1930s, Michigan's few limited welfare programs were handled by the counties, but the relief load during the Depression shifted the burden to the state and federal levels. In 2004, about 462,000 people received unemployment benefits, with the average weekly unemployment benefit at $289. In fiscal year 2005, the estimated average monthly participation in the food stamp program included about 1,047,594 persons (469,976 households); the average monthly benefit was about $87.41 per person. That year, the total of benefits paid through the state for the food stamp program was over $1 billion.

Temporary Assistance for Needy Families (TANF), the system of federal welfare assistance that officially replaced Aid to Families with Dependent Children (AFDC) in 1997, was reauthorized through the Deficit Reduction Act of 2005. TANF is funded through federal block grants that are divided among the states based on an equation involving the number of recipients in each state. Michigan's TANF program is called the Family Independence Program (FIP). In 2004, the state program had 212,000 recipients; state and federal expenditures on this TANF program totaled $416 million in fiscal year 2003.

In December 2004, Social Security benefits were paid to 1,716,290 Michigan residents. This number included 1,059,530 retired workers, 179,870 widows and widowers, 226,060 disabled workers, 99,620 spouses, and 151,210 children. Social Security beneficiaries represented 17% of the total state population and 95.6% of the state's population age 65 and older. Retired workers received an average monthly payment of $1,029; widows and widowers, $967; disabled workers, $950; and spouses, $514. Payments for children of retired workers averaged $519 per month; children of deceased workers, $660; and children of disabled workers, $277. Federal Supplemental Security Income payments in December 2004 went to 219,337 Michigan residents, averaging $424 a month.

40 HOUSING

In 2004, there were an estimated 4,433,482 housing units in Michigan, 3,923,135 of which were occupied. That year, Michigan ranked second in the nation (after Minnesota) for the highest percentage of owner-occupied housing units, at 74.7%. About 70.5% of all units were single-family, detached homes. Most homes rely on utility gas for heating. It was estimated that 218,182 units lacked telephone service, 8,787 lacked complete plumbing facilities, and 12,705 lacked complete kitchen facilities. The average household had 2.51 members.

In 2004, 54,700 privately owned units were authorized for construction. The median home value was $145,177. The median monthly cost for mortgage owners was $1,137. Renters paid a median of $628 per month. In September 2005, the state received grants of $849,997 from the US Department of Housing and Urban Development (HUD) for rural housing and economic development programs. For 2006, HUD allocated to the state over $36.3 million in community development block grants (CDBG). The city of Detroit received over $38.8 million in CDBG grants. A limited amount of state aid for low-income housing is available through the State Housing Development Authority.

41 EDUCATION

Historically, Michigan has strongly supported public education. In 2004, 87.9% of Michigan residents age 25 and older were high school graduates, and 24.4% had obtained a bachelor's degree or higher.

The total enrollment for fall 2002 in Michigan's public schools stood at 1,785,000. Of these, 1,254,000 attended schools from kindergarten through grade eight, and 531,000 attended high school. Approximately 72.7% of the students were white, 20.1% were black, 4.1% were Hispanic, 2.2% were Asian/Pacific Islander, and 1% were American Indian/Alaskan Native. Total enrollment was estimated at 1,786,000 in fall 2003 and was expected to be 1,728,000 by fall 2014, a decline of 3.2% during the period 2002 to 2014. Expenditures for public education in 2003/04 were estimated at $19.2 billion. Since 1969, the National Assessment of Educational Progress (NAEP) has tested public school students nationwide. The resulting report, *The Nation's Report Card,* stated that in 2005 eighth graders in Michigan scored 277 out of 500 in mathematics compared with the national average of 278.

In fall 2003 there were 160,049 students enrolled in 983 private schools. The largest number of these students were enrolled in Catholic schools. Lutherans, Seventh-Day Adventists, and Reformed and Christian Reformed churches also have maintained schools for some time; in the 1970s, a number of new Christian schools, particularly those of fundamentalist Baptist groups, were established.

As of fall 2002, there were 605,835 students enrolled in college or graduate school; minority students comprised 18.9% of total postsecondary enrollment. In 2005 Michigan had 110 degree-granting institutions. The oldest state school is the University of Michigan, originally established in Detroit in 1817; its Ann Arbor campus was founded in 1835, and classes there began in 1841. Among the public universities are the University of Michigan, including the Dearborn and Flint campuses, Michigan State University, and Wayne State University. Among the state's private colleges and universities, the University of Detroit Mercy, a Jesuit school, is one of the largest. Kalamazoo College (founded in 1833), Albion College (1835), Hope College (1866) and Alma College (1886) are some of the oldest private liberal arts colleges in the state.

42 ARTS

Michigan's major center of arts and cultural activities is the Detroit area. The city's refurbished Orchestra Hall is the home of the Detroit Symphony Orchestra as well as chamber music concerts and other musical events. The Detroit Symphony has a long history having been founded in 1914; in the 1920s and 30s the symphony hosted several famous guest artists including Igor Stravinsky, Isadora Duncan, Richard Strauss, and Anna Pavlova. The Music Hall and the Masonic Auditorium present a variety of musical productions; the Fisher Theater and the Masonic Temple Theater are the major home for Broadway productions; and the Detroit Cultural Center supports a number of cultural programs. In 2006, the Masonic Temple Theater featured the three-time Tony Award winning *Wicked.* The new Detroit Opera House is sponsored by the Michigan Opera Theatre. Nearby Meadow Brook, in Rochester, has a summer music program. At the University of Michigan, in Ann Arbor, the Power Center for the Performing Arts and Hill Auditorium host major musical, theatrical, and dance presentations.

Programs relating to the visual arts tend to be academically centered; the University of Michigan, Michigan State, Wayne State, and Eastern Michigan University have notable art schools. The Cranbrook Academy of Arts, which was created by the architect Eliel Saarinen, is a significant art center, and the Ox-bow School at Saugatuck is also outstanding. The Ann Arbor Art Fair, established in 1960, is the largest and most prestigious summer outdoor art show in the state hosting over 500,000 annual attendees. As of 2006, the Ann Arbor Art Fair had won four awards, including being named as the number one art fair in the country by *AmericanStyle* magazine in 2004. The Waterfront Film Festival in Saugatuck and the touring Ann Arbor Film Festival promote the art of independent filmmaking.

The Meadow Brook Theater in Rochester, founded on Oakland University's campus is the largest nonprofit professional theater company in the state. In the 2004/05 season Meadow Brook won a series of local awards including a Lawrence Devine Award, an OPie, and a Wilde Award—all recognizing either outstanding performances or distinguished career achievements. Detroit features a number of little theater groups and successful summer theaters include the Cherry County Playhouse at Traverse City and the Star Theater in Flint.

The Detroit Symphony Orchestra, founded in 1914, is nationally known. Grand Rapids and Kalamazoo have regional orchestras that perform on a part-time, seasonal basis. The National Music Camp at Interlochen is a mecca for young musicians in the summer, and a prestigious private high school for the arts year round. As of 2006 the Interlochen music camp included over 400 presentations that incorporated more than 2,000 students and 25 special guest performances, annually.

There are local ballet and opera groups in Detroit and in a few other communities. Michigan's best-known contribution to popular music was that of Berry Gordy Jr., whose Motown recording company in the 1960s popularized the "Detroit sound" and featured such artists as Diana Ross and the Supremes, Smokey Robinson and the Miracles, Aretha Franklin, the Four Tops, the Temptations, and Stevie Wonder, among many others. In the 1970s however, Gordy moved his operations to California.

The state of Michigan generates federal and state funds for its arts programs. In 2005, the Michigan Council for the Arts and other Michigan arts organizations received 33 grants totaling $1,322,745 from the National Endowment for the Arts. Private sources also provided funding for the activities of the Council. The Michigan Humanities Council (MHC) was founded in 1974. One of its ongoing programs is the Michigan's Arts and Humanities Touring Program, which includes performing artists and cultural interpreters/educators. In 2006, the MHC awarded grants totaling $36,847 to support the touring program that season, which then included 146 live artistic and cultural presentations. In 2005, the National Endowment for the Humanities contributed 33 grants totaling $3,083,441 to state programs.

43 LIBRARIES AND MUSEUMS

As of September 2001, Michigan had 381 public library systems, with a total of 654 libraries, of which 278 were branches. In that same year, the system had a total of 27,188,000 volumes of books and serial publications, and a total circulation of 51,773,000. The system also had 1,445,000 audio and 839,000 video items, 78,000 electronic format items (CD-ROMs, magnetic tapes, and disks), and 17 bookmobiles. The Library of Michigan in Lansing functions as the coordinator of library facilities in the state. The largest public library is the Detroit Public Library, which in 1999 had over 2.5 million books and print materials in its main library and 26 branches. Outstanding among its special collections are the Burton Historical Collection, a major center for genealogical research, the National Automotive History Collection, and the E. Azalia Hackley Collection, a notable source for material pertaining to African Americans in the performing arts, especially music. Grand Rapids, Kalamazoo, Lansing, Flint, and Ann Arbor are among the larger public libraries. In fiscal year 2001, operating income for the state's public library system totaled $329,283,000 and included $548,000 in federal grants and $16,031,000 in state grants.

Among academic libraries, the University of Michigan at Ann Arbor, with 6,283,385 volumes and 56,663 periodical subscriptions in 1999, features the William L. Clements collection of books and manuscripts on the colonial period, the Labadie Collection

relating to the history of American radicalism, and the Bentley Library's distinctive collection of books and manuscripts, particularly the one on Michigan, the largest such collection.

In 1980, the Gerald R. Ford Presidential Library was opened on the University of Michigan's Ann Arbor campus. The Michigan State University Library at East Lansing had 4,274,375 volumes and 27,314 periodical subscriptions in 1999. At Wayne State University in Detroit, the Walter P. Reuther Library houses the largest collection of labor history records in the United States, as well as primary materials relating to social, economic, and political reform and urban affairs.

The Detroit Institute of Arts is the largest art museum in the state and has an outstanding collection of African art. It is located in the Detroit Cultural Center, along with the Public Library and the Detroit Historical Museum, one of the largest local history museums in the country. The Kalamazoo Institute of Art, the Flint Institute of Art, the Grand Rapids Art Museum, and the Hackley Art Gallery in Muskegon are important art museums. The University of Michigan and the Cranbrook Academy of Arts in Bloomfield Hills also maintain important collections.

The Detroit Historical Museum heads 229 museums in the state, including the State Historical Museum in Lansing and museums in Grand Rapids, Flint, Kalamazoo, and Dearborn. In the latter city, the privately run Henry Ford Museum and Greenfield Village are leading tourist attractions. In 1996 the world's largest museum of African American history was established in Detroit. A major Holocaust Memorial Center is located in the West Bloomfield Hills area of metropolitan Detroit.

The major historical sites open to the public include the late-18th-century fort on Mackinac Island and the reconstructed early-18th-century fort at Mackinaw City. The latter site has also been the scene of an archaeological program that has accumulated one of the largest collections of 18th-century artifacts in the country. Major investigations of prehistoric Indian sites have also been conducted in recent years.

44 COMMUNICATIONS

Michigan's remote position in the interior of the continent hampered the development of adequate communications services, and the first regular postal service was not instituted until the early 19th century.

Telephone service began in Detroit in 1877. By 2004, 93.7% of the occupied housing units in the state had telephones. Additionally, by June of that same year there were 5,430,637 mobile wireless telephone subscribers. In 2003, 59.9% of Michigan households had a computer and 52.0% had Internet access. By June 2005, there were 1,359,079 high-speed lines in Michigan, 1,256,759 residential and 102,320 for business.

Michigan had 62 major AM radio stations and 110 major FM stations in 2005. Radio station WWJ, originally owned by the Detroit News, began operating in 1920 as one of the country's first commercial broadcasting stations, and the News also started Michigan's first television station in 1947. As of 2005 there were 33 major television stations in the state. In the Detroit area, 68% of 1,855,500 television households had cable, and in the Grand Rapids-Kalamazoo-Battle Creek area, 62% of 671,320 television households had cable in 1999.

By 2000, a total of 145,596 Internet domain names had been registered in Michigan.

45 PRESS

The first newspaper to appear in Michigan was Father Richard's *Michigan Essay or Impartial Observer*, published in August 1917. Continuous newspaper coverage in Michigan dates from the appearance of the weekly *Detroit Gazette*, also in 1817. The state's oldest paper still being published is the *Detroit Free Press*, founded in 1831 and the state's first daily paper since 1835.

In 2005 there were 48 daily newspapers in Michigan, with 27 Sunday editions published in the state. Two of the state's largest newspapers—Knight Ridder's *Detroit Free Press* and Gannett's *Detroit News*—entered into a joint operating agreement (JOA) in 1989. The advertising, business, delivery, and production of each paper joined forces in a company called Detroit Newspapers; the editorial and news operations remain separate and report to their respective parent companies. During the struggle, the *Detroit Journal* was published weekly by locked-out newspaper workers. The *News* had the sixth-largest daily circulation of any paper in the United States in 1994. By 2004, however, the *News* had dropped to number 46 in daily circulation among newspapers nationwide and the *Free Press* was at number 21.

The following table shows leading daily newspapers in Michigan with average daily and Sunday circulation in 1998:

AREA	NAME	DAILY	SUNDAY
Detroit	*News* and *Free Press* (m,S)	510,736	710,036
Flint	*Journal* (e,S)	84,313	102,154
Grand Rapids	*Press* (e,S)	138,126	189,690
Kalamazoo	*Gazette* (e,S)	62,350	72,945
Lansing	*State Journal* (m,S)	70,725	90,502
Pontiac	*Oakland Press* (m,S)	78,213	80,737
Saginaw	*News* (e,S)	46,439	55,690

46 ORGANIZATIONS

In 2006, there were over 11,310 nonprofit organizations registered within the state, of which about 7,137 were registered as charitable, educational, or religious organizations. The most important trade association headquartered in Michigan is the Motor Vehicle Manufacturers Association, with offices in Detroit. Its labor union counterpart—the United Automobile, Aerospace and Agricultural Implement Workers of America (UAW)—also has its international headquarters in that city.

Others with headquarters in the state include the American Concrete Institute, the Detroit; Society of Manufacturing Engineers, Dearborn; American Society of Agricultural Engineers, St. Joseph; the American Board of Emergency Medicine, East Lansing, and the National Association of Investment Corporations, Madison Heights.

Organizations for arts and education include the Association of College Honor Societies, the Children's Literature Association, the American Guild of Music, Interlochen Center for the Arts, and the Institute for Social Research There are also a number of municipal and regional arts groups and historical societies. State organizations of art and culture include the Michigan Humanities Council, the Michigan Historical Society, and the Michigan Historic Preservation Network. Several organizations focus on regional environmental issues, including the Great Lakes Maritime Institute and the Great Lakes Commission. The United Kennel Club is a hobby organization with national memberships.

Charitable organizations include the Good Fellows, based in Detroit. Founded in 1914, the organization was called the Newsboys, since its first members were newspaper carriers. Though the group participates in a number of charitable causes, its primary program is A Christmas for Every Needy Child. There are chapters of Good Fellows nationwide. The W. K. Kellogg Foundation based in Battle Creek also supports a number of community, national, and international projects. The Islamic Assembly of North America, which serves as a coordinating body for US Islamic centers and organizations, is based in Ann Arbor.

47 TOURISM, TRAVEL, AND RECREATION

Tourism has been an important source of economic activity in Michigan since the 19th century and now rivals agriculture as the second most important segment of the state's economy. About 54% of all travel is in the form of day trips for state residents or visitors from neighboring states. In 2003, Michigan had 150,000 people employed in tourism.

Michigan's tourist attractions are diverse and readily accessible to much of the country's population. The opportunities offered by Michigan's water resources are the number one attraction; no part of the state is more than 85 mi (137 km) from one of the Great Lakes, and most of the population lives only a few miles away from one of the thousands of inland lakes and streams. Southwestern Michigan's sandy beaches along Lake Michigan offer sunbathing and swimming on 8,000 mi (5,000 km) of Great Lakes coastline. Inland lakes numbering 11,000 in southern Michigan are favored by swimmers while the Metropolitan Beach on Lake St. Clair, northeast of Detroit, claims to be the largest artificial-lake beach in the world. Camping has enjoyed an enormous increase in popularity; in addition to the extensive public camping facilities, there are many private campgrounds. The beach towns of Silver Lake, Sand Dunes, Holland, South Haven, and St. Joseph receive most of their tourists in the summer months. Ann Arbor and Grand Rapids share the presidential library of Gerald R. Ford. Ann Arbor also hosts the country's oldest art fair in July.

Although the tourist and resort business has been primarily a summer activity, the rising popularity of ice fishing, skiing, and other winter sports, autumn scenic tours, hunting, and spring festivals has made tourism a year-round business in many parts of the state. Historic attractions have been heavily promoted in recent years, following the success of Dearborn's Henry Ford Museum and Greenfield Village; such as the Motown Historical Museum. Tours of Detroit automobile factories and other industrial sites, such as Battle Creek's breakfast-food plants, are also important tourist attractions. The Spirit of Ford, a 50,000 sq ft center in Dearborn, offers a "behind the scenes" look at how the automaker designs, engineers, tests, and produces cars and trucks.

Camping and recreational facilities are provided by the federal government at three national forests comprising 2.8 million acres (1.1 million hectares), three facilities operated by the National Park Service (Isle Royale National Park, the Pictured Rocks National Lakeshore, and Sleeping Bear Dunes National Lakeshore), and several wildlife sanctuaries. A wild African-style village covering 70 acres (28.3 hectares) at the Binder Park Zoo in Battle Creek features giraffes, zebras, and ostrich, plus a variety of endangered

African species roaming freely on the grassy savannah. Michigan is the only state divided into two parts—the Upper Peninsula and the Lower Peninsula—which are connected by the well-known Mackinac Bridge.

State-operated facilities include 64 parks and recreational areas with 172,343 acres (69,747 hectares), and state forests and wildlife areas totaling 4,250,000 acres (1,720,000 hectares). Holland and Warren Dunes state parks, located on Lake Michigan, have the largest annual park attendances; Ludington State Park, also on Lake Michigan, attracts the largest number of campers.

48 SPORTS

Michigan has five major professional sports teams, all of them centered in Detroit: the Tigers of Major League Baseball, the Lions of the National Football League, the Pistons of the National Basketball Association, the Shock of the Women's National Basketball Association, and the Red Wings of the National Hockey League. The Tigers won the World Series in 1935, 1945, 1968, and 1984. The Pistons won the NBA Championship in 1989, 1990, and 2004. The Red Wings, arguably the most renowned hockey club ever, won the Stanley Cup in 1936, 1937, 1943, 1950, 1952, 1954, 1955, 1997, 1998, and 2002.

The state also has minor league hockey teams in Detroit, Flint, Grand Rapids, Motor City, Muskegon, Kalamazoo, Plymouth, Port Huron, and Saginaw; and baseball teams in Grand Rapids, Battle Creek, Lansing, and Traverse City.

Horse racing, Michigan's oldest organized spectator sport, is controlled by the state racing commissioner, who regulates thoroughbred and harness-racing seasons at tracks in the Detroit area and at Jackson. Attendance and betting at these races is substantial, although the modest purses rarely attract the nation's leading horses. Auto racing is also popular in Michigan. The state hosts four major races: the Tenneco Automotive Grand Prix of Detroit, the Michigan 500 Indy car race on the CART circuit, and two NASCAR Nextel Cup races.

Interest in college sports centers on the football and basketball teams of the University of Michigan and Michigan State University, which usually are among the top-ranked teams in the country. The University of Michigan football team was named national champion in 1901 (with Harvard), 1902, 1903, 1904 (with Penn), 1918 (with Pittsburgh), 1923 (with Illinois), 1932, 1933, 1947, 1948, and 1997. The team won the Rose Bowl in 1948, 1951, 1965, 1981, 1989, 1993, and 1998, the Citrus Bowl in 1999, and the Orange Bowl in 2000. Michigan State won the Rose Bowl in 1954, 1956, and 1988, and was named national champion in 1952 (with Georgia Tech), 1965 (with Alabama), and 1966 (with Notre Dame). The University of Michigan basketball team won the National Collegiate Athletic Association (NCAA) tournament in 1989, and Michigan State won it in 1979 and 2000. Michigan also advanced to the championship game in 1965, 1976, 1992, and 1993.

Other colleges also have achieved national rankings in basketball, hockey, baseball, and track. Elaborate facilities have been built for sporting competitions in Michigan; for example the University of Michigan's football stadium, seating 107,501, is one of the largest college-owned stadiums in the country.

Other annual sporting events include the Snowmobile Poker Runs in St. Ignace and, in July, the yacht races from Chicago and Port Huron to Mackinac Island.

49 FAMOUS MICHIGANIANS

Only one Michiganian has held the offices of US president and vice president. Gerald R. Ford (Leslie King Jr., b.Nebraska, 1913), the 38th US president, was elected to the US House as a Republican in 1948 and served continuously until 1973, becoming minority leader in 1965. Upon the resignation of Vice President Spiro T. Agnew in 1973, President Richard M. Nixon appointed Ford to the vice-presidency. When Nixon resigned on 9 August 1974, Ford became president, the first to hold that post without having been elected to high national office. Ford succeeded in restoring much of the public's confidence in the presidency, but his pardoning of Nixon for all crimes he may have committed as president helped cost Ford victory in the presidential election of 1976. Ford subsequently moved his legal residence to California.

Lewis Cass (b.New Hampshire, 1782–1866), who served as governor of Michigan Territory, senator from Michigan, secretary of war and secretary of state, is the only other Michigan resident nominated by a major party for president; he lost the 1848 race as the Democratic candidate. Thomas E. Dewey (1902–72), a native of Owosso, was the Republican presidential nominee in 1944 and 1948, but from his adopted state of New York.

Two Michiganians have served as associate justices of the Supreme Court: Henry B. Brown (b.Massachusetts, 1836–1913), author of the 1896 segregationist decision in *Plessy v. Ferguson;* and Frank Murphy (1890–1949), who also served as US attorney general, mayor of Detroit, governor of Michigan, and was a notable defender of minority rights during his years on the court. Another justice, Potter Stewart (1915–85), was born in Jackson but appointed to the court from Ohio.

Other Michiganians who have held high federal office include Robert McClelland (b.Pennsylvania, 1807–80), secretary of the interior; Russell A. Alger (b.Ohio, 1836–1907), secretary of war; Edwin Denby (b.Indiana, 1870–1929), secretary of the Navy, who was forced to resign because of the Teapot Dome scandal; Roy D. Chapin (1880–1936), secretary of commerce; Charles E. Wilson (b.Ohio, 1890–1961), and Robert S. McNamara (b.California, 1916), secretaries of defense; George Romney (b.Mexico, 1907–96), secretary of housing and urban development; Donald M. Dickinson (b.New York, 1846–1917) and Arthur E. Summerfield (1899–1972), postmasters general; and W. Michael Blumenthal (b.Germany, 1926), secretary of the treasury.

Zachariah Chandler (b.New Hampshire, 1813–79) served as secretary of the interior but is best remembered as a leader of the Radical Republicans in the US Senate during the Civil War era. Other prominent US senators have included James M. Couzens (b.Canada, 1872–1936), a former Ford executive who became a maverick Republican liberal during the 1920s; Arthur W. Vandenberg (1884–1951), a leading supporter of a bipartisan internationalist foreign policy after World War II; and Philip A. Hart Jr. (b.Pennsylvania, 1912–76), one of the most influential senators of the 1960s and 1970s. Recent well-known US representatives include John Conyers Jr. (b.1929) and Martha W. Griffiths (b.Missouri, 1912–2003), a representative for 20 years who served as the state's lieutenant governor from 1983–91.

In addition to Murphy and Romney, important governors have included Stevens T. Mason (b.Virginia, 1811–43), who guided Michigan to statehood; Austin Blair (b.New York, 1818–94), Civil War governor; Hazen S. Pingree (b.Maine, 1840–1901) and Chase S. Osborn (b.Indiana, 1860–1949), reform-minded governors; Alexander Groesbeck (1873–1953); G. Mennen Williams (1911–88); and William G. Milliken (b.1922), governor from 1969 to January 1983. From 1974 to 1994, Detroit's first black mayor, Coleman A. Young (b.Alabama, 1918–97), promoted programs to revive the city's tarnished image.

The most famous figure in the early development of Michigan is Jacques Marquette (b.France, 1637–75). Other famous historical figures include Charles de Langlade (1729–1801), a leader of the Ottawa people and a French-Indian soldier in the French and Indian War and the American Revolution; the Ottawa chieftain Pontiac (1720?–69), leader of an ambitious Indian uprising; and Gabriel Richard (b.France, 1769–1832), an important pioneer in education and the first Catholic priest to serve in Congress. Laura Haviland (b.Canada, 1808–98) was a noted leader in the fight against slavery and for black rights, while Lucinda Hinsdale Stone (b.Vermont, 1814–1900) and Anna Howard Shaw (b.England, 1847–1919) were important in the women's rights movement.

Nobel laureates from Michigan include diplomat Ralph J. Bunche (1904–71), winner of the Nobel Peace Prize in 1950; Glenn T. Seaborg (1912–99), Nobel Prize winner in chemistry in 1951; and Thomas H. Weller (b.1915) and Alfred D. Hershey (1908–97), Nobel Prize winners in physiology or medicine in 1954 and 1969, respectively. Among leading educators, James B. Angell (b.Rhode Island, 1829–1916), president of the University of Michigan, led that school to the forefront among American universities while John A. Hannah (1902–91), longtime president of Michigan State University, successfully strove to expand and diversify its programs. General Motors executive Charles S. Mott (b.New Jersey, 1875–1973) contributed to the growth of continuing education programs through huge grants of money.

In the business world, William C. Durant (b.Massachusetts, 1861–1947), Henry Ford (1863–1947) and Ransom E. Olds (b.Ohio 1864–1950) are the three most important figures in making Michigan the center of the American auto industry. Ford's grandson, Henry Ford II (1917–87), was the dominant personality in the auto industry from 1945 through 1979. Two brothers, John Harvey Kellogg (1852–1943) and Will K. Kellogg (1860–1951), helped make Battle Creek the center of the breakfast-food industry. William E. Upjohn (1850–1932) and Herbert H. Dow (b.Canada, 1866–1930) founded major pharmaceutical and chemical companies that bear their names. James E. Scripps (b.England, 1835–1906), founder of the *Detroit News,* was a major innovator in the newspaper business. Pioneer aviator Charles A. Lindbergh (1902–74) was born in Detroit.

Among prominent labor leaders in Michigan were Walter Reuther (b.West Virginia, 1907–70), president of the United Automobile Workers, and his controversial contemporary, James Hoffa (b.Indiana, 1913–1975?), president of the Teamsters Union, whose disappearance and presumed murder remain a mystery.

The best-known literary figures who were either native or adopted Michiganians include Edgar Guest (b.England, 1881–1959), writer of enormously popular sentimental verses; Ring Lardner (1885–1933), master of the short story; Edna Ferber (1885–1968), best-selling novelist; Paul de Kruif (1890–1971), popular writer on scientific topics; Steward Edward White (1873–1946), writer of adventure tales; Howard Mumford Jones (1892–1980), critic and scholar; and Bruce Catton (1899–1978), Civil War historian.

Other prominent Michiganians past and present include Frederick Stuart Church (1842–1924), painter; Liberty Hyde Bailey (1858–1954), horticulturist and botanist; Albert Kahn (b.Germany, 1869–1942), noted architect and innovator in factory design; and (Gottlieb) Eliel Saarinen (b.Finland, 1873–1950), architect and creator of the Cranbrook School of Art, and his son Eero (1910–61), designer of the General Motors Technical Center in Warren and many distinctive structures throughout the United States. Malcolm X (Malcolm Little, b.Nebraska, 1925–65) developed his black separatist beliefs while living in Lansing.

Popular entertainers born in Michigan include Danny Thomas (Amos Jacobs, 1914–91), David Wayne (1914–91), Betty Hutton (b.1921), Ed McMahon (b.1923), Julie Harris (b.1925), Ellen Burstyn (Edna Rae Gilhooley, b.1932), Della Reese (Dellareese Patricia Early, b.1932), William "Smokey" Robinson (b.1940), Diana Ross (b.1944), Bob Seger (b.1945), and Stevie Wonder (Stevland Morris, b.1950), along with film director Francis Ford Coppola (b.1939).

Among sports figures who had notable careers in the state were Fielding H. Yost (b.West Virginia, 1871–1946), University of Michigan football coach; Joe Louis (Joseph Louis Barrow, b.Alabama, 1914–81), heavyweight boxing champion from 1937 to 1949; "Sugar Ray" Robinson (1921–89), who held at various times the welterweight and middleweight boxing titles; and baseball Hall of Famers Al Kaline (b.Maryland, 1934) and Tyrus Raymond ("Ty") Cobb (b.Georgia, 1886–1961), who won 12 batting titles, were Detroit Tigers stars. Earvin "Magic" Johnson (b.1959), who broke Oscar Robertson's record for most assists, was born in Lansing, Michigan.

⁵⁰BIBLIOGRAPHY

Ashlee, Laura Rose (ed.). *Traveling through Time: A Guide to Michigan's Historical Markers.* Ann Arbor: University of Michigan Press, 2005.

Bak, Richard. *A Distant Thunder: Michigan in the Civil War.* Ann Arbor, Mich.: Huron River Press, 2004.

Browne, William Paul. *Michigan Politics and Government: Facing Change in a Complex State.* Lincoln: University of Nebraska Press, 1995.

Council of State Governments. *The Book of the States, 2006 Edition.* Lexington, Ky.: Council of State Governments, 2006.

Dunbar, Willis F., and George S. May. *Michigan: A History of the Wolverine State.* 3rd rev. ed. Grand Rapids: Eerdmans, 1995.

Fine, Sidney. *Civil Rights and the Michigan Constitution of 1963.* Ann Arbor: Bentley Historical Library, University of Michigan, 1996.

Folsom, Burton W. *Empire Builders: How Michigan Entrepreneurs Helped Make America Great.* Traverse City, Mich.: Rhodes & Easton, 1998.

Hershock, Martin John. *Liberty and Power in the Old Northwest: Michigan, 1850–1867.* N.p., 1996.

Kenyon, Amy Maria. *Dreaming Suburbia: Detroit and the Production of Postwar Space and Culture.* Detroit: Wayne State University Press, 2004.

LeBeau, Patrick Russell. *Rethinking Michigan Indian History.* East Lansing, Mich.: Michigan State University Press, 2005.

Loepp, Daniel. *Sharing the Balance of Power: An Examination of Shared Power in the Michigan House of Representatives, 1993–94.* Ann Arbor: University of Michigan Press, 1999.

Moore, Elizabeth. *The State We're In: A Citizen's Guide to Michigan State Government.* Lansing: League of Women Voters of Michigan, 1995.

Poremba, David Lee. *Michigan.* Northampton, Mass.: Interlink Books, 2005.

Rubenstein, Bruce A. *Michigan, A History of the Great Lakes State.* Wheeling, Ill.: Harlan Davidson, 1995.

Sugrue, Thomas J. *The Origins of the Urban Crisis: Race and Inequality in Postwar Detroit.* Princeton. N.J.: Princeton University Press, 2005.

US Department of Commerce, Economics and Statistics Administration, US Census Bureau. *Michigan, 2000. Summary Social, Economic, and Housing Characteristics: 2000 Census of Population and Housing.* Washington, D.C.: US Government Printing Office, 2003.

MINNESOTA

State of Minnesota

ORIGIN OF STATE NAME: Derived from the Sioux Indian word *minisota,* meaning "sky-tinted waters." **NICKNAME:** The North Star State. **CAPITAL:** St. Paul. **ENTERED UNION:** 11 May 1858 (32nd). **SONG:** "Hail! Minnesota." **MOTTO:** *L'Etoile du Nord* (The North Star). **FLAG:** On a blue field bordered on three sides by a gold fringe, a version of the state seal is surrounded by a wreath with the statehood year (1858), the year of the establishment of Ft. Snelling (1819), and the year the flag was adopted (1893). Five clusters of gold stars and the word "Minnesota" fill the outer circle. **OFFICIAL SEAL:** A farmer, with a powder horn and musket nearby, plows a field in the foreground, while in the background, before a rising sun, a Native American on horseback crosses the plains; pine trees and a waterfall represent the state's natural resources. The state motto is above, and the whole is surrounded by the words "The Great Seal of the State of Minnesota 1858." Another version of the seal in common use shows a cowboy riding across the plains. **BIRD:** Common loon. **FISH:** Walleye. **FLOWER:** Pink and white lady slipper. **TREE:** Red (Norway) pine. **GEM:** Lake Superior agate. **LEGAL HOLIDAYS:** New Year's Day, 1 January; Birthday of Martin Luther King Jr., 3rd Monday in January; Presidents' Day, 3rd Monday in February; Memorial Day, last Monday in May; Independence Day, 4 July; Labor Day, 1st Monday in September; Veterans' Day, 11 November; Thanksgiving Day, 4th Thursday in November plus one day; Christmas Day, 25 December. By statute, schools hold special observances on Susan B. Anthony Day, 15 February; Arbor Day, last Friday in April; Minnesota Day, 11 May; Frances Willard Day, 28 September; Leif Erikson Day, 9 October. **TIME:** 6 AM CST = noon GMT.

¹LOCATION, SIZE, AND EXTENT

Situated in the western north-central United States, Minnesota is the largest of the Midwestern states and ranks 12th in size among the 50 states.

The total area of Minnesota is 84,402 sq mi (218,601 sq km), of which land accounts for 79,548 sq mi (206,029 sq km) and inland water 4,854 sq mi (12,572 sq km). Minnesota extends 406 mi (653 km) N–S; its extreme E–W extension is 358 mi (576 km).

Minnesota is bordered on the N by the Canadian provinces of Manitoba and Ontario (with the line passing through the Lake of the Woods, Rainy River, Rainy Lake, a succession of smaller lakes, the Pigeon River, and Lake Superior); on the E by Michigan and Wisconsin (with the line passing through Lake Superior and the St. Croix and Mississippi rivers); on the s by Iowa; and on the w by South Dakota and North Dakota (with the line passing through Big Stone Lake, Lake Traverse, the Bois de Sioux River, and the Red River of the North).

The length of Minnesota's boundaries totals 1,783 mi (2,870 km). The state's geographic center is in Crow Wing County, 10 mi (16 km) sw of Brainerd.

²TOPOGRAPHY

Minnesota, lying at the northern rim of the Central Plains region, consists mainly of flat prairie, nowhere flatter than in the Red River Valley of the west. There are rolling hills and deep river valleys in the southeast; the northeast, known as Arrowhead Country, is more rugged and includes the Vermilion Range and the Mesabi Range, with its rich iron deposits. Eagle Mountain, in the extreme northeast, rises to a height of 2,301 ft (702 m), the highest point in the state; the surface of nearby Lake Superior, 601 ft (183 m) above

sea level, is the state's lowest elevation. The mean elevation of the state is approximately 1,200 ft (366 m).

With more than 15,000 lakes and extensive wetlands, rivers, and streams, Minnesota has more inland water than any other state except Alaska. Some of the inland lakes are quite large: Lower and Upper Red Lake, 451 sq mi (1,168 sq km); Mille Lacs, 207 sq mi (536 sq km); and Leech Lake, 176 sq mi (456 sq km). The Lake of the Woods, 1,485 sq mi (3,846 sq km), is shared with Canada, as is Rainy Lake, 345 sq mi (894 sq km). A total of 2,212 sq mi (5,729 sq km) of Lake Superior lies within Minnesota's jurisdiction.

Lake Itasca, in the northwest, is the source of the Mississippi River, which drains about three-fifths of the state and, after meeting with the St. Croix below Minneapolis–St. Paul, forms part of the eastern boundary with Wisconsin. The Minnesota River, which flows across the southern part of the state, joins the Mississippi at the Twin Cities. The Red River of the North, which forms much of the boundary with North Dakota, is part of another large drainage system; it flows north, crosses the Canadian border above St. Vincent, and eventually empties into Lake Winnipeg in Canada. North River is the source of the St. Lawrence River.

Most of Minnesota, except for small areas in the southeast, was covered by ice during the glacial ages. When the ice melted, it left behind a body of water known as Lake Agassiz, which extended into what we now call the Dakotas and Canada and was larger than the combined Great Lakes are today; additional melting to the north caused the lake to drain away, leaving flat prairie in its wake. The glaciers also left behind large stretches of pulverized limestone, enriching Minnesota's soil, and the numerous shallow depressions that have developed into its modern-day lakes and streams.

³CLIMATE

Minnesota has a continental climate, with cold, often frigid winters and warm summers. The growing season is 160 days or more in the south-central and southeastern regions, but 100 days or less in the northern counties. Average temperatures range from 8°F (-13°C) in January to 66°F (18°C) in July for Duluth, and from 12°F (-11°C) in January to 74°F (23°C) in July for Minneapolis–St. Paul, often called the Twin Cities. The lowest temperature recorded in Minnesota was -60°F (-51°C), at Tower on 2 February 1996; the highest, 114°F (46°C), at Moorhead on 6 July 1936.

Annual precipitation is at about 31 in (79 cm) at Duluth and 29.4 in (75 cm) at Minneapolis–St. Paul. Precipitation is lightest in the northwest, where it averaged 19 in (48 cm) per year. Heavy snowfalls occur from November to April, averaging about 70 in (178 cm) annually in the northeast and 30 in (76 cm) in the southeast. Blizzards hit Minnesota twice each winter on the average. Tornadoes occur mostly in the south; on average there are 18 tornadoes in the state each year.

⁴FLORA AND FAUNA

Minnesota is divided into three main life zones: the wooded lake regions of the north and east, the prairie lands of the west and southwest, and a transition zone in between. Oak, maple, elm, birch, pine, ash, and poplar still thrive although much of the state's woodland has been cut down since the 1850s. Common shrubs include thimbleberry, sweetfern, and several varieties of honeysuckle. Familiar among some 1,500 native flowering plants are puccoon, prairie phlox, and blazing star; the pink and white (showy) lady slipper is the state flower. White and yellow water lilies cover the pond areas, with bulrushes and cattails on the shore. Three plant species were listed as threatened by the US Fish and Wildlife Service in April 2006—Leedy's roseroot, prairie bush-clover, and western prairie fringed orchid; the Minnesota dwarf trout lily was listed as endangered that year.

Among Minnesota's common mammals are the opossum, eastern and starnose moles, little brown bat, raccoon, mink, river otter, badger, striped and spotted skunks, red fox, bobcat, 13-lined ground squirrel (also known as the Minnesota gopher, symbol of the University of Minnesota), beaver, porcupine, eastern cottontail, moose, and white-tailed deer. The common loon (the state bird), western meadowlark, Brewer's blackbird, Carolina wren, and Louisiana water thrush are among some 240 resident bird species; introduced birds include the English sparrow and ring-necked pheasant. Teeming in Minnesota's many lakes are such game fishes as walleye, muskellunge, northern pike, and steelhead, rainbow, and brown trouts. The two poisonous snakes in the state are the timber rattler and the massasauga.

Classification of rare, threatened, and endangered species is delegated to the Minnesota Department of Natural Resources. Among rare species noted by the department are the white pelican, short-eared owl, rock vole, pine marten, American elk, woodland caribou, lake sturgeon, and paddlefish; threatened species include the bobwhite quail and piping plover. Nine species of animals occurring within the state (vertebrates and invertebrates) were listed as threatened or endangered in 2006 by the US Fish and Wildlife Service, including the gray wolf, bald eagle, piping plover, Topeka shiner, and Higgins' eye pearlymussel.

⁵ENVIRONMENTAL PROTECTION

The state's northern forests have been greatly depleted by fires, lumbering, and farming, but efforts to replenish them began as early as 1876, with the formation of the state's first forestry association. In 1911, the legislature authorized a state nursery, established forest reserves and parks, and created the post of chief fire warden to oversee forestry resources and promote reforestation projects. Minnesota divides its environmental programs among three agencies: the Minnesota Pollution Control Agency, the Department of Natural Resources, and the Office of Environmental Assistance. The Conservation Department, created in 1931, evolved into the present Department of Natural Resources, which is responsible for the management of forests, fish and game, public lands, minerals, and state parks and waters. The department's Soil and Water Conservation Board has jurisdiction over the state's 92 soil and water conservation districts. A separate Pollution Control Agency enforces air and water quality standards and oversees solid waste disposal and pollution-related land-use planning. The Environmental Quality Board coordinates conservation efforts among various state agencies.

Minnesotans dump 4,400 tons of waste a year (0.99 tons per capita) into 53 municipal landfills. In 1994, the state implemented the Minnesota Landfill Cleanup Program to ensure the proper care of 106 closed or closing municipal landfills. Beginning in 1996, the state began construction on 25 new municipal landfills and instituted a planning effort to manage all existing and closed sites. In 2003, Minnesota had 81 hazardous waste sites listed in the US Environment Protection Agency (EPA) database, 24 of which were on the National Priorities List as of 2006. In 2005, the EPA spent over $1.9 million through the Superfund program for the cleanup of hazardous waste sites in the state. The same year, federal EPA grants awarded to the state included $19.8 million for the state clean water revolving fund and $16.4 million for the drinking water revolving fund. To control the state's solid waste stream, Minnesotans have established 488 curbside recycling programs. The Reserve Mining Co. complied with a court order in 1980 by ending the dumping of taconite wastes, a possible carcinogen, into Lake Superior.

Other pollution problems came to light during the 1970s with the discovery of asbestos in drinking water from Lake Superior, of contaminants from inadequately buried toxic wastes at St. Louis Park, and of the killing by agricultural pesticides of an estimated 100,000 fish in two southeastern Minnesota brooks. During the early 1980s, the state's Pollution Control Agency approved plans by FMC, a munitions maker, to clean up a hazardous waste site at Fridley (near Minneapolis), which the EPA claimed was the country's most dangerous hazardous waste area. The Minnesota Mining and Manufacturing Co. in 1983 began to remove chemical wastes from three dumps in Oakdale (a suburb of St. Paul), where the company had disposed of hazardous wastes since the late 1940s. Each cleanup project was to cost the respective companies at least $6 million. In 2003, 31.4 million lb of toxic chemicals were released in the state.

In 1997, the state had some 9.5 million acres (3.8 million hectares) of wetlands. The Wetlands Conservation Act of 1991 set the ambitious goal of no wetland loss in the future.

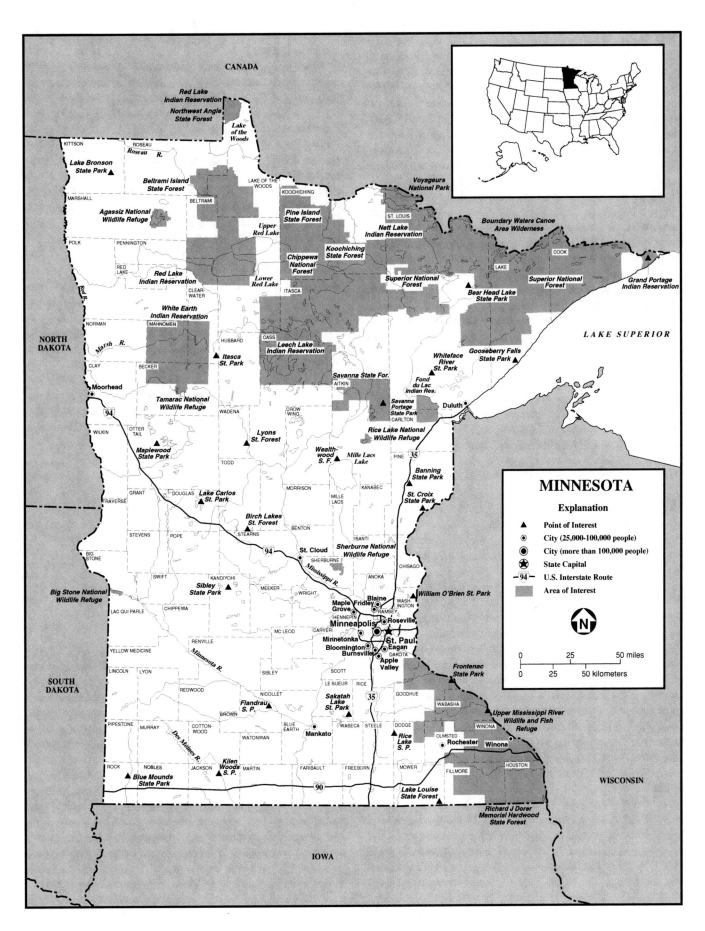

CANADA

Red Lake
Indian Reservation
Northwest Angle
State Forest

Lake
of the
Woods

KITTSON | ROSEAU
Roseau R.

Lake Bronson
State Park ▲

Beltrami Island
State Forest

MARSHALL

BELTRAMI

LAKE OF THE
WOODS

KOOCHICHING

Voyageurs
National Park

Agassiz National
Wildlife Refuge

Pine Island
State Forest

ST. LOUIS

Boundary Waters Canoe
Area Wilderness

POLK

PENNINGTON

Upper
Red Lake

Nett Lake
Indian Reservation

Chippewa
National
Forest

Koochiching
State Forest

COOK

RED
LAKE

Red Lake
Indian Reservation

CLEAR-
WATER

Lower
Red Lake

ITASCA

Superior National
Forest

LAKE

Superior National
Forest

Grand Portage
Indian Reservation

NORMAN

White Earth
Indian Reservation

MAHNOMEN

HUBBARD

CASS

Bear Head Lake
State Park ▲

LAKE SUPERIOR

NORTH
DAKOTA

Marsh R.

CLAY

▲ Itasca
St. Park

BECKER

Leech Lake
Indian Reservation

Savanna State For.

AITKIN

Whiteface
River
St. Park

Gooseberry Falls
State Park ▲

Moorhead ⊙

Tamarac National
Wildlife Refuge

WADENA

CROW
WING

Fond
du Lac
Indian Res.

Savanna
Portage
State Park

Duluth ⊙

WILKIN

Lyons
St. Forest ▲

CARLTON

Rice Lake National
Wildlife Refuge

OTTER
TAIL

Maplewood
State Park ▲

TODD

Wealth-
wood
S. F. ▲

Mille Lacs
Lake

PINE

⑨④

35

Banning
State Park ▲

GRANT

DOUGLAS

Lake Carlos
St. Park ▲

MORRISON

MILLE
LACS

KANABEC

St. Croix
State Park ▲

TRAVERSE

STEVENS

POPE

Birch Lakes
St. Forest ▲

STEARNS

BENTON

ISANTI

94

Sherburne National
Wildlife Refuge

CHISAGO

BIG
STONE

SWIFT

KANDIYOHI

St. Cloud ⊙

SHERBURNE

ANOKA

Big Stone National
Wildlife Refuge

Mississippi R.

LAC QUI PARLE

CHIPPEWA

Sibley
State Park ▲

MEEKER

WRIGHT

William O'Brien St. Park ▲

Blaine ⊙
Maple Fridley ⊙
Grove ⊙ RAMSEY
HENNEPIN ⊙ Roseville
Minneapolis ⊙
Minnetonka ⊙
Bloomington ⊙
Burnsville ⊙

WASH-
INGTON

RENVILLE

MC LEOD

CARVER

★ St. Paul
⊙ Eagan
DAKOTA

YELLOW MEDICINE

Minnesota R.

SIBLEY

Apple
Valley

SOUTH
DAKOTA

LINCOLN

LYON

REDWOOD

SCOTT

LE SUEUR RICE

Sakatah
Lake
St. Park ▲

35

GOODHUE

Frontenac
State Park ▲

NICOLLET

WABASHA

Flandrau
S. P. ▲

BROWN

BLUE
EARTH

WASECA

STEELE

DODGE

Upper Mississippi River
Wildlife and Fish
Refuge ▲

Des Moines R.

PIPESTONE

MURRAY

COTTON-
WOOD

WATONWAN

Mankato ⊙

▲ Rice
Lake
S. P.

OLMSTED

WINONA

Rochester ⊙

Winona ⊙

ROCK

NOBLES

JACKSON

Kilen
Woods
S. P. ▲

MARTIN

FARIBAULT

FREEBORN

MOWER

FILLMORE

HOUSTON

Blue Mounds
State Park ▲

90

Lake Louise
State Forest

WISCONSIN

Richard J Dorer
Memorial Hardwood
State Forest

IOWA

MINNESOTA

Explanation

▲ Point of Interest
⊙ City (25,000-100,000 people)
◉ City (more than 100,000 people)
★ State Capital
─94─ U.S. Interstate Route
▨ Area of Interest

Ⓝ

0   25   50 miles
0   25   50 kilometers

6 POPULATION

Minnesota ranked 21st in population in the United States with an estimated total of 5,132,799 in 2005, an increase of 4.3% since 2000. Between 1990 and 2000, Minnesota's population grew from 4,375,099 to 4,919,479, an increase of 12.4%. The population was projected to reach 5.6 million by 2015 and 6.8 million by 2025. The population density in 2004 was 64.1 persons per sq mi.

Minnesota was still mostly wilderness until a land boom in 1848 attracted the first substantial wave of settlers, mainly lumbermen from New England, farmers from the Middle Atlantic states, and tradespeople from eastern cities. The 1850 census recorded a population of 6,077 in what was then Minnesota Territory. With the signing of major Indian treaties and widespread use of the steamboat, large areas were opened to settlement, and the population exceeded 150,000 by the end of 1857. Attracted by fertile farmland and enticed by ambitious recruitment programs overseas, large numbers of European immigrants came to settle in the new state from the 1860s onward. In 1880, the state population totaled 780,733; by 1920 (when overseas immigration virtually ceased), the state had 2,387,125 residents. Population growth leveled off during the 1920s and has fallen below the national average since the 1940s. As of 2004, Minnesotans had a median age of 36.6 years. Nearly 24.3% of the population was under age 18, while 12.1% was age 65 or older.

The Minneapolis–St. Paul–Bloomington metropolitan area had an estimated population of 3,116,206 in 2004, up from an estimated 2,723,137 in 1995. The city of Minneapolis itself had an estimated 373,943 residents in 2004; St. Paul had an estimated 276,963. Other leading cities include Duluth and Rochester.

7 ETHNIC GROUPS

Minnesota was settled during the second half of the 19th century, primarily by European immigrants, chiefly Germans, Swedes, Norwegians, Danes, English, and Poles, along with the Irish and some French Canadians. The Swedish newcomers were mainly farmers; Norwegians concentrated on lumbering, while the Swiss worked for the most part in the dairy industry. In 1890, Finns and Slavs were recruited to work in the iron mines; the state's meatpacking plants brought in Balkan nationals, Mexicans, and Poles after the turn of the century. By 1930, 50% of the population was foreign-born. Among first- and second-generation Minnesotans of European origin, Germans and Scandinavians are still the largest groups. The state has more ethnic Norwegians than any other, and is second in number of ethnic Swedes, behind California. The other ethnic groups are concentrated in Minneapolis–St. Paul or in the iron country of the Mesabi Range, where ethnic enclaves still persist. As of 2000, foreign-born residents of Minnesota numbered 260,463, or 5.3% of the state total, up from 113,039 (2.5%) in 1990.

As of 2000 there were 54,967 American Indians in Minnesota, with 35,282 living on 13 of the state's 14 Indian reservations (one was unpopulated). Besides those living on reservations and in villages, a cluster of Indian urban dwellers (chiefly Ojibwa) lived in St. Paul. The reservation with the largest 2000 population was Leech Lake, with 10,205 people. Other reservations included Fond du Lac (3,728) and Mille Lacs (4,704). Indian lands totaled 764,000 acres (309,000 hectares) in 1982, of which 93% were trib-

al lands. In 2004, 1.2% of the state's population was composed of American Indians.

There were only 39 black Americans in Minnesota in 1850; by 1990, blacks numbered 95,000, or 2.1% of the total population, and as of 2000, the black population had jumped to 171,731 (3.5%). In 2004, 4.1% of the population was black. In 2000 there were 141,968 Asian and Pacific residents, including 41,800 Hmong (second-largest total in the United States), 18,824 Vietnamese, 16,887 Asian Indians, 16,060 Chinese, 12,584 Koreans, and 9,940 Laotians. In 2000, Pacific Islanders numbered 1,979. In 2000, there also were 143,382 Hispanics and Latinos, 2.9% of the state population. In 2004, 3.4% of the population was Asian, 0.1% of Pacific Island origin, and 3.5% Hispanic and Latino. That year, 1.4% of the population reported origin of two or more races.

8 LANGUAGES

Many place-names echo the languages of the Yankton and Santee Sioux Indian tribes and of the incoming Algonkian-language Ojibwa, or Chippewa, from whom most of the Sioux fled to Dakota Territory. Such place-names as Minnesota itself, Minnetonka, and Mankato are Siouan in origin; Kabetogama and Winnibigoshish, both lakes, are Ojibwan.

The following table gives selected statistics from the 2000 Census for language spoken at home by persons five years old and over. The category "African languages" includes Amharic, Ibo, Twi, Yoruba, Bantu, Swahili, and Somali. The category "Scandinavian languages" includes Danish, Norwegian, and Swedish.

LANGUAGE	NUMBER	PERCENT
Population 5 years and over	**4,591,491**	**100.0**
Speak only English	4,201,503	91.5
Speak a language other than English	389,988	8.5
Speak a language other than English	**389,988**	**8.5**
Spanish or Spanish Creole	132,066	2.9
Miao, Hmong	41,673	0.9
German	35,072	0.8
African languages	24,747	0.5
Vietnamese	16,503	0.4
French (incl. Patois, Cajun)	15,744	0.3
Scandinavian languages	12,722	0.3
Chinese	12,578	0.3
Russian	9,629	0.2
Laotian	7,987	

English in the state is essentially Northern, with minor infiltration of Midland terms because of early movement up the Mississippi River into southern Minnesota and also up the Great Lakes into and beyond Duluth. Among older residents, traces of Scandinavian intonation persist, and on the Iron Range several pronunciation features reflect the mother tongues of mine workers from eastern Europe.

Although some minor variants now compete in frequency, on the whole Minnesota speech features such dominant Northern terms as *andirons, pail, mouth organ* (harmonica), *comforter* (tied and filled bedcover), *wishbone, clingstone peach, sweet corn, angleworm* (earthworm), *darning needle or mosquito hawk* (dragonfly), and *sick to the stomach*. Minnesotans call the grass strip between street and sidewalk the *boulevard* and a rubber band a *rubber binder,* and many *cook coffee* when they brew it. Three-fourths of a sample population spoke *root* with the vowel of *put;* one third, through school influence, pronounced /ah/ in *aunt* instead of the usual Northern short /a/, as in *pants*. Many younger speakers pronounce *caller* and *collar* alike.

9 RELIGIONS

Minnesota's first Christian church was organized by Presbyterians in Ft. Snelling in 1835; the first Roman Catholic church, the Chapel of St. Paul, was dedicated in 1841 at a town then called Pig's Eye but now known by the same name as the chapel. Immigrants arriving in subsequent decades brought their religions with them, with Lutherans and Catholics predominating.

The Roman Catholic Church reported a statewide membership of 1,185,980 in 2004; with about 730,989 members belonging to the archdiocese of St. Paul and Minneapolis. As of 2000, predominant Protestant groups included the Evangelical Lutheran Church in America, 853,448 adherents, and the Lutheran Church–Missouri Synod, 203,863 adherents. In 2004, the United Methodist Church had 83,755 members. In 2005, the United Church of Christ reported a statewide membership of 33,901. Other Lutheran, Presbyterian, and Baptist denominations were also somewhat prominent. The Episcopal Church had 30,547 adherents in 2000. The Church of Jesus Christ of Latter-Day Saints (Mormons) reported 27,524 members in 71 congregations in 2006. A Mormon temple was opened in St. Paul in 2000. In 2000, there were about 42,000 adherents to Judaism and 12,300 adherents of Islam. That year, over 1.8 million people (about 38.3% of the population) were not counted as members of any religious organization.

Minnesota is the headquarters for three national Lutheran religious groups: the American Lutheran Church, the Church of the Lutheran Brethren, and the Association of Free Lutheran Congregations. The Temple of Eckankar (est. 1990) and the Eckankar Spiritual Center (est. 2004) are located in Chanhassen, which is considered to be the spiritual home of the faith. Eckankar, called "a religion of the light and sound of God" by its followers, was introduced by Paul Twitchell, an American journalist, in 1965.

10 TRANSPORTATION

The development of an extensive railroad network after the Civil War was a key factor in the growth of lumbering, iron mining, wheat growing, and other industries. By 2003, Minnesota had a total of 5,923 rail mi (9,536 km). In that same year, metallic ores were the top commodity transported by rail that originated within the state. As of 2006, Amtrak provided east–west service from Chicago to Seattle/Portland to six stations in Minnesota, including Minneapolis–St. Paul, via its Empire Builder train.

Planning and supervision of mass transportation in the Twin Cities metropolitan area are under the jurisdiction of the Metropolitan Transit Commission, a public corporation. The national Greyhound bus line was founded in Hibbing in 1914.

Minnesota had 131,937 mi (212,418 km) of public roads and streets in 2004. Minneapolis–St. Paul is linked by I-35 to Duluth, and I-94 connects the Twin Cities with Moorhead and Fargo, North Dakota. In 2004, there were 2.490 million automobiles, 2.046 million trucks of all types, and 7,000 buses registered with the state. In that same year, the state had 3,083,007 licensed drivers.

The first settlements grew up around major river arteries, especially in the southeast; early traders and settlers arrived first by canoe or keelboat, later by steamer. The port of Duluth-Superi-

or, at the western terminus of the Great Lakes–St. Lawrence Seaway (officially opened in 1959) was the state's busiest port, handling 45.392 million tons of domestic and international cargo in 2004, making it the 19th-busiest port in the United States. The port of Two Harbors was the state's second busiest port that same year and the nation's 48th busiest, handling 13.472 million tons. The ports of Minneapolis and St. Paul handle a combined cargo greater than seven million tons each year, with agricultural products and scrap iron moving downstream and petroleum products, chemicals, and cement moving upstream. Minnesota in 2004 had 258 mi (415 km) of navigable inland waterways. In 2003, waterborne shipments totaled 47.687 million tons.

In 2005, Minnesota had a total of 520 public and private-use aviation-related facilities. This included 384 airports, 58 heliports, one STOLport (Short Take-Off and Landing), and 77 seaplane bases. Minneapolis–St. Paul International is the state's largest and busiest airport. In 2004, the airport had 17,482,627 enplanements, making it the ninth-busiest airport in the United States.

11 HISTORY

People have lived on the land that is now Minnesota for at least 10,000 years. The earliest inhabitants—belonging to what archaeologists classify as the Paleo-Indian (or Big Game) culture—hunted large animals, primarily bison, from which they obtained food, clothing, and materials for shelter. A second identifiable cultural tradition, from around 5000 BC, was the Eastern Archaic (or Old Copper) culture. These people hunted small as well as large game animals and fashioned copper implements through a cold hammering process. The more recent Woodland Tradition (1000 BC– AD 1700) was marked by the introduction of pottery and of mound burials. From the 1870s to the early 1900s, more than 11,000 burial mounds were discovered in Minnesota—the most visible remains of prehistoric life in the area. Finally, overlapping the Woodland culture in time was the Mississippian Tradition, beginning around AD 1000, in which large villages with permanent dwellings were erected near fertile river bottoms; their residents, in addition to hunting and fishing, raised corn, beans, and squash. There are many sites from this culture throughout southern Minnesota.

At the time of European penetration in the 17th and early 18th centuries, the two principal Indian nations were the Dakota, or Minnesota Sioux, and, at least after 1700, the Ojibwa, or Chippewa, who were moving from the east into northern Minnesota and the Dakota homelands. Friendly relations between the two nations were shattered in 1736, when the Dakota slew a party of French missionaries and traders (allies of the Ojibwa) and their Cree Indian guides (distant relatives of the Ojibwa) at the Lake of the Woods, an act the Ojibwa viewed as a declaration of war. There followed more than 100 years of conflict between Dakota and Ojibwa, during which the Dakota were pressed toward the south and west, with the Ojibwa establishing themselves in the north.

Few scholars accept the authenticity of the Kensington Rune Stone, found in 1898, the basis of the claim that Minnesota was visited in 1362 by the Vikings. The first white men whose travels through the region have been documented were Pierre Esprit Radisson and his brother-in-law, Médart Chouart, Sieur de Groseilliers, who probably reached the interior of northern Minnesota in the 1650s. In 1679, Daniel Greysolon, Sieur Duluth, held council with the Dakota near Mille Lacs and formally claimed the region for King Louis XIV of France. The following year, Duluth negotiated the release of three captives of the Dakota Indians, among them a Belgian explorer and missionary, Father Louis Hennepin, who named the falls of the Mississippi (the site of present-day Minneapolis) after his patron saint, Anthony of Padua, and returned to Europe to write an exaggerated account of his travels in the region.

Duluth was in the vanguard of the French, English, and American explorers, fur traders, and missionaries who came to Minnesota during the two centuries before statehood. Among the best known was Nicolas Perrot, who built Ft. Antoine on the east side of Lake Pepin in 1686. In 1731, Pierre Gaultier de Varennes, Sieur de la Verendrye, journeyed to the Lake of the Woods, along whose shores he erected Ft. St. Charles; subsequently, he or his men ventured farther west than any other known French explorer, reaching the Dakotas and the Saskatchewan Valley. His eldest son was among those slain by Dakota Indians at the Lake of the Woods in 1736.

Competition for control of the upper Mississippi Valley ended with the British victory in the French and Indian War, which placed the portion of Minnesota east of the Mississippi under British control; the land west of the Mississippi was ceded by France to Spain in 1762. Although the Spanish paid little attention to their northern territory, the British immediately sent in fur traders and explorers. One of the best known was Jonathan Carver, who spent the winter of 1766–67 with the Dakota on the Minnesota River. His account of his travels—a mixture of personal observations and borrowings from others—quickly became a popular success.

There was little activity in the region during the Revolutionary War, and for a few decades afterward, the British continued to pursue their interests there. The North West Company built a major fur-trading post at Grand Portage, which quickly became the center of a prosperous inland trade, and other posts dotted the countryside. The company hired David Thompson away from the Hudson's Bay Company to map the area from Lake Superior west to the Red River; his detailed and accurate work, executed in the late 1790s, is still admired today. After the War of 1812, the US Congress passed an act curbing British participation in the fur trade, and the North West Company was eventually replaced by the American Fur Company, which John Jacob Astor had incorporated in 1808.

Under the Northwest Ordinance of 1787, Minnesota east of the Mississippi became part of the Northwest Territory; most of western Minnesota was acquired by the United States as part of the Louisiana Purchase of 1803. The Red River Valley became a secure part of the United States after an agreement with England on the northern boundary was reached in 1818.

In 1805, the US War Department sent Lt. Zebulon Pike and a detachment of troops to explore the Mississippi to its source. Pike failed to locate the source, but he concluded a treaty with a band of Dakota for two parcels of land along the river. Later, additional troops were sent in to establish US control, and in 1819, a military post was established in part of Pike's land, on a bluff overlooking the junction of the Mississippi and Minnesota rivers. First called Ft. St. Anthony, it was renamed in 1825 for Col. Josiah Snelling, who supervised the construction of the permanent fort. For three decades, Ft. Snelling served as the principal center of civilization in Minnesota and the key frontier outpost in the northwest.

In 1834, Henry H. Sibley was appointed a manager of the American Fur Company on the upper Mississippi. He settled comfortably at Mendota, a trading post across the river from Ft. Snelling, and enjoyed immediate success. The company's fortunes took a downward turn in 1837, however—partly because of a financial panic but, even more important, because the first of a series of treaties with the Dakota and Ojibwa transferred large areas of Indian land to the US government and thus curtailed the profitable relationship between fur traders and Indians. The treaties opened the land for lumbering, farming, and settlement. Lumbering spawned many of the early permanent settlements, such as Marine and Stillwater, on the St. Croix River, and St. Anthony (later Minneapolis) at the falls of the Mississippi. Another important town, St. Paul (originally Pig's Eye), developed as a trading center at the head of navigation on the Mississippi.

In 1849, Minnesota Territory was established. It included all of present-day Minnesota, along with portions of North and South Dakota east of the Missouri River. Alexander Ramsey, a Pennsylvania Whig, was appointed as the first territorial governor, and in 1851, the legislature named St. Paul the capital. Stillwater was chosen for the state prison, while St. Anthony was selected as the site for the university. As of 1850, the new territory had slightly more than 6,000 inhabitants, but as lumbering grew and subsequent Indian treaties opened up more land, the population boomed, reaching a total of more than 150,000 by 1857, with the majority concentrated in the southeast corner, close to the rivers.

On 11 May 1858, Minnesota officially became the 32nd state, with its western boundaries pruned from the Missouri to the Red River. Henry Sibley, a Democrat, narrowly defeated Alexander Ramsey, running as a Republican, to become the state's first governor. But under Ramsey's leadership, the fast-growing Republican Party soon gained control of state politics and held it firmly through the early 20th century. In the first presidential election in which Minnesota participated, Abraham Lincoln, the Republican candidate, easily carried the state, and when the Civil War broke out, Minnesota was the first state to answer Lincoln's call for troops. In all, Minnesota supplied more than 20,000 men to defend the Union.

More challenging to the defense of Minnesota was the Dakota War of 1862. Grieved by the loss of their lands, dissatisfied with reservation life, and ultimately brought to a condition of near starvation, the Dakota appealed to US Indian agencies without success. The murder of five whites by four young Dakota Indians ignited a bloody uprising in which more than 300 whites and an unknown number of Indians were killed. In the aftermath, 38 Dakota captives were hanged for "voluntary participation in murders and massacres," and the Dakota remaining in Minnesota were removed to reservations in Nebraska. (Some later returned to Minnesota.) Meanwhile, the Ojibwa were relegated to reservations on remnants of their former lands.

Also during 1862, Minnesota's first railroad joined St. Anthony (Minneapolis) and St. Paul with 10 mi (16 km) of track. By 1867, the Twin Cities were connected with Chicago by rail; in the early 1870s, tracks crossed the prairie all the way to the Red River Valley. The railroads brought settlers from the eastern states (many of them Scandinavian and German in origin) to every corner of

Minnesota; the settlers, in turn, grew produce for the trains to carry back to the cities of the east. The railroads soon ushered in an era of large-scale commercial farming. Wheat provided the biggest cash crop, as exports rose from 2 million bushels in 1860 to 95 million in 1890. Meanwhile, the falls of St. Anthony became the major US flour-milling center; by 1880, 27 Minneapolis mills were producing more than 2 million barrels of flour annually.

Despite these signs of prosperity, discontent grew among Minnesota farmers, who were plagued by high railroad rates, damaging droughts, and a deflationary economy. The first national farmers' movement, the National Grange of the Patrons of Husbandry, was founded in 1867 by a Minnesotan, Oliver H. Kelley, and spread more rapidly in Minnesota than in any other state. The Farmers' Alliance movement, joining forces with the Knights of Labor, exerted a major influence on state politics in the 1880s. In 1898, the Populist Party—in which a Minnesotan, Ignatius Donnelly, played a leading role nationwide—helped elect John Lind to the governorship on a fusion ticket.

Most immigrants during the 1860s and 1870s settled on the rich farmland of the north and west, but after 1880 the cities and industries grew more rapidly. When iron ore was discovered in the 1880s in the sparsely settled northeast, even that part of the state attracted settlers, many of them immigrants from eastern and southern Europe. Before 1900, Duluth had become a major lake port, and by the eve of World War I, Minnesota had become a national iron-mining center.

The economic picture changed after the war. As the forests were depleted, the big lumber companies turned to the Pacific Northwest. An agricultural depression hit the region, and flour mills moved to the Kansas City area and to Buffalo, New York. Minnesotans adapted to the new realities in various ways. Farmers planted corn, soybeans, and sugar beets along with wheat, and new food-processing industries developed. To these were added business machines, electronics, computers, and other high-technology industries. In 1948, for the first time, the dollar value of all manufactured products exceeded total cash farm receipts. In 1950 the state's urban population exceeded its rural population for the first time. Minnesota was becoming an urban commonwealth.

In addition to heightened demand for its agricultural products, Minnesota prospered as a result of new defense-related, high-technology, and other industries that grew up following World War II. Over $1 billion was invested in plants to process low-grade iron ore, called taconite, after the state's supply of high-grade ore declined. By the 1970s, environmentalists were targeting the ore producers for polluting Lake Superior with mineral wastes, and in 1978 the Minnesota Supreme Court ordered Reserve Mining Company to comply with pollution-control standards.

A successful merger of Minnesota's Farmer-Labor and Democratic parties, engineered in 1943–44 by both local and national politicians, revived the state's progressivist tradition after World War II. Hubert Humphrey (later US vice president) and his colleagues Orville Freeman, Eugene McCarthy, and Eugenie Anderson emerged as leaders of this new coalition. Their political heir, Walter Mondale, was vice president in 1977–81 but, as the Democratic presidential candidate in 1984, lost the election in a Republican landslide, carrying only his native state and the District of Columbia.

In the 1990s, Minnesota continued its economic diversification as service industries, including finance, insurance, and real estate, became increasingly important. As a result, it closed the decade with a low unemployment rate of 2.8% (when the national average was just over 4%). Though Minnesota, led by the Twin Cities, enjoyed an unprecedented decade of economic prosperity, it was generally acknowledged that agriculture across the Great Plains was in crisis by the end of the 1990s.

For many farmers, their problems had been exacerbated by weather conditions. In 1988, Minnesota's agricultural producers suffered from the worst drought since the 1930s. As a result of the severe flooding of the Mississippi River in 1993, almost half of Minnesota's counties were designated as disaster areas. Again in 1997, some of the most severe flooding in the century occurred in the Red River and Minnesota River valleys.

The state legislature closed its 1999 session having passed the largest permanent tax cut and one-time rebate in the state's history, amounting to $2.9 billion in tax relief. Though the accomplishment was hailed as a result of a multipartisan effort, discord soon befell Minnesota government. By October, activists were attempting to recall Governor Jesse Ventura, elected the previous year the Reform Party candidate, only to align himself with the Independence Party of Minnesota shortly after taking office. The following legislative session (in 2000) saw more veto overrides than in any other session of the last half century.

Republican Tim Pawlenty, elected governor in 2002, sponsored an Internet privacy bill early in his term and stressed the need for higher education standards and attracting more high-tech jobs to the state. In 2003, Minnesota faced the largest budget deficit in its history, $4.2 billion. The legislature that year passed a $28.3 billion budget marked by spending cuts and no new taxes. Democrats, farmers, and labor leaders feared Pawlenty's commitment to no new taxes would amount to large spending cuts in education, health care, and other areas. However, by 2005 Pawlenty had balanced the state's budget without cutting funding for K–12 education. Under Pawlenty's leadership, an overhaul of the state's education standards, welfare reform, lawsuit reform, and a large transportation package were passed.

As of 2005, the state had a $10 billion per year tourism industry. As such, it was focusing attention on its water resources, which provide jobs, drive quality of life, and support fish and wildlife. Development, pollution, and growing demands for safe drinking water are all pressures placed on the future health of Minnesota waters.

12 STATE GOVERNMENT

The constitutional convention that assembled at St. Paul on 13 July 1857 was marked by such bitter dissension that the Democrats and Republicans had to meet in separate chambers; the final draft was written by a committee of five Democrats and five Republicans and then adopted by a majority of each party, without amendment. Since Democrats and Republicans were also unwilling to sign the same piece of paper, two separate documents were prepared, one on blue-tinted paper, the other on white. The constitution was ratified by the electorate on 13 October and approved by the US Congress on 11 May 1858. An amendment restructuring the constitution for easy reference and simplifying its language was approved in 1974; for purposes of constitutional law, however, the original document (incorporating numerous other amendments) remains authoritative. Through January 2005 there were 118 amendments.

As reapportioned by court order after the 1970 census, the Minnesota legislature consists of a 67-member Senate and a 134-member House of Representatives. Legislative sessions begin in January and are limited to 120 legislative days or to the first Monday after the third Saturday in May. Sessions are to be held in only odd-numbered years, but the legislature may divide and meet in even-numbered years as well. Only the governor may call for special sessions. Senators serve four years and representatives two, at annual salaries of $31,140 as of 2004, unchanged from 1999. Representatives must be at least 18 years old and senators 21; they must be qualified voters, and must have resided in the state for one year and in the legislative district for six months preceding election.

The governor and lieutenant governor are jointly elected for four-year terms; both must be US citizens at least 25 years old, qualified voters, and must have been residents of Minnesota for a year before election. Other constitutional officers are the secretary of state, auditor, and attorney general, all serving for four years. Numerous other officials are appointed by the governor, among them the commissioners of government departments and many heads and members of independent agencies. As of December 2004, the governor's salary was $120,311.

Once a bill is passed by a majority of both houses, the governor may sign it, veto it in whole or in part, or pocket-veto it by fail-ing to act within 14 days of adjournment. (When the legislature is in session, however, a bill becomes law if the governor fails to act on it within three days.) A two-thirds vote of the members of both houses overrides a veto. Constitutional amendments require the approval of a majority of both houses of the legislature and are subject to ratification by the electorate. Those voting in state elections must be at least 18 years old, US citizens, and state residents for at least 20 days prior to election day. Restrictions apply to convicted felons and those declared mentally incompetent by the court.

[13] POLITICAL PARTIES

The two major political parties are the Democratic-Farmer-Labor Party (DFL) and the Republican Party (until 1995 called the Independent-Republican Party). The Republican Party dominated Minnesota politics from the 1860s through the 1920s, except for a period around the turn of the century. The DFL, formed in 1944 by merger between the Democratic Party and the populist Farmer-Labor Party, rose to prominence in the 1950s under US Senator Hubert Humphrey; it functions as the state chapter of the US Democratic Party.

The DFL is the heir to a long populist tradition bred during the panic of 1857 and the early days of statehood, a tradition perpetuated by a succession of strong, though transient, third-party movements. The Grange, a farmers' movement committed to the cause of railroad regulation, took root in Minnesota in 1868; it withered in the panic of 1873, but its successors, the Anti-Monopoly Par-

Minnesota Presidential Vote by Political Parties, 1948–2004

YEAR	ELECTORAL VOTE	MINNESOTA WINNER	DEMOCRAT[1]	REPUBLICAN[2]	PROGRESSIVE	SOCIALIST	SOCIALIST LABOR[3]
1948	11	*Truman (D)	692,966	483,617	27,866	4,646	2,525
1952	11	*Eisenhower (R)	608,458	763,211	2,666	—	2,383
						SOC. WORKERS	
1956	11	*Eisenhower (R)	617,525	719,302	—	1,098	2,080
1960	11	*Kennedy (D)	779,933	757,915	—	3,077	962
1964	10	*Johnson (D)	991,117	559,624	—	1,177	2,544
							AMERICAN IND.
1968	10	Humphrey (D)	857,738	658,643	—	—	68,931
					PEOPLE'S		AMERICAN
1972	10	*Nixon (R)	802,346	898,269	2,805	4,261	31,407
					LIBERTARIAN		
1976	10	*Carter (D)	1,070,440	819,395	3,529	4,149	13,592
						CITIZENS	
1980	10	Carter (D)	954,173	873,268	31,593	8,406	6,136
1984	10	Mondale (D)	1,036,364	1,032,603	2,996	1,219	—
					MINNESOTA PROGRESSIVE		SOCIALIST WORKERS
1988	10	Dukakis (D)	1,109,471	962,337	5,109	5,403	2,155
					IND. (Perot)		CONSTITUTION
1992	10	*Clinton (D)	1,020,997	747,841	3,373	562,506	3,363
							GREEN (Nader)
1996	10	*Clinton (D)	1,120,438	766,476	8,271	257,704	24,908
					REFORM		
2000	10	Gore (D)	1,168,266	1,109,659	5,282	22,166	126,696
					THE BETTER LIFE (Nader)		GREEN (Cobb)
2004	10**	Kerry (D)	1,445,014	1,346,695	4,639	18,683	4,408

*Won US presidential election.
**Minnesota has 10 electoral votes. One electoral vote was cast for John Edwards.
1 Called Democratic-Farmer-Labor Party in Minnesota.
2 **IND.**-Republican party called Republican Party as of 1995.
3 Appeared as Industrial Government Party on the ballot.

ty and the Greenback Party, attracted large followings for some time afterward. They were followed by a new pro-silver group, the Farmers' Alliance, which spread to Minnesota from Nebraska in 1881 and soon became associated with the Minnesota Knights of Labor. The Populist Party also won a foothold in Minnesota, in alliance with the Democratic Party in the late 1890s.

The Farmer-Labor Party, the most successful of Minnesota's third-party movements, grew out of a socialist and isolationist movement known at first as the Non-Partisan League. Founded in North Dakota with the initial aim of gaining control of the Republican Party in that state, the league moved its headquarters to St. Paul and competed in the 1918 elections under the name Farmer-Labor Party, hastily adopted to attract what party leaders hoped would be its two main constituencies. The party scored a major success in 1922 when its candidate, Henrik Shipstead, a Glenwood dentist, defeated a nationally known incumbent, Republican Senator Frank B. Kellogg; Farmer-Labor candidate Floyd B. Olson won the governorship in 1930. The decline of the party in the late 1930s was hastened by the rise of Republican Harold Stassen, an ardent internationalist, who won the governorship in 1938 and twice won reelection.

The first DFL candidate to become governor was Orville Freeman in 1954. The DFL held the governorship from 1963 to 1967 and from 1971 to 1978, when US Representative Al Quie (IR) defeated his DFL opponent, Rudy Perpich; however, Perpich regained the governorship for the DFL in 1982. Perpich served four terms. He lost to Independent-Republican Arne Carlson in 1990, and Carlson was reelected in 1994. The 1998 gubernatorial election in Minnesota made national headlines; it was won by Reform candidate and former World Wrestling Federation personality Jesse Ventura. After gaining office, Ventura switched allegiances to the Independence Party of Minnesota. Tim Pawlenty, a Republican, won the governorship in 2002.

Minnesota is famous as a breeding ground for presidential candidates. Governor Harold Stassen contended seriously for the Republican nomination in 1948 and again in 1952. Vice President Hubert Humphrey was the Democratic presidential nominee in 1968, losing by a narrow margin to Richard Nixon. During the same year, US Senator Eugene McCarthy unsuccessfully sought the Democratic presidential nomination on an antiwar platform; his surprising showings in the early primaries against the incumbent, Lyndon B. Johnson, helped persuade Johnson to withdraw his candidacy. Eight years later, McCarthy ran for the presidency as an independent, drawing 35,490 votes in Minnesota (1.8% of the total votes cast) and 756,631 votes (0.9%) nationwide. Walter Mondale, successor to Hubert Humphrey's seat when Humphrey became Johnson's vice president in 1964, was chosen in 1976 by Jimmy Carter as his vice-presidential running mate; he again ran with Carter in 1980, when the two lost their bid for reelection. In the 1984 election, Minnesota was the only state to favor the Mondale-Ferraro ticket. Minnesotans gave the Republican Party a majority in the state's House of Representatives for the first time since 1970, but the Democrats retained control of the state Senate.

In 2000, Democrat Al Gore won 48% of the presidential vote; Republican George W. Bush gained 46%; and Green Party candidate Ralph Nader received 5%. In 2004, Democratic challenger John Kerr garnered 51% of the vote to Bush's 48%. In 2004 there were 2,977,000 registered voters; there is no party registration in

the state. The state had 10 electoral votes in the 2004 presidential election.

In 2000, Democrat Mark Dayton was elected to the Senate. In 1996 Democrat Paul Wellstone successfully defended his Senate seat against a challenge by Republican Rudy Boschwitz, from whom he had won the seat in 1990. Wellstone died in a plane crash in October 2002, along with his wife and daughter, three staff members, and two pilots. Republican Norm Coleman won Wellstone's Senate seat in 2002, defeating Democrat and former vice president Walter Mondale, who stepped in to run after Wellstone's death. Following the 2004 elections, Minnesota's delegation to the US House was split between four Democrats and four Republicans. In mid-2005, there were 36 Democrats, 29 Republicans, and 1 Independent serving in the Minnesota state Senate. Party representation in the state House consisted of 66 Democrats, and 68 Republicans.

[14] LOCAL GOVERNMENT

As of 2005, Minnesota was divided into 87 counties, 854 municipal governments, 415 school districts, and 403 special districts. In 2002 there were also 1,793 townships.

Each of Minnesota's counties is governed by a board of commissioners, ordinarily elected for four-year terms. Other elected officials include the auditor, treasurer, recorder, sheriff, attorney, and coroner; an assessor and engineer are customarily appointed. Besides administering welfare, highway maintenance, and other state programs, the county is responsible for planning and development and, except in large cities, for property assessment. During the 1970s, counties also assumed increased responsibility for solid waste disposal and shoreline management.

Each regional development commission, or RDC, consists of local officials (selected by counties, cities, townships, and boards of education in the region) and of representatives of public interest groups (selected by the elected officials). RDCs prepare and adopt regional development plans and review applications for loans and grants.

Cities either have home-rule charters or are statutory cities, which are restricted to the systems of government prescribed by state law. In either case, the mayor-council system is the most common. Besides providing such traditional functions as street maintenance and police and fire protection, some cities operate utilities, sell liquor, or run hospitals, among other services. Each township is governed by a board of supervisors and by other elected officials.

In 2005, local government accounted for about 194,995 full-time (or equivalent) employment positions.

[15] STATE SERVICES

To address the continuing threat of terrorism and to work with the federal Department of Homeland Security, homeland security in Minnesota operates under the authority of executive order; the public safety commissioner is designated as the state homeland security advisor.

Minnesota's ombudsman for corrections investigates complaints about corrections facilities or the conduct of prison officials. The Campaign Finance and Public Disclosure Board supervises the registration of lobbyists, monitors the financing of political campaigns, and sees that elected and appointed state officials observe regulations governing conflict of interest and disclosure of personal finances. Minnesota law also provides that legislative meetings of any kind must be open to the public.

The state-aided public school system is under the jurisdiction of the Department of Education, which carries out the policies of an 11-member Board of Teaching appointed by the governor. Responsible for higher education are the University of Minnesota Board of Regents, elected by the legislature; the boards of trustees of the Minnesota State Colleges and Universities (MNSCU), appointed by the governor; and other agencies. The Department of Transportation maintains roads and bridges, enforces public transportation rates, inspects airports, and has responsibility for railroad safety.

Minnesota's Department of Health investigates health problems, disseminates health information, regulates hospitals and nursing homes, and inspects restaurants and lodgings. Health regulations affecting farm produce are administered by the Department of Agriculture. State facilities for the developmentally disabled are operated by the Department of Human Services, which administers state welfare programs and provides social services to the aged, the handicapped, and others in need.

The Department of Public Safety registers motor vehicles, licenses drivers, enforces traffic laws, and regulates the sale of liquor. The Department of Military Affairs has jurisdiction over the Minnesota National Guard, and the Department of Corrections operates prisons, reformatories, and parole programs. The Housing Finance Agency aids the construction and rehabilitation of low- and middle-income housing. Laws governing occupational safety, wages and hours, and child labor are enforced by the Department of Labor and Industry, while the Department of Employment and Economic Development supervises public employment programs and administers unemployment insurance. Other departments focus on agriculture, commerce, employee relations, finance, natural resources, public service, and revenue.

16 JUDICIAL SYSTEM

Minnesota's highest court is the Supreme Court, consisting of a chief justice and six associate justices; all are elected without party designation for six-year terms, with vacancies being filled by gubernatorial appointment. The district court, divided into 10 judicial districts with 254 judges in 1999, is the court of original jurisdiction. Each judicial district has at least three district judges, elected to six-year terms. The governor designates a chief judge for a three-year term.

County courts, operating in all counties of the state except two—Hennepin (Minneapolis) and Ramsey (St. Paul), which have municipal courts—assume functions formerly exercised by probate, family, and local courts. They exercise civil jurisdiction in cases where the amount in contention is $5,000 or less, and criminal jurisdiction in preliminary hearings and misdemeanors. They also hear cases involving family disputes, and have concurrent jurisdiction with the district court in divorces, adoptions, and certain other proceedings. The probate division of the county court system presides over guardianship and incompetency proceedings and all cases relating to the disposing of estates. All county judges are elected for six-year terms.

As of 31 December 2004, a total of 8,758 prisoners were held in Minnesota's state and federal prisons, an increase (from 7,865) of 11.4% over 2003. As of year-end 2004, a total of 544 inmates were female, up 25.1% (from 435) from the year before. Among sentenced prisoners (one year or more), Minnesota had an incarceration rate of 171 per 100,000 population in 2004.

According to the Federal Bureau of Investigation, in 2004 Minnesota had a violent crime rate (murder/nonnegligent manslaughter; forcible rape; robbery; aggravated assault) of 269.6 reported incidents per 100,000 population, or a total of 13,751 reported incidents. Crimes against property (burglary; larceny/theft; and motor vehicle theft) in that same year totaled 155,019 reported incidents or 3,039 reported incidents per 100,000 people. Minnesota has no death penalty. The state's Crime Victims Reparations Board offers compensation to innocent victims of crime or to their dependent survivors.

In 2003, Minnesota spent $119,675,678 on homeland security, an average of $24 per state resident.

17 ARMED FORCES

In 2004, there were 9,076 Defense Department personnel, 1,607 active-duty military personnel and 479 civilian personnel in Minnesota. In 2004 Minnesota firms received about $1.33 billion in defense contracts, and Defense Department payroll amounted to $708 million.

As of 2003, there were 426,591 veterans of US military service living in Minnesota. Of these, 59,307 served in World War II; 52,341 in the Korean conflict; 140,907 during the Vietnam era; and 51,141 in the Gulf War. Expenditures on veterans exceeded $1.0 billion in 2004.

As of 31 October 2004, the Minnesota Highway Patrol employed 545 full-time sworn officers

18 MIGRATION

A succession of migratory waves began in the 17th and 18th centuries with the arrival of the Dakota and Ojibwa, among other Indian groups, followed during the 19th century by New England Yankees, Germans, Scandinavians, and finally southern and eastern Europeans. Especially since 1920, new arrivals from other states and countries have been relatively few, and the state experienced a net loss from migration of 80,000 between 1970 and 1980. The trend was almost halted in the 1980s when immigration nearly equaled emigration. Between 1990 and 1998, Minnesota had net gains of 71,000 in domestic migration and 47,000 in international migration. In 1998, 6,981 foreign immigrants entered the state. Minnesota's overall population increased 8% between 1990 and 1998.

Within the state, there has been a long-term movement to metropolitan areas, especially to the suburbs of major cities; from 1970 to 1983, the state's metropolitan population grew by nearly 1% annually. The urban population increased from 66.8% to 69.9% during the 1980s and, leveling off somewhat, ranged between 68.8% and 69.7% in the 1990s. From 1980 to 1990, the population of the Minneapolis–St. Paul metropolitan area grew 15.5%; it grew another 8.9% between 1990 and 1996. In the period 2000–05, net international migration was 70,800 and net internal migration was -16,768, for a net gain of 54,032 people.

¹⁹INTERGOVERNMENTAL COOPERATION

Relations with the Council of State Governments are conducted through the Minnesota Commission on Interstate Cooperation, consisting of five members from each house of the state legislature and five administrative officers or other state employees; in addition, the governor, the president of the Senate, and the speaker of the House are nonvoting members. Minnesota also participates in the Great Lakes Charter, which it formed with seven other states in 1985 to preserve the lakes' water supply, and in other regional compacts. Minnesota is a party to the Boundary Compact Between Michigan, Wisconsin, and Minnesota; the Great Lakes Commission; the Midwest Interstate Low-Level Radioactive Waste Compact Commission; and the Midwestern Higher Education Compact. Minnesota received $5.493 billion in federal grants in fiscal year 2005, an estimated $5.154 billion in fiscal year 2006, and an estimated $5.783 billion in fiscal year 2007.

²⁰ECONOMY

Furs, wheat, pine lumber, and high-grade iron ore were once the basis of Minnesota's economy. As these resources diminished, however, the state turned to wood pulp, dairy products, corn and soybeans, taconite, and manufacturing, often in such food-related industries as meat-packing, canning, and the processing of dairy products. The leading sources of income in Minnesota have shifted again in the late 1990s. Manufacturing as a percent of total state output fell from 18.5% in 1997 to 13.7% in 2004, although there was net growth in manufacturing output from 1997 to 2001 of 5.8% compared to an output growth of 32.5% from general services; 27.9% from the trade sector; 26.1% from financial services; and 25.8% from government services. Minnesota's economy grew robustly at the end of the 1990s—7% in 1997, 5.2% in 1999, and 8.5% in 2000, but the annual growth rate plummeted to 1% in the recession of 2001. In 2002, employment declined more rapidly than in the country as a whole because of the large share of Minnesota workers in sectors most affected by the national slowdown: manufacturing, information technology, and airline industries. Office vacancy rates in metropolitan areas increased from 12.2% in 2001 to 19.6% in 2002, above the national average of 16.5%. On the other hand, having escaped the drought conditions that afflicted many other states, corn and soybean harvests were large in 2002, and Minnesota growers were in a position to benefit from drought-induced higher prices for both crops. The dairy sector, however, faced historically low prices, increasing the number of dairy producers leaving the industry.

Minnesota's gross state product in 2005 was $233 billion, up from $223.822 billion in 2004, when manufacturing accounted for the largest share at $30.670 billion (13.7% of GSP), followed by the real estate sector at $24.875 billion (11.1% of GSP), and healthcare and social assistance at $17.637 billion (7.8% of GSP). In that same year, there were an estimated 464,946 small businesses in Minnesota. Of the 134,438 businesses that had employees, an estimated total of 131,674 or 97.9% were small companies. An estimated 15,167 new businesses were established in the state in 2004, up 3.5% from the year before. Business terminations that same year came to 15,209, down 15.2% from 2003. There were 1,374 business bankruptcies in 2004, down 0.4% from the previous year. In 2005, the state's personal bankruptcy (Chapter 7 and Chapter 13) filing rate was 391 filings per 100,000 people, ranking Minnesota as 40th in the nation.

²¹INCOME

In 2005 Minnesota had a gross state product (GSP) of $233 billion which accounted for 1.9% of the nation's gross domestic product and placed the state at number 17 in highest GSP among the 50 states and the District of Columbia.

According to the Bureau of Economic Analysis, in 2004 Minnesota had a per capita personal income (PCPI) of $36,184. This ranked eighth in the United States and was 109% of the national average of $33,050. The 1994–2004 average annual growth rate of PCPI was 4.6%. Minnesota had a total personal income (TPI) of $184,413,901,000, which ranked 17th in the United States and reflected an increase of 6.4% from 2003. The 1994–2004 average annual growth rate of TPI was 5.7%. Earnings of persons employed in Minnesota increased from $138,475,249,000 in 2003 to $147,971,949,000 in 2004, an increase of 6.9%. The 2003–04 national change was 6.3%.

The US Census Bureau reports that the three-year average median household income for 2002 to 2004 in 2004 dollars was $55,914, compared to a national average of $44,473. During the same period an estimated 7.0% of the population was below the poverty line as compared to 12.4% nationwide.

²²LABOR

According to the Bureau of Labor Statistics (BLS), in April 2006 the seasonally adjusted civilian labor force in Minnesota numbered 2,946,100, with approximately 119,600 workers unemployed, yielding an unemployment rate of 4.1%, compared to the national average of 4.7% for the same period. Preliminary data for the same period placed nonfarm employment at 2,756,800. Since the beginning of the BLS data series in 1976, the highest unemployment rate recorded in Minnesota was 9% in November 1982. The historical low was 2.5% in April 1999. Preliminary nonfarm employment data by occupation for April 2006 showed that approximately 4.7% of the labor force was employed in construction; 12.5% in manufacturing; 19.3% in trade, transportation, and public utilities; 6.6% in financial activities; 11.3% in professional and business services; 14.2% in education and health services; 9.1% in leisure and hospitality services; and 15.2% in government.

The history of unionization in the state includes several long and bitter labor disputes, notably the Iron Range strike of 1916, the Teamsters' strike of 1934, and the Hormel strike of 1985–86. The earliest known unions—two printers' locals, established in the late 1850s—died out during the Civil War, and several later unions faded in the panic of 1873. The Knights of Labor were the dominant force of the 1880s. The next decade saw the rise of the Minnesota State Federation of Labor, whose increasing political influence bore fruit in the landmark Workmen's Compensation Act of 1913 and the subsequent ascension of the Farmer-Labor Party. The legislature enacted a fair employment practices law in 1955 and passed a measure in 1973 prescribing collective-bargaining procedures for public employees and granting them a limited right to strike.

The BLS reported that in 2005, a total of 392,000 of Minnesota's 2,494,000 employed wage and salary workers were formal members of a union. This represented 15.7% of those so employed, down from 17.5% in 2004, but still above the national average of 12%. Overall in 2005, a total of 410,000 workers (16.4%) in Minnesota were covered by a union or employee association contract, which includes those workers who reported no union affiliation. Minnesota is one of 28 states that does not have a right-to-work law.

As of 1 March 2006, Minnesota had a state-mandated minimum wage rate of $6.15 per hour for employers having annual receipts of $625,000 or more, and a rate of $5.25 per hour for employers under that total. In 2004, women in the state accounted for 47.5% of the employed civilian labor force.

23AGRICULTURE

Cash receipts from farm marketings totaled over $9 billion in 2005, placing Minnesota sixth among the 50 states; crops made up about 47% of the total value. For 2004, Minnesota ranked first in the production of sugar beets, sweet corn for processing, and green peas for processing; second in spring wheat, third in alfalfa hay; fourth in corn, oats, soybeans, and flaxseed; and sixth in barley and durum wheat.

The early farmers settled in the wooded hills and valleys in the southeastern quarter of the state, where they had to cut down trees and dig up stumps to make room for crops. With the coming of the railroads, farmers began planting the prairies with wheat, which by the late 1870s took up 70% of all farm acreage. In succeeding decades, wheat prices fell and railroad rates soared, fanning agrarian discontent. Farmers began to diversify, with dairy farming, oats, and corn becoming increasingly important. Improved corn yields since the 1940s have spurred the production of hogs and beef cattle and the growth of meat-packing as a major industry.

As of 2004, the state had 79,800 farms, covering 27,600,000 acres (11,200,000 hectares), or 51% of the state's total land area; the average farm had 346 acres (140 hectares). The number of people living on farms steadily declined from 624,000 in 1960 to 482,000 in 1970, and by 2002 there were only 66,996 persons residing on the farms they operated. The value of farmland rose between 2000 and 2004, from $1,320 per acre to $1,800. Minnesota's farmers faced acute financial troubles during the early 1980s as a result of heavy debts, high interest rates, and generally low crop prices.

The main farming areas are in southern Minnesota, where corn, soybeans, and oats are important, and in a Red River Valley along the western border, where wheat, barley, sugar beets, and potatoes are among the chief crops.

Agribusiness is Minnesota's largest basic industry, with about one-fourth of the state's labor force employed in agriculture or agriculture-related industries, most notably food processing.

24ANIMAL HUSBANDRY

Excluding the northeast, livestock-raising is dispersed throughout the state, with cattle concentrated particularly in west-central Minnesota and in the extreme southeast, and hogs along the southern border.

In 2005, the state had an estimated 2.4 million cattle and calves, valued at nearly $2.3 billion. The state had 6.5 million hogs and pigs, valued at $780 million in 2004. Minnesota produced more turkey in 2003 than any other state: 1.2 billion lb (0.55 billion kg), worth $425.3 million. Also during 2003, the state produced 13.8

million lb (6.3 million kg) of sheep and lambs, which brought in a total of nearly $13.3 million.

The state's total of 8.3 billion lb (4 billion kg) of milk outproduced all but five states in 2003. Production of broilers in 2003 was 228.5 million lb (103.4 million kg), worth around $77.7 million, and egg output in the same year was 2.9 billion, worth $146.4 million.

25FISHING

Commercial fishermen in 2004 landed 323,000 lb (146,800 kg) of fish valued at $187,000. The catch included herring and smelts from Lake Superior, whitefish and yellow pike from large inland lakes, and carp and catfish from the Mississippi and Minnesota rivers. In 2001, the commercial fleet had about 25 boats and vessels.

Sport fishing attracts some 1.5 million anglers annually to the state's 2.6. million acres (1.1 million hectares) of fishing lakes and 7,000 mi (11,000 km) of fishing streams, which are stocked with trout, bass, pike, muskellunge, and other fish by the Division of Fish and Wildlife of the Department of Natural Resources. Federal funds allocated for sport fish restoration projects totaled $10.8 million in 2005/06. In 2004, there were 1,467,677 sports fishing licenses issued in the state, second highest after Texas.

26FORESTRY

Forests, which originally occupied two-thirds of Minnesota's land area, have been depleted by lumbering, farming, and forest fires. As of 2004, forestland covered 16,230,000 acres (6,568,000 hectares), or over 30% of the state's total land area. Most of the forestland is in the north, especially in Arrowhead Country in the northeast. Of the 14,723,000 acres (5,958,000 hectares) of commercial timberland, less than half is privately owned and more than one-third is under state, county, or municipal jurisdiction. In 2004, lumber production totaled 265 million board feet, 45% hardwoods and 55% softwoods. Over half of the timber that is harvested is used in paper products, and about one-third for wood products. Mills that process raw logs account for half of all forest and forest-product employment in Minnesota.

The state's two national forests are Superior (2,094,946 acres/847,825 hectares) and Chippewa (666,541 acres/269,749 hectares). The Department of Natural Resources, Division of Forestry, promotes effective management of the forest environment and seeks to restrict forest fire occurrence to 1,100 fires annually, burning no more than 30,000 acres (12,000 hectares) in all.

More than 3 million acres (1.2 million hectares) are planted each year with trees by the wood fiber industry, other private interests, and federal, state, and county forest services—more than enough to replace those harvested or destroyed by fire, insects, or disease.

27MINING

According to preliminary data from the US Geological Survey (USGS), the estimated value of nonfuel mineral production by Minnesota in 2003 was $1.23 billion, a decrease from 2002 of about 5%. The USGS data ranked Minnesota as 11th among the

50 states by the total value of its nonfuel mineral production, accounting for around 3% of total US output.

By value (in descending order), Minnesota's top nonfuel mineral commodities in 2003 were iron ore, construction sand and gravel, crushed stone, industrial sand and gravel, dimension stone, and lime. Minnesota in 2003 was the nation's top producer of iron ore, was third in peat, and sixth in construction sand and gravel.

According to preliminary data for 2003, production of usable iron ore totaled 34.8 million metric tons and was valued at $969 million, while construction sand and gravel output that year stood at 47 million metric tons and was valued at $188 million. Crushed stone output in 2003 totaled 9.8 million metric tons and was valued at $57.3 million. Minnesota in 2003 was also a producer of common clays and dimension stone.

28 ENERGY AND POWER

As of 2003, Minnesota had 179 electrical power service providers, of which 125 were publicly owned and 47 were cooperatives. Of the remainder, five were investor owned, one was federally operated, and one was an owner of an independent generator that sold directly to customers. As of that same year there were 2,410,903 retail customers. Of that total, 1,398,351 received their power from investor-owned service providers. Cooperatives accounted for 675,996 customers, while publicly owned providers had 336,550 customers. There were five federal customers and only one independent generator or "facility" customer.

Total net summer generating capability by the state's electrical generating plants in 2003 stood at 11.486 million kW, with total production that same year at 55.050 billion kWh. Of the total amount generated, 90.1% came from electric utilities, with the remainder coming from independent producers and combined heat and power service providers. The largest portion of all electric power generated, 35.655 billion kWh (64.8%), came from coal-fired plants, with nuclear plants in second place at 13.413 billion kWh (24.4%) and other renewable power sources in third at 2.410 billion kWh (4.4%). Natural gas power plants accounted for 3.3% of all power generated, followed by petroleum fueled plants at 1.6%, hydroelectric at 1.5%, and other types of generating facilities at 0.1%.

As of 2006, Minnesota had two nuclear power plants: the Monticello plant near Monticello and the Prairie Island plant in Red Wing.

Minnesota's 7 million acres (2.8 million hectares) of peat lands, the state's only known fossil fuel resource, constitute nearly half of the US total (excluding Alaska). If burned directly, the accessible fuel-quality peat deposit could substantially supplement Minnesota's energy needs. As of 2004, the state had no proven reserves or production of crude oil and natural gas. As of 2005, Minnesota's two refineries had a capacity of 335,000 barrels per day.

29 INDUSTRY

Minnesota's vast wealth of natural resources, especially the state's extensive timberlands and fertile prairie, was the basis for Minnesota's early industrial development. In the late 19th century, Minneapolis was the nation's flour milling center. By the early 20th century, canning and meat packing were among the state's largest industries.

While food and food products remain an important part of the state's economy, the state's economy has diversified significantly from these early beginnings. As of the early 2000s, the state looks primarily to high technology industries such as computer manufacturing, printing and publishing, scientific instrument manufacturing, and fabricated metal production, for revenues.

According to the US Census Bureau's Annual Survey of Manufactures (ASM) for 2004, Minnesota's manufacturing sector covered some 20 product subsectors. The shipment value of all products manufactured in the state that same year was $88.472 billion. Of that total, food manufacturing accounted for the largest share at $16.841 billion. It was followed by computer and electronic product manufacturing at $11.898 billion; fabricated metal product manufacturing at $7.357 billion; transportation equipment manufacturing at $7.105 billion; and machinery manufacturing at $7.080 billion.

In 2004, a total of 325,601 people in Minnesota were employed in the state's manufacturing sector. Of that total, 214,788 were actual production workers. In terms of total employment, the computer and electronic product manufacturing industry accounted for the largest portion of all manufacturing employees at 44,845, with 20,519 actual production workers. It was followed by food manufacturing at 42,337 employees (32,182 actual production workers); fabricated metal product manufacturing at 39,238 employees (27,531 actual production workers); machinery manufacturing at 31,238 employees (18,790 actual production workers); and printing and related support activities with 29,224 employees (19,967 actual production workers).

ASM data for 2004 showed that Minnesota's manufacturing sector paid $14.210 billion in wages. Of that amount, the computer and electronic product manufacturing sector accounted for the largest share at $2.631 billion. It was followed by fabricated metal product manufacturing at $1.768 billion; food manufacturing at $1.513 billion; machinery manufacturing at $1.472 billion; and printing and related support activities at $1.161 billion.

30 COMMERCE

Access to the Great Lakes, the St. Lawrence Seaway, and the Atlantic Ocean, as well as to the Mississippi River and the Gulf of Mexico, helps make Minnesota a major marketing and distribution center for the upper Midwest.

According to the 2002 Census of Wholesale Trade, Minnesota's wholesale trade sector had sales that year totaling $108.3 billion from 8,884 establishments. Wholesalers of durable goods accounted for 5,022 establishments, followed by nondurable goods wholesalers at 2,749 and electronic markets, agents, and brokers accounting for 1,113 establishments. Sales by durable goods wholesalers in 2002 totaled $46.7 billion, while wholesalers of nondurable goods saw sales of $46.6 billion. Electronic markets, agents, and brokers in the wholesale trade industry had sales of $14.9 billion.

In the 2002 Census of Retail Trade, Minnesota was listed as having 21,129 retail establishments with sales of $60.01 billion. The leading types of retail businesses by number of establishments were: gasoline stations (2,605); food and beverage stores (2,551); motor vehicle and motor vehicle parts dealers (2,461); miscellaneous store retailers (2,447); and clothing and clothing accessories stores (2,298). In terms of sales, motor vehicle and motor vehicle parts stores accounted for the largest share of retail sales at $14.8 billion, followed by general merchandise stores at $8.6 billion; food and beverage stores at $8.5 billion; and building material/garden equipment and supplies dealers at $6.1 billion. A total of 306,571 people were employed by the retail sector in Minnesota that year.

Exports of manufactured goods to foreign countries amounted to $14.7 billion in 2005. Manufactured exports included computers and computer software, electronic equipment, scientific instruments, and transportation equipment. Dairy products, feed grains, soybeans, and wheat were the largest agricultural commodity exports by total value.

31 CONSUMER PROTECTION

The Minnesota Attorney General's Office enforces Minnesota's laws against false advertising, consumer fraud, and deceptive trade practices. The Consumer Protection Division answers consumer questions and mediates consumer complaints, attempting to resolve the complaints through a voluntary mediation program. The Attorney General's office also produces brochures and booklets on a wide variety of consumer topics, including landlords and tenants, new-car buying, home building, credit, and debt collection.

When dealing with consumer protection issues, the state's Attorney General's Office can initiate civil but not criminal proceedings; represent the state before state and federal regulatory agencies; administer consumer protection and education programs; handle formal consumer complaints; and exercise limited subpoena powers. In antitrust actions, the Attorney General's Office can act on behalf of those consumers who are incapable of acting on their own; initiate damage actions on behalf of the state in state courts; and initiate criminal proceedings. However, the Attorney General cannot represent counties, cities and other governmental entities in recovering civil damages under state or federal law.

The Consumer Protection Division is located in St. Paul. Also, the Hennepin County Attorney's Office in Minneapolis offers consumer protection services, as does the Minneapolis Division of Licenses and Consumer Services.

32 BANKING

As of June 2005, Minnesota had 470 insured banks, savings and loans, and saving banks, plus 102 state-chartered and 69 federally chartered credit unions (CUs). Excluding the CUs, the Minneapolis-St. Paul-Bloomington market area accounted for the largest portion of the state's financial institutions and deposits in 2004, with 176 institutions and $56.362 billion in deposits. As of June 2005, CUs accounted for 16.5% of all assets held by all financial institutions in the state, or some $12.948 billion. Banks, savings and loans, and savings banks collectively accounted for the remaining 83.5% or $65.360 billion in assets held.

As of 2004, the median net interest margin (the difference between the lower rates offered to savers and the higher rates charged on loans) stood at 4.37%, up from 4.33% in 2003; by 2005 the rate was 4.46%. The median percentage of past-due/nonaccrual loans to total loans was 1.44% in 2005, up slightly from 1.38% in 2004 but down from 1.65% in 2003.

33 INSURANCE

Minnesotans held over 2.8 million life insurance policies valued at about $268 billion as of 2004; total value for all categories of life insurance (individual, group, and credit) was over $469 billion. The average coverage amount is $94,900 per policy holder. Death benefits paid that year totaled $969.6 million.

As of 2003, there were 49 property and casualty and 13 life and health insurance companies incorporated or organized in the state. In 2004, direct premiums for property and casualty insurance totaled $8.7 billion. That year, there were 8,391 flood insurance policies in force in the state, with a total value of $1.2 billion. About $2.79 billion of coverage was held through FAIR plans, which are designed to offer coverage for some natural circumstances, such as wind and hail, in high risk areas.

In 2004, 64% of state residents held employment-based health insurance policies, 7% held individual policies, and 19% were covered under Medicare and Medicaid; 9% of residents were uninsured. Minnesota has the lowest percentage of uninsured residents in the nation; the state also ranks as having the highest percentage of employment-based insureds. In 2003, employee contributions for employment-based health coverage averaged at 16% for single coverage and 25% for family coverage. The state offers an 18-month health benefits expansion program for small-firm employees in connection with the Consolidated Omnibus Budget Reconciliation Act (COBRA, 1986), a health insurance program for those who lose employment-based coverage due to termination or reduction of work hours.

In 2003, there were over 3.4 million auto insurance policies in effect for private passenger cars. Required minimum coverage includes bodily injury liability of up to $30,000 per individual and $60,000 for all persons injured in an accident, as well as property damage liability of $10,000. Personal injury protection, underinsured, and uninsured motorist coverage are also mandatory. In 2003, the average expenditure per vehicle for insurance coverage was $836.12.

34 SECURITIES

The Minneapolis Grain Exchange, founded in 1881 as the Minneapolis Chamber of Commerce, is the state's major commodity exchange. The MGE is used primarily for the pricing of grains. Enforcement of statutes governing securities, franchises, and corporate takeovers (as well as charitable organizations, public cemeteries, collection agencies, and bingo) is the responsibility of the Securities Division of the Department of Commerce.

In 2005, there were 1,400 personal financial advisers employed in the state and 7,410 securities, commodities, and financial services sales agents. In 2004, there were over 225 publicly traded companies within the state, with over 115 NASDAQ companies, 45 NYSE listings, and 7 AMEX listings. In 2006, the state had 19 Fortune 500 companies; Target (based in Minneapolis) ranked first in the state and 29th in the nation with revenues of over $52.6 billion, followed by UnitedHealth Group (Minnetonka), Best Buy (Richfield), St. Paul Travelers Co. (St. Paul), and 3M (St. Paul). All five companies are listed on the NYSE.

³⁵PUBLIC FINANCE

Minnesota spends a relatively large amount on state government and local assistance, especially on a per capita basis. The state budget is prepared by the Department of Finance and submitted biennially by the governor to the legislature for amendment and approval. The fiscal year (FY) runs from 1 July to 30 June.

Fiscal year 2006 general funds were estimated at nearly $16.7 billion for resources and $15.8 billion for expenditures. In fiscal year 2004, federal government grants to Minnesota were $7.2 billion.

Minnesota—State Government Finances

(Dollar amounts in thousands. Per capita amounts in dollars.)

	AMOUNT	PER CAPITA
Total Revenue	29,708,220	5,828.57
General revenue	24,217,043	4,751.23
Intergovernmental revenue	6,379,798	1,251.68
Taxes	14,734,921	2,890.90
General sales	4,066,790	797.88
Selective sales	2,317,528	454.68
License taxes	941,783	184.77
Individual income tax	5,709,584	1,120.19
Corporate income tax	637,183	125.01
Other taxes	1,062,053	208.37
Current charges	1,903,656	373.49
Miscellaneous general revenue	1,198,668	235.17
Utility revenue	–	–
Liquor store revenue	–	–
Insurance trust revenue	5,491,177	1,077.34
Total expenditure	28,831,675	5,656.60
Intergovernmental expenditure	9,638,153	1,890.95
Direct expenditure	19,193,522	3,765.65
Current operation	13,399,569	2,628.91
Capital outlay	1,312,133	257.43
Insurance benefits and repayments	3,346,880	656.64
Assistance and subsidies	756,958	148.51
Interest on debt	377,982	74.16
Exhibit: Salaries and wages	3,928,883	770.82
Total expenditure	28,831,675	5,656.60
General expenditure	25,383,736	4,980.13
Intergovernmental expenditure	9,638,153	1,890.95
Direct expenditure	15,745,583	3,089.19
General expenditures, by function:		
Education	9,872,467	1,936.92
Public welfare	8,047,983	1,578.96
Hospitals	191,650	37.60
Health	516,458	101.33
Highways	1,823,163	357.69
Police protection	212,528	41.70
Correction	411,061	80.65
Natural resources	465,387	91.31
Parks and recreation	160,839	31.56
Government administration	655,093	128.53
Interest on general debt	377,982	74.16
Other and unallocable	2,649,125	519.74
Utility expenditure	101,059	19.83
Liquor store expenditure	–	–
Insurance trust expenditure	3,346,880	656.64
Debt at end of fiscal year	6,665,669	1,307.76
Cash and security holdings	50,533,430	9,914.35

Abbreviations and symbols: – zero or rounds to zero; (NA) not available; (X) not applicable.

SOURCE: *U.S. Census Bureau, Governments Division, 2004 Survey of State Government Finances,* January 2006.

On 5 January 2006 the federal government released $100 million in emergency contingency funds targeted to the areas with the greatest need, including $4.2 million for Minnesota.

³⁶TAXATION

In 2005, Minnesota collected $15,881 million in tax revenues or $3,094 per capita, which placed it sixth among the 50 states in per capita tax burden. The national average was $2,192 per capita. Property taxes accounted for 3.9% of the total, sales taxes 26.5%, selective sales taxes 15.3%, individual income taxes 39.9%, corporate income taxes 5.9%, and other taxes 8.5%.

As of 1 January 2006, Minnesota had three individual income tax brackets ranging from 5.35 to 7.85%. The state taxes corporations at a flat rate of 9.8%.

In 2004, state and local property taxes amounted to $4,920,174,000 or $965 per capita. The per capita amount ranks the state 27th nationally. Local governments collected $4,312,311,000 of the total and the state government $607,863,000.

Minnesota taxes retail sales at a rate of 6.50%. In addition to the state tax, local taxes on retail sales can reach as much as 1%, making for a potential total tax on retail sales of 7.50%. Food purchased for consumption off-premises is tax exempt. The tax on cigarettes is 123 cents per pack, which ranks 14th among the 50 states and the District of Columbia. Minnesota taxes gasoline at 20 cents per gallon. This is in addition to the 18.4 cents per gallon federal tax on gasoline.

According to the Tax Foundation, for every federal tax dollar sent to Washington in 2004, Minnesota citizens received $0.69 in federal spending.

³⁷ECONOMIC POLICY

Minnesota's Department of Employment and Economic Development (DEED) offers a variety of programs to encourage expansion of existing industries and to attract new industry to the state. The department extends loans to small businesses for capital investments that create or retain jobs. It awards grants to new or expanding companies in rural areas and provides limited guarantees to private lenders for loans given to start-up companies. The Minnesota Trade Office assists with the financing of small business exports. The state offers grants to depressed communities to help them retain or attract business or to rebuild their infrastructure. Minnesota's corporate income tax is structured to favor companies having relatively large payrolls and property (as opposed to sales) within the state. In 2006, an initiative called Positively Minnesota was guiding economic development efforts. The primary goal was to capture a great share of business expansions. As a group, Positively Minnesota included economic developers, utilities and private firms as well as the DEED. Beginning in 2004, the Job Opportunity Building Zones (JOBZ) project was launched: it is a rural economic development stimulus program. The program provides substantial tax relief to companies that start up or expand in targeted areas of Minnesota. The program identifies 10 zones encompassing more than 300 communities in every region of the state (except in the seven Twin Cities metropolitan counties). The program was to expire in 2015.

38 HEALTH

Shortly after the founding of Minnesota Territory, promoters attracted new settlers partly by proclaiming the tonic benefits of Minnesota's soothing landscape and cool, bracing climate; the area was trumpeted as a haven for retirees and for those afflicted with malaria or tuberculosis.

The infant mortality rate in October 2005 was estimated at 5.2 per 1,000 live births. The birth rate in 2003 was 13.9 per 1,000 population. The abortion rate stood at 13.5 per 1,000 women in 2000. In 2003, about 86.5% of pregnant woman received prenatal care beginning in the first trimester. In 2004, approximately 85% of children received routine immunizations before the age of three.

The crude death rate in 2003 was 7.1 deaths per 1,000 population. As of 2002, the death rates for major causes of death (per 100,000 resident population) were: heart disease, 171.4; cancer, 183.5; cerebrovascular diseases, 53.9; chronic lower respiratory diseases, 39.3; and diabetes, 26.2. The mortality rate from HIV infection was 1.1 per 100,000 population. In 2004, the reported AIDS case rate was at about 4.3 per 100,000 population. In 2002, about 57.6% of the population was considered overweight or obese. As of 2004, about 20.6% of state residents were smokers.

In 2003, Minnesota had 131 community hospitals with about 16,400 beds. There were about 615,000 patient admissions that year and 9.1 million outpatient visits. The average daily inpatient census was about 11,300 patients. The average cost per day for hospital care was $1,109. Also in 2003, there were about 425 certified nursing facilities in the state with 39,336 beds and an overall occupancy rate of about 92.1%. In 2004, it was estimated that about 79.7% of all state residents had received some type of dental care within the year; this was the second-highest dental care percentage in the nation (following Connecticut). Minnesota had 283 physicians per 100,000 resident population in 2004 and 962 nurses per 100,000 in 2005. In 2004, there were a total of 3,069 dentists in the state.

About 19% of state residents were enrolled in Medicaid and Medicare programs in 2004. Approximately 9% of the state population was uninsured in 2004; representing the lowest uninsured rate in the country. In 2003, state health care expenditures totaled $6.9 million.

The Mayo Clinic, developed by Drs. Charles H. and William J. Mayo in the 1890s and early 1900s, was the first private clinic in the United States and became a world-renowned center for surgery. In 2005, it was ranked second on the Honor Roll of Best Hospitals 2005 by *U.S. News & World Report*. In the same report, it ranked second for best care in heart disease and heart surgery and fifth for best care in cancer. The separate Mayo Foundation for Medical Education and Research, founded and endowed by the Mayo brothers in 1915, was subsequently affiliated with the University of Minnesota, which became the first US institution to offer graduate education in surgery and other branches of clinical medicine.

39 SOCIAL WELFARE

In 2004, about 147,000 people received unemployment benefits, with the average weekly unemployment benefit at $318. In fiscal year 2005, the estimated average monthly participation in the food stamp program included about 259,937 persons (124,398 households); the average monthly benefit was about $88.16 per person. That year, the total of benefits paid through the state for the food stamp program was about $274.9 million.

Temporary Assistance for Needy Families (TANF), the system of federal welfare assistance that officially replaced Aid to Families with Dependent Children (AFDC) in 1997, was reauthorized through the Deficit Reduction Act of 2005. TANF is funded through federal block grants that are divided among the states based on an equation involving the number of recipients in each state. Minnesota's TANF program is called Minnesota Family Investment Program (MFIP). In 2004, the state program had 88,000 recipients; state and federal expenditures on this TANF program totaled $193 million in fiscal year 2003.

In December 2004, Social Security benefits were paid to 775,050 Minnesota residents. This number included 517,510 retired workers, 76,260 widows and widowers, 84,830 disabled workers, 44,770 spouses, and 51,680 children. Social Security beneficiaries represented 15.2% of the total state population and 93.8% of the state's population age 65 and older. Retired workers received an average monthly payment of $955; widows and widowers, $925; disabled workers, $879; and spouses, $480. Payments for children of retired workers averaged $505 per month; children of deceased workers, $673; and children of disabled workers, $260. Federal Supplemental Security Income payments in December 2004 went to 70,745 Minnesota residents, averaging $398 a month. An additional $7.7 million of state-administered supplemental payments were distributed to 40,320 residents.

40 HOUSING

In 2004, Minnesota had an estimated 2,212,701 housing units, of which 2,054,900 were occupied. That year, Minnesota had the highest rate of homeownership in the nation with 75.3% of all housing units being owner-occupied. About 68% of all units were single-family, detached homes. Most units rely on utility gas and electricity for heating. It was estimated that 53,332 units lacked telephone service, 9,065 lacked complete plumbing facilities, and 9,270 lacked complete kitchen facilities. The average household had 2.41 members.

In 2004, 41,800 new units were authorized for construction. The median home value was $181,135. The median monthly cost for mortgage owners was $1,260. Renters paid a median of $673 per month. In September 2005, the state received a grant of $362,500 from the US Department of Housing and Urban Development (HUD) for rural housing and economic development programs. For 2006, HUD allocated to the state over $20.9 million in community development block grants.

41 EDUCATION

Minnesota's first public school system was authorized in 1849, but significant growth in enrollment did not occur until after the Civil War. In 2004, 92.3% of Minnesotans age 25 or older were high school graduates, far exceeding the national average of 84%. Some

32.5% had obtained a bachelor's degree or higher, compared to the national average of 26%.

The total enrollment for fall 2002 in Minnesota's public schools stood at 847,000. Of these, 568,000 attended schools from kindergarten through grade eight, and 279,000 attended high school. Approximately 80.2% of the students were white, 7.8% were black, 4.6% were Hispanic, 5.4% were Asian/Pacific Islander, and 2.1% were American Indian/Alaskan Native. Total enrollment was estimated at 836,000 in fall 2003 but was expected to be 826,000 by fall 2014, a decline of 2.5% during the period 2002 to 2014. Expenditures for public education in 2003/04 were estimated at $8.6 billion. In fall 2003, there were 93,935 students enrolled in 568 private schools. Since 1969, the National Assessment of Educational Progress (NAEP) has tested public school students nationwide. The resulting report, *The Nation's Report Card*, stated that in 2005, eighth graders in Minnesota scored 290 out of 500 in mathematics compared with the national average of 278.

As of fall 2002, there were 323,791 students enrolled in college or graduate school; minority students comprised 11.7% of total postsecondary enrollment. In 2005 Minnesota had 113 degree-granting institutions. The state's public postsecondary education system is overseen by Minnesota State Colleges and Universities (MNSCU) and includes three areas: the state university system—with campuses at Bemidji, Mankato, Marshall, Minneapolis–St. Paul, Moorhead, St. Cloud, and Winona; the community college system, and a statewide network of area vocational-technical institutes. The University of Minnesota (founded as an academy in 1851) has campuses in the Twin Cities, Duluth, Morris, and Crookston. The state's oldest private college, Hamline University in St. Paul, was founded in 1854 and is affiliated with the United Methodist Church. There are more than 20 private colleges, many of them with ties to Lutheran or Roman Catholic religious authorities. Carleton College, at Northfield, is a notable independent institution.

Minnesota has an extensive program of student grants, work-study arrangements, and loan programs, in addition to reciprocal tuition arrangements with Wisconsin, North Dakota, and South Dakota.

42 ARTS

State and regional arts groups as well as individual artists are supported by state and federal grants administered through the Minnesota State Arts Board, an 11-member panel appointed by the governor. In 2005, the Minnesota State Arts Board and other Minnesota arts organizations received 57 grants totaling $3,319,100 from the National Endowment for the Arts. The State Arts Board was also given funding from the state and from private sources. The Minnesota Humanities Commission (MHC) was founded in 1971. As of 2006 the MHC offered public programs such as the "Humanities Foundations," which provided family literacy programs and Teacher Institutes and "Learning in Retirement," which promoted adult learning through senior organizations. In 2005, the National Endowment for the Humanities contributed $1,503,460 to 19 state programs.

The Ordway Music Theater in St. Paul, which has two concert halls, opened in January 1985. The Ordway is the home of the Minnesota Orchestra, the Minnesota Opera Company, and the St. Paul Chamber Orchestra. The privately owned nonprofit theater was built for about $45 million and was founded with funding from the Minnesota Mining and Manufacturing Corp. and other private sources. In 1999, the Ordway received funding from the National Endowment for the Arts to use interactive video-conferencing technology to develop an "electronic field trip" accessible to student audiences across the state.

The St. Olaf College Choir, at Northfield, has a national reputation. The Tyrone Guthrie Theater, founded in Minneapolis in 1963, is one of the nation's most prestigious repertory companies; it moved to a location overlooking the Mississippi River in 2006. The Minnesota Ballet is based in Duluth.

Literary arts are active in the state. The Loft, founded in 1974 in Minneapolis, is considered to be one of the nation's largest and most comprehensive literary centers and offers programs for readers, mentoring programs for writers, grants and awards for writers, and publications, among other services.

The Walker Art Center in Minneapolis is an innovative museum with an outstanding contemporary collection. The Minneapolis Institute of Arts exhibits more traditional works with a permanent collection of over 100,000 pieces spanning 5,000 years of world history. The Weisman Art Museum of the University of Minnesota is in Minneapolis, and the Minnesota Museum of Art is in St. Paul.

43 LIBRARIES AND MUSEUMS

In 2001, Minnesota had an estimated 140 public library systems, with a total of 359 libraries, of which 232 were branches. The total number of books and serial publications that year was 14,414,000 volumes, with audio and video items totaling 651,000 and 488,000, respectively. Library circulation reached 43,843,000. The system also operated 17 bookmobiles. The largest single public library system is the 15-library Minneapolis Public Library and Information Center (founded in 1885); its new Central Library opened in 2006. The leading academic library, with 5,747,805 volumes, is that maintained by the University of Minnesota at Minneapolis. Special libraries include the James Jerome Hill Reference Library (devoted to commerce and transportation) and the library of the Minnesota Historical Society, both located in St. Paul. Nearly all public, academic, school, and special libraries participate in one of the seven library system networks that facilitate resource sharing. In 2001, operating income for the state's public library system was estimated at $149 million, including $642,000 in federal grants and $10 million in state grants.

There are more than 164 museums and historic sites. In addition to several noted museums of the visual arts, Minnesota is home to the Mayo Medical Museum at the Mayo Clinic in Rochester. The Minnesota Historical Society Museum offers rotating exhibits on varied aspects of the state's history. In May 1996, the Mille Lacs Indian Museum and Trading Post opened its doors. Historic sites include the Split Rock Lighthouse on the north shore of Lake Superior, Historic Fort Snelling in the Twin Cities, the boyhood home of Charles Lindbergh in Little Falls, and the Sauk Centre home of Sinclair Lewis.

44 COMMUNICATIONS

As of 2004, 97.1% of Minnesota's occupied housing units had telephones. Additionally, by June of that same year there were 2,832,079 mobile wireless telephone subscribers. In 2003, 67.9%

of Minnesota households had a computer and 61.6% had Internet access. By June 2005, there were 723,484 high-speed lines in Minnesota, 655,837 residential and 67,647 for business.

Commercial broadcasting began with the opening of the first radio station in 1922; as of 2005 there were 135 major radio stations—33 AM and 102 FM—and 20 major television stations. The Minneapolis–St. Paul metropolitan area had 1,481,050 television households, 54% of which received cable as of 1999.

As of 2000, a total of 116,792 Internet domain names had been registered in Minnesota.

⁴⁵PRESS

The *Minnesota Pioneer,* whose first issue was printed on a small hand press and distributed by the publisher himself on 28 April 1849 in St. Paul, vies with the *Minnesota Register* (its first issue was dated earlier but may have appeared later) for the honor of being Minnesota's first newspaper. Over the next 10 years, in any case, nearly 100 newspapers appeared at locations throughout the territory, including direct ancestors of many present-day publications. In April 1982, Minneapolis's daily newspapers were merged into the *Minneapolis Star Tribune.* As of 2005, the state had 15 morning dailies, 10 evening dailies, and 15 Sunday papers.

The following table lists the leading dailies, with their average circulations in 2005:

AREA	NAME	DAILY	SUNDAY
Duluth	*News Tribune* (m,S)	46,460	69,471
Minneapolis	*Star Tribune* (m,S)	381,094	678,650
St. Paul	*Pioneer Press* (m,S)	191,264	254,078

As of 2005, 333 weekly newspapers were being published in Minnesota. Among the most widely read magazines published in Minnesota were *Family Handyman,* appearing 11 times a year; *Catholic Digest,* a religious monthly; and *Snow Goer,* published six times a year for snowmobile enthusiasts.

⁴⁶ORGANIZATIONS

In 2006, there were over 8,805 nonprofit organizations registered within the state, of which about 5,694 were registered as charitable, educational, or religious.

The Minnesota Historical Society, founded in 1849, is the oldest educational organization in the state and the official custodian of its history. The society is partly supported by state funds, as are such other semistate organizations as the Academy of Science (which promotes interest in science among high school students), the Minnesota State Horticultural Society, and the Humane Society. The Sons of Norway and American Swedish Institute, both with headquarters in Minneapolis, seek to preserve the state's Scandinavian heritage. The Czechoslovak Genealogical Society International is based in St. Paul.

The American Board of Physical Medicine and Rehabilitation is based in Rochester. The National Scholastic Press Association is based in Minneapolis. The Organic Consumers Association, established in 1998, is based in the town of Finland.

Hobbyist and sport associations with headquarters in Minnesota include the American Coaster Enthusiasts, the North American Fishing Club, and North American Hunting Club.

The National Marrow Donor Program is based in Minneapolis, as is the National Council of the United States, International Organization of Good Templars.

⁴⁷TOURISM, TRAVEL, AND RECREATION

In 2004, the state hosted some 28.6 million travelers, with 50% of all tourist activity involving Minnesota residents touring their own state. About 11.7 million visitors were from out of state, primarily from one of the following states: Wisconsin, Iowa, North Dakota, Illinois, California, South Dakota, Michigan, Texas, Missouri, and Florida. Shopping was the most popular tourist activity for out-of-state visitors. Total travel expenditures for 2004 reached $9.2 billion, which included support for over 233,000 jobs. More than 40% of tourists visited the twin cities of Minneapolis and St. Paul..

With its lakes and parks, ski trails and campsites, and historical and cultural attractions, Minnesota provides ample recreational opportunities for residents and visitors alike. Minnesota's attractions include the 220,000-acre (80,000-hectare) Voyageurs National Park near the Canadian border; Grand Portage National Monument, in Arrowhead Country, a former fur-trading center with a restored trading post; and Pipestone National Monument, in southwestern Minnesota, containing the red pipestone quarry used by Indians to make peace pipes. Lumbertown USA, a restored 1870s lumber community, is in Brainerd, and the US Hockey Hall of Fame is in Eveleth. The city of Ely has the International Wolf Center. Harmony features Niagara Cave with an underground waterfall. Minneapolis is famous for the Mall of America, a huge indoor commercial and entertainment center featuring stores, rides, a beach, skating rink, movies, and restaurants. The Minnesota Zoo is located about 20 mi (30 km) south of Minneapolis–St. Paul. Between Redwood Falls and Jackson, tourists can view the Jeffers Petroglyphs dating from 3000 BC.

The state maintains and operates 66 parks, 9,240 mi (14,870 km) of trails, 10 scenic and natural areas, 5 recreation areas, and 18 canoe and boating routes. Minnesota also has 288 primary wildlife refuges. Many visitors hunt deer, muskrat, squirrel, beaver, duck, pheasant, and grouse. Others enjoy boating each year on Minnesota's scenic waterways. Winter sports have gained in popularity, and many parks are now used heavily all year round. Snowmobiling, though it has declined somewhat since the mid-1970s, still attracts enthusiasts annually, and cross-country skiing has rapidly accelerated in popularity.

⁴⁸SPORTS

Five of the major professional sports currently have teams in Minnesota: the Twins of Major League Baseball, the Vikings of the National Football League, the Lynx of the Women's National Basketball Association, the Wild of the National Hockey League, and the Timberwolves of the National Basketball Association. The Twins won the World Series in 1924, 1987, and 1991. The Vikings have gone to the Super Bowl four times, losing each one. The Minnesota North Stars of the National Hockey League moved to Dallas in 1993, but a new NHL team, the Minnesota Wild, began play in 2000.

In collegiate sports, the University of Minnesota Golden Gophers compete in the Big Ten Conference. The football team won the Rose Bowl in 1962, while the basketball team won the Big Ten title and advanced to the National Collegiate Athletic Association (NCAA) Final Four in 1997. The university is probably best known for its ice hockey team, which won the NCAA title in 1974, 1976, 1979, 2002, and 2003, and supplied the coach, Herb Brooks, and many of the players for the gold medal–winning US team in the 1980 Winter Olympics.

Other annual sporting events include the John Beargrease Sled Dog Race between Duluth and Grand Marais in January or early February, and auto racing at the Brainerd International Raceway in July and August. Alpine and cross-country skiing are popular.

Tracy Caulkins, Roger Maris, and Kevin McHale, past stars in swimming, baseball, and basketball, respectively, were all born in Minnesota.

49 FAMOUS MINNESOTANS

No Minnesotan has been elected to the US presidency, but several have sought the office, including two who served as vice president. Hubert Horatio Humphrey (b.South Dakota, 1911–78) was vice president under Lyndon Johnson and a serious contender for the presidency in 1960, 1968, and 1972. A onetime mayor of Minneapolis, the "Happy Warrior" entered the US Senate in 1949, winning recognition as a vigorous proponent of liberal causes; after he left the vice presidency, Humphrey won reelection to the Senate in 1970. Humphrey's protégé, Walter Frederick "Fritz" Mondale (b.1928), a former state attorney general, was appointed to fill Humphrey's Senate seat in 1964, was elected to it twice, and after an unsuccessful try for the presidency, became Jimmy Carter's running mate in 1976; four years later, Mondale and Carter ran unsuccessfully for reelection, losing to Ronald Reagan and George Bush. Mondale won the Democratic presidential nomination in 1984 and chose US Representative Geraldine A. Ferraro of New York as his running mate, making her the first woman to be nominated by a major party for national office; they were overwhelmingly defeated by Reagan and Bush, winning only 41% of the popular vote and carrying only Minnesota and the District of Columbia. Warren Earl Burger (1907–95) of St. Paul was named chief justice of the US Supreme Court in 1969. Three other Minnesotans have served on the court: Pierce Butler (1866–1939), William O. Douglas (1898–1980), and Harry A. Blackmun (b.Illinois, 1908–97).

Senator Frank B. Kellogg (b.New York, 1856–1937), who as secretary of state helped to negotiate the Kellogg-Briand Pact renouncing war as an instrument of national policy (for which he won the 1929 Nobel Peace Prize), also served on the Permanent Court of International Justice. Other political leaders who won national attention include governors John A. Johnson (1861–1909), Floyd B. Olson (1891–1936), and Harold E. Stassen (1907–2001), a frequent presidential candidate beginning in 1948. Eugene J. McCarthy (1916–2005), who served in the US Senate, was the central figure in a national protest movement against the Vietnam war and, in that role, unsuccessfully sought the 1968 Democratic presidential nomination won by Humphrey. McCarthy also ran for the presidency as an independent in 1976.

Several Minnesotans besides Kellogg have served in cabinet posts. Minnesota's first territorial governor, Alexander Ramsey (1815–1903), later served as a secretary of war, and Senator William Windom (1827–91) was also secretary of the treasury. Others serving in cabinet posts have included William DeWitt Mitchell (1874–1955), attorney general; Maurice H. Stans (1908–98), secretary of commerce; James D. Hodgson (b.1915), secretary of labor; and Orville Freeman (1918–2003) and Bob Bergland (b.1928), both secretaries of agriculture. The first woman ambassador in US history was Eugenie M. Anderson (Iowa, 1909–97), like Humphrey an architect of the Democratic-Farmer-Labor Party.

Notable members of Congress include Knute Nelson (b.Norway, 1843–1923), who served in the Senate from 1895 to his death; Henrik Shipstead (1881–1960), who evolved into a leading Republican isolationist during 24 years in the Senate; Representative Andrew J. Volstead (1860–1947), who sponsored the 1919 prohibition act that bears his name; and Representative Walter Judd (1898–1994), a prominent leader of the so-called China Lobby.

The Mayo Clinic was founded in Minnesota by Dr. William W. Mayo (b.England, 1819–1911) and developed through the efforts of his sons, Drs. William H. (1861–1939) and Charles H. (1865–1939) Mayo. Oil magnate J. Paul Getty (1892–1976) was a Minnesota native, as was Richard W. Sears (1863–1914), founder of Sears, Roebuck.

Prominent literary figures, besides Sinclair Lewis, include Ignatius Donnelly (b.Pennsylvania, 1831–1901), a writer, editor, and Populist Party crusader; F. Scott Fitzgerald (1896–1940), well known for classic novels including The Great Gatsby; and Ole Edvart Rølvaag (b.Norway, 1876–1931), who conveyed the reality of the immigrant experience in his Giants in the Earth. The poet and critic Allen Tate (b.Kentucky, 1899–1979) taught for many years at the University of Minnesota.

Journalist Westbrook Pegler (1894–1969) and cartoonist Charles Schulz (1922–2000) were both born in Minnesota as was radio personality and author Garrison Keillor (b.1942), who gained nationwide fame playfully satirizing his home state through the fictitious town of Lake Wobegon. Architects LeRoy S. Buffington (1847–1937) and Cass Gilbert (b.Ohio, 1859–1934) and economist Thorstein Veblen (b.Wisconsin, 1857–1929) influenced their fields well beyond the state's borders, as did Minnesota artists Wanda Gag (1893–1946) and Adolph Dehn (1895–1968).

Minnesota-born entertainers include Judy Garland (Frances Gumm, 1922–69) and Bob Dylan (Robert Zimmerman, b.1941). Football star William "Pudge" Heffelfinger (1867–1954) was a Minnesota native, and Bronislaw "Bronco" Nagurski (b.Canada, 1908–1990) played for the University of Minnesota.

Daniel Greysolon, Sieur Duluth (b.France, 1636–1710), Father Louis Hennepin (b.Flanders, 1640?–1701), and Jonathan Carver (b.Massachusetts, 1710–80) were among the early explorers and chroniclers of what is now the State of Minnesota. Fur trader Henry H. Sibley (b.Michigan, 1811–91) was a key political leader in the territorial period and became the state's first governor; he also put down the Sioux uprising of 1862. Railroad magnate James J. Hill (b.Canada, 1838–1916) built one of the greatest corporate empires of his time, and Oliver H. Kelley (b.Massachusetts, 1826–1913), a Minnesota farmer, organized the first National Grange. John Ireland (b.Ireland, 1838–1918) was the first Roman Catholic archbishop of St. Paul, while Henry B. Whipple (b.New York, 1822–1901), longtime Episcopal bishop of Minnesota, achieved particular recognition for his work among Indians in the region.

The first US citizen ever to be awarded the Nobel Prize for literature was Sinclair Lewis (1885–1951), whose novel Main Street (1920) was modeled on life in his hometown of Sauk Centre. Philip S. Hench (b.Pennsylvania, 1896–1965) and Edward C. Kendall (b.Connecticut, 1886–1972), both of the Mayo Clinic, shared the 1950 Nobel Prize for medicine, and St. Paul native Melvin Calvin (1911–97) won the 1961 Nobel Prize for chemistry.

50 BIBLIOGRAPHY

Council of State Governments. *The Book of the States, 2006 Edition.* Lexington, Ky.: Council of State Governments, 2006.

Lewis, Anne Gillespie. *The Minnesota Guide.* Golden, Colo.: Fulcrum Pub., 1999.

Meyer, Roy (revision ed.). *History of the Santee Sioux: United States Indian Policy on Trial.* Lincoln: University of Nebraska Press, 1993.

Perich, Shawn. *Wild Minnesota: A Celebration of Our State's Natural Beauty.* Stillwater, Minn.: Voyageur Press, 2005.

Radicalism in Minnesota, 1900–1960: A Survey of Selected Sources. St. Paul: Minnesota Historical Society Press, 1994.

Radzilowski, John. *Minnesota.* New York: Interlink Books, 2004.

Risjord, Norman K. *A Popular History of Minnesota.* St. Paul: Minnesota Historical Society Press, 2005.

Rueter, Theodore. *The Minnesota House of Representatives and the Professionalization of Politics.* Lanham, Md.: University Press of America, 1994.

Stuhler, Barbara. *Gentle Warriors: Clara Ueland and the Minnesota Struggle for Woman Suffrage.* St. Paul: Minnesota Historical Society Press, 1994.

US Department of Commerce, Economics and Statistics Administration, US Census Bureau. *Minnesota, 2000. Summary Social, Economic, and Housing Characteristics: 2000 Census of Population and Housing.* Washington, D.C.: US Government Printing Office, 2003.

MISSISSIPPI

State of Mississippi

ORIGIN OF STATE NAME: Derived from the Ojibwa Indian words *misi sipi,* meaning great river. **NICKNAME:** The Magnolia State. **CAPITAL:** Jackson. **ENTERED UNION:** 10 December 1817 (20th). **SONG:** "Go, Mississippi." **MOTTO:** *Virtute et armis* (By valor and arms). **COAT OF ARMS:** An American eagle clutches an olive branch and a quiver of arrows in its talons. **FLAG:** Crossed blue bars, on a red field, bordered with white and emblazoned with 13 white stars—the motif of the Confederate battle flag—cover the upper left corner. The field consists of three stripes of equal width, blue, white, and red. **OFFICIAL SEAL:** The seal consists of the coat of arms surrounded by the words "The Great Seal of the State of Mississippi." **BIRD:** Mockingbird; wood duck (waterfowl). **FISH:** Largemouth or black bass. **FLOWER:** Magnolia. **TREE:** Magnolia. **LEGAL HOLIDAYS:** New Year's Day, 1 January; Birthdays of Robert E. Lee and Martin Luther King Jr., 3rd Monday in January; Washington's Birthday, 3rd Monday in February; Confederate Memorial Day, last Monday in April; Memorial Day and Jefferson Davis's Birthday, last Monday in May; Independence Day, 4 July; Labor Day, 1st Monday in September; Veterans' Day and Armistice Day, 11 November; Thanksgiving Day, 4th Thursday in November; Christmas Day, 25 December. **TIME:** 6 AM CST = noon GMT.

¹LOCATION, SIZE, AND EXTENT

Located in the eastern south-central United States, Mississippi ranks 32nd in size among the 50 states.

The total area of Mississippi is 47,689 sq mi (123,514 sq km), of which land takes up 47,233 sq mi (122,333 sq km) and inland water 456 sq mi (1,181 sq km). Mississippi's maximum E–W extension is 188 mi (303 km); its greatest N–S distance is 352 mi (566 km).

Mississippi is bordered on the N by Tennessee; on the E by Alabama; on the S by the Gulf of Mexico and Louisiana; and on the W by Louisiana (with the line partially formed by the Pearl and Mississippi rivers) and Arkansas (with the line formed by the Mississippi River). Several small islands lie off the coast.

The total boundary length of Mississippi is 1,015 mi (1,634 km). The state's geographic center is in Leake County, 9 mi (14 km) WNW of Carthage.

²TOPOGRAPHY

Mississippi lies entirely within two lowland plains. Extending eastward from the Mississippi River, the Mississippi Alluvial Plain, popularly known as the Delta, is very narrow south of Vicksburg but stretches as much as a third of the way across the state farther north. The Gulf Coastal Plain, covering the rest of the state, includes several subregions, of which the Red Clay Hills of northcentral Mississippi and the Piney Woods of the south and southeast are the most extensive. Mississippi's generally hilly landscape ascends from sea level at the Gulf of Mexico to reach its maximum elevation, 806 ft (246 m), at Woodall Mountain, in the extreme northeastern corner of the state. The mean elevation of the state is approximately 300 ft (92 m).

The state's largest lakes—Grenada, Sardis, Enid, and Arkabutla—are all manmade. Numerous smaller lakes—called oxbow lakes because of their curved shape—extend along the western edge of the state; once part of the Mississippi River, they were formed when the river changed its course. Mississippi's longest inland river, the Pearl, flows about 490 mi (790 km) from the eastern center of the state to the Gulf of Mexico, its lower reaches forming part of the border with Louisiana. The Big Black River, some 330 mi (530 km) long, begins in the northeast and cuts diagonally across the state, joining the Mississippi about 20 mi (32 km) below Vicksburg. Formed by the confluence of the Tallahatchie and Yalobusha rivers at Greenwood, the Yazoo flows 189 mi (304 km) southwest to the Mississippi just above Vicksburg.

³CLIMATE

Mississippi has short winters and long, humid summers. Summer temperatures vary little from one part of the state to another. Biloxi, on the Gulf coast, averages 82°F (28°C) in July, while Oxford, in the north-central part of the state, averages 80°F (27°C). During the winter, however, because of the temperate influence of the Gulf of Mexico, the southern coast is much warmer than the north; in January, Biloxi averages 51°F (10°C) to Oxford's 44°F (6°C). The lowest temperature ever recorded in Mississippi was -19°F (-28°C) on 30 January 1966 in Corinth; the highest, 115°F (46°C), was set on 29 July 1930 at Holly Springs.

Precipitation in Mississippi increases from north to south. The north-central region averages 53 in (135 cm) of precipitation a year; the coastal region, 62 in (157 cm). Annual precipitation at Jackson is about 56 in (142 cm). Some snow falls in northern and central sections. Mississippi lies in the path of hurricanes moving northward from the Gulf of Mexico during the late summer and fall. On 17–18 August 1969, Hurricane Camille ripped into Biloxi and Gulfport and caused more than 100 deaths throughout the state. In August 2005, Hurricane Katrina swept through the same region causing floodwater surges of over 30 ft (9 m). Biloxi and Gulfport suffered severe damage to homes and businesses. As of late 2005, the estimated death toll for the cities and the rest of the county was over 100 people. One month later, Hurricane Rita passed through the area, causing severe flooding inland as well as near the coastal regions of the state. Two tornado alleys cross Mississippi from the southwest to northeast, from Vicksburg to Oxford and McComb to Tupelo.

⁴FLORA AND FAUNA

Post and white oaks, hickory, maple, and magnolia grow in the forests of the uplands; various willows and gums (including the tupelo) in the Delta; and longleaf pine in the Piney Woods. Characteristic wild flowers include the green Virginia creeper, black-eyed Susan, and Cherokee rose. In April 2006, the US Fish and Wildlife listed Price's potato-bean as a threatened species. The Louisiana quillwort, pondberry, and American chaffseed were listed as endangered plant species the same year.

Common among the state's mammals are the opossum, eastern mole, armadillo, coyote, mink, white-tailed deer, striped skunk, and diverse bats and mice. Birds include varieties of wren, thrush, warbler, vireo, and hawk, along with numerous waterfowl and seabirds, Franklin's gull, the common loon, and the wood stork among them. Black bass, perch, and mullet are common freshwater fish. Rare species in Mississippi include the hoary bat, American oystercatcher, mole salamander, pigmy killifish, Yazoo darker, and five species of crayfish. Listed as threatened or endangered in 2006 were 30 species of animals (vertebrates and invertebrates), including the American and Louisiana black bears, eastern indigo snake, Indiana bat, Mississippi sandhill crane, bald eagle, Mississippi gopher frog, brown pelican, red-cockaded woodpecker, five species of sea turtle, and the bayou darter.

⁵ENVIRONMENTAL PROTECTION

Except for the drinking water program, housed in the State Health Department, and regulation of noncommercial oil field waste disposal activities, assigned to the State Oil and Gas Board, the Mississippi Department of Environmental Quality (MDEQ) is responsible for environmental regulatory programs in the state. MDEQ regulates surface and groundwater withdrawals through its Office of Land and Water Resources and surface mining reclamation through its Office of Geology. All other environmental regulatory programs, including those federal regulatory programs delegated to Mississippi by the US Environmental Protection Agency (EPA), are administered through MDEQ's Office of Pollution Control. The state has primacy for almost all federally delegable programs; the one notable exception is the federal hazardous waste corrective action program (under the federal Hazardous and Solid Waste Amendments of 1984). MDEQ implements one of the premier Pollution Prevention programs in the nation.

In 1996, wetlands accounted for 13% of the state's lands. The Natural Heritage Program helps manage these wetlands.

In 2003, 63.1 million lb of toxic chemicals were released in the state. In 2003, Mississippi had 83 hazardous waste sites listed in the EPA database, three of which were on the National Priorities List as of 2006, including American Creosote Works, Inc, Davis Timber Company, and Picayune Wood Treating Site. In 2005, the EPA spent over $1.5 million through the Superfund program for the cleanup of hazardous waste sites in the state. The same year, federal EPA grants awarded to the state included $9.7 million for

the clean water revolving loan fund, as well as over $9 million dollars in funds for other water quality and protection projects.

⁶POPULATION

Mississippi ranked 31st in population in the United States with an estimated total of 2,921,088 in 2005, an increase of 2.7% since 2000. Between 1990 and 2000, Mississippi's population grew from 2,573,216 to 2,844,658, an increase of 10.5%. The population was projected to reach 3.01 million by 2015 and 3.06 million by 2025.

After remaining virtually level for 30 years, Mississippi's population during the 1970s grew 13.7%, but increased only 2.1% from 1980 to 1990. In 2004, the median age of Mississippians was 34.9. In the same year, 25.8% of the on under the age of 18 while 12.2% was age 65 or older. The population density in 2004 was 23.9 persons per sq km (61.9 persons per sq mi).

Mississippi remains one of the most rural states in the United States, although the urban population has increased fivefold since 1920, when only 13% of state residents lived in cities. Mississippi's largest city, Jackson, had an estimated 2004 population of 179,298, down from 193,097 in 1994. Biloxi and Gulfport are other major cities with large populations. The Jackson metropolitan area had an estimated population of 517,275 in 2004.

⁷ETHNIC GROUPS

Since 1860, blacks have constituted a larger proportion of the population of Mississippi than of any other state. By the end of the 1830s, blacks outnumbered whites 52% to 48%, and from the 1860s through the early 20th century, they made up about three-fifths of the population. Because of out-migration, the proportion of black Mississippians declined to about 36% in 2000 (still the highest in the country). By 2004, 36.8% of the population was black. In 2000, the state had 1,746,099 whites, 1,033,809 blacks, 18,626 Asians, 11,652 American Indians, and 667 Pacific Islanders. In 2000, there were 39,569 (1.4%) Hispanics and Latinos. In 2004, 0.7% of the population was Asian and 1.7% Hispanic or Latino. That year, 0.6% of the population reported origin of two or more races.

Until the 1940s, the Chinese, who numbered 3,099 in 2000, were an intermediate stratum between blacks and whites in the social hierarchy of the Delta Counties. There also were 5,387 Vietnamese and 2,608 Filipinos in 2000. Although the number of foreign-born almost tripled in the 1970s, Mississippi still had the nation's smallest percentage of foreign-born residents (1.4%, or 39,908) in 2000.

Mississippi has only a small American Indian population— 0.4% of the state's population in 2000 (11,652). Many of them live on the Choctaw reservation in the east-central region. In 2004, 0.5% of the population was American Indian.

⁸LANGUAGES

English in the state is largely Southern, with some South Midland speech in northern and eastern Mississippi because of population drift from Tennessee. Typical are the absence of final /r/ and the lengthening and weakening of the diphthongs /ai/ and /oi/ as in *ride* and *oil*. South Midland terms in northern Mississippi include *tow sack* (burlap bag), *dog irons* (andirons), *plum peach* (clingstone peach), *snake doctor* (dragonfly), and *stone wall* (rock fence). In the eastern section are found *jew's harp* (harmonica)

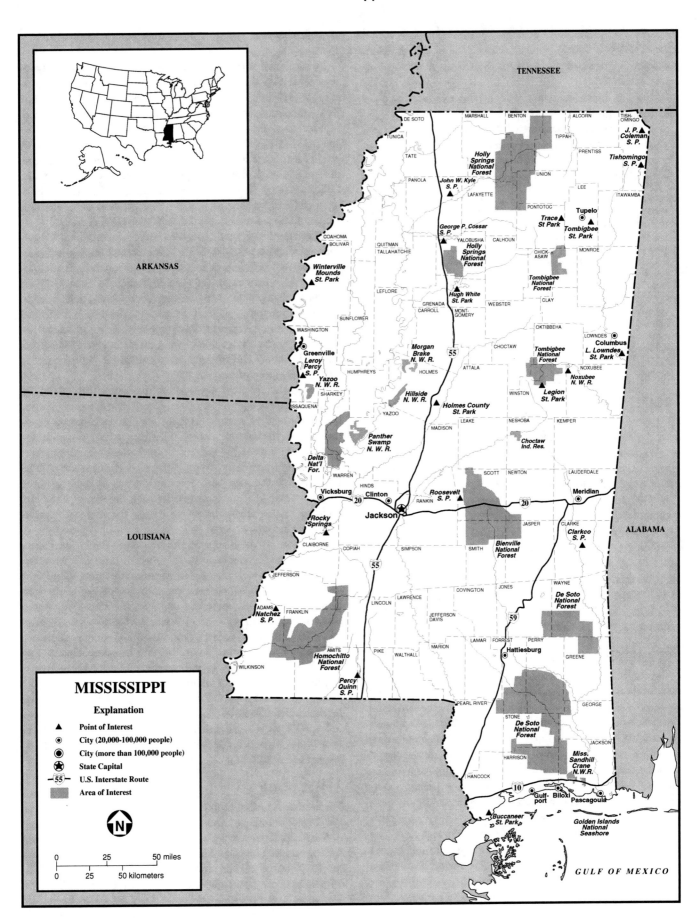

TENNESSEE

DE SOTO
MARSHALL   BENTON   ALCORN   TISH-OMINGO
TUNICA   TIPPAH   J. P. Coleman S. P.
TATE   Holly   UNION   PRENTISS   Tishomingo S. P.
PANOLA   Springs
                        National   LEE   ITAWAMBA
John W. Kyle S. P.   Forest   PONTOTOC
COAHOMA   QUITMAN   LAFAYETTE   Trace St Park   Tupelo
BOLIVAR   TALLAHATCHIE   George P. Cossar S. P.   Tombigbee St. Park
            YALOBUSHA   CALHOUN   CHICK-ASAW   MONROE
Winterville   Holly Springs National Forest   Tombigbee National Forest
Mounds St. Park   Hugh White S. P.   GRENADA   WEBSTER   CLAY
LEFLORE   CARROLL   MONT-GOMERY
WASHINGTON   OKTIBBEHA
SUNFLOWER   CHOCTAW   LOWNDES   Columbus
Greenville   Morgan Brake N. W. R.   Tombigbee National Forest   L. Lowndes St. Park
Leroy Percy S. P.   HUMPHREYS   HOLMES   ATTALA   WINSTON   NOXUBEE
Yazoo N. W. R.   Hillside N. W. R.   Legion St. Park   Noxubee N. W. R.
SHARKEY   YAZOO   Holmes County St. Park
ISSAQUENA   LEAKE   NESHOBA   KEMPER
                     Panther Swamp N. W. R.   MADISON
                     Delta Nat'l For.   Choctaw Ind. Res.
WARREN   HINDS   SCOTT   NEWTON   LAUDERDALE
Vicksburg   Clinton   Roosevelt S. P.
            Jackson   RANKIN   20   Meridian
Rocky Springs   20   JASPER   CLARKE   Clarkco S. P.
CLAIBORNE   COPIAH   SIMPSON   SMITH   Bienville National Forest
JEFFERSON   55   WAYNE
LINCOLN   LAWRENCE   COVINGTON   JONES   De Soto National Forest
ADAMS   Natchez S. P.   FRANKLIN   JEFFERSON DAVIS   59   PERRY   GREENE
AMITE   Homochitto National Forest   LAMAR   FORREST   Hattiesburg
WILKINSON   PIKE   WALTHALL   MARION   GEORGE
Percy Quinn S. P.   PEARL RIVER   STONE   De Soto National Forest
                    JACKSON
HARRISON   HANCOCK   Miss. Sandhill Crane N.W.R.
            10   Gulf-port   Biloxi   Pascagoula
Buccaneer St. Park   Golden Islands National Seashore

ARKANSAS

LOUISIANA

ALABAMA

GULF OF MEXICO

MISSISSIPPI

Explanation

▲ Point of Interest
◉ City (20,000-100,000 people)
◉ City (more than 100,000 people)
★ State Capital
—55— U.S. Interstate Route
▨ Area of Interest

N

0   25   50 miles
0   25   50 kilometers

and *croker sack* (burlap bag). Southern speech in the southern half features *gallery* for porch, *mosquito hawk* for dragonfly, and *press peach* for clingstone peach. Louisiana French has contributed *armoire* (wardrobe).

In 2000, 96.4% of Mississippi residents five years old and older spoke only English in the home, down from 97.2% in 1990.

The following table gives selected statistics from the 2000 Census for language spoken at home by persons five years old and over. The category "Other Native North American languages" includes Apache, Cherokee, Choctaw, Dakota, Keres, Pima, and Yupik.

LANGUAGE	NUMBER	PERCENT
Population 5 years and over	**2,641,453**	**100.0**
Speak only English	2,545,931	96.4
Speak a language other than English	95,522	3.6
Speak a language other than English	**95,522**	**3.6**
Spanish or Spanish Creole	50,515	1.9
French (incl. Patois, Cajun)	10,826	0.4
Other Native North American languages	5,654	0.2
German	5,501	0.2
Vietnamese	4,916	0.2
Chinese	2,506	0.1
Tagalog	2,005	0.1
Korean	1,485	0.1
Italian	1,336	0.1
Arabic	1,081	0.0

⁹RELIGIONS

Protestants have dominated Mississippi since the late 18th century. The Baptists are the leading denomination and many adherents are fundamentalists. Partly because of the strong church influence, Mississippi was among the first states to enact prohibition and among the last to repeal it.

In 2000, the Southern Baptist Convention was the largest denomination in the state with 916,440 known adherents; there were 14,947 new members in 2002. The United Methodist Church is considered to be the second-largest denomination in the state, with 189,149 members in 2004. Also in 2004, the Roman Catholic Church reported a statewide membership of about 124,150. In 2000, there were an estimated 3,919 Muslims and about 1,400 Jews. Over 1.2 million people (about 45.4% of the population) did not claim any religious affiliation in 2000.

¹⁰TRANSPORTATION

At the end of 2003, there were 2,658 rail mi (4,279 km) of mainline railroad track in Mississippi, including 2,016 mi (3,245 km) operated by five Class I railroads, which in 2003, were the Burlington Northern Santa Fe, CSX, Illinois Central Gulf, Kansas City Southern, and Norfolk Southern lines. As of 2006, Amtrak provided rail passenger service via its City of New Orleans train, serving the cities of Greenwood, Yazoo, Jackson, Hazlehurst, Brookhaven, and McComb on its route between Chicago and New Orleans, and the Crescent, serving Meridian, Laurel, Hattiesburg, and Picayune in Mississippi, on its route between Atlanta and New Orleans.

Mississippi had 74,129 mi (119,347 km) of public roads as of 2004. Interstate highways 55, running north–south, and 20, running east–west, intersect at Jackson. I-220 provides a loop from I-55 north of Jackson to I-20 west of Jackson. I-10 runs across the Mississippi Gulf Coast, and I-110 provides a connector from I-10 to US Highway 90 in Biloxi. I-59 runs diagonally through the southeastern corner of Mississippi from Meridian to New Orleans.

Development of four-lane highways was financed by a "pay-as-you-go" public works program passed by the Mississippi legislature in 1987 to provide a four-lane highway within 30 minutes or 30 mi (48 km) of every citizen in the state. Originally, the $1.6 billion, three-phase agenda called for the creation of four lanes for 1,077 mi (1,733 km) of highway as of 2001. During the 1994 regular legislative session, an additional 619 mi (996 km), known as Phase IV, were added to the program at an expected cost of $1.3 billion. In 2004, there were 1,896,008 licensed drivers in Mississippi and 1.159 million registered motor vehicles, including some 1.113 million automobiles and 815,000 trucks of all types.

Mississippi's ports and waterways serve a surrounding 16-state market where nearly 40% of the nation's total population is located. Mississippi has two deepwater seaports, Gulfport and Pascagoula, both located on the Gulf of Mexico. In 2004, Gulfport handled 2.374 million tons of cargo, and Pascagoula handled 34.099 million tons, making it the 22nd-busiest port in the United States. Much of Pascagoula's heavy volume consists of oil and gas imports. Other ports located on the Gulf include Port Bienville in Hancock County and Biloxi in Harrison County. Biloxi handled 2.670 million tons of cargo in 2004.

The Mississippi River flows along the western border of the state, linking the Gulf of Mexico to inland river states as far away as Minneapolis, Minnesota. The Mississippi is the largest commercial river in the country and the third-largest river system in the world, and it carries the majority of the nation's inland waterway tonnage. Approximately 409 mi (658 km) of the Mississippi River flow through the state, with ports in Natchez, Vicksburg, Yazoo County, Greenville, and Rosedale. In 2004, the Port of Vicksburg handled 3.922 million tons of cargo, while the Port of Greenville handled 3.045 million tons.

To the east of Mississippi lies the Tennessee-Tombigbee (Tenn-Tom) Waterway, completed in 1984, which links the Tennessee and Ohio rivers with the Gulf of Mexico. Stretching 95 mi (153 km) through Mississippi from the northeast corner of the state down to a point just south of Columbus, the Tenn-Tom Waterway's overall length is 232 mi (373 km). Five local ports are located on the waterway: Yellow Creek, Itawamba, Amory, Aberdeen, and Columbus-Lowndes County. In 2004, Mississippi had 873 mi (1,405 km) of navigable inland waterways. In 2003, waterborne shipments totaled 47.446 million tons.

In 2005, Mississippi had a total of 243 public and private-use aviation-related facilities. This included 191 airports, 51 heliports, and 1 STOLport (Short Take-Off and Landing). Jackson-Evers International Airport is the state's main air terminal. In 2004, the airport had 639,947 enplanements.

¹¹HISTORY

The earliest record of human habitation in the region that is now the state of Mississippi goes back perhaps 2,000 years. The names of Mississippi's pre-Columbian inhabitants are not known. Upon the appearance of the first Spanish explorers in the early 16th century, Mississippi Indians numbered some 30,000 and were divided into 15 tribes. Soon after the French settled in 1699, however, only three large tribes remained: the Choctaw, the Chickasaw, and the Natchez. The French destroyed the Natchez in 1729–30 in retaliation for the massacre of a French settlement on the Natchez bluffs.

Spanish explorers, of whom Hernando de Soto in 1540–41 was the most notable, explored the area that is now Mississippi in the first half of the 16th century. De Soto found little of the mineral wealth he was looking for, and the Spanish quickly lost interest in the region. The French explorer Robert Cavelier, Sieur de la Salle, penetrated the lower Mississippi Valley from New France (Canada) in 1682. La Salle discovered the mouth of the Mississippi and named the entire area Louisiana in honor of the French king, Louis XIV.

An expedition under French-Canadian Pierre Lemoyne, Sieur d'Iberville, established a settlement at Biloxi Bay in 1699. Soon the French opened settlements at Mobile (1702), Natchez (1716), and finally New Orleans (1718), which quickly eclipsed the others in size and importance. After losing the French and Indian War, France ceded Louisiana to its Spanish ally in 1762. The following year, Spain ceded the portion of the colony that lay east of the Mississippi to England, which governed the new lands as West Florida. During the American Revolution, the Spanish, who still held New Orleans and Louisiana, marched into Natchez, Mobile, and Pensacola (the capital) and took West Florida by conquest.

Although the United States claimed the Natchez area after 1783, Spain continued to rule it. However, the Spanish were unable to change the Anglo-American character of the settlement. Spain agreed to relinquish its claim to the Natchez District by signing the Treaty of San Lorenzo on 27 October 1795, but did not evacuate its garrison there for another three years.

The US Congress organized the Mississippi Territory in 1798. Between 1798 and 1817, the territory grew enormously in population, attracting immigrants mainly from the older states of the South but also from the Middle Atlantic states and even from New England. During this period, the territory included all the land area that is today within the borders of Mississippi and Alabama. However, sectionalism and the territory's large size convinced Congress to organize the eastern half as the Alabama Territory in 1817. Congress then offered admission to the western half, which became the nation's 20th state-Mississippi on 10 December.

Until the Civil War, Mississippi exemplified the American frontier; it was bustling, violent, and aggressive. By and large, Mississippians viewed themselves as westerners, not southerners. Nor was Mississippi, except for a few plantations around Natchez, a land of large planters. Rather, Mississippi's antebellum society and government were dominated by a coalition of prosperous farmers and small landowners. At the time of statehood, the northern two-thirds of Mississippi, though nominally under US rule since 1783, remained in the hands of the Choctaw and Chickasaw and was closed to settlement. Under intense pressure from the state government and from Andrew Jackson's presidential administration, these tribes signed three treaties between 1820 and 1832, ceding their Mississippi lands and agreeing to move to what is now Oklahoma.

The opening of fertile Indian lands for sale and settlement produced a boom of speculation and growth unparalleled in Mississippi history. Cotton agriculture and slavery—introduced by the French and carried on by the British and Spanish, but hitherto limited mostly to the Natchez area—swept over the state. As the profitability and number of slaves increased, so did attempts by white Mississippians to justify slavery morally, socially, and economically. The expansion of slavery also produced a defensive attitude, which focused the minds of white Mississippians on two dangers: that the slaves outnumbered the whites and would threaten white society unless kept down by slavery; and that any attack on slavery, whether from the abolitionists or from Free-Soilers like Abraham Lincoln, was a threat to white society. The danger, they believed, was so great that no price was too high to pay to maintain slavery, even secession and civil war.

After Lincoln's election to the US presidency, Mississippi became, on 9 January 1861, the second southern state to secede. When the war began, Mississippi occupied a central place in Union strategy. The state sat squarely astride the major Confederate east–west routes of communication in the lower South, and the Mississippi River twisted along the state's western border. Control of the river was essential to Union division of the Confederacy. The military campaign fell into three phases: the fight for northeastern Mississippi in 1862, the struggle for Vicksburg in 1862–63, and the battle for east Mississippi in 1864–65. The Union advance on Corinth began with the Battle of Shiloh (Tenn.) in April 1862. The first Union objective was the railroad that ran across the northeastern corner of Mississippi from Corinth to Iuka and linked Memphis, Tenn., to Atlanta, Ga. Losses in the ensuing battle of Shiloh, which eventually led to the occupation of Corinth by Union troops, exceeded 10,000 men on each side.

The campaign that dominated the war in Mississippi—and, indeed, along with Gettysburg provided the turning point of the Civil War—was Vicksburg. Perched atop high bluffs overlooking a bend in the Mississippi and surrounded by hills on all sides, Vicksburg provided a seemingly impregnable fortress. Union forces maneuvered before Vicksburg for more than a year before Grant besieged the city and forced its surrender on 4 July 1863. Along with Vicksburg went the western half of Mississippi. The rest of the military campaign in the state was devoted to the fight for the east, which Union forces still had not secured when the conflict ended in 1865. Of the 78,000 Mississippians who fought in the Civil War, nearly 30,000 died.

Ten years of political, social, and economic turmoil followed. Reconstruction was a tumultuous period during which the Republican Party encouraged blacks to vote and hold political office, while the native white Democrats resisted full freedom for their former slaves. The resulting confrontation lasted until 1875, when, using violence and intimidation, the Democrats recaptured control of the state from the Republicans and began a return to the racial status quo antebellum. However, reconstruction left its legacy in minds of Mississippians: to the whites it seemed proof that blacks were incapable of exercising political power; to the blacks it proved that political and social rights could not long be maintained without economic rights.

The era from the end of Reconstruction to World War II was a period of economic, political, and social stagnation for Mississippi. In many respects, white Mississippians pushed blacks back into slavery in all but name. Segregation laws and customs placed strict social controls on blacks, and a new state constitution in 1890 removed the last vestiges of their political rights. Mississippi's agricultural economy, dominated by cotton and tenant farming, provided the economic equivalent of slavery for black sharecroppers. As a continuing agricultural depression ground down the small white farmers, many of them also were driven into the sharecropper ranks; in 1890, 63% of all Mississippi farmers were tenants. Whether former planter-aristocrats like John Sharp Williams or small-farmer advocates like James K. Vardaman (1908–12) and Theodore Bilbo (1916–20 and 1928–32) held office as governor, political life was dominated by the overriding desire to keep the blacks subservient. From Reconstruction to the 1960s, white political solidarity was of paramount importance. Otherwise, the whites reasoned, another Reconstruction would follow. According to the Tuskegee Institute, 538 blacks were lynched in Mississippi between 1883 and 1959, more than in any other state.

The Great Depression of the 1930s pushed Mississippians, predominantly poor and rural, to the point of desperation, and the state's agricultural economy to the brink of disaster. In 1932, cotton sank to five cents a pound, and one-fourth of the state's farmland was forfeited for nonpayment of taxes. World War II unleashed the forces that would later revolutionize Mississippi's economic, social, and political order, bringing the state its first prosperity in a century. By introducing outsiders to Mississippi and Mississippians to the world, the armed forces and the war began to erode the state's insularity. It also stimulated industrial growth and agricultural mechanization and encouraged an exodus of blacks to better-paying jobs in other states. By the early 1980s, according to any standard, Mississippi had become an industrial state. In the agricultural sector, cotton had been dethroned and crop diversification accomplished. Politics in Mississippi also changed considerably after World War II. Within little more than a generation, from 1945 to 1975, legal segregation was destroyed, and black people exercised their political rights for the first time since Reconstruction. The "Mississippi Summer" (also called Freedom Summer) civil rights campaign—and the violent response to it, including the abduction and murder of three civil rights activists in June 1964—helped persuade white Mississippians to accept racial equality. Charles Evers, the brother of slain civil rights leader Medgar Evers, was elected mayor of Fayette in 1969, becoming Mississippi's first black mayor since Reconstruction.

Following the 1990 redistricting that boosted the number of blacks in the Mississippi House of Representatives, the Mississippi legislature was nearly 23% black in a state in which blacks constituted 33% of the population. In 1998 African Americans accounted for 36% of the state's population.

In 1988 reformist governor Ray Mabus, elected in 1987, enacted the nation's largest teacher pay increase by that date. Nevertheless, teacher salaries in 1992 were still, on average, the second-lowest in the nation and public education remained a priority for the state in the early 2000s. Democratic Governor Ronnie Musgrove, elected in 2000, was able to win additional teacher pay increases from the legislature in 2001. Education was Musgrove's main focus in his 2003 State of the State Address, as he proposed a program that would place children in school two months before kindergarten and one that would attempt to keep top faculty members at Mississippi's state colleges and universities.

Mississippi's economy was hard hit by the 1986 decline in oil and gas prices. Unemployment in the state rose to 13%. By 1992 it had fallen to about 8%. The 1990s saw increasing industrial diversification and rising personal incomes, although many agricultural workers in the Mississippi Delta area remained jobless due to the increasing mechanization of farm work. By 1999 the jobless rate had dropped to 5.1%, though still above the national average of 4.2%. Nevertheless, the state remained among the nation's poorest, with nearly 18% of its population living below the poverty level as of 1998, a poverty rate that persisted into the early 2000s. Only three states had higher poverty rates. In 2003, Mississippi was facing a budget shortfall of at least $500 million.

Former chairman of the Republican National Committee, Haley Barbour, was elected governor in November 2003. Upon becoming governor, Barbour focused on job creation, job training, workplace development efforts, and tort reform. He launched "Momentum Mississippi," a long-range economic development strategy group composed of the state's business and community leaders. In 2005, he introduced comprehensive education reform legislation to reward teacher and school performance, reduce state bureaucracy, and strengthen discipline in the state's public schools. With regard to the abortion debate, Barbour introduced and passed six pro-life laws in 2004.

Southern Mississippi was devastated by Hurricane Katrina in August 2005. A 30-ft (10-m) storm surge came ashore, destroying 90% of buildings along the Biloxi-Gulfport coastline. Casino barges in the area were washed ashore. About 800,000 people suffered power outages in Mississippi in the aftermath of the storm.

¹²STATE GOVERNMENT

Mississippi has had four state constitutions. The first (1817) accompanied Mississippi's admission to the Union. A second constitution (1832) was superseded by that of 1869, redrafted under Republican rule to allow Mississippi's readmission to the Union after the Civil War. The state's present constitution, as amended, dates from 1890. By January 2005 it had 123 amendments.

Mississippi's bicameral legislature includes a 52-member Senate and a 122-member House of Representatives. Annual sessions begin in January and extend 90 calendar days, except in the first year of a gubernatorial administration, when they run 125 calendar days. All state legislators are elected to four-year terms. State representatives must be at least 21 years old and senators 25. Representatives must be qualified voters and must have been Mississippi residents for four years and residents of their district for at least two years before election. Senators must have been qualified voters and state residents for at least four years and residents of their district for at least two years before election. The legislative salary was $10,000 in 2004, unchanged from 1999.

The governor and lieutenant governor (separately elected), secretary of state, attorney general, state treasurer, state auditor, commissioner of insurance, and the commissioner of agriculture and commerce all serve four-year terms. (Voters also elect three transportation commissioners and three public service commissioners, who also serve four-year terms.) The governor and lieutenant governor must be qualified voters, at least 30 years old, US citizens for 20 years, and Mississippi residents for 5 years before election. As of December 2004, the governor's salary was $122,160. The governor is limited to a maximum of two consecutive terms.

A bill passed by both houses is sent to the governor, who has five days to veto or sign it before it becomes law. If the legislature adjourns, the governor has 15 days after the bill was presented to him to act on it before the measure becomes law. The governor's veto can be overridden by a two-thirds vote of the elected members of both houses. Constitutional amendments must first receive the approval of two-thirds of the members of each house of the legislature. The electorate may also initiate amendments, provided petitions are signed by 12% of total votes for all candidates for governor at the last election. A majority of voters must approve the amendment on a statewide ballot.

Every US citizen over the age of 18 may vote in Mississippi upon producing evidence of 30 days of residence in the state and county (and city, in some cases). Restrictions apply to those convicted of certain crimes and to those judged by the court as mentally incompetent to vote.

¹³POLITICAL PARTIES

Mississippi's major political parties are the Democratic Party and the Republican Party, each an affiliate of the national party organization. Mississippi Democrats have often been at odds with each other and with the national Democratic Party. In the 1830s, party affiliation in the state began to divide along regional and economic lines: woodsmen and small farmers in eastern Mississippi became staunch Jacksonian Democrats, while the conservative planters in the western river counties tended to be Whigs. An early demonstration of the power of the Democrats was the movement of the state capital from Natchez in 1821 to a new city named after Andrew Jackson. During the pre–Civil War years, the secessionists were largely Democrats; the Unionists, western Whigs.

During Reconstruction, Mississippi had its first Republican governor. After the Democrats returned to power in 1875, they systematically deprived blacks of the right to vote, specifically by inserting into the constitution of 1890 a literacy clause that could be selectively interpreted to include illiterate whites but exclude blacks. A poll tax and convoluted residency requirements also restricted the electorate. Voter registration among blacks fell from 130,607 in 1880 to 16,234 by 1896.

In 1948, Mississippi Democrats seceded from the national party over the platform, which opposed racial discrimination. That November, Mississippi voters backed the States' Rights Democratic (Dixiecrat) presidential ticket. At the national Democratic convention in 1964, the black separatist Freedom Democratic Party asked to be allotted 40% of Mississippi's seats but was turned down. A further division in the party occurred during the 1960s between the (black) Loyalist Democrats and the (white) Regular Democrats, who were finally reunited in 1976. During the 1950s and early 1960s, the segregationist White Citizens' Councils were so widespread and influential in the state as to rival the major parties in political importance.

Since the passing of the federal Voting Rights Act of 1965, black Mississippians have registered and voted in substantial numbers. According to estimates by the Voter Education Project, only 5% of voting-age blacks were registered in 1960; by 1992, 23% were registered.

Mississippi was one of the most closely contested states in the South during the 1976 presidential election, and that again proved to be the case in 1980, when Ronald Reagan edged Jimmy Carter by a plurality of fewer than 12,000 votes. In 1984, however, Reagan won the state by a landslide, polling 62% of the vote. In the 2000 election, Republican George W. Bush won 57% of the vote; Democrat Al Gore received 42%; and Independent Ralph Nader garnered 1%. In 2004 Bush won 59.6% to Democrat John Kerry's 39.6%. In 2002 there were 1,754,560 registered voters; there is no party registration in the state. The state had seven electoral votes in the 2000 presidential election.

Elected in 1991, Mississippi's governor Kirk Fordice was the first Republican governor since Reconstruction. But a Democrat soon regained the office: David Ronald Musgrove was elected governor in 1999. In 2003, former chairman of the Republican

Mississippi Presidential Vote by Political Parties, 1948–2004

YEAR	ELECTORAL VOTE	MISSISSIPPI WINNER	DEMOCRAT	REPUBLICAN	STATES' RIGHTS DEMOCRAT	SOCIALIST WORKERS	LIBERTARIAN
1948	9	Thurmond (SRD)	19,384	4,995	167,538	—	—
1952	8	Stevenson (D)	172,553	112,966	—	—	—
					IND.		
1956	8	Stevenson (D)	144,453	60,683	42,961	—	—
					UNPLEDGED		
1960	8	Byrd**	108,362	73,561	116,248	—	—
1964	7	Goldwater (R)	52,616	356,512	—	—	—
					AMERICAN IND.		
1968	7	Wallace (AI)	150,644	88,516	415,349		
					AMERICAN		
1972	7	*Nixon (R)	126,782	505,125	11,598	2,458	—
1976	7	*Carter (D)	381,309	366,846	6,678	2,805	2,788
					WORKERS' WORLD		
1980	7	*Reagan (R)	429,281	441,089	2,402	2,240	4,702
1984	7	*Reagan (R)	352,192	582,377	—	—	2,336
1988	7	*Bush (R)	363,921	557,890	—	—	3,329
					IND. (Perot)	**NEW ALLIANCE**	
1992	7	Bush (R)	400,258	487,793	85,626	2,625	2,154
1996	7	Dole (R)	394,022	439,838	52,222	—	2,809
					(Nader)	**REFORM**	
2000	7	*Bush, G. W. (R)	404,614	572,844	8,122	2,265	2,009
					REFORM (Nader)	**CONSTITUTION (Peroutka)**	
2004	6	*Bush, G. W. (R)	458,094	684,981	3,177	1,759	1,793

*Won US presidential election.
** unpledged electors won plurality of votes and cast Mississippi's electoral votes for Senator Harry F. Byrd of Virginia.

National Committee, Haley Barbour, was elected governor. Following the 2004 elections, the state's two US senators were Republicans Trent Lott and Thad Cochran. Lott became majority leader of the Senate in 1996 following the departure of Bob Dole (R-Kansas); he stepped down from that post in December 2002 following controversy over remarks he made praising former South Carolina senator Strom Thurmond's 1948 segregationist campaign for the presidency. Until the 1994 midterm elections all of Mississippi's US representatives were Democrats; in that election, Republican Roger Wicker won a House seat that had been in Democratic hands since Reconstruction. Following the 2004 elections, the House delegation was comprised of two Democrats and two Republicans. Following the 2004 elections, the state Senate comprised 28 Democrats and 24 Republicans; the state House had 75 Democrats and 47 Republicans.

14 LOCAL GOVERNMENT

Each of Mississippi's 82 counties is divided into 5 districts, each of which elects a member to the county board of supervisors. As of 2005, Mississippi had 296 municipal governments (incorporated as cities, towns, or villages), typically administered by a mayor and council. Some smaller municipalities were run by a commission or by a city manager, appointed by council members. There were 152 public school districts and 458 special districts in 2005.

In 2005, local government accounted for about 132,139 full-time (or equivalent) employment positions.

15 STATE SERVICES

To address the continuing threat of terrorism and to work with the federal Department of Homeland Security, homeland security in Mississippi operates under the authority of executive order; the homeland security director is designated as the state homeland security advisor.

The Mississippi Ethics Commission, established by the state legislature in 1979, is composed of eight members who administer a code of ethics requiring all state officials and elected local officials to file statements of sources of income.

The Mississippi Department of Education is primarily a planning and service organization whose role is to assist local schools from kindergarten through junior college and adult education. A separate Board of Trustees of State Institutions of Higher Learning administers Mississippi's public college and university system. The Department of Health administers a statewide system of public health services, but other bodies, including the Department of Mental Health, also have important functions in this field. The Department of Human Services provides welfare services in the areas of assistance payments, child support, food stamp distribution, and such social services as foster home care.

Public protection is afforded by the Office of the Attorney General, Military Communities Council, Bureau of Narcotics, Department of Public Safety (including the Highway Safety Patrol), and Department of Corrections.

16 JUDICIAL SYSTEM

The Mississippi Supreme Court consists of a chief justice, two presiding justices, and eight associate justices, all elected to eight-year terms. The constitution stipulates that the Supreme Court must hold two sessions a year in the state capital; one session is to commence on the second Monday of September; the other on the first Monday of March. A new Court of Appeals was created in 1995. It consists of one chief judge, two presiding judges, and seven judges. Principal trial courts are the circuit courts, which try both civil and criminal cases; their 49 judges are elected to four-year terms. Municipal court judges are appointed. Small-claims courts are presided over by justices of the peace, who need not be lawyers.

As of 31 December 2004, a total of 20,983 prisoners were held in Mississippi's state and federal prisons, an increase of 1.9% (from 20,589) from the previous year. As of year-end 2004, a total of 1,796 inmates were female, up 2.3% (from 1,755) from the year before. Among sentenced prisoners (one year or more), Mississippi had an incarceration rate of 669 per 100,000 population in 2004, the third-highest in the United States.

According to the Federal Bureau of Investigation, Mississippi in 2004, had a violent crime rate (murder/nonnegligent manslaughter; forcible rape; robbery; aggravated assault) of 295.1 reported incidents per 100,000 population, or a total of 8,568 reported incidents. Crimes against property (burglary; larceny/theft; and motor vehicle theft) in that same year totaled 100,980 reported incidents or 3,478.5 reported incidents per 100,000 people. Mississippi has a death penalty, of which lethal injection is the sole method of execution. Following capital punishment's reinstatement in 1977, the state has executed seven persons (as of 5 May 2006); one execution was carried out in 2005. As of 1 January 2006, Mississippi had 65 inmates on death row.

In 2003, Mississippi spent $217,949,581 on homeland security, an average of $75 per state resident.

17 ARMED FORCES

In 2004, there were 17,917 active-duty military personnel and 4,514 civilian personnel stationed in Mississippi. There were two major US Air Force bases, Keesler (Biloxi) and Columbus. Among the four US naval installations were an oceanographic command at Bay St. Louis, an air station at Meridian, and a construction battalion center at Gulfport. In 2004, Mississippi received about $1.86 billion in federal defense contracts, and $708 million in Defense Department payroll outlays.

There were 240,109 veterans of US military service living in Mississippi as of 2003. Of those who served in wartime, 29,837 were veterans of World War II; 25,845 of the Korean conflict; 66,717 of the Vietnam era; and 44,950 during the Persian Gulf War. Expenditures on veterans amounted to some $844 million during 2004.

As of 31 October 2004, the Mississippi Highway State Patrol employed 531 full-time sworn officers.

18 MIGRATION

In the late 18th century, most Mississippians were immigrants from the South and predominantly of Scotch-Irish descent. The opening of lands ceded by the Indians beginning in the 1820s brought tens of thousands of settlers into northern and central Mississippi, and a resulting population increase between 1830 and 1840 of 175% (including an increase of 197% in the slave population).

After the Civil War, there was little migration into the state, but much out-migration, mainly of blacks. The exodus from Mississippi was especially heavy during the 1940s and 1950s, when at least 720,000 people, nearly three-quarters of them black, left the state. During the 1960s, between 267,000 and 279,000 blacks departed, while net white out-migration came to an end. Black out-migration slowed considerably during the 1970s, and more whites settled in the state than left. Also during the 1970s there was considerable intrastate migration to Hinds County (Jackson) and the Gulf Coast. Between 1980 and 1990, Mississippi had a net loss from migration of 144,128 (38% whites). Only 12 of the state's 82 counties recorded a net gain from migration during the 1980s, mostly in Rankin, DeSoto, Madison, and Hancock counties. Between 1990 and 1998, Mississippi had net gains of 43,000 in domestic migration and 6,000 in international migration. In 1998, the state admitted 701 foreign immigrants. Between 1990 and 1998, Mississippi's overall population increased 6.9%. In the period 2000–05, net international migration was 10,653 and net internal migration was -10,578, for a net gain of 75 people.

[19]INTERGOVERNMENTAL COOPERATION

The Mississippi Commission on Interstate Cooperation oversees and encourages the state's participation in interstate bodies, especially the Council of State Governments and the National Conference of State Legislatures. Mississippi also participates in the Appalachian Regional Commission, Arkansas-Mississippi Great River Bridge Construction Compact, Highway 82 Four Lane Construction Compact, Mississippi-Alabama Railroad Authority Compact, Gulf States Marine Fisheries Commission, Southeastern Forest Fire Protection Compact, Southern Growth Policies Board, Southern States Energy Board, Southern Regional Education Board, and Tennessee-Tombigbee Waterway Development Authority. Mississippi received $4.532 billion in federal aid in fiscal year 2005, an estimated $4.746 billion in fiscal year 2006, and an estimated $4.876 billion in fiscal year 2007.

[20]ECONOMY

Between the Civil War and World War II, Mississippi's economy remained poor, stagnant, and highly dependent on the market for cotton—a bitter legacy from which the state took decades to recover. As in the pre–Civil War years, Mississippi exports mainly raw materials and imports mainly manufactures. In the 1930s, state leaders began to realize the necessity of diversifying the economy. By the mid-1960s, many more Mississippians recognized that political and economic inequality and racial conflict did not provide an environment attractive to the industries the state needed.

Once the turmoil of the 1950s and early 1960s had subsided, the impressive industrial growth of the immediate postwar years resumed. By the mid-1960s, manufacturing—attracted to the state, in part, because of low wage rates and a weak labor movement—surpassed farming as a source of jobs. During the following decade, the balance of industrial growth changed somewhat. The relatively low-paying garment, textile, and wood-products industries, based on cotton and timber, grew less rapidly in both value added and employment than a number of heavy industries, including transportation equipment and electric and electronic goods. The debut of casino gambling in the state in 1992 stimulated Mississippi's economy in the early and mid-1990s, and by 2002 accounted for 2.7% of total state employment (close to 31,000). In early 1995, however, the manufacturing sector began losing jobs, contributing to a deceleration in annual growth rates in the late 1990s. These losses created stress in other sectors, particularly in the retail trade and transportation and public utilities sectors. Ar-

eas of moderate growth in 2002 were business services and government. The number of personal bankruptcies in the state set a record in 2002, but the growth rate in filings moderated to 1.2%, down from 19.5% in 2001. The opening of a $1.4 billion Nissan plant near Jackson boosted the state's economy. Southern Mississippi, where the Ship System division of Northrop Grumman, Keesler Air Force Base, and the Stennis Space Center are located, should also benefit from increased national defense spending.

Mississippi's gross state product (GSP) in 2004 was $76.166 billion, of which manufacturing (durable and nondurable goods) accounted for the largest share at $12.161 billion or 15.9% of GSP, followed by the real estate sector at $7.221 billion (9.4% of GSP) and healthcare and social assistance at $5.497 billion (7.2% of GSP). In that same year, there were an estimated 197,586 small businesses in Mississippi. Of the 54,117 businesses that had employees, an estimated total of 52,403 or 96.8% were small companies. An estimated 6,141 new businesses were established in the state in 2004, up 2% from the year before. Business terminations that same year came to 7,380, up 1.6% from 2003. There were 170 business bankruptcies in 2004, down 39.7% from the previous year. In 2005, the state's personal bankruptcy (Chapter 7 and Chapter 13) filing rate was 765 filings per 100,000 people, ranking Mississippi as the ninth-highest in the nation.

[21]INCOME

In 2005 Mississippi had a gross state product (GSP) of $80 billion, which accounted for 0.6% of the nation's gross domestic product and placed the state at number 36 in highest GSP among the 50 states and the District of Columbia.

According to the Bureau of Economic Analysis, in 2004 Mississippi had a per capita personal income (PCPI) of $24,518. This ranked 51st in the United States and was 74% of the national average of $33,050. The 1994–2004 average annual growth rate of PCPI was 4.2%. Mississippi had a total personal income (TPI) of $71,122,091,000, which ranked 33rd in the United States and reflected an increase of 6.1% from 2003. The 1994–2004 average annual growth rate of TPI was 5.0%. Earnings of persons employed in Mississippi increased from $47,031,531,000 in 2003 to $49,796,304,000 in 2004, an increase of 5.9%. The 2003–04 national change was 6.3%.

The US Census Bureau reported that the three-year average median household income for 2002–04 in 2004 dollars was $33,659, compared to a national average of $44,473. During the same period an estimated 17.7% of the population was below the poverty line, as compared to 12.4% nationwide.

[22]LABOR

According to the Bureau of Labor Statistics (BLS), in April 2006 the seasonally adjusted civilian labor force in Mississippi numbered 1,314,300, with approximately 101,000 workers unemployed, yielding an unemployment rate of 7.7%, compared to the national average of 4.7% for the same period. Preliminary data for the same period placed nonfarm employment at 1,133,400. Since the beginning of the BLS data series in 1976, the highest unemployment rate recorded in Mississippi was 13.7% in May 1983. The historical low was 4.9% in January 2001. Preliminary nonfarm employment data by occupation for April 2006 showed that 4.8% of the labor force was employed in construction; 15.5% in manufacturing; 19.8% in trade, transportation, and public utilities; 7.9% in professional and business services; 10.8% in education and health services; 10.2% in leisure and hospitality services; and 21.4% in government.

The US Department of Labor's Bureau of Labor Statistics reported that in 2005, a total of 77,000 of Mississippi's 1,089,000 employed wage and salary workers were formal members of a union. This represented 7.1% of those so employed, up from 4.9% in 2004, but still below the national average of 12%. Overall in 2005, a total of 105,000 workers (9.7%) in Mississippi were covered by a union or employee association contract, which includes those workers who reported no union affiliation. Mississippi is one of 22 states with a right-to-work law.

As of 1 March 2006, Mississippi did not have a state-mandated minimum wage law. However, employees in that state were covered under federal minimum wage statutes. In 2004, women in the state accounted for 47.3% of the employed civilian labor force.

23 AGRICULTURE

In 2005, Mississippi ranked 26th among the states in income from agriculture, with marketings of over $3.85 billion; crops accounted for $1.24 billion and livestock and livestock products for $2.61 billion.

The history of agriculture in the state is dominated by cotton, which from the 1830s through World War II was Mississippi's principal cash crop. During the postwar period, however, as mechanized farming replaced the sharecropper system, agriculture became more diversified. During 2000–04, Mississippi ranked third in cotton and fourth in rice production, among the 50 states. About 2,370,000 bales of cotton worth $591 million were harvested in 2004 (second after Texas). Soybean output in 2004 totaled 62,320,000 bushels, worth $367.7 million, and rice production was 16,146,000 hundredweight in 2004, with a value of $117.9 million.

Federal estimates for 2004 showed some 42,200 farms with a total area of 11 million acres (4.5 million hectares. The richest soil is in the Delta, where most of the cotton is raised. Livestock has largely taken over the Black Belt, a fertile area in the northwest.

24 ANIMAL HUSBANDRY

Cattle are raised throughout the state, though principally in the Black Belt and Delta. The main chicken-raising area is in the eastern hills.

In 2005, there were around 1.07 million cattle and calves, valued at $834.6 million. In 2004, there were around 315,000 hogs and pigs, valued at $34.6 million. Mississippi is a leading producer of broilers, ranking fifth in 2003; some 4.3 billion lb (2 billion kg) of broilers, worth $1.51 billion, were produced in that year.

25 FISHING

In 2004, Mississippi ranked ninth among the 50 states in size of commercial fish landings, with a total of 183.7 million lb (83.5 million kg) valued at $43.8 million. Of this total, 162.8 million lb (74 million kg) was landed at Pascagoula-Moss Point, the nation's eighth-largest port for commercial landings. Shrimp and blue crab made up the bulk of the commercial landings. The saltwater catch also includes mullet and red snapper; the freshwater catch is dominated by buffalo fish, carp, and catfish. In 2003, the state had 35

processing and 31 wholesale plants employing about 2,706 people. In 2002, the commercial fishing fleet had 1,365 boats and vessels.

Mississippi is one of the leading states in catfish farming, mostly from ponds in the Yazoo River basin. There are 410 catfish farms in operation, covering about 101,000 acres (48,900 hectares) of water surface, with a combined 2006 inventory of 641 million fingerlings and 346 million stocker-sized catfish. Sales of catfish in 2004 totaled $275 million. In 2004, the state issued 369,252 sport fishing licenses. The Mississippi Department of Wildlife, Fisheries, and Parks operates 21 fishing lakes. The National Fish Hatchery System stocks more than 1.5 million fish annually to support fish resources in the coastal rivers of the Gulf of Mexico.

26 FORESTRY

Mississippi had approximately 18,605,000 acres (7,529,000 hectares) of forested land in 2004, over 60% of the total land area of the state. Six national forests extend over 1.1 million acres (445,000 hectares). The state's most heavily forested region is the Piney Woods in the southeast. Of the state's total commercial timberland, 90% is privately owned. Some of this land was also used for agricultural purposes (grazing). Lumber production in 2004 totaled 2.74 billion board feet (sixth in the United States).

27 MINING

According to preliminary data from the US Geological Survey (USGS), the estimated value of nonfuel mineral production by Mississippi in 2003 was $174 million, a decrease from 2002 of about 2%.

According to the preliminary data, Mississippi's top nonfuel mineral by value in 2003 was construction sand and gravel, which accounted for around 40% of all nonfuel mineral output by value. It was followed by fuller's earth, crushed stone, portland cement, and industrial sand and gravel. More than 65% by value of all nonfuel mineral production by Mississippi in 2003 was accounted for by construction sand and gravel, crushed stone, and portland cement.

Construction sand and gravel production in 2003 totaled 12.8 million metric tons and was valued at $69.1 million, while fuller's earth output that year totaled 411,000 metric tons and was valued at $29.9 million, according to the preliminary data from the USGS. The data also showed that crushed stone output in 2003 totaled 2.5 million metric tons and was worth $26.8 million.

The data listed Mississippi as ranking second among the states in production of fuller's earth, third in bentonite, and fourth in ball clay, by volume.

28 ENERGY AND POWER

As of 2003, Mississippi had 51 electrical power service providers, of which 23 were publicly owned and 25 were cooperatives. Of the remainder, two were investor owned, and one was federally operated. As of that same year there were 1,420,571 retail customers. Of that total, 605,653 received their power from investor-owned service providers. Cooperatives accounted for 683,124 customers, while publicly owned providers had 131,787 customers. There were seven federal customers.

Total net summer generating capability by the state's electrical generating plants in 2003 stood at 17.282 million kW, with total production that same year at 40.148 billion kWh. Of the total amount generated, 78.1% came from electric utilities, with the remainder coming from independent producers and combined heat and power service providers. The largest portion of all electric power generated, 17.082 billion kWh (42.5%), came from coal-fired plants, with nuclear power plants in second place at 10.902 billion kWh (27.2%) and natural gas fired plants in third place at 9.477 billion kWh (23.6%). Other renewable power sources accounted for 2.5% of all power generated, with petroleum fired plants at 4.1% and plants using other types of gases at 0.1%.

The Grand Gulf Nuclear Station boiling-water reactor, built by Mississippi Power Company in Claiborne County, continues to provide power to consumers within Mississippi. As of 2006, it was the state's sole nuclear power plant.

Mississippi is a major petroleum producer. As of 2004, the state had proven crude oil reserves of 178 million barrels, or 1% of all proven US reserves, while output that same year averaged 47,000 barrels per day. Including federal offshore domains, the state that year ranked 14th (13th excluding federal offshore) in proven reserves and 13th (12th excluding federal offshore) in production among the 31 producing states. In 2004 Mississippi had 1,412 producing oil wells. As of 2005, the state's four refineries had a combined crude oil distillation capacity of 364,800 barrels per day.

In 2004, Mississippi had 437 producing natural gas and gas condensate wells. In that same year, marketed gas production (all gas produced excluding gas used for repressuring, vented and flared, and nonhydrocarbon gases removed) totaled 145.692 billion cu ft (4.13 billion cu m). As of 31 December 2004, proven reserves of dry or consumer-grade natural gas totaled 995 billion cu ft (28.2 billion cu m). Most production comes from the south-central part of the state.

Mississippi in 2004 had one producing coal mine, a surface operation. Coal production that year totaled 3,586,000 short tons, down from 3,695,000 short tons in 2003. One short ton equals 2,000 lb (0.907 metric tons).

29 INDUSTRY

According to the US Census Bureau's Annual Survey of Manufactures (ASM) for 2004, Mississippi's manufacturing sector covered some 19 product subsectors. The shipment value of all products manufactured in the state that same year was $43.862 billion. Of that total, transportation equipment manufacturing accounted for the largest share at $7.694 billion. It was followed by food manufacturing at $5.798 billion; chemical manufacturing at $4.832 billion; furniture and related product manufacturing at $3.678 billion; and petroleum and coal products manufacturing at $3.412 billion.

In 2004, a total of 169,947 people in Mississippi were employed in the state's manufacturing sector, according to the ASM. Of that total, 134,189 were actual production workers. In terms of total employment, the food manufacturing industry accounted for the largest portion of all manufacturing employees at 28,815, with 25,274 actual production workers. It was followed by furniture and related product manufacturing at 26,292 employees (20,094 actual production workers); transportation equipment manufacturing at 25,689 employees (19,568 actual production workers); wood product manufacturing at 11,894 employees (9,934 actual production workers); and fabricated metal product manufacturing with 11,532 employees (9,118 actual production workers).

ASM data for 2004 showed that Mississippi's manufacturing sector paid $5.545 billion in wages. Of that amount, the transportation equipment manufacturing sector accounted for the largest share at $1.003 billion. It was followed by furniture and related product manufacturing at $709.476 million; food manufacturing at $655.124 million; fabricated metal product manufacturing at $390.577 million; and wood product manufacturing at $368.544 million.

30 COMMERCE

According to the 2002 Census of Wholesale Trade, Mississippi's wholesale trade sector had sales that year totaling $19.2 billion from 2,948 establishments. Wholesalers of durable goods accounted for 1,758 establishments, followed by nondurable goods wholesalers at 1,040 and electronic markets, agents, and brokers accounting for 150 establishments. Sales by durable goods wholesalers in 2002 totaled $5.9 billion, while wholesalers of nondurable goods saw sales of $11.6 billion. Electronic markets, agents, and brokers in the wholesale trade industry had sales of $1.5 billion.

In the 2002 Census of Retail Trade, Mississippi was listed as having 12,561 retail establishments with sales of $25.01 billion. The leading types of retail businesses by number of establishments were: gasoline stations (2,009); motor vehicle and motor vehicle parts dealers (1,664); food and beverage stores (1,513); clothing and clothing accessories stores (1,476); and miscellaneous store retailers (1,220). In terms of sales, motor vehicle and motor vehicle parts dealers accounted for the largest share of retail sales at $6.4 billion, followed by general merchandise stores at $5.1 billion; gasoline stations at $3.2 billion; and food and beverage stores at $2.8 billion. A total of 135,838 people were employed by the retail sector in Mississippi that year.

Exports from Mississippi totaled $4 billion in 2005.

31 CONSUMER PROTECTION

The Consumer Protection Division of the Office of the Attorney General, and the Bureau of Regulatory Services under the Department of Agriculture and Commerce, are each responsible for a range of consumer protection activities within the state of Mississippi. The Consumer Protection Division, established in 1974, may investigate complaints of unfair or deceptive trade practices and, in specific cases, may issue injunctions to halt them. Under 1994 amendments, a violation of the Consumer Protection Act is now a criminal misdemeanor. The Bureau of Regulatory Services consumer protection activities are centered on its Petroleum Products Inspection Division and its Weights and Measures Division, which respectively check petroleum product quality and pump calibration at the retail level, and scales and measurement equipment used in commerce and trade.

When dealing with consumer protection issues, the state's Attorney General's Office can initiate civil and criminal proceedings, but cannot represent the state before state and federal regulatory agencies. The office administers consumer protection and education programs, handle consumer complaints and has broad subpoena powers. In antitrust actions, the Attorney General's Office can act on behalf of those consumers who are incapable of acting on their own; initiate damage actions on behalf of the state in state courts; initiate criminal proceedings; and represent counties, cities and other governmental entities in recovering civil damages under state or federal law.

Offices of the Consumer Protection Division and the Bureau of Regulatory Services are each located in the state capitol of Jackson.

32 BANKING

As of June 2005, Mississippi had 100 insured banks, savings and loans, and saving banks, plus 30 state-chartered and 81 federally chartered credit unions (CUs). Excluding the CUs, the Memphis market area (which included portions of Tennessee, Mississippi, and Arkansas accounted for the largest portion of the state's financial institutions and deposits in 2004, with 52 institutions and $26.946 billion in deposits, followed by Jackson with 24 institu-

tions and $7.492 billion in deposits for that same year. As of June 2005, CUs accounted for 5.8% of all assets held by all financial institutions in the state, or some $2.720 billion. Banks, savings and loans, and savings banks collectively accounted for the remaining 94.2% or $43.960 billion in assets held.

In 2004, median past-due/nonaccrual loan levels stood at 2.38% of total loans, down from 2.79% in 2003. The median net interest margin (the difference between the lower rates offered to savers and the higher rates charged on loans) in that same year stood at 4.18%, unchanged from the previous year.

The Banking Division of the Mississippi Department of Banking and Consumer Finance is responsible for regulating state-chartered financial institutions.

33 INSURANCE

In 2004 there were over 2.1 million individual life insurance policies in force with a total value of over $99.8 billion; total value for all categories of life insurance (individual, group, and credit) was about $149 billion. The average coverage amount was $45,800 per policy holder. Death benefits paid that year totaled $526 million.

At the end of 2003, 26 life and health and 18 property and casualty insurance companies were domiciled in Mississippi. In 2004, direct premiums for property and casualty insurance totaled $3.6 billion. That year, there were 42,320 flood insurance policies in force in the state, with a total value of $5.2 million. About $1.6 billion of coverage was in force through beach and windstorm insurance.

In 2004, 47% of state residents held employment-based health insurance policies, 4% held individual policies, and 30% were covered under Medicare and Medicaid; 18% of residents were uninsured. In 2003, employee contributions for employment-based health coverage averaged 15% for single coverage and 29% for family coverage. The state offers a 12-month health benefits expansion program for small-firm employees in connection with the Consolidated Omnibus Budget Reconciliation Act (COBRA, 1986), a health insurance program for those who lose employment-based coverage due to termination or reduction of work hours.

In 2003, there were over 1.6 million auto insurance policies in effect for private passenger cars. Required minimum coverage includes bodily injury liability of up to $25,000 per individual and $50,000 for all persons injured in an accident, as well as property damage liability of $25,000. In 2003, the average expenditure per vehicle for insurance coverage was $709.45.

34 SECURITIES

There are no securities exchanges in Mississippi. In 2005, there were 420 personal financial advisers employed in the state and 610 securities, commodities, and financial services sales agents. In 2004, there were over 27 publicly traded companies within the state, with over eight NASDAQ companies, eight NYSE listings, and three AMEX listings.

35 PUBLIC FINANCE

Two state budgets are prepared annually—one by the State Department of Finance and Administration, for the executive branch; and one by the Joint Legislative Budget Committee, for the legis-

---

Mississippi—State Government Finances

(Dollar amounts in thousands. Per capita amounts in dollars.)

	AMOUNT	PER CAPITA
Total Revenue	15,351,077	5,291.65
General revenue	12,196,208	4,204.14
Intergovernmental revenue	5,424,813	1,869.98
Taxes	5,124,730	1,766.54
General sales	2,482,908	855.88
Selective sales	908,294	313.10
License taxes	318,488	109.79
Individual income tax	1,061,704	365.98
Corporate income tax	243,846	84.06
Other taxes	109,490	37.74
Current charges	1,211,257	417.53
Miscellaneous general revenue	435,408	150.09
Utility revenue	–	–
Liquor store revenue	193,518	66.71
Insurance trust revenue	2,961,351	1,020.80
Total expenditure	14,330,205	4,939.75
Intergovernmental expenditure	3,880,446	1,337.62
Direct expenditure	10,449,759	3,602.12
Current operation	7,786,087	2,683.93
Capital outlay	966,268	333.08
Insurance benefits and repayments	1,339,387	461.70
Assistance and subsidies	157,645	54.34
Interest on debt	200,372	69.07
Exhibit: Salaries and wages	1,868,768	644.18
Total expenditure	14,330,205	4,939.75
General expenditure	12,833,368	4,423.77
Intergovernmental expenditure	3,880,446	1,337.62
Direct expenditure	8,952,922	3,086.15
General expenditures, by function:		
Education	4,310,712	1,485.94
Public welfare	4,048,627	1,395.60
Hospitals	695,350	239.69
Health	297,655	102.60
Highways	1,012,320	348.96
Police protection	75,257	25.94
Correction	306,477	105.65
Natural resources	235,490	81.18
Parks and recreation	45,853	15.81
Government administration	283,352	97.67
Interest on general debt	200,372	69.07
Other and unallocable	1,321,903	455.67
Utility expenditure	–	–
Liquor store expenditure	157,450	54.27
Insurance trust expenditure	1,339,387	461.70
Debt at end of fiscal year	4,274,977	1,473.62
Cash and security holdings	23,288,104	8,027.61

Abbreviations and symbols: – zero or rounds to zero; (NA) not available; (X) not applicable.

SOURCE: *U.S. Census Bureau, Governments Division, 2004 Survey of State Government Finances,* January 2006.

lative branch—and submitted to the legislature for reconciliation and approval. The fiscal year runs from 1 July through 30 June.

Fiscal year 2006 general funds were estimated at $4.3 billion for resources and $4.0 billion for expenditures. In fiscal year 2004, federal government grants to Mississippi were $5.3 billion.

In the fiscal year 2007 federal budget, Mississippi was slated to receive: $5 million to replace the air traffic control tower at Gulfport-Biloxi International Airport.

36 TAXATION

In 2005, Mississippi collected $5,432 million in tax revenues or $1,860 per capita, which placed it 39th among the 50 states in per capita tax burden. The national average was $2,192 per capita. Property taxes accounted for 0.8% of the total, sales taxes, 47.6%; selective sales taxes, 17.2%; individual income taxes, 21.6%; corporate income taxes, 5.2%; and other taxes, 7.5%.

As of 1 January 2006, Mississippi had three individual income tax brackets ranging from 3.0% to 5.0%. The state taxes corporations at rates ranging from 3.0% to 5.0% depending on tax bracket.

In 2004, state and local property taxes amounted to $1,859,756,000, or $641 per capita. The per capita amount ranks the state 40th nationally. Local governments collected $1,819,515,000 of the total and the state government $40,241,000.

Mississippi taxes retail sales at a rate of 7%. In addition to the state tax, local taxes on retail sales can reach as much as 0.25%, making for a potential total tax on retail sales of 7.25%. Food purchased for consumption off-premises is taxable. The tax on cigarettes is 18 cents per pack, which ranks 49th among the 50 states and the District of Columbia. Mississippi taxes gasoline at 18.4 cents per gallon. This is in addition to the 18.4 cents per gallon federal tax on gasoline.

According to the Tax Foundation, for every federal tax dollar sent to Washington in 2004, Mississippi citizens received $1.77 in federal spending, which ranks the state fourth nationally.

37 ECONOMIC POLICY

In 1936, the state began implementing a program called Balance Agriculture with Industry (BAWI), designed to attract manufacturing to Mississippi. The BAWI laws offered industry substantial tax concessions and permitted local governments to issue bonds to build plants that would be leased to companies for a 20-year period, after which the company would own them. Mississippi continues to offer low tax rates and numerous tax incentives to industry.

The Mississippi Development Authority is charged with encouraging economic growth in the specific fields of industrial development, marketing of state products, and development of tourism. A high-technology asset is the John C. Stennis Space Center (SSC) in Hancock County, which is NASA's largest rocket engine test facility.

In September 2005, President George W. Bush announced he would create a Gulf Opportunity Zone for Louisiana, Mississippi, and Alabama in the aftermath of the devastation wrought by Hurricane Katrina. Congress passed the Gulf Opportunity Zone Act in December 2005, which provides a number of tax incentives to encourage the rebuilding of areas ravaged by Hurricanes Katrina, Rita, and Wilma.

38 HEALTH

The infant mortality rate in October 2005 was estimated at 9.6 per 1,000 live births, representing the second-highest rate in the country that year (following the District of Columbia). The birth rate in 2003 was 14.7 per 1,000 population. The abortion rate stood at 5.9 per 1,000 women in 2000. In 2003, about 84.9% of pregnant woman received prenatal care beginning in the first trimester. In 2004, approximately 84% of children received routine immunizations before the age of three.

The crude death rate in 2003 was 9.9 deaths per 1,000 population. As of 2002, the death rates for major causes of death (per 100,000 resident population) were: heart disease, 315.5; cancer, 211.3; cerebrovascular diseases, 67.1; chronic lower respiratory diseases, 48; and diabetes, 23.4. Mississippi ranked third in the nation for the highest death rates by heart disease, following West Virginia and Oklahoma. The state also had the third-highest homicide rate at 10.6 per 100,000 (following the District of Columbia and Louisiana). The accidental death rate of 57.2 per 100,000 is also one of the highest in the country. The mortality rate from HIV infection was 6.4 per 100,000 population. In 2004, the reported AIDS case rate was at about 16.5 per 100,000 population. In 2002, about 60.8% of the population was considered overweight or obese; this represented the third-highest rate in the country, following West Virginia and Alabama. As of 2004, about 24.4% of state residents were smokers.

In 2003, Mississippi had 92 community hospitals with about 13,000 beds. There were about 416,000 patient admissions that year and 4 million outpatient visits. The average daily inpatient census was about 7,400 patients. The average cost per day for hospital care was $882. Also in 2003, there were about 204 certified nursing facilities in the state with 18,149 beds and an overall occupancy rate of about 88.5%. In 2004, it was estimated that about 59.4% of all state residents had received some type of dental care within the year; this was the lowest percentage for dental care in the nation. Mississippi had 182 physicians per 100,000 resident population in 2004 and 889 nurses per 100,000 in 2005. In 2004, there was a total of 1,159 dentists in the state.

About 30% of state residents were enrolled in Medicaid and Medicare programs in 2004. Approximately 18% of the state population was uninsured in 2004. In 2003, state health care expenditures totaled $4.2 million.

39 SOCIAL WELFARE

In 2004, about 60,000 people received unemployment benefits, with the average weekly unemployment benefit at $172. In fiscal year 2005, the estimated average monthly participation in the food stamp program included about 391,485 persons (158,539 households); the average monthly benefit was about $98.55 per person. That year, the total of benefits paid through the state for the food stamp program was about $462.9 million.

Temporary Assistance for Needy Families (TANF), the system of federal welfare assistance that officially replaced Aid to Families with Dependent Children (AFDC) in 1997, was reauthorized through the Deficit Reduction Act of 2005. TANF is funded through federal block grants that are divided among the states based on an equation involving the number of recipients in each state. In 2004, the state TANF program had 42,000 recipients; state and federal expenditures on this TANF program totaled $67 million in fiscal year 2003.

In December 2004, Social Security benefits were paid to 545,710 Mississippians. This number included 289,380 retired workers, 56,860 widows and widowers, 103,870 disabled workers, 25,310 spouses, and 70,290 children. Social Security beneficiaries represented 18.7% of the total state population and 92.5% of the state's population age 65 and older. Retired workers received an average monthly payment of $875; widows and widowers, $765; disabled workers, $835; and spouses, $422. Payments for children of retired workers averaged $423 per month; children of deceased workers, $552; and children of disabled workers, $244. Federal Supplemental Security Income payments in December 2004 went to 125,180 Mississippi residents, averaging $369 a month.

⁴⁰HOUSING

In 2004, Mississippi had an estimated 1,221,240 housing units, of which 1,074,503 were occupied; 69.6% were owner-occupied. About 69.4% of all units were single-family, detached homes; 13.7% were mobile homes. Utility gas and electricity were the most common energy sources to all units. It was estimated that 92,908 units lacked telephone service, 8,325 lacked complete plumbing facilities, and 9,387 lacked complete kitchen facilities. The average household had 2.61 members.

In 2004, 14,500 privately owned units were authorized for construction. The median home value was $79,023, the second-lowest in the country (above Arkansas). The median monthly cost for mortgage owners was $843. Renters paid a median of $529 per month. In September 2005, the state received grants of $949,098 from the US Department of Housing and Urban Development (HUD) for rural housing and economic development programs. For 2006, HUD allocated to the state over $30.3 million in community development block grants. Also in 2006, HUD offered an additional $5 billion to the state in emergency funds to rebuild housing that was destroyed by Hurricanes Katrina, Rita, and Wilma in late 2005.

⁴¹EDUCATION

In 2004, 83% of Mississippians age 25 and older had completed high school, almost reaching the national average of 84%. Some 20.1% had obtained a bachelor's degree or higher, below the national average of 26%.

Mississippi's reaction to the US Supreme Court decision in 1954 mandating public school desegregation was to repeal the constitutional requirement for public schools and to foster the development of segregated private schools. In 1964, the state's schools did begin to integrate, and compulsory school attendance was restored 13 years later. As of 1980, 26% of minority (nonwhite) students were in schools in which minorities represented less than 50% of the student body, and 19% were in 99–100% minority schools—a considerable degree of de facto segregation, but less so than in some northern states. In 1982, the compulsory school age was raised to 14, and as of 2001, it was 17; also in 1982, a system of free public kindergartens was established for the first time.

The total enrollment for fall 2002 in Mississippi's public schools stood at 493,000. Of these, 360,000 attended schools from kindergarten through grade eight, and 132,000 attended high school. Approximately 47.3% of the students were white, 50.7% were black, 1.1% were Hispanic, 0.7% were Asian/Pacific Islander, and 0.2% were American Indian/Alaskan Native. Total enrollment was estimated at 489,000 in fall 2003 and was expected to be 469,000

by fall 2014, a decline of 4.8% during the period 2002–14. There were 49,729 students enrolled in 240 private schools in fall 2003. Expenditures for public education in 2003/04 were estimated at $3.4 billion or $6,237 per student, the fifth-lowest among the 50 states. Since 1969, the National Assessment of Educational Progress (NAEP) has tested public school students nationwide. The resulting report, *The Nation's Report Card,* stated that in 2005 eighth graders in Mississippi scored 262 out of 500 in mathematics compared with the national average of 278.

As of fall 2002, there were 147,077 students enrolled in college or graduate school; minority students comprised 39.1% of total postsecondary enrollment. In 2005 Mississippi had 40 degree-granting institutions including 9 public 4-year institutions, 17 public 2-year institutions, and 11 nonprofit private 4-year schools. Important institutions of higher learning in Mississippi include the University of Mississippi, established in 1844, Mississippi State University, and the University of Southern Mississippi. Predominantly black institutions include Tougaloo College, Alcorn State University, Jackson State University, and Mississippi Valley State University.

⁴²ARTS

The Mississippi Arts Commission was founded in 1968 and supports and promotes the arts in community life as well as education. In 2005, the Mississippi Arts Commission and other Mississippi arts organizations received seven grants totaling $701,500 from the National Endowment for the Arts. The commission also receives significant sums from the state and private sources. In 2005, the National Endowment for the Humanities contributed $891,547 to eight state programs.

Jackson has two ballet companies, a symphony orchestra, and two opera companies. Opera South, an integrated but predominantly black company, presents free operas during its summer tours and mounts two major productions yearly. The Mississippi Opera was incorporated in 1947 and is noted as the 11th-oldest continuously producing professional opera company in the nation. There are local symphony orchestras in Meridian, Starkville, Tupelo, and Greenville.

The established professional theaters in the state are the Sheffield Ensemble in Biloxi and the New Stage in Jackson. The Greater Gulf Coast Arts Center has been very active in bringing arts programs into the coastal area.

A distinctive contribution to US culture is the music of black sharecroppers from the Delta, known as the blues. The Delta Blues Museum in Clarksdale has an extensive collection documenting blues history. The annual Mississippi Delta Blues and Heritage Festival is held in Greenville. In September 2005 the 28th annual festival was held showcasing performances by artists such as Shirley Brown and Bobby Rush. Past performers include B.B. King, Muddy Waters, and Stevie Ray Vaughn.

⁴³LIBRARIES AND MUSEUMS

As of September 2001, Mississippi had 49 public library systems, with a total of 237 libraries, of which 189 were branches. In that same year, there were 5,615,000 volumes of books and serial publications in Mississippi libraries, and a total circulation of 8,898,000. The system also had 138,000 audio and 168,000 video items, 7,000 electronic format items (CD-ROMs, magnetic tapes, and disks), and two bookmobiles. The finest collection of Mississippiana is at the Mississippi State Department of Archives and History in Jackson. In the Vicksburg-Warren County Public Library are collections on the Civil War and state history and oral history collections. Tougaloo College has special collections of African materials, civil rights papers, and oral history. The Gulf Coast Research Library of Ocean Springs has a marine biology collection. In fiscal year 2001, operating income for the state's public library system totaled $37,393,000, including $746,000 in federal grants and $7,084,000 in state grants.

There are 65 museums, including the distinguished Mississippi State Historical Museum at Jackson. Pascagoula, Laurel, and Jackson all have notable art museums. The Mississippi Museum of Natural Science in Jackson has been designated the state's official natural science museum by the legislature. Also in Jackson is the Mississippi Agriculture and Forestry Museum. In Meridian is a museum devoted to country singer Jimmie Rodgers, and in Jackson one to pitcher Dizzy Dean.

Beauvoir, Jefferson Davis's home at Biloxi, is a state shrine and includes a museum. The Mississippi governor's mansion—completed in 1845, restored in 1975, and purportedly the second-oldest executive residence in the United States—is a National Historical Landmark.

44 COMMUNICATIONS

In 2004, only 89.6% of Mississippi's occupied housing units had telephones, the second-lowest rate in the United States. In addition, by June of that same year there were 1,411,277 mobile wireless telephone subscribers. In 2003, 48.3% of Mississippi households had a computer and 38.9% had Internet access, the lowest in the United States in both categories. By June 2005, there were 191,768 high-speed lines in Mississippi, 165,095 residential and 26,673 for business.

In 2005, the state had 64 major operating radio stations (7 AM, 57 FM) and 14 major television stations. A total of 17,234 Internet domain names had been registered in Mississippi as of 2000.

45 PRESS

In 2005, Mississippi had 23 daily newspapers: 8 morning dailies and 15 evening dailies. There were 18 Sunday papers in the state. The state's leading newspaper, located in Jackson and owned by the Gannett Company, is *The Clarion–Ledger,* a morning daily with a weekday circulation of 94,938 (107,865 Sunday).

Other leading dailies with approximate 2005 circulation rates are:

AREA	NAME	DAILY	SUNDAY
Biloxi-Gulfport	Sun Herald (m,S)	46,598	55,582
Tupelo	NE Mississippi Daily Journal	35,490	35,841

A monthly, *Mississippi Magazine,* is published in Jackson.

46 ORGANIZATIONS

In 2006, there were over 1,789 nonprofit organizations registered within the state, of which about 1,057 were registered as charitable, educational, or religious organizations.

The National Association for the Advancement of Colored People (NAACP), the Congress of Racial Equality, the Southern Christian Leadership Conference, and the Student Nonviolent Coordinating Committee (SNCC, later the Student National Coordinating Committee) were among the organizations that played key roles in the civil rights struggles in Mississippi during the 1950s and 1960s.

Other organizations with headquarters in Mississippi are the American Association of Public Health Physicians (Greenwood), the Sons of Confederate Veterans (Hattiesburg), the Sacred Heart League (Wallis), the National Band Association (Hattiesburg), and the Amateur Field Trial Clubs of America (Hernando). The International Dodge Ball Federation has a base in Gulfport.

47 TOURISM, TRAVEL, AND RECREATION

In 2004, there were 30 million overnight travelers in Mississippi, with 83% of all visitors traveling from out of state. In 2002 tourists spent an estimated $6.4 billion, which supported over 126,500 travel-related jobs. Jobs in the gaming industry represented about one-third of the total.

Among Mississippi's major tourist attractions are its floating riverboat casinos and its mansions and plantations, many of them in the Natchez area. Tunica, 30 miles south of Memphis, Tennessee, has Las Vegas-style casinos with hotels and entertainment, generating a significant source of revenue for the state. McRaven Plantation in Vicksburg was built in 1797. The Delta and Pine Land Co. plantation near Scott is one of the largest cotton plantations in the United States. At Greenwood is the Florewood River Plantation, a museum recreating 19th-century plantation life. The Mississippi State Fair is held annually in Jackson during the second week in October. Natchez Trace Parkway is a scenic route, running 444 mi (740 km) from Natchez, Mississippi, to Nashville, Tennessee. Among the tourist attractions along this route is the Emerald Mound, the second-largest Indian ceremonial earthwork. The city of Oxford was the home of William Faulkner and visitors can tour his former home, Rowan Oak. Although Memphis, Tennessee, is the site of Elvis Presley's home (Graceland), Tupelo is the site of his birthplace. As of 2006, many attractions had not yet recovered from the damage caused by Hurricane Katrina in 2005.

National parks include the Natchez Trace Parkway, Gulf Islands National Seashore, and Vicksburg National Military Park. There are also 6 national forests and 24 state parks.

48 SPORTS

There are no major professional sports teams in Mississippi. There are minor league hockey teams in Biloxi and Jackson. The University of Mississippi has long been prominent in college football. "Ole Miss" teams won the Sugar Bowl in 1958, 1960, 1961, 1963, and 1970, and the Cotton Bowl in 1956. The Rebels play in the Southeastern Conference, as do the Mississippi State Bulldogs. Southern Mississippi is a member of Conference USA.

Other annual sporting events of interest include the Dixie National Livestock Show and Rodeo, held in Jackson in February, and the Southern Farm Bureau Classic, held in Madison in October and November.

Football greats Walter Payton and Jerry Rice, along with boxing legend Archie Moore, were born and raised in Mississippi.

49 FAMOUS MISSISSIPPIANS

Mississippi's most famous political figure, Jefferson Davis (b.Kentucky, 1808–89), came to the state as a very young child, was educated at West Point, and served in the US Army from 1828 to 1835. He resigned a seat in Congress in 1846 to enter the Mexican War from which he returned home a hero after leading his famous regiment, the 1st Mississippi Rifles, at the Battle of Buena Vista, Mexico. From 1853 to 1857, he served as secretary of war in the cabinet of President Franklin Pierce. Davis was representing Mississippi in the US Senate in 1861 when the state withdrew from the Union. In February 1861, he was chosen president of the Confederacy, an office he held until the defeat of the South in 1865. Imprisoned for two years after the Civil War (though never tried), Davis lived the last years of his life at Beauvoir, an estate on the Mississippi Gulf Coast given to him by an admirer. There he wrote *The Rise and Fall of the Confederate Government*, completed eight years before his death in New Orleans.

Lucius Quintus Cincinnatus Lamar (b.Georgia, 1825–93) settled in Oxford in 1855 and only two years later was elected to the US House of Representatives. A supporter of secession, he served as Confederate minister to Russia in 1862. After the war, Lamar was the first Mississippi Democrat returned to the House; in 1877, he entered the US Senate. President Grover Cleveland made Lamar his secretary of the interior in 1885, later appointing him to the US Supreme Court. Lamar served as associate justice from 1888 until his death.

Some of the foremost authors of 20th-century America had their origins in Mississippi. Supreme among them is William Faulkner (1897–1962), whose literary career began in 1924 with the publication of *The Marble Faun*, a book of poems. His novels included such classics as *The Sound and the Fury* (1929), *Light in August* (1932), and *Absalom, Absalom!* (1936). Faulkner received two Pulitzer Prizes (one posthumously), and in 1949 was awarded the Nobel Prize for literature.

Richard Wright (1908–60), born near Natchez, spent his childhood years in Jackson. He moved to Memphis as a young man, and from there migrated to Chicago; he lived his last years in Paris. A powerful writer and a leading spokesman for the black Americans of his generation, Wright is best remembered for his novel *Native Son* (1940) and for *Black Boy* (1945), an autobiographical account of his Mississippi childhood.

Other native Mississippians of literary renown (and Pulitzer Prize winners) are Eudora Welty (1909–2001), Tennessee Williams (Thomas Lanier Williams, 1911–83), and playwright Beth Henley (b.1952). Welty's work, like Faulkner's, is set in Mississippi; her best-known novels include *Delta Wedding* (1946), *The Ponder Heart* (1954), and *Losing Battles* (1970). Although Tennessee Williams spent most of his life outside Mississippi, some of his most famous plays are set in the state. Other Mississippi authors are Hodding Carter (b.Louisiana, 1907–72), Shelby Foote (1916–2005), Walker Percy (b.Alabama, 1916–1990), and Willie Morris (1934–99).

Among the state's numerous musicians are William Grant Still (1895–1978), a composer and conductor, and Leontyne Price (Mary Leontine Price, b.1927), a distinguished opera singer. Famous blues singers are Charlie Patton (1887–1934), William Lee Conley "Big Bill" Broonzy (1898–1958), Howlin' Wolf (Chester Arthur Burnett, 1910–1976), Muddy Waters (McKinley Morganfield, 1915–83), John Lee Hooker (1917–2001), and Riley "B. B." King (b.1925). Mississippi's contributions to country music include Jimmie Rodgers (1897–1933), Conway Twitty (1933–1994), and Charley Pride (b.1939). Elvis Presley (1935–77), born in Tupelo, was one of the most popular entertainers in US history.

50 BIBLIOGRAPHY

Alampi, Gary (ed.). *Gale State Rankings Reporter.* Detroit: Gale Research, Inc., 1994.

Ballard, Michael B. *Civil War Mississippi: A Guide.* Jackson: University Press of Mississippi, 2000.

Bond, Bradley G. *Mississippi: A Documentary History.* Jackson: University Press of Mississippi, 2003.

———. *Political Culture in the Nineteenth-century South: Mississippi, 1830–1900.* Baton Rouge: Louisiana State University, 1995.

Brinkley, Douglas. *The Great Deluge: Hurricane Katrina, New Orleans, and the Mississippi Gulf Coast.* New York: Morrow, 2006.

Busbee, Westley F. *Mississippi: A History.* Wheeling, Ill.: Harlan Davidson, 2005.

Cities of the United States. 5th ed. Farmington Hills: Thomson Gale, 2005.

Coleman, Mary DeLorse. *Legislators, Law, and Public Policy: Political Change in Mississippi and the South.* Westport, Conn.: Greenwood Press, 1993.

Council of State Governments. *The Book of the States, 2006 Edition.* Lexington, Ky.: Council of State Governments, 2006.

Dittmer, John. *Local People: The Struggle for Civil Rights in Mississippi.* Urbana: University of Illinois Press, 1994.

Ferris, William (ed.). *The South.* Vol. 7 in *The Greenwood Encyclopedia of American Regional Cultures.* Westport, Conn.: Greenwood Press, 2004.

Nelson, Lawrence J. *King Cotton's Advocate: Oscar G. Johnston and the New Deal.* Knoxville: University of Tennessee Press, 1999.

Norman, Corrie E., and Don S. Armentrout (eds.). *Religion in the Contemporary South: Changes, Continuities, and Contexts.* Knoxville: University of Tennessee Press, 2005.

Saikku, Mikko. *This Delta, This Land: An Environmental History of the Yazoo-Mississippi Floodplain.* Athens: University of Georgia Press, 2005.

US Department of Commerce, Economics and Statistics Administration, US Census Bureau. *Mississippi, 2000. Summary Social, Economic, and Housing Characteristics: 2000 Census of Population and Housing.* Washington, D.C.: US Government Printing Office, 2003.

US Department of Education, National Center for Education Statistics. Office of Educational Research and Improvement. *Digest of Education Statistics, 1993.* Washington, D.C.: US Government Printing Office, 1993.

US Department of the Interior, US Fish and Wildlife Service. *Endangered and Threatened Species Recovery Program.* Washington, D.C.: US Government Printing Office, 1990.

Welty, Eudora. *One Time, One Place: Mississippi in the Depression.* New York: Random House, 1971.

MISSOURI

State of Missouri

ORIGIN OF STATE NAME: Probably derived from the Iliniwek Indian word *missouri,* meaning "owners of big canoes." **NICKNAME:** The Show Me State. **CAPITAL:** Jefferson City. **ENTERED UNION:** 10 August 1821 (24th). **SONG:** "Missouri Waltz." **MOTTO:** *Salus populi suprema lex esto* (The welfare of the people shall be the supreme law). **COAT OF ARMS:** Two grizzly bears stand on a scroll inscribed with the state motto and support a shield portraying an American eagle and a constellation of stars, a grizzly bear on all fours, and a crescent moon, all encircled by the words "United We Stand, Divided We Fall." Above are a six-barred helmet and 24 stars; below is the roman numeral MDCCCXX (1820), when Missouri's first constitution was adopted. **FLAG:** Three horizontal stripes of red, white, and blue, with the coat of arms encircled by 24 white stars on a blue band in the center. **OFFICIAL SEAL:** The coat of arms is surrounded by the words "The Great Seal of the State of Missouri." **BIRD:** Bluebird. **FLOWER:** White Hawthorn blossom. **TREE:** Flowering dogwood. **LEGAL HOLIDAYS:** New Year's Day, 1 January; Birthday of Martin Luther King Jr., 3rd Monday in January; Lincoln's Birthday, 12 February; Washington's Birthday, 3rd Monday in February; Harry S. Truman's Birthday, 8 May; Memorial Day, last Monday in May; Independence Day, 4 July; Labor Day, 1st Monday in September; Columbus Day, 2nd Monday in October; Veterans' Day, 11 November; Thanksgiving Day, 4th Thursday in November; Christmas Day, 25 December. Though not a legal holiday, Missouri Day, the 3rd Wednesday in October, is commemorated in schools each year. **TIME:** 6 AM CST = noon GMT.

¹LOCATION, SIZE, AND EXTENT

Located in the western north-central United States, Missouri ranks 19th in size among the 50 states.

The total area of Missouri is 69,697 sq mi (180,516 sq km), of which land takes up 68,945 sq mi (178,568 sq km) and inland water 752 sq mi (1,948 sq km). Missouri extends 284 mi (457 km) E-w; its greatest N-s extension is 308 mi (496 km).

Missouri is bounded on the N by Iowa (with the line in the extreme NE defined by the Des Moines River); on the E by Illinois, Kentucky, and Tennessee (with the line passing through the Mississippi River); on the s by Arkansas (with a "boot heel" in the SE bounded by the Mississippi and St. Francis rivers); and on the w by Oklahoma, Kansas, and Nebraska (the line in the NW being formed by the Missouri River).

The total boundary length of Missouri is 1,438 mi (2,314 km). The state's geographic center is in Miller County, 20 mi (32 km) sw of Jefferson City.

²TOPOGRAPHY

Missouri is divided into four major land regions. The Dissected Till Plains, lying north of the Missouri River and forming part of the Central Plains region of the United States, comprise rolling hills, open fertile flatlands, and well-watered prairie. The Osage Plains cover the western part of the state, their flat prairie monotony broken by low rounded hills. The Mississippi Alluvial Plain, in the southeastern corner, is made up of fertile black lowlands whose floodplain belts represent both the present and former courses of the Mississippi River. The Ozark Plateau, which comprises most of southern Missouri and extends into northern Arkansas and northeastern Oklahoma, constitutes the state's largest single region. The Ozarks contain Taum Sauk Mountain, at 1,772 ft (540 m) the highest elevation in the state. Along the St. Francis River, near Cardwell, is the state's lowest point, 230 ft (70 m). The mean elevation is approximately 800 ft (244 m).

Including a frontage of at least 500 mi (800 km) along the Mississippi River, Missouri has more than 1,000 mi (1,600 km) of navigable waterways. The Mississippi and Missouri rivers, the two largest in the United States, respectively form the state's eastern border and part of its western border; Kansas City is located at the point where the Missouri bends eastward to cross the state, while St. Louis developed below the junction of the two great waterways. The White, Grand, Chariton, St. Francis, Current, and Osage are among the state's other major rivers. The largest lake is the artificial Lake of the Ozarks, covering a total of 93 sq mi (241 sq km).

Missouri's exceptional number of caves and caverns were formed during the last 50 million years through the erosion of limestone and dolomite by melting snows bearing vegetable acids. Coal, lead, and zinc deposits date from the Pennsylvanian era, beginning some 250 million years ago. The Mississippi Valley area is geologically active: massive earthquakes during 1811 and 1812 devastated the New Madrid area of the southeast.

³CLIMATE

Missouri has a continental climate, but with considerable local and regional variation. The average annual temperature is 50°F

(10°C) in the northwest, but about 60°F (16°C) in the southeast. Kansas City has an average temperature of 56°F (13°C), ranging from 30°F (-1°C) in January to 80°F (26°C) in July; St. Louis has an annual average of 56°F (13°C) with 30°F (-1°C) in January and 79°F (26°C) in July.

The coldest temperature ever recorded in Missouri was -40°F (-40°C), set at Warsaw on 13 February 1905; the hottest, 118°F (48°C), at Warsaw and Union on 14 July 1954. A 1980 heat wave caused 311 heat-related deaths in Missouri, the highest toll in the country; most were elderly residents of St. Louis and Kansas City. Fifty-one more heat-related deaths occurred in St. Louis during a 1983 heat wave.

The average annual precipitation for Kansas City is about 36 in (100 cm), with some rain or snow falling about 110 days a year. The heaviest precipitation is in the southeast, averaging 48 in (122 cm); the northwest usually receives 35 in (89 cm) yearly. Snowfall averages 20 in (51 cm) in the north, 10 in (25 cm) in the southeast. During the winter, northwest winds prevail; the air movement is largely from the south and southeast during the rest of the year. Springtime is the peak tornado season.

⁴FLORA AND FAUNA

Representative trees of Missouri include the shortleaf pine, scarlet oak, smoke tree, pecan (Carya illinoensis), and peachleaf willow, along with species of tupelo, cottonwood, cypress, cedar, and dogwood (the state tree). American holly, which once flourished in the southeastern woodlands, is now considered rare; various types of wild grasses proliferate in the northern plains region. Missouri's state flower is the hawthorn blossom; other wild flowers include Queen Anne's lace, meadow rose, and white snakeroot. Showy and small white lady's slipper, green adder's-mouth, purslane, corn salad, dotted monarda, and prairie white-fringed orchid are rare in Missouri. Among the eight threatened or endangered plants listed by the US Fish and Wildlife Service in 2006 were the decurrent false aster, running buffalo clover, pondberry, Missouri bladderpod, and western prairie fringed orchid.

Indigenous mammals are the common cottontail, muskrat, white-tailed deer, and gray and red foxes. The state bird is the bluebird; other common birds are the cardinal, solitary vireo, and the prothonotary warbler. Wetlands covering about 1.4% of the state are important wintering grounds for hundreds of thousands of migratory birds and waterfowl, including the endangered bald eagle. A characteristic amphibian is the plains leopard frog; native snakes include garter, ribbon, and copperhead. Bass, carp, perch, jack salmon (walleye), and crayfish abound in Missouri's waters. The chigger, a minute insect, is a notorious pest.

In 2006, 17 species of animals (vertebrates and invertebrates) were listed as threatened or endangered in Missouri, including three species of bat (Ozark big-eared, gray, and Indiana), pallid sturgeon, gray wolf, and three varieties of mussel.

⁵ENVIRONMENTAL PROTECTION

Missouri's first conservation law, enacted in 1874, provided for a closed hunting season on deer and certain game birds. In 1936, the state established a Conservation Commission to protect the state's wildlife and forest resources. Missouri's Department of Conservation manages the state forests and fish hatcheries and maintains wildlife refuges and the Department of Natural Resources is re-

sponsible for state parks, energy conservation, and environmental quality programs, including air pollution control, water purification, land reclamation, soil and water conservation, and solid and hazardous waste management. The State Environmental Improvement and Energy Resources Authority, within the Department of Natural Resources, is empowered to offer financial aid to any individual, business, institution, or governmental unit seeking to meet pollution control responsibilities.

An important environmental problem is soil erosion; the state loses 71 million tons of topsoil each year. Residents approved a 0.1% sales tax in 1984 and 1988 to create a fund to address this problem. As of 1982, 42 sites in Missouri were found to have unsafe concentrations of dioxin, a highly toxic by-product of hexachlorophene, manufactured in a Verona chemical plant; in that year, an evacuation was begun (completed in 1985) of the 2,000 residents of Times Beach, a community 30 mi (48 km) west of St. Louis that was declared a federal disaster area. St. Louis ranked high among US cities for the quantities of lead and suspended particles found in the atmosphere, but conditions improved between the mid-1970s and early 1980s. In 2003, 102.5 million lb of toxic chemicals were released in the state.

In 2003, Missouri had 503 hazardous waste sites listed in the US Environment Protection Agency (EPA) database, 26 of which were on the National Priorities List as of 2006. In 1996, it had 643,000 acres (260,000 hectares) of wetlands, or about 1.4% of the state's lands. In 2005, the EPA spent over $11.9 million through the Superfund program for the cleanup of hazardous waste sites in the state. The same year, federal EPA grants awarded to the state included $12 million for the drinking water state revolving fund, plus an addition $12 million grant for other safe drinking water projects.

⁶POPULATION

Missouri ranked 18th in population in the United States with an estimated total of 5,800,310 in 2005, an increase of 3.6% since 2000. Between 1990 and 2000, Missouri's population grew from 5,117,073 to 5,595,211, an increase of 9%. The population is projected to reach 6 million by 2015 and 6.3 million by 2025. The population density in 2004 was 83.5 persons per sq mi.

In 1830, the first year in which Missouri was enumerated as a state, the population was 140,455. Missouri's population just about doubled each decade until 1860, when the growth rate subsided; the population surpassed the 2 million mark at the 1880 census, 3 million in 1900 (when it ranked fifth in the United States), and 4 million during the early 1950s.

In 2004, the median age for Missourians was 37.3. In the same year, 24.1% of the on under age 18 while 13.3% was age 65 or older.

More than half of all Missourians live in urban areas. The largest cities and their estimated 2004 populations are Kansas City, 444,387, and St. Louis, 343,279—both well below the 1980 figures. The St. Louis metropolitan area, embracing parts of Missouri and Illinois, comprised an estimated 2,764,054 people in 2004 while metropolitan Kansas City, in Missouri and Kansas, had a population of 1,925,319.

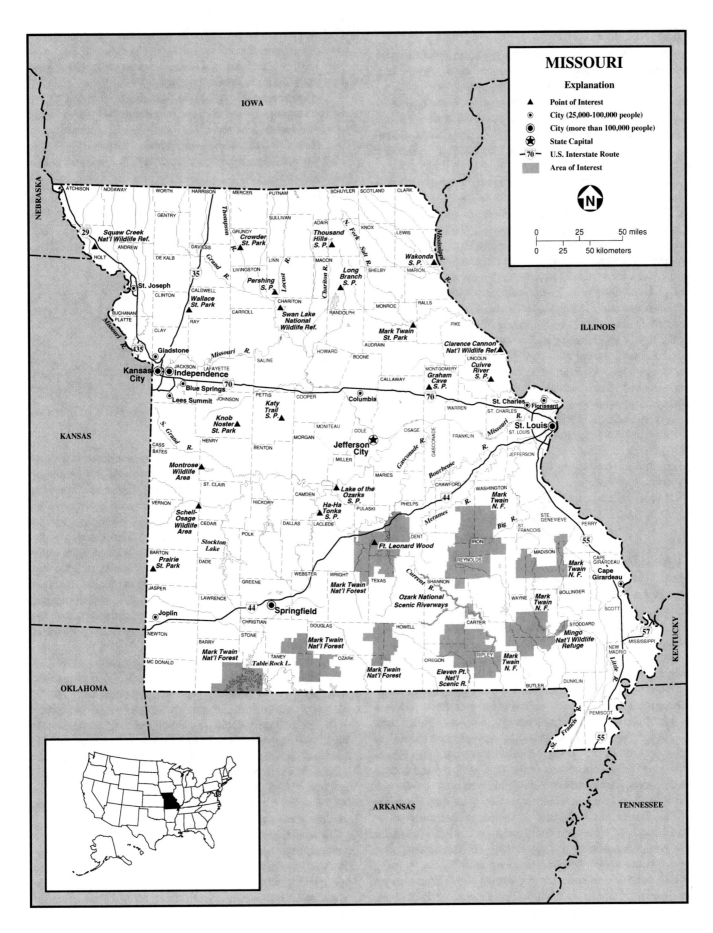

MISSOURI

Explanation

▲ Point of Interest
◉ City (25,000-100,000 people)
◎ City (more than 100,000 people)
★ State Capital
—70— U.S. Interstate Route
▨ Area of Interest

Ⓝ

0   25   50 miles
0   25   50 kilometers

IOWA

NEBRASKA

29 Squaw Creek Nat'l Wildlife Ref.
St. Joseph
Crowder St. Park
Thousand Hills S.P.
Wakonda S.P.
Long Branch S.P.
Pershing S.P.
Wallace St. Park
35
Swan Lake National Wildlife Ref.
Mark Twain St. Park
Clarence Cannon Nat'l Wildlife Ref.
Cuivre River S.P.
Gladstone
Kansas City
Independence
Blue Springs
Lees Summit
Katy Trail S.P.
Columbia
Graham Cave S.P.
St. Charles
Florissant
St. Louis
Knob Noster St. Park
Jefferson City
Montrose Wildlife Area
Lake of the Ozarks S.P.
Ha-Ha Tonka S.P.
Schell-Osage Wildlife Area
Mark Twain N.F.
Stockton Lake
Ft. Leonard Wood
Meremec
Big R.
Mark Twain N.F.
55
Cape Girardeau
Prairie St. Park
Mark Twain Nat'l Forest
Ozark National Scenic Riverways
Mingo Nat'l Wildlife Refuge
57
Joplin
44
Springfield
Mark Twain Nat'l Forest
Mark Twain N.F.
Table Rock L.
Mark Twain Nat'l Forest
Eleven Pt. Nat'l Scenic R.
55

ILLINOIS

KANSAS

OKLAHOMA

ARKANSAS

KENTUCKY

TENNESSEE

Counties labeled: ATCHISON, NODAWAY, WORTH, HARRISON, MERCER, PUTNAM, SCHUYLER, SCOTLAND, CLARK, GENTRY, SULLIVAN, ADAIR, KNOX, LEWIS, ANDREW, DE KALB, DAVIESS, GRUNDY, LINN, MACON, SHELBY, MARION, HOLT, BUCHANAN, CALDWELL, LIVINGSTON, CHARITON, RANDOLPH, MONROE, RALLS, PLATTE, CLINTON, CLAY, RAY, CARROLL, HOWARD, AUDRAIN, PIKE, LINCOLN, JACKSON, LAFAYETTE, SALINE, BOONE, CALLAWAY, MONTGOMERY, WARREN, ST. CHARLES, ST. LOUIS, PETTIS, COOPER, JOHNSON, CASS, BATES, HENRY, BENTON, MORGAN, MONITEAU, COLE, OSAGE, GASCONADE, FRANKLIN, JEFFERSON, ST. CLAIR, MILLER, MARIES, CRAWFORD, VERNON, CEDAR, HICKORY, CAMDEN, PULASKI, PHELPS, WASHINGTON, STE. GENEVIEVE, PERRY, DALLAS, LACLEDE, DENT, IRON, ST. FRANCOIS, MADISON, BARTON, DADE, POLK, WEBSTER, WRIGHT, TEXAS, REYNOLDS, BOLLINGER, CAPE GIRARDEAU, JASPER, GREENE, SHANNON, WAYNE, SCOTT, LAWRENCE, CHRISTIAN, DOUGLAS, HOWELL, CARTER, STODDARD, NEWTON, STONE, TANEY, OZARK, OREGON, RIPLEY, NEW MADRID, MISSISSIPPI, MC DONALD, BARRY, DUNKLIN, BUTLER, PEMISCOT

Rivers: Thompson R., Grand R., Locust R., Chariton R., N. Fork Salt R., Mississippi R., Missouri R., S. Grand R., Gasconade R., Bourbeuse R., Meremec R., Big R., Current R., Eleven Pt. Nat'l Scenic R., St. Francis R., Little R.

7 ETHNIC GROUPS

After the flatboat and French traders and settlers had made possible the earliest development of Missouri and its Mississippi shore, the river steamer, the Civil War, the Homestead Act (1862), and the railroad changed the character of the state ethnically as well as economically. Germans came in large numbers, developing small diversified industries, and they were followed by Czechs and Italians. The foreign-born numbered 151,196 in 2000, up from 83,633 in 1990.

Black Americans have represented a rising proportion of Missouri's population in recent decades: 9% in 1960, 10.3% in 1970, 10.5% in 1980, 10.7% in 1990, 11.2% in 2000, and 11.5% in 2004. Kansas City's black community supported a flourishing jazz and urban blues culture between the two world wars, while St. Louis was the home of Scott Joplin and W. C. Handy in the early years of the 20th century. Of the 629,391 black residents of Missouri in 2000, 178,266 lived in St. Louis, which was 51.2% black. In 2000 Missouri also had 118,592 Hispanics and Latinos, nearly double the 1990 figure of 62,000, and including 77,887 of Mexican ancestry. In 2004, 2.6% of the population was of Hispanic or Latino origin. The total Asian population as of 2000 was 61,595; in that year there were 13,667 Chinese, 7,735 Filipinos, 6,767 Koreans, 3,337 Japanese, and 12,169 Vietnamese (triple the 1990 figure of 4,030). Pacific Islanders numbered 3,178. In 2004, 1.3% of the population was Asian, and 0.1% of Pacific Island origin.

Only a few American Indians remained in Missouri after 1836. The 2000 census showed an Indian population of 25,076. The state has no Indian reservations. In 2004, 0.5% of the population was American Indian.

Of those claiming descent from at least one specific ancestry group in 2000, 1,313,951 named German, 528,935 English, and 711,995 Irish.

8 LANGUAGES

White pioneers found Missouri Indians in the northern part of what is now Missouri Osage in the central portion, and Quapaw in the south. Long after these tribes' removal to Indian Territory, only a few place-names echo their heritage: Missouri itself, Kahoka, Wappapello.

Four westward-flowing language streams met and partly merged in Missouri. Northern and North Midland speakers settled north of the Missouri River and in the western border counties, bringing their Northern *pail* and *sick to the stomach* and their North Midland *fishworm* (earthworm), *gunnysack* (burlap bag), and *sick at the stomach*. But *sick in the stomach* occurs along the Missouri River from St. Louis to Kansas City and along the Mississippi south of St. Louis. South of the Missouri River, and notably in the Ozark Highlands, South Midland dominates, though with a few Southern forms, especially in the cotton-growing floodplain of the extreme southeast. *Wait on* (wait for), *light bread* (white bread), and *pullybone* (wishbone) are critical dialect markers for this area, as are *redworm* (earthworm), *towsack* (burlap bag), *snap beans* (string beans), *how* and *now* sounding like /haow/ and /naow/, and Missouri ending with the vowel of *me* rather than the final vowel of /uh/ heard north of the Missouri. In the extreme southeast are Southern *loaf bread, grass sack* (burlap bag), and *cold*

drink as a term for a soft drink. In the eastern half of the state, a soft drink is generally *soda* or *sody*; in the western half, *pop*.

In 2000. 94.9% of state residents five years old or older spoke only English at home, down from 96% in 1990.

The following table gives selected statistics from the 2000 Census for language spoken at home by persons five years old and over. The category "African languages" includes Amharic, Ibo, Twi, Yoruba, Bantu, Swahili, and Somali. The category "Other West Germanic languages" includes Dutch, Pennsylvania Dutch, and Afrikaans.

LANGUAGE	NUMBER	PERCENT
Population 5 years and over	**5,226,022**	**100.0**
Speak only English	4,961,741	94.9
Speak a language other than English	264,281	5.1
Speak a language other than English	**264,281**	**5.1**
Spanish or Spanish Creole	110,752	2.1
German	30,680	0.6
French (incl. Patois, Cajun)	30,680	0.4
Chinese	11,631	0.2
Vietnamese	9,420	0.2
Serbo-Croatian	8,350	0.2
Italian	6,710	0.1
Russian	5,469	0.1
Arabic	5,137	0.1
African languages	5,117	0.1
Other West Germanic languages	4,822	0.1
Korean	4,753	0.1
Tagalog	4,645	0.1

9 RELIGIONS

Beginning in the late 17th century, French missionaries brought Roman Catholicism to what is now Missouri; the first permanent Roman Catholic church was built about 1755 at St. Genevieve. Immigration from Germany, Ireland, Italy, and Eastern Europe swelled the Catholic population during the 19th century and Roman Catholicism remains the largest single Christian denomination, though the Evangelical Protestants collectively outnumber Catholics. Baptist preachers crossed the Mississippi River into Missouri in the late 1790s, and the state's first Methodist church was organized about 1806. Immigrants from Germany included not only Roman Catholics, but also many Lutherans, the most conservative of whom organized the Lutheran Church—Missouri Synod in 1847.

In 2004, Missouri had 844,102 Roman Catholics; with 550,000 belonging to the archdiocese of St. Louis. The next largest religious group is the Southern Baptist Convention, with 797,732 adherents in 2000 and 13,646 newly baptized members reported in 2002. The United Methodist Church had 176,022 members in 2004. In 2000, the Lutheran Church–Missouri Synod had 140,315 members and the Christian Church (Disciples of Christ) had 105,583. The same year, the estimated number of Jews was 62,315 and Muslims numbered about 19,359. About 2.7 million people (48.3% of the population) were not counted as members of any religious organization.

The administrative offices of the Baptist Bible Fellowship International, along with its affiliated Baptist Bible College and Baptist Bible School of Theology, are located in Springfield. The world headquarters for the Fellowship of Christian Athletes and the international headquarters of the Church of the Nazarene are located in Kansas City.

¹⁰TRANSPORTATION

Centrally located, Missouri is the leading US transportation center. Both St. Louis and Kansas City are hubs of rail, truck, and airline transportation.

In 1836, delegates from 11 counties met in St. Louis to recommend construction of two railroad lines and to petition Congress for a grant of 800,000 acres (324,000 hectares) of public land on which to build them. More than a dozen companies were incorporated by the legislature, but they all collapsed with the financial panic of 1837. Interest in railroad construction revived during the following decade, and in 1849 a national railroad convention was held in St. Louis at which nearly 1,000 delegates from 13 states recommended the construction of a transcontinental railroad. By 1851, three railroad lines had been chartered, and construction by the Pacific Railroad at St. Louis was under way. The Pacific line reached Kansas City in 1865, and a bridge built over the Missouri River four years later enabled Kansas City to link up with the Hannibal and St. Joseph Railroad, providing a freight route to Chicago that did not pass through St. Louis. In 2003, there were 4,791 rail mi (7,713 km) of track within the state, including 4,087 rail mi (6,580 km) of Class I track. In 2006, Amtrak provided passenger train service running directly from Chicago to St. Louis and to Kansas City, en route to San Antonio and Los Angeles, to 11 stations in Missouri.

The first road developed in colonial Missouri was probably a trail between the lead mines and Ste. Genevieve in the early 1700s. A two-level cantilever bridge—the first in the world to have a steel superstructure—spanning the Mississippi at St. Louis was dedicated on 4 July 1874. By 1940, no place in Missouri was more than 10 mi (16 km) from a highway. In 2004, there were 125,923 mi (202,736 km) of public roads in Missouri. The main interstate highways were: I-70, linking St. Louis with Kansas City; I-44, connecting St. Louis with Springfield and Joplin; I-55, linking St. Louis with Chicago, Illinois, to the north and paralleling the course of the Mississippi between St. Louis and Memphis, Tennessee; I-35, connecting Kansas City with Des Moines, Iowa; and I-29, paralleling the Missouri River north of Kansas City. Motor vehicle registration for the state in 2004 totaled some 4.855 million vehicles of all types, including 2.690 million passenger cars, 2.084 million trucks of all types, and 4,000 buses. In that same year, there were 4,047,652 licensed drivers in the state.

The Mississippi and Missouri rivers have long been important transportation routes. Pirogues, keelboats, and flatboats plied these waterways for more than a century before the first steamboat, the *New Orleans*, traveled down the Mississippi in 1811. The Mississippi still serves considerable barge traffic, making metropolitan St. Louis an active inland port area, with 33.386 million tons of cargo handled in 2004. For that same year, Missouri had 1,033 mi (1,663 km) of navigable inland waterways. In 2003, waterborne shipments totaled 34.050 million tons.

Pioneering aviators in Missouri organized the first international balloon races in 1907 and the first US-sponsored international aviation meet in 1910. Five St. Louis pilots made up the earliest US Army air corps, and a barnstorming pilot named Charles A. Lindbergh, having spent a few years in the St. Louis area, had the backing of businessmen from that city when he flew his *Spirit of St. Louis* across the Atlantic in 1927. In 2005, Missouri had a total of 539 public and private-use aviation-related facilities. This included 404 airports, 129 heliports, 2 STOLports (Short Take-Off and Landing), and four seaplane bases. Kansas City International Airport and Lambert-St. Louis International Airport are the state's most important airports. In 2004, Kansas City International had 5,040,595 enplanements, while Lambert-St. Louis International had 6,377,628 enplanements that same year, making them the 39th- and 34th-busiest airports in the United States, respectively.

¹¹HISTORY

The region we now call Missouri has been inhabited for at least 4,000 years. The prehistoric Woodland peoples left low burial mounds, rudimentary pottery, arrowheads, and grooved axes; remains of the later Mississippian Culture include more sophisticated pottery and finely chipped arrowheads. When the first Europeans arrived in the late 17th century, most of the few thousand Indians living in Missouri were relatively recent immigrants, pushed westward across the Mississippi River because of pressures from eastern tribes and European settlers along the Atlantic coast. Indians then occupying Missouri belonged to two main linguistic groups: Algonkian-speakers, mainly the Sauk, Fox, and Iliniwek (Illinois) in the northeast; and a Siouan group, including the Osage, Missouri, Iowa, Kansas, and other tribes, to the south and west. Of greatest interest to the Europeans were the Osage, among whom were warriors and runners of extraordinary ability. The flood of white settlers into Missouri after 1803 forced the Indians to move into Kansas and into what became known as Indian Territory (present-day Oklahoma). During the 1820s, the US government negotiated treaties with the Osage, Sauk, Fox, and Iowa tribes whereby they surrendered, for the most part peaceably, all their lands in Missouri. By 1836, few Indians remained.

The first white men to pass through land eventually included within Missouri's boundaries apparently were Jacques Marquette and Louis Joliet, who in 1673 passed the mouth of the Missouri River on their journey down the Mississippi; so did Robert Cavelier, Sieur de la Salle, who claimed the entire Mississippi Valley for France in 1682. Probably the first Frenchman to explore the Missouri River was Louis Armand de Lom d'Arce, Baron de Lahontan, who in 1688 claimed to have reached the junction of the Missouri and Osage rivers. The French did little to develop the Missouri region during the first half of the 18th century, although a few fur traders and priests established posts and missions among the Indians. A false report that silver had been discovered set off a brief mining boom in which no silver but some lead—available in abundance—was extracted. Missouri passed into Spanish hands with the rest of the Louisiana Territory in 1762, but development was still guided by French settlers; in 1764, the French fur trader Pierre Laclède established a trading post on the present site of St. Louis.

Although Spain fortified St. Louis and a few other outposts during the American Revolution and beat back a British-Indian attack on St. Louis in 1780, the Spanish did not attempt to settle Missouri. However, they did allow Americans to migrate freely into the territory. Spanish authorities granted free land to the new settlers, relaxed their restrictions against Protestants, and welcomed slaveholding families from southern states—especially important after 1787, when slavery was banned in the Northwest Territory. Pioneers such as Daniel Boone arrived from Kentucky, and the Chouteau fur-trading family gained a lucrative monopoly among the Osage. Spanish rule ended abruptly in 1800 when Napoleon forced Spain to return Louisiana to France. Included in the Louisiana Purchase, Missouri then became part of the United States in 1803. After the Lewis and Clark expedition (1804–06) had successfully explored the Missouri River, Missouri in general—and St. Louis in particular—became the gateway to the West.

Missouri was part of the Louisiana Territory (with headquarters at St. Louis) until 1 October 1812, when the Missouri Territory (including present-day Arkansas, organized separately in 1819) was established. A flood of settlers between 1810 and 1820 more than tripled Missouri's population from 19,783 to 66,586, leading Missourians to petition the US Congress for statehood as early as 1818. But Congress, divided over the slavery issue, withheld permission for three years, finally approving statehood for Maine and Missouri under the terms of the Missouri Compromise (1820), which sanctioned slavery in the new state but banned it in the rest of the former Louisiana Territory north of Arkansas. Congress further required that Missouri make no effort to enforce a state constitutional ban on the immigration of free Negroes and mulattos; once the legislature complied, Missouri became the 24th state on 10 August 1821. Alexander McNair became the state's first governor and Thomas Hart Benton was one of the state's first two US senators; Benton remained an important political leader for more than three decades.

Aided by the advent of steamboat travel on the Mississippi and Missouri rivers, settlers continued to arrive in the new state, whose population surpassed 1 million by 1860. The site for a new capital, Jefferson City, was selected in 1821, and five years later the legislature met there for the first time. French fur traders settled the present site of Kansas City in 1821 and established a trading post at St. Joseph in 1827. Mormons came to Independence during the early 1830s but were expelled from the state and crossed the Mississippi back into Illinois. For much of the antebellum period, the state's economy flourished, with an emphasis on cotton, cattle, minerals (especially lead and zinc), and commerce—notably the outfitting of wagon trains for the Santa Fe and Oregon trails. On the eve of the Civil War, more than half the population consisted of Missouri natives; 15% of the white population was foreign-born, chiefly German and Irish. Black slaves represented only 9% of the total population—the lowest proportion of any slave state except Delaware—while only about 25,000 Missourians were slave holders. Nevertheless, there was a great deal of proslavery sentiment in the state, and thousands of Missourians crossed into neighboring Kansas in the mid-1850s to help elect a proslavery government in that territory. State residents were also active in the guerrilla warfare between proslavery forces and Free Staters that erupted along the border with "bleeding Kansas." The slavery controversy was exacerbated by the US Supreme Court's 1857 decision in the case of Dred Scott, a slave formerly owned by a Missourian who had temporarily brought him to what is now Minnesota, where slavery was prohibited; Scott's suit to obtain his freedom was denied by the Court on the grounds that it was unconstitutional to restrict the property rights of slave holders, in a decision that voided the Missouri Compromise reached 37 years earlier.

During the Civil War, Missouri remained loyal to the Union, though not without difficulty. When the conflict began, Governor Claiborne Fox Jackson called out the state militia "to repel the invasion" of federal forces, but pro-Union leaders such as Francis P. Blair deposed Jackson on 30 July 1861. Missouri supplied some 110,000 soldiers to the Union and 40,000 to the Confederacy. As devastating as the 1,162 battles or skirmishes fought on Missouri soil—more than in any other state except Virginia and Tennessee—was the general lawlessness that prevailed throughout the state; pro-Confederate guerrilla bands led by William Quantrill and Cole Younger, as well as Unionist freebooters, murdered and looted without hindrance. In October 1864, a Confederate army under Maj. Gen. Sterling Price was defeated at the Battle of Westport, on the outskirts of Kansas City, ending the main military action. Some 27,000 Missourians were killed during the war. At a constitutional convention held in January 1865, Missouri became the first slave state to free all blacks.

During Reconstruction, the Radical Republicans sought to disfranchise all citizens who failed to swear that they had never aided or sympathized with the Confederacy. But the harshness of this and other measures caused a backlash, and Liberal Republicans such as Benjamin Gratz Brown and Carl Schurz, allied with the Democrats, succeeded in ousting the Radicals by 1872. The subsequent decline of the Liberal Republicans inaugurated a period during which Democrats occupied the governorship uninterruptedly for more than three decades.

The 1870s saw a period of renewed lawlessness, typified by the exploits of Jesse and Frank James, which earned Missouri the epithet of the "robber state." Of more lasting importance were the closing of the frontier in Missouri, the decline of the fur trade and steamboat traffic, and the rise of the railroads, shifting the market economy from St. Louis to Kansas City, whose population tripled during the 1880s, while St. Louis was eclipsed by Chicago as a center of finance, commerce, transportation, and population. Missouri farmers generally supported the movement for free silver coinage, along with other Populist policies such as railroad regulation. Reform Governor Joseph W. Folk (1905–09) and his immediate successors in the statehouse, Herbert S. Hadley (1909–13) and Elliott W. Major (1913–17), introduced progressive policies to Missouri. However, the ideal of honest government was soon subverted by Kansas City's corrupt political machine, under Thomas J. Pendergast, the most powerful Democrat in the state between the two world wars. Machine politics did not prevent capable politicians from rising to prominence—among them Harry S. Truman, Missouri's first and only (as of 2006) native son to serve in the nation's highest office.

The state's economy increasingly shifted from agriculture to industry, and Missouri's rural population declined from about three-fourths of the total in 1880 to less than one-third by 1970. Although the overall importance of mining declined, Missouri remained the world's top lead producer, and the state ranked as second only to Michigan in US automobile manufacturing. Postwar prosperity was threatened beginning in the 1960s by the deterioration of several cities, notably St. Louis, which lost 47% of its population between 1950 and 1980; both St. Louis and Kansas City subsequently undertook urban renewal programs to cope with the serious problems of air pollution, traffic congestion, crime, and substandard housing. During the early 1980s, millions of dollars in federal, state, and private funds were used to rehabilitate abandoned and dilapidated apartment buildings and houses.

Missouri was affected by the farm crisis of the 1980s, and many farms in the state failed. With the weakening of trade restrictions, the state's industries also suffered during this period. However, Missouri's economy improved in the 1990s, initially at a rate that outpaced much of the country. By 1999 the state's jobless rate had fallen below the national average to 3.4%. Due largely to the weak US economy in the early 2000s, Missouri's unemployment rate rose to 5.8% by July 2003, albeit below the national average of 6.2%. However, from September 2004 to September 2005, the state's unemployment rate declined from 5.9% to 4.8%, when it stood below the national average of 5.1%.

Times Beach and other parts of the state were found to be contaminated by high levels of dioxin in the early 1980s. The federal government purchased the homes and businesses that had to be abandoned by community residents and in 1991 began a several-year cleanup program; in 1999 a state park opened there.

In the spring and summer of 1993, Missouri was hit by devastating floods. The Illinois, Mississippi, and Missouri rivers reached record crests, rising in some areas to twice the height considered to be flood level. Over half the state was declared a disaster area, and 19,000 people were evacuated from their homes. Damage to the state was estimated at $3 billion.

In 2000, the state's popular governor, Mel Carnahan, died in a plane crash while running for the US Senate. He was replaced by Democrat Bob Holden, who became the first governor to appoint a state head of homeland security following the 11 September 2001 terrorist attacks on the United States. In 2003, Missouri legislators adopted a measure requiring women seeking abortions to consult a doctor and comply with a 24-hour waiting period. Holden vetoed the measure, but both houses of the Missouri legislature voted to override his veto, making the measure law. Twenty-two states as of 2006 had enacted 24-hour waiting periods for abortions. (Indiana's waiting period is 18 hours.)

Republican Matt Blunt was elected governor in November 2004. He campaigned on a platform pledging to make education the state's top priority, to reform the state's social welfare programs, to address the state's health care crisis, to improve the entrepreneurial climate, and to hold the line on taxes.

12 STATE GOVERNMENT

Missouri's first constitutional convention met in St. Louis on 12 May 1820, and on 19 July a constitution was adopted. The constitution was rewritten in 1865 and again in 1875, the latter document remaining in effect until 1945, when another new constitution was enacted and the state government reorganized. A subsequent reorganization, effective 1 July 1974, replaced some 90 independent agencies with 13 cabinet departments and the Office of Administration. The 1945 constitution is still in effect today, with a total of 105 amendments through January 2005.

The legislative branch, or General Assembly, consists of a 34-member Senate and a 163-seat House of Representatives. Annual sessions begin in early January and must conclude by 30 May. Special sessions may be called by petition of three-quarters of the members of each house; such sessions are limited to 30 calendar days. Senators are elected to staggered four-year terms, representatives for two; the minimum age for a senator is 30, for a representative 24. Legislators must have been residents of their districts for one year prior to election; senators must have been qualified voters for a minimum of three years, representatives a minimum of two years. The legislative salary was $31,351 in 2004.

The state's elected executives are the governor and lieutenant governor (who run separately), secretary of state, auditor, treasurer, and attorney general; all serve four-year terms. The governor is limited to two terms in office, consecutive or not. The governor must be at least 30 years old and must have been a US citizen for 15 years and a Missouri resident for 10 years prior to election. As of December 2004, the governor's salary was $120,087.

A bill becomes law when signed or not vetoed by the governor within 15 days of legislative passage. A two-thirds vote by the elected members of both houses is required to override a gu-

Missouri Presidential Vote by Political Parties, 1948–2004

YEAR	ELECTORAL VOTE	MISSOURI WINNER	DEMOCRAT	REPUBLICAN	PROGRESSIVE	SOCIALIST
1948	15	*Truman (D)	917,315	655,039	3,998	2,222
1952	13	*Eisenhower (R)	929,830	959,429	—	—
1956	13	Stevenson (D)	918,273	914,289	—	—
1960	13	*Kennedy (D)	972,201	962,218	—	—
1964	12	*Johnson (D)	1,164,344	653,535	—	—
					AMERICAN IND.	
1968	12	*Nixon (R)	791,444	811,932	206,126	—
1972	12	*Nixon (R)	698,531	1,154,058	—	—
1976	12	*Carter (D)	998,387	927,443	—	—
					LIBERTARIAN	SOC. WORKERS
1980	12	*Reagan (R)	931,182	1,074,181	14,422	1,515
1984	11	*Reagan (R)	848,583	1,274,188	—	—
						NEW ALLIANCE
1988	11	*Bush (R)	1,001,619	1,084,953	434	6,656
						IND. (Perot)
1992	11	*Clinton (D)	1,053,873	811,159	7,497	518,741
1996	11	*Clinton (D)	1,025,935	890,016	10,522	217,188
						GREEN
2000	11	*Bush, G. W. (R)	1,111,138	1,189,924	7,436	38,515
						CONSTITUTION (Peroutka)
2004	11	*Bush, G. W. (R)	1,259,171	1,455,713	9,831	5,355

*Won US presidential election.

bernatorial veto. The governor has 45 days to act on a bill if the House adjourns. If he fails to do so, the bill becomes law. Except for appropriations or emergency measures, laws may not take effect until 90 days after the end of the legislative session at which they were enacted. Constitutional amendments require a majority vote of both houses or may be proposed by 8% of the legal voters for all candidates at the last election. Ratification by the voters is required.

To vote in Missouri, one must be a US citizen, at least 18 years old, and a state resident. Restrictions apply to convicted felons and those declared mentally incompetent by the court.

13 POLITICAL PARTIES

The major political groups in Missouri are the Democratic Party and the Republican Party, each affiliated with the national party organization. Before 1825, the state had no organized political parties, and candidates ran as independents; however, each of Missouri's first four governors called himself a Jeffersonian Republican, allying himself with the national group from which the modern Democratic Party traces its origins. Except for the Civil War and Reconstruction periods, the Democratic Party held the governorship from the late 1820s to the early 1900s. Ten Democrats and seven Republicans served in the statehouse from 1908 through 1985. The outstanding figures of 20th century Missouri politics were both Democrats: Thomas Pendergast, the Kansas City machine boss whose commitment to construction projects bore no small relation to his involvement with a concrete manufacturing firm, and Harry S. Truman, who began his political career as a Jackson County judge in the Kansas City area and in 1945 became 33rd president of the United States.

After voting consistently for Republican presidential candidates in the 1980s, Missouri was carried by Democrat Bill Clinton in 1996. In the 2000 presidential election, Missourians once again voted Republican, with George W. Bush receiving 51% of the vote to Democrat Al Gore's 47%. Green Party candidate Ralph Nader won 2% of the vote. In 2004, Bush garnered 53.4% to Democratic challenger John Kerry's 46.1%. In 2004 there were 4,194,000 registered voters; there is no party registration in the state. The state had 11 electoral votes in the 2004 presidential election.

Democrat Mel Carnahan was reelected to the governorship in 1996. In October 2000, Carnahan was running for the US Senate against Republican John Ashcroft when he died in a plane crash with his son and a political aide. Carnahan was elected posthumously to the Senate in November, and his wife Jean accepted an appointment to his seat. She served until 2002, when she was defeated by former US Representative and Republican Jim Talent in an extremely close race. As of 2005, Missouri's US senators were both Republicans—Talent, and Christopher Bond, reelected in 2004. In 2004, Republican Matt Blunt was elected governor. Following the 2004 elections, four of the state's US representatives were Democrats and five were Republicans. In the state Senate in mid-2005, there were 11 Democrats and 23 Republicans; in the state House, there were 66 Democrats and 97 Republicans.

14 LOCAL GOVERNMENT

As of 2005, Missouri had 115 counties, 946 municipalities, 524 public school districts, and 1,514 special districts. In 2002 there were also 312 townships. Elected county officials generally include commissioners, a public administrator, a prosecuting attorney, a sheriff, a collector of revenue, an assessor, a treasurer, and a coroner. The city of St. Louis, which is administratively independent of any county, has an elected mayor, a comptroller, and a board of aldermen; the circuit attorney, city treasurer, sheriff, and collector of revenue, also elected, perform functions analogous to county officers. Most other cities are governed by an elected mayor and council. The state was the first in the union to grant home rule to cities.

In 2005, local government accounted for about 226,571 full-time (or equivalent) employment positions.

15 STATE SERVICES

To address the continuing threat of terrorism and to work with the federal Department of Homeland Security, homeland security in Missouri operates under executive order; a homeland security director is appointed to oversee the state's homeland security activities.

Under the 1974 reorganization plan, educational services are provided through the Department of Elementary and Secondary Education and the Department of Higher Education. Within the former's jurisdiction are the state schools for the deaf, the blind, and the severely handicapped; adult education programs; teacher certification; and the general supervision of instruction in the state. The department is headed by a board of education whose eight members are appointed by the governor to eight-year terms; the board, in turn, appoints the commissioner of education, the department's chief executive officer. The Department of Higher Education—governed by a nine-member appointive board that selects the commissioner of higher education—sets financial guidelines for state colleges and universities, authorizes the establishment of new senior colleges and residency centers, and establishes academic, admissions, residency, and transfer policies. Transportation services are under the direction of the Department of Transportation, which is responsible for aviation, railroads, mass transit, water transport, and the state highway system. The Department of Revenue licenses all road vehicles and motor vehicle operators and is responsible for the administration of all state taxes and local-option sales taxes.

Health and welfare services are provided primarily through the Department of Social Services, which oversees all state programs concerning public health (including operating a chest hospital and a cancer hospital), public assistance, youth corrections, probation and parole, veterans' affairs, and the aging. The Department of Mental Health operates state mental hospitals, community mental health centers, and other facilities throughout the state, providing care for the emotionally disturbed, the developmentally disabled, alcoholics, and drug abusers. Among the many responsibilities of the Attorney General are consumer protection, enforcement of antidiscrimination laws, and agricultural and environmental issues. In 1984, a constitutional amendment created a new Department of Economic Development, which inherited many of the responsibilities of the Attorney General.

Administered within the Department of Public Safety are the Missouri State Highway Patrol, Emergency Management Agency, and civil defense, veterans' affairs, highway and water safety, and alcoholic beverage control programs. The Department of Labor and Industrial Relations (DOLIR) administers unemployment insurance benefits, workers' compensation, and other programs. The Department of Corrections is responsible for corrections, probation, and parole of adult offenders. The Department of Agriculture enforces state laws regarding agribusiness products, and the Department of Conservation provides environmental aid. The lieutenant governor is designated as state ombudsman and volunteer coordinator.

[16]JUDICIAL SYSTEM

The Missouri Supreme Court, is the state's highest court. It consists of seven judges and three commissioners. Judges are selected by the governor from three nominees proposed by a nonpartisan judicial commission; after an interval of at least 12 months, the appointment must be ratified by the voters on a separate nonpartisan ballot. The justices, who serve 12-year terms, select one of their number to act as chief justice. The mandatory retirement age is 70 for all judges in state courts.

The Court of Appeals, consisting of 32 judges in three districts, assumed its present structure by constitutional amendment in 1970. All appellate judges are selected for 12-year terms in the same manner as the supreme court justices.

The circuit courts are the only trial courts and have original jurisdiction over all cases and matters, civil and municipal. Circuit court judges, numbering 135 in 1999, serve 6-year terms. Although many circuit court judges are still popularly elected, judges in St. Louis, Kansas City, and some other areas are selected on a nonpartisan basis. Many circuit courts have established municipal divisions, presided over by judges paid locally.

As of 31 December 2004, a total of 31,081 prisoners were held in Missouri's state and federal prisons, a decrease of 2.6% (from 30,303) from the previous year. As of year-end 2004, a total of 2,507 inmates were female, up 12% (from 2,239) from the year before. Among sentenced prisoners (one year or more), Missouri had an incarceration rate of 538 per 100,000 population in 2004.

According to the Federal Bureau of Investigation, Missouri in 2004, had a violent crime rate (murder/nonnegligent manslaughter; forcible rape; robbery; aggravated assault) of 490.5 reported incidents per 100,000 population, or a total of 28,226 reported incidents. Crimes against property (burglary; larceny/theft; and motor vehicle theft) in that same year totaled 224,629 reported incidents or 3,903.5 reported incidents per 100,000 people. Missouri has a death penalty, of which lethal injection or lethal gas are the prescribed methods. However, the state law is unclear about who shall decide which method to use: the Director of the Missouri Department of Corrections; or the inmate. From 1976 through 5 May 2006, the state has carried out 66 executions, 5 in 2005. As of 1 January 2006, Missouri had 53 inmates on death row.

In 2003, Missouri spent $133,539,014 on homeland security, an average of $23 per state resident.

[17]ARMED FORCES

Missouri has played a key role in national defense since World War II, partly because of the influence of Missouri native Stuart Symington, first as secretary of the Air Force (1947–50) and later as an influential member of the Senate Armed Services Committee. In 2004, there were 27,520 active-duty military personnel and 2,749 civilian personnel stationed in the state. Installations include Ft. Leonard Wood, near Rolla, and Whiteman AFB, Knob

Noster. The Defense Mapping Agency Aerospace Center is in St. Louis. Defense contract awards for 2004 totaled more than $6.5 billion, ninth-highest in the United States for that year. In addition, there was another $2.1 billion in defense payroll outlays, including retired military pay.

There were about 554,531 veterans living in the state as of 2003. Of these, 77,373 served in World War II; 65,882 in the Korean conflict; 169,346 during the Vietnam era; and 78,798 during the Persian Gulf War. Expenditures on veterans amounted to about $1.6 billion in 2004.

As of 31 October 2004, the Missouri State Highway Patrol employed 1,070 full-time sworn officers.

[18]MIGRATION

Missouri's first European immigrants, French fur traders and missionaries, began settling in the state in the early 18th century. Under Spain, Missouri received few Spanish settlers but many immigrants from the eastern United States. During the 19th century, newcomers continued to arrive from the South and the East—slave-owning Southerners (with their black slaves) as well as New Englanders opposed to slavery. They were joined by a wave of European immigrants, notably Germans and, later, Italians. By 1850, one out of three St. Louis residents was German-born; of all foreign-born Missourians in the late 1800s, more than half came from Germany.

The state has lost population through migration—322,000 people were lost to net migration between 1940 and 1970, followed by a net gain of 22,000 during the 1970s and a net loss of nearly 100,000 during the 1980s. Between 1990 and 1998, Missouri had net gains of 94,000 in domestic migration and 34,000 in international migration. In 1998, some 3,588 foreign immigrants arrived in the state. The dominant intrastate migration pattern has been the concentration of blacks in the major cities, especially St. Louis and Kansas City, and the exodus of whites from those cities, initially to the suburbs and later to small towns and rural areas. As of 1996, 82.4% of the population lived in metropolitan areas while 17.6% lived in non-metropolitan areas, up from 17.2% in 1990. Missouri's overall population increased 6.3% between 1990 and 1998. In the period 2000–05, net international migration was 42,690 and net internal migration was 26,979, for a net gain of 69,669 people.

[19]INTERGOVERNMENTAL COOPERATION

The Commission on Interstate Cooperation, established by the state legislature in 1941, represents Missouri before the Council of State Governments and its allied organizations. Regional agreements in which the state participates include boundary compacts with Arkansas, Iowa, Nebraska, and Kansas, and various accords governing bridges across the Mississippi and Missouri rivers. The state is a signatory to the Bi-State Development Agency Compact with Illinois. Representatives from both Missouri and Kansas take part in the Kansas City Area Transportation Authority, which operates public transportation in the metropolitan region, the Metropolitan Culture District Compact, and the Kansas-Missouri Waterworks Compact. Missouri also belongs to the Southern States Energy Board, Southern Growth Policies Board, Midwest Interstate Low-Level Radioactive Waste Compact Commission, and many other multistate bodies. Federal grants to state and local governments in fiscal year 2005 amounted to $7.045 billion, an estimated $7.023 billion in fiscal year 2006, and an estimated $7.581 billion in fiscal year 2007.

20 ECONOMY

Missouri's central location and access to the Mississippi River contributed to its growth as a commercial center. By the mid-1700s, the state's first permanent settlement at Ste. Genevieve was shipping lead, furs, salt, pork, lard, bacon, bear, grease, feathers, flour and grain, and other products to distant markets. The introduction of steamboat traffic on the Mississippi, western migration along the Santa Fe and Oregon trails, and the rise of the railroads spurred the growth of commerce during the 19th century. Flour mills and gristmills, breweries and whiskey distilleries, and meat-packing establishments were among the state's early industrial enterprises. Lead mining has been profitable since the early 19th century. Grain growing was well established by the mid-18th century, and tobacco was a leading crop 100 years later.

Missouri's economy remains diversified, with manufacturing, farming, trade, tourism, services, government, and mining as prime sources of income. Automobile and aerospace manufacturing are among the state's leading industries, while soybeans and meat and dairy products are the most important agricultural commodities. The state's historic past, varied topography, and modern urban attractions—notably the Gateway Arch in St. Louis—have made tourism a growth industry. Mining, employing less than 1% of the state's nonagricultural workers, is no longer as important as it once was. Missouri posted moderate growth rates in the late 1990s. Although manufacturing output has fallen, output from financial services, including insurance and real estate, have increased. In the first quarter of 2001, Missouri began losing jobs, four months ahead of the United States as a whole, with manufacturing accounting for 62% of the loss that year. Unemployment peaked at 5.4% in June 2002, but manufacturing unemployment has continued above 6%. Office vacancy rates in St. Louis and Kansas City in 2002 stood at 17.7% and 18.6%, respectively, above the national average of 16.5%. Missouri's farm sector was also afflicted by drought in 2002, which contributed to a 22% decrease in corn production and a 17% decrease in soybean production compared to 2001. Cattle production was also disrupted by the drought-induced shortages of hay and pasture. Stress on the farming sector persisted into the winter of 2002–03 as drought conditions continued.

Missouri's gross state product (GSP) was $203.294 billion in 2004, of which manufacturing (durable and nondurable goods) accounted for the largest share at $31.481 billion, or 15.4% of GSP, followed by the real estate sector at $19.529 billion (9.6% of GSP), and health care and social assistance at $15.149 billion (7.4% of GSP). In that same year, there were an estimated 461,259 small businesses in Missouri. Of the 134,448 businesses that had employees, an estimated total of 131,405 or 97.7% were small companies. An estimated 16,155 new businesses were established in the state in 2004, up 1.3% from the year before. Business terminations that same year came to 17,924, down 11.2% from 2003. There were 354 business bankruptcies in 2004, down 6.3% from the previous year. In 2005, the state's personal bankruptcy (Chapter 7 and Chapter 13) filing rate was 660 filings per 100,000 people, ranking Missouri 15th in the nation.

21 INCOME

In 2005, Missouri had a gross state product (GSP) of $216 billion, which accounted for 1.7% of the nation's gross domestic product and placed the state 20th among the 50 states and the District of Columbia.

According to the Bureau of Economic Analysis, in 2004 Missouri had a per capita personal income (PCPI) of $30,475. This ranked Missouri 31st in the United States and was 92% of the national average of $33,050. The 1994–2004 average annual growth rate of PCPI was 3.9%. Missouri had a total personal income (TPI) of $175,524,474,000, which ranked 20th in the United States and reflected an increase of 5.1% from 2003. The 1994–2004 average annual growth rate of TPI was 4.7%. Earnings of persons employed in Missouri increased from $128,893,590,000 in 2003 to $135,403,221,000 in 2004, an increase of 5.1% compared with 6.3% for the nation as a whole.

The US Census Bureau reported that the three-year average median household income for 2002–04 in 2004 dollars was $43,988 compared to a national average of $44,473. During the same period an estimated 10.9% of the population was below the poverty line as compared to 12.4% nationwide.

22 LABOR

According to the Bureau of Labor Statistics (BLS), in April 2006 the seasonally adjusted civilian labor force in Missouri numbered 3,057,200, with approximately 141,700 workers unemployed, yielding an unemployment rate of 4.6%, compared to the national average of 4.7% for the same period. Preliminary data for the same period placed nonfarm employment at 2,757,500. Since the beginning of the BLS data series in 1976, the highest unemployment rate recorded in Missouri was 10.5% in April 1983. The historical low was 2.6% in January 2000. Preliminary nonfarm employment data by occupation for April 2006 showed that approximately 5.2% of the labor force was employed in construction; 11% in manufacturing; 19.8% in trade, transportation, and public utilities; 6% in financial activities; 11.7% in professional and business services; 13.5% in education and health services; 10% in leisure and hospitality services; and 15.6% in government.

As early as the 1830s, journeyman laborers and mechanics in St. Louis, seeking higher wages and shorter hours, banded together to form trade unions and achieved some of their demands. Attempts to establish a workingman's party were unsuccessful, however, and immigration during subsequent decades ensured a plentiful supply of cheap labor. Union activity increased in the 1870s, partly because of the influence of German socialists. The Knights of Labor took a leading role in the labor movement from 1879 to 1887, the year that saw the birth of the St. Louis Trades and Labor Assembly; one year later, the American Federation of Labor came to St. Louis for its third annual convention, with Samuel Gompers presiding. The Missouri State Federation of Labor was formed in 1891, at a convention in Kansas City. By 1916, the state had 915 unions. Union activity in Missouri declined in the 1990s and early 2000s.

The US Department of Labor's Bureau of Labor Statistics reported that in 2005, a total of 290,000 of Missouri's 2,532,000 employed wage and salary workers were formal members of a union. This represented 11.5% of those so employed, down from 12.4%

in 2004, and below the national average of 12%. Overall in 2005, a total of 319,000 workers (12.6%) in Missouri were covered by a union or employee association contract, which includes those workers who reported no union affiliation. Missouri was among the 28 states that did not have a right-to-work law.

As of 1 March 2006, Missouri had a state-mandated minimum wage rate of $5.15 per hour. In 2004, women in the state accounted for 47.9% of the employed civilian labor force.

23 AGRICULTURE

Missouri had 106,000 farms (second in the United States) covering 30.1 million acres (12.2 million hectares) in 2004. About 12.4 million acres (5 million hectares) were actually harvested that year. Missouri's agricultural income reached $5.57 billion in 2005, 15th among the 50 states.

In 2004, Missouri was fourth among the states in grain sorghum production, fifth in soybean, and sixth in rice production. Soybean production is concentrated mainly in the northern counties and in the extreme southeast, with Mississippi County a leading producer. Stoddard County is a major source for corn and wheat production, as is New Madrid for grain sorghum.

The cash value of all crops totaled $2.5 billion in 2005, including $1.1 billion from soybeans, $510 million from hay, $887 million from corn, $155 million from wheat, $27 million from grain sorghum, and $161.4 million from cotton. The value of rice production in 2004 was $92.8 million. Farmers harvested 223.2 million bushels of soybeans, 466 million bushels of corn, 48.4 million bushels of wheat, 15.7 million bushels of grain sorghum, 820,000 bales of cotton, and 9.4 million tons of hay in 2004. That year, 13.2 million hundredweight (494.9 million kg) of rice was harvested. Tobacco, oats, rye, apples, peaches, grapes, watermelons, and various seed crops are also grown in commercial quantities.

24 ANIMAL HUSBANDRY

In Missouri, hog raising is concentrated north of the Missouri River, cattle raising in the western counties, and dairy farming in the southwest.

In 2005, Missouri farms and ranches had an estimated 4.5 million cattle and calves, valued at $3.8 billion. In 2004, there were around 2.9 million hogs and pigs, valued at $246.5 million. During 2003, Missouri farmers produced 816.2 million lb (371 million kg) of turkey (ranked third in the nation), valued at around $285.7 million. Also in 2003, poultry farmers produced 1.9 million eggs, valued at $100 million. The state's 129,000 milk cows yielded nearly 1.9 million lb (0.86 million kg) of milk in 2003.

25 FISHING

Commercial fishing takes place mainly on the Mississippi, Missouri, and St. Francis rivers. In 2005, there were 24 catfish farms covering 1,320 acres (534 hectares), with sales of $1.4 million in 2004. Sport fishing is enjoyed throughout the state, but especially in the Ozarks, whose waters harbor walleye, rainbow trout, bluegill, and largemouth bass. In 2004, Missouri issued 844,318 sport fishing licenses. The Neosho National Fish Hatchery stocks rainbow trout to Lake Taneycomo, as well as sites in Kansas and Iowa. There are eleven state hatcheries, four of which include trout parks.

26 FORESTRY

At one time, Missouri's forests covered 30 million acres (12 million hectares), more than two-thirds of the state. As of 2004, Missouri had 15,010,000 acres (6,075,000 hectares) of forestland (about one-third of the land area in the state), of which more than 95% was commercial forest, 82% of it privately owned. Most of Missouri's forestland is in the southeastern third of the state. Of the commercial forests, approximately three-fourths are of the oak/ hickory type; shortleaf pine and oak/pine forests comprise about 5%, while the remainder consists of cedar and bottomland hardwoods.

According to the Forestry Division of the Department of Conservation, Missouri leads the United States in the production of charcoal, red cedar novelties, gunstocks, and walnut bowls and nutmeats; railroad ties, hardwood veneer and lumber, wine and bourbon casks, and other forest-related items are also produced. Lumber production in 2004 totaled 575 million board feet, 97% of it hardwoods.

Conservation areas managed by the Forestry Division are used for timber production, wildlife and watershed protection, hunting, fishing, and other recreational purposes. A state-run nursery sells seedling trees and shrubs to Missouri landowners. Missouri's one national forest, Mark Twain in the southeast, encompassed 1,489,000 acres (603,000 hectares) of National Forest System lands as of 2005.

27 MINING

According to preliminary data from the US Geological Survey (USGS), the estimated value of nonfuel mineral production by Missouri in 2003 was $1.29 billion, an increase from 2002 of about 2%. The USGS data ranked Missouri as eighth among the 50 states by the total value of its nonfuel mineral production, accounting for almost 3.5% of total US output.

According to the preliminary data for 2003, by value and in descending order, crushed stone, portland cement, lead, and lime were the state's top nonfuel minerals. Collectively, these commodities accounted for almost 90% of all nonfuel mineral output, by value. However, while lead ranked third among the state's top nonfuel minerals, by value of production, Missouri was the top lead-producing state in the United States, accounting for over 50% of the nation's output. The state was also ranked (by value) in 2003 as first in the production of lime and in fire clay, third in zinc and fuller's earth, fifth in crushed stone and portland cement, and sixth in silver.

According to the preliminary data, crushed stone production in 2003 totaled 73.3 million metric tons and was valued at $381 million, while portland cement output that year totaled 5 million metric tons and was valued at $350 million. Construction sand and gravel production in 2003 totaled 10.2 million metric tons and was valued at $43.4 million, while fire clay output stood at 340,000 metric tons, and had a value of $7.36 million, according to the USGS data.

In 2003, Missouri was also an important producer of construction and industrial sand and gravel, common clays, masonry cement, and by value, gemstones.

²⁸ENERGY AND POWER

As of 2003, Missouri had 137 electrical power service providers, of which 88 were publicly owned and 44 were cooperatives. Of the remainder, four were investor owned, and one was an owner of an independent generator that sold directly to customers. As of that same year there were 2,918,563 retail customers. Of that total, 1,858,353 received their power from investor-owned service providers. Cooperatives accounted for 665,489 customers, while publicly owned providers had 394,720 customers. There was only one independent generator or "facility" customer.

Total net summer generating capability by the state's electrical generating plants in 2003 stood at 19.976 million kW, with total production that same year at 87.225 billion kWh. Of the total amount generated, 98.7% came from electric utilities, with the remainder coming from independent producers and combined heat and power service providers. The largest portion of all electric power generated, 74.211 billion kWh (85.1%), came from coal-fired plants, with nuclear plants in second place at 9.699 billion kWh (11.1%) and natural gas fueled plants in third at 2.624 billion kWh (3%). Other renewable power sources, hydroelectric and petroleum fueled plants accounting for the remainder.

As of 2006, Missouri had one operating nuclear power facility, the Callaway plant located in Callaway County.

Fossil fuel resources are limited. Reserves of bituminous coal totaled 6 billion short tons in 1998, but only a small portion (3 million short tons) was considered recoverable. In 2004, the state had three producing coal mines, all of them surface operations. Coal production that year totaled 578,000 short tons, up from 533,000 short tons in 2003. One short ton equals 2,000 lb (0.907 metric tons).

Small quantities of crude petroleum are also produced commercially. As of 2004, Missouri had proven crude oil reserves of less than 1% of all proven US reserves, while output that same year averaged 241 barrels per day. Including federal offshore domains, the state that year ranked 30th (29th excluding federal offshore) in production among the 31 producing states. In 2004 Missouri had 271 producing oil wells. There are no refineries in Missouri.

As of 2004, Missouri had no proven reserves or production of natural gas.

²⁹INDUSTRY

According to the US Census Bureau's Annual Survey of Manufactures (ASM) for 2004, Missouri's manufacturing sector covered some 20 product subsectors. The shipment value of all products manufactured in the state that same year was $102.803 billion. Of that total, transportation equipment manufacturing accounted for the largest share at $33.158 billion. It was followed by food manufacturing at $14.572 billion; chemical manufacturing at $13.137 billion; machinery manufacturing at $6.219 billion; and fabricated metal product manufacturing at $5.226 billion.

In 2004, a total of 302,906 people in Missouri were employed in the state's manufacturing sector, according to the ASM. Of that total, 228,857 were actual production workers. In terms of total employment, the transportation equipment manufacturing industry accounted for the largest portion of all manufacturing employees with 55,659 (46,554 actual production workers). It was followed by food manufacturing, with 37,306 (29,642 actual production

workers); machinery manufacturing, with 32,513 (21,676 actual production workers); fabricated metal product manufacturing, with 31,053 (22,690 actual production workers); and plastics and rubber products manufacturing, with 20,539 (15,510 actual production workers).

ASM data for 2004 showed that Missouri's manufacturing sector paid $12.706 billion in wages. Of that amount, the transportation equipment manufacturing sector accounted for the largest share at $3.453 billion. It was followed by machinery manufacturing at $1.307 billion; food manufacturing at $1.190 billion; fabricated metal product manufacturing at $1.183 billion; and chemical manufacturing at $798.137 billion.

³⁰COMMERCE

Missouri has been one of the nation's leading trade centers ever since merchants in Independence (now part of the Kansas City metropolitan area) began provisioning wagon trains for the Santa Fe Trail.

According to the 2002 Census of Wholesale Trade, Missouri's wholesale trade sector had sales that year totaling $95.6 billion from 8,491 establishments. Wholesalers of durable goods accounted for 5,019 establishments, followed by nondurable goods wholesalers at 2,697 and electronic markets, agents, and brokers accounting for 775 establishments. Sales by durable goods wholesalers in 2002 totaled $37.8 billion, while wholesalers of nondurable goods saw sales of $47.1 billion. Electronic markets, agents, and brokers in the wholesale trade industry had sales of $10.6 billion.

In the 2002 Census of Retail Trade, Missouri was listed as having 23,837 retail establishments with sales of $61.8 billion. The leading types of retail businesses by number of establishments were: motor vehicle and motor vehicle parts dealers (3,160); gasoline stations (3,136); miscellaneous store retailers (2,825); and clothing and clothing accessories stores (2,665). In terms of sales, motor vehicle and motor vehicle parts stores accounted for the largest share of retail sales at $16.6 billion, followed by general merchandise stores at $10.3 billion; food and beverage stores at $7.1 billion; gasoline stations at $6.8 billion; and building material/garden equipment and supplies dealers at $5.3 billion. A total of 311,593 people were employed by the retail sector in Missouri that year.

Foreign exports of Missouri products exceeded $10.4 billion in 2005.

³¹CONSUMER PROTECTION

The Missouri Department of Insurance handles consumer complaints related to insurance matters. The office has a consumer services division that accepts complaints regarding violations of state insurance laws and regulations, unfair claim practices, advertising, and mandated benefits, policy language, and offers. The Attorney General's office has a Consumer Protection Division which investigates and prosecutes allegations of fraud in connection with the sale or offer for sale (advertising) of goods and services. The Office of the Public Counsel represents utility consumers in proceedings before and appeals from the Missouri Public Service Commission (PSC), which regulates the rates and services of utilities.

When dealing with consumer protection issues, the state Attorney General's Office can initiate civil and criminal proceedings;

represent the state before state and federal regulatory agencies; administer consumer protection and education programs; handle consumer complaints; and exercise broad subpoena powers. In antitrust actions, the Attorney General's Office can act on behalf of those consumers who are incapable of acting on their own; initiate damage actions on behalf of the state in state courts; and initiate criminal proceedings. However, the office cannot represent counties, cities and other governmental entities in recovering civil damages under state or federal law.

³²BANKING

The first banks in Missouri, the Bank of St. Louis (established in 1816) and the Bank of Missouri (1817), had both failed by the time Missouri became a state, and the paper notes they had distributed proved worthless. Not until 1837 did the Missouri state government again permit a bank within its borders, and then only after filling its charter with elaborate restrictions. The Bank of Missouri, chartered for 20 years, kept its reputation for sound banking by issuing notes bearing the portrait of US Senator Thomas Hart Benton, nicknamed "Old Bullion" because of his extreme fiscal conservatism.

As of June 2005, Missouri had 372 insured banks, savings and loans, and saving banks, plus 157 state-chartered and 14 federally chartered credit unions (CUs). Excluding the CUs, the St Louis market area accounted for the largest portion of the state's bank deposits in 2004 at $48.005 billion, while it ranked second in the number of financial institutions at 138. The Kansas City market area had the most financial institutions at 152, but ranked second in deposits at $32.593 billion. As of June 2005, CUs accounted for 8.2% of all assets held by all financial institutions in the state, or some $8.372 billion. Banks, savings and loans, and savings banks collectively accounted for the remaining 91.8% or $94.030 billion in assets held.

In 2004, the median past-due/nonaccrual loan level as a percentage of total loans stood at 1.37%, down from 1.66% in 2003, although in the fourth quarter 2005, the level rose to 1.59%. For the year 2004, the median net interest margin (the difference between the lower rates offered to savers and the higher rates charged on loans) stood at 4.01%, up from 3.93% in 2003. In fourth quarter 2005, the median NIM rate was 4.07%.

Regulation of state-chartered financial institutions is the responsibility of the Department of Development's Division of Finance.

³³INSURANCE

In 2004, there were over 3.5 million individual life insurance policies in force with a total value of over $242.9 billion; total value for all categories of life insurance (individual, group, and credit) was about $420 billion. The average coverage amount is $67,600 per policy holder. Death benefits paid that year totaled $1.2 billion.

In 2003, 36 life and insurance companies were domiciled in Missouri, as were 49 property and casualty insurance companies. Direct premiums for property and casualty insurance in Missouri totaled $8.7 billion in 2001. That year, there were 22,397 flood insurance policies in force in the state, with a total value of $2.6 billion. About $484 million of coverage was held through FAIR plans, which are designed to offer coverage for some natural circumstances, such as wind and hail, in high risk areas.

In 2004, 56% of state residents held employment-based health insurance policies, 5% held individual policies, and 26% were covered under Medicare and Medicaid; 12% of residents were uninsured. In 2003, employee contributions for employment-based health coverage averaged at 17% for single coverage and 25% for family coverage. The state offers a nine-month health benefits expansion program for small-firm employees in connection with the Consolidated Omnibus Budget Reconciliation Act (COBRA, 1986), a health insurance program for those who lose employment-based coverage due to termination or reduction of work hours.

In 2003, there were over 3.8 million auto insurance policies in effect for private passenger cars. Required minimum coverage includes bodily injury liability of up to $25,000 per individual and $50,000 for all persons injured in an accident, as well as property damage liability of $10,000. Uninsured motorist coverage is also mandatory. In 2003, the average expenditure per vehicle for insurance coverage was $701.67.

³⁴SECURITIES

The Missouri Uniform Securities Act, also known as the "Blue Sky Law" and administered by the Securities Division of the Office of Secretary of State, requires the registration of stocks, bonds, debentures, notes, investment contracts, and oil, gas, and mining interests intended for sale in the state. In cases of fraud, misrepresentation, or other failure to comply with the act, the Missouri investor has the right to sue to recover the investment, plus interest, costs, and attorney fees. Government securities, mutual funds, stocks listed on the principal national exchanges, and securities sold under specific transactional agreements are exempt from registration.

In 2005, there were 1,580 personal financial advisers employed in the state and 5,130 securities, commodities, and financial services sales agents. In 2004, there were over 117 publicly traded companies within the state, with over 40 NASDAQ companies, 50 NYSE listings, and 5 AMEX listings. In 2006, the state had ten Fortune 500 companies; Emerson Electric (based in St. Louis) ranked first in the state and 126th in the nation with revenues of over $17.3 billion, followed by Express Scripts in Maryland Hts. and Anheuser-Busch, Ameren, and Monsanto in St. Louis. Express Scripts is listed with NASDAQ; the other four companies are listed on the NYSE.

³⁵PUBLIC FINANCE

The Missouri state budget is prepared by the Office of Administration's Division of Budget and Planning and submitted annually by the governor to the General Assembly for amendment and approval. The fiscal year runs from 1 July to 30 June. Missouri's constitutional revenue and spending limit provides that over time, the growth in state revenues and spending cannot exceed the growth in Missouri personal income.

Fiscal year 2006 general funds were estimated at $7.5 billion for resources and $7.1 billion for expenditures. In fiscal year 2004, federal government grants to Missouri were $8.7 billion

In the fiscal year 2007 federal budget, Missouri was slated to receive $96.6 million for exterior repairs, hazardous material abatement, and modernization efforts at the Richard Bolling Federal

Building in Kansas City; $25.8 million to replace an operating suite at a veterans' hospital in Columbia; and $7 million for a veterans' medical care center renovation and national cemetery expansion in St. Louis.

³⁶TAXATION

In 2005, Missouri collected $9,544 million in tax revenues or $1,645 per capita, which placed it 46th among the 50 states in per capita tax burden. The national average was $2,192 per capita. Property taxes accounted for 0.2% of the total, sales taxes 31.8%, selective sales taxes 16.4%, individual income taxes 42.1%, corporate income taxes 2.3%, and other taxes 7.2%.

As of 1 January 2006, Missouri had 10 individual income tax brackets ranging from 1.5% to 6.0%. The state taxes corporations at a flat rate of 6.25%.

In 2004, state and local property taxes amounted to $4,304,387,000 or $747 per capita. The per capita amount ranks the state 37th highest nationally. Local governments collected $4,281,624,000 of the total and the state government $22,763,000.

Missouri taxes retail sales at a rate of 4.225%. In addition to the state tax, local taxes on retail sales can reach as much as 4.5%, making for a potential total tax on retail sales of 8.725%. Food purchased for consumption off-premises is taxable, but at lower rate. The tax on cigarettes is 17 cents per pack, which ranks 50th among the 50 states and the District of Columbia. Missouri taxes gasoline at 17.55 cents per gallon. This is in addition to the 18.4 cents per gallon federal tax on gasoline.

According to the Tax Foundation, for every federal tax dollar sent to Washington in 2004, Missouri citizens received $1.29 in federal spending.

³⁷ECONOMIC POLICY

Primary responsibility for economic development is vested in the Department of Economic Development (DED). Its Enterprise Zone Program provides a variety of tax credits, exemptions, and other incentives to businesses that locate in designated areas. The division also offers grants, information, technical aid, and other public resources to foster local and regional development. Special programs are provided for the Ozarks region and to rehabilitate urban neighborhoods. Agencies affiliated with the DED include: the Division of Business and Community Services; the Division of Credit Unions; the Division of Finance; the Division of Tourism; the Missouri Arts Council; the Missouri Housing Development Commission; the Missouri Development Finance Board; and the Division of Workforce Development.

³⁸HEALTH

The infant mortality rate in October 2005 was estimated at 7.6 per 1,000 live births. The birth rate in 2003 was 13.5 per 1,000 population. The abortion rate stood at 6.6 per 1,000 women in 2000. In 2003, about 88.4% of pregnant woman received prenatal care beginning in the first trimester. In 2004, approximately 82% of children received routine immunizations before the age of three.

The crude death rate in 2003 was 9.7 deaths per 1,000 population. As of 2002, the death rates for major causes of death (per 100,000 resident population) were: heart disease, 294.5; cancer, 217.2; cerebrovascular diseases, 68.5; chronic lower respiratory diseases, 50.5; and diabetes, 28.6. The mortality rate from HIV infection was 2.2 per 100,000 population. In 2004, the reported AIDS case rate was at about 6.8 per 100,000 population. In 2002, about 58.4% of the population was considered overweight or obese. As of 2004, about 24.1% of state residents were smokers.

In 2003, Missouri had 119 community hospitals with about 19,300 beds. There were about 831,000 patient admissions that year and 15.7 million outpatient visits. The average daily inpatient census was about 11,900 patients. The average cost per day for hospital care was $1,403. Also in 2003, there were about 534 certified nursing facilities in the state with 54,415 beds and an over-

Missouri—State Government Finances

(Dollar amounts in thousands. Per capita amounts in dollars.)

	AMOUNT	PER CAPITA
Total Revenue	26,320,416	4,569.52
General revenue	20,287,403	3,522.12
Intergovernmental revenue	7,412,108	1,286.82
Taxes	9,119,664	1,583.28
General sales	2,950,055	512.16
Selective sales	1,518,453	263.62
License taxes	605,590	105.14
Individual income tax	3,720,749	645.96
Corporate income tax	224,366	38.95
Other taxes	100,451	17.44
Current charges	1,966,875	341.47
Miscellaneous general revenue	1,788,756	310.55
Utility revenue	–	–
Liquor store revenue	–	–
Insurance trust revenue	6,033,013	1,047.40
Total expenditure	22,038,965	3,826.21
Intergovernmental expenditure	5,260,101	913.21
Direct expenditure	16,778,864	2,913.00
Current operation	11,428,958	1,984.19
Capital outlay	1,505,282	261.33
Insurance benefits and repayments	2,551,924	443.04
Assistance and subsidies	653,594	113.47
Interest on debt	639,106	110.96
Exhibit: Salaries and wages	3,101,488	538.45
Total expenditure	22,038,965	3,826.21
General expenditure	19,487,011	3,383.16
Intergovernmental expenditure	5,260,101	913.21
Direct expenditure	14,226,910	2,469.95
General expenditures, by function:		
Education	6,868,317	1,192.42
Public welfare	5,657,912	982.28
Hospitals	1,041,370	180.79
Health	665,345	115.51
Highways	1,853,322	321.76
Police protection	134,869	23.41
Correction	609,300	105.78
Natural resources	325,328	56.48
Parks and recreation	52,556	9.12
Government administration	616,591	107.05
Interest on general debt	639,106	110.96
Other and unallocable	1,022,995	177.60
Utility expenditure	30	.01
Liquor store expenditure	–	–
Insurance trust expenditure	2,551,924	443.04
Debt at end of fiscal year	16,218,362	2,815.69
Cash and security holdings	59,430,937	10,317.87

Abbreviations and symbols: – zero or rounds to zero; (NA) not available; (X) not applicable.

SOURCE: *U.S. Census Bureau, Governments Division, 2004 Survey of State Government Finances*, January 2006.

all occupancy rate of about 68.6%. In 2004, it was estimated that about 64% of all state residents had received some type of dental care within the year. Missouri had 241 physicians per 100,000 resident population in 2003 and 940 nurses per 100,000 in 2004.

In 2005, the Barnes-Jewish Hospital of Washington University ranked sixth on the Honor Roll of Best Hospitals 2005 by *U.S. News & World Report*. In the same report, it ranked ninth for best care in heart disease and heart surgery.

About 26% of state residents were enrolled in Medicaid and Medicare programs in 2004. Approximately 12% of the state population was uninsured in 2004. In 2003, state health care expenditures totaled $7.7 million.

39 SOCIAL WELFARE

In 2004, about 166,000 people received unemployment benefits, with the average weekly unemployment benefit at $205. In fiscal year 2005, the estimated average monthly participation in the food stamp program included about 766,425 persons (298,380 households); the average monthly benefit was about $80 per person, the second-lowest average payment in the nation (above Wisconsin). That year, the total of benefits paid through the state for the food stamp program was about $735.7 million.

Temporary Assistance for Needy Families (TANF), the system of federal welfare assistance that officially replaced Aid to Families with Dependent Children (AFDC) in 1997, was reauthorized through the Deficit Reduction Act of 2005. TANF is funded through federal block grants that are divided among the states based on an equation involving the number of recipients in each state. Missouri's TANF program is called Beyond Welfare. In 2004, the state program had 100,000 recipients; state and federal expenditures on this TANF program totaled $130 million in fiscal year 2003.

In December 2004, Social Security benefits were paid to 1,046,110 Missouri residents. This number included 642,970 retired workers, 102,730 widows and widowers, 153,570 disabled workers, 54,680 spouses, and 92,160 children. Social Security beneficiaries represented 18.2% of the total state population and 93.9% of the state's population age 65 and older. Retired workers received an average monthly payment of $944; widows and widowers, $891; disabled workers, $872; and spouses, $469. Payments for children of retired workers averaged $477 per month; children of deceased workers, $619; and children of disabled workers, $254. Federal Supplemental Security Income payments in December 2004 went to 116,131 Missouri residents, averaging $386 a month. An additional $2.2 million of state-administered supplemental payments were distributed to 8,865 residents.

40 HOUSING

In 2004, Missouri had an estimated 2,564,340 housing units, of which 2,309,205 were occupied; 70.8% were owner-occupied. About 69.3% of all units were single-family, detached homes. Utility gas and electricity were the most common energy sources for heating. It was estimated that 89,522 units lacked telephone services, 11,971 lacked complete plumbing facilities, and 12,264 lacked complete kitchen facilities. The average household had 2.42 members.

In 2004, 32,800 new privately owned units were authorized for construction. The median home value was $117,033. The median monthly cost for mortgage owners was $954. Renters paid a median of $567 per month. In September 2005, the state received a grant of $360,898 from the US Department of Housing and Urban Development (HUD) for rural housing and economic development programs. For 2006, HUD allocated to the state over $24.2 million in community development block grants.

The Missouri Housing Development Commission of the Department of Economic Development is empowered to make and insure loans to encourage the construction of residential housing for persons of low or moderate income; funds for mortgage financing are provided through the sale of tax-exempt notes and bonds issued by the commission. Construction of multi-unit public housing stagnated during the 1970s. In 1972, municipal authorities ordered the demolition of two apartment buildings in St. Louis's Pruitt-Igoe public housing complex, built 18 years earlier and regarded by many commentators as a classic case of the failure of such high-rise projects to offer a livable environment; the site remained vacant in the early 1980s. Only 5.5% of St. Louis's housing units in 1990 had been built during the 1980s; during the 1970s, many units were abandoned.

41 EDUCATION

Although the constitution of 1820 provided for the establishment of public schools, it was not until 1839 that the state's public school system became a reality through legislation creating the office of state superintendent of common schools and establishing a permanent school fund. Missouri schools were officially segregated from 1875 to 1954, when the US Supreme Court issued its landmark ruling in *Brown v. Board of Education;* the state's school segregation law was not taken off the books until 1976. In that year, nearly 37% of all black students were in schools that were 99–100% black, a condition fostered by the high concentration of black Missourians in the state's two largest cities. In 1983, a desegregation plan was adopted for St. Louis-area public schools that called for 3,000 black students to be transferred from city to county schools.

In 2004, 87.9% of all Missourians 25 years of age or older were high school graduates, and 28.1% had obtained bachelor's degrees or higher. The total enrollment for fall 2002 in Missouri's public schools stood at 924,000. Of these, 653,000 attended schools from kindergarten through grade eight, and 272,000 attended high school. Approximately 77.7% of the students were white, 18% were black, 2.6% were Hispanic, 1.4% were Asian/Pacific Islander, and 0.4% were American Indian/Alaskan Native. Total enrollment was estimated at 917,000 in fall 2003 and expected to be 910,000 by fall 2014, a decline of 1.6% during the period 2002–14. In fall 2003, there were 119,812 students enrolled in private schools. Expenditures for public education in 2003/04 were estimated at $7.8 billion. Since 1969, the National Assessment of Educational Progress (NAEP) has tested public school students nationwide. The resulting report, *The Nation's Report Card,* stated that in 2005, eighth graders in Missouri scored 276 out of 500 in mathematics, compared with the national average of 278.

As of fall 2002, there were 348,146 students enrolled in college or graduate school; minority students comprised 16.5% of total postsecondary enrollment. As of 2005, Missouri had 123 degree-granting institutions including, 14 public 4-year schools, 20 public 2-year schools, and 54 nonprofit private 4-year schools. The University of Missouri, established in 1839, was the first state-supported university west of the Mississippi River. It has four campuses: Columbia (site of the world's oldest and one of the best-known journalism schools), Kansas City, Rolla, and St. Louis. The Rolla campus, originally founded in 1870 as a mining and engineering school, is still one of the nation's leading universities specializing in technology.

Lincoln University, a public university for blacks until segregation ended in 1954, is located in Jefferson City. There are five regional state universities, at Warrensburg, Maryville, Cape Girardeau, Springfield, and Kirksville, and three state colleges, at St. Louis, St. Joseph, and Joplin. Two leading independent universities, Washington and St. Louis, are located in St. Louis, as is the Concordia Seminary, an affiliate of the Lutheran Church–Missouri Synod and the center of much theological and political controversy during the 1970s. The Department of Higher Education offers grants and guaranteed loans to Missouri students.

42 ARTS

The Missouri Arts Council is a state agency consisting of 15 citizens directly appointed by the director of the Department of Economic Development. In 2005, Missouri arts organizations received 34 grants totaling $2,251,800 from the National Endowment for the Arts. In 1994, the Missouri General Assembly established the Missouri Cultural Trust, a state endowment for the arts, with the goal of building it into a $200 million operational endowment in 10 years. The Trust was one of only a few such trusts in the nation, and the only one that received dedicated annual tax revenues. In 2006, the Missouri Arts Council canceled its Capital Incentive Program associated with the Cultural Trust due to insufficient funding. In effect, it was projected that the trust fund would hold only $35,000 by June 2007.

The Missouri Humanities Council (MHC) was founded to provide opportunities for families and communities to broaden their appreciation for subjects such as history and literature. The MHC sponsors "Chautauqua" an annual weeklong summer history festival on various themes and in 2006 the council launched its "Young Chautauqua" program. The festival is generally in a different community each year. In 2005, the National Endowment for the Humanities contributed $1,947,100 for 15 state programs.

Theatrical performances are offered throughout the state, mostly during the summer. In Kansas City, productions of Broadway musicals and light opera are staged at the Starlight Theater, which seats 7,860 in an open-air setting. The Missouri Repertory Theater or Kansas City Repertory Theater, on the University of Missouri campus in Kansas City, also has a summer season. As of 2006, construction of a new downtown theater was still in process. The new theater was expected to house about 320 people, creating a smaller and more intimate performance space option. In 2006, the Kansas City Repertory Theater announced that their new downtown theater would be named Copaken Stage; the first performance was scheduled to take place in winter 2007. In St. Louis, the 12,000-seat Municipal Opera puts on outdoor musicals, while the Goldenrod, built in 1909 and said to be the largest showboat ever constructed (seating capacity 289), is used today for vaudeville, melodrama, and ragtime shows. Other notable playhouses are the 8,000-seat Riverfront Amphitheater in Hannibal, and the 344-seat Lyceum Theater in Arrow Rock (population 89).

Leading orchestras are the St. Louis Symphony and Kansas City Symphony; Independence, Liberty, Columbia, Kirksville, St. Joseph, and Springfield also have orchestras. The Opera Theatre of St. Louis and the Lyric Opera of Kansas City are distinguished musical organizations. In 2000, the Opera Theatre of St. Louis was one of only two US opera companies to receive a grant from the Ford Foundation. The Ford Foundation grant totaled $1.5 million, to be matched 4 to 1 over the next five years. Springfield has a regional opera company.

Between World Wars I and II, Kansas City was the home of a thriving jazz community that included Charlie Parker and Lester Young; leading bandleaders of that time were Benny Moten, Walter Page, and, later, Count Basie. Country music predominates in rural Missouri in places like the Ozark Opry at Osage Beach. The city of Branson is center to numerous live music and performance shows. As of 2006 there were 40 performing venues in Branson, with over 100 shows.

43 LIBRARIES AND MUSEUMS

For the fiscal year ending in June 2001, Missouri had 150 public library systems, with a total of 363 libraries, of which 216 were branches. In that same year, the state's public libraries had 18,716,000 volumes of books and serial publications on their shelves, with a combined total circulation of 38,767,000. The system also had 674,000 audio and 413,000 video items, 17,000 electronic format items (CD-ROMs, magnetic tapes, and disks), and 30 bookmobiles. The Missouri State Library, in Jefferson City, is the center of the state's interlibrary loan network. It also serves as the only public library for the population who live in areas without public libraries; it has 79,761 books. The largest public library systems, those of Kansas City and St. Louis County, had 1,204,992 and 2,777,056 volumes, respectively; the public library system of the city of St. Louis had 2,505,182 in 15 branches. The University of Missouri-Columbia has the leading academic library, with 2,850,747 volumes in 1998. The State Historical Society of Missouri Library in Columbia contains 453,000 volumes. The federally-administered Harry S. Truman Library and Museum is at Independence. In fiscal year 2001, operating income for the state's public libraries came to $153,728,000 and included $1,888,000 in federal grants and $3,954,000 in state grants.

Missouri has well over 162 museums and historic sites. The William Rockhill Nelson Gallery/Atkins Museum of Fine Arts in Kansas City and the St. Louis Art Museum each house distinguished general collections, while the Springfield Art Museum specializes in American sculpture, paintings, and relics of the westward movement. The Mark Twain Home and Museum in Hannibal has a collection of manuscripts and other memorabilia. Also notable are the Museum of Art and Archaeology, Columbia; the Kansas City Museum of History and Science; the Pony Express Stables Museum, St. Joseph; and the Jefferson National Expansion Memorial, Missouri Botanical Garden, St. Louis Center Museum of Science and Natural History and McDonnell Planetarium, National Museum of Transport, and a zoo, all in St. Louis. Kansas City, Springfield, and Eldon also have zoos.

44 COMMUNICATIONS

In 1858, John Hockaday began weekly mail service by stagecoach between Independence and Salt Lake City, and John Butterfield,

Missouri

with a $600,000 annual appropriation from Congress, established semi-monthly mail transportation by coach and rail from St. Louis to San Francisco. On 3 April 1860, the Pony Express was launched, picking up mail arriving by train at St. Joseph and racing it westward on horseback; the system ceased in October 1861, when the Pacific Telegraph Co. began operations. The first experiment in airmail service took place at St. Louis in 1911; Charles Lindbergh was an airmail pilot on the St. Louis-Chicago route in 1926.

As of 2004, Missouri had approximately 93.7% of all state residences had telephone service. Additionally, by June of that same year there were 2,859,953 mobile wireless telephone subscribers. In 2003, 60.7% of Missouri households had a computer and 53.0% had Internet access. By June 2005, there were 710,812 high-speed lines in Missouri, 653,590 residential and 57,222 for business.

Radio broadcasting in Missouri dates from 1921, when a station at St. Louis University began experimental programming. On Christmas Eve 1922, the first midnight Mass ever to be put on the air was broadcast from the Old Cathedral in St. Louis. The voice of a US president was heard over the air for the first time on 21 June 1923, when Warren G. Harding gave a speech in St. Louis. FM broadcasting began in Missouri during 1948. As of 2005 there were 36 major commercial AM stations and 97 major FM stations in service. Missouri's first television station, KSD-TV in St. Louis, began in 1947, with WDAF-TV in Kansas City following in 1949. As of 2005, Missouri had 25 major television stations. The St. Louis area had 1,114,370 television households, and only 56% of those received cable (one of the lowest penetration rates of all cities) in 1999. Kansas City had a 65% penetration rate in 802,580 television households in that same year.

A total of 84,512 Internet domain names had been registered in Missouri as of 2000.

45 PRESS

The *Missouri Gazette*, published in St. Louis in 1808 by the politically independent and controversial Joseph Charless, was the state's first newspaper; issued to 174 subscribers, the paper was partly in French. In 1815, a group of Charless's enemies raised funds to establish a rival paper, the *Western Journal*, and brought in Joshua Norvell from Nashville to edit it. By 1820 there were five newspapers in Missouri.

Since that time, many Missouri newspapermen have achieved national recognition. The best known is Samuel Clemens (later Mark Twain), who started out as a "printer's devil" in Hannibal at the age of 13. Hungarian-born Joseph Pulitzer began his journalistic career in 1868 as a reporter for a German-language daily in St. Louis. Pulitzer created the *St. Louis Post–Dispatch* from the merger of two defunct newspapers in 1878, endowed the Columbia University School of Journalism in New York City, and established by bequest the Pulitzer Prizes, which annually honor journalistic and artistic achievement.

The following table shows Missouri's leading dailies with their approximate 2005 circulations:

AREA	NAME	DAILY	SUNDAY
Kansas City	*Kansas City Star* (m,S)	275,747	388,425
St. Louis	*St. Louis Post–Dispatch* (m,S)	286,310	449,845

Periodicals include the St. Louis-based *Sporting News,* the bi-monthly "bible" of baseball fans; *VFW Magazine,* put out month-ly in Kansas City by the Veterans of Foreign Wars; and the *Missouri Historical View,* a quarterly with offices in Columbia. As of 2005 there were 13 morning newspapers, 29 evening dailies, and 23 Sunday papers.

46 ORGANIZATIONS

In 2006, there were over 7,460 nonprofit organizations registered within the state, of which about 4,647 were registered as charitable, educational, or religious organizations.

Among the national and international organizations with headquarters in Kansas City are the Veterans of Foreign Wars of the USA, the American Gulf War Veterans Association, Camp Fire USA., People-to-People International, the American Academy of Family Physicians, the American Business Women's Association, the American Nurses Association, the Fellowship of Christian Athletes, the National Association of Intercollegiate Athletics, the American Humor Studies Association, and Professional Secretaries International.

Headquartered in St. Louis are the American Association of Orthodontists, the American Optometric Association, the Catholic Health Association of the United States, the Danforth Foundation, the International Consumer Credit Association, National Garden Clubs, and the National Hairdressers and Cosmetologists Association. Children International and DeMolay International are based in Kansas City. Two major religious organizations based in the state are the Baptist Bible Fellowship International and the Gospel Missionary Union. The General Society, Sons of the Revolution is based in Independence.

State culture is represented in part by the Kansas City Barbeque Society and the Scott Joplin International Ragtime Foundation, both of which have national memberships. The Negro Leagues Baseball Museum is located in Kansas City. The Missouri Arts Council is based in St. Louis.

Other organizations include the Accrediting Council on Education in Journalism and Mass Communications (Columbia), the National Christmas Tree Association (St. Louis), and the American Cat Fanciers Association (Branson).

47 TOURISM, TRAVEL, AND RECREATION

In 2004, the state hosted some 37.7 million domestic travelers, an all-time high, with 69% of all visitors coming from out-of-state. About 42% of all visitors came to visit family or friends. Of those traveling strictly for leisure activities, shopping was the major attraction. Total travel revenues were $8.3 billion and the industry supported over 284,916 jobs. The most popular vacation areas are the St. Louis region (40% of all visits) and the Kansas City area (23%).

The principal attraction in St. Louis is the Gateway Arch, at 630 feet (192 meters) the tallest man-made national monument in the United States. Designed by Eero Saarinen in 1948 but not constructed until three years after his death in 1964, the arch and the Museum of Westward Expansion form part of the Jefferson National Expansion Memorial on the western shore of the Mississippi River.

In the Kansas City area are the modern Crown Center hotels and shopping plaza, Country Club Plaza, the Truman Sports Complex, Ft. Osage near Sibley, Jesse James's birthplace near Excelsior Springs, and Harry Truman's hometown of Independence, where his presidential library and museum are housed. Memorabilia of Mark Twain are housed in and around Hannibal in the northeast, and the birthplace and childhood home of George Washington Carver, a national monument, is in Diamond.

The Lake of the Ozarks, with 1,375 mi (2,213 km) of shoreline, is one of the most popular vacation spots in mid-America. Other attractions are the Silver Dollar City handicrafts center near Branson; the Pony Express Stables and Museum at St. Joseph; Wilson's Creek National Battlefield at Republic, site of a Confederate victory in the Civil War; and the "Big Springs Country" of the Ozarks, in the southeast. The state fair is held in Sedalia each August. The city of Gallatin contains the history of the famous outlaw Jesse James and his gang. Walt Disney modeled his rendition of Main Street, Disneyland, after his hometown of Marcelline.

Missouri has 27 state parks. Operated by the Department of Natural Resources, they offer camping, picnicking, swimming, boating, fishing, and hiking facilities. Lake of the Ozarks State Park is the largest, covering 16,872 acres (6,828 hectares). Branson hosts a musical resort and theater which attracts many visitors. There are also 27 historic sites; state parks and historic sites cover 105,000 acres (43,050 hectares). Hunting and fishing are popular recreational activities in state parks.

48 SPORTS

There are six major professional sports teams in Missouri: the Kansas City Royals and St. Louis Cardinals of Major League Baseball; the Kansas City Chiefs and St. Louis Rams of the National Football League; the St. Louis Blues of the National Hockey League; and the Kansas City Wizards of Major League Soccer.

The Cardinals won the World Series in 1926, 1931, 1934, 1942, 1944, 1946, 1964, 1967, and 1982. The Royals have won the World Series once, in 1985, against their cross-state rivals, the St. Louis Cardinals. The Chiefs appeared in Super Bowl I in 1967, losing to the Green Bay Packers. They won the Super Bowl in their next appearance, in 1970. The Rams moved to St. Louis from Los Angeles after the 1994 season and now play in the 66,000-seat Edward Jones Dome, which opened in 1995. They won the Super Bowl in 2000 with a dramatic 23–16 victory over the Tennessee Titans.

Horse racing has a long history in Missouri. In 1812, St. Charles County sportsmen held two-day horse races; by the 1820s, racetracks were laid out in nearly every city and in crossroads villages.

In collegiate sports, the University of Missouri competes in the Big Twelve Conference.

49 FAMOUS MISSOURIANS

Harry S Truman (1884–1972) has been the only native-born Missourian to serve as US president or vice president. Elected US senator in 1932, Truman became Franklin D. Roosevelt's vice-presidential running mate in 1944 and succeeded to the presidency upon Roosevelt's death on 12 April 1945. The "man from Independence"—whose tenure in office spanned the end of World War II, the inauguration of the Marshall Plan to aid European economic recovery, and the beginning of the Korean conflict—was elected to the presidency in his own right in 1948, defeating Republican Thomas E. Dewey in one of the most surprising upsets in US political history. Charles Evans Whittaker (b.Kansas, 1901–73) was a federal district and appeals court judge in Missouri before his ap-

pointment as Supreme Court associate justice in 1957. Among the state's outstanding US military leaders are Generals John J. Pershing (1860–1948) and Omar Bradley (1893–1981).

Other notable federal officeholders from Missouri include Edward Bates (b.Virginia, 1793–1869), Abraham Lincoln's attorney general and the first cabinet official to be chosen from a state west of the Mississippi River; Montgomery Blair (b.Kentucky, 1813–83), postmaster general in Lincoln's cabinet; and Norman Jay Colman (b.New York, 1827–1911), the first secretary of agriculture. Missouri's best-known senator was Thomas Hart Benton (b.North Carolina, 1782–1858), who championed the interests of Missouri and the West for 30 years. Other well-known federal legislators include Francis P. Blair Jr. (b.Kentucky, 1821–75), antislavery congressman, pro-Union leader during the Civil War, and Democratic vice-presidential nominee in 1868; Benjamin Gratz Brown (b.Kentucky, 1826–85), senator from 1863 to 1867 and later governor of the state and Republican vice-presidential nominee (1872); Carl Schurz (b.Germany, 1829–1906), senator from 1869 to 1875 and subsequently US secretary of the interior, as well as a journalist and Union military leader; William H. Hatch (b.Kentucky, 1833–96), sponsor of much agricultural legislation as a US representative from 1879 to 1895; Richard P. Bland (b.Kentucky, 1835–99), leader of the free-silver bloc in the US House of Representatives; James Beauchamp "Champ" Clark (b.Kentucky, 1850–1921), speaker of the House from 1911 to 1919; W. Stuart Symington (b.Massachusetts, 1901–88), senator from 1953 to 1977 and earlier the nation's first secretary of the Air Force; and Thomas F. Eagleton (b.1929), senator since 1969 and, briefly, the Democratic vice-presidential nominee in 1972, until publicity about his having received electroshock treatment for depression forced him off the ticket. (Eagleton announced in 1984 that he would not seek reelection to the Senate in 1986.)

Outstanding figures in Missouri history included two pioneering fur traders: William Henry Ashley (b.Virginia, 1778–1838), who later became a US representative, and Manuel Lisa (b.Louisiana, 1772–1820), who helped establish trade relations with the Indians. Meriwether Lewis (b.Virginia, 1774–1809) and William Clark (b.Virginia, 1770–1838) explored Missouri and the West during 1804–6; Lewis later served as governor of Louisiana Territory, with headquarters at St. Louis, and Clark was governor of Missouri Territory from 1813 to 1821. Dred Scott (b.Virginia, 1795–1858), a slave owned by a Missourian, figured in a Supreme Court decision that set the stage for the Civil War. Missourians with unsavory reputations include such desperadoes as Jesse James (1847–82), his brother Frank (1843–1915), and Cole Younger (1844–1916), also a member of the James gang. Another well-known native was Kansas City's political boss, Thomas Joseph Pendergast (1872–1945), a power among Missouri Democrats until convicted of income tax evasion in 1939 and sent to Leavenworth prison.

Among notable Missouri educators were William Torrey Harris (b.Connecticut, 1835–1909), superintendent of St. Louis public schools, US commissioner of education, and an authority on Hegelian philosophy; James Milton Turney (1840–1915), who helped establish Lincoln University for blacks at Jefferson City; and Susan Elizabeth Blow (1843–1916), cofounder with Harris of the first US public kindergarten at St. Louis in 1873. Distinguished scientists include agricultural chemist George Washington Carver

(1864–1943), astronomers Harlow Shapley (1885–1972) and Edwin P. Hubble (1889–1953), Nobel Prize-winning nuclear physicist Arthur Holly Compton (b.Ohio, 1892–1962), and mathematician-cyberneticist Norbert Wiener (1894–1964). Engineer and inventor James Buchanan Eads (b.Indiana, 1820–87) supervised construction during 1867–74 of the St. Louis bridge that bears his name. Charles A. Lindbergh (b.Michigan 1902–74) was a pilot and aviation instructor in the St. Louis area during the 1920s before wining worldwide acclaim for his solo New York-Paris flight.

Prominent Missouri businessmen include brewer Adolphus Busch (b.Germany, 1839–1913); William Rockhill Nelson (b.Indiana, 1847–1915), who founded the *Kansas City Star* (1880); Joseph Pulitzer (b.Hungary, 1847–1911), who merged two failed newspapers to establish the *St. Louis Post-Dispatch* (1878) and later endowed the journalism and literary prizes that bear his name; and James Cash Penney (1875–1971), founder of the J. C. Penney Co. Noteworthy journalists from Missouri include newspaper and magazine editor William M. Reedy (1862–1920), newspaper reporter Herbert Bayard Swope (1882–1958), and television newscaster Walter Cronkite (b.1916). Other distinguished Missourians include theologian Reinhold Niebuhr (1892–1971), civil rights leader Roy Wilkins (1901–81), and medical missionary Thomas Dooley (1927–61).

Missouri's most popular author is Mark Twain (Samuel Langhorne Clemens, 1835–1910), whose *Adventures of Tom Sawyer* (1876) and *Adventures of Huckleberry Finn* (1884) evoke his boyhood in Hannibal. Novelist Harold Bell Wright (b.New York, 1872–1944) wrote about the people of the Ozarks; Robert Heinlein (1907–88) is a noted writer of science fiction, and William S. Burroughs (1914–97) an experimental novelist. Poet-critic T(homas) S(tearns) Eliot (1888–1965), awarded the Nobel Prize for literature in 1948, was born in St. Louis but became a British subject in 1927. Other Missouri-born poets include Sara Teasdale (1884–1933), Marianne Moore (1887–1972), and Langston Hughes (1902–67). Popular novelist and playwright Rupert Hughes (1872–1956) was a Missouri native, as was Zoe Akins (1886–1958), a Pulitzer Prize-winning playwright.

Distinguished painters who lived in Missouri include George Caleb Bingham (b.Virginia, 1811–79), who also served in several state offices; James Carroll Beckwith (1852–1917); and Thomas Hart Benton (1889–1975), the grandnephew and namesake of the state's famous political leader. Among the state's important musicians are ragtime pianist-composers Scott Joplin (b.Texas, 1868–1917) and John William "Blind" Boone (1864–1927); W(illiam) C(hristopher) Handy (b.Alabama, 1873–1958), composer of "St. Louis Blues," "Beale Street Blues," and other classics; composer-critic Virgil Thomson (1896–1989), known for his operatic collaborations with Gertrude Stein; jazzman Coleman Hawkins (1907–69); and popular songwriter Burt Bacharach (b.1929). Photographer Walker Evans (1903–75) was a St. Louis native.

Missouri-born entertainers include actors Wallace Beery, (1889–1949), Vincent Price (1911–93), and Edward Asner (b.1929); actresses Jean Harlow (Harlean Carpenter, 1911–37), Jane Wyman (b.1914), Betty Grable (1916–73), and Shelley Winters (1922–2006); dancers Sally Rand (1904–79) and Josephine Baker (1906–75); actress-dancer Ginger Rogers (1911–95); film director John Huston (1906–84); and opera stars Helen Traubel (1903–72), Gladys Swarthout (1904–69), and Grace Bumbry (b.1937). In popular music, the state's most widely known singer-songwriter is Charles "Chuck" Berry (b.California, 1926), whose works had a powerful influence on the development of rock and roll.

St. Louis Cardinals stars who became Hall of Famers include Jerome Herman "Dizzy" Dean (b.Arkansas, 1911–74), Stanley Frank "Stan the Man" Musial (b.Pennsylvania, 1920), Robert "Bob" Gibson (b.Nebraska, 1935), and Louis "Lou" Brock (b.Arkansas, 1939). Among the native Missourians who achieved stardom in the sports world are baseball manager Charles Dillon "Casey" Stengel (1890–1975), catcher Lawrence Peter "Yogi" Berra (b.1925), sportscaster Joe Garagiola (b.1926), and golfer Tom Watson (b.1949).

50 BIBLIOGRAPHY

Burnett, Robyn. *German Settlement in Missouri: New Land, Old Ways*. Columbia: University of Missouri Press, 1996.

Christensen, Lawrence O. et al. (ed.). *Dictionary of Missouri Biography*. Columbia: University of Missouri Press, 1999.

Council of State Governments. *The Book of the States, 2006 Edition*. Lexington, Ky.: Council of State Governments, 2006.

Greene, Lorenzo J., et al. *Missouri's Black Heritage*. Rev. ed. Columbia: University of Missouri Press, 1993.

Hall, Leonard. *Stars Upstream: Life along an Ozark River*. Columbia: University of Missouri Press, 1991.

Larsen, Lawrence Harold. *Federal Justice in Western Missouri: The Judges, the Cases, the Times*. Columbia: University of Missouri Press, 1994.

Mobil Travel Guide. Great Plains 2006: Iowa, Kansas, Missouri, Nebraska, Oklahoma. Lincolnwood, Ill.: ExxonMobil Travel Publications, 2006.

McAuliffe, Emily. *Missouri Facts and Symbols*. Mankato, Minn.: Hilltop Books, 2000.

Stone, Jeffrey C. *Slavery, Southern Culture, and Education in Little Dixie, Missouri, 1820–1860*. New York: Routledge, 2006.

US Department of Commerce, Economics and Statistics Administration, US Census Bureau. *Missouri, 2000. Summary Social, Economic, and Housing Characteristics: 2000 Census of Population and Housing*. Washington, D.C.: US Government Printing Office, 2003.

MONTANA

State of Montana

ORIGIN OF STATE NAME: Derived from the Latin word meaning "mountainous." **NICKNAME:** The Treasure State. **CAPITAL:** Helena. **ENTERED UNION:** 8 November 1889 (41st). **SONG:** "Montana;" "Montana Melody." **MOTTO:** *Oro y Plata* (Gold and silver). **FLAG:** A blue field, fringed in gold on the top and bottom borders, surrounds the center portion of the offical seal, with "Montana" in gold letters above the coat of arms. **OFFICIAL SEAL:** In the lower center are a plow and a miner's pick and shovel; mountains appear above them on the left, the Great Falls of the Missouri River on the right, and the state motto on a banner below. The words "The Great Seal of the State of Montana" surround the whole. **BIRD:** Western meadowlark. **FISH:** Black-spotted (cutthroat) trout. **FLOWER:** Bitterroot. **TREE:** Ponderosa pine. **GEM:** Yogo sapphire and Montana agate. **LEGAL HOLIDAYS:** New Year's Day, 1 January; Birthday of Martin Luther King Jr., 3rd Monday in January; Presidents' Day, 3rd Monday in February; Memorial Day, last Monday in May; Independence Day, 4 July; Labor Day, 1st Monday in September; Columbus Day, 2nd Monday in October; State Election Day, 1st Tuesday after the 1st Monday in November in even-numbered years; Veterans' Day, 11 November; Thanksgiving Day, 4th Thursday in November; Christmas Day, 25 December. **TIME:** 5 AM MST = noon GMT.

¹LOCATION, SIZE, AND EXTENT

Located in the northwestern United States, Montana is the largest of the 8 Rocky Mountain states and ranks fourth in size among the 50 states.

The total area of Montana is 147,046 sq mi (380,849 sq km), of which land takes up 145,388 sq mi (376,555 sq km) and inland water 1,658 sq mi (4,294 sq km). The state's maximum E–W extension is 570 mi (917 km); its extreme N–S distance is 315 mi (507 km).

Montana is bordered on the N by the Canadian provinces of British Columbia, Alberta, and Saskatchewan; on the E by North Dakota and South Dakota; on the S by Wyoming and Idaho; and on the W by Idaho. The total boundary length of Montana is 1,947 mi (3,133 km). The state's geographic center is in Fergus County, 12 mi (19 km) W of Lewistown. Nearly 30% of the state's land belongs to the federal government.

²TOPOGRAPHY

Montana, as mountainous in parts as its name implies, has an approximate mean elevation of 3,400 ft (1,037 m). The Rocky Mountains cover the western two-fifths of the state, with the Bitterroot Range along the Idaho border; the high, gently rolling Great Plains occupy most of central and eastern Montana. The highest point in the state is Granite Peak, at an elevation of 12,799 ft (3,904 m), located in south-central Montana, near the Wyoming border. The lowest point, at 1,800 ft (549 m), is in the northwest, where the Kootenai River leaves the state at the Idaho border. The Continental Divide passes in a jagged pattern through the western part of the state, from the Lewis to the Bitterroot ranges.

Ft. Peck Reservoir is Montana's largest body of inland water, covering 375 sq mi (971 sq km); Flathead Lake is the largest natural lake. The state's most important rivers are the Missouri, rising in southwest Montana and Red Rock Creek and flowing north

and then east across the state, and the Yellowstone, which crosses southeastern Montana to join the Missouri in North Dakota near the Montana border. Located in Glacier National Park is the Triple Divide, from which Montana waters begin their journey to the Arctic and Pacific oceans and the Gulf of Mexico. The total length of the Missouri River is 2,540 mi (4,088 km); it is the longest river in the country.

³CLIMATE

The Continental Divide separates the state into two distinct climatic regions: the west generally has a milder climate than the east, where winters can be especially harsh. Montana's maximum daytime temperature averages 27°F (-2°C) in January and 85°F (29°C) in July. Great Falls has an average temperature of 45°F (7°C), ranging from 21°F (-6°C) in January to 69°F (21°C) in July. The all-time low temperature in the state, -70°F (-57°C), registered at Rogers Pass on 20 January 1954, is the lowest ever recorded in the conterminous US; the all-time high, 117°F (47°C), was set at Medicine Lake on 5 July 1937. During the winter, Chinook winds from the eastern Rocky Mountains can bring rapid temperature increases of 40–50°F within a few minutes. Great Falls receives an average annual precipitation of 15.3 in (38 cm), but much of north-central Montana is arid. About 59.1 in (150 cm) of snow descends on Great Falls each year.

⁴FLORA AND FAUNA

Montana has three major life zones: subalpine, montane, and plains. The subalpine region, in the northern Rocky Mountains, is rich in wild flowers during a short midsummer growing season. The montane flora consists largely of coniferous forests, principally alpine fir, and a variety of shrubs. The plains are characterized by an abundance of grasses, cacti, and sagebrush species. Three plant species were threatened as of April 2006: Ute ladies'-tresses, Spalding's catchfly, and water howellia.

Game animals of the state include elk, moose, white-tailed and mule deer, pronghorn antelope, bighorn sheep, and mountain goat. Notable among the amphibians is the axolotl; rattlesnakes and other reptiles occur in most of the state. Eleven species of animals (vertebrates and invertebrates) were listed as threatened or endangered in 2006 by the US Fish and Wildlife Service, including the grizzly bear, black-footed ferret, Eskimo curlew, two species of sturgeon, gray wolf, and whooping crane.

5 ENVIRONMENTAL PROTECTION

Montana's major environmental concerns are management of mineral and water resources and reclamation of strip-mined land. The 1973 Montana Resource Indemnity Trust Act, by 1975 amendment, imposes a coal severance tax of 30% on the contract sales price, with the proceeds placed in a permanent tax trust fund. This tax, in conjunction with the Montana Environmental Policy Act (1971) and the Major Facilities Siting Act (1973) reflects the determination of Montanans to protect the beauty of the Big Sky Country while maintaining economic momentum. The Water Quality Bureau of the Montana Department of Health and Environmental Sciences is responsible for managing the small number of state wetlands. In 2005, federal EPA grants awarded to the state included $50,000 for wetland protection projects.

In 2003, 45.2 million lb of toxic chemicals were released in the state. In 2003, Montana had 71 hazardous waste sites listed in the US Environment Protection Agency (EPA) database, 14 of which were on the National Priorities List as of 2006. In 2005, the EPA spent over $26.4 million through the Superfund program for the cleanup of hazardous waste sites in the state. The same year, the state received a federal EPA grant of $10 million for projects to establish and maintain safe drinking water supplies.

6 POPULATION

Montana ranked 44th in population in the United States, with an estimated total of 935,670 in 2005, an increase of 3.7% since 2000. Between 1990 and 2000, Montana's population grew from 799,065 to 902,195, an increase of 12.9%. The population is projected to reach 999,489 by 2015 and 1.03 million by 2025. The population density in 2004 was 6.4 persons per sq mi, the third-lowest in the country (after Alaska and Wyoming). In 2004, the median age of all Montana residents was 39.6. In the same year, 22.5% of the populace was under the age of 18 while 13.7% was age 65 or older.

In 2004, the largest metropolitan area was Billings, with an estimated population of 144,472. The Missoula metropolitan area had an estimated population of 99,018 and the Great Falls area had a population of about 79,849.

7 ETHNIC GROUPS

According to the 2000 census, there were approximately 56,068 American Indians in Montana, of whom the Blackfeet and Crow are the most numerous. The Blackfeet and Crow reservations had populations of, respectively, 10,100 and 6,894 in 2000. In 2004, 6.4% of the population was American Indian.

The foreign born, numbering 16,396, made up 1.8% of Montana's 2000 Census population, a decrease of 24% since 1980. Canada, Germany, the United Kingdom, and Mexico were the leading places of origin. As of 2000, the black and Asian populations were just 2.692 and 4,691, respectively. In 2000, 18,081 residents were Hispanic or Latino, representing 2% of the total population. In 2004, 0.4% of the population was black, 0.5% Asian, 0.1% Pacific Islander, and 2.4% Hispanic or Latino. That year, 1.5% of the population reported origin of two or more races.

8 LANGUAGES

English in Montana fuses Northern and Midland features, the Northern proportion declining from east to west. Topography has given new meaning to *basin, hollow, meadow,* and *park* as kinds of clear spaces in the mountains.

In 2000, the number of Montanans who spoke only English at was 803,031, representing about 95% of the resident population five years of age or older. There was no change in the overall percentage of English speakers from 1990 to 2000.

The following table gives selected statistics from the 2000 Census for language spoken at home by persons five years old and over. The category "Other Native North American languages" includes Apache, Cherokee, Choctaw, Dakota, Keres, Pima, and Yupik. The category "Scandinavian languages" includes Danish, Norwegian, and Swedish. The category "Other Slavic languages" includes Czech, Slovak, and Ukrainian.

LANGUAGE	NUMBER	PERCENT
Population 5 years and over	847,362	100.0
Speak only English	803,031	94.8
Speak a language other than English	44,331	5.2
Speak a language other than English	**44,331**	**5.2**
Spanish or Spanish Creole	12,953	1.5
German	9,416	1.1
Other Native North American languages	9,234	1.1
French (incl. Patois, Cajun)	3,298	0.4
Scandinavian languages	1,335	0.2
Italian	759	0.1
Japanese	711	0.1
Russian	610	0.1
Other Slavic languages	570	0.1
Chinese	528	0.1

9 RELIGIONS

In 2000, there was a nearly equal number of Protestants versus Catholics within the state. The Roman Catholic Church is the largest single Christian denomination with about 103,351 adherents in 2004. Leading Protestant denominations (with 2000 data) were the Evangelical Lutheran Church in America, 50,287; the United Methodist Church, 17,993; Assemblies of God, 16,385; the Lutheran Church—Missouri Synod, 15,441; and the Southern Baptist Convention, 15,318. In 2006, the Church of Jesus Christ of the Latter-day Saints (Mormons) reported a statewide membership of 13,384 in 116 congregations; there is a Mormon temple in Billings (est. 1999). There were about 850 Jews and 614 Muslims in the state in 2000.

Though relatively small in terms of membership, several religious groups within the state experienced significant growth throughout 1990–2000. Friends–USA (Quakers) reported a membership growth from 77 in 1990 to 160 in 2000. The Free Lutheran Congregations grew from 75 members to 427 members and the Salvation Army reported a total of 1,414 members in 2000, up from 551 in 1990. About 493,703 people (55% of the population) did not report affiliation with any religious organization in 2000.

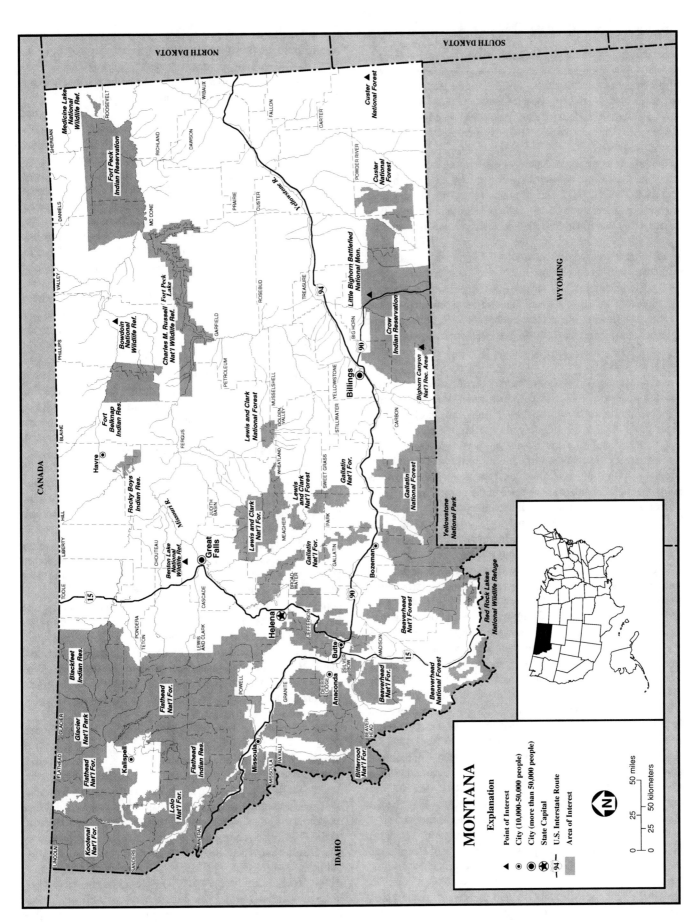

NORTH DAKOTA

SOUTH DAKOTA

Custer National Forest

SHERIDAN

Medicine Lake National Wildlife Ref.

ROOSEVELT

DANIELS

Fort Peck Indian Reservation

RICHLAND

WIBAUX

DAWSON

MC CONE

PRAIRIE

FALLON

CARTER

Yellowstone R.

Custer National Forest

94

POWDER RIVER

VALLEY

Fort Peck Lake

GARFIELD

ROSEBUD

TREASURE

Little Bighorn Battlefield National Mon.

PHILLIPS

Charles M. Russell Nat'l Wildlife Ref.

Bowdoin National Wildlife Ref.

BIG HORN

Crow Indian Reservation

90

BLAINE

Fort Belknap Indian Res.

PETROLEUM

MUSSELSHELL

YELLOWSTONE

Billings

STILLWATER

CARBON

Bighorn Canyon Nat'l Rec. Area

HILL

Havre

Rocky Boys Indian Res.

Missouri R.

FERGUS

JUDITH BASIN

Lewis and Clark National Forest

GOLDEN VALLEY

WHEATLAND

SWEET GRASS

Gallatin Nat'l For.

Gallatin National Forest

Yellowstone National Park

LIBERTY

TOOLE

15

CHOUTEAU

CASCADE

Benton Lake National Wildlife Ref.

Great Falls

Lewis and Clark Nat'l For.

MEAGHER

Lewis and Clark Nat'l Forest

PARK

GALLATIN

Gallatin Nat'l For.

Bozeman

Beaverhead Nat'l Forest

Red Rock Lakes National Wildlife Refuge

PONDERA

TETON

LEWIS AND CLARK

BROAD WATER

Helena

JEFFERSON

Butte

SILVER BOW

MADISON

15

Beaverhead National Forest

Blackfeet Indian Res.

POWELL

GRANITE

DEER LODGE

Anaconda

Beaverhead Nat'l For.

GLACIER

Glacier Nat'l Park

Flathead Nat'l For.

Flathead Indian Res.

BEAVER-HEAD

FLATHEAD

Kalispell

Flathead Nat'l For.

MISSOULA

Missoula

RAVALLI

Bitterroot Nat'l For.

LINCOLN

Kootenai Nat'l For.

Lolo Nat'l For.

SANDERS

CANADA

WYOMING

IDAHO

MONTANA

Explanation

▲ Point of Interest

⊙ City (10,000–50,000 people)

◉ City (more than 50,000 people)

✪ State Capital

—94— U.S. Interstate Route

Area of Interest

N

0   25   50 miles

0   25   50 kilometers

10 TRANSPORTATION

Montana's first railroad, the Utah and Northern, entered the state in 1880. Today, Montana is served by two Class I railroads (the Burlington Northern Santa Fe, and the Union Pacific), plus two regional railroads, and two local railroads, operating on 3,291 rail mi (5,298 km) of track. As of 2006, Amtrak operated one long-distance route (Chicago–Seattle/Portland) through the state, which served 12 stations.

Because of its large size, small population, and difficult terrain, Montana was slow to develop a highway system. In 2004, the state had 69,452 mi (111,817 km) of public roads, streets, and highways. There were around 1.031 million registered motor vehicles in that same year, including some 427,000 automobiles, approximately 555,000 trucks of all types, and some 1,000 buses. There were 712,880 licensed drivers in 2004.

In 2005, Montana had a total of 276 public and private-use aviation-related facilities. This included 241 airports, 31 heliports, 2 STOLports (Short Take-Off and Landing), and two seaplane bases. The state's leading airport is at Billings. In 2004, Billings–Logan International airport had 395,086 passenger enplanements.

11 HISTORY

Much of Montana's prehistory has only recently been unearthed. The abundance of fossils of large and small dinosaurs, marine reptiles, miniature horses, and giant cave bears indicates that, from 100 million to 60 million years ago, the region had a tropical climate. Beginning some 2 million years ago, however, dramatic temperature changes profoundly altered what we now call Montana. At four different times, great sheets of glacial ice moved south through Canada to cover much of the north. The last glacial retreat, about 10,000 years ago, did much to carve the state's present topographic feature. Montana's first humans probably came from across the Bering Strait; their fragmentary remains indicate a presence dating between 10,000 and 4000 BC.

The Indians encountered by Montana's first white explorers—probably French traders and trappers from Canada—arrived from the east during the 17th and 18th centuries, pushed westward into Montana by the pressure of European colonization. In January 1743, two traders, Louis-Joseph and Francois Vérendrye, crossed the Dakota plains and saw before them what they called the "shining mountains," the eastern flank of the northern Rockies. However, it was not until 1803 that the written history of Montana begins. In that year, the Louisiana Purchase gave the United States most of Montana, and the Lewis and Clark expedition, dispatched by President Thomas Jefferson in 1804 to explore the upper reaches of the Missouri River, added the rest. On 25 April 1805, accompanied by a French trapper named Toussaint Charbonneau and his Shoshoni wife, Sacagawea, Meriwether Lewis and William Clark reached the mouth of the Yellowstone River near the present-day boundary with North Dakota. Shortly thereafter, the first American trappers, traders, and settlers entered Montana.

The fur trade dominated Montana's economy until 1858, when gold was discovered near the present community of Drummond. By mid-1862, a rush of miners from the gold fields of California, Nevada, Colorado, and Idaho had descended on the state. The temporary gold boom brought not only the state's first substantial white population but also an increased demand for government.

In 1863, the eastern and western sectors of Montana were joined as part of Idaho Territory, which, in turn, was divided along the Bitterroot Mountains to form the present boundary between the two states. On 26 May 1864, President Abraham Lincoln signed the Organic Act, which created Montana Territory.

The territorial period was one of rapid and profound change. By the time Montana became a state on 8 November 1889, the remnants of Montana's Indian culture had been largely confined to federal reservations. A key event in this transformation was the Battle of the Little Big Horn River on 25 June 1876, when Lieutenant Colonel George Custer and his 7th US Cavalry regiment of fewer than 700 men were overwhelmed as they attacked an encampment of 15,000 Sioux and Northern Cheyenne led by Crazy Horse and Chief Gall. The following year, after a four-month running battle that traversed most of the state of Montana, Chief Joseph of the Nez Percé tribe surrendered to federal forces, signaling the end of organized Indian resistance.

As the Indian threat subsided, stockmen wasted little time in putting the seemingly limitless open range to use. By 1866, Nelson Story had driven the first longhorns up from Texas, and by the mid-1870s, sheep had also made a significant appearance on the open range. In 1886, at the peak of the open-range boom, approximately 664,000 head of cattle and nearly a million sheep grazed Montana's rangeland. Disaster struck during the "hard winter" of 1886/87, however, when perhaps as many as 362,000 head of cattle starved trying to find the scant forage covered by snow and ice. That winter marked the end of a cattle frontier based on the "free grass" of the open range and taught the stockmen the value of a secure winter feed supply.

Construction of Montana's railroad system between 1880 and 1909 breathed new life into mining as well as the livestock industry. Moreover, the railroads created a new network of market centers at Great Falls, Billings, Bozeman, Missoula, and Havre. By 1890, the Butte copper pits were producing more than 40% of the nation's copper requirements. The struggle to gain financial control of the enormous mineral wealth of Butte Hill led to the "War of the Copper Kings," in which the Amalgamated Copper Co., in conjunction with Standard Oil gave up its copper holdings. The new company, Anaconda Copper Mining, virtually controlled the press, politics, and governmental processes of Montana until changes in the structure of the international copper market and the diversification of Montana's economy in the 1940s and 1950s reduced the company's power. Anaconda Copper was absorbed by the Atlantic Richfield Co. in 1976, and the name was changed to Anaconda Minerals in 1982.

The railroads also brought an invasion of agricultural homesteaders. Montana's population surged from 243,329 in 1900 to 548,889 by 1920, while the number of farms and ranches increased form 13,000 to 57,000. Drought and a sharp drop in wheat prices after World War I brought an end to the homestead boom. By 1926, half of Montana's commercial banks had failed. Conditions worsened with the drought and depression of the early 1930s, until the New Deal—enormously popular in Montana—helped revive farming and silver mining and financed irrigation and other public works projects.

The decades after World War II saw moderate growth in Montana's population, economy, and social services. Although manufacturing developed slowly, the state's fossil fuels industry grew rapidly during the national energy crisis of the 1970s. However, production of coal, crude oil, and natural gas leveled off after the crisis and even declined in the early 1980s.

In 1983 the Anaconda Copper Mining Company shut down its mining operations in Butte. Farm income also suffered in the 1980s as a result of falling prices, drought, and insect damage. Growth in manufacturing and construction and recovery in the agricultural sector, improved Montana's economy in the 1990s. However, even in the midst of a sustained economic boom, the state had the eighth highest unemployment rate in the nation, 5.2% as of 1999. Other indicators also showed the state was not benefiting from the sustained national economic expansion of recent years. Montana faced a $230 million budget deficit in 2003, but lawmakers were able to balance the budget with a series of program reductions, new taxes, and budget transfers. Montana's unemployment rate in September 2005 was 4.5%, below the national average of 5.1%. However, in 2004 the poverty rate was 14.3% (measured as a three-year average estimate from 2002–04) above the national average of 12.7%.

Tourism, air quality, and wildlife in parts of Montana were affected by the 1988 forest fires that burned for almost three months in Yellowstone National Park. Some Montana residents had to be evacuated from their homes. The state was among those afflicted by raging wildfires the summer of 2000, the worst fire season in more than a decade. In the summer of 2002, wildfires burned over 7.1 million acres of public and private land in the United States, most of it in the west. By August 2003, 36 wildfires had destroyed over 400,000 acres in Montana, equivalent to half the state of Rhode Island. Both Yellowstone and Glacier National Parks had to close sections of the parks due to fires.

In 1992 Montana's delegation to the US House of Representatives was reduced from two members to one, based on the results of the 1990 Census. The state remains one of the least populated in the nation, with an estimated 902,195 residents in 2000—or about six people per square mile. In 2004, there were an estimated 926,865 residents in Montana.

In November 2004, Brian Schweitzer was elected the state's first Democratic governor since 1988.

12 STATE GOVERNMENT

Montana's original constitution, dating from 1889, was substantially revised by a 1972 constitutional convention, effective 1 July 1973. Under the present document, which had been amended 30 times by January 2005, the state legislature consists of 50 senators, elected to staggered four-year terms, and 99 representatives, who serve for two years. Legislators must be at least 18 years old and have lived in the state for a year and in their district for six months prior to election. In 2004 legislators received $78.60 per diem during regular sessions. Sessions are held only in odd-numbered years, beginning the first Monday of January and lasting no more than 90 legislative days. An amendment passed by voters in 2002 requires the governor to give advance notice of special sessions, which have no time limit and may be called by petition of a majority in each house.

The only elected officers of the executive branch are the governor and lieutenant governor (who run jointly), secretary of state, attorney general, superintendent of public instruction, and auditor; each serves a four-year term. Without exception, the governor

is limited to serving eight out of every 16 years. A candidate for governor must be at least 25 years old and a citizen and resident of both the United States and Montana. As of December 2004, the governor's salary was $93,089.

To become law, a bill must pass both houses by a simple majority and be signed by the governor, remain unsigned for 10 days (25 days if the legislature adjourns), or be passed over the governor's veto by a two-thirds vote of the members present in both houses. The state constitution may be amended by constitutional convention, by legislative referendum (a two-thirds vote of both houses), or by voter initiative (10% of qualified electors, as determined by number of votes cast for governor at the last election). To be adopted, each proposed amendment must be ratified at the next general election.

To vote in Montana, one must be a US citizen, at least 18 years old, and a state and county resident for 30 days prior to election day. Restrictions apply to convicted felons and those declared of unsound mind.

13 POLITICAL PARTIES

Since statehood, Democrats generally dominated in contests for the US House and Senate, and Republicans in elections for state and local offices and in national presidential campaigns (except during the New Deal years). Although the erosion of Montana's rural population since the 1920s diluted the Republicans' agrarian base, the party has gained increasing financial and organizational backing from corporate interests, particularly from the mining and energy-related industries.

The strength of the Democratic Party, on the other hand, lies in the strong union movement centered in Butte and its surrounding counties, augmented by smaller family farms throughout the state. Urbanization also benefited the Democrats. Montanans voted overwhelmingly for Republican President Ronald Reagan in November 1984 and for Republican George Bush in 1988, but Democrat Bill Clinton carried the state in 1992. However, in 1996 Clinton lost the state to Republican Bob Dole. In 2000, Republican George W. Bush won an overwhelming victory over Democrat Al Gore, 58% to 34%. Green Party candidate Ralph Nader

Montana Presidential Vote by Major Political Parties, 1948–2004

YEAR	ELECTORAL VOTE	MONTANA WINNER	DEMOCRAT	REPUBLICAN
1948	4	*Truman (D)	119,071	96,770
1952	4	*Eisenhower (R)	106,213	157,394
1956	4	*Eisenhower (R)	116,238	154,933
1960	4	Nixon (R)	134,891	141,841
1964	4	*Johnson (D)	164,246	113,032
1968	4	*Nixon (R)	114,117	138,835
1972	4	*Nixon (R)	120,197	183,976
1976	4	Ford (R)	149,259	173,703
1980	4	*Reagan (R)	118,032	206,814
1984	4	*Reagan (R)	146,742	232,450
1988	4	*Bush (R)	168,936	190,412
1992**	3	*Clinton (D)	154,507	144,207
1996**	3	Dole (R)	167,922	179,652
2000	3	*Bush, G. W. (R)	137,126	240,178
2004	3	*Bush, G. W. (R)	173,710	266,063

*Won US presidential election.
**IND. candidate Ross Perot received 107,225 votes in 1992 and 55,229 votes in 1996.

won 6% of the vote. In 2004, Bush again won a decisive victory over Democratic challenger John Kerry, 59% to 39%. In 2004 there were 638,000 registered voters; there is no party registration in the state. The state had three electoral votes in the 2004 presidential election.

Montana Governor Marc Racicot, Republican, was elected in 1992 and reelected in 1996. Republican Judy Martz was elected Montana's first female governor in 2000. In 2004, Democrat Brian Schweitzer won the governorship, becoming the first Democrat since 1988 to win the office. Republican Conrad Burns was elected to the Senate in 1988 and reelected in 1994 and 2000, and Democrat Max Baucus won reelection in 2002. The state's sole seat in the US House was retained by a Republican in the 2004 election. In mid-2005, there were 23 Republicans and 27 Democrats in the state Senate. The state House was split, with 50 seats held by Republicans and 50 by Democrats.

14 LOCAL GOVERNMENT

As of 2005, Montana had 56 counties, 129 municipalities, 592 special districts, and 453 public school districts. Typical elected county officials are three county commissioners (or a city manager), attorney, sheriff, clerk and recorder, school superintendent, treasurer, assessor, and coroner. Unified city-county governments include Anaconda-Deer Lodge and Butte-Silver Bow.

In 2005, local government accounted for about 35,946 full-time (or equivalent) employment positions.

15 STATE SERVICES

To address the continuing threat of terrorism and to work with the federal Department of Homeland Security, homeland security in Montana operates under state statute; the emergency management director is designated as the state homeland security advisor.

The Citizens' Advocate Office, established in 1973, serves as a clearinghouse for problems, complaints, and questions concerning state government. The commissioner of higher education administers the state university system, while the superintendent of public instruction is responsible for the public schools. The Department of Transportation is the main transportation agency. Health and welfare programs are the province of the Department of Public Health and Human Services. Other departments deal with agriculture, commerce, justice, labor and industry, livestock, and natural resources and conservation.

16 JUDICIAL SYSTEM

Montana's highest court, the Montana Supreme Court, consists of a chief justice and six associate justices. District courts are the courts of general jurisdiction. Justice of the peace courts are essentially county courts whose jurisdiction is limited to minor civil cases, misdemeanors, and traffic violations. Montana has seven supreme court justices elected on nonpartisan ballots for eight-year terms and 37 district court judges elected for six years.

As of 31 December 2004, a total of 3,877 prisoners were held in Montana's state and federal prisons, an increase from 3,620 of 7.1% from the previous year. As of year-end 2004, a total of 473 inmates were female, up from 419 or 12.9% from the year before. Among sentenced prisoners (one year or more), Montana had an incarceration rate of 416 per 100,000 population in 2004.

According to the Federal Bureau of Investigation, Montana in 2004, had a violent crime rate (murder/nonnegligent manslaughter; forcible rape; robbery; aggravated assault) of 293.8 reported incidents per 100,000 population, or a total of 2,723 reported incidents. Crimes against property (burglary; larceny/theft; and motor vehicle theft) in that same year totaled 27,215 reported incidents or 2,936.2 reported incidents per 100,000 people. Montana has a death penalty, of which lethal injection is the sole method of execution. From 1976 through 5 May 2006, the state has executed only two persons. The most recent execution was carried out in February 1998. As of 1 January 2006, Montana had four inmates on death row.

In 2003, Montana spent $37,553,219 on homeland security, an average of $37 per state resident.

17 ARMED FORCES

In 2004, there were 3,789 active-duty military personnel and 1,274 civilian personnel stationed in Montana. The principal military facility in Montana is Malmstrom Air Force Base (Great Falls), a Strategic Air Command facility. Total defense contracts in 2004 amounted to $206.8 million, and total Defense Department payroll outlays were $403 million.

An estimated 102,605 veterans of US military service were living in Montana in 2003. Of these, 13,746 served in World War II; 11,049 in the Korean conflict; 33,814 during the Vietnam era; and 14,703 in the Gulf War. For the fiscal year 2004, total Veterans Affairs expenditures in Montana exceeded to $291 million.

As of 31 October 2004, the Montana Highway Patrol employed 206 full-time sworn officers.

18 MIGRATION

Montana's first great migratory wave brought Indians from the east during the 17th and 18th centuries. The gold rush of the 1860s and a land boom between 1900 and 1920 resulted in surges of white settlement. The economically troubled 1920s and 1930s produced a severe wave of out-migration that continued through the 1960s. The trend reversed between 1970 and 1980, however, when Montana's net gain from migration was 16,000; from 1980 to 1989, the state had a net loss of 43,000 residents from migration. Between 1990 and 1998, Montana had net gains of 48,000 in domestic migration and 3,000 in international migration. In 1998, the state admitted 299 foreign immigrants. Between 1990 and 1998, the state's overall population increased 10.2%. In the period 2000–05, net international migration was 2,141 and net internal migration was 18,933, for a net gain of 21,074 people.

19 INTERGOVERNMENTAL COOPERATION

Among the interstate agreements in which Montana participates are the Interstate Oil and Gas Compact, Western Interstate Corrections Compact, Western Interstate Energy Compact, Western Interstate Commission for Higher Education, Interstate Compact for Juveniles, Northwest Power and Conservation Council (with Idaho, Oregon, and Washington), and Yellowstone River Compact (with North Dakota and Wyoming). Federal grants to the state and local governments in fiscal year 2005 totaled $1.263 billion, an estimated $1.269 billion in fiscal year 2006, and an estimated $1.289 billion in fiscal year 2007.

20 ECONOMY

Resource industries—agriculture, mining, lumbering—traditionally dominated Montana's economy, although they have declined during the past decade. A lawsuit with the federal government over the federal lands which supplied much of the state's timber placed the timber industry's future in question, as did the selling by Champion International of its two mills and of its timber lands. While Stimson Lumber purchased the mills from Champion, it rehired only two-thirds of the employees. The mining industry in western Montana was hurt by low international price levels. The closure of Troy Mine, which produced silver, lead and zinc, resulted in the idling of 300 workers. Employment in the services industries overtook manufacturing and mining during the 1990s. Diversification into business, engineering, health, and tourism services has stimulated the economy. Annual growth rates averaged 4.67% from 1998 to 2000, and the state economy was little affected by the national recession and slowdown in 2001, posting a growth rate of 4.3%. In November 2002, Montana's nonagricultural employment was up 1.1% above the year before, above the national rate. Employment increased in construction, financial and general services, and fell slightly in the manufacturing and transportation and utilities sectors. The announced closing of Stimson Lumber in Libby is expected to cost 300 mill jobs, and another 410 related jobs. Montana's farm sector, contributing directly less than 3% to gross state product, has been severely stressed by a four-year drought. Wheat crop yields in 2002 were the lowest since 1988. Government subsidy payments to Montana farmers, the fourth highest in the country, amounted to 157% of their net income (that is, net income would have been negative without the subsidies).

Montana's gross state product (GSP) in 2004 was $27.482 billion, of which the real estate sector accounted for the largest share at $3.229 billion or 11.7% of GSP, followed by healthcare and social assistance, at $2.491 billion (9% of GSP), and construction, at $1.627 billion (5.9% of GSP). In that same year, there were an estimated 106,789 small businesses in Montana. Of the 34,570 businesses that had employees, an estimated total of 33,801 or 97.8% were small companies. An estimated 4,588 new businesses were established in the state in 2004, up 0.9% from the year before. Business terminations that same year came to 4,896, up 4.6% from 2003. There were 109 business bankruptcies in 2004, up 11.2% from the previous year. In 2005, the state's personal bankruptcy (Chapter 7 and Chapter 13) filing rate was 471 filings per 100,000 people, ranking Montana as the 32nd highest in the nation.

21 INCOME

In 2005 Montana had a gross state product (GSP) of $30 billion which accounted for 0.2% of the nation's gross domestic product and placed the state at number 48 in highest GSP among the 50 states and the District of Columbia.

According to the Bureau of Economic Analysis, in 2004 Montana had a per capita personal income (PCPI) of $27,657. This ranked 42nd in the United States and was 84% of the national average of $33,050. The 1994–2004 average annual growth rate of PCPI was 4.5%. Montana had a total personal income (TPI) of $25,635,394,000, which ranked 46th in the United States and reflected an increase of 6.7% from 2003. The 1994–2004 average annual growth rate of TPI was 5.2%. Earnings of persons employed in Montana increased from $17,162,093,000 in 2003 to $18,423,659,000 in 2004, an increase of 7.4%. The 2003–04 national change was 6.3%.

The US Census Bureau reports that the three-year average median household income for 2002 to 2004 in 2004 dollars was $35,201, compared to a national average of $44,473. During the same period an estimated 14.3% of the population was below the poverty line, as compared to 12.4% nationwide.

22 LABOR

According to the Bureau of Labor Statistics (BLS), in April 2006 the seasonally adjusted civilian labor force in Montana numbered 502,800 with approximately 18,300 workers unemployed, yielding an unemployment rate of 3.6%, compared to the national average of 4.7% for the same period. Preliminary data for the same period placed nonfarm employment at 428,600. Since the beginning of the BLS data series in 1976, the highest unemployment rate recorded in Montana was 8.7% in May 1983. The historical low was 3.4% in March 2006. Preliminary nonfarm employment data by occupation for April 2006 showed that approximately 6.9% of the labor force was employed in construction; 4.5% in manufacturing; 4.5% in trade, transportation, and public utilities; 5% in financial activities; 8.4% in professional and business services; 13% in leisure and hospitality services; and 20.2% in government. Data were unavailable for education and healthcare services.

The US Department of Labor's Bureau of Labor Statistics reported that in 2005, a total of 42,000 of Montana's 391,000 employed wage and salary workers were formal members of a union. This represented 10.7% of those so employed, down from 11.7% in 2004, and below the national average of 12%. Overall in 2005, a total of 48,000 workers (12.2%) in Montana were covered by a union or employee association contract, which includes those workers who reported no union affiliation. Montana is one of 28 states that does not have a right-to-work law.

As of 1 March 2006, Montana had a two-tiered state-mandated minimum wage rate. Businesses with gross annual sales of $110,000 or less were subject to a $4.00 per hour rate. All others were subject to a $5.15 per hour rate. In 2004, women in the state accounted for 47.6% of the employed civilian labor force.

23 AGRICULTURE

Montana's farms numbered 28,000 in 2004, with average acreage of 2,146 (869 hectares). Farm income totaled nearly $2.38 billion in 2005. In 2004, Montana was the nation's third-leading wheat producer, with an output of 173.2 million bu, valued at $612 million. Other major crops were barley (third in the United States) with 48.9 million bu, valued at $139.6 million; sugar beets (sixth) with 1.1 million bu, valued at $56.2 million; and hay with 4.7 million tons, valued at $362.1 million.

24 ANIMAL HUSBANDRY

In 2005, Montana's farms and ranches had around 2.4 million cattle and calves, valued at $2.5 million. There were an estimated 165,000 hogs and pigs, valued at $18.2 million in 2004. During 2003, Montana farmers produced around 24.6 million lb

(11.2 million kg) of sheep and lambs that grossed $22.6 million in income.

25 FISHING

Montana's designated fishing streams offer some 10,000 mi (16,000 km) of good to excellent freshwater fishing. In 2004, the state issued 379,252 sport fishing licenses.

Montana is home to the Creston and Ennis National Fish Hatcheries as well as the Bozeman Fish Technology Center and the Bozeman Fish Health Center. Creston specializes in rainbow trout, westslope cutthroat trout, kokanee salmon, and bull trout. Ennis works as part of the National Broodstock Program, producing about 20 million rainbow trout eggs annually for research facilities, universities and federal, state and tribal hatcheries in 23 states.

26 FORESTRY

As of 2004, 23,500,000 acres (9,510,000 hectares) in Montana were classified as forestland. There were 11 national forests, comprising 16,932,447 acres (6,852,561 hectares) in 2005. The lumbering industry produced 1.09 billion board feet in 2004.

27 MINING

According to preliminary data from the US Geological Survey (USGS), the estimated value of nonfuel mineral production by Montana in 2003 was $492 million, an increase from 2002 of about 4%. The USGS data ranked Montana 26th among the 50 states by the total value of its nonfuel mineral production, accounting for over 1% of total US output.

According to the preliminary data for 2003, metallic minerals accounted for almost 63% of Montana's nonfuel mineral production, by value. Higher average prices and a two-fold increase in production, made gold the state's top nonfuel mineral by value, overtaking palladium. Following gold were platinum, construction sand and gravel, cement (portland and masonry), and bentonite. Montana in that same year was the only state to have primary platinum and palladium mine production and ranked fourth in the output of gold, according to the preliminary data. In 2003 Montana was first in the production of talc, second in bentonite, fourth in zinc and lead, and seventh in silver. The state was also ranked eighth in the production of gemstones (by value).

Preliminary data for 2003, showed palladium output at 14,600 kg, with a value of $98.3 million, while platinum output that year totaled 4,100 kg, with a value of $86.5 million. Construction sand and gravel production in 2003 totaled 18 million metric tons, with a value of $81.9 million, while bentonite clay output totaled 181,000 metric tons, with a value of $14.9 million. Crushed stone output in that same year stood at 2.5 million metric tons, with a valued of $10.8 million.

Montana was also a producer of dimension stone in 2003.

28 ENERGY AND POWER

As of 2003, Montana had 44 electrical power service providers, of which one was publicly owned and 30 were cooperatives. Of the remainder, five were investor owned, three were federally operated, four were generation-only suppliers and one was a delivery-only provider. As of that same year there were 518,380 retail customers. Of that total, 325,008 received their power from inves-

tor-owned service providers. Cooperatives accounted for 172,439 customers, while publicly owned providers had 923 customers. There were 18,652 federal customers and there were1,358 generation-only customers. There was no data on the number of delivery-only customers.

Total net summer generating capability by the state's electrical generating plants in 2003 stood at 5.210 million kW, with total production that same year at 26.268 billion kWh. Of the total amount generated, 22.9% came from electric utilities, with the remainder (77.1%) coming from independent producers and combined heat and power service providers. The largest portion of all electric power generated, 17.048 billion kWh (64.9%), came from coal-fired plants, with hydroelectric plants in second place at 8.701 billion kWh (33.1%) and petroleum fueled plants in third at 402.164 million kWh (1.5%). Other renewable power sources accounted for 0.3% of all power generated, with natural gas fueled plants and those using other types of gases at 0.1% each.

As of 2004, Montana had proven crude oil reserves of 364 million barrels, or 1% of all proven US reserves, while output that same year averaged 68,000 barrels per day. Including federal offshore domains, the state that year ranked tenth (ninth excluding federal offshore) in proven reserves and 11th (10th excluding federal offshore) in production among the 31 producing states. In 2004 Montana had 3,627 producing oil wells, accounting for 1% of US production. As of 2005, the state's four refineries had a combined crude oil distillation capacity of 181,200 barrels per day.

In 2004, Montana had 4,971 producing natural gas and gas condensate wells. In that same year, marketed gas production (all gas produced excluding gas used for repressuring, vented and flared, and nonhydrocarbon gases removed) totaled 96.762 billion cu ft (2.74 billion cu m). As of 31 December 2004, proven reserves of dry or consumer-grade natural gas totaled 995 billion cu ft (28.2 billion cu m).

In 2004, Montana had six producing coal mines, five surface operations and one underground. Coal production that year totaled 39,989,000 short tons, up from 36,994,000 short tons in 2003. Of the total produced in 2004, the surface mines accounted for 39,831,000 short tons. Recoverable coal reserves in 2004 totaled 1.14 billion short tons. One short ton equals 2,000 lb (0.907 metric tons).

29 INDUSTRY

According to the US Census Bureau's Annual Survey of Manufactures (ASM) for 2004, Montana's manufacturing sector covered some six product subsectors. The shipment value of all products manufactured in the state that same year was $6.468 billion. Of that total, wood product manufacturing accounted for the largest share at $960.445 million. It was followed by food manufacturing at $666.718 million; nonmetallic mineral product manufacturing at $216.365 million; and fabricated metal product manufacturing at $196.782 billion.

In 2004, a total of 17,311 people in Montana were employed in the state's manufacturing sector, according to the ASM. Of that total, 12,709 were actual production workers. In terms of total employment, the wood product manufacturing industry accounted for the largest portion of all manufacturing employees, with 4,109 (3,568 actual production workers). It was followed by food manufacturing, with 2,464 employees (1,547 actual production workers); miscellaneous manufacturing, with 1,447 (976 actual production workers); and nonmetallic mineral product manufacturing, with 1,405 (1,093 actual production workers).

ASM data for 2004 showed that Montana's manufacturing sector paid $664.859 million in wages. Of that amount, the wood product manufacturing sector accounted for the largest share at $147.640 million. It was followed by food manufacturing at $81.157 million; fabricated metal product manufacturing at $48.872 million; machinery manufacturing at $48.438 million; and miscellaneous manufacturing at $44.878 million.

30 COMMERCE

According to the 2002 Census of Wholesale Trade, Montana's wholesale trade sector had sales that year totaling $7.2 billion from 1,485 establishments. Wholesalers of durable goods accounted for 839 establishments, followed by nondurable goods wholesalers at 571 and electronic markets, agents, and brokers accounting for 75 establishments. Sales by durable goods wholesalers in 2002 totaled $2.4 billion, while wholesalers of nondurable goods saw sales of $3.9 billion. Electronic markets, agents, and brokers in the wholesale trade industry had sales of $833.7 million.

In the 2002 Census of Retail Trade, Montana was listed as having 5,145 retail establishments with sales of $10.1 billion. The leading types of retail businesses by number of establishments were: motor vehicle and motor vehicle parts dealers (743); miscellaneous store retailers (679); building material/garden equipment and supplies dealers (612); gasoline stations (597); and food and beverage stores (496). In terms of sales, motor vehicle and motor vehicle parts dealers accounted for the largest share of retail sales at $2.7 billion, followed by general merchandise stores at $1.6 billion; food and beverage stores at $1.3 billion; and gasoline stations at $1.2 billion. A total of 52,891 people were employed by the retail sector in Montana that year.

Montana's foreign exports in 2005 totaled $710 million, second to last in the nation above only Wyoming.

31 CONSUMER PROTECTION

Montana's consumer protection laws are administered by the state's Department of Justice's Office of Consumer Protection. The office enforces Montana's consumer protection laws and regulations relating to telemarketing, the sales and repair of automobiles and trucks, credit management services, deceptive and misleading advertising, door-to-door sales, gasoline pricing, online commerce, and unfair business acts under the state's Telemarketing Registration and Fraud Act, the New Vehicle Warranty Act, the Consumer Protection Act, the Personal Solicitation Sales Act, and the Unfair Trade Practices Act.

When dealing with consumer protection issues, the state's attorney general (who heads the state's Department of Justice) is extremely limited in terms of what it is authorized to do, and can only exercise its authority regarding consumer protection in cooperation with the state's Department of Administration. The attorney general cannot initiate civil or criminal proceedings; represent the state before state and federal regulatory agencies; administer consumer protection and education programs; handle formal consumer complaints; or exercise subpoena powers. In antitrust actions, the attorney general can only act on behalf of those consumers who are incapable of acting on their own and initiate

damage actions on behalf of the state in state courts. It cannot initiate criminal proceedings or represent counties, cities and other governmental entities in recovering civil damages under state or federal law.

The offices of the state's Department of Justice's Office of Consumer Protection are located in the state capital, Helena.

32 BANKING

As of June 2005, Montana had 82 insured banks, savings and loans, and saving banks, plus 12 state-chartered and 56 federally chartered credit unions (CUs). Excluding the CUs, the Billings market area accounted for the largest portion of the state's bank deposits at $1.966 billion and was second in the number of financial institutions at 12 in 2004, while the Missoula market area that same year, ranked first in the number of institutions, with 13 and was second in bank deposits at $1.278 billion. As of June 2005, CUs accounted for 14.3% of all assets held by all financial institutions in the state, or some $2.511 billion. Banks, savings and loans, and savings banks collectively accounted for the remaining 85.7% or $15.090 billion in assets held.

As of fourth quarter 2005, median percentage of past-due/non-accrual loans to total loans stood at 1.99%, down from 2.21% in 2004 and 2.26% in 2003. The median net interest margin (the difference between the lower rates given to savers and the higher rates charged on loans) was 4.95% in fourth quarter 2005, up from 4.63% in 2004 and 4.57% in 2003.

Regulation of Montana's state-chartered banks, savings and loans, credit unions, trust companies, consumer finance and escrow companies, deferred deposit loan companies, title loan lenders, mortgage brokers and loan originators, is the responsibility of the state's Division of Banking and Financial Institutions.

33 INSURANCE

In 2004 there were 373,000 individual life insurance policies in force with a total value of about $35.9 billion; total value for all categories of life insurance (individual, group, and credit) was about $50 billion. The average coverage amount is $96,300 per policy holder. Death benefits paid that year totaled $127.7 million.

As of 2003, there were four property and casualty and three life and health insurance companies domiciled in the state. Direct premiums for property and casualty insurance totaled $1.4 billion in 2004. That year, there were 3,364 flood insurance policies in force in the state, with a total value of $413 million.

In 2004, 45% of state residents held employment-based health insurance policies, 8% held individual policies, and 26% were covered under Medicare and Medicaid; 19% of residents were uninsured. Montana ties with four other states as having the fourth-highest percentage of uninsured residents in the nation. In 2003, employee contributions for employment-based health coverage averaged at 14% for single coverage and 28% for family coverage. The state does not offer a health benefits expansion program in connection with the Consolidated Omnibus Budget Reconciliation Act (COBRA, 1986), a health insurance program for those who lose employment-based coverage due to termination or reduction of work hours.

In 2003, there were 696,263 auto insurance policies in effect for private passenger cars. Required minimum coverage includes bodily injury liability of up to $25,000 per individual and $50,000 for all persons injured in an accident, as well as property damage liability of $10,000. In 2003, the average expenditure per vehicle for insurance coverage was $674.22.

34 SECURITIES

There are no securities exchanges in Montana. In 2005, there were 390 personal financial advisers employed in the state and 390 securities, commodities, and financial services sales agents. In 2004, there were at least 11 publicly traded companies within the state, with at least 2 companies listed on the NASDAQ (Semitool, Inc. and United Financial Corp.) and at least 1 listed on the NYSE (Touch America Holdings).

35 PUBLIC FINANCE

The Montana state budget is prepared biennially by the Office of Budget and Program Planning and submitted by the governor to the legislature for amendment and approval. The fiscal year runs from 1 July to 30 June. Effective fiscal year 1995, certain public school revenues were to be deposited in a general fund, increasing general fund revenues and public school appropriations.

Fiscal year 2006 general funds were estimated at $1.8 billion for resources and $1.6 billion for expenditures. In fiscal year 2004, federal government grants to Montana were nearly $2 billion

In the fiscal year 2007 federal budget, Montana was slated to receive: $15.5 million in State Children's Health Insurance Program (SCHIP) funds to help the state provide health coverage to low-income, uninsured children who do not qualify for Medicaid. This funding is a 23% increase over fiscal year 2006; and $6.6 million for the HOME Investment Partnership Program to help Montana fund a wide range of activities that build, buy, or rehabilitate affordable housing for rent or homeownership, or provide direct rental assistance to low-income people. This funding was an 11% increase over fiscal year 2006.

36 TAXATION

In 2005, Montana collected $1,788 million in tax revenues or $1,910 per capita, which placed it 35th among the 50 states in per capita tax burden. The national average was $2,192 per capita. Property taxes accounted for 10.4% of the total, selective sales taxes 25.5%, individual income taxes 39.9%, corporate income taxes 5.5%, and other taxes 18.8%.

As of 1 January 2006, Montana had seven individual income tax brackets ranging from 1.0% to 6.9%. The state taxes corporations at a flat rate of 6.75%.

In 2004, state and local property taxes amounted to $958,779,000 or $1034 per capita. The per capita amount ranks the state 20th nationally. Local governments collected $774,842,000 of the total and the state government $183,937,000.

Montana taxes gasoline at 27 cents per gallon. This is in addition to the 18.4 cents per gallon federal tax on gasoline.

According to the Tax Foundation, for every federal tax dollar sent to Washington in 2004, Montana citizens received $1.58 in federal spending.

37 ECONOMIC POLICY

The Economic Development Advisory Council of the state's Department of Commerce offers a variety of programs aimed at improving and enhancing Montana's economic and business climate.

Montana—State Government Finances

(Dollar amounts in thousands. Per capita amounts in dollars.)

	AMOUNT	PER CAPITA
Total Revenue	5,451,685	5,881.00
General revenue	4,245,305	4,579.62
Intergovernmental revenue	1,705,088	1,839.36
Taxes	1,625,692	1,753.71
General sales	–	–
Selective sales	437,051	471.47
License taxes	233,372	251.75
Individual income tax	605,582	653.27
Corporate income tax	67,723	73.06
Other taxes	281,964	304.17
Current charges	493,458	532.32
Miscellaneous general revenue	421,067	454.23
Utility revenue	–	–
Liquor store revenue	49,524	53.42
Insurance trust revenue	1,156,856	1,247.96
Total expenditure	4,691,318	5,060.75
Intergovernmental expenditure	955,378	1,030.61
Direct expenditure	3,735,940	4,030.14
Current operation	2,476,317	2,671.32
Capital outlay	522,585	563.74
Insurance benefits and repayments	528,430	570.04
Assistance and subsidies	85,160	91.87
Interest on debt	123,448	133.17
Exhibit: Salaries and wages	708,831	764.65
Total expenditure	4,691,318	5,060.75
General expenditure	4,119,927	4,444.37
Intergovernmental expenditure	955,378	1,030.61
Direct expenditure	3,164,549	3,413.75
General expenditures, by function:		
Education	1,377,921	1,486.43
Public welfare	762,029	822.04
Hospitals	39,467	42.57
Health	227,881	245.83
Highways	537,810	580.16
Police protection	45,940	49.56
Correction	121,156	130.70
Natural resources	279,892	301.93
Parks and recreation	14,523	15.67
Government administration	226,112	243.92
Interest on general debt	123,448	133.17
Other and unallocable	363,748	392.39
Utility expenditure	271	.29
Liquor store expenditure	42,690	46.05
Insurance trust expenditure	528,430	570.04
Debt at end of fiscal year	3,048,862	3,288.96
Cash and security holdings	11,724,183	12,647.45

Abbreviations and symbols: – zero or rounds to zero; (NA) not available; (X) not applicable.

SOURCE: U.S. Census Bureau, Governments Division, 2004 Survey of State Government Finances, January 2006.

Working closely with other state agencies and federal and private programs, the department's aim is to assist start-up and existing businesses with the technical and financial assistance necessary for their success. Relationships with local development groups, chambers of commerce, and similar organizations help Montana communities develop their full potential. Montana microbusiness companies with fewer than 10 full-time equivalent employees and annual gross revenues under $500,000 can receive loans of up to $35,000. Other qualifying businesses can borrow under several other state and federal development loan programs. The Economic Development Advisory Council's trade program assists businesses in pursuing domestic and worldwide trade. The Small Business Development Center (SBDC) program and the State Data Center program both operate statewide networks of service centers.

38 HEALTH

The infant mortality rate in October 2005 was estimated at 6.7 per 1,000 live births. The birth rate in 2003 was 12.4 per 1,000 population. The abortion rate stood at 13.5 per 1,000 women in 2000. In 2003, about 84.4% of pregnant woman received prenatal care beginning in the first trimester. In 2004, approximately 78% of children received routine immunizations before the age of three.

The crude death rate in 2003 was 9.2 deaths per 1,000 population. As of 2002, the death rates for major causes of death (per 100,000 resident population) were: heart disease, 213.8; cancer, 210.1; cerebrovascular diseases, 70.3; chronic lower respiratory diseases, 63.3; and diabetes, 23.1. The accidental death rate of 57.6 per 100,000 was one of the highest in the nation. The mortality rate from HIV infection was not available. In 2004, the reported AIDS case rate was at about 0.8 per 100,000 population, the lowest rate in the country. In 2002, about 54.1% of the population was considered overweight or obese. As of 2004, about 20.3% of state residents were smokers.

In 2003, Montana had 53 community hospitals with about 4,300 beds. There were about 107,000 patient admissions that year and 2.7 million outpatient visits. The average daily inpatient census was about 2,900 patients. The average cost per day for hospital care was $733. Also in 2003, there were about 101 certified nursing facilities in the state with 7,489 beds and an overall occupancy rate of about 76.6%. In 2004, it was estimated that about 65.9% of all state residents had received some type of dental care within the year. Montana had 224 physicians per 100,000 resident population in 2004 and 800 nurses per 100,000 in 2005. In 2004, there was a total of 513 dentists in the state.

About 26% of state residents were enrolled in Medicaid programs and Medicare programs in 2004. Approximately 19% of the state population was uninsured in 2004. In 2003, state health care expenditures totaled $941,000.

39 SOCIAL WELFARE

Montana played an important role in the development of social welfare. It was one of the first states to experiment with workers' compensation, enacting a compulsory compensation law in 1915. Eight years later, Montana and Nevada became the first states to provide for old age pensions.

In 2004, about 22,000 people received unemployment benefits, with the average weekly unemployment benefit at $197. In fiscal year 2005, the estimated average monthly participation in the food stamp program included about 80,870 persons (34,573 households); the average monthly benefit was about $91.95 per person. That year, the total of benefits paid through the state for the food stamp program was about $89.2 million.

Temporary Assistance for Needy Families (TANF), the system of federal welfare assistance that officially replaced Aid to Families with Dependent Children (AFDC) in 1997, was reauthorized through the Deficit Reduction Act of 2005. TANF is funded through federal block grants that are divided among the states based on an equation involving the number of recipients in each state. Montana's TANF program is called Families Achieving Independence in Montana (FAIM). In 2004, the state program had 14,000 recipients; state and federal expenditures on this TANF program totaled $35 million in fiscal year 2003.

In December 2004, Social Security benefits were paid to 165,910 Montana residents. This number included 106,970 retired workers, 16,770 widows and widowers, 19,070 disabled workers, 10,780 spouses, and 12,320 children. Social Security beneficiaries represented 17.9% of the total state population and 93.9% of the state's population age 65 and older. Retired workers received an average monthly payment of $916; widows and widowers, $883; disabled workers, $863; and spouses, $459. Payments for children of retired workers averaged $430 per month; children of deceased workers, $605; and children of disabled workers, $249. Federal Supplemental Security Income payments in December 2004 went to 14,558 Montana residents, averaging $377 a month.

40 HOUSING

In 2004, Montana had an estimated 423,262 housing units, of which 368,530 were occupied; 68.5% were owner-occupied. About 69.8% of all units were single-family, detached homes; about 12.8% were mobile homes. Utility gas and electricity were the most common energy sources for heating. It was estimated that 18,156 units lacked telephone service, 1,780 lacked complete plumbing facilities, and 2,143 lacked complete kitchen facilities. The average household had 2.45 members.

In 2004, 5,000 new privately owned units were authorized for construction. The median home value was $119,319. The median monthly cost for mortgage owners was $974. Renters paid a median of $520 per month. In September 2005, the state received grants of $1.15 million from the US Department of Housing and Urban Development (HUD) for rural housing and economic development programs. For 2006, HUD allocated to the state over $6.8 million in community development block grants.

41 EDUCATION

In 2004, 91.9% of Montana residents age 25 and older were high school graduates, far above the national average of 84%. Some 25.5% had obtained a bachelor's degree or higher, slightly below the national average of 26%.

The total enrollment for fall 2002 in Montana's public schools stood at 150,000. Of these, 101,000 attended schools from kindergarten through grade eight, and 49,000 attended high school. Approximately 85.1% of the students were white, 0.7% were black, 2.1% were Hispanic, 1% were Asian/Pacific Islander, and 11% were American Indian/Alaskan Native. Total enrollment was estimated at 147,000 fall 2003 and expected to reach 141,000 by fall 2014, a decline of 5.9% during the period 2002 to 2014. In fall 2003 there were 8,924 students enrolled in 104 private schools. Expenditures for public education in 2003/04 were estimated at $1.2 billion. Since 1969, the National Assessment of Educational Progress (NAEP) has tested public school students nationwide. The resulting report, *The Nation's Report Card,* stated that in 2005, eighth graders in Montana scored 286 out of 500 in mathematics compared with the national average of 278.

As of fall 2002, there were 45,111 students enrolled in college or graduate school; minority students comprised 11.7% of total postsecondary enrollment. In 2005 Montana had 23 degree-granting institutions. The University of Montana has campuses at Missoula, Montana Tech, and Western Montana College. Montana State University encompasses the Bozeman, Billings, and Northern campuses.

42 ARTS

The Montana Arts Council was established in 1967 to promote and expand the significance of arts and culture in the lives of Montanans. In 2005, the Montana Arts Council and other Montana arts organizations received 12 grants totaling $812,900 from the National Endowment for the Arts (NEA). The Council has also received funding from state and private sources.

The Montana Committee for the Humanities (MCH) was founded in 1972. In 2000, the MCH sponsored its first annual Montana Festival of the Book in downtown Missoula, bringing together writers, readers, and entertainers from across the state. In 2005, the National Endowment for the Humanities contributed $662,437 to 11 state programs.

The C. M. Russell Museum in Great Falls honors the work of Charles Russell, whose mural *Lewis and Clark Meeting the Flathead Indians* adorns the capitol in Helena. Other fine art museums include the Museum of the Rockies in Bozeman, Yellowstone Art Center at Billings, and the Missoula Art Museum. The Missoula Art Museum emphasizes artwork relevant to the American West culture, especially contemporary pieces by Montana artists. Orchestras are based in Billings and Bozeman and the Equinox Theater Company is also a popular attraction in Bozeman.

43 LIBRARIES AND MUSEUMS

In 2001, Montana had 79 public library systems, with a total of 107 libraries, of which there were 28 branches. The combined book and serial publication stock of all Montana public libraries that same year was 2,625,000 volumes, and their combined total circulation was 4,812,000. The system also had 62,000 audio and video items, each, and 3,000 electronic format items (CD-ROMs, magnetic tapes, and disks), and four bookmobiles. Distinguished collections include: those of the University of Montana (Missoula), with over 850,000 volumes; Montana State University (Bozeman), 597,609; and the Montana State Library and Montana Historical Society Library, both in Helena. In fiscal year 2001, operating income for the state's public library system was $15,425,000, including $49,000 in federal grants and $344,000 in state grants.

Among the state's 74 museums are the Montana Historical Society Museum, Helena; World Museum of Mining, Butte; Western Heritage Center, Billings; and Museum of the Plains Indian, Browning. National historic sites include Big Hole and Little Big Horn battlefields and the Grant-Kohrs Ranch at Deer Lodge, west of Helena.

44 COMMUNICATIONS

In 2004, 93.5% of the state's households had telephone service. In addition, by December 2003 there were 373,947 mobile wireless telephone subscribers. In 2003, 59.5% of Montana households had a computer and 50.4% had Internet access. By June 2005, there were 90,563 high-speed lines in Montana, 79,658 residential and 10,905 for business. There were 43 major commercial radio stations (14 AM, 29 FM) in 2005, and 16 major television stations.

A total of 15,300 Internet domain names were registered in Montana in 2000.

45 PRESS

As of 2005, Montana had eight morning dailies, three evening dailies, and seven Sunday newspapers. The leading papers were the *Billings Gazette* (47,105 mornings, 52,434 Sundays), *Great Falls Tribune* (33,434 mornings, 36,763 Sundays), and the *Missoulian* (30,466 mornings, 34,855 Sundays).

46 ORGANIZATIONS

In 2006, there were over 1,495 nonprofit organizations registered within the state, of which about 1,075 were registered as charitable, educational, or religious organizations. National professional and business organizations and associations based in Montana include the American Indian Business Leaders and the American Simmental Association.

Regional arts, history, and culture are represented in part through the Boone and Crockett Club, the Butte Jazz Society, the Custer Battlefield Historical and Museum Association, and the Lewis and Clark Trail Heritage Foundation. Conservation and outdoors recreation organizations include the Greater Yellowstone Coalition, Montana Outfitters and Guides Association, the National Forest Foundation, the Greater Yellowstone Coalition, Our Montana (Billings), and the Great Bear Foundation (Missoula). The national Adventure Cycling Association is based in Missoula.

The Indian Law Resource Center, founded in 1978 and based in Helena, serves as a legal, environmental, and human rights organization promoting the welfare of Indian tribes and other indigenous peoples in North America.

47 TOURISM, TRAVEL, AND RECREATION

Many tourists seek out the former gold rush camps, ghost towns, and dude ranches. Scenic wonders include all of Glacier National Park, covering 1,013,595 acres (410,202 hectares), which is the US portion of Waterton-Glacier International Peace Park; part of Yellowstone National Park, which also extends into Idaho and Wyoming; and Bighorn Canyon National Recreation Area. Bozeman, the gateway to Yellowstone Park also is a research area for dinosaurs. The Museum of the Rockies sponsors a dig in Choteau near Glacier National Park.

Montana is home to several Indian tribes; the Crow, the Sioux, and the Plains Indians reside here. Montana is the site of Custer's Last Stand, the Battle of Little Bighorn. There is a national monument to Custer there. Bighorn Canyon National Recreation Area is one of the largest outdoor recreation area in the United States. Glacier County has the Ninepipes Museum and the Flathead Indian Reservation. The Rocky Mountain Elk Wildlife Foundation is the newest of the conservation education facilities. In June 2005, Montana opened the Northeastern Plains Birding Trail. This trail links 12 birding sites and is populated by large numbers of migratory birds.

In 2002, some 10 million nonresident travelers spent $1.8 billion on visits to the state. The tourist industry sponsors over 33,500 jobs. Tourism promotion and development were funded primarily through a 4% lodging tax, which generated $11 million per year. Tourism payroll generated $358 million in tax revenue. Montana was observing the bicentennial of the Lewis and Clark expedition during 2003–06, with festivities scheduled throughout the state.

⁴⁸SPORTS

There are no major professional sports teams in Montana, although there are minor league baseball teams in Billings, Great Falls, Helena, and Missoula. The University of Montana Grizzlies and Montana State University Bobcats both compete in the Big Sky Conference. Skiing is a very popular sport. The state has world-class ski resorts in Big Sky. Other annual sporting events include the Seeley-Lincoln 100/200 Dog Sled Race between Seely Lake and Lincoln in January and many rodeos statewide.

⁴⁹FAMOUS MONTANANS

Prominent national officeholders from Montana include US Senator Thomas Walsh (b.Wisconsin, 1859–1933), who directed the investigation that uncovered the Teapot Dome scandal; Jeannette Rankin (1880–1973),the first woman member of Congress and the only US representative to vote against American participation in both world wars; Burton K. Wheeler (b.Massachusetts, 1882–1975), US senator from 1923 to 1947 and one of the most powerful politicians in Montana history; and Michael Joseph "Mike" Mansfield (b.New York, 1903–2001), who held the office of majority leader of the US Senate longer than anyone else.

Chief Joseph (b.Oregon, 1840?–1904), a Nez Percé Indian, repeatedly outwitted the US Army during the late 1870s; Crazy Horse (1849?–77) led a Sioux-Cheyenne army in battle at Little Big Horn. The town of Bozeman is named for explorer and prospector John M. Bozeman (b.Georgia, 1835–67).

Creative artists from Montana include Alfred Bertram Guthrie Jr. (b.Indiana, 1901–91), author of *The Big Sky* and the Pulitzer Prize-winning *The Way West;* Dorothy Johnson (b.Iowa, 1905–84), whose stories have been made into such notable Western movies as *The Hanging Tree, The Man Who Shot Liberty Valance,* and *A Man Called Horse;* and Charles Russell (b.Missouri, 1864–1926), Montana's foremost painter and sculptor. Hollywood stars Gary Cooper (Frank James Cooper, 1901–61) and Myrna Loy (1905–

93) were born in Helena. Newscaster Chet Huntley (1911–74) was born in Cardwell.

⁵⁰BIBLIOGRAPHY

Council of State Governments. *The Book of the States, 2006 Edition.* Lexington, Ky.: Council of State Governments, 2006.

Elison, Larry M. *The Montana State Constitution: A Reference Guide.* Westport, Conn.: Greenwood Press, 2001.

Howard, Joseph Kinsey. *Montana, High, Wide, and Handsome.* Lincoln: University of Nebraska Press, 2003.

Malone, Michael P., and Richard B. Roeder. *Montana: A History of Two Centuries.* Rev. ed. Seattle: University of Washington Press, 1991.

Parzybok, Tye W. *Weather Extremes in the West.* Missoula, Mont.: Mountain Press, 2005.

Preston, Thomas. *Rocky Mountains: Montana, Wyoming, Colorado, New Mexico,* 2nd ed. Vol. 3 of *The Double Eagle Guide to 1,000 Great Western Recreation Destinations.* Billings, Mont.: Discovery Publications, 2003.

Rowles, Genevieve (ed.). *Adventure Guide to Montana.* Edison, N.J.: Hunter, 2000.

Sateren, Shelley Swanson. *Montana Facts and Symbols.* Mankato, Minn.: Hilltop Books, 2000.

Small, Lawrence F. (ed.). *Religion in Montana: Pathways to the Present.* Billings, Mont.: Rocky Mountain College, 1992.

US Department of Commerce, Economics and Statistics Administration, US Census Bureau. *Montana, 2000. Summary Social, Economic, and Housing Characteristics: 2000 Census of Population and Housing.* Washington, D.C.: US Government Printing Office, 2003.

Wright, John B. *Montana Ghost Dance: Essays on Land and Life.* Austin: University of Texas Press, 1998.

Wyckoff, William. *On the Road Again: Montana's Changing Landscape.* Seattle: University of Washington Press, 2006.

ISBN-13: 978-1-4144-1121-7
ISBN-10: 1-4144-1121-9

Alabama

Alaska

Arizona

Arkansas

California

Hawaii

Idaho

Illinois

Indiana

Iowa

Massachusetts

Michigan

Minnesota

Mississippi

Missouri

New Mexico

New York

North Carolina

North Dakota

Ohio

South Dakota

Tennessee

Texas

Utah

Vermont

Puerto Rico

District of Columbia

United States